P9-DNT-930

Sa 3
V. 2

ENCYCLOPEDIA OF AFRICAN-AMERICAN CULTURE AND HISTORY

ENCYCLOPEDIA OF AFRICAN-AMERICAN CULTURE AND HISTORY

Edited by

JACK SALZMAN
DAVID LIONEL SMITH
CORNEL WEST

Volume 2

MACMILLAN LIBRARY REFERENCE USA
SIMON & SCHUSTER MACMILLAN
NEW YORK

SIMON & SCHUSTER AND PRENTICE HALL INTERNATIONAL
LONDON   MEXICO CITY   NEW DELHI   SINGAPORE   SYDNEY   TORONTO

Simon & Schuster Macmillan
866 Third Avenue, New York, NY 10022

PRINTED IN THE UNITED STATES OF AMERICA

printing number

1 2 3 4 5 6 7 8 9 10

LIBRARY OF CONGRESS CATALOGING-IN-PUBLICATION DATA
Encyclopedia of African-American culture and history /
    edited by Jack Salzman, David Lionel Smith, Cornel West.
        p.   cm.
    Includes bibliographical references and index.
    ISBN 0-02-897345-3 (set)
    1. Afro-Americans—Encyclopedias.   2.
Afro-Americans—History—Encyclopedias.   I. Salzman,
Jack. II. Smith, David L., 1954–   III. West, Cornel.
E185E54   1995
973'.0496073'003—dc20   95-33607
                                                 CIP

This paper meets the requirements of ANSI/NISO Z39.48-1992
(Permanence of Paper)

C

(Continued)

Civil Rights Congress. The Civil Rights Congress (CRC) was founded in 1946 with the merger of the International Labor Defense, the NATIONAL NEGRO CONGRESS and the National Federation for Constitutional Liberties—three organizations closely associated with the COMMUNIST PARTY OF THE U.S.A. During the late 1940s and early '50s, the CRC fought for the civil rights and liberties of African Americans, labor leaders, and suspected communists. They believed that the defense of communists was the first line in the defense of civil liberties generally and sought to overturn the Smith Act (1940) and the McCarran Act (1950), both designed to stifle dissent and harass left-wing organizations.

Like the NATIONAL ASSOCIATION FOR THE ADVANCEMENT OF COLORED PEOPLE (NAACP), the CRC pursued legal cases to challenge the racism and inequality in American society. However, the CRC did not rely on legal strategy alone but combined it with political agitation, massive publicity campaigns, and large demonstrations to mobilize public opinion to demand an end to racist attacks. In the early 1950s the CRC launched a campaign to raise public awareness about the systemic violence and segregation that African Americans faced by presenting a petition to the United Nations that charged the United States government with genocide.

In one of its earliest cases, Rosa Lee Ingram, a black tenant farmer and widowed mother of twelve children, together with two of her sons, was convicted in 1947 of the murder of John Stratford and sentenced to death. Stratford, a white tenant farmer, had been sexually harassing Ingram when her sons came to her defense and hit Stratford on the head.

The CRC, under the leadership of its women's auxiliary, Sojourners for Truth and Justice, fought a public battle to free the Ingrams. They filed a petition with the United Nations, named Rosa Ingram Mother of the Year, started the National Committee to Free the Ingram Family, which raised money for family members, and sent a delegation armed with 100,000 signatures to the Department of Justice and the White House. As a result of the CRC's efforts and the resulting press coverage, Rosa Ingram and her sons were freed in 1954.

In another well-publicized effort, the CRC defended the Martinsville Seven, seven young black men in Virginia sentenced to death in 1949 by an all-white jury for raping a white woman. Civil rights organizations were outraged by the harshness of the sentence as well as the judge's refusal to grant a change of venue to ensure that the men received a fair trial. Deferring the legal case to the NAACP, the CRC focused on the publicity campaign. They conducted a massive international letter campaign, organized a prayer vigil, picketed the White House, held demonstrations in Richmond, and demanded a pardon from the governor. Although the NAACP and the CRC failed to save the lives of the Martinsville Seven, they succeeded in exposing the racism of the legal system in the United States.

The CRC fought tenaciously to defend the civil rights of the persecuted. They were not, however, strict civil libertarians. For example, they opposed free speech for the KU KLUX KLAN and other racists, which brought them into conflict with an organization such as the American Civil Liberties Union. In addition, recurring tension with the NAACP made

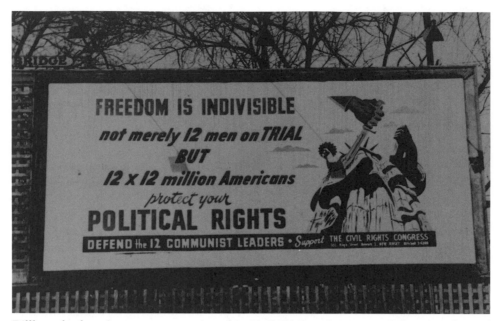

Billboard advertisement supporting the Civil Rights Congress. (Photographs and Prints Division, Schomburg Center for Research in Black Culture, The New York Public Library, Astor, Lenox and Tilden Foundations)

an alliance difficult, but at times the two organizations were able to achieve behind-the-scenes cooperation. Nevertheless, the CRC's unyielding opposition to racism won it support among some sectors of the African-American community. At its peak, the CRC reached a membership of ten thousand, with its strongest base in large cities. William PATTERSON, lawyer and Communist party leader, served as executive secretary of the organization during its existence. Other prominent leaders included Paul ROBESON, Dashiell Hammett, and Louise Thompson Patterson.

The CRC was active during the McCarthy period, and the U.S. government tried persistently to repress the organization. In the mid-1950s the organization was under investigation by the Internal Revenue Service, New York State, and the House Committee on Un-American Activities. Government officials impounded CRC records, conducted an audit, and demanded lists of contributors. In 1954 the organization's leaders refused to give up the names of supporters and were arrested on contempt charges. Two years later, the Subversive Activities Control Board concluded that the CRC was "substantially controlled" by the Communist Party, U.S.A. Although many Communist party members and sympathizers were active in the CRC, the organization was always independent of the party. Nevertheless, in 1956 the CRC was forced to close its doors because of the increasing legal costs of the government investigations and a decline in the number of contributors. Despite its short-lived existence, CRC succeeded in

bringing to international attention the injustice prevalent in the American legal system and the racism endemic to American society.

REFERENCE

HORNE, GERALD. *Communist Front? The Civil Rights Congress, 1946–56.* Rutherford, N.J., 1987.

PAM NADASEN

Civil Rights and the Law.   Civil rights, in the broadest sense, are the constitutional and legal rights enjoyed by citizens. Throughout most of the nation's history, civil rights have varied according to one's status: men enjoyed rights that women did not possess; propertied men possessed rights denied their poorer brothers; and whites had rights denied persons of color. Since the early nineteenth century, African Americans and their white allies have forcefully demanded an end to discrimination in civil rights on account of race. Stretching well into the second half of the twentieth century, this campaign has dramatically transformed American law and life, pushing the nation closer to its ideal of civil equality.

From the Revolution to the Civil War

Before the American Revolution, the law of every colony permitted persons of color to be held as slaves (*see also* SLAVERY; SLAVE TRADE) and discriminated against African-Americans, whether slave or free, in a variety of ways. With its emphasis on equality and natural rights, the Revolution unleashed a powerful antislavery movement that achieved abolition in the northern states by the middle decades of the nineteenth century. However, in the South, where the vast majority of slaves lived, the political dominance of slaveholders precluded serious consideration of abolition. Southern leaders' determination to protect slavery was also felt at the Constitutional Convention in 1787. Eager to win southern support for creation of a stronger national government, northern delegates made a variety of concessions to slavery: they strengthened the slave states' political power in Congress by basing representation in the House of Representatives on a state's free population and three-fifths of its slaves; prohibited Congress from interfering with the importation of slaves for twenty years; provided for the return of FUGITIVE SLAVES who escaped across state lines; and insulated slavery from congressional influence in any state the chose to make it lawful.

In the decades after the Constitution was ratified, slavery and racial discrimination in the South became more deeply entrenched. Southern legislators and judges steadily eroded the rights of free blacks, whom they viewed as potential agents of abolitionism. The few southern states that had permitted free blacks to vote disfranchised them, courts in many states ruled that they were not citizens, and legislatures adopted laws requiring them to register periodically with local authorities, excluding them from certain trades and subjecting them to humiliating punishments like whipping.

Discrimination against free blacks also became more common in the North as the nineteenth century progressed. At the time the constitution was ratified, every northern state allowed all free men who owned sufficient property to vote, regardless of race. By 1860, however, three of these states had limited suffrage to whites, as had all but two of the new states admitted since ratification. Six northern states denied African Americans the right to testify against whites, five others barred the entry of black migrants or required them to post bonds, many permitted or required local school authorities to establish segregated schools, and most prohibited interracial marriage.

As discrimination intensified in the 1830s and '40s, northern blacks and white abolitionists developed a powerful Constitutional argument for equality and federal protection of civil rights. They contended that African Americans—by virtue of their birth—were citizens of both the United States and the state in which they resided. In a republic founded on the egalitarian principles of the Declaration of Independence, the insisted, all citizens were entitled to equal rights, irrespective of race. They also argued that the U.S.

Constitution's privileges and immunities clause ("the Citizens of Each State shall be entitled to all Privileges and Immunities of Citizens in the Several States" [Article IV, Sec. 2]) created a body of fundamental rights that all citizens possessed and that no state could violate.

Although these arguments would profoundly influence those who framed the Reconstruction Amendments in the 1860s, they produced few immediate results. Before the Civil War, the Constitution gave states almost unlimited authority to define the rights of individuals. It contained few provisions protecting individual rights against state infringement. Moreover, the Supreme Court, in *Barron* v. *Baltimore* (1833) and later rulings, held that because the Bill of Rights had been adopted to restrain the national government, its provisions did not constrain state action. Most legal authorities rejected the abolitionists' broad reading of the privileges and immunities clause, insisting that it merely guaranteed a citizen of one state who entered another state whatever rights that state accorded its own citizens. And many influential political and legal figures asserted that the framers had intended to limit U.S. citizenship to whites and that persons of color had no rights under the federal Constitution. In 1857, a southern-dominated U.S. Supreme Court endorsed this position in *Dred Scott* v. *Sandford* (*see* DRED SCOTT DECISION).

At the state level, proponents of equal citizenship achieved mixed results. Their arguments generally did not prevail in state courts. In 1849, for example, when African Americans in Boston challenged segregation in the city's schools, contending that it violated the state constitution's guarantee of equality, the state supreme court rejected their argument. However, African Americans and their white allies occasionally scored victories in the political arena. After failing in court, abolitionists convinced the Massachusetts legislature to ban school segregation in 1855. In several other northern states, antislavery politicians scored legislative victories that eased legal discrimination against blacks.

The Civil War and Reconstruction Era

The CIVIL WAR and RECONSTRUCTION effected a revolution in civil rights. Northern Republicans embraced EMANCIPATION as a war aim, striking at slavery through the Confiscation Act (1862), the Emancipation Proclamation (1863), and the THIRTEENTH AMENDMENT (1865). When the war ended, slavery was dead, yet the legal status of former slaves remained unclear. During the winter of 1865–1866, southern legislatures adopted the BLACK CODES—harshly discriminatory laws designed to maintain white hegemony. Viewing the black codes as measures to defeat emancipation, the Republican majority in Congress concluded that if former slaves were to enjoy genuine freedom, they must possess equal civil rights, something that could only be secured by federal power.

During the late 1860s and '70s, Congress established the principle of color-blind citizenship and provided broad national protection for civil rights. The Civil Rights Act of 1866 stipulated that all persons were entitled to the same legal rights as whites and authorized federal courts to enforce its provisions when state officials refused to comply. The FOURTEENTH AMENDMENT (1868) settled the debate over African-American citizenship, proclaiming that "all persons born . . . in the United States are citizens of the United States and the State wherein they reside." It also established broad national guarantees for indi-

vidual rights, stipulating that no state could deprive any person of the privileges or immunities of United States citizens or deny any person life, liberty, or property without due process of law or the equal protection of the laws.

Other civil rights measures quickly followed. In the Reconstruction Act (1867), congressional Republicans extended the right to vote to southern black men. The FIFTEENTH AMENDMENT (1870) prohibited denial of the right to vote on the basis of race. When southern whites employed terrorism to deter African Americans from voting, Congress adopted the Enforcement Acts (1870–1871). Dramatically extending federal protection for individual rights, these measures authorized federal supervision of elections and established criminal penalties for state officials and individuals who employed violence to deny anyone

An illustration of South Carolina's Rep. Robert B. Elliot's January 6, 1874, speech in support of new civil rights legislation. Though the bill was later enacted as the Civil Rights Act of 1875, the U.S. Supreme Court in the civil rights cases (1883) declared the bill's prohibition of discrimination unconstitutional. (Prints and Photographs Division, Library of Congress)

the right to vote or any right secured by the Constitution or federal law. Congressional Republicans also insisted that access to public places was a common law right to which all citizens were entitled, a principle embodied in the Civil Rights Act of 1875. It banned racial discrimination in public transportation, restaurants, hotels, and theaters, as well as on juries.

Even before the congressional program reached its zenith, the U.S. Supreme Court had begun to circumscribe national power to protect civil rights. In *The Slaughter-House Cases* (1873), the Court held that the privileges and immunities of U.S. citizens were decidedly limited. State citizenship, not U.S. citizenship, the Court insisted, was the source of most individual rights. The ruling eviscerated the Fourteenth Amendment's privileges and immunities clause, significantly reducing federal power to protect individual rights. The justices also adopted a narrow interpretation of Congress's authority to reinforce the Fourteenth Amendment. By holding that the Amendment applied only to state action denying persons equal protection or due process, the Court made it difficult for the federal government to protect African Americans from private acts of discrimination and violence. Indeed, in *The Civil Rights Cases* (1883), the Court declared unconstitutional the Civil Rights Act of 1875.

While the Court was reducing federal power to protect civil rights, white Democrats were regaining control of the southern states, where 90 percent of the African Americans lived. Although the laws they enacted seldom discriminated openly against blacks, Democrats nonetheless used government and law to preserve white control. Democratic state and local officials reinforced plantation owners' authority over black laborers, excluded blacks from jury service, overzealously prosecuted criminally accused blacks, and generally ignored crimes against blacks. As lynching became epidemic in the 1880s and '90s, state and local officials generally refused to protect victims or bring perpetrators to justice.

Beginning in the late 1880s, as federal power to protect civil rights waned, southern states adopted laws requiring potential visitors to pay poll taxes and/or pass literacy tests. Although these measures also kept many poor whites from voting, discriminatory enforcement by hostile white officials effectively disfranchised blacks. By 1910, registration among black males ranged from 15 percent in Virginia to less than 2 percent in Alabama and Mississippi. These years also saw the rise of legally enforced segregation. Beginning with laws requiring separate but equal accommodations for black and white railroad passengers, JIM CROW (as this system of *de jure* segregation was popularly known) extended to most areas of life in the South by the 1910s.

African Americans challenged these measures, insisting that they stigmatized them and denied them rights guaranteed by the Constitution. In a series of highly formalistic rulings, however, the Supreme Court rejected their challenges. In *Plessy* v. *Ferguson* (1896), it upheld a railroad segregation law, ruling that it did not deny African Americans equal protection because it required railroads to provide blacks and whites "equal but separate" accommodations. Three years later, in *Cumming* v. *School Board of Richmond County, Ga.*, the Court upheld a county's decision to close its only black high school while continuing to operate several white high schools, indicating that it would be lax in requiring that segregated facilities be equal. In *Williams* v. *Mississippi* (1898), the Court upheld the state's poll tax and literacy test, ruling that they did not restrict the right to vote on the basis of race and therefore did not violate the Fifteenth Amendment. By the turn of the century, the Reconstruction Amendments' guarantee of color-blind citizenship and equal civil rights was little more than an empty promise for black Southerners.

Blacks in the North fared somewhat better. They faced few barriers to voting, and laws requiring segregation were rare. Indeed, in the years following *The Civil Rights Cases,* most northern states had prohibited discrimination in public accommodations. However, these laws went largely unenforced, and it was common for white-owned hotels, theaters, and restaurants to deny African Americans service.

The Challenge to Segregation

In the early twentieth century a small group of northern black leaders and white reformers kept alive the Reconstruction-era vision of equal citizenship. Meeting in New York in 1909, a small group of these men and women formed the NATIONAL ASSOCIATION FOR THE ADVANCEMENT OF COLORED PEOPLE (NAACP). Dedicated to "assuring to each and every citizen, irrespective of color, the equality of opportunity and equality before the law which underlie our American institutions and are guaranteed by the Constitution," the NAACP pursued a campaign of publicity, lobbying, and litigation to restore life to the Reconstruction amendments.

During its first two decades, the NAACP enjoyed limited success. Although its campaign for a federal antilynching law (1918–1922) raised public consciousness, a threatened filibuster by southern Democrats in the Senate killed the bill. NAACP attorneys fared better in the U.S. Supreme Court. In *Guinn* v. *U.S.* (1915), the Court struck down the grandfather clause, a device that many southern states used to exempt white voters from literacy tests. Two years later, in *Buchanan* v. *Warley,* it ruled that laws requiring segregation of residential neighborhoods violated the Fourteenth Amendment. Such victories did not, however, produce significant change. The demise of the grandfather clause left poll taxes and literacy tests in place. Moreover, residential segregation—which was largely the result of private agreements, the practices of realtors, and violence—became even more entrenched, even in the North. In *Corrigan* v. *Buckley* (1926), the Court rejected the NAACP's challenge to restrictive covenants (provisions put in deeds to prohibit the sale of real estate to blacks), holding that they were private agreements and therefore did not violate the Fourteenth Amendment.

In the 1930s, Charles Hamilton Houston, who became the NAACP's chief counsel in 1934, and Thurgood MARSHALL, his protégé and successor who would later become a justice of the U.S. Supreme Court, developed a legal strategy to force fundamental change. Focusing on education, they used *Plessy*'s separate-but-equal doctrine to challenge the gross inequities permeating the South's dual school system. By compelling states to make white and black schools equal, the NAACP (and after 1939, the NAACP Legal Defense Fund, Inc.) hoped to make segregation too expensive for poor southern states to maintain.

The campaign targeted graduate and professional education, where discrimination was clearest. Southern states typically denied African Americans admission to white graduate and professional schools, yet established no comparable programs at black colleges. At best, they offered to help African Americans attend schools in other states. In *Missouri* ex rel. *Gaines* v. *Canada* (1938), NAACP attorneys challenged these policies. While not questioning the legitimacy of segregation, the Supreme Court held that a state that provided legal education within its borders for whites must do the same for blacks. When states created segregated graduate and professional schools for blacks, the Court demanded that they be fully equal to those available to whites. In *Sweatt* v. *Painter* (1950), it ordered a black applicant admitted to the University of Texas School of Law after finding the state's Jim Crow law school inferior to the white school. Because the Court emphasized the importance of intangible factors such as the school's reputation, *Sweatt* implicitly questioned whether segregated education could be truly equal.

Harlem demonstration for the passage of the Anti-Lynching Bill, 1936. (Photographs and Prints Division, Schomburg Center for Research in Black Culture, The New York Public Library, Astor, Lenox and Tilden Foundations)

Herbert L. Bruce (right foreground) leads P.W.A. pickets, 1936. (Photographs and Prints Division, Schomburg Center for Research in Black Culture, The New York Public Library, Astor, Lenox and Tilden Foundations)

By the late 1940s, the Supreme Court gave other indications of impatience with segregation. In *Smith* v. *Allwright* (1944), it struck down the white primary, a device used by southern Democrats to bar registered black voters from voting in the only election that counted in the one-party South. The Court also attacked restrictive covenants, holding in *Shelley* v. *Kraemer* (1948) that the equal protection clauses prohibited courts from enforcing them. Moreover, relying on the Constitution's commerce clause and the Interstate Commerce Act, it banned segregation on interstate buses and trains (*Morgan* v. *Virginia* [1946] and *Henderson* v. *U.S.* [1950].)

As the Court chipped away at segregation, African Americans broadened the civil rights agenda, which traditionally had emphasized political and legal rights. During the 1920s and '30s, A. Philip RANDOLPH and other black leaders had urged greater attention to improving the economic position of black workers. In 1941, as the nation moved toward war, Randolph used the threat of a mass march on Washington to prod President Franklin D. Roosevelt to issue an executive order banning employment discrimination in the defense industry and establishing a powerful COMMITTEE ON FAIR EMPLOYMENT PRACTICES (FEPC) to hear complaints and impose sanctions on employers found guilty of discrimination. Although it did not survive the war, FEPC brought federal protection of civil rights into the workplace for the first time.

The 1940s also saw growing support for civil rights among northern Democrats. Liberals, whose strength in the party had grown during the 1930s, urged more aggressive support for civil rights as a matter of principle. Hard-headed political realism reinforced their position. During the 1930s, most African-American voters had joined the DEMOCRATIC PARTY. After WORLD WAR II, as northern

Democrats faced a stiff Republican challenge, they adopted a more aggressive stance on civil rights to keep black voters in the Democratic camp. In 1948, President Harry S. Truman issued Executive Order 9981 to begin the desegregation of the armed forces. Truman also sent sweeping civil rights legislation to Congress, providing tough federal sanctions against lynching, banning segregation in interstate transportation, and (using the model of Roosevelt's wartime FEPC) establishing federal sanctions against discrimination in the workplace. Although southern Democrats and conservative Republicans killed the program, Truman's initiatives brought civil rights to the forefront of American politics.

As political support for civil rights broadened, Thurgood Marshall and his colleagues intensified the campaign against segregated education. Shifting their focus from unequal facilities, they directly challenged the constitutionality of segregation in BROWN V. BOARD OF EDUCATION (1954). The Supreme Court accepted their argument, unanimously ruling that "separate educational facilities are inherently unequal." However, in an effort to dampen white resistance, the Court ordered gradual implementation of *Brown,* instructing lower federal courts to devise plans to desegregate schools "with all deliberate speed" or, in other words, to cautiously proceed with local desegregation plans.

The Civil Rights Movement

Although *Brown* shattered the legal basis for southern segregation, the old order died hard. Southern states and localities devised a variety of subterfuges to evade school desegregation, and occasionally defied federal court orders. Federal judges charged with implementing *Brown* proceeded very cautiously. At best, they approved desegregation plans that gradually implemented token integration; at worst, they blocked desegregation altogether. Moreover, state and local governments continued to enforce laws segregating virtually all other areas of southern life. In the face of this resistance, the Supreme Court refused to back down. It extended its ban against segregation from public education to public parks, buses, golf courses, and beaches. When Arkansas officials defied court-ordered segregation, a unanimous Court ruled in *Cooper* v. *Aaron* (1958) that state recalcitrance would not be permitted to delay desegregation. Yet in school cases the justices refused to push the lower federal courts to move beyond token desegregation.

Congress and the executive branch were less aggressive than the Court. Although he ordered troops to Little Rock in 1957 to overcome state officials' defiance of a federal court's desegregation order, President Dwight D. Eisenhower neither endorsed *Brown* nor pressed Congress for legislation to dis-

mantle segregation. In Congress, liberal Democrats initiated legislation to speed up school desegregation, ban segregation in public accommodations, provide effective remedies against voting discrimination, and prohibit employment discrimination. But southern Democrats and conservative Republicans allied to block these efforts. Consequently, the measures that did pass—the Civil Rights Act of 1957 and 1960—only modestly increased federal power to protect voting rights.

Citizen action finally broke the logjam on civil rights, dramatically accelerating the pace of change in the 1960s. Beginning with student SIT-INS in 1960, civil rights activists challenged segregation and voting discrimination through mass protest and civil disobedience. Culminating in the massive demonstrations led by Dr. Martin Luther King, Jr., in Birmingham, Alabama in 1963 and Selma, Ala., in 1965, this campaign forced the hand of the President and Congress. The Birmingham Crisis finally moved President John F. Kennedy to appear on national television to announce his support for legislation to eradicate segregation.

Skillfully pushed through Congress by Kennedy and his successor, Lyndon B. Johnson, the Civil Rights Act of 1964 translated into law most of the goals of the early civil rights movement. It struck a powerful blow against school segregation, authorizing the justice department to bring school desegregation suits, directing federal agencies to adopt guidelines banning discrimination in programs receiving federal funds, and stopping the flow of federal dollars when school districts failed to comply. Relying on its power to regulate interstate commerce (thereby circumventing the Supreme Court's state-action limitation on the Fourteenth Amendment), Congress also prohibited discrimination by restaurants, hotels, motels, gas stations, theaters, stadiums, concert halls, and other places of entertainment.

The Civil Rights Act also addressed the problem of employment discrimination. Again relying on the commerce power, it banned discrimination on the basis of race, religion, national origin, or sex by employers, labor unions, and employment agencies. To enforce the law, Congress created the Equal Employment Opportunity Commission (EEOC). Liberal Democrats wanted to empower the Commission to issue cease-and-desist orders against those it found guilty of discrimination. But Republicans, whose votes were necessary to pass the bill, objected, and the Commission received only limited enforcement powers.

The Civil Rights Act nevertheless had dramatic consequences. Although it by no means ended discrimination, the law was remarkably effective in opening public accommodations to African Ameri-

Students and local residents crowd and shout at African-American student Elizabeth Eckford as she tries to pass through the lines of National Guardsmen in an effort to gain entrance to Little Rock's Central High School, September 4, 1957. (UPI/Bettmann)

cans. It also destroyed the South's dual school system. The Department of Health, Education, and Welfare adopted guidelines requiring actual desegregation and threatened to cut off federal funds to school districts that failed to comply. Simultaneously, the Supreme Court ruled that school districts that had been segregated by law had an obligation to achieve integration, not merely to adopt nondiscriminatory attendance policies. Moreover, it indicated that the time for "deliberate speed" had ended, ordering school districts to adopt desegregation plans that "promise . . . to work, and promise . . . to work *now*." (*Green* v. *County School Board* [1968]) The guidelines, reinforced by *Green,* produced results, especially in towns and rural areas of the South. Despite the flight of many white pupils to segregated private schools, by 1972 southern schools were the most integrated in the nation.

In 1965, Congress struck at disfranchisement in the Voting Rights Act. Targeting the literacy test, the act

suspended any "test or device" as a prerequisite for voting in any state or county in which fewer than 50 percent of adults were registered. To prevent these jurisdictions from developing new measures to disfranchise African Americans, it required preclearance from the attorney general or a federal court in Washington, D.C., before they could change voting procedures. Only if measures had neither the intent nor effect of discriminating were they to be approved. The act also authorized the federal government to appoint officials to register voters in any county where there was substantial evidence of discrimination. Aggressively enforced by the Johnson administration, the act swept away the principal barriers to black voting in the South. In Mississippi, where only 7 percent of African-American adults had been registered to vote in 1964, black registration rose to 67 percent in 1969.

The 1960s also revived federal power to punish the perpetrators of racist violence. White southerners of-

Martin Luther King, Jr., being arrested in Montgomery, Ala., 1958. (© Charles Moore/Black Star)

ten attacked and even murdered black and white civil rights activists. State officials generally were unwilling to bring the perpetrators to justice. Reconstruction-era statutes still on the books authorized federal prosecution of persons who conspired to prevent anyone from exercising rights secured by the Constitution or laws of the United States. The state-action limitation on the Fourteenth Amendment, however, suggested that these measures did not reach private conspiracies to deny persons equal protection or due process. Nevertheless, in two 1966 rulings, *U.S.* v. *Price* and *U.S.* v. *Guest,* the Supreme Court upheld use of the Reconstruction statutes to prosecute private individuals charged with murdering civil rights workers. The rulings established Congress's authority to punish state and private action that threatened those rights that were secured by the Fourteenth Amendment. In 1968, Congress used this power to define federally protected rights more precisely and to authorized federal prosecution of persons who forcefully interfered with the exercise of these rights.

After 1965, the focus of the civil rights movement shifted from the South to northern cities, where segregated housing had become a principal concern. In the North, as in the South, custom, the policies of realtors and lending agencies, and threats of violence had created rigid residential segregation. Consequently, African Americans were forced into substandard but expensive housing in areas with inferior schools or inadequate public services. Residential segregation also created segregated schools. In 1968, Congress belatedly enacted a federal fair housing statute, expanding the range of federally protected civil rights, but the white backlash after the LOS ANGELES WATTS RIOT OF 1965 persuaded legislators to strip the bill of tough enforcement provisions. Consequently, it did little to alleviate the problem of housing discrimination.

The Post–Civil Rights Era

During the 1970s and '80s, activists built on the achievements of the 1960s, developing important legal tools to transform the promise of equality into reality. Their strategies moved beyond the early civil rights movement's goal of making law color-blind; now they sought color-conscious remedies to deal with the more subtle forms of discrimination that survived the demise of Jim Crow and to root out the consequences of the nation's long history of racism.

Residential segregation and the movement of whites to the suburbs meant that urban schools,

In 1962, reacting to opposition to James Meredith entering the University of Mississippi, which included recalcitrance by Gov. Ross Barnett and local rioting, President John F. Kennedy federalized the Mississippi National Guard. Meredith, accompanied by federal marshals, is escorted into the university. (Prints and Photographs Division, Library of Congress)

North and South, were highly segregated. In the cities, therefore, integration could only be achieved through busing children from minority neighborhoods to schools in white neighborhoods and vice versa. In *Swann* v. *Charlotte-Mecklenburg Board of Education* (1971), the Supreme Court endorsed the use of busing in districts that had been segregated by law and that therefore had an obligation to integrate. Although northern states had not imposed segregation by law, school officials in the North had often adopted policies consciously designed to segregate pupils. In 1973, the Court ruled that these policies amounted to state-imposed segregation and authorized the use of busing to achieve integration.

As busing spread to northern cities, opposition to it increased. In 1974, whites in South Boston responded to a court-ordered busing plan with violence, and the Senate defeated by one vote a measure that would have barred the federal courts from issuing busing orders. The Supreme Court placed tight restrictions on busing, ruling in *Milliken* v. *Bradley* (1974) that courts could not order transportation of students between a city and its suburbs unless the suburban district was guilty of policies that contributed to segregation. This dealt a crippling blow to efforts to achieve integration in most metropolitan areas, where city school districts were predominantly black and the surrounding suburban districts were largely white. By 1990, schools in large cities were more segregated than they had been in 1968.

Civil rights advocates were more successful in winning new remedies against discrimination in the workplace. In *Griggs* v. *Duke Power* (1971), the Supreme Court held that employers must show that requirements for employment which disproportionately exclude African Americans (e.g., a high school diploma or passing scores on standardized examinations) are actually job-related. The decision freed civil rights attorneys from proving intentional discrimination in these cases and removed a serious barrier to equal employment opportunity. In 1972, Congress strengthened the hand of EEOC, giving it authority to sue employers whom it found guilty of discrimination. Coupled with steady growth in the agency's budget, this strengthened the 1964 Civil Rights Act's ban on job discrimination. Moreover, in *Runyon* v. *McCrary* (1976), the Court ruled that persons denied employment because of their race could sue under the Civil Rights Act of 1866. Unlike the 1964 act, the Reconstruction-era law allowed plaintiffs monetary damages, giving aggrieved parties a powerful weapon against employers guilty of willful discrimination.

The 1970s also witnessed the expansion of AFFIRMATIVE ACTION programs designed to bring African Americans and women into positions historically closed to them. Developed in the late 1960s by the Labor Department to guarantee nondiscrimination by firms doing business with the federal government, affirmative action was incorporated into the EEOC's guidelines in the early 1970s. Affirmative action required employers to be conscious of the racial mix of their workforce and to take positive steps to include minorities by developing strategies for recruitment, setting goals for hiring, and establishing timetables to reach those goals. Affirmative action programs adopted by employers and universities generated a number of lawsuits charging that they amounted to "reverse discrimination" against white men and violated the Fourteenth Amendment and the Civil Rights Act of 1964.

The Supreme Court proved generally supportive of affirmative action. Although in *Regents of the University of California* v. *Bakke* (1978), the Court struck down a state medical school program which set aside a specified number of seats for minority applicants, it

Lyndon B. Johnson signs the Civil Rights Bill, April 11, 1968. (Prints and Photographs Division, Library of Congress)

emphasized that schools might take race into account in the admissions process in order to create a more diverse student body. The Court looked more favorably on voluntary affirmative action plans adopted by private employers. In *Weber* v. *United Steel Workers* (1979), it upheld a plan setting aside one-half of the places in a craft training program for African Americans, emphasizing that the plan involved no state action, was temporary, and had been adopted to redress a long history of discrimination. The Court also consistently upheld court-ordered affirmative action programs that established hiring quotas to redress long-standing, intentional discrimination. Even during the 1980s, as the administration of President Ronald Reagan urged the Court to repudiate affirmative action, the justices continued to accept voluntary affirmative action programs and to endorse judicially imposed hiring quotas as remedies for wanton discrimination.

The 1970s and '80s also witnessed a strengthening of the Voting Rights Act. The Supreme Court ruled that all changes in electoral laws that made it more difficult for African Americans to elect candidates of their choice—such as at-large elections—must be rejected. This blocked a widespread effort by whites to subvert the Voting Rights Act by manipulating elec-

toral procedures to minimize the number of black elected officials. Although this ruling applied only to newly adopted laws, Congress amended the act in 1982, prohibiting any electoral practice that reduced minorities' ability to elect representatives of their choice. Civil rights attorneys used the amended law effectively to attack existing at-large election schemes and to force state legislatures to create black-majority legislative and congressional districts. The result was a dramatic increase in the number of African-American elected officials. Black membership in Congress, for example, grew from six in 1965 to sixteen in 1975 to twenty in 1985 to thirty-nine in 1993.

As a decade of conservative appointments tilted the Court to the right, civil rights advocates encountered growing resistance from the Supreme Court at the end of the 1980s. In 1989, the Court substantially weakened the *Griggs* ruling of 1971, restricted the ability of victims of employment discrimination to sue under the Civil Rights Act of 1866, and challenged the finality of consent decrees (i.e., court orders enforcing agreements reached out of court by parties to a lawsuit) in job discrimination cases. Because these rulings were based on interpretations of federal statutes, Congress amended the relevant laws in the Civil Rights Act of 1991, thereby reversing the effect of the Court's decisions. Although the act merely served to protect earlier gains, it demonstrated the continued clout of civil rights advocates in the face of a hostile Court.

REFERENCES

BARDOLPH, RICHARD. *The Civil Rights Record: Black Americans and the Law, 1849–1970.* New York, 1970.

BELKNAP, MICHAEL R. *Federal Law and Southern Order: Racial Violence and Constitutional Violence in the Post-Brown South.* Athens, Ga., 1987.

BELL, DERRICK. *And We Are Not Saved: The Elusive Quest for Racial Justice.* New York, 1987.

BERRY, MARY FRANCES. *Black Resistance/White Law: A History of Constitutional Racism in America.* New York, 1971.

FEHRENBACHER, DON E. *The Dred Scott Case: Its Significance in American Law and Politics.* New York, 1978.

HYMAN, HAROLD M., and WILLIAM WIECEK. *Equal Justice Under Law: American Constitutional Development, 1835–1875.* New York, 1982.

KLUGER, RICHARD. *Simple Justice.* New York, 1975.

KOUSSER, J. MORGAN. *Dead End: The Development of Nineteenth-Century Litigation on Racial Discrimination in the Schools.* Oxford, U.K., 1986.

LAWSON, STEPHEN F. *In Pursuit of Power: Southern Blacks and Electoral Politics, 1965–1982.* New York, 1985.

LOFGREN, CHARLES. *The Plessy Case.* New York, 1987.

MCNEIL, GENNA RAE. *Groundwork: Charles Hamilton Houston and the Struggle for Civil Rights.* Philadelphia, 1983.

NIEMAN, DONALD G. *Promises to Keep: African-Americans and the Constitutional Order, 1776 to the Present.* New York, 1991.

WIECEK, WILLIAM. *The Sources of Antislavery Constitutionalism in America, 1760–1848.* Ithaca, N.Y., 1977.

DONALD G. NIEMAN

Civil Rights Movement.

The African-American civil rights movement has roots in the earliest resistance by blacks to their involuntary arrival in America and their unequal treatment. As slaves in America, blacks protested through work slowdowns and sabotage, escapes, and rebellions; while free blacks in the North opposed racial discrimination through petitions, litigation, and more aggressive nonviolent tactics such as boycotts from 1844 to 1855 that pressured Boston authorities to desegregate public schools.

The South, where slavery endured until 1865 and where at least 90 percent of black Americans lived until 1910, posed the crucial testing ground for civil rights activism. The newly freed slaves asserted their rights in ways ranging from participation in southern electoral politics, as voters and public officials, to nonviolent protests against segregated horsecars. These protests triumphed in New Orleans, Richmond, Va., and Charleston, S.C., in 1867, in Louisville in 1871 (all involving confrontations with passengers and police), and in Savannah, Ga., in 1872 (through a boycott that placed economic pressure on the traction company).

The rise of JIM CROW laws throughout the South beginning in the late nineteenth century triggered black resistance in every state of the former Confederacy; most of this resistance centered on boycotts of segregated streetcars. These protests postponed the spread of segregation in some cities, but ultimately they failed everywhere amid a surge of white racial violence and legal repression, including disfranchisement of most southern blacks by 1900. Black civil rights activity also succumbed to a national resurgence of racism, evident in the Supreme Court verdict in PLESSY V. FERGUSON (1896) that sustained a Louisiana segregation statute for affording blacks separate-but-equal facilities. The preeminent southern black spokesman, Booker T. WASHINGTON, accommodated these bleak trends by appealing to whites for economic toleration and racial peace while publicly renouncing agitation for social and political rights.

Because of the long odds and mortal risks facing black dissidents in the South, civil rights militance in the early twentieth century remained chiefly the province of northern blacks such as the Massachusetts natives William Monroe TROTTER and W. E. B. DU BOIS. In 1905 Du Bois began a movement in Niagara Falls, N.Y., to urge redress of racial injustices. Poorly attended and funded, the NIAGARA MOVEMENT lived four years in obscurity before dissolving into a new, interracial organization that formed in the wake of white racial rioting in Springfield, Ill., the city of Abraham Lincoln's youth. In 1910 the NAACP began its long crusade for racial equality, operating through the courts and the trenchant pen of Du Bois, the group's first black officer and the editor of a new journal for black rights, the *Crisis.*

In the 1915 case *Guinn* v. *United States,* attorneys for the NAACP persuaded a unanimous Supreme Court to declare unconstitutional the "grandfather clause," by which some states had disfranchised blacks through harsh registration tests while exempting citizens—almost invariably whites—whose grandfathers had voted. This ruling did not clearly exhaust the South's legal stratagems for denying blacks the ballot, but it encouraged the NAACP's reliance on the courts—the branch of government best insulated from political pressures—and on constitutional appeals for colorblind justice.

During the 1930s the NAACP sued for equal school facilities for blacks, in accord with the Supreme Court sanction of separate-but-equal treatment. In this way the NAACP secured the desegregation of all-white law or graduate schools in Maryland, Missouri, and other states unable to convince federal courts of an equal commitment to black and white students. The NAACP also beat down the formal exclusion of blacks from party primary elections in the South, through litigation culminating with the Supreme Court case *Smith* v. *Allright* in 1944.

Beginning in the 1930s elected officials received increasingly vigorous tutoring from the NAACP and other black groups on the need for protection of civil rights. Strong federal anti-lynching bills passed the House of Representatives in 1937 and again in 1940, though each time succumbing to southern filibusters in the Senate. In 1941 the black union leader A. Philip RANDOLPH planned a march on Washington to protest racial discrimination in the armed forces and defense industries. To persuade Randolph to call off the march, President Franklin Roosevelt in July 1941 created an advisory committee, the FAIR EMPLOYMENT PRACTICES COMMITTEE, to promote racial integration in munitions factories. A limited step, it was also the first presidential order for civil rights since RECONSTRUCTION—and the first intended chiefly to quiet an emerging black mass movement.

Civil rights activity quickened after the end of WORLD WAR II, in 1945, in an increasingly open society that could not easily justify segregation after years of propaganda denouncing Nazi Germany for its vicious racial policies. The registration of over two million blacks by the late 1940s, many of them migrants from the rural South to northern cities, further undermined the racial status quo. So did the growing numbers of religious, civil, labor, intellectual, and white minority leaders who termed racism a challenge to national democratic values. Their words gained added force from the competition between the United States and the Soviet Union for support from emerging nonwhite nations, which made evidence of American racism a damaging embarrassment.

In December 1946 President Harry Truman appointed a committee to investigate violations of black rights. Three months later he endorsed the resulting report, entitled "To Secure These Rights," which prescribed a comprehensive federal assault on Jim Crow. In 1948 Truman acceded to a strong civil rights plank that liberal delegates had inserted in the Democratic national platform. He then weathered

March on Washington, D.C., August 28, 1963. (© Fred Ward/Black Star)

defections by a minority of southern whites to win a second term, aided by 70 percent of the northern black vote. Two years later he began desegregation of the armed forces to heighten military efficiency for the KOREAN WAR and to quiet restive black leaders.

By the late 1940s the NAACP's chief legal counsel, Thurgood MARSHALL, felt emboldened to attack directly the principle of segregation in public education. In several cases before the Supreme Court, Marshall argued that segregation denied blacks "equal protection of the laws" as guaranteed by the Fourteenth Amendment to the Constitution. In 1954 Chief Justice Earl Warren wrote for a unanimous Court, in BROWN V. TOPEKA, KANSAS BOARD OF EDUCATION, that in the area of public education "the doctrine of 'separate but equal' has no place."

By threatening white supremacy the Brown case intensified southern resistance to civil rights progress. The KU KLUX KLAN and other fringe hate groups experienced overnight revivals, congressmen and governors vowed "massive resistance," and state district attorneys sought injunctions to ban NAACP branches (they were entirely successful in Alabama by 1957). In May 1955 the Supreme Court tempered its original ruling in *Brown* by requiring no timetable for school desegregation, only that school districts move "with all deliberate speed." Compliance proved minimal, and when President Dwight D. Eisenhower sent federal troops in 1957 to guard nine blacks attending a formerly all-white high school in Little Rock, Ark., the prolonged furor discouraged further national intervention for desegregation.

Despite its limited tangible impact, *Brown* did confer a symbol of legitimacy on black activists, who prepared bolder assaults on segregation in the South. In December 1955 blacks in Montgomery, Ala., organized a bus boycott after a former NAACP secretary, Rosa PARKS, was arrested for refusing to yield her seat on a segregated bus to a white man (*see* MONTGOMERY BUS BOYCOTT). The boycott leader was a twenty-six-year-old, northern-educated minister originally from Atlanta, the Rev. Dr. Martin Luther KING, Jr. King gained national attention for the protest against segregation by invoking Christian morality, American ideals of liberty, and the ethic of nonviolent resistance to evil exemplified by Mohandas Gandhi of India in his campaign against British colonial rule. Like Gandhi, King advocated confronting authorities with a readiness to suffer rather than inflict harm, in order to expose injustice and impel those in power to end it. In November 1956, despite growing white violence, the boycott triumphed with aid from the NAACP, which secured a Supreme Court decision (in *Gayle* v. *Browder*) that overturned Montgomery's laws enforcing bus segregation.

The signs of growing black restiveness in the South encouraged new civil rights initiatives. In January 1957 King organized the SOUTHERN CHRISTIAN LEADERSHIP CONFERENCE (SCLC), a network of nonviolent civil rights activists drawn mainly from the black church. In September of that year Congress passed the first Civil Rights Act since Reconstruction; the act created a commission to monitor civil rights violations and authorized the Justice Department to guard black voting rights through litigation against discriminatory registrars. This act (and a follow-up measure in April 1960) nonetheless failed to curb the widespread disfranchisement of southern blacks.

The failure to implement federal civil rights edicts increasingly spurred blacks to shift their struggle for

March on Washington, D.C., (left to right, interlocked hands) Whitney Young, Roy Wilkins, A. Philip Randolph, Walter Reuther. (Moorland-Spingarn Research Center, Howard University)

equality from the courts and cloakrooms to the streets. During the late 1950s blacks, often affiliated with local NAACP youth chapters, conducted scattered, short-lived SIT-INS at lunch counters that served whites only. On February 1, 1960, a sit-in by four students at the Woolworth's lunch counter in Greensboro, N.C., triggered a host of similar protests throughout the South, targeting Jim Crow public accommodations from theaters to swimming pools. Strict conformity to nonviolent Christian and Gandhian tenets characterized the demonstrators, many of whom courted arrest and even imprisonment in order to dramatize the evils of segregation (*see* SIT–INS).

In April 1960 several hundred student activists gathered in Raleigh, N.C., at the invitation of Ella BAKER, the executive director of the Southern Christian Leadership Conference. Baker urged the students to preserve their grass-roots militancy by remaining independent of established civil rights groups, and they responded by forming the STUDENT NONVIO-LENT COORDINATING COMMITTEE (SNCC, pronounced "snick") to promote Gandhian resistance to Jim Crow. By the summer of 1960 the sit-ins, which were often reinforced by boycotts of offending stores, had desegregated dozens of lunch counters and other public accommodations, mainly in southern border states.

Black protests intensified during the presidency of John F. Kennedy, a Democrat elected in 1960 with heavy black support. Kennedy early directed the Justice Department to step up litigation for black rights, but he avoided bolder commitments that he feared would trigger southern white racial violence and political retaliation. Civil rights leaders therefore increasingly designed campaigns to pressure their reluctant ally in the White House. In May 1961 James FARMER, who had cofounded the CONGRESS OF RA-CIAL EQUALITY (CORE) nearly two decades earlier, led fourteen white and black CORE volunteers on a freedom ride through the South, testing compliance with a Supreme Court order to desegregate interstate bus terminal facilities. White mobs abetted by police beat the riders in Birmingham, Ala., on May 14; six days later federal marshals saved the riders from a mob in Montgomery. As the freedom rides proliferated, Kennedy quietly persuaded southern communities to desegregate their bus terminals.

Although the Kennedy administration strove to balance the competing pressures of black activists and their southern white opponents, growing racial tensions impelled the president to take stronger civil rights initiatives. In October 1962 Kennedy sent federal marshals to protect a black student, James MER-EDITH, who had registered at the all-white University of Mississippi at Oxford. After mobs killed two

"The Selma March," 1965. Dr. Martin Luther King, Jr., and Coretta Scott King are accompanied by Bayard Rustin, A. Philip Randolph, Ralph Abernathy, and Ralph Bunche, among others. (Photographs and Prints Division, Schomburg Center for Research in Black Culture, The New York Public Library, Astor, Lenox and Tilden Foundations)

people at the campus and besieged the marshals, the president reluctantly troops to restore order.

Racial polarization worsened in 1963, as demonstrations throughout the South precipitated 15,000 arrests and widespread white violence. On May 3 and for several days afterward, police in Birmingham beat and unleashed attack dogs on nonviolent black followers of Dr. King, in full view of television news cameras. The resulting public revulsion spurred President Kennedy to address the nation on June 11, to confront a "moral issue" that was "as old as the Scriptures" and "as clear as the American Constitution." He urged Congress to enact a strong civil rights law that would allow race "no place in American life."

A coalition of African-American groups and their white allies sponsored a march on Washington on August 28, 1963, to advance the civil rights bill then before Congress. Reflecting the growing national stature of the civil rights movement, the rally secured the participation of diverse political, cultural, and religious figures. Standing before the Lincoln Memorial, Dr. King told several hundred thousand blacks and whites at this event of his "dream" for interracial brotherhood. Afterward President Kennedy praised the goals and peaceful character of the march.

When Lyndon B. Johnson succeeded to the presidency on November 22, 1963, he made passage of the civil rights bill his top priority and effectively linked this goal to the memory of the martyred President Kennedy. A broad-based federation called the Leadership Conference on Civil Rights coordinated the lobbying efforts of over a hundred groups on behalf of the legislation, centered on extraordinary activity by Protestant, Catholic, and Jewish ministers. On July 2, 1964, Johnson signed the omnibus Civil Rights Act, which barred segregation in public accommodations, ended federal aid to segregated institutions, outlawed racial discrimination in employment, sought to strengthen black voting rights, and extended the life of the UNITED STATES COMMISSION ON CIVIL RIGHTS (see also CIVIL RIGHTS AND THE LAW).

SNCC remained in the vanguard of civil rights activism in 1964 by organizing rural blacks in Mississippi, a state whose history was pockmarked with the casual shootings of black people. About a thousand college students, most of them white, volunteered for the FREEDOM SUMMER project to further the nonviolent, integrationist ideals of the civil rights movement. The project workers set up "Freedom Schools" to give black children a positive sense of their history and identity, and an interracial party, the "Freedom Democrats," to give otherwise disfranchised blacks a political voice. The project also exposed the extreme dangers daily facing civil rights workers, after a federal manhunt recovered the bodies of three volunteers—Michael Schwerner, Andrew Goodman, and James CHANEY (see also CHANEY, SCHWERNER, GOODMAN)—who had been murdered by a mob led by the deputy sheriff of Philadelphia, Miss. In late August the project workers helped the Freedom Democrats try to unseat Mississippi's lily-white delegation at the Democratic national convention. Despite considerable northern support, their challenge failed because of strong resistance by President Johnson, who feared the loss of southern white voters in an election year. This harsh coda to the Freedom Summer spurred younger black activists to question the wisdom of alliances with white liberals and to stress instead the importance of black solidarity.

The fraying civil rights coalition rallied in 1965 behind Dr. King's campaign in Selma, Ala., for equal voting rights. On March 7 black marchers setting out from Selma toward Montgomery suffered assaults by state and local police. The televised scenes of violence galvanized national support for protection of blacks seeking the ballot, a view that President Johnson reinforced in a special appearance before Congress on March 15. Ten days later twenty-five thousand black and white marchers reached Montgomery escorted by federal troops. On August 6, 1965, Johnson signed a strong VOTING RIGHTS ACT, which authorized the attorney general to send federal examiners to supersede local registrars and regulations wherever discrimination occurred. The act also directed the attorney general to challenge poll taxes for state and local elections in the courts (the Twenty-fourth Amendment to the Constitution, adopted in 1964, had already banned such taxes in national elections).

After 1965 the civil rights movement fragmented in the absence of an overriding goal to unify and inspire it. During a march with King through Mississippi in June 1966, SNCC's Stokely CARMICHAEL ridiculed faith in nonviolence and white good will and demanded "black power," a militant slogan that alienated white liberals and divided blacks. As the focus of the civil rights movement increasingly turned from de jure segregation, to economic inequality and patterns of de facto segregation in the North, agreement on a strategy for addressing and solving these problems became more elusive. Ghetto riots, including a six-day rampage in South Central Los Angeles (Watts—see LOS ANGELES, WATTS RIOT) in August 1965, further split the movement by harming its nonviolent image and by shifting its focus from constitutional rights to problems of slum housing and poverty, for which no reform consensus existed. On April 4, 1968, the assassination of King in Memphis, Tenn., touched off riots that left Washington, D.C., in flames for three days. The following week, partly in tribute to the slain King, Congress passed the Civil Rights Act of 1968, which banned discrimination in the sale and rental of most housing.

The 1970s witnessed the emergence of expressly race-conscious government programs to redress the legacy of racial discrimination. In the 1971 case *Swann* v. *Charlotte-Mecklenburg* the Supreme Court acknowledged the failures of earlier approaches to school desegregation by sanctioning the busing of children to other neighborhoods as a tool to achieve racial balance. The federal government also promoted AFFIRMATIVE ACTION to afford blacks (and, increasingly, other minorities and women) preference in school admissions and employment. These developments reflected the limitations of civil rights legislation in affording access to the economic mainstream; but they provoked fierce opposition. Violence in Boston and other cities over racial busing confirmed that the race problem was truly national rather than southern. And in *Regents of University of California* v. *Bakke* in 1978 the Supreme Court reflected the national acrimony over affirmative action by ruling five to four to strike down racial quotas in medical school admissions while allowing (by an equally slim margin) some race-conscious selection to achieve educational "diversity."

During the 1980s a conservative shift in national politics frustrated civil rights leaders, especially in the NAACP and the Urban League, who relied on federal activism to overcome state, municipal, and private acts of discrimination. Ronald Reagan, a Republican who won the presidency for the first of two terms in 1980, sought to trim federal authority in racial matters. From 1981 to 1985 his administration reduced the number of lawyers in the Justice Department's Civil Rights Division from 210 to 57, and also vainly attempted to disband altogether the United States Commission on Civil Rights. On January 8, 1982, Reagan restored the federal tax exemptions for segregated private schools that had been ended in 1970. The following year the Supreme Court, by an eight-to-one vote, overturned this ruling as a violation of the Civil Rights Act of 1964; in 1986 Reagan appointed the lone dissenter, William Rehnquist, to be Chief Justice of the Supreme Court.

The Rehnquist Court increasingly chipped away at government safeguards of black rights, a pattern evident from several employment discrimination cases in 1989: in *Patterson* v. *McLean Credit Union* the Court ruled that the Civil Rights Act of 1866 protected blacks merely in contracting for jobs but did not protect them from racial harassment by employers; in *Wards Cove Packing Co.* v. *Atonio* the Court shifted the burden of proof from employers to employees regarding job discrimination; in *City of Richmond* v. *J. A. Croson Co.* the Court rejected a program setting aside 30 percent of city contracts for minority businesses in the absence of flagrant evidence of discrimination, although Richmond had a history of official segregation and although minority contractors held fewer than 1 percent of the city contracts in Richmond, where minorities constituted half the population; in *Price Waterhouse* v. *Hopkins* the Court exonerated an employer who had committed acts of racial discrimination but who also cited other, legitimate reasons for such actions. In October 1990 the Republican president, George Bush, vetoed a civil rights bill that expressly restored the earlier, tougher curbs on job discrimination, and the Senate sustained his veto by a single vote. In November 1991, President Bush signed a milder version of this same bill while restating his opposition to quotas to promote minority hiring.

The central goal of the civil rights movement—full equality between blacks and whites—remains a distant vision. Residential segregation, seen in the persistence of inner-city black ghettos and lily-white suburbs, has easily survived federal open-housing statutes (*see* HOUSING DISCRIMINATION). De facto segregation of churches, social centers, and private schools also remains routine; and wealth, too, is largely segregated along racial lines, with the median family income of blacks in 1990 barely three-fifths that of whites, and with blacks three times as likely to be poor. Many civil rights leaders have urged comprehensive government remedies; but black political power remains limited with regard to national office holding and access to the circles that make foreign and domestic policy.

Despite its limitations, the civil rights movement has in key respects transformed American race relations. In communities throughout the South during the 1960s, "whites only" signs that had stood for generations suddenly came down from hotels, rest rooms, theaters, and other facilities. School desegregation by the mid-1970s had become fact as well as law in over 80 percent of all southern public schools (a better record than in the North, where residential segregation remains pronounced). The federal government has also vigorously checked groups promoting racial hatred: Beginning in 1964 the FBI infiltrated the Ku Klux Klan so thoroughly that by 1965 perhaps one in five members was an informant; federal indictments and encouragement of private lawsuits helped reduce Klan membership from 10,000 in 1981 to less than 5,500 in 1987.

Protection of the suffrage represents the civil rights movement's greatest success: When Congress passed the Voting Rights Act in 1965 barely 100 blacks held elective office in the country; by 1989 there were more than 7,200, including 24 congressional representatives and some 300 mayors. Over 4,800 of these officials served in the South, and nearly every Black

Belt county in Alabama had a black sheriff. Mississippi, long the most racially repressive state, experienced the most dramatic change, registering 74 percent of its voting-age blacks and leading the nation in the number of elected officials (646). The unexpectedly strong showing by the Reverend Jesse JACKSON in seeking the Democratic presidential nomination in 1984 and 1988 reflected the growing participation by blacks in mainstream politics.

Having leveled the formal barriers of a legal caste system during the early 1960s, the civil rights movement has since expanded its aims to include substantive equality of opportunity in all areas of American life. The NAACP and the Urban League have for decades urged federal measures to reconstruct the inner cities, create jobs, extend job training to all poor Americans, and strengthen affirmative action to help minorities overcome a legacy of exclusion. Beginning in the 1980s, however, a growing minority of blacks have gained national influence (highlighted by the appointment of Clarence Thomas to the Supreme Court in 1991) by emphasizing private rather than government initiatives and by deploring quotas and other race-conscious programs as politically divisive. The movement for racial equality is now struggling to forge a program that can both unify black activists and also capture the nation's moral high ground and its reform impulses as convincingly as earlier civil rights campaigns.

REFERENCES

HOWELL, RAINES, ed. *My Soul Is Rested: Movement Days in the Deep South Remembered.* New York, 1983.

KLUGER, RICHARD. *Simple Justice.* New York, 1977.

SELLERS, CLEVELAND, with Robert Terrell. *The River of No Return: The Autobiography of a Black Militant and the Life and Death of SNCC.* New York, 1973.

SITKOFF, HARVARD. *The Struggle for Black Equality, 1954–1980.* New York, 1981.

WEISBROT, ROBERT. *Freedom Bound: A History of America's Civil Rights Movement.* New York, 1991.

WILLIAMS, JUAN, with the "Eyes on the Prize" Production Team. *Eyes on the Prize: America's Civil Rights Years, 1954–1965.* New York, 1987.

ROBERT WEISBROT

Civil War. On April 12, 1864, three years to the day after the Civil War began with the firing on Fort Sumter in Charleston harbor, George W. Hatton, a former slave who had risen to the rank of sergeant in Company C, First Regiment, United States Colored Troops, encamped near New Bern, N.C., sat down to write a letter and reflect upon the circumstance in which he found himself. Hatton, his fellow soldiers, and their families had lived generations as slaves in the American South. Now they were part of a liberating army and serving a government that, through a combination of intent and necessity, waged total war on the South in order to destroy SLAVERY. Hatton struggled to find the right words for his sentiments. "Though the Government openly declared that it did not want the Negroes in this conflict," he wrote, "I look around me and see hundreds of colored men armed and ready to defend the Government at any moment; and such are my feelings, that I can only say, the fetters have fallen—our bondage is over."

A month later, Hatton's regiment was encamped close to Jamestown, Va., when several African-American freedwomen entered their lines showing evidence that they had been severely whipped. Members of Hatton's company managed to capture "a Mr. Clayton," the man who had allegedly administered the beatings. The white Virginian was stripped to the waist, tied to a tree, and given twenty lashes by one of his own former slaves, a William Harris, now a member of the Union army. In turn, each of the women Clayton had beaten was given her chance to lay the lash on the slaveholder's back. The women were given leave to, in Sgt. Hatton's words, "remind him that they were no longer his, but safely housed in Abraham's bosom, and under the protection of the Star Spangled Banner, and guarded by their own patriotic, though once down-trodden race." Again Hatton felt almost lost for words to describe the transformations he witnessed. "Oh that I had the tongue to express my feelings," he declared, "while standing on the banks of the James River, on the soil of Virginia, the mother state of slavery, as a witness of such a sudden reverse! The day is clear, the fields of grain are beautiful, and the birds are singing sweet melodious songs, while poor Mr. C. is crying to his servants for mercy."

Such acts of violent retribution by ex-slaves against their former masters were rare in the wake of Emancipation. Most freedpeople simply sought a portion of land, freedom of movement, and security for their families in circumstances of hardship and uncertainty. But Hatton's eloquence allows us to see many elements in the meaning of the Civil War in African-American history. It was the extraordinary time when blacks, free and ex-slave alike, came to identify their own fate closely with the fate of the Union—the United States "Government" (blacks frequently capitalized the word as Hatton did) and its military and political fortunes. Because the war to save the Union became the war to free the slaves, and because so many southern blacks liberated themselves when the opportunity came, many thousands serving as soldiers and sailors in Union uniforms, the Civil War and black Emancipation became inextricable parts of the same epic event. Because the sectional balance of political and economic power was fundamentally altered for a century in great part out of the destruction of slavery, and because, simply put, the terrible conflict would not have happened were it not for the presence of over four million slaves and the array of contradictions they caused for the meaning of America, the Civil War may rightly be considered, as many historians now consider it, the "Second American Revolution."

The drama of Emancipation—four million people liberated from chattel slavery in the midst of the world's first total war—is all the more striking because for black leaders the 1850s had been a decade of discouragement and division combined with unpredictable political crisis. Some black abolitionists like Martin DELANY, Henry Highland GARNET, and Mary Ann Shadd struggled to organize emigration plans by which free blacks could start life over again in Africa, the Caribbean, or Canada. Most antebellum free blacks living in the North (a quarter million in the 1850s) followed the lead of Frederick DOUGLASS, James McCune SMITH, or Sojourner TRUTH, who insisted that the future for African Americans lay in America. This was not an easy position to sustain by the late 1850s, especially in the wake of the DRED SCOTT DECISION in 1857, wherein Chief Justice of the U.S. Supreme Court Roger B. Taney proclaimed that blacks were "beings of an inferior order . . . so far inferior, that they had no rights which the white man was bound to respect." But black and white abolitionists condemned such ideas, and hope could also be found in the mounting sectional conflict over the expansion of slavery into the West, and in the new antislavery REPUBLICAN PARTY to which it gave birth. Blacks welcomed the news of JOHN BROWN'S RAID on Harpers Ferry in 1859; some had actively participated in the ill-planned and ill-fated raid on a federal arsenal in northern Virginia. Plotting slave insurrections, however, had always been easier in theory than in practice, as many fugitive slaves in the North knew from experience. Larger hopes rested in the idea that somehow the conflict between North and South would boil into disunion and political confrontation sufficient enough to cause the federal government to move, militarily and legally, against slavery.

So, after the election of Abraham Lincoln in 1860, the secession crisis the following winter, and the outbreak of war in the spring of 1861, African Americans could take heart that the longed-for "jubilee" of black freedom that they had sung and written about for years might now happen. Although prophecy and reality would not meet easily, nor without ghastly bloodshed, most would have agreed with Douglass's

editorial of March 1861. "The contest must now be decided, and decided forever," he wrote, "which of the two, Freedom or Slavery, shall give law to this Republic. Let the conflict come." In a few short years and through untold suffering, the rest of the American people, with differing degrees of satisfaction or resistance, would be forced to see in the war the same meaning that Douglass proclaimed. In the wake of the outbreak of war, Douglass captured the anxiety and the hopes of his people as well as their antislavery friends: "For this consummation we have watched and wished with fear and trembling. God be praised! that it has come at last."

Black responses to the outbreak of war ranged from an ecstatic willingness to serve to caution and resistance. Across the North, free black communities sent petitions to state legislatures, organized militia companies, and wrote to the secretary of war offering their services on the battlefield. Only two days after President Lincoln's call for volunteers, the Twelfth Baptist Church in Boston hosted a meeting that the abolitionist William Wells BROWN called "crowded as I had never seen a meeting before." In one resolution after another, these black Bostonians declared their support. "Our feelings urge us to say to our countrymen," they announced, "that we are ready to stand by and defend the Government with our lives, our fortunes, and our sacred honor." From Pittsburgh came the offer of a black militia company called the "Hannibal Guards," who insisted on being considered "American citizens." Although "deprived of all our political rights," this group of eager soldiers understood the moment as a historic main chance: They wished "the government of the United States sustained against the tyranny of slavery." From Philadelphia came the news that the sizable black population of that city would raise two full regiments of infantry. In New York City, blacks rented a hall to hold meetings and drill their own militia in preparation for service. In Albany, Ohio, a militia company organized, calling itself the "Attucks Guards" and flying a handmade flag presented by the black women of the town. In Detroit a full black military band under the command of a Capt. O. C. Wood sought to enlist. And from Battle Creek, Mich., a black physician, G. P. Miller, wrote to the War Department asking for the privilege of "raising from 5,000 to 10,000 freemen to report in sixty days to take any position that may be assigned to us (sharpshooters preferred)."

But as promptly as blacks volunteered, their services were denied during the first year of the war. Most states explicitly prohibited black participation in their militias. The policy of the federal government reflected widespread white public opinion: that the war was for the restoration of the Union and not the destruction of slavery. On a deeper level, most white Northerners held the view that "this is a white man's war," as the police in Cincinnati told a large gathering of blacks attempting to find a hall in which to hold their patriotic meetings. Amid this fear, confusion, and bravado, the deep-seated racism of the mid–nineteenth century prevailed as the United States Congress and the War Department made it federal policy to deny enlistment to black soldiers. All of this occurred amid widespead assumptions in the North that secession and rebellion would be easily put down in one summer. But underneath all such social currents rested the fear that white men simply would not shoulder muskets next to black men. Soon, a tragically divided people would be forced to see how historical forces had been unleashed that would compel them to act both because of and above their prejudices.

A vigorous debate about support for the war ensued among blacks during the first year of the conflict. Stung by the rejection of their early enthusiasm for enlistment, some blacks turned away in anger, declaring—as did a man in Troy, N.Y.—that "we of the North must have all the rights which white men enjoy; until then we are in no condition to fight under the flag which gives us no protection." An "R.H.V." from New York City was even more explicit in opposing black participation. "No regiments of black troops," he said, "should leave their bodies to rot upon the battle-field beneath a Southern sun, to conquer a peace based upon the perpetuity of human bondage." Black newspaper editors divided over the issue. The *Anglo-African* (New York) vehemently urged support for the war as a crusade against the slaveholding South, and therefore in blacks' long-term interests. Frederick Douglass, in his *Douglass Monthly* (Rochester, N.Y.), demanded black enlistment from the first sounds of war. The exclusion policy angered him deeply, and by September 1861, he attacked the Lincoln administration's "spectacle of blind, unreasoning prejudice," accusing it of fighting with its "white hand" while allowing its "black hand to remain tied." The *Christian Recorder,* the African Methodist Episcopal Church newspaper in Philadelphia, dissented from Douglass's call for troops. "To offer ourselves now," wrote its editor Elisha Weaver, "is to abandon self-respect and invite insult." Blacks should not fight, said Weaver, in a war where "not only our citizenship, but our common humanity is denied." The war was not yet the social revolution it would become; and no black leader could see the end from the beginning.

In the South, the bulk of African Americans found themselves living in the Confederate States of America, a hastily created nation mobilizing for war on a scale no one had imagined, determined to preserve slavery as the basis of its socioeconomic system, and soon under siege and invasion. All of these circumstances made for what would eventually become—especially when the Yankee armies came in large numbers to Virginia, the coast of the Carolinas, the Mississippi River Valley, and the Tennessee-Georgia region—a mass exodus of both military and self-emancipation from 1862 to 1865 (*see* EMANCIPATION). But at the outset of the war, motivated by local pride, protection of the home place, or fear of reprisal, some southern blacks actually offered their services to the Confederate armies. Two Louisiana regiments of blacks were enlisted in 1861, but were never allowed to serve in active duty.

In March 1861, in a speech in Savannah, Ga., Vice President of the Confederacy Alexander H. Stevens stated, at least implicitly, what all Southerners would come to know—that it was black Southerners who might have the most at stake in this war. Comparing the Confederacy to the federal government created in 1787, Stevens declared that the South's move for independence "is founded upon exactly the opposite ideas; its foundations are laid, its cornerstone rests, upon the great truth that the Negro is not equal to the white man; subordination to the superior race is his natural and moral condition." Stevens knew, as did the masses of slaves anticipating "de Kingdom comin' an' de year ob Jubilo," that the status of slavery was central to the war. Before it was over in 1865, that founding Constitution of 1787 would undergo the beginnings of a process of fundamental change.

One of the few economic strengths in the Confederacy's war-making capacity was its huge supply of black labor. Tens of thousands of slaves were pressed into service to build fortifications and to work as teamsters, cooks, boatmen, blacksmiths, laundresses, and nurses. Slaves had long performed these tasks in the South; so, as the massive mobilization took place all across the Confederacy, black forced labor became one of the primary means by which the South waged war. Blacks were "hired out" by their owners to work in ordnance factories, armories, hospitals, and many other sites of military production and transport. In Georgia alone, an estimated ten thousand blacks worked on Confederate defenses. In some twenty-nine hospitals across northern Georgia in 1863, blacks comprised 80 percent (nearly one thousand people) of the workers, especially the nurses, cooks, and laundresses. Early in the war many slaveholders were quite willing to offer the labor of their slaves to the South's cause. But as the conflict endured, and the displacement of people became ever more chaotic, many owners began to transfer (or, as this process became known, "refugee") their slaves to the interior.

Huge numbers of slaves were set in motion by these removals. Many blacks experienced separation of families as men were forced into Confederate labor gangs and women and children were often left to their own devices back on the home place, or themselves were eventually caught up in refugee movement in the face of advancing Union armies. But especially for males, this social flux, however great the hardship, provided enormous opportunity for escape to Union lines. Especially in the upper South and along the coasts, but eventually in the South's heartland as well, many slaves would find freedom by slipping away from Confederate railroad crews or joining Union forces after decisive battles.

Indeed, thousands of blacks were "employed" (not always with compensation) as military laborers on the Union side as well. Wherever Union forces advanced into the South, so important were blacks as foragers, wagon masters, construction workers for fortifications and bridges, and cooks and camp hands that a visitor to any Yankee army camp would see hundreds and sometimes thousands of black faces. Ex-slaves who were familiar with the southern countryside also served numerous Union officers as spies and sources of military intelligence. Harriet TUBMAN, famous for her earlier career as a "conductor" on the UNDERGROUND RAILROAD, was one of the countless blacks who served the Union cause as guides and spies. She was formally commended by the secretary of war and at least five high-ranking Union officers for her two years' work in the Sea Islands as a nurse and a daring scout.

Driven by human will and military necessity, an enormous exodus of liberation ensued throughout the first three years of the war. The black Union soldier and later historian George Washington WILLIAMS observed both motivations. "Whenever a Negro appeared with a shovel in his hands," wrote Williams, "a white soldier took his gun and returned to the ranks." "It was an exodus whose Moses was multiple," wrote historian Benjamin QUARLES, "an Odyssey whose Ulysses was legion."

Nothing so typified the eventual antislavery character of the Civil War as the black soldier in Union blue. As the war dragged on, events moved so quickly that Emancipation and black enlistment became inseparable realities. From the first designation of fugitive slaves as "contrabands" (confiscated property of war) in 1861, abolitionists demanded that blacks be recruited as soldiers. The initial exclusion policy proved untenable in the face of total war, and by 1862, due to mounting white casualties, northern public opinion was increasingly favorable to the employment of black troops. That sentiment grew even stronger in the spring of 1863, when the federal government instituted a much-despised conscription law.

Harriet Tubman. (Prints and Photographs Division, Library of Congress)

In the wake of the bloody and unsuccessful Peninsular campaign in July 1862, Congress enacted the Second Confiscation Act, empowering Lincoln to "employ . . . persons of African descent . . . for the suppression of the rebellion." Under vague authority, initial black regiments had already been organized by zealous Union commanders in Louisiana and Kansas. But by August 1862, the War Department authorized the recruitment of five regiments of black infantry in the Sea Islands of South Carolina and Georgia. By Thanksgiving Day, Thomas Wentworth Higginson, the commander of the FIRST SOUTH CAROLINA VOLUNTEERS (the first regiment of ex-slaves), looked out of the broken windows of an abandoned plantation house in the Sea Islands, "through avenues of great live oaks," and observed that "all this is the universal Southern panorama; but five minutes walk beyond the hovels and the live oaks will bring one to something so un-Southern that the whole Southern coast at this moment trembles at the suggestion of such a thing—the camp of a regiment of freed slaves."

Following Lincoln's Emancipation Proclamation in January 1863, the governors of Massachusetts, Connecticut, and Rhode Island were authorized to

Escaped slaves, known as contrabands, played a vital role in undermining the economy of the Confederacy. The contrabands photographed here were at Yorktown, Va., in 1862. (Prints and Photographs Division, Library of Congress)

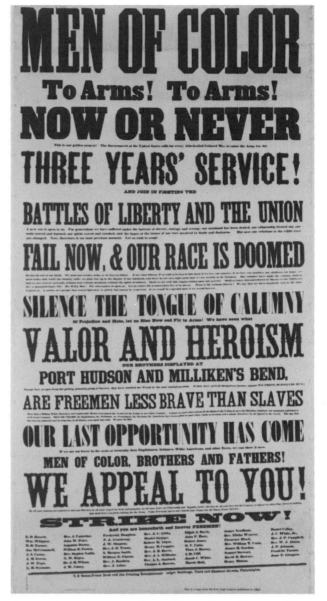

A recruitment poster for African-American soldiers during the Civil War. Of the 178,000 black soldiers that fought for the Union during the war, over 80 percent came from the slave states. (Photographs and Prints Division, Schomburg Center for Research in Black Culture, The New York Public Library, Astor, Lenox and Tilden Foundations)

raise black regiments. Gov. John Andrew of Massachusetts had been especially instrumental in convincing the Lincoln administration to make such moves. Abolitionist George L. Stearns was commissioned to organize black recruiters, and by April black abolitionists such as Douglass, Martin Delany, Henry Highland Garnet, John Mercer LANGSTON, William Wells Brown, Charles Lenox REMOND, and O. S. B. Wall were enlisting young free blacks from across the North and sending them to Readville, Mass., where they became part of the FIFTY-FOURTH MASSACHUSETTS COLORED REGIMENT. That spring, as a recruiting document, Douglass published his "Men of Color to Arms!," a pamphlet that captured the revolutionary character of the war now imagined in black communities. "I urge you to fly to arms and smite with death the power that would bury the government and your liberty in the same hopeless grave," Douglass demanded of young recruits, of whom his own first two were his sons Lewis and Charles.

The Fifty-fourth Massachusetts became the famous test case of what the northern press still viewed as the experiment with black troops. Its valorous assault on Fort Wagner on the sands around Charleston harbor in South Carolina, July 18, 1863, where the regiment suffered 100 dead or missing and 146 wounded, served as a tragic but immensely symbolic demonstration of black courage (*see* FORT WAGNER, BATTLE OF). Indeed, many white Northerners, as well as Confederate soldiers, discovered that black men would and could fight. Blacks who served in the

Union army and navy during the Civil War fought for many reasons. They fought for the simplest and deepest of causes: their own freedom and that of their families. They fought because events had seemed to provide an opening to a new future, to the achievement of the birthright of *citizenship* through military service. They also fought for the right to fight, for a sense of human dignity. They fought because they lived in a world that so often defined "manhood" as that recognition gained by the act of soldiering.

Sergeant W. H. Carney of the 54th Massachusetts Volunteers. (Photographs and Prints Division, Schomburg Center for Research in Black Culture, The New York Public Library, Astor, Lenox and Tilden Foundations)

In May 1863 the War Department established the Bureau of Colored Troops, and from then until the end of the war, quartermasters and recruiting agents labored competitively to maximize the number of black soldiers throughout the South. The manpower needs of the Union armies were endless, and black enlistment became the most direct way to undermine and destroy slavery. By the end of the war in April 1865, the nearly 180,000 blacks in the Union forces included 33,000 from the northern free states. The border slaveholding states of Delaware, Maryland, Missouri, and Kentucky provided a total of 42,000, half that number from Kentucky alone. Tennessee sent 20,000; Louisiana, 24,000; Mississippi, nearly 18,000; and the remaining states of the Confederacy, almost 40,000. These statistics demonstrate that Emancipation and black enlistment became twin functions of the Union war effort. Wherever northern armies arrived first and stayed the longest, there the greatest numbers of black men became Yankee soldiers.

In desperation, some slaveholders offered wages and other privileges in order to induce their slaves to stay. As the war dragged on, some black men eagerly enlisted with the Union, but others were forced into service by impressment gangs—sometimes composed of black soldiers—as a means of filling the ranks. Like their white comrades, black soldiers suffered untold hardships. But they sometimes received inadequate medical care compared with white troops, faced possible re-enslavement or execution if captured, and encountered several overt forms of discrimination within the Union ranks. Virtually all commissioned officers in black units were white, and though promises had been made to the contrary during the early recruiting period, the federal government capitulated to racism with an explicitly unequal pay system for black soldiers. White privates in the Union army received $13 per month plus $3 for clothing, while black men received only $7 plus clothing. As a matter of both principle and dire hardship for their families, the unequal pay issue angered black soldiers and recruiters more than any other form of discrimination. During 1863 many black regiments resisted the policy, refusing to accept any pay until it was equalized. Open revolt resulted in at least one regiment, the Third South Carolina Volunteers, being led by black sergeant William Walker. Walker led his company in stacking their arms at their commanding officer's tent in protest of unequal pay. After a lengthy court-martial, Walker was convicted of mutiny, and in February 1864 he was executed by a firing squad before the audience of his own brigade. The strictures of military law, mixed with racism, made war in this instance an extremely unforgiving business.

Black families, especially women, suffered not only the dislocations of war, but tremendous physical and financial hardship as well. Many, like Rachel Ann Wicker of Piqua, Ohio, wrote in protest to governors and President Lincoln. In September 1864, Wicker informed Governor Andrew of Massachusetts (her husband was in the Fifty-fifth Massachusetts) that "i speak for myself and Mother and i know of a great many others as well as ourselve are suffering for the want of money to live on." She demanded that Andrew explain "why it is that you Still insist upon them taking 7 dollars a month when you give the Poorest White Regiment that has went out 16 dollars." Under pressure from such women, from black communities, abolitionists, and governors, Congress enacted equal pay for blacks and whites in June 1864.

In spite of ill treatment, black soldiers—motivated by their own sense of freedom, feeling a sense of dignity that perhaps only military life could offer, and politicized as never before—participated in some 39 major battles and 410 minor engagements during the last two years of the war. Many vocal white critics were silenced when black units fought heroically

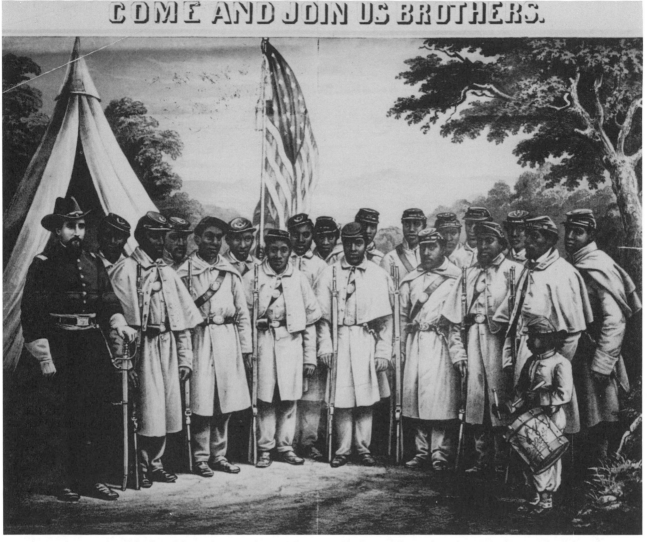

COME AND JOIN US BROTHERS.

Poster used to recruit black soldiers during the Civil War. (Photographs and Prints Division, Schomburg Center for Research in Black Culture, The New York Public Library, Astor, Lenox and Tilden Foundations)

and suffered terrible casualties in such battles as Port Hudson, La., in May 1863; Milliken's Bend in June 1863; Fort Wagner the next month; and various stages during the siege of Petersburg, Va., in 1864. Sometimes Confederate troops gave no quarter to their captured black opponents. At FORT PILLOW, TENNESSEE, in April 1864, Confederate general Nathan Bedford Forrest gave orders that led to the massacre of at least 200 black soldiers. In all, nearly 3,000 blacks died in battle during the Civil War, and another staggering 33,000 died of disease. Again and again, many of the white officers who led black units testified to the courage and devotion of their men. Higginson declared that he never had to "teach the principles of courage" to his regiment of freed slaves. And he especially marveled at one of his black sergeants, Prince Rivers, who had been a "crack coachman" in Beaufort, S.C., before Emancipation.

"There is not a white officer in this regiment," wrote Higginson, "who has more administrative ability, or more absolute authority over the men; they do not love him, but his mere presence has controlling power over them. He writes well enough . . . if his education reached a higher point, I see no reason why he should not command the Army of the Potomac." By the time Abraham Lincoln spoke of a "new birth" of freedom at Gettysburg in November 1863, and called Emancipation the "result so fundamental and astounding" in his second inaugural address in March 1865, there was no better symbol emerging of that regeneration than the anguished sacrifices of black soldiers and their families in the crusade for their own freedom.

With the passage of the THIRTEENTH AMENDMENT in February 1865, slavery was legally abolished in America; the institution from which all blacks had been forced to derive social identity had been de-

Christian Fleetwood, sergeant of the 4th S. Colored Troops, received the Congressional Medal of Honor for action at Chapin's Farm on September 29, 1864, near Richmond, Va. Sixteen other African-American soldiers were awarded this honor for bravery during the Civil War. (Prints and Photographs Division, Library of Congress)

welcomed them in what the black newspaper correspondent T. Morris Chester called "a spectacle of jubilee." Jubilant black folk also welcomed Lincoln when he visited Richmond on April 4, only two days after Confederate evacuation. There was "no describing the scene along the route," reported Chester. "The colored population was wild with enthusiasm." There were whites in the crowd, but "they were lost in the great concourse of American citizens of African descent." To the black soldiers, many of whom were recently slaves, as well as to the masses of freedpeople, such a revolutionary transformation, such an apocalyptic moment, could only be the work of God in union with his people. Garland H. White, a former Virginia slave who had escaped to Ohio before the war, now marched into Richmond as the chaplain of the Twenty-eighth United States Colored Troops. After making a triumphant speech "amid the shouts of ten thousand voices" on Broad Street, White, overcome by joyful tears, wandered the streets of Richmond, where later that day he found his mother, whom he had not seen in twenty years. Even more telling, though, was the liberation of Richmond's remaining slave pens and auction rooms. As the black troops approached the abandoned "Lumpkin's Jail" (owned by the notorious slave trader Robert Lumpkin), the prisoners behind the barred windows began to chant:

> Slavery chain done broke at last!
> Broke at last! Broke at last!
> Slavery chain done broke at last!
> Gonna praise God till I die!
>
> Now no more weary trav'lin',
> 'Cause my Jesus set me free,
> An' there's no more auction block for me
> Since he give me liberty.

REFERENCES

BERLIN, IRA, et al., eds. *Freedom: A Documentary History of Emancipation, 1861–1867.* Series 2, *The Black Military Experience.* New York, 1983.

BLIGHT, DAVID W. *Frederick Douglass' Civil War: Keeping Faith in Jubilee.* Baton Rouge, La., 1989.

LITWACK, LEON F. *Been in the Storm So Long: The Aftermath of Slavery.* New York, 1979.

MCPHERSON, JAMES M. *The Negro's Civil War: How American Negroes Felt and Acted during the War for the Union.* New York, 1965.

QUARLES, BENJAMIN. *The Negro in the Civil War.* New York, 1953.

DAVID W. BLIGHT

stroyed. For blacks the ending of the Civil War was a season of great hope and anxiety. Freedom, and at least the promise of the right to vote and equality before the law, was now possible. Millions of ex-slaves dreamed of land ownership amid their ambiguous new status in the conquered and devastated South. The years ahead during RECONSTRUCTION and beyond would bring great advancement in black politics, civil rights, and institution-building, as well as great disappointment and betrayal. But Emancipation had come at last.

In its own context, the meaning of the Civil War for African Americans had no more poignant illustration than the fall of Richmond, the capital of the Confederacy, in the first week of April 1865. Black troops were among the first Union forces to triumphantly occupy the city, and the freed population

Clark, Edward, Jr. (May 26, 1926–), painter. Born in New Orleans in 1926 to Merion Hutchingson, a seamstress, and Edward Clark, a waiter, Ed

Clark, Jr., left with his family for Chicago in 1933. Educated in Catholic schools, he always received encouragement for drawing. After serving with the ground crew in the Army Air Force from 1944 to 1946, Clark studied at the school of the Chicago Art Institute until 1951. He then went to Paris on the G.I. Bill and studied at the Grande Chaumière Academy. Although support ended in 1952, Clark stayed until 1956. Returning to New York and remaining for ten years, Clark began developing as an abstract expressionist, with a particular interest in action painting. Clark sees painting "as a purely visual experience in which color and movement are primary factors in that experience." Movement particularly interests him, and he is credited by some art critics as being the first to do shaped paintings, in 1956 when he was in the Tenth Street Brata Group. (Shaped paintings are those in which the picture continues beyond the confines of the framed canvas.)

In Paris from 1966 to 1969, Clark experimented with the ellipse, a form he believes best expresses such movement. Since 1952 he has exhibited almost every year nationally and internationally: Paris, Tokyo, Yugoslavia, and Mexico. The Studio Museum in Harlem held a retrospective in 1980. In 1975 he was awarded a grant from Creative Artists Public Service Program (CAPS), and he received grants from the National Endowment for the Arts in 1972 and 1982. Clark has been a visiting artist at Syracuse University, the Art Institute of Chicago, and the Skowhegan School of Painting, among others. His paintings are in collections in New York, Los Angeles, Massachusetts, Brazil, and Switzerland.

Ed Clark's *Untitled* (Paris Series), 1987, acrylic on canvas. (The Studio Museum in Harlem)

REFERENCES

Interview with the artist, October 5, 1992.
ROBINS, CORRINE. *The Pluralist Era: American Art, 1968–1981.* New York, 1984.

BETTY KAPLAN GUBERT

Clark, Kenneth Bancroft (July 24, 1914–), psychologist. Born in the Panama Canal Zone, Kenneth Bancroft Clark, the son of Hanson and Miriam Clark, had a direct influence on the U.S. Supreme Court decision in the case of BROWN V. BOARD OF EDUCATION OF TOPEKA, KANSAS in 1954. The Court cited Clark's psychological research on race relations in its favorable ruling outlawing segregation. Clark attended Howard University (B.A., 1935; M.S. 1936), and earned a Ph.D. from Columbia in 1940. He had a distinguished career at the City College of New York, where he taught from 1942 to 1975, retiring as professor emeritus of psychology. During his City College career, he also served as visiting professor at Columbia, the University of California at Berkeley, and Harvard. A writer as well as scholar, Clark is the author of *Dark Ghetto: Dilemmas of Social Power* (1965), *Crisis in Urban Education* (1971), and, with Talcott Parsons, *The Negro American* (1966). He was also one of the chief organizers of Harlem Youth Opportunities Unlimited. He has been recognized for his scholarship and his contributions to the black community, most notably as the winner of the SPINGARN MEDAL in 1961. Since his retirement from academia, he has served as president of Kenneth B. Clark and Associates, a consulting firm specializing in affirmative action in race relations.

REFERENCES

POLSKI, HARRY A., and JAMES WILSON, eds. *The Negro Almanac: A Reference Work on the African American.* 5th ed. Detroit, 1989.
CLOYD, IRIS, ed. *Who's Who Among Black Americans 1990–91.* Detroit, 1990.

CHRISTINE A. LUNARDINI

Clark, Peter Humphries (March 1829–June 21, 1925), educator and socialist. Peter Humphries Clark was born in Cincinnati, Ohio, in 1829. His grandfather, William Clark of the Lewis and Clark expedition, freed and moved his black mistress and their five children from Kentucky to Cincinnati in 1804, shortly before beginning his journey. Clark feared for the family's safety if they stayed in the slave state while he was away. Since Cincinnati had no public schools for African Americans, Peter Humphries Clark was educated at the newly established Gilmore High School, a private school for blacks. By the end of his tenure there, he had advanced rapidly enough to become an assistant teacher.

Disheartened by antiblack violence in the city—antiblack riots in 1829 and 1841 forced numerous African Americans to flee the city—Clark considered emigrating to Liberia. In 1853 he served as National Secretary of the Colored Convention in Rochester, N.Y., and on the editorial board of Frederick Douglass's *North Star*. He briefly published his own abolitionist newspaper, the *Herald of Freedom*, in 1855.

In 1857 Clark returned to Cincinnati and became involved in helping to establish public schooling for African Americans. Most of his efforts were sidetracked by the outbreak of the CIVIL WAR. During the war, Clark was involved in the formation of the Black Brigade, an all African-American non-combat unit that remained in Cincinnati. Clark wrote *The Black Brigade of Cincinnati* (1864), the brigade's history.

Between 1857 and 1866, Clark and other black educators fought with the city school board for funding for a black high school. As Superintendent of the Colored Schools for several years, Clark was eventually able to convince the school board of the necessity of a high school. Founded in 1866, the Gaines High School functioned as a normal school for teacher education; within two decades it had over one hundred students. Clark remained its principal until 1887, the same year in which the public schools integrated.

After the Civil War, Clark became known for his increasingly radical and changing political ideals. While he was a supporter of the REPUBLICAN PARTY as late as 1876, Clark left the party when President Rutherford B. Hayes removed federal troops from the South in 1877. Clark then denounced all of the mainstream parties and called for democratic socialism. He is often credited with being the first African-American socialist.

For Clark, seeing what he perceived as "the miserable condition into which society has fallen," the only remedy was socialism. He adopted the standard of the recently reorganized Workingmen's party and was one of a number of candidates on the party's slate in the elections of fall 1877. As a candidate for state Superintendent of Schools, Clark received more votes than any other candidate from his party. A powerful orator, Clark always counseled peaceful action. At the same time, he wholly and vigorously advocated a major readjustment of capitalism. During the 1877 national railroad strike, he addressed strikers, espousing nationalization of key businesses

such as the railroads and calling for a redistribution of wealth.

It is unclear at what point Clark became, in turn, disillusioned with socialism, but by the early 1880s, he had thrown his support behind the Democrats. One benefit of this support was that Democratic influence secured Clark an appointment as the first black on the Board of Trustees of Ohio State University in 1883. In 1887, after being dismissed by the Republican-dominated school board, which leveled allegations of corruption against him, Clark moved to St. Louis, where he taught at Sumner High School until his retirement in 1908. Perhaps finally disillusioned by the few outlets for political participation for blacks, Clark was never again active in regional or local politics. He remained in St. Louis, increasingly an invalid, until his death there at the age of ninety-six.

REFERENCES

FONER, PHILIP S. *The Great Labor Uprising of 1877*. New York, 1977.

GERBER, DAVID A. "Peter Humphries Clark: The Dialogue of Hope and Despair." In Leon Litwack and August Meier, eds., *Black Leaders of the Nineteenth Century*. Urbana, Ill., 1988, pp. 173–190.

GUTMAN, HERBERT. "Peter H. Clark: Pioneer Negro Socialist." *Journal of Negro Education* 34 (Fall 1965): 413–418.

LYDIA MCNEILL

Clark, Septima Poinsette

Clark, Septima Poinsette (May 3, 1898–December 15, 1987), educator and civil rights activist. Septima Poinsette was born and reared in Charleston, S.C. Her mother, Victoria Warren Anderson, was of Haitian descent and worked as a laundress, and her father, Peter Porcher Poinsette, was a former slave who worked as a cook and a caterer. Her parents deeply influenced Poinsette and instilled in her a willingness to share one's gifts and a belief that there was something redeeming about everyone. In addition, Poinsette's early education, which brought her into contact with demanding black teachers who insisted that students have pride and work hard, left a positive and lasting impression on her. Partly as a result of these influences, Poinsette pursued a career in education. In 1916, she received her teaching certificate from AVERY NORMAL INSTITUTE, a private school for black teachers founded after the end of the Civil War by the AMERICAN MISSIONARY ASSOCIATION in Charleston.

Poinsette's first teaching position was on Johns Island, S.C., from 1916 to 1919, because African

Two of the leading figures in the post–World War II struggles for black equality in the South: Septima Clark (left), from South Carolina, and Rosa Parks (right), from Montgomery, Ala., meet at the Highlander School in Monteagle, Tenn., in the 1950s. An interracial institute for labor and political activists, the Highlander School played an important role in developing effective strategies for grass-roots organizing for the civil rights movement. (Highlander Research and Education Center)

Americans were barred from teaching in the Charleston public schools. She tried to address the vast educational, political, and economical inequities that faced Johns Island blacks by instituting adult literacy classes and health education and by working with the NAACP. In 1919, she returned to Charleston to work at Avery and spearheaded a campaign against Charleston's exclusionary education system that resulted, one year later, in the overturning of the law barring black teachers from teaching in public schools. In May 1920, Poinsette married Nerie Clark, a back Navy cook. She had two children, one of whom died at birth. After her husband died in 1924, Clark sent her other child, Nerie, Jr., to live with his paternal grandmother because she could not support him financially.

Shortly thereafter, Clark returned to Columbia, S.C., became active in various civic organizations, and continued her education, receiving a B.A. from Benedict College (1942) and an M.A. from Hampton Institute (1945). She led the fight for equal pay for black teachers in South Carolina. Her efforts attracted the attention of the NAACP, which initiated litigation and won a 1945 ruling mandating equal pay for black teachers in South Carolina. In 1947, Clark returned to Charleston to teach in public schools and continued her civic activities until she was fired in 1956 because of her membership in the NAACP. Unable to find another position in South Carolina, Clark moved to the Highlander Folk School, in Monteagle, Tenn., an interracial adult education center founded by Myles Horton in 1932 to foster social activism and promote racial equality. There Clark became director of education. Together with Horton and South Carolina black activists such as Esau Jenkins from Johns Island, she devised educational strategies to challenge black illiteracy and encourage black voter registration. Clark, guided by the belief that literacy was integral to black equality, instituted the citizenship school program, an adult literacy program that focused on promoting voter registration and empowering people to solve their own problems through social activism.

The first citizenship school, founded on John's Island in 1957, was a success, and Clark traveled throughout the deep South, trying to make links with other local activists to foster the expansion of the schools. In 1961, the citizenship school program was transferred to the SOUTHERN CHRISTIAN LEADERSHIP CONFERENCE (SCLC) after the Tennessee legislature's persistent efforts to disrupt Highlander activities resulted in the school's charter being revoked and its property being confiscated. Clark joined SCLC to oversee the newly renamed Citizen Education Project, and by 1970 over 800 Citizenship schools had been formed that graduated over 100,000 African Americans who served as a key grass-roots base for the civil rights movement throughout the deep South. In 1971, however, she retired from SCLC because long-term commitment to the schools had faded.

Clark remained an outspoken spokesperson for racial, as well as gender, equality. She chronicled her life of activism in her autobiography, *Echo in My Soul,* in 1962. In 1966, she spoke at the first national meeting of the National Organization of Women (NOW) about the necessity of women challenging male dominance. In 1976, she was elected to the Charleston, S.C., school board. Three years later, she was awarded the Living Legacy award from President Jimmy Carter in honor of her continuing dedication to black empowerment through education. In 1987, she received an American Book Award for her second autobiography, *Ready from Within: Septima Clark and the Civil Rights Movement.* Later that year, Septima Clark died in Charleston, S.C.

REFERENCES

CLARK, SEPTIMA. *Echo in My Soul,* 1962.

CLARK, SEPTIMA, with Cynthia Stokes Brown. *Ready from Within: Septima Clark and the Civil Rights Movement.* Navarro, Calif., 1986.

CRAWFORD, VICKI, JACQUELINE ROUSE, and BARBARA WOODS, eds. *Trailblazers and Torchbearers: Women in the Civil Rights Movement.* Brooklyn, N.Y., 1990.

CHANA KAI LEE

Clark-Atlanta University.   In 1988, two historic black colleges, Clark College and Atlanta University, merged to form Clark-Atlanta University. Atlanta University was founded on October 16, 1867, when the trustees of Atlanta University received a charter from the state of Georgia. Edmund Ware, appointed by the AMERICAN MISSIONARY ASSOCIATION (AMA) to head up freedmen's education in Atlanta in 1866, was encouraged to find a black school already in operation when he arrived. The school had been founded in 1865 by two former slaves who turned it over to the leadership of newly arrived northern missionaries. Under Ware's guidance, enrollment grew and a new school house was built.

After the charter was granted and funds were raised (including $10,000 from the Freedman's Bureau), fifty acres were purchased and the cornerstone of the first building was set in June 1869. The first completed building housed the Normal School, which opened in October 1869. Both a grammar and secondary school were maintained on the premises until after the turn of the century.

Academic standards were high and the curriculum was patterned after the model of New England colleges. The educators were committed to the belief that African Americans deserved and were capable of an education equal to that offered to white students. Atlanta University was open to students of all races and colors. Initially, both black and white children attended (the white students were the children of faculty members). White and black faculty and students dined together in the tradition of the New England colleges. This scandalized Atlanta whites, who boycotted the university and everyone connected with it. In 1887 the state of Georgia cut off the land grant appropriations because of the interracial mixing.

After the turn of the twentieth century, the missionary societies did not get the contributions they once had received and so they were no longer able to provide much financial support to black colleges. The philanthropic organizations that gradually took the missions societies' place as the primary benefactor of black colleges and universities were skeptical of higher education for African Americans. As a result, Atlanta University experienced a constant battle for financial stability. This situation led to the affiliation with MOREHOUSE COLLEGE and SPELMAN COLLEGE in 1929. Part of the agreement stipulated that Spelman and Morehouse would remain undergraduate institutions while Atlanta University would function solely as a graduate school. (The first graduate degree, an M.A., was awarded in 1931.) This affiliation eventually grew into the ATLANTA UNIVERSITY CENTER in 1957. In 1988 Clark College and Atlanta University merged to form Clark-Atlanta University.

Atlanta University's most famous professor was W. E. B. DU BOIS, who taught there twice, from 1897 to 1910 and from 1932 to 1944. In addition to his many other responsibilities and accomplishments, Du Bois headed up the Atlanta University Studies program. This program began in 1896 as a sociological study of the urban condition of black Americans by a white businessman, George Bradford. Bradford began his study in response to the annual conference on the needs of rural black Americans, which was hosted by HAMPTON and TUSKEGEE institutes. Du Bois took the project over in 1897 and completely changed its focus. Instead of continuing the theme of the first two conferences—that African-American urban life would improve if blacks worked harder and improved their moral character—Du Bois sought to systematically study all possible sociological topics of African-American urban life. Topics and studies of the two-day conferences included "The Negro in Business" (1899), "The Negro Artisan" (1902), "The Negro Church" (1903), and "The Negro American Family" (1908). The proceedings from most of these conferences were published.

The conferences grew in prestige and fame and many experts from around the world participated in them. Max Weber, the great German sociologist, joined in the conference on crime in 1904. In spite of the tremendous financial difficulties of the program, Du Bois, almost singlehandedly, placed the Atlanta University Studies program in the forefront of American social science research on African Americans.

In addition to the contract of affiliation, 1929 also saw another milestone for Atlanta University. John HOPE was selected as the first African-American president of the university. Hope was already the president of Morehouse College. He served as president of both schools until 1931 when he retired from Morehouse (after a twenty-five-year tenure as its president) and devoted the rest of his life (he died in 1936) to the presidency of Atlanta University.

The many distinguished graduates from Atlanta University include James Weldon JOHNSON, appointed U.S. Consul in Venezuela in 1906 by President Theodore Roosevelt and executive secretary of the NATIONAL ASSOCIATION FOR THE ADVANCEMENT OF COLORED PEOPLE (NAACP) from 1920 to 1930, and Walter WHITE, who was the Executive Secretary of the NAACP from 1931 to 1955.

Clark College was founded in 1869 as the Summerhill School by the Freedmen's Aid Society of the Methodist Episcopal Church. It became Clark University in 1870, named after Bishop Davis W. Clark the first president of the Freedmen's Aid Society. The school was chartered by the state of Georgia in 1877.

Clark was a coeducational institution which taught elementary and secondary levels exclusively in its early years. The first baccalaureate degree was issued in 1883. It remained a private, undergraduate liberal arts institution committed to providing its students with the intellectual knowledge and skills necessary to excel in the field they chose to pursue.

In 1883 a department of theology was opened which separated from Clark University in 1886 and became Gammon Theological Seminary. Though not a party to the original contract of affiliation between Atlanta University, Morehouse College, and Spelman College in 1929, Clark began to participate in closer relations with the new university system, thereafter. In 1940 Clark University changed its name to Clark College and in 1957, it became one of the six founding members of the Atlanta University Center. In 1992 Clark-Atlanta University had an enrollment of 4,480 students, 86 percent of whom were African American.

REFERENCES

BACOTE, CLARENCE A. *The Story of Atlanta University*. Atlanta, 1969.

LEWIS, DAVID LEVERING. *W. E. B. Du Bois: Biography of a Race, 1868–1919*. New York, 1993.

McPHERSON, JAMES M. *The Abolitionist Legacy*. Princeton, N.J., 1975.

ROEBUCK, JULIAN B., and KOMANDURI S. MURTY. *Historically Black Colleges and Universities*. Westport, Conn., 1993.

DEBI BROOME

Clarke, Kenneth Spearman "Kenny" (January 9, 1914–January 26, 1985), jazz drummer, bandleader. Born in Pittsburgh, Clarke was a member of a musical family, and studied piano, trombone, drums, vibraphone, and music theory in Pittsburgh public schools. From 1929 to 1933 he gained his first experience as a professional drummer with Leroy Bradley's band, and later with Roy ELDRIDGE. In 1934, he left Pittsburgh to perform with the St. Louis–based Jeter-Pillars Band. A year later, Clarke moved to New York, where he joined the Edgar Hayes Orchestra in 1936. The next year he made his recording debut and first European tour. In 1938, while in Stockholm, Clarke made his first record as leader, playing vibraphone with a quartet comprising other Hayes band members.

After an eight-month stint with the Claude Hopkins Orchestra, Clarke joined Teddy Hill's band, which also included trumpeter Dizzy GILLESPIE. Together, Clarke and Gillespie helped develop the fundamental rhythmic and melodic concepts of bebop. Clarke used a continuous four-part polyrhythmic structure in which the main pulse was maintained on the cymbals, while the drums themselves provided accents and punctuation. This freed the drums from their traditional time-keeping role of earlier jazz drumming styles, and lightened the overall timbral character of drum accompaniment. Clarke's irregular rhythmic accents and drum punctuations became known as "dropping bombs" and "klook-mops," and "Klook" became Clarke's nickname. In February 1940, Clarke documented his new style in the closing choruses of the recording "One O'Clock Jump" with Sidney BECHET. Later that year he was hired to lead the house band at Minton's Playhouse, which hosted popular late-night jam sessions with Thelonius MONK on piano and Charlie CHRISTIAN on electric guitar.

In addition to his many original compositions, Clarke is believed to have helped write two of the earliest and most enduring compositions in modern jazz: "Salt Peanuts" (1942), with Dizzy Gillespie; and "Epistrophy" (a.k.a. "Fly Right," 1941), with Thelonious Monk.

In 1943 Clarke was drafted into the Army. He served in Europe until 1946, when he returned to New York and resumed his career. He recorded "Epistrophy" as a leader, and worked as a sideman on Dizzy Gillespie's recording of "Cubana Be/Cubana Bop" (1947). Over the next ten years Clarke toured internationally and recorded extensively (including with Miles DAVIS's "Birth of the Cool" band in 1949). In 1952 he cofounded the MODERN JAZZ QUARTET (*La Ronde*, 1952). He also continued to work as a leader of small groups (*Bohemia After Dark,* 1955; *Klook's Clique,* 1956).

In 1956 Clarke settled in Paris, where he performed, recorded, established a drum school, and appeared in and wrote scores for films. From 1959 to 1962 he coled a group called the Three Bosses, which included fellow expatriates Bud POWELL and Oscar PETTIFORD. From 1960 to 1973 Clarke joined with the Belgian pianist Francy Boland to lead the Clarke-Boland Big Band, which toured internationally and recorded prolifically (*Francy Boland Big Band,* 1963). In his last years, Clarke worked with the drum quartet Pieces of Time. Clarke, who was occasionally known by his Islamic name, Liaquat Ali Salaam, died near Paris, where he had lived for many years.

REFERENCES

BROWN, ANTHONY. "The Development of Modern Jazz Drumset Artistry," *The Black Perspective in Music* 18, nos. 1,2 (1990): 39–58.
GITLER, IRA. *Jazz Masters of the Forties.* 1966. Reprint. New York, 1983, p. 174.
MATTINGLY, R. "In Memoriam Kenny Clarke," *Modern Drummer* 9, no. 4 (1985): 64.

ANTHONY BROWN

Class. *See* Race, Caste, and Class.

Class and Society.   The basic social and political contours that defined the cultural status of African Americans from the late nineteenth century through the mid-twentieth century were the products of the racist exclusion of blacks from positions of power. The very weak position of blacks in all kinds of job markets, housing, public schooling, higher education, and political participation from the turn of the century to the 1960s was the outcome of racial-caste marginalization, a virulent form of nativism. Despite continuing obstacles due to anti-black nativism both from white Anglo-Saxon Protestants (WASPs) and white ethnics (who participated at various time in such marginalization and whose social status was automatically raised by a "political culture of whiteness" that permitted assimilation through the assertion of a white identity), the class position of black Americans has been fundamentally altered since World War II.

Apart from Native Americans and Hispanic Americans, black Americans had the weakest social patterns among American ethnic groups in the era prior to the transformations of the 1940s through the 1960s. Virtually coerced into low-paying and rugged farm labor in the decades following the Emancipation and well into the early 1900s, a majority of African Americans at the start of World War II were still tied to low-paying farm occupations. Some 75 percent of black men were identified by census data in the early 1940s as employed as domestic servants and farm laborers. Such employment at the low-paying end of the job market translated into widespread poverty among black families, a poverty that had been gravely worsened, like that of their white counterparts, by the Great Depression. For instance, while some 48 percent of the white families were below the federal poverty line by 1939, 87 percent of black families were victims of poverty.

Within this impoverished group was a small black middle class of ministers, doctors, lawyers, businessmen, and professionals, who operated almost exclusively within the black community, providing services blacks were unable to secure from whites. Their associations, like the National Negro Business League (founded in 1900 by Booker T. WASHING-

TON), functioned protectively—shielding bourgeois blacks from the pressures of white supremacy and shoring up ghetto markets.

Among the elements distinguishing the black bourgeoisie was a strong sense of racial uplift. The doctrine of black ethnic uplift extends back to the church-based charities among antebellum free black communities and, after Emancipation, to the black churches and fraternal orders that organized mutual-assistance societies and founded black colleges and some elementary and secondary schools. W. E. B. DU BOIS spoke eloquently of the duty of members of the Talented Tenth—the elite minority of black society—to educate themselves for a mission as black leaders, and to involve themselves with the advancement of less fortunate blacks.

African-American sociologist E. Franklin FRAZIER's book, *The Black Bourgeoisie* (1957), presented a famous and devastating critique of the old-guard bourgeoisie, considered on the basis of its snobbishness and vested interest in segregation. Frazier discussed the black bourgeoisie as victims of a ghetto mentality—a sense of being beleaguered, marginal, and inferior. In compensation, he claimed, the bourgeoisie was consumed with status-seeking desire, expressed in showy, vulgar bursts of consumerism and conspicuous consumption. Frazier believed that "the exclusion of the middle-class Negro from [equal] participation in the general life of the American community"—American racism, in short—was at the root of this high-society mania among bourgeois blacks.

At the core of Frazier's blistering critique of the old-guard black bourgeoisie in the early 1950s was his belief that the obsessive high-society orientation blocked members of the old-guard elite from seeing their obligation to the large poor and marginalized sector of black Americans—an obligation to use some of their bourgeois resources as instruments of broader ethnic uplift:

> It has meant that whites did not take Negroes seriously; that whites did not regard the activities of Negroes as of any real consequence in American life. It has tended to [therefore] encourage a spirit of irresponsibility or an attitude of 'play' or make-believe among them. Consequently Negroes have 'played' at conducting their schools, at running their businesses, and at practicing their professions. The spirit of play or make-believe has tended to distort or vitiate the ends of their most serious activities. . . . Since [members of] the black bourgeoisie live largely in a world of make-believe, the masks which they wear to play their sorry roles conceal the feelings of inferiority . . . that haunt their inner lives. . . . Their escape into a world of make-believe with its sham 'society' [conspicuous status-seeking] leaves them with a feeling of emptiness and futility.

Although Frazier's book was published in the 1950s, his description clearly applied more precisely to the prewar bourgeoisie. Economic and social change for the black community began in the 1940s. The impact of World War II on the economic standing of all Americans was enormous, but black families were particularly affected. Postwar black per capita income was about four times higher than in 1939, though it remained just 50 percent of per capita white income. The postwar era also saw black families in poverty fall from 87 percent in 1939 to 36 percent at war's end (white poverty fell to 9 percent).

In the postwar era black labor shifted away from farm labor in the South to blue-collar industrial work. Commenting on these postwar occupation data, the National Research Council's monumental survey of blacks' status observed that

> Comparing the employment situation of black men in 1973 with that of 1940 shows that the proportion of labor force participants who were unemployed, on public emergency jobs, or working on farms declined from 52 to 11 percent; those working machine operators, factory laborers, or blue-collar craftsmen rose from 31 to 50 percent. During the same period, black women moved from domestic service and farm labor into factories, shops, offices, and some professional and managerial positions.

The most significant factor in this economic shift was the creation of a new black bourgeoisie. White-collar occupations for blacks expanded enormously, especially in the postwar decades of the 1960s and 1970s. This growth can be seen from data organized by the U.S. Department of Labor. While the overall number of employed blacks increased by 1.3 million (17.3 percent) between 1972 and 1980, the largest relative gains for blacks were in white-collar occupations (nearly 1.2 million or 55 percent). Within that category, the sharpest increases were in professional/technical jobs (354,000 or 55.4 percent) and in managerial/administrative jobs (168,000 or 69.1 percent). By 1980, there were some 13,000 black doctors and dentists, 22,000 accountants, 25,000 engineers, and 191,000 managers and administrators. At the same time, the numbers of skilled, well-paid blue-collar workers increased by 217,000 or 32.3 percent.

This white-collar growth overlapped with and in part resulted from the civil rights revolution. An equally important qualitative aspect of the growth of white-collar, middle-class occupations for African Americans in the latter postwar era was the occupational rise of black women. Both at the lower and top ranks of white-collar occupations, black women strengthened their position relative to their white counterparts, more so, in fact, than did black men.

For example, according to Diane Westcott by 1980 some 14 percent of black women held professional/technical jobs compared to 17 percent of white women, while 8 percent of black males held such jobs compared to 16 percent of white males. The data for specific professional and technical occupations are worth noting in regard to black female/male participation by 1980. Black women made up 7.4 percent of women accountants (black males, 3.6 percent of male accountants); 9.4 percent of women computer specialists were black (black males, 4.1 percent); 10.8 percent of women personnel and labor specialists were black (black males, 7.9 percent); 0.5 percent of women medical/dental practitioners were black (black males, 2.1 percent); 9.2 percent of women health technicians were black (black males, 3.3 percent); 10.2 percent of women schoolteachers were black (black males, 6 percent); 4.6 percent of women banking/financial officials were black (black males, 2.6 percent); 6.7 percent of women engineers and science technicians were black (black males, 5.6 percent), and 7.1 percent of women lawyers and judges were black (black males, 3.1 percent).

Progress and Crisis: A Two-tier Black Society

As has been demonstrated, African Americans in the latter postwar era were able to make substantial progress into the middle-class or bourgeois occupational sector, and a full-fledged mainstream black bourgeoisie was created for the first time. This progress was far from universal, however, and an analysis of the status of the black middle class requires some understanding of the larger black economy. Indeed, black economic progress has occurred as part of a dominant cyclical pattern, with steeply growing numbers of blacks in poverty accompanying the rising numbers of middle-class blacks. The poverty level for blacks declined from 90 percent in 1939 to 55 percent in 1959, and then declined again to 30 percent in 1974 (in contrast to a 9 percent white poverty rate). Between 1974 and 1985, there was an increase in black poverty, which reached 35 percent during the recession in the early 1980s. The rate settled down by 1985 to 32 percent, where it more or less remained through the early 1990s.

Distinguished economist Reynolds Farley suggests that there are "three major factors" in this progression: First, the wages of employed blacks rose faster than those of whites from the end of the depression until the early 1970s. This made it possible for many blacks to rise out of poverty. After the early 1970s, however, average overall male wages have fallen (in constant dollar amounts), while those of women have stagnated or increased just a little. Although the earnings of blacks relative to those of whites improved a bit in the 1970s and 1980s, the economic circumstances are such that it would now take very sharp increases in earnings to minimize existing poverty levels, black or white.

Second, there have been major changes in labor supply. As Farley explains, "Declines in employment are evident among men of both races, but the drops have been much greater among blacks. There is agreement about this shift, but much controversy about the causes, with William Wilson arguing the absence of jobs—especially near the black ghettos—explains the change, while Lawrence Mead stresses . . . the reluctance of black men to accept menial work [combined] with the availability of transfer payment to depress [black] employment."

Farley also points to changes in family structure, namely the explosion of female-headed households, as an important element in black poverty. Beginning in the 1960s, while black fertility rates as a whole remained largely constant, increasing numbers of out-of-wedlock births (mainly among teenagers) occurred. The percentage of out-of-wedlock births by blacks in 1970 was nearly twice the 1960 figure (37.6 percent compared with 23.6 percent), and by 1980 more than half of black births (56.4 percent) were out of wedlock. As a result, female-headed households, almost all of them poor, multiplied. More than one-third of black households in 1970 were headed by women; the figure exploded to 58 percent of black households by 1991. (Other nonwhite ethnic groups, such as Puerto Ricans, Mexican Americans, Native Americans, and Hawaiians, have mirrored this growth.) Since female-headed black households have twice the poverty rate of two-parent black households, the explosion of female-headed households since 1970 has brought a concomitant explosion of numbers of black children reared in poverty. Some 58 percent of all poor black children resided in female-headed households by 1970, and by the end of the 1980s nearly 80 percent lived in such households (compared to 36 percent of poor white children). By 1990 some 45 percent of black children lived in poverty, compared to some 16 percent of white children.

The pattern of rising and falling poverty levels among blacks has served to institutionalize class divisions between rich and poor blacks. African Americans since the early 1970s have developed a two-tier class structure—one, a top tier of "mobile blacks" (stable working-class, middle-class, and upper-class), and a second, lower tier of "static blacks" (weak working-class, poor and subpoor, or underclass). In a recent observation on the seemingly intractable problem of the growing fissure in the class structure of black America, Gerald Jaynes and Robin Williams—directors of the National Research Council's massive survey of African-American status—remarked:

An important aspect of this polarization in the incomes of black men and black families has been the growth, during the years since 1960, of female-headed black families. It is among such families that the incidence of poverty is highest. While some female-headed families are middle-class just as some two-parent families are poor, it is not an exaggeration to say that the two most numerically important components of the black class structure have become a lower class dominated by female-headed families and a middle-class largely composed of families headed by a husband and wife.

Of course, both the top-tier and bottom-tier of the class structure that has evolved since the 1970s have affected the overall American society and the capacity of blacks to influence institutional and political processes in this society. It has been particularly the dynamics surrounding the mainstreaming of the mobile-black sector (especially the middle-class and elite) that are empowering black Americans within the overall American society. Not surprisingly, the overall social and cultural mainstreaming of African Americans since the civil rights revolution has been demographically located among the mobile-stratum black families.

Emergence of Viable Black Bourgeoisie

BLACK INCOME GROWTH

The civil rights revolution of the 1960s, which put an end to legal discrimination, occurred simultaneously with a period of strong economic growth, especially between 1964 and 1970. During this period, some 13 million new jobs were produced, some three-quarters of which were middle-class jobs. Between 1964 and 1970 the black middle class expanded between 8 percent and 12 percent annually. This meant that, while only 13 percent of black Americans held middle-class occupations in 1960, there would be 27 percent middle-class black job-holders in 1970.

Though the job-growth rate of middle-class blacks during the 1970s slowed to 3 percent annually, there was still an overall expansion of middle-class, black job-holders, resulting in 3.5 million middle-class black job-holders—about 40 percent of employed blacks—by 1980. Black middle-class growth was notable not only for its rapid rate, but for the range of occupations that blacks entered. A major motor of black middle-class growth has been government employment, which accounted for the jobs of 30 percent of the heads of black families by the late 1970s (compared with 16 percent of the heads of white families).

The expansion of middle-class jobs translated into an increase in blacks with income at the middle and upper levels. In 1986, for example, household-income surveys by the Bureau of Census found some

45 percent of black households falling within middle-income brackets and above—that is, from $22,000 per year and above per household. When this proportion of black households is combined with that of black households with incomes between $15,000 and $22,000, some 63 percent of black households can be categorized as "mobile-stratum" households (the remaining households might be termed "static-stratum" households.

When viewed in aggregate terms, 1990 black-household-income data further indicate a rigidification of the two-tier class dynamic among black Americans. Some two-thirds of black households still fall within what we term the "mobile-stratum." For instance, out of 10,488,000 black families, some 246,000 households earned between $50,000 and $54,000; 92,000 households earned more than $70,000; and 8,000 households earned more than $100,000.

These mobile-stratum families are overwhelmingly two-parent families. This type of black family has sustained overall mobility and wealth advances, unlike most of the 56 percent of black families that are female-headed. For example, some 67 percent of two-parent families own their homes and have enjoyed steady increases in household income, nearly closing the income gap dividing them from similarly situated white families. Two-parent black families (about 44 percent of all black families) earn $85 for every $100 earned by the average white family.

JOB-MARKET DEGHETTOIZATION

The expansion of white-collar occupations among blacks has occurred alongside a demographic dispersion of the locale of white-collar employment for blacks—from a ghetto job market to a national (white) job market; that is, from the provision of professional services in black areas to jobs in national banks, insurance companies, retail firms, industries, universities, and government agencies.

The significance of this occupational dispersion of mobile-stratum blacks can be seen in the doubling of the proportion of black managers and technicians in top-level Fortune 500 firms by the late 1970s and early 1980s. For example, AT&T had 12 percent minority managers (mainly black) by 1981; Exxon had 3.4 percent minority managers in 1977 and 8.9 percent minority professionals; Gannett Publications had 7 percent minority managers and 8.5 percent minority professionals in 1980; Equitable Life Assurance Society had 6.2 percent minority managers, 10.2 percent professionals, and 16.3 percent technicians in 1981; Hewlett-Packard had 9.7 percent minority managers and 14.6 percent professionals in 1981, and IBM had, out of a total of 197,000 employees in 1981, some 15,600 black employees (about 8 percent) and about 8 percent black managers and professionals.

The role of affirmative-action policy was important in the extensive job-market deghettoization among the black bourgeoisie from the 1970s onward, and nowhere was this policy's impact more fundamental and apparent than in the officer and noncommissioned officer ranks of the United States armed forces. Studies by Northwestern University sociologist Charles Moskos show that while barely 2 percent of armed-forces officers were black in the 1970s, by the late 1980s some 12 percent of officers were black (7,000), which include 7 percent of all generals and 11 percent of colonels. Furthermore, while in the 1970s only 5 percent of noncommissioned officers were black, by the middle 1980s there were 85,000 black noncommissioned officers in the armed forces. This includes 24 percent of master sergeants and 31 percent of sergeant major rank.

The occupational dispersion of middle-class blacks away from ghetto job markets has been reinforced by the increasing shift to suburban living among the mobile stratum of black Americans. As Frank Wilson has observed, by the 1970s the numbers of blacks moving to the suburbs exceeded net central city movement. Between 1980 and 1990, the black suburban population increased by 2 million—from 6.2 million to 8.2 million (32 percent). Seventy-three percent of this growth occurred between 1986 and 1990. It is, then, the synergetic interplay between the new occupational dispersion of middle-class blacks, on the one hand, and their residential suburbanization on the other that define the essential ingredients of a mainstream black bourgeoisie.

We have no better source for a graphic documentation of the mainstreaming of the black bourgeoisie than the journal *Black Enterprise,* the first black-oriented magazine for businesspeople and entrepreneurs. Owned by Earl Graves, a former army officer turned entrepreneur, its circulation is around one million. For more than two decades each monthly issue of *Black Enterprise* has carried a column entitled, "Making It," which consists of a job profile of a person who exemplifies the mainstreaming process among the black bourgeoisie.

FROM STATUS-SEEKING TO POWER-SEEKING

The importance of massive occupational dispersion to the functional dimensions of the new black bourgeoisie—a mainstream, nonghetto bourgeoisie—cannot be overemphasized. First, it diminishes the historic ghetto mentality of the black bourgeoisie—the sense of being beleaguered, marginal, or inferior—that Frazier described in *The Black Bourgeoisie* (1957). The new black bourgeoisie holds a much more assertive self-concept. Second, the new black bourgeoisie's broad-based entrance into the American political economy—corporate structures and power networks—enables it to surmount its ideological and social segregation. Third, it forces the new black bourgeoisie to shed the hyper-consumerism of the old black bourgeoisie that Frazier vividly critiqued and replace it with a focus on acquiring power.

There have been two developmental aspects of the new black bourgeoisie that have defined its cultural metamorphosis from what Frazier called in the 1950s an indulgent status-seeking bourgeoisie to what we might call a power-seeking bourgeoisie: first, the growth of a new network of professional associations, and second, the growth of numerous magazines that carry a black version of what R. H. Tawney called the acquisitive ethos.

The black bourgeoisie's transition from a ghetto-based to a nationwide occupational milieu was not an instantaneous development. Rather, it was associated with the growth of a network of professional associations that mediated much of the job-market deghettoization and then ensured its institutionalization. Since the early 1970s, the new black bourgeoisie began to fashion a new generation of professional associations, the best documentary guide to which are the pages of *Black Enterprise* and a catalog of some 200 black professional associations called *A Guide to Black Organizations* (1984), produced by the Philip Morris public-affairs department. Among the new-guard block associations are the National Association of Black Manufacturers (founded in 1971), National Associations of Black Accountants (1970), National Black Media Coalition (1973), National Black Network (1973), Council of Concerned Black Executives (1975), National Associations of Black Contractors (1972), and Organization of Black Airline Pilots (1976), to name just a representative few. Major metropolitan areas also spawned new-guard black associations, like the Dallas Alliance for Minority Enterprise (circa 1974), the Durham [Black] Business and Professional Chain (c. 1975), and New York City's One Hundred Black Men (c. 1968).

The growth of new-guard associations was supported and articulated by a new black political class of elected and appointed officials. In the early 1990s, there were some forty black Congresspersons, who possessed a high average seniority rate. The Congressional Black Caucus, formed in the early 1970s to give strategic organization to black Congress persons, was followed by the National Black Caucus of State Legislators, the National Association of Minority County Officials, and the National Caucus of Black Schoolboard Members.

Though all-black in composition like the old-guard (pre-1970s) bourgeois associations, the new-guard associations have a different relationship to America's power processes. Where the old-guard worked self-protectively, the new-guard associations function integratively, opening broad opportunities for mobile-stratum blacks throughout American economic and institutional life. The integrative process nationalizes the black bourgeoisie's networks. As a result, power structures among blacks and whites increasingly intersect, and various aspects of black and white attitudinal and ideological patterns merge.

The integration of the black bourgeoisie into mainstream power networks has led a growing proportion of bourgeois blacks to acquire social, professional, and political orientations that are more class-linked than race-linked. This is analogous to the protracted but steady intertwining, from the 1950s onward, of overall ideological orientation among Irish, Jewish, Italian, and other white-ethnic bourgeoisies with the hegemonic values embraced by the white Protestant establishment.

The second major dynamic involved in the metamorphosis of the black bourgeoisie from a status-seeking identity toward a power-seeking demeanor has been the growth of nationwide network of magazines that carry a black version of the acquisitive ethos. By the early 1980s, the most prominent of these organs with nationwide circulations were *Black Enterprise* (circulation 250,000 in the early 1980s and around 1 million in the 1990s), *Essence* (600,000 circulation in the early 1980s), *Black Collegian: The National Magazine of Black College Students* (250,000 circulation in the early 1980s), and *Dollars and Sense* (110,00 circulation in the early 1980s).

These nationwide journals were supplemented at the local level (city and state) by an array of other acquisitive-ethos-bearing magazines. Among these journals are *New City* (Washington, D.C.), *Washington Living* (Washington, D.C.), *Pride* (St. Louis), *About Time* (Rochester, N.Y.), *Black Family* (Chicago), *New England Weekly* (Boston), and *Sun Belt* (a black state magazine in Mississippi).

These national and local new black journals have become the prominent purveyors of power-seeking lifestyles among bourgeois blacks, devoted to black entrepreneurial growth and to the strategic position of black professions broadly in American life. This purpose is heralded in the subtitle of *Dollars and Sense:* "the compendium of information for black business and professional men and women." *Black Enterprise* carries a variety of articles every month that chronicle successful entrepreneurial careers among the new bourgeoisie and supply a wide range of technical and strategic information regarding investments, financial management, and market dynamics. No previous generation of middle-class blacks has been exposed to this type of black media, inundating blacks with a message on the need to penetrate American

power networks. This has facilitated the mainstreaming of the black bourgeoisie.

Persistent Bourgeois High-Society Patterns

While it is clear that the new black bourgeoisie has skillfully fashioned a power-mustering ethos and network since the late 1960s, it is also clear that it has not fully vanquished the old-guard bourgeoisie's consumerist, status-seeking ("high-society") patterns. This is apparent, for example, in the persistence of high-society agencies among bourgeois blacks like the Greek letter fraternities, now again captivating students not only at black colleges (where they reigned supreme in the pre-1960s era), but on white campuses as well. While skillful at publicly packaging themselves as community-service organizations, black fraternities are essentially good-time and consumerist-oriented agencies of black bourgeois life.

The persistence of the high-society mindset is reflected in the rise of national black magazines dedicated to marketing a gaudy use of leisure time. Founded in the late 1970s, the monthly *Black Odyssey: A Magazine on Travel and Leisures* is typical of this trend. *Odyssey* also deviates occasionally from its ultra-consumerist message, offering instead a leisure perspective for the more spartan, noting in an editorial in its Summer 1979 issue that

> Some of us want to know where the nearest picnic area is located. Where can we learn to swim and snorkel? What and where are the museums in the cities in which we live and visit? Where are the respectable single clubs? Where are the not so respectable singles clubs? Where are the jazz concerts and discos?

A content analysis of EBONY in recent years also suggests, despite its attempt to change into a power-centered publication, the persistence of gaudy consumerist patterns among the black bourgeoisie. A typical instance of this was an *Ebony* cover story that portrayed the affluent lifestyle of wealthy black families in industry and finance. The article also featured the family of the late singer Nat "King" Cole, whose widow lives in a multimillion dollar home in Bel Air, Calif., has a house staff, and owns several luxury automobiles. Another cover story carried by *Ebony* depicted the gaudy consumerist lifestyle of a major rap singer who, in addition to owning a stable of thoroughbred racehorses, is building a $20 million home. Numerous other entertainers' high-society lifestyles have been given special layout-coverage in *Ebony* (like a recent eight-page treatment of Eddie Murphy's wedding celebration).

An interesting and new feature surrounding the persistence of ultra-consumerist patterns among the black bourgeoisie is that there is now a new locale for this pattern, one much farther afield residentially than the ghetto neighborhoods of the old black bourgeoisie that Frazier criticized. The new home of the black bourgeoisie is in the affluent new suburbs on the metropolitan rim of the former ghetto neighborhoods, which are now mainly the habitat of the weak working-class and poor black households. The 1990 census found some 8.2 million blacks in the suburbs—some 32 percent of blacks—including the model, super-affluent black suburban community in Prince George's County, Md. Some 37 percent of black households in Prince George's County have $50,000 income or more, which is only 8 percent points below the 45 percent of white households in this income bracket, but 12 percentage points greater than the national proportion of black households in the $50,000 or more bracket (25 percent). Prince George's County has just under 730,000 population, of which 51 percent is black, 43 percent white, and about 7 percent other groups. More than half of the census tracts are either mainly white or mainly black. Though this concentration resulted partly from illegal racial-steering practices by real-estate firms, reporter David J. Dent discovered that many of the bourgeois black families openly favor living among other affluent blacks. As a senior contract administrator in the federal government put it: "I don't want to come home and always have my guard up." Another bourgeois black family member elaborated on this preference for a race-specific affluent neighborhood: "We always wanted to make sure our child had many African-American children to play with, not just one or two. We always wanted to be in a community with a large number of black professionals and to feel part of that community." In short, it seems that an important segment of the new black bourgeoisie prefers to associate intraethnically, like the generation of bourgeois Jews and Irish after World War II (and bourgeois Italians since the early 1960s) who developed networks of ethnically-consolidated bourgeois affluence in suburbs such as New York's Scarsdale and New Rochelle.

Moreover, just as the post–World War II Jewish and Irish suburban bourgeoisie went in for consumerist display outlets like lush country clubs and grand religious edifices, wealthy churches as objects of bourgeois consumerist display have been particularly evident in the new, affluent black bourgeois suburbs like Prince George's County, where the oldest black congregation—Ebenezer African Methodist Episcopal Church—built a $10 million edifice as part of its rapid growth from 100 members in 1983 to 7,000 today. Another affluent neighborhood congregation—St. Paul United Methodist Church—commenced erecting a $3 million edifice for just 100 members.

As discussed above, E. Franklin Frazier was an important critic of the old-guard bourgeoisie's high-society pretensions. On the one hand, Frazier overstated the extent to which these patterns differentiated the old-guard black bourgeoisie from its white-ethnic counterparts (Irish, Jewish, Italian, etc.). The high-society pretensions that Frazier critiqued among the black bourgeoisie were, in reality, common to American bourgeoisie in general. Thorstein Veblen and other critical observers of mainstream bourgeoisie America considered this a condition of American success—the tacky leveler among our multiethnic bourgeois strivers. It was an easy route to what might be called an "elite consensus"—the lowest common denominator of such consensus—rather than the more ethnically rigorous quest for an identity that would meld bourgeois status with continuing action toward the incorporation of less affluent group members into egalitarian society. All continue to share a vibrant appetite for conspicuous and gaudy consumerist patterns. Though today the old-guard bourgeoisie's high-society outlook is complemented and, to some degree, challenged by its concern for power-mustering, it is not yet time to write the obituary of gaudy consumerist patterns.

Just as Frazier savaged the traditional black bourgeoisie for inattention to black community uplift, it is far from clear that the new black bourgeoisie that has emerged since the civil rights revolution is ready to rekindle an ethnic-uplift obligation, still less to forge a multilayered programmatic attack on the cultural disarray (especially among the children of poor households, who increasingly spend most of their childhood in poverty, surrounded by numerous forms of societal and cultural dislocation and chaos) that plagues some one-third of African-American households. The persistence of the consumerist-oriented high-society pattern among the new black bourgeoisie is, in its current format, inconsistent with a renewal of the old black bourgeoisie's ethnic-uplift and cultural helping-hand obligation, despite the fact that the financial capacity and overall institutional capacity of today's black bourgeoisie to launch a program of outreach to the black poor is superior to that of its predecessor.

A partial exception to the patterns of integrationist power-seeking and consumerism has been the behavior of blacks in the political arena, the main arena of society in which ethnic uplift of a sort has continued. Owing to the fact that today's mainstream black bourgeoisie remains dependent upon broad-gauged black political support for consolidating its own power within the American system, the professional political sector of the black bourgeoisie retains a fundamentally pro-black tilt, especially in its influence upon both Democratic and Republican party politics.

For example, as the new black political class penetrated the mainstream legislative coalitions in Congress during the 1970s and 1980s, it spearheaded policy initiatives on behalf of a variety of black policy needs, both domestic and foreign, regarding Africa in particular. Within the Republican sector of the black political class, Attorney William T. Coleman played a crucial role during his tenure as Secretary for Transportation under President Gerald Ford (1973–1976), initiating numerous policy advances such as affirmative action. Similarly at the state level, black Republican politicians like Leonard S. Coleman (commissioner for energy in New Jersey Gov. Thomas Kean's first administration and commissioner for community affairs in the second [1980–1988]) advanced New Jersey's affirmative-action practices.

In contrast, the small sector of militant conservatives within the black bourgeoisie (e.g., Thomas Sowell, Clarence Thomas, Glenn Loury, and Shelby Steele) do not tend to function within an organized black voter constituency. Instead, they function within the power milieu of conservative power networks (think-tanks and foundations like Heritage Foundation, Olin Foundation, American Enterprise Institute) and right-wing intellectual networks linked to organs like *The National Review, Commentary Magazine,* and *Policy Review.*

The Future of African-American Society

While the Frazierian model of an isolated and fantasy-bound black bourgeoisie no longer applies to the black middle class, neither does a pure integrationist model that ignores the obstacles to assimilation posed by residual nativism and by the continuing problem of the black underclass. One possible model for the status of African Americans in the American social order might be called a transitional integrationist perspective. This perspective posits that the current status of African Americans is characterized by a new transracial capability across a variety of fundamental institutional patterns in American life—industry, commerce, professions, universities, politics, and government, and the cultural sphere (including entertainment, sports, etc.). In these basic institutions of American life, the pre-1960 era's formalized racist (legally segregated) patterns dominated by culturally legitimate anti-black nativism, while far from dissolved, are now actively challenged. It is precisely because of the ongoing challenge to America's pre-1960 racist patterns by blacks and their white allies (especially the feminist or women's movement) that the dynamics now facilitating an emergent transitional-integrationist milieu also bring to the surface latent racial tension or discord. Surveys conducted in recent years in schools, colleges, and workplaces, reveal this latent racial tension, which sometimes turns militant and violent (as in South Boston High School in Boston, Mass., in May 1993). Yet this is not tension within the rigid racial milieu of the past—tension and violence in support of racist oppression, barriers, and constraints. This is racial tension within a changing racial milieu, a milieu that functions as the forerunner of an emergent transitional integrationist era.

There is, above all, a new sociopolitical dynamic associated with African-American life. First, there are the new sociological dynamics associated with the expanded ranks of bourgeois and stable working-class black families (some 65 percent of black families). For the first time, many white Americans have opportunities for interpersonal professional or residential ties with class peers among blacks. These bonds facilitate a reduction of status anxiety toward African Americans. Some whites will seize these new opportunities for interpersonal ties with black class peers and are doing so, though we do not have hard data for this. Some will hesitate, but entertain this new option. Many, of course, will resist, as we can infer from the National Opinion Research Center's survey that shows 53 percent of whites viewing blacks as "less intelligent than whites." Still, no such generic metamorphosis in a nation's historical patterns of status rigidity and exclusion has been a majority-led process, so we expect a minority of whites to seize new opportunities for class-peer ties with blacks in America's emergent transitional-integrationist era.

The second dynamic that is driving this transitional-integrationist milieu relates to the rise of a full-fledged political class among the new black mobile stratum—a political class now comprising some 8,000 elected officials nationally, reinforced by perhaps 40,000 black appointed and civil-service officials. This new political class has experienced a major expansion of its political authority and influence through the growth of what some observers call crossover black politicians—that is, black politicians who derive a major part of their electoral support not from black voters, but from white voters. The leading crossover or transracial congresspersons include Rep. Allan Wheat (Democrat-Mo.), Rep. Ron Dellums (Democrat-Calif.), and Rep. Gary Franks (Republican-Conn.). There are also growing numbers of black mayors who have achieved crossover or transracial electoral capacity—in Seattle, Denver, New Haven, Cleveland, and elsewhere—as well as one very important crossover black politician at the state executive level, Gov. L. Douglas Wilder of Virginia. It should also be noted that at the congressional level, another feature of this class's expanding political influence is the benefit that accompanies its high aggregate seniority level. The long tenure of black congresspersons has meant that they hold a significant number of chairmanships of congressional committees. As of 1992, twenty-six black congresspersons chaired committees—out of a total of thirty-nine black congresspersons—and four of these chairmanships involved standing committees, one was a select committee, and thirteen were subcommittees. Thus, when viewed in aggregate terms, the growing clout of the new black political class can be expected to facilitate the emergent transitional integrationist era.

Meanwhile, the African-American contribution to an evolving transitional integrationist milieu is, all things being equal, likely to remain a cutting-edge or wedge factor in this development. We say this because, although there are strong nativistic tendencies among blacks toward whites (with anti-Semitism being a highly visible facet of this black nativism), African Americans are still distinctly less prone to nativism than white Americans. Data based on a 1988 *Newsweek* poll show that blacks are very favorably disposed to transracial housing patterns. Another *Newsweek* poll (April 1991) revealed additional strong transracial preferences among black Americans when compared with whites. For instance, some 84 percent of blacks report that they "work with many members of another race," compared with 51 percent of whites who report the same. Only 17 percent of blacks say they are "uncomfortable working with members of another race." Also, some 63 percent of blacks report that they "socialize regularly with members of another race."

Furthermore, data from a National Academy of Science 1980 survey suggest a broad pragmatic readiness among African Americans to expand prevailing integrationist patterns in American society. Thus, some 58 percent of blacks replied "disagree" or "strongly disagree" to the statement, "Blacks should always vote for black candidates when they run." Some 58 percent replied "disagree" or "strongly disagree" to the statement, "Black women should not date white men." Finally, some 56 percent of blacks replied "disagree" or "strongly disagree" to the statement, "Black men should not date white women." We know of no comparable data on these and related issues covering Jews, Italians, Irish, WASPs and other white groups, but a similarly strong cosmopolitan or integrationist American system will clearly depend on a similar pragmatic attitudinal transformation among white Americans.

As the expanding mobile stratum among black families provides more whites with the opportunity to forge interpersonal ties with class peers among blacks, so the expanding influence of the black political class enables white politicians to intersect their interests (and those of white voters) with the policy dynamics relating to black Americans. A study of 1990 census data that concluded that median household income for blacks in Queens County, N.Y., exceeded that of whites hinted at the expansion of the black middle class on a hitherto unsuspected scale. The eventual fruition of an emergent transitional-integrationist paradigm in American life will depend upon the steady expansion of these new avenues of transracial interpersonal networking among blacks and whites.

REFERENCES

BALTZELL, E. DIGBY. *The Protestant Establishment.* New York, 1964.

BILLINGSLEY, ANDREW. *Climbing Jacob's Ladder: The Enduring Legacy of African-American Families.* New York, 1993.

BOND, HORACE MANN. *The Education of the Negro in the American Social Order.* New York, 1934.

DENT, DAVID J. "The New Black Suburbs." *New York Times Magazine* (June 14, 1992): 18–25.

FARLEY, REYNOLDS. "The Common Destiny of Blacks and Whites: Observations about the Social and Economic Status of the Races." In Herbert Hill and James E. Jones, *Race in America: The Struggle for Equality.* Madison, Wis., 1993.

FRAZIER, E. FRANKLIN. *Black Bourgeoisie.* New York, 1957.

JAYNES, GERALD, and ROBIN M. WILLIAMS. *A Common Destiny: Blacks and American Society.* Washington, D.C., 1989.

KILSON, MARTIN. "Anatomy of Black Conservatism." *Transition* 59, 1993.

LANDRY, BART. "The New Black Middle Class." *Focus: Journal of Joint Center for Political and Economic Studies* 15 (September 1987): 5–7.

SKLARE, MARSHALL. *Jewish Identity on the Suburban Frontier.* Chicago, 1979.

WESTCOTT, DIANE. "Blacks in the 1970s: Did They Scale the Job Ladder?" *Monthly Labor Review* 100 (June 1982): 29–38.

WILSON, FRANK HAROLD. "The Changing Distribution of the African American Population in the United States, 1980–1990." *Urban League Review* 15 (Winter 1991/1992): 53–74.

MARTIN KILSON

Classical Music. *See* Concert Music; Music; Opera.

Clay, Cassius. *See* Ali, Muhammad.

Clay, William Lacy (April 30, 1931–), congressman. Born in St. Louis, Mo., William Clay was the son of Luella and Irvin Clay, a welder. He attended the city's public schools, helping to support himself by working as a tailor and clothing store salesman. He then attended St. Louis University, graduating with a B.A. in 1953. Following his graduation, Clay was drafted into the army. After his discharge in 1955, he returned to St. Louis, and worked several years at such jobs as insurance salesman and bus driver. Meanwhile, he became active in civil rights efforts in association with the St. Louis branch of the CONGRESS OF RACIAL EQUALITY (CORE) and with the NAACP. In 1959, with aid from group members, Clay was elected to the St. Louis Board of Alderman. During his first term, Clay sponsored passage of the city's first Fair Employment Act. Reelected in 1963, Clay proposed an ordinance banning discrimination in public accommodations, but he resigned from the board shortly after, and was selected for the more influential post of Democratic ward committeeman.

Clay became involved in political organizing while on the Board of Aldermen. In 1961 he was named business representative for the city branch of the state, county, and municipal employees' union. He also engaged in civil rights work, and spent four months in prison in 1963 following a demonstration at the city's Jefferson Bank and Trust Company. In 1966 he became election coordinator for the local branch of the powerful steamfitters' union.

In 1968 a black majority congressional district opened up in St. Louis following redistricting. Clay won a five-person Democratic primary by 6,500 votes, then handily defeated his white Republican opponent in the general election to became Missouri's first black member of Congress. Initially Clay was assigned to the Education and Labor Committee, where he called for a raise in the minimum wage and for stronger fair employment laws. As head of the Labor-Management Relations Subcommittee, he began a long-standing effort to pass legislation requiring employers to hire back striking workers following settlement of labor disputes. As head of the Subcommittee on Pensions, Clay obtained changes in laws that allowed workers to be vested in the system after fewer years of experience.

In 1975 Clay was the target of investigations following charges that he had engaged in drug trafficking and evaded income taxes. Although exonerated of any drug charges by the Justice Department, he sharply criticized what he claimed were politically motivated attacks on his character. He was also embarrassed in 1992 by revelations that he had overdrawn 290 checks on his account in the House bank.

Despite both attacks, Clay was easily reelected in 1976 and 1992.

Long a member of the House Post Office and Civil Service Committee, Clay was named chair in December 1990, a post he held for four years. During his tenure he sponsored legislation extending job safety protections to post office workers, and worked to amend the Hatch Act to permit lobbying and voluntary political action by federal workers.

Clay is the author of two books: *Thoughts on the Death Penalty* (1976), an investigation of capital punishment; and *Just Permanent Interests* (1992), a history of blacks in Congress.

REFERENCES

CHRISTOPHER, MAURINE. *Black Americans in Congress.* New York, 1976.

CLAY, WILLIAM L. *Just Permanent Interests: Black Americans in Congress, 1870–1991.* New York, 1992.

GREG ROBINSON

Claytor, William Waldron Schieffelin (January 4, 1908–July 14, 1967), mathematician. William Claytor was born in Norfolk, Va. A graduate of Dunbar High School in Washington, D.C., he briefly attended Hampton Institute before matriculating at Howard University in 1925. A mathematics major, he graduated with a B.S. in 1929. During the 1929–1930 academic year, he was enrolled in Howard's graduate division, pursuing advanced studies in mathematics.

In 1930 Claytor transferred to the University of Pennsylvania. There, he held the Harrison Scholarship (1931–1932) and the Harrison Fellowship (1932–1933); he earned a Ph.D. in mathematics in 1933. His research specialty, topology, involved the analysis of intrinsic properties that distinguish shapes. Part of his doctoral work, on "immersion of Peanian continua in a spherical surface," was presented at a meeting of the American Mathematical Society on April 14, 1933. He was the first to propose a complete solution to the problem of the immersion of a continuous curve in the Euclidean plane. His work was highly regarded by his professor, J. R. Kline. In ranking students who earned Ph.D.s under him, Kline considered Claytor to be second only to Leo Zippin (who later helped solve Hilbert's fifth problem: which kinds of manifolds admit a Lie group structure).

Claytor taught at West Virginia State College (1933–1935) before receiving a fellowship from the Julius Rosenwald Fund for postdoctoral research in mathematics at the University of Michigan. While affiliated with Michigan, he presented another study—a continuation of his interest in topology—before the American Mathematical Society on December 30, 1936. He taught in the extension department at Michigan until 1941, when he went into service in the army. A private in Company G at Fort George, Md., he rose to the rank of first lieutenant. After World War II, Claytor resumed teaching. He held faculty posts at Southern University (1945–1946), Hampton Institute (1946–1947), and Howard University (1947–1967). His topological studies, published in *Annals of Mathematics* (1934 and 1937), were cited regularly by subsequent mathematicians.

REFERENCE

NEWELL, VIRGINIA K., et al., eds. *Black Mathematicians and Their Works*. Ardmore, Pa., 1980, pp. 69–84, 282.

KENNETH R. MANNING

Cleaver, Eldridge Leroy (August 31, 1935–), writer, political activist. Eldridge Cleaver was born in Wabbaseka, Ark., where he attended a junior college. From 1954 to 1957 and again from 1958 to 1966 he was incarcerated on drug and rape charges, and furthered his education while in prison. In 1965, Cleaver became the most prominent "Black Muslim" prisoner to break with Elijah MUHAMMAD's NATION OF ISLAM after MALCOLM X's assassination. Just as FBI director J. Edgar Hoover had begun to target the BLACK PANTHERS as the nation's "greatest threat," Cleaver became the party's minister of information in 1966, calling for an armed insurrection to overthrow the United States government and replace it with a black socialist government. During the late 1960s and early '70s, he also was an assistant editor and contributing writer to *Ramparts* magazine.

In 1968, Cleaver published *Soul on Ice,* which remains his primary claim to literary fame. A collection of autobiographical and political essays in the form of letters and meditations, *Soul on Ice* articulated the sense of alienation felt by many black nationalists who refused to work within an inherently corrupt system. Cleaver viewed his own crimes as political acts and spelled out how racism and oppression had forged his revolutionary consciousness.

Later that year, while on parole, Cleaver was involved in a shootout with Oakland police during which a seventeen-year-old Black Panther, Bobby Hutton, was killed; Cleaver and a police officer were wounded. Cleaver's parole was revoked and he was charged with assault and attempted murder. Although he received worldwide support and was chosen to run as the presidential candidate for the Peace

Eldridge Cleaver (left) at the Black Panther party rally, Oakland, Calif., July 1968. (© Bob Fitch/Black Star)

and Freedom Party (*see* Dick GREGORY for discussion of another 1968 black antiwar presidential candidate), Cleaver feared for his safety if he surrendered to the authorities. He fled the country, jumping a $50,000 bail, and lived for the next seven years in Cuba, France and Algiers. He also visited the Soviet Union, China, North Vietnam, and North Korea during these years of exile. But in 1975 he returned to the United States and struck a deal with the FBI. Although he faced up to seventy-two years in prison, he was sentenced instead to 1,200 hours of community service.

In 1978, Cleaver published *Soul on Fire,* a collection of essays on his newly acquired conservative politics, and in 1979 he founded the Eldridge Cleaver Crusades, an evangelical organization. In 1984 he ran as an independent candidate for Congress in the eighth Congressional District in California. In the 1980s, he lectured on religion and politics, and published his own poetry and polemical writings. In March 1994, his struggle with drugs came to national attention when he underwent brain surgery after he had been arrested in Berkeley, Calif., late at night with a serious head injury, in a state of drunkenness and disorientation.

Cleaver has been a prolific writer and speaker and was seen by some in the late 1960s as a black leader capable of organizing and leading a mass movement. *Soul on Ice* won the Martin Luther King Memorial Prize in 1970. Most of his work consists of nonfiction writing: *Eldridge Cleaver: Post-Prison Writings and Speeches* (1969), *Eldridge Cleaver's Black Papers* (1969), the introduction to Jerry Rubin's *Do It!* (1970), and contributions to *The Black Panther Leaders Speak: Huey P. Newton, Bobby Seale, Eldridge Cleaver, and Company Speak Out Through the Black Panther Party's Official Newspaper* (1976) and to *War Within: Violence or Nonviolence in Black Revolution* (1971). He has also authored and coauthored numerous pamphlets for the Black Panther party and the People's Communication Network. Some of his work has also appeared in anthologies such as the *Prize Stories of 1971: The O. Henry Awards*.

Cleaver has had both his critics and his followers. There are those who felt that his commitment to violence and his use of rape as a political weapon in the 1960s had no place within society. Others have questioned the sincerity and credibility of his later *volte face* to right-wing politics and fundamentalist Christianity, and Cleaver has often felt compelled to explain and defend himself. According to him, combined with his growing disenchantment with communism and radical politics was a mystical vision resulting in his conversion to Christianity. When accused of having mellowed with age, Cleaver replied, "That implies that your ideas have changed because of age. I've changed because of new conclusions."

REFERENCES

BARANSKI, LYNNE, and RICHARD LEMON. *People* (March 22, 1982).
HUNTER, CHARLAYNE. "To Mr. and Mrs. Yesterday," *New York Times Book Review* (March 24, 1968): 3.

AMRITJIT SINGH

Clement, Rufus Early (June 26, 1900–November 7, 1967), educator. Rufus Early Clement was born in Salisbury, N.C., the son of George Clinton Clement, a bishop of the African Methodist Episcopal Church. In 1919 Clement graduated as valedictorian from Livingstone College in Salisbury. He earned a Bachelor of Divinity degree at Garrett Theological Seminary, Evanston, Ill., in 1922. That same year he received an M.A. at Northwestern University, where in 1930 he was awarded a Ph.D. for his dissertation on the history of black education in North Carolina between 1865 and 1928.

In the fall of 1922, Clement began his teaching career as an instructor in history at Livingstone College in Salisbury, N.C. Three years later, at the age of twenty-five, he was made professor and was chosen dean of the college. Clement left Livingstone in 1931 to become the first dean of Louisville Municipal College in Kentucky, a new all-black educational institution affiliated with the University of Louisville. He remained there until 1937, when he was elected by the board of directors of Atlanta University to succeed John HOPE as president.

Clement served as president of Atlanta University until 1967. While there he developed several professional schools and programs designed to increase employment among blacks, including a school for library service and the People's College, an adult education program, both founded in 1941. In 1944 the School of Education was founded, followed by the School of Business Administration in 1946.

Clement was also a leader in the Atlanta black community, and challenged segregation throughout his career. In 1953 he was elected to the Atlanta Board of Education by a sweeping majority, which made him the first African American to be elected to public office in that city since RECONSTRUCTION; he served until 1967. As a school board member, Clement devised a plan in 1960 to integrate Atlanta's public schools under a federal court decree. As a member of the Commission on Inter-racial Cooperation, Clement was instrumental in efforts to secure voting rights for blacks. Along with the Rev. Dr. Martin Luther KING, Jr. and other civil rights leaders, he helped negotiate an end to a boycott of downtown Atlanta businesses by Atlanta University students and local citizens in 1961 that effectively forced them to desegregate.

Clement also participated in a number of national organizations including the Advisory Council on African Affairs to the State Department. In 1964 he was chosen by President Lyndon Johnson to represent the United States in Malawi (formerly known as Nyasaland) on the occasion of its independence. Clement died in 1967 while in New York City attending a series of meetings with Atlanta University trustees.

REFERENCES

BRANCH, TAYLOR. *Parting the Waters: America in the King Years 1954–63.* New York, 1988.
MAYS, BENJAMIN E. *Born to Rebel: An Autobiography.* 1971. Reprint. Athens, Ga., 1972.
Obituary. *New York Times.* November 8, 1967, p. 40.

JOSEPH W. LOWNDES
SUSAN MCINTOSH

Clemente, Roberto (August 18, 1934–December 31, 1972), baseball player and humanitarian. The seventh and youngest child of Luisa (Walker) and Melchor Clemente, a sugar-mill foreman in Carolina, Puerto Rico, Roberto Clemente became his island's most illustrious native son. Playing with a skill and a verve that won the acclaim of fans throughout the Western Hemisphere, Clemente became major league BASEBALL's first pan-Caribbean star. He was respected off the field as much as he was on it.

After debuting with the Puerto Rican Santurce Cangrejeros in 1952, Clemente signed with the Brooklyn Dodgers. Drafted out of the Dodger organization by the Pittsburgh Pirates a year later, the 5'11", 185-pound ball player soon became a graceful fixture in right field at Forbes Field.

In his eighteen seasons with the Pirates, Clemente won four National League batting titles, hit 240 home runs, and compiled a lifetime .317 batting average. A perennial all-star and the 1966 National League Most Valuable Player, the rifle-armed Clemente won twelve Gold Gloves for his fielding.

Clemente was a star on the Pirates' 1960 championship club, and his inspired play led the team back from a two-games-to-none deficit in the 1971 World Series. He hit safely in all fourteen series games he played in, with a cumulative .362 average.

On September 30, 1972, Clemente doubled in what turned out to be his last regular season at-bat. It was his three thousandth hit, making him only the eleventh major leaguer to reach that plateau.

Following that season, Clemente managed the Puerto Rican team in the world amateur championships in Nicaragua. When Managua was struck by an earthquake after his return to Puerto Rico, he plunged into relief efforts. Upon hearing reports of the Nicaraguan National Guard plundering relief supplies, Clemente set forth for Managua on New Year's Eve, 1972. His plane never made it, disappearing into the Caribbean soon after takeoff. His body was never recovered.

A proud man, Clemente protested the discrimination that Latin and black ball players encountered. Before his death, he had begun work on Ciudad Deportiva, a sport city for Puerto Rican youth. His wife, Vera Clemente de Zabala, has since made his dream into a multisport reality. Clemente's death led the Hall of Fame to waive its five-year rule; he was elected only weeks after his untimely death.

REFERENCE

WAGGENHEIM, HAL. *Clemente!* New York, 1973.

ROB RUCK

Roberto Clemente, a veteran of eighteen seasons with the Pittsburgh Pirates, died in a plane crash coming to the assistance of victims of the 1972 Managua, Nicaragua, earthquake. In 1973, he was elected the first Latino member of the Baseball Hall of Fame. (AP/Wide World Photos)

Cleveland, James Edward (1931–1991), gospel singer. Born in Chicago, James Cleveland was educated in public schools and began piano lessons at the age of five. Three years later he became a soloist in Thomas A. DORSEY's Junior Gospel Choir at Pilgrim Baptist Church. At age fifteen he joined a local group, the Thorne Crusaders, with whom he remained for the next eight years. He began composing, and at age sixteen wrote "Grace Is Sufficient," recorded by the Roberta MARTIN Singers and now a part of the standard gospel repertory.

After leaving the Thornes, Cleveland served as pianist and arranger for Albertina Walker's Caravans and recorded with them. He later joined the Gospel Chimes and the Gospel All-Stars, and eventually organized the James Cleveland Singers. In 1963 he joined Rev. Lawrence Roberts and his choir at First Baptist Church in Nutley, N.J., to make a number of recordings beginning with "Peace, Be Still" (1962). Cleveland liked a treble sound and dispensed with the bass voice in the gospel choir. He also preferred the call-and-response delivery to singing in concert, and on choir recordings played the role of preacher to the choir as congregation. He felt that gospel needed a congregation present, and made all his choir recordings live.

During the 1950s and 1960s, Cleveland wrote over five hundred songs, including "Oh, Lord, Stand By Me" (1952), "He's Using Me" (1953), "Walk On by Faith" (1962), and "Lord, Help Me to Hold Out" (1973). He continued to compose into the 1980s, and scored a success with the Mighty Clouds of Joy recording of "I Get a Blessing Everyday" (1980).

The Cleveland style was one of half-crooning, half-preaching the verses and then moving into sung refrains. His hard gospel technique of singing at the extremes of his register created a contrast with the falsetto he employed. He was fond of the vamp—a section of the song, usually toward the end, when the choir repeated one phrase, over which he extemporized variations. Like Dorsey, Cleveland wrote and sang in the everyday language of his audiences, dealing with such common subjects as paying rent and buying food.

In August 1968 he formed the Gospel Music Workshop of America, an organization with several hundred thousand members by the mid-1980s. Each year's convention released a recording; one of the better known was with his protégée Aretha FRANKLIN ("Amazing Grace," 1971), who studied his style when he was director of the Radio Choir at Detroit's New Bethel Baptist Church, where her father, Rev. C. L. FRANKLIN, was pastor.

Known as the "Crown Prince of Gospel" and "King of Gospel," Cleveland won several gold records and three Grammy Awards, appeared at Carnegie Hall, worked with Quincy JONES in the TV production of *Roots,* and recorded the opera *Porgy and Bess* with Ray CHARLES and Cleo Laine. In 1980, along with Natalie Cole, he starred in the television special *In the Spirit,* filmed in England for Grenada Television (BBC). In November 1970, Cleveland organized and became pastor of Cornerstone Institutional Baptist Church in Los Angeles, with sixty charter members. At his death in 1991, membership totaled over seven thousand.

REFERENCES

BOYER, HORACE CLARENCE. "A Comparative Analysis of Traditional and Contemporary Gospel Music." In *More than Dancing: Essays on Afro-American Music and Musicians.* Westport, Conn., 1985.

HEILBUT, ANTHONY. *The Gospel Sound: Good News and Bad Times.* New York, 1975.

HORACE CLARENCE BOYER

Cleveland, Ohio. Cleveland has had African-American connections from its earliest days. The city and the surrounding Western Reserve area were founded in 1798 by explorers from the Connecticut Land Company, who brought along an African American, "Black Joe," as guide and interpreter. While a fugitive slave named Ben spent several months in Cleveland in 1806, the first African-American Clevelander, George Peake, arrived with his family in 1809. Peake, a farmer and ex-soldier from Maryland, later invented an improved hand mill for grinding corn. Few blacks settled in the growing community, however. In 1820 there were only fifty-four blacks in the vicinity, and just three were within city limits. White residents were not particularly friendly to them, though in 1819 a Cleveland jury convicted two white men on kidnapping charges for the attempted recapture of a FUGITIVE SLAVE from Virginia. In 1827, despite strong black opposition, the Cuyahoga County Colonization Society was formed to support efforts at sending blacks to Africa.

There were still only seventy-six blacks in Cleveland in 1830, most of them living in the town's eastern section, when Cleveland's first black church, St. John's African Methodist Episcopal (AME) Church, was organized. During the next two decades, the area's black population grew to over three hundred. Under the leadership of John Malvin, a sailor and merchant from Cincinnati, the city's black community organized the School Fund Society, which ran schools intermittently until city funding was granted in 1843. In 1839 the Young Men's Union Society (later the Colored Young Men's Lyceum), a literary and political club, was founded.

During this period, Cleveland, along with the rest of the surrounding Western Reserve, was settled by masses of white New Englanders, many of whom were reformers and evangelicals with powerful antislavery convictions. In 1833 the Cleveland (later the Cuyahoga County) Anti-Slavery Society was formed. Cleveland soon became a center of abolitionist activity and a primary station on the UNDERGROUND RAILROAD. Black activists included John Malvin, William Howard Day, editor of Cleveland's first black newspaper, the *Alienated American* (1853–1855), and barber John Brown, the city's wealthiest African American. They joined whites such as Joshua Giddings (elected to Congress on the Free Soil ticket in 1850) to aid fugitive slaves and lobby for civil rights and suffrage. In 1849 they helped bring about the repeal of most of the state's Black Laws (see BLACK CODES).

Under abolitionist influence, Cleveland's white population developed a distinctive racial liberalism, and a large part of its white population supported black equality. By the end of the 1840s, the city's public schools and most of its churches were integrated. Segregation in public places was rare, and blacks were able to find housing throughout the city. Numerous African Americans found jobs as skilled laborers. Others entered the professions; notable among them was Robert Boyd Leach, one of the few antebellum black doctors. A few African Americans, such as Brown, cattle dealer Alfred Greenbrier, and contractor Madison Tilley, occupied prominent places in the city economy.

An important result of Cleveland's racial tolerance was that the city's black population shared the facilities of the larger community, and separate black institutions were thus few and poorly supported. While a National Emigration Convention of Colored Men was organized in the city in 1854, most community leaders were integrationist.

The outbreak of the CIVIL WAR in 1861 prompted widespread excitement in Cleveland, and black leaders called for the Union Army to accept black soldiers. However, it was not until 1863 that blacks were accepted into the Army. As many as fifteen hundred blacks fought in the 127th Ohio Volunteer Infantry (later absorbed into the Fifth Ohio United States Colored Troop). In honor of African-American contributions to the victory, a black soldier is depicted in the city's Soldiers & Sailors Monument, dedicated in 1894.

In the years after the Civil War, a modest number of blacks, largely from the Upper South, migrated to Cleveland, but African Americans remained less than 2 percent of the total population. In 1870 all black males in Ohio were enfranchised, and three years later Republican John P. Green was elected justice of the peace, becoming Cleveland's first black officeholder. In 1882, with the aid of white votes, he won election to the state legislature. In 1891 Green was elected to the state senate. However, at the same time, Cleveland's tradition of racial tolerace began to decline. Discrimination restricted black job prospects. Between 1865 and 1890, the proportion of black homeowners fell from over 33 percent to 15 percent. Segregation of public facilities grew increasingly common despite the 1887 Ohio civil rights law.

As housing segregation increased, the East Side's Central Avenue district became largely a black area. In the face of exclusion, black Clevelanders organized within their own community. St. John's AME church grew in size, and three more churches, including Mount Zion Congregational Church and Cory Methodist Church, were established by 1890. Institutions such as the Cleveland Home for Aged Colored People (1896) were created.

Cleveland also featured a lively black cultural scene at the end of the nineteenth century. Lyceums and debating clubs, such as the Coral Builders Society and the Wide Awake Literary Society, sprang up. In 1883 Harry Clay Smith, a twenty-year-old from West Virginia, founded the *Cleveland Gazette,* a weekly black newspaper that became the voice of black Cleveland. Despite competition from various short-lived journals, it remained in circulation for over seventy years. Black theater, beginning in the 1850s with the Dramatic Temple, remained popular. Many important musicians came from Cleveland, including Charles McAfee, bassoonist with the Cleveland Orchestra and also the leader of the Excelsior Band and the McAfee and Bowman Orchestra; concert singer Rachel Turner Walker, "the Creole Nightingale"; opera composer Harry Lawrence FREEMAN; and Justin Miner Holland, famed for his guitar instruction manual.

The most eminent black Clevelander of the late nineteenth century was lawyer/novelist Charles W. CHESNUTT, who came to the city in 1883. Admitted to the Ohio bar in 1887, he made his living as a lawyer and court reporter. Meanwhile, he became nationally known for his speeches, novels, and short stories. Chesnutt was the first African-American member of the Cleveland Chamber of Commerce, and in 1912 he helped found the Cleveland branch of the NATIONAL ASSOCIATION FOR THE ADVANCEMENT OF COLORED PEOPLE (NAACP). Another notable resident was Garrett Morgan, who came to Cleveland in 1895; a businessman and newspaper editor, he was best known for his inventions.

Cleveland's black population doubled during the 1890s as large-scale migration from the South began, and the city continued to receive migrants during the first part of the century. However, white immigrants from Europe also settled in Cleveland, and the proportion of blacks in the population remained under 2 percent. Although Cleveland managed to avoid the extremes of racial violence that occurred elsewhere, the city became heavily segregated. While the public schools remained integrated, industrial jobs were closed to blacks due to employer and union exclusion, and most poor blacks were forced into low-paying menial labor. Middle-class African Americans were denied equal access to civil service and white-collar jobs, and black businessmen were forced to redirect their services towards an all-black market. A few wealthy blacks, such as barber George Myers, continued to be accepted among the city's elite.

The concentration of blacks in the Central Avenue area heightened black influence in politics. The leading black politicians were George Myers and Harry Clay Smith, two disciples of Republican political boss Mark Hanna. Smith, who founded the Afro-American Republican Club in 1892, served three terms in the state assembly, while Myers (son of Baltimore labor leader Isaac Myers) served as a delegate to three Republican national conventions. In 1910 Thomas Fleming, an African American, was appointed to Cleveland's city council, and with the aid of saloonkeeper and political boss "Starlight" Boyd, he was elected to a regular term five years later. Meanwhile, in 1901 the First Johnson Negro Democratic Club, headed by Walter L. Brown, was formed. Although blacks were unable to win Democratic support for citywide office until the 1920s, in 1909 Brown won the party's nomination for justice of the peace.

During the Great Migration, beginning around 1915, Cleveland was a principal destination of southern black migrants. By 1930 the black population was almost nine times larger than it had been in 1910. The migration had wide-reaching economic, political, and social consequences for black Cleveland. The civilian labor shortage that occurred during World War I forced industrial employers to hire black male workers; by 1920 a higher percentage of African Americans worked in industry in Cleveland than in any other city except DETROIT. While blacks remained largely excluded from unions and were unable to move beyond low-level positions, median family income increased. The wages of these workers made possible a growing black middle class. In 1921 Herbert Chauncey founded the Empire Savings & Loan Company, the city's first black-owned bank.

At the same time, the migration strained scarce city housing resources. Blacks were forced into already crowded and unhealthy housing in the Central-Woodland district. The migrants paid high rents for space in the district's tenements and apartment houses (many of which were owned by middle-class blacks). Attempts by blacks to move outside the district were met by violence. In 1925, when Charles Garvin, a black doctor and community leader, bought a house in an all-white neighborhood, it was destroyed by a bomb.

The growing population increased black political power and assertiveness. Under the leadership of Claybourne George, the Cleveland NAACP, which boasted sixteen hundred members by 1922, instituted dozens of civil rights suits to challenge black exclusion and campaigned for the hiring of black workers by city business. Marcus GARVEY's UNIVERSAL NEGRO IMPROVEMENT ASSOCIATION also had a powerful Cleveland chapter, organized by Leroy Bundy.

Black institutions were formed to aid the migrants. The most notable were the Negro Welfare Association (later the Cleveland Urban League), founded in 1917, and the Phillis Wheatley Association, a settlement house for black women, founded in 1913. Another institution was the *Cleveland Call & Post* newspaper, formed by the merger of two small journals in 1927 and still in publication in the 1990s.

At the same time, black representation and influence on the city council increased. By 1929 a "black triumvirate" of George, Bundy, and Lawrence Payne had been elected. Since the three controlled the balance of power in an often deadlocked council, they were able to trade votes during the following three years for the integration of City Hospital and for committee chairmanships. Over the subsequent decade, they used these chairmanships to obtain welfare aid and city services for the black community as well as the appointment of blacks to city commissions.

Despite the unpleasant conditions in the Central-Woodland district, a strong entertainment culture developed in the "Roaring 3rd" section in the 1920s and '30s. Dance halls, such as the Golden Slipper (later the Trianon), and jazz dance clubs, such as Val's in the Valley (renowned during the early 1930s for the presence of pianist Art TATUM), grew up in the area. Cleveland also launched the careers of jazz artists such as violinist Hezekiah "Stuff" SMITH. Another important cultural resource was the nationally known Karamu House, a white-run interracial theater and settlement house founded as the Playhouse Settlement in 1915. The Karamu Theater, opened in 1927, sponsored dance and acting classes as well as amateur theatrical productions written by such African Americans as Shirley Graham and Langston HUGHES (who spent some of his youth in Cleveland).

Sports were also a popular pastime. Cleveland fielded several professional black baseball teams, notably the Cleveland Buckeyes, Negro American League champions of the 1940s. The city's most celebrated athlete was Jesse OWENS, who became a national hero after winning four gold medals in track and field in the 1936 Olympics.

The GREAT DEPRESSION led to widespread unemployment among Cleveland's blacks, and the African-American population declined slightly as residents left the city in search of work. Many black businesses, including the Empire Savings & Loan, were forced to close. Several insurance companies developed financial problems, and in 1936 four companies merged into the Dunbar Mutual Insurance Company, which became the city's largest black-owned business. Despite the efforts of such groups as the Future Outlook League, which successfully used boycotts to fight job discrimination, inequality remained a chronic problem. During the decade, many blacks were able to find emergency employment through New Deal social programs, and the community's political allegiance swung to the Democratic party.

The industrial surge that accompanied WORLD WAR II and the postwar prosperity drew new waves of black migrants to Cleveland in search of industrial employment. The city's black population grew from 84,504 to 250,818 in twenty years. With help from the federal FAIR EMPLOYMENT PRACTICES COMMITTEE, blacks were able to find jobs and to advance into previously all-white positions. The migration also made possible advances in black political power; by 1960 there were ten blacks on Cleveland's city council, and blacks were active in city commissions. No large city had a higher level of black political representation. Civil rights activity also increased. By 1945 the NAACP's membership jumped to ten thousand. The same year, the Cleveland Community Relations Board was founded. It drafted a city ordinance, enacted in 1946, revoking the licenses of public facilities which were found to have excluded blacks.

The new migration prompted recurring housing shortages in the deteriorating Central-Woodland area where most blacks were forced to live. In the years after the war, blacks began to expand into the Glenville and Mount Pleasant neighborhoods, which had long had black residents. During the 1950s blacks began to move into the once fashionable, previously all-white Hough neighborhood. The area became largely black within ten years. Black residents in these areas of Cleveland were faced with poor city services, deteriorating schools, and police repression. (A warrantless police search of the home of Dollree Mapp, a black woman, led to the landmark 1961 U.S. Supreme Court case *Mapp* v. *Ohio*.)

The CIVIL RIGHTS MOVEMENT dramatically expanded in Cleveland during the 1960s. In 1963 the NAACP organized the United Freedom Movement (UFM), an alliance of some fifty groups. In 1963 and 1964 the UFM launched a campaign against de facto school segregation. Leaders sued to halt construction of new schools, and interracial contingents demonstrated at schools in white areas that segregated black students bused from inner-city areas. On several occasions violence erupted when white mobs confronted the protesters, and in April 1964 a small riot broke out after a white demonstrator was accidentally killed during a construction site protest. Leaders organized a school boycott, but Mayor Ralph Lochner and city leaders refused to meet with UFM representatives. Split by factionalism, by 1966 the UFM had virtually disintegrated.

On July 18, 1966, the frustration over inequality that had been building up in black Cleveland overflowed, and full-scale rioting broke out in the Hough

neighborhood. A crowd of blacks destroyed a tavern after an altercation inside. Police were called in, but the rioting intensified. Mayor Lochner called in units of the Ohio National Guard and closed all the city's bars, but the rioting continued for six nights. Four people were killed, thirty were injured, and three hundred were arrested.

In 1967 Carl STOKES, a state legislator who had run for mayor as an independent two years previously and narrowly lost, ran again, this time on the Democratic ticket. Stokes's narrow victory, based on a near-unanimous black vote (African Americans made up about a third of the city's population) and one-fourth of the white vote, made him the first black mayor of a large city. The following year his brother, Louis STOKES, ran for Congress from a newly created black-majority district and was elected Cleveland's first black congressman. The victories of the Stokes brothers were important symbols of black political power in the city. Carl Stokes put through important reforms; he implemented affirmative action through an equal employment opportunity ordinance, increased spending for housing and welfare (with the help of federal funding frozen under previous administrations), and created Cleveland:Now! a joint public-private program for community rehabilitation, which raised more than $100 million in funds.

However, Stokes's administration was crippled by the Glenville Shootout of July 23, 1968, a gun battle in Glenville between police and black militants led by Fred "Ahmad" Evans. It left seven dead (including three policemen) and set off rioting by local blacks. Stokes called in National Guard troops, then cordoned off the area, ordering only black police and community leaders inside to calm rioters. However, the rioting continued for three days, demonstrating that the election of a black mayor was not sufficient to eliminate racial tension and violence. Cleveland: Now! was discredited when it was revealed at Evans's trial that he had purchased guns with money obtained indirectly through the program. Stokes was reelected in 1969, but he was unable to persuade voters to approve higher income taxes for better city services or to reform the city police department. He declined to run again in 1971. Though blacks continued to occupy positions of power on the city council, it was not until 1990 that the city elected another black mayor, Michael White.

Since the end of the 1960s, Cleveland has had many of the same problems as other deindustrializing cities. The poor economy and racial tension have led whites and middle-class blacks to migrate to nearby suburbs. (As a result, Shaker Heights has developed a large black population.) By 1990 the city of Cleveland had a near majority of blacks in its population. Most of Cleveland's blacks, concentrated in East

Cleveland, faced decrepit housing and schools. A 1983 report identified Cleveland as one of the nation's three most segregated cities. (In 1976 a U.S. District Court ordered busing to assure desegregated schools.) The city economy remained sluggish. In 1978 Cleveland briefly went into default on its obligations. Despite economic development through such programs as the Gateway Project, a nonprofit public construction firm with significant minority participation, black unemployment remained high. The closing of the First National Bank Association in 1990 was a blow to black business in Cleveland.

Barriers to advancement notwithstanding, there have been many black success stories. In 1974 Frank ROBINSON of the Cleveland Indians was hired as major league baseball's first black manager. In 1990 Thomas Greer became editor of the *Cleveland Plain Dealer,* the city's main newspaper. Clevelanders, in fact, have achieved some success in many fields in recent decades. Notable figures include musicians Tadd DAMERON and jazz avant-gardist Albert Ayler, stage figures Dorothy DANDRIDGE and Ruby DEE, promoter Don KING, and writers Chester HIMES and Russell Atkins.

The city's complex black history has been preserved at the city's Afro-American Cultural and Historical Society Museum, founded in 1953 and established in a permanent building in 1983.

REFERENCES

BLACK, LOWELL DWIGHT. *The Negro Volunteer Militia Units in the Ohio National Guard, 1870–1954.* Cleveland, 1976.
DAVIS, RUSSELL H. *Black Americans in Cleveland.* Washington, D.C., 1972.
KUSMER, KENNETH. *A Ghetto Takes Shape: Black Cleveland, 1870–1930.* Urbana, Ill., 1976.
PORTER, PHILIP W. *Cleveland: Confused City on a Screw.* Columbus, Ohio, 1976.
VAN TASSEL, DAVID D., and JOHN J. GRABOWSKI, eds. *The Encyclopedia of Cleveland History.* Bloomington, Ind., 1987.

GREG ROBINSON

Clifton, Thelma Lucille (June 27, 1936–), poet, author, and educator. Born in Depew, N.Y., to Samuel L. Sayles, Jr., and Thelma Moore Sayles, Lucille Sayles attended Howard University and Fredonia State Teachers College, where she met her husband, Fred J. Clifton, and author Ishmael REED, who publicized her poetry. Clifton's first book of poetry, *Good Times: Poems,* published in 1969, was cited by the *New York Times* as one of the ten best books of that year.

Clifton, a prolific writer, is the author of seven books of poetry, a memoir, and numerous contributions to magazines and anthologies. She has also written, in both prose and verse, twenty-one books for children. Her "Everett Anderson" series tells of the adventures of a young black boy. Clifton's 1983 book *Everett Anderson's Goodbye* won the Coretta Scott King Award of the American Library Association (1984). She has also received the Discovery Award from YM/YWHA Poetry Center of New York (1969); National Endowment for the Arts awards (1970, 1972); and the Juniper Prize (1980). She served as Poet Laureate of the State of Maryland from 1979 to 1982, and she was nominated for the Pulitzer Prize in 1980 for *Two-Headed Woman* and in 1988 for *Next: New Poems.* Clifton has received honorary doctorates from the University of Maryland and from Towson State University. She has been a visiting writer at Columbia University and at George Washington University, has served as Poet in Residence at Coppin State College, and since 1985 has taught at the University of California at Santa Cruz.

Clifton's work has been described as exemplifying "endurance and strength through adversity." She writes of family, ghetto life, and the role of the poet. Her poetry makes use of a creative mix of black dialects and standard English in order to capture and encompass different voices. In her children's books, Clifton uses urban settings and nontraditional relationships as a way of considering family issues and matters of concern to African Americans.

REFERENCES

METZGER, LINDA, ed. *Black Writers: A Selection of Sketches from Contemporary Authors.* Detroit, 1989.
ROLLOCK, BARBARA. *Black Authors and Illustrators of Children's Books: A Biographical Dictionary.* Westport, Conn., 1988.

LILY PHILLIPS

Clinton, George (July 22, 1941–), funk musician. Born in Kannapolis, N.C., George Clinton grew up in Plainfield, N.J., and learned to sing as a child. When he was fourteen he formed a doo-wop group, the Parliaments, while working full-time, first in a hula hoop factory, and then as a hairdresser at a local hair salon. The Parliaments recorded "Sunday Kind of Love" (1956), "Party Boys" (1957), and "Cry" (1958), but none of these recordings were successful. Nonetheless, Clinton came to the attention of Berry GORDY, who in 1962 hired him as a writer for MOTOWN Records, but was unimpressed by the music of the Parliaments. In 1966 the Parliaments recorded "I Want to Testify," a performance that signaled a new direction for Clinton. In 1967 he expanded the ensemble to include loud horns and electric instruments, and incorporated hard, spare rhythms that became known as funk. In 1968 Bernard Worrell joined the band to record *Whatever Makes My Baby Feel Good*. The next year Clinton organized Funkadelic, a group made up of many of the new Parliaments, playing in the same style. Funkadelic recorded *Music for My Mother* (1969).

In the 1970s Clinton worked simultaneously with these two groups, Parliament (as it was now known) and Funkadelic, to become the major exponent of funk music, presiding over a virtual empire of costumed, wildly imaginative singers, instrumentalists, songwriters, and producers, among them Bootsy Collins, who joined in 1972. Among Parliament's recordings are *Up for the Down Stroke* (1974), the 1975 million-sellers *Chocolate City* and *Mothership Connection*, *The Clones of Dr. Funkenstein* (1976), *Funkentelechy vs. the Placebo Syndrome* (1977), and *Gloryhallastoopid* (1979). Funkadelic's recordings from the 1970s include *Free Your Ass and Your Mind Will Follow* (1970), *Maggot Brain* (1971), *America Eats*

George Clinton, the mastermind behind the Parliaments and the Funkadelics, was as noted for his outrageous costumes as for his ingenious combinations of soul, funk, and jazz. (Frank Driggs Collection)

Its Young (1972), *Cosmic Slop* (1973), *Standing on the Verge of Getting It On* (1974), *Hardcore Jollies* (1976), the million-selling *One Nation Under a Groove* (1978), and *Uncle Jam Wants You* (1979). During the 1970s Clinton led a collective of his two groups, called Parliament Funkadelic, which gave rise to spinoff bands such as Bootsy's Rubber Band and the Brides of Funkenstein.

After a massive 1978–1979 tour called the Parliafunkadelicment Mothership Connection Tour, Clinton was embroiled in legal actions that prevented him from playing in Parliament or Funkadelic. Clinton moved to an estate outside Detroit, retired from performing, and made solo recordings, often using Parliament or Funkadelic musicians. His solo albums from the 1980s include *The Electric Spanking of War Babies* (1981); *Computer Games* (1982), which included the hit "Atomic Dog" and revealed an obsession with technological advances, including sampling, sequencing, and digital remixing; *You Shouldn't Nuf-Bit Fish* (1983); *Some of My Best Jokes Are Friends* (1985); and *George Clinton Presents Our Funky Gang* (1989). In the late 1980s Clinton resolved his legal problems and once again began touring with Parliament Funkadelic.

Since the late 1980s Clinton's pioneering role in developing funk music has been recognized by young musicians paying homage to him through numerous quotes, remakes, and samplings of his recordings. Prince released two of Clinton's records, *The Cinderella Theory* (1989) and *Hey Man, Smell My Finger* (1992), on his record label, and Clinton produced the Red Hot Chili Peppers' *Freaky Styley* (1985). Clinton has also appeared in the films *House Party* (1989) and *P.C.U.* (1994)

REFERENCE

FRICKE, DAVID. "George Clinton Interview." *Rolling Stone* (September 20, 1990): 74–77.

JONATHAN GILL

Coasters, The, vocal group. The Coasters, with their unrestrained vocals on comic songs, were one of the most popular rhythm and blues vocal groups of the 1950s. Founded in 1949 as the Robins, the group first achieved major commercial success with "Riot in Cell Block no. 9" (1954) and "Smokey Joe's Café" (1955), both featuring Richard Berry. In 1955 they officially changed their name to the Coasters, a reference to their Los Angeles origins. In the mid-1950s the group consisted of lead tenor Carl Gardner (1928–   ), bass Bobby Nunn (1925–1986), and the midrange voices of Billy Guy (1936–   ) and Leon Hughes (1938–   ).

The Coasters, one of the premier "doo-wop" groups of the 1950s, were especially effective in comic songs such as "Yakety Yak" and "Along Came Jones." They are performing here at New York City's Madison Square Garden in 1974. (AP/Wide World Photos)

Starting in the mid-1950s, the Coasters had numerous hit records, most of them humorous tunes, though often with sardonic undertones, written by white songwriters Jerry Leiber and Mike Stoller. These songs, which rejected the sweeter, crooning style of most doo-wop groups for a rougher, more energetic style, included "Framed" (1955), "Down in Mexico" (1956), "Searchin'" (1957), "Young Blood" (1957), "Yakety Yak" (1958), "Charlie Brown" (1958), "Poison Ivy" (1959), "Shopping for Clothes" (1960), and "Little Egypt" (1961). During their heyday in the mid-to-late 1950s, the group underwent complicated personnel changes, with Hughes being replaced by Young Jessie, who gave way to Cornell Gunter (1936–1990) and then Earl "Speedo" Carroll (1937–   ). Nunn was replaced by Will "Dub" Jones (1939–   ), who was featured on "Along Came Jones" (1959) before being replaced by Ronnie Bright (1939–   ).

Since the 1960s the Coasters have failed to maintain the popularity they achieved in the late 1950s, but they have continued to tour with a lineup consisting of Gardner, Carroll, Bright, and Jimmy Noonan. Their albums include *It Ain't Sanitary* (1972), *On Broadway* (1973), *Wake Me, Shake Me* (1980), *Thumbin' a Ride* (1985), and *Poison Ivy* (1991). The Coasters were inducted into the Rock and Roll Hall of Fame in 1987.

REFERENCE

MILLAR, B. *The Coasters*. London, 1975.

JONATHAN GILL

Cobb, Jewel Plummer (January 17, 1924–   ), scientist and educator. The daughter of Frank V. Plummer, a physician, and Carribiel Cole Plummer, who taught physical education and dance, Jewel Plummer Cobb cultivated an interest in biology as a high school student in Chicago, where she was born. Cobb matriculated as a freshman at the University of Michigan at Ann Arbor in the fall of 1941. The following year, she transferred to Talladega College in Alabama, where she earned a B.A. in biology in 1944. A budding researcher in a male-dominated profession, she acquired an M.A. and a Ph.D. in cell physiology in 1947 and 1950, respectively, from New York University. Her thesis "Mechanisms of Pigment Formation" outlined the basic research format for her subsequent investigations of melanomas (cancerous pigment cells) and chemotherapeutic agents. Shortly after her appointment as a National Cancer Institute Post-Doctorate Fellow at Harlem Hospital, Cobb assumed her first major teaching position as an anatomy instructor at the University of Illinois Medical School in 1952. She married Roy R. Cobb in 1954.

In 1955, just one year after the Supreme Court forced the desegregation of the nation's schools in *Brown* v. *Board of Education*, Cobb established a Tissue Culture Research Laboratory at the New York University–Bellevue Hospital Medical Center. Over the next three decades, she served as a professor, researcher and administrator at New York University, Sarah Lawrence College, and Connecticut College. As dean at Connecticut, she inaugurated a program to enhance science education for women and minorities. In 1974, she worked to establish a task force on women and minorities in science as a member of the National Science Foundation's National Science Board. Currently president emeritus of California State University at Fullerton, Cobb holds numerous honorary doctorates and awards, as well as memberships and affiliations with the American Association for the Advancement of Science, the NATIONAL ASSOCIATION FOR THE ADVANCEMENT OF COLORED PEOPLE (NAACP), and the National Academy of Sciences.

REFERENCE

COBB, JEWEL PLUMMER. "A Life in Science: Research and Service." *Sage: A Scholarly Journal on Black Women* 6 (Fall 1989): 39–43.

GERARD FERGERSON

Cobb, William Montague (October 12, 1904–November 20, 1990), physician. W. Montague Cobb was born in Washington, D.C., the son of William

Elmer and Alexzine Montague Cobb. A graduate of Dunbar High School (1921), he pursued a liberal-arts program at Amherst College and earned an A.B. there in 1925. Cobb's special talent for science earned him the Blodgett Scholarship for work at the Marine Biological Laboratory in Woods Hole, Mass., where he studied embryology in the summer of 1925. He entered Howard University Medical College that fall, earning an M.D. in 1929.

During his final year at Howard, Cobb taught embryology to medical students. This was the start of a lifelong career in teaching and research. Following a year's internship at FREEDMEN'S HOSPITAL, he enrolled in the doctoral program at Western Reserve University and was awarded a Ph.D. in anatomy and physical anthropology in 1932.

Cobb taught anatomy at HOWARD UNIVERSITY for forty-one years. Starting as an assistant professor in 1932, he attained the rank of full professor in 1942. He served as chairman of the Department of Anatomy from 1947 to 1969. In 1969, he became the first to hold a distinguished professorship at Howard. Following his official retirement in 1973, he served as visiting professor at several institutions, including Stanford University, the University of Maryland, and Harvard University.

Cobb's research interests were wide-ranging. He contributed the chapter on the skeleton to the third edition (1952) of E. V. Cowdry's *Problems of Aging: Biological and Medical Aspects.* Other work of his was cited in *Gray's Anatomy,* Sir Henry Morris's *Human Anatomy,* and *Cunningham's Manual of Practical Anatomy.* He is said to have been the first black scientist cited in all three of these standard medical texts. Cobb's work on the "physical anthropology of the American Negro," published in the *American Journal of Physical Anthropology* and other periodicals, was recognized as authoritative.

Along with Julian H. LEWIS, Cobb pioneered efforts to counteract the myths that had evolved among scientists concerning the biological inferiority of black people. In all, he published over six hundred articles in professional journals. His prominence brought him terms as president of the Anthropological Society of Washington (1949–1951) and of the American Association of Physical Anthropologists (1958–1960), at a time when it was almost unheard of for an African American to hold such posts within predominantly white organizations.

Cobb is perhaps best remembered, both within the medical community and beyond, for his civil rights activities. During the 1940s, he represented the NAACP before the U.S. Senate in testimony supportive of a national health-insurance program. Under the auspices of the NATIONAL ASSOCIATION FOR THE

William Montague Cobb. (Photographs and Prints Division, Schomburg Center for Research in Black Culture, The New York Public Library, Astor, Lenox and Tilden Foundations)

ADVANCEMENT OF COLORED PEOPLE (NAACP), he prepared two seminal monographs, *Medical Care and the Plight of the Negro* (1947) and *Progress and Portents for the Negro in Medicine* (1948), which helped raise public awareness of how discriminatory practices had adversely influenced the access of blacks to health-care services and professional opportunities. Cobb served as NAACP president from 1976 to 1982.

In his capacity as president (1945–1947, 1951–1954) of the all-black Medico-Chirurgical Society of the District of Columbia, Cobb led two important campaigns: the racial integration of Gallinger Hospital (later, D.C. General Hospital) in 1948 and the admission, in 1952, of black physicians to membership in the all-white Medical Society of the District of Columbia. He also served a term as president of the National Medical Association in 1964. It was in his role, however, as editor of the *Journal of the National Medical Association* (1949–1977) that he found his primary forum, both for discussing contemporary issues of health-care access and for portraying the rich historical heritage to which blacks—going back beyond colonial America to prehistoric times—can lay claim.

REFERENCES

COBB, W. MONTAGUE. *The First Negro Medical Society: A History of the Medico-Chirurgical Society of the District of Columbia.* Washington, D.C., 1939.

LAWLAH, JOHN W. "The President-Elect." *Journal of the National Medical Association* 55 (November 1963): 551–554.

KENNETH R. MANNING

COFO. *See* Council of Federated Organizations.

Coincoin (c. August 24, 1742–1816), plantation owner. Coincoin was born a slave in Natchitoches, La. Though named Marie Therese at her baptism, she was commonly referred to by the African name her parents called her, Coincoin—a name given to second-born daughters by the Ewe tribe of western Africa. When Coincoin was a teenager, her owner rented her to Claude Thomas Pierre Metoyer, a French merchant on Isle Brevelle in the Red River Valley of Louisiana. For two decades, Coincoin lived with Metoyer as his servant and mistress. She bore ten children with him, of whom six were sold to other owners. (Five of her children who were born before she was rented to Metoyer were also sold away.) When the relationship became the focus of a local scandal, Metoyer purchased Coincoin and freed her.

In 1786, when the two separated, Coincoin was left with a small plot of land and an annuity of 120 piasters. She established an independent plantation on the land, growing tobacco and indigo, raising cattle and turkeys, and trapping bear for grease and hides. Coincoin later set up a cattle range on a nearby 640-acre land grant received from the Spanish government. Beginning in 1786, with the income from her agricultural holdings, Coincoin set out to manumit her family. Over the next decade, she traveled throughout the South to track down and purchase her enslaved children and grandchildren. Coincoin successfully manumitted ten of her eleven enslaved children and many of her grandchildren.

In the early nineteenth century, Coincoin expanded her economic assets by purchasing slaves and additional acreage. By the time of her death in 1816, she owned sixteen slaves and more than 800 acres of land. Her offspring expanded on Coincoin's holdings and eventually controlled an agricultural empire on Isle Brevelle. By the Civil War, the Metoyers had become the largest African-American slaveholding family in American history, with holdings that included nearly 20,000 acres of land and 500 slaves.

REFERENCES

MILLS, GARY B. *The Forgotten People: Cane River's Creoles of Color.* Baton Rouge, La., 1976.

WOODS, FRANCES JEROME. *Marginality and Identity: A Colored Creole Family Through Ten Generations.* Baton Rouge, La., 1972.

THADDEUS RUSSELL

Coker, Daniel (1780–1846), minister and abolitionist. Born Isaac Wright in Maryland to an African slave father and an English indentured-servant mother, Daniel Coker received a rudimentary education while attending school as his white half-brother's valet. He escaped to New York while still a youth and took his new name to avoid detection. In New York, Coker met Bishop Francis Asbury, who ordained him to the METHODIST CHURCH ministry around 1800. Coker returned shortly after to Baltimore and, with his freedom recently purchased, spoke out against SLAVERY, writing an abolitionist pamphlet, *A Dialogue Between a Virginian and an African Minister,* in 1810. He became the leader of a society of black Methodists who desired independence from white Methodists because of discrimination, and ran the African School in connection with this society.

Coker's Methodist society evolved into the independent African Bethel Church. In 1816, delegates, including Coker and Richard ALLEN, from five black Methodist societies gathered in Philadelphia to establish the independent AFRICAN METHODIST EPISCOPAL CHURCH. Elected as the first bishop of the new denomination, Coker declined the post—perhaps because of dissension over his light skin color—and Allen became the first bishop. Coker returned to his Baltimore pastorate, but was expelled from the ministry from 1818 to 1819 for an unknown offense. He left for Africa in 1820 as a missionary with the assistance of the Maryland Colonization Society. After spending some time in Liberia, he settled in Sierra Leone, where he was the superintendent of a settlement for "recaptured" Africans and helped found the West African Methodist Church.

REFERENCES

COKER, DANIEL. *Journal of Daniel Coker.* Baltimore, 1820.

PAYNE, ALEXANDER. *History of the African Methodist Episcopal Church.* Nashville, Tenn., 1891.

TIMOTHY E. FULOP

Cole, Nat "King" (Cole, Nathaniel Adams)

(March 17, 1919–February 15, 1965), singer and pianist. Born in Montgomery, Ala., Nat Cole moved with his family to Chicago when he was two years old. His father, the Rev. Edward James Cole, Sr., was a pastor at the True Light Baptist Church. His parents encouraged the musical talents of young Cole and his four brothers. All but one eventually became professional musicians. Cole had his earliest musical experiences in his father's church, where he sang and played the organ. While in high school, he played in the Rogues of Rhythm, a band led by his brother Eddie, at a Chicago night spot called the Club Panama. In 1936 he played piano in a touring production of Noble SISSLE and Eubie BLAKE's *Shuffle Along.* The tour ended in Long Beach, Calif., in 1937. Cole stayed in southern California, and played piano in Los Angeles–area clubs.

In 1938 he organized a trio with Oscar Moore on guitar and Wesley Prince on bass. About this time he adopted the name Nat "King" Cole. The trio began to gain popularity largely due to Cole's sophisticated, swinging piano style. In 1943 Cole signed a contract with the newly organized record company Capitol.

Though pianist Nat "King" Cole and his trio were one of the most distinctive jazz ensembles of the early 1940s, his increasing success as a singer led to a second career as a pop vocalist. (AP/Wide World Photos)

On his first hit recording "Straighten Up and Fly Right" (1943), Cole sang for the first time. The song, based on a sermon of his father's, was taken from a traditional black folktale. In 1944, Cole achieved a national reputation as a pianist, taking part in "Jazz at the Philharmonic," a series of touring jazz concerts.

Eventually, Cole's singing came to dominate his piano playing. His 1946 recording of "The Christmas Song," which added a string section to Cole's singing, was a turning point in the evolution of his career. By 1949 he was recording primarily with orchestral accompaniment, and his piano playing was relegated to a secondary role. Cole achieved great success with such vocal recordings as "Mona Lisa" (1950) and "Unforgettable" (1951). Cole's singing style was, like his piano playing, relaxed, disarming, and authoritative. His performances remained impressive even with the most banal material, and they always retained their integrity, shunning both pseudodramatic straining for effects and coy mannerisms. His singing had an immense popularity with both white and black audiences. Cole's was the first black jazz combo to have its own sponsored radio program (1948–1949), and in 1956 and 1957 he became the first black performer to have his own series on network television. (The program was canceled, however, because of the difficulty in finding sponsors for it.) Cole also made several films, including *St. Louis Blues* (1958, a life of W. C. HANDY), and *Cat Ballou* (1965).

In the early 1960s Cole was sometimes criticized by black activists for his failure to actively participate in the struggle for civil rights. Cole resented the accusations, noting that he had made substantial financial contributions to civil rights organizations. By this time, Cole was a headliner at Las Vegas casinos and was one of the most financially successful performers in popular music. He died of lung cancer in 1965 at the height of his popularity. He was the most successful black performer of the postwar era. The appreciation of his contribution to popular music has increased since his death. His television show has been syndicated and many of his recordings have been reissued.

Cole's first marriage, to Nadine Robinson in 1937, ended in divorce. He married Maria Ellington (no relation to Duke Ellington) in 1948. They had four children, and also adopted Maria's niece. One of their children, Natalie Cole, has had a successful career as a pop singer. In 1991, Natalie Cole achieved considerable recognition for her album *Unforgettable,* an ingeniously recorded album of duets with her late father, which won Grammies for best album and best song.

ROBERT W. STEPHENS

Cole, Rebecca J. (March 16, 1846–August 14, 1922), physician and social reformer. Born in Philadelphia in 1846 (three years before the first American woman, Elizabeth Blackwell, received an M.D.), Rebecca Cole attended the city's prestigious Institute for Colored Youth before pursuing advanced medical studies. The institute had maintained an academic department from its founding by Quakers in 1837 and counted numerous African-American leaders among its alumni. Cole matriculated at the Woman's Medical College of Pennsylvania in 1866 and received an M.D. in 1867 after the submission of her thesis, "The Eye and Its Appendages." Upon graduation, Cole became the second black woman to receive an M.D. in the United States and the first to graduate from the Woman's Medical College. She accepted an invitation from Elizabeth Blackwell to be a "sanitary visitor" at Blackwell's New York Infirmary for Women and Children to help spread knowledge of public health among the urban poor. A dedicated advocate for the disfranchised, Cole also practiced in Philadelphia, Columbia, S.C., and Washington, D.C., where she held her last major appointment as superintendent of the Home for Destitute Colored Women and Children. Throughout her medical career, which spanned over half a century, Cole remained active in the black club women's movement and lectured widely on ways to improve the health status of African Americans. She died in Philadelphia.

REFERENCES

MOLDOW, GLORIA. *Women Doctors in Gilded-Age Washington: Race, Gender, and Professionalization.* Chicago, 1987.

STERLING, DOROTHY. *We Are Your Sisters: Black Women in the Nineteenth Century.* New York, 1984

GERARD FERGERSON

Cole, Robert Allen "Bob" (July 1, 1868–August 2, 1911), entertainer. Bob Cole was born in Athens, Ga. to Robert Allen Cole, Sr., and Isabella Thomas Weldon. He was the oldest child and only boy in a musically active family of six children. He played the banjo, guitar, piano, and cello. Cole completed elementary school and may have attended high school in Atlanta, but never attended college, though he took a position at Atlanta University. After a period of playing cello in a string quartet, working in a hotel as a "singing bellboy," and working in clubs as an entertainer, around 1891 Cole signed with Sam T. Jack's Creole Show in Chicago as comedian, writer, and stage manager.

He later organized the All-Star Stock Company in New York, which became a training ground for black performers. Cole was involved in the first shows of M. Sissieretta JONES, whose troupe was known as Black Patti's Troubadours (1896). He wrote a skit for the Troubadours, "At Jolly Coon-ey Island," which he starred in and stage managed. When his request for higher pay was ignored, he left the show. He and Billy Johnson wrote and produced *A Trip to Coontown,* which toured from 1897 to 1901. This was the first full-length musical (nonminstrel) show written, produced, and staged by blacks. It received critical acclaim on Broadway.

In 1899 Cole met the Johnson brothers, James Weldon JOHNSON and J. Rosamond JOHNSON, and they formed a musical team. James Weldon later became a diplomat, and J. Rosamond and Cole became partners until Cole's retirement from the stage in 1911. Between 1900 and 1910, they produced over 150 songs, which were used in their vaudeville acts and were also often incorporated into Broadway shows with white casts like *The Sleeping Beauty and the Beast* (1901) and *Sally in Our Alley* (1902). Among their best-known songs were "Under the Bamboo Tree" and "Oh, Didn't He Ramble" (written under the pseudonym of Will Handy). Cole and Johnson produced several musical comedies, including *The Shoo-Fly Regiment* (1906) and *The Red Moon* (1908), which were produced on Broadway by all-black casts. In 1910, Cole and Johnson returned to New York and renewed their vaudeville act until 1911, when Cole died. Cole was the most versatile performer/composer of his day and greatly influenced the development of black musical theater.

REFERENCES

RIIS, THOMAS L. "Bob Cole: His Life and His Legacy to Black Musical Theater." *Black Perspective in Music* 13, no. 2 (Fall 1985): 136–150.

———. *Just Before Jazz: Black Musical Theatre in New York, 1890–1915.* Washington, D.C., 1989.

MARVA GRIFFIN CARTER

Cole, William Randolph "Cozy" (October 17, 1906–January 29, 1981), jazz drummer. Born in East Orange, N.J., and raised in a musical family, Cole's musical education was influenced by his three brothers, all of whom were jazz musicians. In high school, Cole continued to study the drums, and he attended Wilberforce College in Ohio for two years. In 1926, he moved to New York, where he studied percussion with Billy Gladstone and Charlie Brooks while taking on odd jobs, including barber and shipping clerk.

Cole began playing professionally in 1928 with Wilbur Sweatman, and then led his own group before joining the bands of Jelly Roll MORTON (1930), Blanche Calloway (1931–1933), Benny CARTER (1933–1934), Willie Bryant (1934–1936), and Jonah Jones (1936–1938). National fame and recognition as a versatile drummer and showman came to Cole during four years with Cab CALLOWAY ("Crescendo in Drums," 1939), and then with the CBS Orchestra (1943–1944). In 1944, Cole worked in the stage production of *Seven Lively Arts*. That year he also recorded "Thru for the Night" and "Concerto for Cozy" as a leader, and "St. Louis Blues" with Roy ELDRIDGE. Cole made his film debut in *Make Mine Music* (1945), played for the soundtrack of *The Strip* (1951), and appeared in *The Glenn Miller Story* (1953). From 1949 through 1953 he played and recorded with Louis ARMSTRONG's All-Stars. Cole also recorded as a leader ("Drum Fantasy," 1954), and as a sideman with Benny Goodman, and studied percussion with Saul Goodman at the Juilliard School of Music.

Along with Sid CATLETT, Cole was one of the most influential drummers of the swing era, particularly noted for his ability to perform in every musical style, from New Orleans to bebop. Cole's drum solos, well grounded in the rudiments of jazz drumming, were always exciting showstoppers. In 1953, he left Armstrong to manage a drum school in Manhattan with Gene Krupa. Cole resumed touring with an all-star band led by Jack Teagarden and Earl HINES in 1957, and the next year reached the pinnacle of his commercial success with a hit recording of "Topsy." He toured Africa in 1962–1963, and his own group was a popular attraction in New York nightclubs throughout the 1960s. In 1969 Cole toured with the Jonah Jones Quintet, performed in the Calloway reunion band at the Newport Jazz Festival in 1973, and toured Europe with Benny Carter's Quartet in the show *A Night in New Orleans* (1976). He died in Columbus, Ohio.

REFERENCES

DANCE, STANLEY. *The World of Swing*. New York, 1974.
VACHER, P. "Cozy Conversing." *Mississippi Rag* 5, no. 6 (1978): 10.

ANTHONY BROWN

Coleman, Bessie (January 26, 1892–April 30, 1926), aviator. Bessie Coleman was the first African-American female aviator. She was born in Atlanta, Tex., but her family moved to Waxahachie, Tex., when she was still an infant. When she was 7, her parents separated. Her father, who was a Choctaw Indian, returned to the reservation in Oklahoma, and her mother supported the large family by picking cotton and doing laundry, jobs in which she was aided by her children. Because she wanted Coleman

to attend college, her mother allowed her to keep her income from her laundry work, but this money only financed one semester at the Colored Agricultural and Normal University in Langston, Okla. (now Langston University). After this semester, she returned to Waxahachie briefly; and between 1915 and 1917, she went to Chicago, where she took a course in manicuring and worked at the White Sox barbershop until the early years of World War I. She then managed a small restaurant.

Coleman became interested in the burgeoning field of aviation, which had entered the national consciousness as a consequence of its role in WORLD WAR I, but all her applications to aviation schools were rejected on the basis of her race and/or gender, until Robert S. ABBOTT, founder and editor of the *Chicago Defender*, advised her to study aviation abroad. She took a course in French, went to Paris in November 1920, and attended an aviation school in Le Crotoy. She returned to the United States in September 1921 with a pilot's license and went back to Europe in 1922, this time obtaining an international pilot's license, the first African-American woman to obtain these licenses. When she returned to the United States after her second sojourn in Europe, Coleman made a name for herself in exhibition flying, performing at shows attended by thousands. She barnstormed throughout the United States and became known as "Brave Bessie." She lectured in schools and churches on the opportunities in aviation wherever she performed, and she saved the money she earned from these lectures and performances in the hope of opening an aviation school for African Americans. On April 30, 1926, during a practice run in Jacksonville. Fla., Coleman's plane somersaulted out of a nosedive, and Coleman fell 2,000 feet to her death.

REFERENCES

KING, ANITA. "Brave Bessie: First Black Pilot." *Essence* (May 1976): 36; (June 1976): 48.
SMITH, JESSIE CARNEY, ed. *Notable Black American Woman*. Detroit, 1992.
"They Take to the Sky." *Ebony* (May 1977): 88–90.

SIRAJ AHMED

Coleman, Ornette (c. March 9, 1930–), jazz saxophonist and composer. Born in Fort Worth, Tex., on a date that remains in dispute, Ornette Coleman's early musical influences included gospel, rhythm and blues, and bebop. Coleman, whose father was a singer, began playing saxophone at age sixteen, and had little formal music instruction. His earliest performances were in local churches, and he was expelled from his high school band for improvising during a performance of John Philip Sousa's "Wash-

Bessie Coleman. (See previous page.) (Photographs and Prints Division, Schomburg Center for Research in Black Culture, The New York Public Library, Astor, Lenox and Tilden Foundations)

ington Post March." Coleman at first played tenor saxophone in a honking rhythm-and-blues style influenced by Illinois JACQUET and Big Jay McNeely. His first professional work came in 1949 with the Silas Green Minstrels, a tent show that toured the South and Midwest. Coleman also traveled with blues singer Clarence Samuels, and blues singer and guitarist "Pee Wee" Crayton. By this time, Coleman had been inspired by bebop to start playing with a coarse, crying tone, and a frantic, unrestrained sense of rhythm and harmony. The reception in the jazz community to his controversial style kept him from working for a decade.

In 1950 Coleman moved to Los Angeles and began to recruit a circle of associates, including drummers Edward Blackwell and Billy Higgins, trumpeters Don CHERRY and Bobby Bradford, bassist Charlie Haden, and pianist Paul Bley. Coleman married poet Jayne CORTEZ in 1954; unable to support himself as a musician, he took a job as a stock boy and elevator operator at a Los Angeles department store. Despite his reputation as an eccentric who had unusually long hair, wore overcoats in the summer, and played a white saxophone, in 1958 Coleman was invited to make his first recording, *Something Else!* which in-

cluded his compositions "Chippie" and "When Will the Blues Leave." Pianist John LEWIS brought Coleman and Cherry to the Lenox (Mass.) School of Jazz in 1959, which led to a famous series of quartet performances at New York's Five Spot nightclub.

The albums Coleman made over the next two years, including *Tomorrow Is the Question, The Shape of Jazz to Come, This Is Our Music,* and *Free Jazz,* were vilified by traditionalists, who heard the long, loosely structured, collective improvisations and adventurous harmonies as worthless cacophony. However, among his admirers, those performances, which included his compositions "Focus on Sanity," "Peace," "Lonely Woman," and "Beauty Is a Rare Thing," were also recognized as the first significant development in jazz since bebop. Although modeled on the wit and irreverence of bebop, Coleman's pianoless quartets broke out of traditional harmonies, as well as rigid theme-and-improvisation structures. Coleman began to call this style "harmolodics," referring to a musical system, since developed in a vast, unpublished manuscript, in which improvised melodies need not obey fixed harmonies.

In the 1950s Coleman had been shunned by the jazz world, but in the 1960s he found himself hailed as one of the greatest and most influential figures in jazz. Yet Coleman, who was divorced from Cortez in 1964, scaled back his activities in order to study trumpet and violin. In the mid-1960s Coleman most frequently appeared in trio settings (*At the Golden Circle,* 1965–1966), often including bassist David Izenzon and drummer Charles Moffett. In 1967 Coleman became the first jazz musician to win a Guggenheim fellowship. During the late 1960s and early 1970s, Coleman often played with the members of his old quartet, plus tenor saxophonist Dewey Redman, with whom he had first become acquainted in Fort Worth (*Science Fiction,* 1971).

Coleman, who had been composing classical music since the early 1950s, also saw performances in the 1960s of his string quartet *Dedication to Poets and Writers* (1961), his woodwind quintet *Forms and Sounds* (1967), and *Saints and Soldiers* (1967), a chamber piece. Coleman's *Skies of America* symphony was recorded in 1972 with the London Symphony Orchestra. In 1973 he traveled to Morocco to record with folk musicians from the town of Joujouka.

Coleman's next breakthrough came in 1975, when he began to play a style of electric dance music that recalled his early career in rhythm-and-blues dance bands. Using Prime Time, a new core group of musicians that often included his son, Denardo, a drummer, born in 1956, Coleman recorded *Dancing in Your Head,* an album-length elaboration of a theme from *Skies of America* in 1975, and recorded *Of Human Feelings* in 1979. During this time Coleman also founded Artists House, a collective that helped introduce guitarists James "Blood" Ulmer and bassist Jamaaladeen Tacuma.

The mid-1980s brought a revival of interest in Coleman. His hometown, Fort Worth, honored him with a series of tributes and performances, including the chamber piece *Prime Design/Time Design* (1983). A documentary by Shirley Clarke, *Ornette: Made in America,* was released in 1984, and Coleman collaborated with jazz-rock guitarist Pat Metheny (*Song X,* 1985), and rock guitarist Jerry Garcia (*Virgin Beauty,* 1987). On *In All Languages* (1987) he reunited with his 1959 quartet, and in 1991 Coleman, who had composed and performed on the film soundtracks for *Chappaqua* (1965) and *Box Office* (1981), recorded the score for *Naked Lunch.* Coleman, who has lived in Manhattan since the early 1960s, continues to compose regularly, though performing and recording only sporadically with Prime Time.

REFERENCES

DAVIS, FRANCIS. *In the Moment: Jazz in the 1980s.* New York, 1986.

LITWEILER, JOHN. *Ornette Coleman: The Harmolodic Life.* London, 1992.

SPELLMAN, A. B. *Four Lives in the Bebop Business.* New York, 1970.

BILL DIXON

Coleman, William Thaddeus, Jr. (July 7, 1920–), lawyer and cabinet secretary. Born in Germantown, Pa., to an elite African-American family, William T. Coleman graduated summa cum laude from the University of Pennsylvania in 1941. He entered Harvard Law School, but spent only one year before his studies were interrupted by his enlistment in the Army Air Corps. There he began his brilliant legal career. Assigned as defense counsel in eighteen court-martial cases, he won sixteen of them. After the end of World War II, Coleman returned to Harvard Law School, where he graduated magna cum laude in 1946. He clerked one year for U.S. Court of Appeals Judge Herbert F. Goodrich. In 1948, he clerked for Justice Felix Frankfurter, becoming the first African-American Supreme Court law clerk.

During the 1950s, Coleman became involved with the NAACP LEGAL DEFENSE AND EDUCATIONAL FUND (LDF), and was involved in a number of sig-

Former Secretary of Transportation William Coleman (right) gives testimony before the Senate Judiciary Committee during confirmation hearings for Supreme Court Associate Justice designee Robert Bork. Rep. Barbara Jordan is seated to Coleman's right, September 21, 1987. (Photographs and Prints Division, Schomburg Center for Research in Black Culture, The New York Public Library, Astor, Lenox and Tilden Foundations)

nificant civil rights cases. He was one of the co-authors of the brief in the *Brown* v. *Board of Education* school desegregation case. In 1952, he joined the law firm of Dilworth Paxson Kalish Levy, and in 1956 he became a partner, the first African-American partner of a prominent white Philadelphia law firm. An expert in transportation law, he was special counsel on transportation for the Southeastern Pennsylvania Transit Authority from 1952 to 1963. In 1957, he joined the Board of the LDF, and he was named chairman in 1964.

By the 1960s, Coleman began to move into public service. In 1964, he served as assistant counsel on the Warren Commission. In 1965, he was appointed chairman of the White House Conference on Civil Rights, "To Fulfill These Rights." The same year, he was cocounsel in *McGlaughlin* v. *Florida,* which established the constitutionality of interracial marriage in Florida. He was also retained by Gov. William Scranton of Pennsylvania in connection with the state's desegregation of Girard College.

Although he served as a member of the U.S. delegation to the United Nations in 1969, Coleman repeatedly refused offers of government positions. He turned down an appellate judgeship and in 1973 declined the job of Watergate special prosecutor. Coleman, a longtime Republican, was named secretary of transportation by President Gerald Ford in 1975. He was only the second African-American cabinet secretary. During his brief tenure, Coleman established the nation's first comprehensive transportation policy. Since 1977, Coleman has been in private law practice in Washington, D.C. as a senior partner at O'Melveny and Meyer. He remains active in civil rights matters through his work with the LDF, and he was influential in the creation of the 1991 Civil Rights Act.

REFERENCE

SALPUKAS, AGIS. "Coleman Heads Effort to Rescue Pan Am." *New York Times Biographical Service,* Vol. 18, pp. 1396–1397.

JAMES BRADLEY

Coles, Charles "Honi" (April 2, 1911–November 12, 1992), tap dancer. Honi Coles's high-speed rhythm tapping (*see* TAP DANCE) was developed in contests on the streets of his native Philadelphia, where he was born in 1911. Coles first came to New York in 1931 as one of the Three Millers, who tap-danced on top of pedestals, executing difficult steps such as barrel turns, wings, and over-the-tops on tiny platforms.

When the act folded, Coles returned to Philadelphia to perfect his technique. He came back to New York in 1934, opening at the APOLLO THEATER. He quickly earned the reputation of having the "fastest feet in show business," and was hailed as an extraordinarily graceful dancer. From 1936 to 1939, he was a member of the Lucky Seven Trio who, somewhat like the Three Millers, tapped on large cubes made to look like dice.

In 1940, when Coles was dancing with Cab Calloway's swing band, he met Charles "Cholly" ATKINS and after World War II they formed the class act of Coles & Atkins. In their routine they opened with a fast-paced song and tap number, followed by a precision swing dance, a soft shoe, and a tap chal-

Charles "Honi" Coles. (Photographs and Prints Division, Schomburg Center for Research in Black Culture, The New York Public Library, Astor, Lenox and Tilden Foundations)

lenge. Their best-known soft shoe, which has become one of the classic routines of tap, was danced to "Taking a Chance on Love," played at an extremely slow tempo; this piece was preserved on the 1963 *Camera Three* television program, "Over the Top with Bebop." As a result of the tempo, Coles and Atkins seem suspended in slow motion as they toss off gliding turns and smooth slides, all with crystal-clear taps.

Coles's dancing was known for its speed, meticulousness, and swinging-rhythmic complexity. He anticipated the prolonged cadences of the great jazz musicians by extending the duration of the steps past the usual eight-bar unit to build more sustained combinations. From 1945 to 1949 Coles and Atkins appeared with the big bands of Cab CALLOWAY, Louis ARMSTRONG, Lionel HAMPTON, Charlie Barnet, Billy ECKSTINE, and Count BASIE. On Broadway they appeared in a show-stopping routine they choreographed for the musical *Gentlemen Prefer Blondes* in 1949.

By the time Coles and Atkins last danced together in 1959, the Big Band era was over, and Broadway was no longer interested in tap dance. For the next sixteen years, Coles worked as the production manager at the Apollo Theater. He served as president of the Negro Actors' Guild and in 1949 was a founder of the tap dancers' fraternity, the Copasetics.

In the early 1960s Coles helped spark a new interest in tap dancing, starting with his appearance at the Newport Jazz Festival in 1962. In 1978 he firmly placed tap in the world of concert art when he performed in the Joffrey Ballet's production of Agnes DeMille's "Conversations about the Dance." He returned to Broadway in *Bubblin' Brown Sugar* (1976), *Black Broadway* (1979), and received both the Tony and the Drama Desk awards as Best Featured Actor and Dancer in a Musical for *My One and Only* (1983). During the 1980s, Coles taught dance and dance history at Yale, Cornell, Duke, and George Washington University.

Coles received the New York City Award of Honor for Arts and Culture in 1986, and the 39th Annual Capezio Dance Award for lifetime achievement in dance in 1988. His films include *The Cotton Club* (1984) and *Dirty Dancing* (1987). A television special, "The Tap Dance Kid" (1980), and a video, "Master of Tap" (1990), record Coles's wit and his art. He was awarded the National Medal of Arts, for outstanding contribution to American cultural life, in 1991. Coles appeared for the last time only a few months before his death as master of ceremonies at a 1992 tap festival in Colorado, along with his old partner Cholly Atkins.

Singer Lena HORNE once said of Coles, "Honi makes butterflies look clumsy. He was my Fred Astaire." A tapper of grace and elegance, Coles was also a singer, composer, raconteur, a renowned master of ceremonies admired for his quick wit, a choreographer, and teacher. He was a dancer whose personal style and technical precision epitomized what is known in the community of tap dance as the "class act" dancer.

REFERENCES

SOMMER, SALLY. "Smooth and Mellow." *International Tap Association Journal* 2, no. 3 (Spring 1990): 7.
STEARNS, MARSHALL, and JEAN STEARNS. *Jazz Dance: The Story of American Vernacular Dance.* New York, 1968.

CONSTANCE VALIS HILL

Colescott, Robert H. (August 26, 1925–), painter. Robert Colescott was born in Oakland, Calif., and studied at the University of California at Berkeley, where he received his A.B. and M.A. degrees. He moved to Paris in the late 1940s, and studied at Fernand Léger's studio. In 1950 he exhibited in the Salon de Mai in Paris. From 1964 to 1967, he lived in Cairo, Egypt, serving as artist-in-residence at the American Research Center (1964–1965) and teaching at the American University (1966–1967). In Egypt, Colescott viewed art shaped by non-European influences, and in response he tried to expand the cultural sources for his own work. While his paintings in the early 1960s focused on the relationship between the figure and landscape (*Negress by the Window,* 1963), and many of his paintings of the mid-1960s were influenced by Pop Art and Minimalism (*Peek-a-Boo,* 1964), Colescott began to develop his own stylistic language after living in Egypt, creating the humorous and politically charged paintings for which he is best known.

Borrowing images from European paintings and mimicking their stylistic conventions, Colescott appropriated their narrative content to create compositions that used irony and exaggeration to challenge racial and gender stereotypes. He injected his cartoonlike, blackfaced figures into the setting of famous European paintings, often altering the original figures' race, gender, facial expression, or occupation. Two of his best-known works in this style are *Eat Dem Taters* (1975) and *Natural Rhythm: Thank You Jan Van Eyck* (1976). Colescott's *Eat Dem Taters* (1975), which was modeled after Vincent Van Gogh's *The Potato Eaters,* transformed the diners into poor black sharecroppers, portraying them as "happy darkies," and thereby making connections between the economic exploitation of American blacks and

Robert Colescott displays his abiding interest in art history in his charcoal drawing *Auver-sur-Oises,* 1982, conceived as a tribute to Vincent van Gogh. In recent years Colescott has produced a series of sardonic revisions of classic paintings, incorporating African-American subject matter. (The Studio Museum in Harlem)

nineteenth-century European peasants. In *Natural Rhythm,* Colescott altered the *Arnolfini Wedding Portrait* of Flemish painter Jan Van Eyck (1370–1440) by replacing the pregnant white bride with a pregnant black bride and representing an interracial couple. Colescott continued to draw upon well-known European images to challenge viewers' ideas about race in *George Washington Carver Crossing the Delaware: Page from an American History Textbook* (1975), *Homage to Delacroix; Liberty Leading the People* (1976), and *Sunday Afternoon with Joaquin Murietta* (1980).

In the late 1970s and early 1980s, Colescott began focusing on the depiction of women in his paintings, while continuing to use cultural stereotypes to address issues of race and sexuality (*Tin Gal,* 1976; *École de Fountainbleau,* 1978; *I Gets A Thrill When I Sees De Koo,* 1978; *Christina's Day Off,* 1983). He also began to create humorous satires of American landscape painting by depicting images filled with a pile of chocolate cake slices or hot dogs (*Le Cubisme: Chocolate Cakescape,* 1981; *Hot Dawg! An Impression,* 1981). By the mid-1980s, Colescott was exploring religious subjects (*Temptation of St. Anthony,* 1983; *Knowledge of the Past Is Key to the Future [St. Sebastian],* 1986) and returned to his interest in using European paintings as a source for visual puns and social commentary (*Les Demoiselles d'Alabama,* 1985).

Colescott's work has been shown at the San Francisco Museum of Modern Art (1976, 1977), the Smithsonian Institute (1976), the Corcoran Gallery of Art in Washington, D.C. (1983), and in a traveling retrospective organized by the San José Museum of Art (1989). Colescott's work was featured in the 1978 Whitney Museum of American Art exhibition "Art About Art."

REFERENCES

DOUGLAS, ROBERT. "Robert Colescott's Searing Stereotypes." *New Art Examiner* (June 1989): 34–37.
JOHNSON, KEN. "Colescott on Black & White." *Art in America* (June 1989): 148–153.
Robert Colescott: A Retrospective, 1975–1986. San Jose. 1976

RENEE NEWMAN

Collins, Leon (192?–April 1985), tap dancer. Born and raised in Chicago, Leon Collins soon abandoned his early ambition to be a prizefighter in favor of a career in music and dance. His first job in the theater was playing guitar for "The Three Dukes." His career in tap began when he danced with the Jimmie LUNCEFORD and Count BASIE orchestras in Chicago and New York during the late 1930s; he moved on to dance with Erskine Hawkins, Earl HINES, and Glen Gray. Collins performed throughout the United States and Europe during the 1940s and early 1950s, dancing both in clubs and in larger venues.

Inspired by the fast bebop rhythms of Charlie PARKER and Dizzy GILLESPIE, Collins expressed with his feet what they played on their horns. Along with hoofers Baby Laurence and Teddy Hale, Collins became a pioneer of the high-speed, packed tempos of bebop-style tap dancing. Tapping to such jazz standards as Dizzy Gillespie's "A Night in Tunisia," he also interpreted Nicolai Rimsky-Korsakov's "Flight of the Bumblebee" and J. S. Bach's "Prelude and Fugue in C Minor," dancing with disarming ease and shimmering speed.

During the 1960s, tap's leanest years, Collins stayed active, teaching young, eager, mostly white students at summer sessions at Radcliffe College and Harvard University. In the 1970s he opened the Leon Collins Dance School in Brookline, Mass., where he taught Diane WALKER, Pamela Raff, and C. B. Heatherington, important tap artists and teachers of the next generation. In 1983 Collins was awarded the Massachusetts Foundation Fellowship for choreography. He appeared with Count Basie at the Summer Olympics in Los Angeles in 1984. Collins's technique, his spirit, and his gift for improvisation are captured on the posthumous 1989 video documentary, *Songs Unwritten: A Tap Dancer Remembered.*

REFERENCE

MARX, TRINA. *Tap-Dance: A Beginner's Guide.* New York, 1983.

CONSTANCE VALIS HILL

Colorado.   Black people have been part of Colorado history since the days of the Spanish *conquistadores.* One of the earliest recorded instances of blacks in what became Colorado occurred in 1776, when the Franciscan friar Silvestre Vélez de Escalante, who was exploring the region, recorded the drowning of one of his black assistants. The first Anglo-American blacks, such as James E. Beckwourth and Edward Rose, came to Colorado as part of the early exploratory parties, as participants in fur-trading expeditions of the early nineteenth century, after the discovery of gold on the banks of Cherry Creek in 1858, and as laborers to staff new communities. Some in the late 1850s and early '60s were slaves, especially those who were part of the fortune-seeking groups that originated in the Southern states. In 1859 a group

of whites from Georgia brought enslaved blacks to Colorado to work gold mines around Pike's Peak. While slavery was never officially legal in Colorado, the slaves were accepted without incident, though they returned to Georgia shortly after the CIVIL WAR began.

By the 1860s, several free blacks had come to Colorado looking to improve their lives, and the population increased to 456 by 1870. "Aunt" Clara BROWN arrived in Colorado in 1859. She opened a laundry in Central City, becoming the town's first African-American female resident and the only nurse in Gilpin County. Another African American, Barney Ford, an ex-slave from Virginia, struck it rich at Breckinridge, then settled in Denver and opened a chain of hotels. "Professor" Lorenzo Bowman, whose nickname stemmed from his expertise in smelting ore, arrived from the Missouri lead mines. J. G. Sims, a migrant from Cincinnati, ran the Eldorado Saloon in Denver. Edward J. Sandelin, a wealthy New Orleans mulatto, arrived in Denver in 1859, where he set up a barbershop and became active in civil rights activities. In 1860, when the first census of population was conducted in the new territory, free African Americans numbered 46 persons.

Aunt Clara Brown, who arrived in Colorado in 1859 as part of a wagon train, was a leader of Colorado's small black community as well as an entrepreneur who made considerable sums of money from mining claims. (Colorado Historical Society)

Although they were few in number, even in the new land they encountered attitudes not unlike those they thought they had left behind. For example, a clause in the act of February 27, 1861, establishing the territory, limited the elective franchise only to those "free, white male U.S. citizens of twenty-one years, who had been residents of the area on the date of the act's passage." Though subject to taxation, blacks were denied access to the territory's new public school system. In 1865, following the Civil War, the legislature reaffirmed its ban on black suffrage.

In 1866, Colorado applied for statehood. African Americans led by Barney Ford and William Jefferson Hardin, a mulatto originally from Kentucky, petitioned Congress for suffrage rights. In 1867 Colorado's application for statehood was denied by the Radical Republican Congress, which meanwhile enfranchised Colorado's blacks. Black lobbying efforts may well have had some effect in the confusing political process by which statehood was denied, and African Americans were held responsible for the failure by many statehood advocates.

After winning suffrage, blacks struggled successfully for civil rights. In 1869 Central City blacks won a court order admitting them to public schools, and in 1873 the Denver schools integrated. Three years later, Colorado gained statehood. The state constitution provided for integrated schools and black suffrage. Shortly thereafter, the first black police officers and jurors appeared, although housing and many areas remained segregated for another ninety years. Black soldiers were also stationed in Colorado. In 1879 the all-black 9th Cavalry Company D rushed to the rescue of a white regiment besieged by Indians at Milk Creek, and won a notable victory.

By the time statehood was finally achieved in 1876, Ford and Hardin had each served terms in the territorial legislature, and the state had a thriving black middle class of new immigrants such as Denver barber Moses Hanner; Lewis Douglass and Frederick Douglass, Jr., civil rights leaders who were sons of abolitionist Frederick DOUGLASS; Lewis Price, a future real estate magnate; tavern owner and Republican stalwart Henry O. Wagoner, whose son was named American Consul in Lyons, France; and Ed Sanderson. Dr. V. B. Spratlin, a graduate of the University of Denver Medical College, later became Denver's first chief medical inspector. In 1877 Nash Walker, a former Alabama slave and Union army veteran, arrived from Kansas and instituted a short-lived Back-to-Africa movement.

The opening of the "Leadville" gold and silver mining area, and the arrival of the railroads in Denver and other areas, brought additional black people to the West. In the 1880s the collapse of Radical Reconstruction brought many EXODUSTERS who could not make a success of high plains agriculture in the western part of Kansas. Looking for easier times in a more hospital environment, they found their way to Colorado. By 1910 about 70 percent of the black population had settled in Denver; others went to live in such towns as Colorado Springs and Pueblo.

In 1890 the white *Denver Republican* observed that the city had a rather prosperous black community that was better situated than many comparable places in the more established regions of the country. A wealthy black elite, whose members lived in the Capitol Hill district, set up community institutions, including two newspapers, the *Denver Star* and the *Colorado Statesman*. Education remained partly integrated and of fairly good quality, and such social organizations as the elite Eureka Literary Club promoted learning by black people. The community also sponsored plays and concerts. In 1894 the prominent vocalist Emma Azalia HACKLEY settled in Denver with her husband, lawyer Edwin Hackley. The *Republican*'s article noted in conclusion that "the tendency of the colored people of Denver is to get ahead and stick solidly to whatever they acquire."

However, the article focused on a small number of the almost six thousand black residents of the city at the time. The remainder were isolated, underemployed and discriminated against in most areas of life. Despite civil rights laws passed in 1885, 1895, and 1912, the authorities declined to ensure equality.

Barney Ford. (Colorado Historical Society)

Blacks were routinely forced into ghettos such as Denver's "Five Points" area. They were excluded from theaters and restaurants, barred from militia companies, and subject to police harassment and random arrest. Forced into job competition with Mexican-Americans—arguably even lower than blacks in the social order—blacks were mainly confined to menial labor and domestic service jobs.

There were also some ugly incidents. When the Colorado Coal and Iron Company hired black miners at Walsenburg and Engleville in the mid-1880s, whites walked off the job and rioted. The turn of the century brought several lynchings. In 1898 the Denver police chief claimed the city needed "a regular old Kentucky lynching." In 1903, twenty-two murders were committed in Denver. Only three defendants, all black, were convicted. In 1915, after the opening of D. W. Griffith's controversial film THE BIRTH OF A NATION, the Denver City Council banned films and plays which "cast racial aspersions" in response to black protest of the film, though the film continued to be shown. By the 1920s, Colorado was a center of the KU KLUX KLAN.

From the turn of the century until the beginning of World War II, there was little black migration, and black population growth was largely a result of natural increase. Blacks responded to discrimination in different ways over the decades. Some, led by O. T. Jackson, founded the black town of Deerfield, near Greeley. Begun in 1911, it reached a peak of 700 residents in 1921, then quickly died out. Others protested. During the 1920s, Denver blacks sued unsuccessfully for open access to hotels and city swimming pools outside Five Points. In the 1930s and '40s, however, protest activity led to the opening of theaters, clubs, and restaurants to black patrons. The city boasted a modest black entertainment scene, including George Morrison's band, a touring orchestra from which sprang such well-known musicians as Denver natives Andy Kirk and Jimmie LUNCEFORD.

The coming of WORLD WAR II brought an enormous shift in the condition of Colorado's African Americans. Government employment quotas brought about the hiring of massive numbers of skilled and unskilled laborers in war industries, as well as in government jobs. Large numbers of blacks took advantage of military pay and benefits to acquire homes and education. The state's black population boomed as a consequence of the new job opportunities, as well as of the construction and expansion of extant and new military facilities. Most of the growth occurred in Denver and Colorado Springs. From 1940 to 1950, the African-American population of Colorado almost doubled, and it nearly doubled again by 1960. In the following ten years it slowed somewhat, but leaped ahead again between 1970 and 1980 as a re-

sult of renewed economic expansion. By 1990, African Americans represented just over 4 percent of the state's population. Due largely to the migration of skilled blacks in response to economic opportunities, black people in Colorado are above median United States black educational and occupational levels. By 1960, black income in the state was up to 75 percent of white income, and the gap narrowed somewhat thereafter.

The road to black equality in Colorado was gradual. In the 1960s, when Denver blacks tried to expand from Five Points into suburban Park Hill, violence erupted on the streets and in schools. Eventually local whites formed the Park Hill Action Committee to ease the pace and tensions of integration, and by 1970 the area was one of the most integrated in the nation. Still, the *Keyes* school busing case brought some of the residual resistance to integration into the open. In 1969 the Denver School Board adopted by a wide margin a school integration plan that included busing. White parents sued to cancel the plan, and the question went through the courts. In 1973 the U.S. Supreme Court, in *Keyes v. Denver School District No. 1*, ruled in favor of the school board. Desegregation was met by violence, as school buses were bombed. An antibusing referendum was passed by 69 percent of voters, and many Republicans were elected to local and state office on antibusing platforms. During the following years, many white Denverites moved from the city to nearby suburbs.

Many Colorado African Americans reached high levels of prominence and achievement in the last half of the twentieth century. Some notable residents have included author Clarence MAJOR, dancer/choreographer Cleo Parker Robinson, athletes Michael Ray Richardson, Larry Farmer, Jerome Biffle, Edwin MOSES, and Tom Jackson, National Earthquake Information Center head Waverly Person, and Colorado Supreme Court Justice Greg Scott. In 1973 George Brown, the third black graduate of the University of Colorado Law School and the first black state senator, was elected to a term as the state's lieutenant governor. The same year, Penfield Tate was elected mayor of Boulder, and Wellington Webb was elected as a state representative. In 1991 Webb became Denver's first black mayor.

By the early 1990s, blacks in Colorado had developed a strong community infrastructure comprised of numerous social and fraternal organizations, churches, and small businesses. They held leadership positions in a number of areas, including government, finance, education, and the military. In commemoration of the contributions of African Americans to the state, Colorado has several black history monuments, the most notable being the Black American West Museum in Denver.

REFERENCES

ABBOTT, CARL, STEVEN J. LEONARD, and DAVID MC-COMB. *Colorado: A History of the Centennial State.* Boulder, Colo., 1982.

BRUYN, KATHLEEN. *"Aunt" Clara Brown: The Story of a Black Pioneer.* Boulder, Colo., 1970.

GILMORE, IRIS. *Barney Ford, Black Baron.* New York, 1973.

HARVEY, JAMES R. "Negroes in Colorado." *Colorado Magazine* 26 (July 1949): 165–176.

KING, WILLIAM M. "Black Children, White Law: Black Efforts to Secure Public Education in Central City, Colorado, 1864–1869." *Essays and Monographs in Colorado History* (1984): 55–81.

———. *Going to Meet a Man: Denver's Last Legal Public Execution, 27 July, 1886.* Niwot, Colo., 1991.

WAYNE, GEORGE H. "Negro Migration and Colonization in Colorado, 1870–1930." *Journal of the West* (January 1976): 102–140.

WILLIAM KING

Colter, Cyrus (January 8, 1910–), novelist. Cyrus Colter's free black forebears emigrated from North Carolina to Park County, Ind., in the 1830s to escape repressive legislation. Colter was born and raised in Noblesville, Ind. His mother died in 1916. Colter's childhood and youth were marked by the learning and accomplishments of his father, a traveling organizer for the fledgling NATIONAL ASSOCIATION FOR THE ADVANCEMENT OF COLORED PEOPLE (NAACP). Colter attended high school in Youngstown, Ohio, then studied at Ohio State University and at Kent Law School of the Illinois Institute of Technology in Chicago (J.D., 1939). Beginning in 1940, he practiced law in Chicago.

Colter entered the U.S. Army in 1942, was assigned to field artillery, was later commissioned a lieutenant and promoted to captain, and served in combat in Italy until the end of World War II. In 1942 he married Imogene Mackay. When in 1946 he returned to Chicago, he embarked on a political career, winning appointment by Democratic Gov. Adlai Stevenson to the Illinois Commerce Commission, on which he served under six governors, three Democratic and three Republican. In 1973 Colter retired from the commission and from the active practice of law and was appointed Chester D. Tripp Distinguished Professor at Northwestern University, where he built the Afro-American Studies Department, teaching until his retirement in 1979.

Beginning to write at the age of fifty, Colter published his first book ten years later. *The Beach Umbrella,* a collection of short stories issued in 1970, won

the first Iowa Fiction Award, judged that year by Kurt Vonnegut. These stories in a predominantly realist mode chronicle the lives of lower- and middle-class African Americans in Chicago. His first novel, *The Rivers of Eros* (1972), is a study of insurmountable contradictions—social, political, and psychological—in the lives of working-class black men and women.

It was followed by *The Hippodrome* (1973), a work very like a French existentialist novel in its depiction of extreme circumstances and dilemmas of individual choice in a social context without conventional moral points of reference. The novel takes place in a private pornographic theater, although the narrative concentrates on moral quandary outside of the moments of performance. *Night Studies* (1979), a novel on a nineteenth-century scale, presents the spiritual and psychological crisis of the leader of a black political movement. Colter's fourth novel, *A Chocolate Soldier* (1988), is a textured tour de force of narration, its central figure a quixotic black student revolutionary, its narrator a complicated and unreliable witness of his doomed one-man uprising who looks back on it late in life. *The Amoralist* (1988) is an expanded edition of *The Beach Umbrella.*

REFERENCES

CROSS, GILTON GREGORY, FRED SHAFER, CHARLES JOHNSON, and REGINALD GIBBONS. "Fought for It and Paid Taxes Too: Four Interviews with Cyrus Colter." *Callaloo* 14, no. 4 (Fall 1991): 855–897.

GIBBONS, REGINALD. "Colter's Novelistic Contradictions." *Callaloo* 14, no. 4 (Fall 1991): 898–906.

REGINALD GIBBONS

Coltrane, John William (September 23, 1926– July 17, 1967), jazz tenor and soprano saxophonist. Born in Hamlet, N.C., Coltrane moved with his family to High Point, N.C., when he was only a few months old. His father was a tailor, and his mother was an amateur singer. Coltrane received his first instrument, a clarinet, when he was twelve, though he soon began to play the alto saxophone, which was his primary instrument for a number of years.

After high school, Coltrane moved to Philadelphia, where he studied at the Ornstein School of Music and the Granoff Studios, where he won scholarships for both performance and composition. He played in the Philadelphia area until 1945, when he entered the Navy for two years, playing in Navy bands. His exposure at this time to bebop and the playing of Charlie PARKER proved a major and lasting influence on Coltrane's music. Coltrane was so awed by Parker's abilities on the alto saxophone that he switched to playing the tenor saxophone, on which he felt he wouldn't be intimidated by the comparison. When Coltrane returned to Philadelphia, he started playing in blues bands, and in 1948 he was hired by Dizzy GILLESPIE. But Coltrane began drinking heavily and using drugs, and in 1951 he lost his job with the Gillespie band.

The recognition of Coltrane as a major jazz figure dates from his joining the Miles DAVIS Quintet in 1955, an association that would last, on and off, until 1959. In 1957, Coltrane overcame his drinking and narcotics problem, and in the process underwent a spiritual rebirth. Also in 1957 he began to play with Thelonious MONK, and recorded his first album as a leader, *Blue Train*. Other important albums from this period include *Giant Steps* and *Coltrane Jazz,* both from 1959.

Coltrane left Davis in 1959 and thereafter led his own ensemble. The key personnel in Coltrane's definitive quartet of the period, which stayed together from 1961 to 1965, included McCoy Tyner on piano, Elvin JONES on the drums, and Reggie Worhman on

Jazz saxophonist John Coltrane with his wife, Alice Coltrane. John Coltrane's extended solo improvisations and adventurous harmonies inspired countless musicians in the 1960s, as did his interest in expressing spiritual concerns through music. (© Chuck Stewart)

bass. Alto saxophonist Eric DOLPHY played regularly with the ensemble until his death in 1964. In 1959 Coltrane started playing the soprano saxophone (an instrument that, except for Sidney BECHET, had been rarely used by jazz musicians). He soon recorded his most famous soprano sax solo, "My Favorite Things." Coltrane developed a distinctive soprano style, different from the one he favored on the tenor saxophone. His best-known works of this period include *A Love Supreme* (1964) and the collective free jazz improvisation *Ascension* (1965). In 1965 Coltrane's band underwent another change. His regular band members included Rashied Ali on drums, Pharoah SANDERS as a second tenor saxophone, and on the piano, his second wife, Alice Coltrane. With this ensemble, Coltrane explored free jazz improvisation until his death from cancer on July 17, 1967.

In the little more than ten years of his active career, Coltrane's music underwent a number of metamorphoses. He first achieved renown as bluesy hard-bop tenor saxophonist. After 1957 he began to develop a new approach in which his solos were filigreed with myriad broken scales and arpeggios played extremely rapidly—this became known as his "sheets of sound" approach. In 1961 Coltrane began to play solos of unprecedented length, often lasting twenty or thirty minutes. If some found these solos to be soporific and self-indulgent, others were mesmerized by their sweep and intensity, and Coltrane acquired a number of avid fans. His best solos in the early 1960s were often gentle and powerfully introspective. By the mid-1960s Coltrane was playing free jazz, where his former lyrical style was often replaced by a harsh and turbulent soloing.

Coltrane, often simply called "Trane," was by far the most popular jazz musician to emerge from the New York City jazz avant-garde of the late 1950s and 1960s. His personal and communicative style, his spiritual quest, and his early death, in addition to the virtuosity and grace of his solos, contributed to a Coltrane "cult" that has not abated in the decades since his passing. His influence on subsequent musicians, which has been immense, includes not only his musical ideas but his taking of extended solos and his view of jazz as an ongoing quest for spiritual knowledge and self-wisdom.

REFERENCES

SIMPKINS, C. O. *Coltrane: A Musical Biography*. New York, 1975.

TAYLOR, CECIL. "John Coltrane." *Jazz Review* (January 1959): 34.

THOMAS, JOHN. *Chasin the Trane: The Music and Mystique of John Coltrane*. Garden City, N.Y., 1975.

WILLIAM S. COLE

Comedians. In any culture, comedians serve complicated functions as both entertainers and social critics. For African-American comedians, this has been further complicated by the burden of American racism and the historical legacy of racial comedy in this culture. Racially grounded humor has been both a means of denigrating black people—reinforcing their degradation and justifying their oppression by white society—and a repository of folk wisdom, a popular tradition of criticism and self-criticism, and a means by which black people could affirm and enjoy their own view of the world. Black comedians have derived much of their humor from the precarious balance between these two tendencies.

African-American comedy as a professional genre originated with blackface minstrelsy (*see* MINSTRELS/ MINSTRELSY), which remained the province of white performers until around the time of the CIVIL WAR. According to Robert Toll, the performance of "alleged Negro songs and dances" in these shows emerged as a popular genre in the 1820s. When all-black troupes such as Callender's Georgia Minstrels were formed after the war, they continued to perform the same kind of material. These early black minstrels, unlike their white rivals, usually did not perform in burnt cork (except for the end men), so that the audience could recognize them as authentic African Americans. As the years passed, however, more and more of these performers reverted to using burnt cork.

The fact that many performers continued to use burnt cork, as late as the 1920s and '30s, supported by a predominantly black clientele, attests to the powerful and paradoxical legacy of the minstrel tradition. Other conventions of minstrelsy persisted in the styles of black comedians as well: for example, the use of ludicrous attire, grotesque facial expressions and body movements, and song-and-dance routines. Favorite minstrel subjects also persisted, such as linguistic maladroitness and misunderstandings, differences in racial behavior, romantic mismatches and misadventures, overindulgence in alcohol and other pleasures, and the common folk's views of current events. Black comedy teams often maintained the basic structure of minstrelsy, generating comic effects from the interaction between a "straight" person (the minstrel "interlocutor") and a foolish companion (the end men, Mr. Tambo and Mr. Bones). As scholars such as Constance Rourke and Walter Blair have demonstrated, these subjects and most minstrel conventions derived from old traditions of European comedy. Nevertheless, the racial elaborations of the traditions were distinctly American.

In the twentieth century, after the collapse of traditional minstrel shows, black performers continued to practice their craft on the TOBA circuit (Theater Owners Booking Association, which controlled tours of black theaters and clubs around the country) and in black musical comedies, such as *Shuffle Along* (1921) and *Hot Chocolates* (1929). Often performing in blackface, these comedians did skits, sang, and danced. The greatest of them was Bert WILLIAMS, a magnificent performer whose ability to range from the hilarious to the heartrending eventually made him the first black star of the Ziegfeld Follies.

The establishment of Harlem's APOLLO THEATRE in 1934 was an important event for black performers. It provided a black equivalent of Carnegie Hall or the Grand Ole Opry: a venue where amateurs could gain recognition and where stars could compete for preeminence. In subsequent decades other venues, such as the Roberts Show Club in Chicago, performed a similar function. From the beginning, comedians were a staple at the Apollo. As in smaller clubs and theaters, they performed both as filler between acts and as headliners when they gained sufficient popularity. One of the most popular acts of the 1930s was Butterbeans and Susie. This husband-and-wife team (Joe and Susie Edwards) specialized in risqué, sexually suggestive humor. Ted Fox, a historian of the Apollo, describes their song "I Want a Hot Dog for My Roll" as typical of their material, which delighted their audiences and outraged censorious middle-class black critics.

Among their contemporaries at the Apollo, Fox lists Dewey "Pigmeat" MARKHAM, Dusty FLETCHER, Tim "Kingfish" MOORE, and Jimmy Baskette. These men were among the leading comedians of the day. Their routines—again, often in blackface—included skits, songs, and dances, much in the minstrel tradition. Markham is best remembered for his routine "Heah Come de Judge," created in 1929, which was resurrected and popularized by Sammy DAVIS, Jr., on the television show *Laugh-In* in the 1960s. Markham also claimed to have invented "truckin'," a comic dance that is now best known from Robert Crumb's underground comic strips. No comedy routine of those years was better known or more loved than Dusty Fletcher's "Open the Door, Richard." Playing a bumbling drunk in minstrel attire attempting to enter a house, Fletcher would stagger repeatedly up a stepladder, falling off again and again, as he wailed piteously: "Open the door, Richard!" This line entered the vernacular as a self-sufficient punch line.

Jackie "Moms" MABLEY is a crucial transitional figure, both because her popularity spanned from these early days through the 1970s and because stylistically she represents a new form of comedy. Like other early comics, Moms played a character, a "dirty old

Dewey "Pigmeat" Markham. (Photographs and Prints Division, Schomburg Center for Research in Black Culture, The New York Public Library, Astor, Lenox and Tilden Foundations)

Jackie "Moms" Mabley was one of the best loved and most durable of black comics. From the 1920s through the '70s, she entertained audiences with her witty and mordant observations on life. Widespread recognition of her talents in the mainstream media came only in the late 1960s. (Photographs and Prints Division, Schomburg Center for Research in Black Culture, The New York Public Library, Astor, Lenox and Tilden Foundations)

lady," who dressed in oversize, faded cotton dresses, baggy cotton stockings, large brogans—or, in later years, sneakers—and droopy hats. Her signature line was "An old man can't do nothing for me but show me which way a young man went." But Moms was a stand-up monologuist rather than a skit performer. In this, she anticipated the dominant style of later comedians. Her forte remained sexual comedy about the failings of old men and the appeal of young ones, but in the 1960s she turned increasingly to political commentary. For instance, in the early 1960s she composed an "opera," rewriting the words of traditional songs and children's rhymes to praise the Rev. Dr. Martin Luther KING, Jr., and satirize segregationists. She sang these songs in her gravelly voice, with a piano accompanist—naturally, a young man.

In the 1950s and 1960s the work of comedians was often disseminated on recordings called "party records." These records usually featured "adult" humor, and they ranged in style from madcap, minstrel-style skits by acts like Skillet and Leroy to the nightclub acts of comedians like George Kirby, Melvin "Slappy" White, and Redd FOXX. All of these performers used sexual humor, with Kirby inclined more toward wit and Foxx more toward raunchiness and profane language. Slappy White, Foxx's partner when the two began performing in the late 1940s, was simultaneously witty and raunchy. All three of these comedians made their reputations on the nightclub circuit and eventually made television appearances. Redd Foxx, the most popular of the group, gained mainstream success in the 1970s as star of the television series *Sanford and Son*. Compared with

Foxx's scathing nightclub persona, the mildly naughty Fred Sanford was a pussycat.

A remarkable group of young stand-up comics emerged in the early 1960s, and most of them went on to very successful careers that included work in television and movies: Nipsey RUSSELL, Godfrey CAMBRIDGE, Scoey MITCHELL, Flip WILSON, and, most important, Dick GREGORY, Bill COSBY, and Richard PRYOR. Russell, noted for his quick, razor-sharp wit, was very popular in New York City. He soon developed a lucrative career as a headliner in Las Vegas nightclubs and as a regular on the television show *Hollywood Squares*. Cambridge, a very large man, combined gentleness, vulnerability, and moral fervor in his routines about race relations, obesity, international politics, and contemporary culture. Like Dick Gregory, he was an outspoken supporter of the civil rights movement. Flip Wilson, due to the popularity of his weekly television comedy show in the early 1970s, became, for a time, perhaps the most familiar of all these comedians. On *The Flip Wilson Show,* he played a variety of amusing characters, most memorably a saucy woman named Geraldine.

Nonetheless, Gregory, Cosby, and Pryor are clearly the most talented and enduringly important of this group. One could hardly imagine three more sharply contrasting comedians. Gregory, the impassioned and blunt-spoken social activist; Cosby, the cool, politely middle-class comedian of family relations; and Pryor, the manic, whimsical, outrageous improviser on every aspect of human and animal life. Collectively, these three represent the finest achievements of modern African-American comedy.

Dick Gregory, more than any other comedian, has used his celebrity as an entertainer to advance social causes. His style employs deadpan understatement and understated exaggeration to great satirical effect. For example, he commented in one of his routines: "I know the South very well. I spent twenty years there one night." Gregory joined the voter-registration marches in Greenwood, Miss., in 1963, becoming the first celebrity to participate in that struggle. During the 1960s he was a popular speaker on college campuses and television talk shows. His unique ability to combine social satire and moral fervor with a compassionate humor regarding the foibles of people from all backgrounds made him a compelling, immensely popular comedian. In the 1970s Gregory began to devote most of his energy to research, writing, and consulting on issues of health, nutrition, and obesity.

Though not an activist, Bill Cosby has also made a significant social impact, both through the content of his television shows and through his philanthropy, as a donor of millions of dollars to Spelman and other black colleges. Cosby first gained national fame in the early 1960s as costar of the television series *I Spy*. His brilliance as a comedian, however, was established by a series of recordings that revealed him to be a versatile, broadly appealing entertainer. Avoiding "blue" humor and political commentary, Cosby's albums focused on childhood, movies, animals, sports, and various whimsies, such as "Why is there air?"

His reminiscences about a childhood friend called Fat Albert eventually developed into a very successful television cartoon series. A significant amount of Cosby's work has been not only about but for children. The ultimate popularity of Fat Albert notwithstanding, however, Cosby's most famous routine of the 1960s was "Noah," a series of exchanges between God and Noah regarding the ark. When Noah, exasperated by animal care and neighbors' ridicule, threatens to dismantle the ark, God asks him: "How long can you tread water?" After a pause, Noah recants with his characteristic, deadpan refrain: "Riiight!" Like Dusty Fletcher's "Open the door, Richard," these lines quickly entered the vernacular.

In the early 1970s, Cosby appeared with Sidney POITIER in a series of popular movies, including *Uptown Saturday Night*. Though entertaining, these did

Bill Cosby during his opening night performance at New York's Radio City Music Hall, March 1987. (AP/Wide World Photos)

nothing to advance Cosby's reputation as a comic. In the 1980s he returned to television with *The Cosby Show,* a series about a physician, his lawyer wife, and their several children. This show was designed to break the stereotype of black families as ghetto-dwelling buffoons with unmarried parents. The backbone of the show, of course, was Cosby's wise and gentle humor, as he dealt with the family's problems and adventures. This was the most successful television show of the decade, gaining top ratings even in South Africa. It brought an unprecedented dignity to blacks in television comedy, and it introduced a new generation to the benevolently mischievous, family-oriented humor of Bill Cosby. Cosby decided to conclude the show in 1992.

Despite the brilliance of Dick Gregory and Bill Cosby, Richard Pryor must be acknowledged as the preeminent African-American comedian of the past two decades. The uniqueness of Pryor's comic genius lies not just with his extraordinary ability to make people laugh but, more important, with the emotional complexity of his humor. Pryor is the most frighteningly confessional of all comedians, and much of his humor derives from his own failed relationships, his personal fears, misfortunes, angers, and addictions. His unprecedented willingness to expose everything, combined with his childlike ability to find wonderment in common things, produces a comedy of breadth and profundity, encompassing emotions from moral horror to sheer exhilaration.

From the beginning of his career in the early 1960s, Pryor had the reputation of being a crazy, unpredictable performer, one who would do or say anything, no matter how profane or taboo. Even then, however, his routines were tempered by moments of poignant self-revelation. Pryor's reputation as America's top stand-up comedian was consolidated in the 1970s and 1980s with the release of several live performances as full-length theatrical films (and subsequently as LP recordings). In these concerts, Pryor demonstrates the full range of his art. He does impersonations of white people, women, dogs, monkeys, and children; he portrays Mudbone, an old black storyteller from the South; and he discusses his misadventures with women, his heart attack, his drug addiction, and even his horrible self-immolation in a freebasing accident.

After this close brush with death Pryor's comedy mellowed somewhat, causing some critics to complain that he had lost his comic edge. Nevertheless, his spellbinding narrative of his addiction, his accident, and his convalescence clearly epitomizes the combination of pain and humor, confession and moral reflection, that has always made him unique. Throughout his career, the conflict between desire and restraint has been central to Pryor's comedy. In

Richard Pryor, April 1982. (AP/Wide World Photos)

his late work, this continues to be the case, except that he has gained a sharper understanding of moral consequences in the failure of restraint. By traditional aesthetic criteria, this discovery of wisdom must be considered a deepening and not a diminution of his art.

Of the African-American comedians to emerge since the 1970s, three are clearly preeminent: Arsenio HALL, Eddie MURPHY, and Whoopi GOLDBERG. Hall, due to his nightly monologues on his popular late-night program, *The Arsenio Hall Show,* has become the most familiar of the three as a stand-up comic. Early in his career, Hall toured with popular soul-music bands, including Patti LABELLE's, as a warm-up act. He gained national television exposure as a regular on *Solid Gold,* a popular soul-music show of the late 1970s and early 1980s. Hall's monologues are reminiscent of Johnny Carson's, drawing heavily on current news stories and celebrities. Aside from his television work, Hall has received critical accolades for his comic roles in two Eddie Murphy films: *Coming to America* and *Harlem Nights.*

Eddie Murphy created an immediate sensation when he joined the cast of *Saturday Night Live* in the late 1970s. Distinguished by his exceptional talents as a mimic, Murphy created several memorable caricatures for the show, including portrayals of Buckwheat and Stevie Wonder. Several of those performances were compiled on a videocassette, *The Best of*

Whoopi Goldberg in *Jumpin' Jack Flash* (1986). Since the late 1980s, she has been the leading black female film star in Hollywood, winning an Academy Award for best supporting actress for her role in *Ghost* (1990). (AP/Wide World Photos)

Saturday Night Live: Eddie Murphy. Many critics consider him the heir apparent to Richard Pryor. In the 1980s, Murphy gained stardom in a series of immensely popular movies, such as *Beverly Hills Cop* and *48 Hours,* that capitalized on his biting repartee and derisive cockiness. He also filmed a pair of live-performance movies, *Eddie Murphy Live* and *Raw.* Murphy's monologues focus primarily on family and sexual relations, but they lack the shifting perspectives and self-critical insight of Pryor's routines. The caustic edge of Murphy's humor has rarely been tempered by compassion.

Whoopi Goldberg incorporates elements of several earlier comedians. Goldberg's stage persona—dreadlocks, athletic shoes, guttural voice—brings to mind Moms Mabley. Like Richard Pryor, she portrays characters facing personal crises with a combination of humor and pathos. Like Dick Gregory, she has incorporated political activisim into her career. Goldberg's one-woman show on Broadway in the early 1980s brought her instant acclaim. Her characters, such as a Valley girl who attempts abortion with a coat hanger and a black girl who wears a mop as a

wig, yearning for blond hair, were at once funny, poignant, and politically charged. Goldberg's greatest triumph came with her portrayal of Celie in the movie *The Color Purple* (1985), but her first memorable comic role came in *Ghost* (1990), in which she played a phony psychic who suddenly begins to communicate with real ghosts. Though Goldberg brings flashes of brilliance to all her work, she has not consistently played roles commensurate with her talent.

Earlier black comedians faced limited options as performers, depending primarily on work in nightclubs and traveling shows. Since the late 1960s, opportunities in television and movies have greatly increased their options, and the growing popularity of comedy clubs and televised comedy workshops in the early 1990s has substantially increased the number and variety of professional comedians. Whether these changes will result ultimately in a flowering of comedic art or a deluge of mediocrity remains to be seen. With Richard Pryor in retirement due to illness, and most of the other major comedians preoccupied with television, movie, and other responsibilities, the comedy stage of the early 1990s appears ready for new stars. In any case, the greatest challenge for comedians will always be the creation of a humor that taps deep emotions, provoking a laughter intensified by moral outrage and tempered with tears.

REFERENCES

BLAIR, WALTER, and HAMLIN HILL. *America's Humor from Poor Richard to Doonesbury.* New York, 1978.

ELLISON, RALPH. "Change the Joke and Slip the Yoke." In *Shadow and Act.* New York, 1972, pp. 45–59.

FOX, TED. *Showtime at the Apollo.* New York, 1983.

LEVINE, LAWRENCE. *Black Culture and Black Consciousness.* New York, 1977.

ROURKE, CONSTANCE. *American Humor: A Study of the National Character.* New York, 1931.

TOLL, ROBERT. *Blacking Up.* New York, 1974.

TRAVIS, DEMPSEY. *An Autobiography of Black Jazz.* Chicago, 1983.

DAVID LIONEL SMITH

Comer, James Pierpont (September 25, 1934–), physician and educator. James Comer was born in East Chicago, Ind., the son of Hugh and Maggie Nichols Comer. A graduate of Indiana University (A.B., 1956), he attended Howard University College of Medicine, where he earned an M.D. in 1960. In 1964, following an internship at St. Catherine's Hospital in his native city and assignments with the Chronic Disease Division of the U.S. Public

Health Service, he earned a master's in public health at the University of Michigan.

While at Michigan, Comer decided on a career in psychiatry. This decision was influenced by his experience and observation of urban social problems and the belief that psychiatry offered, if not a solution, at least a forum within which to address such problems. He trained in psychiatry at Yale University. After a year working with the National Institute of Mental Health in Washington, D.C., he returned to Yale in 1968 as director of a project that applied the principles of psychiatry to the problems of inner-city schools. His approach to behavioral problem solving—essentially a sympathetic probing for the causes underlying disruptive or antisocial behavior—was conceived as an innovative alternative to negative methods of discipline. The "Comer Process" was adopted by numerous school districts nationwide.

On the Yale faculty since 1968, Comer became the Maurice Falk Professor of Child Psychiatry in 1976. A cofounder of Black Psychiatrists of America, he served on the National Board to Abolish Corporal Punishment in the Schools.

REFERENCES

COMER, JAMES P. *Maggie's American Dream: The Life and Times of a Black Family*. New York, 1988.
———. "The Social Power of the Negro." *Scientific American* 216 (April 1967): 21–27.

PHILIP N. ALEXANDER

Comic Books.   In the early years of comic books, African Americans sometimes appeared as minor characters, usually in the demeaning guise of familiar stereotypes. Not until the 1960s did blacks begin to appear as important figures in mass-circulation comic books. African-American artists and writers, meanwhile, did not gain a significant presence in the comic book industry until the 1970s, and their numbers have remained very small.

In important respects, comic books have always reflected tendencies in other popular genres, including COMIC STRIPS, radio shows, movies, and television. Thus, the depictions of black Americans in comic books have often reflected established popular cultural norms. In the 1940s, for example, Will Eisner's series *The Spirit* included a black sidekick named Ebony White. Reflecting the transition between traditional racial stereotypes and an incipient realism during that decade of World War II, Eisner drew Ebony with some stereotypical features, such as exaggerated lips, but also portrayed him as a sympathetic character, no more the butt of low humor than *The Spirit*'s other characters.

In the 1960s, television shows like *I Spy* and *Julia* began to incorporate black characters as educated middle-class professionals—for example, as intelligence agents and nurses. Correspondingly, the *Spiderman* comic book introduced Joe Robertson as city editor at the *Daily Bugle,* the newspaper where Spiderman's alter ego, Peter Parker, worked as a freelance photographer. This trend continued in the 1970s, especially in the Marvel Comics universe. For example, *Silver Surfer* #5 (1969) featured a black scientist named Al B. Harper, who used his technical skills and ultimately sacrificed his life to help the Silver Surfer save humanity from extermination by the Stranger, an intergalactic misanthrope.

Marvel also introduced the first major black superhero, the Black Panther, in 1966. The ruler of a fictional African nation called Wakanda, T'Challa, the Black Panther, wore a skintight black costume that

This illustration, by Will S. Watkins IV, depicts Akil (background) and Onyxx, two of the most prominent characters from Flatline Comics, Inc. Flatline Comics was founded in 1992 by Kemp Powers, Will S. Watkins IV, and Ornette Coleman. (Flatline Comics, Inc.)

invoked his namesake and personal totem. Though he lacked true superpowers, the Panther possessed the enhanced strength, quickness, and agility that his name suggested. Wakanda maintained a combination of traditional culture and advanced technology; reflecting this cosmopolitanism, the Black Panther often traveled to America, becoming involved with superhero groups. He first appeared in *The Fantastic Four* No. 52 and eventually became a regular member of *The Avengers*. He gained his own series, titled *Jungle Action,* beginning in 1973.

Marvel's first and most successful black title, however, was *Luke Cage, Superhero for Hire* (1972). In an accident involving a combination of electric shock and immersion in chemicals, Cage acquired impenetrable skin and greatly magnified strength (though not "superhuman" power on the scale of Marvel's the Hulk or DC Comics' Superman). A comic book equivalent of popular "blaxploitation" movie heroes, Cage lived in Harlem and fought various criminals, usually working on a "for hire" basis. Later in the 1970s, as the popularity of martial-arts films began to eclipse blaxploitation, Marvel teamed Luke Cage with a martial-arts superhero, Iron Fist. The Luke Cage series was significant as the first major black feature to be drawn by a black artist, Billy Graham. Graham also drew some issues of the Black Panther series.

Subsequent black characters in Marvel Comics have included Black Goliath, who briefly had his own title; Storm, an African woman who joined the New X-Men, a group of mutant superheroes; and the Falcon, who became the partner of Captain America in the 1970s. There have been fewer black characters in DC comics, and nearly all have been minor figures. These have included John Stewart, who occasionally appeared in *Green Lantern,* and Mal, a sidekick of the Teen Titans. In the 1970s, a special DC collectors' series included a duel between Superman and Muhammad Ali. In the 1980s DC introduced *Cloak and Dagger,* a pair of symbiotically linked superheroes. Cloak is a black man, Dagger a white woman.

Also worthy of note is *Sabre,* a series produced by Eclipse Publications, a small comics company. Created by Don MacGregor, who wrote the Black Panther series for Marvel, *Sabre* features a protagonist modeled visually on the rock guitarist Jimi Hendrix. This is not a superhero comic. Rather, it is a philosophical, post–nuclear holocaust fiction, somewhat like the *Mad Max* movies. Sabre's adventures are secondary to his meditations, and, despite his appearance, his blackness has no ethnic content. The series originally appeared in an extended, black-and-white graphic-novel format, drawn by Paul Gulacy, in 1978. Subsequent issues have been in conventional full-color comic format, drawn by Billy Graham.

In the 1980s, the proliferation of specialty comic-book stores and other economic factors led to fundamental changes in the comics industry. The creation of new outlets undermined the power wielded by the major companies through their control of newsstand space. New comics companies developed, marketing their titles through specialty stores, often to more mature and selective clienteles than traditional comic books had targeted. This created opportunities for people with special genre interests (social realism, fantasy, SCIENCE FICTION, horror, etc.), women, ethnic minorities, and others to produce and consume a greater variety of comics than ever before. Even the major companies began to produce graphic novels and other special projects, designed for this new comic book market. In the early 1990s, some independently produced black comic books have appeared, such as *Brotherman* by David, Jason, and Guy Sims, and *Black Thunder* by Ernest Gibbs, Jr. African Americans currently working for the major companies include the writer Dwayne McDuffie and Marcus McLaurin, an editor at Marvel. These exceptions notwithstanding, black people remain underrepresented in the world of comic books, both as subject matter and as producers.

REFERENCES

DANIELS, LES. *Marvel: Five Fabulous Decades of the World's Greatest Comics.* New York, 1991.
RILEY, ROCHELLE. "The Dictator of Discipline: Superhero Brotherman." *Emerge* (February 1991): 24–26.

DAVID LIONEL SMITH

Comic Strips.   From its very beginnings in 1895, the American comic strip has reflected the nation's rich ethnic mixture, with such features as *The Katzenjammer Kids* (1897–), *Alphonse and Gaston* (1902), *Bringing Up Father* (1911–), and *Abie the Agent* (1914–1940) focused on characters of German, French, Irish, and Jewish backgrounds, respectively. The African American, however, generally served as a background character in early strips and was consistently portrayed in the mainstream press in the stereotyped minstrel-show style that had become commonplace in films, cartoons, advertising, and other media of the period. This was true even of the early work of the brilliant creator of *Krazy Kat,* George HERRIMAN, who was only recently discovered to have been of African ancestry.

As it became evident after the turn of the twentieth century that the comic strip was a permanent part of the newspaper, many black NEWSPAPERS encouraged the development of comic strips by black staff artists, often only for local consumption but more sensitive to the nuances of black character and life. The best known and longest lived of them was the CHICAGO DEFENDER's *Bungleton Green* (1920–1963), first created by Leslie L. Rogers and continued under the hands of Henry Brown from 1929 to 1934, Jay Jackson from 1934 to 1954, and Chester Commodore until its end. Bung, the central character, was an inept opportunist and con man, much in the pattern of such mainstream characters as Mutt and Jeff and Barney Google, and the humor derived from his unsuccessful efforts to make a quick buck by hustling someone. Since his economic woes were not far from the situations of most of his readers, he struck a responsive chord in his faithful following, who approved of his spunk, if not his methods. During the 1940s, the strip became a predominantly adventure tale before returning to the gag format, though it continued, from time to time, to deal in satiric and indirect ways with racial themes.

Other African-American strips to emerge in the wake of *Bungleton Green* in the 1930s were *Sunnyboy Sam* by Wilbert Holloway, *Bucky* by Sammy Milai, and *Susabelle* by Elton FAX, the last two beginning a tradition of features about black children drawn with honesty and humor. Ollie HARRINGTON, who has been called America's greatest black cartoonist, earned prominence and popularity in the black community in the mid-1930s through his candid *Bootsy* cartoons for the AMSTERDAM NEWS, and in the mid-1940s for the World War II adventure strip about a black aviator, *Jive Gray*. The last was distributed nationally by the Continental Features Syndicate, established by the black entrepreneur Lajoyeaux H. Stanton and one of the first to handle black features.

In the 1940s and 1950s, Mel Tapley's *Breezy* was about teenagers, Chester Commodore's *The Sparks* satirized middle-class black family life, and Tom FEELINGS's *Tommy Traveler in the World of Negro History* took the young hero back to witness some of the proud achievements of the black past. The panel *Cuties* by Elmer Simms CAMPBELL began mainstream syndication in 1943, but here, as in his work for *Esquire* and later *Playboy*, Campbell specialized in drawing beautiful white women in romantic situations. Most readers never knew he was black. The most important feature to appear at the time was *Torchy Brown* by Jackie Ormes, a distinctively drawn strip about an independent, aggressive, and attractive woman who becomes involved in fighting racism and sexism, among other social problems, in exciting adventure narratives. Torchy was a powerful role model for young black women.

The first African-American strip to achieve mainstream national distribution by a major syndicate was *Wee Pals* by Morrie Turner, in 1964. California-born Turner had first drawn an all-black strip about children modeled after *Peanuts* called *Dinky Fellas* for two black papers, the Berkeley *Post* and the Chicago *Defender,* in 1963. With the encouragement of Charles Schulz and Dick GREGORY, the strip was integrated with children of different races and dispositions— Anglo-, Asian-, and Native American, Chicano, Jewish, intellectual, feminist, militant, etc. The charm of Turner's style and his gently satiric treatment of racial and political themes made the strip a great success during the years of the civil rights movement, and he turned the characters to educational advantage by using them in children's books, television shows, and campaigns in support of social improvement and racial harmony.

Turner's success in breaking the racial barrier in mainstream syndication was emulated by two more features about children. *Luther* (named after the Rev. Dr. Martin Luther KING, Jr.) was begun by Brumsic Brandon, Jr., in 1968 with the intent of finding humor in the lives of working-class blacks in the urban

In 1964 Morrie Turner's *Wee Pals* became the first comic strip by an African American to achieve mainstream distribution. (Photographs and Prints Division, Schomburg Center for Research in Black Culture, The New York Public Library, Astor, Lenox and Tilden Foundations)

ghetto without gloss or glamour. In addition to Luther, it featured such young characters as Hardcore and Oreo and the white teacher Miss Backlash. In 1970, the Jamaica-born Ted Shearer began another racially mixed strip called *Quincy,* which was more sentimental and gentle-natured than *Luther.* Shearer's style was distinctive and the humor engaging, but *Quincy* was like too many other children's strips of the time and seldom reflected on the social and economic problems of blacks. Both *Luther* and *Quincy* ended in 1986. Three integrated adventure strips appeared during this period, but none lasted very long: *Dateline Danger* began in 1968, *The Badge Guys* in 1971, and *Friday Foster* in 1972, the last featuring a glamorous black heroine.

Once Turner, Brandon, and Shearer had demonstrated a national interest in comic strips about blacks, the syndicates soon began to search out African-American talents and nurture their work. Between 1980 and 1982, Ray Billingsley, a young cartoonist from North Carolina, created a popular feature about a black inner-city family called *Lookin' Fine;* more widespread success came in 1988 with the appearance of *Curtis.* This strip also features a typical black family, but Billingsley succeeds in balancing the ethnic humor with generalized situations of family conflict. Occasionally the strip ventures into controversial areas such as drugs, drinking, smoking, and discrimination, which sometimes generates letters to the newspaper editors.

While a young, hardworking black couple are at the center of *Jump Start* by Philadelphia-born Robb Armstrong—Joe is a policeman and Marcy a nurse—this strip, begun in 1988, takes in through numerous subsidiary characters an entire urban community. The stresses of their action-oriented careers and the strains of married life are major sources of comedy. In 1989, Stephen Bentley of Los Angeles began *Herb & Jamaal,* featuring two mature and experienced men, former high school buddies, who have opened an ice cream parlor. The ethnicity of the strip resides less in its humor than in its authentic feel for black streetwise inner-city relationships.

In 1991, Barbara Brandon, the daughter of Brumsic Brandon, Jr., nationally syndicated a feature she had first developed in 1989 called *Where I'm Coming From.* Using an open panel style and talking heads rather than full figures (in order to reverse the traditional emphasis on the female body), Brandon had created a small community of women characters who observe social attitudes, politics, and gender behavior through the prism of their experience as black women in America. The humor is acerbic and often provocative to male readers, but it is nevertheless realistically and sensitively attuned to contemporary social issues.

Another sign of an African-American presence in the comics is the number of black characters that have been added to popular features since the 1960s. A selective list of these includes Franklin in *Peanuts* by Charles Schulz, Lieutenant Flap in *Beetle Bailey* by Mort Walker, Morrie (after Morrie Turner) in *Family Circus* by Bil Keane, Clyde and Ginny in *Doonesbury* by Garry Trudeau, and Oliver Wendell Jones in *Bloom County* by Berke Breathed. While they may appear to be token presences, these are characters who have moved beyond stereotypes and become integrated in the larger community of the world of comic art.

REFERENCES

ERICSSON, MARY KENTRA. *Morrie Turner: Creator of "Wee Pals."* Chicago, 1986.

GOULART, RON, ed. *The Encyclopedia of American Comics.* New York, 1990.

HARDY, CHARLES, and GAIL F. STERN, eds. *Ethnic Images in the Comics.* Philadelphia, 1986.

HORN, MAURICE, ed. *The World Encyclopedia of Comics.* New York, 1976.

STEVENS, JOHN D. " 'Bungleton Green': Black Comic Strip." *Journalism Quarterly* 51 (Spring 1974): 122–124.

M. THOMAS INGE

Communist Party of the United States.

When the Communist Party of the United States (CPUSA) was founded in 1921, few people realized the critical role it would play in African-American politics and culture. The product of several splinter groups emerging out of the Socialist party's left wing in 1919, it was founded by people who (like the Socialists before them) viewed the plight of African Americans as inseparable from the class struggle. However, pressure from the newly formed "Third" International, or Comintern, and popular support for black nationalist movements within African-American communities compelled the CPUSA to reconsider its approach to the "Negro question." In 1921, V. I. Lenin assailed the American Communist leadership for neglecting the plight of black workers; one year later, Comintern officials insisted that African Americans were a "nationality" oppressed by worldwide imperialist exploitation and called on American Communists to work within the Garvey movement (*see* UNIVERSAL NEGRO IMPROVEMENT ASSOCIATION). In 1928 the Comintern, with input from Harry Haywood and South African Communist James La Guma, passed a resolution asserting that African Americans in the southern Black Belt counties constituted an oppressed nation and therefore possessed an inherent right of self-determination.

An emerging black Left, deeply touched by the Bolshevik revolution as well as by postwar workers' uprisings and racial violence, also shaped the Communist position toward African Americans in the 1920s. The AFRICAN BLOOD BROTHERHOOD (ABB), founded in 1918 by Cyril BRIGGS, eventually joined the CPUSA en masse during the early 1920s. Formed as a secret, underground organization of radical black nationalists, the ABB supported collective working-class action, and advocated armed defense against lynching as well as racial equality and self-determination for Africans and peoples of African descent. After being absorbed by the CPUSA, the ABB ceased to exist as an independent entity. In its place the party in 1925 created the American Negro Labor Congress (ANLC), an organization led chiefly by ex-ABB leaders intent on building interracial unity in, and black support for, the labor movement. When the ANLC disintegrated after failing to gain popular support, it was replaced by the League of Struggle for Negro Rights in 1930. This proved to be somewhat more successful due to the popularity of its newspaper, the LIBERATOR. Under the editorship of Cyril Briggs, it became a journal of black news tailor-made for the African-American community and a forum for radical black creative writers.

The self-determination slogan may have inspired a few black intellectuals already in the CPUSA, but it was not the key to building black working-class support during the 1930s. However, the party's fight for the concrete economic needs of the unemployed and working poor, its role in organizing sharecroppers in Alabama, its militant opposition to racism, and its vigorous courtroom battles in behalf of African Americans through the International Labor Defense (ILD) attracted a considerable section of America's black working class and intelligentsia. In particular, the ILD's defense of nine young black men falsely accused of raping two white women in Alabama, known as the SCOTTSBORO CASE, crystallized black support for the CPUSA in the 1930s.

Black support during this period typified black working-class life and culture, and many rank-and-file Communists were churchgoing Christians who combined the party's politics and ideology with black folk culture. Moreover, in spite of the CP's highly masculine language of class struggle and self-determination, black women played central roles in both the leadership and the rank and file. African-American working women participated in relief demonstrations, resisted evictions, confronted condescending social workers, and fought utilities shutoffs. The Communist party produced a significant group of black women leaders, including Louise Thompson PATTERSON, Claudia Jones, Audley MOORE, and Bonita Williams.

In 1935, in accordance with the Comintern's Seventh World Congress, the CPUSA called for a Popular Front against fascism, deemphasized its Marxist ideology, and eventually supported Roosevelt's New Deal coalition. While southern Communists chose to play down race in order to build alliances with southern white liberals, the Popular Front led to more support from African Americans in the urban North. The party gained a larger black following in such places as Harlem and Chicago because of its opposition to Italy's invasion of Ethiopia in 1935, and when African-American radicals were unable to join Haile Selassie's army, because of U.S. government restrictions against the enlistment of U.S. citizens in a foreign army, many closed ranks with the Left and fought in the Spanish Civil War. Communists were also the primary force behind the NATIONAL NEGRO CONGRESS (1935–1946) and the Southern Negro Youth Congress (1937–1948), both of which represented hundreds of black organizations. Finally, during the Popular Front black Communist labor organizers—among them, Hosea HUDSON, Ebb COX, James Hart, and Ferdinand C. Smith—played a critical role in the formation of the Congress of Industrial Organizations (CIO), particularly in the steel, mining, marine transport, and meat-packing industries.

During this period the party attracted a considerable number of black artists, including Paul ROBESON

Benjamin J. Davis, Jr., marching beneath a Communist party banner in New York City. Davis, a member of the New York City Council from 1943 to 1947, was one of the few persons elected to a public office as a member of the Communist party. (Photographs and Prints Division, Schomburg Center for Research in Black Culture, The New York Public Library, Astor, Lenox and Tilden Foundations)

and Langston HUGHES. Communist cultural critics collected African-American music, began to write jazz criticism, and insisted that black culture was the clearest expression of "American culture." This newfound appreciation of black culture opened up potential space for creative expression within CPUSA circles. Communist papers published poems and short stories by black writers and carried articles and cartoons on black history; CPUSA auxiliaries sponsored plays by black playwrights, art exhibits, benefit jazz concerts, and dances. Nevertheless, many projects were constrained by ideological imperatives or failed due to lack of support. In 1932, for example, the Soviet Union invited a group of black artists (including Langston Hughes) to make a film about African-American life, but the Soviets soon abandoned the project.

The Nazi-Soviet Pact of 1939, the CPUSA's sudden shift to an extreme antiwar position, the Dies Committee's investigation into "un-American" activities, and the rising anticommunism among CIO leaders weakened the party's base of support on the eve of World War II, but its relationship to black workers and artists remained fairly strong, especially in Harlem. Between 1939 and 1940, for instance, black Communists led a boycott of the film *Gone with the Wind*, initiated a campaign to "End Jim Crow in Sports" and collected 10,000 signatures to demand the integration of blacks in major league BASEBALL, organized numerous plays and jazz concerts, and persuaded blues composer W. C. HANDY to lecture at the Workers School.

When Communists shifted to a prowar position after Germany invaded Russia in 1941, the African-American leadership, for the most part, adopted an uncompromising stance vis-à-vis the war effort, insisting on a "double victory" against racism at home and fascism abroad. While the CPUSA essentially opposed the "Double V" campaign, arguing that too much black militancy could undermine the war effort, rank-and-file Communists continued to fight on the civil rights front throughout the war, demanding, among other things, the full integration of the armed forces and implementation of the FAIR EMPLOYMENT PRACTICES COMMITTEE. In spite of these measures, the party's opposition to the Double V slogan left many African Americans feeling that it had abandoned them for the sake of the war.

After the war, the Communists worked to rebuild ties to black working-class communities, a strategy that included resurrecting the self-determination thesis. The Civil Rights Congress, led by Communist William L. Patterson, gained notoriety for its militant defense of African Americans falsely accused of crimes and Communists accused of "un-American" activities, and for its historic petition to the United

Hosea Hudson. (Photographs and Prints Division, Schomburg Center for Research in Black Culture, The New York Public Library, Astor, Lenox and Tilden Foundations)

Nations charging the U.S. government with genocide against African Americans. However, McCarthyite repression and the party's leftward turn in the wake of Secretary Earl Browder's expulsion and William Z. Foster's rise to power weakened the CPUSA considerably. As the state arrested Communists for violating the Smith Act (including black leaders such as Henry Winston, Ben J. DAVIS, Jr., Claudia JONES, and Pettis Perry), the party experienced its own factional disputes and expulsions. As the country moved right, the party under Foster moved farther left and further into isolation. By 1956, the CPUSA had become a shadow of its former self, never to achieve the status it had enjoyed in the 1930s and 1940s.

During the next three decades, black Communists and ex-Communists such as Jack O'Dell, Mae Mallory, Abner Berry, and Hosea Hudson (to name but a few) participated in various civil rights organizations, antiwar movements, labor unions, and black nationalist struggles. As an organization, however, the CPUSA maintained a significant black constituency only in New York City, Detroit, and California—with the latter regarded as a renegade state by the CPUSA Central Committee. While the national leadership attacked black nationalism during the height of the Black Power movement, the California cadre, under the guidance of leaders such as Charlene Mitchell and Dorothy Healey, not only gave support to various nationalist movements but established an all-black youth unit called the Che-Lumumba Club, in defiance of Central Committee directives. The movement to free Angela DAVIS, the last nationally renowned black Communist of the twentieth century, further strengthened the CPUSA's black support in California.

With the collapse of the Soviet Union in 1991, the CPUSA practically fell apart. Virtually every leading African-American cadre member, including Angela Davis, James Jackson, and Charlene Mitchell, quit the party altogether with the hope of reconstituting a new democratic left-wing movement.

REFERENCES

ALLEN, JAMES S., and PHILIP FONER, eds. *American Communism and Black Americans: A Documentary History, 1919–1929.* Philadelphia, 1987.

HAYWOOD, HARRY. *Black Bolshevik: Autobiography of an Afro-American Communist.* Chicago, 1978.

HORNE, GERALD. *Communist Front? The Civil Rights Congress, 1946–1956.* London and Toronto, 1988.

KELLEY, ROBIN D. G. *Alabama Communists During the Great Depression.* Chapel Hill, N.C., 1990.

NAISON, MARK D. *Communists in Harlem during the Depression.* Urbana, Ill., 1983.

ROBIN D. G. KELLEY

Compromise of 1850. The Compromise of 1850 actually consists of five separate legislative acts that affected African Americans. These included a new FUGITIVE SLAVE LAW, the admission of slaves into some of the new western territories, the admission of California to the Union as a free state, and the prohibition of the public sale of slaves in Washington, D.C.

In 1850 the United States faced its greatest sectional crisis since the MISSOURI COMPROMISE. The Mexican-American War had led to the acquisition of vast new western territories and to virtual political paralysis over the status of SLAVERY in those territories. Meanwhile, southern dissatisfaction over the Fugitive Slave Act of 1793 and the Supreme Court decision in *Prigg* v. *Pennsylvania* led to demands for stronger federal support for the return of runaway slaves, while northern hostility to slavery led to calls for secession in the South. Meanwhile, the population boom in California that came as a result of the discovery of gold there led to a demand for immediate statehood.

In early 1850, Sen. Henry Clay of Kentucky tried to resolve these problems with his "omnibus bill." This bill had provisions designed to appease the South, including a new fugitive slave law, and provisions to please the North, such as the immediate admission of California as a free state. Clay hoped legislators from both sections would support the bill. However, in July Congress defeated it, with members from each section opposing the law because of what it gave to the other.

In September, Sen. Stephen A. Douglas of Illinois guided the compromise through Congress, not as a single bill but as a series of five separate laws—two antislavery, three proslavery.

The most significant antislavery provision was the admission of California as a free state. For the first time since the Missouri Compromise, the Union would have a majority of free states. While not immediately changing the balance of power in the nation, this was an enormous potential threat to the South and to slavery. Thereafter the North would have a permanent and growing majority in the Senate. The compromise also abolished the SLAVE TRADE in the District of Columbia. This was an important moral victory for antislavery northerners but one with little practical impact; private sale of slaves in the district remained legal, while slave trading still existed in neighboring Maryland and Virginia.

Two statutes allowed slavery in the newly created Utah and New Mexico territories, although few slaves were actually brought to either place. More important was the new fugitive slave law, which simplified the process of returning fugitive slaves to their masters and provided federal protection and support for masters seeking their escaped slaves.

The compromise was an abject failure. Some northern compromisers, like Daniel Webster of Massachusetts, were vilified for their votes in favor of the new fugitive slave law. Like the compromise it symbolized, the fugitive slave law failed in its purpose while exacerbating sectional tensions. It failed to secure the return of significant numbers of slaves, while leading to violent confrontations in the North and to northern states openly refusing to cooperate with the federal government. The compromise helped preserve the Union for another decade, while at the same time underscoring the impossibility of solving the problem of slavery through the political process.

REFERENCES

FREEHLING, WILLIAM. *Secessionists at Bay: 1776–1854.* New York, 1991.

POTTER, DAVID. *The Impending Crisis.* New York, 1976.

PAUL FINKELMAN

Compromise of 1877. The Compromise of 1877 refers to the settlement which resolved the disputed presidential election of 1876. The REPUBLICAN candidate for president, Rutherford B. Hayes, was declared elected in exchange for the national Republican administration's promise to remove federal troops from southern states. The bargain represented the end of RECONSTRUCTION and the end of substantial black participation in southern politics.

In the presidential election of 1876, the DEMO-CRATIC candidate, Samuel J. Tilden, in fact won a majority of the popular vote. However, 184 undisputed votes in the electoral college left him one vote short of a necessary majority. The outcome would be determined by the results in three southern states—Louisiana, South Carolina, and Florida, still under Republican state governments. Republican-dominated election officials in all three states declared majorities for Hayes, after invalidating returns reflecting intimidation and fraud against black voters. At the same time, new Democratic state regimes, claiming election in the 1876 canvass, announced that their states had voted for Tilden. As the electoral college prepared to meet in Washington to name the president, the possibility of a violent confrontation over the disputed succession loomed—and the memory of the recent CIVIL WAR made that possibility palpable.

The procedures for counting electoral votes under the Twelfth Amendment to the federal Constitution were ambiguous. To resolve the crisis, Congress established a bipartisan Electoral Commission in January 1877 to determine the actual returns. It soon became apparent that the Republicans enjoyed a narrow majority on the commission, and that Hayes would be declared the winner. Fearing a continuing constitutional crisis, Hayes moved to reassure southern Democrats that if inaugurated, he would prove amenable to their interests.

The precise content of the numerous private meetings between Hayes's intermediaries and southern Democrats is not known. On February 26, the most important of these meetings occurred at the Wormley House, a black-owned Washington, D.C., hotel. Hayes's personal representative announced that if inaugurated, Hayes would recognize the Democratic gubernatorial candidates as elected, and pursue a policy of noninterference in affairs in the southern states. Other Republican promises were made regarding federal sponsorship of a proposed southern railroad line to the Pacific; southern Democrats abandoned congressional obstruction of the final electoral count to secure Hayes's election, and he was peacefully inaugurated on March 4, 1877.

The following month Hayes withdrew the last federal troops sustaining the Reconstruction governments, which immediately dissolved in the face of a possible bloodbath. In essence, Hayes left southern Republicans—who had helped make him President—to fend for themselves in the future. This marked the end of Reconstruction and the eclipse of federal efforts to secure voting and other civil rights for the southern freedpeople.

REFERENCES

FONER, ERIC. *Reconstruction, America's Unfinished Revolution, 1863–1877.* New York, 1988.
WOODWARD, C. VANN. *Reunion and Reaction: The Compromise of 1877 and the End of Reconstruction.* Rev. ed. Garden City, N.Y., 1956.

MICHAEL W. FITZGERALD

Concert Music. While most of the world's music involves an audience (even if some degree of participation is expected from that group), "concert music" is generally regarded as that which belongs to a written tradition, and which can then be performed more or less as originally created, even if the composer is no longer present.

Composers

The existence of composers of written-down concert music among figures of African heritage manifests acculturation with European practice; oral tradition was the common African custom. As a result, those encountering the concert legacy of composers and performers are sometimes astonished to realize that this tradition is considerably older than the more expected idioms of BLUES, JAZZ, and GOSPEL. Even in contemporary Africa, concert composers have been active: Ephraim Amu (1899–), Fela Sowande (1905–1987), Akin Euba (1935–), Ayo Bankole (1935–1976), Francis Bebey (1929–), and Duro Ladipo (1931–1978) serve as immediate examples.

That highly significant talent had already existed within the race prior to the nineteenth century is evidenced by examples of the Chevalier de Saint-Georges (1749–1799, from Guadeloupe), Felipe Gutiérrez y Espinosa (1825–1899, from Puerto Rico), José Maurício Nunes-García (1767–1830), and Antônio Carlos Gomes (1836–1896), with their many compatriots from Brazil, the Haitians Justice Elie (1883–1931) and Robert Geffrard (1860–1894), Samuel Coleridge-Taylor (1875–1912, from England), and José Silvestre de los Dolores White Lafitte (1836–1918, from Cuba).

It was the visit of Antonín Dvořák that stimulated the aspirations of American talents. He had been brought to New York to direct the National Conservatory of Music in 1892. This Czech musician had minority status in the Austro-Hungarian Empire and was a musical nationalist in Wagner's Europe. The advice he gave American composers was to base a musical vocabulary on black and Native American traditions, rather than on the common German models. Among the many talents he identified were Harry T. BURLEIGH and Will Marion Cook. Dvořák's final symphony (*From the New World*) and his F major string quartet (*American*) were suggestive models, with international reference to the spirituals.

At this time, individual black American musical creativity (as distinct from that which produced SPIRITUALS) was restricted to the creation of repertory for minstrelsy (*see* MINSTRELS/MINSTRELSY) (e.g., James BLAND and Ernest HOGAN) to nonethnic sentimental ballads for the parlor (Gussie Lord Davis, 1863–1899), SOCIAL DANCE music (Newport Gardner,

Classically trained Will Marion Cook was a leading theatrical composer in the early twentieth century and an inspiration and mentor to several generations of black musicians. (Photographs and Prints Division, Schomburg Center for Research in Black Culture, The New York Public Library, Astor, Lenox and Tilden Foundations)

1746–1826, from Africa, and Joseph POSTLEWAITE) and character pieces for piano in the new style of RAGTIME (Scott JOPLIN). The careers of bandsman Frank JOHNSON and his associates from Philadelphia, and the phenomenal Blind Tom (*see* Thomas Green Wiggins BETHUNE) were among the few earlier exceptions, which also included Basile Barès (1845–1902), Edmund Dédé (1827–1903), and the Lambert family, all from New Orleans. Working with the stimulus provided by Dvořák, Cook helped open the door in New York for black musical theater (especially with his *In Dahomey* from 1902). Burleigh took the spiritual out of the oral tradition, setting it as an art song for voice and piano (thus providing concert repertory for his own singing and for Marian ANDERSON and those singers that followed).

A second major stimulus from abroad was the visit in 1904 and thereafter of the Afro-British Samuel Coleridge Taylor (1875–1912). Already a celebrity in London, he conducted his cantata, *Hiawatha's Wedding Feast,* to enthusiastic audiences in Washington, D.C., and Baltimore, verifying his status as a cultural hero. Buoyed by this impetus, William Grant STILL evolved as this country's first generally acknowledged black composer, bringing into the HARLEM RENAISSANCE his interests in the blues, which perhaps culminated in his *Afro-American Symphony* (1931), the initial work of its type by a black American. (Still wrote four other subsequent symphonies.) The list of first-time accomplishments in black American music has Still's name cited in most instances. He had many contemporaries of note, including Clarence Cameron WHITE, John W. WORK III, R. Nathaniel DETT (1882–1943), Florence PRICE, and William Levi DAWSON (not to be confused with an unrelated Chicago politician of the same name), who demonstrated parallel talents with somewhat more specialized interests or restricted opportunities. Still's *Negro Folk Symphony* (1934) was premiered and later championed by Leopold Stokowski.

World War II brought a new variety of European stimulus to the United States: neoclassicism (a musical counterpart of nondiscrimination), which generally ignored the romantic atmosphere of ethnicity. Paul Hindemith left Nazi Germany for political and artistic reasons, and encountered an eager disciple in Ulysses KAY at Yale University. Despite having an encouraging uncle in jazzman King OLIVER, Kay's interest in the vernacular and folkloric was minimal. As more liberal sentiments began to manifest, he encountered fewer restrictions than Still had faced. This was also true in the instance of Julia Perry (1924–1979), who, like other contemporaries, studied after the war in Europe. More recent are the cases of Alvin Singleton (1940–) and Maurice Weddington (1941–).

Thomas "Blind Tom" Bethune, born a Georgia slave, was a noted concert pianist of the late nineteenth century and was acclaimed for his transcriptions and improvisations as well as for his original compositions. (Left: Prints and Photographs Division, Library of Congress; above: Photographs and Prints Division, Schomburg Center for Research in Black Culture, The New York Public Library, Astor, Lenox and Tilden Foundations)

From that same generation appeared George T. WALKER, who first gained recognition as an outstanding pianist. With the issue in the 1970s by Columbia Records of *The Black Composers Series* and the Desto label anthology *Natalie Hinderas Plays Music of Black Composers,* the vitality of Walker's creative imagination became widely documented and respected. His music, although rooted in the formal disciplines of neoclassicism, has highly idealized references to jazz, blues, and the spirituals. A similar case is that of Howard SWANSON, who particularly excelled as a song composer and whose *Short Symphony* (1948) was widely acclaimed.

Earlier figures for whom performance opportunities were not readily available opted for careers in education, training composers, performers, and scholars whose generation had greater latitude. Among those who thus served, limited though their work was in composition, were Kemper Harrell

(1885–1971), Walter Dyett (1901–1969), Mark Fax (1911–1974), Frederick Hall (1898–1982), Llewellyn Wilson (1887–1950), A. Jack Thomas (1884–1962), and N. Clark Smith (1877–1933). One of many who created his own opportunities to perform was Harry Lawrence FREEMAN, who established opera companies in Denver, Chicago, Cleveland, and New York.

By the time of the CIVIL RIGHTS MOVEMENT, even those composers with international orientations adopted a new spirit of ethnic nationalism, proudly alert to the developments of socially aware jazz (e.g., Billie HOLIDAY, Charles MINGUS, and John COLTRANE) and third world concerns. This was enhanced by the composers' disinterest in stereotypic labels and encouraged by the freedom that resulted from not being fully accepted in a more regimented musical environment. Jazz figures had already explored larger forms (e.g., Scott Joplin, James P. JOHNSON, and Duke ELLINGTON) and were now joined by David

Baker (1931–), who ventured into cantatas and concertos; Valerie Capers (1937–), who has explored the world of opera; Yusef LATEEF, Ornette COLEMAN, with his monumentally Ivesian orchestral soundscape *Skies of America* (1973); William Fischer (1935–); and Muhal Richard ABRAMS, who, like his colleagues from the ASSOCIATION FOR THE ADVANCEMENT OF CREATIVE MUSICIANS, including Anthony BRAXTON, was never comfortable with the jazz label. Quite notable is Anthony DAVIS, whose operatic efforts are landmarks equivalent to the earlier milestones of Cook and Joplin. The other side of these crossovers included Noel Da Costa (1929–); Carman Moore (1936–), who studied with European avant-gardist Stefan Wolpe but accepted overt stimuli from gospel music; Talib Rasul Hakim (1940–1988, *ne* Stephen Chambers), whose interests included Islamic mysticism; Frederick Tillis (1930–); Adolphus Hailstork (1941–), who has expressed ardent social concerns in a basically traditional idiom; Wendell Logan (1940–); and especially Olly WILSON, a significant composer and intellectual whose Africanisms, jazz, electronic explorations, and RHYTHM AND BLUES influences are blended with a penetrating sensibility of the concert heritage.

Arthur P. Cunningham (1928–), a Fisk University alumnus, evidences ethnic influences in his often-performed *Lullabye for a Jazz Baby* (1970), written for André Kostelanetz, and in the choral works in his gospel-infused *Harlem Suite*. Somewhat related is Roger Dickerson (1934–), who readily blended ethnic and concert traditions as well as James Furman (1937–1989), and Leslie Adams (1932–), with his facile melodic gift.

Performance opportunities and the expectations of academic employment diverted Undine Smith MOORE, whose vanguard essays for piano played little influence in her choral contributions, an area in which Betty Jackson King (1928–), Lena McLin (1928–), Noah RYDER, and Eva JESSYE also gave attention. Moore's stimulus came from the spiritual tradition she came to know at Fisk University, where she studied with John Work III, while Jessye's impetus was interrelated with Gershwin's *Porgy and Bess,* for whose performances she regularly served as choral director. In that same tradition were Hall JOHNSON and his former associates, Jester HAIRSTON and Leonard De Paur (1914–), as well as Carl Diton (1886–1962), who, in later times, might have had a much more extensive career as pianist and baritone.

Hale SMITH proved himself expert in functional music (notable arrangements of earlier black music and educational music for piano and for band), without such influences necessarily affecting his highly original creativity. No less is true of Coleridge-

Taylor Perkinson (1932–), whose art-for-art's sake creativity is balanced by commissions for film and television. Those who are best known only for the music they write for the visual media would include Quincy JONES and Oliver Nelson (1932–1975).

The music of T. J. ANDERSON absorbs influences and even brief quotations from others (e.g., Herbie HANCOCK) within his pointillistic and venturesome textures. He has created works calling for ensembles within which one finds children's toy noisemakers, yet it was he who, in 1972, introduced Scott Joplin's opera, *Treemonisha*.

Within this mélange of ideas appear also Primous Fountain III (1949–), an autodidact with a rich awareness of many heritages; the free-spirited Jalalu-Kalvert Nelson (1951–), who is passionately expressive of humanistic concerns, often with mixed media; and Dorothy Rudd Moore (1940–), who has secured wide recognition for her chamber and stage works.

Roque Cordero (1917–), although from Panama, has spent most of his creative life in the United States. Interested in liberal applications of dodecaphonic technique, he successfully merged the style of Alban Berg with Panamanian nationalism, especially in his dramatic violin concerto of 1962. A similarity exists in the instance of Halim El-Dabh (1921–), whose instrumental and electronic works exhibit Egyptian and Ethiopian backgrounds.

Performers

Music making was one of the duties assigned to slaves of such talents, which is abundantly clear in written accounts, illustrations, and advertisements for the return of escapees (the majority of whom were violinists). Many of the early musicians are known only by an assigned single name (Cuff, for example). The major exceptions in slavery were pianist-composer Blind Tom and his contemporary, soprano Elizabeth Taylor GREENFIELD, both of whom had some experience in Europe, and those free-born instrumentalists associated in Philadelphia with Francis Johnson (1792–1844).

Once slavery was abolished, progress toward the liberation of concert talent gradually became evident. With singers, that process began with Greenfield and was continued with Marie Selika (1849–1937) and M. Sissieretta JONES, although their principal venue was the minstrel stage, not the concert platform. The history of formal recitals begins with tenor Roland HAYES. Stimulated by his success and opportunities available because of her great talents, contralto Marian ANDERSON opened many doors, including those of the Metropolitan Opera in 1955. Recitals, and sometimes recordings and concerts with orchestra, were available to Inez Matthews (1907–1950), Ella-belle Davis (1907–1960), and Dorothy MAYNOR; but Catherine Yarborough (1903–1986) appeared in the United States only in musical comedy, having to save *Aida* for Europe, where she was known as Caterina Jarboro. The next generation saw the births of Muriel Rahn (1911–1961) and Carol Brice (1918–1985), with Rahn's major opportunity coming in an ebonized version of *Carmen* (sharing the stage with Muriel Smith, 1923–1985). Brice became one of the many to benefit from the casting obligations of George Gershwin's *Porgy and Bess* and Virgil Thomson's *Four Saints in Three Acts,* and recordings of the same. Those born in the 1920s generally enjoyed greater freedom. Mattiwilda DOBBS, briefly with the Metropolitan Opera, was a leading soprano in Europe, and contralto Louise Parker (1925–1986) was a personal favorite of both Leopold Stokowski and Paul Hindemith, but it was Leontyne PRICE who was the major heir to Marian Anderson's legacy, even if this was claimed first in Europe and only later (1961) with the Metropolitan Opera. Margaret Tynes (1929–) claimed the European stage, although she had been featured in *A Drum Is a Woman* by Duke Ellington. Those born in the 1930s included such great artists as Betty Allen (1930–) and Hilda HARRIS, Shirley VERRETT, Reri Grist (1932–), who had been originally in Leonard Bernstein's *West Side Story*), Martina ARROYO, and Grace BUMBRY. The next decade saw the births of Gwendolyn Killebrew (1942–), Esther Hinds (1943–), Faye Robinson (1943–), Carmen Balthrop (1948–), Barbara Hendricks (1948–), and Leona Mitchell (1949–). Despite the aforementioned singers' excellence, crowns were clearly won by Kathleen BATTLE and especially Jessye NORMAN. A younger generation of established talents includes Marietta Simpson (a member of a remarkably musical family from Philadelphia) and Elvira Green.

These are all women, which is not to suggest that men were less gifted. The problem has been one of casting. Based on Anglo anxieties, while it was acceptable in some circles for the woman to be, willingly or not, in a mixed-race situation, the male was a threat. Despite that obstacle, which sent many tenors and baritones to Europe for their careers, Jules BLEDSOE, Paul ROBESON, and William Warfield (1920–) found the role of Joe in Jerome Kern's *Showboat* an entrée to the recital and concert stage, as did Todd DUNCAN and Donnie Ray Albert (1950–) with *Porgy and Bess,* along with many other singers, especially after the opera's debut in 1985 with the Metropolitan Opera. Charles Holland (1910–1987) and Lawrence Winters (1915–1965) spent their careers in Europe. (In earlier times, Holland sang with Fletcher HENDERSON and Benny CARTER.) Robert

MCFERRIN, SR., was the first black male to sing with the Metropolitan Opera, where he appeared as Rigoletto, Valentine (in *Faust*), and Amonasro (in *Aida*) during his three seasons there. Seth McCoy (1928–) has been active with the Metropolitan Opera, but also enjoys a major career in oratorio. Musical theater for the most part claimed Rawn Spearman (1924–), while Andrew Frierson's (1927–) operatic career came into focus at the New York City Opera. McHenry Boatwright (1928–) appeared with other companies and as recitalist. Thomas Carey (1931–) and Eugene Holmes (1934–) found careers in Europe more promising, as initially did Simon ESTES. Recitalist and operatic baritone Ben Holt (1955–1990) had his brilliant career cut short, as did Leonore Lafayette (1926–1959). Among the most promising of the younger generation are Kevin Short (1960–) of the Metropolitan Opera and Antonio Green (1966–). The underrepresentation of male vocal talents continues to be a cause for concern for both managements and singers.

Opportunities for conductors have been brighter. First to be cited is Dean DIXON, whose rare appear-

Dean Dixon was the director of orchestras in Germany and Sweden as well as a guest conductor with the New York Philharmonic in 1970 and the Philadelphia Orchestra in 1975. (Prints and Photographs Division, Library of Congress)

ances in his native country were compensated by engagements and recordings abroad, and Everett LEE, who looked mainly to Europe and South America for his career. A modest degree of social sensibility forced urban American orchestras to seek black conductors for children's and pop concerts in the 1960s, thus aiding the hopes of Paul FREEMAN and James DEPREIST (both found their first posts as music directors in Canada). Henry Lewis (1932–) established himself largely in opera, as did Calvin Simmons (1950–1982), who died tragically in a boating accident. The younger figures include Isaiah Jackson (1945–), Kay George Roberts (1950–), Michael Morgan (1957–), Leslie Dunner, and Alfred Duckett.

The history of concert pianists begins with Hazel HARRISON, the first American-trained musician to appear with a European orchestra (1904, in Berlin), with later figures including the exceptional prodigy Philippa Duke SCHUYLER (killed in 1969 while rescuing orphans in Vietnam), Frances Walker (1924–), Natalie HINDERAS, Raymond Jackson (1933–), Robert Jordan (1940–), André WATTS,

After initial acclaim as a young teenage piano prodigy, André Watts has gone on to a major career as a solo pianist, specializing in the music of Franz Liszt and other masters of the romantic piano repertory. (AP/Wide World Photos)

Pianist Natalie Hinderas recorded a pathbreaking multidisk collection of compositions by African-American classical composers in 1970. (Photographs and Prints Division, Schomburg Center for Research in Black Culture, The New York Public Library, Astor, Lenox and Tilden Foundations)

and Leon Bates (1949–). Also important is the duo piano team of Wilfred Delphin and Edwin Romain, whose international tours began in the 1970s and continue to the present.

It is generally true that few orchestral instrumentalists have careers as recitalists, with the exception of violinists (who often were also composers). Among these must be cited the Chevalier de Saint-Georges (1749–1799) and his contemporary, the Chevalier Meude-Monpas, followed by George Bridgetower (1779–1860), who premiered Beethoven's *Kreutzer Sonata,* José Silvestre de los Dolores White LaFitte, a.k.a. José White (1836–1918), and Amadeo Roldán (1900–1939), none of whom were born in the United States. Apart from the many slave violinists, concert careers were attempted by Will Marion Cook, Joseph Douglass (1871–1935, grandson of abolitionist Frederick DOUGLASS, who was an amateur violinist), Clarence Cameron WHITE, and Louia Vaughan Jones (1895–1964), with great success secured by Sanford Allen (1939–) whose recording of the violin concerto by Panamanian-American Roque Cordero won an award from the Koussevitsky Foundation, but whose career has been too rarely enhanced by solo engagements.

The relative absence of black performers in American orchestras has long been a concern of socially aware ensembles, but even today some major orchestras have never had a black member. Many talented black performers who were classically trained have abandoned concert music in favor of the more open arenas of jazz and popular music. There have undoubtedly been others who, earlier on, abandoned even preliminary classical training in favor of other venues.

REFERENCES

GRAY, JOHN. *Blacks in Classical Music: A Bibliographical Guide to Composers, Performers, and Ensembles.* Westport, Conn., 1988.

SOUTHERN, EILEEN. *Biographical Dictionary of Afro-American and African Musicians.* Westport, Conn., 1982.

———. *The Music of Black Americans: A History.* New York 1983.

DOMINIQUE-RENÉ DE LERMA

Conductors, Black Orchestral.   *See* Concert Music.

Cone, James Hal

Cone, James Hal (August 5, 1938–), theologian. Born in Fordyce, Ark., in 1938, and raised in Bearden, Ark., James H. Cone received degrees from Philander Smith College (B.A.), Garrett Theological Seminary (B.D.), and Northwestern University (M.A., Ph.D.). His intellectual, emotional, and racial identities developed out of two childhood experiences. First, the wholesome encouragement and support of the AFRICAN METHODIST EPISCOPAL CHURCH and Bearden's black community reinforced fundamental beliefs in Cone's self-worth and Christian convictions. Second, the negative effects of segregation and white racism left an instinctive intolerance for discrimination.

Born into a family of modest means (his father cut wood), Cone experienced poverty and grew to appreciate the problems of the poor in American society. Within this context, his father became the decisive role model for what it meant to be a poor, proud African-American man in a predominantly white society.

Cone's theological reflections are products of both the CIVIL RIGHTS and BLACK POWER movements of the 1950s and 1960s. Though he earned his Ph.D. in 1965 and taught at Philander Smith College and Adrian College, Cone's theological creativity bore fruit with his first book, *Black Theology and Black Power* (1969). This text catapulted Cone, then a little-known college professor, to the prestigious and internationally recognized faculty at Union Theological Seminary, New York.

Black Theology and Black Power was the first scholarly work on black theology. Cone contended that the 1960s Black Power movement was the revelation of Jesus Christ. Conversely, North American white churches represented the Antichrist, and, therefore, were non-Christian. Similarly, all black churches siding with white Christianity were evil. Basically, religious institutions could find God's presence only in urban rebellions and community organizing of poor black Americans. Only when the poor obtained their full humanity could everyone be free; hence the universal dimension of black theology.

A further systematic treatment of the poor and the Christian faith appeared in Cone's next book, *A Black Theology of Liberation* (1970). This work marked the first attempt to develop a black theology by investigating major church doctrines through the eyes of the African-American poor. Black religious studies became a systematic theology. In reaction to his over-reliance on white religious systems of thought, *The Spirituals and the Blues: An Interpretation* (1972), Cone's third book, indicates black theology's major turn toward religious sources created by the African-American church and community. If black theology was a faith expression of poor African Americans, Cone believed, then such a theology must arise organically from the African-American experience itself.

His fourth text, *God of the Oppressed* (1975), marks Cone's second systematic black theology of liberation, this time based on his personal experiences and black resources.

Cone closed out the decade of the 1970s by co-editing (with Gayraud Wilmore) *Black Theology: A Documentary History, 1966–1979* (1979). After *My Soul Looks Back* (1982), *For My People* (1984), and *Speaking the Truth* (1986), Cone published *Martin & Malcolm & America* (1991), a pioneering advancement of black theology into mainstream popular discussion.

REFERENCES

CONE, JAMES H. *For My People: Black Theology and the Black Church.* Maryknoll, N.Y., 1984.

———. *God of the Oppressed.* San Francisco, 1975.

HOPKINS, DWIGHT N. *Shoes That Fit Our Feet: Sources for a Constructive Black Theology.* Maryknoll, N.Y., 1993.

DWIGHT N. HOPKINS

Confessions of Nat Turner (Novel).   *See* Nat Turner Controversy.

Congressional Black Caucus.   The Congressional Black Caucus was a product of the growth in black political power in the 1960s and '70s. The cre-

ation of an institutional base for black Americans within the U.S. Congress had been encouraged by the passage of the Civil Rights Act of 1964 and the VOTING RIGHTS ACT of 1965. In 1969 Rep. Charles DIGGS (D-Mich.) formed the Democratic Select Committee (DSC), the precursor of the Congressional Black Caucus, as a means by which the nine black members of the House of Representatives could address their common political concerns. Later that year Diggs and his colleagues played a role in defeating the nomination of Clement Haynesworth to the U.S. Supreme Court, and they investigated the killings of BLACK PANTHER party members in Chicago. They boycotted President Richard Nixon's 1970 State of the Union Address and pressured Nixon into meeting with the DSC concerning civil rights, antidrug legislation, welfare reform, and Vietnam.

On June 18, 1971, at its first annual dinner in Washington, D.C., the group was formally organized as the Congressional Black Caucus (CBC), and Diggs became its first chairman. In March 1972 the CBC helped sponsor the National Black Political Convention in Gary, Ind., but distanced itself from the convention because of its dominance by militant activist groups. In June of that year, in order to make the 1972 Democratic national convention more attentive to black concerns, the CBC drafted the Black Declaration of Independence and the Black Bill of Rights. The Black Declaration of Independence demanded that the DEMOCRATIC PARTY and its nominee commit themselves to full racial equality. The Black Bill of Rights called for, among other items, a full employment program; a guaranteed-annual-income system; an end to American military involvement in Vietnam and all African countries; and a setting aside of 15 percent of all government contracts for the use of black businesses. However, the CBC failed to win the official support of the Democratic party or its nominee, George McGovern, for these demands.

In 1973 Rep. Louis STOKES (D-Ohio) succeeded Diggs as caucus chairman. Stokes worked to get individual CBC members greater seniority and more powerful committee chairs in Congress. Rep. Charles RANGEL (D-N.Y.) became the CBC chair in 1974, serving until 1976. Over the next twenty years, Rangel became one of the leading congressional authorities on urban housing and narcotics control. During that same period, the CBC extended its influence both within and outside of Congress. CBC members became chairs of seven out of twenty-seven congressional committees. It developed nationwide networks of black voters and business leaders and "brain trust" networks addressing education, health, the justice system, and foreign affairs. In 1976 it es-

Black Caucus senators and members of Congress, 1971. (© Fred Ward/Black Star)

tablished the Congressional Black Caucus Foundation, which conducts and funds studies relating congressional politics to the concerns of the black community. In 1977 the CBC established TransAfrica; headed by Randall ROBINSON, TransAfrica became the major lobbying body in Washington on behalf of the ANTI-APARTHEID MOVEMENT in South Africa and of other African policy issues. The CBC was also involved in the successful efforts to pass the 1977 Full Employment Act, the 1982 Martin Luther King Holiday legislation, and the 1986 sanctions against South Africa.

The growth of black political power has expanded the size of the CBC. In 1992 an unprecedented forty African Americans were elected to Congress. This increase in size has tested and transformed the CBC in other ways as well. In 1993 Carol Moseley-Braun (D-Ill.) became the first black senator in fourteen years and one of ten black women in Congress. In 1990 Gary Franks (R-Conn.) became the first black Republican elected to the House of Representatives since 1932. A conservative Republican, Franks has been at odds with the policies of the CBC and has attacked it for its liberal slant and allegiance to the DEMOCRATIC PARTY.

There has been a growing ideological diversity within the CBC, its chairs ranging from such centrists as Charles RANGEL (D-N.Y.) and Edolphus "Ed" Towns (D-N.Y.) to such left-liberals as Ron DELLUMS (D-Calif.). In 1993, Kweisi Mfume (D-Md.) became chair and has been active in publicizing the activities of the CBC. He has also been its most controversial chair. In 1993 he advocated the formation of a "sacred covenant" between the CBC and the NATION OF ISLAM with its leader, Louis FARRAKHAN. The other members of the CBC subsequently renounced this covenant, and Mfume eventually followed the rest of the Black Caucus in doing so.

Although controversial, Mfume helped to make the CBC more aggressive in influencing domestic and foreign policy. When the House of Representatives, without consulting the CBC, moved to give President Clinton the line-item veto (a tool that governors had used in the past to keep civil rights measures out of legislative bills), Mfume led the CBC in blocking the effort. Mfume also helped change President Clinton's policy toward Haiti. Mfume's pressure persuaded Clinton to extend more aid to Haitian refugees, place stronger sanctions on Haiti's military government, and consider returning Haiti's democratic government to power by force.

The Congressional Black Caucus has become one of the most influential voting blocks within Congress. While it has been divided on certain issues, such as the 1993 North American Free Trade Agreement (NAFTA), on many other issues, such as health care, African and Caribbean issues, and crime, the CBC has emerged as a shrewd and pragmatic advocate for African-American interests.

REFERENCES

BARNET, MARGUERITE ROSS. "The Congressional Black Caucus." In Harvey C. Mansfield, ed., *Congress Against the President: Proceedings of the Academy of Political Science*. New York, 1975.

CLAY, WILLIAM L. *Just Permanent Interests: Black Americans in Congress, 1870–1991*. New York, 1992.

RUFFIN, DAVID C., and FRANK DEXTER BROWN. "Clout on Capitol Hill." *Black Enterprise* 14 (October 1984): 97–104.

DURAHN TAYLOR

Congress of National Black Churches, Inc.,

interdenominational religious organization. The Congress of National Black Churches (CNBC) is an umbrella organization of eight major African-American denominations that represents 65,000 churches and over 15 million individuals. Based in Washington, D.C., CNBC was founded in 1978 by Bishop John Hurst Adams of the AFRICAN METHODIST EPISCOPAL CHURCH to establish dialogue within the African-American community across denominational lines and to facilitate collective church action. It unites the following denominations: African Methodist Episcopal, AFRICAN METHODIST EPISCOPAL ZION, CHRISTIAN METHODIST EPISCOPAL, CHURCH OF GOD IN CHRIST, National Baptist Convention of America, Inc., the NATIONAL BAPTIST CONVENTION, USA, INC., National Missionary Baptist Convention of America, and Progressive National Baptist Convention, Inc. The board of directors of CNBC is made up of four representatives from each denomination and meets twice a year. A staff of approximately twenty people, headed by an executive director, implements policy and keeps the organization running on a day-to-day basis.

The platform of the CNBC has two goals. First, it strives to provide moral leadership for African Americans, enhance spirituality, and strengthen values. Second, the Congress operates as a social service agency, providing material assistance to meet the needs of the poor and augment the power of the African-American community. It holds seminars and award fellowships to those interested in the ministry as a career. In the past, the Congress initiated an Anti-Drug Campaign to provide assistance and information to community groups that want to rid their neighborhood of drugs, and discussed the possibility of providing health insurance for larger numbers of African Americans. In 1993, in cooperation with Africare, it raised over $100,000 for the starving people of Somalia. According to Bishop Adams, the vision includes "organizing the institutional power of the black church to address the pragmatic needs of the black community. It is to use power to relieve pain; to use power to enhance possibilities."

One of CNBC's most well-known and successful ventures, which combines both these goals, is Project SPIRIT (Strength, Perseverance, Imagination, Responsibility, Integrity, and Talent). Launched in 1985, SPIRIT has as its central component an after-school tutoring and morale-building program. Other aspects of this project, which is designed to strengthen the black family, are a weekly session for parents on child rearing, and counseling sessions to prepare pastors to deal with family problems. Another major project of CNBC was the creation in 1984 of the Church Insurance Partnership Agency, an alliance between churches and insurance companies, which provides churches with property and liability coverage. More recently, CNBC has begun a dialogue about sexuality to examine AIDS, sexually transmitted diseases, homosexuality, male-female relationships, and birth control within the black community.

REFERENCES

"Economic Salvation." *Black Enterprise* (June 1984): 56.

"Health Debate Rages On." *Black Enterprise* (May 1992): 20.

POINSETT, ALEX, and AVERY RUSSELL. "Black Churches: Can They Strengthen the Black Family?" *American Visions* (October 1988): 9–10.

Visions: The Congress of National Black Churches, Inc. (newsletter) 3, no. 1 (Spring 1993).

PAM NADASEN

Congress of Racial Equality (CORE), civil rights organization. With a political and ideological legacy that spans six decades from interracial nonviolent direct action in the 1940s and '50s, militant black nationalist separatism in the late '60s, and black capitalism in the '70s, '80s, and '90s, the Congress of Racial Equality (CORE) is one of the most important civil rights organizations in the history of the United States. It was founded in Chicago in 1942 as the Committee of Racial Equality (the name was changed to the present one in 1943) by a group of ten white and five black student activists who were influenced by the Christian Youth Movement, rising industrial unionism, and the antiracist political activism of black and white communists in the 1930s. The founders of CORE were staunch believers in pacifism. Many of them were members of the Chicago chapter of the Fellowship of Reconciliation (FOR), an interracial and pacifist civil rights organization committed to social change through the transformation of racist attitudes, led by A. J. Muste (1885–1967). Deeply influenced by the strategies of social change championed by Indian activist Mahatma Gandhi as described in Krishnalal Shridharani's *War Without Violence* (1939), CORE founders believed that through interracial organizing and nonviolent direct action they could attack racism at its "core."

CORE was an informal, decentralized organization. Members drafted a "Statement of Purpose" and "CORE Action Discipline," both of which served as a constitution for the organization and proclaimed the members' commitment to working for social change through nonviolent direct action in a democratic, nonhierarchical organization. Guidelines for new members demanded familiarity with Gandhian ideas and active participation in the organization. Voluntary contributions from the members served as the organization's only source of funding. The leadership of CORE was shared by George Houser, a white student at the University of Chicago, and James FARMER, a black Methodist student activist. James Robinson, a white Catholic pacifist, and Bernice Fisher, a white divinity student at the University of Chicago, also provided inspirational and organizational leadership.

In their first year, CORE activists organized SIT-INS and other protests against segregation in public accommodations, but white recalcitrance and a weak membership base left them with few victories. In 1942, at a planning conference to discuss organizational growth, CORE activists declared their commitment to expanding nationally by forming alliances with local interracial groups working to defeat racism through nonviolent direct action. Farmer argued that CORE would not grow as a mass-based activist organization unless it severed its ties to FOR and disassociated itself from the organization's pacifism. Under the rubric of FOR's Department of Race Relations, he and Bayard RUSTIN, a black FOR field secretary, traveled around the country and met with activists sympathetic to Gandhian ideology, to foster interest in forming CORE chapters among those present at FOR events.

As a result of their efforts, CORE had seven affiliates by the end of 1942. Most chapters were located in the Midwest; they contained fifteen to thirty members who were usually middle-class college students and were predominantly white. Local groups retained primary membership affiliation and control over local funds. As a result, chapter activities varied widely and were not centrally coordinated. Chapters where pacifists dominated focused almost entirely on educating and converting racists, rather than on direct action. The repressive atmosphere of the South in the 1940s severely curtailed the activity of CORE's few southern affiliates. New York, Chicago, and Detroit were the most active and militant chapters, conducting training workshops in nonviolent direct action for volunteers in selected northern cities as well. They also organized SIT-INS—a tactic pioneered by CORE activists—and picket lines at segregated restaurants, swimming pools, movie theaters, and department stores.

CORE had some success in integrating public accommodations and recreational areas, but it was clear to CORE's founders that to mount a sustained assault on racism they would have to create a stronger national structure. In 1943, Farmer was elected the first chairman of CORE and Bernice Fisher was elected secretary-treasurer. By 1946, due to both the reluctance of local chapters to relinquish their independence or share their funds and to the infrequency of national planning meetings, CORE faced an organizational crisis. After much debate, CORE revamped its national structure: Farmer resigned and George Houser occupied the newly created leadership position of executive secretary. Houser played a central role in defining the ideology of CORE as editor of the *CORE-lator,* the organizational newsletter, and author of almost all CORE literature. He focused CORE's organizational energy and limited resources on a closer coordination of local activities among its thirteen affiliates, with the ultimate goal of building a mass movement.

The culmination of Houser's efforts was CORE's first nationally coordinated action, the Journey of Reconciliation—a two-week trip into the upper South to test the 1946 *Morgan* decision by the U.S. Supreme Court outlawing segregation in interstate travel. In April of 1947, sixteen men—eight white and eight black—traveled by bus through the region challenging segregated seating arrangements that relegated blacks to the back of the bus. The protesters were confronted by some violence and overt hostility, but in general they were faced with apathy from most whites, who were unaware of the Morgan decision. In many instances, black passengers on the bus followed suit when they saw racial mores being successfully challenged. The arrest of four of the pro-

testers in Chapel Hill, N.C.—with three of them, Bayard Rustin, Igal Roodenko, and Joe Felmet forced to serve thirty days on a chain gang—catapulted CORE and the Journey of Reconciliation to national attention.

In 1947, CORE took further steps to strengthen their organizational structure by creating an office of field secretaries to travel around the country to organize new CORE chapters. Two year later they created the National Council—a policy-making body with one representative from each local chapter—to improve communication between the local and the national chapters. In 1951, CORE hired James Robinson to coordinate fund-raising efforts. Despite these efforts, the early fifties marked another period of organizational decline for CORE, as the number of affiliated chapters dropped from a high of twenty at the end of the 1940s and fluctuated around eleven during the early 1950s.

Weakened by continuing debates over the role of pacifism and the national organizational structure, CORE's growth was further stunted by anticommunism. Although CORE's executive committee had drafted a "Statement on Communism" in 1948 saying that it would not work with communists,

Andrew Young (third from left, foreground) with members of CORE at a break in the march to Enid campsite, June 12, 1966. (© Charmian Reading)

CORE's civil rights activities were attacked as "subversive" and "un-American" in the hostile racial climate of the 1950s. At this organizational nadir, Houser resigned and the national structure was once again reorganized to divide his duties among three people: Billie Ames, a white activist from CORE's St. Louis chapter, became group coordinator and took charge of organizational correspondence; James Peck, a white Journey of Reconciliation veteran, was in charge of editing the CORE-lator; and James Robinson continued to serve as treasurer. Wallace Nelson, who had held the salaried position of field secretary, was replaced by four volunteers.

CORE found a renewed sense of purpose in the mid-1950s. In 1954, the BROWN V. BOARD OF EDUCATION OF TOPEKA, KANSAS decision declared separate but equal educational facilities unconstitutional. One year later, the Montgomery bus boycott mobilized thousands of African Americans to challenge segregated buses. CORE activists—as pioneers of the strategy of nonviolent direct action—provided philosophical resources to the boycott and dispatched LeRoy Carter, a black field-secretary, to Montgomery to provide support. Electrified by rising black protest, CORE decided to channel the majority of the organization's energy into expanding into the South.

To facilitate this expansion, there was a revival of the national staff. In 1957, James Robinson, whose tireless fund-raising efforts had boosted organizational finances, was appointed executive secretary. He worked closely with the National Action Committee, comprising influential members based in New York who made policy decisions. CORE created a staff position for a public relations coordinator, who was in charge of promoting CORE as a major civil rights organization alongside the NAACP and the SOUTHERN CHRISTIAN LEADERSHIP CONFERENCE (SCLC), which was founded after the Montgomery bus boycott. In addition, the CORE-lator was transformed from an organizational organ into an informative newsmagazine that reported on the social movements emerging in the South.

Most importantly, CORE directly confronted its relationship to the black community for the first time. Although its predominantly white leadership structure remained firmly in place, African Americans such as James McCain, who was appointed field secretary in 1957, were sought out for prominent and visible positions. Publicity for CORE also was sought in the black press. Nonetheless, CORE'S ideological commitment to interracialism continued to be unwavering. McCain, for example, worked closely with James Carey, a white field secretary, to demonstrate the viability of interracial organizing to potential new affiliates. However, the fundamental nature of the organization had begun to change. Interracialism—which had been defined since CORE's inception as racial diversity within chapters—was redefined on a regional level. To reflect the probability of minimal white support for CORE in the South, as well as the continued inability of majority white chapters on the West Coast to secure a black membership base, the interracial requirement for chapters was removed from the constitution. In addition, although CORE retained its base among white and black middle-class college students, its class and age composition was radically altered as many younger and poorer African Americans, with few ideological links to pacifism, joined its ranks.

By 1960, the number of CORE chapters had risen to twenty-four, with new chapters springing up in Virginia, Tennessee, South Carolina, Florida, Kentucky. With a stable national structure, growing income, new constituencies, and increased visibility, CORE finally seemed poised to join the ranks of the major civil rights organizations. In February 1960, when four college students sat in at a lunch counter in Greensboro, N.C., to protest segregation and ignited a wave of student protest that spread throughout the South, CORE activists scrambled to provide guidance. In Florida, CORE members pioneered the "jail-in" technique when five members chose to serve out their sentences rather than pay bail after being arrested for sitting in at a department store counter. One year later, CORE activists organized another "jail-in" in Rock Hill, S.C., which received national attention, helped galvanize the black community, and set a precedent of "jail-no bail" that became an important direct action strategy in the civil rights movement. In the North, affiliates started sympathy demonstrations for the student demonstrators and called for nationwide boycotts to attempt to place economic pressure on national chains to desegregate their facilities.

In May 1961, CORE mounted its most militant challenge to segregation: the Freedom Rides. Modeled on the earlier Journey of Reconciliation, the Freedom Rides were protests against segregated interstate buses and terminals in the South. Seven white and six black activists, including James Farmer (who had been appointed CORE executive director earlier that year), participated in the Freedom Rides. After successfully challenging segregation in Virginia and North Carolina, the Freedom Riders faced harassment, intimidation, and violence from racist southern whites in the deep South. Two riders were attacked in Rock Hill, S.C.; two were arrested in Winnesboro, S.C.; and in a violent climax, riders were beaten and their bus bombed by a white mob near Birmingham, Ala. After this event, which was recorded by the press for a shocked nation to see, CORE terminated the rides. SNCC activists resumed

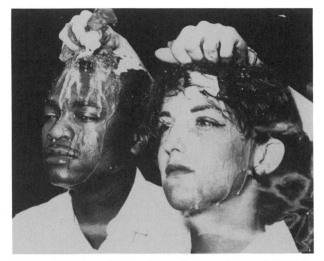

Richard Siller and Lois Bonzell, members of CORE, learning how to cope with violent responses to demonstrations during a practice session in San Francisco in 1963. (AP/Wide World Photos)

the Freedom Rides in Mississippi, unleashing a white backlash so virulent that the Kennedy administration was forced to intervene with federal protection. Though SNCC activists—with some resentment on the part of CORE officials—took the leadership of the protest and received most of the credit for the remaining Freedom Rides, CORE continued to provide guidance to the freedom riders and stationed field secretaries in key southern cities to assist riders. Many CORE activists, including Farmer, rejoined the rides when SNCC continued them. The freedom riders finally triumphed in September 1961 when the Interstate Commerce Commission issued an order prohibiting segregated facilities in interstate travel.

The Freedom Rides placed CORE in the vanguard of the civil rights movement. As a result of the national attention that the rides had generated, James Farmer joined SNCC's John LEWIS and SCLC's Rev. Dr. Martin Luther KING, Jr., as a national spokesperson for the CIVIL RIGHTS MOVEMENT. By the end of 1961, CORE—with fifty-three affiliated chapters, rising income, and increased visibility—was able to mount new activities. CORE was an active participant in the wave of direct action protest that swept through the South in 1962 and 1963. In 1962, CORE worked closely with the local NAACP to launch the Freedom Highways project to desegregate Howard Johnson hotels along North Carolina highways. Faced with retaliatory white violence, and locked into increasingly contentious competition with the other civil rights organizations, CORE broadened the scope of its activities. In 1962, CORE joined the VOTER EDUCATION PROJECT (VEP) initiated by President John F. Kennedy and mounted vigorous voter

registration campaigns in Louisiana, Florida, Mississippi, and South Carolina.

CORE activists played a pivotal role in many of the leading events of the civil rights movement. In 1963, CORE joined the NAACP, SCLC, and SNCC in sponsoring the March on Washington. As a part of the COUNCIL OF FEDERATED ORGANIZATIONS (COFO), a statewide coalition of civil rights organizations engaged in voter registration, CORE played a crucial role in the FREEDOM SUMMER in 1964 in Mississippi. James CHANEY and Michael Schwerner, two of three civil rights workers killed in June 1964 by racist whites in the infamous case that focused national attention on the South, were members of CORE.

By 1963, CORE activities—severely curtailed by arrests and racial violence—shifted from the South to the North. Two thirds of CORE's sixty-eight chapters were in the North and West, concentrated mainly in California and New York. In the North, CORE chapters directly confronted discrimination and segregation in housing and employment, using tactics such as picketing and the boycott. As they began to address some of the problems of economically disadvantaged African Americans in the North—among them, unemployment, housing discrimination, and police brutality—they began to attract more working class African-American members. To strengthen their image as a black-protest organization, leadership of northern chapters was almost always black, and CORE chapters moved their headquarters into the black community. As member composition changed and CORE acquired a more militant image, CORE's deeply held ideological beliefs and tactics of social change were increasingly challenged by black working-class members. These members were willing to engage in more confrontational tactics, such as resisting arrest, obstructing traffic, all night sit-ins, and other forms of militant civil disobedience. Drawing on different ideological traditions, they viewed nonviolence as a tactic to be abandoned when no longer expedient—not as a deeply held philosophical belief. They often identified with MALCOLM X, who preached racial pride and black separatism, rather than with Gandhian notions of a beloved community.

By 1964, the integrationist, southern-based civil rights coalition was splintering, and consensus over tactics and strategy within CORE was destroyed. Vigorous debates emerged within CORE about the roles of whites (by 1964 less than 50 percent of the membership) in the organization. Infused with heightened black pride and nationalism, angered by the paternalism of some white members, and believing that black people should lead in the liberation of the black community, many black CORE members pushed for the diminution of the role of whites within the organization; an increasingly vocal minority called for the expulsion of whites.

As CORE struggled for organizational and programmatic direction, old tensions between rank and file members of the national leadership resurfaced as local chapters, operating almost autonomously, turned to grass-roots activism in poor black communities. In the South, CORE activities centered on building self-supporting community organizations to meet the needs of local communities. Activists organized projects that ranged from job discrimination protests, to voter registration, to securing mail delivery for black neighborhoods. In the North, CORE activists continued in the tradition of direct action. They fostered neighborhood organizations with local leadership, started community centers and job placement centers, and organized rent strikes and welfare rights protests.

In 1966, the National CORE convention endorsed the slogan of Black Power. Under the leadership of Farmer and Floyd MCKISSICK—elected in 1963 as CORE national chairman—CORE adopted a national position supporting black self-determination, local control of community institutions, and coalition politics. In 1967 the word "multiracial" was deleted from the constitution, and whites began an exodus from the organization. One year later, Roy INNIS, a dynamic and outspoken leader of CORE's Harlem chapter, replaced Farmer and under the new title of national director took control of the organization. Innis staunchly believed in separatism and black self-determination and argued that blacks were a "nation within a nation." He barred whites from active membership in CORE and centralized decision-making authority to assert control over local chapter activities. By this point, however, CORE was a weakened organization with a handful of affiliated chapters and dwindling resources.

Innis's economic nationalism and support for black capitalism led to an extremely conservative political stance for CORE on issues ranging from civil rights legislation and foreign policy to gun control and welfare. In 1970 he met with southern whites to promote separate schools as a viable alternative to court imposed desegregation and busing. In the late 1970s and early '80s, almost all CORE activities ground to a halt as Innis and CORE came under increasing criticism. In 1976, Farmer severed all ties with CORE in protest of Innis's separatism and his attempt to recruit black Vietnam veterans to fight in Angola's civil war on the side of the South-African-backed National Union for the Total Independence of Angola (UNITA). In 1981, after being accused by the New York State attorney general's office of misusing charitable contributions, Innis agreed to contribute $35,000 to the organization over a three-year period in exchange for not admitting to any irregularities in handling funds. In the early 1980s, former CORE members, led by Farmer, attempted to transform CORE into a multiracial organization, but Innis remained firmly in command. In 1987, Innis supported Bernhard Goetz, a white man who shot black alleged muggers on the subways in New York; and Robert Bork, a conservative Supreme Court nominee.

CORE chapters have mounted only sporadic activities in the 1990s, but Innis—at this point, one of the leading black conservatives—has maintained visibility as national director of the organization.

REFERENCES

BELL, INGE POWELL. CORE and the Strategy of Nonviolence. New York, 1968.
FARMER, JAMES. Lay Bare the Heart: An Autobiography of the Civil Rights Movement. New York, 1985.
MEIER, AUGUST, and ELLIOT RUDWICK. Black Protest in the Sixties. Chicago, 1970.
———. CORE: A Study in the Civil Rights Movement. New York, 1975.
PECK, JAMES. Cracking the Color Line: Nonviolent Direct Action Methods of Eliminating Racial Discrimination. New York, 1962.
VAN DEBURG, WILLIAM. New Day in Babylon: The Black Power Movement and American Culture, 1965–1975. Chicago, 1992.

CAROL V. R. GEORGE

Conley, William Lee. See Broonzy, William Lee Conley "Big Bill."

Connecticut. Africans in Connecticut originally arrived as a result of the triangular trade in rum, slaves, and molasses that linked New England, West Africa, and the Caribbean. As early as 1679, a governor of Connecticut recorded the importation of several Africans by the northern SLAVE TRADE—numbers that would gradually increase during the next century. By 1750, the black population of Connecticut had grown to 3,010, comprising 3 percent of the population. In 1790, black population was 5,473, or 2.6 percent of the population of the state. At this time, nearly half of the black population was concentrated in the cities of New London and Fairfield.

The particular form of "family slavery" practiced in Connecticut—and throughout New England—meant that Connecticut's black population was peripheral to the economy. Blacks occupied a distinctly subordinate position within the social, political, and religious life of the state. In spite of these restrictions, however, blacks in Connecticut managed to organize their own institutions—beginning with the practice of electing kings and governors of their own, a custom which began in the mid-eighteenth century and continued in some towns until the 1850s.

In 1784, Connecticut passed a gradual emancipation law that allowed for a slave's freedom at the age of twenty-five. Thus by 1820 the number of slaves in the state had decreased to less than one hundred. As the free black population increased in the state, so did the movement of blacks from rural towns to urban centers—primarily to meet the demand for services created by a growing urban population. As narratives by ex-slaves like Venture SMITH, James Mars, William Grimes, and others make clear, however, the experiences of free blacks in Connecticut from the late eighteenth century to the eve of the Civil War were often difficult, and their lives were circumscribed by racial discrimination. The 1818 Connecticut Constitution made it plain that only white male citizens were entitled to vote—a clause which was not amended until 1876. Blacks in Connecticut also encountered racial discrimination in employment, housing, transportation, and education. In 1830, for example, whites in New Haven voted overwhelmingly against a plan to establish an academic and vocational school for blacks—even though the funds would be provided by private sources.

During the period from the 1830s through the Civil War, Connecticut citizens revealed an ambivalent and contradictory attitude toward blacks—an ambivalence captured in two major events of the period. In 1833, the attempts by Prudence Crandall to admit black women to her previously all-white girls' academy in Canterbury, Conn., were met with ferocious opposition by the white residents of the community. Crandall's school was repeatedly vandalized, and she was ultimately arrested and imprisoned.

In marked contrast to the Prudence Crandall affair was the reaction of many Connecticut residents to the celebrated *Amistad* affair. In 1839, fifty-four Africans being transported on the Spanish schooner *Amistad* rebelled off the coast of Cuba, killed many of the crew, and forced the survivors to sail back to Africa. By a series of ruses the crew managed to guide the *Amistad* to the Long Island Sound, where the Africans were captured in 1839. The *Amistad* case was a complicated one, involving international legal questions, and was finally settled by the Supreme Court, with former President John Quincy Adams successfully arguing the case for the Africans. During their sojourn in Connecticut, the *Amistad* Africans were the subject of considerable attention by aboli-

tionists and ordinary citizens alike. As Africans who would not remain in Connecticut, they received considerably more sympathy and support from white citizens than did black residents of the state.

Blacks in the cities challenged these racist practices by organizing their own churches, schools, lodges, and self-help organizations. The first of these institutions were the churches, such as the Talcott Street Church in Hartford, founded in 1826, and the Temple Street Congregational Church in New Haven, founded by Simeon Jocelyn, a white minister, and four black colleagues in 1829. Blacks also petitioned for separate schools for their children—as they did in Hartford when they established African schools during the 1830s. The leaders of these institutions played a prominent role in the struggle against slavery and racial injustice in the decades preceding the CIVIL WAR. The ministers Amos BEMAN (1812–1874) of New Haven and James W. C. PENNINGTON of Hartford were particularly effective leaders during this period.

Although two all-black regiments from Connecticut fought during the Civil War, returning home to the accolades of the governor and residents of the state, the material conditions of blacks did not significantly improve during the years following the Civil War. The practice of racially segregated schools did not end until 1868, for example, when James Ralston, a Hartford resident and the Grand Master of the Prince Hall Masons, petitioned the legislature. In spite of the passage of the THIRTEENTH, FOURTEENTH, and FIFTEENTH AMENDMENTS, blacks in Connecticut continued to experience racial discrimination in virtually every area of public life. Having secured the right to vote, Connecticut black residents began to seek inroads into the political system—most notably through the State Sumner Union League, named after the radical Republican Senator Charles Sumner (1811–1874)—which sought to influence the politics of the REPUBLICAN PARTY in the 1880s and '90s. At the same time, the black population continued to grow, from approximately 10,000 in 1873 to over 15,000 by the early twentieth century.

World War I marked the beginning of a major transformation of Connecticut's black population. The migration of southern blacks to northern cities dramatically escalated at the outbreak of the war, when northern industries experienced a sharp decline in the supply of immigrant workers. In 1914 and 1915, Connecticut factories began recruiting southern black workers. Other heavy industries in Connecticut soon followed suit. By 1930, the black population had grown to approximately 30,000. A similar dramatic change occurred in the years following World War II, when the black population in the state grew to 54,000 in 1950, 107,000 in 1960, and

181,000 in 1970. According to the 1990 U.S. Census, blacks constituted 269,000, or 8.2 percent, of the population of Connecticut—the highest percentage of blacks in any New England state.

The growth of the black population in Connecticut cities during the twentieth century led to renewed efforts by the black community to challenge deeply entrenched patterns of racial discrimination in the state. In the years following World War II, inspired by the southern CIVIL RIGHTS MOVEMENT, black communities in cities throughout Connecticut mobilized to struggle against chronic unemployment, inferior housing, political powerlessness, and persistent racism. The growing militancy of the black population culminated in a series of riots that swept Hartford, New Haven, and other cities throughout the state in 1967, 1968, and 1969. Blacks also began to make inroads into the political system during this period. Gerald Lamb became the first black elected to statewide office when he successfully ran for state treasurer on the Democratic party ticket in 1963. Thirman L. Milner of Hartford became the first popularly elected black mayor in New England in 1981, and his success was followed by the election of John Daniels as mayor of New Haven. Carrie Saxon Perry became the first black woman mayor of the city of Hartford in 1987, and Gary Franks of Waterbury, a conservative Republican, was elected to Congress in 1990.

From the early nineteenth century to the present, blacks in Connecticut have been closely associated with urban settings, and in the twentieth century in particular, the cities of Connecticut have been arenas in which the black population has waged its steady and persistent quest for equality.

REFERENCES

BONTEMPS, ARNA, ed. *Five Black Lives*. Middletown, Conn., 1971.

FRASER, BRUCE. *The Land of Steady Habits: A Brief History of Connecticut*. Hartford, Conn., 1988.

GREENE, LORENZO J. *The Negro in Colonial New England*. New Haven, 1942.

PIERSON, WILLIAM D. *Black Yankees: The Development of an Afro-American Subculture in Eighteenth Century New England*. Amherst, Mass., 1988.

WHITE, DAVID O. "Blacks In Connecticut." In David M. Roth and Judith Arnold Grenier, eds., *Connecticut History and Culture: An Historical Overview and Resource Guide for Teachers*. Hartford, 1985.

JAMES A. MILLER

Conservatism.   The recorded history of African-American conservative thought may well begin with the perplexing figure of the late-eighteenth-century black poet Jupiter HAMMON. A Long Island, New York, slave, Hammon urged his fellow blacks to be obedient to authority and to refrain from vices such as profanity and stealing. For slaves wishing an end to their servitude, he counseled patience, Christian forbearance, obedience to their masters, and exemplary moral character. Underlying Hammon's view of slavery and freedom was an intense evangelical Christianity that reduced temporal events to moments of little consequence.

Although few subsequent African Americans were as publicly supportive of the institution of slavery, Hammon's conservative principles had many adherents over the next two centuries. Chief among these principles is social conservatism, characterized by respect for existing political and social hierarchies, strong patriotism, and support for capitalist enterprise. Though not all black social conservatives have been middle class, most have endorsed middle-class Christian standards of propriety.

Social conservatism has often been in direct opposition to liberalism, which has traditionally supported the working class and organized labor. Given the traditional hostility of labor to blacks and black unionism, it is hardly surprising that many blacks have defined their concerns as opposed to those of the white working class, and have identified themselves as political conservatives.

Another component of black conservatism is what can be called racial circumspection, characterized by a fear of social unrest and support of a slow, incremental approach to political change. Rather than castigating white America for its racism, black conservatives have emphasized an internal critique of African-American society, maintaining that many existing problems could be ameliorated if blacks worked to better themselves. Black conservatives also argue that the status of blacks can improve within existing political institutions without antagonizing whites.

Nevertheless, there has been much divergence of opinion within black conservatism. Some black conservatives are committed to full racial equality, while others have been willing to accommodate a racial caste system. There have been militant integrationists, and equally militant separatists, and black nationalists. In their diversity, black conservatives mirror the complexity of black society itself.

A common view of black conservatism is that it is self-contradictory or hypocritical. The Russian anarchist Pyotr Kropotkin, on being told that Booker T. WASHINGTON was a conservative, wondered what blacks in the United States had to conserve. This view is understandable but unfair. Few black conservatives have complacently upheld the status quo, and almost all have acknowledged the pervasiveness of some degree of racial inequality.

Antebellum Conservatism

In the United States before the CIVIL WAR, African American political leaders supported the more conservative factions in American politics—the Federalists, the Whigs, and the Republicans. As early as 1786 Prince HALL, the leader of Boston's black community, offered to raise troops to help put down Shays' Rebellion. The black New England clergyman Lemuel HAYNES, a conservative Congregationalist best known for upholding orthodox doctrines of salvation against the innovations of Unitarians, remained a fervent Federalist until the end of his life. In New York City, the NEW YORK MANUMISSION SOCIETY was dominated by Federalists. It established a common school for blacks, and maintained close ties with local black residents, who perhaps played a role in carrying New York City for the Federalists in the 1813 gubernatorial race.

African-American political support was in part reciprocated by northern conservatives. In the 1821 New York State constitutional convention, the Bucktail faction of the Democratic party supporting "universal" male suffrage, successfully imposed steep restrictions on black voting, while conservatives, including doughty old Federalists such as Chancellor Kent, opposed racial distinctions in voting requirements. In the 1830s and '40s Whigs such as Philip Hone and Horace Greeley tried in vain to reopen the voting restrictions imposed by the 1821 Constitution. In Rhode Island in the 1840s a similar configuration of political forces found blacks supporting the conservative, limited-franchise faction in the so-called "Dorr war." In Pennsylvania the situation was somewhat more murky, since there were some prominent Republican supporters of black interests such as Benjamin Rush, but most of the old Quaker abolitionists were Federalists, and it was largely Democratic pressure that successfully ended black suffrage in Pennsylvania in 1838. In state after state in the East and the Midwest, a faction of the Whig Party provided the only significant support for black interests, while Jacksonian Democrats were generally united in their opposition to any form of black advancement.

However, given the limitations on African-American political participation—in 1860 only five of the thirty-three states permitted unrestricted male black suffrage—party politics was relatively unimportant in forming the ideology of free northern blacks. More important was a middle-class culture that emphasized the development of an educated leadership class dedicated to self-improvement. Religious bodies such as the African Methodist Episcopal Church often aspired to middle-class refinement, and its leaders, such as Daniel PAYNE, looked with disdain on emotional "African" forms of worship such

as the ring shout. Part of the emphasis on "uplift" was also economic. Denied access to most artisanal crafts, most free blacks were either menial laborers or small entrepreneurs, who were unlikely to have much sympathy with the radical workingmen's critique of salaried labor as "wage slavery" or "white slavery." The abolitionist-nationalist Martin DELANEY argued in 1852 that until blacks developed their own business and became producers, their calls for equality were bound to be fruitless. The bold assertion of antebellum blocks the ability of blacks to function effectively in a white-dominated world is often joined to relatively conventional standards of appropriate behavior and societal organization. Consider the resolutions of the National Negro Convention of 1832, which after a stirring condemnation of slavery called on African Americans to "be righteous, be honest, be just . . . [but] offend not the laws of your country."

Historian David Brion Davis has argued that the opposition of white abolitionists to slaveholders and southern society often led them to embrace the industrial capitalist order of the North without regard for the plight of northern labor. But for black abolitionists as well, the revulsion of blacks toward the slave South usually made them hospitable to the social order of the North (if not to its racial caste system). The political maturation of Frederick DOUGLASS was closely related to his enthusiastic embrace of the Constitution, his acceptance of conventional political activity, and his distaste at how white abolitionists often raised issues he thought irrelevant to the slavery question, such as socialism and the status of private property. Unlike some white abolitionists such as William Lloyd Garrison, Douglass had no vested interest in being a professional outsider. While he demanded that America live up to its highest aspirations, there was an underlying patriotism and social conservatism in Douglass's views that only became more pronounced later in his life.

Whatever the general impact of abolitionism on black thought, within black abolitionism there was a coterie of moderates, including Samuel CORNISH, Peter WILLIAMS, Jr., Mary Ann Shadd Cary and her father, Abraham SHADD, William WHIPPER, and the leaders of the AMERICAN MORAL REFORM SOCIETY. These abolitionists were generally strong integrationists who had close ties with white evangelical abolitionists and stressed the importance of temperance and other middle-class moral values.

Another strain of conservatism was found among nationalists who despaired of the possibility of blacks achieving full civic equality in the United States and who looked elsewhere to establish black sovereignty free of white domination. Political and cultural elitism was central to the political thought of Martin Delaney and James HOLLY, and later in the century to

Alexander CRUMMELL and Henry McNeal TURNER. The most influential nationalists were interested in reestablishing under black control the basic civic and economic institutions of the United States in an autonomous society where blacks could produce an elite of equal attainments to whites. This conservative nationalism led in fact to the establishment of the Republic of Liberia.

Civil War and Reconstruction

After the Civil War the core of black political concern shifted to the 4.5 million recently emancipated slaves in the South. The political questions that blacks faced were momentous and the range of responses of southern blacks was wide, often determined by class and prewar status. There were a large number of freed slaves who demanded radical land reform and confiscation of Confederate estates, and used organizations such as the UNION LEAGUE to press their claims. Opposed to them were not only whites but many blacks as well. The bulk of elected southern black officials took a more cautious view than the black electorate as a whole. Indeed, on issues such as the confiscation of Confederate land, most black leaders were more forgiving than white Radical Republicans such as Charles Sumner or Thaddeus Stevens. Certainly the best-known black politicians to emerge from RECONSTRUCTION were convinced that the way to retain political power was to balance defenses of black rights with conciliatory gestures toward whites. By the end of Reconstruction in 1876 many of the most prominent black southern politicians, such as former Louisiana governor P. B. S. PINCH-BACK, Congressman John R. LYNCH, Robert SMALLS, John Mercer LANGSTON, and Senator Blanche BRUCE, looked upon President Rutherford B. Hayes's policy of reconciliation with southern whites as one that would restore calm to the South and provide African Americans with a needed respite from conflict.

Some southern black leaders grudgingly assented to the progressive erosion of black rights. Isaiah MONTGOMERY, the only black at the Mississippi Constitutional Convention of 1890, voted for laws that almost entirely eliminated black suffrage in that state. He was widely criticized for this by Frederick Douglass, T. Thomas FORTUNE, and others, but his actions were in keeping with the temper of a conservative segment of the black middle class and elite in the late nineteenth century that asserted that blacks had important things to do, and this required social peace rather than a dangerous and apparently fruitless fight for full equality. Montgomery himself was the main promoter of MOUND BAYOU, MISS., probably the most successful of almost one hundred black towns founded in the South between 1880 and 1920.

Most of the black towns had similar conservative sponsorship.

The nadir of black political power from 1880 through 1920 was nevertheless a golden age for founding black institutions. Organizations created at the time ranged from the highly political to those that were inward-looking, such as some fraternal organizations. Through the upheavals of the 1960s, black institutional life as manifested in fraternal societies, historically black colleges and universities and college organizations, women's clubs, and many of the professional organizations gathered under the umbrella of the NATIONAL NEGRO BUSINESS LEAGUE (founded in 1990), served as a redoubt of African-American social conservatism.

This conservatism can be seen in the politics of individual accommodationists. Benjamin ARNETT, an African Methodist Episcopal bishop in Ohio, befriended powerful politicians such as William McKinley, developed a reputation as a moderate, and had some success in reversing the antiblack legislation in his home state. Some, such as William STEWARD of Louisville, acquiesced in the broader forms of JIM CROW discrimination, but had success in preventing some of its less controversial manifestations, such as streetcar segregation.

Crucial to post-Reconstruction conservatism was the emphasis placed on self-help, and the elevation of blacks through their own endeavors. This is often associated with Booker T. Washington, whose works are filled with metaphors of "rising up," but the appeal of this philosophy of self-help was quite wide. Frederick Douglass in the post-Reconstruction period often lectured on his own career as emblematic of the "self-made man." And while Douglass never moderated his commitment to full equality, the emphasis on self-help was compatible with a growing social conservatism. Douglass's politics in his last decades were characterized by a hostility to the working class and labor unions, a fear of radicalism, and a powerful loyalty to the REPUBLICAN PARTY and support of its probusiness policies. Nannie BURROUGHS, the influential leader of the Woman's Convention Auxiliary of the National Baptist Convention, also combined the social conservatism of self-help philosophy with militance on civil rights questions. In her social teaching Burroughs advocated instructing women in the "three B's" of the "Bible, bath, and broom," and had as her motto "Work, Support Thyself, to Thine Own Powers Appeal."

Alexander Crummell was another influential African-American conservative thinker of the late nineteenth century. He shared with Douglas the belief in self-help and economic improvement, as well as a unwavering commitment to full racial equality.

Unlike Douglass, who viewed separate black institutions as a concession to racism, Crummell, an Episcopal priest who lived in Washington, D.C., was a committed nationalist. (He had lived twenty years in Liberia.) In his politics, Crummell was starkly reactionary, and was a throwback to the black Federalists of the early nineteenth century. He was a believer in theocracy, a supporter of strong rulers, and an avowed Hamiltonian who criticized the DECLARATION OF INDEPENDENCE for permitting an excess of democracy. He was opposed to labor unions, and socialism, and wanted blacks to be "ranked among conservative men in this land." Rather than expend fruitless energy in agitation, Crummel recommended that blacks develop institutions that would rival and imitate those present among Christian whites. His commitment to an intellectual elite was instrumental in the founding of the AMERICAN NEGRO ACADEMY in 1897.

The best-known black conservative at the turn of the twentieth century was Booker T. Washington, in whose career many of the strains of late-nineteenth-century conservatism coalesced. Washington advocated coexistence with whites and a concentration on self-help. Washington's vision of the future of African Americans was in a largely rural South, dominated by whites, in which most blacks would be either farmers or small businessmen. In the 1895 ATLANTA COMPROMISE speech, Washington argued that separate development of the races was better for both blacks and whites. He urged whites to accept blacks, who had "without strikes and labor wars, tilled your fields, cleared your forests." According to Washington, higher education was superfluous to all but a select few, emphasizing instead industrial and vocational education.

Washington's message and underlying social conservatism had widespread support among blacks, and not just among the middle class. The black church was profoundly influential in disseminating both social and political conservatism. Although some, such as Crummell, came to conservatism from a hierarchical High Church Episcopalianism, there was an alternative popular form of religious conservatism, or what might be better called political indifference, deeply rooted in southern black life. Most outside observers of the black church at the turn of the century criticized the black clergy for narrowness, otherworldliness, and inattention to political issues. Though there were exceptions, the black church in the late nineteenth century preached a predominantly conservative message.

Black educator Benjamin MAYS once reminisced that when he was growing up in rural South Carolina around 1900 his pastor never criticized lynching and in his sermons emphasized obedience to authority.

In Mays's study *The Negro's Church* (1939), more than 90 percent of those interviewed on the early twentieth-century black church said their pastors either ignored social conditions or urged that whites be treated with deference and respect. Only a handful remembered their pastors teaching them to demand their rights. Nonetheless, as Mays and most of the people he interviewed acknowledged, black Christian belief provided a sense of pride, self-worth, and self-confidence, maintaining that the ultimate source of authority was not of this world. If this could lead to a challenge of temporal power such as that of NAT TURNER'S REBELLION, it could just as easily lead to a proudly, defiantly quietist version of Christianity, perhaps best exemplified by the title character in Harriet Beecher Stowe's UNCLE TOM'S CABIN.

Twentieth-Century Conservatism

In many ways what is distinctive about African-American thought in the twentieth century developed out of a critique of Booker T. Washington. Though from the outset there were unfavorable responses to Washington and the Atlanta Compromise speech, much of the early reaction was positive. As Louis Harlan has written, "Washington's speech reflected a drift in Negro thought that had been going on since the end of Reconstruction, toward the economic approach, toward accommodation with the white South." Individuals as ideologically diverse as T. Thomas Fortune, T. McCants STEWART, W. E. B. DU BOIS, and Edward Wilmot BLYDEN initially approved of his speech. In time the anti-Washington sentiment increased. There were two main reasons for this. Washington's emphasis on industrial education angered people such as Crummell and Du Bois, who were committed to an educated black elite. And Washington's apparent support for segregation stretched the conservative philosophy of befriending whites to its limits. In truth, Washington's position on segregation was never consistent, and he was never as supportive of it as his most notorious comments seemed to indicate. He criticized some accommodationists, such as his fellow Alabama educator William H. COUNCILL, who joined the DEMOCRATIC PARTY after Reconstruction, as a sycophant and a toady. Washington privately challenged and helped fund lawsuits against segregation. Toward the end of his life, perhaps prodded by critics, he became somewhat more forthright in his attacks on Jim Crow. But his record in opposing segregation was uneven at best, and his public statements and his great influence in black political circles made him a tempting target.

The first of Washington's major critics was the Harvard-educated and Boston-based William Monroe TROTTER. Trotter was unremittingly hostile to any compromise with segregation, and his lambasting of Washington's accommodationist politics was ferocious. But Trotter had much in common with the older Frederick Douglass, maintaining a conservatism on most social issues, including a pronounced hostility to organized labor. As his biographer noted, Trotter "demanded full equality for Negroes and proposed practically nothing else for the basic American economic and governmental system."

The movement of Marcus GARVEY cannot easily be classified along any conventional liberal-to-conservative spectrum. Certainly the emphasis on building black businesses and opposition to organized labor were fully compatible with Washington's ideals. J. Raymond JONES, the future Tammany boss, remarked that when he first came to New York City from the Virgin Islands in the 1920s he found the Garveyites, with their emphasis on private entrepreneurship to be the most "American" of the political alternatives in Harlem, compared to the socialists and other radicals, and felt that Garveyism fostered his own integration into American society. A number of former associates of Washington, including T. Thomas Fortune and Washington's former secretary Emmett J. SCOTT, supported Garvey. Garvey himself chose to emphasize the more conservative aspects of his racial separatism after he became ensnarled during the 1920s in legal problems, such as attempts to establish a dialogue with white segregationists. However, Garvey's rejection of both white America and the political institutions of the United States unsettled many observers, both black and white, and it places him outside the standard benchmarks of black conservatism. Still, if it is Garvey's cultural militance that has made him a hero to later generations of decidedly unconservative African Americans, his appeal at the time, and success among the middle class, were in part due to his strong underlying social conservatism.

After Washington's death in 1915, the conservative views he fostered remained an important part of black intellectual life. However, for his latter-day conservative supporters, industrial education became less of a panacea, and attacks on segregation were more direct. By the 1930s Washingtonism was slowly losing its distinctiveness. This can be seen in Robert Mussa MOTON, Washington's successor at Tuskegee Institute (now TUSKEGEE UNIVERSITY), whose *What the Negro Thinks* (1931) criticized segregation fairly forcefully, but argued that its worst excesses were being eliminated and that whites were coming to understand its futility. In the North, Robert A. VANN, editor of the PITTSBURGH COURIER, accepted many of the tenets of Washington, as when he claimed that "Negro business [is] the bulwark of our racial progress." Vann generally condemned organized labor, accused Samuel Gompers of having Communist sympathies, and thought blacks were far more patriotic citizens and workers than recently arrived "hyphenated Americans." But Vann also regularly criticized the federal and state governments for shortcomings on racial justice, supported the formation of the INTERNATIONAL BROTHERHOOD OF SLEEPING CAR PORTERS (though he later called for the outster of A. Philip RANDOLPH as its head because of Randolph's socialist background), and moved from the Republican to the Democratic party in the 1930s.

Vann had southern counterparts in P. B. YOUNG and Gordon Blaine HANCOCK. P. B. Young, editor of the *Norfolk Journal and Guide,* argued that racial problems could be solved if southern whites and blacks worked together to solve their mutual problems, and he remained an adherent of Washington's social and economic philosophy, emphasizing the need for business development, racial elevation, and "sober and intelligent" African-American spokesmen. Young was opposed to the mass movement of blacks to the North, and worried that blacks accustomed to "southern habits and traditions" were in for grief in the North. Yet like Vann, Young supported the NEW DEAL, and in 1943, in part because of his reputation as a racial moderate, he was appointed to the FAIR EMPLOYMENT PRACTICES COMMISSION (FEPC) during WORLD WAR II, investigating discrimination among defense contractors.

Gordon Blaine Hancock, a professor at Virginia Union University in Richmond, held similar views. During the GREAT DEPRESSION Hancock urged blacks to hold on to their jobs and support black businesses rather than agitate, and tried to start a "Back to the Farm" movement in the 1930s, in an effort to keep blacks in the rural South. Yet Hancock was also one of the leaders of the Durham (N.C.) Conference in 1942, which resolved that it was "fundamentally opposed to the principle and practice of compulsory segregation in our American society," though it called for its gradual rather than immediate elimination. The DURHAM MANIFESTO is evidence of the narrowing gaps among black conservatives, liberals, and even radicals on the need for some sort of government intervention to end racial discrimination.

The twenty-five years after the end of World War II probably mark the nadir of black conservatism, either before or since. It is the relative absence of black conservatives from black political debate during the 1950s and 1960s that made their subsequent reappearance so noteworthy. Most black moderates supported the desegregation decision in BROWN V. BOARD OF EDUCATION OF TOPEKA (1954) and its aftermath, and the incrementalist vision of civil rights promoted by mainstream organizations such as the NATIONAL ASSOCIATION FOR THE ADVANCEMENT OF

COLORED PEOPLE and the NATIONAL URBAN LEAGUE. At the same time, the reborn conservative movement of the 1950s was at best skeptical of the decisions of the Warren Court, federal interventions in southern states, and congressional civil rights legislation, viewing them as illegitimate extensions of government authority and violations of the principles of federalism. Such views did not find much favor with African Americans. In 1964, rejecting the conservative Republican candidate Barry Goldwater, who opposed the Civil Rights Act of 1964, an estimated 99 percent of African Americans voted for the Democrat, Lyndon Johnson.

However muted, black conservatism remained a presence within black political debate during these years. The main issue that galvanized conservatives, black and white, was anticommunism. Like their white counterparts, most prominent black anticommunists were either former leftists or were persons who had considerable familiarity with left-wing circles, and tended to be journalists or writers, instead of the respectable upholders of social order who had previously characterized black conservatives. While there were many black liberals who were strongly anticommunist, such as Walter WHITE, Ralph BUNCHE, and Roy WILKINS, conservative anticommunists made communism the central political issue in their lives, often leading to breaks with the major civil rights organizations. One of the first prominent anti-communists was Max YERGAN, a one time close ally of Paul ROBESON and cofounder of the left-wing and anti-imperialist COUNCIL ON AFRICAN AFFAIRS (CAA). In 1947 Yergan dramatically broke with the CAA, charging that the organization was dominated by communists. Within a few years Yergan was a strong supporter of the Cold War, and later became a supporter of the white-dominated regimes of South Africa and Rhodesia as bulwarks against the spread of communism through Africa.

One of the most outspoken black conservatives in the postwar period was the novelist Zora Neale HURSTON. She had always been suspicious of the left-wing inclinations of many of her HARLEM RENAISSANCE colleagues. By the time she left New York City for Florida in the 1940s, she had become strongly anticommunist, was active in George Smathers's notorious red-baiting campaign for the U.S. Senate in 1950, and believed that the NAACP was a communist-front organization. In 1955, in a letter to the *Orlando Sentinel,* she criticized the recent *Brown* decision as an example of communist-inspired thinking because it implied that blacks could learn only when tethered to whites. Though Hurston's fears of communist infiltration and domination bordered on the obsessive, her criticism of *Brown* was also rooted in her cultural pride, and the conviction that liberal and left-wing attempts to help African Americans started from the premise that black families, institutions, and community life were badly flawed and needed massive intervention and transformation to be salvaged.

A fierce anticommunism also inspired George SCHUYLER, a one time colleague of Hurston during the Harlem Renaissance, who became the most prominent black conservative in the middle decades of the century. A journalist, satirical novelist, and longtime editorial writer for the *Pittsburgh Courier,* Schuyler was always an opponent of communism (though he went through an idiosyncratic radical phase in the 1930s), and by the 1940s had emerged as a determined anticommunist, the author of pamphlets such as *The Communist Conspiracy Against the Negroes.* Schuyler found that Cold War liberal organizations such as the Congress for Cultural Freedom were too liberal, and in the 1950s adopted a laissez-faire critique of the liberal state, similar to that of William F. Buckley, Jr. Like Hurston, Schuyler felt that white liberals' interest in African Americans was invariably condescending, and that attempts to legislate social attitudes were futile. (Schuyler's daughter, Philippa Duke SCHUYLER, was also active in anticommunist efforts in the Third World, and wrote several books on the subject before her death in a helicopter crash in South Vietnam in 1967.)

George Schuyler was active in organizations that tried to bring attention to communist participation in anticolonial movements. Like Yergan, Schuyler was active in the American Committee for Aid to Katanga Freedom Fighters in 1961 in the Congolese civil war, and later supported white minority regimes in Africa. Schuyler thought the CIVIL RIGHTS MOVEMENT had tarnished the achievements of the black middle class by focusing on black failures, and that civil rights efforts carried too far were in danger of causing a genocidal backlash. Of the era of civil rights activism, he wrote of "supposedly intelligent young Negroes . . . sprawling on Court House steps yammering spirituals and the slogan 'We Shall Overcome,' first popularized by the Castro forces."

Another leading black opponent of the civil rights movement was Joseph H. JACKSON, the longtime leader of the NATIONAL BAPTIST CONVENTION, U.S.A., INC., the largest black organization in the United States. Jackson's conservatism was more Washingtonian than anticommunist, and represented traditional black social conservatism. Jackson said of the sit-in movement, "they talk too much about racial integration and not enough about racial elevation," and later called Martin Luther KING, Jr., a "hoodlum" and a "crook." Though sentiments such as Schuyler's and Jackson's undoubtedly had a constituency among blacks, it was not until black and white conservatives accepted the achievements of King and the civil rights movement that black conservatism began to find a new intellectual and social base.

Black Conservatism Since the Civil Rights Movement

A new black conservatism first emerged out of internal disputes within the civil rights movement. One part of the movement, comprised of anti-communist, prolabor liberals such as A. Philip Randolph, Ralph Bunche, and Bayard RUSTIN were dismayed by militant black politics after 1965. They viewed calls for Black Power as separatist, ill-informed, and detrimental to the working alliance they had established with organized labor and the Democratic party. Still committed to a vigilant anti-communism, they remained supporters of President Johnson and the war in Vietnam. In later years they remained loyal to integrated unionism, supporting, for example, the United Federation of Teachers against black advocates of community control during the bitterly divisive New York City teachers' strike of 1969. Unlike earlier black conservatives, Rustin and Randolph were both prolabor, and wholeheartedly committed to the reforms of the New Deal and the achievement of the civil rights movement, and unlike later black conservatives, they were committed to massive support for the black urban poor. But as rightward-moving anticommunist liberals (sometimes labeled neoconservatives), Randolph and Rustin, like later black conservatives, were convinced that something had gone terribly wrong with the struggle for black freedom around 1965.

By the mid-1970s, the opposition to affirmative action would become, as Stephen Carter has argued, the main shibboleth in the division between black conservatives and liberals. The main argument of black conservatives held that the civil rights legislation of the 1960s mandated equality of opportunity, and that affirmative action was a step backward from a "color-blind" society. Other black conservative arguments against affirmative action held that it reinforced a notion of blacks as victims, and unfairly stigmatized black achievers as beneficiaries of extra assistance. The black argument against affirmative action gained its first widely recognized spokesmen in Thomas Sowell, whose *Race and Economics* (1975) and *Preferential Politics* (1980) received wide recognition, and was furthered by Shelby Steele, Stephen Carter, Glenn Loury, and Stanley Crouch, among others.

In time the argument against affirmative action was broadened by some black conservatives into a more general critique of what was often called the "civil rights establishment." This was fed by a growing sense among all blacks that the civil rights movement of the 1960s had not solved underlying problems of poverty in the urban ghetto, and that new freedoms made possible an ever greater differentiation between a growing black middle class and the lumpenproletariat of the "underclass." Progressives such as Jesse JACKSON tended to blame urban poverty primarily on government underfunding and the persistence of systemic discrimination. When black conservatives looked at the same problem, they saw individual and collective moral and cultural failings, and viewed inner-city blacks as complicit in their own poverty. Government programs addressing poverty were a failure, they concluded; African Americans had to help themselves.

During and since the 1980s a number of African Americans have attained recognition as conservative advocates of self-help, often strongly supporting black institutional and economic development. These include the eccentric nationalist and head of CORE Roy INNIS and the nationally syndicated talk-show host Tony Brown. An unusual "conversion" to conservatism in the late 1980s, which provoked much comment, was the emergence of former civil rights activist James MEREDITH as an aide to the extremely right-wing North Carolina senator Jesse Helmes. Colin POWELL, chairman of the Joint Chiefs of Staff under Presidents Bush and Clinton, though carefully avoiding domestic politics or even hinting at his party affiliation, was a striking example of the success possible to African Americans, and an exemplification of the traditional values of social conservatism.

Some scholars, such as Martin Kilson and Cornel West, have argued that recent black conservatism is inauthentic, without true roots in the black community, and that black conservatives have been promoted by their white counterparts in an effort to create a dialogue within the black community that does not really exist. Certainly black conservative candidates have not done particularly well among black voters. Running against white opponents, William Lucas won only 21 percent of the black vote in the Michigan gubernatorial election in 1985, and Allen Keyes garnered only 30 percent in his run for the senate from Maryland in 1988. There have been only two black Republican members of the House of Representatives since the end of World War II, both conservative, and both were elected from predominantly white districts, Gary Franks of Connecticut, first elected in 1990, and J. C. Watts, from Oklahoma, elected in 1994.

Undoubtedly the most prominent and controversial black conservative of the 1990s has been Clarence THOMAS, who has become a shibboleth in his own right. Thomas was appointed chair of the Equal Opportunity Employment Commission in 1983 by President Reagan, and his career was advanced by conservatives who were eager to demonstrate an alternative to the liberalism of civil rights leaders. Thomas was named a federal district court judge in 1990. In the fall of 1991 President Bush nominated Thomas for the U.S. Supreme Court to replace Thurgood MARSHALL. Thomas's controversial confirmation hearings, which often touched only tangentially on his politics, still managed to focus attention on black conservatism. Thomas argued that his views represented a natural evolution from the civil right movement, and looked toward an America in which race would no longer dominate its politics or its courts; however, many of his critics have felt that he dishonored the legacy of Thurgood Marshall.

The Republican victory in the 1994 congressional election is likely to heighten the debate on the role of blacks in the Republican party, and the appropriateness of conservatism for African Americans. Though conservatism remains a decidedly minority point of view among African Americans, its constituency is genuine, and in some ways the basic question has changed little since the time of Jupiter Hammon—how can blacks best prosper in a society dominated by whites? The conservative answer—working within existing institutions for personal and collective betterment—will likely always have its share of adherents.

REFERENCES

ANDREWS, WILLIAM L. "The Politics of African-American Ministerial Autobiography from Reconstruction to the 1920s." In Paul E. Johnson, ed. *African-American Christianity*. Berkeley, Calif., 1994.

BUCKLEY, WILLIAM F., JR., ed. *Did You Ever See a Dream Walking? American Conservative Thought in the Twentieth Century*. Indianapolis, Ind., 1970.

BUNI, ANDREW. *Robert L. Vann of the Pittsburgh Courier: Politics and Black Journalism*. Pittsburgh, Pa., 1974.

CARTER, STEPHEN L. *Reflections of an Affirmative Action Baby*. New York, 1991.

CROUCH, STANLEY. *Notes of a Hanging Judge: Essays and Reviews, 1979–1989*. New York, 1990.

CRUMMELL, ALEXANDER. *Destiny and Race: Selected Writings, 1840–1898*. Wilson J. Moses, ed., 1989.

DAVIS, DAVID BRION. "Reflections on Abolitionism and Ideological Hegemony." *American Historical Review* 92 (1987): 797–812.

FOX, STEPHEN R. *The Guardian of Boston: William Monroe Trotter*. New York, 1970.

GATEWOOD, WILLARD B. *Aristocrats of Color: The Black Elite, 1880–1920*. Bloomington, Ind., 1990.

GAVINS, RAYMOND. *The Perils and Prospects of Southern Leadership: Gordon Blaine Hancock, 1884–1970*. Durham, N.C., 1977.

HARLAN, LOUIS R. *Booker T. Washington: The Making of a Black Leader, 1856–1901*. New York, 1972.

———. *Booker T. Washington: The Wizard of Tuskegee, 1901–1915*. New York, 1983.

HEMENWAY, ROBERT E. *Zora Neale Hurston: A Literary Biography*. Urbana, Ill., 1980.

KAPLAN, SIDNEY, and EMMA NOGRADY KAPLAN. *The Black Presence in the Era of the American Revolution*. Amherst, Mass., 1989.

KILSON, MARTIN. "Anatomy of Black Conservatism." *Transition* 59 (1993): 4–18.

LITWACK, LEON, and AUGUST MEIER, eds. *Black Leaders of the Nineteenth Century*. Urbana, Ill., 1988.

LOGAN, RAYFORD W., ed. *What the Negro Wants*. Chapel Hill, N.C., 1944.

MCFEELY, WILLIAM. *Frederick Douglass*. New York, 1991.

MOSES, WILSON J. *Black Messiahs and Uncle Toms: Social and Literary Manipulations of a Religious Myth*. University Park, Pa., 1982.

PEASE, JANE H., and WILLIAM H. PEASE. *They Who Would Be Free: Blacks' Search for Freedom, 1830–1861*. Urbana, Ill., 1990.

PORTER, DOROTHY. *Early Negro Writing, 1760–1837*. Boston, 1971.

ROEDIGER, DAVID R. *The Wages of Whiteness: Race and the Making of the American Working Class*. London, 1991.

SCHUYLER, GEORGE S. *Black and Conservative: The Autobiography of George S. Schuyler*. New Rochelle, N.Y., 1966.

WALTER JOHN C. *The Harlem Fox: J. Raymond Jones and Tammany, 1928–1970*. Albany, N.Y., 1989.

WEST, CORNELL. *Race Matters*. New York, 1993.

WILSON, WILLIAM JUNIUS. *The Declining Significance of Race*. Chicago, 1980.

PETER EISENSTADT

Constitution (U.S.), Amendments to. See Fifteenth Amendment; Fourteenth Amendment; Thirteenth Amendment.

Contagious Diseases. See Diseases and Epidemics.

Conwell, Kathleen (March 18, 1942–September 1988). Kathleen Conwell was raised in New Jersey. Her father, Frank Conwell, was the principal of a high school and later elected the first African-American state assemblyman in New Jersey. Kathleen Conwell's skill as a speaker became apparent while she was in high school. Upon graduation from Skidmore College in Saratoga Springs, N.Y., with a degree in philosophy and religion, she joined the Student Nonviolent Coordinating Committee (SNCC) to help register black voters in the South.

As a graduate student at the Sorbonne in France, she became interested in telling stories through film. After completing her M.A. degree in 1966, she returned to the United States, working on the editorial and production staff of WNET in New York as she began her writing career. Her first short stories reflected experiences in SNCC, France, and the dilemmas of a young married woman. Shortly after the end of her marriage to Douglas Collins, she joined the faculty of City College at the City University of New York in 1974 as a professor of film history and screenwriting.

In 1980, she wrote the screenplay for an adaptation of a Henry Roth short story and also produced and directed her first film, *The Cruz Brothers and Mrs. Malloy,* about the struggle of three Puerto Rican brothers to survive in a small country town. The film won first prize at the Sinking Creek Film Festival and led to invitations to appear at the Berlin, Venice, Munich, and Montreal film festivals. Later it was optioned by the Learning Channel for its *Likely Stories* series.

In 1981, *In the Midnight Hour,* her full-length drama about a black family in turmoil at the beginning of the civil rights movement, was produced by the Richard Allen Center for Culture and Art. Her second play, *The Brothers,* opened at the American Place Theatre and was named one of the twelve outstanding plays of the 1982 season by the Theatre Communications Group. It earned Collins a grant in playwriting from the National Endowment for the Arts. Collins's second feature film, *Losing Ground* (1982), was a comedy about a black philosophy professor's quest for "ecstasy" free of the constraints of academia. It won first prize at Portugal's Figueroa da Foz International Film Festival and was broadcast on PBS.

Subsequent plays included *The Reading* (1984), a one-act play about the conflict between white and black women, commissioned by the American Place Theatre; *Begin the Beguine* (1985), a collection of one-act plays produced at the Richard Allen Center; *Only the Sky Is Free* (1985), about the first black aviator, Bessie Coleman; *While Older Men Speak* (1986), about two old friends who meet for dinner and try to unravel the past; and *Looking for Jane,* a full-length play about black and white sexuality as seen through the eyes of a white woman.

In 1987, she married Alfred E. Prettyman and completed her screenplay *Madame Flor.* Her novel *Lollie: A Suburban Tale* was completed in the spring of 1988, followed that summer by another screenplay, *Conversations with Julie,* about a mother and daughter coming to terms with separation. She died of cancer in September of that year.

REFERENCES

BROWN, JANET. *Taking Center Stage: Feminism in Contemporary U.S. Drama.* Metuchen, N.J. 1991.
KLOTMAN, PHYLLIS RAUCH, ed. *Screenplays of the African American Experience.* Bloomington, Ind. 1991
TIME-LIFE BOOKS, ed. *African Americans' Voices of Triumph: Creative Fire.* New York, 1994.
WILLIAMS, JOHN. "Re-Creating Their Media Image: Two Generations of Black Women Filmmakers." *Cineaste* 20, no. 3 (1994).

SERET SCOTT

Conwill, Houston (1947–), artist. Fusing backgrounds in spiritualism and art, Houston Conwill creates work with a social and political message. Born in Louisville, Ky., he initially studied to be a Catholic monk at St. Meinrad Seminary in St. Meinrad, Ind. His interest in becoming an artist, however, led him after one year of study there to Howard University (1970–1973) and the University of Southern California, Los Angeles (1974–1976); both institutions have since bestowed on Conwill distinguished alumnus awards. In 1980 he moved to New York, where he lives with his wife, Kinshasha Holman Conwill.

Throughout his career Conwill has aimed to tell the story of his heritage through images and ideas from his own culture and from an African-American perspective. Abandoning earlier paintings and prints influenced by the ritualistic subjects of Romare BEARDEN and the shaped canvases of his teacher Sam GILLIAM, in 1975 he began to make ritual objects. Cast-latex juju bags embossed with symbolic emblems were assembled with other major objects into art environments that also served as ceremonial spaces for his performances, the first of which was *JuJu Funk* (1975). These were followed by petrigraphs—scroll-shaped objects with pictographic cultural references placed in niches.

In his major earthwork, *Passages: Earth/Space H-3* (1980; Nexus Contemporary Art Center, Atlanta), Conwill constructed the niches in an underground chamber. This initiated an architectural direction for his work that continued in his collaborations. Since 1984 he has made cosmograms with his sister, the poet Estella Conwill Majozo, and the architect Joseph De Pace. Cosmograms are floor diagrams of black history. The first of these were the "Cakewalk" series, which includes such important projects as *The New Cakewalk* (1988; High Museum of Art, Atlanta) and *The New Cakewalk Humanifesto: A Cultural Libation* (1989; Museum of Modern Art, New York). A blend of history, folklore, dance, sermon, and polit-

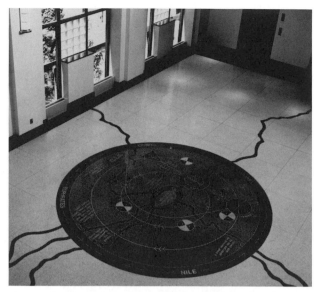

Rivers, by Houston Conwill, located in the floor of the Langston Hughes Auditorium, Schomburg Center for Research in Black Culture, New York City. (© Sherman Bryce)

ical manifesto, these multilayered installations continued Conwill's mix of African and Western image as well as spiritual and secular texts.

As temporary, site-specific installations, such as *Markings on the Sand* (1989; Hirshhorn Museum and Sculpture Garden, Washington, D.C.), these works derived their subject from the place where they were found. Some, also, like the "Cakewalk" series, owed their form in part to that of a dance: *The New Charleston* (1991; Spoleto Festival U.S.A., Charleston, S.C.) dealt with the Middle Passage as told through the journey of captured Africans to Charleston Harbor; *The New Merengue* (1992; Brooklyn Museum) was about the centuries-old journey of Brooklyn's Caribbean and African-American population.

Conwill, Majozo, and De Pace have been commissioned to create permanent public works, including *Rivers* (1990; Schomburg Center for Research in Black Culture, New York), *Revelations* (1991; Martin Luther King, Jr., Memorial, San Francisco), and *DuSable's Journey* (1991; Harold Washington Library Center, Chicago).

REFERENCES

JACOB, MARY JANE. "Houston Conwill, Estella Conwill Majozo, and Joseph De Pace." In *Places with a Past: New Site-Specific Art at Charleston's Spoleto Festival.* New York, 1991, pp. 146–151.

WILSON, JUDITH. "Creating a Necessary Space: The Art of Houston Conwill, 1975–1983." *International Review of African American Art* 6, no. 1 (1984): 50–62.

MARY JANE JACOB

Conyers, John, Jr. (May 16, 1929–), congressman. John Conyers, Jr., was born in Detroit to John and Lucille Conyers. He graduated from Wayne State University (B.A., 1957) and Wayne State Law School (J.D., 1958). From December 1958 to May 1961, he served as a legislative assistant to Michigan Rep. John D. Dingell. During these years, he was also a senior partner in the law firm of Conyers, Bell & Townsend. In October 1961, Conyers was appointed by Gov. John B. Swainson to be Referee for the Workman's Compensation Department. When redistricting created a second black-majority congressional district in Detroit in 1964, Conyers entered the race. Running on a platform of "Equality, Jobs, and Peace," he won his first election by a mere 108 votes and became the second black to serve as congressman from Michigan (he followed Democrat Charles C. DIGGS, Jr., from the Thirteenth District, who had been elected in 1954). In subsequent years, Conyers gained reelection by ever increasing margins, winning his fifteenth term, in 1992, with 84 percent of the vote.

In his long tenure as representative of Michigan's First District, and as a founding member of the Congressional Black Caucus (CBC), Conyers has worked to promote social welfare and civil rights causes. Soon after his arrival in Washington, he supported President Lyndon Johnson's Medicare program and the VOTING RIGHTS ACT (1965). Just four days after the assassination of the Rev. Dr. Martin Luther KING, Jr., in April 1968, Conyers submitted a bill to create a national holiday on the birthday of the slain civil rights leader. Getting federal approval for the holiday proved to be an arduous task; fifteen years passed before President Ronald Reagan signed the bill into law on November 22, 1983. In the interim, Conyers had convinced a number of mayors and governors throughout the country to declare January 15 a local or state holiday.

While Conyers has advocated independent black political movements, he has avoided aligning himself with black separatists. At the National Black Political Convention held in Gary, Ind., in March 1972, Conyers was critical of those who advocated forming an independent black political party, saying, "I don't think it is feasible to go outside the two-party system. I don't know how many of us blacks could be elected without white support."

During the 1980s, Conyers was often an opponent of the administrations of Ronald Reagan and George Bush. He spoke out against Bush's efforts to keep Haitian refugees from entering the United States in 1992, and opposed the appointment of conservative African American Clarence THOMAS to the Supreme Court. While a lifelong Democrat, Conyer was also at times critical of President Jimmy Carter, as he was when Carter dismissed U.N. Ambassador Andrew YOUNG. In fact, relations between Carter—who had also failed to support the King holiday bill—and Conyers grew so strained that the congressman launched a "dump Jimmy Carter for President" campaign on the eve of the 1980 primaries.

Conyers has served as chairman of the Government Operations Committee, and has been a senior member of the Judiciary Committee. He has also served on the House Small Business Committee and the Speaker's Task Force on Minority Set-Asides.

REFERENCE

EHRENHALT, ALAN, ed. *Politics in America: Members of Congress in Washington and at Home.* Washington, D.C., 1984.

CHRISTINE A. LUNARDINI

Cook, Charles "Cookie"

Cook, Charles "Cookie" (1917–August 8, 1991), tap dancer. Born in Chicago and raised in Detroit, Cook grew up in a boardinghouse for black performers run by his mother, which was located next door to the Copeaum Theatre. Infatuated with the theater from an early age, Cook performed with "Garbage and His Two Cans" and toured with Sarah Venable's "Mammy and Her Picks," where he met his performing partner, Ernest Brown. In 1930 they formed Cook & Brown, a slapstick comedy act that combined acrobatic stunts with humor and eccentric dancing.

In their act, the six-foot-tall Cook would attempt to discipline the outbursts of the diminutive four-foot-ten Brown; when knocked down, Brown slid the full length of the stage and bounced up in a reverse split, ready for more. After appearing in 1930 with Ben Bernie's orchestra at the College Inn in Chicago, they opened at the COTTON CLUB in New York City in 1934, and quickly became highly popular comic performers.

For over forty years, Cook & Brown headlined in vaudeville, and played in venues all over the country with Duke ELLINGTON, Count BASIE, Lena HORNE, and Bill ROBINSON. On Broadway in *Kiss Me Kate* (1948), they stopped the show with their routine "Too Darn Hot." Cook's style later evolved toward less flashy but more intricate floor work. A founding member in 1949 of the Copasetics, a tap dance fraternity, Cook later appeared at the Newport Jazz Festival, the Brooklyn Academy of Music, the Jacob's Pillow Dance Festival, and the 1984 Summer Olympic Games, and in the film *The Cotton Club* (1984). During the 1970s and the '80s, Cook remained active as a dance teacher in New York City, where he died at the age of seventy-seven. The most accessible of

tap masters, he was unselfish in passing on the routines he so wanted to preserve.

REFERENCES

GOLDBERG, JANE. "Charles 'Cookie' Cook." *Village Voice,* August 27, 1991.
GOLDBETTER, SUSAN. "In Memoriam." *International Tap Association Newsletter* 2, no. 4 (November–December 1991).
STEARNS, MARSHALL. "Frontiers of Humor: American Vernacular Dance." *Southern Folklore Quarterly* 30, no. 3 (September 1966): 227–235.

CONSTANCE VALIS HILL

Cook, Mercer

Cook, Mercer (March 30, 1903–October 4, 1987), educator and ambassador. The son of composer Will Marion COOK and singer Abbie Mitchell, Mercer Cook was born in Washington, D.C., and given the full name of Will Mercer Cook. He received his B.A. from Amherst College in 1925, a diploma from the University of Paris in 1926, and an M.A. and Ph.D. from Brown University in 1931 and 1936. He served as assistant professor at Howard University from 1927 until 1936; he then joined the faculty at Atlanta University as a professor of French, where he taught for seven years. From 1943 to 1945 Cook was supervisor of English at the University of Haiti in Port-au-Prince, after which he returned to Howard University, where he taught until 1960. During these years he wrote and edited books in English and French, most prominently *Le Noir* (1934), *Portraits americains* (1939), and *Five French Negro Authors* (1943). He also translated Léopold Senghor's *African*

Mercer Cook (shown here in 1978), professor of Romance languages at Howard University and U.S. ambassador to the Republic of Niger and the Republic of Senegal, is the translator of several African authors, including Leopold Sédar Senghor and Cheik Anta Diop. (© Leandre Jackson)

Socialism (1959), Mamadou Dia's *The African Nations and World Solidarity* (1961), and Cheikh A. Diop's *The African Origins of Civilization* (1974).

In 1961 President John F. Kennedy appointed Cook ambassador to the Republic of Niger, a position he held for three years. From 1964 to 1966, he was the envoy to Senegal and Gambia. Cook also occupied leadership positions in the American Society for African Culture and the Congress of Cultural Freedom. In 1963 he represented the United States as alternate delegate to the United Nations General Assembly.

Cook returned to Howard University in 1966 to head its department of romance languages. In 1969, he coauthored with Stephen Henderson *The Militant Black Writer in Africa and the United States*. The following year he retired from active teaching. Cook died of pneumonia in Washington, D.C. on October 4, 1987.

REFERENCES

Low, Augustus W., and Virgil A. Cliff, eds. *Encyclopedia of Black America*. New York, 1981.

Rush, Theresa Gunnels. *Black American Writers Past and Present: A Biographical and Bibliographical Dictionary*. Metuchen, N.J., 1975.

Shockley, Ann Allen. *Living Black American Authors: A Biographical Directory*. New York, 1973.

STEVEN J. LESLIE

Cook, Will Marion (January 27, 1869–July 19, 1944), composer and arranger. Will Cook was born in Washington, D.C., the son of John Cook, the treasurer of Howard University. In 1882 he went to Oberlin College to study violin. He returned to Washington in 1885 to give his first recitals, one of which was sponsored by Frederick DOUGLASS. Later that year Cook left for Berlin to study with Joseph Joachim, the greatest violinist of the era. On returning to the United States in 1890, Cook began a career as a concert violinist, and five years later he performed at Carnegie Hall.

Cook then moved to New York to attend the National Conservatory of Music, studying with Antonín Dvořák. However, Cook's classical career was frustrated by racial discrimination. He turned to black musical comedies, working with singer Bob Cole at the All-Star Stock Company. In 1898 Cook collaborated with Paul Laurence DUNBAR on the ragtime operetta *Clorindy; or, The Origin of the Cakewalk,* the first black musical comedy to play at a major Broadway theater. The following year Cook married soprano Abbie Mitchell who often appeared in his shows. Cook again worked with Dunbar on *Jes' Lak White Fo'ks* (1899) and *The Cannibal King* (1901). During the next decade many of Cook's musicals featured the vaudeville team of Bert Williams and George Walker. These shows include *The Sons of Ham* (1900) and *In Dahomey* (1903). In 1904 Cook wrote the music for *The Southerners,*the first Broadway show with an interracial cast. Williams and Walker's *In Abyssinia* came in 1906, followed in 1908 by *In Bandanna Land*. In that year Cook also separated from Mitchell, although they continued to work together. Cook also gained renown for his songs, including "Who Dat Say Chicken" (1902), "Darktown Is Out Tonight" (1902) and "Bon Bon Buddy" (1908), which were among the first songs recorded by the Victor Talking Machine Co. Cook was also active as conductor of the Nashville Students, later known as the Memphis Students, a syncopated orchestra and vaudeville troupe that toured Europe in 1905, and one of the first black ragtime groups to perform for whites in New York. In addition, Cook composed "Swing Along," "Exhortation," and "Rain Song" for James Reese EUROPE's Clef Club Orchestra's Carnegie Hall concert (1912), where he played violin. In 1913 Cook composed music for *The Traitor,* and two years later he helped write *Darkeydom*.

Also in the early teens, Cook organized the New York Syncopated Orchestra, which toured the United States with a varied repertory of classical music and early jazz. In 1918 he took the group, then known as the Southern Syncopated Orchestra, on tour in the United States and Europe, including a command performance in 1919 for King George V of Britain. The ensemble included clarinetist Sidney BECHET, trumpeter Arthur Briggs, drummer Bennie Peyton, Abbie MITCHELL, and conductor and composer Will Tyers. The ensemble played a diverse repertory, including classical waltzes, marches, blues, and spirituals, as well as Cook's compositions "Rain Song" and "Exhortation," and was largely responsible for the initial introduction of early jazz to European audiences. The group also made Cook a figure of signal importance in both jazz and black musical theater, responsible for translating ragtime music and cakewalk dancing to the popular stage.

After the orchestra disbanded, Cook returned to the United States in 1922, settling in New York. There he organized a new Clef Club Orchestra, which included singer Paul ROBESON. During the 1920s he served as a mentor to Duke ELLINGTON and continued to write for the stage, including *Runnin' Wild* (1923), *I'm Coming Virginia* (1927), *Troubled in Mind* (1929), *Swing Along* (1929), with Will Vodery, and *St. Louis Woman* (1929). Cook, who was the father of Mercer Cook, died of cancer in New York in 1944.

REFERENCES

CARTER, MARVA GRIFFIN. *The Life and Music of Will Marion Cook.* Ph.D. diss., University of Illinois, 1988.
SOUTHERN, EILEEN. *The Music of Black Americans: A History.* New York, 1971.

MARVA GRIFFIN CARTER

Cooke, Lloyd M. (June 7, 1916–), chemist. Lloyd M. Cooke was born in LaSalle, Ill. He received a B.S. from the University of Wisconsin in 1937. At the advice of his father, who told him his was a hopeless profession for an American black, Cooke abandoned aeronautical engineering and earned a Ph.D. in organic chemistry from McGill University in 1941. His research in carbohydrate chemistry focused on the structure of lignin.

After lecturing at McGill for one academic year, in 1942, Cooke took a job with the Corn Products Refining Company in Argo, Ill. In 1946, he became a group leader with the Visking Corporation, which was acquired by Union Carbide in 1956. Cooke served Union Carbide in many capacities, most notably as the company's New York City Director of Urban Affairs (1970–1978). In the 1970s, Cooke was also Union Carbide's Corporate Director of University Relations (1973–1976) and its Corporate Director of Community Affairs (1976–1977).

In addition to his work in the private sector, Cooke served two terms as a member of the National Science Board (1970–1982). He also held various posts within the American Chemical Society, and was responsible for the organization and preparation of its book, *Cleaning Our Environment—The Chemical Basis for Action,* which was intended for lay readers in environmental administration, but became widely used in university curricula. Between 1972 and 1979 he was a consultant to the U.S. Congress's Office of Technical Assessment. He was vice chairman of the Economic Development Council of New York from 1978 to 1981, and from 1981 to 1983 he served as president of the National Action Council on Minorities in Engineering. He also served as a trustee of the Chicago Chemical Library Foundation and the McCormick Theological Seminary.

REFERENCES

BENDER, MARYLIN. "A Solver of Problems: Cooke Studies Urban Crises for Carbide." *New York Times,* April 25, 1971, Sec. 3, p. 7.
SAMMONS, VIVIAN OVELTON. *Blacks in Science and Medicine.* New York, 1990.

PETER SCHILLING

Cooke, Samuel "Sam" (January 22, 1935–December 11, 1964), singer and songwriter. The son of a Baptist minister, Cooke began his musical career singing GOSPEL with his seven brothers. In 1950, he replaced R. H. Harris, an influential gospel singer, as lead tenor of the Soul Stirrers, the leading male group in the field; he refined Harris's style, adding a smoother falsetto and purifying the tone, and soon became one of the most important figures in gospel, touring and recording with the group for more than five years. In 1956 Cooke turned to secular music and made a series of pop recordings for Keen Records; "You Send Me" (1957), his first hit, sold more than two million copies worldwide. "You Send Me" was still marked by his gospel style, as were the successful singles that followed, including "I Love You for Sentimental Reasons," "Everybody Likes to Cha Cha Cha," "Only Sixteen," and "Win Your Love for Me." In 1960 Cooke signed with RCA Records, where he wrote songs that, though still popular, were slightly closer to the RHYTHM AND BLUES tradition (among them "Wonderful World," "Chain Gang," "Sad Mood," "Having a Party," "Bring It on Home to Me," "Another Saturday Night," and "Twistin' the Night Away"). In addition to writing and performing, Cooke also produced records for his Star label and ran Kags Music, a publishing company.

Cooke was shot to death on December 11, 1964, at a motel in Hollywood by a white woman who claimed he had tried to attack her; his funeral was one of the largest in Chicago's history, attended by fans of both his gospel and his pop music. His final recording, "A Change Is Gonna Come," is a successful blend of gospel and pop styles, an indication of the growing importance of social themes and black awareness in popular music. Cooke's vocal style and his songwriting have exerted considerable influence on numerous performers, among them Marvin GAYE, Otis REDDING, Curtis MAYFIELD, and Rod Stewart.

ROBERT W. STEPHENS

Cooper, Anna Julia Haywood (August 10, 1858–February 27, 1964), educator and writer. Anna Julia Haywood was born a slave in Raleigh, N.C. While still a child, she was hired out as a nursemaid and developed a love for books and learning. In 1867 she entered St. Augustine's Normal and Collegiate Institute in Raleigh, where she soon began to tutor and teach other students. While there, she met George A. C. Cooper, a teacher of Greek. The couple married in 1877, but George Cooper died two years later.

In the fall of 1881, Anna Cooper entered Oberlin College. She received a B.A. in 1884 and an M.A. three years later. She taught for a short while at Wilberforce College in Ohio and at St. Augustine's in Raleigh before going to the M Street (now Paul Laurence Dunbar) High School in Washington, D.C., in 1887. In 1902 Cooper became principal of M Street High School.

Cooper believed that African Americans needed to pursue not only industrial training, but academic education as well. During her tenure as head of M Street, she successfully expanded college prep courses, attracted academically oriented black students, and increased the proportion of M Street graduates attending Ivy League schools. Cooper's commitment to classical studies for African Americans clashed with Booker T. WASHINGTON's philosophies, which dominated black higher education at the time. Her unconventional approach resulted in charges of misconduct and insubordination. Because of the charges leveled against her, the school board decided not to reappoint

A woman of immense accomplishments over the course of her long life, educator Anna Julia Cooper is perhaps best remembered for her treatise *A Voice from the South,* one of the earliest works of black feminism. (Anna J. Cooper Papers, Moorland-Spingarn Research Center, Howard University)

her as principal in 1906. Cooper then taught for four years at Lincoln University in Missouri before returning to M Street to teach Latin.

At the age of fifty-three, Cooper began doing graduate work. She studied at La Guilde Internationale, Paris (1911–1912) and at Columbia University (1913–1916), working toward her Ph.D., which she received from the Sorbonne in Paris in 1925. Her dissertation, *L'attitude de la France à l'égard de l'esclavage pendant la révolution* (translated as "The Attitude of France Toward Slavery During the Revolution") was published in 1925.

Much of the rest of Cooper's career revolved around Frelinghuysen University in Washington, D.C., an institution of adult education offering evening classes in academic, religious, and trade programs. She served as president of Frelinghuysen from 1930 to 1940. Because of financial difficulties, the university lost its charter in 1937, becoming the Frelinghuysen Group of Schools for Colored Working People, and Cooper became its registrar. Cooper continued to be centrally involved with the school, offering her home for classes and meetings, when necessary.

Throughout her career, Cooper was a staunch defender of African-American rights and a relentless proponent of education for females. She believed that race and sex were inseparable and that both racism and sexism affected the social status of black women. She also argued that the struggles of all oppressed people were "indissolubly linked" together. In her book *A Voice from the South,* published in 1892, she asserted that African-American women were a distinct political and social force, and that they could act as spokespersons for their race and as advocates for women.

Cooper believed that the key to achieving social equality for women was education, and she fought for women's collective right to higher education. During her early years at St. Augustine, she protested the exclusion of females from courses for ministerial studies, and argued that boys and girls should have equal access to education. She believed that education would widen women's horizons and make them less dependent on marriage and love. She was one of the earliest advocates for women's rights and one of the most tenacious supporters of women's suffrage. Cooper was also the only woman elected to the American Negro Academy, was a participant in the 1900 Pan African Conference, and was elected to its executive committee.

Although Cooper never had children of her own, she adopted and raised five great-nieces and nephews. The death in 1939 of her niece and namesake, Annie Cooper Haywood Beckwith, who had lived with her since 1915, when she was six months old, devastated Cooper. Shortly after Beckwith's death in 1939, Cooper's public activity diminished. Nevertheless, she continued to write and work at home. She was a prolific writer, publishing on a wide variety of subjects, such as *Le Pélerinage de Charlemagne* (*Charlemagne's Pilgrimage*) (1925), *Equality of Race and the Democratic Movement* (1945), *The Life and Writings of the Grimké Family* (1951), and essays on "College Extension for Working People" and "Modern Education." Cooper died in her sleep in 1964 at the age of 105.

REFERENCES

COOPER, ANNA J. *A Voice from the South by a Black Woman of the South.* New York, 1969.
GABEL, LEONA G. *From Slavery to the Sorbonne and Beyond: The Life and Writings of Anna J. Cooper.* Northampton, Mass., 1982.
HUTCHINSON, LOUISE DANIEL. *Anna J. Cooper, A Voice from the South.* Washington, D.C., 1982.

PAM NADASEN

Cooper, Charles "Chuck" (September 29, 1926–February 5, 1984), basketball player and government official. The Boston Celtics broke the National Basketball Association's color line when they selected Chuck Cooper as their second-round draft pick on April 25, 1950. Though Cooper hesitated to accept acclaim as a pioneer in sport, arguing that "any black coming after Jackie [ROBINSON], in any sport, had it easy compared to the turmoil he lived through," the tenacious defender "had to go through hell," according to his coach, Red Auerbach.

The son of Daniel Cooper, a postmaster, and Emma Cooper, Chuck played basketball at Westinghouse High School in his native Pittsburgh and attended all-black West Virginia State for a year before entering the Navy during World War II. The 6'5", 215-pound Cooper then attended Duquesne University, where he starred as one of college basketball's first black All-Americans.

After graduation from Duquesne, Cooper played six years in the NBA, including four with the Celtics, which he led in rebounding. Along with fellow rookie and roommate Bob Cousy, Cooper revitalized a mediocre Boston team. He then played a season each for the Milwaukee/St. Louis Hawks and the Fort Wayne Pistons, before finishing his basketball career outside the NBA with the Harlem Magicians. Cooper later earned a Master of Social Work degree from the University of Minnesota, served on Pittsburgh's school board, and became the city's first black department head as director of parks and rec-

reation. He also worked as supervisor of Pittsburgh National Bank's affirmative action program. Bob Cousy remembered Cooper as a "man of class, intelligence, and sensitivity," on and off the court.

REFERENCE

ASHE, ARTHUR R., JR. *A Hard Road to Glory: A History of the African-American Athlete Since 1946.* New York, 1988.

ROB RUCK

Cooper, Ralph (c. 1910–August 4, 1992), master of ceremonies, actor, and dancer. Ralph Cooper was born in New York City, the fourth child of Solomon Cooper, a coachman, and his wife. Cooper attended public school in New York and enrolled in college at New York University (NYU). He left NYU after one semester to pursue a career as a dancer.

With Eddie RECTOR, Cooper formed the dance team Rector and Cooper. The duo performed at the COTTON CLUB in Manhattan and the Granada Theatre in Chicago in the late 1920s. In the early 1930s Cooper returned to New York City from Chicago and assembled a band, Ralph Cooper and His Kongo Knights. Cooper played saxophone, sang, and danced with the band, which performed at such venues as the Harlem Opera House. In April of 1933 he became master of ceremonies at the Lafayette Theatre, where he initiated the show "Wednesday Night Auditions," a weekly amateur night. On January 26, 1934, Cooper left the Lafayette Theatre to host the inaugural show at the rival APOLLO THEATER.

His "Wednesday Night Auditions" became "Wednesday Amateur Night," a popular weekly talent contest. In 1935 the show began broadcasting live on New York's WMCA radio. Cooper served as talent scout, coordinator, and host for the Apollo, providing a polished and soothing presence for the rambunctious crowd. The amateur show was a harsh testing ground, and performers were often booed by the audience. If crowd reaction to a performer was sufficiently vehement, the "executioner," a jesterlike character, escorted the performer offstage. A successful performance proved the launching ground for the career of many aspiring musicians, including Ella FITZGERALD, Sarah VAUGHAN, and Pearl BAILEY.

Cooper took a hiatus from the Apollo beginning in the mid-1930s to work in Hollywood, choreographing the film *Poor Little Rich Girl* (1936), which starred Shirley Temple. As an aspiring actor, he did not find any film roles to his liking and consequently formed an independent film production company, Million Dollar Productions, with a group of friends. Cooper wrote, produced, and starred in many of its films, most of which were moderate successes. One, *The Duke Is Tops* (1938), featured Lena HORNE as Cooper's costar in her first film role.

Cooper returned to New York in the early 1940s and resumed his role as host of "Amateur Night at the Apollo." During that time he booked and managed musical acts, and hosted a radio show from the Palm Club on the now-defunct New York City station WOV.

At the end of the 1940s Cooper reunited for a short time with his old partner Eddie Rector before becoming involved in local politics. In addition to continuing his work at the Apollo, he eventually served as a field representative for the State Division of Human Rights in 1967, as well as appearing at political rallies and fund-raisers. When the Apollo closed in the mid-1970s, Cooper increased his time at WOV, working as a disc jockey and radio show host. In the early 1980s, when the Apollo reopened, he resumed his role as master of ceremonies.

In 1990 Cooper cowrote (with Steve Dougherty) *Amateur Night at the Apollo,* a history of his career in the entertainment business. He served as the host of "Amateur Night at the Apollo" until shortly before his death from cancer in his Harlem home.

REFERENCES

COOPER, RALPH, with Steve Dougherty. *Amateur Night at the Apollo.* New York, 1990.

FOX, TED. *Showtime at the Apollo.* New York, 1983.

SUSAN MCINTOSH

Copasetics, The. The Copasetics is a dance fraternity of mostly African-American tap dancers established in 1949 in memory of Bill "Bojangles" ROBINSON. The name of the club is taken from Robinson's famous catchphrase, "Everything's copasetic" (i.e., fine or tip-top), which has been incorporated into American dictionaries as a legitimate word. This group was founded after Robinson's death by Charles "Cookie" COOK. Leroy Myers, Luther Preston, musician Billy STRAYHORN, and James Walker. Early members of the Copasetics included Elmer "Youngblood" Waters, Charles "Honi" COLES, and Charles "Cholly" ATKINS. All of these men were well-known performers during the golden years of tap in the 1920s and 1930s.

In the mid-1950s, when tap dance went into decline with the demise of vaudeville and tap's loss of

The Copasetics (from left to right) Charles C. Cook, Charles "Babba" Gaines, Henry "Baby" Phace Roberts, Honi Coles, Louis Simms Carpenter, Buster Brown. (© George West)

appeal on Broadway and in film, and the subsequent popularity of rock and roll and pop music, these tappers were forced into early retirement. With the re-emerging popularity of tap in the 1970s and especially in the 1980s, tap veterans of the Copasetics were suddenly in demand as teachers and performers throughout the United States and Europe, and the club started performing as a group. As a result of the Copasetics' excellence in performing and technical skills, future tappers had standards by which to define what tap had been and to set foundations for tap's future. This group was the living repository of tap history, and from their ranks, most of the teachers of the next generation would come.

Members of the Copasetics include Louis Simms Carpenter, Leon COLLINS, Harold Cromer, Steve Condos, James "Stumpy" Cross, Billy Ekstein, Albert "Gip" Gibson, Norman Gillian, Francis Goldberg, Frank Goldberg, Milton and Tippy Larkin, Jan Micken, Pete NUGENT, Charles Pendleton, Henry "Baby" Phace Roberts, Timmy Rogers, and Charles "Chazz" Young.

CONSTANCE VALIS HILL

Coppin, Frances "Fanny" Jackson

Coppin, Frances "Fanny" Jackson (1837–1913), educator. Fanny Jackson Coppin was born a slave in Washington, D.C. When she was approximately twelve years old, her freedom was bought for $125 by her aunt Sarah Orr Clark, who saved the purchase price from her $6-a-month salary. Coppin went to live with another aunt in Newport, R.I., but felt she was a strain on her relative's limited resources. At the age of fourteen, she went to live as a domestic servant with a white couple. She used her salary to pay for a private tutor and piano lessons. In 1859 she entered the Rhode Island State Normal School in Bristol. From 1860 to 1865 she attended Oberlin College, earning a B.A., and was named class poet at graduation. While at the college, Coppin had sixteen private music students, and established an evening adult-education class for freed blacks, which she taught voluntarily four nights a week. The publicity she received for this class prompted Oberlin to name her a student teacher for preparatory classes. She was the first African-American student named to this position.

In 1865, Coppin became principal of the girls' division of the Institute for Colored Youth in Philadelphia (later known as Cheyney State College). The institute had been founded in 1837 by the Society of Friends to counter anti-abolitionist claims that blacks were incapable of acquiring a classical education. In 1869, Coppin was named principal of the entire institute, becoming the first black American female to head an institution of higher learning.

In 1889, the institute opened an industrial department, for which Coppin had vigorously campaigned, wanting to train black men and women in the technical skills and trades from which they were often excluded by trade unions. In her 1913 autobiography, *Reminiscences of School Life, and Hints on Teaching,* she wrote, "In Philadelphia, the only place at the time where a colored boy could learn a trade, was in the House of Refuge, or the Penitentiary!"

Coppin actively campaigned to earn women the right to vote. She wrote a column for the *Christian Recorder,* the newspaper of the African Methodist Episcopal Church. After her retirement in 1902, she traveled with her husband, an AME minister, as a missionary to South Africa. Coppin State College in Baltimore is named in her honor.

REFERENCES

COPPIN, FANNY JACKSON. *Reminiscences of School Life, and Hints on Teaching.* Philadelphia, 1913.

PERKINS, LINDA M. *Fanny Jackson Coppin and the Institute for Colored Youth, 1865–1902.* New York, 1987.

JUALYNNE DODSON

Coppin, Levi Jenkins

Coppin, Levi Jenkins (December 24, 1848–June 25, 1924), bishop. A native of Fredrickstown, Md., Levi Jenkins Coppin spent his childhood in Baltimore and in Wilmington, Del. It took Coppin only a short time to rise in the AFRICAN METHODIST EPISCOPAL (AME) Church after receiving his license to preach in 1876. Twelve years later, the denomination chose him as editor of its major publication, the *AME Church Review,* a post he held until 1888, when he ran unsuccessfully for the bishopric. He then returned to Philadelphia, where he had previously resided, to serve as pastor of the historic Bethel Church.

Coppin became a bishop in the AME Church in 1900. From 1990 to 1904, he served in South Africa, where he worked to spread the influence of the denomination in that area and in Ethiopia. Coppin, a devoted Mason, also established the Masonic Lodge of Capetown, which had an affiliation with the Philadelphia Jurisdiction of the Prince Hall Masons. After his return to the United States, he served most of his remaining years in the South.

Coppin was a moderately conservative theologian on the issue of race. Although he counseled patience, hard work, and thrift, he did hold membership in social protest groups such as the Afro-American Council and the National Association for the Advancement of Colored People. Coppin is remembered best for the influence he had upon the church as editor of the *Review* and for his work in Africa.

REFERENCE

WRIGHT, RICHARD R. *The Bishops of the African Methodist Episcopal Church.* Nashville, 1963.

JIMMIE LEWIS FRANKLIN

CORE. *See* Congress of Racial Equality.

Cornely, Paul Bertau (March 9, 1906–), physician and educator. Paul Cornely was born in Pointe-à-Pitre, Guadeloupe, the son of Eleodore and Adrienne Mellon Cornely. After receiving early schooling in Santurce, Puerto Rico, he migrated with his family to the United States in 1920. He attended schools in New York City and Detroit before entering the College of the City of Detroit in 1924. A transfer student to the University of Michigan, he received an A.B. (1928) and an M.D. (1931). In 1934, he became the first African American to earn a doctorate in public health, also at Michigan.

Cornely interned at Lincoln Hospital in Durham, N.C. (1931–1932), and joined the faculty of HOWARD UNIVERSITY in 1934, serving until his retirement in 1973. At Howard, he helped develop programs in preventive medicine, public health, and physical medicine and rehabilitation. Cornely was one of the first to use scientific survey techniques to assess the status of the black health professional in America. In 1951, he published a seminal study demonstrating that with a comparable or even heavier patient load, the average black physician's income was 25 percent to 30 percent lower than that of the average white physician.

Cornely produced numerous studies on the distribution and supply of health personnel and on access to health services among minorities and the economically disadvantaged. He was medical director of FREEDMEN'S HOSPITAL (1947–1958) and a consultant to the NATIONAL URBAN LEAGUE (1944–1947). A member (1947–1967) of the board of directors of Physicians' Forum, which advocated progressive health-care reform in the United States, he served as the group's president in 1954. He became the first black president of the American Public Health Association in November 1969.

REFERENCE

CORNELY, PAUL B. "The Economics of Medical Practice and the Negro Physician." *Journal of the National Medical Association* 43 (March 1951): 84–92.

PHILIP N. ALEXANDER

Cornish, Samuel Eli (1795–November 6, 1858), abolitionist and newspaper editor. Born of free parents in Sussex County, Del., Samuel E. Cornish was raised in Philadelphia and New York City, and graduated from the Free African School in Philadelphia. Shortly thereafter he began training for the ministry under John Gloucester, pastor of the First African Church, Presbyterian, in Philadelphia. Licensed to preach as a Presbyterian minister in 1819, Cornish spent six months serving as a missionary to slaves on Maryland's Eastern Shore before returning to New York to organize the New Demeter Street Presbyterian Church. He was ordained in 1822 and continued there until 1828. Throughout his life Cornish remained involved in religious activities, working as a preacher and missionary to African Americans in New York, Philadelphia, and Newark, N.J.; in 1845 or 1846 he organized Emmanuel Church in New York City, remaining as its pastor until 1847.

Beyond his role as a clergyman, Cornish was noted as a journalist. His most significant contribution was the founding of FREEDOM'S JOURNAL, the first African-American newspaper in the United States. Cornish began the weekly journal in New York on March 16, 1827, serving as senior editor while another young African American, John B. RUSSWURM, held the position of junior editor. As fathers of the African-American press, the two men stated in their first editorial that "we wish to plead our own cause. Too long others have spoken for us." Under Cornish's control, *Freedom's Journal* became a popular protest vehicle and an instrument for promoting racial pride, as well as an advocate of education and emancipation.

Cornish resigned as editor of the *Journal* in September 1827 and became an agent for the New York Free African schools, but under Russwurm's editorship the paper declined. In 1829 Cornish revived it, changing the name to *The Rights of All*, and sustained publication for one year. Cornish went on to serve in

A pioneer African-American journalist and New York City Presbyterian minister, Samuel Cornish founded the first African-American newspaper, *Freedom's Journal*. Cornish also helped to establish the American and Foreign Anti-Slavery Society and was active in numerous antebellum abolitionist and moral reform organizations. (Photographs and Prints Division, Schomburg Center for Research in Black Culture, The New York Public Library, Astor, Lenox and Tilden Foundations)

various positions in missionary and benevolent societies. From 1837 to 1839 he served as the sole or joint editor of the *Colored American*. In 1840 Cornish wrote *The Colonization Scheme Considered*, a powerful pamphlet against colonization, which he felt was unjust and failed to provide a solution to the problem of slavery.

In addition to his religious and journalistic efforts, Cornish served antislavery and other reform causes through a number of benevolent organizations. Among his other efforts, he helped found and served as an executive committee member of the AMERICAN ANTI-SLAVERY SOCIETY (1835–1837), was vice president of the AMERICAN MORAL REFORM SOCIETY (1835–1836), and served on the executive committee of the New York City Vigilance Committee (1835–1837) and the AMERICAN AND FOREIGN ANTI-SLAVERY SOCIETY (1840–1841; 1847–1848). By the 1850s, Cornish, who had been at one time both a

founding member of the American Missionary Association and a fervent Garrisonian, grew impatient with anticlericalism and black exclusiveness in antislavery efforts. He remained active in AMERICAN MISSIONARY SOCIETY efforts as a member of the executive committee (1846–1855) and vice president (1848–1858), but essentially ceased active participation in the abolitionist movement. In poor health in his later years, he moved to Brooklyn in 1855, and died there in 1858.

REFERENCES

BENNETT, LERONE, JR. "Founders of the Black Press." *Ebony* (February 1987): 96–100.
HUTTON, FRANKIE. *The Early Black Press in America, 1827–1860.* Westport, Conn., 1993.

GREG ROBINSON

Cortez, Jayne (May 10, 1936–), poet. Born in Fort Huachuca, Ariz., Cortez moved with her family to Watts in Los Angeles when she was seven. Jazz was one of her earliest and most significant artistic influences. In 1954, while still a teenager, she married avant-garde saxophonist Ornette COLEMAN. The two were divorced in 1960, and afterward Cortez began to pursue her childhood dream of becoming an actress by studying drama and attending acting workshops. At around the same time she began to write poetry.

In 1963 she met James FORMAN, the executive secretary of the Student Nonviolent Coordinating Committee (SNCC), who persuaded her to go to Mississippi to help register voters. She spent the summer of 1963 in Greenwood and the summer of 1964 in Jackson, and returned, by her own account, transformed: "I saw history being made." Cortez continues to be a highly political poet.

Upon her return to California, Cortez founded the Watts Repertory Theater Company, a writers' and actors' workshop, and publicly began to read her poetry there. In 1967, Cortez moved to New York, where she founded Bola Press and later published her first collection of poetry, *Pissstained Stairs and the Monkey Man's Wares* (1969). In 1975 she married artist Melvin Edwards, and from 1977 to 1983 she served as writer-in-residence at Livingston College of Rutgers University. Cortez has traveled widely, reading her poetry in North America, Latin America, Africa, Europe, and the Caribbean.

Music permeates Cortez's poetry. She abruptly changes line lengths and frequently repeats words and lines, establishing rhythms evocative of the spectrum of the African-American musical tradition, from the blues to experimental jazz. She often performs and has on occasion recorded with jazz musicians. African imagery, poetic forms, and language are also an important force in Cortez's work, which is collected in the volume *Coagulations: New and Selected Poems* (1984). Most of her books and records have been published by Bola Press.

REFERENCES

DeVeaux, Alexis. "A Poet's World: Jayne Cortez Discusses Her Life and Her Work." *Essence* 8, no. 11 (March 1978): 77–79, 106, 109.

Lee, Don L. "Toward a Definition: Black Poetry of the Sixties." In Addison Gayle, Jr., ed., *The Black Aesthetic*. Garden City, N.Y., 1972.

Melhem, D. H. *Heroism in New Black Poetry: Introductions and Interviews*. Lexington, Ky., 1990.

Redmond, Eugene B. *Drumvoices: The Mission of Afro-American Poetry, A Critical History*. Garden City, N.Y., 1976.

Woodson, Jon. "Jayne Cortez." In Trudier Harris and Thadious M. Davis, eds., *Afro-American Poets Since 1955: Dictionary of Literary Biography*. Vol. 41. Detroit, 1985, pp. 69–74.

LOUIS J. PARASCANDOLA

Cortor, Eldzier (January 10, 1916–), painter and poet. Known for painting elongated nude figures in intimate settings full of evocative objects, Eldzier Cortor has had many influences on his work. Cartoons and cartoonists (E. Simms CAMPBELL), African sculpture (introduced by Kathleen Blackshear), and Dutch and Flemish genre paintings all influenced him to create sensuous and surreal paintings in which color and composition meld mystery and ordinary life.

Born in Richmond, Va., Cortor was taken to live in Chicago when he was one year old by his parents, John and Ophelia. After high school he studied at the school of the Art Institute of Chicago, where Kathleen Blackshear was an instructor. He also studied with Laszlo Moholy-Nagy at the Chicago Institute of Design, and was a fellow student of Charles SEBREE and Charles WHITE. He taught at the Southside Community Art Center and worked on the WPA's easel project. In 1944 and 1945, Cortor received Rosenwald grants to paint in the Sea Islands off Georgia. He then went to New York to study printmaking at Columbia and at Bob Blackburn's workshop. A Guggenheim fellowship in 1949 permitted him to travel to Cuba, Haiti, and Jamaica for two years.

Cortor's works are in the collections of the Studio Museum of Harlem and the National Museum of American Art. Thirty-four of his paintings, spanning

Dance Figure by Eldzier Cortor, mezzotint on paper, c.1986. (The Studio Museum in Harlem)

more than fifty years, were exhibited by the Kenkeleba Gallery in 1988.

REFERENCE

Jennings, Corinne L. "Eldzier Cortor: The Long Consistent Road." In *Three Masters: Eldzier Cortor, Hughie Lee-Smith, Archibald John Motley, Jr.,* New York, 1988, pp. 12–22.

BETTY KAPLAN GUBERT

Cosby, William Henry, Jr. "Bill" (July 12, 1937–), comedian and philanthropist. Bill Cosby was born in Germantown, Pa., to William and Annie Pearle Cosby. After a stint in the Navy (1956–1960),

Cosby studied at Temple University in Philadelphia, but dropped out to pursue a career as a stand-up comic.

During the 1960s, Cosby worked in network television as a comedian featured on late-night talk shows. In 1965 he became the first African-American network television star in a dramatic series when producers named him to costar with Robert Culp in *I Spy* (1965–1968). Cosby's character, Alexander Scott, did not usually address his blackness or another character's whiteness. As with other forms of popular entertainment with black characters at the time, Cosby's character was portrayed in a manner in which being black merely meant having slightly darker skin. He won Emmy awards for the role in 1966 and 1967.

From 1969 through 1971, Cosby appeared as Chet Kincaid, a bachelor high school coach, on the situation comedy series *The Bill Cosby Show.* Cosby portrayed Kincaid as a proud but not militant black man. The series was moderately successful. A few years later, Cosby and CBS joined forces in a television experiment, *Fat Albert and the Cosby Kids* (1972–1977), a cartoon series for children. The series set the course for television in the vital new area of ethics, values, judgment, and personal responsibility. By the end of its three-year run, *Fat Albert* had inspired a number of new directions in children's television.

In 1972 and 1973, Cosby starred in *The New Bill Cosby Show,* a comedy-variety series. Cosby's Jemin Company, which he had recently established, produced the shows, allowing him to have more control over the productions. As he did in all his television series, Cosby made great use of other black artists who had had few opportunities to practice their craft elsewhere.

For a few months in late 1976, largely because of his success as a regular guest on the PBS educational series *The Electric Company,* where he demonstrated great skill at working with and entertaining youngsters, ABC hired Cosby to host a prime time hour-long variety series oriented toward children, *Cos.* It did not catch on with viewers, however, and was canceled after a few months.

In the fall of 1984, *The Cosby Show* began on NBC, featuring Cosby as Cliff Huxtable, an obstetrician living with his wife and four children in a New York City brownstone. Their fifth child, away at college most of the time, appeared sporadically in featured parts. The show put black images on the screen that many people admired. The characters on *The Cosby Show* represented a real African-American upper-middle-class family, rarely seen on American television. Cosby sought black artists who had not been seen on network television in years for cameo roles (Dizzy GILLESPIE and Judith JAMISON, for example). He also included black writers among his creative staff, and by the third year, he insisted on using a black director for some of the episodes. In its first year, *The Cosby Show* finished third in the ratings; from the second season through the fourth season, it was the number-one-rated show in the United States.

Conscious of the need to lead the networks toward more equitable treatment of African Americans, Cosby used his position to require that more doors be opened. He had a presence in almost every area of television programming: He was a mass volume spokesman and star presenter for advertisements and public relations image campaigns that included Jello, Coca-Cola, Delmonte, Kodak, and E. F. Hutton. He appeared in drama, action-adventure stories, comedies, and children's programs. In 1992 he also entered into prime time syndication with Carsey-Werner Productions with a remake of the old Groucho Marx game series, *You Bet Your Life.* The show lasted only one season. That same year, however, Cosby made public his bid to purchase the National Broadcasting Corporation (NBC-TV), a television network worth $9 billion. Cosby was determined to call attention to the proliferation of negative images of black people and the titillation of viewers with sex and violence. All television viewers, he argued, were diminished by the spate of "drive-by-images" that reinforced shallow stereotypes.

Throughout his career, Cosby appeared at highly popular concert performances across the United

Stand-up comedian Bill Cosby in 1965. That year, in the series *I Spy,* Cosby was the first African American to have a starring role in a television dramatic series whose cast was not largely black. (Prints and Photographs Division, Library of Congress)

States. His comedy focused on his own life as a reflection of universal human needs. He also produced more than twenty comedy/musical record albums, many of which have won Grammy awards, including *Bill Cosby Is a Very Funny Fellow* (1963), *I Started Out as a Child* (1964), *Why Is There Air?* (1965), *Wonderfulness* (1966), *Revenge* (1967), *To Russell, My Brother, Whom I Slept With* (1968), *Bill Cosby 1969*, *Bill Cosby Talks to Children About Drugs* (1971), and *Children, You'll Understand* (1986). Cosby has written many best-selling books, including *The Wit and Wisdom of Fat Albert* (1973), *You Are Somebody Special* (1978), *Fatherhood* (1986), *Time Flies* (1987), and *Love and Marriage* (1989). He has served on numerous boards, including the NAACP, OPERATION PUSH, the UNITED NEGRO COLLEGE FUND, and the National Sickle Cell Foundation (*see* SICKLE CELL DISEASE).

Cosby, who in 1993 was listed in *Forbes* magazine as one of the 400 richest people in the world with a net worth of more than $315 million, has been one of the most important benefactors to African-American institutions. In 1986 he and his wife gave $1.3 million to FISK University; the following year they gave another $1.3 million to be divided equally among four black universities—Central State, HOWARD, Florida A & M, and Shaw; in 1988 they divided $1.5 million between Meharry Medical College and Bethune Cookman College. In 1989 Bill and Camille Cosby announced that they were giving $20 million to SPELMAN College, the largest personal gift ever made to any of the historically black colleges and universities. In 1994 the couple donated a historic landmark building in downtown Washington, D.C. to the NATIONAL COUNCIL OF NEGRO WOMEN to help them establish a National Center for African-American Women. Cosby himself has been the recipient of numerous awards, including the NAACP's SPINGARN MEDAL (1985). He holds an M.A. (1972) and a doctorate (1976) in education from the University of Massachusetts at Amherst. In 1976 he also finally received a B.A. from Temple University. Cosby, who married Camille Hanks in 1964, has lived in rural Massachusetts since the early 1970s.

REFERENCES

LANE, RANDALL. "Bill Cosby, Capitalist." *Forbes* (September 28, 1992): 85–86.
SMITH, RONALD L. *Cosby.* New York, 1986.
ZOGLIN, RICHARD. "Cosby Inc." *Time* (September 28, 1987): 56–60.

JANNETTE L. DATES

Cotten, Elizabeth (c. January 1895–June 29, 1987), folk musician. Elizabeth Cotten was born in Chapel Hill, N.C., on a date that is not known for certain. She learned to play banjo and guitar as a child and wrote what is one of her most enduring compositions, "Freight Train," at the age of twelve. For most of her adulthood, Cotten did not perform professionally. In the early 1940s she moved to Washington, D.C., and worked as a maid for Charles Seeger, the famous ethnomusicologist, and his wife, composer Ruth Crawford-Seeger. At the urging of Seeger's family, Cotten began to perform professionally, and when FOLK MUSIC gained wide popularity in the late 1950s, she became one of its prime exponents. Her unusual performance style—she played the guitar left-handed, holding it upside-down and using only two fingers—and her spry voice made her a favorite at folk and BLUES festivals throughout the United States over the next three decades. Many of Cotten's songs, including "Freight Train" (recorded in 1958), "Going Down the Road Feeling Bad" (1958), "Oh Babe It Ain't No Lie" (1958), and "Shake Sugaree" (1965), with their somber evocations of rural life and the disappointments of love, became classics of the folk genre. Her 1984 album *Elizabeth Cotten Live!* won a Grammy Award. Cotten lived in Washington, D.C., until her final years, when she moved to Syracuse, N.Y., where she died in 1987.

REFERENCE

PARELES, JOHN. "Elizabeth Cotten at 90, Bigger Than the Tradition." *New York Times,* January 7, 1983, p. C18.

JONATHAN GILL

Cotton Club.   First opened in 1920 as the Club Deluxe, the venue at Lenox Avenue and West 142nd Street in HARLEM took on new ownership and its permanent name in 1922. Owney Madden, who bought the club from heavyweight boxing champion Jack JOHNSON, intended the name Cotton Club to appeal to whites, the only clientele permitted until 1928. The club made its name by featuring top-level black performers and an upscale, downtown audience. It soon became a leading attraction for white "tourists" from high society wanting to see the much publicized, risqué Harlem cultural life.

Following the death in 1927 of Andy Preer, leader of the house band, the Cotton Club Syncopators, Duke ELLINGTON and his orchestra were brought in as replacements and began a four-year rise to prominence on the Cotton Club's stage. Soon after Ellington took over as bandleader, the Cotton Club Orchestra was broadcast nightly over a national radio network.

Responding to local protests, the club's management opened its doors to black patrons for the first time in the winter of 1928. Nonetheless, prices were kept prohibitively high and the club's audience remained virtually all white. The nightly revues, which were generally more popular than the orchestra, featured scantily clad, light-skinned women dancing to Ellington's "jungle music."

In 1931 Ellington and his orchestra left the club and were replaced by Cab CALLOWAY's Missourians. Calloway, like Ellington, established himself as a major figure in mainstream JAZZ during his Cotton Club years. Calloway's Missourians remained the house band until 1934, when they were replaced by Jimmie Lunceford's acclaimed swing band. Most of the renowned jazz performers of the period appeared at the Cotton Club, including Louis ARMSTRONG, Ethel WATERS, and dancers Bill "Bojangles" ROBINSON and the NICHOLAS BROTHERS.

Following riots in Harlem in 1935, the club was forced to close due to a widespread perception among whites that the area was unsafe. It reopened in 1936 downtown at 200 West 48th Street, where it remained until its final closing in 1940.

REFERENCES

CHARTERS, SAMUEL BARCLAY, and LEONARD KUNSTADT. *Jazz: A History of the New York Scene.* 1962. Reprint. New York, 1981.

SCHULLER, GUNTHER. *The Swing Era: The Development of Jazz, 1930–1945.* New York, 1989.

THADDEUS RUSSELL

Council on African Affairs.   The Council on African Affairs (CAA), the most important Pan-Africanist group of the 1940s, was founded on January 28, 1937, by a group led by Paul ROBESON and Max YERGAN, a former YMCA secretary. Originally named the International Committee on African Affairs, it was a small information and lobbying group. Anticolonialist in nature, it was dedicated to increasing Americans' awareness of conditions in Africa, to expose the "ruthless exploitation of the people; repressive legislation . . . and the growing poverty of the Africans." For many years it was the only organization dedicated to African problems. It was funded largely by Frederick V. Field (of the Chicago department store family), who had communist leanings, as did many of the CAA's leaders. Its seventy-member board, however, included such noncommunist luminaries as Adam Clayton POWELL, JR., Alain LOCKE, Channing TOBIAS, Herbert Delany, and Mary McLeod BETHUNE. Two other board members,

Ralph BUNCHE and Mordecai JOHNSON, decided shortly after joining that the CAA was too left-wing in its politics and resigned. In 1941, the group had fourteen active committee members who met three times per year.

In 1942, the organization, renamed the CAA, set up offices at 23 West 26th Street in New York City, and in August published its first two-page newsletter, *News of Africa.* In 1943, Alphaeus Hunton, a Howard University English professor, became the CAA's educational director. He began a monthly bulletin, *New Africa* (later called *Spotlight on Africa,* 1944), which was part of a program to influence mass opinion, especially on the U.S. role in Africa as exploiter of cheap labor and raw materials. In April 1944, the CAA sponsored a conference on "Africa—New Perspectives" with Kwame Nkrumah of the Gold Coast (now Ghana) as the guest speaker.

During World War II, Hunton and Yergan conferred with the U.S. State Department's Division of African Affairs about economic and political questions, advocating a program of postwar liberation and self-determination for African colonies. In 1945, CAA chairman Paul Robeson lobbied President Harry S. Truman and Secretary of State Edward Stettinius to support African decolonization at the United Nations Conference in San Francisco. Hunton was an accredited observer, and he attended meetings of the Ad Hoc Committee on Non-Self-Governing Territories. He prepared reports for UN delegates on South Africa. When Jan Smuts, the prime minister of South Africa, applied for permission to annex South-West Africa, the CAA led the successful fight at the UN to block the measure.

By 1946, the CAA had seventy-two members, some 80 percent of whom were African Americans. Often the only source of information on Africa, the CAA provided news releases to sixty-two foreign and sixty-seven U.S. newspapers. Its *African Bibliography* was published from January 1945 to February 1950. It publicized apartheid, starvation, and exploitation of black Africans in South Africa, and supported the African National Congress. So influential was the CAA that *New Africa* was banned in British-held Kenya. CAA activities included mass meetings, picketing of the South African embassy, and a food drive.

The last big CAA event was an April 1947 meeting at the 71st Regimental Armory in New York. Paul Robeson spoke, comparing the United States unfavorably to the U.S.S.R., citing the latter's aid to Third-World countries. That year, as the Cold War heated up, the CAA was placed on the attorney general's list of subversive organizations.

In February 1948, a major schism occurred. Executive Director Max Yergan insisted that the CAA

Council should declare its "nonpartisan" character, while Robeson and his followers claimed this would aid anti-Soviet reactionaries. The dispute was referred to a policy committee headed by W. E. B. DU BOIS, who had become active in the CAA following his departure in 1948 from the NATIONAL ASSOCIATION FOR THE ADVANCEMENT OF COLORED PEOPLE (NAACP). In March, the CAA board defeated Yergan's motion and censured him for alleged financial irregularities. Yergan claimed the CAA had been taken over by communists, and formed his own rump faction. That summer, the CAA leadership expelled him. This action cost the organization the support of Powell, Tobias, Delany, and Bethune. Robeson remained as chairman, Du Bois became vice chairman, and Hunton became executive secretary. Louise Thompson PATTERSON, a prominent communist, became the director of organization, and with Robeson organized fund-raising concerts and local chapters. The CAA became Robeson's power base, and supporters demonstrated in 1950 after he was denied a passport.

In 1953, the CAA was ordered to register under the McCarran Act as a subversive organization, and in 1955 Hunton was called before a federal grand jury to testify about whether the CAA was a foreign agent, given its ties with the African National Congress and the South African Indian Congress. Funding soon dried up, and in 1955 the CAA ceased most activities. The U.S. government's Subversive Activities Control Board finally shut it down for good in 1956.

REFERENCES

DUBERMAN, MARTIN B. *Paul Robeson.* New York, 1988.

HORNE, GERALD. *Black and Red: W. E. B. Du Bois and the Afro-American Response to the Cold War, 1947–1963.* Albany, N.Y., 1986.

HUNTON, DOROTHY. *Alphaeus Hunton: The Unsung Valiant.* Self-published. 1986.

LYNCH, HOLLIS R. *Black American Radicals and the Liberation of Africa: The Council on African Affairs, 1937–1955.* Ithaca, N.Y., 1978.

ALANA J. ERICKSON

Council of Federated Organizations, civil rights organization. The Council of Federated Organizations (COFO)—a coalition of the CONGRESS OF RACIAL EQUALITY (CORE), the NATIONAL ASSOCIATION FOR THE ADVANCEMENT OF COLORED PEOPLE (NAACP), and the STUDENT NONVIOLENT COORDINATING COMMITTEE (SNCC)—was founded in 1962 to attack racial discrimination and segregation in Mississippi. SNCC activists formed an overwhelming majority within COFO. SNCC's Robert MOSES provided inspirational leadership as director of the organization, with CORE's David Dennis serving as assistant director and NAACP activist Aaron Henry serving as president. Supported by funds from the VOTER EDUCATION PROJECT, COFO activists mounted voter registration campaigns in Mississippi in 1962 and 1963. However, due to white terrorism and harassment, they were able to register few African-American voters.

In 1963, COFO activists, assisted by approximately one hundred northern white student volunteers, sponsored a mock gubernatorial election with alternative candidates to prove the willingness and desire of black Mississippians to vote. Thousands of blacks participated in this successful Freedom Vote campaign and one year later COFO activists launched FREEDOM SUMMER—an intensive summer-long voter registration and education campaign in Mississippi modeled on the Freedom Vote. The COFO-sponsored Freedom Summer focused national attention on the plight of African Americans in the South and became one of the most important milestones in the civil rights movement. COFO disbanded soon after the Freedom Summer ended.

REFERENCES

CARSON, CLAYBORNE. *In Struggle: SNCC and the Black Awakening of the 1960s.* Cambridge, Mass., 1981.

MCADAM, DOUG. *Freedom Summer.* New York, 1988.

ROBYN SPENCER

Councill, William Hooper (July 12, 1849–April 17, 1909), educator and leader. William Hooper Councill was born a slave in Fayetteville, N.C. When he was eight years old, he, his mother, and his youngest brother were sold to an Alabama planter. His father, having escaped to Canada, had been unable to secure the family's freedom. During the CIVIL WAR, Councill escaped with his mother and brother behind Union lines. From 1865 to 1867, Councill's only formal education took place when he attended a freedman's school in Stevenson, Ala. He continued to study on his own at night while he taught in black public schools and worked in restaurants and hotels. He was admitted to the Alabama bar in 1883, although he never practiced law.

Ambitious and driven to succeed, Councill found the path of least resistance through accommodation. He became a Democrat in 1875 and soon thereafter became the principal in the new State Normal and

Industrial School at Huntsville. Under Councill's leadership, by the mid-1880s the school became one of the largest, most prestigious industrial schools in the South. He accomplished this in part by publicly proclaiming acceptance of segregation and black civil and political inequality.

In 1885 Councill was accused of raping a twelve-year-old girl and then shooting at her uncle. Though he was acquitted, African Americans in Huntsville used the incident to demand his removal as principal, while northern philanthropists responded by diverting their money over to Tuskegee Institute (*see* TUSKEGEE UNIVERSITY). Councill encountered further controversy in 1887, when, uncharacteristically, he decided to sue a railroad after he was forced out of a first-class car.

Councill regained his position as principal in 1888, and in 1891, he managed to obtain the majority of federal land-grant funds (received under the provisions of the second Morrill Act of 1890), and the school's name was changed to the Alabama State Agricultural and Mechanical College for Negroes. Councill's pronouncements on race relations were so extreme that even Booker T. WASHINGTON hesitated to appear with him in public because of Councill's reputation for "toadying to the Southern white people." His rivalry with Washington faded after Washington attained national prominence after 1895. Councill died at his college in 1909.

Councill's public accommodationist pronouncements about race relations seem to be in conflict with his early efforts toward equality and some of his later writings. In an article published in July 1899, recognizing that racial equality in the United States was not a realistic expectation, he openly endorsed Bishop Henry TURNER's philosophy of emigration to Africa, where black nationality could exist without the specter of racism.

REFERENCES

HARLAN, LOUIS R. *Booker T. Washington.* Vol. 1, *The Making of a Black Leader.* New York, 1972.

LOGAN, RAYFORD W. and MICHAEL R. WINSTON. eds. *Dictionary of American Negro Biography.* New York, 1982.

MEIER, AUGUST. *Negro Thought in America, 1880–1915.* Ann Arbor, Mich., 1963.

DEBI BROOME

Count Basie.   *See* Basie, William James "Count."

Couvent Institute.   Located in New Orleans, the Couvent Institute was one of the most spectacular educational establishments founded by and for blacks in the United States. It was named for Madame Justine Couvent, born Justine Fervin around 1757, probably in Africa, and brought as a slave to America. Her husband, Gabriel Bernard Couvent, a carpenter by trade, bought her freedom; she received no formal education. In 1829, she inherited her husband's estate, and her priest at confession persuaded her not to forget indigent children in her own will. She stipulated in her will that her estate go to a school supervised by the Catholic clergy.

After her death in 1837, the money went to the Institution for Indigent Orphans, which in 1848 created a primary school for black orphans of the Third District, providing free classroom instruction. Color prejudice in the Catholic Church played a part in delaying the opening of the school until 1852, and Father Manehault, who supervised it, had to show considerable tact, since teaching free blacks was risky in Louisiana. Education was provided free of tuition, and the teaching was both in French and English, with separate classes for boys and girls. Later, Spanish classes were added.

Possibly due to the tastes of principal Armand LANUSSE, the syllabus emphasized the French classics—Boileau, Corneille, and La Fontaine. Starting with Félicie Cailloux, there were six black instructors. The school played a key role, not only in the primary education of free people of color, but in bringing together enlightened and progressive teachers who played important cultural roles: Paul Trévigne, a writer and editor; Samuel Snaër, a composer; and Joanni Questi, a poet.

The quality of the school was such that, even in antebellum days, the state legislature and the city of New Orleans provided funds for its maintenance. Mostly, however, black leaders provided support in money and time, as did Thomy Lafon, Aristide Mary, and Rodolphe Desdunes. Reconstruction saw attendance drop off because black children were then allowed to attend public schools in the city together with whites. By 1885, the school was about to close when community leaders, spurred by Rodolphe Desdunes, rescued it. The Couvent school later became the Holy Redeemer School. Located on Dauphine Street, it is now run by the Sisters of the Holy Ghost.

REFERENCE

BLASSINGAME, JOHN W. *Black New Orleans, 1860–1880.* Chicago, 1973.

MICHEL FABRE

Covan, William McKinley "Willie" (March 4, 1897–May 7, 1989), tap dancer. Willie Covan's extraordinarily long career is a microcosm of tap dance history. Born in Savannah, Ga., Covan grew up in Chicago, mimicking street dancers and earning pennies by tapping to street rhythms. By the time he was twelve, he was performing on what was called the "pickaninny circuit" (in which young African-American children performed as backup choruses for "headliner" vaudeville. These acts featured performers such as Bill "Bojangles" ROBINSON, Mayme Remington, and Mae West). In the early part of the 1900s, large black touring shows, such as "Black Pattie and Her Troubadors" or "Old Kentucky" traveled throughout the United States. Friday night dance competitions were featured attractions of these shows, and at sixteen, Covan won the "Old Kentucky" contest—and gained a reputation as an excellent tap dancer—when he performed syncopated buck-and-wings instead of the standard time steps. In New York City during the 1920s, he danced in the first all-black Broadway musicals *Shuffle Along* (1921), *Runnin' Wild* (1922), *Liza* (1923), and *Dixie to Broadway* (1924), and teamed with Ulysses "Slow Kid" Thompson, choreographing a swinging blend of taps, acrobatics, and Russian dancing (a blend that included fast-paced and fast-moving squat-kicks, similar to the squat-kicks seen in Russian folk dancing). With partner Leonard Ruffin, Covan tapped an elegant soft shoe, paving the way for later class acts.

Covan later organized the Four Covans, consisting of Willie himself, his brother Dewey, and their respective wives, Flore and Corita Harbert. Their dance routines incorporated a variety of styles—jazz dance, speed tapping, precision dancing, challenge dances, and flash acrobatics. In 1927, after working with Lionel HAMPTON at the Sebastian Club in Los Angeles, the Four Covans jumped from the Orpheum vaudeville syndicate to the Keith and Lowe Circuits—and to New York's Palace Theater, the crown jewel among vaudeville's venues, where they were a great success. Covan's influence widened when he opened the Covan Dance School in Los Angeles in 1936, and then, in the 1950s, when he became the master tap instructor at MGM Studios. In that capacity he taught and coached, among others, Eleanor Powell, Vera Ellen, Mickey Rooney, Shirley Temple, Mae West, Ann Miller, and Debbie Reynolds. Yet he received no film credit. Covan was known for his distinct taps and elegant soft-shoe work, and for his pioneering role as an acrobatic dancer. In command of a wide range of styles, he used them all throughout his very long dance career.

In retirement during the 1970s and 1980s, as one of the eldest members of the tap community, Covan was revered as a source of tap history. An engaging raconteur, he shared memories with many tap dancers. Cowan is credited with inventing one of the most demanding of all tap steps, the double around the world with no hands—the tap equivalent of two consecutive aerial barrel turns, framed at its beginning and ending with perfect, in-tempo tapping. Remembered as a nearly impossible feat, it stands as a lasting monument in the ephemeral world of dance—a tiny moment of movement, remembered as a split-second image in a performance long past.

REFERENCES

BLEEDEN, JOE. "Legendary Dancer Willie Covan." *International Tap Association Journal* 2, no. 1 (Fall 1989): 26.
FRANK, RUSTY. *TAP!* New York, 1991.
STEARNS, MARSHALL, and JEAN STEARNS. *Jazz Dance: The Story of American Vernacular Dance.* New York, 1968.

CONSTANCE VALIS HILL

Cox, Elbert Frank (December 5, 1895–November 28, 1969), mathematician. Elbert Cox was born in Evansville, Ind., the son of Johnson D. and Eugenia Talbott Cox. A 1917 graduate of Indiana University, he taught high-school mathematics in Henderson, Ky., and served with the American Expeditionary Forces in France during World War I. In 1919, he was appointed head of the Department of Natural Sciences at Shaw University, a post he held until 1922, when he enrolled for graduate study in mathematics (with a minor in physics) at Cornell University. He studied briefly at McGill University in 1924. At Cornell, he held the prestigious Erastus Brooks fellowship.

When Cox was awarded a Ph.D. at Cornell in 1925, he became the first African American to earn a doctorate in pure mathematics. His research focused on polynomial solutions of difference equations. In September 1925, he was elected to membership in the Mathematical Association of America. He was mentioned twice (1930 and 1932) in the "Problems and Solutions" column of *American Mathematical Monthly* as having solved problems proposed by readers of the journal. An abridgment of his doctoral thesis was published in *Tohoku Mathematical Journal* (1934). Subsequently, he developed a research interest in differential equations and interpolation theory. In 1947, he published a study of "interpolation functions for systems of grading" in the *Journal of Experimental Education*.

Cox devoted himself primarily to the teaching of mathematics. He served as professor of physics and mathematics at West Virginia State College (1925–1929); in 1929, he became associate professor of mathematics at HOWARD UNIVERSITY. Following his promotion to full professor in 1947, he held the department chairmanship until 1961. He retired in 1966 and died several years later.

REFERENCE

"Cox, Elbert Frank." In *Who's Who in Colored America,* Supplement. Yonkers, N.Y., 1950, p. 8.

KENNETH R. MANNING

Cox, Ida Prather (c. 1896–November 10, 1967), singer. Ida Cox was born in Tuccoa, Ga. As a child she sang in the African Methodist Episcopal Church choir in Cedartown, Ga., but in 1910 she left home to tour with White & Clark's Black & Tan Minstrels. While traveling with the Florida Orange Blossom Minstrels, she married trumpeter Adler Cox. By 1920, she was an established solo performer in the THEATRE OWNERS' BOOKING ASSOCIATION (TOBA) listings.

From 1923 to 1929, Cox was under exclusive contract to the Paramount recording company, which promoted her as the "Uncrowned Queen of the Blues." Usually accompanied by pianist Lovie Austin, she recorded seventy-eight titles for the label. During this period, she also recorded for the Harmograph and Silvertone labels, using the pseudonyms Julia Powers, Velma Bradley, Jane Smith, and Kate Lewis. From 1929 Cox toured with her own show, the Raisin' Cain revue, which was so popular that it was chosen as the first TOBA show to open at the APOLLO THEATER in Harlem.

Changing musical tastes and a weak economy led to the breakup of the troupe, which had been reorganized as the Darktown Scandals, in the early 1940s. Cox continued to work in small houses throughout the country. In 1939 she appeared at Carnegie Hall in John Hammond's "From Spirituals to Swing" concert. After suffering a stroke while performing in a nightclub in Buffalo in 1945, Cox retired. In 1961 she made a final recording, "Blues for Rampart Street," with the Coleman HAWKINS band.

Although she lacked the power of her contemporaries Ma RAINEY and Bessie SMITH, Cox's voice was penetrating and emotionally intense. Her classic blues style is best exemplified on songs of her own composition such as "Graveyard Dream Blues" and "Wild Women Don't Have the Blues."

REFERENCE

HARRISON, DAPHNE D. *Black Pearls: Blues Queens of the 1920s.* New Brunswick, N.J., 1988.

GENETTE MCLAURIN

Cox, Oliver Cromwell (August 24, 1901–September 4, 1974), sociologist. Born in Port of Spain, Trinidad, Oliver Cox was the son of Virginia Blake and William Raphael Cox. His father, a customs officer and the captain of a revenue schooner, was too busy to supervise the education of Cox and his eight siblings, and so it was entrusted to his uncle, Reginald W. Vidale, a teacher and headmaster of St. Thomas Boys' School in Port of Spain.

Cox came to the United States in 1919 to work and be educated. In 1925 he entered Lewis Institute in Chicago, where he majored in history and economics. He received an associate degree in spring 1927, and that fall entered Northwestern University, where he graduated with a bachelor of science in law degree in 1929. Shortly thereafter, he was stricken with polio. He spent eighteen months recovering, and thereafter always walked with crutches.

After abandoning thoughts of practicing law in Trinidad, Cox decided to go into academic work, which would, he said, "not require too much legwork." In fall 1930, he entered the University of Chicago as a graduate student in economics, earning an M.A. in 1932. Soon after, however, he switched to sociology, claiming that economists had not explained the causes of the GREAT DEPRESSION. His dissertation, entitled "Factors Affecting the Marital Status of Negroes in Chicago," was based on the study of a massive quantity of statistical data. Cox received his Ph.D. in August 1938.

Despite his degrees in both economics and sociology, Cox was unable, then as later, to find a job at a white institution. He took a position in the Economics Department at Wiley College in Marshall, Tex. After five years at Wiley, Cox accepted a more lucrative post at Tuskegee Institute (*see* TUSKEGEE UNIVERSITY in Alabama). Tuskegee's vocational approach to education frustrated him, however, and he joined the faculty of LINCOLN UNIVERSITY in Jefferson City, Mo., in 1949. He stayed at Lincoln until 1970, when he joined the faculty at Wayne State University in Detroit, Mich., where for a short time he was a Distinguished Visiting Professor.

Cox is best known for his attack on the "caste school of race relations," of which W. Lloyd Warner was the most articulate member. Cox argued, first in his article "The Modern Caste School of Race Relations" (1942), and at greater length in his major work, *Caste, Race, and Class* (1948), that to view race relations in America as analogous to caste systems such as that of Hindu India ignored historical differences in the development of the two systems, and discounted the political and economic basis of American race relations. Cox insisted that racism in America was a product of class conflict. In later years, Cox elaborated his Marxist view of capitalism and race relations in three books: *Foundations of Capitalism* (1959), *Capitalism and American Leadership* (1962), and *Capitalism as a System* (1964). Cox underlined the importance of international trade and uneven global development in the history of European capitalism.

Oliver C. Cox. (Photographs and Prints Division, Schomburg Center for Research in Black Culture, The New York Public Library, Astor, Lenox and Tilden Foundations)

Cox's final work, "Jewish Self-Interest and 'Black Pluralism'" (1974), dealt with the problem of black nationalism. His assertion that ethnic pluralism was promoted by Jews for their own benefit caused a storm of criticism.

Only at the end of his life did Cox achieve limited professional recognition. His work, despite its originality, remains curiously overlooked.

REFERENCES

BLACKWELL, JAMES, and MORRIS JANOWITZ, eds. *Black Sociologists: Historical and Contemporary Perspectives.* Chicago, 1974.

HUNTER, HERBERT M., and SAMEER Y. ABRAHAM, eds. *Race, Class, and the World System: The Sociology of Oliver C. Cox.* New York, 1987.

GREG ROBINSON

Craft, Ellen (1826–1891) and **William** (1824–February 1900), fugitive slaves. Ellen and William Craft were fugitive slaves known for their dramatic escape to freedom. Ellen Smith was born in Clinton, Ga., the daughter of a mulatto slave, Maria, and her owner, Major James Smith. At age eleven, Ellen was given as a wedding gift to one of Smith's daughters living in Macon, Ga. Ellen soon met William Craft, a fellow slave and cabinetmaker, and within a few years they began to plot their escape from bondage.

Escape from the deep South was a rare and dangerous undertaking. The Crafts' plan was indeed bold, creative, and worked out in detail. They first procured passes to visit friends during the Christmas season, when discipline was known to be lax. Their pass was good for several days, so they had time to travel some distance before they were noticed. Ellen, of fair complexion, posed as a white male slave-owner, an invalid traveling north to consult doctors; William impersonated her black slave. She cut her hair, wrapped her head in a bandage, and practiced imitating a man's gait. As a final touch, she wore eyeglasses to disguise her appearance, and because she was illiterate, she held her writing arm in a cast to avoid having to sign her name. The final part of the disguise would be crucial when they were forced to sign hotel registers.

The couple left for freedom on December 21, 1848, and traveled by train, steamer, and ferry through Georgia, South Carolina, North Carolina, Virginia, and Maryland, in a journey that involved several near discoveries. Finally, they arrived in free territory in Philadelphia on Christmas day, 1848.

In Philadelphia, Ellen and William Craft stayed with free blacks and Quakers. They were befriended by abolitionist luminaries such as William Wells BROWN and William Lloyd Garrison (*see* ABOLITION), and the Crafts frequently lectured on their dramatic escape on the antislavery circuit.

In 1850, however, national events changed their lives dramatically. In that year the FUGITIVE SLAVE LAW was passed and the Crafts were literally hunted down in Boston by southern slavehunters and driven into exile in England. Their plight became a national issue when President Millard Fillmore insisted that if the laws of the land were not obeyed in Boston and the Crafts were not shipped back to the South, he would use the United States Army to force the issue.

While in England, the Crafts remained active in the abolitionist movement. They went on a speaking tour with abolitionist William Wells Brown, and in 1851 they took a post teaching at the Ockham School, a pioneering trade school that combined classroom work in traditional subjects with farming, carpentry, and other crafts. William Craft also gained a reputation as a public spokesman against slavery and made several return trips to the United States to speak out against the Confederacy during the Civil War. Ellen was active in the British and Foreign Freedmen's Aid Society, a missionary organization that organized "civilizing" work in British colonies in Africa and the Caribbean. The Crafts published the story of their escape from slavery, *Running a Thousand Miles for Freedom,* while in London in 1860. Between 1863 and 1867, William was in Dahomey in West Africa with the Company of African-American Merchants, where he started a school and established commercial ties.

In 1868, the Crafts returned to the United States with two of their five children and settled in Bryan County, Ga., where they opened an industrial school for black youths. They purchased a plantation in Woodville in 1871, where they continued their school and hired tenant farmers to grow rice, cotton, corn, and peas which they sold in the Savannah area. By 1877 they had seventy-five pupils, but were suffering from the financial burden of keeping up the school.

William became a leader in the local REPUBLICAN PARTY, ran for State Senate in 1874, and in 1876 represented his district at the state and national Republican conventions. He also spent a good part of his time in the North, raising funds for the school and lecturing to church groups on the conditions in the South. Ellen managed the plantation while he was away, negotiated the annual contracts with tenants, and drove their crops to market. But the plantation never prospered, and Northerners, in the mood for reconciliation with the South, were less forthcoming with donations to the experimental school. Rumors spread by the Crafts' enemies suggesting that they were living off the largess of naive northern philanthropists did not help their project, and they eventually gave up the school. Around 1890 they left the Woodville plantation and moved to Charleston, S.C., where they remained for the rest of their lives.

REFERENCES

BLACKETT, R. J. M. *Beating the Barriers: Biographical Essays in Nineteenth-Century Afro-American History.* Baton Rouge, La., 1986.

LOGAN, RAYFORD W., and MICHAEL R. WINSTON, eds. *Dictionary of American Negro Biography.* New York, 1982.

SMITH, JESSIE CARNEY, ed. *Notable Black American Women.* Detroit, 1992.

STERLING, DOROTHEY. *Black Foremothers.* New York, 1988.

SABRINA FUCHS

Creed, Courtlandt Van Rensselaer (April 1835–August 8, 1900), physician. Courtlandt Van Rensselaer Creed was born in New Haven, Conn., the son of John William Creed, a West Indian immi-

grant who worked as a waiter and janitor at Yale College, and his wife, Vashti Elizabeth Duplex. After attending the Lancasterian School in New Haven, Creed was employed briefly as a book agent prior to entering Yale Medical School in 1854. He earned an M.D. in 1857, the first African American to earn a degree at Yale.

Creed opened an office in his family home, a spacious residence purchased by his father in 1848. There, in a predominantly white part of town, he built a successful general practice that included several prominent citizens. During the CIVIL WAR, he volunteered as secretary for a local Colored Freedmen's Aid Society. In 1864, following several fruitless attempts to offer his services to the Union Army, he was appointed acting surgeon of the 30th Connecticut Volunteers, a black regiment. He was one of a few black physicians to receive officers' commissions. Although little is known about his wartime service, he may have worked for a period on the staff of the Knight U.S. Army General Hospital in New Haven. He was mustered out of the Army on November 7, 1865.

Creek settled in New York, but found life difficult there and returned to New Haven in 1873. The remainder of his life was passed in relative poverty and obscurity. The family house was sold to pay off debts and legal expenses. While continuing to practice medicine, Creed lodged in dingy rooming houses in New Haven and, briefly in the early 1890s, in Brooklyn, N.Y. On August 8, 1900, he died of kidney disease while attending to a patient.

REFERENCES

"Cortland [*sic*] Van Rensselaer Creed." In *Obituary Record of Graduates of Yale University, 1900–1910.* New Haven, 1910, pp. 91–92.

DANIELS, DARYL KEITH. African-Americans at the Yale University School of Medicine: 1810–1960. M.D. thesis, Yale University, 1991.

KENNETH R. MANNING

Creole. The word "creole" is used throughout the world, although primarily in the Caribbean and in Mauritius and La Réunion islands in the Indian Ocean. In the United States, it generally designates cultural elements to be found in the former French colony of Louisiane; the adjective "creole" is widely applied to food habits and cuisine, artifacts, songs, music, and so on.

The word, it is generally agreed, is derived from the Portuguese *crialla,* akin to the Spanish *criar,* meaning "to raise" (as cattle or children); hence the sense of "born on the plantation, in the colonies," as opposed to both aboriginal or native and to originating in Europe or Africa. "Creole" thus designated the descendants of European settlers and/or their slaves. In the French West Indies, the term *nègres créoles* was reserved for plantation-reared slaves to distinguish them from *nègres bossales* (= *d'eau salée,* i.e., saltwater) brought from Africa; Creole is now reserved there to the colored population, the white planter stock being the *békés* (a term related to *buckra*). In Mauritius and La Réunion, the respectable white families are called *créoles* and the blacks are called *population de couleur* or *population générale*.

In Louisiana, the term has long been applied to the generally Catholic offspring of French and Spanish settlers and/or blacks, to distinguish them from immigrants and "Americans." It took on an exotic dimension in the eighteenth century, not only in the United States, where Anglos viewed the leisurely, refined style of life of the Creoles as dissolute, although appealing, but also in France, where it gave rise to the fashion of *"les inc'oyables"*—dandies who slurred their r's in Saint-Dominique fashion—possibly because Empress Joséphine was herself a Creole.

Although the descendants of the Cajuns qualify as Creoles according to the above definition, these twice-removed descendants of French settlers in Nova Scotia were called "Cajuns" (a deformation of "Acadians") by the host population when they settled the bayou region west of New Orleans in the late eighteenth century. With time, the term "Creole" became associated locally with the "aristocratic" families of French-speaking whites. This was largely due to the pressure of the racial barriers imposed by Anglo-Saxons who did not distinguish between Negroes and mulattos, while "mulâtres" enjoyed a special status in the three-tiered Latin societies of the West Indies.

The early recordings made by Joe "King" Oliver and his Creole Jazz Band remain the definitive statement of New Orleans jazz. Among the band members who made their recording debuts with King Oliver's 1923 band was the young second cornetist Louis Armstrong. In this highly staged photograph of the band are (from left) Honoré Dutrey, trombone; Warren "Baby" Dodds, drums; King Oliver, cornet; Louis Armstrong, kneeling, slide cornet; Lil Hardin, piano; Bill Johnson, banjo; and Johnny Dodds, clarinet. (Frank Driggs Collection)

Legal efforts were thus made by the white Creoles to prevent free people of color from defining themselves as such. Whereas baptismal registers reveal that "Creole" also designated black children in the seventeenth century, legal action was taken and registers sometimes "rectified." The best-known court case of such denial was that of a mulatto woman, illustrated in *Toucoutou,* a novel by Edward Laroque-Tinker. This move toward legal exclusion of an important, cultured, and socially respectable group by those who often were their siblings was graphically evoked by George Washington Cable, whose half dozen novels on that theme (notably *The Grandissimes)* aroused the ire of local white Creoles whose foibles he exposed.

The term was retained by the descendants of the free people of color, however, and used by all Louisianans with an adjective, as in "Negro Creole," or "Creole Negro." Between the two world wars, when the French-speaking white population dwindled, "Creole" designated more frequently, and soon, nearly exclusively, the descendants of free people of color. These either sometimes "passed" when migrating west and north, or intermarried more freely with darker-skinned African Americans. One should emphasize that genealogy, personal achievement, and social status—*not* skin color—are the in-group criteria for belonging. For instance, the distinctly African features and dark complexion of classical composer and director Edmond Dédé were no obstacle to his being proudly claimed as one of the Creoles.

Linguistically, a creole language—or (when spoken by a restricted group) a creole dialect—is the result of the interface of European, African, and East Indian languages. Broadly speaking, the syntax and grammar retain strongly West African structures, while most of the vocabulary is French, Spanish, English, Dutch, etc., according to which country colonized a given area of the Caribbean or of the Indian Ocean. One could say that "creole" corresponds to "pidgin," with the difference that it evolved in a geographical context new to both Europeans and slaves while pidgin evolved in Africa. In creole-speaking areas, there is a continuum of dialects, each with distinctive local features, yet retaining enough in common to permit at least limited understanding as they range from Louisiana to Surinam and Guiana.

Long regarded as inadequate renderings of standard European languages, or as an inferior *patois,* creole dialects have been spoken by the masses sometimes exclusively of other languages, and were refused language status by colonizers or local elites for ideological, not scientific, reasons. As a result, speaking creole played an important part in cultural resistance, notably during the U.S. occupation of Haiti from 1915 to 1930, when creole became a "national" language.

In Louisiana, literature in creole has existed since Jean-Jacques Rousseau quoted it, and it is still flourishing, although in a limited way, in the plays and poetry of Sybil Kein, after having regained importance during the HARLEM RENAISSANCE. In the Caribbean, a large body of important literature is written in creole, including verse by Jamaican Louise Bennett and Trinidadian Edward K. BRATHWAITE, several plays by Derek WALCOTT from St. Lucia, and in calypso songs and dub poetry.

Among cultural anthropologists, "creole" is used in a wider sense, and the concept of creolization is being opposed to that of the "melting pot" as a paradigm of a kind of cultural interchange in which so-called "purity" is not considered superior to "intermixture." Daniel Crowley defines it as "the process of adaptation which Melville Herskovits synthesized as retention, reinterpretation, and syncretism," in areas where "a culture neither aboriginal nor alien but a mixture of these two with retentions on both sides and ample borrowing from other outside sources is in the process of becoming dominant" (Whitten 38). This is equally applicable to the completion of any self-referential cultural or linguistic system or to "the fusion of fragmented traditions from a variety of origins into a new, functioning grammar."

REFERENCE

WHITTEN, NORMAN E., and JOHN F. SZWED, eds. *Afro-American Anthropology.* New York, 1970.

MICHEL FABRE

Crichlow, Ernest (June 19, 1914–), artist. Ernest Crichlow was born in Brooklyn to Barbadian parents. He studied art in the early 1930s at the Art Students' League and also at New York University, and later in the 1930s he traveled to Greensboro, N.C., as a WORKS PROJECT ADMINISTRATION (WPA) artist. It was not until the 1950s that he returned to New York.

Crichlow is best known for founding the Cinque Gallery on Lafayette Street in New York City with Romare BEARDEN and Norman LEWIS in 1969. The Gallery was named after the African leader of the 1839 AMISTAD MUTINY in which a Spanish slave ship was seized by its cargo of Africans who tried to navigate it back to their homeland. The gallery provided exhibition space for black artists who are under thirty years of age.

Crichlow is also a painter and an illustrator of children's books. His work is representational in style and addresses social issues, particularly as they relate to the lives of urban children (see his paintings *The*

White Fence and *White Fence #2*). He explained that he focused on children to say "what I want to say about Negroes. I have seen so much sadness and hope in the faces of Negro children. I have tried to capture this sadness . . . in order to explain it." Crichlow has also illustrated many children's books on the subjects of African-American culture and history, including *Freedom Train: The Story of Harriet Tubman* (1963), *Lift Every Voice* (1964), *Let Them Live in Peace* (1968), and *African Folk Tales* (1969).

Crichlow has taught since the 1930s at such institutions as the Harlem Art Center, the George Washington Carver School, Shaw University, SUNY at New Paltz, and the City College of New York. He exhibited at the Federal Art Gallery and ACA Gallery in New York City, the Newark Museum, and Smith College Museum of Art.

REFERENCES

Afro-American Artists New York and Boston. Boston, 1970.
"Ernest Crichlow." *Freedomways* 4 (Summer 1964): 455.
FINE, ELSA HONIG. *The Afro-American Artist: A Search for Identity.* New York, 1973.

RENEE NEWMAN

Crime. The association between blacks and "crime" is all too familiar in today's America. It is fed by the worsening round of ghetto drugs and violence, and by robbery, theft, and genocidal rates of homicide among young black men. In turn it feeds fear and stereotypes among men and women of all races, creating a classic vicious circle by blighting all attempts to rebuild the nation's urban economies, and building frustration among African-American men and women unable to find the jobs needed to escape from dangerous neighborhoods. But while all of this is passionately felt, it is rarely understood. And what seems familiar to those looking at this country now may appear quite different from the broader perspectives offered by a glance first at American history and second at the problems of the new global economy.

Any analysis of "crime" and blacks must begin with the historical fact that the institution of black slavery was not simply our nation's equivalent of original sin, but also quite literally a crime in itself. Historians are unclear about the exact status of the first Africans unloaded at Jamestown in 1619, but they were not "slaves," as that term was later defined, simply because British law did not then allow such a condition. Indentured servants, voluntary or involuntary, were supposed to enjoy specified pro-

tections and limited terms. But it was easy for masters in the loosely governed American colonies, motivated by some combination of racism and greed, to cheat captives who knew neither the law nor the language, and strip them of all rights. Colonial legislatures simply ratified these crimes after the fact, later in the seventeenth century, by decreeing not only that those of uniquely African ancestry must remain slaves for life, but that so must their descendants through the female line forever.

To trace the amount and nature of "crime" committed by or against peoples so enslaved over the next two centuries is complicated by the fact that they had virtually no legal rights nor access to "law." Most jurisdictions, over time, outlawed the most extreme forms of brutality by white masters. But rape, for example, was never made illegal, and in any case, the laws were rarely invoked, and slaves themselves had no power to invoke them. Conversely, a few slave offenses, such as the murder of a white, required formal intervention by the state. But this, too, was rare. The justice system as applied to slaves was mostly designed to prevent or suppress insurrection, a "crime" almost as rare as it was terrifying for masters to imagine. Otherwise, in plantation country, the authorities were not much concerned with the ordinary crimes of vice, theft, and violence, except when, in some places, a poor white underclass traded liquor and other forbidden goods to slaves for stolen items or sexual favors, a traffic worrisome less because it was criminal than because it subverted the lines of caste and allowed a dangerous taste of freedom.

Ordinarily, then, it was left to masters themselves to define what among free people would be "crimes" and to punish as they saw fit. In practice, slave behavior was governed in part by these external sanctions and in part by slaves' own sense of morality. The variations among both external and internal codes were enormous. Masters could be brutal or benign, much or little concerned about behavior that did not directly concern them; slave quarters might be policed internally, either by a humane consensus or by powerful bullies, who themselves knew no sanctions except force.

The only two offenses masters consistently complained about, across the generations and the variations, were the two common to any slave regime— that is, petty theft and sabotage. Both resulted from differences between codes. Thomas Jefferson himself noted that any people themselves defined as "property" could hardly be expected to regard property rights as sacred, and many distinguished between acceptable "taking" from whites and unacceptable "stealing" from each other. Acts of revenge, ranging from tool breakage to arson, were equally inevitable.

The only other generalization possible about "crime" among slaves—or their masters—is that in time the convergence of several influences, including the humane eighteenth-century Enlightenment, Christian missionary work, and the end of the (legal) importation of new, uncomprehending, and often rebellious Africans, had the effect of "softening" a plantation regime under increasing attack from outside. Such crimes against humanity as murder or torture by owners were more often condemned, either by southern white "public opinion," or, however rarely, by the justice system itself. By the mid-nineteenth century, too, both races had long shared the same space, with the language, codes, and behavior of each mutually affecting those of the other. There were, of course, always differences about matters directly involving caste and slavery itself. Otherwise, given the obvious variations in perspective and opportunities, there is no evidence that the descendants of Africans either thought about or committed the usual common-law crimes in ways very different from other southerners.

Developments in urban areas, meanwhile, ran along different but roughly parallel lines. In the North, slaves and later free blacks tended always to live in towns and cities; in the South, freedmen and hired slaves, although far fewer than those who worked in agriculture, made up an important fraction of the urban population. So long as slavery existed, and with it the threat of revolt, all blacks were objects of periodic waves of fear, and subjects of special surveillance. At all times, those who were not live-in servants settled in the poorer areas of town, where they often shared the usual habits of marginalized peoples with their immigrant or misfortunate white neighbors. A few, however, managed against the odds to win places in the urban middle class as skilled artisans or shopkeepers, and sometimes as ministers.

The African-American experience with urban crime was, then, never simple. Observers noted early on that blacks were heavily represented among those accused of offenses ranging from prostitution, petty theft, and vagrancy to homicide; by the early nineteenth century, the more sophisticated were explaining this in essentially modern terms as the expected results of poverty, even desperation, aggravated by racism. In the meantime, however, a small but vital middle class was by the early nineteenth century establishing a very different set of habits and attitudes, represented by such leaders as the shipowner Paul CUFFE, the manufacturing sailmaker James FORTEN, and Richard ALLEN, the blacksmith who founded the AFRICAN METHODIST EPISCOPAL (AME) Church. Much like their white counterparts, they adopted the ideology of republican virtue (later Victorian respectability), and not only proclaimed but lived up to the virtues of hard work, self-help, and moral restraint. Virtually all these men and women fiercely condemned such sections of the criminal code as the FUGITIVE SLAVE LAWS, and many took great risks to break it. Beyond that, as usual, the spectrum of behavior from the criminal to the law-abiding tended to run along lines of economic class rather than race.

Crime, however, when compounded by racism, did contribute to two great differences between the black and white middle classes. First was the stereotyping which has always chained churchgoers and criminals together on the basis of shared color alone. Second, and related, was the fact that urban blacks were continually victimized by individual assault and mob riot, some of it sparked by abolitionist activity, most of it by sheer racial hostility and sometimes economic jealousy. And if rural slavery was somewhat "softened" with time, these urban atrocities were not. Mob activity, rarely punished by the justice system, tended instead to increase as the mid-nineteenth century decades brought both greater fears that abolitionism might lead to CIVIL WAR and a huge influx of violent, drunken refugees from Irish famine, who easily turned their frustrations against those who competed for jobs as domestics, sailors, and laborers.

By the time of the Civil War, then, problems arising out of slavery, poverty, and racism had given African Americans a distinctive experience with crime and justice, more as victims than as perpetrators. In the South, theft on the plantation was more an annoyance than a real problem, and while masters feared mass insurrection, they almost never experienced it. Physical danger was a far greater threat from within the dominant caste than from without, as white tolerance for and even approval of violence contributed to notorious rates of southern murder and mayhem. In the North, a relatively small number of economically insecure free blacks were inevitably involved in many kinds of illegal activity, but this was not out of proportion to their population.

The Civil War and the end of formal bondage brought a new era. But for the 90 percent of African Americans who still lived in the South, disillusionment followed quickly. Without legal slavery, white caste dominance, politically, economically, and psychologically, could be maintained only through illegal violence. Once kept from the polls and denied political power, the freedmen were pushed into second-class citizenship. As former masters no longer protected those who had earlier been valuable property, black men and women were for the first time fair game for a poor white majority frustrated by its own poverty and defeats. As the era of RECONSTRUCTION faded into the heyday of LYNCHING, beginning in the 1880s, the always weak and decentralized southern justice system offered little defense. Black victims of crime committed either by whites or by favored bullies of their own race soon learned that sheriffs were rarely helpful. And the new "chain gang" system, which let county justices turn a profit from renting out the bodies of convicts, not only crippled faith in the legal process, but contributed to the growing number of young men who worked in isolated gangs, building railroads or cutting timber, without any of the social restraints imposed by membership in communities. The standard white justification for repression—an alleged black lust for white women, a charge rarely leveled in the antebellum era—may have had some dim basis in a changed social reality. Even if the specific fear was misplaced, a new black generation was in fact growing up freed from slavery's tight surveillance, with access to guns, and with some sense of their own potential power.

Between the Civil War and World War II, however, the more usual response to the JIM CROW regime was not to retaliate, but simply to move. Even as, like slavery before it, that regime was softened in time without losing its fundamental character, African Americans continued to move out of the rural South and into the city. And there, especially in the North, their experience with crime and justice was, as always, more complex.

The city was where the future lay. And it was the city, in the decades after the Civil War, that was the scene of a long series of historic triumphs: several incomplete but important victories over segregation, the growth of a new professional class, worldwide recognition of outstanding individual artists and athletes, dramatic gains in literacy, and some political leverage. But underneath all this the majority continued to live in relative poverty, plagued by racism. And beginning in the late nineteenth century, a new development made this black poverty more ominous than ever, and different from that of any other group.

The difference is simply that in the period between the Civil War and World War II, racial prejudice, then at its virulent height, barred African Americans from the new economic frontier opened by the contemporary urban industrial revolution. Except for a few places (e.g., Birmingham and Detroit) and a few times (notably around World War I), not only store and office jobs but factory jobs were held to be too good for blacks. Both men and women were then overwhelmingly confined to just two occupational categories: domestic or personal service, and wholly unskilled labor. One obvious result was a chronic poverty that undermined the new professional class—blacks could not afford doctors and lawyers of their own race, and whites would not go to them, making years of sacrifice economically irrelevant and eventu-

ally leading to cynicism about education as a path to opportunity. Another effect was heavy dependence on the government as an employer, particularly for those with the skills to score well on civil service tests. A third was that many, both the desperate and the ambitious, turned to crime.

Criminal statistics are notoriously had to interpret, but an analysis of homicide rates in Philadelphia underlines what was distinctive about the black experience. While in the mid-nineteenth century Irish immigrants (and in the early twentieth, Italians) had murder rates far higher than those of African Americans, rates for both white groups dropped sharply once they were absorbed into the economic mainstream. The urban industrial revolution brought not only relative security, the opportunity for family life, and hope for the future, but also an unprecedented demand for disciplined behavior. As work required more careful cooperation than ever before, the rate of drunken, impulsive, violent behavior dropped all over the western world. But this and other benefits of the industrial revolution came mostly to those allowed to participate in it. For many African Americans the factory system meant no more than cheaper manufactured handguns. The long habit of carrying weapons, or stashing them in bedrooms or kitchens, was first meant for protection against hostile whites, but as usual, it simply raised the stakes in arguments among family and acquaintances. As a result, while white murder rates dropped between the mid-nineteenth century and the mid-twentieth, black rates, while not especially high to begin with, climbed upward.

Crime for profit, as well as purely impulsive violence, contributed to rising rates. Even as white attacks declined and black neighborhoods grew too big to be invaded, there was no letup in the felt need for weapons. Politically weak and dependent on government for employment and other benefits, African Americans could not resist when white politicians, all over the country, informally "zoned" their localities as red light districts. The underside of the famous black success in entertainment is that HARLEM, Beale Street, and the South Side were places where white visitors came not only to hear music but to gamble, to drink, and to pick up black women. Both business disputes and personal quarrels among strangers looking for action were then typically settled with violence.

The underworld of commercial vice was historically among the most integrated milieus in America, but it offered little equal opportunity. For some groups, criminal entrepreneurship served as a temporary step up on the American ladder of success, a source of capital to pass on to another, more legitimate generation. But among African Americans, only the prostitutes were generally able to overcome the biggest challenge of black business: not simply to take money from their own, but to bring it in from far richer white customers. Otherwise, black men and women typically took bets, sold drinks at retail, and profited from some numbers operations in places like Harlem; unlike their white counterparts, they did not go into liquor wholesaling, or build new cities (like Las Vegas) in the desert. The reckless nature of their lives and work prevented them from successfully establishing families. And in addition to their direct contribution to climbing crime rates, their total effect on the black community was doubly negative. The fact that residential segregation did not allow law-abiding men and women to move away from high-crime areas meant that children were continually exposed to the flamboyant high style of illegal enterprise. And criminals not only brought in little money from outside; they prevented others from doing so, as legitimate businesses withered in the absence of white patrons fearful of entering ever bigger and more dangerous ghettos.

WORLD WAR II brought in another era and broke this vicious pattern for a time. The wartime need for black hands and brains finally opened the doors to factories and offices all over the United States, and the 1940s and 1950s were a kind of golden age for African Americans, as the long migration out of the rural South finally led to promising employment in the cities not only for a small elite, but for the great majority. A vigorous CIVIL RIGHTS MOVEMENT brought other gains in the same years, and by 1960, more blacks than whites, proportionately, were both living in cities and working in factories. And one effect of this broad move toward inclusion in the social and economic mainstream was for the first time a drop in black murder rates, and a closing of the gap between black and white rates of violence generally.

But the promise was short-lived. African Americans were admitted into the urban industrial revolution only in its last stages. In the later twentieth century, as older cities began the long process of losing people and jobs, vulnerable blacks were the hardest hit. And as inner city unemployment rates soared higher, the murder rate, too, reversed itself to zigzag up again.

The current situation is, then, simply the result of a progressive economic deterioration among the poorest members of the African-American community, and directly parallels the long death of the old urban industrial economy and its incomplete replacement by a new one. What made the impact of crime more destructive than ever were two differences from older patterns. One was that after World War II, the use of illegal drugs, once far more common among whites, grew rapidly in the urban ghetto. While the sale of drugs, like prostitution, is one of the businesses that brings in retail profits from white customers, the black community reaps little of the big money from wholesaling and importing, but does reap much of the misery from addiction. The other, ironically, was the success of the long black battle for civil rights, and the decline of racism in its stark, older forms. The price paid for the fact that skilled and educated members of the community have been able to move out of the ghetto is that those who cannot escape have been left without legitimate leadership or examples of success. And many, caught up in the worldwide consumer culture without legitimate means of paying for it, feel that criminal enterprise is not simply an attractive outlet for their ambitions, but the only one.

The figures from the FBI's Uniform Crime Reports tell the resulting story: for 1990, the African-American population of the United States, roughly 10 percent of the whole, accounted for 55 percent of all arrests for murder and manslaughter, 43 percent of those for forcible rape, 61 percent for robbery, 30 percent for burglary and larceny, and 39 percent for prostitution and commercialized vice.

A wider perspective suggests two different ways in which to view these depressing figures. One is that, after generations in which the white population directly dominated the black, first through slavery and then through racism, the work of racial subordination is now possible with a minimum of direct interference, as the great majority of black crime is directed inward, destroying the poorest members of the community itself, while the indirect effects in blighting neighborhoods and perpetuating fearful or contemptuous stereotypes reach far beyond those victimized directly. The other is that while African Americans were long kept out of the "mainstream" during the preindustrial era by slavery, and during the industrial era by racism, in this postindustrial era, many are now unhappily caught up in a destructive undertow that has trapped them together with others of all creeds and races. That is, recent ghetto experience with crime and violence is not atypical but archetypical, and simply represents in extreme form what much of the developed world is now facing.

No group or nation has in fact solved the problems of transition from the old manufacturing to the new service economy, with its extreme educational demands and its job losses among the less skilled. The African-American pattern is all too familiar, with its widening gap between those who are prospering as never before and those who are left behind. So are rising rates of crime, not only among new Asian, European, and Hispanic immigrants to the United States, but among all peoples dislocated by change across the globe. And it grows harder to throw stones at a native black "underclass" for behavior and attitudes increasing worldwide: "crime" is only part of a wider complex involving an emphasis on immediate personal gratification at the expense of savings, investment, education, and shared public goals.

A historical perspective, then, suggests that the African-American experience with crime has changed several times. Under the regime of slavery, from the mid-seventeenth century to the mid-nineteenth, it was both unique and extreme; under the regime of overt racism, during the urban industrial revolution from the mid-nineteenth century to the mid-twentieth, it was unique but less extreme; in the current era of milder racism but wrenching economic transition, it is simply extreme, and no longer unique. This perspective offers no clear guide to the future. But it does suggest that since the black experience is not isolated, no dramatic reduction in crime and associated behavior can occur without a solution to problems that plague the whole of the nation, and indeed the world.

REFERENCES

BERRY, MARY FRANCES. *Black Resistance, White Law: A History of Constitutional Racism.* New York, 1971.

BRUNDAGE, W. FITZHUGH. *Lynching in the New South: Georgia and Virginia, 1880–1930.* Urbana and Chicago, 1993.

DRAKE, ST. CLAIR, and HORACE R. CLAYTON. *Black Metropolis: A Study of Negro Life in a Northern City.* New York, 1945.

GENOVESE, EUGENE. *Roll, Jordan, Roll: The World the Slaves Made.* New York, 1974.

GURR, TED ROBERT, ed. *Violence in America.* Vol. 1. *The History of Crime.* Newbury Park, Calif., 1989.

HACKER, ANDREW. *Two Nations: Black and White, Separate, Hostile, and Unequal.* New York, 1992.

KOLCHIN, PETER. *American Slavery, 1619–1877.* New York, 1993.

LANE, ROGER. *Roots of Violence in Black Philadelphia, 1860–1900.* Cambridge, Mass. 1986.

———. *William Dorsey's Philadelphia and Ours: On the Past and Future of the Black City in America.* New York, 1991.

SILBERMAN, CHARLES. *Criminal Violence, Criminal Justice.* New York, 1978.

WILBANKS, WILLIAM. *The Myth of a Racist Criminal Justice System.* Belmont, Calif., 1987.

ROGER LANE

Crisis, The.   *The Crisis* magazine is the official organ of the NATIONAL ASSOCIATION FOR THE ADVANCEMENT OF COLORED PEOPLE (NAACP) founded in 1910 by its first editor, W. E. B. DU BOIS. The publication's original title for many years was

The Crisis: A Record of the Darker Races, and its contents throughout time have reflected its historical importance as the chronicler of African-American history, thought, and culture. The title, Du Bois later wrote, was the suggestion of William English Walling, a founder of the NAACP.

Du Bois said his object in publishing *The Crisis* was "to set forth those facts and arguments which show the danger of race prejudice, particularly as manifested today toward colored people. It takes its name from the fact [that] the editors believe that this is a critical time in the history of the advancement of men." The monthly issues contained subject matter ranging from literary works, editorial commentary, feature stories, and reports on NAACP activities to articles on current events. In the first decades two

THE CRISIS
A RECORD OF THE DARKER RACES

Volume One   NOVEMBER, 1910   Number One

Edited by W. E. BURGHARDT DU BOIS, with the co-operation of Oswald Garrison Villard, J. Max Barber, Charles Edward Russell, Kelly Miller, W. S. Braithwaite and M. D. Maclean.

CONTENTS

Along the Color Line   3

Opinion   7

Editorial   10

The N. A. A. C. P.   12

Athens and Brownsville   13
By MOORFIELD STOREY

The Burden . . .   14

What to Read . .   15

PUBLISHED MONTHLY BY THE
National Association for the Advancement of Colored People
AT TWENTY VESEY STREET   NEW YORK CITY

TEN CENTS A COPY

Cover of *The Crisis,* volume one, number one, November 1910. (Photographs and Prints Division, Schomburg Center for Research in Black Culture, The New York Public Library, Astor, Lenox and Tilden Foundations)

regular features were "American Negroes in College" and "Along the NAACP Battlefront."

Du Bois served as editor for twenty-four years before retiring in 1934. By that time, *The Crisis* could boast among its contributors such luminaries as George Bernard Shaw, Mahatma Gandhi, Sinclair Lewis, Langston HUGHES, and James Weldon JOHNSON. Although founded with the objective of being the official organ of the NAACP, it was also intended to be as self-supporting as possible. But when Du Bois retired as editor in 1934, its circulation had dropped from 100,000 (1918) to only 10,000. His successor as editor was Roy WILKINS, who served in that role until 1949 before being succeeded by James W. Ivy (1949–1967), who was at the helm during the peak civil rights era years.

During the transition years, *The Crisis* shifted its focus from the issues of wartime discrimination against African Americans in the U.S. armed forces, lynchings, and other manifestations of JIM CROW policies, to the courts, where rights were being upheld in voter registration, school desegregation, and housing discrimination. By 1988 circulation had risen to 350,000 subscribers. The magazine's basic editorial philosophy changed little over time from that established by Du Bois, but it had attracted enough major national corporate advertisers to place it on solid financial footing. Moreover, the NAACP had changed its policy to require both members and nonmembers to pay the subscription fee.

The Crisis continues with contributors from all walks of African-American life, including leadership in the clergy, academe, business, law, medicine, and other professions. It continues the tradition of serving as the cultural and social "record of the darker races."

REFERENCES

DU BOIS, W. E. B. *The Autobiography of W. E. Burghardt Du Bois.* New York, 1968.

Douglass Square, Boston, by Allan Crite. (See following page.) (National Archives)

EMERY, EDWIN, and MICHAEL EMERY. *The Press and America*. Englewood Cliffs, N.J., 1978.

CLINT C. WILSON II

Crite, Allan Rohan (March 20, 1910–), painter, illustrator, and art historian. Although Allan Rohan Crite was born in Plainfield, N.J., his career is indelibly linked with Boston, where he moved as a young child and has resided ever since. After showing early talent, he studied at Boston's School of the Museum of Fine Arts from 1929 to 1939 and at other local institutions. His works of the 1930s and 1940s chronicled the black working- and middle-class residents of his Roxbury neighborhood. Their dignified realism reveals the sensitivity of an artist working within his community; they contrast sharply with the corrosively negative depictions of blacks that were prominent at the time.

A deeply committed EPISCOPALIAN, Crite in the late 1930s began to produce religious works in a variety of media. Best known are illustrated books that were radical in their day for depicting biblical characters as black. In strongly drawn images he attempted not just to illustrate traditional SPIRITUALS but to re-create their rhythmic mood by repeating complete and partial images throughout the text, suggesting musical themes and variations. He also created murals and devotional objects for churches throughout the United States.

Crite has exhibited in the United States and abroad, including several exhibitions of sacred art.

REFERENCE

NATIONAL MUSEUM OF AMERICAN ART. THE SMITHSONIAN INSTITUTION. "Allan Rohan Crite." In Regina A. Perry, *Free Within Ourselves*. Washington, D.C., 1992, pp. 50–53.

HELEN M. SHANNON

Criticism, Feminist. The term "black feminist criticism" was first used in Barbara Smith's landmark essay "Towards a Black Feminist Criticism (*Conditions*, 1977). Claiming that the academic segments of the black and women's movements of the 1960s and 1970s had failed to include African-American women's perspectives, Smith argued that critics needed to demonstrate how the literature of black and other Third World women exposes "the complex system of sexism, racism, and economic exploitation" affecting the lives of African-American women. By 1977,

Smith had been a major actor in the founding of black feminist activist groups such as the Comachee River Collective. Her essay passionately argued that such activism would be neither remembered nor analyzed if a corresponding black feminist criticism did not exist. Smith's essay pointed to the relationship between political action and knowledge production—a missing relationship, at that time, in the black feminist movement.

Because educational institutionalization of African-American women's thought had not occurred even in historically black academic institutions, Barbara Smith could not have known that a black feminist critical approach had been simmering for more than a century. As early as the 1830s, in her speeches and essays, African-American activist Maria STEWART initiated the articulation of the relationships among race, class, and gender in American society, that these categories were not discrete categories but were always in relation to each other for both dominant and minority groups. From the 1850s till the end of the nineteenth century, African-American intellectual, activist, and writer Frances HARPER forcefully charted a black feminist perspective in her voluminous works: poetry, fiction, essays, and speeches. In her essay collection *The Voice from the South by a Black Woman of the South* (1892), Anna J. COOPER firmly established the existence of a black women's oppositional intellectual tradition as she critiqued the racism of white American liberals and the sexism of black middle-class men. The literary criticism of HARLEM RENAISSANCE writers such as Jessie Redmon FAUSET as well as the first scholarly study of African-American women's poetry, Frances Collier Durden's thesis *Negro Women in Poetry: From Phillis Wheatley to Margaret Walker* (1947), are early examples of a developing black women's literary/scholarly tradition. But because a black feminist perspective had not been codified as a field of study in the American academy, there was not a systematic approach to the study of black women, nor a passing on of their achievements and concerns in educational institutions. As a result, Barbara Smith's essay represents a turning point in the development of the field of black feminist criticism.

Ironically, the tremendous impact on intellectual inquiry of the black and women's movements of the 1960s and '70s—movements that Smith criticized in her essay—was a decisive factor as to why the responses to her call would result in a new field of study. Her essay was preceded by a least four important publications about black women that had been substantively influenced by these movements. The fiction writer Toni Cade (later BAMBARA) edited the far-ranging anthology *The Black Woman* (1970), a volume that critiqued both the male-focused cultural

One of the highest-ranking black women trade unionists of her time, Maida Springer Kemp (second from left) from the International Ladies' Garment Workers' Union (ILGWU), was a member of a 1945 mission to study the psychological effects of the war on British workers. (Photographs and Prints Division, Schomburg Center for Research in Black Culture, The New York Public Library, Astor, Lenox and Tilden Foundations)

nationalist movement and the (white) women's liberation movement of the 1960s even as it gathered together the points of view of contemporary African-American women from different strata. Historian Gerda Lerner's *Black Women in White America* (1973), the first book-length documentary history of black women in the United States, stressed the uniqueness of black women's history, which the author saw as shaped by intersections of sex, race, and class. Alice WALKER's classic essay "In Search of Our Mothers' Gardens" (*Ms.*, May 1974) explored the restrictive historical contexts of early African-American women writers such as Phillis WHEATLEY and Zora Neale HURSTON and theorized about the creative legacy of black women in the past, most of whom had no access to "high" forms of expression. Walker suggested that supposedly "low" black women's folk forms such as quilting, gardening, and storytelling could also be models of creativity upon which African-American women writers and artists could draw, thus transforming the very concept of what was considered to be artistic production.

A few months later, in August 1974, *Black World,* the premier black intellectual publication of that period, featured on its cover the picture of the then little-known writer Zora Neale Hurston. In that issue, poet and essayist June JORDAN compared and contrasted Hurston's life and work to that of Richard WRIGHT, possibly the best-known black writer of that time. Mary Helen Washington, who would become a major black feminist critic, argued in that same issue that African-American women writers had been neglected, even as she analyzed recurring themes in the works of contemporary African-American women writers such as Paule MARSHALL, Toni MORRISON, and Alice Walker. Understanding the need to make available contemporary African-American women's writing to a general public and to teachers, Washington edited *Black-eyed Susans: Classic Stories by and About Black Women* (1975), the first collection of 1970s African-American women writers. Cade and Washington's anthologies, Walker's essay, and the focus of African-American women writers in *Black World* prepared the ground for literary scholarship on black women writers, which would increase significantly in the next decade.

While these publications of the early 1970s laid the basis for Smith's call in 1977, it is unlikely that her essay would have had the impact on academic inquiry it did, if as a result of the black and women's movements, a small but significant number of black women had not gained entry into mainstream white universities, where they experienced how their histories, ideas, or concerns were nonexistent in the academy. As well, the direction of the first phase of responses to Smith's call would have been quite different if controversial fiction such as Toni Morrison's *The Bluest Eye* (1970) and *Sula* (1974), Alice Walker's *The Third Life of Grange Copeland* (1970) and *In Love with Trouble* (1973), or poetry collections such as Audre LORDE's *From a Land Where Other People Live* (1973) and June Jordan's *Things That I Do in the Dark: Selected Poetry* (1977) had not been circulating among black women academics. Contemporary African-American women writers provided much of the impetus for the beginnings of a contemporary black feminist approach. Thus, much of the initial scholarship using black feminist critical approaches came primarily from literary scholars.

In the 1980s, major anthologies in specific disciplines, the means by which new fields in the academy were often initially charted, were published by and about black women, an indication that a black women-centered studies were coming into being. The literary anthology *Sturdy Black Bridges: Visions of Black Women in Literature* (1979) edited by Roseann Bell, Bettye Parker, and Beverly Guy-Sheftall (the premier black feminist in historically black institutions), included not only African-American women writers but also the writings and criticism of contemporary Caribbean and African women pointed to the need for comparative studies of women in the African diaspora. In 1984 the poet Mari Brown edited *Black Women Writers: A Critical Evaluation, 1950–1980,* a collection of essays that clearly indicated the existence of many literary critics who specialized in African-American women's writing. *Changing Our Own Words: Essays on Criticism, Theory, and Writing by Black Women,* edited by Cheryl Wall (1990), summed up much of black feminist literary critical scholarship of the 1980s, for it included not only a history of that direction but also self-reflective essays on its value to significant academic debates on race, sexuality, the family, community, tradition, and power.

African-American women scholars also were immersed in the social context of their sisters in the past and the present. Important social science anthologies of that period were: *The Black Woman* (1980), edited by La Frances Rodgers-Rose, which employed a so-ciological methodology to emphasize differences between African-American and European-American women, while *The Black Woman Cross-Culturally* (1981), edited by Filomina Chiomka Steady, relied heavily on an anthropological approach as a way of comparing societal contexts of black women in the diaspora. The developing interdisciplinary orientation of a black woman-centered scholarly perspective culminated in the anthology *All the Women Are White, All the Blacks Are Men, but Some of Us Are Brave* (1982), in which the editors Gloria Hull, Patricia Bell Scott, and Barbara Smith proposed the need for the field of black women's studies, for which the contributors provided perspectives, since African-American women's contributions and issues were generally excluded in black (male) studies and (white) women's studies.

At the same time, individual black women scholars published major studies. Major historical studies were published as scholars began to see the necessity for excavating the voices of African-American women of the past if they were to situate black women in the present. In the area of history, Sharon Harley and Rosalyn Terborg-Penn's collection of essays *The African-American Woman* (1978), laid the basis for a black feminist approach, since that study analyzed the roles that African-American women had played not only in the abolitionist movement but also the women's rights movement of the nineteenth century, and explored the ways in which African-American women experienced sexism as well as racism in both these movements. That study was followed by Angela DAVIS's *Women, Race, and Class* (1981), which synthesized a Marxist and black feminist approach to the history of African-American women, so that the intersections of gender, race, and class could be directly analyzed. By the mid-1980s the studies in black women's histories reached a level of sophistication as different approaches began to emerge. Paula Giddings' popular historical study *When and Where I Enter: The Impact of Black Women on Race and Sex in America* (1984) revised previous African-American historical studies that had been primarily male-centered by demonstrating the considerable impact African-American women had had on the black struggles for freedom in the United States. Dorothy Sterling's *We Are Your Sisters: Black Women in the Nineteenth Century* (1984) is a primary sourcebook for black women's feminist activity in the nineteenth century. Jacqueline Jones's *Labor of Love, Labor of Sorrow: Black Women, Work, and Family, from Slavery to the Present* (1985) employed the labor history approach to detail the work and family lives of black women. Deborah Gray White's *Ar'n't I a Woman? Female Slaves in the Plantation South* (1985) is what black historian Cheryl Townsend Gilkes calls

Forty-six women employees of male-dominated *Newsweek* magazine conduct a press conference to announce their intent to sue the magazine under the 1964 Civil Rights Act. Charging discrimination in jobs and hiring, they said they are "forced to assume a subsidiary role simply because of their sex." Seated (from left to right) are employees Patricia Lunden, Mary Pleshette, Eleanor Holmes Norton, and ACLU legal director Lucy Howard, March 16, 1970. (UPI/Bettmann)

an ethnohistory in that it presented an empirical analysis of slave women's experience to establish the ways in which slave women were agents of history and shapers of culture.

Important literary studies also helped to chart the field of black feminist criticism. While Barbara T. Christian's *Black Women Novelists: The Development of a Tradition* (1980)—the first book-length study of African-American women novelists—emphasized the writings of contemporary novelists Paule Marshall, Toni Morrison, and Alice Walker, that study used an interdisciplinary approach as the framework for claiming an identifiable African-American literary tradition dating back to nineteenth-century writer Frances Harper. Christian approached their novels as one means by which African-American women situated themselves as subjects within their cultural/artistic context even as they responded to the restrictions of sexism, racism, and class exploitation. That concept of a specific African-American women's literary tradition was further extended in *Conjuring: Black Women, Fiction, and Literary Tradition* (1985), edited by Marjorie Pryse and Hortense Spillers.

Spillers's provocative "Afterword" forecast a shift in the scope and structural nature of black feminist criticisms, since she enunciated the ruptures and multiplicities in what had been regarded as an apparently monolithic tradition.

While these historical and literary critical studies implied a black feminist perspective, they did not specifically name black feminist criticism as their subject. In the 1980s a second epistemological moment in feminist criticism occurred. It was a clearly defined shift as black women scholars intentionally studied black women from the perspective of a developing black feminist ideology. Again a major essay signaled that shift. As opposed to Smith's essay "Towards a Black Feminist Criticism," which was published in *Conditions,* a nonacademic journal, Deborah McDowell's essay "New Directions for Black Feminism" (1980) was published in the academic journal *Black American Literature Forum,* an indication that black feminist criticism was beginning to take hold in the academy. In that essay, McDowell made distinctions between scholarship on black women, and a specifically black feminist criticism that might be applied to writings by groups other than African-American women. What was "black feminist criticism," as opposed to a black women-centered academic focus that accepted all African-American women who might or might not employ a feminist approach? Could a black feminist inquiry include black male critics such as Henry Louis Gates, Jr., who was already writing essays about Zora Neale Hurston and Alice Walker's texts, which would be published in his award-winning *The Signifying Monkey* (1988)? Were white feminist inclusions of black feminism analyses in such volumes as *Feminist Criticism and Social Change* (1985), edited by Judith Newton and Deborah Rosenfelt, to be considered instances of black feminist criticism? In other words, could only black women do black feminist criticism? McDowell interrogated issues of identity and territoriality into the debates that attempted to define black feminist criticism. Her essay forecast difficult issues about power relations in the academic as black male critics and white female critics became "experts" on black women's literature and theory, as exemplified by Gates's editing of a collection of critical essays, *Reading Black, Reading Feminist* (1990), which included readings by black and white women and men, and by Houston A. Baker's critical study *Workings of the Spirit: The Poetics of Afro-American Women's Writing* (1991).

McDowell suggested parameters for black feminist criticism—that it must be contextually informed and that it must pay close attention to individual texts. What did her insistence on a close reading of texts mean for a black feminist interdisciplinary approach? In 1980, bell hooks, who would become a major black feminist cultural critic, published *Ain't I a Woman: Black Women and Feminism* (1980), which raised theoretical questions about the sociopolitical framework within which black women might be studied. And in popular culture, Michele Wallace published *Black Macho and the Myth of the Superwoman* (1980), which analyzed both sexism in the Black Power movements of the 1960s and African-American women's internalization of their oppression. A controversial book, *Black Macho,* along with Ntozake SHANGE's play *for colored girls who have considered suicide/when the rainbow is enuf* (1977) and Alice Walker's novel *The Color Purple* (1983) thrust issues of intersection of sexism and racism, the twin oppressions that have historically and presently plagued black women, into the public arena. On the academic front, Christian answered McDowell's queries, and Wallace and Shange's works with *Black Feminist Criticism* (1985), a collection of essays that stressed the practice and process of the black feminist critic within and without the university, and that black feminist criticism was situated at the points at which the acad-

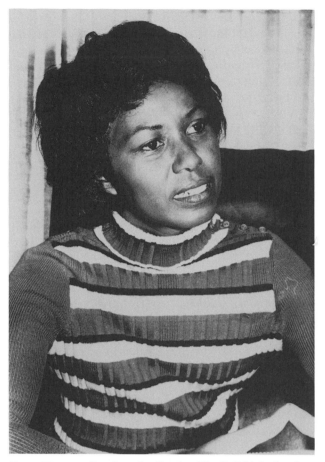

Rep. Yvonne Brathwaite Burke (D–Calif.) is the first member of Congress to receive maternity leave. She was granted the leave by House Speaker Carl Albert (D–Okla.) in November 1972. (AP/Wide World Photos)

emy and "the world" converged. The interdisciplinary approaches launched by black feminists during the early 1980s culminated in *Reconstructing Womanhood: The Emergence of the Afro-American Novelist, of the Afro-American Woman* (1985), in which Hazel Carby focused on the conditions affecting the production of nineteenth-century texts, and therefore on these texts as representations.

At the same time that black feminist scholars began to form alliances with other U.S. women of color feminists, Dexter Fisher's anthology *The Third Woman: Minority Women Writers of the United States* (1980) and *This Bridge Called My Back* (1981), edited by Chicana feminists Gloria Anzaldua and Cherrie Moraga and introduced by African-American writer Toni Cade, acknowledged cultural differences even as they demonstrated how racism, sexism, and class exploitation were commonalities shared by women of color in the United States. *This Bridge* would forecast the importance that the concept of difference would have in the late 1980s on the direction of black feminist criticisms. The culmination of that perspective is evident in the anthology *Making Face, Making Soul,* edited by Gloria Anzaldua (1993), a sophisticated presentation of the development of women of color thought, especially in the West.

One major challenge to the development of a black feminist criticism has been the omission of black lesbian inquiry. Barbara Smith's anthology of black lesbian writing, *Home Girls* (1983), and poet Audre Lorde's collection of essays *Sister Outsider* (1984) and her automythobiography *Zami* (1982) provided the theoretical grounding for the exploration of black lesbian thought and expression. At the same time, creative writer Alice Walker's *The Color Purple* (1983), which included a black lesbian relationship at the center of the novel, won a Pulitzer Prize for fiction. A new writer, Gloria NAYLOR, included in her prize-winning volume *The Women of Brewster Place* a segment on black lesbians. The result was that analyses of sexual preference and of homophobia were increasingly included in black feminist criticisms. Such a shift in perspective was indicated by scholarly essays such as Barbara T. Christian's "No More Buried Lives: The Theme of Lesbianism in Audre Lorde's *Zami*"; Gloria Naylor's *The Women of Brewster Place;* Ntozake Shange's *Sassafras, Cypress, and Indigo;* and Alice Walker's *The Color Purple* (1984) and by Barbara Smith's "The Truth That Never Hurts: Black Lesbians in Fiction in the 1980s" (1990).

The title of hooks's second book, *From Margin to Center: Black Feminism* (1984), delineated the shift that was taking place among black feminist academic critics in the 1980s. Rather than conceiving of black feminist theory as a marginal epistemology, hooks demonstrated the ways in which it transformed supposedly central ways of thinking. In *Black Feminist Thought: Knowledge Consciousness and the Politics of Empowerment* (1990), sociologist Patricia Hill Collins sought to explore the necessary connections among an epistemology, praxis, and empowerment. Her project established the fact "that African-American women [had] created an independent, viable yet subjugated knowledge concerning [their] own subordination," even as she explored the ways in which "contemporary Black women intellectuals are engaged in the struggle to reconceptualize all dimensions of the dialectic of oppression and activism as it applies to African-American women." Because her critique emphasized the unique qualities that African-American women have had to develop as well as the structural foundations of racism, sexism, and class exploitation at which black women have been the vortex, she also demonstrates the ways in which black feminist thought is central, rather than marginal, to the transformation of the production of knowledge.

As Hill's work indicated, one raging debate in black feminist academic circles was the questioning of definitions of "theory." What is considered theory, what are its purposes, and what are the relationships among definitions of theory, academic and nonacademic audiences, and the use of language. In the late 1980s, analyses such as Barbara I. Christian's "The Race for Theory" (1988), and hooks's *Talking Black: Thinking Feminist, Thinking Black,* wrestled with definitions of "theory" as well as with the relationship of theory to practice. A recent example of this concern is the collection *Theorizing Black Feminisms: The Visionary Pragmatism of Black Women* (1994), edited by Stanlie James and Abena Busia.

In the introduction to *Feminist Theory in Practice and Process* (*Signs,* 1989), the editors noted that "just as one of the first acts in the development of a feminist theory was to reject the standpoint and experience of white men as normative, so too one of the first acts in developing black feminist theory has been to reject the perspectives of white women as normative. . . ." Perhaps the major epistemological change that black feminist criticism effected was that it challenged the concept of a universalized woman. It also became increasingly clear that the field was not monolithic and had evolved into a multiplicity of approaches that explore the ways in which black women have affected and been affected by historical, sociological, literary, and cultural phenomena. A crucial text of the 1980s was Audre Lorde's *Sister Outsider.* In essays such as "Age, Race, Class, and Sex: Women Redefining Difference," Lorde used the poetic possibilities of language to theorize about how structural oppressions stem from the same source: "an inability to recognize the notion of difference as a dynamic human force which is enriching rather than threatening to the defined self."

That epistemological shift would affect the ways in which not only African-American women but also women throughout the world would insist that they be studied. There were at least two directions for black feminist criticism that resulted from this epistemological development: black women's diasporic studies and postcolonial feminist studies. At least two other related fields, black men's studies and cultural studies, have been greatly influenced by the concepts and methodologies of black feminist criticism.

Black women-centered studies about African, Caribbean, and British black women writers started appearing in mid-1980s with the publication of numerous critical essays on contemporary African women writers, and with Elaine Savory Fido's *Out of the Kumbla: Caribbean Women and Literature* (1990), a collection of critical essays on Caribbean women writers. Studies by individual scholars also appeared, such as Lloyd Brown's *Women Writers in Black Africa*

(1981), Oladele Taiwo's *Female Novelists in Modern Africa* (1984), and Rudo B. Gaidzanwa's *Images of Women in Zimbabwean Literature* (1985). Evelyn O'Callaghan's *Woman Version: Theoretical Approaches to West Indian Fiction by Women* (1994) is an example of the ways in which critics are beginning to use different theoretical approaches to black diasporic women's writings. At the same time, collections such as *Unheard Words* (1985), edited by Mineke Schipper, and essays such as Gayatri Spivak's "Three Women's Texts and a Critique of Imperialism" (1985) and Chandra Mohantry's "Under Western Eyes: Feminist Scholarship and Colonial Discourses" (1988), introduced the concept of colonial discourses as a necessary element in studying black women outside the United States. Postcolonial feminist critics insisted that feminist scholarship "is not the mere production of knowledge. . . . It is a political praxis which counters and resists the totalizing imperative of age-old 'legitimate' and 'scientific' bodies of knowledge" (Chandry, 1988). That approach is evident in *Wild Women in the Whirlwind: Afra-American Culture and the Contemporary Literary Renaissance* (1990), edited by Joanne M. Braxton and Andree Nicola McLaughlin, which collected essays focused on the oral tradition—the folk culture as well as the literary production of black women throughout the world.

By the late 1980s black feminist criticisms had developed into other strains besides that of literary studies: gender studies that emphasized *difference* as the central trope of investigation, and the interdisciplinary academic field of cultural studies. A derivative of gender studies, black men's studies, is a developing area in which black men have begun to explore the ways in which constructions of masculinity in relation to race were often camouflaged in U.S. society. Again, creative writers were the impetus for this movement. Major contemporary African-American male writers such as John WIDEMAN and Clarence MAJOR credited African-American women's intellectual questions in the 1970s with opening spaces for them to investigate themselves as men in relationships with family, and female and male lovers as opposed to the white/black border wars to which many black male writers of the past had been restricted. Again, anthologies are important in charting this new field: Joseph Beane's *Brother to Brother* (1993), Richard Myers and Jacob Gorden's *The African-American Black Male, His Person, Status, and Family,* and most recently Robert Allen and Herb Boyd's *Brother Man* (1995).

The interdisciplinary though diverse field of cultural studies is unified by the desire of scholars and critics to see "culture, not as a 'canon' or a 'tradition' but as the embodiment and site of antagonistic rela-

tions of domination and subordination, that is as a productive network of power relations" (*Differences*, p. 19), a point of view central to the development of black feminist criticism since black women's cultural production had fallen so completely outside the "canon," and since it was impossible to study black women without investigating issues of domination and subordination. What the field of cultural studies emphasizes, however, is the analysis, specifically of domination and subordination, in cultural production. Examples of cultural studies from a black feminist perspective are bell hooks's *Outlaw Culture: Resisting Representations* (1994) and Karla Holloway's *Codes of Conduct: Race, Ethics, and the Color of Our Character* (1994).

Because black feminist criticism has been positioned at the vortex of so many discourses and because black women are often characterized as the "quintessential site of difference," black feminist criticism has had much influence on race, gender, women of color, postcolonial, and queer theories. It might appear that it is alive and well in the academy. In 1994, however, two essays were published that question that happy ending. In "Diminishing Returns: Can Black Feminism(s) Survive the Academy?" Barbara Christian wondered why it is that while black feminist criticism's central concept, the relations among race, class, and gender, has become so integral to academic production, fewer and fewer blackwomen are receiving Ph.D.s or becoming academic. What are the ramifications for black feminist thought? What does this phenomenon have to do with academic culture in historically white institutions in relation to race and gender? And in "The Occult of True Black Womanhood: Critical Demeanor and Black Feminist Studies" (*Signs*), Ann DuCille examines "the implications and consequences of the current explosion of interest in black women as literary and historical subjects even as this interest . . . increasingly marginalizes both the black women critics and scholars who excavated the fields in question and their black feminist 'daughters' who would further develop those fields." In a sense Christian and DuCille's essays turned on its head the call Barbara Smith issued in her landmark essay. Having established a framework through which studies of black women's thought have greatly influenced other significant fields of thought, black feminist critics are increasingly aware of how these oppressions have heightened rather than decreased since the mid-1980s for black women in the United States, and have affected their positions as thinkers both within and without the academy.

That awareness was central to the calling of the conference "Black Women in the Academy: Defending Our Name," 1894–1994," which was convened

January 13–15, 1994, at Massachusetts Institute of Technology. In her essay "The Territory Between Us: A Report on 'Black Women in the Academy: Defending Our Name, 1894–1994,' " Saidiya Hartman tells us that the conference planners, Evelyn Hammonds and Robin Kilson, assistant professors at MIT, "recognized the need for a public forum of black women academics in order to address issues of research survival in the academy and the repressive political climate of the 1980s and 1990s, in which black people had been constructed as the domestic enemy and black women, in particular as welfare queens, whores, breeders, and quota queens." The conveners were amazed when more than two thousand black women in the academy responded. While Hartman's essay focused n the difficulties inherent in a "too easy" definition of community, her report is a testimony to the crisis black women in the academy are experiencing. While black feminist criticism development since the mid-1970s may have been a successful academic field in that it has become so much a part of academic inquiry in many disciplines that it occupies an almost invisible space, its continued development may well depend on the extent to which black women in the society are themselves visibly empowered by it.

REFERENCES

BAKER, HOUSTON A. *Workings of the Spirit: The Poetics of Afro-American Women's Writing*. Chicago, 1991.

BAMBARA, TONI CADE, ed. *The Black Woman*. New York, 1970.

BELL, ROSEANN P., BETTYE J. PARKER, BEVERLY GUY-SHEFTALL, eds. *Sturdy Black Bridges: Visions of Black Women in Literature*. Garden City, N.Y., 1979.

BROWN, MARI. *Black Women Writers: A Critical Evaluation, 1950–1980*. 1984.

CARBY, HAZEL. *Reconstructing Womanhood: The Emergence of the Afro-American Novelist*. New York, 1985.

CHRISTIAN, BARBARA T. *Black Feminist Criticism*. 1985.

———. *Black Women Novelists: The Development of a Tradition*. Westport, Conn., 1980.

COLLINS, PATRICIA HILL. *Black Feminist Thought: Knowledge Consciousness and the Politics of Empowerment*. Boston, 1990.

DAVIS, ANGELA. *Women, Race, and Class*. New York, 1981.

GATES, HENRY LOUIS. *The Signifying Monkey*. New York, 1988.

GIDDINGS, PAULA. *When and Where I Enter: The Impact of Black Women on Race and Sex in America*. New York, 1984.

HOLLOWAY, KARLA. *Codes of Conduct: Race, Ethics, and the Color of Our Character*. New Brunswick, N.J., 1995.

HOOKS, BELL. *Ain't I a Woman: Black Women and Feminism*. Boston, 1981.

———. *Outlaw Culture: Resisting Representations*. New York, 1994.

JAMES, STANLIE, and ABENA BUSIA. *Theorizing Black Feminisms: The Visionary Pragmatism of Black Women*. 1994.

PRYSE, MARJORIE, and HORTENSE SPILLERS, eds. *Conjuring: Black Women, Fiction, and Literary Tradition*. Bloomington, Ill., 1985.

SMITH, BARBARA. *Home Girls*. New York, 1983.

———. "Towards a Black Feminist Criticism." In *Conditions*. New York, 1977.

STEADY, FILOMINA CHIOMKA, ed. *The Black Woman Cross-Culturally*. Cambridge, Mass., 1981.

WALKER, ALICE. "In Search of Our Mother's Gardens." *Ms.* (May 1974).

WALL, CHERYL, ed. *Changing Our Own Words: Essays on Criticism, Theory, and Writing by Black Women*. New Brunswick, N.J., 1989.

WASHINGTON, MARY HELEN, ed. *Black-Eyed Susans: Classic Stories by and About Black Women*. Garden City, N.Y., 1975.

BARBARA T. CHRISTIAN

Criticism, Literary. In his *Notes on the State of Virginia*, Thomas Jefferson, to illustrate his assertions of Negro inferiority, remarked, "Religion indeed has produced a Phyllis Whately [*sic;* reference is to Phillis WHEATLEY], but it could not produce a poet. The compositions published under her name are below the dignity of criticism" (p. 189). Jefferson's attitude of dismissal extended equally to the writers Jupiter HAMMON and Ignatius Sancho and to every other black person. Though his discussion of Wheatley's work falls short, by his own admission, of literary criticism, it initiates a tradition of disparagement in which European-American critics use ideology as a grounds for judging African-American writing inferior. Not surprisingly, the work of African-American critics has often been conceived, at least implicitly, in response to such critical chauvinism.

African-American literary criticism should be understood to comprise several interlocking categories of writing: criticism of works by African Americans, criticism by African Americans, and criticism of African-American works by African-American critics. Furthermore, criticism includes literary biography, literary history, literary theory, and cultural theory as well as analyses of specific literary works. Thus African-American literary criticism is a broadly defined genre, and because the racial category "black" or "African American" has always been heavily laden with social values, literary criticism has been one of the realms in which questions of racial values and racial identity have always been articulated and contested.

The explicitly Euro-chauvinist tradition that uses literary criticism as a pretext for assertions of white supremacy and black inferiority, initiated by Jefferson and perpetuated through the late twentieth century, has its vigorously antagonistic counterpart in the tradition that commits itself to demonstrating through criticism the distinctiveness and integrity of African-American artists and culture. Despite their sharp disagreements, these two traditions hold in common the premise that the race of the author should be a major consideration for the critic. This presumption, needless to say, has not generally been inflicted upon European-American authors, and such differential treatment has provoked anger or anxiety in many black writers. Ironically, this passion or its absence has manifested itself in writers' works and has in turn shaped the critical responses to their works. Such are the literary burdens of race.

In one sense, Jefferson's overtly dismissive comments are anomalous to the critical tradition. If work is "below the dignity of criticism," why would a critic lower himself to it? More typically, racial chauvinism has been expressed in the form of condescending praise. For example, in 1926, just as the HARLEM RENAISSANCE was beginning, John Nelson published *The Negro Character in American Literature,* the first full-length study of this subject. Nelson took particular delight in the comic and sentimental portraits of black people in works by turn-of-the-century writers such as Thomas Nelson Page, Irwin Russell, and Joel Chandler Harris:

> [the Negro's] irresistible gaiety, his gift for dance and song, his spontaneity and childish delight in gay colors and all forms of display, his love of high-sounding words, his fondness for chicken and watermelon, his gullibility, his excuse-making powers, his whimsicality, his illogicalness and superstition, his droll philosophy, his genial shiftlessness and laziness, his "superb capacity for laughter"—these traits were appreciated as never before, were revalued and pronounced delightful.

In other words, Nelson loved minstrelsy. Nelson's comments are noteworthy because they both reflect the attitudes of many critics and indicate implicitly the kind of portrayals of black people that critics found acceptable, even in works by black writers: colorful and comical.

The impatience of such critics with black writers who rendered more serious or realistic depictions of African-American life is articulated by David Littlejohn in *Black on White: A Critical Survey of Writing by American Negroes* (1966):

> A white reader is saddened, then burdened, then numbed by the deadly sameness, the bleak wooden round of ugly emotions and situations; the same frustrated dreams, the same issues and charges and formulas and events repeated over and over, in book after book . . . the responding spirit is dulled, finally, bored by the iteration of hopelessness, the sordid limitation of the soul in the tight closet of the black imagination.

By contrast, Littlejohn praises Gwendolyn BROOKS because she is "far more a poet than a Negro." The implication, clearly, is that "Negro" and "poet" are somehow antithetical. Such remarks illustrate the continuity of racially dismissive and condescending attitudes in American literary criticism over a span of two centuries. African-American writers and critics have produced their work fully cognizant that many highly educated white Americans continue to espouse such views.

Not surprisingly, then, the most conspicuous African-American critical tradition has been polemical. This polemical tradition has been primarily concerned to use literary criticism as a means of addressing social issues, not as a form of aesthetic engagement. In the nineteenth century, African-American criticism belonged almost exclusively to this genre; but there was relatively little of it, since the quantity of African-American literature was small and was primarily limited to the black periodical press. Not until after the turn of the century did the social and economic conditions exist to support a class of black professional critics. Thus the criticism published during the nineteenth century was generally the work of activists who published work in various genres. Frederick DOUGLASS, for example, sometimes commented on books, but he was not a literary critic. Similarly, characters in the fiction of Frances E. W. HARPER and Pauline HOPKINS sometimes discuss books, but this is not what we mean by literary criticism, either.

Kelly MILLER, a professor and administrator at HOWARD UNIVERSITY, published fine, erudite, vigorously argued, and elegantly balanced essays on a broad range of topics. His collection *Race Adjustments* (1908) includes essays on Thomas Dixon's *The Leopard's Spots* and Walt Whitman. The essay on *The Leopard's Spots,* a novel that sold over a million copies, challenges the racist views and historical accuracy of Dixon's narrative about RECONSTRUCTION. Furthermore, Miller contests Dixon's bigoted and inaccurate depiction of African Americans and racial politics at the turn of the century. In this essay, the critic appears in the guise of racial spokesman and defender. By contrast, "What Walt Whitman Means to the Negro" allows Miller to display his literary erudition and sensibility as well as to make a social point. He celebrates Whitman's work because of its democratic inclusiveness, such that "all are welcome; none are denied, shunned, avoided, ridiculed, or made to feel ashamed" (p. 204). Furthermore, he asserts:

> Whitman has a special meaning to the Negro, not only because of his literary portrayal; he has lessons also. He inculcates the lesson of ennobling self-esteem. He teaches the Negro that "there is no sweeter fat than sticks to his own bones." He urges him to accept nothing that "insults his own soul" (p. 208).

These comments reflected Miller's own grounding in a late nineteenth-century culture in which moral issues were a paramount concern for literary critics.

That same predisposition is conspicuous in the literary criticism of the most influential African-American literary critic of Miller's generation: W. E. B. DU BOIS. Du Bois is not generally regarded as a literary critic, but in judging intellectuals trained in the late nineteenth century, disciplinary categories of the late twentieth century can be misleading. Like Kelly Miller and Charles Waddell CHESNUTT, Du Bois was a "man of letters." He published distinguished writing in virtually every genre. As editor of the CRISIS for twenty-five years, he was easily the most widely read African-American writer of the early twentieth century. In his articles, columns, and commentaries, Du Bois addressed virtually every issue, event, and publication of relevance to African Americans.

It was not merely the quantity of his output nor the size of his audience, however, that made Du Bois so influential. Rather, Du Bois's accomplishments as a scholar and activist, his incomparable erudition, his elegant writing style and refined literary sensibility, and his intense passion for truth, justice, and beauty all combined to make him authoritative and compelling. Thus his judgments about particular artists or works carried extraordinary weight. Du Bois used his enormous prestige to endorse and publicize the works of black writers, including HARLEM RENAISSANCE figures such as Countee CULLEN, Langston HUGHES, and Jessie FAUSET.

The essay that best represents Du Bois as a visionary and inspirational critic is his "Criteria of Negro Art" (1926). In it he reiterates his belief, earlier expressed in *The Souls of Black Folk* (1903), that black people have a special calling to revive in a debased, materialist nation an appreciation for beauty and higher values:

> Who shall let this world be beautiful? Who shall restore to men the glory of sunsets and the peace of quiet sleep? We black folk may help for we have within us as a race new stirrings; stirrings of the beginning of a new appreciation of joy, a new desire to create, of a new will to be; as though in this morning of group life we had awakened from some sleep that at once dimly mourns the past and dreams a splendid future. . . .

After declaring the unity of beauty with truth and justice, Du Bois concludes with a prophecy: "The ultimate art coming from black folk is going to be just as beautiful, and beautiful largely in the same ways, as the art that comes from white folk, or yellow, or red; but the point today is that until the art of the black folk compells recognition they will not be rated as human." For Du Bois, then, the creation of black art and the struggle for social justice were inseparable, and by implication, artists should be understood as warriors in this struggle, not deserters from it. This formulation encourages young artists to pursue their own aesthetic visions and offers them protection against charges of irrelevance or frivolity, such as political pragmatists have often advanced against art. While Du Bois did not hesitate to criticize particular works bluntly and even harshly, his broader critical impact was as a champion of literary art. As a critic, he exerted a major influence on artists of the Harlem Renaissance; and as a model of intellectual activism, he influenced the radical critics of the 1930s and 1960s.

Though Du Bois was the preeminent African-American critic and intellectual life of the Harlem Renaissance decade (the 1920s), several other notable critics of African-American writing emerged during that period. James Weldon JOHNSON deserves to be remembered alongside Du Bois as a truly exemplary figure who exerted influence in several fields. He was a poet, novelist, essayist, songwriter, civil rights leader, and diplomat, and though he is not usually described as a literary critic, his preface to the first edition of *The Book of American Negro Poetry* (1921) is one of the seminal essays on African-American poetry.

Johnson's preface serves a number of purposes at once. It identifies the major styles and tendencies of African-American artistic expression and assesses the relationship of black culture to the broader American and international cultures. It considers the relationship between vernacular culture and fine art traditions and does so with a refreshingly uncondescending appreciation of black popular arts such as the

BLUES and the cakewalk. And not least, it provides a concise historical overview of African-American poetry from Jupiter HAMMON and Phillis WHEATLEY to Langston Hughes and other poets born about the turn of the century. In effect, the essay sets a broad context with its detailed discussions of eighteenth- and nineteenth-century poets and other aesthetic forms, though the anthology actually begins with Paul Laurence DUNBAR. In its time *The Book of American Negro Poetry* was important for introducing many poets who were unfamiliar to the reading public. Its preface endures, however, as one of the best and most insightful discussions of the African-American poetic tradition.

Another distinguished and influential critic of the 1920s was Alain Leroy LOCKE, a philosopher, essayist, editor, art collector, critic, and the first African-American Rhodes scholar. Like Du Bois, Locke was a man of broad interests and influence. He is most commonly remembered as the editor of the NEW NEGRO (1925), a volume that announced and sought to define the cultural explosion known subsequently as the Harlem Renaissance. At the time it was more often called "the New Negro Movement," and Alain Locke was regarded as its midwife and intellectual leader.

Locke's literary essays of the 1920s reflect a fundamental conflict between two antagonistic intellectual tendencies. On the one hand, Locke was deeply committed to empirical social science and to an understanding of race in social and cultural terms. This tendency is expressed in his introductory essay, "The New Negro," when he argues that the Negro Renaissance should be understood in relation to recent migration from the rural South, the black response to urban social conditions, and a political consciousness developed from struggles over race, labor, economics, and related issues. In this sense, he argues, developments in Harlem should be understood in the context of national and international developments, and Harlem would become a "race capital" because "Harlem has the same role to play for the New Negro as Dublin has had for the New Ireland or Prague for the New Czechoslovakia" (p. 7).

On the other hand, Locke's thinking also reveals a strain of romantic primitivism, a tendency that some scholars attribute to his close association with the white philanthropist and Negrophile Charlotte Osgood Mason. "Godmother," as she insisted she be called, believed that white civilization was decadent and doomed unless it could be infused with the vitality inherent in "primitive" cultures, such as black and Native American. Thus she undertook to subsidize African-American artists, and with Locke as her talent scout, she became a patroness to Langston

Hughes, Zora Neale HURSTON, Aaron DOUGLAS, and others. Locke, himself, received considerable largesse from Godmother, enabling him to travel to Europe annually and helping him to acquire what developed into a major collection of African art. "Negro Youth Speaks," Locke's introduction to the literature section of the volume, argues:

> Art cannot disdain the gift of a natural irony, of a transfiguring imagination, of rhapsodic Biblical speech, of dynamic musical swing, of cosmic emotion such as only the gifted pagans knew, of a return to nature, not by way of the forced and worn formula of Romanticism, but through the closeness of an imagination that has never broken kinship with nature (p. 52).

Since Locke published this primitivist manifesto in 1925 and did not meet Mrs. Mason until 1926, perhaps their relationship would be more aptly described as a confluence of like minds. Mrs. Mason doubtless encouraged this aspect of Locke's thinking, but she did not initiate it.

By the late 1930s Locke repudiated primitivism, returning to an emphasis on social experience as the basis of black cultural expression. Locke might be more aptly described as a cultural critic than as a literary critic, strictly speaking. Nevertheless, his literary influence was substantial because of his essays, anthologies, correspondence, social activity, and his role as a procurer of patronage. In addition to *The New Negro,* he also published *Plays of Negro Life* (1927), coedited with T. Montgomery Gregory.

Another influential anthologist of this period was William Stanley BRAITHWAITE. Unlike Locke, Braithwaite was himself a creative writer—a poet—and his purview was not exclusively or even primarily African American. Raised by very fair-skinned parents who encouraged young William not to associate with black people, Braithwaite eventually developed into a poet whose work betrayed virtually no evidence of his African-American background. He developed a substantial reputation as an essayist and reviewer for leading literary magazines such as *Atlantic Monthly, North American Review,* and *Scribner's.* His greatest fame and influence, however, accrued from his several poetry anthologies, such as *The Book of Elizabethan Verse,* and the series of annual compilations that he edited from 1913 to 1929, called *Anthology of Magazine Verse.* In this editorial capacity, he helped to bring national attention to such younger writers as Carl Sandburg, Edgar Lee Masters, and Vachel Lindsay. Though he was celebrated by African-Americans—for example, he won the SPINGARN MEDAL in 1918—many of his readers were unaware that he was black. Braithwaite was unique in enjoying a successful literary career in which his race was neither a stigma nor a premise of his professional identity.

During the 1920s the first serious histories of black literature began to appear. Foremost among them was Benjamin BRAWLEY's *The Negro Genius* (1937), originally published in 1918 as *The Negro in Literature and Art*. Benjamin Griffith Brawley was a professor of literature with degrees from Chicago and Harvard, who spent the bulk of his teaching career at Shaw University and Howard. He published textbooks on English literature and a biography of Paul Laurence Dunbar, but *The Negro Genius* was his most enduring work. As its original title suggests, *The Negro Genius* was actually a history of African Americans in all of the arts: literature, drama, visual arts, and music. Brawley's objective was to trace the various manifestations of African-American creative talent, and his book is virtually an encyclopedia of black artists, offering brief introductory essays on each, in chronological order.

The Negro Genius has embedded within it a kind of racial theory, distinguishing between the inherent gifts of "people of mixed blood" and "blacks":

> People of mixed blood have given us the college presidents, the administrators, the Government employees; but the blacks are the singers and seers. Black slaves gave us the spirituals; modern composers of a lighter hue transcribe them. . . . In other words, the mixed element in the race may represent the Negro's talent, but it is upon the black element that he must rely for his genius (pp. 8–9).

"Negro genius" is, according to Brawley, "lyrical, imaginative, subjective." Though Brawley makes such claims in a spirit of race pride, vindicating dark-skinned people, racial theory cuts in both directions. If the aesthetic is black, the scientific must be white. If genius is racial, the lack of genius must also be racial. Brawley's larger intention is to celebrate African-American achievement; but framing the argument in racial terms simply perpetuates the basis for invidious hierarchies, which has always been the primary function of racial ideology. As a critical premise this notion is also flawed, because it encourages the critic to appreciate the lyricism of black artists but not their formal designs. It stereotypes black artists even as it celebrates them. Nevertheless, *The Negro Genius* did a valuable service by providing a broad, concise, and readily accessible account of African-American artistic achievement.

Another notable work of this period was *The Negro Author and His Development* (1930) by Vernon Loggins, which unlike Brawley's work focused exclusively on black literature. The most sophisticated history of African-American literature published during this era, however, was *To Make a Poet Black* (1939) by J. Saunders REDDING. Indeed, no book is more deserving to be regarded as the classic African-American literary history. Redding's book is distinguished by its literary style, its conceptual design, its high aesthetic standards, and its vigorous critical argument. Unlike Brawley, who was constrained by the essentially apologetic conception of *The Negro Genius* to praise the authors he discussed in order to persuade a doubting audience that black people are capable of creating serious art, Redding defined for himself a critical agenda, committed to analyzing and evaluating the work of black writers.

Redding begins with an acknowledgment of the conflicting social imperatives that have bedeviled black writers, the sharply opposed expectations of black and white audiences. As a consequence of this conflict, Redding argues, "Negro writers have been obliged to have two faces." These two impulses Redding defines as, first, the aesthetic quest for honest, well-crafted self-expression, and second, the political quest to contribute to the advancement of one's oppressed race. In Redding's own concise description, "these two necessities can be traced with varying degrees of clarity—now one and now the other predominant—like threads through the whole cloth" (p. 3). This describes aptly a trait that has characterized African-American writing throughout its history, and accordingly it provides a set of terms that Redding can use cogently and consistently to analyze texts from Jupiter Hammon to Sterling BROWN.

While he addresses the writers' work with a sympathetic understanding of their circumstances and an appreciation of their particular talents and achievements, Redding never relinquishes his commitment to the primacy of aesthetic concerns. For him this means that literature should be not just skillfully wrought but also honest, passionate, and purposeful. Thus, while he acknowledges Phillis Wheatly as a talented and important poet, he deplores her glib religiosity, her acceptance of slavery, and her failure to identify with the plights of other slaves as attitudes that undermine her art:

> It is this negative, bloodless, unracial quality in Phillis Wheatley that makes her seem superficial, especially to members of her own race. Hers is a spirit-denying-the-flesh attitude that somehow cannot seem altogether real as the essential quality and core of one whose life should have made her sensitive to the very things she denies. In this sense none of her poetry is real (p. 11).

For similar reasons, he criticizes the work of William Stanley Braithwaite, dismissing it as "the most outstanding example of perverted energy that the period from 1903 to 1917 produced" (p. 89). Braithwaite's work, he argues, "is pretty and skillful poetry, but it is not poetry afire with the compelling necessity for expression. No passion (even slightly remembered in tranquility) of pain or joy, no spring of pure personal knowledge or conviction justifies it" (p. 91). For Redding, neither deficient literary technique nor deficient moral fervor is acceptable, and both of these poets lack the latter.

In the early fiction of Charles Chesnutt, Redding finds work that meets his high standards. He declares: "His early career was a great artistic success, for he did the one thing needful to the American Negro writer: He worked dangerous, habit-ridden material with passive calm and fearlessness. . . . He exposed the Negro to critical analysis" (p. 76). The terms that he uses to convey praise reflect Redding's insistence on originality, honesty, and cogency. The poems and prefaces of James Weldon Johnson, especially in *God's Trombones,* also embody for Redding the mature achievement of African-American writing:

> Aside from the beauty of the poems, the essay which prefaces them is of the first importance for it definitely hails back from the urban and sophisticated to the earthy exuberance of the Negro's kinship with the earth, the fields, the suns and rains of the South. Discarding the "mutilations of dialect," Mr. Johnson yet retains the speech forms, the idea patterns, and the rich racial flavor (p. 121).

Revealingly, Redding places Johnson out of chronological sequence at the end of the book, just before Sterling Brown and Zora Neale Hurston. These writers represent for him the most promising achievements of African-American writing. *To Make a Poet Black* is a monumental work of African-American literary criticism because it is the first book-length history of African-American literature that breaks entirely with the tradition of racial apologetics, devoting itself instead to a sustained examination of how social pressures, cultural traditions, and personal sensibility interact in the making of African-American literary art.

Sterling A. Brown was a major poet of his generation and a major critic as well. *The Negro in American Fiction* (1937) and *Negro Poetry and Drama* (1937) are exhaustive works on their respective topics. Brown's critical approach is primarily that of descriptive bibliography. His books are immensely useful, but they provide concise summaries or assessments rather than detailed discussions of individual works. A major concern of both books is "to show how attitudes to Negro life have developed in American thinking" (*Negro Poetry,* p. 2). Thus Brown surveys both black

and white writers, assessing how African Americans have been depicted in literary works. Unlike Redding, he does not emphasize aesthetic evaluation. Nevertheless, these are works of formidable scholarship, and they have remained important to students of race in American literature, though they are not so pertinent to theoretical or evaluative concerns as *To Make a Poet Black.*

In 1939 the College Language Association (CLA) was formed to provide a professional outlet for African-American literary scholars, who were in effect excluded from the Modern Language Association (MLA). Like the MLA, the CLA held annual meetings and published a journal, which for many years was the primary outlet for scholarship by black critics. The formation of the CLA was an important event, since it marked the emergence of African-American literary scholars as a professional class. Two of the most prominent of the black academic critics during this period were Nick Aaron Ford (1904–1982), author of *The Contemporary Negro Novel* (1936), and Hugh Gloster (1911–), who wrote *Negro Voices in American Fiction* (1948). Blyden Jackson (1910–) is also a member of this generation, but he did not publish his most important book, the first volume of a general history of African-American writing, until 1989, after his retirement. *A History of Afro-American Literature: The Long Beginning, 1746–1895* is a monumental achievement. A model of thorough and detailed scholarship, it supersedes all other histories of African-American literature and establishes Jackson as a preeminent scholar in the field at a time when others of his generation are regarded as forebears, not contemporaries. Jackson's lengthy bibliographical essay alone, which encompasses the entire fields of historical and literary scholarship on African Americans from the beginnings to the 1980s, makes his book an indispensable reference work.

These scholars of the 1930s and 1940s taught in black colleges, and the heavy course loads in those institutions limited their opportunities for research and writing. Thus, with a few exceptions, the literary scholars of this generation exerted their influence primarily through their articles, professional associations, and teaching, not through books. Ironically, however, most black colleges did not offer courses on black literature. (Sterling Brown at Howard was a pioneering exception.) English professors were expected to do research and writing on "canonical" (i.e., white) authors; and this remained the case even through the 1960s. The work of a few outstanding critics notwithstanding, then, the volume of criticism on African-American writers remained limited. Only in the 1980s, with the full integration of American universities, the gradual development of African-American literature courses as regular components in

English department curricula, and the erosion of racist and elitist attitudes within the academy did it become possible for a generation of scholars to turn their full attention to the study of African-American literature.

Meanwhile, during the next two decades, the most important works of African-American criticism were written by literary artists, such as Richard WRIGHT, James BALDWIN, and Ralph ELLISON; and their most famous literary essays were polemical pieces that echoed the larger debate between Marxists and liberals over the value and function of art. For instance, Richard Wright's essay "Blueprint for Negro Writing" (1937), rejecting black nationalist attitudes and most previous black literature, declares a Marxist agenda for African-American fiction. By the time he wrote "How Bigger Was Born" (1940), his meditation on *Native Son,* Wright's thinking had begun to manifest existentialist ideas that would dominate his work of the late forties and fifties. Wright's most sustained treatment of black writers, and one of his finest critical essays, is "The Literature of the Negro in the United States," which was published in a French periodical and later included in his book *White Man, Listen!* (1957). In any case, the unprecedented success of *Native Son* made Wright the preeminent African-American literary figure of the 1940s. His forthright identification with the left seemed to convey an imperative for all black writers.

Not surprisingly, some writers took exception. James Baldwin's essays "Everybody's Protest Novel" (1949) and "Many Thousands Gone" (1951) reject the entire tradition of protest fiction, from UNCLE TOM'S CABIN to *Native Son.* In Baldwin's view, protest fiction dehumanizes characters by subsuming individual psychology and experience to sociological generalizations. Baldwin argues instead for fiction that foregrounds the individual perspective. One may debate how accurately Baldwin describes Wright and other protest writers, but clearly these two essays anticipate the character of Baldwin's own fiction and essays.

Ralph Ellison also distanced himself from Wright, but he did so by asserting his own alternative, humanist vision rather than by attacking Wright. Ellison's most famous skirmish was an exchange with the leftist critic Irving Howe, whose "Black Boys and Native Sons" (1963) chided with Baldwin, Ellison, and others for deviating from the activist model of Wright's fiction. Ellison's two-installment rejoinder, combined in his collection *Shadow and Act* into a single essay called "The World and the Jug," is a devastating deflation of Howe's argument. Ellison's importance as a critic, however, transcends such debates. With a few exceptions, Ellison's essays are not concerned with African-American literature but rather with issues of literary art more broadly framed. He does, however, give detailed attention to African-American music and comic traditions. As a theorist of the relationship between vernacular culture and high art, Ellison has been among our most sophisticated thinkers. Essays such as "Change the Joke and Slip the Yoke" and "The Little Man at Chehaw Station" are classic inquiries into African-American sensibility and the nature of American culture. The work collected in *Shadow and Act* and *Going to the Territory* demonstrates that Ellison was unsurpassed as a literary essayist.

The prominence of Baldwin and Ellison notwithstanding, the 1950s and early 1960s was a relatively moribund period in the history of African-American literary criticism. Though many talented black critics were active during this period, surprisingly little was published on African-American literature. One exceptional critic whose work, ironically, corresponds to this quiescent period is Nathan A. Scott, Jr. (1925–). A brilliant and prolific critic with degrees in both divinity and literature, Scott used his books to explore the manifestations of moral, psychological, and existential conflicts in modern literature. His works include *Rehearsals of Discomposure: Alienation and Reconciliation in Modern Literature* (1952); *The Tragic Vision and the Christian Faith* (1957); and *Negative Capability: Studies in the New Literature and the Religious Situation* (1969). Scott taught at Howard from 1948 to 1955, at the University of Chicago for twenty years, and subsequently at the University of Virginia. Though he published a splendid essay on Richard Wright, "The Dark and Haunted Tower of Richard Wright" (1964), Scott, arguably the most acclaimed and distinguished African-American literary critic of his generation, seldom turned his attention to black writers.

Several other critics of this generation were instrumental in moving the study of black literature from black colleges, where heavy teaching and administrative demands made the completion of book projects very difficult, to the major and predominantly white research universities. That group includes Richard Barksdale (University of Illinois), George Kent (University of Chicago), Charles T. Davis (Yale), and Darwin T. Turner (University of Iowa). Though all of these critics published important essays, they were most influential as teachers, mentors, and professional colleagues—daunting scholarly models who set very high standards and proposed collective agendas for the future study of African-American literature. All of them published books after they moved to the universities, but Kent, Davis, and Turner all died prematurely, leaving major scholarly manuscripts unfinished. Nevertheless, the scholars who established black literary studies in the universities in the 1970s laid the basis for the blossoming of that field in the late 1980s and 1990s.

Mainstream academic critics, however, were not the only important critics of African-American literature during that period, and they were certainly not the most conspicuous. During the late 1960s a school of black nationalist criticism developed, and it was for a time predominant in setting the canon and shaping critical attitudes. The most influential critics of this group included Hoyt Fuller, the editor of *Negro Digest:* creative writers such as Amiri BARAKA, Carolyn RODGERS, Haki MADHUBUTI, and Larry NEAL; and academics such as Addison Gayle and Stephen Henderson. These black aesthetic critics shared a belief that literature and criticism should be socially relevant, providing a critique of racist white society and advancing the struggle for black consciousness, black solidarity, and black liberation. They favored writing that addressed political and racial issues and preferred polemics to introspection, collectivity to subjectivity, and didacticism to humor.

The critics of this movement exercised their influence through conventional publications, but because of the vogue for public meetings during this era of heightened political passions, lectures and conferences were frequent and heavily attended. Thus the oral presentation of literary arguments acquired a special importance during the BLACK ARTS MOVEMENT. The social and political conditions created a large and avid audience for books on black topics, and this resulted in a proliferation of anthologies, new works, and reissues. Anthologies such as *Black Fire* by Amiri Baraka and Larry Neal, *Black Expression* and *The Black Aesthetic* by Addison Gayle, and *Understanding the New Black Poetry* by Stephen Henderson were very influential in shaping critical opinion. Furthermore, literary criticism and literary polemics were prominent features of important intellectual journals such as *Negro Digest/Black World* and *The Black Scholar* as well as literary magazines such as *Cricket* and *The Journal of Black Poetry.* Suddenly African-American literary critics had more outlets and a broader audience than had ever existed before.

Even serious scholarly books began to be directed toward a general audience. George Kent's *Blackness and the Adventure of Western Culture* (1972), a collection of essays on twentieth-century black writers, was published by THIRD WORLD PRESS in Chicago as the first book of literary scholarship to be issued by a black publisher. Full-scale literary histories such as Addison Gayle's *The Way of the New World* (1975) and Eugene B. Redmond's *Drumvoices: The Mission of Afro-American Poetry* (1976) were published by major publishing houses and issued in mass market paperback editions. The Black Arts movement made literary criticism a popular genre.

At the same time, the Black Arts movement provoked opposition among academic critics that was soon to repudiate black aesthetic criteria as the basis of critical discourse. Black Arts critics succeeded in articulating critical principles that were appropriate to the concerns of a black nationalist politics, but unfortunately these principles, seeking to incorporate only those works that seemed properly "black," defined a very narrow literary canon that excluded most extant African-American writing. Black Arts critics were especially concerned with the relationship between vernacular culture and literary expression. Ironically, this had been the predominant preoccupation of the African-American critical tradition, most of which the Black Arts critics rejected. Despite their dismissive attitude toward their critical forebears, the Black Arts critics were not able to develop a black aesthetic theory that could respond adequately to the complexities of sophisticated literary texts. Consequently, critics who wished to take seriously the black literary tradition were obliged to move beyond the narrow limits imposed by Black Arts theory.

This process of critical rebellion was marked by several publications of the late 1970s, most notably, the anthology of *Chant of Saints* (1979), edited by Michael S. HARPER and Robert B. Stepto, and *Afro-American Literature: The Reconstruction of Instruction* (1979), edited by Dexter Fisher and Robert B. Stepto. The latter was especially important. It developed from a two-week seminar on African-American literature sponsored by the Modern Language Association in 1977, and like the seminar, it was intended to reappropriate and reformulate the teaching and scholarship in the field. The volume features essays by Stepto, Melvin DIXON, Henry Louis Gates, Jr., Sherley Anne WILLIAMS, Robert Hemenway, and Robert G. O'Meally, all of whom would gain recognition in the 1980s as major critics of African-American literature. This book, which includes designs for courses and recommends areas for future inquiry, represents the successful coup that displaced black nationalist hegemony over African-American literary studies. By focusing attention on questions of narrative structure, generic convention, literary form, and rhetorical design, *Reconstruction* redirected black literary critics into the academic mainstream.

The book was also notable because it represented the emergence of Henry Louis Gates, Jr., whose three essays in this collection brought him national prominence within the profession. Gates was the most conspicuous and arguably the most influential African-American literary critic of the 1980s and early 1990s. His most important work of criticism was *The Signifying Monkey: A Theory of African-American Literary Criticism* (1988), a synthetic work that used ethnolinguistic scholarship, folklore studies, and literary theory to explore "the relation of the black vernacular tradition to the Afro-American literary tradition. The book attempts to identify a theory of criticism that is inscribed within the black vernacular tradition and that in turn informs the shape of the Afro-American literary tradition" (p. xix). Gates argues that the signifying monkey derives from the messenger and trickster figure Esu-Elegbara (Legba) of the Yoruba tradition and manifests itself in literature as "Signifyin(g)," which represents "moments of self-reflexiveness" (p. xxi). Gates identifies this self-reflexiveness in the "intertexuality" through which black texts speak to and signify upon each other. Ironically, though Gates explicitly rejects the Black Arts critics, his endeavor to derive from African-American culture a theory of black literature represents the most thorough, scholarly, and intellectually compelling realization of what the Black Arts critics attempted and failed to achieve.

Despite the singularity and importance of *The Signifying Monkey,* Gates has exerted his greatest influence through his extensive editorial work and his vast energies as a publicist and entrepreneur for African-American literary studies. His compilations of literary criticism, such as *Black Literature and Literary Theory* (1984), and "The Schomburg Library of Nineteenth-Century Black Women Writers," of which he is general editor, have shaped the work of a generation of graduate students.

While Gates has clearly been the most influential African-American literary critic in the final two decades of this century, the books published by Houston A. Baker, Jr., constitute the most sustained, wide-ranging, and detailed inquiry into African-American literature by any critic. In a series of books beginning with *Long Black Song* (1972), Baker has addressed nearly all of the major African-American texts, authors, and literary movements, as well as the most compelling issues associated with the study of African-American writing and culture. Furthermore, Baker has been an assiduous student of literary theory, and each of his books has reflected his careful engagement with current and emerging forms of theory or interpretive method, seeking always to examine the pertinence of such academic trends to the study of black expressive culture. Baker's distinctive combination of vernacular culture and high theory in the reading of black texts is most compellingly demonstrated in *The Journey Back* (1980) and *Blues, Ideology, and Afro-American Literature* (1984).

Beginning his career during the era of the Black Arts critics, Baker shared many of their basic concerns and priorities; yet his work always displayed a scholarly thoroughness and theoretical sophistication that distinguished it from that group. Baker's work represents both the continuity of African-American

critical traditions and the integration of black critics into the professional discourse of European-American criticism. Baker's unique position within the academy was aptly acknowledged when in 1992 he became the first African-American president of the Modern Language Association.

Though literary theory was the preeminent concern of academic critics from the late 1970s to the early 1990s, distinguished work continued to be done in literary history and literary biography. Two of the most significant scholarly events of this period were the publications of two exemplary biographies: Robert Hemenway's *Zora Neale Hurston: A Literary Biography* (1977) and Arnold Rampersad's two volume biography *A Life of Langston Hughes* (1986 and 1988). Also during these years the number of black Ph.D.s increased dramatically, and correspondingly. African-American literary scholars found employment at virtually all of the major colleges and universities. Given the emphasis on scholarly publication as a necessity of professional survival, it was inevitable that the quality and quantity of publications by black critics would also increase dramatically. Thus the critics who have published excellent work in this field since 1980 are far too numerous to enumerate. Two journals were the primary venues for black literary scholarship during these years: *African-American Review* (originally called *Negro American Literature Forum* and subsequently *Black American Literature Forum*) and *Callaloo.* Furthermore, the study of black writers became surprisingly fashionable during the early 1990s, and for the first time, journals on American literature began to publish work on black literature with some frequency.

The most significant and pervasive new direction of African-American literary studies from the mid-1980s to the mid-1990s was the entry of large numbers of black women into the profession and the proliferation of work on black women writers. During the 1970s a small group of black women began to acquire national reputations as literary scholars, notably Barbara Christian, Thadious Davis, Trudier Harris, Nellie McKay, Hortense Spillers, Eleanor Taylor, and Kenny Williams. By the mid-1990s the black women entering the profession outnumbered the black men substantially. Black women writers such as Harriet JACOBS, Frances E. W. Harper. Zora Neale Hurston, Alice WALKER, and Toni MORRISON, too long undervalued, began to acquire a secure place in American literature syllabi and in the pages of scholarly journals.

The creative capacity of African-Americans is no longer open to dispute, nor is it necessary to justify the study of African-American texts. Thus African-American literary criticism has at last escaped the onus of racial apologetics. In general, black critics remain deeply interested in the relationship between social experience—whether this means racial and gender identity or cultural knowledge and conditioning—and literary expression. This will likely remain the case as long as black critics experience social pressures that distinguish them from their white counterparts. Nevertheless, as awareness increases of various possibilities of African-American racial experience, critical judgments regarding the relationship between race and writing will doubtless become more and more vexed.

REFERENCES

BAKER, HOUSTON A., JR. *Blues, Ideology, and Afro-American Literature: A Vernacular Theory.* Chicago, 1984.

———. *The Journey Back: Issues in Black Literature and Criticism.* Chicago, 1980.

BAKER, HOUSTON A., JR., and PATRICIA REDMOND, eds. *Afro-American Literary Study in the 1990s.* Chicago, 1989.

BELL, BERNARD W. *The Afro-American Novel and Its Tradition.* Amherst, Mass., 1987.

BRAWLEY, BENJAMIN. *The Negro Genius.* New York, 1937.

BROWN, STERLING A. *The Negro in American Fiction.* Washington, D.C., 1937.

———. *Negro Poetry and Drama.* Washington, D.C., 1937.

CARBY, HAZEL V. *Reconstructing Womanhood: The Emergence of the Afro-American Woman Novelist.* New York, 1987.

CHRISTIAN, BARBARA. *Black Feminist Criticism: Perspectives on Black Women Writers.* New York, 1985.

DAVIS, ARTHUR P. *From the Dark Tower: Afro-American Writers, 1900–1960.* Washington, D.C., 1974.

FISHER, DEXTER, and ROBERT B. STEPTO, eds. *Afro-American Literature: The Reconstruction of Instruction.* New York, 1979.

GATES, HENRY LOUIS, JR. *Black Literature and Literary Theory.* New York, 1984.

———. *Figures in Black: Words, Signs, and the "Racial" Self.* New York, 1987.

———. *Reading Black, Reading Feminist: A Critical Anthology.* New York, 1990.

GAYLE, ADDISON, JR., ed. *The Black Aesthetic.* Garden City, N.Y., 1971.

HENDERSON, STEPHEN. *Understanding the New Black Poetry: Black Speech and Black Music as Poetic References.* New York, 1973.

JACKSON, BLYDEN. *A History of Afro-American Literature.* Vol. 1, *The Long Beginning, 1746–1895.* Baton Rouge, La., 1989.

PRYSE, MARJORIE, and HORTENSE J. SPILLERS, eds., *Conjuring: Black Women, Fiction, and Literary Tradition.* Bloomington, Ind., 1985.

REDDING, J. SAUNDERS. *To Make a Poet Black.* Ithaca, N. Y., 1988.

REDMOND, EUGENE B. *Drumvoices: The Mission of Afro-American Poetry.* Garden City, N.Y., 1976.

STEPTO, ROBERT B. *From Behind the Veil: A Study of Afro-American Narrative.* Urbana, Ill., 1979.

TURNER, DARWIN T. "Afro-American Literary Critics." *Black World* 19, no. 9 (1970): 54–67.

WEIXLMANN, JOE, and HOUSTON A. BAKER, eds. *Studies in Black American Literature 3: Black Feminist Criticism and Critical Theory.* Greenwood, Fla., 1988.

DAVID LIONEL SMITH

Crosswaith, Frank Rudolph (July 16, 1892–June 17, 1965), labor organizer and political activist. Frank Crosswaith was born in Fredericksted, St. Croix, Danish West Indies (now the U.S. Virgin Islands), the son of William I. and Anne Eliza Crosswaith. Educated at the University Preparatory School in Fredricksted, Crosswaith emigrated to the United States in his late teens and studied at the socialist Rand School of Social Science in New York City while working as an elevator operator. Upon graduating from the Rand School, Crosswaith began his career as a pioneer in the field of black labor organization. Dubbed the "Negro Debs" because his fiery oratorical style and his struggle on behalf of African-American workers were reminiscent of Socialist leader Eugene V. Debs (*see* SOCIALISM), Crosswaith helped form unions for mechanics, barbers, laundry workers, and motion picture operators.

In the early 1920s Crosswaith began his long collaboration with A. Philip RANDOLPH when he joined with the MESSENGER magazine in opposing Marcus GARVEY. As "economic radicals," the *Messenger* group worked for a class alliance of black and white workers and believed that Garvey's race alliance undercut their efforts at making the African-American masses class conscious. In 1925 Crosswaith helped found and was elected executive secretary of the short-lived Trade Union Committee for Organizing Negro Workers, which ceased to exist when, later in the year, Crosswaith became a full-time organizer for Randolph's BROTHERHOOD OF SLEEPING CAR PORTERS (BSCP).

Crosswaith left the BSCP to become a general organizer for the International Ladies' Garment Workers Union in the 1930s. He championed the formation of the Harlem Labor Committee in 1934. Made chairman of the committee, Crosswaith planned to work through American Federation of Labor (AFL) unions (*see* LABOR AND LABOR UNIONS) that were seeking to organize black workers. As a consequence of the committee's efforts, a number of union locals such as the Motion Picture Operators, the Cleaners, Dyers, Pressers and Drivers Union, and

Frank R. Crosswaith. (Photographs and Prints Division, Schomburg Center for Research in Black Culture, The New York Public Library, Astor, Lenox and Tilden Foundations)

mostly low-wage, low-skilled unions began admitting African Americans. Crosswaith was also instrumental in organizing the integrated Negro Labor Committee in 1935, which had as its chief goals organizing black workers into unions and "to establish the solidarity of Negro and White labor." As chairman, Crosswaith supported the successful strike by black members of the newly formed American Newspaper Guild against the *New York* AMSTERDAM NEWS, in 1935.

Also involved in politics, Crosswaith was vice chairman of the first American Labor party during the LaFollette presidential campaign in 1924. He became a lecturer on behalf of the Socialist party and the League for Industrial Democracy, in which capacity he made national tours of college campuses. A frequent but unsuccessful candidate for office, Crosswaith ran as the Socialist candidate for New York City aldermanic president, state secretary of state, and lieutenant governor. Supported by the American Labor party, he also made an unsuccessful bid for the office of president of the city council.

Unlike most other left-leaning West Indian blacks, Crosswaith did not side with the COMMUNIST PARTY at the time of the Socialist party split in 1919. Instead, bitter over the Communist role in breaking up the *Messenger* group and attempting to infiltrate the porters union, he remained with Randolph's black Socialist faction and became a virulent anti-Communist. In 1941, as a leader of the liberal right wing of the

American Labor party, he joined in an appeal to party members to keep "free of control and eventual disintegration at the hands of the Communists." He later left the American Labor party to join the Liberal party, and he served as a member of its executive board.

Upon the recommendation of Randolph, in 1942, Mayor Fiorello H. LaGuardia appointed Crosswaith a member of the New York City Housing Authority, a job that was then part-time and unsalaried, and which he held until 1947. Through the years, Crosswaith cooperated with Randolph in the latter's civil rights activities. He was involved in the organizing of Randolph's proposed march on Washington in 1941 which resulted in President Franklin D. Roosevelt's Executive Order 8802 establishing the wartime FAIR EMPLOYMENT PRACTICES COMMITTEE. He was one of the featured speakers at the march on Washington movement's Madison Square Garden rally on June 16, 1942. Crosswaith served as one of the chairmen of Randolph's Youth March for Integrated Schools in Washington, D.C. in 1958. A journalist as well, Crosswaith was editor of *Negro Labor News* for twelve years and coauthored, with Alfred Baker Lewis, *True Freedom for Negro and White Workers* and *Discrimination Incorporated*. He died in Chicago.

REFERENCES

FRANKLIN, CHARLES LIONEL. *The Negro Labor Unionists of New York*. New York, 1936.
LOGAN, RAYFORD W., and MICHAEL R. WINSTON, eds. *Dictionary of American Negro Biography*. New York, 1982.
Obituary. *New York Times*, June 18, 1965, p. 35.

PAULA F. PFEFFER

Crouch, Andrae Edward (July 1, 1942–), gospel singer. Andrae Crouch was born in Los Angeles, where his father was a minister in a Holiness church. He sang in the choir as a youth, began playing piano for the church at age eleven, and played on his father's weekly radio broadcasts. He was educated at the San Fernando Valley High School and Valley Junior College, and also studied at Life Bible College in Los Angeles. In his formative years, Crouch formed a group called the Crouch Trio, which included his twin sister, Sandra, and a brother. In the early 1960s he formed a group, the COGICS (an acronym drawn from Church of God in Christ), which included Billy Preston, Sandra Crouch, Blinky Williams, Gloria Jones, Frankie Spring, and Edna Wright. The group's first recording, on Vee Jay Records, was critically acclaimed.

Andrae Crouch. (AP/Wide World Photos)

In the late 1960s, Crouch formed another group, the Disciples, with whom he recorded and performed around the world. Crouch's work with the Disciples won him wide recognition; along with Edwin HAWKINS, he became a primary figure of contemporary GOSPEL MUSIC in the late 1960s and the '70s. Of his more than three hundred compositions, many have become standard repertory for gospel performers; among them are "Take Me Back," "My Tribute," "Soon and Very Soon," and "The Blood Will Never Lose Its Power." Crouch's compositions are varied, embodying both traditional gospel and secular styles, and feature electronic instrumentation.

REFERENCES

CROUCH, ANDRAE. *Through It All: A Biography.* Waco, Tex., 1974.

HEILBUT, ANTHONY. *The Gospel Sound: Good News and Bad Times.* 1971. Reprint. New York, 1985.

GUTHRIE P. RAMSEY, JR.

Crowdy, William Saunders (1847–August 4, 1908), religious leader. William Crowdy was born a slave at Charlotte Hall, Saint Mary's County, Maryland, and served in the Union Army during the Civil War. Little is known about his early life, but by the early 1890s, he had acquired a farm in Guthrie, Oklahoma Territory, and joined the local Baptist church.

For a time he also worked as a cook in Kansas City, Mo., where he married Lovey Yates Higgins. In 1893, Crowdy began to experience visions instructing him on the founding of a new church to be called the Church of God and Saints of Christ. He began to preach on the streets of Guthrie, and in 1895–1896 he carried out preaching tours of Texas and Chicago. In 1896, he went to Lawrence, Kans., where he formally organized his church. Crowdy established church doctrine in a series of sermons, holding that blacks were the descendants of the lost tribes of Israel and incorporating a number of Jewish elements (including the observance of Jewish holidays and the Saturday sabbath), together with practices retained from his Baptist background.

In 1900, Crowdy moved to Philadelphia, where he assembled a large congregation and established the headquarters of the church. In Philadelphia, the Church of God and Saints of Christ began to celebrate Passover and incorporate other aspects of Jewish worship. While in Philadelphia, Crowdy married Saint Hallie Brown, a leading member of the church. Later, however, he repudiated the practice of remarriage, left his second wife, and brought his first wife to live with him. In 1903, Crowdy moved to Washington, D.C. In 1907, while visiting followers in Newark, N.J., he suffered a stroke, and he died the following year. After his death, his followers continued to revere him as a prophet.

REFERENCE

WYNIA, ELLY M. *The Church of God and Saints of Christ: The Rise of Black Jews.* New York, 1994.

DANIEL SOYER

Crum, William D. (February 9, 1859–December 7, 1912), diplomat. William Crum was the first African-American collector of customs for the port of Charleston, S.C. His father was a white plantation owner in Orangeburg, S.C., where Crum was born. Crum graduated from the Avery Normal Institute in Charleston in 1875 and studied for a short time at the University of South Carolina before receiving an M.D. from Howard University in 1880. He practiced in Charleston and was head of the local African-American hospital.

He became involved in REPUBLICAN politics and was nominated postmaster of Charleston by President Benjamin Harrison in 1892, but the nomination was successfully opposed by white Charlestonians. Booker T. WASHINGTON, along with other prominent African Americans, persuaded President Theodore Roosevelt to nominate Crum, who was a delegate to every Republican National Convention from 1884 to 1904, for the position of collector of customs for Charleston. Because of bitter opposition to the appointment of a black, the Senate did not confirm Crum until 1905, at least two years after the nomination (Roosevelt gave him interim appointments while he awaited confirmation). Unwilling to undertake another difficult confirmation struggle, President William Howard Taft, who succeeded Roosevelt, refused to renominate Crum as customs collector, but nominated him instead as minister resident and consul-general to Liberia in 1910. Crum died in Liberia in 1912. His career displays the limits of political power available to African Americans in the turn-of-the-century South. Despite his accommodationist sympathies and his long service as a Republican stalwart, his political advance was harried at every step by whites who resented his political success.

REFERENCE

GATEWOOD, WILLIAM B. "William D. Crum: A Negro in Politics." *Journal of Negro History* (October 1968): 301–320.

SIRAJ AHMED

Alexander Crummell. (Photographs and Prints Division, Schomburg Center for Research in Black Culture, The New York Public Library, Astor, Lenox and Tilden Foundations)

Crummell, Alexander (March 3, 1819–September 19, 1898) nationalist, abolitionist, and missionary. Alexander Crummell was the son of Boston Crummell, who had been kidnapped from his homeland in Temne country, West Africa, and enslaved in New York. Boston Crummell was never emancipated, his son later wrote, but obtained his freedom simply by announcing to his master that "he would serve him no longer." Boston Crummell married Charity Hicks, a freeborn woman from Long Island, and established an oyster house in lower Manhattan. It was in the Crummell home that the African-American newspaper FREEDOM'S JOURNAL was founded.

The Crummells were members of the Protestant Episcopal church, and Alexander came early under the influence of Rev. Peter WILLIAMS, Jr. Williams was a supporter of back-to-Africa movements, and had been friendly with the repatriationists Paul CUFFE and John RUSSWURM. Crummell attended school in Williams's church and in the African Free School until his early teens, when he enrolled in the Noyes Academy in Canaan, N.H. Shortly after it opened, the academy was closed by mob violence and Crummell resumed his studies at the Oneida Institute in Whitesboro, N.Y.

Encouraged by Williams to become a candidate for ordination, Crummell applied to the General Theological Seminary in New York City but was rejected. He informally attended lectures at Yale University, and studied privately with clergymen in New England. While in New England he married Sarah Mabritt Elston of New York, ministered to congregationists in New Haven and Providence, and worked as a correspondent for the *Colored American*. Crummell was ordained to the Episcopal priesthood in 1842, and labored with small congregations in Philadelphia and New York. He went to England in 1848, ostensibly to raise funds for his parish; almost immediately, however, he began preparing with a tutor to enter Cambridge University. His familial obligations and lecturing activities detracted from his academic performance, and he failed his first attempt at the university examinations, but he was among the eleven out of thirty-three candidates who passed the "additional examination," and he was awarded the bachelor's degree in 1853.

Desiring to bring up his children "under black men's institutions," he embarked on his missionary career in West Africa under the auspices of the Protestant Episcopal church. Over the ensuing decades he was often in conflict with his immediate superior,

Rev. John Payne, the bishop of Cape Palmas, especially when Crummell attempted to organize another diocese in the Liberian capital city of Monrovia. Crummell at first showed little interest in working with the native population. Many of his writings during these years addressed such statesmanlike topics as "God and the Nation" and "The Relations and Duties of Free Colored Men in America to Africa." These, along with a number of his other essays on black-nationalist themes, were collected for his first book, *The Future of Africa* (1862).

Crummell spent sixteen years between 1853 and 1872 in Liberia, although he returned to the United States twice during those years for fund-raising purposes. The assassination of Liberian president Edward James Royce and threats against Crummell's own life led to his hasty and final departure in 1872. Sarah Crummell died in 1878 and he was remarried, to Jennie M. Simpson, on September 23, 1880. Crummell established St. Luke's Episcopal Church in Washington in 1879, and retained the pastorate until 1894, when he retired. He continued to write and lecture actively until his death in 1898. Among his important writings during the Washington years were "The Destined Superiority of the Negro" and "The Black Woman of the South, Her Neglects and Her Needs" (1883). These and other sermons were collected in his books *The Greatness of Christ and Other Sermons* (1882) and *Africa and America* (1891).

Crummell's theological writings are dominated by the idea that salvation cannot be achieved solely by the acceptance of grace. He believed that God works actively in history and that the good are punished and the evil rewarded in this life. Crummell was contemptuous of enthusiastic revivalism and believed that the struggle for salvation must remain an arduous task, even after the Christian has experienced conversion. Although a notorious Anglophile, and hostile to the cultural expressions of the black masses, he never wavered in his black-nationalist chauvinism, apparently seeing no contradictions in his position. His essay "The Destined Superiority of the Negro" revealed his confidence that the African race was a "chosen people."

In the year before his death, Crummell organized the AMERIAN NEGRO ACADEMY, which was dedicated to the pursuit of the higher culture and civilization for black Americans. He influenced W. E. B. DU BOIS, whose sentimental and somewhat inaccurate eulogy, "Of Alexander Crummell," was reprinted in *The Souls of Black Folk* (1903). Other Crummell protégés were William H. Ferris and John E. Bruce, both of whom became prominent Garveyites during the 1920s.

Crummell's papers are widely scattered, and a complete bibliographic survey is beyond the scope of this article. The main repository is in the Schomburg Collection of the New York Public Library. A number of important letters are in the American Colonization Society Papers in the Library of Congress and in the Domestic and Foreign Missionary Society Papers in the Archives of the Episcopal Church at Austin, Tex. Additional important materials are in the Massachusetts and Maryland State Historical Societies.

REFERENCES

MOSES, WILSON J. *Alexander Crummell: A Study of Civilization and Discontent.* 1989.
OLDFIELD, JOHN. *Alexander Crummell and the Creation of an African-American Church in Liberia.* 1990.
RIGSBY, GREGORY U. *Alexander Crummell: Pioneer in Nineteenth Century Pan-African Thought.* 1987.
SCRUGGS, OTEY M. *We the Children of Africa in This Land.* 1972.

WILSON J. MOSES

Cruse, Harold Wright (March 18, 1916–) writer and educator. Harold Cruse is primarily known for his authorship of a single influential book, *The Crisis of the Negro Intellectual* (1967). Relatively little is known of Cruse's life. He was born in 1916 in Petersburg, Va., where his parents separated when he was young. He moved with his father to New York, where the elder Cruse became a cleaning supervisor on the Long Island Railroad. Cruse studied in New York's public schools, and worked at a variety of jobs after his graduation. He dates his intellectual life from 1940, when he attended a book party/lecture by author Richard WRIGHT in Harlem. Cruse served in the quartermaster division of the Army during World War II. Following his discharge, he attended City College of New York on the G.I. Bill, but dropped out after less than a year.

During the following fifteen years, Cruse became involved in Harlem left-wing circles, although he has long refused to give details of his involvement with the COMMUNIST PARTY. He attempted to write articles and plays, and held a variety of part-time jobs. Eventually, he became a bitter opponent of the Communist party. Around 1963, he began work on *The Crisis of the Negro Intellectual*, which was completed four years later. The book was a massive historical study that criticized many black leaders and thinkers for their failure to give expression to nationalist consciousness. Cruse argued that Harlem culture had been dominated by a "clique" of writers and artists affiliated with left-wing groups such as the Communist party, which had systematically opposed the creation of black intellectual or cultural autonomy. As a result, they had no black intellectual or political program to offer as an alternative to integration and assimilation into white America. The book, published in the midst of the BLACK POWER movement, stirred up enormous controversy among both blacks and whites. In 1968, Cruse published a book of essays on black nationalism, *Rebellion or Revolution?*

In fall 1968, Cruse was hired as a visiting professor by the University of Michigan in Ann Arbor, Mich. The following year, he helped found the university's Center for Afro-American and African Studies. In 1977 Cruse became the first African-American professor without an academic degree to be named full professor at an American university. In 1982, he published a second full-length work, *Plural but Equal*, a critique of the effects of integration on African-American education and life. In 1987 Cruse was named professor emeritus.

REFERENCES

CRUSE, HAROLD. *The Crisis of the Negro Intellectual* 1967. Reprint. New York, 1984.
—— *Plural but Equal: A Critical Study of Blacks and Minorities and America's Plural Society.* New York, 1987.

GREG ROBINSON

Cruz, Emilio (March 15, 1938–   ), artist. Emilio Cruz was born in New York City and received his early education as an artist from his Cuban-born father, who studied at the National Academy of Art in New York and worked with the WORKS PROJECT ADMINISTRATION (WPA) there. Cruz graduated from the High School of Industrial Art in 1955 and during that year began working as a commercial artist and taking classes at the Art Students' League. In the late 1950s through the mid-1960s, he began to receive recognition as an artist for his figurative expressionist work as a part of a movement of artists—including Jan Mueller, Lester Johnson, Gandy Brody, and Bob Thompson—who reintroduced the human figure in American art, combining it with abstract elements. In the mid-1960s he was awarded a John Hay Whitney Fellowship (1964) and a Cintas Foundation Fellowship (1965). In 1966 he was an American representative to the First World Festival of Negro Arts in Dakar, Senegal. In 1969 Cruz continued his figurative work, predating the neoexpressionist movement, with paintings and a series of small drawings created in St. Louis as a visiting artist on a Rockefeller-Danforth fellowship. This work, done in response to the assassination of the Rev. Dr. Martin Luther KING, Jr., the riots that followed, and the subsequent violence of unleashed attack dogs and fire hoses, reflected Cruz's repugnance for political and racial conflict and for the destruction of the environment.

In 1970 Cruz received one of the first fellowships awarded by the National Endowment for the Arts (NEA), and he moved to Chicago, where he taught drawing and painting at the Art Institute of Chicago for twelve years. During this period Cruz continued his exploration of the human figure, integrating it into large-scale paintings in which he experimented with surface textures and with the introduction of geometric shapes and patterns. The figuration in these works included representations of the human form as well as of birds and other animals. These works reflected Cruz's continuing concern with the symbiotic relationships that exist between human beings and other creatures within the planetary whole. He also constructed large fiberglass sculptures that were based on the structure of the rib cage and constructed cutouts that incorporated the human figure, animals, and mirrors in ways that reflected and expanded upon his paintings of the same period. Cruz combined these works in installations that included paintings, cutout constructions, and fiberglass sculptures. Simultaneously he wrote and published poetry and began to mount performances in which he integrated the visual imagery with his written text, music, and movement. Returning to New York in 1982, Cruz created a series of paintings based on his drawings of 1969, which were exhibited at the Alternative Museum in 1985. Two years later, Cruz received his second NEA fellowship.

Cruz's current work includes the "Homo Sapiens Series," which continues to reflect his personal history of involvement with the human figure. Of these works Cruz has stated, "The exposed bone structure and vertebra connects the human being with other biological creatures in our planetary biosphere exemplifying our oneness while displaying our fragile physiological construction."

Cruz has had solo exhibitions at the Zabriskie Gallery in New York City (1963, 1964, 1965), the Dayton Art Institute (1974), the Walter Kelley Gallery in Chicago (1973, 1975, 1976, 1978), the Alternative Museum (1985), the Studio Museum in Harlem (1987), the California African American Museum (1988), the Anita Shapolsky Gallery (1986, 1990) and the Galerie Françoise et Ses Frères in Baltimore (1991).

In 1976 Cruz returned to performance, a form he had experimented with since the 1960s, and created a work entitled *Musical Homage to Arts and Other Symbiotic Creatures,* which he presented in Chicago at the NAME Gallery and the Illinois Institute of Technol-

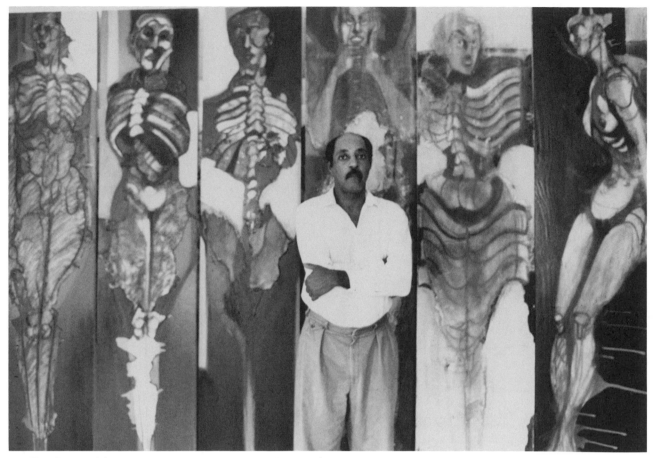

Emilio Cruz with *Homo Sapiens Series,* 1994. (© Emilio Cruz)

ogy. In 1981 Cruz founded Spectacle Inc., a multimedia theater production company that featured actors, musicians, and dancers who performed works written and directed by Cruz, among them *Homeostasis: Once More the Scorpion* and *The Absence Held Fast to Its Presence,* in Chicago and New York. That year Cruz was selected to represent the United States in the Festival Mondial du Théâtre in France and toured *Homeostasis* and *The Absence* in Paris, Milan, and Turin. Cruz has continued to mount performances that he has written and directed; they include *Cage,* 1987; *Get Down Perfume,* 1990; *Trilogy for a Distant God,* 1993; and *Plum,* 1994.

REFERENCES

FINE, ELSA HONIG. *The Afro-American Artist: A Search for Identity.* New York, 1973.
RAND, HARRY. *Emilio Cruz: Recent Paintings and Drawings.* New York, 1984.

RENEE NEWMAN

Cuffe, Paul (January 17, 1759–September 9, 1817), merchant and emigrationist. Paul Cuffe was born on

Cuttyhunk Island in the Massachusetts Bay Colony to Cuffe Slocum, a former slave who had purchased his freedom, and Ruth Moses, a Wampanoag Native American. Growing up near the busy port of New Bedford, Mass., Cuffe shipped out on whaling expeditions while still a teenager. On one voyage, at the beginning of the American Revolution, his ship was seized by the British in the Bay of Mexico, and Cuffe was imprisoned in New York City for three months. After returning to Massachusetts in 1776, he resumed self-education and farming before returning to a maritime career.

Early in his life Cuffe—like most of his nine siblings, he used his father's African name as a surname—showed disdain for racial discrimination. In 1780, he and his brother John refused to pay taxes to protest a clause in the state constitution which forbade blacks suffrage. Their petition to the Massachusetts General Court alluded to the injustice of taxation without representation. While Cuffe was again briefly imprisoned, this time by Massachusetts's authorities for civil disobedience, the bold action successfully reduced the family's taxes.

On February 25, 1783, Cuffe married Alice Pequit. They had seven children. Throughout the American

Wood engraving of Paul Cuffe, black ship builder and sea captain, who, at the age of twenty-one, petitioned the Massachusetts legislature to relieve African Americans from paying taxes since they had "no vote or influence in the election of those who tax us." (Photographs and Prints Division, Schomburg Center for Research in Black Culture, The New York Public Library, Astor, Lenox and Tilden Foundations)

Revolution, Cuffe continued his maritime activities, captaining several boats to Nantucket Island past patrolling British privateers. He began family-based businesses which included farming, fishing, and whaling, as well as coastal and international commerce. He built at least seven vessels at his Westport, Mass. docks, including the schooner *Ranger,* the bark *Hero,* the brig *Traveler,* and the ship *Alpha.* His own ship's crews were identified by their African ancestry. They were customarily drawn from extended family members, mainly offspring from the marriage of his sister Mary and her Native-American husband Michael Wainer. Cuffe amassed a fortune in trade, despite ostracism and periodic encounters with arriving slavers. His property in 1806 was valued at approximately $20,000, making him Westport's wealthiest resident.

In 1808 Cuffe was received into the Society of Friends. He became a devout Quaker, contributed over $500 toward the building of meetinghouse, and entered into business ventures with leading Friends such as William Rotch, Jr. Religious affiliations also linked Cuffe to the Anglo-American abolitionist movement to end the transatlantic slave trade. Cuffe received requests from members of the Royal African Institution to visit Sierra Leone, England's West African asylum for ex-slaves. The possibility of Cuffe's involvement in resettling American blacks in Africa became the subject of letters between James Pemberton, Benjamin Rush, and James Brain of the Pennsylvania and Delaware Abolition Societies and William Wilberforce, Thomas Clarkson, and Zachary Macauley of Britain's abolitionist coalition in Parliament.

Cuffe made two trips to the English colony of Sierra Leone. The first left Westport on January 1, 1811, with a crew of nine black sailors. Disembarking on the West African coast from his brig *Traveller,* Cuffe became intrigued with the possibilities of beginning a three-way trade between the United States, England, and Sierra Leone. The trade route, he imagined, would bond together African descendants and their benefactors on three continents. On this trip, Cuffe also sailed to England where he protested the effects of Britain's trading monopoly upon aspiring black settler merchants. Nevertheless, he was warmly received by English abolitionists and lionized by the British press as the "African Captain."

Cuffe's efforts—he hoped to bring skilled immigrants for settlement on annual trips to Africa—were inhibited by the War of 1812. Both the United States and England, naturally, forbade trade with one another. Cuffe's petitions to allow continuance of his peaceful traffic, which he made both to the United States Congress and to the British Parliament, were refused.

After the war's end, Cuffe sailed again for Sierra Leone—this time leaving on December 10, 1815, with nine families consisting of thirty-eight people. Two of the families were headed by Congolese and Senegalese men returning home. America's urban black elite, particularly Philadelphia's James FORTEN, Absalom JONES, and Richard ALLEN, endorsed Cuffe's emigration scheme.

Upon his return to the U.S., Cuffe became increasingly convinced of the need for a mass emigration of blacks. He even gave his support to the AMERICAN COLONIZATION SOCIETY—an organization led by white Southerners and widely suspected by abolitionists—after they courted his endorsement. Cuffe's death in 1817 came before he could fulfill his own emigration plan, which he hoped would lessen the plight of black Americans and bring a measure of prosperity to Africa. He is considered by some to be the father of black nationalism.

REFERENCES

DIAMOND, ARTHUR. *Paul Cuffe*. New York, 1989.
HARRIS, SHELDON H. *Paul Cuffe, Black America, and the African Return*. New York, 1972.
SALVADOR, GEORGE. *Paul Cuffe, the Black Yankee, 1759–1817*. New Bedford, Mass., 1969.
THOMAS, LAMONT D. *Paul Cuffe, Black Entrepreneur and Pan-Africanist*. Urbana, Ill., 1988.

LAMONT D. THOMAS

Cullen, Countee (March 30, 1903–January 9, 1946), poet, novelist, and playwright. It has been difficult to place exactly where Countee Cullen was born, with whom he spent the very earliest years of his childhood, and where he spent them. New York City and Baltimore have been given as birthplaces by several scholars. Cullen himself, on his college transcript at New York University, listed Louisville, Ky., as his place of birth. A few years later, when he had achieved considerable literary fame during the era known as the NEW NEGRO or HARLEM RENAISSANCE, he was to assert that his birthplace was New York City, a claim he continued to make for the rest of his life. Both Cullen's second wife, Ida, and some of his closest friends, including Langston HUGHES and Harold Jackman, all said he was born in Louisville, although one Cullen scholar, Beulah Reimherr, in her M.A. thesis, claims that Ida Cullen gave her husband's place of birth as Baltimore. As James Weldon JOHNSON wrote in *The Book of American Negro Poetry* (revised edition, 1931), "There is not much to say about these earlier years of Cullen—unless he himself should say it." And Cullen—revealing a temperament that was not exactly secretive but private, less a matter of modesty than a tendency toward being encoded and tactful—never in his life said anything more clarifying.

What we know for certain is that he was born on March 30, 1903, and that sometime between his birth and 1918 he was adopted by the Rev. Frederick A. and Carolyn Belle (Mitchell) Cullen of the Salem Methodist Episcopal Church in Harlem. It is impossible to state with any degree of certainty how old Cullen was at the time, or how long he knew the Cullens before he was adopted. Apparently, he went by the name of Countee Porter until 1918. He became Countee P. Cullen by 1921, and eventually just Countee Cullen. According to Harold Jackman, the adoption was never really "official"; that is to say, it was never formally consummated through the proper state-agency channels. It is difficult, indeed, to know whether Cullen was ever legally an orphan at any stage in his childhood.

Frederick Cullen was one of the pioneer black activist-ministers; he moved his Salem Methodist Episcopal Church from a storefront mission—where it was in 1902, when he first arrived in New York City—to the site of a former white church in Harlem in 1924, where he could boast of a membership of over 2,500. Since Countee Cullen himself stated in his 1927 anthology of black American poetry. *Caroling Dusk*, that he was "reared in the conservative atmosphere of a Methodist parsonage," it is clear that his foster father, particularly, was a strong influence. The two men were very close, often traveling abroad together. But as Cullen evidences a decided unease in his poetry over his strong and conservative Christian training and the attraction of his pagan inclinations, his feelings about his father may have been somewhat ambivalent. Frederick Cullen was, on the one hand, a puritanical Christian patriarch, and Countee was never remotely that. On the other hand, it has been suggested that Frederick was also something of an effeminate man. (He was dressed in girl's clothing by his poverty-stricken mother well beyond the acceptable boyhood age for such a practice and was apparently effeminate in his manner as an adult.) Some scholars, especially Jean Wagner, have argued that Countee Cullen's homosexuality, or decidedly ambiguous sexual nature, may have been attributable to his foster father's contrary influence as both fire-breathing Christian and latent or covert transsexual. To be sure, in his poetry Cullen equated paganism with various sensual postures, including homosexuality. Cullen was a devoted and obedient son, and the fact that the Cullens had no other children made this attachment much easier to achieve.

Cullen was an outstanding student both at DeWitt Clinton High School (1918–1921)—where he not only edited the school's newspaper but also assisted in editing the literary magazine, *Magpie*, and wrote his first poetry that achieved notice—and at New York University (1921–1925), where he wrote most of the major work that was to make up his first two volumes, *Color* (1925) and *Copper Sun* (1927). It was also while at NYU that he wrote *The Ballad of the Brown Girl* (1927). In high school Cullen won his first contest, a citywide competition, with the poem "I Have a Rendezvous with Life," a nonracial poem inspired by Alan Seeger's "I Have a Rendezvous with Death." If any event signaled the coming of the Harlem Renaissance, it was the precocious success of this rather shy black boy who, more than any other black literary figure of his generation, was being touted and bred to become a major crossover literary figure. Here was a black man with considerable academic training who could, in effect, write "white" verse—ballads, sonnets, quatrains, and the like—much in the manner of Keats and the British Romantics (albeit, on more than one occasion, tinged with racial concerns), with genuine skill and compelling power. He was certainly not the first African American to attempt to write such verse, but he was first to do so with such extensive education, with such a complete understanding of himself as a poet, and producing poetry that was not trite or inferior. Only two other black American poets before Cullen could be taken so seriously as self-consciously considered and proficient poets: Phillis WHEATLEY and Paul Laurence DUNBAR.

If the aim of the Harlem Renaissance was, in part, the reinvention of the native-born African American as a being who could be assimilated while decidedly retaining something called a "racial self-consciousness," then Cullen fit the bill better than virtually any other Renaissance writer. And if "I Have a Rendezvous with Life" was the opening salvo in the making of Cullen's literary reputation, then the 1924 publication of "Shroud of Color" in H. L. Mencken's *American Mercury* confirmed the advent of the black boy wonder as one of the most exciting American poets on the scene. After graduating Phi Beta Kappa from NYU, Cullen earned a master's degree in English and French from Harvard (1927). Between high school and graduation from Harvard he had become the most popular black poet—virtually the most popular black literary figure—in America. It was after one of his poems and his popular column appeared in OPPORTUNITY magazine that A'Lelia WALKER (heiress of Madame C. J. WALKER's hair-care-products fortune) named her salon, where the black and white literati gathered in the late 1920s, the Dark Tower.

Cullen won more major literary prizes than any other black writer of the 1920s: the first prize in the Witter Bynner Poetry Contest in 1925; *Poetry* magazine's John Reed Memorial Prize; the Amy Spingarn Award of *The Crisis* magazine; second prize in *Opportunity* magazine's first poetry contest; second prize in the poetry contest of *Palms*. He was the second African American to win a Guggenheim Fellowship. His first three books—*Color, Copper Sun,* and *The Ballad of the Brown Girl*—sold well and made him a hero for many blacks. Lines from Cullen's popular poems, such as "Heritage," "Incident," "From the Dark Tower," and "Yet Do I Marvel," were commonly quoted.

Cullen was also at the center of one of the major social events of the Harlem Renaissance; on April 9, 1928, he married Yolande Du Bois, only child of W. E. B. DUBOIS, in one of the most lavish weddings in black New York history. This wedding was to symbolize the union of the grand black intellectual patriarch and the new breed of younger African Americans who were responsible for much of the excitement of the Renaissance. It was an apt meshing of personalities, as both Cullen and Du Bois *père* were conservative by nature and ardent traditionalists. That the marriage turned out so disastrously and ended so quickly—Yolande and Cullen divorced in 1930—probably adversely affected Cullen. (He remarried in 1940.) Cullen published *The Black Christ and Other Poems* in 1929, receiving lukewarm reviews from both black and white presses. He was bitterly disappointed that *The Black Christ*, his longest and in many respects his most complicated poem, the product of over two years' work, was considered by most critics to be his weakest and least distinguished.

From the 1930s until his death, Cullen wrote a great deal less, partly hampered by his job as a French teacher at Frederick Douglass Junior High (his most famous student was James BALDWIN). But he wrote noteworthy, even significant work in a number of genres. His novel *One Way to Heaven,* published in 1934, rates among the better black satires, and is one of the three important fictional retrospectives of the Harlem Renaissance, the others being Wallace THURMAN's *The Infants of the Spring* and George SCHUYLER's *Black No More;* his translation of *The Medea* is the first major translation of a classical work by a twentieth-century black American writer; the children's books *The Lost Zoo* and *My Lives and How I Lost Them* are among the more clever and engaging books of children's verse, written at a time when there was not much work published for children by black writers; and his poetry of the period includes perhaps some of his best, certainly some of his more darkly complex, sonnets. He was also working on a musical with Arna BONTEMPS called *St. Louis Woman* (based on Bontemps's novel, *God Sends Sunday*) at the time of his death from high blood pressure and uremic poisoning.

For many years after his death, Cullen's reputation was eclipsed by those of other Harlem Renaissance writers, particularly Langston Hughes and Zora Neale HURSTON, and his work had gone out of print. More recently, however, there has been a resurgence of interest in his life and work, and his books are being reissued.

REFERENCES

BONTEMPS, ARNA, ed. *The Harlem Renaissance Remembered.* New York, 1972.

DAVIS, ARTHUR P. *From the Dark Tower: Afro-American Writers, 1900 to 1960.* Washington, D.C., 1974.

EARLY, GERALD, ed. *My Soul's High Song; The Collected Writings of Countee Cullen, Voice of the Harlem Renaissance.* New York, 1991.

FERGUSON, BLANCHE F. *Countee Cullen and the Negro Renaissance.* New York, 1966.

HUGGINS, NATHAN. *Harlem Renaissance.* New York, 1971.

WAGNER, JEAN. *Black Poets of the United States: From Paul Laurence Dunbar to Langston Hughes.* Translated by Kenneth Douglas. Champaign, Ill. 1973.

GERALD EARLY

Cummings, Blondell

Cummings, Blondell (November 194?–), modern dancer, choreographer, and arts advocate. Born in Effingham, S.C., but raised in Harlem as the oldest of three girls. Cummings began dance study in the New York public schools. She attended New York University's School of Education, did graduate work in film and photography at Lehman College, and continued serious dance study at the schools of Martha Graham, José Limon, and Alvin AILEY. Cummings founded the Video Exchange to document danceworks, and at the same time began dancing with the companies of Richard Bull, Kai Takei, the New York Chamber Dance Company, the New Jersey Repertory Company, and Rod RODGERS. In 1969 she joined Meredith Monk/The House, where critics identified her virtuostic abilities to project character through gestures and sounds, most notably as the Dictator in Monk's *Quarry* (1976). In 1978 Cummings formed the Cycle Arts Foundation, a discussion/performance workshop focused on familial issues including menopause, the bonding and sharing rituals of lifestyle, and art-making. This effort underscored Cummings's commitment to relate the arts to everyday life, and to "create a new ritual of empowerment to uplift the family."

Cummings also created several experimental dances that featured her remarkably concentrated solo abilities, including "The Ladies and Me" (1979), a "visual diary" set to the music of Ma RAINEY, Billie HOLIDAY, Sister Rosetta THARPE, Mary Lou WILLIAMS, Ella FITZGERALD, and others; "Chicken Soup" (1981), a portrait of lifetime domesticity; and "For J.B." (1990), dedicated to Josephine BAKER. Among her arresting multimedia collaborations are *The Art of War/Nine Situations* (1984), a meditation on connections between military strategy and daily life, created with Jessica Hagedorn; and *Omadele and Giuseppe* (1991), a contemplation of interracial living, created with Tom Thayer. Cummings's workshop/performance practice often invited audience participation, confirming her belief that "choreography is always the act of sharing."

REFERENCES

DIXON, BRENDA. "Blondell Cummings: The Ladies and Me." *TDR* 24, no. 4 (1980): 37–44.

SMALL, LINDA. "Blondell Cummings." *Village Voice,* March 10, 1980, p. 35.

THOMAS F. DEFRANTZ

Cuney, Norris Wright

Cuney, Norris Wright (1846–1898), politician. Born of a prominent planter and a slave woman near Hempstead, Tex., and formally educated in the North. Settling in Galveston, Tex., in 1865, Norris Wright Cuney by the early 1870s had secured a place in the federal customhouse and in REPUBLICAN PARTY councils. Though he was favored by radical governor Edmund J. Davis, and later by prominent northern Republicans, it was Cuney's cultivation of a sizable black constituency that guaranteed his prominence. African Americans provided the bulk of the Texas Republican party's support, leaving Cuney its most powerful member after Davis's death in 1883. Elected to the Republican National Committee in 1886, Cuney was one of a number of black Southerners who retained some prominence in the party's organization in the post-RECONSTRUCTION decades—even as the influence of African Americans in the politics of the southern states waned. In 1889 Cuney was appointed collector of customs in Galveston, the foremost federal position in Texas and one of the highest offices then held by an African American in the South.

As party leader, Cuney denounced segregation of railroad cars, exclusion of blacks from jury service, and armed intimidation of Black Belt Republicans, while seeking expanded educational and social services. For over a decade, he stymied "lily white" Republicans who argued that the party could attract more white voters if its black leadership was overthrown. At the same time, he earned the respect of many white Galvestonians, as evidenced by his being elected alderman twice (1883, 1885) from a white majority district. His interests in black advancement and in cultivating the local business community proved not to be mutually exclusive: In 1885, he allowed black longshoremen he employed to break a strike, but on condition that blacks thereafter be granted an equal share of work on Galveston's docks. Cuney never placed undue faith in the liberality of Texas's white majority, however. His party rarely nominated blacks for state offices. It often endorsed independents or third-party dissidents rather than field a ticket, hoping to enhance its power by becoming the keystone of an anti-Democratic majority coalition. In 1892, however, Cuney ignored the agrarian reformers in the Populist party, allying the Republicans with a powerful faction of conservative Democrats organizing against their own party's comparatively progressive incumbent governor. The failure, and seemingly mercenary expedience, of this maneuver eroded Cuney's authority. The Democrats' return to the White House in 1893 curtailed his patronage powers; at the same time, "lily white" agitation intensified. His opposition to the nomination of William McKinley in 1896 finally allowed rivals to depose him. Eighteen months later, Cuney died. Black leadership of Texas's Republican party did not long survive his passing.

REFERENCE

HARE, MAUD CUNEY. *Norris Wright Cuney: A Tribune of the Black People.* New York, 1913.

PATRICK G. WILLIAMS

Curtis, Austin Maurice (January 15, 1868–1939), surgeon. Austin Maurice Curtis was born in Raleigh, N.C., during Reconstruction. Educated in the public schools there, he attended Lincoln University in Pennsylvania, receiving a B.A. in 1888. Lincoln would also award him an honorary Sc.D. in 1929. In 1891 he received an M.D. from Northwestern University Medical School in Chicago and began graduate training in surgery at PROVIDENT HOSPITAL in Chicago, the first surgical intern appointed by Provident. After training under Daniel Hale WILLIAMS for two years, Curtis established a private practice in Chicago, where he practiced for four years. In 1895, he accepted an appointment to the attending staff at Chicago's Cook County Hospital—the first African-American surgeon to receive such an appointment.

In 1897, Curtis's former teacher Williams recruited him to Washington, D.C. Recognized as a specialist in abdominal surgery, Curtis became a professor at HOWARD UNIVERSITY's College of Medicine. He also joined the staff of Washington's FREEDMEN'S HOSPITAL as chief surgeon, a position he held from 1898 until 1902, though he continued there as an attending surgeon for more than thirty years. Throughout his years in Washington, Curtis consulted as a surgical specialist to white and black hospitals in the District of Columbia, Maryland, and Virginia.

In 1925 he founded the Curtis Private Surgical Sanitarium with his son, and in 1928 he became the first African-American chair of Howard's Department of Surgery, a position he held until his retirement in 1936. Curtis died in Washington in 1939. In 1941, Howard University established the Austin M. Curtis Memorial Lectureship in recognition of his contributions to the university.

REFERENCES

ORGAN, CLAUDE H., JR., and MARGARET M. KOSIBA, eds. *A Century of Black Surgeons: The USA Experience,* Norman, Okla., 87.

SAMMONS, VIVIAN OVELTON. *Blacks in Science and Medicine.* New York, 1990.

CLAUDE H. ORGAN, JR.
VERNON J. HENDERSON

D

Daddy Grace. *See* Grace, Charles Emmanuel "Daddy Grace."

Dafora, Asadata (August 4, 1890–March 4, 1965), dancer. Asadata Dafora was born in Freetown, Sierra Leone, the great-grandson of a former slave who returned from Nova Scotia to his homeland. His birth name is uncertain but was probably Austin Asadata Dafora Horton. Dafora attended Wesleyan High School in Freetown and moved to Europe in 1910. His life in Europe is not well documented, but he is believed to have studied opera in Germany and Italy from 1910 through 1912. Dafora is also reported to have been a member of the British Army during World War I.

In 1929, Dafora arrived in New York intending to pursue a career in opera. He began working with a group of African men who frequented the National African Union, a social club. From these initial efforts he formed Shogola Oloba, an African troupe of performers. His troupe performed scenes from *Zoonga,* a dance opera of his composition, at the Communist Party Bazaar at Madison Square Garden in New York City in 1933. The following year Dafora premiered the dance opera *Kykunkor* (Witch Woman) at the Little Theater in New York City. A novelty in the United States because of its African theme, *Kykunkor* told the story of a bridegroom who had been cursed by a scorned lover. The performance was a critical success, and by 1935 the group had become the African Dance Troupe of the Federal Theatre Project. It was featured in Orson Welles's production of *Macbeth.*

In 1938, Shogola Oloba performed *Zunguru,* a work in the style of *Kykunkor.* It was revived in 1940 and again in 1958 with the participation of Esther Rolle (best known for her portrayal of Florida Evans on the 1970s television sitcom *Good Times*).

In 1960, Dafora returned to Freetown and passed directorship of his troupe to Rolle. The following year he once again returned to the United States, where he died in Harlem Hospital in 1965.

REFERENCES

HUGHES, LANGSTON, and MILTON MELTZER. *Black Magic: A Pictorial History of the African-American in the Performing Arts.* Englewood Cliffs, N.J., 1967.

LONG, RICHARD A. *The Black Tradition in American Dance.* New York, N.Y., 1989.

SOUTHERN, EILEEN. *Biographical Dictionary of African-American and African Musicians.* Westport, Conn., 1982.

STEARNS, MARSHALL, and JEAN STEARNS. *Jazz Dance: The Story of American Vernacular Dance.* New York, N.Y., 1968.

THORPE, EDWARD. *Black Dance.* New York, 1990.

MARCIA ETHEL HEARD

Dailey, Ulysses Grant (August 3, 1885–April 22, 1961), surgeon. Born in Donaldsville, La., Grant Dailey grew up in Fort Worth, Tex., where his fa-

709

ther, Tony, owned a successful hand-laundry. Dailey acquired a taste for classical music and was a locally accomplished pianist and bandleader; he even dreamed of becoming an orchestra conductor, but instead pursued a medical career. He attended Straight College (now Dillard University) in New Orleans, where he completed the eighth grade in 1900. Dailey thereupon began work as an office assistant for a doctor in Fort Worth. He proved so helpful that the doctor soon let him assist in operations. Dailey pored over medical texts during his spare time and, without a high school diploma, in 1902 passed the entrance exam to Northwestern University's medical school in Chicago, earning his M.D. four years later. The youngest in his class, he worked at Northwestern as an assistant demonstrator of anatomy from 1906 to 1908.

Completing postgraduate work in Paris and Berlin in 1912, Dailey practiced surgery until 1926 at Provident Hospital, the leading African-American medical institution in Illinois. He also taught at the Chicago Medical College and worked as attending surgeon at Fort Dearborn Hospital during the early 1920s. In 1926 he founded the fifty-bed Dailey Hospital and Sanitarium in Chicago, treating primarily tuberculosis patients. Dailey was forced to close the hospital in 1932 because of funding problems. He returned to Provident Hospital in 1933 as its chief surgeon, following the death of Dr. Daniel Hale WILLIAMS.

Dailey published widely on both medical and scientific topics, and on issues that concerned African Americans studying and practicing medicine. In 1916 Dailey was president of the National Medical Association, the professional organization for black physicians. During the GREAT DEPRESSION, he wrote a column for the Chicago *Defender,* "Until the Doctor Comes," which brought health knowledge to a popular audience. He also held leading positions in organizations such as the American College of Surgeons and the International College of Surgeons.

World War II and the postwar years marked Dailey's increasing concern with world health problems. In 1942 he was appointed an honorary emissary to Haiti, where he accompanied the United Nations Technical Assistance Program. In 1946 in Lima, Peru, Dailey became the first African American to address the International College of Surgeons. He also edited the National Medical Association's *Journal* from 1948 to 1949. Daily was awarded the Distinguished Service Medal of the National Medical Association in 1949. He retired in 1956 and died in 1961.

REFERENCES

ORGAN, CLAUDE H., and MARGARET M. KOSIBA. *A Century of Black Surgeons: The U.S.A. Experience.* Norman, Okla., 1987.

PRESTON, DONALD. *The Scholar and the Scalpel: The Life Story of Ulysses Grant Dailey.* Chicago, 1966.

SUSAN MCINTOSH
ALLISON X. MILLER

Daly, Marie Maynard (April 16, 1921–), biochemist. Marie Daly was born in New York City. In 1942 she received a B.S. from Queens College and earned an M.S. in 1943 from New York University. She received a Ph.D. in chemistry from Columbia University in 1947, thereby becoming the first black woman to earn a doctorate in chemistry.

Daly began her career as an instructor in physical science at Howard University in 1947–1948, and then moved to the Rockefeller Institute, where she was visiting investigator, an American Cancer Society Fellow from 1948 to 1951, and a research assistant from 1951 to 1955. For the next four years (1955–1959), Daly was an associate at the Columbia University Research Service at the Goldwater Memorial Hospital. Daly concluded her career at the Albert Einstein College of Medicine (1960–1986), where she taught biochemistry and did research on nucleic acids, arterial smooth muscle, and creatine transport metabolism.

REFERENCES

American Men & Women of Science 1922–93, Vol. 2. New Providence, N.J., 1992.
CLOYD, IRIS. *Who's Who Among Black Americans.* Detroit, Mich., 1990.

SIRAJ AHMED

Dameron, Tadley Ewing Peake "Tadd" (February 21, 1917–March 8, 1965), jazz pianist and composer. Dameron was born and raised in Cleveland, Ohio. He received his first music lessons from his older brother. He also studied with Louis Bolden, a local pianist, before working professionally with bands led by Freddie Webster, Zack Whyte, and Blanche Calloway. In 1940 he worked briefly as an arranger, then performed in New York with Vido Musso. Dameron joined Harlan Leonard's band in Kansas City ("400 Swing," 1940), and then worked in a war plant before moving to New York.

In New York, Dameron quickly became a popular and successful big band composer and arranger. His most important work from this time was with Dizzy GILLESPIE's big band, but he also wrote for Jimmie LUNCEFORD, Benny CARTER, Teddy Hill, Billy ECKSTINE, and Sarah VAUGHAN. By the mid-1940s

Dameron was a fixture of the burgeoning bebop scene, and it was during this time that he wrote his best-known compositions, "Good Bait" (1945), "Hot House" (1945), and "Our Delight" (1946). In 1948 Dameron led his own bebop quintet, including trumpeter Fats NAVARRO, in an extended gig at New York's Royal Roost nightclub. In 1949 Dameron traveled to Paris, and performed and recorded there with trumpeter Miles DAVIS. He remained in Europe after the engagement was finished and found work in Paris and London as an arranger for Ted Heath and other bandleaders. He returned to the United States to perform with "Bull Moose" Jackson's band during 1951–1952 and in the next year led a band that included Clifford BROWN and Philly Joe JONES. Despite a heroin addiction that began to interfere with his ability to work, he wrote and recorded one of the founding works of "Third Stream" jazz—a fusion of classical music and jazz—*Fontainebleau,* in 1956. That piece, an elegant, fully composed jazz tone poem, displayed Dameron's sophisticated and ambitious sense of harmony.

Dameron was arrested on drug charges in 1958 and served a two-year sentence. Upon his release in 1961, he began to write again, composing for Milt JACKSON and Sonny Stitt. He also wrote arrangements for Benny Goodman. During this time, however, his health began to fail him. He made a final appearance at a 1964 benefit and died of cancer in New York the following year.

REFERENCES

GITLER, IRA. *Jazz Masters of the 40's.* 1966. Reprint. New York, 1983.
WILMER, VALERIE. "The Magic Touch: A Swan Song for Tadd Dameron." *Jazz Beat* 2, no. 5 (1965): 20.

GUTHRIE P. RAMSEY, JR.

Dance. *See* Ballet; Breakdancing; Tap Dance; Theatrical Dance.

Dance Theater of Harlem, classical dance company. The Dance Theater of Harlem (DTH) was founded on August 15, 1969, by Arthur Mitchell and Karel Shook as the world's first permanent, professional, academy-rooted, predominantly black ballet troupe. Mitchell created DTH to address a threefold mission of social, educational, and artistic opportunity for the people of Harlem, and to prove that "there are black dancers with the physique, temperament and stamina, and everything else it takes to produce what we call the 'born' ballet dancer." Dur-

Arthur Mitchell (center), with his Dance Theater ballet dancers. Mitchell created a racially integrated dance and music school in Harlem. (UPI/Bettmann)

ing its official 1971 debut, DTH triumphantly debunked opinions that black people could not dance ballet. By 1993 DTH had become a world-renowned company with forty-nine dancers, seventy-five ballets in its repertory, an associated school, and an international touring schedule.

DTH's extensive repertory has included technically demanding neoclassic ballets (George Balanchine's 1946 *The Four Temperaments*); programmatic works (Mitchell's 1968 *Rhythmetron* and Alvin AILEY's 1970 *The River* to music by Duke ELLINGTON); and pieces that explore the African-American experience (Louis Johnson's 1972 *Forces of Rhythm* and Geoffrey Holder's 1974 *Dougla* created in collaboration with DTH conductor-composer Tania Leon). DTH also excels in its own versions of classic ballets, including a sumptuous, Geoffrey Holder–designed production of Stravinsky's *Firebird* (1982) choreographed by John Taras, and a stunning Creole-inspired staging of *Giselle* (1984) created by Mitchell, designer Carl Mitchell, and artistic associate Frederic Franklin. This highly acclaimed *Giselle* set the Romantic-era story in the society of free black plantation owners in pre–Civil War Louisiana. DTH is perhaps best known for its revivals of dramatic ballets, including Agnes de Mille's 1948 *Fall River Legend* and Valerie Bettis's 1952 *A Streetcar Named Desire,* both of which have starred principal ballerina Virginia JOHNSON. Other important classical dance artists associated with DTH include Lydia Arbaca, Karen Brown, Stephanie Dabney, Robert Garland, Lorraine Graves, Christina Johnson, Ronald Perry, Walter Raines, Judith Rotardier, Paul Russell, Eddie J. Shellman, Lowell Smith, Mel Tomlinson, and Donald Williams.

In 1972 the DTH school moved to its permanent home at 466 West 152nd Street, where training in dance, choreography, and music supplemented outreach programs bringing dance to senior citizens and children of the Harlem community with special needs. The international celebrity achieved by DTH began with a Caribbean performance tour in 1970, an engagement at the Spoleto Festival in 1971, and an auspicious 1974 London debut at Sadler's Wells. In 1988 DTH embarked on a five-week tour of the U.S.S.R., playing sold-out performances in Moscow, Tbilisi, and Leningrad, where the company received a standing ovation at the famed Kirov Theatre. In 1992, DTH successfully performed in Johannesburg, South Africa.

In 1990, faced with a $1.7 million dollar deficit, DTH was forced to cancel its New York season and lay off dancers, technicians, and administrative staff for a six-month period. Mitchell and the board of directors responded with increased efforts to enlarge corporate support and strengthen their African-American audience base. In 1994 DTH completed a $6 million expansion and renovation project, which doubled classroom and administrative space and confirmed the DTH commitment to provide access to the disciplined training necessary for a career in classical ballet.

REFERENCES

KENDALL, ELIZABETH. " 'Home' to Russia: Dance Theatre of Harlem on Tour in the Soviet Union." *Ballet Review* V. 16 No. 4, Winter 1989:3–49.

MAYNARD, OLGA. "Dance Theatre of Harlem: Arthur Mitchell's 'Dark and Brilliant Splendor.' " *Dance Magazine* (May 1975): 52–64.

THOMAS F. DEFRANTZ

Dandridge, Dorothy (c. November 1923–September 8, 1965), actor and singer. The daughter of a minister and a stage entertainer, Dorothy Dandridge was born in Cleveland, Ohio, and was groomed for a stage career by her mother, Ruby Dandridge, who separated from her husband and began touring the country as a performer shortly after her second daughter was born. While still a child, Dandridge sang, danced, and did comedy skits as part of her mother's show. When their mother settled in Los Angeles, she and her older sister Vivian—together they had been billed as "The Wonder Kids"—attended school and appeared in bit parts in films, including the Marx Brothers comedy *A Day at the Races* (1937). During the 1940s, Dorothy and Vivian joined with another young African-American woman, Etta Jones, to form an act called "The Dandridge Sisters," and embarked on a tour with the Jimmie LUNCEFORD band. Dandridge met her first husband, Harold NICHOLAS (of the Nicholas Brothers dancing team), while she was performing at the COTTON CLUB in Harlem. A brain-damaged daughter, Harolyn, was born to the couple before they divorced.

During this time, Dandridge managed to secure a few minor Hollywood roles, and appeared in such films as *Drums of the Congo* (1942), *The Hit Parade of 1943, Moo Cow Boogie* (1943), *Atlantic City* (1944), *Pillow to Post* (1946), and *Flamingo* (1947). The early 1950s witnessed the flowering of her movie career, as she acquired leading roles in the low-budget films *Tarzan's Perils, The Harlem Globe-Trotters,* and *Jungle Queen* (all made in 1951). Dandridge, who was exceptionally beautiful, worked actively at cultivating a cosmopolitan, transracial persona, brimming with sexual allure. She also became increasingly well known as a nightclub singer. Indeed, Dandridge's performances at New York's La Vie En Rose (1952) were in such demand that the club—then on the brink of bankruptcy—was saved from financial collapse. She was one of the first African Americans to perform at the Waldorf-Astoria's Empire Room, and appeared at such prestigious clubs as Ciro's (Los Angeles), the Cafe de Paris (London), the Copacabana (Rio de Janeiro), and the Chi Chi (Palm Springs).

Dandridge's big break as a motion picture actress came in 1954, when she secured the title role in Otto Preminger's all-black production *Carmen Jones.* That year, she became the first black actor to be nominated for an Oscar for a leading role. That she had achieved celebrity stature was evidenced by her appearances on the cover of *Life,* as well as in feature articles in national and international magazines. However, three years were to pass before Dandridge made another film, largely because, in racist Hollywood, she was not offered roles commensurate with her talent and beauty, and she could no longer settle for less. Her next film, *Island in the Sun* (1957), was the first to feature an interracial romance (between Dandridge and white actor John Justin); the film was poorly received, as were *The Decks Ran Red* (1958), *Tamango* (1959), and *Malaga* (1962), all of which touched on interracial themes. Although Dandridge won acclaim in 1959 for her portrayal of Bess (opposite Sidney POITIER) in Otto Preminger's film of *Porgy and Bess,* she received fewer and fewer film and nightclub offers as time passed. After divorcing her second husband, white restaurant-owner Jack Dennison, she was forced to file for bankruptcy and lost her Hollywood mansion. Her sudden death in 1965 was attributed to an overdose of antidepressants; she was forty-one years old. Dandridge's autobiography, *Everything and Nothing,* was published posthumously in 1970; in 1977, she was inducted into the Black Filmmakers Hall of Fame.

REFERENCES

DANDRIDGE, DOROTHY and EARL CONRAD. *Everything and Nothing: The Dorothy Dandridge Tragedy.* New York, 1970.

Obituary. *New York Times,* September 9, 1965, p. 41.

PAMELA WILKINSON

Danner, Margaret Essie (January 12, 1915–), poet. Born in Pryorsburg, Ky., Margaret Danner grew up in Chicago and attended Roosevelt, Loyola, and Northwestern in Chicago. Encouraged by poets Karl Shapiro and Paul Engle, Danner published poems in *Poetry* magazine, and worked there from 1951 to 1957 as the magazine's first black staff member. Her first book of poems, *Impressions of African Art Forms,* came out in 1960. She was poet in residence at Wayne State University in Detroit in 1961 and 1962, and while there, founded the community arts center referred to in her poem "Boone House." As its director, Danner nurtured the burgeoning of creative expression in Detroit's black community in the 1960s. She published *To Flower: Poems* in 1963, and in 1964 worked with Langston HUGHES on a recording, *Writers of the Revolution.* In 1966, Danner collaborated with poet Dudley RANDALL on *Poem Counterpoem,* and that year visited Senegal. She published *Iron Lace* in 1968, and served in 1968–1969 as poet in residence at Virginia Union University in Richmond. She served as poet in residence at LeMoyne-Owen College, in Memphis, Tenn., from 1970 to 1975. Danner published *The Down of a Thistle* In 1976. Danner's poems have appeared in many anthologies and small magazines. Her poetry evokes the spirit of racial protest, but it is not overtly political. Rather, her verses use African imagery to celebrate the cultural heritage of African Americans.

REFERENCES

KING, WOODIE, ed. *The Forerunners: Black Poets in America.* Washington, D.C., 1975.

REDMOND, EUGENE. *Drumvoices: The Mission of Afro-American Poetry.* Garden City, N.Y. 1976.

JONATHAN GILL

Dash, Julie (October 22, 1952–), filmmaker. Born and raised in New York City, Julie Dash began studying film as a teenager in 1969 at the Studio Museum of Harlem. After receiving a B.A. in film production from the City College of New York, Dash moved to Los Angeles to attend the Center for Advanced Film Studies at the American Film Institute, the youngest fellow ever to attend this institution. Later, she did graduate work at the University of California at Los Angeles.

Dash's films are sensitive, complex portrayals of the dilemmas confronting a diverse group of black women. While at the American Film Institute, she directed *Four Women,* an experimental dance film inspired by the Nina Simone song of the same title (1977 winner of the Golden Medal for Women in Film at the Miami International Film Festival); and *Diary of an African Nun,* based on a short story by Alice Walker (1977 winner of the Director's Guild Award). Her 1983 black-and-white short *Illusions,* the story of a fair-skinned black woman film executive set in 1942, was nominated for a Cable ACE Award in art direction, and is permanently archived at Indiana University and at Clark College in Atlanta.

In 1986, Dash relocated to Atlanta from Los Angeles and began work on *Daughters of the Dust.*

Generally regarded as the first feature-length film by an African-American woman, *Daughters of the Dust* opened in 1992 to critical acclaim. "Its nonlinear narrative, focusing on the Gullah culture of the South Carolina Sea Islands, centers on the lives of African-

Filmmaker Julie Dash. (Allford/Trotman Associates)

American women. They are the bearers of the culture, tellers of the tales, and most important, spectators for whom she created the film. Dash's approach to filmmaking has been "to show black women at pivotal moments in their lives . . . [to] focus on and depict experiences that have never been shown on screen before."

After *Daughters,* Dash moved to London to collaborate on a screenplay with Maureen Blackwood of Sankofa. She also began work on a series of films depicting black women in the United States from the turn of the twentieth century to the year 2000.

REFERENCES

BAKER, HOUSTON. "Not Without My Daughters." *Transition* 57: 150–166.
DAVIS, ZEINABU IRENE. "An Interview with Julie Dash." *Wide Angle* 13, no. 3 and 4: 120–137.
KLOTMAN, PHYLLIS RAUCH. "Julie Dash." In Phyllis Klotman, ed., *Screenplays of the African-American Experience,* pp. 191–195. Bloomington, Ind., 1991.
MILLS, DAVID. "A Dash of Difference." *Washington Post,* February 28, 1992, p. C1.

FARAH JASMINE GRIFFIN

Davidson, Olivia America

Davidson, Olivia America (June 11, 1854–May 9, 1889), educator. Olivia Davidson was born in Tazewell County, Va. She moved to Athens, Ohio, as a child, and attended common schools until the age of fifteen. In 1870 she began teaching in state schools and continued for several terms.

In 1874 Davidson moved to Spencer, Miss., and then Memphis, Tenn., where she taught for four years. In 1878, while she was at home in Ohio, an epidemic of yellow fever broke out in Memphis. Rather than return to her teaching job, she decided to enter HAMPTON INSTITUTE in Virginia, from which she graduated with highest honors in 1879.

While at Hampton she met Mary Hemenway, a philanthropist from Boston. Impressed by Davidson's distinction in school, Hemenway offered to pay for the continuation of Davidson's education in New England. Davidson accepted the offer and attended the State Normal School in Framingham, Mass., from 1879 to 1881, once again graduating with high honors.

Upon graduation, Davidson was invited by Booker T. WASHINGTON to work as assistant principal and teacher at the newly established Tuskegee Normal and Industrial School in Alabama, later the Tuskegee Institute (*see* TUSKEGEE UNIVERSITY). Despite her frail health, she proved to be a hard worker and a dedicated teacher, instructing in a variety of subjects such as mathematics, astronomy, and bot-

any. Davidson also successfully solicited money to help purchase permanent buildings for the school. Her projects, which included benefit suppers, student literary entertainment, and speaking tours in the North, raised enough money within one year to buy the farm on which Tuskegee was located and to construct classrooms and dormitories for students. Though rarely acknowledged, Davidson's efforts were crucial in establishing Tuskegee as one of the most prominent African-American educational institutions in the country.

Davidson's unwavering commitment to black education included a special concern for girls, whom she called the "hope of the race." In addition, she believed that a teacher's responsibility was not confined to the classroom. She felt teachers had an obligation to take an interest in the living conditions of their students. She urged educators to pay attention to personal hygiene, degrading home influences, and what she considered inappropriate student behavior, such as tying cloth on their heads. Underlying Davidson's advocacy of better living conditions were confidence in the strategy of moral uplift and an adherence to liberal assimilationist beliefs.

In 1886 Davidson and Booker T. Washington married. Together the couple had two sons, Booker T., Jr., and Ernest Davidson. Olivia Davidson's new familial responsibilities and indefatigable administrative efforts began to take their physical toll. Although she was not diagnosed with tuberculosis until 1889, her health continued to deteriorate throughout the 1880s and she suffered a series of relapses. Two days after her second son was born in 1889, a fire broke out in the house, forcing her out into the cold. This led to a steady decline in her health from which she was unable to recover. Davidson died at the early age of thirty-five, abruptly ending a career of service and devotion to African-American education.

REFERENCES

DORSEY, CAROLYN A. "Despite Poor Health: Olivia Davidson Washington's Story." *Sage: A Scholarly Journal on Black Women* 2 (Fall 1985): 69–72.
HARLAN, LOUIS R., ed. *The Booker T. Washington Papers, Volume 2, 1860–1889.* Urbana, Ill., 1972.
HUNTER, WILMA KING. "Three Women at Tuskegee, 1882–1925: The Wives of Booker T. Washington." *Journal of Ethnic Studies* 3 (September 1976): 76–89.

SABRINA FUCHS
PAM NADASEN

Davidson, Shelby James

Davidson, Shelby James (May 10, 1868–1931), inventor and lawyer. Shelby J. Davidson was born in 1868 in Lexington, Ky. There he attended public elementary and high school and received teacher's training. He enrolled at State University in Louisville (a racially segregated institution managed by African-American Baptists), but transferred to Howard University in Washington, D.C., where he earned an A.B. degree in 1893. Later that year he began a nineteen-year career at the post office department in Washington.

When the treasury department commissioned Davidson to study the operation and use of adding machines at its office in Detroit, Mich., Davidson developed his own improvement. He patented an attachment to adding machines that rewound the roll of paper so that the back of the paper would be reused. Davidson also developed a coin-machine counting attachment, and a mechanism for automatically calculating totals for the money orders submitted to the postmaster.

Davidson began to receive legal training in the offices of Col. William A. Cook of Washington in 1893. He was admitted to the bars of Kentucky and Washington in 1900. Three years later he was admitted to practice before the D.C. Court of Appeals. In 1912 he was admitted to the bar of the U.S. Supreme Court, when Belva A. Lockwood, the first woman granted privileges to practice before the high court, nominated Davidson. In the same year Davidson resigned from government service, continuing his private law practice and entering the real estate business in Washington. Davidson was also a trustee of the Bureau of the Baptist Church, and a member of the Colored Bar Association. He died in 1931 in the Washington area.

REFERENCES

JAMES, PORTIA P. *The Real McCoy: African-American Invention and Innovation, 1619–1930.* Washington, D.C., 1989.

MATHER, FRANK LINCOLN, ed. *Who's Who of the Colored Race.* Chicago, 1915.

PETER SCHILLING

Davis, Angela Yvonne (January 26, 1944–), political activist. Angela Davis lived in a section of Birmingham, Ala., known as "Dynamite Hill" because of the violent attacks by white nightriders intent on maintaining the residential demarcation line between blacks and whites. Both of her parents were educators, worked actively for the NAACP, and taught their children not to accept the socially segregated society that existed at the time. She attended Brandeis University, where she was influenced by the teachings of Marxist philosopher Herbert Marcuse. After graduating in 1961, she spent two years in Eu-

Angela Davis was implicated in the aborted 1970 rescue of George Jackson from incarceration, and the effort to free her was one of the most celebrated radical causes in the early 1970s. After her acquittal on all charges in 1972, Davis was an active leader of the Communist party and was their vice presidential candidate in 1980 and 1984. (© Mel Rosenthal, Impact Visuals)

rope, where she was exposed to student political radicals. Her own radicalism, however, came into focus with the murder in 1963 of four young black Sunday school children in a Birmingham, Ala., church bombing. In California, where she went to pursue graduate study with Marcuse (who was now at the University of California, San Diego), Davis began working with the STUDENT NONVIOLENT COORDINATING COMMITTEE (SNCC), the Black Panthers (see BLACK PANTHER PARTY FOR SELF–DEFENSE), and the Communist party, of which she became a member in 1968 (see COMMUNIST PARTY OF THE U.S.A.).

Hired in 1969 by UCLA to teach philosophy, Davis not long after was fired by the Board of Regents and then-Governor Ronald Reagan because of her Communist party affiliation. Ultimately, her case went to the Supreme Court, which overturned the dismissal. By that time, however, Davis herself was in hiding as a result of an incident at the Soledad state prison. In August 1970, George Jackson, a prisoner and member of the Black Panthers, assisted by his brother Jonathan, attempted to escape using smuggled guns. Both brothers were killed, and some of the guns were traced to Davis. Fearful for her safety and distrustful of the judicial system, Davis went underground. For two months she was on the FBI's Ten Most Wanted list before being apprehended and incarcerated. She remained in jail for sixteen months before being tried for murder and conspiracy. In June 1972 she was acquitted of all charges against her. Davis resumed her academic career at San Francisco State University and again became politically active, running as the Communist party candidate for vice president in 1980 and 1984. In 1991 she joined the faculty of the University of California, Santa Cruz, as professor of the history of consciousness. She is the author of several books, including *If They Come in the Morning* (1971), *Women, Race, and Class* (1983), and *Women, Culture, and Politics* (1989). Her autobiography, *Angela Davis: An Autobiography*, originally published in 1974, was reissued in 1988.

REFERENCE

LANKER, BRIAN. *I Dream a World: Portraits of Black Women Who Changed America.* New York, 1989.

CHRISTINE A. LUNARDINI

Davis, Anthony (February 20, 1951–), composer and pianist. Anthony Davis has received international recognition for his compositions as well as his virtuoso performances, both as a solo pianist and as a leader of his ensemble, Episteme. He was born in Paterson, N.J., the son of Charles T. Davis, the first black professor at Princeton University and a pioneer in the field of black studies. Davis grew up in New York and studied at Yale University (B.A. 1975). During this time he also worked with JAZZ ensembles led by trumpeter Leo Smith, saxophonist Anthony BRAXTON, and trombonist George Lewis.

Davis moved to New York in 1975 and worked with Smith's trio, which consisted of flutist James Newton, cellist Abdul Wadud, and Lewis. In 1981, Davis formed his own ensemble, Episteme, to present jazz improvisation within a rigorously composed framework that often uses ostinato-based figures. Episteme's music was noted for juxtaposing opposing repeated rhythms as the basis of compositions, a technique that stemmed from Davis's interest in South Indian and Balinese music. Davis also draws influence from the Western European tradition and jazz. In the early 1980s, Davis served as Yale's first Lustman Fellow, teaching piano and Afro-American Studies.

Davis was a Pulitzer Prize nominee for the piano concerto *Wayang No. 5,* which he premiered with the San Francisco Symphony in 1984. His commissions include *Middle Passage,* a programmatic work about the SLAVE TRADE, for pianist Ursula Oppens, which Davis performed himself on his 1985 album of the same name, and *Still Waters* for the Brooklyn Philharmonic, recorded as a trio with Newton and Wadud on *I've Known Rivers* (1982), and again as a septet on his album *Undine* (1987). In 1988, Davis's violin concerto, *Maps,* was premiered by Shem Guibbory, who commissioned the work with assistance from the Kansas City Symphony.

Davis is probably best known for his opera *X: The Life and Times of Malcolm X* with a scenario by his brother Christopher and a libretto by his cousin Thulani Davis. It was first produced by the American Music Theater Festival in Philadelphia in 1985 and had its premiere at the New York City Opera in 1986. Davis's second opera, *Under the Double Moon,* was premiered by the Opera Theater of St. Louis in 1989. A SCIENCE FICTION opera, it is based on a novel by Davis's former wife, Deborah Atherton, who also wrote the libretto. *Tania,* Davis's third opera, based on the story of Patty Hearst and the Symbionese Liberation Army, premiered in 1992 at the American Music Theater Festival in Philadelphia. Commissioned by the Lyric Opera of Chicago and the American Music Theater Festival of Philadelphia, Davis's fourth opera, *Amistad,* will receive its premiere in 1997. *Amistad* tells the story of the 1839 capture of the slave ship and the subsequent overthrow of their captors. The Africans were jailed but won their freedom through the efforts of President John Quincy Adams and other abolitionists (*see* AMISTAD MUTINY).

REFERENCES

ROCKWELL, JOHN. "Malcolm X—Hero to Some, Racist to Others—Is Now the Stuff of Opera." *New York Times,* September 28, 1986, Sec. 2, p. 1.

SCHWARTZ, K. ROBERT. "A Composer Between Two Worlds." *New York Times,* June 7, 1992, Sec. 2, p. 1.

STRICKLAND, EDWARD. *American Composers: Dialogue on Contemporary Music.* Bloomington, Ind., 1991.

RAE LINDA BROWN

Davis, Benjamin Jefferson, Jr. (September 8, 1903–August 22, 1964), lawyer and politician. Born in Dawson, Ga., Benjamin Davis, the son of a prominent Republican newspaper publisher, grew up in Atlanta. He graduated from Amherst College in 1925, and received his law degree from Harvard Law School in 1929. He then returned to Atlanta, and three years later agreed to take the case of Angelo HERNDON, an African-American communist accused of "inciting insurrection" for organizing a demonstration. The trial experience radicalized him. Forced by threats to his life to leave Atlanta shortly after Herndon's conviction, he joined the COMMUNIST

PARTY OF THE U.S.A. and moved to Harlem. Davis became active in party affairs, editing the *Daily Worker* and helping to organize and influence the policies of the National Negro Congress. Davis also became active in the Harlem boycott movement, organizing demonstrations for equal job opportunity. Through his work he developed ties to influential leaders, notably the Rev. Adam Clayton POWELL, JR.

In 1942, Powell gave up his New York City Council seat to run for Congress, and chose Davis as his successor. Running on the Communist ticket, Davis was elected to the city council. He was reelected in 1945 by a wide margin. In 1948, at the height of the Cold War, Davis was convicted of violating the Smith Act, which prohibited membership in organizations that advocated the violent overthrow of the government. The next year, Davis was defeated in his bid for reelection. The Supreme Court upheld the Smith Act convictions in *Dennis* v. *United States,* and Davis spent three years in prison. Released in 1955, he returned to Communist party activities, never swerving from a hard-line position during the various party splits after 1956. Davis served on the national committee, served as chairman of the New York State district, and was selected as national chairman in 1959. In 1962 he was indicted with Gus Hall under the McCarran Internal Security Act, but he died of lung cancer in 1964 before he could be tried. His autobiography was published posthumously.

REFERENCE

DAVIS, BENJAMIN J. *Communist Councilman for Harlem.* New York, 1969.

SARAH M. KEISLING

Davis, Benjamin Oliver, Jr.

Davis, Benjamin Oliver, Jr. (December 18, 1912–), general. Benjamin O. Davis, Jr., son of the first African-American general in the U.S. Army (*see* Benjamin Oliver DAVIS, SR.), had a long and distinguished career of his own in the U.S. Air Force. Following his long MILITARY service, he spent a number of years working as an important administrator in the Department of Transportation.

The younger Davis was born in Washington, D.C. He spent many of his early years watching or participating in his father's military activities. In the 1920s, he lived with his parents and attended school in Tuskegee, Ala., and Cleveland, Ohio. One of his most vivid memories from those days involved his father facing down a KU KLUX KLAN march while the family lived at Tuskegee. As an adolescent, Davis, Jr., was an excellent scholar and displayed leadership qualities. He was one of the few African-American

students at Central High School in Cleveland and was elected president of his graduating class. He attended college at Western Reserve University (Cleveland, Ohio) and the University of Chicago, but then decided on a military career. Despite the handicaps that had faced his father, he felt that it was a profession where he could advance on his merits. In 1932 his father asked the assistance of Oscar DePriest, congressman from Illinois, who nominated Davis, Jr., to the United States Military Academy. Subsequently he passed the entrance examination and entered West Point in 1932.

Life at the military academy had change little since the last African-American had graduated in the 1880s. The presence of blacks was resented, and almost all the cadets ignored Davis. The only time he had any companionship was when he was allowed to leave West Point. During his years at the academy he began to develop an interest in flying, an area the Army had closed to African Americans. When he graduated in 1936, ranking thirty-fifth in a class of 276, he requested assignment to the Army Air Corps. The Army refused because there were no African-American flying units and they would not assign a black officer to a white unit.

During the next few years he performed a variety of duties, similar to those of his father. In 1938 he received an appointment as Professor of Military Science at Tuskegee Institute. Two years later he was detached to work as an aide to his father, who was then commanding the 2nd Cavalry Brigade at Fort Riley, Kans.

His interest in flying never waned, and in 1941, he received his opportunity. Bowing to pressure, the Army decided to allow African Americans into the Army Air Corps, established a flight training program at Tuskegee Institute, and ordered Davis to command the first class. After he graduated in 1942, he was rapidly promoted to the rank of major and given command of the 99th Pursuit Squadron, the first African-American air unit. In April 1943, the unit was transferred to North Africa and in June flew its first combat mission. Most of the ensuing missions were rather routine, but not everyone was persuaded of their effectiveness. A number of white officers were convinced that no African-American air unit could ever measure up to the quality of the white units.

Later in the year Davis was ordered back to the United States and assigned command of the 332nd Fighter Group, a larger all-black flying unit. More important, he was able to answer the many questions that army staff officers posed about the effectiveness of the 99th Squadron. Enough of these officers were convinced to the extent that they decided to continue the African-American flying program and transferred

Major Benjamin Oliver Davis, Jr., commanding officer of the 99th Pursuit Squadron about to enter his plane. (Prints and Photographs Division, Library of Congress)

the 332nd to the Italian theater. During the last year of the war, Davis was promoted to the rank of colonel, flew sixty combat missions, mainly escorting bombers, and received several awards, including the Distinguished Flying Cross. At the end of the war he returned to the United States and was placed in command of the 477th Composite Group. Among the problems he had to face in his new assignment were segregated base facilities, poor morale, and continued evidence of the detrimental impact of segregation.

During the next few years Davis continued to deal with those problems while advocating an end to segregation. When President Harry S. Truman issued Executive Order 9981 in 1948, ending racial discrimination in the armed forces, Davis became a key officer in the Air Force. He helped draft desegregation plans and put them into practice at Lockbourne Air Base. Subsequently he was assigned to the new Air War College. During the Korean War he served at the Pentagon as deputy for operations in the Fighter Branch. Later he was given a variety of command assignments throughout the world, including Formosa, Germany, and the Philippines. In 1965 he was promoted to lieutenant general, the first African American to reach that rank. He retired from the Air Force in 1970.

During the following years he served in a variety of positions within civilian government. For several months in 1970 he was director of public safety in

Cleveland, Ohio, but found he could not work well with Mayor Carl STOKES. Adapting to the world of urban politics proved to be quite difficult for a man who had spent the previous thirty years in the military. In June 1970 Davis became a member of the President's Commission on Campus Unrest. From 1970 to 1975, he served as an administrator in the Department of Transportation. As assistant secretary of transportation, he headed the federal programs developed to deal with air hijacking and highway safety. In 1978 he became a member of the Battle Monuments Commission, a position his father had held twenty-five years earlier. During the next few years, he remained busy with a variety of activities, including programs designed to tell people about the role of African Americans in aviation, and the writing of his autobiography, which was eventually published in 1991.

REFERENCES

DAVIS, BENJAMIN O., JR. *American: An Autobiography.* Washington, D.C., 1991.
NALTY, BERNARD C. *Strength for the Fight: A History of Black Americans in the Military.* New York, 1986.

MARVIN E. FLETCHER

Davis, Benjamin O., Sr. (May 28, 1880–November 26, 1970), general. Benjamin O. Davis, Sr., was born in Washington, D.C. During his fifty years of duty as an enlisted man and officer in the United States Army, he strove to help others surmount the barrier of racism.

Davis, the youngest of three children, grew up in Washington, D.C. After graduating from high school, he volunteered for service in the SPANISH-AMERICAN WAR. The Army appointed him a second lieutenant in the Eighth United States Volunteer Infantry. After the unit was deactivated at the end of the war in 1899, Davis decided to continue his military career and joined the regular army. Two years later, he successfully passed a competitive examination and became an officer. On October 22, 1902, he married his childhood sweetheart, Elnora Dickerson. During the next few decades he served in a variety of positions, usually removed from active duty with his regiment. This included duty as military attaché to Liberia (1909–1911), teacher of military science at Wilberforce University (1906–1911, 1915–1917, 1929–1930, 1937–1938), instructor with the Ohio National Guard (1924–1928), and professor of military science at Tuskegee Institute (1921–1924, 1931–1937). In 1912 a son, Benjamin O. DAVIS, JR., was born. The elder Davis's wife died in 1917 after the birth of their third child, and three years later he married Sadie Overton. In late October 1940, President Franklin D. Roosevelt appointed Davis as brigadier general, making him the first African American to reach that rank.

During World War II, Davis carried out a variety of assignments in Washington and Europe, all generally connected with racial issues. For much of the period he was assistant inspector general. He conducted investigations of racial incidents, tried to encourage the advancement of African-American soldiers and officers, and made efforts to convince the Army to face the consequences of its policies of segregation and discrimination. As a member of the Committee on Negro Troop Policies, Davis quietly worked toward these ends. In 1942 and again in 1944–1945, he served in England and dealt with racial problems in the European theater of operations. One of his most notable contributions occurred as a result of the manpower shortage created by the German attack in the Ardennes in December 1944. He advanced a proposal for retraining black service troops as combat soldiers and inserting these men into white units on an individual basis. Though Gen. Dwight Eisenhower, the theater commander, found this unacceptable, he was forced to accept integration of African-American platoons into white units. It was a significant breakthrough in the wall of segregation.

Benjamin O. Davis, Sr., the first black general in the U.S. Army, during World War II. (Prints and Photographs Division, Library of Congress)

Following the conclusion of the war, Davis served in a variety of positions before his retirement in 1948. He continued to stress the inequities of segregation and was pleased when President Harry Truman ordered its removal. In the next decade he worked for the government of the District of Columbia and the American Battle Monuments Commission. He resided in Washington with Sadie until her death in 1966, and spent the last years of his life with his younger daughter, Elnora McLendon, in her home in Chicago.

REFERENCES

FLETCHER, MARVIN E. *America's First Black General: Benjamin O. Davis, Sr., 1880–1970.* Lawrence, Kans., 1989.

NALTY, BERNARD C. *Strength for the Fight: A History of Black Americans in the Military.* New York, 1986.

MARVIN E. FLETCHER

Davis, Charles Rudolph "Chuck" (January 1, 1937–), dancer, choreographer, instructor. Charles Rudolph Davis was born to Annie and Tony Davis of Raleigh, N.C., and began dancing with his friends at an early age. After graduation from J. W. Ligon High School in Raleigh, Davis served two years in the Navy, received nursing training at George Washington University Hospital, and studied theater and dance at Howard University before going to New York in 1958 to study dance.

A large man, 6′ 5″ and weighing over 200 pounds, Davis became interested in traditional African dance in part through his anger at depictions of Africans in the mass media. After his move to New York City, he danced with the companies of Klara Harrington, Olatunji, Raymond Sawyer, Eleo POMARE, Bernice Johnson, and Joan MILLER. In 1968 he organized his own dance troop, the New York–based Chuck Davis Dance Company, which until 1987 was a leading exponent of traditional African dance in America. Davis's choreography was informed by nearly annual trips to Africa. While maintaining a busy schedule of teaching, lecturing, and choreographing, Davis found time to study with master teachers of various African dance styles, including Momodou Job of Senegal, Ibrahiem Camara of Guinea, Rose Marie Giraud of the Côte d'Ivoire (Ivory Coast), and American-born Nana Dinizulu and Pearl PRIMUS.

In 1980 Davis returned to North Carolina where he founded the African-American Dance Ensemble and the Alayanfe Children's Dance Company in Durham. In 1977 Davis created the DanceAfrica festival, an annual event celebrating African dance held at New York's Brooklyn Academy of Music.

REFERENCES

EMERY, LYNNE FAULEY. *Black Dance from 1619 to To-day.* 2nd rev. ed. Princeton, N.J., 1988, pp. 305–306.

STEARNS, MARSHALL, and JEAN STEARNS. *Jazz Dance : The Story of American Vernacular Dance.* New York, 1968.

JULINDA LEWIS-FERGUSON

Davis, John Henry (January 12, 1921–July 1984), weightlifter. John Davis was born in Smithtown, N.Y. He attended public schools in Brooklyn and soon became active in weightlifting competitions. At the age of seventeen, he entered and won his first world championship (1938), in addition to placing first in the U.S. junior nationals and second in the senior nationals. For the next fifteen years (1938–1953), he remained undefeated in national, international, and Olympic competitions. Davis, who competed first as a light heavyweight and then as a heavyweight, was only five feet, nine inches tall and weighed 230 pounds (at his peak), so small by weightlifting standards that his competitors often outweighed him by as much as 100 pounds.

Davis would likely have dominated the heavyweight class of international weightlifting had the world championship and the Olympics been held during WORLD WAR II. Still, after serving in the U.S. Army during the war, he won gold medals in the 1948 London Olympics as well as in the 1952 Helsinki games. At the 1951 Pan American Games in Buenos Aires, Davis set a world record with a 330-pound press, a 330-pound snatch, and a 402-pound clean and jerk (total: 1,062).

The American public never recognized Davis for his accomplishments, and he turned down the few offers he received for strongman-type promotional work. Europeans, on the other hand, celebrated him for his achievements. One of his most celebrated feats was lifting the cumbersome Appollon Railway Wheels in Paris (1949).

During his nineteen years as a competitive weightlifter, Davis also took voice lessons and contemplated a singing career, though he never sang professionally. In his later years, he worked as a prison guard in New York City. He died of cancer in 1984. In 1989 Davis was inducted into the Olympic Hall of Fame.

REFERENCES

ASHE, ARTHUR R., JR. *A Hard Road to Glory: A History of the African-American Athlete Since 1946.* New York, 1988.

"Former Olympic Hero, World's Strongest Man, Losing Battle to Cancer." *Jet* (May 7, 1984): 50.

PORTER, DAVID L., ed. *Biographical Dictionary of American Sports: Basketball and Other Indoor Sports.* Greenwood, N.Y., 1988.

PETER SCHILLING

Davis, John Preston (c. 1905–September 10, 1973), civil rights activist and editor. Little is known about John Davis's early life. In 1926, he graduated from Bates College in Maine and later entered Harvard Law School, earning a degree in 1933. After law school, Davis cofounded and led the Joint Committee on National Recovery, a coalition of African-American organizations working to guarantee equality in New Deal programs.

In 1935, Davis and the committee, along with Ralph BUNCHE, the chair of Howard University's social science division, and James FORD of the COMMUNIST PARTY, organized the Conference on the Status of the Negro in the New Deal at Howard. The conference, which included civil rights leaders from various organizations, resulted in the establishment of the NATIONAL NEGRO CONGRESS (NNC). The NNC advocated the mobilization of African Americans to fight for decent wages, educational opportunities, unemployment insurance without discrimination, adequate welfare relief, as well as governmental assistance to black farmers and sharecroppers. The NNC also combated lynching, police brutality, and fascism. A. Philip RANDOLPH was elected national secretary of the NNC.

Through the late 1930s, the NNC increasingly came under Communist party control, alienating many of its non-Communist leaders, including Randolph. Davis publicly denied Communist party associations at the time, but later testified before the Civil Service Commission that, from 1935 to 1942, he considered himself "agreeable to carry out a Communist program" and had been a Communist party member. In 1940, Randolph resigned in protest over the NNC's Communist domination and was replaced by Davis, who oversaw the decline of the organization through World War II. The NNC disbanded in 1945, and Davis moved into publishing. He worked as editor of *Our World,* "a picture magazine for the Negro family," until the magazine folded in 1953.

In 1956, Davis was hired by the Phelps-Stokes Fund as editor of special publications. Davis edited the *American Negro Reference Book,* published in 1966 by the Phelps-Stokes Fund. Davis died in New York City in 1973.

REFERENCES

KLEHR, HARVEY. *The Heyday of American Communism: The Depression Decade.* New York, 1984.

"John P. Davis Dies at 68, Negroes Congress Officer." *New York Times.* September 12, 1973, p. 50.

THADDEUS RUSSELL

Davis, John Warren (February 11, 1888–July 12, 1980), educator. John Warren Davis was born in Milledgeville, Ga., in 1888. When Davis was four, his family moved to Savannah, Ga. While his parents remained there, John went to Americus, Ga., in 1895 to care for an elderly couple who had raised his mother. Upon finishing grade school in 1902, Davis was directed to Morehouse College by one of his teachers, a Morehouse alumnus. Davis would remain in Atlanta for the next fifteen years.

In the early twentieth century, Morehouse maintained both secondary and collegiate programs. After eight years at Morehouse, Davis received his B.A. degree in 1911. He worked his way through college—toiling in Chicago's stockyards in the summers and in the business office at Morehouse during the academic year. After receiving his degree, Davis remained at Morehouse for six additional years, serving as a faculty member and administrator.

Davis left Atlanta in 1917 and went to Washington, D.C., to work for the YMCA for two years. When historian Carter WOODSON, one of Davis's friends, was offered the opportunity to become the president of a fledgling state land-grant college in West Virginia, he declined, but suggested Davis instead. Upon Woodson's recommendation, John W. Davis became the president of West Virginia State College.

When Davis and his wife arrived in Institute, W. Va., in 1919, they found only about twenty students whom Davis characterized as college-level pupils; several hundred high school students were also attending the school. Within a short time, however, Davis began to revamp the school. He emphasized aggressive construction and fund raising. Other projects included attempts to improve the quality of both the student body and the faculty.

By 1952, West Virginia State had almost 2,000 students and was completely accredited; the high school program had been discontinued earlier in Davis's tenure. Late that year, at President Harry Truman's request, Davis agreed to become director of technical services to Liberia, a U.S. State Department position that provided assistance and consultation to Liberians. While Davis enjoyed his work in Liberia and was recognized by the Liberian government for his efforts, he was replaced in late 1954 by President Dwight Eisenhower.

Thurgood MARSHALL, an attorney for the NAACP's Legal Defense and Educational Fund (LDF), asked Davis upon his return to assess the state of education for African Americans, especially in the southern states. For the next year, Davis toured the South, emphasizing in his reports the importance of resolving several of the most serious crises in southern education—funding, discriminatory wage practices for teachers, and the need for incentives for black youths to attend college. One result of Davis's crusade was the Herbert Lehman Education Fund, which provides scholarships for African Americans attending state universities. Another legacy of his work with the LDF is the Earl Warren Legal Training Fund, which provides support for black law students.

Davis worked with the LDF for twenty-five years. Although he had moved to Englewood, N.J., in semiretirement, he never stopped traveling, giving speeches, and raising money for various African-American causes. He died in New Jersey in 1980.

REFERENCES

DAVIS, JOHN WARREN. "Reminiscences of John W. Davis." October 1975–June 1976. In the Columbia University Oral History Collection.

GLOSTER, HUGH. "In Memoriam: John W. Davis." *Journal of Negro History* 66, no. 1 (Spring 1981): 78–80.

WESLEY, CHARLES H. "In Memoriam: John W. Davis." *Journal of Negro History* 66, no. 1 (Spring 1981): 76–78.

JOHN C. STONER

Davis, Miles Dewey, III (May 26, 1926–September 28, 1991), jazz trumpeter and composer. One of the most influential musicians in America in the 1950s and 1960s, Davis was a restlessly innovative performer, a central figure in several post-bebop jazz styles, including cool, hard-bop, modal, fusion, and electric jazz. Born in Alton, Ill., Davis grew up in East St. Louis. His mother was a classically trained pianist and violinist. Davis received his first trumpet at the age of thirteen from his father, a successful dentist. In high school he studied with Elwood Buchanan. Trumpeter Clark TERRY also served as a mentor. Davis began playing dates in the St. Louis area in his mid-teens, and in 1943 and 1944 he played with Eddie Randle's Rhumboogie Orchestra. He also performed with Adam Lambert's Six Brown Cats in

Chicago, and with Billy ECKSTINE in St. Louis, before moving to New York in 1944. Davis's ostensible reason for coming to New York was to study at the Juilliard School, but he gained his real education in the jazz clubs of Harlem and 52nd Street.

Once in New York, Davis began associating with the young musicians beginning to popularize bebop. He made his first recordings in 1945 with vocalist Rubberlegs Williams. Later that year he recorded with alto saxophonist Charlie PARKER ("Billie's Bounce," "Now's the Time"). Parker became Davis's mentor and roommate, and over the next few years the two made many important and influential bebop recordings, including "Yardbird Suite," "Ornithology," A Night in Tunisia," "Donna Lee," "Chasin' the Bird," and "Parker's Mood." On these recordings Davis distinguished himself by his intimate tone and sparse, hesitant style of improvisation. During this time Davis was a fixture on 52nd Street, performing and recording with pianist Tadd DAMERON, pianists Bud POWELL and Thelonious MONK, vocalist Billy Eckstine, and saxophonist Coleman HAWKINS. He first recorded as a band leader in 1947 ("Milestones" and "Half Nelson," with Parker on tenor saxophone), and the next year left Parker to form an experimental nine-piece group in collaboration with arranger Gil Evans. The ensemble, which included a French horn and tuba and featured advanced harmonies and unusual compositional forms, was short-lived, performing at the Royal Roost nightclub for only two weeks. Nonetheless, its recordings from 1949–1950 ("Move," "Venus de Milo," "Boplicity," and "Israel") spawned the cool jazz movement of the 1950s, and became particularly popular upon their 1954 rerelease in LP form as *The Birth of the Cool.*

Despite a period of heroin addiction from 1949 to 1953, Davis continued to perform and record in a cool style, often with saxophonist Sonny ROLLINS ("Morpheus," "Dig," "The Serpent's Tooth," "Tune Up," and "Miles Ahead"). His career took another leap forward with the 1954 recording of "Walkin'." That recording, with its more extroverted approach, inaugurated hard bop, a rugged and bluesier version of bebop. In 1955 Davis formed his first significant quintet, including tenor saxophonist John COLTRANE, bassist Paul Chambers, pianist Red Garland, and drummer Philly Joe JONES. They recorded the landmark *Round About Midnight* (1955) and performed and recorded until 1957, when Davis added alto saxophonist Cannonball ADDERLEY to the group. In 1957 Davis went to France to record the soundtrack for Louis Malle's film *Elevator to the Gallows.* Back in the United States the next year, Davis recorded *Milestones,* which introduced the concept of modal jazz, in which modes or scales, as opposed to

chord changes, determine a song's harmonies. In 1959 Davis recorded perhaps his greatest record, *Kind of Blue,* which included the modal compositions "So What," "All Blues," and "Freddie Freeloader," with an ensemble that included drummer Jimmy Cobb and pianists Wynton Kelly and Bill Evans. In the late 1950s Davis also renewed his association with arranger Gil Evans. They produced three acclaimed orchestral works, *Miles Ahead* (1957), *Porgy and Bess* (1958), and *Sketches of Spain* (1959–1960). During this time Davis achieved his mature instrumental style, delicate and tentative on ballads, boldly lyrical on up-tempo numbers.

Davis's trumpet style resembled, in a famous description, "a man walking on eggshells," but he was often belligerent and profane, on stage and off. He refused to announce titles, walked off the stage when sidemen soloed, and rarely acknowledged applause. Nonetheless, he openly demanded the respect he felt was appropriate to jazz musicians. During the 1950s Davis also became an internationally known public figure noted for his immaculate attire, his interest in sports cars, and for taking up boxing as a hobby.

In 1960, Adderley and Coltrane left the ensemble, which underwent a number of personnel shifts until

Miles Davis in New York City, 1949. (Popsie Randolph/© Frank Driggs Collection)

1963, when Davis hired pianist Herbie HANCOCK, bassist Ron CARTER, and drummer Tony WILLIAMS. With saxophonist Wayne SHORTER's arrival the next year, Davis began featuring churning, lengthy improvisations built around Shorter's quirky compositions (*E.S.P.,* 1965; *Miles Smiles,* 1966).

During the late 1960s Davis became disenchanted with the poor reception his music found among black audiences, and he began to search for a new, more commercially appealing style. He found inspiration in the funk rhythms of James BROWN and Sly Stone, as well as in Karlheinz Stockhausen's vast electric-mystic soundscapes. Davis added Keith Jarrett and Chick Corea on electric pianos and John McLaughlin on electric guitar to his regular ensemble, and recorded *In a Silent Way* (1969) and the bestselling *Bitches Brew* (1969), albums that introduced the style that has become known as jazz-rock or "fusion," using loud rock instruments and funk rhythms to accompany extended solo and group improvisations. Davis continued in this vein on *Big Fun* (1969), *Live-Evil* (1970), *On the Corner* (1972), *Agharta* (1975) and *Pangea* (1975). Although Davis gained many fans of rock music, jazz fans were perplexed and unsympathetic. Health problems due to drug abuse and a 1972 car accident convinced Davis to retire in 1975.

In 1980 Davis returned to music, but to the disappointment of many of his fans he continued using popular forms of electric instruments. In his best performances, Davis still communicated with the intensity and fire he had in the 1950s, but his recordings, including *The Man with the Horn* (1981), *Star People* (1982), *Tutu* (1986), and *Amandla* (1989), were largely panned by critics, who were particularly harsh on his undistinguished accompanists. Davis, who lived in New York and Malibu, continued to perform and record in the late 1980s and early 1990s. In 1982 Davis married his third wife, the actress Cicely TYSON; they were divorced in 1989.

He published an outspoken memoir, *Miles, the Autobiography,* in 1989. After many years of battling alcoholism, drug addiction, and circulatory and respiratory ailments, Davis died in 1991 in New York.

REFERENCES

CARR, IAN. *Miles Davis: A Critical Biography.* London, 1982.
CHAMBERS, JACK. *Milestones,* 2 vols. Toronto, 1983, 1985.
COLE, BILL. *Miles Davis: A Musical Biography.* New York, 1974.
DAVIS, MILES, with Quincy Troupe. *Miles, the Autobiography.* New York, 1989.

WILLIAM S. COLE

Davis, Ossie (December 18, 1917–), actor and playwright. Ossie Davis was born in Cogdell, Ga., to Kince Charles Davis, a railroad construction worker, and Laura Cooper Davis. After finishing high school in Waycross, Ga., he hitchhiked north and attended Howard University. In 1937, Davis left Howard and went to New York City, where he worked at odd jobs before joining Harlem's Rose McClendon Players in 1939.

Davis was drafted into the Army in 1942, and after his discharge in 1945, he again pursued his acting career. In 1946, he successfully auditioned for Robert Ardrey's *Jeb,* in which he starred opposite actress Ruby DEE. Davis and Dee were married in 1948.

In 1953, Davis wrote *Alice in Wonder,* a one-act play, produced in Harlem, that dealt with the politics of the McCarthy era. Blacklisted for left-wing associations, Davis and Dee supported themselves by staging readings at colleges. In 1955, Davis starred in a television production of Eugene O'Neill's *The Emperor Jones,* and two years later appeared on Broadway opposite Lena HORNE in *Jamaica!*

In the 1960s, Davis achieved broad success in the performing arts. In 1960, he replaced Sidney POITIER and appeared with Ruby Dee in Lorraine HANSBERRY's play *A Raisin in the Sun.* The following year, his play *Purlie Victorious,* a satire on southern racism, opened on Broadway to an enthusiastic response. Davis also wrote and starred in the film version of *Purlie Victorious,* entitled *Gone Are the Days* (1963). He appeared in several other films during this period, including *The Cardinal* (1963), *The Hill* (1964), *The Scalphunters* (1968), and *Slaves* (1969). He also appeared on several television shows, wrote an episode for the popular series *East Side/West Side,* and narrated National Education Television's *History of the Negro People* (1965). In 1969, Davis was nominated

Ossie Davis. (Sharon C. Farmer/Moorland–Spingarn Research Center, Howard University)

for an Emmy award for his performance in the Hallmark Hall of Fame special *Teacher, Teacher.* That same year Davis directed, cowrote, and acted in the film *Cotton Comes to Harlem,* based on a novel by Chester HIMES.

During these years, Davis continued his political activities. In 1962, he testified before Congress on racial discrimination in the theater, and joined the advisory board of the CONGRESS OF RACIAL EQUALITY (CORE). The following year, he wrote a skit for the 1963 March on Washington, and in 1965 Davis delivered a eulogy at the funeral of his friend, MALCOLM X. In 1972, he served as chairman of the Angela Davis Defense Fund. While Davis has strong affinities with black nationalism, he has nonetheless rejected black racism and separatism.

Through the 1970s, '80s, and early '90s, Davis continued his performing career, notably in a radio series, the *Ossie Davis and Ruby Dee Hour* (1974–1976); in the public television series *With Ossie and Ruby* (1981); in the role of Martin Luther King, Sr., in Abby Mann's television miniseries *King* (1977); and in the Spike LEE films *Do the Right Thing* (1989) and *Jungle Fever* (1991). Throughout the early 1990s, he was a semiregular on the television series *Evening Shade.* Davis also has written several children's books, which include plays based on the lives of Frederick DOUGLASS and Langston HUGHES, and a novel, *Just Like Martin* (1992), about a southern boy, inspired by the life of the Rev. Dr. Martin Luther KING, Jr.

REFERENCES

LANDAY, EILEEN. *Black Film Stars.* New York, 1973.
McMURRAY, EMILY J., and OWEN O'DONNELL, eds. *Contemporary Theater, Film and Television.* Detroit, 1992.

SUSAN McINTOSH
GREG ROBINSON

Davis, Sammy, Jr. (December 8, 1925–May 19, 1990), singer, dancer, and actor. Sammy Davis, Jr., was born in Harlem in New York and began performing with his father, a vaudeville entertainer, before his fourth birthday. Davis made his first film, *Rufus Jones for President* (1933) when he was eight years old. By the time he was fifteen, he had traveled widely throughout the United States as a full partner in the Will Mastin Trio, comprised of Davis, his father, and Davis's adopted "uncle" Will Mastin. Although they often played at white venues, the trio was compelled to eat and room at Negro establishments; yet Davis, who had received an informal ed-

ucation at the hands of family and friends, was unprepared for the virulent racism he encountered upon joining the Army in 1943. During his tenure in the military, he produced and performed in shows with other service personnel, including the singer and songwriter George M. Cohan, Jr.

Following WORLD WAR II, Davis returned to the Will Mastin Trio. The group played to segregated audiences and, despite their rising popularity, were forbidden to sleep or socialize in the hotels and casinos where they worked. Davis began recording songs for Capitol Records in 1946; one of his first cuts, "The Way You Look Tonight," was named *Metronome*'s Record of the Year. An extremely versatile performer, adept at tap dancing, singing, impersonations, and comic and serious acting, he received his first big break when Frank Sinatra asked the trio to open for his show at Manhattan's Capitol Theater. Davis went on to perform at Slapsie Maxie's and Ciro's in Los Angeles and at the Copacabana in New York, in addition to appearing on *The Ed Sullivan Show* and Eddie Cantor's *The Colgate Comedy Hour.*

In November 1954, Davis, who had become a celebrity with white and black audiences alike, was involved in a near-fatal car accident while driving from Las Vegas to Los Angeles. He lost his left eye and was hospitalized for several months; during this time, he was visited by a rabbi, who urged him to reflect on the consequences of the accident and the meaning of his previous actions. After a period of intense study, Davis, who claimed to have found an "affinity" between blacks and Jews as oppressed peoples, converted to Judaism.

Davis's popularity was much enhanced by his brush with death. He performed in Philadelphia, Chicago, and Los Angeles, before taking the lead role in *Mr. Wonderful,* a musical comedy that opened on Broadway in 1956. Two years later, Davis, who had been nicknamed "Mr. Wonderful" after the Broadway show, was featured in a serious dramatic role in the movie *Anna Lucasta.* In the 1959 film of *Porgy and Bess,* Davis gave a memorable performance as the character Sportin' Life. That year, he married Loray White, an African-American dancer whom he later left for the Swedish actress Mai Britt. Davis's interracial romance with Britt was highly publicized, and the couple married in 1960.

Davis is perhaps best known for the films he made during the 1960s, when he worked and socialized with the "Rat Pack," a group of Hollywood actors that included Sinatra, Dean Martin, Peter Lawford, and Joey Bishop, who were featured, along with Davis, in such films as *Oceans Eleven* (1960), *Sergeants Three* (1962), *Robin and the Seven Hoods* (1964), *Salt and Pepper* (1968), and *One More Time* (1970). Davis also appeared in such films as *Johnny Cool* (1963), *A*

Sammy Davis, Jr. (center), with James Baldwin (left), and Martin Luther King, Jr. (right), at the Majestic Theater, New York, 1964. (© George West)

Man Called Adam (1966), *Sweet Charity* (1969), and the German remake of *The Threepenny Opera* (1964), in which he sang "Mack the Knife." In addition, he continued to perform in clubs and on Broadway, where he was praised for his rendering of the title character in *Golden Boy,* Clifford Odets's play about an African-American boxer struggling to free himself from the constrictions of ghetto life. Davis appeared on television in numerous comic and guest-artist roles, as well as in serious dramatic series like the *Dick Powell Theatre* and *General Electric Theater.* In 1966, he hosted a television variety and talk show called *The Sammy Davis Jr. Show,* which ran for less than a year. He also continued to record albums and produced such hit songs as "Candy Man," "Hey There," "Mr. Bojangles," and "The Lady Is a Tramp."

Throughout the 1960s, Davis worked to promote civil rights and African-American/Jewish relations by giving benefit performances and substantial donations. His first autobiography, *Yes I Can,* was published in 1965; three years later, he was awarded the Spingarn Medal by the NAACP for his work in civil rights. Davis's marriage to Mai Britt ended in 1968, and two years later, he married the African-American actress Altovise Gore. In 1971, he was awarded an honorary doctorate of fine arts by Wilberforce Uni-

versity in Ohio. A controversy erupted the following year when Davis, a registered Democrat and supporter of left-wing causes, allowed himself to be photographed with President Richard Nixon at the 1972 Republican Convention; he publicly endorsed Nixon for a time but then renounced their affiliation in 1974.

During the early 1970s, Davis, by then almost as well known for his extravagant spending habits and hard-drinking lifestyle as for his stage presence and vitality, began to experience liver and kidney problems, for which he was eventually hospitalized in 1974. However, he rebounded fairly quickly and was back onstage a few months later in a revue called *Sammy on Broadway.* From 1975 to 1977, he starred in the television show *Sammy and Company.* He performed regularly on the Las Vegas club circuit, and in 1979, became the first recipient of *Ebony* magazine's Lifetime Achievement Award.

Davis's second autobiography, *Hollywood in a Suitcase,* was published in 1980; throughout the decade he continued to appear, albeit less frequently, in films, on television, and onstage. In 1986, he received an honorary degree from Howard University. Two years later, he embarked on a national tour with Frank Sinatra, Dean Martin, and Liza Minnelli. Davis was featured in the movie *Taps* (1989), a tribute to showbiz entertainers, and published a third autobiographical work, *Why Me?* (1989), before dying of throat cancer in spring 1990.

REFERENCES

DAVIS, SAMMY, JR. *Yes I Can.* New York, 1980.

MORTIZ, CHARLES, ed. *Current Biography Yearbook,* New York, 1978.

JESSE RHINES

Davis, William Allison (October 14, 1902–November 21, 1983), educator. Born in Washington, D.C., Allison Davis attended Williams College in Williamstown, Mass., where he graduated in 1924. The following year, he received an M.A. degree in English from Harvard University. Soon after, Davis switched his focus to anthropology; he received an M.A. in anthropology from Harvard in 1932. From 1933 to 1935, Davis was a field researcher for social anthropologist W. Lloyd Warner, studying class/caste relations in a southern town. The project ultimately resulted in the well-known study, *Deep South* (1941). In 1935 Davis was hired as Professor of Anthropology at Dillard University in New Orleans, La., and in 1939, after a brief period at Yale University, he moved on to the University of Chicago, where he was named an assistant professor by the University's Center for Child Development. Soon after, Davis and colleague John Dollard collaborated on *The Children of Bondage: The Personality Development of Negro Youth in the Urban South* (1940), a study of the destructive psychological effects of segregation on southern black children. In 1942 Davis received his Ph.D. in education from the University of Chicago, and was named an assistant professor of education. Over the following years, Davis did exhaustive research on racial bias in intelligence testing, and in 1948 he published his most notable book, *Social-Class Influences Upon Learning.* In the work, Davis argued that black children's lower scores on IQ tests were not based on their lower intelligence, but resulted from middle-class cultural bias in the questions posed.

In 1948 Davis was granted tenure and promoted to full professor at the University of Chicago, the first African American to hold such a position at a major integrated university. During the next twenty years, he continued his work in psychology and education. He devised the Davis-Ellis intelligence test, a relatively bias-free measure of mental development, and wrote several important studies of the influence of social and class factors in the education of children, including *Psychology of the Child in the Middle Class* (1960) and *Compensatory Education for Cultural Devel-*opment (1964), as well as numerous articles in professional journals.

Davis received many tributes for his work. He was the first scholar from the field of education elected to the American Academy of Arts and Sciences. In 1965 he was elected a Distinguished Professor at the University of Illinois. In 1966 he was appointed the President's Commission on Civil Rights, and in 1968 served as vice-chair of the U.S. Labor Department's Commission on Manpower Retraining. In 1970 Davis became the University of Chicago's first John Dewey Distinguished Service Professor.

Davis retired from teaching in 1978, and was named professor emeritus. He devoted his last years to writing *Leadership, Love, and Aggression* (1983), a study of the psychological forces governing four African Americans—Frederick DOUGLASS, W. E. B. DU BOIS, the Rev. Dr. Martin Luther KING, Jr., and Richard WRIGHT—and the role of anger and love in their leadership efforts. In November 1983, shortly after the book was published, Davis died following heart surgery. In 1993 the U.S. Postal Service honored him with an Allison Davis postal stamp.

REFERENCE

DAVIS, ALLISON. *Leadership, Love, and Aggression.* New York, 1983.

GREG ROBINSON

Dawson, Mary Cardwell (February 14, 1894–March 19, 1962), musician. Mary Cardwell Dawson was a teacher of voice, a pianist, and the founder/director of the National Negro Opera Company. She grew up in Pittsburgh, Pa., her family having moved there from Meridian, N.C., early in her life. Her musical training included study at the New England Conservatory, in Boston, and at the Chicago Musical College. She taught voice, at first in a private studio and later at the Cardwell School of Music, which she established in Pittsburgh in 1927. In the 1930s, she toured as director of the Cardwell Dawson Choir, a prize-winning organization that made appearances at the Century of Progress Exposition in Chicago and at the New York World's Fair. Dawson served as president of the NATIONAL ASSOCIATION OF NEGRO MUSICIANS from 1939 to 1941.

After presenting *Aida* at a National Association of Negro Musicians convention in the summer of 1941, Dawson officially launched her National Negro Opera Company at Pittsburgh in the following October with a production of the same opera. The star was La Julia Rhea, one of many black singers who found with this company an otherwise unavailable opportunity to sing opera in the United States (see OPERA). Other cast members were Minto Cato, Carol Brice, Robert MCFERRIN, and Lillian Evanti. During its twenty-one years, the company had a difficult existence financially, but it mounted productions in Pittsburgh, Washington, D.C., New York, Chicago, and Philadelphia. The Washington production of *La Traviata* starring Lillian Evanti drew audiences totaling more than thirty thousand and was favorably reviewed. Dawson spent her final years in Washington, D.C.

REFERENCE

STORY, ROSALYN M. *And So I Sing: African-American Divas of Opera and Concert.* New York, 1990.

DORIS EVANS MCGINTY

Dawson, William Levi (September 26, 1899–May 2, 1990), composer and educator. Born in Anniston, Ala., Dawson developed a strong interest in music, especially after he was encouraged to play the trombone by his teacher, S. W. Gresham. He began studies in 1914 at Tuskegee Institute, where he played in the band and orchestra. After completing his education there in 1921, he continued studies at Washburn College in Topeka, Kans., the Horner Institute of Fine Arts in Kansas City, Mo. (B.M., 1925), the American Conservatory of Music in Chicago (M.M., 1927), the Chicago Musical College, and the Eastman School of Music in Rochester, N.Y.

From 1921 to 1925 he held music teaching positions in Kansas and in Kansas City, Mo. In Chicago he directed the Ebenezer A.M.E. Church Choir, played first trombone in the Chicago Civic Symphony, and performed as jazz trombonist with several jazz groups.

In 1931 he returned to Tuskegee Institute as Director of the School of Music, a position he held until 1955. During his years at Tuskegee he developed the Tuskegee Institute Choir into a nationally acclaimed choral ensemble of one hundred voices. The Tuskegee Choir was the main attraction at the 1932 opening of Radio City Music Hall in New York. Numerous performances were given by the choir over national radio including ABC, CBS, and NBC, as well as at the White House for President Herbert Hoover and at a birthday celebration for President-elect Franklin Roosevelt in 1933.

Dawson became well known for his choral arrangements of spirituals filled with rich harmonies and rhythmic energy. His *Negro Folk Symphony,* written in a postromantic style utilizing black folksong, was premiered by Leopold Stokowski and the

Philadelphia Orchestra in 1934. Thirty years later Stokowski recorded the symphony with the newly founded American Symphony Orchestra in New York City.

In 1953 Dawson took a sabbatical to travel to West Africa, where he studied traditional music. In 1956, after he retired from Tuskegee, the Department of State sent Dawson to Spain to conduct choral groups. After his retirement, he conducted choral ensembles in the United States and abroad. He was elected to the Alabama Arts Hall of Fame in 1975 and was given an American Choral Directors Association Award that same year.

(This William Levi Dawson should not be confused with the Chicago congressman William Levi DAWSON whose entry immediately follows this one. They were not related.)

REFERENCES

MALONE, M. H. *William Levi Dawson: American Music Educator.* Diss., Florida State University, 1981.
SOUTHERN, EILEEN, ed. "William Levi Dawson." *Biographical Dictionary of Afro-American and African Musicians.* Westport, Conn., 1982.
TISCHLER, ALICE. *Fifteen Black American Composers.* Detroit, 1981.

LUCIUS R. WYATT

Dawson, William Levi (1886–1970), congressman. Born in Albany, Ga., Dawson was raised in Georgia, and later attended FISK UNIVERSITY, graduating in 1909. He moved to Chicago in 1912, one of the vast number of southern blacks who migrated to that city during the decade. He served in the army in WORLD WAR I, was injured in combat, and eventually rose to the rank of first lieutenant.

Returning to Chicago, he received his law school degree from Northwestern University and became a member of the Illinois bar in 1920. He entered local politics and in 1928 unsuccessfully challenged white veteran Congressman Martin B. Madden. In 1933, running as a Republican, he was elected as an alderman to the Chicago City Council. In 1939 he joined the Democratic party and was first elected to the House of Representatives in 1942. Dawson controlled political patronage on Chicago's South Side for many years and was a vital cog in Chicago's Democratic machine. He was instrumental in the election of Richard J. Daley as Chicago's mayor in 1955, but the emergence of Daley marked the end of Dawson's uncontested control of his political base.

In 1949 Dawson assumed the chair of the House Committee on Governmental Operations, the first

From 1943 to 1970, Democratic party stalwart William Levi Dawson served his Chicago district in the House of Representatives. (Prints and Photographs Division, Library of Congress)

African-American chairman of a congressional committee. Dawson's career was controversial. His supporters praised his service to constituents as well as his ability to secure patronage and government assistance for his district. But his relations with the major black political organizations were cautious at best, and his detractors felt he was diffident in his political commitment to the civil rights agenda.

(This William Levi Dawson is not to be confused with the classical composer William Levi DAWSON, whose entry immediately precedes this one. They were not related.)

REFERENCES

CHRISTOPHER, MAURINE. *America's Negro Congressmen*. New York, 1971.
CLAYTON, EDWARD T. *The Negro Politician*. Chicago, 1964.
STONE, CHARLES "CHUCK." *Black Political Power in America*. Revised ed. Philadelphia, 1970.
WILSON, JAMES Q. *Negro Politics*. New York, 1960.

CHRISTOPHER R. REED

Day, Thomas (c. 1800–1860), furniture maker. Thomas Day's date and place of birth, his economic status, and other information on his life are not known with certainty, reflecting the difficulty of obtaining data on the lives of many free blacks in the nineteenth-century South. He was born either in the West Indies island of Nevis, or in the rural area of Caswell County, N.C. It is known that he did most of his work two miles from Caswell County, in Milton, N.C. Day became well known because of his expert craftsmanship in carving mahogany and walnut chairs, tables, and footstools. As a result of his expertise, he was given special privileges: a unique bill in North Carolina was passed which allowed the wives of African Americans with Day's status to remain free when they migrated to the state.

Day began studying woodcarving at an early age in Boston and in Washington, D.C., and by 1818, he had begun to sell his furniture to the local residents of Milton. A prominent family in the region, the Donohos, kept many pieces of Day's work through several generations of the family. The pieces show his classic workmanship and skill as carpenter and woodcarver. Many of his other pieces of furniture are located throughout North Carolina. At Day's death, just before the Civil War, his estate was estimated to be worth more than $100,000.

REFERENCE

SPRADLING, MARY MACE, ed. *In Black and White*. Detroit, 1980.

NEIL GOLDSTEIN

Deacons for Defense and Justice, The (1964–), black self-defense organization. Organized in Jonesboro, La., on July 10, 1964, the Deacons for Defense and Justice was established in the wake of KU KLUX KLAN–inflicted violence against Jonesboro blacks engaged in voter registration activities. Most of the original members of the Deacons were Korean War and World War II veterans, who vehemently opposed the espousal of nonviolence by the Civil Rights movement and advocated black self-defense against white aggression. The Deacons believed they should protect themselves and other African Americans because southern law enforcement officials were unwilling and unable to do so. Although most of their activities consisted of peacefully guarding civil rights workers, the Deacons did not hesitate to retaliate when provoked, as in separate incidents in Louisiana in 1964 and 1965, when they used their weapons after they were fired upon.

In 1965, the headquarters of the Deacons for Defense moved to Bogalusa, La. As more African Americans began to question the nonviolent ideology of the Civil Rights movement, branches of the Deacons were organized in Alabama, Mississippi, Florida, South Carolina, and North Carolina. By June 1965, Charles Sims, President of the Deacons, claimed that there were over fifty chapters throughout the South. In northern cities, the Friends of the Deacons of Defense and Justice was organized, and in April 1966, one of the first northern chapters of the Deacons was established in Chicago.

Although the Rev. Dr. Martin Luther King, Jr., and the Southern Christian Leadership Conference condemned the Deacons for "advocating violence," the Deacons worked with such militant grassroots civil rights organizations as the CONGRESS FOR RACIAL EQUALITY (CORE) and the STUDENT NONVIOLENT COORDINATING COMMITTEE (SNCC). At the invitation of SNCC and CORE, for example, the Deacons protected civil rights marchers during the march led by James MEREDITH in Mississippi in 1966.

After this period, civil rights activities in the South peaked and most of the organization's activities ceased. Two factors in its decline may have been harassment by local police forces and FBI scrutiny. Sporadic chapter activity continued until 1968, when the organization faded from the political landscape.

REFERENCE

PETERSON, FRANKLYN. "The Deacons: They Fight for Survival." *Sepia* (May 1967): 10–14.

MANSUR M. NURUDDIN
ROBYN SPENCER

Deadwood Dick. *See* Love, Nat "Deadwood Dick."

DeBerry, William Nelson (1870–January 20, 1948), Congregational minister. Born to former slaves in Nashville, Tenn., William Nelson DeBerry graduated from Fisk University in 1896 and from Oberlin Seminary in 1899. Following his ordination that same year, he accepted the pastorate of Saint John's Congregational Church in Springfield, Mass. Over the ensuing three decades he transformed a small congregation of about one hundred members into a formidable institutional church with an array of social-service programs: a summer camp for youth, playgrounds, classes in sewing and cooking, an employment service, and a housing project. DeBerry resigned the Saint John's pastorate in 1930 to devote his energies to these various programs, newly separated from the church and reorganized as the Dunbar Community League.

DeBerry's activities in Springfield brought him national recognition. In 1915 he became the first alumnus elected a trustee of Fisk. He was a member of various denominational and mission boards, the Springfield Board of Public Welfare, and the Massachusetts Committee on Racial and Interracial Understanding. In 1927, the Harmon Foundation in New York awarded DeBerry its first medal for "distinguished service in religion among Negroes of the United States." The next year, the city of Springfield honored him with the William Pynchon medal for "distinguished public service."

REFERENCE

Obituary. *New York Times,* January 21, 1948.

RANDALL BALMER

DeCarava, Roy (December 9, 1919–), photographer. Born and raised by his mother in Harlem, Roy DeCarava graduated with a major in art from the Straubenmuller Textile High School in 1938. While still in high school he worked as a sign painter and display artist and in the poster division of the WORKS PROJECT ADMINISTRATION (WPA) project in New York City. In his senior year he won a competition to design a medal for the National Tuberculosis Association's high school essay contest and upon graduation received a scholarship for excellence in art.

Supporting himself as a commercial artist, DeCarava studied painting at Cooper Union with Byron Thomas and Morris Kantor from 1938 to 1940, and lithography and drawing at the Harlem Art Center from 1940 to 1942. He attended the George Washington Carver Art School in 1944 and 1945, studying painting with Charles White. In 1946 his serigraph won the print award at the Atlanta University Fifth Annual Exhibition of Painting and Sculpture (a national juried exhibition for black artists), and the following year he had a one-man show at the Serigraph Gallery in New York.

In 1946, DeCarava began to use photography as a means to sketch ideas for paintings, and by 1947 he had decided to concentrate exclusively on it. Although he lacked formal training, DeCarava approached photography as "just another medium that an artist would use"; he quickly established a distinctive style and chose a subject—the people of Harlem—that engaged him deeply and productively. Some of his strongest work dates from the late 1940s and early 1950s, such as *Graduation* (1949) and *Gittel* (1950). His first photographic exhibition was in 1950 at New York's Forty-fourth Street Gallery, and that year he sold three prints to the Museum of Modern Art. In 1952, DeCarava became the tenth photographer and among the earliest black artists to be awarded a Guggenheim Fellowship. Continuing his work in Harlem during the fellowship year, DeCarava produced over 2,000 images; he wanted to show, he has said, "[African Americans'] beauty and the image that we presented in our being." In 1955 four of his photographs appeared in the Museum of Modern Art's famous *Family of Man* exhibition and best-selling book. In the same year, 141 photographs were published with a text by Langston HUGHES in their much-acclaimed classic *The Sweet Flypaper of Life* (1955), a tale of everyday events in the lives of a fictional yet representative Harlem family.

DeCarava formed his style at a time in photographic history when the social documentary ethos of the 1930s was giving way to a more formalist aesthetic which especially appreciated a photographer's manipulation of the unique qualities of the medium. He was influenced by the French photographer Henri Cartier-Bresson, whose theory of the "decisive moment" credits formal organization equally with factual content in conveying essential meaning in a photograph. Like Cartier-Bresson, DeCarava uses a small camera, avoids contrived settings, often shooting in the street, and achieves important, often metaphorical, effects through composition, as in *Sun and Shade* (1952) and *Boy Playing, Man Walking* (1966). Indeed, DeCarava has taken pains throughout his career to foster interpretations that see more in his style than literal and programmatic documentary. His titles are always brief and uninflected, and he insists that his work is not political and that "the definition of truth is a personal one." Dismayed that so few galleries showed photography as a fine art, DeCarava operated the Photographer's Gallery from 1954 to 1956, exhibiting work by such artists as Berenice Abbott, Harry Callahan, and Minor White.

DeCarava felt keenly that black people were not seen as "worthy subject matter" for art; he was determined that African Americans be portrayed in ways that were "serious," "artistic," and "human." His dual commitment—to content representing the beauty and diversity of the African-American experience and to full formal mastery of his medium—has deeply influenced younger photographers, who have seen him as the first to develop "the black aesthetic" in photography. From 1963 to 1966, he directed the Kamoinge Workshop for black photographers and chaired the Committee to End Discrimination Against Black Photographers of the American Society of Magazine Photographers. In 1968 DeCarava picketed the Metropolitan Museum of Art's controversial *Harlem on My Mind* exhibition, protesting its emphasis on documentary, rather than artistic, representation of the Harlem Community. In 1972 DeCarava received the Benin Award for contributions to the black community.

DeCarava's work was included in six group shows at the Museum of Modern Art during the 1950s and '60s, and he had a one-man show at the Studio Museum in Harlem in 1969. In 1958 he gave up commercial art to support himself as a free lance photographer for magazines, advertising agencies, museums, and nonprofit organizations. From 1968 to 1975, DeCarava was a contract photographer for *Sports Illustrated* magazine, and in 1975 he was appointed associate professor of art at Hunter College, attaining the rank of City University distinguished professor in 1989.

DeCarava's impressive exhibition record continued in the 1970s and '80s with solo shows at the Museum of Fine Arts in Houston, the Corcoran Gallery of Art in Washington, D.C., and the Museum of Modern Art in Sweden. *The Sound I Saw,* an exhibition of 100 jazz photographs at the Studio Museum in Harlem, was accompanied by a publication of the same title (1983). In 1982, the Friends of Photography published *Roy DeCarava: Photographs,* a major monograph with eighty-two pictures.

In the course of his career DeCarava has traveled and photographed in Paris, London, Stockholm, and Bangkok. His developing interest in abstraction has suggested to some critics that DeCarava feels an increasing emotional detachment from his subjects. Most viewers, however, have appreciated the artist's occasional experiment with blur or soft focus in later work as evidence of his ongoing creative exploration of his medium.

An exhibition of DeCarava's works is to be held at the Museum of Modern Art in January 1996.

REFERENCES

BLUE, CARROLL. "Conversations with Roy DeCarava." A 58-minute film distributed by First Run/ Icarus Films. New York, 1983.

COLEMAN, A. D. "Roy DeCarava: 'Thru Black Eyes.' " In *Light Readings: A Photography Critic's Writings 1968–78.* New York, 1979, pp. 18–28.

DeCARAVA, SHERRY TURNER. "Celebration." In *Roy DeCarava: Photographs.* Carmel, Calif., 1981, pp. 7–20.

FRASER, C. GERALD. "For Roy DeCarava, 62, It's Time for Optimism." *New York Times,* June 6, 1982, p. 60.

WALLEN, RUTH. "Reading the Shadows—The Photography of Roy DeCarava." *Exposure* 27, no. 4 (Fall 1990): 13–26.

MAREN STANGE

Declaration of Independence. The Declaration of Independence affected African-American history in two quite different ways. First was the role slavery played in the drafting of the document. Second, the Declaration contains an apparent promise of liberty and equality that was unfulfilled for blacks before the Civil War and only partially fulfilled after the war.

In his original draft of the Declaration, Thomas Jefferson condemned King George III of England for supporting the slave trade and imposing it on Virginians. This provision has led to a myth that Jefferson attempted to attack slavery in the Declaration. Rather, Jefferson's attack focused on the slave trade. In his draft, Jefferson complained that the king had "waged cruel war against human nature itself, violating its most sacred rights of life and liberty" by perpetuating the African slave trade. The African slave trade was "piratical warfare" carried out by "a CHRISTIAN king" who was so "determined to keep open a market where MEN" were bought and sold that he used his "negative" to suppress "every legislative attempt to prohibit or to restrain this execrable commerce."

While condemning the king for supporting the African trade, Jefferson also denounced him for encouraging slaves to enlist in the British army, "exciting those very people to rise in arms among us, and to purchase that liberty of which he has deprived them, by murdering the people on whom he also obtruded them: thus paying off former crimes committed against the LIBERTIES of one people, with crimes which he urges to commit against the LIVES of another." This was a reference to Lord Dunmore, the royal governor of Virginia, who encouraged slaves to enlist in his army in return for their freedom. For Jefferson, former slaves in uniform were far more threatening than the king's white army. British soldiers killed enemies in battle, but slaves in uniform, fighting for their own liberty, were "murderers." Jefferson failed to consider the irony of supporting the American rebellion against England while repressing the liberties of African Americans at home.

The Congress deleted this passage for a variety of reasons, including the complaints of Georgia and South Carolina, still active participants in the transatlantic trade. Northerners such as John Adams called this deleted passage a "vehement philippic against negro slavery." But southern masters easily drew a distinction between the slave trade and slavery itself. The arguments against the African trade were humanitarian, economic, and prudential. Many Southerners opposed the trade because newly imported slaves were dangerous or because more slaves would lower the value of the slaves they already owned. Others considered the trade immoral and cruel, although they did not consider slavery itself to be either. Some Southerners, including Jefferson, wanted to curb the growth of America's black population out of racist fears and prejudices.

The final version of the Declaration, however, did contain Jefferson's condemnation of the king for enlisting black slaves to fight under the English flag. The document asserted that the king had waged war "with circumstances of Cruelty and Perfidy, scarcely paralleled in the most barbarous Ages, and totally unworthy of the Head of a civilized Nation." It is possible that Jefferson here was referring to the enlistment of slaves, for the Declaration further asserted that the king had "excited domestic insurrections against us." For southern slave owners, "domestic insurrections" had only one meaning: slave revolts.

The preamble of the Declaration asserted the "self-evident" truths that all persons "are created equal, and that they are endowed by their Creator with certain unalienable Rights, that among these are Life, Liberty, and the pursuit of Happiness." The meaning of this clause has been variously interpreted, yet for African Americans it has often remained an unfulfilled promise.

It is most likely that Jefferson, the primary author of the Declaration, did not intend "equality" to extend to blacks. When Jefferson wrote the Declaration he owned more than 175 slaves. Historian William M. Wiecek has persuasively argued that for Jefferson and other Southerners, the "self-evident truths contain[ed] an implicit racial exception" and "the lines, properly read in the light of American social conditions in 1776, contain[ed] the word 'white' before the word 'men.'" Not a few Englishmen read the Declaration and wondered, as did Samuel Johnson, "How is it that we hear the loudest *yelps* for liberty among the drivers of negroes?" African-American scientist Benjamin BANNEKER similarly noted the inconsistencies in Jefferson's principles and practices, wondering how he could author such an "invaluable doctrine" while keeping so many under "groaning captivity and cruel oppression." On the other hand, a few states did incorporate the wording of the Declaration of Independence into their constitutions as a means to end slavery. For example, in 1783 the chief justice of Massachusetts interpreted the state constitution's "free and equal clause" to mean that slavery was essentially illegal in the state.

During the antebellum period, some Americans used the Declaration to argue against slavery. Abolitionists saw in it language that rooted their struggle to end slavery in the deepest heritage of the nation. Abraham Lincoln, who was far more moderate on the question of slavery and race, nevertheless argued in his debates with Stephen A. Douglas that blacks were "entitled to all the rights enumerated in the Declaration of Independence—the right of life, liberty, and the pursuit of happiness. I hope that he is as much entitled to these as the white man. . . . [And] in the right to eat the bread without leave of anybody else which his own hand earns, he is my equal and . . . the equal of every other man." At Gettysburg, Lincoln argued that the essence of America was that it "was conceived in Liberty and dedicated to the proposition that all men are created equal." In 1863 the promise of equality remained unfulfilled, and many would argue that for most African Americans it has remained unfulfilled over a century and a quarter later.

REFERENCES

FINKELMAN, PAUL. "Jefferson and Slavery: 'Treason Against the Hopes of the World.' " In Peter S. Onuf, ed. *Jeffersonian Legacies*. Charlottesville, Va., 1993, pp. 181–221.

QUARLES, BENJAMIN. *The Negro in the American Revolution*. Chapel Hill, N.C., 1961.

ROBINSON, DONALD. *Slavery in the Structure of American Politics, 1765–1820*. New York, 1971.

WIECEK, WILLIAM M. *The Sources of Antislavery Constitutionalism in America, 1760–1848*. Ithaca, N.Y., 1977.

PAUL FINKELMAN

Dee, Billy. *See* Williams, William December "Billy Dee."

Actor Ruby Dee has combined a rich and diverse career in the theater and film with deeply felt commitments to the civil rights movement and other progressive causes. (Shawn Walker)

Dee, Ruby (October 27, 1924–), actress. Born Ruby Ann Wallace in Cleveland, Ohio, Dee and her family soon moved to New York City and settled in Harlem. After graduating from high school, Dee attended Hunter College, and from 1941 to 1944, prepared for a stage career at the American Negro Theater. In 1943, she made her Broadway debut with Canada Lee in Harry Rigsby and Dorothy Heyward's *South Pacific* (not to be confused with the later Rodgers and Hammerstein musical of the same name). She had her first starring role on Broadway in *Jeb,* alongside Ossie DAVIS. Two years later she married Davis, who subsequently appeared with her in several productions. Her notable New York theater performances include *A Raisin in the Sun* (1959); *Purlie Victorious* (1961); *Boseman and Lena* (1971), for which she won a 1971 Obie Award; and *Wedding Band* (1972–1973), for which she won a Drama Desk Award (1974).

Dee's film debut was in the role of Rachel Robinson in *The Jackie Robinson Story* (1950). She went on to perform in *St. Louis Blues* (1957), *A Raisin in the Sun* (1961), *Gone Are The Days* (1963), and *Buck and the Preacher* (1971). In 1965, she joined the American Shakespeare Festival in Stratford, Conn., and was the first black actress to play major roles in the company. In 1975, Dee and Ossie Davis received a special award from Actor's Equity for "outstanding creative contributions both in the performing arts and in society at large." Dee collaborated on the screenplay for *Uptight* in 1968, and wrote the Off-Broadway musical *Twin-Bit Gardens* (1979).

Together with Ossie Davis, Dee has long been a participant in civil rights efforts. She has served on national committees of the NATIONAL ASSOCIATION FOR THE ADVANCEMENT OF COLORED PEOPLE (NAACP) and the SOUTHERN CHRISTIAN LEADERSHIP CONFERENCE, and has performed in numerous fundraising benefits. In the late 1960s, she hosted benefits for the BLACK PANTHER PARTY and the Young Lords. In 1970, Dee and Ossie Davis were presented with the Frederick Douglass Award by the New York Urban League. Her other activities include reading for the blind, raising money to fight drug addiction, and helping black women study drama through the Ruby Dee Scholarship in Dramatic Art, established in the late 1960s. A frequent reader of poetry and drama in national tours, she has also written several books of poetry and short stories, including *Glowchild* (1972), *My One Good Nerve* (1987), *Two Ways to Count to Ten* (1988), and *Tower to Heaven* (1991). Dee has contributed columns to the *New York Amsterdam News,* and she was the assistant editor of the magazine *Freedomways* in the early 1960s.

In recent years, Dee has been seen in the films *Cat People* (1982) and *Do the Right Thing* (1989). Television appearances include her Public Television Series *With Ossie and Ruby* (1981), the Negro Ensemble Company's production of *Long Day's Journey into Night* (1983), and the Hallmark Hall of Fame production *Decoration Day* (1991), for which she was awarded an Emmy. In 1990, Dee wrote the script and starred in the AMERICAN PLAYHOUSE production *Zora Is My Name,* a one-woman show based on the life and work of Zora Neale HURSTON.

REFERENCE

MAPP, EDWARD. *Directory of Blacks in the Performing Arts.* New York, 1990.

SUSAN MCINTOSH

DeFrantz, Anita (October 4, 1952–), athlete and lawyer. Anita DeFrantz was born in Philadelphia and then moved with her family to Indianapolis, where her father managed a local branch of the YOUNG MEN'S CHRISTIAN ASSOCIATION (YMCA). DeFrantz had very little athletic training as a child, but after entering Connecticut College in New London, Conn., in 1970, she became interested in rowing. DeFrantz graduated in 1974 with a degree in political philosophy and entered law school at the University of Pennsylvania, where she took up rowing seriously.

DeFrantz maintained an arduous six-day-a-week training schedule, and rowed in her first official competition during the spring of her first year at law school in 1975. In 1976, DeFrantz was captain of the first U.S. women's eight-member rowing team to take part in Olympic competition. At the Montreal Olympics that year, DeFrantz and her teammates won the bronze medal. DeFrantz was a member of the U.S. National Rowing Team from 1975 to 1980, winning national championships in eight-member, four-member, and two-member rowing. In 1978, DeFrantz was a member of the silver-medal team in the world championships.

After earning her law degree in 1977, DeFrantz began working at a public interest law firm in Philadelphia, providing legal services to children. In 1979, she moved to New Jersey to train full-time for the 1980 Olympics, while working part-time as a counselor for prelaw students at Princeton University. President Jimmy Carter's boycott of the Olympic Games in Moscow following the Soviet Union's invasion of Afghanistan, however, prevented DeFrantz from competing. Disappointed and frustrated, DeFrantz filed a suit against the United States Olympic Committee (USOC) and retired from competition shortly thereafter.

In 1980, the International Olympic Committee (IOC) awarded DeFrantz the Olympic Order Medal for her lifetime contributions to rowing. She was chosen as a torchbearer for the 1984 Olympics in Los Angeles. In 1987, DeFrantz was elected to serve as president of the Amateur Athletic Foundation in Los Angeles, an organization dedicated to promoting youth sports through the purchase of athletic equipment, organization of teams, and training of coaches. Serving as an advocate of athletes' rights, DeFrantz was chosen the first African-American woman to serve on the ninety-member IOC in 1988. DeFrantz also served on a variety of other committees and councils, including the President's Council on Physical Fitness and the Los Angeles Organizing Committee for the 1984 Olympics. In 1992, DeFrantz was elected to serve on the IOC's eleven-member executive board, a position that allowed her to play a direct role in shaping policies concerning the Olympic Games.

REFERENCES

ASHE, ARTHUR, R., JR. *A Hard Road to Glory: A History of the African-American Athlete Since 1946.* New York, 1988.
REICH, KENNETH. *Making It Happen: Peter Ueberroth and the 1984 Olympics.* Santa Barbara, Calif., 1986.

CHRISTINE A. LUNARDINI

De Grasse, John Van Surly (June 1825–1868), physician. John De Grasse, the son of a naturalized black immigrant from Great Britain, was born in New York City. He attended private and public schools in the city until 1840, then entered the Oneida Institute in New York. The desire to pursue a medical career took De Grasse to Paris in 1843, where he studied medicine for two years. Upon his return to New York, he continued studying medicine with Dr. Samuel R. Childs.

About this time, the AMERICAN COLONIZATION SOCIETY was sponsoring the education of blacks willing to emigrate to Liberia; De Grasse became a beneficiary of this project, although he never moved to Africa. He was allowed to further his MEDICAL EDUCATION at Bowdoin College in Maine, where he received an M.D. with honors in 1849. Upon graduation, De Grasse again went to Europe, working as a ship surgeon and traveling between voyages in France, Italy, and Switzerland.

De Grasse returned to New York City in 1853 and practiced medicine for two years before settling down in Boston, where he acquired a reputation as a competent, caring doctor. On August 24, 1854, he became the first African American to be admitted to a professional medical association, the Massachusetts Medical Society.

In 1863, with the Civil War raging, De Grasse volunteered in the Union Army and served as assistant surgeon in the 35th U.S. Colored Troops. He was one of the first blacks to be commissioned as a surgeon in the U.S. Army, but was cashiered due to drunkenness on duty. Nevertheless, the Commonwealth of Massachusetts honored his service in the war with a gold-hilted sword, presented to him by Gov. John A. Andrews.

During Reconstruction, De Grasse was a recognized leader of the African-American community in Massachusetts. The circumstances of his death are unknown.

REFERENCES

GLATTHAN, JOSEPH T. *Forged in Battle: The Civil War Alliance of Black Soldiers and White Officers*. New York, 1990.

MORAIS, HERBERT M. *The History of the Negro in Medicine*. New York, 1967.

NELL, WILLIAM. *Colored Patriots of the American Revolution*. Boston, 1855.

QUARLES, BENJAMIN. *Black Abolitionists*. New York, 1969.

WOODSON, CARTER. *The Education of the American Negro*. 1919. Reprint. New York, 1968.

SIRAJ AHMED

Delaney, Beauford (c. 1902–March 26, 1979), painter. Beauford Delaney was born in Knoxville, Tenn., to Samuel Delaney, a Methodist minister, and Delia Johnson Delaney. His younger brother Joseph DELANEY was also a well-known painter. Beauford Delaney's talent was recognized early; Lloyd Branson, an elderly white artist, gave him lessons as well as the financial assistance to obtain further training. From 1924 to 1929 he studied in Boston at the Massachusetts Normal School of Art, the South Boston School of Art, and the Copley Society. Delaney came to New York in 1929, "hopped bells" at night at the Grand Hotel on Broadway and 31st Street, and by day painted the habitués of Billy Pierce's Dancing School on West 46th Street. From February 26 to March 8, 1930, twelve of his portraits in oil and pastels were included in a group show at the Whitney Studio Galleries, just prior to its reopening as the Whitney Museum of American Art. Juliana Force, of the museum, was an early patron and offered him a job, with free studio and living space. He worked at the Whitney about three years as a guard, telephone operator, and gallery attendant. In a *New York Telegram* feature article at the time of the Whitney show, Delaney said, "I never drew a decent thing until I felt the rhythm of New York . . . as distinct as the human heart. And I'm trying to put it on canvas." His first one-man show took place in May 1932 at the 135th Street branch of the New York Public Library.

Delaney, because of his skill and special personality, was soon painting portraits of such musicians as

Beauford Delaney's (untitled) oil on canvas, 1958. (The Studio Museum in Harlem)

Louis ARMSTRONG, Duke ELLINGTON, and Ethel WATERS. During the 1930s and 1940s, he continued to exhibit and to meet people such as James BALDWIN, Henry Miller, Al and Dolly Hirschfeld, Georgia O'Keeffe, and James Jones. Many of them remained lifelong friends. He spent the summers of 1951 and 1952 at the Yaddo Art Colony in Saratoga Springs, N.Y., and in 1953 he sailed for Paris, where he remained for the rest of his life. Despite regular solo and group exhibitions, good reviews, and important friends, Delaney's life was never free of money worries. Always extremely generous to friends and acquaintances, he shared or gave away what he had, including a $5,000 award from the National Council on the Arts in 1968. Earlier, in 1961, on a trip to Greece, he suffered a nervous breakdown, which required lengthy hospitalization. When he recovered, he moved to a new studio on the rue Vercingetorix, where he remained until 1975.

Besides portraits, Delaney painted street scenes using geometric shapes, bright colors, and heavy impato. Filled with energy, they seem to be moving. Delaney also turned to abstractions to capture light in all its variants: *Faded Light, Streaked Light, Light Seeping Through*. Marie-Françoise Sanconie in *Paris Connections* (1992) describes his work as "founded on the matter of a dazzled color, sensuously worked in its echoes and brought to its ultimate point of incandescence." His most important retrospectives were at the Galerie Darthea Speyer in Paris, 1973; the Studio Museum in Harlem, 1978; and the Philippe Briet Gallery, 1991. Delaney was confined to a mental hospital in Paris in 1975, and remained there until his death in 1979.

REFERENCES

Beauford Delaney: A Retrospective. With an essay by Richard A. Long. New York, 1978.
Beauford Delaney: A Retrospective (50 Years of Light). With chronology by Sylvain Briet. New York, 1991.
MOULIN, RAOUL-JEAN. "Paris 1945–1991." In Asake Bonami and Belvie Brooks, eds. *Paris Connections: African American Artists in Paris*. San Francisco, 1992.
"Young Negro Artist Finds New York Noise Inspiring." *New York Telegram*, March 27, 1930.

BETTY KAPLAN GUBERT

Delaney, Joseph (September 13, 1904–November 20, 1991), painter. Joseph Delaney was born in Knoxville, Tenn. Both he and his older brother Beauford DELANEY became painters of contemporary urban African-American life. Joseph Delaney came north after high school, living briefly in Cincinnati, Detroit, Pittsburgh, and Chicago, working at odd jobs along the way. He was captivated by the social life of Chicago in the early 1920s, and remained in that city until 1928, shining shoes, washing windows, waiting tables, and meeting many of the jazz musicians who would become subjects for his paintings. In 1925 he began a three-year term with the National Guard; when he returned to Knoxville for a year in 1928, he organized the city's first Boy Scout troop and sold insurance.

Delaney settled in New York City in 1929 and enrolled at the Art Students League, where he was a student of Thomas Hart Benton and a classmate of Jackson Pollock. During the 1930s, he was a muralist for New York's Federal Art Project (1936–1939), taught art in Brooklyn and Harlem, and cataloged textiles, Chippendale furniture, and Paul Revere silver for the *Index of American Design*.

Delaney's paintings include portraits and street scenes of New York; his most famous works are *V-J Day, Times Square* (1945) and *Penn Station at Wartime* (1945). Both scenes capture the movement of crowds in the metropolis while concentrating on each individual's unique facial expression and physical constitution. His works, which depict the constancy of everyday routines during moments of historical significance, tell a story through the stylistic tendencies of regional realism and German expressionism, influenced by Thomas Hart Benton and Jackson Pollock respectively. While the paintings communicate a concrete sense of place, presenting viewers with recognizable New York terrain and highly individualized characters, the linked elongated figures and the flattened perspective are informed by expressionist techniques.

Delaney exhibited individually through the 1940s at numerous galleries, and during the 1960s and 1970s his work was included in large exhibits that spanned the history of African-American visual arts in the United States. These included The Evolution of Afro-American Artists: 1800–1950 at City College of New York (1968), Invisible Americans, Black Artists of the 1930s at the Studio Museum in Harlem (1969), Fragments of American Life at Princeton University (1975), and Two Centuries of Black Art, which was produced by the Los Angeles County Museum of Art and traveled throughout the United States (1977). Until his death, Delaney continued to operate a studio in Manhattan and showed his paintings at the annual Greenwich Village Art Show near Washington Square in New York.

REFERENCES

DRISKELL, DAVID C. *Two Centuries of Black American Art*. New York, 1976.
FEINSTEIN, SAM. "Joe Delaney." *Art Digest* (March 15, 1953): 31.

FINE, ELSA HONIG. *The Afro-American Artist: A Search for Identity*. New York, 1982.
STOCK, ELLEN. "Roamin' Fever." *New York* (May 26, 1975): 63.

JANE LUSAKA

Delany, Clarissa Scott (May 22, 1901–October 11, 1927), poet and educator. Clarissa Delany was born at Tuskegee Institute (*see* TUSKEGEE UNIVERSITY), Ala., where her father, Emmett J. SCOTT, was secretary to Booker T. WASHINGTON. Delany attended Tuskegee Institute and continued her studies at Bradford Academy and Wellesley College. After receiving her degree from Wellesley in 1923, she taught for three years at the Dunbar High School in Washington, D.C., before deciding that teaching was not a career that she wished to pursue. In 1926 she became the director of the Joint Committee on Negro Child Study in New York City, completing a study of deliquency and neglect among black children in New York City. In the fall of that year she married Hubert Delany and left her position to become a homemaker.

Delany was one of a community of black women poets who contributed to the HARLEM RENAISSANCE, and numerous periodicals published her poetry. Her poem "Solace" is included in many anthologies, including Countee CULLEN's *Caroling Dusk* (1927). Delany's poetry, like that of many contemporary middle-class black women poets, is restrained in tone and theme, often employing natural imagery as a vehicle for personal introspection. Her promising writing career was cut short when she died at the age of twenty-six. She is eulogized in Angelina W. GRIMKÉ's poem "To Clarissa Scott Delany."

REFERENCES

HONEY, MAUREEN, ed. *Shadowed Dreams: Women's Poetry of the Harlem Renaissance*. New Brunswick, N.J., 1989.
ROSES, LORRAINE ELENA, and RUTH ELIZABETH RANDOLPH. *Harlem Renaissance and Beyond: Literary Biographies of 100 Black Women Writers, 1900–1945*. Boston, 1990.

MATTHEW BUCKLEY

Delany, Martin Robison (May 6, 1812–June 24, 1885), abolitionist and writer. Delany was born in Charles Town, Va. (now Charleston, W. Va.); his mother was free, his father a slave. Delany grew up in Chambersburg, Pa., and was educated at the school of the Rev. Louis Woodson in Pittsburgh. His mentor was the well-to-do John B. Vashon. In 1843 he married Catherine Richards and began his career as a medical doctor and abolitionist. Between 1843 and 1847 Delany published the first African-American newspaper west of the Alleghenies, the *Mystery*. In 1847 he joined Frederick DOUGLASS as coeditor of the newly founded *Rochester North Star,* in which his letters provide valuable commentary on antebellum free blacks.

In the 1840s Delany criticized colonizationists who advocated the emigration of free African Americans to Liberia, which he, like most blacks, saw as forcible exile. But as the decade ended, Delany and Douglass grew apart. Delany left the *North Star* in 1849, advocating more black self-reliance than Douglass, who welcomed the support of white reformers. The strengthening of the federal FUGITIVE SLAVE LAWS and his frustration with his fellow blacks prompted Delany to withdraw from reform in 1850 and attend the Harvard Medical School, until forced out in 1851.

The crisis of the 1850s distressed northern blacks, many of whom fled to Canada to avoid reenslavement and harassment. Four years before moving his family from Pittsburgh to Chatham, Canada West (now known as Ontario), Delany published the first book-length analysis of the economic and political situation of blacks in the United States: *The Condition, Elevation, Emigration, and Destiny of the Colored People of the United States, Politically Considered* (Philadelphia, 1852), which is cited for its nationalism and advocacy of emigration out of the United States. In 1859 the *Anglo-African Magazine* and in 1861–1862 the *Weekly Afro-American* published his only novel, *Blake, or the Huts of America,* in serial form.

During the 1850s Delany moved from cautious endorsement of emigration with the Americas to planning African-American colonies in West Africa. He organized emigration conferences in 1854, 1856, and 1858, and in 1854 published a pamphlet, *The Political Destiny of the Colored Race,* that recommended emigration. In late 1858 he sailed to West Africa; he visited Alexander CRUMMELL in Liberia in 1859; in December of that year, in the company of Robert Campbell, a teacher at the Institute for Colored Youth in Philadelphia, he signed a treaty with the Alake of Abeokuta, in what is now western Nigeria, providing for the settlement of educated African Americans and the development of commercial production of cotton using free West African labor. Before the first group of settlers could leave for West Africa, however, the CIVIL WAR broke out and changed everything.

Once the War Department reversed its refusal to enroll black volunteers in the Union Army, Delany became a full-time recruiter of black troops for the

Maj. Martin R. Delany, M.D., author and Freemason. Delany was the first African American to become a commissioned officer in the United States Colored Troops during the War of the Rebellion. (Photographs and Prints Division, Schomburg Center for Research in Black Culture, The New York Public Library, Astor, Lenox and Tilden Foundations)

in Charleston and drifted into conservatism. By the mid-1870s he was criticizing South Carolina blacks and white CARPETBAGGERS (he, too, was a carpetbagger) for demagoguery and corruption. In 1874 he ran unsuccessfully for lieutenant governor on the slate of the Independent Republicans, a coalition of conservative Republicans and moderate Democrats. By 1876 he was supporting the candidacy of the Democratic candidate for governor, Wade Hampton III, who had been the richest slave owner in the South before the war. Hampton and the Democrats were elected, and by 1879 had purged the state of all black officeholders, including Delany.

At sixty-seven, Delany once again dedicated himself to emigration, this time to Liberia, with the ill-fated Liberian Exodus Joint-Stock Steamship Company. His last acts were the publication of *Principia of Ethnology: The Origin of Races with an Archaeological Compendium of Ethiopian and Egyptian Civilization* and selling his book on a lecture tour. He died in Wilberforce, Ohio.

REFERENCES

GRIFFITH, CYRIL E. *The African Dream: Martin R. Delany and the Emergence of Pan-African Thought.* University Park, Pa., 1975.

MILLER, FLOYD J. *The Search for a Black Nationality,* 1975.

PAINTER, NELL IRVIN. "Martin Delany and Elitist Black Nationalism." In August Meier and Leon Litwack, eds. *Black Leaders of the Nineteenth Century.* Urbana, Ill., 1988.

ULLMAN, VICTOR. *Martin R. Delany: The Beginnings of Black Nationalism.* Boston, 1971, pp. 149–172.

NELL IRVIN PAINTER

state of Massachusetts. One of the FIFTY-FOURTH REGIMENT OF MASSACHUSETTS VOLUNTEER INFANTRY's earliest volunteers was Toussaint Louverture Delany, his oldest son. (The Delanys had named each of their seven children after a famous black figure.) In early 1865 Martin Delany was commissioned a major in the Union Army, the first African American to be made a field officer. He ended the war in the South Carolina Low Country and began to work for the BUREAU OF REFUGEES, FREEDMEN, AND ABANDONED LANDS (Freedmen's Bureau).

Immediately after the war, Delany was a popular speaker among the freedpeople, for he symbolized both freedom and blackness. But as the years passed and the South Carolina Republican party became the party of the poor and black, Delany also began to question its ability to govern the state of South Carolina as a whole. He went into the real estate business

Delany, Samuel R. (April 1, 1942–), science fiction writer and critic. Born in Harlem in comfortable circumstances, he graduated from the Bronx High School of Science and briefly attended City College of New York. Despite serious dyslexia, he embarked early on a literary career, publishing his first novel, *The Jewels of Aptor,* in 1962. Delany has been a rather prolific writer, and by the time of his eighth novel, *The Einstein Intersection* (1967), he had already achieved star status in SCIENCE FICTION. He was the first African American to devote his career to this genre. Delany won the Nebula—one of science fiction's two most prestigious awards—in 1967, twice in 1968, and again in 1969. He received the other major science fiction award, the Hugo, in 1968 and 1989 (the latter for his autobiography). Today, he is considered to be one of the wide-ranging masters of the field, having produced books of sword-and-sorcery fantasy as well as science fiction. In addition, he has established himself as a rigorous and erudite theorist and critic of what he calls "the science fiction enterprise."

From a perspective of African-American literary history, Delany is noteworthy in part because he was the first significant black figure in a field with which, previously, African Americans at best had had a tangential relationship. Still, he was not the first writer to introduce black themes or characters into science fiction; indeed, he has written of how startled he was to discover, deep into the novel, that the hero of Robert Heinlein's *Starship Troopers* (1959) was non-Caucasian. Early in his own career, in fact, Delany's blackness certainly was not evident to the majority of his readers. However, his real importance depends, first, upon the way his work has focused on the problematic aspects of desire, difference, and the nature of

Science fiction writer Samuel R. Delany. (Photographs and Prints Division, Schomburg Center for Research in Black Culture, The New York Public Library, Astor, Lenox and Tilden Foundations)

freedom. In his four-volume Nevèrÿon fantasy series (1983–1987), these themes are played out in a mythical past. In *The Tides of Lust* (1973) and *Dhalgren* (1975), the site is a kind of mythical present; and in *Triton* (1976) and *Stars in My Pocket Like Grains of Sand* (1984), the setting is the far future. Many of the same concerns found in his fiction are articulated in his autobiography, *The Motion of Light in Water* (1988). Delany's second major contribution is his successful meshing of postmodern critical thought with the discourses of science fiction and fantasy. He has brought to these often scorned forms a narrative depth and linguistic sophistication they had seldom previously displayed.

In 1961, Delany married the poet Marilyn Hacker. The two separated in 1975. They have a daughter, Iva Alyxander, born in 1974. Delany has taught at the State University of New York at Buffalo, the University of Wisconsin in Milwaukee, and Cornell University. Since 1988, he has been a professor of comparative literature at the University of Massachusetts at Amherst.

REFERENCES

DELANY, SAMUEL R. *The Straits of Messina*. Seattle, 1989.

FOX, ROBERT ELLIOT. *Conscientious Sorcerers: The Black Postmodernist Fiction of LeRoi Jones/Amiri Baraka, Ishmael Reed, and Samuel R. Delany*. Westport, Conn., 1987.

ROBERT ELLIOT FOX

DeLarge, Robert Carlos (March 15, 1842–February 14, 1874), congressman and magistrate. Born a mulatto slave in Aiken, S.C., Robert DeLarge received educational training at a primary school in North Carolina and high school in South Carolina. As a delegate to the 1865 Colored People's Convention immediately after the war, he strongly advocated universal public education as a means of empowering African Americans and making them good citizens. "If there is one place in the State where no distinction should be made, or in this country," he said, "it should be in the school house. . . ." DeLarge also believed that suffrage should only be granted to educated people; therefore, once a sufficient educational system was in place, the illiterate could be excluded. He was a member of the BROWN FELLOWSHIP SOCIETY, an elite fraternal organization restricted to mulattoes.

Rising quickly in REPUBLICAN PARTY circles, DeLarge was chairman of the committee at the South Carolina state Republican convention in 1867, which adopted a platform calling for universal male suf-

Slave-born Robert C. DeLarge, a Reconstruction congressman, generally advocated fairly conservative positions and conciliation with whites during his one term in Congress. (Prints and Photographs Division, Library of Congress)

frage, welfare assistance, and the dissolution of land monopolies. The next year at the state constitutional convention, DeLarge again served as a vocal participant.

Racial reconciliation was, in his opinion, a prerequisite of establishing a harmonious and progressive climate in the state. At the 1868 convention, he unsuccessfully attempted to include a clause ending disfranchisement and political disabilities for former Confederates. On the eve of ratification of the constitution, he asked whites to come together with African Americans to ratify the constitution.

DeLarge's first foray into electoral politics came in 1868 when he won a seat in the South Carolina state legislature. His brief and stormy tenure there was marked by continual debates about Republican corruption and other issues. Appointed land commissioner by the legislature in 1869 and despite seemingly successful efforts to sell plots of land to poorer South Carolinians, DeLarge was accused of land fraud.

DeLarge's commitment to racial reconciliation was very much an issue during his 1870 congressional campaign. Running against a white Republican opponent, Christopher Bowen, DeLarge effectively threatened to desert the party and take the African-American Republicans with him if he was not elected.

He won the controversial election, albeit with a slender majority.

Despite Bowen's challenge of the election results, DeLarge was seated in the Forty-second Congress, which began in March 1871. In Congress, he again championed the removal of disabilities from former Confederates, arguing that if these influential men continued to be penalized, the entire South would suffer. Increasingly an advocate of ACCOMMODATIONISM in his politics, DeLarge was willing to blame both Democrats and Republicans for creating the atmosphere of violence and mistrust that pervaded South Carolinian politics at the time. Striking out at CARPETBAGGERS, agitators, and others who had corrupted the political process, DeLarge desired a return to some sort of humane, genteel, political arena where all differences could be resolved given time and effort.

The House committee investigating DeLarge's elections finally rendered a decision at the end of January 1873. DeLarge had served for twenty-two months, but had spent much of the second session battling accusations about electoral fraud. While the committee ruled that both Bowen and DeLarge were guilty of electoral fraud, they still recommended that DeLarge be removed and Bowen seated for the next two months. DeLarge returned to South Carolina and became a popular magistrate in Charleston. He died of tuberculosis in 1874 at the age of thirty-two.

REFERENCES

CHRISTOPHER, MAURINE. *Black Americans in Congress.* New York, 1976.
MCFARLIN, ANNJENNETTE SOPHIE. *Black Congressional Reconstruction Orators and their Orations, 1869–1879.* Metuchen, N.J., 1976.
WILLIAMSON, JOEL. *After Slavery: The Negro in South Carolina During Reconstruction, 1861–1877.* New York, 1975.

ALANA J. ERICKSON

DeLavallade, Carmen (March 6, 1931–), dancer, choreographer. Carmen deLavallade was born of creole parents in New Orleans and raised in Los Angeles by her aunt. She studied dance as a young child, and at sixteen received a scholarship to study with Lester Horton. She joined the Lester Horton Dance Theater in 1949 and was a lead dancer from 1950 to 1954. Horton believed in broad-based training, so deLavallade was taught ballet, modern and ethnic dance forms, as well as painting, music, sculpting, acting (with Stella Adler), set design, costuming, and lighting. An extraordinarily gifted dancer, she kept ballet as her first love, studying privately with Italian ballerina Carmelita Maracci.

Possessing physical beauty, elegance, and technical polish, deLavallade entranced audiences with the sensual quality of her dancing. The first of many roles Horton created for her was Salome in *The Face of Violence*. It was when they were both with Horton that deLavallade began her long association with Alvin AILEY.

Concurrently, another aspect of her career was taking shape. Lena HORNE had seen her in Los Angeles and had introduced the seventeen-year-old to the filmmakers at 20th Century Fox, and between 1952 and 1955 deLavallade appeared in four movies, including *Carmen Jones* (1955). During the filming, she met Herbert Ross, who asked her to appear as a dancer in the Broadway musical *House of Flowers* (1954), which he choreographed. During that engagement in 1955, deLavallade met and married the dancer and actor Geoffrey HOLDER.

DeLavallade succeeded her cousin, Janet Collins, as *prima ballerina* of the Metropolitan Opera in 1955–56. Shortly after that, deLavallade became a principal in John Butler's company and made her television debut in 1956 in Butler's ballet, *Flight*. She also performed with the New York City Opera, dancing in her husband's works. As a freelancer, she worked with several choreographers and had many roles created for her. Her son was born in February 1957.

With Geoffrey Holder, deLavallade danced in West Indian–influenced style and performed modern dance (he set her signature solo, *Come Sunday,* to black SPIRITUALS, sung by Odetta.) In 1957 she appeared in the television production of Duke ELLINGTON's *A Drum is a Woman*. Her later film credits include *Odds Against Tomorrow* (1959), with Harry BELAFONTE. She has also acted in off-Broadway productions.

Ever since deLavallade worked with Alvin Ailey in Horton's company, Ailey had been one of her major influences. By the early 1960s, deLavallade was an important guest artist in his company, and on the company's first European tour (in 1962), the billing was "deLavallade-Ailey American Dance Company." She danced with Donald McKayle (1963–64), and appeared in Agnes deMille's 1965 American Ballet Theater productions of *The Four Marys* and *The Frail Quarry*. In 1966 she won the coveted *Dance Magazine* award for her contribution to the art of dance. DeLavallade also pursued an acting career and appeared in several off-Broadway productions, including *Othello* and *Death of a Salesman*.

In 1970 deLavallade joined the prestigious Yale School of Drama as a choreographer and performer-in-residence. She staged musicals, plays, and operas, and later became a full professor at Yale and a member of the Yale Repertory Theater. DeLavallade left Yale around 1980, but continues to teach, lecture, and perform. In October 1993 she appeared with the Bill T. JONES/Arnie Zane Dance Co. at the Joyce Theater in New York City, still commanding admiration with her unique stage presence. In the fall of 1993 she also choreographed the dances for a new production of Antonín Dvořák's opera *Rusalka* at the Metropolitan Opera.

DERRY SWAN

Delaware. In 1638, Swedes established the first permanent European settlement in Delaware, at Fort Christina (known today as Fort Christiana). The next year, in a development that marked the beginning of the African-American experience in Delaware, a Swedish ship brought a slave known as "Black Anthony" to Fort Christina from the West Indies. But it was after the Dutch conquest of the Swedish colony in 1655 that the first significant numbers of Africans arrived there. By October 1664, probably 20 percent to 25 percent of Delaware's residents were unfree blacks. At the time, the colony contained a considerably higher percentage of enslaved Africans and was far more dependent on their labor than was either Virginia or Maryland.

The English conquest of Delaware in 1664 was followed by a relative decline in the African population. By 1700, African Americans represented no more than 5 percent of Delaware's total population. In the five decades after the end of Queen Anne's War in 1713, large numbers of enslaved blacks entered Delaware with their masters from the Eastern Shore of Maryland and Virginia. Others were purchased at the slave markets in Philadelphia and Annapolis (*see* SLAVE TRADE). In 1763, with SLAVERY at its height, unfree blacks made up almost 25 percent of Delaware's population.

By the mid-eighteenth century, the switch in Delaware's cash crops from tobacco to corn and wheat caused slave work to move away from the arduous stoop labor required by tobacco to the less arduous, but still demanding, labor of the corn- and wheat fields. Most unfree black Delawareans lived and worked in slave units that contained five to eleven African Americans during the colonial era and three to six in the nineteenth century. The small size of the slave units contributed to making two-parent households and the survival of African culture less evident among Delaware's enslaved blacks than among the enslaved in states further south.

From 1775 to 1810, a strong antislavery movement led by Quakers (*see* SOCIETY OF FRIENDS) and METHODISTS swept through Delaware. By 1810, approximately 75 percent of the state's African Americans were free. Indeed, no other state with a significant slave population could match Delaware's MANUMISSION rate for those years. During the late colonial period, slavery had a strong foothold in all three of Delaware's counties, but by the beginning of the CIVIL WAR, more than 75 percent of the few remaining slaves were concentrated in Sussex, the state's southernmost county. Although only 8 percent of Delaware's African Americans were still enslaved in 1860, it took the passage of the THIRTEENTH AMENDMENT in 1865 to finally end slavery in the state.

Prior to the Civil War, Delaware's growing population of free blacks faced a life that, in many ways, was not much better than slavery. Among the barriers to African-American progress were severe social and governmental restrictions on job and educational opportunities. A representative of the AMERICAN ANTI-SLAVERY SOCIETY visited Delaware in 1837 and reported that free blacks enjoyed "but a mongrel liberty, a mere mock freedom. They are truly neither slaves nor free."

From the Civil War to WORLD WAR I, most black Delawareans continued to live in the countryside, where the men were hired hands or tenant farmers and some women worked as domestics. During those years, however, there developed a small African-American middle class in the rapidly growing industrial city of Wilmington. Because of a dramatic growth in the white population, blacks dropped from 25 percent of Delawareans in 1840 to 15 percent in 1914.

World War I marked the beginning of a subsequently massive immigration into Delaware by rural African Americans from Maryland, Virginia, and the Carolinas, which reached its peak during WORLD WAR II and the three decades that followed. Most of the newcomers were drawn to the promise of blue-collar jobs in Wilmington, where blacks increased from 13 percent of the population in 1940 to 44 percent in 1970 (Wilmington's black population also accounted for 44 percent of the state's African Americans by the latter year). However, because large numbers of whites moved into northern Delaware after 1940, by 1970 black Delawareans represented only 14 percent of the state's total population.

At an early date, Delaware's African Americans responded to white racism by establishing their own institutions free of white control. In the late eighteenth century, many Delaware blacks were drawn to white-controlled Methodist Episcopal Church. Racial slights, however, caused Peter SPENCER to withdraw from that denomination and to found the African Union Church in Wilmington in 1813.

Union became one of the first truly independent black churches in the United States and the parent body of the African Union Methodist Protestant and the Union American Methodist Episcopal churches. Three years later, at a conference in Baltimore, former Delaware slave Richard ALLEN became the key founder of the AFRICAN METHODIST EPISCOPAL CHURCH, which had a number of congregations in Delaware by the late nineteenth century.

Prior to the Civil War, African Americans were excluded from public education in Delaware. Between 1866 and 1876, the Delaware Association for the Moral Improvement and Education of Colored People, a philanthropic organization, established thirty-two elementary schools for black children. It was only after the Delaware Association began to founder and pressure was applied by Washington that the Delaware General Assembly finally, in 1875, created a tax-supported statewide school system for African Americans. However, the black schools were far inferior to the white schools because they received far less financial support. It was not until after black Wilmington attorney Louis Redding openly challenged Delaware's public-school segregation in the courts, in the late 1940s and early 1950s, that real progress toward equal education was made. By 1967, all public schools and most other public facilities in Delaware were integrated. In New Castle County, however, residential patterns and school district boundaries continued de facto segregation until ended by court-ordered busing in the mid-1970s.

Although some black Delawareans, thanks to the Fifteenth Amendment and pressure from Washington, began voting soon after the Civil War, most were kept from exercising that right by an openly racist Democratic party that dominated state politics until the 1890s. Quite understandably, most of Delaware's African Americans supported the REPUBLICAN PARTY until the 1930s, when the attractions of the New Deal gradually began to draw them into the ranks of the DEMOCRATIC PARTY. In 1901, Thomas Postles became the first African American to win public office when he was elected to the Wilmington City Council, but it was not until 1947 that Rep. William J. Winchester became the first black to be elected to the Delaware General Assembly.

Racial tensions, which have always been central to Delaware's history, erupted in a day of arson and looting in Wilmington following the murder of Rev. Martin Luther KING, Jr., in 1968. The incident hastened white flight to Wilmington's suburbs. By 1992, educational and employment opportunities were far more open to blacks than ever before, but poverty and racial tensions continued to play important roles in the lives of Delaware's African Americans.

REFERENCES

DEAN, JOHN GARY. *The Free Negro in Delaware: A Demographic and Economic Study, 1790–1865.* Masters thesis, University of Delaware, 1970.

ESSAH, PATIENCE. *Slavery and Freedom in the First State: The History of Blacks in Delaware from the Colonial Period to 1865.* Ph.D. diss., U.C.L.A., 1985.

HANCOCK, HAROLD B. "Not Quite Men: the Free Negroes in Delaware in the 1830's." *Civil War History* (December 1971): 320–331.

LIVESAY, HAROLD C. "Delaware Negroes, 1865–1915." *Delaware History* (October 1968): 87–123.

MUNROE, JOHN A. "The Negro in Delaware." *South Atlantic Quarterly* (Autumn 1957): 428–444.

WILLIAM H. WILLIAMS

Dellums, Ronald V. "Ron" (November 24, 1935–), congressman. Ron Dellums was born and raised in Oakland, Calif. He received undergraduate degrees from Oakland City College and San Francisco State University before earning an M.S.W. degree in psychiatric social work from the University of California at Berkeley. He served on the Berkeley City Council from 1967 to 1971, and in 1970 mounted a successful campaign for Congress. Dellums's victory in the Democratic primary over longtime representative Jeffrey Cohelan, a white liberal who was slow to oppose the Vietnam War, was largely due to his militant opposition to the war in a district that was a center of the peace movement. Dellums's Eighth District, which encompasses Berkeley, Oakland, and the surrounding suburbs, in 1993 was 70 percent white and the eighth best-educated district in the nation. But the district also includes West and East Oakland, two of the largest and poorest black ghettoes in the western United States. The district has been described as "a mixture of poverty and intellectual ferment."

Dellums's unique constituency has enabled him to maintain his stance as one of the nation's most radical national politicians. Among the legislation he has sponsored were bills to impose sanctions against South Africa, to remove restraints on abortion and marijuana, to create a national health care system, and to grant amnesty to all Vietnam War resisters. Unlike most of his legislation, the South African sanctions bill actually passed, after fifteen annual submittals, in 1986. Dellums has been a consistent and unabashed gadfly from the left. In 1977 he shocked Congress with his characterization of the American class system: "America is a nation of niggers. If you are black, you're a nigger. Blind people, the handi-

Rep. Ronald Dellums (D-Calif.), as chairman of the Congressional Black Caucus, sits in a House Judiciary Subcommittee hearing room after talking about Texas Rep. Mickey Leland's tragic airplane accident. The wreckage of Leland's plane, with fifteen other victims, was found earlier in the day, August 13, 1989. (UPI/Bettmann)

capped, radical environmentalists, poor whites, those too far to the left are all niggers."

Dellums has been the leading congressional dove and has consistently opposed expansion of the military and U.S. intervention abroad. He was the first to introduce legislation to preclude funding for the MX, Pershing II, Midgetman, and B-1 weapons programs. In 1991 he was one of very few members of Congress to remain opposed to the war in the Persian Gulf after it began. Because of his seniority on the House Armed Services Committee, Dellums became chairman of the committee in 1993. He also served as chairman of the Congressional Black Caucus from 1989 to 1991.

REFERENCES

CLAY, WILLIAM L. *Just Permanent Interests: Black Americans in Congress, 1870–1991.* New York, 1992.

SWAIN, CAROL M. *Black Faces, Black Interests: The Representation of African Americans in Congress.* Cambridge, Mass., 1993.

THADDEUS RUSSELL

Demby, William E., Jr. (December 25, 1922–), writer and educator. Born in Pittsburgh, Pennsylvania, William Demby was raised in Clarksburg, W. Va., the basis for the coal-mining town that is the setting of his first novel, *Beetlecreek* (1950). Demby began his collegiate studies at West Virginia State College, but was interrupted by WORLD WAR II. He saw military service in both Italy and North Africa, and wrote for the military magazine *Stars and Stripes*. He returned from the war to FISK UNIVERSITY in Nashville, Tenn., and received a bachelor's degree in 1947.

That same year he returned to Italy, commencing a long expatriation. While a student of art history at the University of Rome, he worked as a jazz musician, a translator, and a writer for film and television. He returned to the United States in 1963 and worked for an advertising agency in New York City before becoming a professor of English at the College of Staten Island in 1969, where he taught until 1989.

Beetlecreek, written in Italy and published in New York in 1950, is based on a short story Demby wrote while at Fisk, in which a bleak small town serves as the setting for an existential tale of spiritual impoverishment, isolation, and murder. In 1965 Demby published *The Catacombs,* a novel set in Rome, which takes time, love, death, and resurrection as its central themes, and intersperses a fictional narrative about characters named Doris, the Count, and Demby, with news briefs about contemporary events. *Love Story Black* (1978), a partly satirical, partly serious portrait of the life of a black middle-aged professor in New York City, ends with a triumphant affirmation of romantic love; the novel's tone and style represented a departure from his first two novels, and it was largely overlooked by critics.

In addition to his teaching and writing, Demby was active in his Sag Harbor, Long Island community. In 1984, along with the writers Betty Friedan and E. L. Doctorow, he founded the Sag Harbor Initiative, an annual two-day town meeting where race issues were discussed. In May 1990, he hosted a fish fry at his home to raise funds for Sag Harbor's 150-year-old St. David's African Methodist Episcopal Zion Church.

REFERENCES

BONE, ROBERT. "William Demby's Dance of Life." *Tri-Quarterly* 15 (Spring 1969): 127–141.

MARGOLIES, EDWARD. *Native Sons: A Critical Study of Twentieth-Century Negro American Authors.* Philadelphia, 1968.

PERRY, MARGARET. "William Demby." *Dictionary of Literary Biography, Vol. 33: Afro-American Fiction Writers after 1955.* Detroit, 1984.

SIRAJ AHMED

Democratic Party. Among the many ironies of African-American history, few are as startling as the transition in the position of blacks in the Democratic party. Throughout the nineteenth century and into the twentieth century, the Democratic party consistently supported white supremacy. While it sometimes courted black support, party leaders never offered more than minor patronage. However, beginning in the 1930s, increasing numbers of African Americans were drawn into the New Deal Democratic coalition. The alliance between blacks and Democrats was cemented in the late 1940s, when the Democrats emerged as the primary civil rights party. By the mid 1960s, blacks voted overwhelmingly for Democratic candidates, and black officeholders and concerns had made important inroads into party policy. Since the 1960s, blacks have consistently been the most loyal supporters of the Democrats, often providing over ninety percent of their votes for the party's candidates. In more recent times, the relationship between blacks and Democrats has been remade by black elected officials and party activists in such efforts as the campaigns of the Rev. Jesse JACKSON.

Prior to the Civil War, the few African Americans who could vote involved themselves with the precursors of the REPUBLICAN party. There were alignments with the Federalists and later the Whigs. On the minor party level, there was identification with the various antislavery parties—i.e., the Liberty party, the Free Soilers, and the Political Abolitionists, some of which had antislavery Democrats—such as former President Martin Van Buren—in active roles. For the most part, these minor parties not only permitted African Americans to attend and participate in their national conventions, but also addressed the issue of slavery. Still, they often ignored other issues, such as suffrage, which had an impact on the roles of black people as citizens of the evolving Republic. The Republican party itself, virtually from its birth, took up the cudgels for the African-American community. In its maiden national effort in 1856, and subsequently in the 1860 presidential election, the Republican party attracted the attention and the support of a considerable segment of the African-American community.

However, the Republican party's chief competitor, the Democratic party, took a negative and inimical position toward the African-American community. It had done so in prior years and continued to do so in later years. In the South, the Democratic majority firmly supported SLAVERY. In the North and later in the midwestern states, Democratic leaders denigrated the entire African-American community and its political aspirations. All during the antebellum period, the Democratic party opposed the extensions of suffrage rights to that portion of the

African-American community that could vote. Historian Phyllis Field, observing the Democrats in New York, wrote: "Whenever the Democratic party was strong . . . there one would find little sentiment to extend the rights of blacks." Similarly, midwestern Democrats' sentiments about suffrage and slavery, epitomized in the rhetoric of Stephen Douglas during the famous Lincoln-Douglas debates in Illinois in 1858, were virtually uniformly negative. Throughout the period, the racist posture of the Democrats pushed the African-American community away from the party.

During the presidential election of 1860, Democratic orators reached new heights of racist demagoguery to stigmatize blacks and their Republican allies, reaching a nationwide audience via newspaper articles, books, and pamphlets. In the 1864 election, Democrats sympathetic to the South, known as "Copperheads," declared that the Republicans favored racial intermarriage, and published political cartoons depicting President Lincoln involved with African-American women at the inaugural ball.

These attitudes continued during RECONSTRUCTION, when the reconstituted southern Democratic party sought to wrest control from the coalition of white and African-American Republicans who headed the local governments. In state after state Democratic "redeemers" used violence and fraud to restore white supremacy. Black Republicans and their white allies were unable to resist without outside intervention, since conservative Democrats controlled the money, the land, and the credit-system. Eventually, white rule was restored in the former Confederate states in the early 1870s, with South Carolina, Louisiana, and Florida in 1876 as the last to be "redeemed." The disputed presidential election of 1876 and the COMPROMISE OF 1877 that followed permitted the southern Democrats to regain these three remaining states and put the fragile Republican coalition to rest as a political force in state governments in the region.

Yet in the post-Reconstruction era in the South, an alliance did begin to take root. It was during this "redemption" drive that African-American Democrats first emerged. During the political struggle for control, white Democrats reached out to the African-American community for voters, political representatives, and finally, political appointees for a few offices. This was a clever maneuver, and here and there it worked. It split the African-American community and drained off crucial support for the Republican coalition. The promise of offices provided another avenue for politically ambitious blacks who had not found rewards or political mobility under the Republican banner. African-American Democrats, such as Thomas Hamilton of South Carolina, were elected to

the state legislature, and held minor political offices on the county and city level. The black voters of their communities provided significant support, although not at the level of that for Republicans.

By 1900, the tenuous African-American Democratic pact with southern white Democrats had dissolved, although a few southern black conservatives, notably William H. COUNCILL and Henry McNeal TURNER, collaborated with the Democrats during the 1890s. For a variety of reasons—ranging from the rising tide of racial bigotry throughout the country to the fears of elite whites of class-based alliances between blacks and poor whites (conservatives beat off Populist challenges, ironically, with the aid of black votes obtained through bribery or fraud)—white candidates campaigned for votes by championing white supremacy, and government officials succeeded in disfranchising almost all black voters.

The second part of this tentative alliance of blacks with the Democratic party—which continued despite the rising tide of racism in the South—was African-American support of national tickets. By the early 1800s, black dissatisfaction with the failure of Republicans outside the South to provide sufficient patronage or support black rights led leaders to seek deals with the Democrats. A few black leaders such as Peter H. CLARK of Cincinnati and Edwin Garrison Walker and James Monroe TROTTER of Boston, left the Republicans and led their followers into the Democratic party. (Such defectors were termed "mugwumps" beginning in 1884.) At the same time, independents such as George T. Downing of Rhode Island, T. Thomas FORTUNE of New York and James Milton Turner of Missouri became involved in Democratic party affairs. The 1884 and 1892 elections of Democrat Grover Cleveland to the presidency provided African Americans with the opportunity to emerge at the national level. Cleveland appointed them to minor, but highly visible, jobs in the national government. What evolved after Cleveland's second election was the creation of two national African-American Democratic organizations, the National Colored Democratic Association and the Negro National Democratic League. These groups functioned in various capacities to sustain the party's evolving position in the African-American community, as well as to sponsor the party's standard bearer, William Jennings Bryan, in two national elections.

In 1912, African Americans became fully involved in the national Democratic party, when presidential candidate Woodrow Wilson reached out in a minor way to secure the African-American vote. Many blacks were disillusioned with the Republicans over patronage discrimination and inaction on civil rights issues and they felt especially betrayed by Presidents Theodore Roosevelt and William Howard Taft,

Roosevelt's secretary of war during the BROWNS-VILLE, TEXAS INCIDENT of 1906. The Wilson strategy was threefold. First, he appealed to key African-American leaders such as William Monroe Trotter and W. E. B. DU BOIS with promises of fair treatment. Second, he recognized several African-American political organizations and groups and their publications as official campaign organs. Finally, he spent money ($52,255.95) to mobilize the northern African-American vote. With these actions, a rudimentary alliance between the African-American community and the national Democratic party took root. Wilson's antiblack actions once in office, such as the segregation of the federal workforce, stalled the emerging alliance, but did not shatter it.

Meanwhile, in the first years of the century, urban African-American communities saw a gradual rebirth of the Democratic party. The migration of African Americans to northern cities to find better opportunities put them into a situation where they could be recruited en masse into the urban Democratic political machines. Local clubs such as St. Louis's Negro Jefferson League (c. 1900) and New York's UNITED COLORED DEMOCRACY (1898) were formed. These organizations tended to be adjuncts of white political clubs which worked to elect Democratic candidates. A new African-American Democratic machine came into being, notably in Chicago and New York. In exchange for electoral support, patronage was dispensed to the African-American community through black leaders, and an occasional black was selected for office at the state and local levels.

This local rebirth led inevitably to a reappearance of African-American Democrats at the national level in the late 1920s and 1930s as full participants in party organizations. The black-Democratic alignment took place slowly in some northern urban areas, in part as a byproduct of involvement in urban and labor union politics, and in a cyclical fashion alternated between fast and slow in other areas. The switch from the Republicans to the Democrats during the depression years was aided by several other factors: First, the Republicans continued during the 1920s to subordinate black concerns to white unity. They provided limited patronage and refused to act against LYNCH-ING. Second, the federal government social welfare programs of the 1930s provided massive aid to African Americans hard hit by the economic crisis and improved their living and working conditions. While sometimes conducted on a discriminatory basis, federal relief and work programs were run more fairly than previous state and local initiatives, and they offered blacks a source of income independent of regional elites. Third, Eleanor Roosevelt and other Democratic reformers spoke out against discrimination and made visible gestures of support for blacks.

However, there was no general shift of Democratic party policy during the 1930s. White Southerners remained a fundamental element in the Democratic coalition, and civil rights was not a part of the central New Deal agenda. Despite this, President Franklin D. Roosevelt did reach out to blacks by appointing a "Black Cabinet" following the 1932 election. For the first time, African Americans received visible appointments at the presidential level. Although they were confined to the narrow role of "Negro advisers," this was an important step beyond the minor appointments of Presidents Wilson and Cleveland.

The culmination of the shift in party allegiance was the election of African-American Democrats to Congress, beginning with Chicago's Arthur MITCHELL in 1934. This was a harbinger of things to come. African-American Democratic congresspersons steadily increased in number, although there were only a handful of blacks in Congress until the 1970s. The rise to power of Adam Clayton POWELL, JR., first elected in 1944, signaled a corresponding gain in black presence in party circles. The achievements of African Americans in national Democratic party politics not only solidified and reconstructed the evolving African-American alliance with the Democrats, but eventually played a large part in pulling remaining African-American Republican voters away from that party and into the Democratic coalition.

Beginning with the election of 1936, a majority of African Americans voted for Democratic candidates for president of the United States and other offices, although a majority still identified themselves as Republicans. The solidification of the black-Democratic alliance followed the Democratic party's emergence as a civil rights party. The Roosevelt administration took a few cautious steps, such as the creation of the FAIR EMPLOYMENT PRACTICES COMMISSION (FEPC) in 1941, but refused to actively challenge its important white southern constituency. It was in the late 1940s, during the presidency of Harry S. Truman, that party leaders first developed a strong civil rights agenda, such as the creation of the Civil Rights Commission in 1946 and the integration of the armed forces in 1948.

By 1948, the majority of blacks identified themselves as Democrats, and black voters, particularly in the urban North and Midwest, were an important source of electoral support. Partly in recognition of northern black support, the national Democratic party adopted a civil rights plank at its convention that year. It prompted a southern walkout, but a strong black vote helped reelect Truman nonetheless.

The election played an important role in shifting the balance of power in the party toward blacks and their white liberal allies. Still, during the 1950s, the

Democratic party rested uneasily between its competing constituencies. It was only gradually, in the shadow of the CIVIL RIGHTS MOVEMENT, that the party began to come to terms with its role as defender of black freedom and advancement. Meanwhile, the liberal racial platform of the national party caused some influential white Southerners, beginning with Strom Thurmond in 1964, to leave the Democrats and join the Republican party. The Republican "southern strategy," pioneered by presidential candidate Richard Nixon in 1968, involved the slowing of desegregation and the downplaying of civil rights activity in return for white support. By the end of the 1960s, the majority of white Southerners were no longer reliably Democratic voters.

The most obvious area of civil rights activity was legislation, notably the 1957, 1960, 1964, and 1972 civil rights acts, which the Democratic party sponsored. The 1972 act was championed by an African-American Democrat, Rep. Augustus F. HAWKINS. When a conservative Supreme Court circumscribed the 1964 and 1972 acts in 1987, the Democratic party sponsored the 1988 and 1991 Civil Rights Restoration Acts. These latter acts maintained the intent and integrity of the original ones and emerged at least to some extent as a result of the influence of African-American Democrats.

Besides these landmark pieces of legislature, the Democrats made major appointments that altered the future for African Americans. Starting with President John Kennedy and continuing through President Bill Clinton, Democratic presidents have made major appointments to the bureaucracy and executive staff and put members of the black community into critical and powerful positions. President Lyndon Johnson, a white Southerner with strong black support, appointed the first African American (Robert WEAVER) to a Cabinet position, and the first African American (Thurgood MARSHALL), to the Supreme Court. The number of African-American appointees increased under another Southerner, President Jimmy Carter, whose election had been assured by a strong black vote, before declining under Presidents Reagan and Bush.

While urban northern blacks remained tied to the Democrats via unions and machine politics, an important element of the absorption of African Americans throughout the South into the Democratic party, once the effort to attach themselves to the national party and its political elites began, was their attempts to reshape and refocus southern "whites only" Democratic state parties. Gradually, African-American satellite Democratic parties began to emerge at the grassroots level. The first major example of this was the South Carolina Progressive Democratic Party (SCPDP), formed in 1944. The SCPDP went to the national Democratic convention that year to urge the party leadership to have the state party in South Carolina change its membership policies, stance, and position on segregation. Although the party did not get far with its challenge, it set the stage for the MISSISSIPPI FREEDOM DEMOCRATIC PARTY (MFDP), organized by African Americans and whites in 1964. That year, the MFDP offered a seating challenge to the "whites only" Democratic party at the National Convention in Atlantic City. While its members had little more success than their predecessors, they received the promise of a study commission, and of an integrated state delegation at the next convention, in Chicago.

The MFDP, in turn, inspired the creation of the National Democratic Party of Alabama in 1968. This party was organized by African Americans in the state who had watched the MFDP on national television in 1964 and then carried their own challenge to the National Convention in 1968. They were seated, and their efforts set off a rash of political organizations in other southern states by African Americans to change the composition, outlook, and procedures of the South's white state Democratic parties.

The efforts of black activists, plus the shift of white conservatives to the Republican party, transformed the Democratic parties of the South. White Democrats with liberal racial views predominated. Strong black support helped elect many U.S. senators and state governors who received a minority of white votes; so, too, in 1976 Jimmy Carter carried the South despite winning only a minority of the white southern vote. Additionally, parties became more inclusive and sponsored black candidates. Mississippi even named an African American, Ed Cole, as state party chair in 1992.

During the seventies and eighties, African-American Democrats made unprecedented gains. As political machines and urban white populations declined, African Americans began to be elected to political office. By 1990, the nation's three largest cities had Democratic African-American mayors. Similarly, African-American community organization, augmented by population shifts and legislative redistricting, made possible the election of thirty-nine African Americans to Congress by 1992.

During this time, there were also new and innovative efforts by African-American Democrats to transform the party and put the alliance on a stronger basis. Black Democratic organizations and caucuses mushroomed in number and size. As early as 1968, there were convention maneuvers to nominate certain delegates as presidential candidates. Efforts were made to nominate Georgia representative Julian BOND as vice president, while Rev. Channing Philips of Washington, D.C., gathered the largest number of presidential delegates among blacks. The effort soon fizzled. In January 1972, Shirley CHISHOLM announced that she would run in the Democratic primaries for president. This novel venture signaled a shift for African-American national politics; previously, blacks had run for the presidency only on minor party tickets, but now an African American launched a major effort on the Democratic ticket. Chisholm ran in nearly half the state primaries and captured more than 350,000 votes and 35 delegates, although she released them during the convention.

Chisholm's efforts foreshadowed the most significant black Democratic effort at remaking the party, the presidential campaigns of Jesse JACKSON in 1984 and 1988. In 1984, Jackson was never in contention for the nomination (the majority of blacks supported front runner Walter Mondale), but ran a strong campaign, capped by a well-received speech at the Democratic Convention. His presence sparked increases in black interest and voter registration. In 1988, Jackson, acting as the leader of a "Rainbow Coalition" of liberals and dispossessed groups, was a serious candidate, and received over seven million votes, winning several primaries. The success of Jackson's 1988 effort was partly responsible for the naming of an African American, Ron BROWN, as national party chairman. Jackson's campaigns established him (and, symbolically, blacks in general) as a powerful though ambiguous figure in the party. While his assistance in rallying voter support was sought, his conservative opponents criticized him for splitting the party and making radical demands. Jackson helped make other African-American candidates credible. In the 1992 primaries, another African American, Gov. L. Douglas WILDER of Virginia, made an abortive effort, withdrawing shortly before the start of the primary season.

The alliance between the African-American community and the Democratic party has been strained in recent years, as blacks resist having their votes taken for granted and white Democrats seeking conservative and moderate white votes distance themselves from black issues at times. Bill Clinton, for example, was accused by black leaders of downplaying black interests in his successful bid for the presidency in 1992. Still, a larger proportion of the black vote than that of any other large ethnic group continued to go to the Democrats. Clinton's own victory in the Democratic primaries was made possible partly by large-scale black electoral support, and in the general election, an estimated 82 percent of blacks who voted did so for the Democratic candidate. Clinton responded by appointing more blacks to his cabinet than any previous president. Whether the black-Democratic alliance will continue or dissolve depends on the new urban crisis and the response of new generation Democrats to the challenges that these issues present. To date, however, African-American Democrats have achieved much in and through their political party.

REFERENCES

BUNCHE, RALPH J. *The Political Status of the Negro in the Age of FDR.* Chicago, 1983.
FIELD, PHYLLIS. *The Politics of Race in New York: The Struggle for Black Suffrage in the Civil War Era.* Ithaca, N.Y., 1982.
FRYE, HARDY. *Black Parties and Political Power: A Case Study.* Boston, 1980.
GROSSMAN, LAWRENCE. *The Democratic Party and the Negro: Northern and National Politics, 1868–1892.* Urbana, Ill., 1976.
HOLT, THOMAS. *Black over White: Negro Political Leadership in South Carolina During Reconstruction.* Urbana, Ill., 1977.
LINK, ARTHUR S. "The Negro as a Factor in the Campaign of 1912." *Journal of Negro History* 32 (January 1947): 81–89.
MILLER, J. ERROLL. "The Negro in National Politics in 1968." In P. W. Romero, ed. *In Black America.* Washington, D.C., 1969.
WALTON, HANES, JR. *Black Politics : A Theoretical and Structural Analysis.* Philadelphia, 1972.
———. "The Democrats and African Americans: The American Idea." In Peter B. Kovler, ed. *Democrats and the American Idea: A Bicentennial Appraisal.* Washington, D.C., 1992, pp. 333–348.
———. "The National Democratic Party of Alabama and Party Failure in America." In Kay Lawson and Peter Merkl, eds. *When Parties Fail.* Princeton, N.J., 1988.
WEISS, NANCY J. *Farewell to the Party of Lincoln: Black Politics in the Age of FDR.* Princeton, N.J., 1983.
WOOD, FORREST G. *Black Scare: The Racist Response to Emancipation and Reconstruction.* Berkeley, Calif., 1983.

HANES WALTON, JR.
MERVYN DYMALLY

Denmark Vesey Conspiracy, The. Denmark Vesey (c. 1767–1822), born in Africa or the Caribbean, was an enslaved carpenter in Charleston when he won $1,500 in a lottery in 1799 and bought his freedom for $600 from slave trader Joseph Vesey. Passing up a chance to return to Africa, he opened a woodworking shop in Charleston and committed himself to the African-American freedom struggle. Vesey was an avid Bible reader, fluent in several languages, and he continually preached to his friends that blacks should be equal to whites. In the winter of 1821–1822 he began organizing for an armed revolt. He recruited enslaved artisans from diverse occupations—carters, sawyers, mechanics, lumberyard workers—and blacks from different religious, ethnic, and language groups within the area's varied community.

Vesey met with his recruits in the carpentry shop and in the local African church, formed several years earlier after whites had expelled blacks from the Methodist Church. He exhorted them to action, using the Bible, the French and Haitian revolutions, and the U.S. congressional debates about slavery in Missouri to support his argument. The planners apparently wrote several letters to Saint-Dominique requesting assistance in the uprising scheduled for mid-July. They planned to take the arsenal and guardhouse in Charleston and then start several fires. As whites left their homes, Vesey and his lieutenants would kill them before they could assemble.

But one recruit approached by Vesey's allies informed his master on May 30, and white authorities, disbelieving at first, questioned suspects until the full outline emerged. When word leaked out, Vesey moved the date forward to the night of Sunday, June 16. The organizers destroyed all papers regarding their design, but it was too late. Further slave confessions and testimony of a black spy in the African Church soon revealed details of the revolt, and arrests began.

During the summer of 1822, the authorities executed thirty-seven black Carolinians and deported forty-three more. Vesey was captured on July 2, after refusing to confess. Gullah Jack Pritchard, the respected conjure man responsible for mobilizing less acculturated African newcomers in the countryside, tried to continue the revolt and free the jailed rebels, but he, too, was captured and hanged. Officials also imposed fines and short prison terms on four white participants found guilty of "inciting slaves to insurrection."

In the year following the revolt, frightened South Carolina legislators passed a series of laws restricting the movement of African Americans, including a Negro Seamen Act ordering all free black sailors to be jailed while their ships were in port. Other southern states followed suit, and when federal courts eventually ruled such laws unconstitutional, it only fueled the debate over states' rights. The fearful white reaction to Vesey's plot has led a few historians to suggest that the conspiracy was imaginary—entirely the product of paranoia among slaveholders. While white hysteria cannot be discounted, neither can the evidence and logic for a well-planned revolt. Some Americans have recalled Vesey as a patriot and martyr; others portray him as a dangerous agitator. Not surprisingly, a proposal in modern Charleston to commemorate Denmark Vesey with a public portrait aroused heated debate.

REFERENCES

APTHEKER, HERBERT. *American Negro Slave Revolts.* New York, 1943.

KILLENS, JOHN OLIVER. *The Trial Record of Denmark Vesey.* Boston, 1970.

LOFTON, JOHN. *Denmark Vesey's Revolt: The Slave Plot That Lit a Fuse to Fort Sumter.* Revised ed. Kent, Ohio, 1983.

WADE, RICHARD C. "The Vesey Plot: A Reconsideration." *Negro Digest* 15 (1966): 28–41.

PETER H. WOOD

Dent, Thomas (March 20, 1932–), dramatist. Born into a New Orleans family committed to social causes, Thomas Dent led a dual career beginning with his student days at Morehouse College in Atlanta, where he earned a bachelor of arts degree in political science and edited the *Maroon Tiger,* a literary journal. In 1959, he was a journalist for the African-American paper *New York Age,* and in 1960 he was copublisher of the political journal *On Guard for Freedom.* In 1962, he cofounded UMBRA WORKSHOP, a collective of black artists, thinkers, and activists who saw no separation between art, society, and black identity. The workshop published *Umbra,* a representative poetry magazine, which was allied with the black arts movement.

From 1966 to 1970, Dent was Associate Director of the Free Southern Theatre (FST) in New Orleans, an organization composed of artists and activists fighting racism and segregation. In New Orleans, his one-act plays "Ritual Murder" (1966), "Negro Study 34A" (1969), and "Snapshot" (1970) were produced. Dent's 1972 *Inner Black Blues,* subtitled *A Poem/Play for Black Brothers and Sisters,* was a bitter denunciation of white oppression of blacks. Within FST, Dent organized BLKARTSOUTH, a community writing and acting workshop. In 1974, he also founded the Congo Square Writers Union of New Orleans, another collective which explored the connections between writers, their communities, and the larger society. Two years later, he published *Magnolia Street* (1976; reprinted 1987), which was followed in 1982 by *Blue Lights and River Songs: Poems.* Through the early 1990s, Dent continued to live and write in New Orleans.

REFERENCES

METZGER, LINDA, ed. *Black Writers. A Selection of Sketches from Contemporary Writers.* Detroit, Mich., 1989.

PETERSON, BERNARD L., JR. *Contemporary Black American Playwrights and Their Plays.* New York, 1988.

SALAAM, KALAMU YA. "Enriching the Paper Trail: An Interview with Tom Dent." *African American Review* 27, no. 2. (1993): 327–344.

MICHAEL PALLER

Dentistry. Dentistry was practiced in 2500 B.C. by the Egyptian priest Imhotep, the father of medicine. Archaeological findings have uncovered instruments and other armamentaria used by West Africans to treat oral diseases and to replace teeth. Emphasis on the oral cavity was manifested by the removal of teeth and the tattooing of the gums for aesthetic reasons. Some of these primitive techniques and treatments survived and were practiced among slaves transported to America. In 1740, an African American named Simon was reputed to be able to "draw and bleed teeth." Peter Hawkins, an African-American preacher, was a "tooth drawer" (Dummett and Dummett 1978).

By 1840, there were 125 African-American dentists. They received their training through apprenticeships, as was customary up to that time. The first dental school in the United States, Baltimore College of Dental Surgery, opened in 1840; in 1869, Robert Tanner FREEMAN graduated from Harvard Dental School, becoming the first African American to receive a dental doctorate and to be licensed to practice dentistry in the United States (Dunning 1981). Ida Gray Nelson Rollins, a graduate of the University of Michigan in 1890, was the first African-American woman to receive a dental degree.

HOWARD UNIVERSITY established a dental department in 1881; in 1886, Meharry Medical College established a dental department as part of its medical school. These two dental schools have educated the majority of African-American dentists (Warren 1988). By 1885, there were 25 licensed African-American dentists out of the country's approximately 15,000 dentists. Organized dentistry for African Americans began in 1895 with the National Medical Association, which comprised physicians, dentists, and pharmacists. The disciplines were divided in 1897, and the dentists established the National Dental Association.

By 1940, the United States had a dentist-to-population ratio of 1:1,865. The African-American dentist-to-population ratio, by contrast, was 1:8,745—and African-American dentists provided most of the dental care to African Americans. Even within the U.S. Public Health Service, there were only fifty-five African-American dentists. By 1945, the dental programs at Howard and Meharry were accredited by the American Dental Association. Arnold Donowa became the first African-American dental dean at Howard University, and Clifton O. Dummett the first at Meharry Medical College. Dummett was the only African American licensed as a specialist by any state board. In the mid-1970s two women, Eugenia L. Mobley at Meharry and Jeanne Sinkford at Howard, were each appointed dean. In 1977, Theodore E. Bolden became the first African American to become dean at a predominantly white dental school, New Jersey College of Medicine and Dentistry. Joseph L. Henry is the only African American to serve as dean of two dental schools: Howard College of Dentistry (1966–1975) and Harvard School of Dental Medicine, where he served as interim dean (1990–1991).

African American oral health is poorer than the oral health of other populations in the United States, due in large part to the lack of available dental professionals, limited geographical and financial access, and other barriers resulting from economic deprivation, racism and discrimination (U.S. Department of Health and Human Services 1991).

In 1990, the U.S. Department of Health and Human Services listed 148,800 active dentists in the United States, of which approximately 2.6% were African Americans. Over the years, this percentage has not significantly changed. Until the social and economic conditions of African Americans in the U.S. improves, the percentage of African-American dentists will remain small.

REFERENCES

DUMMETT, CLIFTON O., and LOIS DOYLE DUMMETT. *Afro-Americans in Dentistry: Sequence and Consequence of Events.* Los Angeles, 1978.
DUNNING, JAMES MORSE. *The Harvard School of Dental Medicine: Phase Two in the Development of a University Dental School.* Boston, 1981.
U.S. Department of Health and Human Services. *Health United States 1990.* Rockville, Md., 1991.
WARREN, RUEBEN C. *Analysis of Student and Practitioner Data, Meharry Medical College, School of Dentistry.* Nashville, Tenn., 1988.

RUEBEN C. WARREN

De Passe, Suzanne (1946?–), entertainment executive. Suzanne de Passe grew up in Harlem. She guards her private life carefully, and as a result little is known about her early life and career. De Passe apparently was working as a booking agent at the Cheetah Disco in New York when she met Berry GORDY, then the head of Motown Records (see MOTOWN). Her strong criticisms of Motown's business operations, delivered directly to Gordy, earned her a position as his creative assistant. Until 1972 she served as road manager, costume designer, and choreographer for the Jackson Five (see Michael JACKSON), then Motown's newest sensation. She was also responsible for signing the Commodores, who went on to become one of Motown's biggest sellers during the 1970s.

In the 1970s de Passe became increasingly involved with Motown's theater, television, and film productions. In 1971 she helped write *Diana,* the first production by Motown's television and theatrical division. That project was so successful that the next year Gordy named de Passe corporate director of Motown's Creative Production division, and vice president of Motown's parent corporation, positions that allowed her to work almost exclusively in television and film. De Passe was nominated for an Academy Award for cowriting the Motown-produced film *Lady Sings the Blues* (1972).

In the late 1970s Gordy began to entrust de Passe with the fastest-growing, most profitable divisions of Motown. In 1977 she was promoted to vice president of Motown Industries, another television and film subsidiary, and in 1981 she was named president of Motown Productions. Under de Passe, the budget for the company grew from $12 million in 1980 to $65 million in 1989. She won Emmy awards for *Motown 25: Yesterday, Today, Forever* (1982–1983) and *Motown Returns to the Apollo* (1984–1985).

By the early 1980s de Passe was considered one of the rising black female Hollywood executives. In 1985 her reputation soared further after she paid $50,000 for the rights to *Lonesome Dove,* the Larry McMurtry novel about a nineteenth-century western cattle drive that had been rejected by every major Hollywood studio. De Passe sold telecast rights to CBS for $16 million, and by 1989 she had produced an eight-hour program that won seven Emmy awards and drew one of the largest audiences ever for a miniseries. In 1990 de Passe produced *Motown 30: What's Goin' On.*

In the early 1990s de Passe started a new company, de Passe Entertainment, and produced the five-hour miniseries *The Jacksons: An American Dream* (1992). In that year she also was co–executive producer of the film *Class Act.* Considered one of the most powerful female black executives in Hollywood, de Passe won a 1989 Essence award, and the next year was inducted into the Black Filmmaker's Hall of Fame. In 1990 de Passe received a Micheaux award for her contribution to the entertainment industry.

REFERENCES

"Motown Executive Brings Western to TV." *Afro-American* (February 4, 1989): 3.

MUSSARI, MARK. *Suzanne de Passe: Motown's Boss Lady.* New York, 1992.

JONATHAN GILL

DePreist, James Anderson (November 21, 1936–), conductor. Born in Philadelphia, James DePreist studied piano and percussion instruments as a child. He received a B.S. degree from the University of Pennsylvania in 1958 and an M.A. in 1961. While in college, he formed the Jimmy DePreist Jazz Quintet. After college, he studied composition with Vincent Persichetti at the Philadelphia Conservatory of Music (1959–1961). DePreist made his conducting debut with the Bangkok Symphony Orchestra during a tour of the Far East for the State Department in 1962. He contracted polio during the tour and had to return to the United States. While recovering, he prepared for the Dmitri Mitropoulos Conducting Competition, in which he reached the semifinals in 1963 and the finals in 1964.

DePreist has held positions with the Bangkok Symphony (1963–1964), the New York Philharmonic (assistant conductor to Leonard Bernstein, 1965–1966), the Symphony of the New World in New York (principal guest conductor, 1968–1970), the National Symphony Orchestra in Washington, D.C. (associate conductor, 1971–1975; principal guest conductor, 1975–1976), the Quebec Symphony (1976–1980), the Oregon Symphony (1980–), and the Malmo Symphony Orchestra (1991–). His recordings include Moses Pergament's oratorio *The Jewish Song,* Witold Lutosławski's *Concerto for Orchestra,* Paul Hindemith's *The Four Temperaments,* Alfred Schnittke's *Faust Cantata,* Dmitri Shostakovich's *Symphony No. 11,* and Easley Blackwood's *Symphony No. 5.* DePreist has written music for concert and ballet and is the author of two volumes of poetry, *This Precipice Garden* (1987) and *The Distant Siren* (1989). DePreist is the nephew of the great contralto Marian ANDERSON, who spent the final year of her life in DePreist's Oregon home.

REFERENCES

CRUTCHFIELD, WILL. "Musician's Own Path to Podium." *New York Times,* July 24, 1984, p. 21.

GRAY, JOHN, comp. *Blacks in Classical Music: A Bibliographical Guide to Composers, Performers, and Ensembles.* Westport, Conn., 1988.

SOUTHERN, EILEEN. *Biographical Dictionary of Afro-American and African Musicians.* Westport, Conn., 1982, p. 100.

WILLIE STRONG

Depression, the Great.   *See* Great Depression and the New Deal.

DePriest, Oscar Stanton (March 9, 1871–May 12, 1951), congressman and businessman. Oscar DePriest was born in Florence, Ala., the child of former slaves. In 1878 the family emigrated to Kansas to escape poverty, as part of the EXODUSTERS migration. DePriest went to Chicago in 1889 and worked as a painter and decorator, trades that led him to become a building contractor and later a successful real estate broker. He also turned out to be a tireless political organizer and established himself as a valuable member of the powerful REPUBLICAN PARTY organization. The party slated him in 1904 for his victorious first race for a public position, a place on the Cook County Board of Commissioners. He won re-election in 1906, but his loss two years later sidelined him from political office until he won election as Chicago's first black alderman in 1915.

Rapid migration of African Americans to Chicago from the South drove up property values in the segregated South Side Black Belt, and DePriest capitalized on the resulting real estate opportunities to amass a considerable fortune. These new immigrants would also refuel DePriest's political career as he became the central black leader in Republican Mayor William ("Big Bill") Thompson's machine—a formidable or-

Oscar DePriest, elected to the House of Representatives from Chicago in 1928, was the first African-American elected to the House in more than a quarter century and the first from a northern state. (Prints and Photographs Division, Library of Congress)

ganization held together by patronage, generosity in political appointments, and extraordinary black party loyalty. DePriests's big political break came in 1928 with the death of his mentor, Congressman Martin Madden. DePriest insisted that the party support his candidacy for Madden's old seat, and with its backing, the district's swelling black majority elected him. When, in 1929, DePriest took his seat in the 71st Congress as the first African-American U.S. representative from a northern state, it was the first time in twenty-eight years that the House had had a black member.

In Congress, DePriest was an energetic, controversial figure who had little success in enacting his frequently introduced civil rights measures. His colleagues defeated his antilynching bill, a measure prohibiting government job discrimination in the South, a proposal to have blacks served in the House restaurant, and a plan for transfer of jurisdiction in criminal cases when a defendant feared local racial or religious prejudice. His most outstanding achievement was an amendment that Congress enacted in March 1933 to prohibit discrimination in the Civilian Conservation Corps. He also secured greater government support of Howard University, and was a strong supporter of immigration restriction, to preserve jobs for African Americans.

DePriest survived the first Democratic electoral sweeps of 1930 and 1932, but he lost two years later to a black Democrat, Arthur MITCHELL, as African-American voters in Chicago gave up their traditional loyalty to the party of Abraham Lincoln and turned to the Democrats. DePriest resumed his real estate career, lost to Mitchell again in 1936, and served once more as a Chicago alderman between 1943 and 1947. He died of a kidney ailment on May 12, 1951.

REFERENCES

CHRISTOPHER, MAURINE. *Black Americans in Congress.* New York, 1976.

DRAKE, ST. CLAIR, and HORACE R. CAYTON. *Black Metropolis: A Study of Negro Life in a Northern City.* 1945. Reprint. New York, 1962.

LOGAN, RAYFORD W., and MICHAEL R. WINSTON, eds. *Dictionary of American Negro Biography.* New York, 1982.

STEVEN J. LESLIE

Dermatology.   The branch of medical science that relates to the skin and its diseases is known as dermatology. Papyruses dating from Egypt in the sixteenth and seventeenth centuries B.C. contained dermatological medical texts, and there is evidence that black African physicians contributed to these treatises. Until the late nineteenth and early twentieth centuries, however, virtually no blacks were allowed formal medical training in the United States. Educational deprivation, discriminatory practices within the profession, and the small number of blacks practicing dermatology are related factors that have tended to limit the contributions of African Americans within this field.

Such circumstances did not, however, preclude the emergence of outstanding dermatologists such as Theodore Kenneth LAWLESS. A 1919 Northwestern medical school graduate, Lawless was the first African American to be certified by the American Board of Dermatology and Syphilology in 1935. Despite struggling against a great deal of racial prejudice which at times impeded his outstanding clinical, pedagogical, and scientific work at Northwestern University in Chicago, he served as a nationally prominent mentor for young black physicians interested in dermatology. He was joined by other pioneer African-American dermatologists such as Ralph H. Scull, certified in 1937; C. Wendell Freeman, certified in 1940; Gerald A. Spencer, certified in 1944; and Joseph G. Gathings, who was certified in 1945. From the mid-1940s to the present, a tiny cadre of African-American dermatologists has developed.

To most African Americans and other "people of color" dermatology's social and cultural impact has outweighed its medical importance. Western science and medicine have often served as vehicles for the social acceptance and legitimization of the negative imagery surrounding black SKIN COLOR in Western-dominated cultures. The prescientific foundations of African dermatology were clinically oriented and disease oriented. Later contributors to Western science and medicine such as Plato (427–347 B.C.), advanced a taxonomic approach to those disciplines. Consequently they inappropriately used their scientific classifications to designate black skin color as a sign of racial inferiority. This trend was reinforced by early non-black icons of Western medicine who resided throughout the Mediterranean basin and the Middle East, including the Greek physician Galen (130–200 A.D.) and the Persian physician Avicenna (980–1037 A.D.). They used dark skin color as a marker and justification for prejudicial diagnoses and treatments of black people. This unfortunate cultural phenomenon has had an adverse impact on both Africans and African Americans from both a scientific and sociocultural perspective.

Although dermatology emerged as a formal medical specialty in the twentieth century, its scientific foundations were laid in Europe in the eighteenth and nineteenth centuries. As the discipline developed, Western scientists and physicians continued to be fascinated with ethnic pigmentation. Anton van Leeuwenhoek, the "father of microscopy"; Marcello Malpighi, the "father of histology"; and Carl Linnaeus, the "father of biological classification"—all lent their names and reputations to pseudoscientific racial-inferiority speculations largely based on black skin color. Although there has been no scientific evidence for race-specific skin diseases, eminent American physicians such as Dr. Benjamin Rush (1745–1813) presented papers at scientific meetings entitled: "Observations intended to favour a supposition that the black Color (as it is called) of the Negroes is derived from Leprosy." Rush prescribed racial segregation until a "cure" for this "skin disease" afflicting an entire race was found. Such prejudicial developments regarding black skin color that permeated the scientific and medical communities in the United States also helped promote and justify for many white physicians the medical assumption of poorer health, shorter lifespans, and inferior potential among people of color.

As formally trained black physicians, such as James McCune SMITH and Martin Robison DELANY appeared in the nineteenth century, scientific presentations and formal treatises refuting the pseudoscientific association between black skin color and racial inferiority appeared for the first time. As twentieth-century dermatology has focused on scientific advance rather than social classifications, there has been no evidence for significant differences in skin disease among races. One important exception is the decreased predilection for certain types of skin cancer due to the protective effect of melanin pigment. Black dermatologists continue to participate and contribute to the field.

REFERENCES

BYRD, W. MICHAEL. "Race, Biology and Health Care: Reassessing a Relationship." *Journal of Health Care for the Poor and Undeserved.* 1 (1990): 278–292.

BYRD, W. MICHAEL, and LINDA A. CLAYTON. "An American Health Dilemma: A History of Blacks in the Health System." *Journal of the National Medical Association* 84 (1992): 189–200.

JONES, JAMES H. *Bad Blood: The Tuskegee Syphilis Experiment.* New York, 1981.

KAUFMAN, M., and TODD SAVITT, eds. *Dictionary of American Medical Biography.* Westport, Conn., 1985.

PUSEY, W. A. *The History of Dermatology.* Springfield, Ill., 1933.

ROSEN, T., and S. MARTIN. *Atlas of Black Dermatology.* Boston, 1981.

VAN SERTIMA, I., ed. *Blacks in Science: Ancient and Modern.* New Brunswick, N.J., 1983.

WASSERMANN, H. P. *Ethnic Pigmentation: Historical, Psychological, and Clinical Aspects.* New York, 1974.

W. MICHAEL BYRD
LINDA A. CLAYTON

Derrick, William Benjamin (July 27, 1843–April 15, 1913), religious leader. William B. Derrick was born in Antigua in the Caribbean. His father was white, of Scottish descent; his mother was West Indian. In 1859, after completing three years of high school, he was apprenticed to a blacksmith. The following year he went to sea. In 1861, Derrick joined the United States Navy, serving for three years on the North Atlantic Squadron's flagship, the *Minnesota.*

Upon leaving the Navy in 1864, Derrick married Mary E. White of Norfolk, Va., and joined St. John's African Methodist Episcopal (AME) Church located in his wife's hometown. In that year, Derrick was licensed to preach. In 1868, the AME Church ordained him a deacon, and in 1870, he became an elder. From the late 1860s through the '70s, he served in various church capacities in Washington, D.C., and later in Virginia. In 1872, he was elected a delegate to the AME General Conference and attended each subsequent General Conference.

In 1879, after the death of his first wife, Derrick visited the West Indies with his second wife, Lillian. When they returned to the United States, he took up ministerial duties first in Salem, N.J., then in Albany, N.Y., and finally in New York City, where after 1890 he served as missionary secretary. In 1896, he became the twenty-third bishop of the AME Church, assigned to the Eighth Episcopal District, comprising Mississippi and Arkansas. In 1900, he was reassigned to the First Episcopal District (Pennsylvania), and from 1904 to 1912, he was in charge of the Third Episcopal District (Ohio, Pittsburgh, the West Indies, South America, West Africa). In 1912, the Third Episcopal District was reconfigured to include Ohio, Pittsburgh, West Virginia, Nova Scotia, and Bermuda. In 1901, Derrick was the AME delegate to the World Methodist Conference in London. In 1911, when the conference was held in Toronto, Derrick was again elected to participate.

Derrick traveled to South Africa in 1906 and successfully gained permission from the South African government for the AME Church to conduct services. While there, Derrick also founded the Lillian Derrick Institute (later renamed the Wilberforce Institute) near Johannesburg. After a period of failing health, Derrick died in Flushing, N.Y., of natural causes on April 15, 1913.

REFERENCES

HARMON, NOLAN R., ed. *The Encyclopedia of World Methodism.* Vol 1. Madison, N.J., 1974, p. 665.
MURPHY, LARRY G., ed. *Encyclopedia of African American Religions.* New York, 1993.
SIMMONS, REV. WILLIAM J. D. D. *Men of Mark: Eminent, Progressive and Rising.* New York, 1887, pp. 88–96.

PETER SCHILLING

Derricotte, Juliette Aline (April 1897–November 7, 1931), YWCA official and college dean. Born in Athens, Ga., Derricotte attended Talledega College, where she served as a representative of the YWCA. After graduating in 1918, she became the Y's traveling secretary. For the next eleven years she spoke at colleges and educational conferences, stressing the need for better relations between black women and white women. In 1922, Derricotte played a major role in organizing the interracial structure of the National Student Council of the YWCA. In 1924, she was one of only two persons of color to attend the World's Student Christian Federation in England.

Derricotte retired as National Student Secretary for the YWCA in 1929 in order to become Dean of Women at FISK UNIVERSITY. In the same year she also became the first woman trustee of Talladega College.

In 1931, on her way to Athens with a group of students, Derricotte was involved in an automobile accident. Blacks were not admitted to the nearest hospital, in Dalton, Ga., and Derricotte received emergency treatment by a white doctor, who then sent her to the segregated Walden Hospital in Chattanooga, Tenn. She died there on November 7, 1931.

REFERENCES

LOGAN, RAYFORD W., and MICHAEL R. WINSTON, eds. *Dictionary of American Negro Biography.* New York, 1982.
PLOSKI, HARRY A., and JAMES WILLIAMS, eds. *The Negro Almanac: A Reference Work of the African American.* 3rd ed. Detroit, Mich., 1989.

ELIZABETH RUBIN
DEREK SCHEIPS

Desdunes, Rodolphe Lucien (November 15, 1849–August 14, 1928), writer. Born in New Orleans, the son of a Haitian cigar-maker and a Cuban woman, Rodolphe Desdunes was educated at the Roman Catholic COUVENT INSTITUTE in New Orleans, where he later served as principal. A self-described "radical," Desdunes formed the short-lived Young Men's Progressive Association (1878) to protest civil rights violations. He entered Straight University's law school, and graduated in 1882. Fluent in both English and French, Desdunes was hired as a U.S. Customs House messenger in 1879, and served there for much of the following thirty-two years. In 1899 he was promoted to weigher.

During this time, Desdunes remained politically active. He helped found the Union Louisianaise in 1888, and two years later founded the American Citizen's Equal Rights Association (ACERA) in an attempt to work with Anglo-American blacks to challenge segregation laws. When the ACERA folded later that year, Desdunes organized the Comité des Citoyens (Citizen's Committee) in New Orleans in 1890 to fight for civil rights and black suffrage. The committee sponsored Homer Plessy's challenge to Louisiana's 1890 transportation segregation law *(see* PLESSY V. FERGUSON*)* and Desdunes's son Daniel argued a parallel suit. Desdunes also wrote for the newspaper *The Daily Crusader,* and was named associate editor in 1895. He published several pamphlets, including *Homage Rendu à la Mémoire d'Alexandre Aristide Mary* (1893), a tribute to his civil rights colleague in which he denounced blacks who used political power for personal aggrandizement; *A Few Words to Doctor Du Bois: "With Malice Towards None"* (1907), a criticism of W. E. B. Du Bois's scathing remarks on the education and cultural attainments of southern blacks; and *À la Mémoire d'Eugène Antoine* (c. 1905), a eulogy for a friend.

In 1911, Desdunes lost much of his sight after dust from some granite he was inspecting as a part of his official duties flew into his eyes. While recovering, Desdunes wrote *Nos Hommes et Notre Histoire* (1911, translated as *Our People and Our History*), a series of biographical sketches of the "creoles," free people of color in New Orleans, along with an essay on Reconstruction in Louisiana and on the history of the *Plessy* v. *Ferguson* segregation case. Desdunes published the work in Montreal. No printer in Louisiana would publish it, because Desdunes insisted on defining "creole" to mean mulatto Louisianans and not white francophone natives. Ironically, Desdunes's tribute to his subjects' contributions was badly received by some of their descendants, who were anxious to conceal any African-American ancestry. Desdunes died in Omaha, Neb., while visiting his son.

REFERENCES

DESDUNES, RODOLPHE. *Our People and Our History.* Trans. by Sister Dorothea Olga McCants. Baton Rouge, La., 1973.

HIRSCH, ARNOLD R., and JOSEPH LOGSDON, eds. *Creole New Orleans: Race and Americanization.* Baton Rouge, La., 1992.

MICHEL FABRE

Destiné, Jean-Leon (March 26, 1928–), dancer, choreographer, teacher. Born in Saint-Marc, Haiti, to a wealthy family, Jean-Leon Destiné spent his career bringing the art of Haiti to the rest of the world. Always interested in the powerful Haitian *vodoun* (*see* VOODOO) and the ritual dances integral to its practice, he studied and danced as a teenager with Lina Mathon-Blanchet, founder of the first Haitian dance company that based its work on its own folk traditions. He came to New York City with Blanchet's troupe in the early 1940s. He stayed in the city as a journalist, but continued to study dance and present solo concerts. In 1946 he joined Katherine DUNHAM's troupe tour, and became known for his performance of the boy possessed in *Shango.*

Haitian-born Jean-Leon Destiné, founder of the Destiné Afro-Haitian Dance Company, was one of the dominant figures in the revival of Haitian and Caribbean dancing in the 1940s and '50s. (Photographs and Prints Division, Schomburg Center for Research in Black Culture, The New York Public Library, Astor, Lenox and Tilden Foundations)

In 1949 Destiné formed the Destiné Afro-Haitian Dance Company. A powerful, authoritative performer, Destiné based his choreography on African, French, and *vodoun* dances. In 1960 the Haitian government requested that he direct the "First Troupe Folklorique Nationale" and appointed him Cultural Attaché for the Republic of Haiti in the United States. Influential and respected, Destiné toured with both companies throughout Europe, North and South America, and the Orient.

Destiné continued to pass on his knowledge and passion for African-Haitian dance, music, and traditions through his teaching. He has taught at the New York Dance Group Studio, the New York University School of the Arts, the Lezly School of Dance, and at UCLA, among other schools. Though most closely affiliated with teaching in California, Destiné continued to tour regularly throughout the United States and to participate in international workshops. In 1993 he appeared at the Dance World Festival in Poland. In all his roles as dancer, choreographer, and folklorist, Destiné has reinforced perspectives about the art inherent within Haitian dance and religion, showing how the study of a culture can vitalize dance.

REFERENCES

EMERY, LYNNE FAULEY. *Black Dance From 1619 to Today*. 2nd ed. Princeton, N.J., 1988.

LONG, RICHARD. *The Black Tradition in American Dance*. New York, 1989.

KIMBERLY PITTMAN

Detroit, Michigan. Detroit was founded in 1701 by Antoine de la Mothe Cadillac, as part of the French Empire in North America. Acquired by the British at the end of the French and Indian War in 1763, the city remained under English control until 1796, when after Jay's Treaty it was turned over to the United States. It is not clear when the first blacks arrived in Detroit, but they began migrating to Michigan in the early 1800s. White Detroiters owned slaves, although the Northwest Ordinance of 1787 officially banned slavery in the territories. The 1810 census reported seventeen slaves in the city. In the 1820s there were sixty-seven blacks in town, 4.7 percent of the population.

In 1827 Michigan passed a Black Code that required all African Americans to have a valid, court-attested certificate of freedom and to register with the county clerk (*see* BLACK CODES). Blacks were required to pay a $300 bond of good behavior, although most actually evaded paying. The law's ostensible purpose was to protect blacks from slavehunters, but its real purpose was to discourage black migration. In 1833 the city had its first major racial disturbance, called the Blackburn riot. After law enforcement officials arrested a fugitive slave couple, Thornton and Ruth Blackburn, in order to return them to Kentucky, blacks attacked the sheriff, who later died from his injuries, and a riot ensued. The Blackburns escaped to Canada. Although more than thirty blacks were arrested, some uninvolved in the conspiracy, none was convicted.

In 1837, the same year that Michigan became a state, its state legislature abolished slavery. The Detroit Anti-Slavery Society was founded that year. Detroit established itself as a major terminal of the UNDERGROUND RAILROAD. Black abolitionists—such as Episcopal Rev. William Monroe, who eventually emigrated to Liberia; George DeBaptiste, a prominent businessman; William Lambert, later a supporter of John Brown; and Henry Bibby, a fugitive slave who eventually sought refuge in Canada—were active in the Colored Vigilance Committee, formed in 1840.

Black migration to Detroit was small until the mid-1840s, but by 1850 there were 587 blacks in the city. The first black community was located on the banks of the Detroit River, at the foot of Woodward Ave. The black area would expand north and a little east over time, but never west across Woodward. The first black church, Second Baptist, was established in 1836, in reaction to segregation in white churches. Bethel African Methodist Episcopal was organized in 1841, and St. Matthew's Episcopal, with Monroe in the pulpit, in 1846. In 1843 the community offered a Young Men's Debating Club, a reading room, a library, and a temperance society. An Afric-American Philharmonic Association opened in 1850. The churches also housed black schools and served as political halls. While blacks were denied suffrage, in 1855 they were given the right to vote in school board elections.

The CIVIL WAR was a turning point in Detroit's history. Many Michiganites opposed slavery, but many were also frankly racist. Detroit had pockets of immigrants from the South, and Confederate sympathizers, but the most hostile forces toward blacks in the city were the group of white immigrants from Ireland and Germany, who resented black labor competition. In 1863, Detroit had a race riot, the West's only major racial disturbance of the war. A black man, William Faulkner, was accused of molesting two nine-year-old girls, one white and one black. Convicted of rape, he was sentenced to life in prison, whereupon a white mob, mostly Irish and German, attempted to lynch him. Militia officers who came to protect Faulkner fired at the mob in self-defense, and one man was killed. The mob, frustrated in its lynch attempt, moved to the black area of Beaubien St., where they beat the residents, killing two and injuring over twenty, and burned down more than thirty of their houses. White Detroiters condemned the mob and reimbursed blacks for their losses, but Frederick DOUGLASS used the defenselessness of Detroit blacks as an example of the need for black soldiers. After 1863, 895 black Michiganites, many from Detroit, joined the Union Army.

Between 1860 and 1870, Detroit's black population increased sevenfold, and continued to climb thereafter, due largely to migrants from Canada, rural Michigan, and elsewhere. Twenty-eight percent of the overall black population, representing the majority of the non–native-born Michiganites, came from Virginia and Kentucky. The migrants from Kentucky had generally been enslaved and had worked in agriculture. Mostly illiterate single people, they found jobs as unskilled laborers. The Virginians were free black family groups, among them a few professionals and many mechanics and tradespeople, who left the industrialized areas of Virginia to escape the state's harsh black codes. Between the two groups there were class tensions, and they frequented different churches.

By 1870, 85 percent of Detroit's blacks lived in the old quarter and an enclave called Kentucky, around Kentucky St., north of Jefferson Ave. Although the neighborhood was not majority black, blacks were confined to shabby tenements and dilapidated houses. Although blacks of mixed ancestry could vote as early as 1866, and some blacks did so illegally, black efforts to secure the vote were repeatedly voted down in Michigan until 1870, when the FIFTEENTH AMENDMENT was passed. The public schools, despite orders of the state legislature, remained segregated until the following year. Once blacks were enfranchised, however, they immediately organized a Colored Republican Club at the ward level. In 1875 and 1876, Samuel Watson became Detroit's first African-American elected official when he was elected to the Board of Estimate, the city legislature's upper house. In 1884, Watson became the first northern black delegate to the Republican National Convention. In 1883, a group of blacks started the weekly *Plaindealer* as the voice of black protest, black business, and black Republicanism (*see* REPUBLICAN PARTY). It was one of the first organs to substitute the term "Afro-American" for "Negro." One of its founders, and the organizer of the protest group Afro-American League, was Robert Pelham, Jr., Detroit's leading black politician in the 1880s. After he left to take a position in the Federal Land Office in 1889, David Augustus Straker became Detroit's chief black leader. Straker, a former dean of Allen University Law School in South Carolina, argued civil rights cases and helped found the Detroit Industrial and Financial Cooperative Association and the National Federation of Colored Men. In 1892 he was elected Wayne County circuit court commissioner (judge). The same year, William W. Ferguson was elected to the Michigan legislature. The seat would be held by blacks until 1900.

After the turn of the century, the demography of black Detroit again shifted, as blacks from the deep South began to migrate. The southern-born population, which had been stable for thirty years, increased by 10 percent, relative to the Michigan-born population, between 1900 and 1910. The automobile and other industries, which hired few blacks, spurred the growth of secondary industries which used black labor. By 1915, increased industrial demand due to World War I, as well as a cutoff of immigration from Europe, induced Henry Ford and other industrialists to employ blacks in large numbers. The availability of jobs at $5 per day, advertised by handbills and by labor agents sent south by Ford, provoked a mass migration to Detroit. Black organizations like the Detroit Urban League were set up to find jobs and housing for the new arrivals. The city's black population, 5,000 in 1910, reached 120,000 in 1930.

While blacks toiled in the most difficult and unpleasant positions in industry, with abysmal housing conditions, the relatively high industrial wages they received, and their separation from white society made possible the growth of an independent black economy. Detroit's black middle class, built on the patronage of black workers, was one of the largest in the nation. Black Republicans, thanks partly to contributions by Henry Ford, were increasingly influential in the party. In 1930, Charles Roxborough was elected to the Michigan state senate, the first African American to serve there.

Competition for jobs and housing sparked widespread racial tension. Detroit was a center of the KU KLUX KLAN in the 1920s. In 1925, when Dr. Ossian Sweet, an African American, bought a house in a white neighborhood, a white mob surrounded his house. Sweet fired out in self-defense and killed a white man. Defended by Clarence Darrow, Sweet and his relatives charged in the shooting were acquitted. During the 1930s, right-wing antiblack leaders Father Coughlin and Gerald L. K. Smith were based in the Detroit area.

The collapse of the economy during the 1930s left many blacks unemployed and ill-housed. Since the flow of friends and relatives from the South looking for work continued, conditions for Detroit blacks worsened. As competition for housing increased, many blacks were forced into the Black Bottom neighborhood, also known as Paradise Alley. The automobile industry cut down its hiring of blacks. Nevertheless, the black community continued to develop. In 1936, publisher/entrepreneur John Sengstacke, who later put together a chain of black newspapers, created the *Michigan Chronicle,* which became the major source of news for black Detroit. Both mainstream and heterodox black religious denominations flourished in Detroit. The Rev. James Francis Marion Jones (Prophet Jones), who arrived in the city in 1938, became a popular cult leader/radio evangelist, although his claim of six million followers seems exaggerated. Of more lasting significance was the NATION OF ISLAM, founded by W. D. FARD about 1930 and led after his death by Elijah MUHAMMAD.

However, by far the best-known black Detroit resident in the first half of the twentieth century was Joe LOUIS, who moved to Detroit at the age of twelve. The heavyweight boxing champion from 1935 through 1949, Louis began his career in local Detroit clubs, and his swift rise to boxing eminence was aided by John Roxborough, a black Detroit businessman.

In 1938, the United Auto Workers (UAW) was able to get a contract with General Motors. Despite the hostility of white workers, the union promoted black unionists such as Horace Sheffield, Robert Battle, Coleman YOUNG, and Sheldon Tappes to leadership positions. In part through union registration drives, blacks in Detroit, as elsewhere, became an important part of Franklin D. Roosevelt's New Deal coalition. In 1936, blacks elected their first Democratic state Representative, Charles Diggs, Sr.

The coming of WORLD WAR II and the awarding of lucrative defense contracts to Detroit industries sparked massive renewed migration to Detroit. Walter WHITE of the NAACP estimated that 350,000 people, including 50,000 blacks, entered the city between March 1942 and June 1943. Hate strikes by white workers against blacks, and the past refusal of many blacks to join unions in strikes, had left great bitterness. In February 1942, blacks turned to protests and violence when the Sojourner Truth Homes, a federal housing project built for blacks, was suddenly reassigned to whites. The change was eventually canceled, but racial tensions grew as job competition and the housing crisis intensified. The tensions finally exploded into the DETROIT RIOT OF 1943.

After the war, the African-American population of Detroit climbed, doubling again between 1940 and 1950, and reaching 482,000 in 1960, 29 percent of the city's population. The black middle class expanded. In 1959 Berry GORDY founded the MOTOWN Record Corporation, which would become a cultural force, and the city's first black-owned multimillion dollar corporation. It created the "Motown sound," tuneful

Local white residents picket in February 1942 to prevent blacks from moving into the Sojourner Truth Homes, a newly opened federal housing project in Detroit. The disturbances at the site were a grim foreshadowing of the massive Detroit riot of June 20, 1943, during which more than thirty people died. (Prints and Photographs Division, Library of Congress)

pop-oriented RHYTHM AND BLUES, and features such groups as the SUPREMES, the TEMPTATIONS, the FOUR TOPS, and the Jackson Five (*see* MICHAEL JACKSON), Black performers such as Diana ROSS, Smokey ROBINSON, and Aretha FRANKLIN became superstars in the music industry. Churches also expanded, and the Rev. C. L. FRANKLIN and the Rev. Charles Hill became legends in their own time. The Rev. Albert Cleague also began the Black Messiah Movement in Detroit in 1952, turning his United Church of Christ into the Shrine of the Black Madonna. Detroit had the largest NATIONAL ASSOCIATION FOR THE ADVANCEMENT OF COLORED PEOPLE chapter in America, and blacks were key members of the DEMOCRATIC PARTY coalition led by the UAW. In 1954, blacks elected Charles DIGGS, Jr., to the U. S. House of Representatives, and in 1957 they elected the first black city councilman, William Patrick.

However, large-scale discrimination persisted. The Interracial Commission, renamed the Detroit Commission on Community Relations (CCR) in 1953, had no enforcement powers, and the UAW failed to win Fair Employment Practices clauses in its contracts. Decentralization in the auto industry led to rising unemployment. Detroit's police, segregated and almost all white, were notorious for bigotry. Only 3 percent of the 300,000 units of new housing built in the 1950s in Detroit were given to blacks. While large numbers of blacks moved into the formerly Jewish neighborhood on 12th Street, those who tried to move into other all-white neighborhoods were met by mobs and brick-throwers.

During the 1960s, Detroit achieved a somewhat undeserved reputation as a "model city" in terms of race relations. Reform Mayor Jerome Cavanaugh, whose 1961 campaign had been supported in large numbers by blacks angered at his incumbent opponent's policy of random police searches, installed a liberal police commissioner. In five years, Cavanaugh brought in an estimated $230 million in federal money for programs, some designed by city officials, for black Detroiters. Groups such as the Citizen's Committee for Equal Opportunity, founded by UAW head Walter Reuther, worked against discrimination. In June 1963, after black militants planned a civil rights protest march, Mayor Cavanaugh persuaded more moderate groups to participate, and invited the Rev. Dr. Martin Luther KING, Jr., to speak. About 125,000 people participated in the Walk to Freedom, making it the largest civil rights protest up to that time. In 1964, a militant black lawyer, John CONYERS, was elected to Congress.

Nevertheless, discrimination persisted. Whites resisted housing integration, and schools were chronically underfunded. Police bigotry proved resistant to change. Poor, unemployed inner-city blacks resented the high prices they faced in stores owned both by whites and by the black middle class, whom they felt were "collaborators" with an oppressive white power structure.

The DETROIT RIOT OF 1967, a gigantic urban rebellion, scarred Detroit physically and destroyed its "model city" image. The alliance of African Americans and white liberals cut, the black community concentrated on electing African-American officials. In 1969, Richard Austin, an African American, ran unsuccessfully for mayor, but in 1973 Coleman YOUNG was elected to the first of five terms as mayor. Mayor Young has reshaped the police force and brought blacks into city government.

Around 1975, Detroit became a black majority city. By 1990, the city had the largest percentage of African Americans of any big city in the United States, but it had lost one-third of its population in the previous twenty years as the auto industry and manufacturing sector declined and more affluent whites and blacks moved to nearby suburbs. Despite the mayor's efforts to stimulate development, symbolized by the Renaissance Center, and revive the local economy through job-creating projects, 34 percent of Detroit's residents were receiving public assistance in 1987. Detroit's large black middle class gave it the highest black median household income in America in the 1980s. Nevertheless, the city experienced chronic double-digit unemployment through the early 1990s as crime rose and neighborhoods decayed.

REFERENCES

ABERBACH, JOEL. *Race in the City: Political Trust and Public Policy in the New Urban System.* Boston, 1973.

FINE, SIDNEY. *Violence in the Model City: The Cavanaugh Administration, Race Relations, and the Detroit Riot of 1967.* Ann Arbor, Mich., 1989.

KATZMAN, DAVID. *Before the Ghetto: Black Detroit in the Nineteenth Century.* Urbana, Ill., 1973.

LEVINE, DAVID ALLA. *Internal Combustion: The Races in Detroit, 1915–1926.* Westport, Conn., 1976.

RICH, WILBUR C. *Coleman Young and Detroit Politics.* Detroit, 1989.

SHOGAN, ROBERT, and TOM CRAIG. *The Detroit Race Riot; A Study in Violence.* Philadelphia, 1964.

THOMAS, RICHARD WALTER. *Life for Us Is What We Make It: Building Black Community in Detroit, 1915–1945.* Bloomington, Ind., 1992.

WILBUR C. RICH

Detroit Riot of 1943.

The beginning of WORLD WAR II brought about large movements of African Americans and whites to Detroit to seek employment in defense industries. The city was unprepared to handle the influx, and racial tensions in Detroit were exacerbated by competition for inadequate city housing and recreational facilities. On June 20, 1943, blacks and whites seeking to escape the heat at Belle Isle, Detroit's municipal resort, came to blows. Rumors of violence spread to Paradise Alley, the city's black section, and to working-class white neighborhoods, and that night the city erupted into a full-fledged racial conflict. It would later be considered the first large-scale "modern" urban riot, since African Americans were not simply victims of mob assaults. Instead of concentrating on self-defense against attack, as previously, they themselves actively attacked property and white bystanders.

Meanwhile, blacks outside their own neighborhoods were also victimized by violence, which the city's police were unable, or unwilling, to stop. City authorities were taken by surprise and were slow to call in outside aid. Federal authorities, conversely, were unsure of their authority to intervene without declaring a state of emergency. Admitting that the city was out of control, they believed, would give America's wartime enemies a powerful propaganda weapon. Finally, late on June 21, military police squads were called in to restore order. The riot claimed 34 victims, of whom 25 were black. There were also some 675 injuries and 1,893 arrests. White investigators such as the governor's Fact-Finding Committee blamed the riots on blacks' "militant appeals for equality." However, in response to the riots Mayor Edward Jeffries set up the Mayor's Interracial Committee—the first government group of its kind in the nation—with authority to investigate complaints and to use the courts to enforce antidiscrimination laws.

See also URBAN RIOTS AND REBELLIONS.

REFERENCES

SHOGAN, ROBERT, and TOM CRAIG. *The Detroit Race Riot: A Study in Violence.* Philadelphia, 1964.

THOMAS, RICHARD WALTER. *Life for Us Is What We Make It: Building Black Community in Detroit, 1915–45.* Bloomington, Ind., 1992.

GAYLE T. TATE

Detroit Riot of 1967. During the 1960s, Detroit enjoyed a somewhat exaggerated reputation as a model city for race relations. Its liberal mayor, Jerome Cavanaugh, attracted federal aid for antipoverty programs, and city authorities, supplemented by private and church groups, made conscious attempts to reach out to black leaders. However, serious problems of economic inequality, poor housing, and police brutality remained unaddressed.

In the early morning of July 23, 1967, police raided a "blind pig," an illegal drinking establishment, on 12th Street. Patrons were led outside, handcuffed, and forced to wait, as police wagons were delayed reaching the site. A crowd, partly aroused by the shouts of black militants, gathered and confronted the police, who withdrew from the area. Aroused blacks rioted, looting and burning large white-owned sections of the 12th Street area, then moving to other parts of the city. Before long, downtown Detroit was in flames. Police and firefighters were soon overwhelmed. At first, police were ordered not to fire on rioters in hopes that tensions would die down, but as the rebellion spread, the order was reversed. The riot continued through July 23 and 24. Mayor Cavanaugh and Michigan Gov. George Romney were reluctant to authorize federal intervention, but on the morning of July 25, National Guard units, later supported by infantry troops, were brought in. Eventually, rioters targeted both black-owned and white-owned stores. The riot wound down over the following two days. In all, there were 43 deaths, 1,189 injuries, and 7,231 arrests. The riot, the largest during the 1960s, ended Detroit's liberal-black coalition. The riots and the slump in the economy prompted large numbers of Detroiters, mostly white, to move from the city to nearby suburbs. By the mid-1970s, Detroit had an African-American majority and a black mayor, Coleman YOUNG, whose main electoral constituency was poor blacks.

See also URBAN RIOTS AND REBELLIONS.

REFERENCE

FINE, SIDNEY. *Violence in the Model City: The Cavanaugh Administration, Race Relations, and the Detroit Riot of 1967.* Detroit, 1989.

GAYLE T. TATE

Dett, Robert Nathaniel (October 11, 1882–October 2, 1943), composer and pianist. Born in Drummondsville, Ontario, R. Nathaniel Dett began studying piano as a child. He performed at churches around Niagara Falls, and at the Cataract Hotel in Niagara Falls, N.Y. He published his first composition, "After the Cake Walk," for piano, in 1900. From 1901 to 1903 Dett studied at the Oliver Willis Halstead Conservatory of Music in Lockport, N.Y. He then studied music at Oberlin College (Ohio) at the time one of the most prominent training grounds for black classical musicians. While at Oberlin he directed the choir of Mt. Zion Baptist Church. He also composed an arrangement for violin and piano of "Nobody Knows the Trouble I've Seen."

After receiving his bachelor's degree in music in 1908, he began teaching, first at Lane College in Jackson, Tenn. While there he composed *Magnolia,* a piano suite. In 1911 he began teaching at the Lincoln Institute in Jefferson, Mo., and in that year he published a book of poems, *Album of the Heart.*

In 1913 Dett was appointed director of music at Hampton Institute in Hampton, Va., a post he held until 1932. While directing the school's choir he revived the tradition of spiritual singing, and took the choir on tours of the United States and Europe. During this time he also composed his best-known work, *In the Bottoms* (1913), a suite that included "Juba Dance." The next year he composed one of his best-known choral settings of a spiritual, "Listen to the Lambs." Dett performed in a series of piano concerts in Chicago from 1914–1916, and in 1916 he married the pianist Elise Smith. In 1919 he founded the National Association of Negro Musicians, and he served as its president from 1924 to 1926. In 1921 he wrote

The Chariot Jubilee, an oratorio based on the spiritual "Swing Low, Sweet Chariot."

Dett, who pursued advanced studies at many American universities, as well as with Nadia Boulanger in Paris in 1929, eventually became famous as a composer of spiritual settings for chorus; he is generally regarded to be one of the most important translators of spirituals into works for the concert stage. Among his best-known arrangements of spirituals are "As by the Streams of Babylon," "Poor Me," and "Steal Away to Jesus." Dett left Hampton in 1932 and settled in Rochester, N.Y. In that year he composed a cantata, *The Ordering of Moses.* Dett taught in the Rochester area until 1937, when he accepted a position at Sam Houston College in Austin, Tex. The next year he composed a piano suite, *Tropic Winter.* Dett later taught at Bennett College, in Greensboro, N.C. During World War II he worked for the United Service Organization (USO), headquartered in Battle Creek, Mich., where he died in 1943.

REFERENCES

McBRIER, VIVIAN F. *R. Nathaniel Dett: His Life and Works, 1882–1943.* Washington, D.C., 1977.
SPENCER, JON MICHAEL, ed. *The R. Nathaniel Dett Reader: A Special Issue of Black Sacred Music: A Journal of Theomusicology.* Durham, N.C., 1991.

DOMINIQUE-RENÉ DE LERMA

R. Nathaniel Dett. (Photographs and Prints Division, Schomburg Center for Research in Black Culture, The New York Public Library, Astor, Lenox and Tilden Foundations)

Deveaux, Alexis (September 24, 1948–), novelist, playwright. Born in New York City, Alexis Deveaux devoted the early years of her adult life to community service. Before attending the State University of New York Empire State College (B.A., 1976) in Saratoga Springs, Deveaux was a community worker for the Bronx Office of Probations, and taught English for the WIN Program of the New York Urban League. She also taught reading and creative writing for Project Create and the Frederick Douglass Creative Arts Center. This concern for the racial and economic inequities facing black Americans and other minorities informs most of her writing. Her book for adolescents, *Na-ni* (1973), and her novel *Spirits in the Streets* (1973), are both set in Harlem, where the realities of poverty, drug addiction, and violence are offset by the characters' strength of will and determination to help each other. *Spirits in the Street* is also noteworthy for its highly effective use of nonstandard black English.

Feminism is another major theme of Deveaux's. In a biographical novel, *Don't Explain: A Song of Billie Holiday* (1980), she portrays the singer not as a victim, but as an independent woman who struggled against the white establishment's ideas of what her music ought to be. Deveaux's one-act play *Circles* (1973) depicts a young black woman's attempts to become a dancer over her family's objections. The full-length *Tapestry* (1976) portrays another black woman coming to terms with her identity. In *A Season to Unravel* (1984), a woman's battle to achieve personal authenticity extends to her sexual identity as a lesbian. *An Enchanted Hair Tale* (1987), Deveaux's second juvenile book, won the Coretta Scott King Honor Award of the American Library Association in 1988.

REFERENCES

DAVIS, THADIOUS M., and HARRIS TRUDIER, eds. *Dictionary of Literary Biography*, Vol. 38: *Afro-American Writers after 1955: Dramatists and Prose Writers*. Detroit, 1985.

TATE, CLAUDIA. *Black Women Writers at Work*. New York, 1983.

MICHAEL PALLER
JEFF ENCKE

Dialect Poetry.   Although it had been written by white and black poets alike, dialect poetry emerged as a significant part of African-American writing in the mid-1890s, with the success of its first well-known black practitioner, Paul Laurence DUNBAR, and played a dominant role in African-American poetry until World War I. It figured prominently in black-edited newspapers and periodicals and in virtually all of the many collections of verse by the black poets of the time. Among its leading creators, in addition to Dunbar, were James Edwin Campbell, Daniel Webster Davis, James D. Corrothers, James Weldon JOHNSON, Elliot Blaine Henderson, and Fenton Johnson.

Much of the earliest African-American dialect poetry was both inspired by and a response to the highly successful work of white plantation-tradition writers, who, evoking nostalgic images of the old South, used dialect in a way that furthered negative racial stereotypes. This plantation-tradition background was apparent in the work by black dialect poets, who drew on it thematically and wrote in a dialect that—rarely going beyond fairly conventionalized misspellings—owed more to that white literary tradition than to actual folk speech. The opening of Dunbar's "Lover's Lane" was fairly typical in its language and tone: "Summah night an' sighin' breeze, / 'Long de lovah's lane; / Frien'ly, shadder-mekin' trees, / 'Long de lovah's lane." Some dialect poets even came close

to their white counterparts in both nostalgia and the use of stereotypes. Davis, for example, penned a tribute to the slave-owning plantation mistress, "Ol' Mistis," fondly describing life on the plantation, and including such lines as "Ub all de plezzun mem'riz' / Dar's one dat fills my heart, / 'Tiz de thought ub dear ol' Mistis, / An' 'twill nebber frum me part."

But most dialect poets, including Dunbar and even Davis, sought to use the problematic plantation-tradition background in a way that rescued both the form and its subjects from the more demeaning aspects of the tradition on which they drew. These poets often made use of actual folk sources, subtly subverting the stereotypes white writers portrayed, as in Dunbar's "An Ante-bellum Sermon," in which a slave preacher turns a message of heavenly freedom into a barely disguised anticipation of the day "when we'se rec'onised as citiz'— / Huh uh! Chillun, let us pray!" or even working to create a dialect poetry of protest against racial oppression, as when Elliot Blaine Henderson wrote of black American life in a South where "Dey lynch him on de lef' / An' dey lynch him on de right." So doing, the poets moved dialect poetry away from caricature and even, in the view of some writers and critics of the time, toward the presentation of a distinctive African-American cultural heritage rooted in the folk life of the rural South.

Following World War I, dialect poetry lost much of its prominence in African-American literature. Many writers, especially during the HARLEM RENAISSANCE, became more troubled by the form's lingering association with plantation-tradition writing while agreeing with the famous 1922 statement of James Weldon Johnson, rejecting his own earlier work, that dialect poetry was severely constrained as a form, limited to little more than humor and pathos. Still, a few poets, notably Langston HUGHES, experimented with it. And, toward the end of the Renaissance period, with the 1932 publication of Sterling BROWN's *Southern Road*, dialect poetry—which Brown strongly defended against Johnson's strictures—received a major, if somewhat isolated, reelaboration.

It would be difficult to argue for any direct connection between the dialect tradition and contemporary African-American poetry. Nevertheless, many of the impulses that took shape within that older body of writing have been notable in more recent work as well. Beginning particularly with the BLACK ARTS MOVEMENT in the 1960s, a number of poets have sought to put distinctively African-American forms of speech to poetic use. Their work, having a flavor that is both urban and militant, is very different from the dialect poetry of Dunbar or even Brown. Growing out of an urban milieu and out of specifically urban speech, this later vernacular poetry represents a self-conscious rejection of dominant literary models, and of dominant cultural models as well. Still, the earlier dialect poets remain important precursors to this more contemporary work. Above all, they help emphasize the length of a tradition into which it fits, a tradition marked by recurring efforts to create a distinctively African-American literature and cultural identity through the possibilities inherent in the representation of a unique folk life and a unique folk speech.

REFERENCES

BELL, BERNARD W. *The Folk Roots of Contemporary Afro-American Poetry*. Detroit, 1974.

GATES, HENRY LOUIS. "Dis and Dat: Dialect and the Descent" and "Songs of a Racial Self: On Sterling A. Brown." In *Figures in Black: Words, Signs, and the "Racial" Self*. New York, 1989, pp. 167–195, 225–234.

REDDING, J. SAUNDERS. *To Make a Poet Black*. Chapel Hill, N.C., 1939.

DICKSON D. BRUCE, JR.

Diaspora. The Greek word for dispersion, *diaspora* is most commonly used in reference to the scattering of Jews from their homeland, and to designate those Jews living outside of Israel. In the late twentieth century it came to serve as a similar referent for people of African origin living outside of AFRICA. The central force in the creation of the African diaspora was the transatlantic SLAVE TRADE, though war and commercial interests have also accounted for other Africans leaving Africa. Voluntary migration has become increasingly important in the latter half of the twentieth century (*see* MIGRATION/POPULATION). The size of the diaspora in the 1990s is difficult to measure. Significant numbers of blacks live in the Caribbean, where the total population stood at roughly 34 million in 1990. The African-American population of the United States was approximately 30 million that same year. Large black populations exist in Central and South American countries, such as Guyana, Panama, and Belize. Brazil, with a total population of 150 million in 1990, reported 6 percent (9 million) of its population were black and 38 percent (57 million) were mixed. Similarly, Colombia, with 33.7 million people in that year, reported 4 percent (1.3 million) were black and 14 percent (4.7 million) were mixed. Significant numbers of peoples with African ancestry also live in a number of European cities, in particular in London and Paris. Smaller, though important, concentrations of African peoples can be found in the Persian Gulf, India, and China. With the African population in 1990 at 642 million (and the sub-Saharan population at 501 million), the African diaspora exceeds 150 million.

The conceptualization of a "diaspora" of African peoples can be traced at least as far back as the late nineteenth century, when West Indian/Liberian scholar Edward W. BLYDEN noted similarities in the dispersion of Jews and Africans away from their homelands. In an address in 1880, Blyden noted that "Africa" was distinguished worldwide for having "served" and "suffered." In this, he said, "her lot is not unlike that of God's ancient people, the Hebrews." The term *African diaspora*, however, did not become popular in the United States until the 1960s and '70s. Some credit George Shepperson, professor of Commonwealth and American History at the University of Edinburgh and author of *Independent African: John Chilembwe and the Origins, Setting and Significance of the Nyassaland Native Uprising of 1915* (Edinburgh, Scotland 1958), with coining the term. The use of *African diaspora*, no doubt, was popularized by black political and intellectual movements, such as the black nationalists of the 1960s, which emphasized the unity of peoples of African ancestry living all over the world. The term was used at the International Congress of African Historians held in Tanzania in 1965. It also appeared in Terrence O. Ranger, ed., *Emerging Themes of African History* (Nairobi, Kenya 1968), and has since been used in a number of book titles. One of the earliest was Martin L. Kilson and Robert I. Rotberg's *The African Diaspora: Interpretive Essays* (Cambridge, U.K. 1976). In the 1980s and '90s, use of the term mushroomed. It was included in more than two dozen book titles on African-American history. It has also been used in several journals, including the *African Diaspora Studies Newsletter* (Howard University 1984–) and *Voices of the African Diaspora* (University of Michigan 1990–).

Interest in the diaspora can be an intensely personal experience. In *Pan Africanism in the African Diaspora: an Analysis of Modern Afrocentric Political Movements* (Detroit 1993), Ronald W. Walters wrote that such studies "taught me about the African dimension of my own identity and about the quality of obligation that this identity implied." More broadly, students of the African diaspora have compared the experiences of peoples of African ancestry living throughout the world, and have tried to understand the relation these people have to Africa and their African heritage.

See also AFRICAN-AMERICAN ORIGINS; AFROCENTRICITY; PAN-AFRICANISM.

REFERENCES

HENDERSON, JOHN P. and HARRY A. REED, eds., *Studies in the African Diaspora: A Memorial to James R. Hooker*. Dover, Mass., 1989.

MURPHY, JOSEPH M. *Working the Spirit: Ceremonies of the African Diaspora.* Boston, 1994.

THOMPSON, VINCENT BAKPETU. *The Making of the African Diaspora in the Americas, 1441–1900.* Harlow, Essex, U.K., 1987.

HARRY A. REED

Dickens, Helen Octavia (February 21, 1909–), physician and medical educator. Helen Octavia Dickens, the first black woman admitted to the American College of Surgeons, was born in Dayton, Ohio, to Charles and Daisy Jane Dickens. Her father, a former slave, worked as a janitor and her mother as a domestic. After attending public schools in Dayton, Dickens enrolled at Crane Junior College in Chicago and later at the University of Illinois, where she earned a B.S. in 1921 and an M.D. in 1934. She was the only black woman in her graduating class of 175. In 1935, after completing her internship and residency at Chicago's Provident Hospital, she moved to Philadelphia to share the family practice established by another African-American woman physician, Virginia ALEXANDER. Dickens left the practice seven years later to obtain additional training in obstetrics and gynecology at Provident Hospital, Harlem Hospital, and the University of Pennsylvania, from which she received the degree of Master of Medical Science in 1945.

Dickens married Purvis S. Henderson, a pediatric neurosurgeon, in 1943. The couple remained together until Henderson's death in 1961 and raised two children, Jayne and Norman. Marriage and children died not impede the progression of Dickens's career: She became certified by the American Board of Obstetrics and Gynecology in 1946. Her admission to the American College of Surgeons came four years later. She served as director of obstetrics and gynecology at Mercy-Douglass Hospital in Philadelphia from 1948 to 1967. In 1965, Dickens joined the faculty of the University of Pennsylvania School of Medicine. Her major achievements there include the creation of one of the nation's first teen-pregnancy clinics and the establishment of a successful program to recruit minority students. Dickens remained an active member of Pennsylvania's faculty as emerita professor of obstetrics and gynecology and associate dean for minority affairs.

REFERENCE

HINE, DARLENE CLARK. "Oral History Interview with Helen Octavia Dickens, M.D." Archives and Special Collections on Woman in Medicine, The Medical College of Pennsylvania, Philadelphia, 1988.

VANESSA NORTHINGTON GAMBLE

Dickerson, Earl Burris (1891–September 3, 1986), lawyer, politician. Earl Burris Dickerson was born in Canton, Miss. and migrated to Chicago when he was fifteen years old. He was educated at the University of Chicago Laboratory School, the Evanston Academy, Northwestern University and the University of Illinois, where he received a B.A. in 1914.

After enlisting in the army during World War I, Dickerson was commissioned as a second lieutenant while serving in France as an interpreter. Returning home, he enrolled at the University of Chicago Law School, and in 1920 became the school's first black graduate. He embarked on a career of law as general counsel with the fledgling black-owned Liberty Life Insurance Company (now Supreme Life) in 1921, and continued in that relationship for more than 50 years.

At the time he began his professional advancement in law, Dickerson defied political tradition and entered Democratic politics on the Republican South Side. Dickerson was appointed assistant corporation counsel during the reform administration of Democratic mayor William E. Dever, the first black assistant attorney general for Illinois (1933–1939), and one of two black members of President Franklin D. Roosevelt's Committee on Fair Employment Practices (FEPC) in 1941. He failed to gain reappointment to the FEPC in 1943 because of his aggressive stand against job discrimination.

Dickerson was elected to the Chicago City Council as its first black Democratic alderman in 1938, and remained in that office until 1943. Courageously breaking political precedents, he conducted hearings into housing discrimination in Chicago and managed to get an antidiscrimination clause added to a public transportation bill. Despite these successes, Dickerson's political ambition to serve in the U.S. Congress representing Illinois's first district was thwarted by his nemesis and former political ally William L. Dawson, who represented the district from 1943 through 1970. Similarly, Dickerson's desire to serve as a federal judge was frustrated in part by his support of unpopular political causes, especially civil rights and the leftist Progressive Party in the late 1940s.

Dickerson was one of the major leaders of both the NAACP and the Urban League, and his affiliation with those associations stretched from the early 1920s to the end of his life. He served on the national board of the NAACP from 1941 through 1980 and helped found the NAACP Legal and Educational Defense Fund in 1939. Dickerson served on the Board of Directors of the Chicago Urban League from 1929 through 1970 and led it as president from 1939 through 1947 and from 1950 through 1955. Additionally, Dickerson served as president of the National Bar Association from 1945 to 1947 and president of the National Lawyers Guild from 1951 to

Earl B. Dickerson. (Photographs and Prints Division, Schomburg Center for Research in Black Culture, The New York Public Library, Astor, Lenox and Tilden Foundations)

1954, when it was under constant attack for its connections to the Communist Party.

Dickerson marched with Dr. Martin Luther KING, Jr., in Washington in 1963 and helped finance King's first northern campaign in Chicago in 1966. In addition to his ongoing involvement with the NAACP and Urban League, Dickerson continued to be active in the civil rights movement in Chicago and nationally in his later years.

REFERENCES

BENNET, LERONE, JR. "The Last Half-Hour," *Ebony* (April 1976).
OBITUARY. *New York Times.* September 4, 1986.
RUCHAMES, LOUIS. *Race, Jobs, and Politics: The Story of the FEPC.* New York, 1953.
STRICKLAND, ARVARH. *History of the Chicago Urban League.* Urbana, Ill., 1966.

CHRISTOPHER R. REED

Dickerson, Glenda (February 9, 1945–), director, playwright, folklorist, and educator. Glenda Dickerson was born in Houston. She received a B.F.A. degree from Howard University in 1966 and an M.F.A. degree from Adelphi University in Garden City, N.Y., in 1969. Dickerson was the artistic director for the Black American Theater and an assistant professor at Howard University from 1969 to 1972. She then became chair of the drama department at Duke Ellington High School for the Performing Arts in Washington, D.C., where she remained until 1976. From 1977 to 1992, she held a number of positions as an instructor and professor of drama at various universities, including Fordham University in New York City, Rutgers University in New Brunswick, N.J., and the State University of New York at Stony Brook. In 1993, Dickerson moved to Atlanta, Ga., to chair the department of theater and drama at SPELMAN COLLEGE.

In addition to teaching, Dickerson has directed, acted, and written throughout her career. In 1983, she founded the Lyric Theater (later renamed the Owen Dodge Lyric Theater), a New York–based traveling company that she directed until 1993. Dickerson's theater emphasizes poetry, myth, and African-American folklore. She has written several plays, among them *Unfinished Song* (1969), a "theatrical collage" of African and African-American spoken poetry, and *Magic and Lions* (1978), a work based on Egyptian mythology and the writings of Ernestine Walker, which won an Audience Development Committee (AUDELCO) award in 1980. She has dramatically adapted several black novels and directed them as video productions for the Living Library series (1967–1976). Dickerson has also produced a number of television dramas, including *For My People* (1972), which won a Peabody Award, and *Wine in the Wilderness* (1971), which was nominated for an Emmy. In 1987–1988, she created *Eel Catching in Setauket: A Living Portrait of a Community,* an oral-history creative performance project that documented the lives of the African-American Christian Avenue community in Setauket on Long Island in New York. In 1992, she was the program director for a similar project for the city of Newark entitled *WELLWATER: Wishes and Words.* With playwright Breena Clarke, Dickinson coauthored the minstrel show *Re/Membering Aunt Jemima (An Act of Magic),* which appeared in the 1993 summer edition of *Women & Performance Journal.*

REFERENCES

BOYD, VALERIE. *Atlanta Constitution Journal,* April 11, 1993.
PETERSON, BERNARD L., JR. *Contemporary Black American Playwrights and Their Plays.* Westport, Conn., 1988.

SHIPHERD REED

Dickinson, Joseph Hunter (June 22, 1855–?),
inventor and legislator. Joseph H. Dickinson was born in Canada West (now Ontario) in 1855 but spent most of his life in Detroit, Mich. He attended school in Detroit and at fifteen began working for the U.S. Revenue Service. Two years later he joined the Clough & Warren Organ Company. Within four years, Dickinson had helped Clough & Warren build an award-winning organ for the 1876 centennial celebration in Philadelphia.

Dickinson married Eva Gould in 1880, and in 1882 he and his father-in-law began their own organ-making firm, the Dickinson-Gould Organ Company. The new company made chapel and parlor organs and even submitted a large organ to the New Orleans Exposition in 1884. In 1886 Dickinson returned to Clough & Warren. The large firm encouraged and helped develop Dickinson's improved designs for both pipe and reed organs, as well as his invention of a mechanism for an automatic piano player. Dickinson held more than a dozen patents for his organ and piano-player inventions and designs. At Clough & Warren, he built and finished two organs for the royal family of Portugal and installed organs of his own design and construction in several Detroit churches.

In 1896 Dickinson was an active participant in the founding of the short-lived National Association for Colored Men. In the same year he received the REPUBLICAN PARTY nomination and was elected to the Michigan state legislature. He was reelected in 1898. In the early 1900s he moved with his family to New Jersey. Records do not indicate the time or place of his death.

REFERENCES

APTHEKER, HERBERT, ed. *A Documentary History of the Negro People in the United States.* Vol. 2. New York, 1951.

JAMES, PORTIA P. *African-American Invention and Innovation, 1619–1930.* Washington, D.C., 1989.

PETER SCHILLING

Dickson, Moses (April 5, 1824–November 28, 1901), political and fraternal leader. Born in Cincinnati, Ohio, Moses Dickson supported himself as a barber from an early age. He took a position on a steamboat in 1840, and his travels through the South over the next three years gave him the opportunity to witness slavery firsthand.

Dickson was profoundly affected by what he saw, and determined to do whatever he could to abolish the slave system. He later claimed to have met with eleven other black men in St. Louis in August 1846, to found a secret organization known as the TWELVE KNIGHTS OF TABOR or the Knights of Liberty. According to Dickson, this organization claimed 47,000 members at its peak, and was actively preparing to do battle against slavery when its work was suspended in 1856 in anticipation of an impending war between the North and the South. Dickson also claimed that the organization helped as many as 70,000 slaves escape to freedom through the UNDERGROUND RAILROAD. In the absence of any other evidence for the order's existence, however, Dickson's account is regarded with skepticism.

Dickson fought in the CIVIL WAR, returning in 1864 to Missouri, where he became active in local politics. He was a delegate to every Republican State Convention in Missouri from 1864 to 1878, and served as an elector for Ulysses S. Grant in 1872. He was also a leading member of the Equal Rights League, an organization which worked to secure the franchise and equality before the law for African Americans in the state. Dickson lobbied for improved education for ex-slaves and their children, and was one of the founders of the Lincoln Institute (now LINCOLN UNIVERSITY) in Jefferson City, Mo., serving as the institution's vice president and as a trustee. In 1866 he joined the AFRICAN METHODIST EPISCOPAL CHURCH, in which he was licensed to preach the following year. In 1878, he became president of the Refugee Relief Board of St. Louis, which provided food and clothing to thousands of people on their way to resettlement in Kansas and elsewhere.

A prominent fraternalist, Dickson served as Grand Master of the Missouri lodge of the Prince Hall Masons. In 1871 he founded a new fraternal order, the International Order of the Twelve Knights and Daughters of Tabor. He wrote an elaborate ritual for this order, combining elements drawn from Masonry and Methodism, and encouraging members to practice Christianity, education, temperance, self-reliance, and economic self-improvement. The organization also provided its members and their families with material assistance in cases of illness or death. In 1907, six years after Dickson's death, the Knights of Tabor claimed 100,000 members in thirty states and several foreign countries.

Moses Dickson died in St. Louis, where he had lived for many years.

REFERENCES

APTHEKER, HERBERT. *A Documentary History of the Negro People in the United States.* New York, 1951.

GREENE, LORENZO JOHN, GARY R. KREMER, and ANTHONY F. HOLLAND. *Missouri's Black Heritage.* St. Louis, 1980.

PIPKIN, J. J. *The Story of a Rising Race; The Negro in Revelation, in History and in Citizenship.* St. Louis, 1902.

WALTON, LESTER. "Moses Dickson: The Great Negro Organizer and Fraternal Leader." *The Colored American Magazine* (April 1902): 354–356.

LYDIA MCNEILL

DANIEL SOYER

Diddley, Bo (McDaniel, Elias) (December 30, 1928–), rhythm and blues singer and guitarist. Bo Diddley was born Otha Ellas (or Elias) Bates in Mc-Comb, Miss., and shortly thereafter was sent to Chicago to live with his cousins, whose last name, McDaniel, he then adopted. He began studying violin while still a child. In his early teens he also taught himself guitar, and was soon playing in informal bands. He also played trombone in Chicago's Baptist Congress Band. He attended Foster Vocational High School, and after graduating was a boxer and construction worker. In 1946 he married Ethel Mae Smith. During this time he performed with the Langley Avenue Jive Cats, a RHYTHM AND BLUES ensemble that included guitarist Earl Hooker.

In the 1950s he adopted the name Bo Diddley, apparently in reference to the diddley bow, a one-string guitar. He has also suggested that his name was slang for a mischievous youngster. In 1955 he recorded "Bo Diddley" and "I'm a Man," appeared on Ed Sullivan's television show, and soon became a significant figure in Chicago's BLUES scene of the late 1950s. His other important recordings from this time include "Crackin' Up" (1959) and "Say Man" (1959). In the 1960s Bo Diddley gained an international reputation for his electrifying live performances, but his recordings, including "You Can't Judge a Book by Its Cover" (1962), "Boss Man" (1966), and "Ooh Baby" (1967), were never hits.

Bo Diddley's notoriety derives largely from a signature syncopated rhythm, related to the "shave and a haircut" and "hambone" figures, which he uses in most of his songs. Bo Diddley has also cultivated a reputation as a powerful and outrageous singer, famous for shouting, growling, and howling boastful lyrics filled with sexual innuendo. His stark and earthy, yet highly experimental guitar playing, combining Chicago electric blues and Afro-Cuban influences, was a prime influence on British rock bands in the 1960s. Bo Diddley appeared in three films during this time, *The Big T.N.T. Show* (1966), the documentary *The Legend of Bo Diddley* (1966), and *Keep on Rockin'* (1969).

Since the 1960s Bo Diddley has maintained a busy schedule. He has performed all over the world, hailed

The best-known recording of Bo Diddley, a rock and roll pioneer of the 1950s, was the eponymous "Hey Bo Diddley." He appeared with his unorthodox guitar at a rock and roll revival concert at New York City's Madison Square Garden in 1975. (AP/Wide World Photos)

as one of the pioneers of ROCK AND ROLL. His recordings include *Black Gladiator* (1971), the soundtrack for the animated film *Fritz the Cat* (1971), *The London Bo Diddley Sessions* (1973), and *I'm a Man* (1977). Bo Diddley's connection with British rockers has continued, with tours alongside The Clash in 1979, and with Rolling Stones guitarist Ron Wood in 1988. In 1987 Bo Diddley was inducted into the Rock and Roll Hall of Fame. In the 1980s he recorded for his own record label, Bokay Productions, a record distribution company based in Hawthorne, Fla. He has occasionally performed with Offspring, a group led by his daughter. In the early 1990s Bo Diddley joined with the athlete Bo JACKSON to make a series of widely seen television advertisements for athletic shoes.

REFERENCES

LODER, KURT. "Bo Diddley Interview." *Rolling Stone* (February 12, 1987): 76–78.

TUCKER, NEELY. "Bo Diddley." *Living Blues* 77 (December 1987): 17–21.

JONATHAN GILL

Diggs, Charles Coles, Jr. (December 2, 1922–), congressman. Born in Detroit, Charles Diggs, Jr., was the only child of Mayne Jones and Charles Coles

Diggs. The senior Diggs was a Michigan legislator and the owner of the state's largest funeral home. Diggs, Jr., studied at the University of Michigan and Fisk University. During World War II, he served as a Tuskegee airman, reaching the rank of lieutenant. After his discharge in 1945, he attended Wayne State University in Detroit, where he obtained a degree in mortuary science. He then went to work in his father's funeral home.

In 1950, Diggs's father, who had been imprisoned for taking bribes, won reelection to his Michigan state senate post in a special election, but the legislature refused to seat him. Diggs, Jr., ran for the seat in a special election, defending his father's record. He won both the primary and the general election by large margins. In the legislature, Diggs allied himself with the policies of Gov. G. Mennen Williams, a friend of the labor movement. In 1951 and 1952, Diggs took night law courses at the Detroit School of Law.

In 1954, Diggs ran for the House of Representatives from Michigan's 13th District. He defeated incumbent George O'Brien in the Democratic primary and defeated a Republican challenger, becoming Michigan's first African-American congressman. Once in the House of Representatives, Diggs pressed for civil rights legislation and enforcement. In 1956, he introduced the measure to establish a Civil Rights Commission. Later, in 1971, he became a founder of the CONGRESSIONAL BLACK CAUCUS. In the 1960s, Diggs backed successful measures to lower the voting age to eighteen and to aid minority businesses. In 1972, Diggs was one of the organizers of the National Black Political Convention in Gary, Ind., an unsuccessful attempt to unify African Americans politically and to form an alternative political party. Diggs established himself on the House District of Columbia Committee, helping to win the district home rule. In 1973, he was named chair of the District Committee.

Diggs also specialized in foreign affairs, particularly in Africa. A champion of foreign aid, in 1959 he became the first African-American member of the House Foreign Affairs Committee, and he later served as Chair of the Committee's Africa Subcommittee. Named by President Richard Nixon to the U.S. delegation to the United Nations, he resigned in December 1971 to protest the U.S. support of South Africa and Portuguese involvement in Africa.

In 1978, Diggs, by then the senior black representative, was convicted of mail fraud and payroll kickbacks involving his office employees. His constituents elected him to a thirteenth term, and he appealed his conviction. Under pressure, he resigned his committee chairmanships, and on July 31, 1979, the House formally censured Diggs, 414–0, for his con-

duct. On June 3, 1980, the Supreme Court refused to hear Diggs's appeal. He resigned his seat and went to prison in Alabama, where he served seven months. Following his release, Diggs served as an aide to the Congressional Black Caucus, and practiced his mortician trade in Maryland. In 1987, Diggs ran unsuccessfully for the Wayne County Commission in Michigan, but that same year he regained the state mortuary license he had lost with his conviction; he has since been working as a mortician.

REFERENCES

CHRISTOPHER, MAURINE. *Black Americans in Congress.* New York, 1976.
"Diggs Released From Prison." *New York Times,* March 7, 1981, p. 38.

STEVEN J. LESLIE

Dill, Augustus Granville (1881–March 9, 1956), sociologist. Born in Portsmouth, Ohio, Augustus Dill attended Atlanta University, where he became a pupil and disciple of W. E. B. DU BOIS, graduating in 1906. With Du Bois's encouragement, Dill then entered Harvard University, where he received a second B.A. degree in 1908. He then returned to Atlanta, where he received an M.A. in sociology and assisted Du Bois in the publication of the Atlanta University sociology studies. In 1910, following Du Bois's departure, Dill was named assistant professor of sociology, and joined Du Bois as coeditor of the Atlanta University studies. Among the works Dill edited were *The College-Bred Negro* (1911), *The Common School and the Negro American* (1912), *The Negro American Artisan* (1913), and *Morals and Manners Among Negro Americans* (1915).

In 1914, Dill moved to New York City and became Du Bois's secretary. Shortly after, he was named editorial assistant and business manager of the NAACP periodical THE CRISIS; he was one of the few black staff members in the organization's early years. With Dill's assistance, *The Crisis* became a profitable and respected African-American journal. In 1920, Dill and Du Bois also began publishing *Brownie's Book,* a short-lived black children's magazine. Dill also pursued an interest in music, becoming an accomplished semiprofessional pianist and organist and accompanying such singers as Roland HAYES in recitals and recordings.

In 1928, Dill was arrested on a morals charge, and his homosexuality was publicly exposed. He was summarily fired from *The Crisis* by Du Bois, whose close relationship with Dill then ceased. During the following twenty-five years, Dill was unable to find a steady job, and supported himself through tutoring, music, and an unsuccessful bookstore. In 1952, Dill moved to his sister's house in Louisville, Ky., where he died four years later.

REFERENCE

KELLNER, BRUCE. *The Harlem Renaissance: A Historical Dictionary for the Era.* New York, 1984.

GREG ROBINSON

Dinkins, David Norman (July 10, 1927–), politician. Born and raised in Trenton, N.J., David Dinkins served in the Marine Corps during World War II. In 1950 he graduated from Howard University and later entered Brooklyn Law School, where he received a degree in 1956. From 1956 through 1975 Dinkins worked as an associate and partner of a law firm.

In the early 1960s, Dinkins joined Harlem's George Washington Carver Democratic Club, then headed by the powerful city councilman J. Raymond Jones. He soon took an active interest in local politics and was elected to the New York State Assembly in 1965 and as a New York State Democratic Party district leader in 1967. He lost his assembly seat as a result of redistricting after only one term, but continued his political career as Harlem's district leader. In 1972, Dinkins became the first African-American President of the Board of Elections, but he resigned a year later in protest when the department failed to enact registration reforms.

In 1973, Dinkins was appointed Deputy Mayor for Planning and Development under newly elected Mayor Abraham Beame. His attempt to become New York City's first black deputy mayor was ended when he disclosed that he failed to pay income taxes for the four previous years. He withdrew his nomination and paid heavy fines, but he continued his career despite this setback. In 1975 he was named city clerk, a position he would hold for ten years. He twice ran for Manhattan borough president, in 1977 and 1981, losing both times to Andrew Stein. Dinkins finally won the office in 1985 and served for one term.

In 1989, Dinkins ran for mayor against incumbent Edward I. Koch. Dinkins presented himself as a civil alternative to the acrimonious Koch and as someone who could better handle the city's racial problems, which he accused the three-term mayor of exacerbating. He defeated Koch in the Democratic primary and in the election defeated Republican Rudolph Giuliani by a slim margin, thereby becoming the first

David Dinkins, a product of Harlem's powerful Democratic clubs, held a number of important city positions, including borough president of Manhattan, before becoming the first African-American mayor of New York City, serving from 1990 to 1994. (© Mel Rosenthal, Impact Visuals)

African-American mayor in New York City's history. His tenure as mayor had its share of budgetary and political problems. He earned the reputation of a cautious and careful administrator, who proved reasonably adept in negotiating the treacherous complexities of New York City's racial and ethnic politics, but was defeated for reelection by Rudolph Giuliani.

REFERENCE

MORITZ, CHARLES ed. *Current Biography Yearbook 1990.* New York, 1990.

JAMES BRADLEY

Diplomats.   *See* Ambassadors and Diplomats.

Disciples of Christ. The Christian Church (Disciples of Christ) has its roots in the religious movements of the early nineteenth century known as the Great Revival and the Restoration. These movements, involving various new Protestant denominations, shared a concern for the restoration of primitive Christianity and a revival of simple piety. These groups wanted to abolish the rigid demarcations between denominations, an attitude that at times drew hostility from rival PRESBYTERIANS, METHODISTS, and BAPTISTS. The Disciples of Christ was formed in 1832, when the Christians in Kentucky, led by Barton W. Stone (1772–1844), joined with the Disciples, led by Thomas Campbell (1763–1854) and his son, Alexander (1781–1866). Groups with similar beliefs, such as the O'Kelly Christians and the Freewill Baptists, spread such doctrines to the South and West in areas that would later attract many of the Disciples of Christ.

The Disciples initially encouraged African Americans' religious participation, both by slaves who joined their masters' congregations and by free blacks. Alexander Campbell was a slave owner and did not allow the church to oppose slavery, but free blacks were encouraged to join the church; they worshipped in his first congregation at Brush Run, Pa., after 1820. Free blacks in the North and South joined the movement and helped establish interracial congregations in such places as Wheatland, Mich.

The position of African Americans in the Disciples of Christ reflected the complex nature of Campbell's attitudes toward slavery. Blacks who were ordained or appointed as deacons could only serve other blacks. While churches with interracial memberships like the one in Uniontown, N.C., flourished, segregation was maintained internally. If permitted inside the churches, free blacks and slaves most often had to sit in the back in a segregated balcony or gallery. The first wholly African-American congregation was organized in 1834 at Midway, Ky. Black membership there had swelled to the point where the white women's missionary group bought a slave (also named Alexander Campbell) and gave him enough education to lead the church. He later earned enough money to buy the freedom of his wife, Rosa Campbell, who became a leader among women Disciples. By 1860, there were probably about 7,000 black Disciples, most of them in North Carolina, Kentucky, and Tennessee. Since the heritage of the Disciples included searching for freedom from restrictive creeds and exclusion from mainstream churches, African Americans may have used the experience of the Disciples to speak to their condition in American society, despite their treatment in the church.

After EMANCIPATION, many African Americans sought to restructure their lives free of white domination. Many black Disciples left the church for denominations with strong African-American constituencies, such as the Baptist or African Methodists. White Disciples were increasingly uneasy in integrated congregations. As a result, the number of African-American independent Disciples congregations increased. Blacks acquired roles of local consequence and developed regional structures to support their churches. In 1878, Preston Taylor (1849–1931) and H. Malcolm Ayers organized a national convention of black Disciples, called the National Convention of Churches of Christ, which met intermittently through the end of the nineteenth century. Born in slavery, Taylor became a preacher and businessman after the Civil War. He mastered stonecutting and managed a mortuary, cemetery, and recreational park besides going about his work building churches and congregations in Kentucky and Tennessee. In the Carolinas, loose associations of black Disciples were organized, and from this base many churches were established in other states in the East. In other places, local prayer meetings grew in size and importance and were formalized as regional state conventions in the 1890s. However, African Americans neither shared leadership on a national level nor became autonomous within the church as an organized group.

Within the official church hierarchy, the group most active in the black community was the Board of Negro Education and Evangelization, founded in 1890 as a subsidiary of the American Christian Missionary Society. Because the developing black congregations were hampered by their lack of trained ministers, the board tried throughout the second half of the nineteenth century to start a college that would draw a national student body to train for the ministry. Southern Christian Institute (SCI) opened in 1881 in Edwards, Miss. Though it trained ministers, it followed the HAMPTON INSTITUTE model of a self-sustaining industrial school and maintained segregation on campus to please its white benefactors. It merged with the Congregationalist Tougaloo College in 1954. The only remaining black Disciples college is Jarvis Christian College at Hawkins, Tex., established in 1912. SCI was able to train evangelical ministers to serve the African-American communities rapidly dispersing throughout the South and Midwest.

The EXODUSTERS of the late 1870s brought new black populations to Texas, Arkansas, Missouri, and Kansas in the West and to Piedmont Virginia, and West Virginia, and the Carolinas in the East. By the end of the nineteenth century, African Americans comprised about 4 to 5 percent of the Disciples of Christ. The great migration of southern blacks to northern cities, which began in 1914, further depopulated southern black congregations. Because the

Disciples of Christ had been an almost entirely rural church, black congregants who left the countryside found few churches in the cities.

The twentieth century brought a gradual restructuring of the church that gave black members more power. African-American congregations were permanently organized as the National Convention of the Disciples of Christ in Nashville in 1917 in response to the formation of the International Convention of the Disciples of Christ, which was established to govern the whole church. The National Convention elected President Taylor its president and agreed to convene once a year as an auxiliary to the International Convention. The convention initiated a period of growth in programs for African Americans in the church, most notably in education; women's groups, and missionary projects. Another prominent leader of the National Convention was Rosa Brown Bracy, who had gained prominence in the church through the Christian Women's Board of Missions. She helped organize the convention and was elected its executive secretary in 1942, the year it changed its name to the National Christian Missionary Convention. In 1945 the body convinced white missionary agencies to work with it collaboratively. This resulted in a large funding increase for work in the black community.

In 1968–1969, the church was restructured and renamed the Christian Church (Disciples of Christ). The formal convention structure merged with the General Assembly (formerly the International Convention) and an all-inclusive National Convocation was created, ensuring African Americans fellowship, leadership training, and discussion of issues related to their church life in the context of the total mission of the church. In addition, the Fund for Reconciliation was established to promote black entrepreneurship and the reintegration of African Americans into the church. In response to James FORMAN's BLACK MANIFESTO in 1969, the church doubled its endowment fund to $4 million. In the 1990s, between 5 and 10 percent of all Disciples are African Americans. They remain active and have served at all levels of church leadership.

REFERENCES

BARBER, WILLIAM JOSEPH. *Disciples Assemblies of Eastern North Carolina*. St. Louis, 1966.

BRACY, ROSA BROWN. *A History of the Negro Disciples*. St. Louis, 1938.

CARDWELL, BRENDA, and WILLIAM K. FOX. *Journey Toward Wholeness: A History of Black Disciples of Christ in Mission of the Christian Churches*. Vol. I, *From Convention to Convocation: No Longer 'Objects of Mission' but 'Partners in the Work' (1700–1988)*. N.p., 1990.

FOX, WILLIAM J., ed. *The Untold Story: A Short History of Black Disciples*. St. Louis, 1976.

HENRY, KENNETH E. "The Black Disciples Heritage: Authentic, Vital and Enduring." *Discipliana* 36, no. 2 (1976).

LYDA, HAP. A History of Black Christian Churches (Disciples of Christ) in the United States Through 1899. Ph.D. Vanderbilt University, 1972.

MCALLISTER, LESTER G., and WILLIAM E. TUCKER. *Journey in Faith*. St. Louis, 1989.

KENNETH E. HENRY

Diseases, Tropical.   *See* Tropical Diseases.

Diseases and Epidemics.   With widespread impact on all segments of American society, diseases and epidemics have taken a higher toll on blacks than on any other group. Several reasons may be cited, including poverty, lack of education, limited access to services, mythologies concerning relative susceptibility of the races, and racial discrimination within the medical profession and health-care institutions. Modern medicine has developed the ability to eliminate, control, or reduce the devastation caused by diseases and epidemics. Nevertheless, the consequences for African Americans remain disproportionately high.

Slaves in the New World suffered from diseases such as malaria, sleeping sickness, and hookworm—all indigenous to their native Africa. In addition, they were exposed to diseases common among American whites, especially smallpox, measles, diphtheria, cholera, yellow fever, dysentery, pleurisy, tuberculosis, and syphilis. These diseases periodically reached epidemic proportions, in urban areas as well as on the plantations. The Philadelphia yellow fever epidemic of 1793 devastated an entire city, across racial and class lines. Epidemics were common because of the primitive state of medical knowledge, and because the role of factors other than disease—overcrowding, poor sanitation, and inadequate diet—was imperfectly understood. (*See* SLAVE TRADE.)

Before the Civil War, economic survival for white Americans depended in large measure on maintaining a healthy slave population. Efforts to control the impact of diseases and epidemics, within the limited means available, were therefore almost as essential within the slave population as among other groups.

When over five thousand people died in a cholera epidemic in Louisiana in 1832, concern over the monetary impact of lost slaves sometimes rivaled the human tragedy of lost friends and relatives. Mortality rates were high for both whites and blacks. The 1850 U.S. census reported the average age of death for blacks as 21.4 years, and for whites as 25.5 years.

The post-Emancipation period coincided with developments in modern medicine that gradually increased life expectancies, alleviated the impact of disease, and reduced the frequency of epidemics. While African Americans benefited from this trend overall, disparities between the races became more pronounced in the late nineteenth and early twentieth centuries. Racial separatism, as formalized in the U.S. Supreme Court's "separate but equal" decision in the case of *Plessy* v. *Ferguson* (1896), combined with the disappearance of urgent economic incentives to promote the health of blacks, often left African Americans to fend for themselves in health care, as in other areas. Black professional associations played an important role in health education and disease control. The National Medical Association, for example, in 1910 established commissions to assess the impact of tuberculosis, hookworm, and pellagra on African Americans. Black physicians founded tuberculosis sanatoria and worked through local black associations, fraternities, churches, and schools to disseminate information on disease control and health maintenance. Under the direction of its resident physician, Tuskegee Institute published occasional health bulletins on subjects ranging from tuberculosis and typhoid fever to "the danger of flies."

In general, the white health-care establishment became involved primarily when the impact of disease on African Americans was perceived as a threat to white communities. This was the case, for example, with sexually transmitted diseases such as syphilis and gonorrhea. Reputable medical texts were known to repeat inaccurate stereotypes of syphilis as a predominantly "Negro" disease (in fact, whites had first given it to blacks), and to warn practitioners that gonorrhea in children, for instance, was "most commonly received from toilet seats soiled by infected members of the household, such as colored maids." The TUSKEGEE SYPHILIS EXPERIMENT, carried out by the U.S. Public Health Service from 1932 to 1972, was based partly on false assumptions about the race-specific impact of the disease.

In the latter half of the twentieth century, federal health-care legislation has done little to modify attitudes or to reduce racial disparities. African Americans developed active tuberculosis during the 1980s at more than six times the rate of whites. Syphilis rates, the highest in the United States since 1950, soared for all groups by 34 percent between 1981 and 1989, with a 50 percent increase among blacks. The so-called "war on cancer," begun in 1972, produced an increasing divergence in death rates for whites and blacks. In 1989, the chance of surviving at least five years past a cancer diagnosis was 50 percent for whites and only 37 percent for blacks. The higher mortality rate for blacks is attributable to their relatively lower level of access to screenings, tests, and treatment. Whites are twice as likely to be admitted to hospitals for cardiac symptoms, and two to four times more likely to undergo coronary artery bypass surgery. Heart researchers have identified a so-called "stroke belt" in the South, where the incidence of untreated high blood pressure among blacks results in a higher than normal risk of death and disability from the disease. In 1989, blacks were nearly three times more likely than whites to develop diabetic end-stage renal disease, even after adjusting for the higher prevalence of diabetes among blacks. While blacks were four times as likely to suffer kidney failure, they waited twice as long as whites for a kidney transplant. Racism, poverty, and lack of access to health services are significant factors in the rapid spread of the AIDS virus through minority groups. In September 1992, minorities (including members of the black, Hispanic, American Indian, and Asian communities) who make up 24.3 percent of the U.S. population, accounted for 43.5 percent of all AIDS cases.

Such failures are offset by promising advances, as in the treatment of sickle-cell anemia. This disease affects about 60,000 people in the United States, primarily African Americans (150 of 100,000 black children are born with the disease). In 1993, researchers found that the underlying factor causing the disease—a lack of fetal hemoglobin—might be rectified by an organic compound called butyrate, which stimulates the dormant gene responsible for producing fetal hemoglobin. Meanwhile, in August 1993, a sickle-cell specialist and expert on minority and community health care, Dr. David Satcher, became the first African American to head the prestigious federal Centers for Disease Control and Prevention, based in Atlanta.

REFERENCES

Centers for Disease Control. *Prevention of Disease, Disability and Death in Blacks and Other Minorities.* Atlanta, 1986.

LEWIS, JULIAN HERMAN. *The Biology of the Negro.* Chicago, 1942.

McBRIDE, DAVID. *From TB to AIDS: Epidemics among Urban Blacks since 1990.* Albany, N.Y., 1991.

MORAIS, HERBERT M. *The History of the Negro in Medicine.* New York, 1967.

KENNETH R. MANNING

Dismukes, William "Dizzy"

Dismukes, William "Dizzy" (March 15, 1890–June 30, 1961), baseball player. Born in Birmingham, Ala., William Dismukes, nicknamed "Dizzy" broke into black baseball as a right-handed pitcher with the West Baden, Ind., Sprudels in 1910. A top pitcher, Dismukes had an unusual underhand pitching style. In 1912 he pitched for the St. Louis Giants; he moved the next year to the Brooklyn Royal Giants. In 1915, Dismukes played for the Indianapolis ABCs, with whom he would be most closely identified. Surviving records state he had a 16–6 record that year, with 52 strikeouts and 4 shutouts in 23 games. During the late teens, while playing for a U.S. Army team, Dismukes showed the white pitcher Carl Mays the "submarine" pitching technique for which Mays was later famous as a member of the New York Yankees.

In 1920, Dismukes rejoined Indianapolis, now in the Negro National League. According to incomplete records, Dismukes pitched for fourteen years, seven in the NNL, and had a lifetime 55–44 record, with 213 strikeouts in 815 innings. During his long baseball career, Dismukes was associated, either as player, coach, manager, and/or executive, with all the above teams, as well as with the Mohawk Giants, Chicago American Giants, Dayton Marcos, Pittsburgh Keystones, Memphis Red Sox, Birmingham Black Barons, St. Louis Stars, Cincinnati Dismukes (his own barnstorming team), Detroit Wolves, Homestead Grays, Columbus Blue Birds, and Kansas City Monarchs. Dismukes retired in the early 1950s after major league integration brought about the demise of the Negro Leagues. He died in Campbell, Ohio.

REFERENCE

HOLWAY, JOHN. *Black Diamonds: Life in the Negro Leagues from the Men Who Lived It.* Westport, Conn., 1989.

GREG ROBINSON

Divine, Father.

Divine, Father. *See* Father Divine.

Dixon, Dean Charles

Dixon, Dean Charles (January 10, 1915–November 4, 1976), conductor. Dean Dixon studied the violin beginning at the age of four. As a teenager, he organized the Dean Dixon Symphony Orchestra and the Dean Dixon Choral Society, both in 1932. He received degrees from the Juilliard School of Music (B.S., 1936) and Columbia University Teachers College (M.A., 1939). He studied conducting privately with Albert Stoessel and made his debut at Town Hall in New York City on May 7, 1938; during this same year he founded the New York Chamber Orchestra. He was the first African American to appear as a guest conductor with Arturo Toscanini's NBC Symphony Orchestra (1941), the New York Philharmonic (1942), and the Philadelphia Orchestra (1943). Even with such impressive credentials, Dixon could not acquire a permanent position in the United States, and consequently spent two decades in Europe (1949–1970).

While engaged in Europe, Dixon conducted the Göteborg Symphony Orchestra in Sweden (1953–1960), the Hessian Radio Symphony Orchestra in Frankfurt, Germany (1961–1964), and the Sydney Symphony Orchestra in Australia (1964–1967). In 1970 he returned to the United States, where he conducted the New York Philharmonic on an extended tour in 1971. Dixon was the first African-American conductor to establish an international reputation and hold long-term conducting positions with major orchestras. His awards and honors include a Rosenwald Fellowship (1945–1947) and the Alice M. Ditson Award for outstanding contributions to American music (1948).

REFERENCES

GRAY, JOHN, comp. *Blacks in Classical Music: A Bibliographical Guide to Composers, Performers, and Ensembles.* Westport, Conn., 1988.
TRUDEAU, N. A. "When the Doors Didn't Open: A Cool Classicist and a Soldier for Social Equality." *High Fidelity/Musical America* 35 (May 1985): 57–58.

WILLIE STRONG

Dixon, Ivan, III

Dixon, Ivan, III (April 6, 1931–), actor and director. Born in Harlem, N.Y., Ivan Dixon is the son of a grocery store owner. When his parents separated, Dixon worked in his father's store while living with his mother until he was sent to boarding school in North Carolina. Dixon began college at North Carolina College at Durham, N.C., but left to attend Western Reserve University in Cleveland, which awarded him a B.A. in political science and history in 1954. Afterwards, he received training in drama at KARAMU PLAYHOUSE of the American Theater Wing in Cleveland.

In 1957 Dixon made his Broadway debut in William Saroyan's "The Cave Dwellers," and in 1958 he began his film career as a stunt double for Sidney POITIER in *The Defiant Ones*. He appeared in the films *Porgy and Bess* (1959) and Lorraine HANSBERRY's *A Raisin in the Sun* (1961), both with Poitier. Dixon's first starring performance came in 1964 as railroad worker Duff Anderson opposite Abbey LINCOLN in the film *Nothing but a Man,* the story of the marriage between a schoolteacher and a laborer nearly torn apart by issues of assimilation and activism. Both Dixon and Lincoln received best actor awards for their performances from the UNESCO-sponsored Black Arts Festival of 1966 in Dakar, Senegal.

Dixon's film career continued with roles in *A Patch of Blue* (1965), *To Trap a Spy* (1966), *Suppose They Gave a War and Nobody Came?* (1970), *Clay Pigeon* (1971), and *Car Wash* (1976). In 1972 Dixon directed his first film, *Trouble Man,* which was followed the next year by the anti-CIA thriller *The Spook Who Sat by the Door*. Both films earned Dixon NAACP Image Awards.

Dixon also appeared regularly on television in the mid-1960s. In 1965 he began the role for which he is best known, Sergeant James Kinchloe in the situation comedy *Hogan's Heroes* (1965–1970). Kinchloe was seldom the focal point of the episodes in the series, about Allied soldiers in a prisoner-of-war camp, but was the faithful stalwart, always handy with the right plan in the right spot. In addition, Dixon appeared in several made-for-television movies, and in 1967 he received an Emmy nomination for his portrayal of a U.S. Army Sergeant in Vietnam in the television film *The Final War of Olly Winter*.

During the late 1970s and '80s, however, Dixon's acting career tailed off, though he directed episodes of such popular television programs as *The Waltons, Starsky and Hutch, Little House on the Prairie,* and *Magnum, P.I.*

In 1993 Dixon built the radio station, KONI-FM in Lanai City, Hawaii.

REFERENCES

BOGLE, DONALD. *Blacks in American Film and Television: An Illustrated Encyclopedia.* New York, 1988.

BOGLE, DONALD. *Toms, Coons, Mulattoes, Mammies & Bucks: An Interpretive History of Blacks in American Film.* New York, 1974.

RULE, SHIELA. "Black Film Portrait Back on Screen." *New York Times,* March 16, 1993, C-13.

KENYA DILDAY

Dixon, Melvin (May 29, 1950–October 26, 1992), novelist and poet. Born in Stamford, Conn., Melvin Dixon received his B.A. from Wesleyan University in 1971 and his Ph.D. in American Studies from Brown University in 1975. He taught African-American literature, modern drama, and creative writing at Fordam University, Williams College, Queens College of the City University of New York, and the CUNY Graduate Center, where he was professor of English from 1986 to 1992. As a critic, Dixon helped to shape the emergent field of comparative African-American literary studies. His major critical work, *Ride Out the Wilderness: Georgraphy and Identity in Afro-American Literature,* was published in 1987. He also translated two important volumes from the French: Geneviève Fabre's *Drumbeats, Masks and Metaphor* (1983), a seminal study of contemporary African-American theater, and *The Collected Poems of Léopold Sédar Senghor* (1987).

In addition to his success as a critic, Dixon was an award-winning creative writer. His collection of his own verse, *Change of Territory* (1983), reflects his spiritual itinerary and development as a black writer; drawing upon diverse travels and sojourns in France, the Antilles, and Senegal, these poems reenact his pilgrimage to many different African-American historical sites. His first novel, *Trouble the Water* (1989)—which received the Charles H. and N. Mildred Nilon Excellence in Minority Fiction Award—poetically chronicles the dramatic homecoming of a black protagonist to his southern roots. By contrast, his second novel, *Vanishing Rooms* (1991), is a terse story set in New York about the agonies and rewards of love and friendship; it is one of the few major works in the African-American literary tradition that focuses on issues of black male homosexuality. Shortly before his death in 1992, Dixon completed a volume of poetry entitled *Love's Instruments,* about his experience of living with AIDS.

REFERENCE

FABRE, MICHEL. *From Harlem to Paris: Black American Writers in France, 1840–1980.* Champaign, Ill., 1991.

MICHEL FABRE

Dixon, Willie (July 1, 1915–January 29, 1992), blues composer, singer. Born in Vicksburg, Miss., Willie Dixon began singing in his early teens, after he heard Charley PATTON and Little Brother Montgomery playing BLUES at local clubs and picnics. He joined the Union Jubilee Singers at the age of fifteen, and remained with the group until he moved to Chicago in 1936. Dixon began to make his living as a boxer, winning the Illinois Golden Gloves championship in the novice heavyweight division in 1937, but his career ended when he was involved in a brawl over wages at the office of the local boxing commissioner.

In the late 1930s Dixon began to play bass, and in 1939 he made his first recordings, singing and playing with the Five Breezes, a GOSPEL vocal group. In the early 1940s Dixon's singing career was interrupted by his antidraft activities. During this time he spoke out forcefully against the conscription of African Americans and was sentenced to ten months in jail for resisting the draft. In 1946 he returned to music, performing with Leonard Caston and either Gene Gilmore or Ollie Crawford, as the Big Three Trio, a RHYTHM AND BLUES vocal group. When the trio, whose recordings included versions of "Signifyin' Monkey" and "Appetite Blues," broke up in 1951, Dixon joined the staff of Chess Records, where he served off and on as musician, producer, and composer for the next two decades. While at Chess, Dixon helped transform the rural, acoustic blues into a style known as the Chicago blues, a harsh urban sound that featured loud, distorted vocals, stinging guitar and harmonica solos, and driving rhythms. Dixon composed, produced, and performed on many of the style's most characteristic recordings, including MUDDY WATERS's "Hoochie Coochie Man" (1954), and LITTLE WALTER's "My Babe" (1955), and served as Chess's talent scout. Dixon left Chess in 1956 and worked with Cobra Records to pioneer the variation on Chicago blues known as the West Side style, which used a guitar-based sound on numerous recordings by Magic Sam, Buddy Guy, and Otis Rush. Dixon formed his own record company, Ghana Music, in 1957, but was unable to maintain the business, and in 1959 he returned to Chess, where he wrote and produced HOWLIN' WOLF's "Back Door Man" (1960) and "Goin' Down Slow" (1961), and Muddy Waters's "Tiger in Your Tank" (1960).

In the early 1960s Dixon began to perform with Memphis Slim, and the two made tours of the United States that helped spark a blues and FOLK revival among white audiences. From 1962 to 1964 they performed in Europe, influencing a generation of white British ROCK AND ROLL bands, including the Rolling Stones and Led Zeppelin. Dixon continued to play, write, and produce for Chess until 1970, when he left to form Yambo records. He toured and made many recordings in the 1970s, including *Peace* (1971), *Maestro Willie Dixon and His Chicago Blues Band* (1973), *Catalyst* (1973), and *What's Happened to My Blues?* (1976). In 1977 Dixon was hospitalized for diabetes, which resulted in one of his feet being amputated, but he remained active. In 1984 he recorded *Mighty Earthquake and Hurricane,* and his 1988 album *Hidden Charms* won a Grammy award. The next year Dixon published his autobiography *I Am the Blues.* In the 1980s Dixon also became involved in film music, producing a new version of "Who Do You Love?" for Bo DIDDLEY in *La Bamba* (1987), and performing "Don't You Tell Me Nothin' " in *The Color of Money* (1986). In 1989 he composed the soundtrack for *Ginger Ale Afternoon.*

In 1987 Dixon, who had long fought for the rights of blues musicians to collect money for their compositions, settled out of court with Led Zeppelin over similarities between their 1969 recording "Whole Lotta Love" and his song "You Need Love." In 1991 Dixon established the Blues Heaven Foundation to help poor musicians and schools buy musical instruments, and assist elderly blues musicians in collecting royalties. The foundation eventually purchased the Chess studios. Dixon remained active until his death of heart failure in 1992 in Burbank, Calif. He was posthumously inducted into the Rock and Roll Hall of Fame in 1994.

REFERENCES

DIXON, WILLIE, with Don Snowden. *I Am The Blues: The Willie Dixon Story.* New York, 1989.
PALMER, ROBERT. *Deep Blues.* New York, 1981.
WATROUS, PETER. "He Made the Blues Worth Listening to Again." *New York Times,* February 9, 1992, p. 27.

JONATHAN GILL

Dobbs, Mattiwilda (July 11, 1925–), soprano. Mattiwilda Dobbs, the daughter of Irene Thompson Dobbs and John Wesley Dobbs, a mail clerk and civil rights leader, grew up in Atlanta, Ga. She received her early music education singing in the First Congregational Church choir and began studying piano at the age of seven. In 1946, Dobbs graduated from Spelman College, where she studied voice with Naomi Maise and Willis James. In 1948, Dobbs received a Master's Degree from Teachers College at Columbia University in Spanish Language and Literature, a degree she pursued because she was unsure of her employment opportunities as a vocalist. However, she continued to study voice at the Mannes College of Music (1948–1949) and with Pierre Bernac in Paris (1950–1952).

Dobbs received worldwide attention as an artist in 1950 when she won first prize in the International Music Competition in Geneva, Switzerland. Following this achievement, she began to appear with orchestras across Europe. Her first operatic success came in 1952, when she appeared at the Holland Festival in Stravinsky's *Le Rossignol.* She was the first black performer to appear at La Scala in Milan (1953), where she played Elvira in Rossini's *L'Italiana in Algeri*. In 1954, Dobbs performed for the British royal family and the king of Sweden at the Royal Opera House at Covent Garden.

In the United States, Dobbs's career began with an appearance in 1954 with the Little Orchestra Society at Town Hall as Zerbinetta in Richard Strauss's *Ariadne auf Naxos*. In 1955, she became one of the first African Americans to sing at the San Francisco Opera House, where she performed the role of the Queen of Shemakha in Rimsky-Korsakov's *Le Coq d'Or*. In 1956 Dobbs made her debut with New York's Metropolitan Opera as Gilda in Verdi's *Rigoletto*. Dobbs, a coloratura soprano, was acknowledged for her finished technique and her voice's buoyancy and flexibility in its upper register.

Dobbs continued to concertize throughout Europe, the United States, Australia, and Israel from 1957 to 1959. She settled in Stockholm in 1959. After 1973, Dobbs returned to the United States periodically to serve as artist-in-residence and professor at various colleges and universities including Spelman College, the University of Texas at Austin, and the University of Illinois. From 1976 to 1991 Dobbs was a professor of voice at Howard University. In 1989 she was elected a member of the Metropolitan Opera Association National Board.

REFERENCES

HINE, DARLENE CLARK, ed. *Black Women in America: An Historical Encyclopedia*. New York, 1993.

SADIE, STANLEY, ed. *New Grove Dictionary of Opera*. New York, 1992.

SOUTHERN, EILEEN. *Biographical Dictionary of Afro-American and African Musicians*. Westport, Conn., 1982.

STORY, ROSALYN M. *And So I Sing: Afro-American Divas of Opera and Concert*. New York, 1990.

JOCELYN BRYANT HARDEN

Doby, Lawrence Eugene "Larry" (December 13, 1923–), baseball player. Larry Doby was the second African American to play major league baseball and the second to manage a major league team. Born and raised in Camden, S.C. Doby moved to Paterson, N.J., in 1938, where he starred in three sports at Eastside High. During his high school years, he also played semipro baseball. In 1942, after graduation, Doby joined the Newark Eagles of the Negro National League, playing under the name "Larry Walker" to protect his amateur status. During the off-season, Doby attended Long Island University and Virginia Union University. Doby's career was interrupted by naval service from 1944 to 1945. In 1946, he returned to the Eagles, made the league all-star team, and helped lead them to the NNL pennant. According to surviving statistics, Doby hit .378 in the NNL, with 25 home runs in 139 games.

Doby played during the winter of 1946 and '47 with the San Juan Senators in Puerto Rico. In spring 1947, while Doby was playing with the Eagles, the Cleveland Indians of the American League recruited him for their outfield and purchased his contract. Doby joined the team on July 4, 1947, several months after Jackie Robinson had broken the color line of major league baseball with the Brooklyn Dodgers of the National League. Although he faced much of the same brutal racist treatment from fans and other players that Robinson did, Doby received little media attention playing in Cleveland. He batted .301 in 1948, and .318 in that season's World Series. In eleven seasons, playing for Cleveland, Chicago, and Detroit, he batted .283, twice led the league in home runs (1952 and 1954, with 32), and made the all-star team six times. In 1962, at age 38, after retiring

Larry Doby, outfielder for the Cleveland Indians, 1948. (UPI/Bettmann)

briefly, Doby went to Japan to play two seasons for the Chunichi Dragons. He was the second American to play in Japan.

After returning from Japan, Doby worked in Cleveland's Center Field Lounge, and operated a liquor store. In 1967, he was appointed Director of Bicycle Safety for Essex County, N.J. When the Montreal Expos were organized in 1969, Doby joined them as a scout and batting coach. In the winter of 1971 and in 1972, Doby managed a team in Venezuela, but lost his job when he refused to throw a game. In 1978 Doby was named manager of the Chicago White Sox, but he held that position for only 87 games, winning 37 and losing 50. In 1980, Doby became director of community relations with the National Basketball League's New Jersey Nets.

REFERENCE

MOORE, JOSEPH THOMAS. *Pride Against Prejudice: The Biography of Larry Doby*. Westport, Conn. 1988.

GREG ROBINSON

Dodds, John M. "Johnny" (April 12, 1892– August 8, 1940), jazz clarinetist. Born and raised in New Orleans, Johnny Dodds grew up in a musical family; his father and uncle played violin and his younger brother was acclaimed jazz drummer Warren "Baby" DODDS (1898–1959).

Dodds began playing the clarinet at seventeen. Partially self-taught, Dodds never learned to read music but received some tutoring from well-known New Orleans clarinetist Lorenzo Tio, Jr. From 1911 until 1917, Dodds was an irregular member of the band of trombonist Kid ORY. Later in 1917, Dodds worked in Fate Marable's riverboat band. After the Storyville district of New Orleans closed in 1917, Dodds toured the country in a vaudeville show and in 1919 was invited to join King OLIVER's Creole Jazz Band in Chicago.

In 1924 Dodds left Oliver to form his own band. For the next six years Dodds recorded extensively with his bands—the Black Bottom Stompers, the Johnny Dodds Trio, and the Washboard Band. Dodds also appeared as a clarinetist on a number of sessions with Jelly Roll MORTON, Louis ARMSTRONG, and blues singer Ida COX. In the 1930s, changing musical tastes and the depression led to a falling-off of his career, and for a while he was forced to drive a taxi to earn a living. The renewed interest in New Orleans jazz in the late 1930s led to a revival of his career, one cut short by a fatal stroke in 1940.

Dodds was a player with a deep resonant tone, an expressive vibrato, and a great feeling for the blues.

He was a vital cog in many of the most important 1920s New Orleans jazz ensembles. Along with Jimmy NOONE and Sidney BECHET, Dodds was in the forefront of New Orleans-style jazz in the 1920s and '30s.

REFERENCES

KERNFIELD, BARRY. *New Grove Dictionary of Jazz*. Vol. 1. London, 1988.
SHAW, ARNOLD. *The Jazz Age*. New York, 1987.
WILLIAMS, MARTIN. *Jazz Masters of New Orleans*. New York, 1967.

MICHAEL A. LORD

Dodds, Warren "Baby" (December 24, 1898– February 14, 1959), jazz drummer. Born in New Orleans, Warren Dodds came from a family of musicians. His father, uncle, and several siblings played musical instruments, and his older brother Johnny became a famous jazz clarinetist. Dodds started drum lessons in his early teens with Dave Perkins, and later studied with Walter Brundy and Louis Cottrell, Sr. Dodds first performed professionally with Willie Hightower, and worked with Papa Celestin and Bunk Johnson before joining Fate Marable's riverboat band in 1918. Dodds left Marable in 1921 and toured California with King OLIVER's Creole Jazz Band, recording with them in Chicago in 1923.

Dodds remained in Chicago for the next twenty years, performing with leading New Orleans musicians such as his brother Johnny Dodds, Honore Dutrey, Charlie Elgar, and Freddie Keppard. However, the 1927 records he made with Louis ARMSTRONG, ("Wild Man Blues"), as well as those with Jelly Roll MORTON ("Billy Goat Stomp") established him as the most influential jazz drummer of the 1920s. Dodds's drum style was rooted in the New Orleans parade tradition, which combined strict timekeeping with explosive displays of virtuosity, often animated by African-derived polyrhythms. Dodds, who specialized in a variety of rolls and special effects grounded in a solid dance beat ["Drum Improvisation 1," "Drum Improvisation 2," (1946)], proved enormously influential to white jazz musicians in the 1920s and 1930s. During the "Dixieland" revival of the 1940s, he returned to his hometown to record with Bunk Johnson ("In Gloryland," 1945), and later toured with Sidney BECHET. He also toured Europe with Mezz Mezzrow in 1948. Health problems forced Dodds to curtail his musical activities starting in 1949, and in 1957 he stopped performing entirely. He died two years later in Chicago.

REFERENCES

GARA, LARRY. *The Baby Dodds Story*. Los Angeles, 1959.

WILLIAMS, MARTIN. *Jazz Masters of New Orleans*. 1967. Revised. New York, 1978.

ANTHONY BROWN

Dodge Revolutionary Union Movement. *See* League of Revolutionary Black Workers.

Dodson, Owen Vincent (November 28, 1914–June 2, 1983), educator and writer. Born in Brooklyn, N.Y., Owen Dodson received his B.A. from Bates College in Lewiston, Maine, in 1936 and an M.F.A. from Yale University in 1939. He began his career in education as drama director at Spelman College, where he worked from 1938 until 1941. In this early phase of his career he also served as an instructor and director of drama at Atlanta University (1938–1942) and at the Hampton Institute in Virginia (1941–1942). His teaching career was briefly interrupted by his enlistment in the Navy (1942–1943). In 1947, Dodson joined the faculty at Howard University. In 1949, he led the Howard University Players on what was both the first State Department–sponsored European tour by a black theater company and the first European tour of any American college theater group; their success influenced Congress to establish a nationally funded cultural exchange program. Dodson directed, produced, and taught drama at Howard for the next twenty-three years, eventually becoming chairman of its drama department (1960–1969). He also lectured at Vassar and Kenyon colleges and at Cornell University, and served as poet-in-residence at the University of Arizona from 1969 to 1970. After his retirement, he returned to New York City, where he died of a heart attack at age sixty-eight.

Dodson was a versatile and prolific writer whose works reflect his acute concern for the problems of racism and injustice, while at the same time evincing a belief in the basic goodness of humanity and in the redemptive power of love. His poetry, in which he characteristically adapts traditional European forms such as the sonnet to the rhythms of black street language, was published in three volumes: *Powerful Long Ladder* (1946), *The Confession Stone* (1968; revised as *The Confession Stone: Song Cycles*, 1970) and *The Harlem Book of the Dead* (1978, with James VanDerZee and Camille Billops). He contributed verse, short stories, and nonfiction to numerous anthologies and periodicals. He also wrote novels, including the semiautobiographical *Boy at the Window* (1951; published in paperback as *When Trees Were Green*, 1967) and its sequel, *Come Home Early, Child* (1977). Together with composer Mark Fax he wrote two operas, *A Christmas Miracle* (1955) and *Till Victory Is Won* (1967).

Dodson also wrote many plays, including the popular *Divine Comedy* (1938), a portrait of religious chicanery first produced at Yale University, and *New World A-Coming: An Original Pageant of Hope* (1944), a work celebrating the black American contribution to the war effort, first produced at Madison Square Garden. His other plays include *The Shining Town* (1937), *The Garden of Time* (1939), *Bayou Legend* (1946), and *The Third Fourth of July* (1946, with Countee Cullen).

Dodson's work brought him a number of awards, including a General Education Board fellowship (1937), a Rosenwald fellowship (1945), a Guggenheim fellowship (1953), a *Paris Review* prize for his short story "The Summer Fire" (1956), an honorary doctorate from Bates College (1967), and a Rockefeller Foundation fellowship (1968).

REFERENCES

HARDY, SALLY W., ed. *Remembering Owen Dodson*. New York, 1984.

HATCH, JAMES V., DOUGLAS A. M. WARD, and JOE WEIXLMANN. "The Rungs of a Powerful Long Ladder: An Owen Dodson Bibliography." *Black American Literature Forum* 14 (1980): 60–68.

METZGER, LINDA, ed. *Black Writers: A Selection of Sketches from Contemporary Authors*. Detroit, 1989.

ALEXIS WALKER

Dolphy, Eric Allan (June 20, 1928–June 29, 1964), jazz musician. Born in Los Angeles, Eric Dolphy began his studies on the clarinet, and later learned alto saxophone. By the time he graduated from junior high school, he was playing saxophone professionally in Los Angeles. From 1948 to 1950 he was an alto saxophonist in Roy Porter's bebop-oriented big band. He attended Los Angeles City College (1948–1950), served two years in the Army (1950–1952), and, after his discharge, continued his studies at the U. S. Naval School of Music in 1952.

Beginning in 1953, Dolphy performed with various groups, including Chico Hamilton (1958). In 1959, he moved to New York, and joined the band of Charles MINGUS (1959–1960), with whom he would continue to play, intermittently, for the rest of his life. An extremely versatile musician, Dolphy became an integral part of New York's jazz scene, recording with John COLTRANE, Ornette COLEMAN, John LEWIS, and George Russell, among others. He was leading his own small combo, in West Berlin, when he died suddenly of a complication from diabetes on June 29, 1964.

Dolphy's short, brilliant career coincided with the development of avant-garde jazz in New York City in the early 1960s. Equally adept on a number of instruments, Dolphy helped establish the flute and bass clarinet as standard jazz instruments. His playing was highly virtuosic, and characterized by gnarled and knotted angular rhythms performed with extraordinary intensity. His best-known recordings include *Outward Bound* (1960) and *Out to Lunch* (1964).

REFERENCE

SIMOSKO, V., and B. TEPPERMAN. *Eric Dolphy: A Musical Biography and Discography*. Washington, D.C., 1974.

EDDIE S. MEADOWS

Domingo, Wilfred Adolphus (1889–February 14, 1968), editor, activist. Born in Kingston, Jamaica, W. A. Domingo was the youngest son of a Jamaican mother and a Spanish father. He was orphaned soon after birth, and he and his siblings were raised by their maternal uncle. Domingo attended Kingston Board School, then took a job as a tailor in Kingston. He wrote newspaper articles and joined the National Club in lobbying for home rule for Jamaica, becoming the club's second assistant secretary. There Domingo met and became close with the first assistant secretary, Marcus GARVEY. In 1912, Domingo came to the United States, settling in Boston, where he intended to enroll in medical school. In 1913, Domingo left Boston and moved to New York, where he began working for Jamaican freedom. In 1917, he formed the British Jamaican Benevolent Association, and he became associated with the SOCIALIST PARTY shortly thereafter.

In 1918, Garvey asked Domingo, who had been peripherally involved in the activities of Garvey's Universal Negro Improvement Association (UNIA), to find him a publisher for a UNIA newspaper. Domingo obliged, and wrote two lead editorials for the first issue of the new *Negro World*. Soon after, Garvey hired him as editor of the journal. Domingo was not passionate about Garvey's back-to-Africa ideology, although he later claimed to have invented the newspaper's tag line, "Africa's Redemption." Instead, he turned the paper into a forum for a discussion of socialist ideas. Domingo warned white labor leaders

to unite with black workers, or become a tool of strikebreaking capitalists. In the summer of 1919, Garvey, displeased, charged Domingo before the UNIA Executive Committee with writing editorials that diverged from the group's program. Domingo resigned, and soon became a bitter critic of Garvey. He began a short-lived socialist paper, the *Emancipator*. After it failed, he began working for A. Philip Randolph's black socialist newspaper, the *Messenger*. In 1923, Domingo broke with Randolph, whom he accused of anti–West Indian prejudice. He joined Cyril Briggs's newspaper, the *Crusader*, and became active in the African Blood Brotherhood.

After 1923, Domingo returned to Jamaica, where he spent several years working as a food importer. In later years, he became active in the Jamaican independence movement, helping to found the Jamaica Progressive League in 1936, and later joining the People's National Party (PNP). He spent the early 1940s in Jamaica, then returned to New York, where he became an enemy of the PNP. Domingo suffered a paralyzing stroke in 1964, and died four years later.

REFERENCE

HILL, ROBERT A., ed. *The Marcus Garvey and Universal Negro Improvement Association Papers*, Vol. 1, Appendix I. Berkeley, Cal., 1983.

GREG ROBINSON

Domino, Antoine, Jr., "Fats" (February 26, 1928–). Rock-and-roll singer, pianist and songwriter. Born in New Orleans, La., Domino taught himself to play piano by the age of nine; in his teens he had already mastered various popular styles, including the boogie-woogie, blues and ragtime that provided the basic materials for his pioneering work in rhythm and blues and rock. By fourteen, Domino had quit school in order to pursue a career in music; he worked in a factory by day and performed at night in bars, developing the stride-like piano playing that became his trademark. At twenty-one he had become house pianist at the Hideaway Club; there he acquired the nickname "Fats" and met trumpeter and bandleader Dave Bartholomew, with whom he recorded "The Fat Man" (1950), a "jump" blues hit that launched Domino's career and introduced many parts of the country to the New Orleans rhythm sound.

Domino's singing and piano playing, backed by Bartholomew's band, established a rhythm-and-blues sound that appealed to both black and white audiences; for twelve years, they turned out more than a dozen Top Ten hits on the Imperial label, including "Ain't That a Shame," "I'm in Love

Fats Domino, with his relaxed singing voice and catchy New Orleans–style piano playing, was one of the first rock-and-roll stars. Among all pop musicians of the 1950s, only Elvis Presley sold more records. (Frank Driggs Collection)

Again," "Blueberry Hill," and "Blue Monday." For a time, Domino and Bartholomew were the most successful songwriting team in pop history. By the mid-1960s, however, their success in creating new music and popularity on the charts faded; Domino worked for a time in Las Vegas and Reno, becoming a fixture on the casino and hotel circuits, and only briefly resumed recording in the late 1960s and early 1970s. Meeting with minimal success, he returned to New Orleans and entered semiretirement. Domino emerged again briefly in the late 1970s and early 80s for several successful tours of Europe. Fats Domino's recordings, which sold over 65 million copies, were an important early example of the "crossover" appeal of rhythm and blues with white audiences.

ROBERT W. STEPHENS

Dorsey, Thomas Andrew "Georgia Tom"
(July 1, 1899–January 23, 1993), gospel composer. Born in Villa Rica, Ga., the oldest of three children of Rev. Thomas Madison and Etta Plant Dorsey, Thomas Dorsey obtained his education in the public schools of Villa Rica and Atlanta. His first piano teacher was his mother, from whom he learned enough by age eight to play the pump organ for church services at which his father preached. In his early teens he began piano lessons, four times weekly,

with a Mrs. Graves, from whom he learned not only piano technique and musical reading but enough music theory to be able to jot down musical ideas he was already creating. He was encouraged in this aspect of musicianship by the band members who accompanied acts at the 81 Theater, a vaudeville house on Atlanta's Decatur Street, where, since age eleven, he had worked selling soda pop. It was in this capacity that, at age thirteen, he met the legendary Ma RAINEY. Other performers he met who were to influence him were pianists Eddie Heywood and Ed Butler, and the comedy team Butterbeans and Susie. Shortly thereafter, Dorsey began playing the house-party circuit in Atlanta.

Desiring a better musical education, Dorsey migrated to Gary, Ind., in 1916, where he worked in a steel mill and played piano in various jazz bands. After returning to Atlanta for the winters of 1917 and 1918, he settled permanently in Chicago in 1919, where he studied for a short while at the Chicago Musical College. From 1923 until 1924, he served as pianist and arranger for Les Hite's Whispering Serenaders. During this time he composed "Riverside Blues" (1923), recorded by King OLIVER's Creole Jazz Band. Around 1924, Dorsey organized his own group, the Wildcats Jazz Band, at the request of J. Mayo ("Ink") Williams of Paramount Records. This group accompanied Ma Rainey on recordings and on tour. While he accompanied Rainey irregularly for a number of years, Dorsey also began a successful association with Tampa Red (born Hudson Whittaker) in 1925. This duo produced the 1928 hit "Tight Like That." It was during this time that Dorsey became known as "Georgia Tom" and "Barrelhouse Tom," because of the raunchy nature of the songs he played.

Although he continued to play in and conduct jazz and blues bands throughout the 1920s, Dorsey's interest was steadily growing toward the new gospel music created by the southern pentecostal churches, and a prominent form of music in Chicago at this time (see GOSPEL MUSIC).

Dorsey then wrote his first gospel song, "If I Don't Get There," which was published in the National Baptist Convention's *Gospel Pearls*. Despite this new conviction, Dorsey returned to the blues world until 1928, when he suffered a nervous breakdown. His second conversion to Christianity—he had been converted as a child in Georgia but in the terminology of the African-American church of the era "backslid" when he began to play secular music—occurred in Chicago, at the 1932 annual meeting of the National Baptist Convention, the largest organization of African-American Christians. During the convention, Rev. A. W. Nix of Birmingham, Ala., delivered a stirring gospel rendition of Edwin O. Excell's

"I Do, Don't You?" Not only did Dorsey join the church again, but he decided that he wanted to dedicate his life to writing gospel music.

In 1930 Dorsey renounced secular music and became a full-time gospel musician, composing gospel pieces and peddling "song sheets" throughout Chicago. The response was discouraging and he was often the butt of jokes. Notwithstanding these initial rejections, Dorsey organized one of the first gospel choirs at Chicago's Pilgrim Baptist Church in 1931, where his accompanist was the young Roberta MARTIN, and whose future members included Eugene Smith, leader of the Roberta Martin Singers, and James CLEVELAND, later known as the "Crown Prince of Gospel." In the next year, Dorsey opened the first publishing house for the exclusive sale of gospel music by African-American composers in the country. The same year, along with Sallie MARTIN and others, he organized the National Convention of Gospel Choirs and Choruses, which, along with Cleveland's Gospel Music Workshop of America (organized in 1968), annually draws the largest number of gospel musicians and music lovers in the United States. In addition to Martin, Dorsey was aided in the early gospel movement by composers Theodore R. Frye and Kenneth Morris and singer Willie Mae Ford SMITH.

In 1932, Dorsey and Frye traveled from Chicago to Indianapolis to organize a gospel choir. When Dorsey arrived in Indianapolis, a telegram informed him that his wife had given birth to a child, but had not survived. Dorsey returned to Chicago, only to find that his newly born daughter had died as well. In his grief, he sat alone in a dark room for three days, emerging to write the song that—after "Amazing Grace"—is the second most popular song in African-American Christendom:

> Precious Lord, take my hand, lead me on, let me stand.
> I am tired, I am weak, I am worn;
> Through the storm, through the night, lead me on to the light.
> Take my hand, precious Lord, lead me on.

Dorsey taught this song to his choir at Pilgrim Baptist, and in less than a year it had moved into the folk category, with congregations singing all three stanzas without the benefit of sheet music. Since then, it has been translated into more than fifty languages, and Dorsey conducted it throughout the world.

Before Thomas A. Dorsey left secular music behind around 1930 to forge the sound of modern gospel music, he was a significant performer of jazz and the blues. During the 1920s, Dorsey had led the band for blues singer Ma Rainey as well as his own ensembles, such as the Wandering Syncopators, as in this 1923 photograph. (AP/Wide World Photos)

"Precious Lord" is not unlike most of Dorsey's compositions, in that the text is that of the poor, disfranchised African-American Christian but also speaks to all people. He has a special penchant for imbuing his songs with catchy phrases, such as "I'm Going to Live the Life I Sing About in My Song," "If We Ever Needed the Lord Before, We Sure Do Need Him Now," and the song written for Mahalia JACKSON, who served as his song demonstrator from 1935 to 1946, "There Will Be Peace in the Valley for Me." His melodies were simple, supported by harmonies that did not detract from the text. Dorsey was so instrumental in the development of gospel music that there was a period during the 1930s and '40s when gospel songs were referred to as "Dorseys." For his contributions he was, early on, dubbed the "Father of Gospel."

Though only a few of Dorsey's songs helped to initiate new trends in gospel music, he is nevertheless remembered as the most important person in gospel music to date. He organized gospel music's first chorus and its first annual national convention, founded its first publishing house, established the gospel-music concert tradition, and in recognition of this, he was celebrated in the 1982 documentary *Say Amen, Somebody.*

REFERENCES

BOYER, HORACE CLARENCE. "Analysis of His Contributions: Thomas A. Dorsey, 'Father of Gospel Music.'" *Black World* 23 (1974): 20.

HEILBUT, ANTHONY. *The Gospel Sound: Good News and Bad Times.* 1971. Reprint. New York, 1985.

HORACE CLARENCE BOYER

Douglas, Aaron (May 26, 1899–February 24, 1979), painter and educator. Born in Topeka, Kans., Aaron Douglas graduated from Topeka High School in 1917, then earned his B.F.A. from the University of Nebraska in 1922. While he taught art at Lincoln High School in Kansas City, Mo. (1923–1925), his social circle included future civil rights leader Roy WILKINS, future classical music composer William Levi DAWSON, and Ethel Ray (Nance), who became Charles S. JOHNSON's assistant at OPPORTUNITY magazine. Ray and Johnson persuaded Douglas to postpone study in France to work in New York. Douglas soon became one of the leading artists of the NEW NEGRO movement, developing a geometric, monochromatic style of depicting African Americans in dynamic silhouettes by synthesizing formal and symbolic elements of West African sculpture with European-American traditions and modern design into a hard-edged, Art Deco–like style.

In 1925, Douglas earned three important distinctions that launched his career—first prize for a front cover illustration of *Opportunity,* first prize in drawing (for *The African Chieftain*) from CRISIS magazine, and a commission to illustrate Alain LOCKE's anthology *The New Negro.* The following year, Douglas married his high school classmate, educator Alta Sawyer, and illustrated *The Emperor Jones* and the short-lived magazine of African-American art and literature *Fire!!* In 1927, he illustrated *Plays of Negro Life,* edited by Locke and Montgomery Gregory, and *God's Trombones: Seven Sermons in Negro Verse* by James Weldon JOHNSON. Six works in the latter book, along with a portrait, were exhibited at the Harmon Foundation in 1928. Over the next decade, Douglas would illustrate books by Charles S. Johnson, Claude MCKAY, Paul Morand, and Andre Salmon, as well as numerous magazine covers.

In the late 1920s, Douglas studied privately with Fritz Winold Reiss, a German-American artist whose modernist work Douglas had admired in the New Negro issue of *Survey Graphic* (edited by Locke in March 1925). Reiss and Locke encouraged Douglas to look to African art for inspiration and develop his own racially representative work. Through their influence, Douglas received a one-year scholarship (1928–1929) to the Barnes Foundation in Merion, Pa., where he studied both African and modern European art.

In 1930, Douglas painted heroic murals of African-American culture and history in the library at Fisk University in Nashville, the Sherman Hotel in Chicago, and Bennett College in Greensboro, N.C. In 1931 he went to Paris for one year to study independently and with Charles Despiau and Othon Friesz at the Académie Scandinave. While Douglas worked diligently, only one piece from his time abroad is known: *Forge Foundry,* a black-and-white illustration published in the French journal *Revue du monde noir* (1931).

In the 1930s, Douglas based himself in New York as an arts leader and muralist. The year after he was elected president of the Harlem Artists' Guild (1935), he addressed the First American Artists Congress. With sponsorship from New Deal art programs and various grants, Douglas completed several murals, most notably *Aspects of Negro Life,* at the 135th Street Harlem Branch of the New York Public Library (1934); those for the Hall of Negro Life exhibited at the Texas Centennial Exposition (1936); and *Education of the Colored Man,* at the Atlanta City Housing Project (1938). In 1938, Douglas received a travel fellowship to the American South and Haiti from the Julius Rosenwald Fund. He exhibited his paintings of Haitian life at the American Contemporary Art Gallery in New York the following year.

Untitled work from *The New Negro* (1925). The distinctive style of Aaron Douglas, embracing both African art and twentieth-century modernism, was an inspiration to many in the Harlem Renaissance. (Prints and Photographs Division, Library of Congress)

In 1939, Douglas began teaching art at FISK UNIVERSITY, where he served as professor and chair of the Department of Art Education for nearly three decades. During this period, he often divided his time between Nashville and New York, where he completed his M.A. in Art Education at Columbia University Teachers College in 1944 (his fraternal affiliations included Sigma Pi Phi and Kappa Alpha Psi) and received a Carnegie teaching grant in 1951. From the 1930s until the '50s, the Douglases frequently entertained artists and writers at their home at 409 Edgecombe Avenue, known as "the White House of Harlem," because the building's residents included prominent intellectuals and civil rights leaders. Douglas painted many of their portraits, in addition to landscapes.

As founder of the Carl Van Vechten Gallery (1949) at Fisk, Douglas acquired a major gift from Georgia O'Keefe, the Alfred Steiglitz Collection (1949), as well as an important series of portraits of African-Americans, the Winold Reiss Collection (1952), and he brought numerous artists to the university for lec-

tures and exhibitions. Noted for these achievements and his art, Douglas was honored by President John F. Kennedy at a White House reception commemorating the centennial of the Emancipation Proclamation in 1963. In 1972 he became a fellow of the Black Academy of Arts and received its outstanding achievement award. The following year, Fisk University awarded Douglas an honorary degree of Doctor of Fine Arts. After retiring as professor emeritus in 1966, Douglas lectured widely and continued to paint until his death in 1979.

Douglas's work has appeared in many major American museums and galleries and in university and community center exhibitions. Additional solo exhibitions were held at D'Caz-Delbo Gallery (1933); University of Nebraska, Lincoln (1941); People's Art Center, St. Louis (1947); Chabot Gallery, Los Angeles (1948); Riley Art Galleries, New York (1955); University of California, Berkeley (1964); and Mulvane Art Center, Topeka (1970).

REFERENCES

DRISKELL, DAVID, DAVID LEVERING LEWIS, and DEBORAH WILLIS RYAN. *Harlem Renaissance: Art of Black America*. New York, 1987.

HUGGINS, NATHAN IRVIN. *Harlem Renaissance*. New York, 1971.

IGOE, LYNN MOODY, with James Igoe. *250 Years of Afro-American Art: An Annotated Bibliography*. New York, 1981.

LEWIS, DAVID LEVERING. *When Harlem Was in Vogue*. New York, 1979.

THERESA LEININGER-MILLER
LINDA NIEMAN

Douglas, Lizzie "Kid."　*See* Memphis Minnie.

Douglass, Anna Murray (c. 1813–August 4, 1882), abolitionist. Anna Murray was born near Denton in eastern Maryland, most likely in 1813. Her parents had been manumitted a month before her birth, making her the first person in her family to be born free. At the age of seventeen she made her way to Baltimore, where at some point in the mid-1830s she met her husband, the future abolitionist Frederick DOUGLASS, then known as Frederick Bailey. After his escape from slavery in 1838, Anna Murray made her way north, and Frederick and Anna were married in New York City shortly thereafter. In New Bedford, Mass., where they then moved, the couple adopted the name Douglass.

Anna Murray Douglass was an activist in her own right. Although she could read and write only a little, she nonetheless participated fully in the circle of Massachusetts reformers in the 1840s that included Wendell Phillips and William Lloyd GARRISON. She met weekly with the antislavery women who mounted the annual Anti-Slavery Fair in Boston's Faneuil Hall. In 1847 the Douglass family moved to Rochester, N.Y., where she continued her abolitionist activities.

This activism was undertaken in addition to the labor necessary to support herself and her five children, especially when her husband traveled to Europe. She worked as a laundress and shoe binder, and managed to set aside part of her earnings for the antislavery cause.

In the words of one of her daughters, the heroism of Frederick Douglass "was a story made possible by the unswerving loyalty of Anna Murray." During their forty-four years of marriage, Anna Murray Douglass supported her famous husband financially and raised their children during his many extended absences. In contrast to the public life of her husband, she was primarily devoted to domestic tasks. Although the couple remained married, they drifted apart in their later years. In 1872 Anna Douglass, her husband, and her family moved to Washington, D.C., where she lived until her death.

REFERENCES

McFEELY, WILLIAM. *Frederick Douglass*. New York, 1992.

SPRAGUE, ROSETTA DOUGLASS. "Anna Murray Douglass—My Mother as I Recall Her." *Journal of Negro History* 8 (1923): 93–101.

YEE, SHIRLEY J. *Black Women Abolitionists: A Study in Activism, 1828–1860*. Knoxville, Tenn., 1992.

MARTHA E. HODES

Anna Murray Douglass, a freeborn Maryland native, helped her future husband, Frederick Douglass, escape slavery in 1838. Married later that year, Anna Douglass was a quiet woman who assumed much of the responsibility for raising the couple's five children. (Prints and Photographs Division, Library of Congress)

Douglass, Frederick (February 1818–February 20, 1895), abolitionist, journalist, orator, and social reformer. Born Frederick Augustus Washington Bailey to Harriet Bailey, a slave, and an unacknowledged father (perhaps his master Aaron Anthony) in Tuckahoe, Md., Frederick Douglass—he assumed this name in 1838 when he escaped north to freedom—soon became the most famous African American of the nineteenth century. Separated from his family while young, he was a personal slave to several whites during his formative years. Consequently, he early learned self-reliance and began honing the arts of survival. At the same time, he found a sense of belonging through his relationships with various families and individuals, white and black, who liked and encouraged the bright and precocious youth. Ultimately, the lure of freedom and equality proved irresistible and propelled him on an extraordinary journey of both individual achievement and service to his people and his nation.

Taken in 1826 to Baltimore—where, as an urban slave, he could expand his horizons greatly—he taught himself how to read and write with the witting and unwitting assistance of many around him. Similarly, this more open urban environment, with its large and expanding free African-American population, further whetted his desire to learn as much as possible about freedom, including runaway slaves and the abolitionist movement.

Around the age of thirteen, he converted to Christianity, but over time he became increasingly disillusioned with a religious establishment that compromised with and supported evil and injustice, especially slavery and racial prejudice and discrimination. Also around that age, he purchased his first book, *The Columbian Orator,* which deepened not only his understanding of liberty and equality but also the enormous power of rhetoric, as well as literacy. Indeed, throughout his life he firmly believed in the power of the written and spoken word to capture and to change reality.

As a rapidly maturing eighteen-year-old, developing spiritually and intellectually as well as physically, he revealed an intensifying longing to be free that led him to plan an unsuccessful runaway scheme with several fellow slaves. Several months previously he fought Covey, the "Negro breaker"—one versed in subduing unruly slaves—another sign of the depth of that longing. He later portrayed his triumph over Covey as a turning point in his struggle to become a free man. With the aid of Anna Murray, a free African-American woman in Baltimore with whom he had fallen in love, he escaped to freedom. They moved to New Bedford, Mass. (1838); Lynn, Mass. (1841); Rochester, N.Y. (1847); and Washington, D.C. (1872).

In the North, Douglass found it very hard to make a living as a caulker because of racial discrimination and often had to resort to menial jobs. Anna worked hard as well, creating a comfortable domestic niche for a family that eventually included five children: Rosetta, Lewis Henry, Frederick, Jr., Charles Remond, and Annie. Frederick's speeches within the local black communities brought him to the attention of the mostly white abolitionists allied with William Lloyd Garrison, and in 1841 they asked him to join them as a lecturer. *(See* ABOLITION.*)* An increasingly powerful lecturer and draw for the Garrisonian Massachusetts Anti-Slavery Society, Douglass learned a great deal from his work with such people as Garrison and Wendell Phillips. Most important, he adopted their pacifism and moral suasionist approach to ending slavery and was deeply influenced by their interrelated perfectionism and social reformism. As a good Garrisonian, he argued for disunion and rejected the political approach to ending slavery as a compromise with a proslavery Constitution.

Douglass also began to come into his own as an activist and a thinker. Drawing upon his experiences as a slave, he lambasted slavery and its notorious effects, most notably antiblack prejudice and discrimination in both North and South. As the living embodiment of a small measure of success in the enormous struggle against slavery, he spoke eloquently with uncommon authority. In 1845, his *Narrative of the Life of Frederick Douglass, an American Slave* was published and its huge success, followed by a successful speaking tour of Great Britain, heightened his celebrity immeasurably. Ever conscious of his public persona and his historical image, he carefully crafted both. *My Bondage and My Freedom* (1855) and *Life and Times of Frederick Douglass* (1881; revised 1892), fuller autobiographies, were likewise crucial in this regard.

Seated are Frederick Douglass and his second wife, Helen Pitts Douglass. (Photographs and Prints Division, Schomburg Center for Research in Black Culture, The New York Public Library, Astor, Lenox and Tilden Foundations)

His stirring narrative and equally stirring oratory derived much of their power and authenticity from Douglass's deep-seated engagement with the plethora of issues confronting blacks north and south, free and slave. His strong involvement in the national Negro convention movement, as well as with various state and local black conferences, furthered his impact and by 1850 made him the principal spokesman for his race. His fierce commitment to egalitarianism, freedom, and justice similarly led him to embrace the women's-rights movement, notably women's suffrage, and to become one of the most important male feminists of the nineteenth century. He attended the first Women's Rights Convention, in Seneca Falls, N.Y., in 1848; on the day of his death, February 20, 1895, he had earlier attended a meeting of the National Council of Women.

Shortly after his return from Great Britain in 1847, Douglass embarked upon a distinguished career in journalism. He edited the *North Star* (1847–1851), *Frederick Douglass' Paper* (1851–1860), *Douglass' Monthly* (1859–1863), and, for a time, the *New National Era* (1870–1874). Complementing the other aspects of his varied public voice and extending its reach and influence, Douglass's work as a journalist furthered his use of the printed word as a tool for agitation and change. Stressing self-reliance, hard work, perseverance, education, and morality, Douglass exemplified the embrace by many African Americans of middle-class values and the American success ethic. Likewise, invoking America's revolutionary tradition, he emphasized the imperative of full black liberation within the confines of the American nation. After 1851, when he formally broke with the Garrisonians and accepted political action against slavery as viable and necessary, he became more politically engaged. By the outbreak of the CIVIL WAR, he supported the REPUBLICAN PARTY.

The tumultuous events of the 1850s convinced Douglass, like untold numbers of his compatriots, that war was unavoidable, the Union cause just, and slave emancipation inevitable. He urged his audience, most notably President Abraham Lincoln, to further ennoble the Union cause by accepting black troops into the Union army and treating them fairly. He exhorted his people to support fully the Union cause and to struggle ceaselessly to ensure that Union victory would mean emancipation and the necessary conditions for black progress. His often arduous efforts to recruit black Union troops, who braved strong white hostility and mistreatment, showed him grappling intensely with the central and complex issue of African-American identity. African Americans, he cogently argued, honored their group as well as national heritage and mission through vigorous support of an abolitionist Union cause.

Douglass emerged from the war even more widely known and respected. He continued to urge his nation to deal justly and fairly with his people, even after the nation reneged on its insufficient and short-lived efforts to do so during RECONSTRUCTION. While many blacks questioned his continuing allegiance to the Republican party, Douglass valiantly—albeit unsuccessfully—endeavored to help the party rediscover its humanistic and moral moorings. Appointed to serve as the United States marshal for the District of Columbia (1877–1881), recorder of deeds for the District of Columbia (1881–1886), and chargé d'affaires for Santo Domingo and minister to Haiti (1889–1891), he remained a stalwart Republican.

Over the years, Douglass's status as a comfortable middle-class elder statesman tended on occasion to blind him to the harsh conditions confronting rural, impoverished, and migrant blacks. Still, as in his fiery condemnation of the alarming growth in the number of lynchings of black men in the 1880s and 1890s (often upon the false accusation of an attack on a white woman), it was clear that his commitment to justice never wavered. Likewise, while many women's-rights advocates criticized him for supporting the FIFTEENTH AMENDMENT, which failed to enfranchise women as it enfranchised black men, Douglass contended that the greater urgency of the black male need for the vote and its greater likelihood of passage made support imperative. After its passage, he continued his efforts on behalf of women's rights and sought to heal the rift within the movement.

When Douglass married Helen Pitts, his white secretary, in January 1884, a year and a half after the death of his first wife, they endured much criticism from many blacks and whites, including close family members. Nonetheless, Douglass, the quintessential humanist, steadfastly articulated his commitment to a composite American nationality, transcending race, as an integral component of his vision of a democratic and egalitarian country. When others criticized him for a lack of race spirit, Douglass, refusing to be imprisoned within a racialist universe, claimed ultimate allegiance to the human race.

Yet he also fully understood and vividly personified his people's struggle from slavery to freedom, from obscurity and poverty to recognition and respectability. His enduring legacy to his people and all Americans is best captured in his lifelong and profound dedication to the imperative of agitation and concerted action: "If there is no struggle," he declared, "there is no progress."

REFERENCES

ANDREWS, WILLIAM L., ed. *Critical Essays on Frederick Douglass.* Boston, 1991.

BLASSINGAME, JOHN W., et. al., eds. *The Frederick Douglass Papers.* New Haven, Conn., 1979–.

BLIGHT, DAVID W. *Frederick Douglass' Civil War: Keeping Faith in Jubilee.* Baton Rouge, La., 1989.

DOUGLASS, FREDERICK. *Life and Times of Frederick Douglass: Written by Himself.* 1892. Reprint. New York, 1962.

———. *The Life and Writings of Frederick Douglass.* 5 vols. New York, 1975.

———. *My Bondage and My Freedom.* 1855. Reprint. New York, 1969.

———. *Narrative of the Life of Frederick Douglass, an American Slave, Written by Himself.* 1845. Reprint. New York, 1968.

MARTIN, WALDO E., JR. "Frederick Douglass: Humanist as Race Leader." In Leon Litwack and August Meier, eds., *Black Leaders of the Nineteenth Century.* Urbana, Ill., 1988, pp. 59–84.

———. *The Mind of Frederick Douglass.* Chapel Hill, N.C., 1984.

MCFEELY, WILLIAM S. *Frederick Douglass.* New York, 1990.

PRESTON, DICKSON J. *Young Frederick Douglass: The Maryland Years.* Baltimore, 1980.

QUARLES, BENJAMIN. *Frederick Douglass.* 1948. Reprint. New York, 1968.

SUNDQUIST, ERIC J., ed. *Frederick Douglass: New Literary and Historical Essays.* New York, 1990.

WALDO E. MARTIN, JR.

Douglass, Sarah Mapps (1806–1882), educator. Sarah Mapps Douglass was born in Philadelphia, the daughter of Robert and Grace Bustill Douglass. She received her education from private tutors. She worked for a brief period in New York, and then returned to Philadelphia to establish a school for young African-American women. In the 1830s, she contributed to the *Liberator* under the pseudonyms "Sophonisba" and "Zillah," and later wrote articles for the *Anglo-African Magazine*. Douglass accepted a position with the Quaker-sponsored Institute for Colored Youth in 1853, and continued her teaching career until 1877. She expanded the traditional studies for young women by lecturing on physiology and hygiene, and held evening classes for adults.

Douglass endured the restrictions and humiliations experienced by black women in antebellum Philadelphia. She attended Quaker meetings with her mother until completely alienated by white religious hypocrisy and the indignity of the "negro pew." She witnessed the mob violence against Philadelphia blacks in 1838. Her sensitive and revealing insights into the personal effects of racial prejudice are recorded in correspondence to her lifelong friends Angelina GRIMKÉ and Sarah GRIMKÉ. She married William Douglass, an Episcopal clergyman, in 1855.

She was involved in several women's reform organizations, including the Philadelphia Female Literary Society and the Philadelphia Women's Anti-Slavery Society. As an officer of the Women's Association, she helped organize fairs to support the black press. After the Civil War, she served as vice president of the Pennsylvania women's auxiliary of the American Freedmen's Aid Commission.

REFERENCES

RIPLEY, C. PETER, et al., eds. *The Black Abolitionist Papers, Volume 3: The United States, 1830–1846.* Chapel Hill, N.C., 1991.
STERLING, DOROTHY, ed. *We Are Your Sisters.* New York, 1984.

MICHAEL F. HEMBREE

Dove, Rita (August 28, 1952–), poet. Rita Dove was born in Akron, Ohio. She graduated *summa cum laude* from Miami University in Oxford, Ohio in 1973, then spent the following year in Tubingen, Germany, as a Fulbright scholar. In 1975 she enrolled in the Writers' Workshop at the University of Iowa, where she received her Master's in Fine Arts degree two years later. In 1981 Dove joined the English Department at Arizona State University, where she continued to teach creative writing until 1989. In that year she accepted a position at the University of Virginia, which named her Commonwealth Professor of English in 1992.

Dove's first volume of poems, *Yellow House on the Corner,* was published in 1980. It was followed in 1983 by *Museum,* which displays a more conscious awareness of the conventions of artistic and historical practice. Three years later, Dove published *Thomas and Beulah* (1986), two versions of the story of two ordinary African Americans. The volume, which loosely narrates the lives of Dove's grandparents, was awarded the Pulitzer Prize in Poetry in 1957. *Thomas and Beulah* is a turning point in Dove's career for more reasons than its award-winning status. Not coincidentally, its narrative style emerges just after Dove's first published foray into fiction, *First Sunday* (1985), a collection of stories. Dove had also published one novel, *Through the Ivory Gate* (1992), the story of a black woman whose work as a puppeteer evokes painful childhood memories of disturbing cultural significance. What *First Sunday* and *Through the Ivory Gate* may lack in believable dialogue and depth of characterization is made up for in the echoes of *Grace Notes* (1989). In these poems, each moment is filled by the persistent ringing of carefully culled metaphor.

More public attention has fallen on Dove's career than on that of any other contemporary African American poet. Recognized for her virtuoso technical ability, Dove represents a generation of poets trained in university writers' workshops who are sometimes chastised for their formal competence at the expense of emotional depth. Dove has distinguished herself in her capacity to filter complex historical and personal information through precise selections of poetic form. In this, she is most closely

Rita Dove, winner of the Pulitzer Prize for poetry, 1987. (AP/Wide World Photos)

allied to black poets such as Gwendolyn BROOKS, Michael S. Harper, and Robert HAYDEN. Her unusual range of subject matter, thematically and geographically, has earned her a reputation as as black writer unafraid to set African-American culture within a global context. Dove's gifts as a poet were most fully acknowledged in 1993 when she was appointed Poet Laureate of the United States, the first black writer and the youngest poet ever to have been so honored.

REFERENCES

RAMPERSAD, ARNOLD. "The Poems of Rita Dove." *Callaloo* 9, no. 1 (Winter 1986): 52–60.

TALEB-KHYAR, MOHAMED B. "An Interview with Maryse Condé and Rita Dove." *Callaloo* 14.2 (Spring 1991): 347–366.

GINA DENT

Dove, Ulysses (January 17, 1947?–) modern dancer and choreographer. Born in Columbia, S.C., the eldest of three children, Ulysses Dove began dance study with Carolyn Tate while a premedical student at Howard University. He transferred to the University of Wisconsin to study with Xenia Chlistowa of the Kirov Ballet, and in 1970 he graduated from Bennington College with a degree in dance. Upon moving to New York, Dove joined the Merce Cunningham company and also performed with Mary Anthony, Pearl Lang, and Anna Sokolow. In 1973 he joined the Alvin AILEY American Dance Theater, where he quickly rose to the rank of principal dancer acclaimed for his commanding presence, bright clarity of movement, and truthful dramatic intensity. Dove turned to choreography at Ailey's urging, and created the 1980 solo "Inside" for Judith JAMISON. He left the Ailey company that year to begin a significant freelance career choreographing dances for the Basel Ballet, Swedish Cullberg Ballet, Dutch National Ballet, London Festival Ballet, American Ballet Theater, New York City Ballet, and Groupe de Recherche Choreographique de l'Opéra de Paris where he spent three years as assistant director. Several Dove ballets have found their definitive, punchy interpretations in performances by the Ailey company, including "Night Shade" (1982) "Bad Blood" (1984), "Vespers" (1986), and "Episodes" (1987). Dove's choreography has been marked by its relentless speed, violent force, and daring eroticism.

REFERENCES

LEWIS, JULINDA. "Inside: A Dance." *Dance Scope* 14, no. 3 (1980).

SUPREE, BURT. "Ulysses Dove: Beginning Again, Again." *Village Voice,* July 17, 1984.

THOMAS F. DEFRANTZ

Dozens, The.   The dozens—also referred to as playing the dozens, sounding, Joning, or woofing—is a verbal game of insult and boasting involving at least two participants and an audience. The dozens are played by males and females across all age groups. Insults can be rhymed or unrhymed, although adult versions rely less on rhyme and more on improvisation. Audience participation is integral, since observers issue the verbal praise that regulates the contest to either a peaceful or violent resolution.

The dozens can be "clean" or "dirty." Performers of the clean or ordinary dozens insult intelligence, achievements, or appearance. For example, "Your lips are so big, they call them soup coolers." Performers of the dirty dozens use obscene language to boast of sexual conquests, frequently of the contender's family members. For example, "I fucked your mother between two cans. Up jumped a baby and hollered, 'Superman' " (quoted in Abrahams 1990, p. 301). The retort "Your mama!" is considered a shorthand form of the dirty dozens.

Early researchers pinned Freudian explanations for the dozens to their perceptions of a dysfunctional community. These patterned insults were interpreted as release valves for a racially repressed group (Dollard 1990) or strategies for African-American males to build masculine identities within a matriarchal society (Abrahams 1990). Later research targeted functional values, citing the dozens's role in promoting community norms and teaching verbal strategies for resolving actual conflicts (Garner 1983).

Origins are uncertain; however, analogs include the verbal duels or "joking relationships" of various African ethnic groups and the derisive exchanges in West Indian calypso and African-American RAP music. Before scholarly attention was accorded them, the dozens were recorded by BLUES performers like Memphis Minnie McCoy, Sweet Peas Spivey, and Lonnie Johnson. The consensus of researchers and performers is that the dozens are entertaining exercises that display cultural competency. Along with other speech acts like preaching, signifying, and rapping, the dozens demonstrate the high value placed on verbal skills across the African DIASPORA.

REFERENCES

ABRAHAMS, ROGER D. "Playing the Dozens." In Alan Dundes, ed. *Mother Wit from the Laughing Barrel.*

1990. Reprinted from *Journal of American Folklore* 75 (1962): 209–220.

DOLLARD, JOHN. "The Dozens: Dialect of Insult." In Alan Dundes, ed. *Mother Wit from the Laughing Barrel.* 1990. Reprinted from *American Imago* 1 (1939): 3–25.

GARNER, THURMON. "Playing the Dozens: Folklore as Strategies for Living." *Quarterly Journal of Speech* 69 (1983): 47–57.

CASSANDRA A. STANCIL

Drake, St. Clair (January 2, 1911–June 14, 1990), sociologist. St. Clair Drake was born in Suffolk, Va., where his father was a Baptist pastor in small rural parishes. Although Drake knew his father only during his first thirteen years, the elder Drake had a decisive influence on his son's later development. John Gibbs St. Clair Drake had been born in Barbados, but studied for the Baptist ministry in Lynchberg, Va. During World War I, Reverend Drake followed his congregation to Pittsburgh, where many had migrated to work in the steel mills.

In Pittsburgh, the family lived in a "middle class" house, with access to a well-stocked library. There Drake formed his habit of wide reading on many subjects. He attended a school where he was the only African-American child, and listened, fascinated, to discussions of religion and race between his father and other preachers.

His parents were divorced in 1924, and Drake accompanied his mother back to Virginia. He attended Booker T. Washington High School in Staunton, Va., where he had his first encounters with southern segregation.

From 1927 through 1931, Drake attended Hampton Institute, in Virginia, where he was an outstanding student. Central to his subsequent career was the influence of a young professor, W. Allison DAVIS, who introduced him to ANTHROPOLOGY. After graduating, Drake taught high school in rural Virginia, traveling to Philadelphia every summer and investing his small earnings in a few books on anthropology. During those summers, he worked and studied with the American Friends Service Committee, a Quaker organization.

In summer 1931, he demonstrated the quiet courage that remained characteristic of him. Some of the Friends initiated a "peace caravan," and Drake and his friend, Enoch Waters, traveled with it through the South, attempting to win support for disarmament and international cooperation. Remarkably, the trek did not terminate in disaster.

In 1935, while still teaching in Virginia, Drake became a member of a research team that was making a social survey of a Mississippi town. Davis had questioned whether the ideas of the white anthropologist, W. Lloyd Warner, concerning class and caste, were applicable to blacks and whites in the South. The outcome was Drake's earliest published research, which was incorporated into Davis's *Deep South.* Working with senior anthropologists, Drake conducted much of the research and prepared the manuscript for publication. After *Deep South,* Drake's closeness to those whom he studied caused him always to describe himself as a "participant-observer."

In 1937 Drake entered the University of Chicago on a Rosenwald Fellowship for further studies in anthropology. Intermittently, he continued to study there over the next fifteen years. In 1942 he married Elizabeth Johns, a white sociologist. *Black Metropolis,* his best-known work, appeared in 1945. Coauthored with Horace CAYTON, it is a pathbreaking work of description and analysis of African-American life in Chicago.

In 1946, Drake joined the faculty of the newly established Roosevelt College (later University) in Chicago, where he remained until 1968. This college had been created as a protest against the racially restrictive Central YMCA College, its predecessor.

Drake was increasingly interested in Africa and the African diaspora. His doctoral dissertation for the University of Chicago, "Value Systems, Social Structure, and Race Relations in the British Isles," involved one year of research of the "colored" community of Cardiff, Wales, placing that community into the larger context of Africa and the South Atlantic. During that year in Britain, Drake became a close associate of George Padmore, the West Indian pan-Africanist and advisor to Kwame Nkrumah. After Ghana's independence, from 1958 to 1961, Drake became Professor of Sociology at the University of Ghana, while still holding his professorship at Roosevelt University.

In 1969 he accepted a long-standing invitation to become Professor of Sociology and Anthropology and Director of African and Afro-American Studies at Stanford University in California. The Stanford period was most notable for the publication of the vast and erudite *Black Folk Here and There* (two vols., 1987–1990). Using an enormous array of sources, it presents the thesis that prejudice against blacks is a relatively recent phenomenon, arising first during the Hellenistic period.

REFERENCES

DRAKE, ST. CLAIR. "In the Mirror of Black Scholarship. W. Allison Davis and *Deep South.*" *Harvard Educational Review,* Monograph #2 (1974): 42–54.

———. Autobiographical manuscripts held in the Schomburg Collection, New York Public Library.

FRANK UNTERMYER

Drama. African-American drama draws from at least two sources: the heritage of Africa and that of Europe. On the North American continent, those cultures met, interacted with Native American traditions and a new physical environment, and produced a culture that, while related to both AFRICA and Europe, is nonetheless distinct from both. For the historian of African-American drama, this heritage poses a series of complex questions: What kinds of events count as drama, in that Europeans have come to define drama primarily as a written text, while Africans have placed more value on the communicative capacity of such ephemeral elements as dance, music, and spectacle? If one focuses on written forms, then for whom have black playwrights written? What are the indicators—in terms of content and/or style—that signify the choice of a primarily black, white, or mixed audience? How have dramatists coded or masked their intentions so as to speak to these different audiences simultaneously?

If emphasis is placed on performance rather than upon a written script, then African-American drama begins on the slave ships, when Africans were forced to sing and dance in order to ensure their health and salability and to provide entertainment for white crewmen. SLAVE NARRATIVES and travelers' accounts attest to the fact that plantation owners encouraged their property to perform because they thought that occasional merry-making increased productivity and lessened the possibility of revolt, and because they seemed genuinely fascinated by the musical idioms, gestures, and the black body itself, all of which were radically different from what they knew of European tradition.

Long before black men were allowed on American stages, a caricature stage Negro made an appearance. The English dramatist Isaac Bickerstaff introduced a lazy, rambunctious West Indian slave in *The Padlock* in 1769; in 1795 the white American James Murdoch followed suit with *The Triumph of Love,* in which a stupid buffoon known as Sambo delighted audiences and initiated a derogatory stereotype that the American public seemingly will not let die. To counter this representation with spectacles more pleasing to "ladies & gentlemen of color," a free black man named Mr. Brown (first name unknown) opened the African Grove Theatre in lower Manhattan in New York City in 1821. This first, professional black theater company mounted productions of Shakespeare,

dance and pantomime interludes, and *King Shotaway* (1823), thought to be the first play written and performed by African Americans. Though no script remains today, records indicate that it concerned a slave insurrection in the Caribbean. Produced within a year of the Denmark Vesey slave insurrection in Virginia, the play roused the ire of white spectators to the extent that a group of rowdies intent on "wanton mischief" destroyed the theatre building and forced the company's closure in 1823. With its demise, Ira ALDRIDGE, who had been inspired to join the group after seeing the West Indian actor James Hewlett in *Richard III,* left for Europe where he eventually won gold medals from the Prussian and Austrian heads of state for his superior artistry in Shakespearean tragedies as well as in popular comedies. Sadly, Aldridge became the first of a long line of African-American expatriate artists who found greater acceptance abroad than at home.

The Sambo stereotype would solidify in the 1840s into the minstrel show. According to conventional theater history, minstrelsy began in 1828 when a young white performer named Thomas D. Rice observed an old, deformed Negro singing and dancing. He is said to have borrowed the man's entire performance (including his clothing), thereby initiating what would become an extremely popular form of entertainment—and a pattern of exploitation repeated by many other white performers who reaped great profit from their imitations of black art. More recent scholarship, however, argues that minstrelsy originated not with Rice and his colleagues who claimed that they were accurately depicting real African-American customs, but with black people themselves. In gathering to sing and dance, enact stories, and mock the cultured pretensions of their masters, slaves were creating a form in which improvisation and ecstatic response based upon the interactions of those assembled were more important than a fixed or written text wherein all elements are related to each other by an inviolable logic that does not give any space to the unplanned or unexplained. They were pioneering a form in which language was treasured for its power to stimulate the imagination and emotions. Given slave conditions, they were projecting a metaphysical stance and style that enabled them to survive with their intelligence, humor, and dignity relatively intact. But in performing for white observers, these slaves masked their behavior so that the owners could interpret their efforts as black incompetence rather than as a critique of what appeared to the slaves as white ridiculousness. Thus, white minstrel performers were offering white audiences a parody of black behavior that was, unbeknownst to them, already a parody of white customs. By the 1860s when black men were allowed to perform onstage, audiences had grown so accustomed to the black-face image that African Americans had to black up—adding yet another layer of parody.

Because of its topicality, improvised quality, and general construction as entertainment aimed at the masses, the minstrel show is usually not considered drama. Yet, it was particularly significant for what would follow, because any playwright wishing to represent African Americans onstage would have to confront the enduring legacy of minstrelsy's grinning darky. Furthermore, it signaled that performance modes rooted in African-American culture were likely to be characterized by masking, evocative language, improvisation grounded in a mastery of technique, episodic structure shaped as much by performer-audience interactions as by logic, as well as by ecstasy, and an ethical/aesthetic stance that seeks to affirm the humane even while it holds opposites in balanced tension.

Masking is at the core of *The Escape; or a Leap for Freedom* by William Wells BROWN, who is generally considered the first African American to have a play published. First read from Northern, abolitionist platforms in 1857 by Brown, who was a successful fugitive, this text appears double-voiced, offering contradictory representations to audience members. Undoubtedly, abolitionist attendees at a reading agreed with the representation of slave owners as exploitative and religiously hypocritical, and they sympathized with the mulatto couple who, in fine diction, vow to seek freedom. They probably also found comic relief in Cato, the stereotypical buffoon who uses nonsensical words, pursues gluttonous pleasures, and apes white mannerisms. But Cato is also a trickster who, when beyond his owners' presence, sings freedom songs (in standard English) and cunningly schemes to turn every situation to his own advantage. Thus, when freedom is almost at hand, he jettisons the grinning mask, helps the runaway couple, and makes his own leap to freedom. In his trickstering, Cato seems to represent an independent spirit that will not be contained by social conventions not of his own making. That position could hardly have been a comforting prospect to those Northerners who, despite their antislavery convictions, believed in black inferiority, and yet, presumably it accurately reflected one attitude found among pre-Civil War blacks. Though the figure of the manipulative buffoon found no place in the theaters patronized by whites, its appearance in one of the earliest black plays identifies masking as an important African-American survival strategy. It is a representation to which African Americans have periodically returned in the musical comedies of Bert WILLIAMS and George Walker (*Abyssinia,* 1906; *Bandanna Land,* 1908), and in dramas as different as Garland Anderson's *Appear-*ances (1925), LeRoi Jones's (Amiri BARAKA's) *The Slave* (1964), Douglas Turner WARD's *Day of Absence* (1965), and Ed BULLINS's *The Gentleman Caller* (1969).

The use of theater as an arena for advancing social change continued in the first decades of the twentieth century, when W. E. B. DU BOIS and others organized the pageant *The Star of Ethiopia.* Seeking to teach history to both blacks and whites, Du Bois and his pageant master Charles Burroughs crafted a series of tableaux linking Egyptian and Yoruba cultures with African-American heroes like Nat Turner and with the quest for freedom. Between 1913 and 1925, this pageant involved approximately three thousand people as performers and was performed in four cities before more than thirty thousand people. Not only did the pageant mobilize often competitive community energies, foster racial pride, and indulge a love of spectacle, but it also provided a model of nonprofessional, socially charged art that others would utilize. Thus, for example, inhabitants of Los Angeles mounted "50 Years of Freedom" in 1915 to combat the negative imagery of D. W. Griffith's film *The Clansman,* and in 1974, people dressed in Ku Klux Klan outfits appeared in San Francisco City Hall chambers as part of an effort to ban the display of regalia of groups advocating hate and genocide.

Angelina Weld GRIMKÉ's *Rachel* is the first twentieth-century full-length play written, performed, and produced by blacks. In this sometimes melodramatic coming-of-age play, a high-spirited young woman rejects marriage and the possibility of motherhood because she fears that future generations will be unable to escape the racism she has personally experienced. The production provoked a storm of controversy when sponsored by the District of Columbia branch of the NATIONAL ASSOCIATION FOR THE ADVANCEMENT OF COLORED PEOPLE (NAACP) in 1916, because it implicitly defied the NAACP philosophy of racial progress led by an educated, black elite, whom Du Bois had termed "the talented tenth." For some, the play reduced art to the level of propaganda. Thus, when Alain LOCKE, one of the leading theoreticians and promoters of the HARLEM RENAISSANCE, and educator Montgomery Gregory founded HOWARD UNIVERSITY's dramatic art department in 1921, they explicitly espoused an aesthetic that privileged technical beauty or art over social concerns. W. E. B. Du Bois took a different position, arguing both in his writings and his organization of the amateur Krigwa Players that the two were not so easily separated. Though short-lived (1925–1927), this drama group was significant because it extended Du Bois's efforts and those of Charles JOHNSON to foster formal cultural production and increase readership through contests and publication in the

NAACP and Urban League magazines, *Crisis* and *Opportunity*. Additionally, the theater's manifesto propounded a standard of evaluation that would be echoed in the militant sixties. Namely, an authentic black theater had to be "about us . . . by us . . . for us . . . and near us."

Also differing with Locke's and Montgomery's emphasis on art divorced from a strong social referent were a number of women who won most of the drama prizes in the *Crisis* and *Opportunity* contests sponsored between 1925 and 1927. Protest against lynching, the lack of birth-control information, and racial discrimination against returning black World War I veterans were some of the issues that women like Alice Dunbar Nelson, Georgia Douglas JOHNSON, Mary Burrill, and May Miller dramatized in plays like *Mine Eyes Have Seen* (1918), *Sunday Morning in the South* (1925), *Safe* (c. 1929), *Blue-Eyed Black Boy* (c. 1930), *Nails and Thorns* (1933), *They That Sit in Darkness* (1919), and *Aftermath* (1919). The antilynching dramas are of particular importance because these women, largely deprived of leadership roles in organizations like the NAACP or the Urban League, seemingly viewed the stage as an arena for advancing an important social agenda. Their work formed a continuum with the direct, antilynching campaigns launched by Ida B. WELLS and other black women active in the Women's Club movement from the turn of the century to the early decades of the twentieth century. Additionally, the antilynch play was a genre in which black women predominated, producing more plays than either black men, white women, or white men.

The GREAT DEPRESSION of the 1930s largely stymied African-American efforts to establish their own theaters. One outlet for theatrical interests was the black church, where folk dramas such as "The Old Ship of Zion," "Heaven Bound," or "In the Rapture" began. Popular throughout the Midwest, East, and South, these dramas took their plots from the Bible. Often a given church would mount the same play over a number of years, so that novelty of story line was not an objective. Rather, dramatic appeal rested in the improvisational space allotted to comic byplay, the artistry with which spirituals were rendered, and the affirmation of a sense of communal solidarity in terms of both religious emotions aroused by the actual event and the creative energies marshalled in preparing costumes, sets, and participants for performance. The aesthetic evident in these folks dramas has parallels with such African traditions as FESTIVALS, for in both instances a community, sharing a set of beliefs and symbols, gathers to enact itself in a performance balancing fixed and fluid elements. That is, the broad parameters of a known plot, familiar spirituals, and performers whose personalities both onstage and offstage are known to the commu-

nity are balanced against fluid performance specifics like the particular placement and rendition of individual songs and narrative episodes, the spontaneous extension of humorous moments, and the emotional dynamic between audience and performers. Through this symbolic practice, a value system is reaffirmed, and the individual is offered an opportunity to experience his or her relationship to a community. Started during the Great Depression, folk dramas like *Heaven Bound, Noah's Ark,* or *The Devil's Funeral* can still be witnessed in some black Baptist and fundamentalist churches.

The government inadvertently became another sponsor for dramatic activity during the Depression. Faced with the collapse of financial markets and the unemployment of millions of Americans, in 1935 the federal government established a relief program known as the Works Progress Administration. It included the Federal Theatre Project (FTP) that during its four years of operation annually employed some thirteen thousand theater workers who performed before approximately 65 million people in theaters, parks, schools, hospitals, and churches. With black units in twenty-two cities, FTP not only offered work to black performers, but also provided many of them with their first formal training in acting, directing, writing, and technical design. Offerings ran the gamut from adaptations of mainstream plays to musicals and dramas addressing contemporary social issues. One of its most popular shows with white and black audiences was a "voodoo" *Macbeth* directed by Orson Welles for the New York Negro unit of FTP. In setting this classic in the tropics, Welles was not only continuing the practice of making Shakespeare accessible to people with varying degrees of formal education, but he was also furthering a theatrical convention in which aspects of African-related culture are used to make mainstream fare more exotic or appealing. "Voodoo" *Macbeth* was soon followed by *Swing Mikado,* a jazz version of the Gilbert and Sullivan light opera; in more recent years, black "remakes" of white standards have resulted in such musicals as *The Wiz* (1975; adapted from *The Wizard of Oz*) and Lee Breuer's *The Gospel at Colonus* (1983; adapted from the fifth-century Greek drama *Oedipus at Colonus*).

In addition to delightful spectacles, the FTP also produced serious drama that questioned the fabric of American life. One such drama, *Big White Fog* by Theodore WARD, is a good example of a play that speaks simultaneously to both white and black audiences. Its realistic style with an immediately recognizable physical setting, operation of cause-and-effect within family relationships, and the hero's movement toward greater self-knowledge locates the text within the mainstream of American dramaturgy. The play's

Playhouse of the Little Negro Theater, Harlem, New York. (Moorland-Spingarn Research Center, Howard University)

cultural specificity resides in it focus on the competing promises of Marcus GARVEY's Back-to-Africa movement, a black capitalism derived from Booker T. WASHINGTON, and socialism within the context of the Depression. Furthermore, its dramatization of intraracial (as well as interracial) color prejudice adds powerful depth, because it captures a reality known painfully well by African Americans, but for the most part hidden from the view of the larger society. Produced first in 1938 by the FTP black unit in Chicago, it aroused a certain degree of controversy because of its seeming support of communism. It was subsequently remounted in New York in 1940 by the short-lived Negro Playwrights Company, which Ward had helped to organize along with other playwrights like Langston HUGHES and Abram Hill (*On Striver's Row*, 1940; *Walk Hard*, 1944). Theodore Ward subsequently found critical praise and limited audience success with his historical drama about Reconstruction, *Our Lan'*. Begun in 1941, it was first produced off-Broadway at the Henry Street Settlement Playhouse in 1946.

Further fueling conservative concern about art and politics was a form of experimental theater known as the Living Newspaper. The format was initially conceived by FTP director Hallie Flanagan, who, like many other white American artists had been impressed by the theatrical experimentation she witnessed in Germany and Russia in the 1920s. The Living Newspaper hired unemployed workers to research current events that were then enacted by large casts in an episodic, panoramic fashion with minimal sets or costumes, in effect producing a kind of theatricalized newsreel. One of the first Living Newspapers to run afoul of its government sponsors was *Ethiopia*, which was closed after an initial preview because of fears that its powerful dramatization of Benito Mussolini's invasion of the African nation of Ethiopia would provoke protests and jeopardize relations with the Italian government, with which the nation was then at peace. Politics also seems to have been the explanation for not producing Abram Hill and John Silvera's script *Liberty Deferred* (1938), which utilized many of the Living Newspaper techniques to dramatize the African-American history. Though FTP fare was very popular with the American public, it nonetheless drew the suspicions of congressmen who regarded this first attempt at subsidized public art as a haven for allegedly anti-American, communist sympathizers. With the economy improving as the nation moved toward active participation in World War II, the Dies Committee killed the Federal Theatre Program in 1939.

Langston Hughes's *Don't You Want to Be Free?* (1937) stands in marked contrast to Ward's *Big White Fog.* While Ward's play had been sponsored by the Federal Theatre, Hughes's was produced by his own leftist-affiliated Harlem Suitcase Theatre. Like much of the agitprop, or agitation-propaganda play writing of the Great Depression, his play utilizes minimal scenery, a small pool of actors to play a large number of roles, and direct address to the audience, designed to encourage them to undertake a specific action. In this case, the text argues for an acceptance of working-class solidarity across racial barriers. The play's distinctiveness is marked by its use of poetry, gospel and blues songs, dance, and vignettes to suggestively chronicle black history from Africa to the United States. The validation of culture that Hughes had begun in experimenting with poetic form in *The Weary Blues* (1926) was here extended to the theater; his use of an episodic structure, knitted together and propelled by the emotional energy of black music as well as by the evocative intensity of language, provided a model that more contemporary playwrights like Amiri Baraka and Ntozake SHANGE would emulate in the 1970s. Hughes's later deployment of religious experience, which found commercial success in *Black Nativity* (1961), helped inaugurate the contemporary gospel drama genre, practiced by such artists as Vinnette CARROLL with *Your Arms Too Short to Box with God* (1975) and Ken Wydro and Vi Higgensen with *Mama I Want to Sing* (1980).

World War II (1939–1945) brought in its wake increased militancy at home and abroad, as African Americans agitated for fair-employment practices, the elimination of restricted housing, and an end to segregated schools, and as Africans mobilized to gain their independence from colonial masters. This new aggressiveness was mirrored in Lorraine HANSBERRY's *A Raisin in the Sun* (1959). Using Langston Hughes's poetic query, "What happens to a dream deferred?", the young playwright explored the conflicting aspirations of the Youngers, a Chicago tenement family eagerly awaiting the arrival of a $10,000 insurance check paid upon the death of the father. Thirty-year-old Walter Lee's dream of owning a liquor store and hence of functioning as a man in terms espoused by the American middle class clashes with Mama's desire to purchase a comfortable house with

a small garden, while Beneatha's medical studies and humanist philosophy come into conflict with her brother's chauvinism and her mother's religiosity. Sister-in-law Ruth's decision to seek an illegal abortion marks the battering that the older generation's Southern, sharecropping values have taken in the industrial North. Paradoxically, Mama's spiritual faith, rooted in the American slave experience, is congruent with Asagai's progressive social commitment based in contemporary, African anticolonial movements, for in wooing Beneatha, this Nigerian student speaks of the necessity of belief in human potential and the consequence struggle for human betterment.

Produced five years after the historic BROWN V. BOARD OF EDUCATION OF TOPEKA, KANSAS decision outlawing segregated schools, *A Raisin in the Sun* seemed to signal the nation's willingness to live up to its credo of equality. It constituted a number of landmarks: the first time that an African-American woman's work had been produced at the Ethel Barrymore Theatre on Broadway; the directorial debut of African-American Lloyd RICHARDS in such a prestigious venue; widespread recognition for actors Claudia MCNEIL, Ruby DEE, Sidney POITIER, and Diana Sands; and encouragement for other artists to articulate their visions of black America. In addition, it won the New York Drama Critics Circle Award, beating out such mainstream competitors as Tennessee Williams's *Sweet Bird of Youth,* Eugene O'Neill's *A Touch of the Poet,* and Archibald MacLeish's *J.B.* Thus, the play's ending was interpreted, for the most part, as a ringing endorsement of integration. But at the time of its twenty-fifth-anniversary production in 1984, optimism had waned; the reinsertion of the character of the chatty neighbor, who brings news of a racial bombing, along with the final action of the play, namely Mama's retrieving her sickly plant for the family's move into a white neighborhood, clarified Hansberry's call for continued struggle for dignity.

In both its content and structure, *Raisin* speaks to the white mainstream and to black audiences. In fact, critics have compared this drama to the Depression-era *Awake and Sing* (1935), written by the white author Clifford Odets, because not only do both feature families dominated by women, but they also deploy ethnic slang and the metaphors of a cramped physical environment as a sign of moral constriction and of money from an insurance check as the vehicle for exercising personal integrity. Ephemeral, performance-based yet nonetheless significant elements, along with the written text, serve, however, to simultaneously locate this drama within an African matrix. Rather than arguing, as did critics influenced by the federally sponsored MOYNIHAN REPORT on black families, that Mama is an emasculating matriarch because the

Ntozake Shange's highly successful *for colored girls who have considered suicide/when the rainbow is enuf* (1976) marked new visibility for black feminist themes in the theater. (Prints and Photographs Division, Library of Congress)

Youngsters do not conform to the 1950s norm of the nuclear family, one can more profitably understand them as fitting the pattern of an extended African family in which great respect is due elders. At moments of extreme crisis, Mama and Walter Lee each evoke the dead patriarch's memory in halting, yet repetitive linguistic rhythms (that are merely suggested in the written script) seemingly to gain access to his moral support in their decision making. Their actions in these instances are akin to African customs of conjuring the spiritual energies of departed relatives in order to solve current, material problems. Similarly, Beneatha and Walter Lee's fanciful creation of a dance welcoming African warriors home from battle constitutes a writing of culture on the body that provides them a dignity denied them by the American environment; as such, it conforms to African assertions that knowledge is kinesthetic and subjective as well as cerebral.

If Hansberry's hero could be aligned with the southern CIVIL RIGHTS MOVEMENT in his attempt to find a place within the American mainstream, then LeRoi Jones's (a.k.a. Amiri Baraka) protagonists in *Dutchman* and *The Slave* were related to the NATION OF ISLAM and its fiery spokesman MALCOLM X, for at the time of the plays' premieres in 1964, spectators saw these characters as determined to destroy the social system. In the former drama, a twentyish African-American man and older, white woman engage in a bizarre dating game on a subway car that never reaches its final destination. Claiming to know both everything and nothing concerning Clay's life history, this stranger named Lula alternately describes a tantalizing sexual liaison that they will enjoy and hurls racial taunts at the would-be poet until he sheds his polite, middle-class demeanor and acknowledges a deep hatred of white America. But Clay fails to act upon his murderous knowledge, preferring instead to use art as a safety valve that tempers rebellious impulses. Once Lula has exposed this rage, she kills Clay and enlists the aid of the hitherto passive onlookers in throwing his body off the train. Like the mythic captain of the *Flying Dutchman,* who was fated to sail the world looking for absolution for his crimes, Lula begins to seek out another young black male as the play closes. Seemingly, the play functioned as a cautionary tale demonstrating to blacks that death was the price for inaction upon their justifiable anger and warning whites of the rage they could expect if they continued to deny full citizenship to African Americans. Largely unnoted at the time was the text's gender politics, which accuses the white woman rather than fingering the actual holders of oppressive power in the United States.

In contrast, the black man is no longer the victim and the white man is visible in *The Slave.* Walker has invaded the home of his white former wife in order to take his daughters to safety behind the lines of his revolutionary army advancing on the city—or, so he alleges, because it seems as though Walker's real purpose is to exorcise those feelings that bind him to Grace and Easley, Grace's present (white) husband and Walker's former professor. In the ensuing literal and figurative battle, Walker kills Easley, a beam fatally hits Grace, and Walker departs, apparently leaving the children upstairs crying.

But social psychiatrist Frantz Fanon, whose writings on anticolonial struggles in Algeria provided intellectuals in the 1960s with an important framework for conceptualizing Black Power movements, has argued that it is easier to proclaim rejection than to reject. Fanon's analysis is pertinent to the Baraka text, for despite his aggressive stance, Walker agonizes that he has no language with which to construct a new world, his sole epistemology or frame of reference is a Western system that enforces hatred of black people.

The ambiguity of his position has, in fact, been signaled at the outset by a prologue in which an actor, dressed as a stereotypical old field slave, addresses viewers directly, arguing that whatever he and they understand as reality may be a lie told for survival purposes. What is needed, he suggests, is a superstructure that will enable communication among blacks and whites by ensuring that their common language has the same undeniable referents; otherwise, a black man's legitimate quest for control over his destiny may be understood by a white man as senseless terrorism. The rest of the play then argues that this enabling structure is violence, undertaken by the exploited black masses in defense, as Fanon argued, against the violence waged upon them by the state. But as a playwright, Baraka is caught in a problematic position, for his primary tool of communication with audiences is language itself, suspect because of its inherent capacity to simultaneously convey multiple references and values. Yet, given the *extra*-theatrical, social backdrop of armed confrontations waged by groups like the BLACK PANTHER PARTY, most spectators and readers at the time of the drama's initial productions focused their attention on the text's revolutionary rhetoric rather than its ambivalence.

At the heart of both these plays is an examination of hegemony or the power of a ruling class to enforce throughout the entire society perspectives that maintain its privileged status through noncoercive means like education, the arts, or certain everyday practices. In *Dutchman* the dominance of the elite, as embodied in Lula, is maintained in part because art functions as a passive mode of resistance that deflects direct confrontation. In *The Slave* and subsequent dramatic works like *Four Black Revolutionary Plays*, *Arm Yrself or Harm Yrself* (1967), or *The Motion of History* (1977), art is defined as counterhegemonic; it is seen as a weapon that can be utilized to attack sociopolitical hierarchies. In rejecting, as Du Bois had done previously, the opposition of art to propaganda, Amiri Baraka became a major proponent of the BLACK ARTS MOVEMENT (1964–1974), functioning as a role model for a younger generation eager to assert a positive sense of their black identity.

In an atmosphere of civil rights demonstrations and urban rebellions, entitlement programs designed to bring about what President Lyndon Johnson termed "the Great Society," Vietnam war protest, and the beginnings of a renewed feminism, African-American drama, with its implicit critique of the dominant social structure, briefly flourished. Playwrights like Ed BULLINS, Richard WESLEY, Clay Goss, Ron MILNER, Ben Caldwell, Sonia SANCHEZ, and MARVIN X followed Baraka's example. Artists like Robert Macbeth, Barbara Ann TEER, and Woodie King, Jr. established companies that advocated a black nationalist position (New York's the New Lafayette, National Black Theatre, and Concept East in Detroit respectively), while more moderate practitioners like Douglas Turner WARD, Hazel BRYANT, C. Bernard Jackson, John Doyle, and Nora Vaughn, and such companies as the Negro Ensemble, the Richard Allen Cultural Center in New York, the Inner City Cultural Center in Los Angeles, and the Grassroots Experience and Black Repertory Group Theatre in the San Francisco Bay Area also found governmental funding and receptive audiences for their efforts.

Another of the most prolific playwrights of this period was Ed Bullins, who has written in a variety of styles, including comedy (*The Electronic Nigger*, 1968), theater of the Absurd (*How Do You Do?* 1965), fictionalized autobiography (*A Son Come Home*, 1968), and a realism whose seemingly photographic accuracy does not reveal the playwright's evaluation of his source material (*Clara's Ole Man*, 1965). Unlike virtually any other black dramatist before him, Ed Bullins placed onstage—and thereby validated—in plays like *Goin' a Buffalo* (1966), *In the Wine Time* (1968), and *The Taking of Miss Janie* (1975) lower-class hustlers, prostitutes, pimps, and unemployed teens as well as lower-middle-class community college students, veterans, musicians, and would-be artists and intellectuals, virtually all of whom aggressively pursue an individually-oriented materialism shorn of any rhetoric of concern for a shared, common good.

In disavowing the espoused social values of the American mainstream, Bullins's playwriting style in his full-length dramas also demanded a mode of criticism that was outside the Aristotelian-derived, mainstream preference for tightly organized, linear dramatic structures. Thus, these dramas may be more productively analyzed in terms of jazz, a musical idiom that originated among African Americans and was until relatively recently held in low regard by the American public. Like a jazz composition in which individual musicians improvise a solo or "riff" off a shared melodic line, a play such as *The Fabulous Miss Marie* (1971) has a basic narrative concerning a group of black Los Angelenos who party unconcernedly while a civil rights demonstration is being broadcast on television. The seemingly endless rounds of drinking, meandering conversations, verbal sparring, and sexual repartee function as a base line from which action is periodically stopped in order for individual characters to step from the shadows into a spotlight and address the audience directly with their own solos on the theme of trying to "make it" in the United States.

Adrienne KENNEDY is another playwright whose work demanded different critical tools. Like Baraka, Kennedy confronts, in plays like *The Owl Answers* (1965) and *Rat's Mass* (1963), questions of representation and identity formation, offering a black woman's account of the cultural schizophrenia induced by American racial constructions. Thus, protagonists like Sarah in *Funnyhouse of a Negro* (1963) are paralyzed by devotion to European culture, symbolized in this text by Queen Elizabeth and the Duchess of Hapsburg, and by psychosexual confusion centered on a father figure, associated here with blackness, encroaching jungles, civilizing missions in Africa, and contradictorily, the anticolonialist Congolese hero Patrice Lumumba. Adding to the ambiguity is Kennedy's consistent decision to distribute the female protagonist's story amongst a number of different characters, thereby producing an identity or voice that does not come together in a single, coherent whole. Though her earliest plays were produced during the same time period as Baraka's, the ideological demand for positive valorization of "the black experience" in the sixties' Black Arts and Black Power movements meant that her frighteningly powerful dramatizations of the anguished sensibility Du Bois had termed "double consciousness" won a few supporters among African-American theatergoers. Notwithstanding, her highly abstract style found positive response within the limited circles of the white avantgarde in New York. Given subsequent critiques of identity and relationships of domination and marginality launched from theorists of feminism, literary deconstruction, postcoloniality, and postmodernism, a space has been cleared, and Kennedy's work is presently garnering from white and black critics alike the attention it deserves.

Exploding on the theatrical scene in 1976 with *for colored girls who have considered suicide/when the rainbow*

Scene from Charles Fuller's *A Soldier's Play*, 1982. (Left to right) Brent Jennings, Steven A. Jones, Eugene Lee, Denzel Washington, Samuel L. Jackson, James Pickens, Jr., Peter Friedman. (Reprinted from *In the Shadow of the Great White Way: Images from the Black Theatre*, Thunder's Mouth Press, © 1957–1989 by Bert Andrews. Reprinted by permission of the Estate of Bert Andrews)

is enuf, Ntozake Shange builds upon examples set by Hughes, Baraka, and Kennedy in black theater as well as those offered by Europe's Antonin Artaud and Bertolt Brecht. Coining the term "choreopoem," Shange creates a total theater in which unscripted elements like music and dance become equal partners with the written word—i.e., poetry. Thus, in *for colored girls . . .* not only do the women talk about their encounters with men, but they also utilize 1960s Motown tunes, Afro-Cuban rhythms, nonsensical chants, and gospel cadences in order to break out of a social world in which they have been devalued as "a colored girl an evil woman a bitch or a nag." With this first text, Shange placed African-American women's experiences of rape, abortion, domestic abuse, sexual desire, and self-affirmation center stage, and she helped fuel an intense debate within black communities concerning the relevance of feminism—understood at that time as the preoccupation of white, middle-class women—to the lives of African Americans. Seeking in *Spell #7* (1979) to confront the power of the minstrel mask that has determined representations of blacks in American popular imagination she crafts a provocative theater whose implications refuse to remain within the illusionary space created by drama. Shange has continued in texts like *Boogie Woogie Landscapes* (1979), *From Okra to Greens/ A Different Kinda Love Story* (1978), and *The Love Space Demands: A Continuing Saga* (1992) to utilize poetry, music, and dance in a nonlinear fashion to explore ways in which a sense of personal integrity and nobility can be harmonized with the realities of racist and sexist social constructions of black (female) identity. Playwrights like Alexis DEVEAUX, Aishah Rahman, and George C. WOLFE have followed Shange's lead in experimenting with dramatic form, while the last has parodied the feminist content of Shange's dramas in *The Colored Museum* (1986).

Closer to the American mainstream's penchant for realism is August WILSON, who has benefited from a virtually unique, creative collaboration with Lloyd Richards, the same director who brought Hansberry's *A Raisin in the Sun* to Broadway some thirty-five years earlier. Each of his plays has been "workshopped" (read aloud by professional actors and a director, critiqued, and re-written) at the National Playwrights Conference of the Eugene O'Neill Theater, run by Richards, before receiving productions (and further revisions) and national media attention at various, mainstream regional theaters and on Broadway.

A skilled storyteller, Wilson has taken on the challenge of writing a play for each decade of the twentieth century. Thus, *Ma Rainey's Black Bottom* (1984) focuses on the renowned 1920s blues singer and her band, who, through their casual reminiscences, reveal a collective history of discrimination. *Fences* (1985) centers on an overbearing man's relationship to his son and other family members at the point in the 1950s when African Americans were being allowed entry into white, professional sports organizations; and *Joe Turner's Come and Gone* (1986) dramatizes the search by various boardinghouse occupants for a sense of wholeness and sustaining purpose in the first decade of the twentieth century, when thousands of rural black people moved north seeking employment in an industrializing economy. In *The Piano Lesson* (1987), set in the 1930s, a brother and sister fight for possession of the family's piano, which seems to symbolize conflicting ideas concerning uses of the past in charting present courses of action; while set against the backdrop of Malcolm X's militancy of the 1960s, *Two Trains Running* (1990) features the regular patrons of a modest diner who pursue their own dreams of advancement by playing the numbers (i.e., illegally betting on the outcome of horse races) or consulting Aunt Esther, a local fortune teller whose alleged, advanced age happens to correspond to the numbers of years African-Americans have lived in the United States.

Like the novelist Toni MORRISON, August Wilson crafts a world in which the pedestrian often assumes grand, mythic proportions, nearly bursting in the process the neat, explanatory rationales implicit in the genre of dramatic realism. Characters regularly fight with ghosts, make pacts with the Devil, or talk to Death; seemingly, they quest for a spiritual center or standpoint from which to confront a material world hostile to their presence. Arguing the importance of blues music in shaping the identity of African Americans, Wilson seems to create characters whose very lives are a blues song: improvisatory, ironic, yet simultaneously affirmative, grounded in a bedrock of belief in the possibility of human integrity.

Seemingly with the post-sixties integration of some public school systems, (sub)urban neighborhoods, job sites, and mass media, the hybrid character of African-American—and indeed, American—culture has accelerated. Those comfortable with a postmodernism that often finds its inspirations in a global eclecticism of "high" and "low" cultures, can enjoy such African-American performance artists as Robbie McCauley (*My Father and the Wars,* 1985; *Sally's Rape,* 1991), and Laurie Carlos who, in the tradition of Ntozake Shange, work individually and collaboratively to fuse personal narratives with larger feminist issues. Also termed a performance artist, Anna Deavere Smith offers in her *On the Road: A Search for American Change* series solo performances of edited interviews with people, both famous and obscure, on topics like gender and racial tensions in

Scene from *Ma Rainey's Black Bottom,* 1984. (Left to right) Scott Davenport-Richards, Charles S. Dutton, Leonard Jackson, Theresa Merritt, Robert Judd, Joe Seneca; (above) Lou Criscuolo, John Carpenter. (Reprinted from *In the Shadow of the Great White Way: Images from the Black Theatre,* Thunder's Mouth Press, © 1957–1989 by Bert Andrews. Reprinted by permission of the Estate of Bert Andrews)

professional organizations, urban neighborhoods, and on university campuses. She has also focused on the increasingly multicultural, fractious character of American cities, for her *Fires in the Mirror: Crown Heights, Brooklyn and Other Identities* (1992) and *Twilight: Los Angeles, 1992* (1994), in which she performs the words of more than thirty women and men within an hour and a half, challenges audiences to grapple with notions of community in the context of competing demands for racial and economic justice. They can also sample dramas by Suzan-Lori PARKS (*The Death of the Last Black Man in the Whole Entire World,* 1990; *Imperceptible Mutabilities in the Third Kingdom,* 1989), who cites the white, American expatriate writer Gertrude Stein and "The Wild Kingdom" television program among her influences; or work by Eric Gupton, Brian Freeman, and Bernard Branner (*Fierce Love: Stories from Black Gay Life,* 1991), collectively known as AfroPomoHomo, a

shortening of the identificatory tags, African-American, postmodernist, and homosexual. Or, spectators can attend a concert by Urban Bush Women, Bill T. JONES/Arnie Zane Dance Company, or David Rousseve, whose mixture of modern dance choreography, pedestrian gestures, athleticism, and narrative communicated through both movement and spoken text blur conventional Western distinctions between drama and dance. What all these artists share is a sensibility that does not reach for some grand, master truth. Rather, juxtaposing elements as diverse as European high art, Georgia Sea Island chants, television programs, West African religions, and popular music, they recognize that African-American identity is varied, and no one can claim to represent black authenticity without doing violence to other perspectives found in these communities.

Indeed, for those theatergoers in the 1990s who find the choreopoem form of an Ntozake Shange, the mythic reach of an August Wilson, or the puzzling symbolism of a Suzan-Lori Parks not to their liking, other options are available. They can attend a performance of *Beauty Shop, Living Room,* or *Beauty Shop, Part 2,* all of which have been written, produced, and directed by Shelly Garrett. Starting in 1987 with the intention of simply creating dramatic pieces that would leave audiences exhausted with laughter, Garrett is said to have targeted his attentions primarily toward an underserved population of black women, ages 25 to 54 who watch soap operas and rarely frequent theater. Thus, his scripts are closer to TV sitcoms in their representations of everyday life; stereotypes abound, with the women portrayed as materialist, classist, sexually repressed or rapacious. Men are represented as self-centered sex objects, financially secure but dull, or flamboyant homosexuals outgossiping the most catty (yet hilarious) women. Seemingly, considerable advertising on black-oriented radio stations, the dramas' verbal play, the performers' zestful aura, a mixture of some recognizable truths, and cheerful confirmation of spectators' misogynist and homophobic attitudes have attracted thousands of spectators, enabling Garrett to tour at least fifty cities nationwide for more than two years with one show. But those disturbed by what they may perceive as rampant sexuality in these shows also have an option in the commercial arena, for producers have created a religious version, like Michael Mathews's *I Need a Man* (1993), wherein some of these lively stereotypes undergo spiritual conversion aided by the performance of gospel music. As with much black art, the form is elastic, so that local, gospel radio personalities occasionally make guest appearances onstage during the performance; the predictability of plot and character types is offset by the dynamics of the performer-viewer interactions. Whether participants undergo a religious experience in this highly commercialized venue depends, as it does in church, upon their own belief systems and sensibilities.

In the early 1990s, approximately 200 companies were dedicated to the production of African-American theater and drama. As the foregoing account suggests, audiences can experience a wealth of themes, perspectives, and styles, all of which seek to articulate aspects of African-American culture. This diversity is indeed a cause for celebration. Yet, given the nation's difficult economic conditions that promise no easy solution, the arts in general and black and other so-called minority expressive cultures in particular will be under intense pressure to obtain the financial resources that enable artistic production. Perhaps artists from earlier generations would have spoken of the economic constraints upon their work, too, and advised their descendants that the challenge remains constant: To create a tasty "soul" food of dramatic fare, one must utilize the diverse materials at hand, seasoning them with attention to technique, intelligence, passion, an occasional bit of humor, openness to inspiration, and most important, grace under pressure.

REFERENCES

ABRAMSON, DORIS E. *Negro Playwrights in the American Theatre, 1925–1959.* New York, 1969.

BOSKIN, JOSEPH. *Sambo: the Rise and Demise of an African Jester.* New York, 1986.

BROWN-GUILLORY, ELIZABETH, ed. *Their Place on the Stage: Black Women Playwrights in America.* Westport, Conn., 1988.

——. *Wines in the Wilderness: Plays by African American Women from the Harlem Renaissance to the Present.* New York, 1990.

CARTER, STEVEN R. *Hansberry's Drama.* Urbana, Ill., 1991.

CRAIG, E. QUITA. *Black Drama of the Federal Theatre Era: Beyond the Formal Horizons.* Amherst, Mass., 1980.

FABRE, GENEVIEVE. *Drumbeats, Masks, and Metaphor.* Translated by Melvin Dixon. Cambridge, Mass. 1983.

FANON, FRANTZ. *Black Skins, White Masks.* Translated by Charles Lam Markmann. New York, 1967.

——. *The Wretched of the Earth.* Translated by Constance Farrington. New York, 1963.

FLETCHER, WINONA L. "Witnessing a 'Miracle': Sixty Years of 'Heaven Bound' at Big Bethel in Atlanta." *Black American Literature Forum* 25, no. 1 (Spring 1991): 83–92.

HARRISON, PAUL CARTER. "Introduction: Black Theater in Search of a Source." In *Kuntu Drama: Plays of the African Continuum.* New York, 1974, pp. 5–29.

——. *Totem Voices: Plays from the Black World Repertory.* New York, 1989.

HATCH, JAMES V., ed. *Black Theater, U.S.A.: Forty-Five Plays by Black Americans, 1847–1974.* New York, 1974.

——. *The Roots of African American Drama.* Detroit, 1991.

HILL, ERROL, ed. *The Theatre of Black Americans:* New York, 1990.

MITCHELL, ANGELA. "Cheap Laughs: Bad Taste, Big Bucks." *Emerge* 4, no. 5 (March 1993): 49–51.

MOLLETTE, CARLTON, and BARBARA MOLLETTE. *Black Theatre: Premise and Presentation.* 1986. Reprint. Briston, Ind., 1992.

NEAL, LARRY. *Visions of a Liberated Future: Black Arts Movement Writings.* New York, 1989.

PERKINS, KATHY A. *Black Female Playwrights: An Anthology of Plays Before 1950.* Bloomington, Ind., 1989.

RAMPERSAD, ARNOLD. *The Life of Langston Hughes, Volume 1, 1902–1941: I, Too, Sing America.* New York, 1986.

SANDERS, LESLIE CATHERINE. *The Development of Black Theater in America.* Baton Rouge, La., 1988.

SCOTT, FREDA L. "The Star of Ethiopia: A Contribution Toward the Development of Black Drama and Theater in the Harlem Renaissance." In Amritijit Singh, William S. Shiver, and Stanley Brodwin, eds. *The Harlem Renaissance: Revaluations.* New York, 1989.

TURNER, DARWIN T., ed. *Black Drama in America: An Anthology.* Washington, D.C., 1993.

WIGGINS, WILLIAM H., JR. "Pilgrims, Crosses, and Faith: The Folk Dimensions of 'Heaven Bound'." *Black American Literature Forum* 25, no. 1 (Spring 1991): 93–100.

WILKERSON, MARGARET B. *Nine Plays.* New York, 1986.

———. "Redefining Black Theatre." *The Black Scholar* 10, no. 10 (July/August 1979): 322–342.

WILLIAMS, MANCE. *Black Theatre in the 1960s and 1970s.* Westport, Conn., 1985.

WOLL, ALLEN. *Black Musical Theatre: From "Coontown" to "Dreamgirls."* Baton Rouge, La., 1989.

SANDRA L. RICHARDS

Dranes, Arizona Juanita (c. 1906–), gospel singer. Little is known of Arizona Dranes's life. She was a poor, blind-from-birth southwestern member of the Church of God in Christ, the Pentecostal denomination, who recorded briefly in the 1920s. She combined a fast, barrelhouse, western piano style with a loud, twangy, unaccented voice to create what is perhaps the most overwhelmingly powerful music in the black gospel tradition. Dranes was born in Dallas, around 1906. Her middle name was Juanita, leading to the suggestion that she might have been part Mexican. She was encouraged to record by Church of God in Christ bishop Samuel M. Crouch.

Despite her religious identity, Dranes's piano style was, in fact, the boogie-woogie ragged march beat with its strong left hand that Wilfred Mellers called "perhaps the most sexy music ever invented" and the "closest early jazz ever came to its African origins" (1986, p. 8). She apparently performed at interracial Sanctified meetings, where the impact of hearing her can only be imagined. Probably speaking of performances in Birmingham, Ala., gospel choir director Alex Bradford recalled, "She'd sing 'Thy Servant's Prayer' and crackers and niggers be shouting *everywhere.*" Rosetta THARPE heard her sing "The Storm Is Passing Over" in St. Louis and came under Dranes's influence, as did Madame Ernestine Washington, Charles "Cow-Cow" Davenport, Meade "Lux" LEWIS, and Roosevelt Sykes the Honeydripper.

Dranes recorded ten sides in Chicago for Okeh Records during two occasions in 1926, one with Sara Martin, the other with Rev. F. W. McGee and the Texas Jubilee Singers. In 1928 she cut six more sides, also in Chicago for Okeh, this time with an unknown female backup choir. Among the titles are "John Said He Saw a Number," "Bye and Bye We're Going to See the King," "Lamb's Blood Has Washed Me Clean," and "I Shall Wear a Crown." Nothing is known about her life after this period.

REFERENCES

HEILBUT, ANTHONY. *The Gospel Sound: Good News and Bad Times.* New York, 1985.

MELLERS, WILFRED. *Angels of the Night: Popular Female Singers of Our Time.* Oxford, U.K., 1986.

RICHARD NEWMAN

Dred Scott v. Sandford. In the Dred Scott decision of 1857 the Supreme Court ruled, in a 7–2 vote, that free blacks were not citizens of the United States and that Congress lacked the power to prohibit SLAVERY in the western territories.

Scott was a Virginia slave, born around 1802, who moved with his master, Peter Blow, to St. Louis in 1830. Blow subsequently sold Scott to Dr. John Emerson, an army surgeon, who took Scott to Fort Armstrong in Illinois, a free state, and Fort Snelling in the Wisconsin Territory, where slavery was prohibited by the MISSOURI COMPROMISE. In 1846, after Emerson's death, Scott sued for his freedom (and that of his family). In 1850 a St. Louis court ruled that Scott became free by residing in Illinois and the Wisconsin Territory. In 1852 the Missouri Supreme Court, articulating the South's proslavery ideology, rejected precedents of its own that went back more than twenty-five years and reversed the lower court decision:

> Times are not as they were when the former decisions on this subject were made. Since then not only individuals but States have been possessed of a dark and fell spirit in relation to slavery, whose gratification is sought in the pursuit of measures, whose inevitable consequence must be the overthrow and destruction of our government.

Thus, Missouri would not recognize the freedom a slave might obtain by living in a free state.

In 1854 Scott began a new suit in United States District Court against John F. A. Sanford, a New Yorker who became the executor of Emerson's estate after Emerson's widow, the initial executor, remarried. Scott claimed he was a citizen of Missouri, suing Sanford in federal court because there was a diversity of state citizenship between the two parties. Sanford answered with a plea in abatement, arguing that no black, free or slave, could ever sue as a citizen in federal court. Federal District Judge Robert W. Wells ruled that *if* Scott was free, he was a citizen of Missouri for purposes of a diversity suit. However, Wells's ruling after the trial was that Scott was still a slave. Scott then appealed to the U.S. Supreme Court. At issue was more than his status: the Missouri Supreme Court's decision challenged the constitutionality of the Missouri Compromise. The central political issue of the 1850s—the power of the federal government to prohibit slavery in the territories—was now before the Supreme Court.

The ardently proslavery Chief Justice Roger B. Taney used *Dred Scott* v. *Sandford* to decide this pressing political issue in favor of the South. Taney asserted that (1) the Missouri Compromise was unconstitutional because Congress could not legislate for the territories; (2) freeing slaves in the territories violated the Fifth Amendment prohibition on taking of property without due process; and (3) blacks, even those in the North with full state citizenship, could never be U.S. citizens. Taney asked: "Can a negro, whose ancestors were imported into this country, and sold as slaves, become a member of the political community formed and brought into existence by the Constitution of the United States, and as such become entitled to all the rights, privileges, and immunities guaranteed by that instrument to the citizens?" Taney answered his own question in the negative. He asserted that at the nation's founding blacks were considered "beings of an inferior order, and altogether unfit to associate with the white race, either in social or political relations; and so far inferior, that they had no rights which the white man was bound to respect; and that the negro might justly and lawfully be reduced to slavery for his benefit." Taney thought his lengthy decision would open all the territories to slavery and destroy the Republican party. In essence, he had constitutionalized racism and slavery. America, in Taney's view, was thoroughly a "white" nation.

Justice Benjamin Robbins Curtis of Massachusetts protested Taney's conclusions. Curtis noted: "At the time of the ratification of the Articles of Confederation [1781], all free native-born inhabitants of the States of New Hampshire, Massachusetts, New York, New Jersey, and North Carolina, though descended from African slaves, were not only citizens of those States, but such of them as had the other necessary qualifications possessed the franchises of electors, on equal terms with other citizens." Curtis concluded that when the Constitution was ratified, "these colored persons were not only included in the body of 'the people of the United States,' by whom the Constitution was ordained and established, but in at least five of the States they had the power to act,

and doubtless did act, by their suffrages, upon the question of adoption." Curtis also argued that under a "reasonable interpretation of the language of the Constitution," Congress had the power to regulate slavery in the federal territories.

Northern Republicans and abolitionists were stunned and horrified. Horace Greeley, writing in the *New York Tribune*, called Taney's opinion "atrocious," "abominable," and a "detestable hypocrisy." The *Chicago Tribune* was repelled by its "inhuman dicta" and "the wicked consequences which may flow from it." Northern Democrats, on the other hand, hoped the decision would destroy the Republican party by undermining its "free soil" platform and by finally ending the national debate over slavery in the territories. The New York *Journal of Commerce* hopefully declared that the decision was an "authoritative and final settlement of grievous sectional issues."

Ultimately, it was neither authoritative nor final. By 1858, northern Democrats faced a politically impossible dilemma. Their answer to the problem of slavery in the territories had been popular sovereignty—allowing the settlers to vote slavery up or down. But Taney's opinion denied both Congress and the settlers of a new territory the power to prohibit slavery. This made popular sovereignty meaningless. Stephen A. Douglas, the most prominent proponent of popular sovereignty, told his Illinois constituents that settlers could still keep slavery out of most of the territories by not passing laws that would protect slave property. This simply led to southern demands for a federal slave code for the territories and a split within the Democratic party in 1860.

Republicans made Taney and the decision the focus of their 1858 and 1860 campaigns. Abraham Lincoln argued in his "house divided" speech (1858) that Taney's opinion was part of a proslavery conspiracy to nationalize slavery. He predicted "another Supreme Court decision, declaring that the Constitution of the United States does not permit a *state* to exclude slavery from its limits." He told Illinois voters that "we shall *lie down* pleasantly dreaming that the people of Missouri are on the verge of making their state *free*; and we shall *awake* to the *reality*, instead, that the Supreme Court has made *Illinois* a *slave* state."

Such arguments helped lead to a Republican victory in 1860. During the Civil War the Lincoln administration gradually reversed many of Taney's assertions about the status of blacks. This Republican policy culminated with the adoption of the FOURTEENTH AMENDMENT, which explicitly overruled *Dred Scott*, declaring, "All persons born or naturalized in the United States . . . are citizens of the United States and of the State wherein they reside."

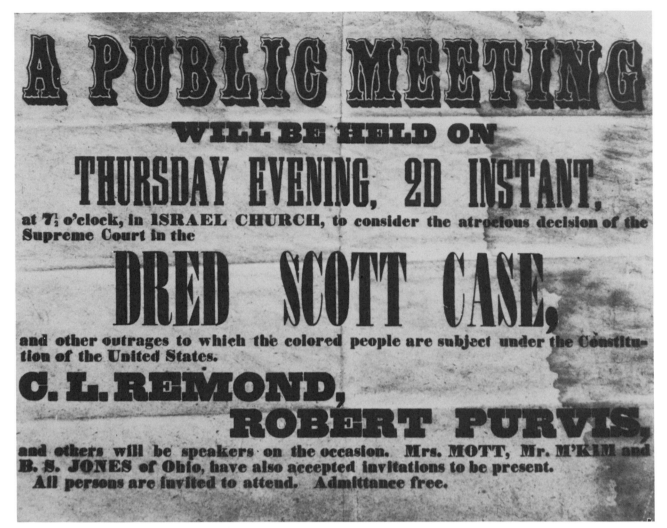

The 1857 decision by the U.S. Supreme Court in the Dred Scott case, which held that African Americans had no right to citizenship, provoked a storm of protest. Free blacks expressed their outrage at numerous meetings, such as this Philadelphia rally. (Photographs and Prints Division, Schomburg Center for Research in Black Culture, The New York Public Library, Astor, Lenox and Tilden Foundations)

REFERENCES

ERLICH, WALTER. *They Have No Rights: Dred Scott's Struggle for Freedom.* Westport, Conn., 1979.

FEHRENBACHER, DON E. *The Dred Scott Case: Its Significance in American Law and Politics.* New York, 1978.

FINKELMAN, PAUL. *An Imperfect Union: Slavery, Federalism, and Comity.* Chapel Hill, N.C., 1981.

———. *Slavery in the Courtroom.* Washington, D.C., 1985.

POTTER, DAVID M. *The Impending Crisis: 1848–61.* New York, 1976.

PAUL FINKELMAN

Drew, Charles Richard (December 6, 1904–April 1, 1950), surgeon. Born and raised in Washington, D.C., Charles Richard Drew graduated from Dunbar High School in 1922. In 1926 he received a B.A. from Amherst College. A first-rate basketball player, on graduation Drew was given an award as best athlete of the college. Between 1926 and 1928, he taught biology and chemistry at Morgan College (now Morgan State University) in Baltimore, where he also served as football coach and as director of athletics.

In 1928, Drew began medical studies at McGill University Medical School in Montreal, Canada. He excelled in medical science courses, won the annual prize in neuroanatomy, was elected to Alpha Phi Omega, the medical honorary scholastic fraternity, and received a prize for the top score in a medical exam competition. In 1933, Drew earned an M.D. and a master in surgery degree. He spent the next two years as an intern and as a resident in medicine at Royal Victoria and Montreal General Hospitals.

As a McGill medical student, Drew was introduced to research on the chemical composition of blood and blood groups by John Beattie, a British medical researcher. A major problem then facing medical science was that quantities of whole, fresh blood large enough to match blood group types between blood donor and blood receiver were not readily available. Drew was bothered by the deaths of seriously ill or injured patients due to blood loss. Learning more about blood and how to preserve it over long periods of time became a research interest that Drew carried with him as he left Montreal to assume a teaching position at HOWARD UNIVERSITY's College of Medicine in 1935.

In 1938, Drew received a research fellowship from the Rockefeller Foundation for study at Columbia-Presbyterian Hospital in New York City. He and John Scudder undertook research that led to the finding that it was blood plasma (the liquid portion of the blood, devoid of blood cells) rather than whole blood that needed to be preserved for transfusions. Drew established an experimental blood bank at Columbia-Presbyterian Hospital. In 1940 Drew was awarded a doctorate at Columbia University with a thesis on "Banked Blood."

Returning to Howard University in 1940, Drew devoted himself to training its medical students in surgery. His teaching was abruptly interrupted, however, by a call for blood plasma needed by wounded soldiers on the battlefields of Europe during World War II. The Blood Transfusion Association in New York City asked Drew to return to help. He was given leave from his instructional duties at Howard University to accept an assignment in the fall of 1940 as Medical Director of the Blood for Britain Program, to supply blood for the British Red Cross. Under Drew's guidance, dried plasma was flown across the Atlantic Ocean to England. Once England had established its own banks, a larger blood program for U.S. military forces was developed. The American Red Cross and the Blood Transfusion Association jointly conducted this program and Drew became its medical director.

In 1941 the military established a system of refusing blood donations from nonwhites to be used by whites. Blood donated by blacks was stored separately and given only to blacks. As director of the Red Cross Blood Bank Program, Drew took a strong stand against the racial separation of banked blood. As a result, he was asked to resign his directorship position. He did, and returned once again to teaching surgery at Howard University, where he became professor and head of the department of surgery and surgeon-in-chief at Freedmen's Hospital.

On March 31, 1950, after working a long day that included performing several operations, Drew agreed to drive with other colleagues to a medical conference in Tuskegee, Ala. He dozed at the wheel, and the car went off the road near Burlington, N.C., and

overturned. Though stories abound that his medical emergency was ignored because of his race, he received prompt medical attention. He died on April 1, 1950 from injuries resulting from the accident.

Drew gained much recognition during his lifetime: He was named Diplomate of Surgery by the American Board of Surgery in 1941; was a recipient of the Spingarn Medal from the NAACP (1944); was granted honorary Doctor of Science degrees from Virginia State College (1945) and Amherst College (1947); and was elected as a Fellow of the International College of Surgery (1946).

REFERENCES

COBB, W. MONTAGUE. "Charles Richard Drew, M.D., 1904–1950." *Journal of the National Medical Association,* 42 (July 1950): 239–245.
WYNES, CHARLES E. *Charles Richard Drew: The Man and the Myth.* Urbana, Ill., 1988.

ROBERT C. HAYDEN

Drew, Timothy.   *See* Noble Drew Ali.

Driskell, David (June 7, 1931–   ), artist and author. David Driskell was born in Eatonton, Ga., but grew up in North Carolina, where he attended public schools. After high school he continued his education at the Skowhegan School of Painting and Sculpture in Maine (1953). Driskell completed his undergraduate study in art at HOWARD UNIVERSITY in 1955. After graduating from Howard, he received an M.F.A. in art from the Catholic University of America (1962), also in Washington, D.C.

Driskell began his teaching career in 1955 at Talladega College in Alabama. In 1962 he returned to Howard as a professor, remaining until 1966 when he became the chair of the Department of Art at Fisk University. In 1978 he left Fisk to chair the Department of Art at the University of Maryland. He remained as chair through 1983, when he stepped down to return to the classroom and devote his time to painting and research.

Driskell has become a prominent scholar of African-American art. He was the curator of several important exhibitions of African-American art, including "Two Centuries of Black-American Art: 1750–1950," at the Los Angeles County Museum of Art in 1976; a touring exhibition entitled "Hidden Heritage: Afro-American Art 1800–1950"; the Studio Museum in Harlem's 1987 exhibition (cocurated with Mary Schmidt-Campbell) "Harlem Renaissance: Art of Black America"; and in Tokyo, "The Art of Black America in Japan." Among the books written by Driskell to accompany these shows are *Two Centuries of Black American Art* (1976) and *Hidden Heritage: Afro-American Art* (1985).

Driskell has also gained a reputation as an artist with exhibitions throughout the United States. The most common theme in his artwork is nature—often as he sees it from his Maine studio. Driskell's art is characterized by his use of brilliant colors as well as by sparing use of figures in his paintings and collages, which reveal both African and Brazilian influences. Some of his pieces in this vein include *The View from the Forest* (1993) and *The Hills Are Moving* (1993).

REFERENCES

BASS, RUTH. *Art News* (October 1993): 166.
COTTER, HOLLAND. *New York Times,* July 16, 1993, p. C25.

TAMARA L. FELTON

Drug, Hospital, and Health Care Employees Union, Local 1199. *See* Local 1199, Drug, Hospital, and Health Care Employees Union.

Drugs. History dates humankind's fascination with addictive drugs from at least three thousand years before Christ and characterizes the allure of intoxicants as one of the most enduring features of human life. While social and behavioral scientists continue their search for an answer to the abuse of drugs, history provides the most compelling explanation: Those groups intensively exposed to these substances fall prey to addiction (Courtwright 1982).

The history of the United States confirms the human dimension of the problem. In this country the addictive potential of opiates (e.g., opium, morphine, heroin, and codeine), cocaine, marijuana, hashish, hallucinogens, and other drugs is no respecter of race, class, gender, or national origin. At one time or another, Americans have perceived drug abuse as a crime, a disease, or a human foible.

Nevertheless, a classic study of drug policy in the United States concludes that there is a peculiarly American response to the problem. "American concern with narcotics is more than a medical or legal problem—it is in the fullest sense a political problem. . . . The most passionate support for legal prohibition of narcotics has been associated with fear of a given drug's effect on a specific minority" (Musto 1972).

The history of drug abuse in the African-American community is the product of this confluence. It reflects an age-old human propensity shaped by periodic episodes of exposure, American society's perception of and response to these episodes, and the community's unique social status. Since the nineteenth century, the course of African Americans' drug history has evolved from relative abstinence to a mass problem affecting every facet of life and culture.

African Americans were freed from bondage in an America some commentators described as a "dope fiend's paradise." Though the addict population is always difficult to measure precisely, opiate abuse was the most prevalent form of addiction in the mid-nineteenth century. The typical habitué was middle-aged, upper-class, white, southern, and female. A large, indeterminate number of Americans were exposed to opium and morphine through hundreds of popular "patent" medicines—packaged remedies available from grocers, druggists, traveling medicine shows, and the family doctor (Courtwright 1982). The smallest group of addicts were Chinese opium smokers.

Systematic studies of drug-maintenance clinics, circa 1912–1924, in more than thirty cities, as well as less reliable surveys of pharmacists and physicians, circa 1870–1902, indicate that until well into the twentieth century, black Americans enjoyed the lowest addiction rate of any national group. One explanation for this low rate was that the slave community was little exposed to opiates, since most addicts were introduced to these drugs through their doctors and self-treatment. Civil War veterans are a case in point. A study of pension files and medical records reveals that after the war, black veterans were rarely addicted, in part because they were less likely to receive painkilling opiates in their poorly equipped hospitals. But sometimes slaves were treated by the same doctors as their masters and given opium-based home remedies like laudanum, paregoric, and Dover's powder. Many were exposed through daily contact with the typical addict of the day, as several published plantation diaries attest.

Slave narratives and biographical and historical studies provide another explanation. They document the slave community's preference for herbal remedies and esteemed "slave doctors." Some historians contend that this cultural healing system offered a small measure of freedom from the masters' power, in addition to opposition to prevailing medical practice (Banks 1991).

Doctors publicized the risk of opiate addiction as early as the 1870s, but prescribing and using opiates was legal, and many continued to administer morphine injections indiscriminately. The growing number of over-the-counter products containing opiates, and later cocaine (circa 1880) and heroin (in 1898), remained unregulated. In 1835, according to estimates extrapolated from opium imports and the minimum average daily dose needed to sustain an addict, there was less than 1 (0.72) addict among 1,000 Americans. By 1894, using these same estimates, the rate was more than 4 (4.59) in 1,000 (Courtwright 1982).

Between 1895 and 1914, low-income white males who smoked opium or sniffed heroin came to dominate the addict population when medically induced addiction declined, opium imports were banned, and patent medicines regulated. From the available evidence, this change brought on a concomitant shift in public concern: Opiate abuse in America became a social problem.

This change in public perception coincided with the view, portrayed in the *New York Times,* that black cocaine use was "a new Southern menace." In 1898, as disfranchisement and "lynch law" became commonplace, a New Orleans physician reported increasing cocaine use among African Americans in that city. Beginning in 1900 and continuing for more than a decade, newspapers in the North and South recounted sensationalized allegations of superhuman feats and violent crimes by "cocainized negroes" reportedly impervious to policemen's bullets. The specter of saloons selling "brain-numbing cocaine" amid allegations of assaults on white women triggered a four-day antiblack riot in Atlanta in 1906 (Banks 1991).

Most drug historians question the validity of these unsubstantiated accounts. Cocaine was widely consumed in many forms and accessible to all groups. A study of Georgia asylum admissions and a survey of drug arrests in Atlanta, New Orleans, and Washington, D.C., confirms the continued underrepresentation of African Americans among those addicted (Banks 1991).

Several historians contend that the Atlanta episode reflects the racial climate more than the prevalence of cocaine abuse among African Americans (Musto 1972). It is reasonable to conclude that some blacks did use cocaine. But no available evidence indicates that they did so at a greater rate than other Americans or that its use inspired a black crime wave.

Nonetheless some southern police departments purchased more potent weapons and antiblack violence continued. Without benefit of supporting evidence, advocates for national drug control successfully exploited the "menace," testifying before Congress that "a great many of the southern rape cases have been traced to cocaine." With passage of the Harrison Act in 1914, the first federal law to control the sale and distribution of narcotics and cocaine, the drug problem in America was transformed into a criminal problem.

In 1915, the first wave of African Americans began to leave the South for jobs and greater racial justice in the North. Instead they found limited opportunities and greater exposure to opium, marijuana, and cocaine, peddled mainly by Italians, Irish, and Jews. The rate of African-American addiction began to increase.

Studies of drug clinics in the 1920s still reported a relatively low rate of African-American addiction. Biographical accounts by James BALDWIN (1985), MALCOLM X (1964), and Milton Mezzrow (1946) and oral histories of abusers testify that at this incipient stage, black drug abuse was an insignificant, invisible phenomenon confined to adults. They recall a widely respected sanction prohibiting African-American youth from any involvement with drugs (Courtwright, Joseph, and Des Jarlais 1989).

African-American music provides another view of drug use. Between 1920 and 1940, the BLUES was a multifaceted discourse addressing drug use, directly and indirectly. The genre records a developing drug culture ranging from sophisticated nightclubs in the North to "jook joints" in the rural South. The blues testifies to the accessiblity of morphine, opium, marijuana, and cocaine despite the law, provides a critical portrayal of drug abusers and the descent to addiction, and comments on the rise in drug-law enforcement and how the GREAT DEPRESSION drove some to sell "dope." Some songs explicitly celebrated a drug-induced escape from misery, but many sounded a cautionary note, as seen in the title of one blues song from Memphis, "Better Leave That Stuff Alone" (1928).

As the Depression deepened and drug enforcement increased in the late 1930s, references to drugs in blues lyrics were fewer and more subtle, but African-American newspapers reported on the drug "peril." Drugs of all kinds were cheap and plentiful, and there was very little crime associated with their use. One study reported disproportionate numbers of black opiate abusers in Chicago. To some analysts, drug arrests are a more accurate measure of public concern than of the actual incidence of abuse. Reports from the Federal Bureau of Narcotics, organized only in 1930, show that in 1940, African Americans represented 10 percent of the population but 24 percent of those arrested for drug violations. But by 1941, the war in Europe disrupted international heroin traffic and drug use declined.

Drug history dates African America's drug problem from the end of World War II—the same period that saw a vigorous challenge to racial discrimination. By 1946, new trafficking routes were organized and an abundance of cheap, pure heroin flowed into the ghettos of New York, Chicago, and Los Angeles, and to smaller cities like Boston and Detroit. Federal arrest records as well as autobiographies by well-known figures such as Billie HOLIDAY (1956) and Malcolm X (1964) recount growing numbers of African Americans involved with drugs. Still, most maintained jobs and families. According to some analysts, the trend inspired little attention outside the black community.

In 1950, the criminal organizations controlling narcotics trafficking adopted a new marketing strategy: the price of heroin went up and its purity went down. Active recruitment by desperate addicts coupled with youthful curiosity, a flood of heroin and increasing exposure to a growing street trade contributed to heroin's allure. Under the weight of these combined factors, the cultural barrier against adolescent use gave way. Claude Brown's *Manchild in the Promised Land* (1965) likened this new phase to a plague that brought personal destruction and a diminishing sense of family and community as African Americans suffered increasing CRIME rates.

Law enforcement's reaction to adolescent addiction was swift. Harry Anslinger, the influential head of the Federal Bureau of Narcotics, was a proponent of the view that heroin abuse was a product of poverty and the slums. Soon media reports echoed this view. Several studies indicate that racially biased news coverage became a vehicle for the enactment of the severest drug penalties in the nation's history (Boggs Act, 1951; Narcotic Drug Control Act, 1956). Statistically, the effects were dramatic. The population of the two federal drug farms, established in 1935, changed from white to black and Hispanic. Between 1940 and 1950 the percentage of African Americans arrested for drug violations more than doubled (from 24 percent to 52 percent). By 1954, when the Supreme Court made its historic ruling against segregated schools, 64 percent of all those arrested for drug violations were black (Courtwright, Joseph, and Des Jarlais 1989).

Calls by national black organizations for government intervention, the Nation of Islam's rehabilitation efforts, and, by some accounts, the racial pride inspired by the civil rights movement between 1957 and 1963 achieved a salutary effect and the arrest rate slowed. But in the 1960s there was a spectacular increase in the quantity and variety of drugs available, and there were major shifts in public concern. When a growing white counterculture began using marijuana, amphetamines, and hallucinogens in the early sixties, public opinion supported rehabilitation as an alternative to imprisonment. But by 1970, as heroin reached unprecedented levels in the inner cities and encroached on the suburbs, as addiction soared among troops in Vietnam and urban riots tore through major cities, the notion of a black drug "contagion" was promoted in mainstream publications such as *Newsweek* and *Look* magazines.

Advocating "law and order," President Richard M. Nixon implemented a "war" on drugs that included distribution of methadone, a synthetic drug that experts claimed would eliminate the crime associated with addiction. African Americans protested the availability of this addictive drug, but opposition faded as the spread of addiction and crime took their toll on black America. Methadone clinics became a part of the urban landscape.

While the proportion of blacks to whites arrested declined in the 1960s, the actual numbers of African Americans sanctioned skyrocketed. *Uniform Crime Reports* (*UCR*) indicated that from 1960 through 1964, the black drug arrest rate averaged 76.4 of every 100,000, increasing from 7,570 to 9,038. However, from 1965 to 1970 the arrest rate increased more than fourfold to 395.7 per 100,000 or 61,223 African Americans. Even a notable decline in heron initiates between 1970 and 1974 proved insufficient in the wake of another critical transformation: The growing number of black independent drug dealers were organizing for a greater share of the wholesale market.

After 1970, increasing exposure and access to a variety of drugs became a major factor in African-American life. So-called designer drugs, potent synthetic substances such as phencyclidine (PCP), were available mainly in urban areas. Snorting cocaine became a popular nonaddictive indulgence for the affluent. After 1979, freebasing, or smoking relatively pure cocaine, proved its addictive potential. The most detrimental change came in 1982–1983 with crack or "rock" cocaine, which provided a cheap, smokable and virulently addictive high that transformed cocaine for mass marketing.

The crack era departed from earlier episodes in significant ways: It engulfed both rural and urban America, the number of female abusers increased dramatically, opportunities for street-level control of the market opened, and black youth gangs became intricately organized drug-dealing networks recruiting progressively younger employees (Williams 1989). One of the most devastating changes was in the increasingly violent nature of drug-related crime.

The proliferation of crack brought a surfeit of powerful automatic weapons and impersonal violence motivated by profit. In the latter half of the 1980s, crack-related murders caused a harrowing increase in the homicide rate of young black males and a concomitant decline in the life expectancy of the entire African-American community.

The dangers of abuse multiplied with the transmission of the AIDS virus through heroin addicts' contaminated hypodermic needles. Equally ominous was the advent of "crack babies," at-risk newborns seriously impaired by their mothers' drug use. Recognizing the trend's life-threatening potential, newly formed community groups as well as established national organizations developed grass-roots prevention and intervention strategies in the late 1980s (Lusane 1991).

Despite periodic claims of approaching victory, federally sponsored drug "wars" contributed to an alarming African-American arrest rate with little effect on the ever-increasing flow of drugs. *UCR* figures report that black drug arrests doubled between 1970 and 1980 (from 61,223 to 125,607) and doubled again between 1985 and 1989 (from 210,298 to 452,574). At its peak in 1989, the rate of black drug arrests was at 1,459.8 per 100,000. African Americans represented approximately 12 percent of the population and reportedly 20 percent of all cocaine users, but 42 percent of all drug arrests.

By 1990, ineffective U.S. drug policies, the growing inaccessibility of jobs combined with increasingly accessible drugs, and changing cultural sanctions made illicit drugs a critical factor in the quality of life in black America. Drugs' insidious effect on family and community is both cause and effect in a spiraling social crisis that victimizes indiscriminately. In stark contrast to its early history, in the waning years of the twentieth century the abuse of addictive drugs is a problem of catastrophic proportions threatening all African-American life and culture.

REFERENCES

BANKS, RAE. "Living the Legacy: Historical Perspectives on African American Drug Abuse." In J. Debro and C. Bolek, eds., *Drug Abuse Research Issues at Historically Black Colleges and Universities.* Tuskegee, Ala., 1991.

COURTWRIGHT, DAVID. *Dark Paradise: Opiate Addition in America Before 1940.* Cambridge, Mass., 1982.

COURTWRIGHT, DAVID, HERMAN JOSEPH, and DON DES JARLAIS. *Addicts Who Survived: An Oral History of Narcotic Use in America, 1923–1965.* Knoxville, Tenn., 1989.

HOLIDAY, BILLIE, with W. Dufty. *Lady Sings the Blues.* Garden City, N.Y., 1956.

LUSANE, CLARENCE. *Pipe Dream Blues: Racism & the War on Drugs.* Boston, 1991.

MEZZROW, MILTON, and B. WOLFE. *Really the Blues.* New York, 1946.

MUSTO, DAVID. *The American Disease.* New Haven, Conn., 1972.

WILLIAMS, TERRY. *The Cocaine Kids: The Inside Story of a Teenage Drug Ring.* Reading, Mass., 1989.

RAE BANKS

Du Bois, Shirley Graham (1896–1977), writer, political activist. Shirley Graham Du Bois was born Lola Bell Graham in 1896 near Indianapolis, Ind., the daughter of an African Methodist Episcopal Church (AME) minister. She studied music at the Sorbonne and Harvard University, and from 1929 to 1931 she headed the music department at Morgan College in Baltimore. In 1931 she enrolled at Oberlin College, where she earned bachelor's and master's degrees. In 1932 her opera *Tom-Tom* was staged at the Cleveland Stadium. She became director of the Chicago unit of the FEDERAL THEATRE PROJECT and then received a Rosenwald Fellowship for creative writing, which she took at Yale from 1938 to 1940.

Graham directed YWCA theater groups until the NAACP employed her as a field secretary in New York, a position she held from 1942 until 1944. During this period she began her series of biographies for young adults of noteworthy African Americans. Graham held a Guggenheim Fellowship in 1945–1947 and a National Institute of Arts and Letters Award in 1950. On February 14, 1951, she married her longtime friend and adviser, W. E. B. DU BOIS, and devoted her energies to causes championed by him.

At the invitation of President Kwame Nkrumah, the couple moved to Ghana in 1961, the year she also became a founding editor of *Freedomways.* Between 1964 and 1966, Graham was the organizing director of Ghana television. When a coup toppled Nkrumah, she moved to Cairo. The U.S. Department of Justice would not permit her to return to the United States, citing her membership in numerous subversive groups. She died of cancer in Beijing in 1977.

REFERENCE

BROWN-GUILLORY, ELIZABETH. "Shirley Graham Du Bois." In Darlene Clark Hine, ed., *Black Women in America: An Historical Encyclopedia.* Brooklyn, N.Y., 1993.

CHRISTINE A. LUNARDINI

Du Bois, William Edward Burghardt (February 23, 1869–August 27, 1963), historian, sociologist, novelist, and editor. W. E. B. Du Bois was born in Great Barrington, Mass. His mother, Mary Burghardt Du Bois, belonged to a tiny community of African Americans who had been settled in the area since before the Revolution; his father, Alfred Du Bois, was a visitor to the region who deserted the family in his son's infancy. In the predominantly white local schools and Congregational church, Du Bois absorbed ideas and values that left him "quite thoroughly New England."

From 1885 to 1888 he attended Fisk University in Nashville, where he first encountered the harsher forms of racism. After earning a B.A. (1888) at Fisk, he attended Harvard University, where he took another B.A. (1890) and a doctorate in history (1895).

Among his teachers were the psychologist William James, the philosophers Josiah Royce and George Santayana, and the historian A. B. Hart. Between 1892 and 1894 he studied history and sociology at the University of Berlin. His dissertation, *The Suppression of the African Slave-Trade to the United States,* was published in 1896 as the first volume of the Harvard Historical Studies.

Between 1894 and 1896, Du Bois taught at Wilberforce University, Ohio, where he met and married Nina Gomer, a student, in 1896. The couple had two children, Burghardt and Yolande. In 1896, he accepted a position at the University of Pennsylvania to gather data for a commissioned study of blacks in Philadelphia. This work resulted in *The Philadelphia Negro* (1899), an acclaimed early example of empirical sociology. In 1897, he joined the faculty at ATLANTA UNIVERSITY and took over the annual Atlanta University Conference for the Study of the Negro Problems. From 1897 to 1914 he edited an annual study of one aspect or another of black life, such as education or the church.

Appalled by the conditions facing blacks nationally, Du Bois sought ways other than scholarship to effect change. The death of his young son from dysentery in 1899 also deeply affected him, as did the widely publicized lynching of a black man, Sam Hose, in Georgia the same year. In 1900, in London, he boldly asserted that "the problem of the Twentieth Century is the problem of the color line." He repeated this statement in *The Souls of Black Folk* (1903), mainly a collection of essays on African-American history, sociology, religion, and music, in which Du Bois wrote of an essential black double consciousness: the existence of twin souls ("an American, a Negro") warring in each black body. The book also attacked Booker T. WASHINGTON, the most powerful black American of the age, for advising blacks to surrender the right to vote and to a liberal education in return for white friendship and support. Du Bois was established as probably the premier intellectual in black America, and Washington's main rival.

His growing radicalism also led him to organize the NIAGARA MOVEMENT, a group of blacks who met in 1905 and 1906 to agitate for "manhood rights" for African Americans. He founded two journals, *Moon* (1905–1906) and *Horizon* (1907–1910). In 1909 he published *John Brown,* a sympathetic biography of the white abolitionist martyr. Then, in 1910, he resigned his professorship to join the new NATIONAL ASSOCIATION FOR THE ADVANCEMENT OF COLORED PEOPLE (NAACP) in New York, which had been formed in response to growing concern about the treatment of blacks. As its director of research, Du Bois founded a monthly magazine, the CRISIS. In

1911 he published his first novel, *The Quest of the Silver Fleece,* a study of the cotton industry seen through the fate of a young black couple struggling for a life of dignity and meaning.

The *Crisis* became a powerful forum for Du Bois's views on race and politics. Meanwhile, his developing interest in Africa led him to write *The Negro* (1915), a study offering historical and demographic information on peoples of African descent around the world. Hoping to affect colonialism in Africa after World War I, he also organized PAN-AFRICAN CONGRESSES in Europe in 1919, 1921, and 1923, and in New York in 1927. However, he clashed with the most popular black leader of the era, Marcus GARVEY of the UNIVERSAL NEGRO IMPROVEMENT ASSOCIATION. Du Bois regarded Garvey's "back to Africa" scheme as ill-considered, and Garvey as impractical and disorganized.

Du Bois's second prose collection, *Darkwater: Voices from Within the Veil* (1920), did not repeat the success of *The Souls of Black Folk* but captured his increased militancy. In the 1920s, the *Crisis* played a major role in the HARLEM RENAISSANCE by publishing early work by Langston HUGHES, Countee CULLEN, and other writers. Eventually, Du Bois found some writers politically irresponsible; his essay "Criteria of Negro Art" (1926) insisted that all art is essentially propaganda. He pressed this point with a novel, *Dark Princess* (1928), about a plot by the darker races to overthrow European colonialism. In 1926 he visited the Soviet Union, then nine years old. Favorably impressed by what he saw, he boldly declared himself "a Bolshevik."

The GREAT DEPRESSION increased his interest in SOCIALISM but also cut the circulation of the *Crisis* and weakened Du Bois's position with the leadership of the NAACP, with which he had fought from the beginning. In 1934, he resigned as editor and returned to teach at Atlanta University. His interest in Marxism, which had started with his student days in Berlin, dominated his next book, *Black Reconstruction in America* (1934), a massive and controversial reevaluation of the role of the freedmen in the South after the Civil War. In 1936, Du Bois commenced a weekly column of opinion in various black newspapers, starting with the PITTSBURGH COURIER. He emphasized his continuing concern for Africa with *Black Folk: Then and Now* (1939), an expanded and updated revision of *The Negro.*

In 1940, Du Bois published his first full-length autobiography, *Dusk of Dawn: An Autobiography of a Concept of Race,* in which he examined modern racial theory against the major events and intellectual currents in his lifetime. In 1944, his life took another dramatic turn when he was suddenly retired by Atlanta University after growing tension between him-

W. E. B. Du Bois in his study. (Photographs and Prints Division, Schomburg Center for Research in Black Culture, The New York Public Library, Astor, Lenox and Tilden Foundations)

self and certain administrators. When the NAACP rehired him that year, he returned to New York as director of special research. In 1945 he was honored at the Fifth Pan-African Congress in Manchester, England, and published a bristling polemic, *Color and Democracy: Colonies and Peace*. A year later, he produced a controversial pamphlet, "An Appeal to the World," submitted by the NAACP on behalf of black Americans to the United Nations Commission on Civil Rights. In 1947 came his *The World and Africa,* an examination of Africa's future following World War II.

By this time Du Bois had moved to the left, well beyond the interests of the NAACP, which generally supported the Democratic party. In 1948, when he endorsed the Progressive party and its presidential candidate, Henry Wallace, he was fired. He then joined Paul ROBESON, who was by this time firmly identified with radical socialism, at the COUNCIL ON AFRICAN AFFAIRS, which had been officially declared a "subversive" organization. In 1950, Du Bois ran

unsuccessfully for the U.S. Senate from New York on the American Labor party ticket. Also that year, in another move applauded by communists, he accepted the chairmanship of the Peace Information Center, which circulated the Stockholm Peace Appeal against nuclear weapons.

Early in 1951, Du Bois and four colleagues from the Peace Information Center were indicted on the charge of violating the law that required agents of a foreign power to register. On bail and awaiting trial, he married Shirley Lola Graham, a fellow socialist and writer (his first wife had died in 1950). At the trial in November 1951, the judge heard testimony, then unexpectedly granted a motion by the defense for a directed acquittal. Du Bois was undeterred by his ordeal. In 1953, he recited the Twenty-third Psalm at the grave of Julius and Ethel Rosenberg, executed as spies for the Soviet Union. For such involvements, he found himself ostracized by some black leaders and organizations. "The colored children," he wrote, "ceased to hear my name."

Returning to fiction, he composed a trilogy, *The Black Flame,* about the life and times of a black educator seen against the backdrop of generations of black and white lives and national and international events (the trilogy comprised *The Ordeal of Mansart,* 1957; *Mansart Builds a School,* 1959; and *World of Color,* 1961). After the government lifted its ban on his foreign travel in 1958, Du Bois visited various countries, including the Soviet Union and China. In Moscow on May 1, 1959, he received the Lenin Peace Prize.

In 1960 Du Bois visited Ghana for the inauguration of Kwame Nkrumah as its first president. He then accepted an invitation from Nkrumah to return to Ghana and start work on an *Encyclopedia Africana,* a project in which he had long been interested. In October 1961, after applying (successfully) for membership in the COMMUNIST PARTY, he left the United States. He began work on the project in Ghana, but illness the following year caused him to go for treatment to Romania. Afterward, he visited Peking and Moscow. In February 1963, he renounced his American citizenship and officially became a citizen of Ghana. He died in Accra, Ghana, and was buried there.

REFERENCES

APTHEKER, HERBERT. *Annotated Bibliography of the Published Writings of W. E. B. Du Bois.* Millwood, N.Y., 1973.
LEWIS, DAVID LEVERING. *W. E. B. Du Bois: Biography of a Race 1868–1919.* New York, 1993.
RAMPERSAD, ARNOLD. *The Art and Imagination of W. E. B. Du Bois.* New York, 1973.

ARNOLD RAMPERSAD

Dumas, Henry Lee (July 20, 1934–May 23, 1968), writer. Born in Sweet Home, Ark., Henry Dumas came to New York City at the age of ten. He received his secondary education at Commerce High School in Harlem and briefly attended the City College of New York before joining the U.S. Air Force, where he served from 1953 until 1957. He attended Rutgers University full-time from 1958 to 1961, and continued to take classes there part-time until 1965, during which time he became increasingly active in the CIVIL RIGHTS MOVEMENT. Dumas was employed as a social worker for the state of New York from 1965 to 1966; in 1967 he worked as assistant director of Upward Bound at Hiram College in Hiram, Ohio and afterwards moved on to become a teacher-counselor and director of language workshops for the Experiment in Higher Education at Southern Illinois University in Carbondale (1967–8). From 1953 to 1968 he was active in the editing, publishing, and distribution of small magazines such as the *Anthologist, Untitled,* and *Camel.* Although Dumas contributed poetry and short stories to these periodicals and others, he did not live to see his work published in book form. While standing on the 125th Street station railroad platform in Harlem on May 23, 1968, Dumas was shot and killed under uncertain circumstances by a transit police officer.

Dumas's posthumous publications, edited by Eugene B. Redmond, a former colleague at Southern Illinois University, include *Poetry for My People* (coedited by Hale Chatfield, 1970; reprinted as *Play Ebony, Play Ivory,* 1974); *Ark of Bones, and Other Stories* (coedited by Chatfield, 1970); *Rope of Wind and Other Stories* (1979); a collection of short fiction, *Goodbye Sweetwater* (1988); and a volume of poetry, *Knees of a Natural Man* (1988). An unfinished novel, *Jonah and the Green Stone* (1976), traces the maturation of a southern black youth and is structured around the biblical stories of Jonah and Noah. Many of Dumas's poems and stories focused on contemporary black experience in the South in the context of the developing civil rights movement. Dumas drew heavily upon historical, cultural, and biblical traditions in his exploration of the African-American struggle to endure and overcome the national legacy of racism and oppression.

REFERENCES

Black American Literature Forum. Henry Dumas Issue. 22, no. 2 (Summer 1988): 143–411.
TAYLOR, CLYDE. "Henry Dumas: Legacy of a Long-Breath Singer." *Black World* 24 (September 1975): 4–16.

CAMERON BARDRICK

Dumas Dramatic Players.   *See* Karamu House.

Dunbar, Paul Laurence (June 27, 1872–February 9, 1906), writer. Dunbar, the child of ex-slaves, was the first African-American writer to attain widespread fame for his literary activities. Known chiefly for his DIALECT POETRY, Dunbar also broke new ground in several ways for the further development of an African-American literary tradition.

Born and raised in Dayton, Ohio, Dunbar showed early signs of literary ambition. He served as editor of his high school newspaper, and at the same time began a short-lived newspaper of his own, the Dayton *Tattler,* focusing on matters of interest to the black community. Like most young black men, and despite a good school record, he confronted upon graduation a world with few opportunities, and had to take work as an elevator operator; but he also became increasingly dedicated to his literary activity, especially to poetry. Encouraged by several white friends in Dayton as well as by the noted popular poet James Whitcomb Riley, Dunbar published locally his first book of poetry, *Oak and Ivy,* in 1892. However, he achieved real fame in 1896, when an expanded and revised collection, *Majors and Minors*—also published mainly for a local audience—came to the attention of the prominent American writer William Dean Howells. Howells admired it and saw to the publication that year of a larger volume, *Lyrics of Lowly Life,* by the established American firm Dodd, Mead. It was the first of five major collections to be published by the company during Dunbar's lifetime.

Singled out for praise by Howells, and serving as the basis for Dunbar's fame, was his dialect verse. Fitting broadly into the popular, mainly white-authored, plantation-tradition literature of the time, Dunbar's dialect poetry created a sentimental portrait of African-American folklife in the antebellum South, treating a variety of themes, from love and courtship to social life and folk ideas. Although the dialect Dunbar used owed more to its literary antecedents than to actual folk speech, he also drew heavily on folk traditions for his own subjects and themes, and thus often succeeded in giving real life to the form, freeing it from the stereotypes that dominated the works of white practitioners. The publication of this work, together with successful public readings of it throughout the United States and abroad, made Dunbar among the most popular poets, regardless of race, in America at the turn of the twentieth century.

Dunbar's success with dialect poetry had a powerful impact on black American literature during its time. He had few black predecessors in the form—although such early black dialect writers as James Edwin Campbell and Daniel Webster Davis were his exact contemporaries—but as his fame grew, so did the volume of dialect poetry in African-American literature. It began to appear frequently in black newspapers and magazines, and few collections of African-American poetry over the next two decades lacked at least some examples of dialect verse. Many were dominated by it.

Dunbar himself was ambivalent about his success with the dialect form. He wrote a great deal of poetry in standard English, and felt that this was his most important work. Much of this verse is significant, especially for its time, as Dunbar not only addressed such contemporary issues as southern racial injustice and violence, but broke notably from conventions of piety and gentility that had earlier dominated poetry by black Americans. Still, it was the dialect poetry that critics, black and white, praised during Dunbar's lifetime, a fact that the poet found greatly frustrating. His frustration spilled over into a personal life marked by real difficulties, including problems in his marriage to the talented writer Alice Moore Dunbar (*see* Alice DUNBAR-NELSON), and the alcoholism and chronic ill health, culminating in tuberculosis, that led to his early death.

Although Dunbar made his reputation as a poet, his literary production during his brief life showed real diversity. It include a large number of short stories that appeared in popular magazines and in four major collections published by Dodd, Mead. Much of this short fiction complemented the popular dialect poetry, some of it written entirely in dialect and most of it featuring dialect-speaking folk characters. A few stories, however, moved in directions of protest, or of exploring issues of urbanization and cultural conflict. Dunbar also did some writing for the theater, including the highly popular musical comedy *Clorindy,* on which he collaborated with the composer William Marion COOK.

But some of his most important work, outside his poetry, lay in his novels. Dunbar published four novels; one, *The Love of Landry* (1900), was a sentimental work set in the American West, but the other three focused on questions of culture and identity in ways that allowed him to explore the issues affecting him as an individual and as an artist. These included *The Uncalled* (1899), tracing a young man's efforts to deal with pressures exerted on him to enter the ministry; *The Fanatics* (1901), a tale of Civil War-era Ohio; and *The Sport of the Gods* (1902), describing the travails of a black family forced to flee the South and to make its

A writer of sensitive lyrics in both black dialect and standard English, Paul Laurence Dunbar had a greater acclaim than any African-American poet since Phillis Wheatley. This photograph is from 1905, the year before his early death. (Prints and Photographs Division, Library of Congress)

way in the more complex setting of urban New York. Only the last novel featured black protagonists, and it has often been considered the pioneering work in literary realism by a black writer. But all, excepting *The Love of Landry,* looked significantly and innovatively at the kinds of forces, cultural and psychological, that confront and constrain the individual in an effort to create a satisfying personal identity, and, at least implicitly, at the meaning of race in American life.

Dunbar's work has not always fared well in the hands of critics in the years after his death. Not without justification, many have found too much of the dialect work, despite the writer's efforts to the contrary, to be uncomfortably close to that of white plantation-tradition writers, contributing to the same stereotypes the plantation tradition helped to spread. But Dunbar's influence and originality remain important milestones in the subsequent evolution of an African-American literary tradition.

REFERENCES

BAKER, HOUSTON A., JR. "The 'Limitless' Freedom of Myth: Paul Laurence Dunbar's *The Sport of the Gods* and the Criticism of Afro-American Literature." In *Blues, Ideology, and Afro-American Literature: A Vernacular Theory*. Chicago, 1984, pp. 114–138.

MARTIN, JAY, ed. *A Singer in the Dawn: Reinterpretations of Paul Laurence Dunbar*. New York, 1975.

REVELL, PETER. *Paul Laurence Dunbar*. Boston, 1979.

WAGNER, JEAN. *Black Poets of the United States from Paul Laurence Dunbar to Langston Hughes*. Translated by Kenneth Douglas. Urbana, Ill., 1973, pp. 73–125.

DICKSON D. BRUCE, JR.

Dunbar-Nelson, Alice (July 19, 1875–September 18, 1935), writer. Alice Dunbar-Nelson was born Alice Ruth Moore in New Orleans, La. From her father, Joseph Moore, a sailor who never lived with the family, she inherited the light-colored skin and hair which enabled her to pass as white when she wished. Her mother, Patricia Wright Moore, an ex-slave who was part black and part Native American, supported the family as a seamstress. After attending public schools, Dunbar-Nelson graduated from the teachers' training program at Straight College (now Dillard University) in her hometown in 1892. In addition to her teaching, she worked as a stenographer and bookkeeper for a black printing firm. She was interested in theater, played the piano and cello, and presided over a literary society. In 1895, *Violets and Other Tales,* her first collection of stories, essays, and poetry, was published.

In 1896 she moved with her family to West Medford, Mass. The following year she moved to New York, where she taught public school in Brooklyn while she helped her friend Victoria Earle Matthews found the White Rose Mission (later the White Rose Home for Girls in Harlem), where she also taught. On March 8, 1898, she married the poet Paul Laurence DUNBAR, and moved to Washington, D.C., where he lived. Their romance had been conducted through letters. He first wrote to her after seeing her picture alongside one of her poems in a poetry review. At their first meeting they agreed to marry.

Although it was a stormy marriage, it significantly aided Dunbar-Nelson's literary career. In 1899 her husband's agent had her second collection, *The Goodness of St. Roque,* published as a companion book to Dunbar's *Poems of Cabin and Field*. The couple separated in 1902 and Dunbar-Nelson moved to Wilmington, Del., where she taught English at the Howard High School. Paul Dunbar died in 1906. In 1910 Dunbar-Nelson married a fellow teacher, Henry Arthur Callis, but that union soon dissolved. In 1916, she married Robert J. Nelson, a journalist with whom she remained until her death in 1935.

Dunbar-Nelson's writings, published continually throughout her life, displayed a wide variety of interests. After studying English literature as a special student at Cornell University, she published "Wordsworth's Use of Milton's Description of Pandemonium" in the April 1909 issue of *Modern Language Notes*. She also published several pedagogical articles, including "Is It Time for the Negro Colleges in the South To Be Put into the Hands of Negro Teachers?" (*Twentieth Century Negro Literature* 1902) and "Negro Literature for Negro Pupils" (*The Southern Workman* February 1922). The *Journal of Negro History* published her historical essay "People of Color in Louisiana" in two parts; the first appeared in October 1916 and the second in January 1917. From 1920 to 1922 she and Nelson published and edited the *Wilmington Advocate*. In addition, she wrote columns for the Pittsburgh *Courier* (1926, 1930) and the Washing-

Alice Dunbar-Nelson. (Photographs and Prints Division, Schomburg Center for Research in Black Culture, The New York Public Library, Astor, Lenox and Tilden Foundations)

ton *Eagle* (1926–1930) in which she reviewed contemporary literature and delivered political analyses.

In 1920, Dunbar-Nelson lost her job at Howard High School due to her political activity on behalf of women's and civil rights. That year she founded the Industrial School for Colored Girls in Marshalltown, Del., which she directed from 1924 to 1928. From 1929 to 1931 she served as Executive Secretary of the American Inter-Racial Peace Committee, a subsidiary of the American Friends (Quakers) Service Committee. She used this position to organize the National Negro Music Festival in 1929, and to engage in a ten-week cross-country speaking tour in 1930. In 1932 she moved to Philadelphia, where her husband was a governor appointee to the Pennsylvania Athletic Commission. Her lifelong interest in the African-American oral tradition prompted her to publish *Masterpieces of Negro Eloquence* in 1914 and *The Dunbar Speaker and Entertainer* in 1920. She was a member of the Delta Sigma Theta sorority and the Daughter Elks. Dunbar-Nelson is often considered a poet of the Harlem Renaissance. Her two most anthologized poems are "Sonnet" (often called "Violets"), and "I Sit and Sew." Her diary, published in 1984, is an invaluable source of information about her life.

REFERENCES

HULL, GLORIA T. *Color, Sex, and Poetry: Three Women Writers of the Harlem Renaissance.* Bloomington, Ind., 1987.

HULL, GLORIA, T., ed. *Give Us Each Day: The Diary of Alice Dunbar-Nelson.* New York, 1984.

MICHEL FABRE

Duncan, Robert Todd (February 12, 1903–), concert singer. Robert Todd Duncan, baritone, was born in Danville, Ky., and raised in Indianapolis. He received a B.A. degree from Butler University and an M.A. from Columbia University Teachers College. From 1925 to 1929 he taught at Simmons University, and from 1931 to 1945 at HOWARD UNIVERSITY, where he also served as head of the music department.

In 1935 Duncan created the role of Porgy in George Gershwin's *Porgy and Bess,* eventually singing the role more than eighteen hundred times through 1944, as well as assuming it in the recording of the 1942 revival. He also performed in many operas, singing the roles of Alfio in a 1934 all-black production of Mascagni's *Cavalleria rusticana,* Amonasro in Verdi's *Aida,* and the title role in Verdi's *Rigoletto.* In 1945 he became the first black male to appear with a major

United States opera company, the New York City Opera. His roles included Tonio in Leoncavallo's *Pagliacci* and Escamillo in Bizet's *Carmen.*

In addition to *Porgy and Bess,* Duncan's theater performances include *The Sun Never Sets* (1938), *Cabin in the Sky* (1940), and *Lost in the Stars* (1950), for which he earned the New York Drama Critics Award and a Tony Award. His film credits include *Syncopation* (1942) and *Unchained* (1955). Television credits include *Todd Duncan: A Mighty Voice* (1982).

Although he never sang at the Metropolitan Opera or recorded in a major studio, between 1940 and his retirement in 1965 Duncan gave more than two thousand recitals around the world and was a soloist with major orchestras. He won awards for his performances in musicals, an NAACP award for his contribution to the theater, and the president of Haiti's Medal of Honor and Merit (1945).

REFERENCES

ALPERT, HOLLIS. *The Life and Times of Porgy and Bess.* New York, 1990.

JABLONSKI, EDWARD. *Gershwin: A Biography.* New York, 1987.

SOUTHERN, EILEEN. *The Music of Black Americans: A History.* 2nd ed. New York, 1983.

JAMES STANDIFER

Duncanson, Robert S. (1821–December 21, 1872), painter. In this thirty-year career from the antebellum era through Reconstruction, Robert S. Duncanson progressed from being a humble housepainter to an artist of international stature who marked the emergence of the African-American practitioner into the Anglo-European art world. Duncanson was the first American artist of African descent to appropriate the landscape as an expression of his cultural identity. He was born into a family of mulatto freepeople who worked as painters, carpenters, and handymen in Fayette, N.Y. The family moved to Monroe, Mich., around 1830; there Duncanson apprenticed in the trade and then worked as a housepainter. By 1841 he had moved to Cincinnati, "the Athens of the West," to learn the art of painting. Throughout the 1840s he worked as an itinerant artist traveling between Cincinnati, Monroe, and Detroit painting portraits, historical subjects, and still lifes.

While working in Detroit, Duncanson received a commission to paint *The Cliff Mine, Lake Superior* (1848)—an event that altered the course of his career. The commission, from the Pittsburgh abolitionist Rev. Charles Avery, launched Duncanson's career as a landscape painter and established a lifelong relationship with abolitionist patrons. In this formative stage of his art, Duncanson was influenced by a group of Cincinnati landscape painters, including T. Worthington Whittredge (1820–1910) and William Louis Sonntag (1822–1900), to pursue the so-called Hudson River School style and create important early landscapes such as *Blue Hole, Flood Waters, Little Miami River* (1851; Cincinnati Art Museum). In 1853, he became the first African-American artist to take the traditional grand tour of Europe when abolitionist patron Nicholas Longworth sponsored his journey. Upon his return, Duncanson emerged as the principal landscape painter in the Ohio River Valley with such important pictures as *Landscape with Rainbow* (1859; National Museum of American Art). At this time he and James Pressley BALL, a daguerreotypist, formed the nucleus of a group of African-American artists in Cincinnati who actively participated in the antislavery movement and created a monumental antislavery panorama that toured the United States.

In the months preceding the Civil War, Duncanson created the largest easel painting of his career, *The Land of the Lotus Eaters* (1861), which prophesied the imminent civil conflict. When he unveiled this vast tropical landscape, critics were moved to proclaim him "the best landscape painter in the West" (*Cincinnati Gazette,* May 30, 1862). Deeply troubled by the war, Duncanson exiled himself from the United States and traveled to Canada in 1863 on a journey to exhibit his "great picture" in England. Canadians warmly received the distinguished African-American painter without any reservations due to his race; he was therefore encouraged to remain there for two years, and contributed to founding a national landscape-painting school. He then toured the British Isles, where he was actively patronized by the aristocracy and where he extensively exhibited *The Lotus Eaters,* which English critics also praised as a "masterwork."

The success of Duncanson's second European tour crowned his career with international acclaim. Upon his return to Cincinnati in 1866, he began a series of Scottish landscapes inspired by English romantic literature, the finest being *Ellen's Isle, Loch Katrine* (1870). In his final years the artist suffered a tragic dementia, perhaps caused by lead poisoning, that led him to believe that he was possessed by the spirit of a master painter. His illness, combined with the pressures of racial oppression and his lofty artistic ambitions, proved too great for the artist to manage; he collapsed while hanging an exhibition in October 1872, dying in a Detroit sanatorium shortly thereafter.

REFERENCES

HARTIGAN, LINDA. "Robert Scott Duncanson." In *Sharing Traditions: Five Black Artists in Nineteenth Century America.* Washington, D.C., 1985, pp. 51–68.

KETNER, JOSEPH D. *The Emergence of the African-American Artist: Robert S. Duncanson 1821–1872.* Columbia, Mo., and London, 1993.

———. "Robert S. Duncanson (1821–1872): The Late Literary Landscape Paintings." *American Art Journal* 15 (Winter 1983): 35–47.

MCELROY, GUY. *Robert S. Duncanson: A Centennial Exhibition.* Cincinnati, 1972.

PORTER, JAMES A. "Robert S. Duncanson: Midwestern Romantic-Realist." *Art in America* 39 (October 1951): 99–154.

PRINGLE, ALLAN. "Robert S. Duncanson in Montreal, 1863–1865." *American Art Journal* 17 (Autumn 1985): 28–50.

JOSEPH D. KETNER

Dunham, Katherine (June 22, 1909–), choreographer and dancer. Born in Chicago, and raised in Joliet, Ill., Katherine Dunham did not begin formal dance training until her late teens. In Chicago she studied with Ludmilla Speranzeva and Mark Turbyfill, and danced her first leading role in Ruth Page's ballet *La Guiablesse* in 1933. She attended the University of Chicago on scholarship (B.A., Social Anthropology, 1936), where she was inspired by the work of anthropologists Robert Redfield and Melville Herskovits, who stressed the importance of the survival of African culture and ritual in understanding African-American culture. While in college she taught youngsters' dance classes and gave recitals in a Chicago storefront, calling her student company, founded in 1931, "Ballet Nègre." Awarded a Rosenwald Travel Fellowship in 1936 for her combined expertise in dance and anthropology, she departed after graduation for the West Indies (Jamaica, Trinidad, Cuba, Haiti, Martinique) to do field research in anthropology and dance. Combining her two interests, she linked the function and form of Caribbean dance and ritual to their African progenitors.

The West Indian experience changed forever the focus of Dunham's life (eventually she would live in Haiti half of the time and become a priestess in the *vodoun* religion), and caused a profound shift in her career. This initial fieldwork provided the nucleus for future researches and began a lifelong involvement with the people and dance of Haiti. From this Dunham generated her master's thesis (Northwestern University, 1947) and more fieldwork. She lectured widely, published numerous articles, and wrote three books about her observations: *Journey to Accompong* (1946), *The Dances of Haiti* (her master's thesis, published in 1947), and *Island Possessed* (1969), underscoring how African religions and rituals adapted to the New World.

And, importantly for the development of modern dance, her fieldwork began her investigations into a vocabulary of movement that would form the core of the Katherine Dunham Technique. What Dunham gave modern dance was a coherent lexicon of African and Caribbean styles of movement—a flexible torso and spine, articulated pelvis and isolation of the limbs, a polyrhythmic strategy of moving—which she integrated with techniques of ballet and modern dance.

When she returned to Chicago in late 1937, Dunham founded the Negro Dance Group, a company of black artists dedicated to presenting aspects of African-American and African-Caribbean dance. Immediately she began incorporating the dances she had learned into her choreography. Invited in 1937 to be part of a notable New York City concert, *Negro Dance Evening,* she premiered "Haitian Suite," excerpted from choreography she was developing for the longer *L'Ag'Ya.* In 1937–1938 as dance director of the Negro Unit of the Federal Theater Project in Chicago, she made dances for *Emperor Jones* and *Run Lil' Chillun,* and presented her first version of *L'Ag'Ya* on January 27, 1938. Based on a Martinique folktale (ag'ya is a Martinique fighting dance), *L'Ag'Ya* is a seminal work, displaying Dunham's blend of exciting dance-drama and authentic African-Caribbean material.

Dunham moved her company to New York City in 1939, where she became dance director of the New York Labor Stage, choreographing the labor-union musical *Pins and Needles.* Simultaneously she was preparing a new production, *Tropics and Le Jazz Hot: From Haiti to Harlem.* It opened February 18, 1939, in what was intended to be a single weekend's concert at the Windsor Theatre in New York City. Its instantaneous success, however, extended the run for ten consecutive weekends and catapulted Dunham into the limelight. In 1940 Dunham and her company appeared in the black Broadway musical, *Cabin in the Sky,* staged by George Balanchine, in which Dunham played the sultry siren Georgia Brown—a character related to Dunham's other seductress, "Woman with a Cigar," from her solo "Shore Excursion" in *Tropics.* That same year Dunham married John Pratt, a theatrical designer who worked with her in 1938 at the Chicago Federal Theater Project, and for the next forty-seven years, until his death in 1986, Pratt was Dunham's husband and her artistic collaborator.

With *L'Ag'Ya* and *Tropics and le Jazz Hot: From Haiti to Harlem,* Dunham revealed her magical mix of dance and theater—the essence of "the Dunham touch"—a savvy combination of authentic Caribbean dance and rhythms with the heady spice of American showbiz. Genuine folk material was presented with lavish costumes, plush settings, and the orchestral arrangements based on Caribbean rhythms and folk music. Dancers moved through fantastical tropical

Katherine Dunham, choreographer and ethnologist, addresses a seminar on the role of art in the lives of African Americans. In the background, Langston Hughes presides. (Photographs and Prints Division, Schomburg Center for Research in Black Culture, The New York Public Library, Astor, Lenox and Tilden Foundations)

paradises or artistically designed juke-joints, while a loose storyline held together a succession of diverse dances. Dunham aptly called her spectacles "revues." She choreographed more than ninety individual dances, and produced five revues, four of which played on Broadway and toured worldwide. Her most critically acclaimed revue was her 1946 *Bal Nègre,* containing another Dunham dance favorite, *Shango,* based directly on *vodoun* ritual.

If her repertory was diverse, it was also coherent. *Tropics and le Jazz Hot: From Haiti to Harlem* incorporated dances from the West Indies as well as from Cuba and Mexico, while the "Le Jazz Hot" section featured early black American social dances, such as the Juba, Cake Walk, Ballin' the Jack, and Strut. The sequencing of dances, the theatrical journey from the tropics to urban black America implied—in the most entertaining terms—the ethnographic realities of cultural connections. In her 1943 *Tropical Revue,* she recycled material from the 1939 revue and added new dances, such as the balletic "Choros" (based on formal Brazilian quadrilles), and "Rites de Passage," which depicted puberty rituals so explicitly sexual that the dance was banned in Boston.

Beginning in the 1940s, the Katherine Dunham Dance Company appeared on Broadway and toured throughout the United States, Mexico, Latin America, and especially Europe, to enthusiastic reviews. In Europe Dunham was praised as a dancer and choreographer, recognized as a serious anthropologist and scholar, and admired as a glamorous beauty. Among her achievements was her resourcefulness in keeping her company going without any government funding. When short of money between engagements, Dunham and her troupe played in elegant nightclubs, such as Ciro's in Los Angeles. She also supplemented her income through film. Alone, or with her company, she appeared in nine Hollywood movies and in several foreign films between 1941 and 1959, among them *Carnival of Rhythm* (1939), *Star-Spangled Rhythm* (1942), *Stormy Weather* (1943), *Casbah* (1948), *Boote e Risposta* (1950), and *Mambo* (1954).

In 1945 Dunham opened the Dunham School of Dance and Theater (sometimes called the Dunham School of Arts and Research) in Manhattan. Although technique classes were the heart of the school, they were supplemented by courses in humanities, philosophy, languages, aesthetics, drama, and speech. For the next ten years many African-American dances of the next generation studied at her school, then passed on Dunham's technique to their students, situating it in dance mainstream (teachers such as Syvilla Fort, Talley BEATTY, Lavinia WILLIAMS, Walter Nicks, Hope Clark, Vanoye Aikens, and Carmencita Romero; the Dunham technique has always been taught at the Alvin AILEY studios).

During the 1940s and '50s, Dunham kept up her brand of political activism. Fighting segregation in hotels, restaurants and theaters, she filed lawsuits and made public condemnations. In Hollywood, she refused to sign a lucrative studio contract when the producer said she would have to replace some of her darker-skinned company members. To an enthusiastic but all-white audience in the South, she made an after-performance speech, saying she could never play there again until it was integrated. In São Paulo, Brazil, she brought a discrimination suit against a hotel, eventually prompting the president of Brazil to apologize to her and to pass a law that forbade discrimination in public places. In 1951 Dunham premiered *Southland,* an hour-long ballet about lynching, though it was only performed in Chile and Paris.

Toward the end of the 1950s Dunham was forced to regroup, disband, and reform her company, according to the exigencies of her financial and physical health (she suffered from crippling knee problems). Yet she remained undeterred. In 1962 she opened a Broadway production, *Bambouche,* featuring fourteen dancers, singers, and musicians of the Royal Troupe of Morocco, along with the Dunham company. The next year she choreographed the Metropolitan Opera's new production of *Aida*—thereby becoming the Met's first black choreographer. In 1965–1966, she was cultural adviser to the President of Senegal. She attended Senegal's First World Festival of Negro Arts as a representative from the United States.

Moved by the civil rights struggle and outraged by deprivations in the ghettos of East St. Louis, an area she knew from her visiting professorships at Southern Illinois University in the 1960s, Dunham decided to take action. In 1967 she opened the Performing Arts Training Center, a cultural program and school for the neighborhood children and youth, with programs in dance, drama, martial arts, and humanities. Soon thereafter she expanded the programs to include senior citizens. Then in 1977 she opened the Katherine Dunham Museum and Children's Workshop to house her collections of artifacts from her travels and research, as well as archival material from her personal life and professional career.

During the 1980s, Dunham received numerous awards acknowledging her contributions. These include the Albert Schweitzer Music Award for a life devoted to performing arts and service to humanity (1979); a Kennedy Center Honor's Award (1983); the Samuel H. Scripps American Dance Festival Award (1987); induction into the Hall of Fame of the National Museum of Dance in Saratoga Springs, N.Y. (1987). That same year Dunham directed the reconstruction of several of her works by the Alvin Ailey American Dance Theater and *The Magic of Katherine Dunham* opened Ailey's 1987–1988 season.

In February 1992, at the age of eighty-two, Dunham again became the subject of international attention when she began a forty-seven-day fast at her East St. Louis home. Because of her age, her involvement with Haiti, and the respect accorded her as an activist and artist, Dunham became the center of a movement that coalesced to protest the United States's deportations of Haitian boat-refugees fleeing to the U.S. after the military overthrow of Haiti's democratically elected President Jean-Bertrand Aristide. She agreed to end her fast only after Aristide visited her and personally requested her to stop.

Boldness has characterized Dunham's life and career. And, although she was not alone, Dunham is perhaps the best known and most influential pioneer of black dance. Her synthesis of scholarship and theatricality demonstrated, incontrovertibly and joyously, that African-American and African-Caribbean styles are related and powerful components of dance in America.

REFERENCES

BECKFORD, RUTH. *Katherine Dunham: A Biography.* New York, 1979.

DUNHAM, KATHERINE. *A Touch of Innocence.* New York, 1969.

SALLY SOMMER

Dunnigan, Alice Allison

Dunnigan, Alice Allison (April 27, 1906–May 6, 1983), journalist. Born in Russellville, Ky., the daughter of sharecroppers, Alice Allison attended Kentucky Normal and Industrial Institute (later renamed Kentucky State College) in 1924 and 1925 and earned a teaching certificate in 1926. She received a bachelor's degree from West Kentucky Industrial College in 1932, but continued to take journalism and library science courses at various colleges, including Louisville Municipal College (1935) and Tennessee State College (1936–1937). In 1930, she was briefly married to Walter Dickinson and in 1932, she married a childhood friend, Charles Dunnigan. From 1925 through 1942, Dunnigan primarily taught in public schools of various towns in Kentucky. During this period, she wrote columns on African-American history and other subjects for such newspapers as the *Kentucky Reporter, Louisville Defender,* and the *Louisville Leader.* She coedited a small journal, *The Informer.*

In 1942, Dunnigan took a civil-service exam, was hired by the War Labor Board, and moved to Washington, D.C. She worked in government positions and, in 1946, resumed her journalistic work as the Washington, D.C., bureau chief of the Associated Negro Press. After a widely publicized fight over her admission to the Senate press gallery, Dunnigan was accredited as the second African-American and first black woman congressional reporter in June 1947. Two months later, after being accredited by the White House Press Association, she became the first black woman to become a White House correspondent. In November, she was appointed by President Harry Truman to the National Committee for the Employment of the Physically Handicapped. In 1948, she was invited as the first black woman reporter to accompany a presidential campaign.

Dunnigan remained a reporter for fourteen years and became a well-known figure in Washington, D.C. She received several honors for her work, including one from the United Press Club. In 1960, she left journalism and worked for Lyndon B. Johnson's presidential campaign. Subsequently, she became an educational consultant for the President's Commission on Equal Employment Opportunity (later renamed the Equal Employment Opportunity Commission). In 1965, she was hired by the U.S. Department of Labor as an information officer. In 1967, she was appointed associate editor for the President's Council for Youth Opportunity. Dunnigan retired from public life in 1970. She subsequently wrote an autobiography, *A Black Woman's Experience* (1964), as well as *The Fascinating Story of Black Kentuckians: Their Heritage and Traditions* (1982), a history of African Americans in Kentucky. Dunnigan died in Washington, D.C.

REFERENCE

DUNNIGAN, ALICE ALLISON. *A Black Woman's Experience: From Schoolhouse to White House.* Philadelphia, Pa., 1974.

GREG ROBINSON

Durham, North Carolina

Durham, North Carolina. Located in a north-central piedmont area of North Carolina, which includes much of the Research Triangle Park, Durham is the state's fifth largest city. In 1990 it had a population of 136,611, about 46 percent African American. A center of black enterprise, it is touted as a beacon of progressive race relations. Its significance is comparable to larger southern cities such as RICHMOND, ATLANTA, and Nashville.

Durham was organized in the 1850s, in the middle of a slave-holding region, the antebellum hamlet boasting scarcely more than a post office and railroad station. Slaves and free people of color helped to cultivate its tobacco and other cash crops. Incorporated in 1866, it drew numerous black residents. Black life centered on the St. Joseph's African Methodist Episcopal and White Rock Baptist Churches.

By the 1880s, tobacco and textile factories and railroads began turning Durham into a model New South town. In 1890 the American Tobacco Company was formed. It soon controlled 75 percent of the national market. In 1898 blacks were hired in large numbers by tobacco factories. Soon after, black entrepreneurs established cotton mills, and in 1902 white tycoon Julian S. Carr opened a cotton mill with all black employees. Compared to many southern factory towns, which shunned black laborers, an unusual number of black Durhamites worked in factories.

A black middle class emerged. John Merrick, an ex-slave barber, bought the rights to the Royal Knights of King David, a fraternal order and used this framework to start an insurance business. After major white insurers like Prudential Life Insurance Company decided during the 1890s to stop accepting black policyholders, Merrick and several business partners formed a syndicate to develop the North Carolina Mutual and Provident Association, chartered in 1898. Mutual was unsuccessful at first, but under the leadership of Charles C. SPAULDING it grew swiftly until it was the largest black-owned business in America. Its directors parlayed its capital and experience into other ventures, including drug stores, a real estate firm, textile mill, and the Mechanics and Farmers Bank, which opened in 1908. The black Durham elite was instrumental in founding North Carolina College (NCC) in 1910 (now North Carolina Central University). Commentators as diverse as Booker T. WASHINGTON and W. E. B. DU BOIS wrote magazine articles hailing the development of black enterprise in Durham. By 1919, when Mutual declared itself the North Carolina Mutual Life Insurance Company, Durham had become virtually the "capital" of the black middle class, a term popularized by sociologist E. Franklin FRAZIER in *The New Negro* (1925). During the 1920s, the Bankers Fire Insurance Company, the Mutual Savings and Loan Association, and the National Negro Finance Corporation were founded there as well.

Despite Durham's reputation for interracial cooperation and economic backing from white businessmen, which buttressed black progress, Jim Crow remained strong in the city through the first half of the twentieth century. Health and labor conditions for black workers were poor. The Durham Committee on Negro Affairs (DCNA), a civil rights organization controlled by the black business elite, was launched in 1935. In 1942, the Durham NAACP, one of the state's oldest branches, joined the DCNA to support a meeting of southern black leaders at North Carolina College, out of which came the "Durham

Manifesto" demanding the abolition of segregation in the South. Five years later, during the Journey of Reconciliation, an early effort by the CONGRESS OF RACIAL EQUALITY (CORE) to test compliance with a Supreme Court decision against segregated interstate buses, Durham police beat and arrested freedom riders. In 1949, black parents won a school equalization suit against the city's board of education, although token school integration did not begin until 1959. The DCNA's voter registration efforts made it a political power.

In 1960, African-American students from NCC sat-in at lunch counters and forced city officials to take steps "quietly" to desegregate downtown stores. Student-led boycotts and mass demonstrations, assisted by Durham attorney Floyd B. MCKISSICK, later head of CORE, led by 1963 to a fair hiring ordinance and nonracial admissions to policy at nearby Duke University. In 1968, Durham was swept by violent African-American protest after the assassination of the Rev. Dr. Martin Luther KING, Jr. Black power advocates recruited hospital workers into unions and struggled to empower poor people. In 1981, black activists formed the National Black Independent Political Party. The DCNA, renamed the Durham Committee on Black Affairs, sponsored the election of blacks to various offices.

In the 1990s, one-fourth of Durham's black residents live in poverty. However, the city remains a hub of black capitalism. North Carolina Mutual is the largest black insurance company in America, while Mechanics and Farmers Bank and Mutual Savings and Loan are nationally prominent. Durham is also a cultural locus, home of the African American Dance Ensemble and the Thelonious Monk Institute of Jazz. In 1992, the predominantly black area of Durham was included in a newly drawn congressional district, and the city's first African-American Representative, Melvin L. Watt, was elected.

REFERENCES

ANDERSON, JEAN BRADLEY. *Durham County: A History of Durham County, North Carolina*. Durham, N.C., 1990.

GAVINS, RAYMOND. "The Meaning of Freedom: Black North Carolina in the Nadir, 1880–1900." In *Race, Class, and Politics in Southern History: Essays in Honor of Robert F. Durden*. Baton Rouge, La. 1989, pp. 175–215.

JONES, BEVERLY W. "Durham, North Carolina" In *The Statistical and Geographical Abstract of the Black Population in the United States*. College Park, Md., 1992.

WEARE, WALTER B. *Black Business in the New South: A Social History of the North Carolina Mutual Life Insurance Company*. Urbana, Ill., 1973.

RAYMOND GAVINS

Durham Manifesto. On October 20, 1942, a group of southern black leaders convened in Durham, N.C., to address the problem of increasing racial tension in the South during WORLD WAR II. The Durham convention, called the Southern Conference on Race Relations, was organized at the suggestion of Jessie Ames, a white moderate and an active member of the Commission on Interracial Cooperation (CIC). Ames, fearing that the voices of white and black moderates in the South were being drowned out by more radical blacks and white supremacists, urged Gordon Blaine HANCOCK, a black sociologist and a moderate on racial issues, to convene the meeting. Ames expressed her hope that the black leaders would propose a "New Charter of Race Relations" for the South that would win the approval and support of white moderates, thereby restoring the role of the increasingly weak CIC and salvaging the possibility of interracial cooperation.

After some disagreement among the organizers (a group of black Virginians) over whether to include northern leaders, Hancock and the others decided to limit the conference to southern blacks. Of the eighty southern black leaders invited to attend the Durham conference, fifty-two accepted. Many of the attendees, including Charles Spurgeon JOHNSON of Fisk University, Benjamin E. MAYS of Morehouse College, and Rufus E. CLEMENT of Atlanta University, were former members of the CIC who had become disenchanted with the hesitant attitude of southern white moderates. In addition to Hancock, who served as the director of the conference, two other blacks from Virginia, Luther Porter JACKSON and P. B. Young, the owner and editor of the Norfolk *Journal and Guide,* assumed leadership positions.

On December 15, 1942, the conference issued the Durham Manifesto, a statement outlining the leaders' demands for improving the position of African Americans in the South. In this statement of purpose, the delegates voiced their fundamental opposition to segregation but avoided a frontal attack on such issues as the desegregation of schools and public accommodations, which might appear to white Southerners as calls for social equality. Instead the leaders expressed their belief that it was more important for the conference to address the "current problems of racial discrimination and neglect." Among the leaders' demands were calls for equal pay and opportunities for blacks in industry, the abolition of poll taxes and white primaries, the protection of civil rights, and a federal antilynching law. The leaders also implored white moderates to take a more active role in helping blacks combat racial discrimination in the South.

White moderates responded by organizing their own conference to address the black leaders' demands, and in June 1943 the two groups met at a collaborative conference in Richmond, Va., where they agreed to disband the former CIC and replace it with the new SOUTHERN REGIONAL COUNCIL. Many of the white leaders, however, objected to the Durham statement as being too aggressive. When the conference finally drafted a common platform, it, like the Durham Manifesto, continued to avoid a direct confrontation on the issue of segregation. Although the Durham Manifesto failed to receive the full support of white moderates, it marked a major step forward in articulating an antisegregationist stance by southern black moderates.

REFERENCES

GAVINS, RAYMOND. *The Perils and Prospects of Southern Black Leadership: Gordon Blaine Hancock, 1884–1970.* Durham, N.C., 1977.
LOGAN, RAYFORD WHITTINGHAM, ed. *What the Negro Wants.* Chapel Hill, N.C., 1944.

LOUISE P. MAXWELL

Du Sable, Jean Baptiste Pointe (c. 1750–1818), founder of Chicago. Jean Baptiste Pointe Du Sable (also spelled Au Sable, De Sable, and De Saible) is thought to have been born in Saint-Domingue (now Haiti) to an African mother and a French mariner father. After his mother's death, his father sent him to Paris, where he was educated. After his stay in Paris, Du Sable worked as a seaman on his father's ships. How he came to North America is not known. According to one account, he immigrated to French Canada and became a fur trapper; another says he immigrated to Louisiana.

What is certain is that by 1779, Du Sable had traveled north to the Chicago River area, where he established trading posts on the sites of Peoria and Michigan City, Ind. That year, he also established a trading post at the mouth of the river, at a place called by local Indians "Checagou," the site of present-day Chicago. He returned that fall to Peoria, where his support of the Americans during the Revolutionary War angered the powerful Mackinac tribe, who were allies of Great Britain. Du Sable was arrested for espionage by British authorities, but his reputation was sufficiently impressive that not only was he released the following year, but the British made him a trader for supplies for their fort and hired him to manage their own trading post.

In 1784, after the British left the region, Du Sable returned to Checagou, where he reestablished his trading post and built a cabin, the first house ever built in Chicago. Du Sable decorated it with French

Jean Baptiste Pointe Du Sable, the first permanent settler of what was to become Chicago. (Photographs and Prints Division, Schomburg Center for Research in Black Culture, The New York Public Library, Astor, Lenox and Tilden Foundations)

furniture and some twenty-three paintings, plus other luxury items. He lived in the region for sixteen years and married a Potawotomi Native-American woman named Catherine, with whom he had two children.

In 1800, after an unsuccessful attempt at being elected chief of the Potawotomi, Du Sable suddenly sold his lucrative Chicago business and land holdings for about $1,200 and moved back to Peoria. Despite owning 800 acres of property there, a claim later upheld in a United States court, Du Sable lost his money and declared bankruptcy in 1814. Ironically, his land holdings in Chicago are now worth more than a billion dollars. Du Sable subsequently moved to St. Charles, Mo., near St. Louis, where he died in poverty in 1818. His grave was discovered in St. Charles in 1991.

As the first permanent non–American Indian resident of the area, Du Sable is honored as the founder of Chicago. Plaques and a large high school in the city bear his name. In 1961, the Du Sable Museum of African-American History opened, the oldest private nonprofit black museum in America. In 1987 Du Sable appeared on a postage stamp.

REFERENCES

BENNETT, LERONE. "The Black Man Who Founded Chicago." *Ebony* (November 1977): 64–78.
KATZ, WILLIAM. *Black People Who Made the Old West.* New York, 1977.

MANSUR M. NURUDDIN
GREG ROBINSON

Dwight, Edward Joseph, Jr. (September 9, 1933–), astronaut candidate and sculptor. Born and raised in Kansas City, Kans., Edward J. Dwight, Jr., grew up near Fairfax Airport, which served as an Army Air Force base during World War II. Fascinated as a child by the fighter planes that flew overhead, he decided on a career with the Air Force.

In 1951 he became the first black male to graduate from Kansas City's Ward Catholic High School, where he excelled in sports and was a member of the National Honor Society. He graduated from Kansas City Kansas Community College in May 1953, and joined the Air Force on August 7, 1953. He was trained to fly jet planes at Williams Air Force Base (AFB) in Arizona. Subsequently commissioned as a second lieutenant, he served as a jet instructor at Williams while studying for his B.S. in aeronautical engineering at Arizona State University (1957). After serving in Japan as a B-57 bomber pilot, he was named the Strategic Air Command's chief of collateral training at Travis AFB in California.

In 1962, at President John F. Kennedy's insistence, the Air Force took its first steps toward racially integrating the Aerospace Research Pilot School at Edwards AFB in California. Dwight was chosen that year as the first black to enroll in the school and thus to receive space-related training as an astronaut designee. He received much press attention as the first potential black U.S. astronaut. However, his application to NASA's Astronaut Selection Board was not accepted. This rejection, along with a disappointing assignment to the Wright-Patterson AFB in Ohio, prompted Dwight to write to the Department of Defense charging that the air force was discriminatory.

In 1966, Dwight resigned from the Air Force, and moved to Denver, Colo., where he cofounded the Jet Training School. He also became a successful real estate agent. In 1977, pursuing a new interest in art and African-American culture, Dwight received an M.F.A. in sculpture from the University of Denver. He has received many prestigious commissions and created sculptures of such significant African Americans as Hank AARON and Martin Luther KING, Jr. In 1987, Dwight was awarded an honorary L.H.D. from Arizona State University.

REFERENCES

ATKINSON, JOSEPH D., JR., and JAY M. SHAFRITZ. *The Real Stuff: A History of NASA's Astronaut Recruitment Program.* New York, 1985.
HAWTHORNE, DOUGLAS B. *Men and Women of Space.* San Diego, Calif., 1992.
WHITE, FRANK. "The Sculptor Who Would Have Gone Into Space." *Ebony* (February 1984): 54–58.

LYDIA MCNEILL

Dyer Bill. In response to mob violence and the frequent brutal lynching of African Americans, the Dyer antilynching bill was first introduced in the United States Congress in April 1918. Leonidas Dyer, a Missouri Republican serving the Twelfth Congressional district, which included the large black electorate in St. Louis's South Side, was the bill's architect and sponsor.

After securing earlier support from the NAACP, which was intensifying its own crusade against lynching at the time, Dyer submitted legislation to make lynching a federal crime. In its original form, the bill invoked the equal-protection-of-the-laws clause of the Fourteenth Amendment to safeguard American citizens against lynching by federal statute. The bill defined a lynch mob as a group of three or more individuals, made them liable to prosecution for a capital crime, and also subjected state officials to fine and imprisonment for failing to prosecute individuals whom they knew were involved in lynching. During the same session, Merrill Moores of Indiana submitted another bill that was also intent on making lynching a federal crime. Neither bill, however, initially satisfied the NAACP. Moorfield Storey, the Association's first president and noted constitutional lawyer, believed both bills were unconstitutional because they employed the Fourteenth Amendment to seek federal redress for the crime of murder, the jurisdiction of which resided with the states. Accordingly, the association failed to lobby vigorously for the bill in 1918, and the matter did not reach a congressional vote.

The following year, however, the NAACP and Storey dropped their opposition and supported Dyer's bill with an intensive lobbying campaign. This resulted partly from Storey's growing recognition that state governments were not punishing lynchers and from his new argument that the federal government could prosecute lynchers under its wartime and national emergency powers. The NAACP's motives stemmed from the worsening conditions facing African Americans in the United States following World War I. Rather than ushering in a new climate of racial tolerance, the war's aftermath had produced more virulent racism and excessive violence. Blacks returning from the war were lynched while still in uniform in some southern communities, and America experienced major race riots during the RED SUMMER of 1919. NAACP support for the Dyer Bill became one facet of a crucial new drive for civil rights in a time of intensified oppression. Despite the turnaround and strenuous campaigning by the NAACP, the bill languished. Dyer faithfully submitted it annually, through 1929, only to have a mixture of constitutional questions, southern filibusters, and general political indifference block a fail vote on its passage.

Although the Dyer Bill never became law, its legacy was revived by the introduction of new antilynching measures, the Costigan-Wagner bill of 1935 and the Wagner-Gavagan bill of 1940, both of which were substantially the same as the Dyer Bill, except that the former sought state rather than federal relief. As President, Franklin D. Roosevelt failed to support these antilynching laws out of fear that his support would cause southern resentment and irrevocably shatter his New Deal coalition. Neither of these measures was successful, but collectively all three proposed bills kept the NAACP active in its antilynching crusade and kept the issue before the nation.

REFERENCE

ZANGRANDO, ROBERT L. *The NAACP Crusade Against Lynching, 1909–1950.* Philadelphia, 1980.

MARSHALL HYATT

E

Early, Jordan Winston (1814–1903), minister. Jordan Early spent the first twelve years of his childhood as a slave in his native Franklin County, Va. His family later moved to St. Louis, Mo., where he was converted to African Methodism in 1828. He learned to read and write and used his knowledge for advancing the AFRICAN METHODIST EPISCOPAL CHURCH (AME). Licensed to preach in 1833, he helped establish the first AME church in St. Louis after Bishop William Paul QUINN introduced Methodism in Missouri. That was the first of many churches Early helped found or build in Missouri, Indiana, Illinois, Louisiana, and Kentucky.

Early's most significant contributions to Methodism came in Tennessee. Before 1865, he pastored churches and served as a missionary in the Midwest and the upper South, except for some brief work in New Orleans during the 1840s where, despite the opposition of some proslavery citizens, he helped erect St. James Chapel. At the 1865 AME annual conference, Bishop J. P. Campbell assigned Early to Nashville, Tenn., where he played a leading role in organizing the AME Church in Tennessee. Early's significance rests with the promotion of African Methodism in the Midwest and South and with reforms within the church, such as greater emphasis upon a trained clergy. He died in 1903 in Nashville.

REFERENCE

EARLY, SARAH J. W. *Life and Labors of Rev. Jordan W. Early . . .* Reprint. Freeport, N.Y., 1971.

JIMMIE LEWIS FRANKLIN

Early African-American Women's Organizations. Beginning in the 1790s, free African-American women in the Northeast began to form mutual relief societies (*see* FRATERNAL ORDERS AND MUTUAL AID ASSOCIATIONS). The first known such women's organization, the Female Benevolent Society of St. Thomas, was founded in Philadelphia in 1793. In 1809 in Newport, R.I., other African-American women organized the African Female Benevolent Society, one year after African-American men had founded the African Benevolent Society there. Although the members welcomed women into that association, the women could not vote or hold office. Letters that passed between the two organizations suggest that the African Female Benevolent Society appreciated its autonomy from the men's organization.

A spate of other African-American women's mutual benefit societies sprang up during the early nineteenth century in Salem, Mass.; Washington, D.C.; Philadelphia; Boston; Troy, N.Y.; Portland, Maine; and New York City. Their surviving record books indicate that dues went toward providing money for sick members or recent widows and for loans for funeral expenses. As a second generation of free women was born to African-born ex-slaves, these societies began to describe themselves as "colored female" associations rather than "African female" societies.

Although working-class African-American women continued to form mutual relief associations well into the nineteenth century, the growth of a small black middle class also prompted some women to change their focus from mutual relief to improvement. In 1831, African-American women established the Female Literary Association of Philadelphia and the Afric-American Female Intelligence Society of Boston to educate themselves and to challenge prejudice and racism. In 1832, African-American women founded the first female antislavery society in Salem, Mass.

REFERENCE

STERLING, DOROTHY, ed. *We Are Your Sisters: Black Women in the Nineteenth Century.* New York, 1984.

MARGARET D. JACOBS

East St. Louis, Illinois, Riot of 1917. The East St. Louis, Ill., riot of 1917 was the first in a number of riots that occurred between 1917 and 1919, a period of economic disruption amid massive black migration northward. East St. Louis, dubbed by some "the Pittsburgh of the West," was a town of sixty-eight thousand people across the Mississippi River from St. Louis, with stockyards and aluminum iron factories. Living conditions were dreadful, and law enforcement was lax in the "open" town. Still, African Americans fleeing the South settled there. The town's black population went from six thousand in 1910 to ten thousand in 1920.

In April 1917, the white labor force went on strike at the Aluminum Ore Company. Employees attempting to form a union were frozen out and replaced by strikebreakers, a small percentage of whom were black. At the same time, during an electoral campaign, local Democratic leaders charged that Republicans were encouraging blacks to settle in East St. Louis to swell the Republican vote. Stories of black vice and crime were prominently reported in newspapers.

On May 28, a labor union delegation called upon the mayor to request that blacks no longer be allowed to migrate to the city. As the delegation was leaving city hall, news reached its members that a black man had accidentally killed a white man during a holdup. Soon rumors spread of white women being insulted and white girls shot. Over three thousand whites gathered to retaliate. Angry mobs invaded the downtown area, attacking African-American residents. Mobs used oil-soaked rags to burn down African-American shanties, and six people were shot, none fatally. Police remained neutral or assisted rioters, and National Guard troops mobilized during the strike refused to intervene. The next day, there were further beatings and a shooting death. Instead of protecting black citizens, police entered blacks' houses to search for concealed weapons.

During the following month, racially motivated crime continued in East St. Louis. Black laborers going to work were attacked and had to get police escorts; blacks crossing the bridge to St. Louis were tormented; and, especially following the calling off of the strike late in June, blacks were randomly beaten. The mayor failed to listen to NATIONAL ASSOCIATION FOR THE ADVANCEMENT OF COLORED PEOPLE (NAACP) warnings of rising racial tension, or even to produce a riot plan. Police and the press cheered on violent whites, and no incidents were investigated or rioters charged. A labor committee sent to investigate the May 28 riot blamed employers for importing "an excessive and abnormal number" of blacks, and on blacks themselves.

On the evening of July 1, as rumors swirled among all races of plans for July 4 uprisings, a carload of whites drove through a black area, spraying bullets into homes. Police remained inactive until the car drove through again, and blacks returned the fire. Blacks, believing a police car was the marauders returning, opened fire, killing two detectives in the process.

On July 2, after viewing the bullet-ridden police car, white crowds marched through the city, beating and shooting blacks. Men were lynched, women and children clubbed. The police refused to act, and some of the National Guard troops and police stationed in the area joined in the rioting. Black houses were set afire, their occupants were shot as they tried to escape, and their corpses were dumped in Chokia Creek. A large crowd of African Americans fled across the bridge to St. Louis. Once the National Guard units left, the violence escalated. At least thirty-nine blacks, and possibly up to a hundred were killed, along with nine whites, making it one of the deadliest riots in African American history. Hundreds were injured, and the black neighborhood was heavily damaged.

The negative publicity the riot generated led Illinois Attorney General C. W. Middlekauf to indict eight-two whites and twenty-three blacks for rioting and murder. Only nine whites were ever sent to prison. Seven police officers charged with murder or assault pleaded guilty to lesser charges and were collectively fined $150. Meanwhile, ten blacks who were arrested in the detectives' deaths received fourteen-year sentences from all-white juries. On July 28, 1917, a silent parade of 10,000, organized by the NAACP, passed through New York City's Harlem neighborhood to protest the riot and killings. The NAACP's relief and protest activities brought it high visibility among African Americans.

The riot demonstrated the defenselessness of black Americans against white violence in the growing urban areas outside the South. It would be only the first in a series of racial incidents in the following two years.

See also URBAN RIOTS AND REBELLIONS.

REFERENCE

RUDWICK, ELLIOTT M. *Race Riot at East St. Louis, July 2, 1917*. 2nd ed. Urbana, Ill., 1982.

GAYLE T. TATE

Eaton, Hubert Arthur (December 2, 1916–), physician and civil rights activist. The son of a physician, Hubert Eaton was born in Fayetteville, N.C. When Eaton was an infant, the family moved to Newport News, Va., and in 1928 settled in Winston-Salem, N.C. As a teenager Eaton became a successful amateur tennis player. In 1933 he won the national junior championship of the American Tennis Association (ATA), the black counterpart to the United States Tennis Association, thereby earning a scholarship to the historically black college, Johnson C. Smith University in Charlotte, where he excelled as a tennis player and student. Following his graduation from Johnson C. Smith in 1937, Eaton enrolled in the University of Michigan as a graduate student in zoology, earning an M.S. degree in one year. He was then admitted to the university's medical school, where he received an M.D. degree in 1942.

After leaving medical school, Eaton served a one-year internship at Kate Bitting Reynolds Memorial Hospital in Winston-Salem. He subsequently moved to Wilmington, N.C., where he established a private practice.

In 1946, while attending the ATA national championship tournament, Eaton discovered the teenaged Althea GIBSON and adopted her as a protégée. That year Gibson moved from Harlem to live with Eaton's family and train with Eaton on his personal tennis court. She stayed with the Eatons for three years while becoming one of the best tennis players in the United States.

In the 1950s Eaton became involved in the civil rights movement in Wilmington. In 1949 he successfully sued to equalize funding for public schools in New Hanover County, where Wilmington is located. In 1956 he initiated a series of law suits against a publicly funded hospital in Wilmington that refused to hire black doctors and discriminated against black patients. After several defeats, including a dismissal by the U.S. Supreme Court, *Eaton et al.* v. *James Walker Memorial Hospital* was upheld by a federal appeals court in 1964, thus establishing legal precedent for the elimination of discrimination in publicly funded hospitals. Eaton also led the successful struggle in 1962 to desegregate Wilmington College, which later became the University of North Carolina at Wilmington. In 1964 Eaton again filed suit against Wilmington's board of education, this time forcing the board to actively integrate its schools.

In the 1970s Eaton directed his political activities toward reform of the medical system. He lobbied for increased funding for Medicare and Medicaid and challenged the centralization and alleged mismanagement of North Carolina's physician training programs.

In 1977 he was elected to the Board of Directors of the University of North Carolina at Wilmington, and in 1981 became the first African-American chairman of the board. In 1984, Eaton published his autobiography, *Every Man Should Try*.

REFERENCE

EATON, HUBERT A. *Every Man Should Try*. Wilmington, N.C., 1984.

THADDEUS RUSSELL

Ebony. Published by the Johnson Publishing Company, *Ebony* is the largest circulation African-American periodical. Founded in 1945, it grew out of an attempt by publisher John H. JOHNSON to please two staff members who wanted to start an entertainment magazine, *Jive*. Johnson agreed to a three-way partnership on the project, but the two staffers were unable to put up money, so Johnson assumed full ownership. Johnson changed the style of the proposed magazine into one whose philosophy would be to highlight the positive side of African-American life, emphasizing black pride and achievements, rather than oppression and poverty. Recognizing the widespread appeal of photos, Johnson planned a monthly glamor magazine on glossy paper, in the style of the popular weekly *Life*, filled with pictures of prominent and successful blacks. The new magazine, which Johnson named *Ebony* (after the beautiful and strong black wood) was planned during World War II, but due to paper restrictions, the first issue did not appear until November 1, 1945. Johnson had pledged to accept no advertisements until circulation reached 100,000; the magazine was an immediate success and the first ads appeared in the May 1946 issue. By May 1947, when *Ebony* became the first African-American periodical large enough to be audited by the Audit Bureau of Circulation, its circulation had reached 309,715. Despite its prestige and large circulation, however, poor advertising revenues made it unprofitable until Johnson secured advertising contracts from white firms previously reluctant to purchase space in African-American publications.

Ebony has drawn some criticism over the years for the showy, escapist nature of its features, and its emphasis on the activities of wealthy blacks, although the magazine took a more activist direction starting in the era of the CIVIL RIGHTS MOVEMENT. Over time, the magazine has added sections on cooking, health, and gossip. The enormous success of *Ebony* has inspired numerous competitors over the years, and the magazine has had numerous spinoffs, including the periodicals *Ebony Man*, the now defunct *Ebony Jr.*, the Ebony Fashion Fair traveling fashion show, and the syndicated television program *Ebony/Jet Showcase*.

In the early 1990s, the magazine's circulation was about 1.9 million, of which 12 percent were white. It was distributed in some forty countries, including many in Africa.

REFERENCES

GRAVES, EARL. "Johnson Celebrates 50th," *Black Enterprise* 23 (November 1992): 26.
JOHNSON, JOHN H., and LERONE BENNETT, JR. *Succeeding Against the Odds,* New York, 1989.

GREG ROBINSON

Eckstine, William Clarence "Billy" (July 8, 1914–March 8, 1993), popular singer and bandleader. Billy Eckstine was born in Pittsburgh, the youngest of three children. His family moved several times in his early childhood, and he attended high school in Washington, D.C., and later attended the St. Paul Normal and Industrial School in Lawrenceville, Va., and Howard University.

Eckstine began his career in show business as a singer and nightclub emcee in Buffalo, Detroit, and Chicago (*see* NIGHTCLUBS). In 1939 he was hired as the main vocalist for the big band of Earl "Fatha" HINES. While with Hines, he introduced Dizzy GILLESPIE, Charlie PARKER, and Sarah VAUGHAN to the Hines band. After a number of hit recordings, including "Jelly, Jelly" (1940) and "Skylark" (1942), he left Hines in 1943.

In 1944 he organized his own big band, with personnel that included many up-and-coming bebop musicians, including Dizzy Gillespie, Miles DAVIS, Charlie Parker, Dexter GORDON, and Art BLAKEY.

When, for financial reasons, he was obliged to abandon the band in 1947, he became a solo singer. His smooth baritone was particularly well suited for ballads. In the late 1940s and early '50s his popularity rivaled that of Frank Sinatra. He was one of the first black singers to transcend the race market and to become a national sex symbol.

Eckstine spent the next several decades as a performer in nightclubs, often accompanied by pianist Bobby Tucker. He also appeared in such films as *Skirts Ahoy* (1953), *Let's Do It Again* (1975), and *Jo Jo Dancer: Your Life is Calling* (1986). "Mr. B," as he was widely known, occasionally played the trumpet but was primarily known as a singer. He influenced several generations of African-American singers, including Joe WILLIAMS, Arthur Prysock, and Lou RAWLS. He died in Pittsburgh.

REFERENCES

GIBSON, F. "The Billy Eckstine Band." *Jazz Journal* 23, no. 5 (1970): 2–3.
SOUTHERN, EILEEN. " 'Mr. B' of Ballad and Bop." *The Black Perspective in Music* 7 (1979): 182–190; 8 (1980): 54–60.

EDDIE S. MEADOWS

Economics. After the Civil War, four million freed slaves joined one-half million free blacks in a twilight status somewhere between full citizenship and slavery. African Americans and their white allies understood that without economic property and voting rights for the ex-slaves, the Emancipation would have little practical meaning for African Americans or American democracy. Political citizenship for African-American men was theoretically achieved in the Thirteenth, Fourteenth, and Fifteenth Amendments to the Constitution and the civil rights acts of 1866 and 1875. Later, however, that status was voided as, state by state, the South disfranchised African-American voters toward the end of the nineteenth century. Moreover, the ex-slaves received no financial reparations for the two and a third centuries of bondage they and their predecessors had endured. In particular, Congress refused to confiscate valuable farmlands from supporters of the Confederacy, who were perceived as a competent managerial elite, for redistribution to the freedmen, who were perceived as unskilled and inexperienced independent farmers. Nor would the federal government risk lending money to plantation owners so that the war-ravaged South could reconstitute its economy on a sound basis.

Reconstruction to 1900

FROM SLAVERY TO SHARECROPPING

Overwhelmingly, the ex-slaves entered freedom with nothing but their labor to sell to former slave owners who were bereft of capital and low on credit and whose prior experience had given them absolute power over that same labor. Between the two groups stood the freed blacks' newfound mobility and the BUREAU OF FREEDMEN, REFUGEES AND ABANDONED LANDS, commonly called the Freedmen's Bureau, which Congress had created as a compromise between forces for and against land confiscation to ensure a smooth and just transition from slave to free labor and a speedy return to large crops of cotton, sugar, tobacco, and rice.

AFRICAN–AMERICAN AGRARIANISM

A complex interaction between politics and African-American self-help was at work throughout the Reconstruction period. Black reconstruction began during the Civil War when thousands of runaway slaves wreaked havoc on the Confederacy's war effort and economy. Many of them were convinced that they had a right to the new homesteads they had established on land abandoned by slave owners in the wake of the advancing Union armies, land from which they were subsequently removed by military force. Blacks now enjoyed the freedom of migration; many former slaves from the upper South and Southeast moved to the Southwest where the fertile cotton lands of Arkansas, Mississippi, and Louisiana allowed planters to offer higher wages than elsewhere. Between 1860

First as slaves and then as free servants, African Americans have been members of the White House maintenance staff since the early nineteenth century. This photograph is from 1877, during the administration of Rutherford B. Hayes. Standing (from left), Jane Humphreys, cook; Henry Harris, waiter; Beverly Lemas, waiter; Mary Monroe, housemaid; Edgar Beckley, messenger; Telemachus Ford, watchman. Seated (from left), Maria Rustin, laundress; Mary Waters, laundress; Winnie Monroe, nurse. (Photographs and Prints Division, Schomburg Center for Research in Black Culture, The New York Public Library, Astor, Lenox and Tilden Foundations)

and 1910 the southern Atlantic states' share of the African-American population declined from 46 percent to 42 percent while the share of the western south central states rose from 15 percent to 20 percent.

Blacks and their Republican allies continued the quest for economic security for the ex-slaves at the state and local levels. African-American politicians in southern state legislatures were strong backers of the rights of labor and the small farmer. They and other Republicans campaigned for homestead laws to enable landless families to acquire unsettled federal land. African-American leaders and their white allies, many of them Union army veterans, started societies that raised money to buy and work land. The legislatures of a number of states passed laws that were decidedly prolabor and as such raised the ire of large owners of property. For example, states such as South Carolina, Alabama, and Georgia passed laws that gave the laborer first right to cotton and other cash crops as a lien on his or her claims for wages or a share of the crop.

FROM GANG LABOR TO FAMILY SHARECROPPING

Sharecropping evolved as a system that neither freedpeople nor planters considered optimal. During the initial years of Reconstruction, former slaves and slave owners faced off in a struggle to determine the new labor-management relations. The ex-slaves rebelled against the attempt by the owners of large plantations to approximate the labor relations of the slave regime. In the immediate postbellum period large cotton plantations would employ several work gangs under the supervision of a headman or overseer; decision making was a hierarchical function. (Such a structure had been typical of the slave economy.) Freedmen (including women and adolescents) were organized into these work gangs, but many refused to work under gang foremen who in many cases had been "drivers" who enforced discipline with whips. African Americans demanded and won more freedom in the performance of their daily tasks and especially in the conduct of their private affairs.

The Freedmen's Bureau adjudicated thousands of labor disputes between planters and laborers. The vast majority involved labor turnover as African Americans attempted to exercise their new rights of mobility. Labor turnover was most frequently due to harsh supervision—whipping and the like—and to the inability of a great many formerly well-to-do planters to pay laborers their wages at the end of the year. Additionally, the bureau was also involved in many arguments over work rules and payment arrangements.

Of the heavily capitalized sugar plantations of Louisiana and, to a lesser extent, the larger rice plantations of South Carolina and Georgia, those that survived Reconstruction intact were generally able to maintain closely supervised work crews that were paid money wages. However, the majority of laborers on tobacco and cotton plantations (usually one-third to one-half their numbers) worked in gangs for a share wage of the net proceeds of a crop that was to be divided between anywhere from ten to fifty workers after it was harvested and sold by the planter. Moreover, in those cases where African Americans did contract to work for money wages, these sums were due in a lump at the end of the crop year. In either case, during the year, laborers obtained subsistence food and clothing (usually on credit) from either plantation stores or independent merchants.

In 1866 and 1868 large-scale crop failures due to disastrous weather conditions left many planters unable to pay their debts to creditors and laborers. As a result, most laborers received only partial wages or no wages at all for a full year's work. This experience led to wholesale abandonment of plantations as laborers searched for employers who could pay them during the harvest season. Furthermore, it led to extreme distrust between African Americans and their employers. These problems of no pay and low pay led to a large reduction in the labor supply of African-American women and children; seeing their work efforts bear little fruit for two years, they reallocated their time to activities such as household chores and school.

At this point the Freedmen's Bureau ruled that, while workers promised money wages were employees and could be paid after the employer had sold the crop, share laborers were part owners of the crop and had the right to demand crop division in the field, after which they could dispose of their share as they wished. Given the huge number of landlords defaulting on payments to laborers, this ruling, which the bureau enforced with the military, led laborers to demand shares because that form of payment provided greater security to the laborer than did postharvest wages. By 1867 only those planters with the greatest reputations for solvency and access to cash or credit could hire labor for wages, since African Americans were as a rule demanding to work where, in their words, they were "part owners of the crop."

But the system of paying laborers one-half the crop while still working them in large gangs led to severe incentive problems and inefficient work. Because all workers received a portion of the entire gang's share, better workers felt that they were being cheated and refused to work with those they considered inefficient. Moreover, some workers recognized that, since they each were just one member of a large work gang, their share of the crop would not be substantially reduced if they shirked their responsibilities. These developments increased absenteeism and other poor work habits, thus causing many arguments. To avoid this problem of the free rider, the size of work gangs was reduced and workers were allowed to choose their coworkers.

During approximately the ten-year period from 1865 to 1875, planters and laborers experimented with many types of labor systems. By the late 1860s many aspects of managerial authority had flowed from planters to laborers as small groups of men and women formed work groups that collectively contracted with planters for a group share of the crop. These work collectives, called variously "squads," "associations," and "clubs," were in a real sense democratic, majority-rule worker collectives that seriously threatened the managerial authority of the planters.

By the mid-to-late 1870s, throughout the cotton and tobacco areas of the South, the scaling down of work-group size to better meet demands for efficiency and equity among workers, the practice of allowing self-selection of coworkers, and African Americans' demand for family autonomy led to the proliferation of share-tenancy for one half the crop by groups of families working a small farm for themselves. Whether the planters anticipated it or not, the individualism inherent in family share-tenancy destroyed the collective esprit of the cotton and tobacco laborers, and unlike the wage hands on sugar plantations who continued to agitate and sometimes lead insurrections against employers and the state for better working conditions, share tenants became a conservative workforce whose deep but unvoiced animosity for its plight only occasionally led to activism.

The agrarianism and political participation among African Americans that preceded full institution of family sharecropping should be understood as twin activities whose common objective was to transfer economic and political power from the landowning and former slaveholder class to the working classes of the South. This attempt to institute economic and political democracy in the South posed a serious threat to the established property interests. The story of their violent reply has often been told. The planters and their allies managed to focus all questions on the issue of race by defining the political and economic contest as one that would determine which *race* as opposed to which *classes* would control the South's political and economic institutions. Extreme violence and terrorism was used by the KU KLUX KLAN and other terrorist organizations to drive African Americans from the political process and from any collective efforts to improve their economic status.

A major cost of the race relations of discrimination and segregation was the failure of blacks and the descendants of the nonslaveholding whites to forge a political bond. Devastated by the Civil War and the credit famine and crop failure of the war's immediate aftermath, small white farmers in the upland regions of the cotton South also became impoverished. The racial segregation of southern life was well illustrated in the geographical division of black and white agricultural labor. From the latter third of the nineteenth century onwards, relatively small farms owned and worked by white families produced increasing quantities of cotton in the piedmont regions of the upper South; labor on large cotton plantations in the lower South, however, was almost exclusively black. White and black cotton producers became victims of a brutal economic system wherein low cotton prices (which persisted into the mid-twentieth century) tied them to a cycle of credit advances, poverty, and debt to landowners and merchants, a cycle that became for many a cruel form of debt peonage.

INDUSTRIAL LABOR

According to the census of 1890, a huge majority of African-American men and women were employed as agricultural laborers or in personal service. In the northern states the discriminatory conditions that had existed before the Civil War persisted. In cities like Chicago, New York, Philadelphia, and Baltimore and in hundreds of smaller towns, blacks, with few exceptions, were proscribed from employment in all but menial laboring and personal-service positions. Blacks with education and skills had to accept employment well below their abilities or had to find some way to operate a business within the segregated African-American community. For example, W. E. B. DU BOIS wrote of a young African American who had graduated from the University of Pennsylvania with a degree in engineering but could only find employment as a restaurant waiter in the Philadelphia of the late 1890s.

By 1900 employment in the South was dominated by a pattern of segregation wherein one race, through economic competition, politics, or violence, essentially drove the other race from the industry or from many occupations within it. The textile industry, which hardly existed in the South before the Civil War, was almost completely staffed by white men, women, and children. Economic segregation exhibited a perverse symmetry—black and white families in cotton production were separated by geography, whereas black and white families in cotton manufacturing were separated by the refusal of textile employers to hire African Americans.

Many African Americans worked outside the plantations. They found employment with the railroads, in coal mining, in the growing lumber mill and turpentine industries that became important to the southern economy, and in the nonfarm tobacco industry centered in the upper South. Moreover, black labor, because it could be obtained cheaply from plantations, was a major factor in the rise of the southern iron and steel industries. Many of these industries managed to keep wages low and working conditions barbarous by hiring convict labor from the state.

TRADE UNIONS

Before the Civil War skilled slaves, hired out by their masters, often competed with white craftsmen for work. Competition from slaves lowered wages and impeded unionization. Southern white workers generally became antagonistic toward the slaves instead of toward the slavery that was responsible for the adverse conditions; even in the North blacks were despised by the white working classes. Expectations that this antagonism between black and white working-class people would continue after emancipation were strengthened during the draft riots of 1863 when thousands of rioting working-class New Yorkers, protesting class-biased draft laws and the Republican party, attacked African Americans, injuring many; subsequently, in 1865, white workers in the Baltimore shipyards and docks staged a long and victorious strike to drive blacks from the better jobs. In Washington, D.C., the white bricklayers' union in 1869 expelled four members found working with blacks on a government job.

Only in industries where large numbers of African Americans had acquired experience as slaves, where there were no significant technological changes in work conditions to disadvantage blacks (i.e., since they were discriminated against when seeking training), and where unionization among whites was not strong were blacks able to maintain an employment presence. Indeed, blacks were often hired specifically to break unions that were forming or were existent but weak. For example, during the decades after 1870, blacks pushed many whites from the iron and coal industries as producers in Georgia, Alabama, and Tennessee recruited black labor for semiskilled jobs in order to break the strength of incipient labor organizations among whites. On the other side of the ledger was the contract construction industry where, throughout the South, thousands of freed slave craftsmen were a strong economic force well into the twentieth century. From their ranks arose many black contractors who, along with the skilled workers, were later gradually squeezed out of the industry mainstream by white contractors and craftsmen, who generally refused to work with or for blacks. Moreover, the discriminatory training and educational opportunities in the private and public sectors prevented African Americans from adapting the skills they had to technologically changing crafts. This was especially true in the newer electrical, plumbing, and mechanical trades, which developed in the late nineteenth and early twentieth centuries.

Such disabilities meant that African Americans were generally forced to compete against white unions or had to accommodate themselves to white dominance of union privileges. Thus, in Baltimore black craftsmen driven from the shipyards organized a cooperative shipbuilding company and operated it successfully for two decades until a combination of changing conditions in the industry and racism caused it to fail. The leader of the Baltimore shipyard workers, Isaac Meyers, became president of the Colored National Labor Union, which sought to organize African-American laborers and was a major national force in black union activity during the late nineteenth century. But the Colored National Labor Union, tied to the Republican party's philosophy that employers and workmen should cooperate and that laborers' greatest achievement was to become business proprietors themselves, largely became a middle-class organization that provided no sound basis for a trade union movement among African Americans.

During the late nineteenth century two disparate philosophies of trade unionism were in conflict to determine the character of the labor movement in the United States. The more conservative craft union philosophy was represented by the American Federation of Labor (AFL), which sought to organize workers into independent (and largely self-interested) craft unions that sought to improve their members' working conditions by erecting barriers to competition. The alternative was to organize workers by industry so that the interests of an industrial union would be tied to every craft practiced therein. This philosophy was represented by the Knights of Labor, who, as they put it, sought to "promote [the] welfare of the masses." In 1893, the AFL national convention unanimously resolved that working people must unite regardless of "creed, color, sex, nationality, or politics." But its organizational structure and philosophy, which gave so much power to local crafts, allowed rabid racism and exclusion of blacks to persist in most locals. Few African Americans gained entry to the AFL. By contrast, the Knights of Labor organized independent of race, but they too could not overcome the specter of racial animosity. Many chapters of the Knights of Labor had separate black and white locals.

Here and there, however, biracial unions arose, suggesting that an accommodation between the races could be reached. Numerous dockworkers along the southeastern seaboard in places such as Charleston, New Orleans, and Mobile had biracial unions that shared employment and union offices through a kind of racial quota system. Frequently whites received more than the share warranted by their numbers. In the coal fields of southern Ohio, western Pennsylvania, and West Virginia, the United Mine Workers arrived at a similar accommodation. Even so, at the end of the nineteenth century, the relationship between the labor movement and African Americans was primarily a contentious and competitive affair that weakened the economic goals of both.

WOMEN'S EMPLOYMENT

African Americans' strongest asset in a discriminatory environment was their willingness to work harder, longer, and for less pay than whites—simply because they had to. The labor market condition of African-American women typified this status. According to the censuses of 1890 and 1900, black women were overwhelmingly employed in domestic service and on farms. The 1900 census showed that 96 percent of African-American women working for wages were employed as field workers, house servants, waitresses, or laundresses. The nationwide discrimination against blacks in general kept African Americans in such poverty that even lower-middle-class whites could afford to hire black women as cooks and housecleaners. These positions involved long hours under close supervision and offered the lowest of wages. In a city such as Cincinnati, Ohio, a typical occupation for African-American women was to set up a business by contracting to wash the clothes of a number of white families each week. This backbreaking labor was often the main support of African-American households.

Black women were also employed in factories to some extent. It appears that in the few instances when African-American women could obtain alternative employment, they chose to abandon domestic service. Along the southeastern seaboard they found seasonal employment, usually involving dirty and difficult working conditions, in various factories in the seafood processing industry. In many seaport towns African-American women and men engaged in the excruciatingly dirty, smelly, and physically demanding task of shucking oysters. During the busy season of September through April, domestic servants in such towns were difficult to hire. However, the seasonality of the work meant that some of the women would have to return to domestic work.

Slaves had been the primary labor source in antebellum Virginia tobacco plants, and after the Civil War African Americans remained a significant factor in the tobacco factories of the upper South. By 1910 the eleven former Confederate states employed over eight thousand African-American women in the least desirable and lowest-paying occupations in tobacco factories. They were primarily restricted to the cigar and chewing-tobacco sectors of the industry. The newer, more mechanized, and higher-paying cigarette industry came to be dominated by white labor. This practice was replicated when black men and women were virtually shut out of the cotton textile industry, which became the major employer of white women.

Labor and Blacks: 1900–1940

THE FIRST URBANIZATION

Between 1880 and 1910 nearly seventeen million Europeans emigrated to the United States. These immigrants overwhelmingly entered the country through the ports of New York and New Jersey and thence spread throughout the northeastern United States, where they swelled the labor force and precipitated a great competition for jobs, housing, and other resources. There was little demand for African-American labor outside the South, and migration of blacks out of the South during this period was relatively low. But the beginning of World War I in 1914 halted the European migration and also created a boom for industry in the United States. Northern employers, starved for labor, turned to the laborers of the South. Black and white southerners responded positively, and a great competition for agricultural labor developed. Hundreds of labor agents from northern and southern factories scoured the rural South for laborers while evading the landlords and local authorities who fought, sometimes with violent extralegal methods, to retain them. Approximately 525,000 African Americans migrated to the urban North between 1910 and 1920 in search of the promised land of the urban labor agents' exaggerated depiction.

Prior to the war African-American migrants to the urban North had mostly found employment as janitors, porters, and servants, but during the war, blacks, both newcomers and older residents alike, were hired for jobs that had previously been restricted to whites. For the most part, however, African-American men were still at best employers' second choice to white labor, and the jobs they could obtain often were in areas "designated" for blacks because they required work in conditions of extreme heat, moisture, dust, or some other undesirable feature. For example, African-American men were typically preferred as asphalt workers, who were required to speedily and efficiently perform heavy and exacting labor with hot asphalt and heated tools during the summer, and in such similar work as the acid bath in the iron and steel industry.

In Chicago in 1910, over 51 percent of African-American men were in domestic and personal service. In 1920 this figure had fallen to 28 percent, even though the black population had increased significantly, because factory work had become the most important source of employment for black men, who had even managed to increase their representation in semiskilled jobs.

Opportunities for African-American women were not so good. While more jobs opened in manufacturing and trade, they were still overwhelmingly restricted to domestic service, where 64 percent of employed African-American women labored. These restrictions applied regardless of skill and qualifications. City-born women with high school and college educations were often no more able to obtain work other than domestic service than were illiterate peasants from a tobacco plantation.

Throughout urban America unionization only benefited white workers, who did their best to exclude blacks from occupations over which unions had control. By the late 1920s in the South—where at the end of the nineteenth century, African Americans could be found in various occupations—growing union control and a resumption of immigration from Europe resulted in losses of jobs for blacks. Railroad work is illustrative: In the late nineteenth and early twentieth centuries blacks had been employed by railroads as firemen, brakemen, and even engineers, but

Working as a porter on passenger trains was one of the few reasonably well-paying jobs open to black males in the early twentieth century. Roy Wilkins, later executive secretary of the NAACP, earned money for his education in the early 1920s by working in the Great Lakes area as a dining car porter. (Prints and Photographs Division, Library of Congress)

unionization led to their ouster in a campaign to make these occupations all white. In some cases, the desire to rid an occupation of black competition led to extreme violence, as when the Brotherhood of Railroad Workers in Memphis, Tenn., placed a bounty of three hundred dollars on the heads of black firemen. Three African-American firemen were kidnapped and murdered for the reward.

Employment conditions for African Americans in New England were no better. In New Haven, Conn., blacks were excluded from all of the city's primary industries. In 1930 not even a dozen African Americans had jobs in the city's clock, rubber, paper and printing, and ammunition factories, although they employed thirteen hundred workers. A study of the area's labor market reported:

> There were none in the cigar and tobacco factories, employing another two hundred and fifty. In the iron and steel industry, a large one in New Haven, the Negroes have had throughout the generation only a few of the two thousand to three thousand semiskilled jobs; at the peak in 1920 their share was less than three-tenths of their due. A smelting plant reported none: "They had always been able to get all the white men they needed, even for the heat jobs." A steel wire manufactory with a force of nearly five hundred employed only one Negro who had insulated himself by serving for a time as a janitor. An informant at a rubber firm said there were no Negroes at all in the new, modern factory, although in the badly ventilated old one both colored men and women had worked in some of the dusty places to which white people objected.

Thus, in 1930, as the Great Depression began, African Americans' economic position had improved to the extent that they were less concentrated in the rural South and were better represented in manufacturing and trade industries. Still, they remained severely underrepresented as artisans and operatives and in clerical, business, and professional positions. Overwhelmingly, African-American women had few opportunities outside domestic and personal service occupations, and black men were relegated to positions as common laborers.

DEPRESSION

Between 1929 and 1932 the real value of the total volume of goods and services produced by the U.S. economy fell by one-third, from $96 billion to $64 billion. This catastrophic event led to hundreds of bank and business failures, mass unemployment on a scale of one in four Americans looking for work, and conditions of poverty that affected the U.S. population in every class. African Americans, who were for the most part at the bottom of the economic order, were destined to face especially bleak prospects. Moreover, the nature of the electoral process further weakened their economic position. The great majority of African Americans were industrially and politically disfranchised. This disability made them an easy target for exclusion from the councils of industrial and political decisions that would affect their economic future. Despite a number of important overtures to black voters by the Democratic party—overtures that ultimately led to increased political representation of African Americans in local and national politics—the economic philosophy of the New Deal may have worsened the suffering that African Americans experienced during the 1930s.

Through most of the decade, the Roosevelt administration believed that the depression was primarily a problem of "ruinous competition" between businesses and workers, which caused prices and wages to be too low to maintain adequate aggregate purchasing power and "American standards of living." Thus, the administration sought to solve this problem. The foundation of the economic policy was the National Industrial Recovery Act (NIRA) of 1933, whose purpose, according to President Roosevelt, "was to put people back to work, . . . to raise the purchasing power of labor by limiting hours (of work) and increasing wages. It was to elevate labor standards by making sure that no employer would suffer competitive disadvantages as a result of paying decent wages or establishing decent working conditions." But the act went far beyond protection of labor and industry from mere business fluctuations to an attack against "unfair competition" by businessmen who took advantage of pools of unemployed, desperate laborers willing to accept jobs at almost any price. This unfair competition consisted in cutting wages and prices to restore profit margins and forcing other firms to follow, willingly or otherwise. Disfranchised African-American men and women had little or no voice in determining the specific policies used to attack these problems. The chosen policies left them highly vulnerable.

Both the rhetoric and the legislation of what historian Arthur Schlesinger, Jr., dubbed the "first" and "second" New Deals aimed at and succeeded for a time in repealing the law of supply and demand. As a consequence, the policy deprived the economically dispossessed of the only weapon they had in the fight to make a living: their ability to offer their labor for lower wages and longer working hours than their more privileged white countrymen could or would. Without this ability African Americans were left with no active agency to force unions and white workers generally to accept black coworkers on terms at least partially determined by blacks. African Americans were forced to apply for employment on the terms set both by employers acting in concert with or in reaction to unions and by the level of discrimination that the public conscience and social institutions would tolerate.

The National Recovery Administration (NRA)—with its voluminous codes of fair competition that legislated minimum prices (for everything from safety pins to automobiles), output quotas, and labor standards—became a bureaucratic, economic, and political failure and was declared unconstitutional by the U.S. Supreme Court in 1935. Nevertheless, its lines of emphasis signaled the major directions that the New Deal would continue to explore. While much attention was given to the argument that price codes hurt small businesses and stifled economic recovery by, in Justice Hugo Black's terms, "making it a crime to produce too much, and to sell too cheaply," no one was listening to the symmetric argument that the legislation robbed the unemployed laborer of his most effective measure for gaining employment precisely because it became a crime to work too much and to sell one's labor cheaper than the competition.

The impact of the new labor market structure upon the black worker was felt immediately, grimly forecasting the shape of things to come. In 1933, after passage of the NIRA, the NAACP reported that "the first effect of the . . . President's agreement was the displacement of many Negro workers throughout the South where employers decided that if they had to pay the minimum wage of twelve dollars a week they would not pay it to Negroes." By way of illustration, the NAACP's journal, the CRISIS, reported the "dismissal of fourteen colored women from a [Memphis] factory where they had been getting seven dollars a week and the employment of fourteen white women to take their places at twelve dollars a week."

If the minority worker faced the problem of being displaced in industries where white workers were willing to enter under the new improved conditions, the new social welfare legislation to protect the American worker was not applicable in just those industries where blacks were so numerically dominant that they could not be feasibly displaced and therefore might benefit from improved conditions. Agriculture, casual, and domestic labor were not covered by social security or fair labor legislation.

Indeed, the Agricultural Adjustment Act of 1933, whose objective was to improve the economic condition of the U.S. farm population, dealt a tremendous blow to the economic condition of African Americans. Landowners were paid by the acre to reduce the amount of land they tilled. A proportion of the funds received was supposed to go to sharecroppers and renters, but the political organizations that oversaw the distributions were in the hands of whites

Stevedores loading a stove on a packet boat in Burrwood, La., in 1938. In New Orleans and elsewhere in Louisiana, dock work was one of the most common occupations of black men. (Prints and Photographs Division, Library of Congress)

and controlled by the landlords, so few croppers or renters received funds. Moreover, the reduction in crop acreage drastically reduced the landowners' need for labor, and many thousands of rural laboring families were thrown out of work. Loans from the government set in motion a demand for farm capital that led to mechanization of plantations, which in turn, by the late 1940s and 1950s, would lead to continuing mass unemployment of southern farm laborers.

Empirical evidence suggests that the very structure of how labor markets allocated jobs and earnings was drastically altered during the 1930s. For example, the infamous two-to-one relationship between nonwhite and white unemployment rates, a relationship that has remained relatively stable for forty years, may well have been a result of labor market intervention in the 1930s. The unemployment rates (in nonfarm industries) for whites and nonwhites respectively were 7.9 percent and 8.6 percent in the spring of 1930, giving a ratio of 1.09. By 1940 the rates were 9.3 percent and 13.4 percent, forming a ratio of 1.44, and the ratio climbed during the next three decades. The inclusion of agricultural unemployment makes the overall nonwhite rate in 1930 lower than that for whites—the last time that result occurred.

The emphasis of the fair labor legislation of the second phase of the New Deal (after 1935)—protection of the market position of the employed—was consistent with the position of the old craft unions, which preached a philosophy of membership exclusion and closed bargaining to maintain and enhance the living standard of a protected few employees. As a consequence, while the labor legislation looked progressive at the time, it allowed the protectionist elements in the union movement, largely represented by the American Federation of Labor (AFL), to gain dominance over the more democratic philosophy of inclusion that was advocated by the Congress of Industrial Organizations (CIO), which had inherited part of the philosophy of unions such as the Knights of Labor. The CIO's attempts to organize black and white labor in the South were brutally crushed during the thirties. It eventually adopted much of the AFL's outlook, though it remained less hostile to black workers than the AFL. In the mid 1950s the AFL and CIO merged.

Thus, in 1934 the marginal position of the black laborer in the New Deal's social compact was determined. The labor market became the province of white laborers who relinquished places to others only on their own terms. These terms increasingly forced African Americans into situations where lack of demand for their services from the private sector made them ever more dependent on the public sector. By 1940 so many African Americans either were working on government works projects or were on welfare relief that in African-American communities the NRA was remembered as the Negro Relief Act.

Poverty was common in the United States at the beginning of the 1940s, but it was far more prevalent among blacks. As a consequence of discrimination in education and in the labor market, black men and women worked long and arduous hours for very little income. Still, four of five black families were headed by two parents; even so, by present-day standards adjusted for inflation, 81 percent of black families, compared with 48 percent of white families, lived in poverty.

1940–1990: An Age of Prosperity and Despair

After substantial economic gains during the era of World War I, African Americans experienced little progress during the interwar period. But since World War II there have been great changes. First, while African Americans' economic status, both in absolute terms and relative to whites, improved during the period from 1940 to 1973, it has since, again relative to whites, leveled off or even deteriorated. Indeed, for many blacks at the lowest economic strata, their absolute economic well-being has deteriorated since the mid-1970s. For example, African Americans' real per capita income and average family income were 58 percent of whites' in the late 1960s and in the late 1980s; the proportion of African-American families with incomes below $10,000 (in constant dollars) rose from 23.9 to 25.6 percent between 1967 and 1990. Second, concurrent with this deterioration has been a drop in the employment of black males; and third, the level of inequality within the black population has heightened.

Changes in the mean annual earnings of men and women and in the relative earnings of blacks to whites at ten-year intervals (plus 1984) are displayed

Chief cook with his assistants at the U.S. Naval Academy in Annapolis, Md., in the 1940s. Until April 1942, almost all of the African Americans in the U.S. Navy were given mess hall duties. (Prints and Photographs Division, Library of Congress)

TABLE 1.   **Mean Annual Earnings of Black and White Women and Men, 1939–1990**

Women

	1939	1949	1959	1969	1979	1984	1990*
Black	$2,070	$3,632	$4,764	$ 8,347	$10,496	$10,252	$14,404
White	5,192	6,647	7,870	9,966	10,420	10,354	15,424
Ratio	.40	.54	.60	.84	1.0	.99	.93

Men

	1939	1949	1959	1969	1979	1984	1990*
Black	$3,833	$6,655	$9,540	$14,177	$15,160	$13,218	$18,783
White	8,745	12,596	18,079	22,860	23,032	20,457	27,630
Ratio	.44	.53	.53	.62	.66	.65	.68

* Earnings for 1939–1979 are standardized to 1984 prices. Earnings in 1990 are for 1990 prices. Source: U.S. Bureau of the Census.

in table 1. Each race-sex group enjoyed substantial increases in real earnings from 1939 into the early 1970s. After 1973, however, growth in real mean earnings stagnated for all groups, and by the middle 1980s real annual earnings had declined below the 1970s peak for each group. Changes in mean weekly wages behaved similarly. Between 1939 and 1984 mean weekly wages for blacks relative to whites increased twenty–six percentage points for males and fifty-six points for females. Overall, black men earned mean weekly wages that had risen to 67 percent of white men's, while mean weekly wages for black women had reached 97 percent of white women's. The rising black-white ratios from 1939 through 1979 indicate that mean earnings for blacks were rising faster than for whites over this time, while the decline in the 1984 ratios indicate that those forces leading to reductions in the real annual earnings of American women and men must have affected labor market opportunities for blacks more severely than for whites. To gain some understanding of these trends in average incomes requires study of the historical conditions that produced them.

During the 1940s African Americans competed in the labor market under very adverse conditions. A majority of white Americans approved of job discrimination against blacks. In a 1944 national survey 55 percent of all white Americans and 80 percent of those living in the South responded that "white people should have the first chance at any kind of job" over blacks. Furthermore, largely because of discrimination in the provision of public education, the median schooling completed by black females and males in 1940 was just 6.2 and 5.4 years, respectively, compared to white female and male medians of 8.8 and 8.7 years, respectively. The primary source of black employment remained agriculture: Two-fifths of black working men labored in agriculture, mostly as sharecroppers, renters, and day laborers, and 50 percent of the black population lived on farms or in farm areas of the South. Nearly three-quarters of employed African-American women were still in domestic or personal service.

Despite these obstacles, black men and women, with higher employment-to-population ratios than whites, were more likely to be working, and they did so for far lower wages. Even so, in 1939 African-American men's mean weekly wage was less than one-half (47%) of the mean wage paid white men and three-quarters (72%) of that paid white women, while black women earned a mean wage a fourth (27%) of white men's and less than one-half (41%) of white women's. Differentials in educational attainment can explain part of the earnings gaps, but striking evidence of the pervasive public sanction of labor market discrimination against African Americans is the fact that in 1939 the mean weekly earnings of black men and women college graduates ($201 and $159 in 1985 prices) were far less than the earnings of white men and women high school graduates ($393 and $270).

A wartime economy again proved to be a source of economic mobility for many African Americans. Pulled by the strong demand for workers in wartime factory production and many other industries, African Americans again left the rural South in search of opportunity. Many found improved job conditions as semiskilled and even some skilled jobs opened to blacks in expanding industries such as munitions and steel. As during World War I, though, equal opportunity did not prevail.

MINORITY EXCLUSION FROM
MID–CENTURY TO 1973
Although labor scarcity and government pressure against discrimination in defense-related industries al-

During World War II many black women entered the industrial labor force for the first time. For most, the experience was short-lived, and they were forced from their positions with the return of GIs after the end of the war. These women worked at the Atchison, Topeka, and Santa Fe rail yard as cleaners of potash cars, Clovis, N.M., 1943. (Prints and Photographs Division, Library of Congress)

leviated the problems somewhat, employers and labor unions remained virtually free to practice systematic and overt discrimination against African Americans during the period from 1940 through the mid-1960s. With few exceptions white-collar clerical jobs and higher-paying blue-collar positions were still unavailable to blacks. Discrimination was invoked against minorities regardless of their qualifications. In the early 1940s, for example, African Americans were so proscribed in labor markets that personal-service and janitorial jobs with elite employers were often positions of high prestige among urban African Americans. Such jobs were held by black graduates of northern high schools and predominantly white colleges. African Americans who had attended "integrated" public schools all their lives and whose families had lived in a city for generations often found access to economic opportunity as blocked as did newly arrived migrants. Thus, while blacks again found themselves much in demand to fill the lower job rungs in many industries—itself a step up from farm work or other work outside the factory—they were still closed off from the better jobs,

and some of the industries providing the best jobs continued to bar African Americans altogether.

For example, from its beginnings the aircraft industry refused to employ African Americans. Even those with the necessary skills and educational requirements for the work found that discrimination barred their way. In the spring of 1940, *Fortune* magazine reported that the aircraft industry had "an almost universal prejudice against Negroes . . . you almost never see Negroes in aircraft factories . . . [and] there is little concealment about the anti-Negro policy." By way of illustration, the article in *Fortune* quoted the president of an aircraft firm called Vultec (shortly afterward a division of General Dynamics, which had a large plant in the Fort Worth, Tex., area) as telling a Negro organization that "it is not the policy of this company to employ people other than of the caucasian race. . . ." Similarly, the president of North American Aviation stated that

we will receive applications from both white and Negro workers. However, the Negroes will be considered only as janitors and in other similar capacities . . . it is against the company policy to employ them as mechanics or aircraft workers. . . . We use none except white workers in the plant . . . at Inglewood [Calif.] and the plant in Dallas and we intend to maintain the same policy in Kansas City. . . .

Throughout the 1940s and into the 1950s, conditions improved somewhat in the North, but in the Southwest plants hired few African Americans, and when they did, they frequently operated segregated facilities. In such plants African Americans were usually refused admittance to training or else given segregated and inferior training. In some cases they were provided training that omitted preparation for key jobs.

During the 1950s, despite three major recessions, the U.S. economy managed to create job growth that raised millions of Americans out of poverty. But during the 1950s and 1960s the rapid mechanization of farming methods throughout the South, encouraged by the improved availability of farm credit due to the Agricultural Adjustment Act created during the New Deal era, greatly decreased the need for farm workers. Thousands of the poorest laborers, black and white, were pushed out of the rural South where they had quickly become an economically redundant population. Spilling into urban areas across the nation, many African Americans found themselves undereducated and discriminated against in an economy plagued with high unemployment.

Government was still a major part of the problem. State employment offices, such as those in the greater Washington, D.C., and Baltimore area, maintained segregated services until the early 1960s. Switchboard operators often asked prospective employers who had failed to request a particular office whether they wanted "white or Negro workers." After the Baltimore office stopped accepting discriminatory requests from employers, the volume of job orders dropped off. Directors of the program attributed this to a "switch by employers from the public to the private employment agencies" where presumably they could still discriminate. However, at the public employment bureaus some personnel acknowledged that they continued to send "discriminating" businesses only the workers they wanted to hire. In the District of Columbia, private agencies proudly touted their ability to avoid black labor. An official audit in the district found that a "substantial proportion (if not a majority) of the job orders placed by private business [were] discriminatory." Similar blatant practices were in place throughout the nation. The U.S. Civil Rights Commission, investigating racial conditions in Cleveland, Ohio, during the late 1960s, found newspaper ads for vacant job positions that required applicants to live on the "West Side only" or specified "West Side residents preferred."

Because of segregation, nearly all blacks lived on the east side of the city.

Discrimination against minorities in public education by state and local governments was equally significant. Inferior, segregated schooling put minorities at a great disadvantage in competing in the labor market. The State Advisory Committees of the U.S. Civil Rights Commission, referring to vocational training, found in 1961 that most communities offered African Americans only inferior, segregated vocational training, if any at all, throughout the United States; even if African Americans did become skilled, discrimination in the skilled trades made black employment difficult or impossible.

A major obstacle to black economic progress during the postwar period was the continued hostility of unions. A study of unions undertaken in the early 1940s discovered that the constitutions or rituals of fourteen national unions explicitly prohibited African-American members. Among these were the machinists' and railroad brotherhoods. Eight others refused admittance to blacks by "tacit consent," and nine more admitted African Americans only in segregated "auxiliary" unions that were affiliated with white parent unions. These segregated relationships put blacks in subordinate positions that gave the white branches most of the best jobs, seniority, and a more than proportionate share of employment. During the 1940s there were many instances when white unions went on strike to protest the hiring or skill upgrading of blacks. In some cases the military had to be called in to desegregate a plant and force white workers back to work so that war production could be continued.

Despite these difficulties, African Americans made inroads into CIO unions. Postwar industrial growth led to an increase in employment in the automobile industry and others that depended on it, such as steel and rubber. By the late 1950s a kind of blue-collar elite of high-wage, unionized workers (belonging to such CIO unions as the United Auto Workers and United Steel Workers) had emerged in many African-American communities. Often these workers, frequently semiliterate migrants from rural communities and farms, were better paid than African-American college graduates; at that time, such educated blacks were restricted to positions serving segregated black communities or in jobs well below their qualifications in the "mainstream" labor market. This desegregation imbalance set up very strong disincentives for young blacks to place a premium on education.

But even among CIO unions black employment was slowed because of racial animosity. During the fifties the CIO's renewed attempts to organize white workers in the South led it to de-emphasize its policies of racial equality, and its 1955 merger with the AFL to create the AFL–CIO implied the tacit acceptance of the discriminatory policies of the AFL's craft unions. In the late 1950s George Meany, then president of the AFL–CIO, acknowledged, "Right here in the District of Columbia . . . there are local unions whose membership . . . [is] closed to Negro applicants." Two-thirds of the way through the twentieth century, minority participation in the craft trades was negligible nationwide. In 1965 the President's Commission on Equal Employment Opportunity surveyed 989 construction industry contractors, 281 employer associations, and 731 unions. In the thirty southern cities surveyed, only 26 of 3,696 persons—less than 1 percent—selected for apprenticeship programs of plumbers', electricians', sheetmetal workers', ironworkers', and carpenters' unions were members of a minority group; 20 of those 26 were in the carpenters' union. In the nonsouthern states and cities, 133 of 5,906 persons (2%) in apprenticeship programs for the same five trades were black; 70 were carpenters. Nevertheless, among industrial unions African Americans' power was growing with their numbers.

ANTIDISCRIMINATION AND
AFFIRMATIVE ACTION

The urban migration of African Americans greatly increased their political power, and with their civil rights organizations they lobbied local, state, and federal officials to end job discrimination. In the 1940s the FAIR EMPLOYMENT PRACTICES COMMITTEE (FEPC) held hearings throughout the nation to investigate allegations of discrimination. Large war contractors, such as steel, aircraft, and shipbuilding firms, were targeted by the FEPC as they were thought to be especially susceptible to federal government coercion. The FEPC was, however, largely an investigative body with limited enforcement powers, and historians have been divided on whether it actually increased opportunities for blacks beyond those jobs that would have arisen anyway due to the wartime shortage of labor. During the 1950s many states and localities passed antidiscrimination legislation, but most economists and historians have assessed these laws as ineffective in reducing job discrimination against minorities.

In the late 1950s President Eisenhower, responding to the findings of discrimination of the Civil Rights Commission (whose members he had appointed) and using the apparatus of the FEPC, created the President's Commission on Equal Employment Opportunity, which was chaired by Vice President Richard Nixon. This commission investigated hiring practices in defense-related industries and used the contracting powers of the federal government to "encourage" contractors to institute affirmative-action hiring programs for blacks. While the commission enjoyed some success, it was largely ineffective against the areas of deepest resistance to equal-employment opportunities for African Americans.

For example, during the 1950s pressure from the federal government persuaded General Electric to desegregate its jet engine facility near Dallas, Tex. Even so, by 1960 the facilities of some large plants were still segregated, and major aircraft companies in the Dallas–Fort Worth area employed few African Americans other than in laboring and service jobs. The African-American proportion of all skilled operatives in the industry in 1968 was 7.5 percent in the Southwest (it was 13.5% nationally). Fort Worth, with a population that was about 16 percent black in 1960, employed a lower percentage of blacks than did Seattle with a 5 percent black population.

Then, in the early 1960s, the government of the United States, swept up in the tide of a national CIVIL RIGHTS MOVEMENT and growing black political power, initiated a series of legislative, executive, and judicial actions designed to redress and correct the effects of over three hundred years of exclusion and discrimination. Strengthening the programs initiated by President Eisenhower, President Kennedy in 1961 banned discrimination by government contractors with executive order 10925, and his administration established guidelines to promote the hiring of minorities by these contractors. Against this background the U.S. Congress, under strong pressure from President Lyndon Johnson and the civil rights coalition of blacks, liberals, and national unions, enacted the Civil Rights Act of 1964, which attempted to remedy discrimination against people of color in employment, housing, access to credit, public accommodation, and association, as well as to promote a more general enjoyment of constitutional rights. Title VII of the act created the Equal Employment Opportunity Commission (EEOC), which became the major antidiscrimination enforcement agency of the federal government in matters of employment. As was the FEPC of the late 1940s, the EEOC was initially limited to fact-finding and conciliation, although it did encourage private parties to sue employers and labor unions and it could recommend that the U.S. Attorney General initiate law suits when a pattern or practice of discrimination was found. In the 1970s Congress gave the EEOC the power to sue alleged discriminators.

In 1965 President Johnson extended legal procedures through executive order 11246, which established rules for nondiscrimination by federal contractors. Contractors with fifty or more employees and contracts of $50,000 or more were required to develop and submit affirmative-action compliance programs with goals and timetables for the hiring and promotion of minorities. In the late 1960s and early 1970s President Richard Nixon—who, it will be recalled, had chaired Eisenhower's commission—institutionalized affirmative-action policies even further through more explicit reliance on the concept of goals and timetables in hiring by federal contractors.

THE KENNEDY–JOHNSON SIXTIES

During the Kennedy and Johnson administrations, expansionary economic policies generally and spending for the war in Vietnam particularly had the economy growing at an unprecedented rate. During the ten-year period between 1963 and 1973, incomes and earnings of the American population reached all-time historical highs. Thus, adjusted for inflation, in 1959 the mean weekly earnings of American white men were $398; that figure had risen to $504 by 1969. The mean weekly earnings of white women rose from $217 to $271 during the same ten years. Nearly all segments of society shared in the economic prosperity. The poverty rate fell from 22.2 percent in 1960 to 12.6 percent in 1970 before reaching its all-time low of 11.1 percent in 1973.

As members of the American population, African Americans shared in this period of economic prosperity. Largely through their own initiative, blacks responded to the growing economy by completing the migration, from south to north and from rural areas to cities, that they began decades earlier, causing a concurrent movement from agricultural employment to other industries. Against a backdrop of high rates of employment, job creation, and growth of real output, there were increases in the schooling of blacks. In addition, through their increasing electoral influence, the moral authority of the civil rights movement, and the urban riots of the 1960s, African Americans forced the political system to afford them greater participation in areas of the economy previously closed to them. Affirmative action and antidiscrimination enforcement were important components, making it possible for more blacks to gain access to "good" jobs, whose numbers had been increased by the steady economic growth.

Perhaps encouraged by the fact that six consecutive presidential administrations, both Democrat and Republican—albeit with varying degrees of vigor—had endorsed a civil rights agenda of fighting employment discrimination and advancing the economic position of minorities towards equality with whites, the U.S. Supreme Court, in a series of cases, strengthened both antidiscrimination forces and affirmative-action policies. In the important 1971 cases, *Griggs* v. *Duke Power Co.*, the Court, arguing that "Congress directed the thrust of the act [title VII] to the consequences of employment practices, not simply the motivation," ruled that employment and hiring practices (such as tests) that led to disparate impact on minorities must be shown to have a strictly business necessity.

Successful litigation against businesses and unions attacked discrimination at its heart while affirmative-action policies in government and the private sector gave African Americans new opportunities. By the mid-1960s strong government pressure against discrimination had opened employment to blacks in the previously all-white southern textile industry. White-collar occupations were opened to black women in many areas of the economy.

The strongest proof of the success of this push for egalitarian race relations was the emergence of a new black middle class. This group was three to four times the size it had been in 1960, but more important, post-1960 entrants were no longer confined to occupations in segregated black society. After the 1960s black ministers, teachers, and the small group of professionals and proprietors serving almost all-black clienteles came to be outnumbered by black professionals and white-collar employees working for organizations and institutions primarily run by whites. This widened job access was matched by increased rates of matriculation at predominantly white colleges. For the first time in American history, the black poor, although numerically significant and highly visible, became a distinct minority of the African-American population.

FROM THE VIETNAM WAR ERA TO 1990

The economics of the 1960s proved to be as much an aberration as its politics. The combination of low-unemployment domestic policies, the War on Poverty, and the expanding Vietnam War defense budgets produced an inflation that by the end of the decade was squeezing the purchasing power of middle-class Americans. Richard Nixon gained the presidency partially on the basis of a promise to bring budgets under control and put a stop to inflation. But the commitment of his administration (and Ford's and Carter's) to fight inflation with high-unemployment policies proved weak. In 1970, one year after the end of the Kennedy-Johnson economic program, inflation and unemployment stood at 5.7 and 4.8 percent, respectively. Ten years later, in 1980, inflation and unemployment were 13.5 and 7 percent, respectively. In between had come a decade of slow economic growth accompanied by the great energy crisis of 1973–1975, when oil and gas shortages increased industrial costs and sent the economy into what was then the worst recession of the postwar period, with unemployment reaching 8.5 percent.

In addition, the European and Japanese economies had fully recovered from the war and were competing effectively with domestic manufactures in the

United States. Hard hit by the competition were autos, steel, rubber, and similar industries. The spectacular economic growth of the sixties—coming on the heels of the modest growth, tempered by three recessions, of the Eisenhower years—camouflaged the shrinking manufacturing base that had alarmed many economists during the 1950s. Thus, manufacturing, which employed a major portion of American middle-income families and practically all middle-income African Americans, was evaporating in many eastern and midwestern cities.

The twenty-seven years of relative economic growth from 1946 to 1973 produced many victories and achievements for African Americans as millions of them reached the middle class. However, the conditions of prosperity did not lift all white Americans out of poverty, nor were they sufficient to do so for all African Americans, who continued to bear the legacy of economic discrimination and inferior schooling. Economic growth, affirmative action, antidiscrimination enforcement, and a determination to make it in the economy had not been enough to overcome inadequate educational and employment incentives, let alone the import-market competition from abroad that reduced the availability of high-paying blue-collar jobs.

THE REAGAN–BUSH YEARS

In the early 1980s Ronald Reagan, elected president on the promise to reinvigorate American society, initiated a policy-induced recession that drove unemployment above 8 percent and slowed the inflation rate. Afterwards, Reagan's much-heralded income tax cut, combined with significant increases in defense spending, created an aggregate demand in service, real estate, and financial markets that led to renewed prosperity for many sectors of the economy. But the economic program also created enormous federal budget deficits, which led to a frenzy of public and private borrowing and spending. In addition, the growth favored those with higher incomes, while the deterioration in the average wages of American men and women continued during the 1980s. As the loss of manufacturing jobs proceeded at a rapid pace, the economy replaced them with service-sector jobs that either required high education and skills or offered very low wages. Changes in U.S. immigration policy in 1965 and again in 1986, as well as substantial increases in illegal immigration, resulted in an unprecedentedly large influx of immigrants, many of whom filled the lower paying jobs. Reductions in real earnings were generally greatest for those men and women with the least education. Black and white men with less than a high school education actually earned real mean weekly wages in 1984 that were less than their respective wages in 1960, and the earnings

of black male high school graduates fell from two-thirds those of black male college graduates in the period from 1939 to 1969 to one-half in 1984.

RACE RELATIONS, FALLING REAL WAGES, AND EMPLOYMENT

Changing employment patterns were similar for black and white men, although declining employment among black men was especially severe. The really significant reductions in labor-force participation and employment occurred between 1970 and 1980. The heralded recovery of the mid-1980s apparently improved the position of white low-skilled men but not black. Thus, although in 1970 there was no difference between the employment rates of black high school and college graduates, by 1985 high school graduates had an employment rate twelve percentage points lower. The employment rate of high school dropouts was nearly thirty points lower.

As a result, the later 1970s and especially the 1980s were times when poor Americans were finding it ever more difficult to escape from poverty. Poverty rates rose dramatically as the American economy faltered. In 1973 the poverty rate among whites was 8.4 percent; in 1992 it was 11.6 percent. For blacks the increase during this period was from 31.5 percent to 33.3 percent. No group was safe: The rate among Latinos went from 21.9 percent in 1973 to 29.3 percent by 1992, and though 1973 figures for Asian Americans are not available, their 12.5 percent poverty rate in 1992 is higher than that of the preceding years. Declining real wages and rising unemployment discouraged many young Americans as successive cohorts of high school graduates entered an economy that appeared to promise them a standard of living worse than that of their parents.

FEMINIZATION OF POVERTY

By the 1990s Americans with poor educations and few skills found it particularly difficult to succeed under these harsh economic conditions. Many gave up the attempt to do so and turned to crime and public assistance as a way of life. Although socially disadvantaged individuals of all racial groups were susceptible to these troubles and temptations, hundreds of thousands of black youths lived in social conditions that made them especially vulnerable. Lack of mainstream economic opportunity and the choice of crime or public assistance spawned a subculture that has now produced two or three generations of low-income, low-skilled African Americans. One-parent black families became nearly as prevalent as two-parent black families. Poverty became highly feminized; overall, a third of black families lived in poverty, but the rate was much higher for mother-only families.

A major factor in this predicament was the continuing discrepancy in economic opportunities available to men and women. Thus, in 1990 black and white women working year-round and full-time earned 58 and 65 percent, respectively, of what white men similarly employed earned. The low mean earnings of women high school graduates working year-round and full-time—$16,026 for black women and $19,356 for white women, compared with $29,257 and $22,644 for white and black men, respectively—made it exceedingly difficult for women heading families with children to escape poverty. For African-American women in this educational group, the poor economic position of similarly educated black men insured continuing high rates of dependence on public assistance.

GOVERNMENT POLICY TOWARD THE POOR DURING THE EIGHTIES

In this economic environment many voters became disgruntled with government policies on affirmative action and aid to the poor. The Reagan administration launched a counterattack on affirmative-action programs. The federal judiciary, whose new appointees were more conservative, rejected the approach to antidiscrimination law that had been followed in the previous decades. Pushed by vigorous lobbying from the Reagan Justice Department, the courts began to shift the burden of proof in discrimination cases back onto employees, weakening the *Griggs* ruling that had set up the standard of disparate impact as prima facie evidence of discrimination. While virtually all white Americans publicly espoused the principle of equal opportunity for all citizens, employment discrimination against African Americans nonetheless remained a significant problem. Using techniques that involved black and white job seekers with identical résumés, researchers in Chicago, Los Angeles, and the District of Columbia found considerable evidence of unequal treatment.

The slowing of economic growth, the continuing shift from heavy manufacturing to service jobs, and a concurrent decline in real wages have produced great economic and social distress. Increased competition for jobs has increased the number of discouraged workers who discontinue an active job search for extended periods. Government transfer programs probably abetted their decisions, but there is little theoretical or empirical evidence for believing that transfers were the major factor. Similarly, activity in the underground economy and crime probably serve as a safety valve for those whose market opportunities have declined most.

The economic history of the United States since Reconstruction shows that the status of blacks and the opportunities available to them and to other minorities have generally moved in a direction consistent with that of the larger American society. This common destiny and the difficult economic conditions since the early 1970s best explain the present conditions among the African-American population.

BIBLIOGRAPHY

DU BOIS, W. E. B. *Black Reconstruction in America, 1860–1880.* New York, 1935.
HARRIS, WILLIAM H. *The Harder We Run: Black Workers Since the Civil War.* New York, 1982.
JAYNES, GERALD. *Branches Without Roots: Genesis of the Black Working Class, 1862–1882.* New York, 1986.
JAYNES, GERALD, and ROBIN M. WILLIAMS, eds. *A Common Destiny: Blacks and American Society.* Washington, D.C., 1989.
JONES, JACQUELINE. *The Dispossessed: America's Underclasses from the Civil War to the Present.* New York, 1992.
———. *Labor of Love, Labor of Sorrow: Black Women, Work, and the Family from Slavery to the Present.* New York, 1988.
MANDLE, JAY R. *Not Slave, Not Free: The African Economic Experience Since the Civil War.* Durham, N.C., 1992.
WOLTERS, RAYMOND. *Negroes and the Great Depression: The Problem of Economic Recovery.* Westport, Conn., 1970.

GERALD D. JAYNES

Ecumenism. African-American history is dotted with movements seeking to preserve the cultural meanings and structures of blacks as an ethnic group. Examples are the PAN-AFRICANISM of W. E. B. DU BOIS, Marcus GARVEY'S UNIVERSAL NEGRO IMPROVEMENT ASSOCIATION and Elijah MUHAMMAD'S NATION OF ISLAM. Each of these movements may be regarded as "ecumenical" in the broad sense of uniting or bringing together the universe or cosmos of African Americans. But the concept of "ecumenism" is more commonly associated with the Christian tradition, and in this century it has taken two primary forms: unity in doctrine and polity, and united social action.

African-American Christians have participated in the international Christian ecumenical movement from its beginning. But they have also created a unique expression of ecumenism in coming together across denominational lines to preserve and strengthen ethnic unity and welfare. Just as secular and quasi-religious movements have been given impetus by the cultural threat posed to the African-American subculture by the philosophy of integration, so, too, with black Christian movements. With the exception of the SOUTHERN CHRISTIAN LEADERSHIP CONFERENCE (SCLC) in its early years, black ecumenical movements reject the cultural negation implicit in assimilation, while assuming proactive roles in seeking social, economic, and political liberation and empowerment.

The first ecumenical movement to emerge out of the black church was the Fraternal Council of Negro Churches. Organized in 1934 by African Methodist Episcopal (AME) bishop Reverdy RANSOM, this organization in important respects anticipated the religiously based black-consciousness organizations of the 1960s and 1970s. In 1934, integration was scarcely a much-discussed solution to the stubborn racial dilemma that haunted American society. The possibility of brotherhood and sisterhood had been implicit, however, in the formation in 1908 of the Federal Council of Churches—an ecumenical association of Protestant denominations in which membership was extended to the major black Methodist and Baptist denominations and conventions.

It was precisely the tarnishing of that possibility through insensitivity to black concerns that prompted Ransom to form a separatist group. Ultimately, and paradoxically, the demise of the Fraternal Council was accelerated by the integration ideology that gained favor in the 1950s as its members disavowed its all-black character, giving allegiance to the National Council of Churches and to new civil rights organizations. Its potency for social change was thus essentially depleted, but in its early years the Fraternal Council was an effective channel for articulating the values and aspirations of the black subculture.

The second ecumenical movement to appear was forged by one of the new civil rights organizations, the SCLC, organized in 1957 with the initial goal of coordinating the many local protest movements springing up around the South. If this organization was not intentionally formed as an ecumenical body, it nevertheless functioned as such, bringing together the religious leadership central to the civil rights movement (Morris, 1984). While initially committed under the leadership of the Rev. Dr. Martin Luther KING, Jr., to integration, beginning in the mid-1960s the SCLC underwent a transition that corresponded to the change in King's own political thought—from a liberal reform stance to advocacy of economic democracy and structural transformation of American society.

This agenda was even more pronounced in the National Committee of Negro Churchmen organized in 1967. (It went through several name changes in subsequent years, becoming the National Conference of Black Christians [NCBC] in 1983.) NCBC membership consisted of some twelve hundred progressive-minded ministers, lay leaders, and scholars who sought to chart a more radical course for the black church and, through the church, the black community in its entirety. Because many of its early members were affiliated with predominantly white denominations and ecumenical organizations, the NCBC's initial task was to interpret in theological terms the Black Power movement, which many white churchpersons, who only lately had come to support the civil rights movement, read as scarcely less than betrayal. Out of that interpretive task, the NCBC became the primary forum for developing black LIBERATION THEOLOGY. It thus became the reflective pole of a continuum defined on the other end by the activism of the SCLC.

Various other ecumenical efforts are located at different points along this continuum. Also at the reflective end is the INTERDENOMINATIONAL THEOLOGICAL CENTER (ITC), a consortium of six seminaries chartered in 1958 in Atlanta. The ITC's primary task is education for ministry, albeit for social ministry. The Black Theology Project convened for the first time in 1976, but sustained consistent activity only from 1984 to 1989. Like the NCBC, it was concerned initially with dialogue with other church sectors—particularly Latin American theologians—but in later years reframed its reflective enterprise to more directly engage the values and priorities of indigenous black communities.

The NATIONAL BLACK EVANGELICAL ASSOCIATION (NBEA) is distinctive in that its constituency represents a segment of the African-American population normally outside the pale of overt proponents of ethnic consciousness. Founded in 1963 at the height of the CIVIL RIGHTS MOVEMENT, the organization was soon caught up in the maelstrom of Black Power and black liberation theology. The primary objective of the NBEA became the cultivation of a social-justice dimension in evangelical urban ministries. In doing so, the group struck a balance between spirituality and social activism that at least initially eluded other ecumenical groups.

Toward the more activist end of the ecumenical continuum is Partners in Ecumenism (PIE). Although structured as a unit of the National Council of Churches, PIE disavowed the agenda of integration in favor of a model of pluralism. From its founding in 1978 to the late 1980s, when it became inactive, PIE sought to raise the consciousness of white church entities and to enlist white churches in a partnership to address urban concerns. At the same time, in actions reminiscent of the Washington bureau of the Fraternal Council, PIE carried on lobbying activity in conjunction with annual conferences held in Washington, D.C.

The CONGRESS OF NATIONAL BLACK CHURCHES (CNBC) was founded the same year as PIE by AME bishop John Hurst Adams. The CNBC departs from the "activism" of other groups in that its primary objective is institution-building through cooperative economic programs and alternative models of support services for the black family. Like the Fraternal Council, it is organized on a conciliar model, with its membership consisting of the officers of eight of the historic black denominations. Alone among the black ecumenical bodies, the CNBC seeks to empower the black community via the collective economic resources of the black church nationally.

Contrasting with this organization was a short-lived group called the National Black Pastors Conference, organized in 1979 and active only through 1981. While it existed, the conference generated widespread enthusiasm among local black clergy of all denominations and persuasions, who embraced its agenda of political activism. A lack of financial resources to support its program, and the disjunction in political ideology between the leadership and rank-and-file members, contributed to its early demise. The initial vision that the Pastors Conference would be the grass-roots adjunct to the more hierarchically oriented CNBC was thereby frustrated.

These ecumenical movements and organizations, introduced here in only the briefest fashion, vary among themselves in tenure, structure, program, and philosophical emphasis. Yet, for all their differences, they hold important features in common: a concern to preserve and celebrate those aspects of black culture having to do with origins and heritage; a concern to clarify, strengthen, and promulgate values indigenous to the black experience in America. The goal of these movements is not only preservation of cultural and religious values, however, but change in the status of African Americans relative to mainstream society. The point is never cooperative religious activity for its own sake, but empowerment of the African-American population: for the SCLC, through political enfranchisement; for the NCBC, via theological formulations; for the CNBC, through economic development.

The yoking of black consciousness, religion, and social activism is evident in this statement by one of the members of the NCBC, which serves accordingly as an apt summary of African-American ecumenism:

> Black ecumenicity must not be simply contrived interdenominationalism. . . . The central thrust must be Black liberation. Anything that does not serve that purpose does not demand serious commitment from Black church[persons].
> The NCBC is not an ecumenical organization alongside others. It is a movement of Black church[persons] committed first to the Church of Jesus the Christ, then to the liberation of the black community. It may save Christianity in the Western World by giving it back to the people. (Watts, 1970, p. 35)

REFERENCES

MORRIS, ALDON D. *The Origins of the Civil Rights Movement.* New York, 1984.
SAWYER, MARY R. "Black Ecumenical Movements: Proponents of Social Change." *Review of Religious Research* 30 (1988): 151–161.
————. *Black Ecumenism.* Philadelphia, 1994.
WILMORE, GAYRAUD. *Black Religion and Black Radicalism.* 2nd edition. Maryknoll, N.Y., 1983.

MARY R. SAWYER

Edelin, Kenneth C. (March 31, 1939–), obstetrician. Born in Washington, D.C., Kenneth Edelin received his B.S. from Columbia College (1939) and his M.D. from Meharry Medical College (1967) in Nashville. After an internship at Wright-Patterson Air Force Base in Ohio and a three-year stint as a medical officer at Lakenheath Air Base Hospital in England, he completed his residency training in obstetrics and gynecology at Boston City Hospital in 1971.

In 1973 Edelin became the first African American to be chief resident in obstetrics and gynecology at Boston City Hospital. While there, he established an adolescent obstetrics and gynecology clinic, an oncology clinic, a methadone maintenance program for heroin-addicted pregnant women, and an ambulatory abortion clinic. In 1978 he was named chairman and professor of obstetrics and gynecology at Boston University School of Medicine and director of obstetrics and gynecology at Boston City Hospital. Edelin established the first midwifery program at Boston City Hospital and became medical director of the Boston Family Planning Project. In July 1989 he left his position as chief resident to become associate dean for student and minority affairs at Boston University School of Medicine and entered private practice. That same year he was elected chairman of the board of Planned Parenthood Federation of America, the largest private family planning agency in the United States, with 850 clinics throughout the country.

Edelin has been active as a board member in a host of professional and civic organizations, both nationally and locally. He has been a fellow of the American College of Obstetricians and Gynecologists, and a member of the American Fertility Society, the Association of Reproductive Health Professionals, and the National Medical Association. He has served as a trustee of Planned Parenthood of Massachusetts, the Solomon Carter Fuller Mental Health Center (Boston), and the Civil Liberties Union of Massachusetts, and as chairman of the New England Committee of the NAACP Legal Defense and Educational Fund.

REFERENCE

"One of America's Leading Black Doctors." *Black Enterprise* (October 1988): 95.

ROBERT C. HAYDEN

Edelman, Marian Wright (June 6, 1939–), attorney and founder of the Children's Defense Fund. The daughter of Arthur Jerome Wright, minister of Shiloh Baptist Church, and Maggie Leola Wright, a community activist, Marian Edelman was born and raised in Bennetsville, S.C. She attended Spelman College, from which she graduated as valedictorian in 1960. During her senior year, Edelman participated in a sit-in at City Hall in Atlanta. Responding to the need for civil rights lawyers, Edelman entered Yale Law School as a John Hay Whitney Fellow in 1960. After graduating from law school in 1963, she became the first black woman to pass the bar in Mississippi. From 1964 to 1968 she headed the NAACP Legal Defense and Education Fund in Mississippi, where she met her husband, Peter Edelman, a Harvard Law School graduate and political activist. In 1971, she became director of the Harvard University Center for Law and Education. She was also the first black woman elected to the Yale University Corporation, where she served from 1971 to 1977.

Edelman is best known for her work with the Children's Defense Fund (CDF), a nonprofit child advocacy organization that she founded in 1973. The CDF offers programs to prevent adolescent pregnancy, to provide health care, education, and employment for youth, and to promote family planning. In 1980, Edelman became the first black and the second woman to chair the Board of Trustees of Spelman College. She has been the recipient of numerous honors and awards for her contributions to child advocacy, women's rights, and civil rights, including the MacArthur Foundation Prize Fellowship (1985) and the Albert Schweitzer Humanitarian Prize from Johns Hopkins University (1988). Edelman has published numerous books and articles on the condition of black and white children in America, including *Children Out of School in America* (1974), *School Suspensions: Are They Helping Children?* (1975), *Portrait of Inequality: Black and White Children in America* (1980), *Families in Peril: An Agenda for Social Change* (1987), and *The Measure of Our Success: A Letter to My Children and Yours* (1992).

REFERENCES

PLOSKI, HARRY A., and JAMES WILLIAM, eds. *The Negro Almanac: A Reference Work on the African American*. 5th ed. Detroit, 1989.
SMITH, JESSIE CARNEY, ed. *Notable Black American Women*. Detroit, 1992.

SABRINA FUCHS

Edmondson, William (c. 1882–1951), sculptor. Edmondson was born in Davidson County, Tenn., one of six children born to George and Jane, slaves of the Edmondson and Compton families. Before 1908 Edmondson worked in shops at the Nashville, Chattanooga, and St. Louis railways; between 1908 and 1931 he worked as a custodian for the Women's Hospital (later the Baptist Hospital) in Nashville. The hospital closed in 1931 and Edmondson lost his job; shortly thereafter he began sculpting, claiming to be inspired by the voice of God first to cut tombstones and later to carve animals, human figures, angels, and crucifixions. Edmondson, who was afflicted with arthritis, fashioned chisels out of railroad spikes and used cast-off limestone for his sculptures. He and his work were discovered in 1937 by the photographer Louise Dahl-Wolfe, who arranged the same year for an exhibition of his work at the Museum of Modern Art—the first solo exhibition of the work of a black artist at the museum. Subsequent interest in his work caused the Works Progress Administration (*see* WORKS PROJECT ADMINISTRATION) to commission two projects from him between 1939 and 1941 and brought about several more exhibitions of his sculpture before he died in Nashville in 1951. His work has since been exhibited at the Tennessee State Museum, the La Jolla Museum of Contemporary Arts in California, the Hirshhorn Museum and Sculpture Garden in Washington, D.C., and the Musée du Jeu de Paume in Paris.

Edmondson's command of abstract sculptural forms enabled him to transcend the boundary between folk and fine art and gave his art a remarkably modern look. The geometric lines that characterize the faces of his figures give them a masklike quality. The animal forms Edmondson created often echo images found in African and African-American mythology and folktales. Like his contemporaries Leslie Bowling and Palmer HAYDEN, Edmondson is considered a "neo-primitive"—an untrained, nonprofessional artist whose style bears striking resemblances to contemporary art. The neo-primitives came to influence artists such as W. H. JOHNSON, Horace PIPPEN, and Jacob LAWRENCE.

REFERENCES

HUDSON, RALPH M. *Black Artists/South*. Huntsville, Ala., 1979

LIVINGSTON, JANE, and JOHN BEARDSLEY. *Black Folk Art in America, 1930–1980*. Jackson, Miss., 1982.

DOROTHY DESIR-DAVIS

Education. The Africans enslaved in the New World were heirs to the rich and varied educational traditions of their homelands. Like young people everywhere, young Africans were given instruction in their artistic, religious, and cultural heritages by their parents, extended kinship networks, and local communities. Africans from different language groups shared much in common with each other, including related forms of social and political organization, marriage and family customs, and sculptural and musical traditions, as well as related folklore and other leisure activities.

At the same time, there were many divisions within the cultures of western and central Africa, the two areas from which slaves were captured and transported to the New World. While most Africans were followers of traditional African religions, some slaves had been Islamicized, and a handful of slaves (primarily from Portuguese areas) had some experience of Christianity in Africa. Most slaves had had no exposure to written language in Africa, but a small number were literate in Arabic. Some copied Islamic legal texts and made phonetic transcriptions of the Gospels.

A continuing debate surrounds the question of the extent to which African cultural and educational traditions have survived in America. "Probably never before in history has a people been so nearly completely stripped of its social heritage as the Negroes who were brought to America," the African-American sociologist E. Franklin FRAZIER wrote in 1939. His contention was vigorously disputed by Melville Herskovits and others and has since largely fallen from favor. Numerous scholars have provided substantial evidence of the continued retention of African folkways and educational traditions among early generations of Africans in the New World. African retentions are most apparent in the arts, in crafts, and in certain aspects of language and family customs. With regard to religious and political organization, however, the evidence is less clear-cut. For slaves in the New World, the role of African traditions had to be balanced against another, less tangible, yet crucial educational concern: the need to learn about the strange and frightening world of the slave owners.

Despite wariness on both sides, slaves and their masters learned about each other informally, and their education was a two-way process. The procedures for South Carolinian rice cultivation were probably taught to planters by slaves familiar with rice agriculture in Africa. Of primary importance to slaves was the acquisition of the English language. Not surprisingly, the slaves who had direct and extended contact with whites gained a more rapid and superior knowledge of standard English, while those with less contact—for instance, the slaves living in the Sea Islands of South Carolina—developed English dialects in which Africanisms were more prominent. Some were forced to learn languages and other aspects of European culture at the bidding of their masters. Numerous slaves were taught the violin, in order to play at dances and cotillions; in many instances, these musicians not only acquired a standard repertory and technique but also were able to incorporate, and introduce to their hearers, elements from their African musical traditions.

Slaves also received other kinds of training. Some were informally apprenticed in various technical disciplines. James Derham, a slave who had been trained as an assistant to a doctor and was later freed, became a practicing physician, and was judged competent in his learning by the late-eighteenth-century Philadelphia abolitionist Benjamin Rush. Rush also praised the abilities of Thomas Fuller, an illiterate Virginia slave who had mastered the principles of "lightning calculation," and astounded his listeners by performing such feats as calculating, without paper and in the space of two minutes, the number of seconds in a year and a half.

Such accomplishments were exceptional. The vast majority of slaves had no opportunity to gain advanced knowledge of European culture because they had no formal education and therefore were unable to acquire the basic tools needed for learning, such as the ability to read. Slave owners were generally made extremely uneasy by the prospect of literate slaves, both for practical reasons—literacy made escapes and insurrections easier to arrange—and for the less tangible ways in which literacy would force slave owners to confront the immorality of human enslavement. Many laws were passed in southern states, banning slave literacy in the aftermath of an insurrectionary scare. In 1740 the STONO REBELLION prompted the institution of antiliteracy laws in South Carolina. In 1770 Georgia made it a crime to teach slaves to read and write, and in the early 1830s, following NAT TURNER'S REBELLION and other alleged provocations, Louisiana, North Carolina, Virginia, and Alabama banned teaching slaves to read, while Georgia and South Carolina reinforced the laws they had previously passed.

The existence of these laws did not prevent slaves from acquiring literacy, and the extent and impact of antiliteracy laws have probably been exaggerated. Very few people were prosecuted for this "crime." The laws appear to have done little more than affirm the common prejudice against slave literacy. Like most aspects of the slave code, enforcement was primarily left in the hands of individual slave owners. Masters could be barbarous in reacting against slaves who gained the ability to read or write; some went so far as to amputate their fingers. These savage gestures did little to curb the hunger for learning of many slaves, and many masters accommodated or even welcomed slave literacy. At least three of the earliest African-American poets—Jupiter HAMMON, Phillis WHEATLEY, and George Moses HORTON—published collections of verse while enslaved, with the tacit approval of their masters. Though accurate figures will probably never be available, it is estimated that 10 percent of slaves could read by 1860.

Before 1800, almost all slaves were largely self-taught. Free blacks—for example, the Maryland astronomer, surveyor, and almanac maker Benjamin BANNEKER—also acquired their knowledge from informal instruction and such printed matter as they were able to acquire. For many slaves, literacy began by finding a friendly white person, often a slave mistress or a generational cohort to the slave (and increasingly, after 1830, a fellow black) who was willing to give instructions in the rudiments of reading. This was usually followed by the careful and intense private reading and rereading of a selected text. At age twelve, Frederick DOUGLASS purchased a copy of *The Columbian Orator* and proceeded to memorize its forms of speech in what was the first step toward his becoming perhaps the most gifted public speaker of his time. For slaves as for their white contemporaries, literacy began with the acquisition of a Bible or a copy of Noah Webster's "blue-black" speller, although the similarities between the ways in which slaves and other students acquired knowledge of reading (and of the even more dangerous art of writing) ended with these texts. For slaves the act was invariably covert. As a former slave related in an interview, many slaves could read but "de kep' dat up deir sleeve, dey played dumb lack dey couldn't read a bit till after surrender." Slaves developed elaborate strategies for hiding reading material from their masters; as Frederick Douglass noted, the fact that such knowledge was forbidden made its acquisition that much sweeter.

Religion

The dissemination of the Christian religion played a major role in providing both the motivation and the practical means for blacks, slave and free, to acquire an education. "The frequent hearing of my mistress reading the Bible aloud," Frederick Douglass wrote in his autobiography, ". . . awakened my curiosity with respect to this *mystery* of reading." In the Protestantism that most African Americans adopted during the antebellum period, great emphasis was placed on the word of God and the biblical text as the center of the religious experience. Many slave owners questioned whether, given the admonitions against slavery in the Bible, a convert to Christianity could legally be owned. This problem was addressed in a number of colonial legislatures—in Maryland as early as 1644—and by various ministers throughout the succeeding two centuries; however, in every instance, a person's religious orientation was found to have no bearing on his or her status as a slave.

No serious institutional effort at proselytizing Africans was made before the establishment of the SOCIETY FOR THE PROPAGATION OF THE GOSPEL IN FOREIGN PARTS (SPG) by the Church of England in 1701. The SPG embraced as its mission the expansion of Christianity to unconverted blacks, Native Americans, and whites, and the expansion of Anglicanism to strongholds of other Christian denominations, such as Congregationalism in New England. Believing that literacy was a requirement for baptism, in 1704 the SPG established the first North American school for educating blacks, in New York. By 1708 its founder, Elias Neau, reported that it had two hundred students, male and female, free and slave. Despite a threat of closure in the aftermath of the NEW YORK SLAVE REVOLT OF 1712, the school survived until the AMERICAN REVOLUTION. Another SPG school, in which two black slaves provided instruction in Christian principles and basic education, was founded in Charleston in 1743, and remained open until 1763.

The conversion of Africans to Christianity did not take place on a large scale until the middle of the eighteenth century, when a movement known as the Great Awakening occurred. Many leaders of the Great Awakening, such as the white Virginian Presbyterian Samuel Davies, emphasized the need for black converts to read the word of God. Throughout the antebellum period a number of white religious leaders, including many staunch defenders of slavery, favored black literacy and the distribution of religious texts as a way of spreading the faith, and doubtless as a means of making slaves more tractable. White ministers, missionaries, and teachers initially believed that they could control the forms and purposes of black literacy; but the emergence of independent black congregations and denominations (which after the end of the eighteenth century usually had literate ministers) soon proved their hopes vain. Throughout and indeed beyond the antebellum period, the church remained a main arena for the advancement of African-American literacy. The ministry was a magnet for literate and ambitious young men, and most congregations tried to foster basic "Bible literacy" among its members.

Schools and Teachers

Not surprisingly, almost all formal education for African Americans in the North and South during the antebellum period was reserved for a small group of free blacks, comprising about 5 percent of the total black population. In New England and the mid-Atlantic colonies or states, schools for blacks became fairly common toward the end of the eighteenth century. Many were founded by abolitionist societies and Quakers. In New York City, the NEW YORK MANUMISSION SOCIETY opened the New York African Free School in 1787. New Jersey Quakers had established schools for blacks in Burlington, Salem, and Trenton by 1800. Philadelphia had seven black schools by 1797. Schools stressing basic literacy were established over a wide range of places, including Newport, R.I.; Charleston, S.C.; Savannah, Ga.; Georgetown, Md.; Wilmington, Del.; Richmond, Alexandria, and Norfolk, Va.

Free blacks also opened a number of schools independently of abolitionist groups. In 1798, Primus Hall, son of the pioneer black Freemason Prince HALL, established a school in his Boston home. Catherine Ferguson, an ex-slave who had purchased her own freedom, opened a school in New York City in 1793. Maria Becraft opened the first boarding school for black girls, in Washington, D.C. Becraft later joined the Sisters of Providence, and by the 1830s, Roman Catholic teaching orders had established schools for black girls in Baltimore, Nashville, and New Orleans. Other late eighteenth-century and early nineteenth-century black mutual aid organizations, such as the African Union Society in Newport and the FREE AFRICAN SOCIETY OF PHILADELPHIA, also established schools. The elite mulatto Brown Fellowship Society in Charleston, S.C., supported two schools, one for the children of its members, another for darker free blacks and orphans. In Philadelphia in 1860, there were fixty-six private schools for blacks, only twelve of which were led by whites.

Schools for blacks were often underfunded, and faced other obstacles as well. In 1829 Daniel PAYNE, who later became the senior bishop of the AFRICAN METHODIST EPISCOPAL CHURCH, opened an innovative school in Charleston and charged his students fifty cents a month. But Payne was obliged to close the school in 1835, after South Carolina had tightened its restrictions against teaching blacks, and whites rioted against the free black community. In 1834 the building housing Noyes Academy in Canaan, N.H., was torn from its foundations and hauled into a swamp by local whites who objected to its integrated student body. Probably the most famous instance of racism of this sort was that encountered by the white Quaker operator of a boarding school in Canterbury, Conn., in 1833. Prudence Crandell lost all of her white students after she admitted a black girl. She then advertised for black girls to attend the school, and thereafter Crandell and the school faced violence by local residents and legal harassment by the state of Connecticut. Crandell refused to post bond and served time in jail. Though she was subsequently vindicated legally, Crandell abandoned the school after 1834.

The establishment of public funding for primary education raised a new series of questions concerning the funding and exclusion of blacks from public schools. Public funding for education began in the 1820s. In some states—as, for instance, Ohio in the 1830s—blacks were excluded altogether from common schools, and they had to fight for a share of tax revenue to establish their own schools in many cities and towns. From 1830 onward, black leaders were divided in their opinions as to whether African Americans should press for admission to the more prestigious and better-funded white schools, or establish public schools of their own. In 1847 Frederick Douglass led an unsuccessful fight for equal funding for a local black public school in Rochester, N.Y. Nine years later, the same black school was closed after the city fathers agreed to integrate the local school system. Lockport, a small New York State city on the Erie Canal, and the northern terminus of the UNDERGROUND RAILROAD, chose to segregate its African-American population and the public schools in 1835. It was not until 1870 that the Rev. C. W. Mossell succeed in renewing the black assault on Lockport's segregated schools. In a series of petitions to the Lockport school board, then to the New York State Superintendent, Mossell, joined by others in the black community, reminded the school board that it was "extravagant to continue the school."

In 1876 the black school "quietly closed its doors and blacks entered the public schools without a murmur of protest from the white community." The most publicized and protracted fight for educational integration of the antebellum period was carried out by prominent black and white abolitionists in Boston, who succeeded in integrating Massachusetts public schools in 1855, after a decade-long struggle.

The Civil War, Emancipation, and the First Schools

In the first half of the nineteenth century, the proliferation of numerous mutual aid societies, fraternal organizations, and black-owned libraries and reading rooms all promoted African-American literacy and education, as did the emergence of the black press and black publishing houses. The hundreds of slave narratives published in antebellum America, many proudly claiming "written by himself or herself," were, among other things, defiant assertions of the importance of literacy. These cultural developments, as well as the formal establishment of schools, contributed to the gathering sectional conflict over the status of slavery, which culminated in the CIVIL WAR.

So great was the need for literacy that efforts on behalf of African-American education persisted even after the country had erupted into war. Indeed, many of the roughly 180,000 black soldiers who served in the Union Army, a large number of them ex-slaves, saw army service as a way of acquiring reading skills. Classes were supervised by the army chaplain, and those who had some reading ability also served as instructors. A number of commanders reported a total reversal of illiteracy rates in their companies and regiments in a period of little more than a year.

The education of freed and runaway slaves who had not enlisted as soldiers also began almost immediately upon contact with the Union Army. Teachers worked in the many "contraband" camps that sprang up behind the Union lines. The earliest of these camps, established by Mary Chase in Alexandria, Va., on September 1, 1861, later became HAMPTON INSTITUTE. When a school for contrabands and freed slaves was established by the AMERICAN MISSIONARY ASSOCIATION (AMA) near Fortress Monroe at Hampton, Va. the AMA's Lewis Lockwood found that Mary S. PEAKE, a black Virginian educated in the private schools of Washington, D.C., already had begun a school for 45 children one month after Confederate forces had evacuated Hampton, Va., in September 1861. Schools were created by the Union Army directly after taking control of rebel territory. One of the best-known examples is the school established on the Sea Islands of South Carolina, at Port Royal, which was captured by Union forces early in 1862. There, both white and black northern teach-

Well into the twentieth century, because of inadequate funds for education and school construction, churches were often used as classrooms, such as this church in Gee's Bend, Ala., in 1937. (Prints and Photographs Division, Library of Congress)

ers—including Charlotte FORTEN, a black teacher from Philadelphia who wrote a widely circulated account of the aptitude of the freedmen as students—participated in what was termed a successful "rehearsal for Reconstruction."

In the aftermath of the Civil War, education emerged as one of the most prominent and basic concerns of the freed slaves. As Booker T. WASHINGTON wrote, "few people who were not right in the midst of the scenes can form any exact idea of the intense desire which the people of my race showed for education . . . it was a whole race trying to go to school. . . . Few were too young, and none too old, to make the attempt." Although many expressed a great interest in reading the Bible, students also saw literacy as the key to full citizenship. Their passion for education remained unchanged throughout the century after EMANCIPATION. It is striking how many African-American leaders in the succeeding century —Washington, W. E. B. DU BOIS, Mary McLeod BETHUNE, Benjamin MAYS, Alain LOCKE, and Anna Julia COOPER, to name a few—were educators. Perhaps the greatest tribute to the tenacity of African-American education is that by 1950, despite inadequate funding, the indifference or outright hostility of most government bodies, and the myriad indignities and injustices of southern segregation, 90 percent of African Americans in the South were literate.

The original Freedmen's Bureau Act of 1865 made no provision for education; however, the Civil Rights Act of 1866 enlarged the bureau's power in this area, and appropriated more than $500,000 for the building and repair of schoolhouses. The extensive educational system that the bureau then established became the framework for African-American common schools. By 1866 the percentage of ex-slaves attending schools in the South was equal to that of blacks in the North, and far above that of southern white students. There were 975 schools with more than 1,400 teachers for freedmen; the number of teachers jumped to 2,000 the following year. Most of the teachers were originally northern, female, and white; however, the Freedmen's Bureau devoted considerable energy to engaging African Americans, and by 1869 a majority of the instructors were black. Many of the whites involved in teaching had backgrounds in ABOLITION and church missionary work, and the underfunded educational efforts of the Freedmen's Bureau were supported by such secular abolitionist organizations as the National Freedmen's Relief Association of New York and the Indiana Emancipation League, as well as religious bodies such as the Scotch Convenanters Church and at least eight regional meetings of the Quakers. After 1868, reconstructed southern state governments also began to contribute to black education. Perhaps the most important alternative source of funding was the AMA, which supported the efforts of the Freedmen's Bureau in addition to establishing its own network of schools. Northern black denominations and organizations such as the AFRICAN CIVILIZATION SOCIETY were also extremely active in sponsoring schools for the freedmen after emancipation.

However, many freed slaves, conscious of their lack of education and its relevance to their new status, founded schools without any prompting from outside authority. When John Alvord, the superintendent of schools for the Freedmen's Bureau, conducted a survey trip to the South in 1865, he discovered that at least 500 schools had been independently established by the freed slaves. Not all of these schools were new; some served as continuations of schools that had operated secretly under slavery. In most areas, blacks were expected to supplement other sources with their own funds. By 1867, the direct and voluntary contributions of blacks greatly augmented, and in some cases far exceeded, the contributions of the Freedmen's Bureau in all southern states. Freed slaves also invested in their schools by purchasing schoolbooks, boarding and protecting teachers, and constructing school buildings.

Whereas the support of public or common schools through taxation had become a fixture of northern society, southern support of education was tenuous at best. Ex-slaves struggled to ensure the political survival of universal public education. As W. E. B. Du Bois wrote, "Public education for all at public expense was, in the South, a Negro idea." Numerous black RECONSTRUCTION era politicians made public education a key element in their political program, and joined with white members of the REPUBLICAN PARTY to include a public school provision in the new state constitutions. Other literacy-related institutions, such as newspapers and printing operations, were established by southern African Americans at this time. "Freedom and school books and newspapers go hand in hand. Let us secure the freedom we have received by the intelligence that can maintain it," admonished an editorial in an 1865 edition of the *New Orleans Black Republican*.

Educating the newly freed slaves was a burden keenly felt by many northern missionaries who regarded education as a key means of regenerating the South. As one Illinois educator remarked in 1865, it was "now up to the teacher to finish the work the soldier had begun." Northern educators sought to inculcate in both white and black Southerners the Protestant values of hard work, sobriety, self-control, and piety. The schools they founded were based on the traditional New England model of liberal education. Arithmetic, reading, writing, Greek, Latin, history, geography, science, music, and phi-

Interior of school on the Mileston Plantation, Mileston, Miss., November 1939. School began very late in the year and attendance was poor until December since the children were needed to pick cotton. (Prints and Photographs Division, Library of Congress)

losophy were all included in the curriculum. In addition, missionary instruction was supplemented by moral teachings, biblical readings, prayer meetings, and other methods designed to shape the ethical as well as the intellectual development of black students.

Many of the missionary educators who went to the South to teach during this period did so at tremendous sacrifice. They frequently taught in inadequate and dangerous conditions and faced indifference or hostility from most southern whites. Although they frequently showed a lack of understanding of the cultural background of their black students, most missionary teachers believed that African Americans were their spiritual equals, and considered education the first step toward achieving political and legal reform.

Colleges

Since the problem of secondary education for African Americans was largely ignored by the southern states, missionary societies concentrated increasingly on creating secondary schools. In the 1870s these societies began to address the need for institutions in which blacks could be trained as teachers; by 1895, more than forty colleges and sixty secondary schools for blacks, most of them supported by northern missionaries, had been established in the South.

Most of the so-called historically black colleges and universities (HBCUs) were founded in the years immediately following the Civil War, and almost all of these were founded by missionary organizations in the North. The American Missionary Association, affiliated with the Congregational Church, established FISK UNIVERSITY (1866), Straight University (1869), Talladega College (1867), Tougaloo College (1869), and Tillotson College (1875). The Freedmen's Aid Society of the Methodist Episcopal Church, North, sponsored Bennett College (1873), CLARK UNIVERSITY (1869), Claflin College (1869), Morgan College (1867), New Orleans University

(1869), Philander Smith College (1877), and Meharry Medical College (1876). The mostly white American Baptist Home Mission Society was responsible for the founding of Benedict College (1870), Bishop College, Hartshorn Memorial College (1884), MOREHOUSE COLLEGE (1867), Shaw University (1865), and Spelman Seminary (1881) (now SPELMAN COLLEGE). The Presbyterian-sponsored colleges were Biddle University (1867), now Johnson C. Smith University, Knoxville College (1875), and Stillman Seminary (1876). Among the colleges founded by black denominations were Allen University (1880), Morris Brown College (1881), Wilberforce College (1856) (now WILBERFORCE UNIVERSITY), Paul Quinn College (1881), Edward Waters College (1888), and Shorter College (1886), all organized by the African Methodist Episcopal Church. The AFRICAN METHODIST EPISCOPAL ZION CHURCH founded Livingstone College (1882), and the Colored Methodist Episcopal Church founded Lane College (1879), Paine College (1884), Texas College (1895), and Miles Memorial College (1907). Black Baptists were responsible for the creation of Arkansas Baptist College (1885), Selma University (1878), and Virginia College and Seminary (1888). Three independent, nondenominational colleges were founded during this time: ATLANTA UNIVERSITY (1872), HOWARD UNIVERSITY (1868), and Leland University (1870). Most African Americans received their higher education at the missionary colleges, despite the fact that these institutions acquiesced to segregation on campus and were controlled financially and administratively by whites.

Private, church-affiliated colleges were supplemented by state colleges and land-grant institutions. The first land-grant school, Alcorn Agricultural and Mining (A&M) College, was authorized in 1871. In 1890 the federal government passed the Second Morrill Act, which extended land-grant provisions to sixteen southern states. In many instances, black colleges were established solely to obtain funding for white colleges under the act. The financial resources of the state land-grant schools were even more limited than those of the private schools. However, unlike the missionary schools, the faculty and administration of the state land-grant institutions were predominantly black. By 1915, sixteen land-grant colleges for African Americans had been established, and almost every southern state supported some type of school for black higher education. Many of these institutions were normal schools, and had as their primary purpose the training of black teachers for a segregated primary education system.

Although this spate of college funding appears impressive, it gives a misleading impression of the state of black collegiate education in the postemancipation period. Most of these colleges and universities were institutes of higher education in name only; very few actually taught courses at the college level. For the most part, these colleges were used for secondary and/or remedial instruction. Many white Southerners feared that higher education would increase the political and economic expectations of African Americans and did all they could to ensure that black colleges obtained as little support as possible from state governments.

As of 1915, only 33 of the nearly 100 black colleges were able to provide college-level courses for their students. A number of early twentieth-century surveys, undertaken by persons of varying ideological perspectives, concluded that the network of black colleges was overextended. In 1900, W. E. B. Du Bois found a total college-level enrollment of only 726 students. Ten years later, in his book *The College Bred Negro,* Du Bois recommended reducing the total number of black colleges from 100 to 32 to strengthen and improve black higher education. In his view, the only "first-grade colored colleges" were Fisk, Howard, Atlanta, Morehouse, and Virginia Union—while Lincoln, Talladega, and Wilberforce served as examples of "second-grade colored colleges." Those who were more skeptical of black higher education, and wished to replace it with industrial training, reached even more sweeping conclusions. Thomas Jesse Jones, the director of the PHELPS-STOKES FUND, visited and studied black institutions over a period of two years, and in 1917 published a two-volume survey that claimed that the only colleges worth saving were Fisk and Howard.

While these debates over state-funded institutions were taking place, private black colleges were forced to seek new sources of funding. The missionary societies had fallen on hard times, and by the end of the century their finances had been greatly curtailed. Their resources were replaced with those of new philanthropies, such as the John T. SLATER FUND (1881); the Anna T. Jeannes Foundation (1907); the Phelps-Stokes Fund (1910); and the Carnegie Foundation, Julius Rosenwald Fund, and Laura Spelman Rockefeller Fund (all founded between 1902 and 1917). Unlike the older missionary societies, the newer philanthropies were predominantly secular in their goals and skeptical of the need for, and possibilities within, black education. Like many northern whites of their era, these philanthropical societies wished to bring about a reconciliation with southern whites; and in their eagerness to be sensitive to southern white concerns, they gave scant consideration to the feelings, needs, and aspirations of southern blacks. To be sure, some northern philanthropies—in particular, the Rosenwald Fund—continued to support serious intellectual work by blacks. Whatever their biases, they performed a vitally needed function at a time when neither the state nor the federal government showed a serious interest in the education of African Americans.

Industrial vs. Academic Education

Chronic lack of funding provided the backdrop for the late nineteenth-century controversy between industrial and academic training, as exemplified by Booker T. Washington and W. E. B. Du Bois, respectively. The concept of industrial education for African Americans was not a new one. Vocational education for artisans had long been favored by both black and white educators. For blacks, the need to acquire an education outside the discriminatory influence of craft unions was a necessity. In 1853, Frederick Douglass had favored industrial schooling as a means of overcoming this problem, and during the post–Civil War period his solution was taken up by such prominent African-American leaders as T. Thomas FORTUNE.

The kind of industrial education favored by Douglass was related to, but differed significantly from, the model of industrial training that became associated with Booker T. Washington. Douglass favored an industrial education that would enable black laborers to become competent in any skill they chose, even if their skills placed them in direct competition with whites. Washington's method, by contrast, consisted primarily in training blacks for teaching in segregated schools and for working in traditionally black occupations (such as agriculture and domestic service).

One of the earliest industrial schools was Hampton Normal Agricultural Institute (now HAMPTON INSTITUTE), founded in 1868 by Gen. Samuel Chapman Armstrong, a Civil War officer who had spent his formative years in Hawaii as the son of missionary parents. There, future teachers worked six days a week to learn "the dignity of labor" before going out to preach the values of hard toil to the South's future labor force. Many white people viewed this form of education as a means of ensuring racial harmony, since it provided blacks with useful skills without challenging the existing racial order.

In 1881 Booker T. Washington, Armstrong's most illustrious pupil, founded Tuskegee Institute (now TUSKEGEE UNIVERSITY) in Alabama. Washington's role in African-American education, like his role in black history in general, remains extremely controversial. His stated goal for his students was to enable them to become economically independent and self-sufficient. Washington advised the Tuskegee students against openly challenging the status quo, and suggested instead that they become responsible citizens by seeking to establish themselves in a job or a trade.

Thereafter, he asserted, white society would concede equality. While Washington was not opposed to academic higher education as such, he looked on it as a secondary task. "It is well to remember," he claimed in a speech in 1904, ". . . that our teachers, ministers, lawyers, and doctors will prosper just in proportion as they have about them an intelligent and skillful producing class."

Washington's great opponent in educational philosophy was W. E. B. Du Bois, the author of *The Souls of Black Folk* (1903) and a Harvard Ph.D. Du Bois, who had begun his undergraduate career at Fisk, was a strong supporter of academic education and the missionary colleges. He placed great emphasis on the importance, within the African-American tradition, of creating what he called "the Talented Tenth," college-educated blacks who would assume leadership roles in the community. For Du Bois, the missionary colleges, and the northern missionaries themselves, had played a critical role in creating educated black college undergraduates. In 1918 Du Bois described the northern missionaries as "men radical in their belief in Negro possibility" who by 1900 had "trained in Greek, Latin, and math 2,000 men, and these men trained fully 50,000 in morals and manners, and they in turn taught the alphabet to 9 million men." Du Bois believed that college-bred African Americans would lead all blacks to an awareness of their full capabilities, and ultimately to equal status with the white population. While he readily acknowledged the faults of the black colleges, he nevertheless insisted on weighing these faults against their potential for creating a black leadership class.

The difference between the philosophies of education for the Negro that were held by Du Bois and Washington became the major source of the debate and enmity between the two Negro educators. Du Bois's major objection to Washington's philosophy was Washington's, and the northern abolitionists', efforts to educate Negro young people for menial jobs and "to farm land that they would seldom own" (Levering Lewis, 1993).

Historian John Hendrik Clarke counsels against taking sides in the Washington–Du Bois debate, since black people were in need of workmen and technicians as well as educators and politicians accountable to the needs of black people.

After 1900, as the influence of missionary societies waned, Booker T. Washington's theories were championed by most of the northern philanthropists. Washington was also supported by an emerging group of white middle-class Southerners who became known as advocates of the "New South." Both groups sought to maintain white supremacy through the creation of a literate and skilled black workforce that would increase economic prosperity without threatening the existing social structure. Hampton and Tuskegee became the well-funded showcases for industrial education. It should be noted, however, that however popular industrial education might have been with white philanthropists, neither the concept nor the institutions were popular among black educators or among southern blacks as a whole. As James Anderson points out in *The Education of Blacks in the South, 1860–1935,* academic education was in greater demand, and it, rather than the few highly publicized examples of industrial education, became the model for almost all of the hundred colleges established in the South.

The controversy between Washington and Du Bois was fueled by the positive reactions of white philanthrophists to Washington's educational views. In a climate in which scientific racism, doubts about the intellectual ability of blacks, and the acceptance of blacks as an inferior, politically negligible caste were nearly universal among the whites in power, the prospect of academic education for blacks was discounted as threatening or irrelevant. Consequently, funding for black academic institutions (e.g., Atlanta University) was curtailed, while Hampton Institute and Tuskegee garnered the larger share of the philanthropists' money.

However, philanthropical discrimination against black colleges, and such criticisms as those expressed by Jones in his 1917 survey, did not force black colleges to close, but led instead to an upgrading of their academic programs. Starting in 1913, accreditation agencies pressured many schools either to eliminate or to separate higher education from their secondary programs of instruction in order to be considered full-fledged colleges or universities. State teaching examinations also caused a number of black colleges —including Hampton and Tuskegee—to introduce a broader liberal arts curriculum so their graduates could pass the teacher certification tests.

The faculties of many black colleges remained predominantly, at times exclusively, white through the end of the nineteenth century. In 1894 only one black faculty member was employed at Fisk, and none at Atlanta University. By 1915, black professors made up 69 percent of the faculty at Howard University, 58 percent at Clark University, 93 percent at Meharry Medical College, and 31 percent at Fisk. Still, most of the presidents of the black colleges were white, and some—who owed their positions to northern philanthropists—were vehemently opposed to political activism and social change. Fayette McKenzie, the president of Fisk after 1915, eliminated the black educators and northern missionaries serving on the Board of Trustees, closed the student government and newspaper, and refused to allow a chapter of the NATIONAL ASSOCIATION FOR THE ADVANCEMENT OF COLORED PEOPLE (NAACP) on campus. In March 1925 a student strike supported by the alumni, the national black press, and local black leaders forced McKenzie to resign. At Hampton in 1929, students forced the president to resign and demanded an academic curriculum. The unrest at these and other black colleges in the 1920s marked a crucial transition in the history of the HBCUs. By the 1930s the colleges were predominantly staffed and administered by black educators and had become increasingly self-conscious with regard to their African-American orientation.

Primary and Secondary Education

Due to the controversy surrounding the Washington-Du Bois debate on black colleges, little attention was paid to primary and secondary education in the late nineteenth and early twentieth centuries. The commitment to African-American education by parents, teachers, and students was not matched by southern state governments, which discriminated against black schools by underfunding them on a regular basis. In 1900 only 36 percent of black children in the South attended school, and of these, 86 percent went for less than six months per year. The gains in school attendance and literacy were fewer for blacks than for whites. From 1876 to 1895 black enrollment increased 59 percent, while white enrollment was up 106 percent. About one-third of all southern blacks were literate by 1900—a sign of both how much had been achieved through black education (from a 90 percent illiteracy rate immediately after the Civil War) and how much was yet to be done.

In *The Common School and the Negro American* (1910), Du Bois accused the U.S. government of not giving sufficient funds and authority to the U.S. Bureau of Education and thereby refusing "to tell the whole truth concerning our efforts to educate the children of freedmen as well as our general educational system." Those black children who did attend school, Du Bois contended, were poorly taught, by teachers who were half prepared, ill-trained, and employed only three to six months a year. Schoolhouses and school equipment were inadequate if not downright wretched. According to Du Bois, the reduction of funds for black schools lowered the efficacy of course studies and served to eliminate competent teachers in favor of instructors who would act as "willing tools who do not and will not complain." Moreover, the introduction of manual and industrial training—however valuable or necessary—had created an excess of ill-considered and unrelated work, which detracted from the time and attention needed for the critical disciplines of reading, writing, and arithmetic. All of these things, Du Bois wrote, were deliberately aimed at "training Negroes as menials and laborers and cutting them off from the higher avenues of life."

Not until the first third of the twentieth century did the majority of black children have access to elementary school. The economic depression of the late nineteenth century and the increasingly virulent racism of most southern whites had prevented further developments in the educational programs initiated by the freedmen and northern missionaries right after the Civil War. What little money was available for public education was spent on the children of poor whites. After 1900, philanthropies such as the General Education Board frequently merged their programs for white and black education into a combined southern education directive—a process that resulted, as Booker T. Washington charged, in money "actually being taken from the colored people and given to the white schools."

Following 1915, a "public" primary education system emerged through the support of local governments, white philanthropies, and black communities. The philanthropies often demanded that black communities pay a large portion of the school costs, through the levying of special taxes and the donation of labor, materials, and land. This practice, documented by Richard R. WRIGHT, Jr., in *Self-Help in Negro Education* (1909), demonstrated yet again the sacrifices African Americans were willing to make for education. Of all the philanthropies, the Rosenwald Fund was the most active in establishing common schools. Between 1913 and 1935, 15 percent of the total costs for school construction in the South were provided by the Rosenwald Fund, and 17 percent were covered by blacks themselves.

While state governments contributed, albeit meagerly and with reluctance, to primary schools, they made a concerted effort to prevent the building of high schools for African Americans. In 1934, 54 percent of southern white children attended high school, as compared to 18 percent of black youth in the South. There were almost no high schools in rural areas until 1915. That blacks were being denied educational opportunities was made clear in the case of *Cumming* v. *School Board of Richmond County, Georgia,* heard by the U.S. Supreme Court in 1899. Upon the closing of the only black high school in the county, local black residents sued for equal segregated facilities. The courts ruled against the plaintiffs, despite the precedent set by the 1896 PLESSY V. FERGUSON decision, which upheld the segregation of railway carriages on interstate lines but asserted that blacks and whites should be accommodated on "separate but equal" terms. A black high school did not reopen in Richmond County until 1945.

In the South as a whole, the building of black high schools did not begin in earnest until 1920. Southern governments and northern philanthropists were determined to develop curricula that would train black youth to become laborers, although in many cases blacks managed to have an academic regimen included in the school programs. County normal schools, modeled on the Hampton and Tuskegee institutions, were cited as an alternative to academic normal schools by most philanthropies until 1930, after which these county normal schools either died out or were converted into public high schools.

Preparatory Elementary and Secondary Schools Founded by African-American Women

In the late nineteenth century and early twentieth century as blacks were migrating from the South to the North, four prominent African-American women founded elementary and secondary preparatory schools for black youths. The schools existed over long periods of time and successfully educated generations of black students.

The Haines Normal and Industrial Institute was chartered in 1886 and closed in 1949. It was founded by Lucy Craft LANEY, the seventh of ten children in a slave family. Lucy Craft Laney was educated by a daughter of the Campbells, a slave-holding family. Later she graduated from Ballard Normal School and, aided by the American Missionary Association, entered Atlanta University, graduating in 1873. For the next ten years she taught in the public schools of several Georgia towns and cities, including Augusta and Savannah.

With the support and help of the Presbyterian Board of Missions, Lucy Craft Laney opened a school in a lecture room of the Christ Presbyterian Church in Augusta. In 1886, the school was chartered by the state of Georgia. By 1931, Haines Institute had grown to 27 teachers, 300 high school students, and 413 elementary school students. Mary McLeod BETHUNE began her teaching career at Haines Institute.

The Palmer Memorial Institute (1902–1971) was founded by Charlotte Hawkins BROWN, an educator and civil rights activist. Charlotte Hawkins was born in rural Henderson, N.C., to parents who had lived with a part of a white family called Hawkins. When she was about seven years old, the family moved to Boston. Charlotte was educated in the public schools of Cambridge (the Allison Grammar School); she was an excellent student, and was chosen graduation speaker. She graduated from the Cambridge English High and Latin School, where the principal became one of her lifelong supporters. She wanted to attend Radcliffe College but her mother was not sympathetic toward Radcliffe, so she decided to prepare for a career in teaching and enrolled in the Massachusetts State Normal School at Salem.

Charlotte Hawkins began her career in teaching at Bethany Institute in McLeansville, N.C. She then returned north for further education at Harvard, Simmons College in Boston, and Temple University in Philadelphia. In 1902, seeking to help break down the walls of segregation in American life, she founded the Palmer Memorial Institute in Sedalia, N.C. The school became known for its emphasis on cultural education.

Charlotte Hawkins Brown also started the movement to establish the State Training School for Negro Girls in Rocky Mount, N.C. This school was organized into elementary, high school, and junior college instruction, with both cultural and academic courses. The campus was one of the first public interracial meeting places in North Carolina, in accordance with Brown's adamant opposition to racial segregation, which also resulted in her frequent ejection from Pullman berths and seats on southern trains.

The National Training School for Girls (1909–1961) was founded by Nannie Helen BURROUGHS, who had a long history of involvement in industrial education and throughout her life was associated with causes related to the African-American working woman.

In 1909 she founded the National Training School for Women and Girls in Washington, D.C. The school became well known for the emphasis Burroughs placed on spiritual training. She stressed the three "B's": the Bible, the bath, and the broom, which she regarded as tools for the advancement of the race.

The school continued to operate in its original format until after Burroughs's death in 1961, although in 1934 its name was changed to the National Trades and Professional School for Women. In 1964 the trade school curriculum was abandoned and the school was reestablished as the Nannie Helen Burroughs School, for students of elementary school age.

A tireless advocate of the education of African Americans, especially women, Burroughs also worked toward securing equality in the workplace for black women. She was a member of the National Association of Colored Women, which later became

A pre–World War I photograph of the National Training School for Women and Girls, Washington, D.C. The school was founded in 1909 by Nannie Burroughs, the school's president for more than half a century. True to its motto, "Bible, bath, and broom," it primarily trained students in domestic science. (Prints and Photographs Division, Library of Congress)

Dr. Mary McLeod Bethune at Bethune-Cookman College in Daytona Beach., Fla., 1943. As president of the National Council of Negro Women (NCNW) from 1935 to 1949 and director of the Negro Division of the National Youth Association (NYA) from 1936 to 1943, she was the most visible and prominent black female of her time. (Prints and Photographs Division, Library of Congress)

the NATIONAL COUNCIL OF NEGRO WOMEN, under the leadership of Mary McLeod Bethune.

Mary McLeod Bethune founded the Daytona Normal and Industrial School in Daytona Beach, Fla., in 1904. The school is now called BETHUNE-COOKMAN COLLEGE.

After serving in national positions under Presidents Calvin Coolidge and Herbert Hoover, Bethune became best known as an adviser to President Franklin D. Roosevelt, Eleanor Roosevelt, and President Harry Truman. Bethune was appointed by President Roosevelt to the directorship of the National Youth Administration. Well-known for her forceful speaking style, she became one of the most sought-after speakers of her day.

The GREAT DEPRESSION of the 1930s marked a turning point in the history of black education. The wholesale firing of blacks in menial positions in order to create work for unemployed whites demonstrated the futility of educating blacks for specifically "black" jobs. A growing militancy, which first found expression in the college disturbances of the previous decade, led blacks to demand control over the staffing and administrative policies of their institutions. In *The Mis-Education of the American Negro*, Carter WOODSON criticized industrial education for short-changing blacks and academic education for its failure to address the specific needs of black students, who were not offered courses in African-American history and culture.

The Educational Impact of the Great Migration

Beginning in the 1920s, blacks began migrating in large numbers to northern states and cities. In 1910, 90 percent of African Americans lived in the South; by 1970, only a bare majority resided in the southeastern and southern states. The movement north was part of a broader transformation from a largely rural into a largely urban population. Cities became the dominant dwelling places for southern as well as northern blacks. These two related migrations, from the South to the North and from the farm to the urban center, changed almost every aspect of African-American life. Migration from rural areas to southern and southwestern cities allowed many blacks to attend school for the first time. In 1910, 46.6 percent of all black children between ages ten and fifteen were working in agriculture, domestic employment, or industry, as compared to 14.3 percent of whites. By 1930, the figures for blacks had dropped to 16.1 percent. Not until 1930 did the percentage of fourteen- and fifteen-year-old blacks attending school reach 78.1 percent, a level approximating that which white children had reached (77.4 percent) two decades earlier. Southern educational authorities, fearful of rural depopulation, started more and somewhat better-funded schools in rural areas after 1915, in hopes of enticing African Americans to stay. (Nonetheless, these new schools remained segregated, under-funded, and were inferior to the schools established for whites.)

Integrated education was possible for those blacks who left the South for the North. By 1910, seven northern states prohibited segregated schools: Illinois, Massachusetts, Nevada, New Jersey, New York, Ohio, and Pennsylvania. Within these systems, differential treatment of black students was hardly a rarity. Nevertheless, there was far less likelihood that black children seeking a fair opportunity for education would be met with instant opposition. The centralization of public schools in northern urban, industrialized areas not only promised lower costs per pupil (as compared to costs in the South overall, and in rural areas in particular) but also precluded the maintenance of racially separate school systems (though not of racially isolated schools).

For African Americans, education in northern cities was in many ways a vast improvement over what was available in the South. Because most northern cities were formally integrated, black students could obtain funding and term lengths that were equal to those of whites, and many were able to excel in this new setting. However, in spite of the fact that segregation was not de jure (as it was in the South), segregated housing patterns often led to de facto segregation and consequently, to the inequitable distribution of funds for predominantly black schools. Blacks were frequently encouraged to take vocational rather than academic courses. In integrated schools they sometimes faced hostility from teachers and fellow students, and were discouraged from participating in extracurricular activities. High-school dropout rates remained higher for blacks than for whites, and

quotas—if not outright bars—limited black entrance and matriculation in northern colleges.

By 1940 the percentage of black students between five and twenty years of age who were attending school had risen from 44.7 percent (in 1910) to 64.4 percent, while white attendance had climbed from 61.3 percent to 71.6 percent during those same years. The median schooling completed by persons aged 25 was 5.7 years for blacks and 8.7 years for whites. This discrepancy was accounted for by the fact that 41.8 percent of blacks had spent fewer than five years in elementary school, as compared to 10.9 percent of whites. By 1950 the percentage of blacks with fewer than five years of primary schooling had dropped to 36.2 percent; not until 1980 would there be a rough parity in the median number of school years completed by blacks (12.2 years) and whites (12.5 years).

During the middle decades of the twentieth century, the federal government became increasingly involved in African-American education. As part of his 1930s New Deal, President Franklin D. Roosevelt created the WORKS PROJECT ADMINISTRATION (WPA), which developed literacy programs and hired black writers to participate in such special projects as documenting the lives of former slaves. WPA classes were attended by more than 100,000 African Americans. From 1936 to 1943, the Division of Negro Affairs of the National Youth Administration (NYA), headed by noted black educator Mary McLeod Bethune, aided hundreds of thousands of black students both in the North and in the still-segregated South. Bethune's was the first federal program to address the needs of black students by providing direct aid, and as such served as an important precedent for later federal educational assistance programs. The federal government continued to voice its support for African-American education throughout the 1940s, and in 1947 the President's Commission on Higher Education issued a report calling for the full integration of all colleges and universities.

Perhaps the most significant indication of the government's commitment to creating educational opportunities for blacks was the appearance of the 1947 report by the Presidential Committee on Civil Rights. The report, titled To Secure These Rights, charged the government with failing to eliminate "prejudice and discrimination from the operation of either our public or our private schools and colleges." After examining the seventeen southern states and the District of Columbia, the committee concluded that "whatever test is used—expenditure per pupil, teachers' salaries, the number of pupils per teacher, transportation of students, adequacy of school buildings and educational equipment, length of school term, extent of curriculum—Negro students are invariably at a disadvantage." A single example of these inequities is the disparity in salaries between white and black teachers in Alabama and Mississippi for the school year 1943–44: In Alabama, white teachers earned $1,158 to black teachers' $661; in Mississippi, white teachers earned $1,107 to black teachers' $342. As the report noted, relatively little had changed since Du Bois cited very similar statistics in his 1911 work *The Common School and the Negro American*.

The Assault of Social Science and Law on "Separate but Equal" Education

The U.S. Supreme Court case of *Plessy* v. *Ferguson*, which upheld segregation by establishing the constitutionality of "separate but equal" facilities for whites and blacks, was decided in 1896, but it was not until

John Saunders Chase stands in line to register for classes as the first African American to be enrolled in the University of Texas, June 7, 1950. He was admitted after the U.S. Supreme Court knocked down a segregation ban. (AP/Wide World Photos)

the late 1930s that segregation became a legal issue in the South. In the subsequent assault on segregation, the great majority of cases involved education, primarily because this was the area in which state-provided facilities were most patently and grossly unequal. Starting with *Missouri ex. rel. Gaines* v. *Canada* (1938), the NAACP LEGAL DEFENSE AND EDUCATIONAL FUND (LDEF) began to chip away at the foundations of segregation on a case-by-case, aspect-by-aspect basis. The rulings in *Gaines* and such cases as *McLaurin* v. *Oklahoma State Regents for Higher Education* (1950) and SWEATT V. PAINTER (1950) forced white institutions to admit black students into their graduate and professional programs because no comparable institutions for blacks existed; however, it was the landmark case of BROWN V. BOARD OF EDUCATION OF TOPEKA (1954) that challenged segregation both in principle and as social policy.

Brown v. Board of Education of Topeka

The case brought to the U.S. Supreme Court by the NAACP Legal Defense and Educational Fund in 1952 was a consolidation of five school cases from the states of South Carolina, Virginia, Kansas, Delaware, and the District of Columbia. Named for the litigants in the Kansas case, the case challenged the legality of segregated public schools, and in so doing, the validity of the ruling in *Plessy* v. *Ferguson* in 1896 (Kluger, *Simple Justice*, 1976; Franklin and Moss, *From Slavery to Freedom*, 1988).

On May 17, 1954, the Court ruled for the plaintiffs, writing, ". . . in the field of public education the doctrine of separate but equal has no place. Separate educational facilities are inherently unequal" (Kluger, *Simple Justice*, p. 707).

The following year, on May 7, 1955, the Court issued its implementation order, directing the desegregation of all public facilities and accommodations ". . . with all deliberate speed."

Sharing Responsibilty: A New Federal Role

Despite the *Brown* decision, and the telling need for massive improvement in elementary and secondary education, the federal government showed a great reluctance to intervene in school desegregation matters. Indeed, President Dwight D. Eisenhower failed to support the opinions expressed in *Brown*, and in so doing subtly encouraged the segregationists in their efforts to limit its impact on state and local policies. However, in 1957 a crisis was precipitated in Little Rock, Ark., when Gov. Orval Faubus openly defied a federal court order by using the Arkansas National Guard to prevent the desegregation of schools. Faubus finally backed down and withdrew the National Guard, but it was promptly replaced by white supremacist mobs, who gathered to stop nine black students from entering the all-white Central High School. Eisenhower responded by federalizing the National Guard and ordering them to protect those students. In the ensuing case, *Cooper* v. *Aaron* (1958), the Supreme Court ruled that state authorities must uphold the *Brown* decision.

The Little Rock incident spurred the passage of the Civil Rights Act of 1957, the first new civil rights legislation since Reconstruction. The 1957 act established the UNITED STATES COMMISSION ON CIVIL RIGHTS, whose duties included the investigation and appraisal of situations that denied blacks equal protection under the law. Although southern senators managed to strip the bill of almost all of its federal enforcement provisions, its enactment marked the first attempt by the federal government to take responsibility for the protection of civil rights.

The real turning point in the establishment of a federal civil rights policy occurred with the passage of the Civil Rights Act of 1964, which allowed the

U.S. attorney general to take legal action in achieving school desegregation and authorized federal assistance for districts desegregating their schools.

President Lyndon B. Johnson's energetic support of the act preceded his administration's landmark Elementary and Secondary Education Act of 1965, authorizing federal assistance in providing teaching materials and special services for school districts with large numbers of poor.

The Elementary and Secondary Education Act of 1965

The Elementary and Secondary Education Act (ESEA) of 1965 was a landmark piece of legislation because its enactment marked a major incursion into state prerogatives and responsibilities for providing elementary and secondary education.

Although the federal government had enacted several statutes affecting the preparation of teachers in elementary and secondary schools and the development of new curricula under the National Defense

Escorted by federal troops, students prepare to enter Central High School in Little Rock, Ark., in October 1957. Prodded by a violent reaction to the attempt to integrate the school, a reluctant President Eisenhower called in the army. Little Rock marked a turning point in the use of federal power to enforce the *Brown* decision. (Prints and Photographs Division, Library of Congress)

Education Act of 1958, it had left control of elementary and secondary education to the states.

The passage of the Elementary and Secondary Education Act of 1965 formally established the doctrine of equal educational opportunity as a national priority and gave millions of dollars to state education and local education authorities (SEAs and LEAs) to use in specified ways under the guidelines of the five titles of the act.

Title I made available an initial allocation of $775 million for the education of children of low-income families (Keppel, *The Necessary Revolution in Education,* 1966). Though allocation of the money was under federal control, it was administered through the states. Title I was changed to Chapter I by the 1981 reauthorization of ESEA. Of the poor children served by Chapter I, an estimated 47 percent have represented the black urban and rural poor. Though an insufficient amount of money was provided to alleviate the "savage inequalities" in local funding between wealthy white suburban school districts and largely black and poor urban school districts (Kozol, *Savage Inequalities,* 1991), Chapter I of ESEA has provided increased educational resources for poor children.

Funds also were provided to strengthen state departments of education (under Title V) in monitoring the spending of federal ESEA allocations by local school districts and to encourage states to provide additional monies for the education of poor pupils. State money was to be used to supplement, not supplant, federal funds.

With the passage of these acts, the federal government obtained the fiscal and legal leverage necessary to overcome the massive resistance to desegregation in the South and in other parts of the country. In 1964, 2.3 percent of southern black students attended integrated schools; percentages increased to 7.5 in 1965 and to 12.5 in 1966. The U.S. Supreme Court's ruling in *Green* v. *County School Board* (1968), ordering the immediate desegregation of schools, succeeded in greatly accelerating this process. Whereas in 1968–69 only 32 percent of southern black students were attending integrated schools, 79 percent were attending integrated schools in 1970–71.

As *de jure* segregation was being brought to an end in the South, civil rights activists turned their attention to the *de facto* segregation persisting elsewhere. While some legislators insisted that *de facto* segregation represented only residential ethnic clustering, and argued against applying civil rights legislation to the affected schools, civil rights advocates noted a more than passing resemblance between the quality of education in largely black inner city schools and the inferior schooling to which blacks were subjected in the segregated South.

Beginning in the mid-1960s, a number of studies were undertaken to assess the overall quality of African-American education. As a consequence of Section 402 of the Civil Rights Act of 1964, the U.S. commissioner of education was required to provide the president and Congress with a report on "the lack of availability of equal educational opportunities for individuals by reason of race, color, religion, or national origin in public educational institutions at all levels in the United States, its territories and possessions, and the District of Columbia." The report, titled *Equality of Educational Opportunity* and delivered on July 2, 1966, concluded that "American public education remains largely unequal in most regions of the country, including all those where Negroes form any significant part of the population." It had been shown that, among minority groups, blacks were subjected most frequently and in the greatest numbers to segregation; when all groups were taken into account, the same held true for white children. Eighty percent of white first-to-twelfth-grade pupils attended schools that were 90 percent to 100 percent white. Segregation also held for teaching staffs nationwide: Where the races of teachers and pupils were not matched, white teachers often taught black children, but black teachers seldom taught white children. Finally, where integration existed, it involved the enrollment of a few black pupils in predominantly white schools, almost never the enrollment of a few whites in predominantly black schools.

The study, which came to be known as the Coleman Report—after James S. Coleman, the Johns Hopkins University professor who headed the research team—found that minority students scored "distinctly lower" than the average white student on tests that measured such basic skills as reading, writing, calculating, and problem-solving. Moreover, findings indicated that "the deficiency in achievement is progressively greater for minority pupils at higher grade levels." Little wonder, then, that in metropolitan areas of the North and West, 20 percent of black students sixteen and seventeen years of age dropped out of school.

In 1967, a year after the Coleman Report appeared, the Commission on Civil Rights issued a report titled *Racial Isolation in the Public Schools,* which stressed that redistricting would have little impact on the *de facto* segregation of housing and schools in large parts of the country. Studies showed that 83 percent of white elementary school students were enrolled in all-white schools, and 75 percent of black children were enrolled in all-black schools. The commission highlighted the liabilities of educating children in racial isolation. Not only did black students achieve less than white students, but also the longer they remained in school, the farther behind they fell. Black students were less likely to attend schools with adequate libraries, strong academic curricula, and competent teachers. Furthermore, black children who attended desegregated schools performed better than those attending racially segregated schools. The commission also recommended that the federal government take action by establishing a uniform standard of racial isolation in schools, and that schools with a black enrollment in excess of 60 percent be judged unsatisfactory.

As a solution to the problem of *de facto* segregation, the Commission on Civil Rights proposed the creation of "magnet schools," which would attract students from a wider area to inner-city schools, and "metropolitan school districts," which would draw on both urban and suburban student populations. Although, in the case of small cities, magnet schools proved successful as part of a citywide desegregation plan, their effectiveness was extremely limited in large cities such as New York, Chicago, Los Angeles, and Philadelphia. In these instances, federal funding was provided at the outset for desegregation planning, but that funding did not cover the costs of constructing new schools or converting large older schools, or of the special programs, equipment, and transportation needed to accommodate all the students who wished to attend. In addition, many poor and minority children lacked the preparation required to pass the entrance standards established for the magnet school programs. As a result, only middle-class children, or the most strongly motivated of the poor, were able to avail themselves of the magnet schools in their system.

The formation of metropolitan school systems has proven even more controversial, and has faced stiff resistance from those who insist on the primacy of neighborhood schools. The intensification of urban-suburban segregation following World War II, when federal programs such as those offered by the Federal Housing Program (FHA) deliberately encouraged the development of all-white suburbs, presented an insuperable barrier to the establishment of integrated metropolitan districts. In *Milliken* v. *Bradley* (1974), the U.S. Supreme Court declared in a 5 to 4 vote that a metropolitan plan for Detroit could not be enforced, since to do so would be punitive to suburban whites, who could not be held responsible for the *de facto* segregation of inner-city schools. However, in *Milliken II* (1977), the Supreme Court overturned *Milliken I* and granted federal courts authority over metropolitan desegregation "when the plans were remedial in nature" and where suburban residents had directly influenced the distribution of races in a particular area. In the appeal of a Delaware case brought by the Delaware NAACP's Louis Redding (*Evans* v. *Buchannan*, 1969, 1978), the Court ruled that Delaware's Educational Advancement Act (1968) had limited school district consolidation to districts with fewer than 15,000 pupils, thereby excluding the possibility of merging Wilmington with any other suburban district. The U.S. District Court found that the state of Delaware and suburban real estate interests had colluded in preventing blacks from moving into the suburban districts bordering on Wilmington. It was impossible, therefore, for the Wilmington school district (which was 84 percent black, 4 percent Hispanic, and 12 percent white) to be desegregated within its own boundaries. The solution proposed by Wilmington for desegregating New Castle County schools resulted in the merging of ten of the eleven suburban school systems in that county with the Wilmington school system into a single consolidated school district.

In a county as small as New Castle County, busing was not too lengthy, since no school destination was more than forty minutes away. The same did not hold true for other states and communities, where busing was opposed on the basis of distance and length of the bus ride.

Gary Orfield and colleagues, in a 1993 study on school desegregation, *The Growth of Segregation in American Schools: Changing Patterns of Separation and Poverty Since 1968,* names Delaware (Wilmington), North Carolina (large county-city desegregation), Virginia (large county desegregation), Kentucky (Louisville), Nevada (Clark County), Indiana (Indianapolis), and Colorado (Denver) as states that have large proportions of African-American students attending integrated schools. He cites metropolitan desegregation orders—usually city with suburbs, or city with adjoining county—as being responsible factors. "When examining the most integrated states for African-American students, it is obvious that there have been long-term impacts of court orders, particularly those that provide for city-suburban desegregation."

In 1995, the U.S. Supreme Court ruled that the U.S. District Court was in error when it held that ". . . Missouri and the Kansas City school system were jointly liable for having run a segregated school system that they had failed to dismantle" (*New York Times,* June 13, 1995, p. 29). The case was remanded to the lower court for solution.

The effect of the ruling was to absolve the state of Missouri of the responsibility for paying for magnet schools and higher teachers' salaries in Kansas City, the remedy that the lower court had prescribed in order to attract white students to the Kansas City schools.

In 1982 the state of Delaware, with permission of the U.S. District Court, was allowed to divide the consolidated school district into four districts radiating from the center of the city of Wilmington, but did not relieve the state of Delaware of the obligation to maintain racial integration across the districts. Now, with the Kansas City ruling, the future of metropolitan solutions (city-suburbs or city-county plans) to help desegregate city school systems looks increasingly dim.

School Busing

Busing, the means by which white and black students were transported from their home neighborhoods to outside schools, became the most popular, and at the same time the most controversial, means of creating integrated school settings in northern cities. In the 1971 case of *Swann* v. *Charlotte-Mecklenburg Board of Education,* the U.S. Supreme Court voted unanimously to direct school authorities in North Carolina to achieve "the greatest possible degree of actual desegregation" by redistributing 14,000 of the 24,000 black students remaining in all-black or nearly all-black schools. The *Swann* case affirmed the Court's pledge, previously articulated in *Green,* to enforce desegregation posthaste, even if—as in this instance—it meant forcing students to travel to schools outside their own district. In the aftermath of *Swann,* many who had been stalwart in their oppo-

sition to *de jure* segregation in the South reversed their position and argued against busing in the North by charging that busing was an infringement on the authority of local school districts and on the prerogatives of parents. Arguments against busing ranged from pragmatic worries about the length and cost of bus trips, to principled concerns as to its effect on the children themselves, since those who were bused had to struggle to adjust in an alien and often hostile environment. The public controversy over busing, which Richard M. Nixon invoked as a central issue in his successful 1968 and 1972 presidential campaigns, peaked in the early 1970s. In 1974–75, a series of violent riots by white residents of South Boston who objected to the busing of blacks to their neighborhood high school attracted national attention and demonstrated the extent of racial animosity in the North.

For many blacks, the busing controversy highlighted the limitations of northern liberals with regard to their commitment to integration. As Carl HOLMAN, president of the National Urban Coalition, observed, "racism comes much more naturally, and to a much broader spectrum of whites, than we could have imagined." Sen. Abraham Ribicoff of Connecticut charged the North with "monumental hypoc-

The Supreme Court decided in *Swann* v. *Charlotte-Mecklenburg Board of Education* (1971) that the primary method used to integrate public schools should be enforced busing. This method was so controversial that police often had to be called in to supervise the process. (Photographs and Prints Division, Schomburg Center for Research in Black Culture, The New York Public Library, Astor, Lenox and Tilden Foundations)

risy" in a speech on segregation that he delivered to the Senate in 1970. Senator Ribicoff's home state, Connecticut, did not adopt a comprehensive state-wide school desegregation plan until 1993, when metropolitan school districts came into being under the forceful leadership of Gov. Lowell Weicker. Attempts to end *de facto* segregation in the North, once *de jure* segregation had been terminated in the South, had a curious result. Statistics from 1971 show a clear predominance of segregated education in northern schools: There, 57 percent of all black students attended largely black schools, while the same might be said of only 32 percent of black students in the South.

Dilemmas of Isolation and Integration

Two major migratory waves following WORLD WAR I and WORLD WAR II brought more than one million African Americans to the major cities of the northern, north-central, and northeastern United States.

After World War II, the movement of blacks into such cities as New York, Boston, Detroit, and Seattle was accompanied by an exodus of whites to newly created suburbs. Because of racially discriminatory lending policies and restricted neighborhoods (Bradford, 1993), it was difficult for blacks to gain access to suburban housing. Neighborhood organizational patterns and the absence of whites in the cities caused urban school systems to become *de facto* racially segregated.

The opposition to school busing by the white majority and the difficulty of proving that *de facto* racial isolation in the North was caused by state or local governmental policies or action brought a growing disenchantment with busing as a means of improving the educational opportunities of black youth.

In the late 1960s and early '70s, a number of black and white liberal educators began to examine the research reporting on the dramatic gains that early childhood education could have on subsequent schooling, as a means of ensuring successful learning for poor urban and rural children, white and black.

Head Start

Head Start, begun in May 1965 and placed in the federal Office of Economic Opportunity, became one of the most durable and successful educational initiatives of President Johnson's administration. It was the most prominent component of Johnson's War on Poverty. Enrolling preschool children aged three to five years, Head Start is a program for poor children—a racially and ethnically diverse group—designed not only to motivate them and improve their conceptual and verbal skills but to motivate parents as well, by involving them in the educational process and educating them as to their children's health and nutritional needs.

Opponents of Head Start claimed it did not bring about the results its creators had supposed—namely, that it would raise IQ levels significantly in as brief a period as eight weeks. In addition, it was feared that the educational advantages of Head Start would tend to "fade out" if they were not reinforced in elementary and secondary education. However, numerous long-term studies have demonstrated Head Start's effectiveness as a preschool program, and despite past and present political opposition, it has been retained as a model for educational spending for successive administrations.

Another preschool program, the Perry Preschool Educational Project, beginning in 1962 with an original group of 123 African-American preschoolers from poor families in Benton Harbor, Mich., has developed a research paradigm that has allowed the project to track the progress of the original group through the twenty-seventh year of the program. The results show greatly reduced rates of delinquency and adolescent pregnancy and higher rates of school completion than those achieved in the nontreatment group.

Community Control of Local Schools

The call for community control of local schools is a more controversial, but not radical, approach to improving education in low-income urban neighborhoods.

When the parents and community called for control of a new intermediate school, I.S. 201, in the East Harlem community of New York City, in whose planning they had participated since 1958, the parents and community reflected the participatory political atmosphere of the 1960s.

As a precedent, parent advisory councils were mandated and had a defined participatory role with professional educators and planners in many federal education programs. Secondly, parents and community representatives were often members of community action agencies and corporations; therefore, while recognizing the professional roles of teachers and school administrators, the parents in the I.S. 201 community sought a similar participatory role in the operation of their new school.

A two-year study by Dr. Kenneth B. CLARK, a professor of psychology at City College of New York—who, with his wife, Mamie Phipps Clark, completed social science research that contributed to the landmark decision in *Brown* v. *Board of Education of Topeka* (1954)—had produced evidence of the significant decrease in academic achievement in the schools in the Harlem Community (*Youth in the Ghetto,* 1964; *Dark Ghetto,* 1965).

Picket march in front of the recently built and soon to open Intermediate School 201 in East Harlem, September 12, 1966. The picketers demanded that African history be taught in the school. (UPI/Bettmann)

Black parents and community members maintained that black schools and black students had suffered gravely under a centralized school system that was unsympathetic to their particular needs.

As a means of improving the performance of black students, they suggested placing schools under the community's jurisdiction and allowing parents, in concert with administrators and teachers, to exert a direct influence on school organization, curriculum, staffing, and policymaking.

In 1958, in one of a series of planning meetings with school officials about the building of a new intermediate school in the East Harlem community, the superintendent of schools, Bernard Donovan, promised parents a role in naming the school and selecting the principal; he said the school would be integrated and would function as a magnet school.

In the fall of 1966, I.S. 201 opened; however, it failed to draw white students from the Bronx or the West Side of Manhattan. When this failure became apparent, and other promises had been broken, the parents and community demanded "control of the school" (D. Jones, 1966). Black groups in New York City and in other parts of the country mobilized to support the East Harlem residents in their call for community action. Preston Wilcox, an assistant professor at the Columbia University School of Social Work, had worked with the parents for many years and suggested that the opening of I.S. 201 should be regarded as an opportunity to experiment with a new approach to relations between the community and the public educational system.

In the spring of 1967, in response to the crisis at I.S. 201, city officials, with planning grants and the help of consultants from the Ford Foundation, created seven demonstration projects designed to "improve the instruction programs for children in the schools concerned by bringing the parents and community into a more meaningful participation with the schools." Three of the projects (I.S. 201; Two Bridges, on Manhattan's Lower East Side; and Ocean Hill-Brownsville, in the East New York section of Brooklyn) included intermediate or junior high schools.

In the spring of 1968, Rhody McCoy, the supervisor of the Ocean Hill-Brownsville project, ordered nineteen teachers and supervisors to report to the city's central Board of Education offices for reassignment. McCoy claimed that these teachers were unsympathetic to the educational reforms advocated by the local school board. His action prompted a power struggle between the Ocean Hill-Brownsville school board and the city teachers' union—the United Federation of Teachers (UFT)—which escalated when the UFT's president, Albert Shanker, called a citywide strike. During the strike, teachers opposed to the UFT tried to keep schools open in Brooklyn and in other parts of the city, with varying degrees of success. Race relations in the city suffered considerably over the next two months as the supporters of Ocean-Hill Brownsville accused their opponents of racism, while the UFT, which was predominantly Jewish, maintained that community control advocates were anti-Semitic. The strike ended after the central school board dismissed McCoy and the Ocean Hill-Brownsville board. It was decided that local schools should not be given the right to transfer teachers; at the same time, however, it was acknowledged that a centralized system could not meet the students' needs, and plans to decentralize New York City's schools were passed by the New York State legislature in the fall of 1969. The decentralization law allowed for the creation of thirty to thirty-three districts of approximately twenty thousand pupils each. The central board retained control over the high schools and citywide educational programs; the community boards were given control over the elementary, middle, and junior high schools within their boundaries. The chancellor was given limited authority over the community boards (N.Y. Education Law, chap. 2590, 1969).

New York City's school system became a model for other metropolitan school systems throughout the nation because decentralization conformed to the requirements of the Elementary and Secondary Education Act of 1965. Title I of the act required organized parental participation—distinct from that of the schools—in the allocation of more than $2.6 billion in funds designed to assist economically disadvantaged children of rural and urban, white and minority groups alike. Despite occasional instances of corruption on local boards and the periodic failure of some schools to lift performance levels (measured by the Board of Education, New York State Regents, and SAT tests), this form of governance, overseen by an active citywide chancellor, continues to be favored in New York City by many parents, community members, teachers, and politicians.

The action of the I.S. 201 parents and community must be evaluated in the political context of the times. This was a period of government-sanctioned, and -aided, community participation in quality of life areas by poor people, mainly black and Latino. The areas of health and education were targeted as those that would reduce crime and welfare dependency. The process was disruptive to the established structure of the school system but resulted in a school system design that brought the system closer to the people it served.

Milwaukee and Chicago are examples of other cities for which New York was a model. The Milwaukee school system was partially decentralized in 1993.

In 1988, the Illinois state legislature enacted into law the School Reform Act, the first in a series of bills designed to decentralize the Chicago public schools. In 1991, the Illinois legislature passed a bill which originated in the State Senate as SB10 and was enacted into law as Public Act 87-454. The legislation determined the governance of the Chicago school system, decentralized the Chicago public schools into local attendance units, or multiattendance units, and designated each Local School Council, previously established, as the policymaking body for each school. The authority of the Local School Councils included responsibility for budget making, for allocation of federal funds to federal and state programs, and for special education and bilingual programs. The design of each school council, the council's authority, and a prescribed mode of operation is described in the publication *LSC Council Sourcebook: Basics for the Local School Council (1993)*.

A declining commitment to integration, evidenced by the controversy over decentralization, was also manifested in federal policy during the Nixon presidency. Presidential adviser Daniel Patrick Moynihan suggested that the administration pursue a policy of noninterference in local affairs and racial matters, which he termed "benign neglect." Nowhere was Nixon's lack of commitment to desegregation more apparent than in the wording of his statement of March 24, 1970, that announced the allocation of $1.5 billion "to mitigate the effects of segregated schools." Although the allocation provided financial assistance to segregated minority school districts or "racially impacted" areas, no effort was made to address the problem of their segregation per se. In 1972 Congress passed the Emergency School Aid Act, aimed at funding minority students according to their special needs. The act supported desegregation in principle; but the passage of the Equal Opportunity Act in 1974 sharply limited the initiatives the federal government could take in ending *de facto* segregation.

Higher Education Since 1954

The *Brown* ruling, which paved the way for drastic changes in public primary and secondary school systems, did little to change the funding and structure of historically black colleges, which continued to subsist on meager funds from state, federal, and private sources. Four years prior to *Brown,* in *Sweatt* v. *Painter* and *McLaurin* v. *Oklahoma State Regents for Higher Education* (1950), two cases involving the admission of African Americans to all-white universities for graduate study, the U.S. Supreme Court ruled that blacks were not receiving the higher educational opportunities to which they were entitled under the "separate but equal" ruling of *Plessy* v. *Ferguson.* The Court's decisions, which ordered that Herman Sweatt be admitted to the all-white University of Texas Law School, and ruled unconstitutional the treatment of George W. McLaurin, who had been admitted to the University of Oklahoma's doctoral program in education on the condition that segregation be maintained (he was obliged to sit in a separate row "for Negroes" in class, eat at a separate table in the cafeteria, and study at a separate desk in the library), anticipated *Brown* insofar as they implied that equality for blacks could not be attained under the segregated state-supported system of higher education. However, the rulings were narrowly applied, and neither law schools nor graduate schools made haste to welcome black students.

During the 1950s and 1960s, HBCUs persisted in their dual function of providing students with a college-level education and offering secondary-level curricula to compensate for the incomplete preparation most graduates of southern public schools received. An emerging generation of well-trained academics, including some whites, brought a newly sustained level of college instruction to many of these institutions. However, only three HBCU's—Atlanta University, the INTERDENOMINATIONAL THEOLOGICAL CENTER, and Meharry Medical College—were devoted solely to graduate study. Meharry and Howard University remained the primary academic institutions for training blacks as doctors, while Howard and Atlanta were the only institutions offering a Ph.D. degree.

Throughout the 1970s and '80s, HBCUs continued to confront the unique problems of providing substantial compensatory education, building and retaining highly trained faculty at salaries lower than the national norm, and attracting student bodies large enough to keep them in operation. Nevertheless, the importance of these institutions increased significantly with the dramatic rise in black college attendance during these two decades. In 1972 an estimated 727,000 black students were enrolled in college and graduate and professional schools. By 1984 this number had risen to 1,274,000, an increase of 75 percent. Black enrollment in higher education programs continued to rise, reaching 1,477,000 in 1991—more than doubling since 1972. At this time, African Americans constituted approximately 11 percent of the nation's total enrollment. Of the 1,480,000 pursuing higher education, roughly 89,000 were in graduate programs and 17,000 in professional schools. Of the 1,330,000 undergraduates, roughly 16 percent (213,904) were attending HBCUs. Also attending HBCUs were 31,085 white, 2,131 Hispanic, 2,009 Asian-American, and 388 Native-American students. While African Americans constitute 8 percent of the total enrollment of non-black institutions of higher education, white students now make up 13 percent of the total enrollment at HBCUs.

In 1992 the U.S. Supreme Court found in *United States* v. *Fordice* that HBCUs had received unequal treatment in Mississippi because the state had not eliminated its dual system of public higher education, first established under segregation. The ruling, which affected eighteen other southern states, had the same impact on public higher education that *Brown* had had on secondary schools; but where *Brown* had been enthusiastically received, *Fordice* elicited widespread skepticism and dismay. According to the Supreme Court, the state of Mississippi had failed to abolish segregation by retaining a system of higher education that favored predominantly white colleges and universities over HBCUs. The state's admissions and funding policies were called into question, as was the number of its institutions, since it was found that programs were being duplicated at white colleges and HBCUs, and that such duplications perpetuated segregation.

The *Fordice* ruling required that action be taken to end *de facto* segregation by integrating Mississippi's eight state-sponsored colleges and universities. At the same time, the Court held that HBCUs should not be accorded preferential treatment in the desegregation process if they intended to remain exclusively black institutions. Many legislators and educators feared that instead of protecting the constitutional rights of African Americans, the Court's call for integration would result in the dismantling of HBCUs in favor of the larger, better-funded, and more "comprehensive" state-sponsored predominantly white schools. The lesson to be learned from *Brown,* opponents to the ruling claimed, was that integration had not been carried out as a two-way process; on the contrary, African Americans had had to bear the burden of adjusting to, and being educated in, white-majority schools. The loss of HBCUs, which African Americans had struggled for more than a century to maintain, would mean the loss of a crucial aspect of their education and history.

In response to the *Fordice* ruling, Mississippi's Board of Trustees of Institutions of Higher Learning proposed closing Mississippi Valley State, a predominantly black university, and merging the other existing black schools. Previously, the Mississippi Black Legislative Caucus had sought a special appropriation of $55 million for academic programs and school renovation at Mississippi Valley State, Alcorn, and Jackson universities; but they were forced to settle for $11 million after failing to obtain legislative support. A similar battle ensued in the Alabama legislature, where internecine competition between Auburn University and the state's two public historically black colleges led to the killing of appropriations of $38 million in educational aid. Decisions regarding the funding and closure of HBCUs continue to be contested as plans for desegregation are decided in these and other states.

The 1990s controversy over desegregation and the budgetary disputes in state legislatures have brought to light the financial inequities against which HBCUs have been struggling since their inception. Reductions in the 1990s in federal as well as state educational budgets have also contributed to the financial difficulties with which HBCUs must contend. It has been shown that HBCUs lag behind other institutions in their reception of specialized funds. For example, in 1990 a study published by the President's Board of Advisers on Historically Black Colleges showed that more than $1.5 billion in research grants had been given to five predominantly white colleges, while $330 million had been divided among 117 predominantly black colleges during that one year. As a means of challenging these inequities, the fledgling Institute for College Research and Development was established by a consortium of six HBCUs. The purpose of the institute, which is supported by the Office of Minority Impact of the Department of Energy, is to increase the number of research grants and thereby diminish the operating costs for these six universities.

Public Education's Perilous New Status

The liberal approach to education, which emerged during the 1960s and received strong federal support, was eroded under the presidential administrations of Richard Nixon (1969–1974) and Gerald Ford (1974–1977), before undergoing a brief revival during the presidency of Jimmy Carter (1977–1981). Under Carter, Head Start received its first budget increase since 1967. However, the administrations of Ronald Reagan (1981–1989) and George Bush (1989–1993) marked a conservative reaction against liberal educational reforms. During his campaign for the presi-

dency, Reagan pledged to abolish the Department of Education, which had been established as a separate arm of the government by Jimmy Carter. Reagan did not succeed in fulfilling his pledge, but he managed to limit the federal government's role in education severely by making the states responsible for many federal assistance programs. In addition to reducing social services and low-income assistance drastically, Reagan's Omnibus Budget Reconciliation Act of 1981 placed state governments in charge of elementary and secondary educational funding, administration, and policies. For the working poor with children in urban school systems, this shift from federal to state control meant larger classrooms and fewer teachers, and reductions in such related services as Aid to Families with Dependent Children (ADFC), Medicaid, food stamps, job training, and compensatory education.

As cuts in federal spending were being implemented, educators and politicians expressed a growing concern over the obvious steady decline in the quality of education that American schools were able to provide. In a 1983 report titled *A Nation at Risk,* the National Commission on Excellence in Education noted that "the educational foundations of our society are presently being eroded by a rising tide of mediocrity that threatens our very future as a nation and a people." The report, which spawned a plethora of national and regional studies (see References), recognized that the poor and minority groups comprised the nation's youth who were most at risk (*A Nation at Risk,* p. 32), but left to the states the responsibility for addressing the specific needs of the most affected groups. The studies noted especially the academic problems of minority students in urban schools. While reporting that American public education must reach higher academic standards and reach higher levels of achievement if America's schoolchildren were to compete successfully with students in other industrial nations of the world, the studies offer no additional funding or funding strategies, such as urging states to develop school funding policies that would provide greater equity in funding between suburban communities and cities, or recommending that corporations and businesses hire and train minority youth.

A comprehensive study of African-American education was carried out by the National Research Council and published under the title *A Common Destiny: Blacks in American Society* (1989). Three of its most important findings were, first, although substantial progress had been made since World War II with regard to some aspects of equality of achievement, participation, and rewards for African Americans, many remained "separated from the mainstream of national life under conditions of great inequality." Second, among the many factors that contribute to measurable gaps between the levels of education, employment, and housing enjoyed by blacks and whites, a remarkable measure of these differences is attributable to the continuation of private and public discrimination. Third, the progress that has been made over the past fifty years in closing these gaps between blacks and whites is the result, in large part, of "purposeful actions and policies by government and private institutions." In the absence of such actions, including national policy initiatives, "further progress is unlikely," the report concludes.

The Resegregation of Public Education

The impact of these years on African-American children in elementary and secondary schools was increasing isolation, whether in predominantly black schools or in desegregated schools, and a decline in the quality of educational opportunity available to them. A statistical analysis based on a 1985–1986 study of the nation's large urban school districts of 15,000 or more students confirms a resegregation in education through ability grouping, curriculum tracking, special education, and discipline. In every

case these result in the placement of most black students in lower academic level groups and few black students in the higher level, "gifted" academic groups. Black students are nearly twice as likely to receive corporal punishment or suspension; they are three times more likely to be expelled. A black student is 18 percent more likely to drop out of school and 27 percent less likely to graduate. "This pattern," say the authors, "is consistent with a denial of equal educational opportunities for black students" (Meir, Steward, and England, 1989). As desegregation was being achieved in the South, segregation increased in the Northeast, now the most segregated region in the country. Studies have shown that because of their racial isolation, black and Hispanic students in urban areas are much less likely to become computer literate—a fact that has serious economic consequences. According to the National Bureau of Economic Research, the inability to use computers accounted for nearly one-third of the increase in the earnings gap between blacks and whites during the period from 1976 to 1990.

Such problems are rooted in early education. Statistics from 1990 show that black fourth graders

Brownie group, part of the Girl Scouts of America, wrapping Christmas presents for the elderly and the sick at a community center in the Crown Heights section of Brooklyn, N.Y., 1988. (Allford/Trotman Associates)

scored 28.6 percent lower than white fourth graders in all areas of mathematics. In that same subject, blacks scored 31.3 percent lower in the eighth grade and 30.9 percent lower in the twelfth grade.

A similar disparity exists in tests reflecting their command of historical information: In 1988, black students scored 15.6 percent lower than whites in the fourth grade, and 31 and 15.4 percent lower in the eighth and twelfth grades, respectively.

Disproportionate Assignments to Special Education for Black and Latino Males: Classification/Placement of African-American and Latino Students

One very significant failing of America's big-city school systems to serve African-American children adequately is the disproportionate assignment of African-American male children to special education classes, especially those for the mentally retarded and for the emotionally disturbed. This pattern of assignment applies also to Latino males and is found in almost every big-city school system.

Many children are placed in special education classes because they perform below their grade in reading and/or for behavioral problems, rather than for organicity. For most children, placement in special education leads to permanent classification, despite state and federal regulations that mandate decertification examinations every three years.

According to a 1991 report (Walter Stafford et al., *Cause for Alarm: The Condition of Black and Latino Males in New York City,* pp. 13–14), "Black males accounted for 28 percent of special education students (33,787 black males, 27,668 Latino males, and 14,309 white males)." Within special education programs, black males (and Hispanic males) were enrolled in two programs: for those with learning disabilities and for those with emotional disturbance. These special education placements are especially damaging to the educational progress of black males, because return to the educational mainstream is virtually impossible; therefore, such placements often lead black male students to drop out of school without sufficient education or educational credentials.

Jay Gottlieb and colleagues, in a 1994 study of special education placements in urban school systems, "Special Education in Urban America: It's Not Justifiable for Many," find that "for children who reside in inner cities, the vast majority of whom are poor and members of minority groups, special education referral, evaluation, and placement practices are not more effective now than they were 25 years ago" (p. 453).

These findings, despite the passage of P.L. 94-142 (1975), legislation generated by the CIVIL RIGHTS MOVEMENT giving people with handicaps the right to be educated in public education and in "the least restricted environment," indicate that urban public school systems continue to misdiagnose and mislabel minority children, black and Latino, and place them in special education classes, when analysis of the placements "reveals the powerful effects of poverty among the minority groups that predominate in urban schools."

Many of these children are classified as learning disabled, a medically oriented categorical designation, to ensure reimbursement for excess costs and special education services and programs. Such assignments are not in conformity with state and federal regulations and demonstrate the necessity for additional reforms in special education placement policies by urban school systems nationwide.

The Gottlieb study concludes:

> . . . the vast majority of children who are classified as learning disabled and placed in special education in many urban school districts are not disabled in the sense demanded by legislation and regulation. Instead, they are children who suffer the many ravages of poverty, not the least of which is its effect on academic performance. (p. 456)

African-American Teachers

The publication of *A Nation at Risk* brought a new focus on the nation's teachers as a critical resource in the performance of the nation's schools and students. Two special studies, *A Nation Prepared: Teachers for the 21st Century,* by the Carnegie Forum on Education and the Economy (1986), and *Tomorrow's Teachers,* a 1986 report of the Holmes Group (a consortium of deans of schools of education in large universities), critically examined the preparation and practice of elementary and secondary teachers. Both reports spoke to the past roles of minority teachers educating children in the nation's public schools, and to the need for minority teachers in the future.

As noted in *A Nation Prepared* and *Teaching's Next Generation* (1993), there is a need to prepare a larger number of minority group members to become teachers. Minority students, mainly black and Latino, represent a majority in twenty-three of twenty-five of the nation's largest cities, but the number of black teachers in the United States is only 8.6 percent. The percentage is expected to decrease to 5 percent if drastic steps are not taken in training and recruitment of black teachers.

By the year 2000, black and Latino students will represent the majority of students in the 25 central cities and metropolitan areas of the United States. The present teaching force is predominantly Caucasian. Many teachers will retire within the next several years, and will have to be replaced with significant numbers of minority teachers.

As the number of minority public school students is rising, the minority teaching force is shrinking in number. The Carnegie report recognized the role that the historically black colleges and state black colleges had performed over the years in the preparation of teachers and teacher educators and proposed collaborative relationships. Both the Carnegie and the Holmes Group reports noted the need to recruit and prepare bright minority students for teaching, now that desegregation had opened many other career choices for them.

A new emphasis now has been placed on teacher preparation. It requires a "knowledge base" in the liberal arts, with concomitant emphasis on the quantitative subjects, and the development of "pedagogical skills": studies in human development and theories of teaching and learning, the knowledge of discrete teaching technologies appropriate to a given subject, as well as knowledge and recognition of a range of student needs.

Throughout the nation, teacher education is being strengthened to meet new state certification requirements by collaborations among education and liberal arts departments in their own colleges and universities and by participation in regional and national teacher education networks.

Preteaching programs and collaborations between and among colleges and high schools are being developed to encourage and recruit students to the teaching profession.

The DeWitt Wallace-Reader's Digest Fund is a major private sponsor of programs to prepare and recruit new minority teachers.

The federal government is providing funds to the states under Chapter V of ESEA, and in separate block grant programs, under Chapter II of the same legislation, for minority teacher education and recruitment.

To be successful, the programs will have to prepare recruits at every level to pass the state examination for certification or the National Teachers Examination from the Educational Testing Service. Failure to pass the required examinations has presented a major barrier to minority candidates in the past.

Bernard Watson and Fasha Traylor express concern about the reform movement in teaching, specifically about the outcome of greater professionalization of teachers. While having no doubt that individual teachers will benefit from the "professionalization" process that the Holmes Group recommends, they warn that greater professionalization of teachers may not necessarily "result in an educational system that is accessible, responsive, and responsible to all American children."

Watson and Traylor offer two bases for this conclusion. First, conceptualization of the National Board for Professional Teaching Standards does not indicate that the board will attend to the specific needs of individual local school districts. Second, given the certainty that the system of rewards for acquiring greater professionalization will find its way into collective bargaining agreements (as they already have in some school systems), it is questionable whether these superbly prepared teachers will seek positions in the schools of minority communities in urban centers or in rural America (Watson and Traylor, "Tomorrow's Teachers: Who Will They Be, What Will They Know?" 1988).

If either the board or the teachers fail to respond appropriately, minority students in the nation's big-city school systems will not benefit from the professionalization of the teaching profession.

Following World War II, large sections of New York City, Philadelphia, Chicago, Detroit, and Atlanta had school subdistricts that enrolled a majority of African-American students. In the late 1960s, the growing percentages of African-American pupils in urban school systems, plus the call for community control of schools, intensified the demand for black administrators in systemwide positions, including the general superintendency.

By March 1974 there were forty-four city or county African-American superintendents, a superintendent of the Virgin Islands (by presidential appointment), and two African-American state superintendents of public instruction, one in Michigan and the other in California (Scott, 1980).

By 1975 Detroit, Washington, D.C., Chicago, Atlanta, and Wilmington, Del., had black superintendents of public schools. New York City appointed its first black chancellor (the title of the system-wide superintendency), Richard Green, in 1985.

The graduate schools of education of Harvard, Columbia, Atlanta, and Fordham Universities, several aided by the Rockefeller and Ford Foundations, among others, recruited to their existing doctoral programs, or developed special programs for the academic and professional preparation of minority candidates for systemwide administrative positions.

Though well prepared, minority superintendents faced the same order of financial and educational problems as did their Caucasian colleagues and predecessors: shrinking budgets, municipal overburden, decaying and asbestos-filled school buildings; and the perpetual problems of racial balance and the underachievement of large numbers of minority pupils.

Afrocentrism and Multiculturalism

A resurgent interest in and support of Afrocentric studies, in part as one form of antidote to alienation from education, has been challenged by some educators as divisive, while the perpetuation of an emphasis on Eurocentric studies is not considered divisive in a culturally pluralistic nation such as ours. But neither an Afrocentric nor a Eurocentric education provides us with the "core around which a truly multicultural education can be developed," Gordon argues.

With increasing frequency we are required, as citizens of our national society, "to function in more than a single language, adapt to the demands of more than a single culture, meet the behavioral demands of more than a single situation, and understand the symbols and rituals of people other than those with whom most of us have been socialized." It is from these multidisciplinary, multiculturalist, multiperspectivist learning experiences that competencies in critical analysis, critical interpretation, and critical understanding will allow for responsibly discharging future decisions and judgments. Gordon concludes that "no matter what core knowledge is chosen as the vehicle . . . educators are beginning to realize that the teaching of dogma (either hegemonic or resistant) is no longer appropriate for the optimal development of learners." ("Conceptions of Africentrism and Multiculturalism in Education: A General Overview").

Where multiculturalism emphasizes the diversity of groups within a particular culture, Afrocentrism insists on the primacy of an African-based cultural tradition. Proponents of this method argue that black youngsters must develop a strong sense of their African heritage if they are to survive in a hostile, white-dominated environment.

One Afrocentric approach is the creation of all-male, Afrocentric schools. Advocates of such schools point to the high levels of violence, and low levels of education, among many black males, and stress the benefits of instilling in young black men a sense of pride in their cultural roots.

The prospect of creating these schools has been hotly debated, with critics charging that a segregated environment would damage students by further alienating them from the cultural mainstream. Not only would the gender exclusive schools be ineligible for federal funding, but evidence suggests that many black male and female students have succeeded academically and developed positive self-images in racially integrated public schools (Clark, *A Possible Reality*, 1972; Edmonds, *Educational Leadership*, 1982).

American blacks have long been divided between Afrocentrist and American nationalist philosophies. Perhaps the time has come for a rapprochement between these two philosophical positions.

W. E. B. Du Bois, in *Souls of Black Folk* (1903), stated the dilemma of the African American: "An American, a Negro; two souls, two thoughts, two unreconciled strivings. . . ."

The dilemma Du Bois described will be resolved when the African heritage of the African American takes its rightful and respected place alongside the other cultures of this intercontinental, international, multicultural nation.

School Choice

There has always been choice in American education, usually divided into three major sectors: public, parochial, and independent. Until choice became an issue in national efforts to improve the academic performance of poor children in public urban and rural schools, the sectors operated as separate islands, with the "separation clause" of the First Amendment to the U.S. Constitution as the arbiter.

The First Amendment to the U.S. Constitution prohibits funding religious schools with public monies. However, according to some legal experts, the "wall" between church and state, private and public schools, has been breached by the "child benefit theory," which was devised by the conceptualizers of the 1965 Elementary and Secondary Education Act to allow funding of poor children in parochial and nonpublic schools, under Title I, now Chapter I, of the act (Hughes and Hughes, 1972).

Under this theory, providing federal money to private schools is legal as long as the money follows the child who otherwise would be eligible in public school. The federal money, or program, therefore benefits the child, not the nonpublic school. A sizable proportion of the American public favors providing public money to private and parochial schools. Rather than equity and access, the battle is being based on quality of education.

There is a general consensus that public schools in city school systems are failing to give poor, racially isolated, language-different students the quality education that will prepare them for a future in the technologically oriented world-society of the twenty-first century. By contrast, suburban schools and private and parochial schools with smaller student bodies (and in the case of wealthy suburbs, different funding formulas) are providing such education.

The implications of choice plans, public and private, are grave for black parents and their children in urban school systems. There is usually an additional monetary cost for the family, if only for transportation to a school in another district or community. At the extreme, the costs are great if the parent has to make up the difference between the public voucher amount and the tuition of the private school.

This is particularly troubling to African Americans who remember that tuition grants for funding private education was the device resorted to in 1955 by Prince Edward County, Va., in defiance of the U.S. Supreme Court's 1954 *Brown* decision. Under this arrangement a system of private schools for white students was established, but none for blacks. Does "school choice" amount to nothing more than a present-day analogue for Prince Edward County's gambit of 1955?

Some educators regard tuition grants or vouchers as flawed policy for dealing with the problems of public education. They argue that school choice allows for winners and losers, and that a national policy that assures there will be losers is unacceptable, unconstitutional, and unsound.

School choice can be exercised within the public schools or outside of public education. The latter is the smaller sector, with a relatively stable 10 to 11 percent of the nation's school-age children in private schools. This sector is augmented slightly by such experiments as Whittle Schools, driven by an interest in both quality in education and the profit to be derived from such educational ventures. A similar experiment is being carried out by Educational Alternatives, Inc., for a group of privatized Baltimore schools and for the public schools of Hartford, Conn. Privatization of public schools raises questions about the equitable distribution of resources and funding among corporation-managed and non-corporation-managed schools. Another important concern is making students and teachers a captive audience for a commercial enterprise paid for with public monies.

Choice within the public sector includes special programs within schools, school pairing (a limited choice), magnet schools, examination schools, choice among schools within a district (a wider choice), choice among districts within a system, and schools funded by business.

Whatever the form of choice, considerations including accountability and governance, effectiveness, equity, and the allocation of resources are inescapable. In matters of accountability and governance, will private schools receiving public money be held to the same accreditation, affirmative action, open records requirements, health and safety statutes (including insurance), and accountability reporting required of the public sector? What is the meaning of claims that "choice works," as President Bush said, when experimental studies over the past twenty years have shown little evidence that choice brings educational improvement, greater parental involvement, or increased pupil learning? With a number of researchers finding that in New York, Chicago, Boston, and Philadelphia choice in education worked to the detriment of low-achieving students, what are the claims to be made for it on the basis of equity? Is it fair that students with learning problems or limited proficiency in English be excluded from magnet schools or that students who simply are average achievers are informally or formally returned to their neighborhood school without recourse? What is to be done about the failure of these schools to educate a student body representative of those cities? Since, according to a wide range of cost estimates and investigations, choice will not be low-cost school improvement, what are the benefits the new investments will bring as a result of choice, that is, benefits that could not be more readily achieved through the expenditure of these new investments on public education alone?

There are those who argue that any such new investments in choice, particularly if it involves public/private school vouchers, violate the long-held belief in the "American social contract," which, it is claimed, makes the entire society responsible for the elementary and secondary education of its children and youth.

There can be serious debits to school choice for black children—and others among the rising number of racial and ethnic minority children—and their parents in urban school systems if, in the name of excellence, better students are siphoned off to magnet and private schools and all other students are dumped into public education. This, as is evident from the history of other forms of tracking, will spawn a self-perpetuating vicious cycle erosive of effective public education.

A number of new academic models have proven to work effectively for black students. The College Board's Equity 2000 project, which has carried out pilot programs in California, Tennessee, Maryland, Rhode Island, Texas, and Wisconsin, trains teachers and guidance counselors to address the special needs of poor and minority students, and maintains a curriculum that emphasizes algebra and geometry as the "gatekeeper" subjects for all middle- and high-school students. A similar and more specialized mathematics program, called the Algebra Project, initiated by Robert P. Moses in the Roxbury neighborhood of Boston, Mass., has been carried out successfully in California and Mississippi.

One of the most celebrated and successful models for developing effective schools was instituted in the New Haven school system by Dr. James Comer, a member of the faculty of psychiatry at Yale University. The School Development Program is a comprehensive school program that involves parents, mental health professionals, teachers, and administrators in a mutually supportive relationship that in turn drives the academic program and assessment in an improved school climate (Comer, 1980).

Each of the programs is skills-based and provides students with the confidence to draw on their per-

Young boys being taught about computers at the George W. Kelson elementary school in Baltimore, Md., in a program designed by Dr. Spencer Holland to educate African-American males. (Allford/Trotman Associates)

sonal experiences to understand and resolve academic problems.

It should be noted, however, that successful models for public education are few, and many public school systems continue to struggle with increasing limitations in financial resources, lower academic standards, lack of discipline, and escalations of violence.

Perhaps the clearest indication of the nation's disillusionment with public education is the currency of school choice—a "public" system that would offer a better education to a select few. This will not respond to a pervasive concern among the nation's parents that their children gain the skills and assurance they will need to sustain themselves in the competitive multinational economy of their adulthood in the twenty-first century. For African Americans especially, the prospects of quality education remain a problem of equal educational rights.

In big cities across the nation attention is being focused on the improvement of public education at all levels. In New York, Chicago, and Philadelphia the Annenberg Foundation is helping principals,

teachers, parents, communities, and boards of education to create smaller, theme-based, alternative primary and secondary schools.

Whatever the structure of the local school system, or the agreed-upon organizing theme of each school, however, preparation for a productive future in the modern world requires that students master the basic skills of English comprehension, writing and mathematics and an understanding of science and computer technology. Public education remains the most certain system for ensuring equity, quality, and personal empowerment. Federal, state, and local education officials, with the help of the private sector, must continue to be held responsible for the effective education of all of the nation's children, whatever their color or socioeconomic status.

REFERENCES

American Council on Education. *Minorities on Campus.* Washington, D.C., 1989.

American Council on Education and Education Commission of the States. *One Third of a Nation.* Washington, D.C., 1988.

ANDERSON, JAMES D. *The Education of Blacks in the South, 1860–1935.* Chapel Hill, N.C., 1988.

ASANTE, MOLEFI K., and MARK T. MATTSON. *Historical and Cultural Atlas of African Americans.* New York, 1992.

ASCHER, CAROL. *Changing Schools for Urban Students.* New York, 1993.

The Atlanta University Publications. 1911. Reprint. Atlanta, 1968.

BERRY, MARY FRANCES. *The Politics of Parenthood.* New York, 1993.

———. "Unfinished Business of Carter G. Woodson." *City Sun,* March 20–26, 1991, p. 31.

BERRY, MARY FRANCES, and JOHN W. BLASSINGAME. *Long Memory.* New York, 1982.

BRACEY, JOHN H., JR., AUGUST MEIR, and ELLIOTT RUDWICK. *Black Nationalism in America.* Indianapolis, Ind., 1970.

BRADFORD, WILLIAM D. "Money Matters: Lending Discrimination in African-American Communities." In *The State of Black America 1993.* New York, 1993, pp. 109–123.

BULLOCK, HENRY ALLEN. *A History of Negro Education in the South.* Cambridge, Mass., 1967.

CARLETON, GEORGE W. *The Suppressed Book About Slavery.* 1863. Reprint. New York, 1968.

CARMICHAEL, STOKELY, and CHARLES V. HAMILTON. *Black Power.* New York, 1967.

Carnegie Forum on Education and the Economy. *A Nation Prepared: Teachers for the 21st Century.* Washington, D.C., 1986.

CARSON, CLAYBORNE. *In Struggle.* Cambridge, Mass., 1981.

CLARK, KENNETH B. *A Possible Reality.* New York, 1972.

———. *Dark Ghetto.* New York, 1965.

———. *Youth in the Ghetto.* New York, 1964.

CLARKE, JOHN HENRIK. *Education for a New Reality in the African World.* New York, 1994.

COMER, JAMES P. *School Power.* New York, 1980.

COMER, JAMES P., ET AL. "School Power: A Model for Improving Black Student Achievement." In Willy DeMarcell Smith and Eva Wells Chunn, eds. *Black Education.* New Brunswick, N.J., 1991.

CORNELIUS, JANET DUITSMAN. *When I Can Read My Title Clear.* Columbia, S.C., 1991.

CREMIN, LAWRENCE A. *American Education: The National Experience, 1783–1876.* New York, 1980.

———. *The Metropolitan Experience, 1976–1980.* New York, 1988.

DAVIDSON, BASIL. *The African Slave Trade: Precolonial History, 1450–1850.* Boston, 1961.

DAVIS, ARTHUR P., J. SAUNDERS REDDING, and JOYCE ANN JOYCE. *The New Calvacade: African-American Writing from 1760 to the Present.* Washington, D.C., 1991.

DOUGLAS, CARLYLE C. "Outlook for Young Black Males Called Bleak." *New York Times,* May 19, 1985, p. 34.

DU BOIS, W. E. B., ed. *The Common School and the Negro American.* Atlanta, Ga., 1911.

EDELMAN, MARIAN WRIGHT. *Families in Peril.* Cambridge, Mass., 1987.

EDMONDS, RON. "Programs of School Improvement: An Overview." *Educational Leadership* (December 1982): 4–11.

FONER, ERIC. *Reconstruction: America's Unfinished Revolution, 1863–1877.* New York, 1988.

FRANKLIN, JOHN HOPE, and ALFRED A. MOSS, JR. *From Slavery to Freedom.* New York, 1994.

GARIBALDI, ANTOINE M. "The Role of Historically Black Colleges in Facilitating Resilience Among African-American Students." *Education and Urban Society* 24 (1991): 103–111.

GORDON, EDMUND W. "Conceptions of Africentrism and Multiculturalism in Education: A General Overview." *Journal of Negro Education* 61, no. 3 (1992): 235–236.

GOTTLIEB, JAY, MARK ALTER, BARBARA W. GOTTLIEB, and JERRY WISHNER. "Special Education in Urban America: It's Not Justifiable for Many." *The Journal of Special Education* 27, no. 4 (1994): 453–465.

GUTMAN, HERBERT G. *The Black Family in Slavery and Freedom, 1750–1925.* New York, 1976.

HACKER, ANDREW. *Two Nations.* New York, 1992.

HARE, BRUCE R. "Black Youth at Risk." In *The State of Black America, 1988.* New York, 1988.

HOLMES GROUP. *Tomorrow's Teachers.* East Lansing, Mich., 1986.

HUGHES, JOHN F., and ANNE O. HUGHES. *Equal Education.* Bloomington, Ind., 1972.

JACKSON, EDWARD M. *Black Education in Contemporary America.* Briston, Ind., 1986.

JAYNES, GERALD DAVID, and ROBIN M. WILLIAMS, JR., eds. *A Common Destiny: Blacks and American Society.* Washington, D.C., 1989.

JONES, DOROTHY S. "Intermediate School 201 Controversy." Report No. 1 to the Church and Race Secretariat of the Protestant Council of the City of New York, September 12, 1966.

JONES, FAUSTINE CHILDRESS. *The Changing Mood in America.* Washington, D.C., 1977.

JONES-WILSON, FAUSTINE C. "Equity in Education: A Low Priority in the School Reform Movement." In Willy DeMarcell Smith and Eva Wells Chunn, eds. *Black Education.* New Brunswick, N.J., 1991.

KEARNEY, C. PHILLIP, and ELIZABETH VANDERPUTTEN, eds. *Grants Consolidation: A New Balance in Federal Aid to Schools?* Washington, D.C., 1979.

KEPPEL, FRANCIS. *The Necessary Revolution in American Education.* New York, 1966.

KLUGER, RICHARD. *Simple Justice.* New York, 1976.

KOZOL, JONATHAN. *Savage Inequalities.* New York, 1992.

LARNER, JEREMEY. "I.S. 201: Disaster in the Schools." *Dissent* 45, no. 1 (1967): 21.

LAZAR, IRVING, and RICHARD B. DARLINGTON. *Lasting Effects After Preschool.* Washington, D.C., 1978.

LIGHTFOOT, SARA LAWRENCE. *The Good High School.* New York, 1993.

LOGAN, RAYFORD W., and MICHAEL R. WINSTON. *Dictionary of America Negro Biography.* New York, 1982.

MANDLE, JAY R. *Not Slave, Not Free: The African-American Experience Since the Civil War.* Durham, N.C., 1992.

MARABLE, MANNING. *How Capitalism Underdeveloped Black America.* Boston, 1983.

———. *Race, Reform, and Rebellion.* Jackson, Miss., 1991.

MEIR, K.J., JOSEPH STEWARD, JR., and ROBERT E. ENGLAND. *Race, Class and Education: The Politics of Second Generation Discrimination.* New York, 1989.

MILLS, JOHNNIE R., JO ANN DAUZAT, and BURNETT JOINER. *Improving Teacher Education: A Conscious Choice.* Dubuque, Iowa, 1989.

MINTER, THOMAS K. *Intermediate School 201, Manhattan: Center of Controversy.* Cambridge, Mass., 1967.

MUNGER, FRANK J., and RICHARD FENNO, JR. *National Politics and Federal Aid to Education.* Syracuse, N.Y., 1962.

NATHAN, RICHARD P., and FRED DOOLITTLE. *The Consequences of Cuts.* Princeton, N.J., 1983.

National Commission on Excellence in Education. *A Nation at Risk: The Imperative for Educational Reform.* Washington, D.C., 1983.

NIANE, D. T., ed. *UNESCO General History of Africa: Africa from the Twelfth to the Sixteenth Century.* London, 1984.

ORFIELD, GARY. *Public School Desegregation in the United States, 1968–1980.* Washington, D.C., 1983.

PORTER, DOROTHY. *Early Negro Writing, 1760–1837.* Boston, 1971.

PRETTYMAN, ALFRED E. "The Ring of *The Bell Curve*: Resonances and Reverberations." New York, 1995.

RAVITCH, DIANE. *The Great School Wars.* 1974. Reprint. New York, 1968.

———. *The Troubled Crusade.* New York, 1983.

ROGERS, DAVID. *110 Livingston Street.* New York, 1968.

SCOTT, HUGH J. *The Black School Superintendent: Messiah or Scapegoat?* Washington, D.C., 1980.

SNOWDEN, FRANK M., JR. *Blacks in Antiquity.* Cambridge, Mass., 1970.

STAFFORD, WALTER, ET AL. *Cause for Alarm: The Condition of Black and Latino Males in New York City.* New York, 1991.

STERLING, DOROTHY, ed. *We Are Your Sisters: Black Women in the Nineteenth Century.* New York, 1984.

SUFFRIN, SIDNEY C. *Administering the National Defense Education Act.* Syracuse, N.Y., 1963.

SWANSON, DENA PHILLIPS, and MARGARET BEALE SPENCER. "Youth Policy, Poverty, and African Americans: Implications for Resilience." *Education and Urban Society* 24 (1991): 148–161.

U.S. Department of Education, National Center for Education Statistics. *America's Teachers: Profile of a Profession.* Washington, D.C., 1993.

———. *The Condition of Education, 1991.* Washington, D.C., 1991.

———. *The Condition of Education, 1992.* Washington, D.C., 1992.

VERGON, CHARLES B. "The Context of School Desegregation Policy." *Education and Urban Society* 23, no. 1 (1990): 3–21.

WATSON, BERNARD C. and TRAYLOR, FASAHA M. "Tomorrow's Teachers: Who Will They Be, What Will They Know?" In *The State of Black America 1988.* New York, 1988.

WEIKERT, DAVID P. *Quality Preschool Programs: A Long-Term Social Investment.* New York, 1989.

WEST, CORNEL. *Race Matters.* Boston, 1993.

WINFIELD, LINDA F., ed. "Resilience, Schooling, and Development in African-American Youth." *Education and Urban Society* 24 (1991): 5.

WOOD, FORREST G. *The Arrogance of Faith.* New York, 1990.

WOODSON, CARTER G., and CHARLES H. WESLEY. *The Education of the Negro Prior to 1861.* Washington, D.C., 1915.

———. *The Miseducation of the Negro.* Washington, D.C., 1933.

———. *The Negro in Our History.* Washington, D.C., 1972.

WRIGHT, DONALD R. *African Americans in the Colonial Era.* Carbondale, Ill., 1990.

———. *African Americans in the Early Republic, 1789–1831.* Carbondale, Ill., 1993.

THOMAS K. MINTER
ALFRED E. PRETTYMAN

Education, Medical. *See* Medical Education.

Education, Religious. *See* Religious Education.

Education, Science. *See* Science Education.

Education, Theological. *See* Theological Education.

Edwards, Lena Frances (September 17, 1900–December 3, 1986), physician. Born in Washington, D.C., Lena Edwards knew from age twelve that she wanted to be a doctor. She attended Dunbar High School, where Carter G. WOODSON was one of her science teachers. She was class valedictorian in 1917.

After completing her undergraduate education at Howard University a year early, she received an M.D. from Howard's College of Medicine in 1924. While in medical school, she married colleague Keith Madison, with whom she had six children. Edwards began a private practice in obstetrics and assisted in many deliveries for women in the Washington area.

Edwards was appointed to the staff of the Margaret Hague Maternity Hospital in Jersey City, N.J., in 1931. One of the few African Americans on the staff, she served there as an assistant gynecologist until 1945. Edwards first applied for a residency in 1936, but was turned down. Despite years of service, her department chair would not consider her for specialized training until a colleague threatened to expose the discriminatory practices. She was subsequently given the promotion and was certified by the American Board of Obstetrics and Gynecology in 1948. Edwards was an early advocate of natural childbirth, believing that anesthetics impaired the health of mother and child. She returned to Howard in 1954 as a member of the medical school faculty.

By 1960, Edwards's children were established in professional careers and no longer needed her financial support. A devout Roman Catholic, she decided, at age fifty-nine, that she wanted the challenge of missionary work. She journeyed to St. Joseph's Mission in the Texas Panhandle town of Hereford to work with Mexican-American migrant workers. Conditions in the migrant camps were crowded and unsanitary; families lived in two-room barracks-style cabins without running water. The workers, some of them undocumented aliens, most without permanent residences, did not have access to local health care facilities. To raise money to build and run the new Our Lady of Guadalupe Maternity Clinic, Edwards campaigned throughout churches in Texas and opened a private practice in Hereford. She learned Spanish and eventually moved into a two-room house. An article in *Ebony* brought her work to the attention of President John F. Kennedy, who appointed her to the Federal Advisory Council on Employment Security and the Federal Manpower Committee—both in 1962. She spoke out on behalf of migrant workers. President Lyndon B. Johnson awarded her the Presidential Medal of Freedom in 1964 for her work in Texas. She left the clinic in 1965 to care for her ailing mother.

Edwards spent the rest of her professional life in New Jersey, where she operated a private practice. She also campaigned for health education and preventive treatment among poor women. She was a member of numerous organizations such as the United Negro College Fund and the American Cancer Society, from which she received an award in 1973 for her work introducing Pap smears to low-income women. She received honorary degrees from the University of Portland in 1960 and Jersey City State College in 1972. The Howard Medical Alumni Association honored her as a "living legend." Lena Edwards died at Lakewood, N.J., in 1986.

REFERENCE

SCALLY, SISTER ANTHONY. "Dr. Lena Edwards: People Lover." *Negro History Bulletin* 39 (May 1976): 592–595.

ALLISON X. MILLER

Edwards, Melvin (May 4, 1937–), sculptor. Mel Edwards was born in Houston, Tex., in 1937. He studied at the Los Angeles City College and the Los Angeles County Art Institute, and received his B.F.A. from the University of Southern California in 1965. Two years later, Edwards moved to New York City, and from 1968 to 1971 he worked on public art projects in Harlem with artists known as the Smokehouse Group. In 1972, Edwards joined the faculty at the art department of Livingston College at Rutgers University in New Jersey, and in 1980 he became a professor at the Mason Gross School of Creative and Performing Arts at Rutgers University.

Edwards has consistently explored infusing African or African-American references into a sculptural language that is firmly founded in modernist idioms. In his large-scale sculpture he has manifested simplified, geometric forms since the late 1960s. Edwards infuses these with anecdote, however, by allowing them to rock in space, or by suspending repeated rows of chains across their spans (*Chains*, 1964; *Curtain for William and Peter*, 1970). Thus the formal aspects of his work that are in step with the contemporary mainstream are filled with content, evoking personal sources such as memories of his grandmother rocking in her chair (*Rockers*, 1970) and his father creating architectural anomalies such as the diagonal hallway in Edwards's boyhood home. He has also entertained anatomical associations in his work, where half-circles and curves recur in set combination to describe various body parts. Edwards has constantly revised his approach to large-scale steel sculpture in response to the inspiration he has garnered over the years in his travels to Africa, particularly to Zimbabwe, and his appreciation of not only the art, but also the architecture in these regions (*Homage to Coco*, 1970).

A persistent iconographic reference in Edwards' work is to slavery. This is first manifest in the use of

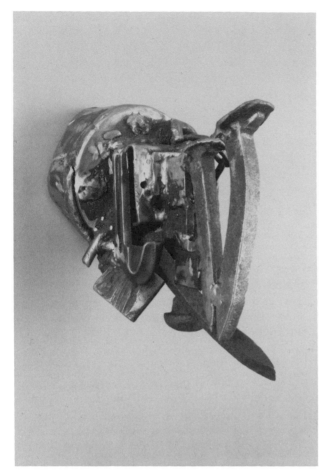

Melvin Edwards's *Working Thought,* part of the Lynch Fragment Series, creates an ominous image of inhumanity from discarded objects of the industrial landscape. (The Studio Museum in Harlem)

chains in his work during the 1960s, which might be suspended in loops from wires set in the ceiling. While Edward might refer in these compositions to concerns such as repetitive serial imagery, or industrial aesthetics, these chains are inescapably grounded in historical specificity. This was manifest in the long-standing series of welded sculptures known collectively as the *Lynch Fragments* (1963–1967). More intimate in scale, and specific in allusion, these works feature intense assemblages of found nuts, bolts, metal tools, and forms that evoke the violation and brutality of lynching, which has punctuated the history of African Americans in this country in their search for social and political equality. These works continue formal and technical approaches to welded sculpture that were established in Europe in the 1930s by Julio Gonzalez and Pablo Picasso, and in this country by David Smith. In Edwards's hands, however, this sculptural statement has become so distinctive for its achievement of the successful fusing of an exquisite formal sensibility with political social commentary.

Edwards has received many awards, such as the John Hay Whitney Fellowship (1964), National Endowment for the Arts and Visual Artist Fellowship (1971), the John Jay Simon Guggenheim Memorial Foundation Award (1975), and a Fulbright Fellowship to Zimbabwe (1988–89). His work has been featured in solo exhibitions at the Santa Barbara Museum of Art (1965), Walker Art Center in Minneapolis (1968), Whitney Museum of American Art (1970), Studio Museum in Harlem (1978), Sculpture Center Gallery, New York (1982), UNESCO in Paris (1984), and the Oklahoma City Art Museum on the Fairgrounds (1991). A retrospective of Edwards's work was shown at the Neuberger Museum of Art and the State University of New York at Purchase, New York in 1993.

REFERENCES

FINE, ELSA HONIG. *The Afro-American Artist: A Search for Identity.* New York, 1973, pp. 265–267.
Gilliam/Edwards/Williams: Extensions. Hartford, Conn., 1974.
Melvin Edwards: Sculpture, A Thirty-Year Retrospective, 1963–1993. New York, 1993.

LOWERY STOKES SIMS

Eikerenkoetter, Frederick J. *See* Reverend Ike.

Elaine, Arkansas, Race Riot of 1919. In 1919, in the midst of the riots of RED SUMMER, a major racial disturbance erupted in Phillips County, Ark., where local blacks worked as sharecroppers and tenant farmers. They were unable to challenge the low wages and cotton prices they received, and many were trapped on the land through debt peonage. In the summer of 1919, Robert L. Hill, an African-American veteran of WORLD WAR I, began to organize the Progressive Farmers and Householders Union, a black self-help organization designed to win blacks fairer treatment and more money for their work. In late September, a group of some sixty-five blacks from the county hired O. S. Bratton, a white Little Rock attorney, to negotiate a fair price for crops and to obtain itemized lists of sums owed to white landowners.

On September 30, the union held a mass meeting at a church in Hoop Spur, a small town near Elaine, Ark. County Deputy Sheriff Charles W. Pratt and W. A. Adkins, a special agent of the Missouri-Pacific Railroad, heard about the meeting and stopped outside the black church. The agents fired into the church, hoping to scare and disperse participants. However, blacks returned the fire, wounding the men.

Word that blacks were planning a race war circulated among whites. Trainloads of armed white men arrived in Elaine. Roving gangs of whites attacked and shot innocent blacks. Federal troops from the Third Division and 57th Infantry arrived to keep peace, but some joined the white rioters. Blacks were arrested in large numbers, and those without special passes were confined in the basement of the local public school. Bratton was arrested and charged with inciting blacks to riot, and the surviving members of the Progressive Farmers and Householders Union and other blacks were rounded up. By the time the rioting was halted, as many as two hundred blacks had been killed, and hundreds more were wounded. There were also five white fatalities.

Twelve members of the union were charged with murder, and sixty-seven more were indicted for insurrection. Blacks in custody were tortured into making incriminating statements. The twelve union members were quickly brought to trial in the presence of a furious mob. Despite Bratton's testimony, all were convicted and sentenced to death, while the other sixty-seven defendants were given harsh prison terms. NATIONAL ASSOCIATION FOR THE ADVANCEMENT OF COLORED PEOPLE (NAACP) leader Walter Francis WHITE conducted an investigation into the riot. The NAACP raised money for the defense and, after sentencing, appealed for a writ of habeas corpus on the grounds that the trials had been mob-dominated and unfair.

In 1921 the NAACP succeeded in having six convictions reversed, but the Arkansas Supreme Court upheld six death penalty convictions. When a federal district court refused to review the sentences, the NAACP hired the distinguished white attorney Moorefield Storey, who appealed to the U.S. Supreme Court. In 1923 the Court ruled 7 to 2 in *Moore v. Dempsey* that mob-dominated state trials violated federal due-process guarantees. The Court overturned the death penalty convictions. In 1923 the governor of Arkansas commuted all the sentences to short terms, and by January 1925 the last prisoners had been released. The decision by the Court was the first important case in which the federal judiciary intervened to curtail the racial biases of "southern justice."

REFERENCE

CORTNER, RICHARD C. *A Mob Intent on Death: The NAACP and the Arkansas Riot Cases.* Middletown, Conn., 1988.

GREG ROBINSON

Elaw, Zilpha (c. 1790–c. 1845), preacher. Zilpha Elaw was a Methodist preacher who wrote a moving autobiography, which remains the only known source of information about her life. She was born in Pennsylvania around 1790 to free parents and grew up in the area near Philadelphia. (Because she only referred to herself by her married name, Elaw, in her *Memoirs,* her original family name is unknown.) After her mother's death in 1802 Elaw went to live with the Mitchels, a Quaker family, as a servant. Distressed about their lack of outward religious expression, she underwent a conversion experience at age fourteen in which, while she milked a cow, Christ appeared to her. She felt this to be a genuine experience because even the cow seemed to sense the vision. She later joined the Methodist Episcopal Church.

Upon leaving the Mitchels in 1808, Elaw continued to practice Methodism. In 1810 she married Joseph Elaw, a garment worker. About two years later she had a daughter. Although she tried to respect her husband's wishes, his lack of piety led to conflicts. He sought to curtail her religious activities and tried to induce her to go to a ballroom in Philadelphia, which she thought sinful. Despite these obstacles, in 1817 she went to a camp meeting. Here she found spiritual companionship with other women and African Americans as pious as she. As time went on, Elaw regularly felt God's presence in her life: she often had visions of angels giving her advice. At one point when she was very ill, Elaw had a vision of a spirit who told her to preach. She hesitated until she attended another camp meeting, when she was moved to preach. Although some of the white clergy encouraged her, the reaction of the black members of her church to the exhorting was less than enthusiastic. A congregation nevertheless grew up around her in Burlington, N.J. Elaw was forced to give up preaching when her husband died in 1823. At first she secured domestic positions for herself and her daughter, but the work proved harmful to her health. She then founded a school for black children in Burlington with the help of Quaker donations.

In 1828, feeling as if she were ignoring the will of God, Elaw resumed preaching. Without denominational or congregational support, she journeyed to the slave states, impressing a widely diverse group of white and black Southerners with her preaching abilities, despite the dangers accompanying her travels as a black woman. After her tour of the South she continued to preach in the Northeast until she responded to a call to preach in England. From 1840 to 1845, Elaw delivered over a thousand sermons in central England. In 1845 Elaw began to make plans to return to the United States. However, since her autobiography breaks off at this point, we have no further information about Elaw's life. Nevertheless, her *Memoirs* remain an exceptional document of African-American women's role in shaping American religion, particularly African-American Christianity.

REFERENCES

ADAMS, HENRY GARDINER, ed. *God's Image in Ebony.* London, 1854.

ANDREWS, WILLIAM L. *Sisters of the Spirit: Three Black Women's Autobiographies of the Nineteenth Century.* Bloomington, Ind., 1986.

BRAXTON, JOANNE M. *Black Women Writing Autobiography: A Tradition Within a Tradition.* Philadelphia, 1989.

ALLISON X. MILLER

Elder, Lonne, III (December 26, 1931–), playwright. Lonne Elder III was born in Americus, Ga. His father, Lonne Elder II, died when Lonne was twelve; his mother, Quincy Elder, was killed in a car accident that same year. He was sent to live with an aunt and uncle in Jersey City, N.J. His uncle ran numbers, and Lonne assisted by carrying the slips.

Elder's formal education after high school was limited. He took classes at the New Jersey State Teachers College, the New School for Social Research, and the Jefferson School (New York City), where he moved when he was nineteen, and he later attended Yale School of Drama (1965–1967). Following two years in the Army (1952–1954), Elder joined the Harlem Writers Guild where the poet Robert HAYDEN encouraged him to commit himself to writing, and Douglas Turner WARD first interested him in the theater.

Elder worked at several jobs in the 1950s and '60s and did some acting: he appeared as Bobo in *Raisin in the Sun* on Broadway and in the national touring company. For the most part, however, Elder concentrated on playwriting. His major work, *Ceremonies in Dark Old Men*, which explored the effects of racism on a Harlem family, premiered in 1965 at Wagner College (Staten Island, N.Y.). A revised version was produced by the Negro Ensemble Company in 1969. It received the Outer Critics Circle and Drama Desk awards for Best Play.

In 1970, Elder moved to Hollywood. His 1972 screenplay for *Sounder* was nominated for an Academy award. Other screenplays include *Melinda* (1972) and *Bustin' Loose* (1981). A television miniseries based on the life of Harriet Tubman, *A Woman Called Moses*, was produced in 1978. Since then, he has devoted himself to producing and writing for television and film.

METZGER, LINDA, ed. *Black Writers. A Selection of Sketches from Contemporary Writers.* Detroit, 1989.

MICHAEL PALLER

Elder, Robert Lee (July 14, 1934–), professional golfer. Born in Dallas, Lee Elder grew up in Texas and Los Angeles. He learned to play GOLF while caddying in country clubs in San Bernadino County in California. After serving in the U.S. Army from 1959 to 1960, Elder joined the African-American United Golf Association Tour in 1961. Elder was the winner of the UGA National Professional title in 1963, 1964, 1966, and 1967. In 1967, Elder raised $6,500 and qualified for the Professional Golfers' Association of America (PGA) Tour, becoming the second African American to play on the regular PGA Tour. Elder performed well during his first year on the tour and in 1968, he faced Jack Nicklaus in a nationally televised five-hole sudden death at the American Golf Classic at the Firestone Country Club in Akron, Ohio. Elder lost. In 1971, he became the first African American invited to play in the South African PGA Open. While in Africa, he won the Nigerian Open. By finishing first at the 1974 PGA Monsanto Open, Elder won a spot in the Masters tournament at Augusta, Ga., in 1975. He was the first African American to do so.

Elder won the 1976 PGA Houston Open, the 1978 PGA Greater Milwaukee Open, and the 1978 Westchester Classic. In 1979, he became the first African-American Ryder Cup team member. During his final year on the PGA Tour in 1984, Elder passed the $1 million career-earning mark. At fifty, Elder began golfing on the Senior Tour, where he had even greater success than he did on the PGA Tour, averaging $300,000 during each of his first three years as a senior. In November 1987, after playing in the Gus Machado Classic in Florida, Elder suffered a severe heart attack. He recovered and the following year won the Machado tournament. In 1994, Elder continued as a regular player on the Senior PGA Tour, along with two other African-American golfers, Jim Dent and Charlie SIFFORD.

REFERENCES

ASHE, ARTHUR R., JR. *A Hard Road to Glory: A History of the African-American Athlete Since 1946.* New York, 1988.

GILDEA, WILLIAM. "Elder Making His Second Shot Stronger and Wiser." *Washington Post,* November 24, 1988, Sec. 3, p. 1.

WALTER FRIEDMAN

Elders, M. Joycelyn Jones (August 13, 1933–), U.S. Surgeon General. Born in Schaal, Ark., Joycelyn Jones was the eldest daughter of Haller and Curtis Jones. She attended Philander Smith College in Little Rock, Ark., where she received her B.A. in 1952. Wishing to become a doctor, she joined the U.S. Army and trained in physical therapy at the Brooke Army Medical Center at Fort Sam Houston, Texas. In 1956 she left the Army and enrolled at the University of Arkansas Medical School, one of the first African Americans to attend, and received her M.D. degree in 1960, the same year she married Oliver Elders. Joycelyn Elders did an internship in pediatrics at the University of Minnesota, then returned to the University of Arkansas in 1961 for her residency period. Elders was ultimately named chief resident, and also received an M.S. in biochemistry in 1967. In 1971 Elders was hired by the University of Arkansas Medical School as an assistant professor in pediatrics, and five years later was named a full professor. Over the succeeding years, she published 138 articles, mostly on child growth problems and diabetes.

In 1987, Arkansas Gov. Bill Clinton named Elders as the Arkansas Health Commissioner. Elders's ad-

Joycelyn Elders as Surgeon General addresses a substance abuse symposium in Washington D.C., September 7, 1993. Elders supports the idea of educating schoolchildren about substance abuse as early as kindergarten. (AP/Wide World Photos)

vocacy of making birth control information and condoms available in schools as ways of fighting teenage pregnancy and AIDS caused a storm of controversy. Conservative critics decried her supposedly permissive attitudes toward sex, and her implementation of a kindergarten-to-college health education program that included sex education as well as the usual information about hygiene, substance abuse, and other matters.

In 1993, Clinton, by then president of the United States, appointed Elders U.S. surgeon general. Despite conservative opposition in Congress over her advocacy of abortion rights and sex education, she was confirmed, and was sworn in on September 10, 1993. During Elders's first year as surgeon general, she faced continued opposition by conservatives to her advocacy of condom distribution and sex education in schools and stirred debate through several controversial stands, such as her support of the medical and compassionate use of marijuana, her warnings to parents against purchasing toy guns for children, and most notably her proposal that the question of legalizing drugs in order to "markedly reduce" the nationwide crime rate be studied. Her supporters claimed that Elders was simply being used as a target by opponents of the administration, and her courageous, forthright style made her a hero to thousands of African Americans and whites throughout the United States. In the wake of continuing controversy, however, President Clinton asked for her resignation; she left the surgeon general's office on December 30, 1994.

REFERENCES

BARNES, STEVE. "The Crusade of Dr. Elders." *New York Times Magazine* (October 15, 1989): 38–41.
ROSELLINI, LYNN. "The Prescriptions of Dr. Yes." *U.S. News and World Report* (July 26, 1993): 60–61.

GREG ROBINSON

Eldridge, Roy David (January 29, 1911– February 26, 1989), jazz trumpeter. Providing a direct link from Louis ARMSTRONG to Dizzy GILLESPIE in the lineage of jazz trumpet playing, Roy Eldridge's melodic style and technical facility influenced all those who followed him. Born in Pittsburgh, he received his first instruction on the trumpet from his older brother Joe, and together they played around the city with small groups. When he was sixteen he toured with a carnival and with other bands throughout the Midwest, then returned home to Pittsburgh for further study. In the early 1930s he moved to New York, where he played with Cecil Scott, Elmer

Snowden, Charles Johnson, and others. It was in the Teddy Hill band that Eldridge won recognition, becoming widely regarded as one of the outstanding soloists of his time. He made his first recording under his own name in 1936, and he joined the Fletcher HENDERSON band soon after, staying with the group until 1938.

Eldridge became one of the first black musicians to work in white orchestras when he played with Gene Krupa in the early 1940s and Artie Shaw in the mid-1940s. Although this was a landmark development, the experience proved difficult. He often had to accept second-class accommodations, and was confronted with so much racism he ultimately decided never to play in a white band again. During his tenure with Krupa, Eldridge recorded outstanding solos on pieces such as "Rockin' Chair," and his performances with singer Anita O'Day, especially "Let Me Off Uptown" (1941), became popular. In 1948, he started a long association with Norman Granz and the Jazz at the Philharmonic series, which lasted until the late 1950s.

Eldridge's style grew out of his love for the sound of the saxophone. He was a gifted melodic player, but could also perform with great power and technical prowess. He tried at one time to play like the bop trumpet players of the 1940s, but he was never able to make the transition from swing to bop. By the late '40s, his playing and singing were considered passé. From the 1950s to 1980, Eldridge performed and recorded with such notable jazz musicians as Benny CARTER, Johnny HODGES, Ella FITZGERALD, and Coleman HAWKINS.

REFERENCES

EVENSMO, J. *The Trumpet of Roy Eldridge 1929–1944.* Hosle, Norway, 1979.
GIDDINS, GARY. "The Excitable Roy Eldridge." In *Rhythm-a-ning.* New York, 1981, p. 68.

WILLIAM S. COLE

Ellington, Edward Kennedy "Duke" (April 29, 1899–May 24, 1974), composer, band leader, jazz pianist. One of the supreme composers of the twentieth century, Edward Kennedy Ellington was born into a comfortable middle class family in Washington, D.C. The son of a butler, Ellington received the nickname "Duke" as a child because of the care and pride he took in his attire. As he grew older, his aristocratic bearing and sartorial elegance made the nickname stick. Although he took piano lessons starting in 1906, he was also a talented painter, and before he finished high school he was offered an NAACP-sponsored painting scholarship for college. By this time, however, his interests were again turning toward music, especially RAGTIME and stride piano. By 1918, when Ellington married Edna Thompson, he was leading a band that played popular tunes in a ragtime style at white "society" events. To support his wife and son, Mercer, who was born in 1919, Ellington also worked as a sign painter.

In 1923, Ellington, encouraged by pianist Fats WALLER, moved to New York as pianist and arranger of the Washingtonians. When the leader of the en-

Duke Ellington Band, on RKO lot, Culver City, Calif., 1930. (Frank Driggs Collection)

semble, Elmer Snowden, left in 1924, Ellington took over and led the band in what were his first appearances on record. The Washingtonians had extensive stays at the Club Hollywood, later called the Kentucky Club, from 1924 to 1927. In this formative period, Ellington's key influence was trumpeter Bubber MILEY, whose guttural, plunger-muted style added a robust, blues-tinged element to Ellington's previously genteel compositions and arrangements. Miley's growling, mournful solos inspired Ellington's most important compositions in the 1920s, including "East St. Louis Toodle-O" (1926), "Black and Tan Fantasy" (1927), and "The Mooche" (1928). Another important composition from this period, "Creole Love Call" (1927), features a wordless obbligato by vocalist Adelaide Hall.

On December 4, 1927, Ellington's band debuted at Harlem's COTTON CLUB, an all-white nightclub. The engagement lasted on and off for four years, and gave Ellington a national radio audience, as well as the chance to accompany a variety of chorus and specialty dance numbers and vocalists, often portraying "primitive" and "exotic" aspects of African-American culture. It was in that environment that he perfected the style, marked by energetic climaxes and haunting sonorities, that became known as his "jungle music."

The Cotton Club engagement made Ellington one of the best-known musicians in jazz, famed not only for his eminently danceable tunes, but also for compositions that attracted the attention of the classical music world. During the 1930s the orchestra toured the U.S. extensively, and made trips to Europe in 1933 and 1939. Ellington's 1930s recordings, which achieved huge success among both white and black audiences, include "Ring Dem Bells" (1930), "Mood Indigo" (1930), "Rockin' in Rhythm" (1931), "It Don't Mean a Thing If It Ain't Got That Swing" (1932), "Sophisticated Lady" (1932), "Daybreak Express" (1933), "Solitude" (1934), "In a Sentimental Mood" (1935), trombonist Juan TIZOL's "Caravan" (1937), "I Let a Song Go out of My Heart" (1938), and "Prelude to a Kiss" (1938). Ellington's early 1940s band is often considered the best he ever led. Bolstered by tenor saxophonist Ben WEBSTER, bassist Jimmy BLANTON, and Ellington's assistant, composer and arranger Billy STRAYHORN, the orchestra recorded a number of masterpieces, including "Ko-Ko" (1940), "Concerto for Cootie" (1940), "In a Mellotone" (1940), "Cotton Tail" (1940), "Perdido" (1942), and "C-Jam Blues" (1942), as well as Strayhorn's "Chelsea Bridge" (1941) and "Take the A Train" (1941). Ellington also recorded in groups led by clarinetist Barney BIGARD, trumpeters Cootie WILLIAMS and Rex STEWART, and saxophonist Johnny HODGES.

In the 1940s Ellington became increasingly interested in extended composition. Though he was the greatest master of the four-minute jazz composition, he chafed against the limitations of the length of a 78-rpm record side. As early as 1934 he wrote the score for the short film Symphony in Black, and the next year recorded Reminiscing in Tempo, a contemplative work taking up four sides. His greatest extended composition was the fifty-minute Black, Brown and Beige, which premiered at Carnegie Hall on January 23, 1943. This work, which included the hymnlike "Come Sunday" passage, depicted African Americans at work and at prayer, with vignettes on aspects of history from emancipation to the development of Harlem as a black community. Other extended works from this period include New World-a-Comin' (1943), The Liberian Suite (1947), and The Tattooed Bride (1948). Ellington continued to issue shorter recordings, but there were fewer memorable short compositions after the mid-1940s, though "The Clothed Woman" (1947) and "Satin Doll" (1953) were notable exceptions. In addition to composing and conducting, Ellington was an excellent pianist in the Harlem stride tradition, and he made memorable duets with bassist Jimmy Blanton in 1940.

During the bebop era of the late 1940s and early '50s, Ellington's band declined in influence. However, their performance at the 1956 Newport Jazz Festival, featuring saxophonist Paul Gonsalves's electrifying solo on "Diminuendo and Crescendo in Blue," reaffirmed their reputation, and earned Ellington a cover article in Time magazine. Ellington thereafter took the orchestra to Europe, Japan, the Middle East, India, South America, and Africa. The orchestra also made albums with Louis Armstrong, Coleman Hawkins, Count Basie, Ella Fitzgerald, and John Coltrane, and as a member of a trio Ellington recorded with Max Roach and Charles Mingus. Among his many later extended compositions are Harlem (1951), A Drum Is a Woman (1956), Such Sweet Thunder (1957), The Queen's Suite (1959), The Far East Suite (1967), and Afro-Eurasian Eclipse (1971). Ellington also composed film scores for Anatomy of a Murder (1959) and the Oscar-nominated Paris Blues (1961). He composed music for ballets by choreographer Alvin AILEY, The River (1970) and Les Trois rois noirs, including a section dedicated to the Rev. Dr. Martin Luther King, Jr., composed in Ellington's final years and premiered in 1976. In his last decade, Ellington also wrote religious music for three events he called "Sacred Concerts" (1965, 1968, 1973), vast productions that evoked his strong sense of spirituality through gospel and choral music, dancing, and thankful hymns.

Starting with the 1943 Black, Brown and Beige, many of Ellington's extended works were tributes to his African-American heritage, and demonstrations of his pride in the accomplishments of African Americans. His many shorter depictions of Harlem range from the elegiac "Drop Me Off in Harlem" (1933) to the boisterous "Harlem Airshaft" (1940). Perhaps his most personal tributes are his two musicals, *Jump for Joy* (including "I Got It Bad and That Ain't Good," 1942), and *My People* (1963), both dealing with the theme of integration. The latter includes the song "King Fit the Battle of Alabam."

Ellington's music was collaborative. Many of his works were written by band members, and many more were written collectively, by synthesizing and expanding riffs and motifs into unified compositions. Ellington's compositions were almost always written with a particular band member's style and ability in mind, and his collaborator Strayhorn remarked that while Ellington played piano, his real instrument was his orchestra. Ellington was an exceptionally original musical thinker, whose orchestral sound was marked by instrumental doublings on reeds, ingenious combinations of instruments, and the carefully crafted use of a variety of muted brasses. The diversity of the band was remarkable, containing an extraordinary variety of masterful and distinctive soloists, ranging from the smooth, sensuous improvisations of saxophonist Johnny Hodges to the gutbucket sounds of trumpeter Cootie Williams and trombonist "Tricky Sam" NANTON.

In the ever-changing world of the big bands, the Ellington orchestra's core roster seldom changed. The most important of his band members, with their tenures parenthetically noted, include trumpeters William "Cat" ANDERSON (1944–1947, 1950–1959, 1961–1971), Bubber Miley (1924–1929), Rex Stewart (1934–1945), Arthur Whetsol (1923–1924, 1928–1936), and Cootie Williams (1929–1940, 1962–1973); violinist and trumpeter Ray NANCE (1940–1963); trombonists Lawrence BROWN (1932–1951, 1960–1970), Joe "Tricky Sam" Nanton (1926–1946), and Juan Tizol (1929–1944, 1951–1953); alto saxophonists Otto Hardwick (1923–1928, 1932–1946), Johnny Hodges (1928–1951, 1955–1970), and Russell Procope (1946–1974); tenor saxophonists Paul Gonsalves (1950–1970, 1972–1974) and Ben Webster (1940–1943, 1948–1949); baritone saxophonist Harry CARNEY (1927–1974); clarinetists Barney Bigard (1927–1942) and Jimmy Hamilton (1943–1968); vocalists Ivy ANDERSON (1931–1942) and Al Hibbler (1943–1951); drummer Sonny GREER (1923–1951); bassist Jimmy Blanton (1939–1941); and composer and arranger Billy Strayhorn (1939–1967).

During his lifetime Ellington was celebrated as a commanding figure in American culture. He cherished the many awards and honorary degrees he earned, including the Spingarn Medal (1959) and eleven Grammy Awards. Ellington remained gracious, though many were outraged by the refusal of a 1965 Pulitzer Prize committee, firmly opposed to recognizing "popular" music, to give him a special award for composition. In 1970 Ellington was awarded the Presidential Medal of Freedom by President Nixon and was feted with a seventieth-birthday celebration at the White House. He died of cancer on May 24, 1974.

Since Ellington's death, his orchestra has been led by his son, Mercer, himself a trumpeter and composer of note. In 1986, Duke Ellington became the first African-American jazz musician to appear on a U. S. postage stamp. The 1980s and '90s have witnessed a growing interest in Ellington among scholars who are increasingly interested in the extended compositions, and among jazz fans gaining access to a wealth of previously unreleased recordings. Such attention inevitably confirms Ellington's status not only as the greatest composer and bandleader in jazz, but as a figure unique in the history of twentieth-century music.

REFERENCES

COLLIER, JAMES LINCOLN. *Duke Ellington*. New York, 1987.
DANCE, STANLEY. *The World of Duke Ellington*. New York, 1970.
ELLINGTON, DUKE. *Music Is My Mistress*. New York, 1973.
SCHULLER, GUNTHER. *Early Jazz*. New York, 1968.
———. *The Swing Era*. New York, 1988.
TUCKER, MARK. *Ellington: The Early Years*. Chicago, 1991.
———, ed. *The Duke Ellington Reader*. New York, 1993.
WILLIAMS, MARTIN. *The Jazz Tradition*. New York, 1983.

MARTIN WILLIAMS

Elliott, Robert Brown (c. 1842–August 9, 1884), politician. Robert Brown Elliott rose to power as an African-American Radical Republican in South Carolina and the nation during RECONSTRUCTION. Elliott was not a native of South Carolina, and his origins remain mysterious. Though he himself claimed to have been born in Boston, no documented trace of his birth or education has been found, although he was clearly well educated. His most recent biographer argues that he was born and raised in Liverpool, England, and arrived in Boston on a steamer, probably after the Civil War. There is evidence he was working as a typesetter in Boston in 1867.

In 1867, Elliott appeared on the South Carolina scene as associate editor of Charleston's *South Carolina Leader,* a Republican newspaper edited by fellow African-American politician Richard CAIN. The next year, after becoming one of the first three African Americans admitted to the state bar, he set up a law practice. Later in 1868, Elliott served as one of seventy-one African-American delegates to the South Carolina Constitutional Convention, was nominated for lieutenant governor, served as the only African American on the Barnwell County Board of Commissioners, and was elected to the state House of Representatives. Elliott chaired the powerful Committee on Railroads, and was even charged with organizing the state militia.

A controversial and outspoken politician, Elliott became known as a "racial militant" for his support of antidiscrimination laws, his opposition to literacy tests and poll taxes for voting, and his advocacy of free health care, legal assistance to the poor, and government regulation of industry.

In 1870, benefiting from the 60 percent black majority in South Carolina, Elliott won election to the U.S. Congress over a white lawyer. He was defeated in an election for the U.S. Senate in 1872, but was easily reelected to his House seat. In Congress, Elliott spoke out against the KU KLUX KLAN, and gave a speech defending Charles Sumner's Civil Rights Bill.

Elliott resigned his seat in 1874 to return to South Carolina and fight political corruption. Between 1874 and 1876 he served as speaker of the state house of representatives. In 1876, he ran for the office of state attorney general. He was defeated, and under the "redeemed" government was unable to find employment. He then practiced law and was appointed Inspector of Customs in Charleston. In 1881, Elliott was transferred to New Orleans, where he was fired a year later. He died of malarial fever, unknown and bankrupt, in 1884.

REFERENCES

LAMSON, PEGGY. *The Glorious Failure: Black Congressman Robert Brown Elliott and the Reconstruction in South Carolina.* New York, 1973.

RABINOWITZ, HOWARD. "Three Reconstruction Leaders: Blanche K. Bruce, Robert Brown Elliott, and Holland Thompson." In Leon Litwack and August Meier, eds. *Black Leaders of the Nineteenth Century.* Chicago, 1988.

MARGARET D. JACOBS

Ellison, Ralph (March 1, 1914–April 16, 1994), writer. Ralph Ellison was born to Lewis and Ida Millsap Ellison in Oklahoma City, Okla., a frontier town with a rich vernacular culture. As a child, he worked at Randolph's Pharmacy, where he heard animal tales and ghost stories. The local all-black high school provided rigorous training in music, and the Aldridge Theatre featured many of the leading blues, ragtime, and jazz musicians of the day. Ellison played in high school jazz bands and in 1933 enrolled as a music major at Tuskegee Institute, Ala. He involved himself in the other arts as well and on his own discovered T. S. Eliot's *Waste Land,* where he found a range of allusions "as mixed and varied as that of Louis Armstrong."

At the end of his third college year, Ellison went to New York to earn money. He never returned to Tuskegee. He met Langston HUGHES, whose poetry he had read in high school, and Richard WRIGHT, who urged him to write for *New Challenge,* which Wright was editing. Ellison wrote a review for the magazine in 1937, his first published work. In 1938 he took a Works Progress Administration job with the New York Writer's Project and worked at night on his own fiction. He read Hemingway to learn style.

Ellison wrote book reviews for the radical periodicals *Direction, Negro Quarterly,* and *New Masses,* which in 1940 printed at least one review by him every month. His first short stories were realistic in the manner of Richard Wright and presented fairly explicit political solutions to the dilemmas of Jim Crow. By 1940 he had begun to find his own direction with a series of stories in the Huck Finn/Tom Sawyer mold—tales of black youngsters who were

Novelist and essayist Ralph Ellison in 1966, giving testimony on urban problems before a U.S. Senate subcommittee. (AP/Wide World Photos)

not so much victims as playmakers in a land of possibility. "Flying Home" (1944) offers wise old Jefferson as a storyteller whose verbal art helps lessen the greenhorn Todd's isolation and teaches him a healthier attitude toward the divided world he must confront. That story set the stage for Ellison's monumental 1952 novel *Invisible Man,* which received the National Book Award the following year.

Set between 1930 and 1950, *Invisible Man* tells of the development of an ambitious young black man from the South, a naïf who goes to college and then to New York in search of advancement. At first Invisible Man, unnamed throughout the novel, wants to walk the narrow way of Booker T. Washington, whose words he speaks at his high school graduation as well as at a smoker for the town's leading white male citizens. At the smoker he is required to fight blindfolded in a free-for-all against the other black youths. In this key chapter, all the boys are turned blindly against one another in a danger-filled ritual staged for the amusement of their white patrons. That night the young man dreams of his grandfather, the novel's cryptic ancestor–wise man, who presents him with "an engraved document" that seems an ironic comment on his high school diploma and its costs. "Read it," the old man tells him. " 'To Whom It May Concern,' I intoned. 'Keep This Nigger Boy Running.' "

Whether a student in the southern college or a spokesman in New York for the radical political movement called the Brotherhood (modeled on the Communist party of the 1930s or some other American political organization that exploited blacks and then sold them out), Invisible Man is kept running. Quintessentially American in his confusion about who he is, he mad-dashes from scene to scene, letting others tell him what his experience means, who he is, what his name is. And he is not only blind, he is invisible—he is racially stereotyped and otherwise denied his individuality. "I am invisible," he discovers, "simply because people refuse to see me. Like the bodiless heads you see sometimes in circus sideshows, it is as though I have been surrounded by mirrors of hard, distorting glass. When they approach me they see only my surroundings, themselves, or figments of their imagination—indeed, everything and anything except me."

After encounters with remarkable adults—some wisely parental, some insane but brilliant, some sly con men—he learns to accept with equipoise the full ambiguity of his history and to see the world by his own lights. "It took me a long time," he says, "and much painful boomeranging of my expectations to achieve a realization everyone else appears to have been born with: That I am nobody but myself. But first I had to discover that I am an invisible man!" He

had to find out that very few people would bother to understand his real motives and values; perhaps not all of these mysteries were knowable, even by himself. And yet in this novel of education and epiphany, Invisible Man decides he can nonetheless remain hopeful: "I was my experiences and my experiences were me," he says. "And no blind men, no matter how powerful they became, even if they conquered the world, could take that, or change one single itch, taunt, laugh, cry, scar, ache, rage or pain of it."

Rich in historical and literary allusions—from Columbus to World War II, from Oedipus and Br'er Rabbit to T. S. Eliot and Richard Wright—*Invisible Man* stands both as a novel about the history of the novel and as a meditation on the history of the United States. In doing so, it presents a metaphor for black American life in the twentieth century that transcends its particular focus. It names not only the modern American but the citizen of the contemporary world as tragicomically centerless (but somehow surviving and getting smarter): *Homo invisibilis.* It is Ellison's masterwork.

Shadow and Act (1964) and *Going to the Territory* (1987) are collections of Ellison's nonfiction prose. With these books he established himself as a preeminent man of letters—one whose driving purpose was to define African-American life and culture with precision and affirmation. The essays on African-American music are insider's reports that reflect Ellison's deep experience and long memory. Whether discussing literature, music, painting, psychology, or history, Ellison places strong emphases on vernacular culture—its art, rituals, and meanings—and on the power of the visionary individual, particularly the artist, to prevail. These books offer a strong challenge to social scientists and historians to consider African-American life in terms not just of its ills and pathologies but of its tested capacity to reinvent itself and to influence the nation and the world.

REFERENCES

BENSTON, KIMBERLY, ed. *Speaking for You: The Vision of Ralph Ellison.* Washington, D.C., 1985.
O'MEALLY, ROBERT G. *The Craft of Ralph Ellison.* Cambridge, Mass., 1980.

ROBERT G. O'MEALLY

Emancipation. Few events in American history can match the drama and the social significance of black emancipation in the midst of the CIVIL WAR. Since the early seventeenth century, when African-born slaves were first brought ashore in Virginia (*see* SLAVERY), through the long development of the

South's plantation economy and its dependence upon slave labor, emancipation had been the dream of African-American people. Beyond the age of the American Revolution, when the northern states freed their relatively small numbers of slaves, and into the antebellum era of abolitionism, the writing of fugitive slave narratives, and increasing free black community development in the North, emancipation became a matter of political and religious expectation. To be a black abolitionist, a fugitive slave desperately seeking his or her way through the mysterious realities of the Underground Railroad, or one of the millions of slaves cunningly surviving on southern cotton plantations was to be an actor in this long and agonizing drama. The agony and the hope embedded in the story of emancipation is what black poet Francis Ellen Watkins tried to capture in a simple verse written in the wake of John Brown's execution in 1859 and only a little over a year before the outbreak of the Civil War:

> Make me a grave where'er you will,
> In a lowly plain, or a lofty hill,
> Make it among earth's humblest graves,
> But not in a land where men are slaves.

Soon, by the forces of total war, which in turn opened opportunities for slaves to seize their own freedom, emancipation became reality in America. Black freedom became the central event of nineteenth-century African-American history and, along with the preservation of the Union, the central result of the Civil War.

On Emancipation day, January 1, 1863 (when Abraham Lincoln's Emancipation Proclamation was to go into effect), "jubilee meetings" occurred all over black America. At Tremont Temple in Boston, a huge gathering of blacks and whites met from morning until night, awaiting the final news that Lincoln had signed the fateful document. Genuine concern still existed that something might go awry; the preliminary proclamation had been issued in September 1862, a mixture of what appeared to be military necessity and a desire to give the war a new moral purpose. Numerous luminaries from throughout antebellum free black leadership spoke during the day; the attorney John ROCK, the minister and former slave John Sella MARTIN, the orator and women's suffragist Anna Dickinson, author William Wells BROWN, and Boston's William Cooper NELL as presiding officer were among them. The most prominent of all black voices, Frederick DOUGLASS, gave a concluding speech during the afternoon session punctuated by many cries of "Amen." In the evening, tension mounted and anxiety gripped the hall, as no news had arrived from Washington. Douglass and Brown provided more oratory to try to quell the changing mood of doubt. Then a runner arrived from the telegraph office with the news: "It is coming!" he shouted, "it is on the wires!" An attempt was made to read the text of the Emancipation Proclamation, but great jubilation engulfed the crowd. Unrestrained shouting and singing ensued. Douglass gained the throng's attention and led them in a chorus of his favorite hymn, "Blow Ye the Trumpet, Blow." Next an old black preacher named Rue led the group in "Sound the loud timbel o'er Egypt's dark sea, Jehovah has triumphed, his people are free!" The celebration lasted until midnight, when the crowd reassembled at pastor Leonard A. GRIMES's Twelfth Baptist Church—an institution renowned among black Bostonians for its role in helping many fugitive slaves move along the road to liberty—to continue celebrating.

From Massachusetts to Ohio and Michigan, and in many Union-occupied places in the South where ex-slaves were now entering the Yankee army or beginning their first year as free people, such celebrations occurred. Full of praise songs, these celebrations demonstrated that whatever the fine print of the proclamation might say, black folks across the land knew that they had lived to see a new day, a transforming moment in their history. At a large "contraband camp" (center for refugee ex-slaves) in Washington, D.C., some six hundred black men, women, and children gathered at the superintendent's headquarters on New Year's Eve and sang through most of the night. In chorus after chorus of "Go Down, Moses" they announced the magnitude of their painful but beautiful exodus. One newly supplied verse concluded with "Go down, Abraham, away down in Dixie's land, tell Jeff Davis to let my people go!" Many years after the Tremont Temple celebration in Boston, Douglass may have best captured the meaning of Emancipation day for his people: "It was not logic, but the trump of jubilee, which everybody wanted to hear. We were waiting and listening as for a bolt from the sky, which should rend the fetters of four millions of slaves; we were watching as it were, by the dim light of stars, for the dawn of a new day; we were longing for the answer to the agonizing prayers of centuries. Remembering those in bonds as bound with them, we wanted to join in the shout for freedom, and in the anthem of the redeemed." For blacks the cruel and apocalyptic war finally had a holy cause.

The emancipation policy of the Union government evolved with much less certitude than the music and poetry of jubilee day might imply. During the first year of the war, the Union military forces operated on an official policy of exclusion ("denial of asylum") to escaped slaves. The war was to restore the Union, but not to uproot slavery. But events overtook such

(Top) Thomas Nast's 1865 engraving "Emancipation" conveyed the hope of many Republicans that with the end of the Civil War, slavery's evil legacy would be overturned. (Bottom) The end of the Civil War and the emancipation of the slaves were annually commemorated by African Americans. This gathering took place in Washington, D.C., on April 19, 1866. (Prints and Photographs Division, Library of Congress)

a policy. Floods of fugitive slaves began to enter Union lines in Virginia, in Tennessee, and along the southern coasts. Thousands were eventually employed as military laborers, servants, camp hands, and even spies. Early in the war, at Fortress Monroe, Va., in May 1861, the ambitious politician-general Benjamin F. Butler declared the slaves who entered his lines "contraband of war." The idea of slaves as confiscated enemy property eventually caught on. In early August 1861, striking a balance between legality and military necessity, the federal Congress passed the First Confiscation Act, allowing for the seizure of all Confederate property used to aid the war effort. Although not yet technically freed by this law, the slaves of rebel masters came under its purview and an inexorable process toward black freedom took root. Into 1862 the official stance of the Union armies toward slaves was a conflicted one: exclusion where the slaveholders were deemed "loyal," and employment as contrabands where the masters were judged "disloyal." Such an unworkable policy caused considerable dissension in the Union ranks, especially between abolitionist and proslavery officers. But wherever Union forces gained ground in the South, the institution of slavery began to crumble.

By the spring and summer of 1862, Congress took the lead on the issue of emancipation policy. In April it abolished slavery in the District of Columbia, and a large sum of money was allocated for the possible colonization of freed blacks abroad. The Lincoln administration, indeed, pursued a variety of schemes for Central American and Caribbean colonization during the first three years of the war. The sheer impracticality of such plans and stiff black resistance notwithstanding, this old idea of black removal from America as the solution to the revolutionary implications of Emancipation died hard within the Lincoln administration and in the mind of the president himself. But Lincoln, as well as many other Americans, would be greatly educated by both the necessity and the larger meanings of Emancipation. A black newspaper in Union-occupied New Orleans declared that "history furnishes no such intensity of determination, on the part of any race, as that exhibited by these people to be free." And Frederick Douglass felt greatly encouraged by an evolving emancipation movement in early 1862, whatever its contradictory motives. "It is really wonderful," he wrote, "how all efforts to evade, postpone, and prevent its coming, have been mocked and defied by the stupendous sweep of events."

In June 1862, Congress abolished slavery in the western territories, a marvelous irony when one remembers the tremendous political crisis over that issue in the decade before the war, as well as the alleged finality of the DRED SCOTT DECISION of 1857. In July,

Congress passed the Second Confiscation Act, which explicitly freed slaves of all persons "in rebellion," and excluded no parts of the slaveholding South. These measures provided a public and legal backdrop for President Lincoln's subsequent Emancipation Proclamation, issued in two parts, maneuvered through a recalcitrant Cabinet, and politically calculated to shape northern morale, prevent foreign intervention (especially that of the British), and keep the remaining four slaveholding border states in the Union. During 1862, Lincoln had secretly maneuvered to persuade Delaware and Kentucky to accept a plan of compensated, gradual Emancipation. But the deeply divided border states bluntly refused such notions. In the preliminary proclamation of September 21, 1862, issued in the aftermath of the bloody battle of Antietam (a Union military success for which Lincoln had desperately waited), the president offered a carrot to the rebellious South: in effect, stop the war, reenter the Union, and slavery would go largely untouched. In his State of the Union address in December, Lincoln dwelled on the idea of gradual, compensated Emancipation as the way to end the war and return a willful South to the Union. None of these offers had any chance of acceptance at this point in what had already become a revolutionary war for ends much larger and higher than most had imagined in 1861.

Lincoln had always considered slavery to be an evil that had to be eliminated in America. It was he who had committed the Republican party in the late 1850s to putting slavery "on a course of ultimate extinction." At the outset of the war, however, he valued saving the Union above all else, including whatever would happen to slavery. But after he signed the document that declared all slaves in the "states of rebellion . . . forever free," Lincoln's historical reputation, as often legendary and mythical as it is factual, became forever tied to his role in the emancipation process. Emancipation did indeed require presidential leadership to commit America to a war to free slaves in the eyes of the world; in Lincoln's remarkable command of moral meaning and politics, he understood that this war had become a crucible in which the entire nation could receive a "new birth of freedom." The president ultimately commanded the armies, every forward step of which from 1863 to 1865 was a liberating step, soon by black soldiers as well. On one level, Emancipation had to be legal and moral, and, like all great matters in American history, it had to be finalized in the Constitution, in the THIRTEENTH AMENDMENT (passed in early 1865). But black freedom was something both given and seized. Many factors made it possible for Lincoln to say by February 1865 that "the central act of my administration, and the greatest event of the nineteenth century," was Emancipation. But none more than the black exodus of self-emancipation when the moment of truth came, the waves of freedpeople who "voted with their feet."

The actual process and timing of Emancipation across the South depended on at least three interrelated circumstances: one, the character of slave society in a given region; two, the course of the war itself; and three, the policies of the Union and Confederate governments. Southern geography, the chronology of the military campaigns, the character of total war with its massive forced movement of people, the personal disposition of slaveholders and Union commanders alike, and the advent of widespread recruitment of black soldiers were all com-

bined factors in determining when, where, and how slaves became free. Thousands of slaves were "hired out" as fortification laborers, teamsters, nurses, and cooks in the Confederate armies, eventually providing many opportunities for escape to Union lines and an uncertain but freer future. Thousands were also "refugeed" to the interior by their owners in order to "protect" them from invading Yankee armies. Many more took to the forests and swamps to hide during the chaos of war, as Union forces swept over the sea islands of the Georgia or South Carolina coast, or the densely populated lower Mississippi Valley region. Many of those slaves eventually returned to their plantations, abandoned by their former masters, and took over agricultural production, sometimes under

In many black communities, the end of slavery was a major holiday. Richmond, Va., the former capital of the Confederacy, was the site of this 1905 parade celebrating the fortieth anniversary of Emancipation. (Prints and Photographs Division, Library of Congress)

the supervision of an old driver, and sometimes by independently planting subsistence crops while the sugar cane rotted.

Many slaves waited and watched for their opportunity of escape, however uncertain their new fate might be. Octave Johnson was a slave on a plantation in St. James Parish, La., who ran away to the woods when the war came. He and a group of thirty, ten of whom were women, remained at large for a year and a half. Johnson's story, as he reported it to the American Freedmen's Inquiry Commission in 1864, provides a remarkable example of the social-military revolution under way across the South. "We were four miles in the rear of the plantation house," said Johnson. His band stole food and borrowed matches and other goods from slaves still on the plantation. "We slept on logs and burned cypress leaves to make a smoke and keep away mosquitoes." When hunted by bloodhounds, Johnson's group took to the deeper swamp. They "killed eight of the bloodhounds; then we jumped into Bayou Faupron; the dogs followed us and the alligators caught six of them; the alligators preferred dog flesh to personal flesh; we escaped and came to Camp Parapet, where I was first employed in the Commissary's office, then as a servant to Col. Hanks; then I joined his regiment." From "working on task" through survival in the bayous, Octave Johnson found his freedom as a corporal in Company C, Fifteenth Regiment, Corps d'Afrique.

For many slaves, the transition from bondage to freedom was not so clear and complete as it was for Octave Johnson. Emancipation was a matter of overt celebration in some places, especially in southern towns and cities, as well as in some slave quarters. But what freedom meant in 1863, how livelihood would change, how the war would progress, how the masters would react (perhaps with wages but perhaps with violent retribution), how freedpeople would find protection in the conquered and chaotic South, how they would meet the rent payments that might now be charged, how a peasant population of agricultural laborers deeply attached to the land might now become owners of the land as so many dreamed, and whether they would achieve citizenship rights were all urgent and unanswered questions during the season of Emancipation. Joy mixed with uncertainty, songs of deliverance with expressions of fear. The actual day on which masters gathered their slaves to announce that they were free was remembered by freedpeople with a wide range of feelings and experience. Some remembered hilarity and dancing, but many remembered it as a sobering, even solemn time. A former South Carolina slave recalled that on his plantation "some were sorry, some hurt, but a few were silent and glad." James Lucas, a former slave of Jefferson Davis in Mississippi, probed

the depths of human nature and ambivalence in his description of the day of liberation: "Dey all had diffe'nt ways o' thinkin' 'bout it. Mos'ly though dey was jus' lak me, dey didn' know jus' zackly what it meant. It was jus' somp'n dat de white folks an' slaves all de time talk 'bout. Dat's all. Folks dat ain' never been free don' rightly know de *feel* of bein' free. Dey don' know de meanin' of it." And a former Virginia slave simply recalled "how wild and upset and *dreadful* everything was in them times."

But in time, confusion gave way to meaning, and the feel of freedom took many forms. For many ex-slaves who followed Union armies freedom meant, initially, life in contraband camps, where black families struggled to survive in the face of great hardship and occasional starvation. But by the end of 1862 and throughout the rest of the war, a string of contraband camps became the first homes in freedom for thousands of ex-slaves. At LaGrange, Bolivar, and Memphis in western Tennessee; at Corinth in northern Mississippi; in "contraband colonies" near New Orleans; at Cairo, Ill.; at Camp Barker in the District of Columbia; on Craney Island near Norfolk, Va.; and eventually in northern Georgia and various other places, the freedpeople forged a new life on government rations and through work on labor crews, and received a modicum of medical care, often provided by "grannies"—black women who employed home remedies from plantation life. For thousands the contraband camps became the initial entry into free labor practices, and a slow but certain embrace of the new sense of dignity, mobility, identity, and education that freedom now meant. Nearly all white Northerners who witnessed or supervised these camps, or who eventually administered private or government work programs on confiscated southern land, organized freedmen's aid societies and schools by the hundreds, or observed weddings and burials, were stunned by the determination of this exodus despite its hardships. In 1863, each superintendent of a contraband camp in the western theater of war was asked to respond to a series of interrogatives about the freedmen streaming into his facilities. To the question of the "motives" of the freedmen, the Corinth superintendent tried to find the range of what he saw: "Can't answer short of 100 pages. Bad treatment—hard times—lack of the comforts of life—prospect of being driven South; the more intelligent because they wished to be free. Generally speak kindly of their masters; none wish to return; many would die first. All delighted with the prospect of freedom, yet all have been kept constantly at some kind of work." All of the superintendents commented on what seemed to them the remarkable "intelligence" and "honesty" of the freedmen. As for their "notions of liberty," the Memphis superintendent answered: "Generally correct. They say they have no rights, nor own anything except as their master permits; but being freed, can make their own money and protect their families." Indeed, these responses demonstrate just what a fundamental revolution Emancipation had become.

Inexorably, Emancipation meant that black families would be both reunited and torn apart. In contraband camps, where women and children greatly outnumbered men, extended families sometimes found and cared for each other. But often, when the thousands of black men across the South entered the Union army they left women and children behind in great hardship, sometimes in sheer destitution, and eventually under new labor arrangements that required rent payments. Louisiana freedwoman Emily Waters wrote to her husband, who was still on duty with the Union army, in July 1865, begging him to get a furlough and "come home and find a place for us to live in." The joy of change mixed with terrible strain. "My children are going to school," she reported, "but I find it very hard to feed them all, and if you cannot come I hope you will send me something to help me get along. . . . Come home as soon as you can, and cherish me as ever." The same Louisiana soldier received a subsequent letter from Alsie Thomas, his sister, reporting that "we are in deep trouble—your wife has left Trepagnia and gone to the city and we don't know where or how she is, we have not heard a word from her in four weeks." The choices and the strains that Emancipation wrought are tenderly exhibited in a letter by John Boston, a Maryland fugitive slave, to his wife, Elizabeth, in January 1862, from Upton Hill, Va. "[I]t is with grate joy I take this time to let you know Whare I am i am now in Safety in the 14th regiment of Brooklyn this Day i can Adres you thank god as a free man I had a little truble in giting away But as the lord led the Children of Isrel to the land of Canon So he led me to a land Whare Fredom Will rain in spite Of earth and hell . . . i am free from al the Slavers Lash." Such were the joys of freedom and the agonies of separation. Boston concluded his letter: "Dear Wife i must Close rest yourself Contented i am free . . . Write my Dear Soon . . . Kiss Daniel For me." The rich sources on the freedmen's experience do not tell us whether Emily Waters ever saw her husband again, or whether the Bostons were reunited. But these letters demonstrate the depth with which freedom was embraced and the human pain through which it was achieved.

The freedpeople especially gave meaning to their freedom by their eagerness for education and land ownership. In the Sea Islands of South Carolina, the PORT ROYAL EXPERIMENT was a large-scale attempt, led by northern philanthropists interested as much in profits as in freedmen's rights, to reorganize cotton production by paying wages to blacks. But amid this combination of abolitionists' good works and capitalist opportunity, thousands of blacks of all ages learned to read. So eager were the freedmen to learn that the teachers from the various freedmen's-aid societies were sometimes overwhelmed. "The Negroes will do anything for us," said one teacher, "if we will only teach them." Land ownership was an equally precious aim of the freedmen, and they claimed it as a right. No one ever stated the labor theory of value more clearly than Virginia freedman Bayley Wyat, in a speech protesting the eviction of blacks from a contraband camp in 1866: "We has a right to the land we are located. For Why? I tell you. Our wives, our children, our husbands, has been sold over and over again to purchase the lands we now locates upon; for that reason we have a divine right to the land. . . . And den didn't we clear the land, and raise de crops ob corn, ob cotton, ob tobacco, ob rice, ob sugar, ob everything?" The redistribution of land and wealth in the South would remain a largely unrealized dream during RECONSTRUCTION, and perhaps its greatest unfinished legacy. But armed with literacy, and an unprecedented politicization, southern blacks accomplished much against great odds in the wake of Emancipation.

By the end of the war in 1865, the massive moving about of the freedpeople became a major factor in Confederate defeat. Thousands of white Union soldiers who witnessed this process of Emancipation became, despite earlier prejudices, avid supporters of the recruitment of black soldiers. And no one understood just what a transformation was under way better than the former slaveholders in the South, who now watched their world collapse around them. In August 1865, white Georgian John Jones described black freedom as the "dark, dissolving, disquieting wave of emancipation." That wave would abate in the turbulent first years of Reconstruction, when the majority of freedmen would resettle on their old places, generally paid wages at first, but eventually working "on shares" (as SHARECROPPING tenant farmers). Reconstruction would bring a political revolution to the South, a great experiment in racial democracy, led by radical Republicans in the federal government and by a new American phenomenon: scores of black politicians. This "disquieting wave" would launch black suffrage, citizenship rights, civil rights, and widespread black officeholding beyond what anyone could have imagined at the outset of the Civil War. That the great achievements in racial democracy of the period 1865–1870 were betrayed or lost by the late nineteenth century does not detract from the significance of such a passage in African-American history. Many of the twentieth-century triumphs in America's never-ending search for racial democracy have their deep roots in the story of Emancipation and its aftermath.

REFERENCES

BERLIN, IRA, et al., eds. *Freedom: A Documentary History of Emancipation, 1861–67.* Series 1, vol. 1, *The Destruction of Slavery.* Series 1, vol. 3, *The Wartime Genesis of Free Labor.* Series 2, *The Black Military Experience.* New York, 1982–1990.

FONER, ERIC. *Nothing but Freedom: Emancipation and Its Legacy.* Baton Rouge, La., 1983.

LITWACK, LEON F. *Been in the Storm So Long: The Aftermath of Slavery.* New York, 1979.

DAVID W. BLIGHT

Emancipation Statutes, Gradual.   *See* Gradual Emancipation Statutes.

Embalmers.   *See* Undertakers, Embalmers, Morticians.

Embry, Wayne (March 26, 1937–), professional basketball player, executive. Wayne Embry was born and raised in Springfield, Ohio. Following his graduation from Tecumseh High School, he enrolled at Miami University in Ohio, where he majored in education, minored in business administration, and played basketball. A 6′8″ center, Embry began a professional basketball career with the Cincinnati Royals in 1958. He later played with the Boston Celtics (1966–1968) and finished his playing career with the Milwaukee Bucks (1968–1969). He was a five-time National Basketball Association (NBA) All-Star.

In 1972 Embry became the first African-American vice president and general manager in the NBA, when he was hired to head the front office of the Milwaukee Bucks. In 1985 he left the Bucks to serve as a vice president and consultant for the Indiana Pacers. The following year, he was named vice president and general manager of basketball operations for the Cleveland Cavaliers and quickly helped the struggling Cavaliers became one of the most successful franchises in the National Basketball Association.

In addition to basketball, Embry has been involved in various business and civic operations. In 1978 he was named president of the Michael Allen Lewis Company and oversaw that company's development into a multimillion-dollar converter and fabricator of materials for the automobile industry. In 1989 he began a six-year term on the board of trustees of the NATIONAL URBAN LEAGUE. For his contributions to the sport of basketball, Embry received the NBA's Schick Life Achievement Award in 1991. He was named the *Sporting News* Executive of the Year in 1992.

REFERENCE

LUPICA, MIKE. "The Wayne and Lenny Show." *Esquire* (June 1989): 61–65.

BENJAMIN K. SCOTT

Emigration.   *See* Immigration; Migration/Population.

Encyclopedia of the Negro, The.   On November 7, 1931, a Conference on the Advisability of Publishing an Encyclopedia of the Negro was held at HOWARD UNIVERSITY. The conference was sponsored by Anson Phelps Stokes, president of the PHELPS-STOKES FUND, which was active in black philanthropy. African-American scholars invited to the conference noted the absence of the two preeminent black historians of the time, W. E. B. DU BOIS and Carter G. WOODSON, and expressed dismay, insisting that these two scholars be invited to the next conference, to be held on January 9, 1932.

Woodson was angered by the presence of whites on the editorial board, especially that of the sociologist Thomas Jesse Jones, who had done his best to hinder the careers of both Du Bois and Woodson. Claiming that his organization, the Association for the Study of Negro Life and History, was putting together its own encyclopedia, Woodson refused to participate in the Phelps-Stokes project.

Du Bois, too, would have preferred an all-black project. He had wanted to produce just such an encyclopedia since 1909, but had not been able to fund it, so he overcame the slight in this instance and attended the second conference. He said in a letter to Woodson, ". . . the enemy has the money and they are going to use it. Our choice, then, is not how the money could be used best from our point of view, but how far without great sacrifice of principle we can keep it from being misused." Du Bois succeeded in having Jones removed from the editorial board and was himself named editor-in-chief. Woodson, however, continued to be hostile to the Phelps-Stokes encyclopedia, writing many acrimonious articles and

Board of Directors and Advisory Board of the *Encyclopedia of the Negro*. (Front row) Otellia Cromwell, Monroe N. Work, Charles H. Wesley, Benjamin Brawley, W. E. B. Du Bois, Eugene Kinckle Jones. (Back row, left to right) W. D. Weatherford, A. A. Schomburg, J. E. Spingarn, Clarence S. Marsh, James Weldon Johnson, Anson Phelps Stokes, W. A. Aery, Charles T. Loram, James H. Dillard, Florence Read, Alain Locke, Mordecai W. Johnson, Waldo G. Leland. (Special Collections and Archives, W. E. B. Du Bois Library, University of Massachusetts-Amherst)

letters regarding the project and Du Bois. No evidence was ever found to show that his own encyclopedia had ever actually been in progress.

Continual in-fighting, along with funding troubles due to the Great Depression, disrupted the project. The only part ever published was the *Preparatory Volume,* which appeared in 1945.

REFERENCES

APTHEKER, HERBERT, ed. *The Correspondence of W. E. B. Du Bois, Volume 1, 1877–1934.* Amherst, Mass. 1973.

MEIER, AUGUST, and ELLIOTT RUDWICK. *Black History and the Historical Profession, 1915–1980.* Urbana, Ill. 1986.

LYDIA MCNEILL

Engineering.   From the early years of the American settlement—in the era of mechanical tinkering—through the computer revolution of the late twentieth century, African Americans have contributed to all of the varied and diverse fields of engineering. Despite the obstacles posed by slavery and by ongoing racial discrimination, the African-American community has participated in the development of such fields as electrical, mechanical, civil, architectural, chemical, industrial/management, and computer engineering.

Although African-American slaves were not allowed to hold patents or develop products under their own names, several free blacks were able to obtain patents in antebellum America. The first black to receive a patent in the United States was Thomas Jennings (1791–1859), who developed a method for the dry scouring of clothes and patented his invention in March 1821. Henry Blair, who invented a labor-saving seed and cotton planter, obtained a patent in October 1836. Ten years later, Norbert RILLIEUX patented a sugar-refining pan that proved to be a major breakthrough in engineering.

African-American engineering discoveries took place in informal surroundings and were largely ignored by the public until the late nineteenth century. After serving as a mechanical engineering apprentice, Elijah J. MCCOY developed an automatic oiling process for railroad engines that was widely used by engineers and mechanics. Granville T. WOODS patented over thirty-five electric devices and obtained over sixty patents for various inventions, beginning in 1872. Woods, who was sometimes referred to as the "Black Edison," made several improvements on the telegraph for which Edison attempted to claim credit. In 1906, William H. Diamond, the first African-American graduate of the University of Pittsburgh, patented a safety light for railroad workers.

Northern colleges and technical schools began admitting African-American students of engineering in the late 1880s, some twenty-five years after the end of the Civil War. One of the first technical schools to enroll blacks was the Massachusetts Institute of Technology (MIT), which granted a degree to Robinson Taylor in 1892; from the year of Taylor's admission through 1930, MIT granted forty technically oriented degrees to African Americans. The first full academic engineering program to be instituted at a black university was implemented at Howard in 1910. Four years later, Manual A. Agosto became the first engineering student to graduate from that university; by 1930, Howard had granted more engineering degrees to African Americans than any other institution in the United States. Howard's degree program was followed by North Carolina's Agricultural and Technical College (now known as North Carolina A&T), and the Hampton Institute in Virginia, from which the first engineers graduated in 1839 and 1845, respectively.

The first African American to earn a doctoral degree in any engineering field was Marron William Fort, who graduated from MIT with a Ph.D. in chemical engineering in 1933. Eight years later, Walter T. Daniels became the second African-American recipient of a doctoral degree in engineering, awarded by Howard University—the first black college to offer a Ph.D. in this field—in 1941. Another African American to achieve distinction in the field was Edward Hope, Jr., who received an M.S. in civil engineering from MIT, and graduated with a Ph.D. in administration from Columbia University in 1942. Hope was subsequently commissioned as a lieutenant in the Civil Engineering Corps of the U.S. Naval Reserve and stationed in Rhode Island.

Opportunities in engineering began to expand for African Americans during World War II, largely as a result of the United States Army's bias against placing blacks in combat situations. Almost 260,000 (segregated) black troops were assigned to the European theater of operations in 1945; of those, approximately one in five were engineer soldiers. While many of these worked as laborers, a number of African Americans did gain firsthand experience in engineering from their military service. In the Pacific theater, several African-American engineers were recognized for their contributions to the war effort. In May 1942, on the eve of the Battle of the Coral Sea, one black aviation engineer battalion worked around the clock in order to complete an airfield in New Caledonia in two days. In Asia, African-American troops helped to build the Burma Road, which became a vital supply link between India and China. Black Navy Sea-

The 41st Engineers on parade at Fort Bragg, N.C., in 1942. The Army was reluctant to have black front-line troops, and a disproportionate number of black soldiers were assigned to noncombat units. Despite this, many engineering units served on the front lines with the responsibility of building and repairing military infrastructure, often while under direct enemy fire. (Prints and Photographs Division, Library of Congress)

Bees also built runways, fueling docks, coastal defense gun mounts and camps (which had to be carved out in thick jungles), often while under fire from enemy bombs.

After the war ended, many African-American veterans were able to obtain a college education in engineering with benefits from the G.I. Bill. Leroy Callender graduated from the City College of New York with a double degree in structural and civil engineering in 1958. Callender, who worked as an engineer on the first nuclear power plant in the East, founded his own firm—Callender Consulting Engineers—in 1969, and took part in such projects as the design and construction of the $63 million Whitney M. Young Housing Complex in Yonkers, N.Y.

Overall, however, the number of African Americans in engineering remained small. Of the 500,000 engineers working in the United States in the early 1960s, less than 1 percent were black. Following World War II, the development of such sophisticated technologies as radar, nuclear reactors, and computers fueled the growth of many new industries. As a response to these and other worldwide technological phenomena—such as the "space race" of the 1960s—the United States expanded its scientific institutions and tried to attract applicants from previously untapped populations. Predominantly white colleges and historically black colleges and universities (HBCUs) organized collaborative programs in order to increase the pool of participants. Whereas by 1972 only 405 African-American engineers had graduated from the American university system, 2,374 blacks received engineering degrees in 1992. Hundreds of additional minority engineering programs were developed throughout the country as a result of partnerships between the government, industry, and institutions of higher learning. As of 1992, over 68,000 African-Americans were participating in the engineering workforce.

Several academic and professional organizations emerged in connection with these aims. The most prestigious professional society, the National Technical Association (NTA), was founded as early as 1926; its establishment was followed by the National Council of Black Engineers and Scientists (NCBES), and the National Society of Black Engineers (NSBE), a university, professional, and community-based organization managed by engineering students. Walter Lincoln HAWKINS, who earned an M.S. in chemical engineering from Howard University in 1934, was the first African-American engineer to be inducted into the (formerly all-white) National Academy of Engineering. In 1958, La Bonnie Ann Bianchi became the first black woman to join a national engineering fraternity, *Tau Beta Pi*. Bianchi also earned the distinction of being the first woman to graduate from the engineering department of Howard University.

Although the African-American presence in engineering has increased substantially, the percentage of women participants remains exceedingly low. The first African-American woman to graduate with a Ph.D. in the field was Jennie Patrick, who was awarded a degree in chemical engineering from MIT in 1979. Patrick went on to become a researcher for two private companies (Dow Chemical and General Electric). In 1983, Christine Darden became the first African-American woman to earn a doctorate of science in mechanical engineering. Darden, who had joined NASA as a data analyst in 1967, received her degree from George Washington University. As of 1986, only 4,400 of the 41,300 employed African-American scientists and engineers were women.

The number of African-American-owned engineering companies is also comparatively small. *Black Enterprise* included thirteen of these in its Top 100 listing of industrial/service companies for 1993. Nevertheless, the thirteen companies represent a full range of services within the profession, from civil engineering through computer design. The most successful business, H. J. Russell & Co., listed assets of $152 million in 1993, and bid successfully for a contract on the Olympic Stadium in Atlanta, Ga.—the projected site of the 1996 summer games. Other top companies include the Maxima Corporation, which designs and produces computer and engineering systems; Digital Systems Research, which specializes in engineering defense systems; and Navcom Systems, a firm that has been involved in electronic engineering since 1986. The combined sales figures for all thirteen black-owned companies totaled almost $500 million in 1994.

REFERENCES

IVES, PATRICIA CARTER. *Creativity and Inventions: The Genius of Afro-Americans and Women in the United States and Their Patents.* Arlington, Va., 1987.

"Minorities in Engineering." *Engineering Workforce Bulletin,* American Association of Engineering Societies, no. 126 (June 1993).

WHARTON, DAVID E. *A Struggle Worthy of Note: The Engineering and Technological Education of Black Americans.* Westport, Conn., 1992.

WILSON, AMY LYLES, W. RALPH EUBANKS, and SANDRA TAMBURRINO, eds. *Blacks in Science and Medicine.* New York, 1990.

CHARLES E. WALKER

Entrepreneurs. African economic practices in food production and distribution provided the basis for the initial entrepreneurial expression of black people in this nation. A vibrant commercial culture existed in western and central Africa during the transatlantic slave trade era. The economic structures of African societies were exceedingly sophisticated. Internal market systems proliferated, regulated by central authorities at the national, regional, and local levels. International trade—including trade in slaves—was controlled by kings and wealthy merchants, while local economies required the participation of men and women as producers, wholesalers, and retailers in markets overseen by guilds.

1619–1789

Africans who were brought to the United States as slaves first made use of the surplus commodities from their own provision grounds—land either allotted to them or surreptitiously appropriated by them for food growing and, occasionally, tobacco cultivation—to create local produce markets where goods were sold or bartered. These were the first business ventures that provided slaves with money. Successful slave entrepreneurs could earn enough money to purchase freedom for themselves and their families and subsequently acquire land. In mid-seventeenth-century Virginia the Anthony Johnson family secured its freedom and opened a commercial farm producing tobacco for both local and international markets. The Johnsons also had a number of indentured servants and slaves.

Although there were relatively few free blacks with holdings in land or slaves, their numbers did increase during the eighteenth century. In colonial cities African Americans were particularly active as entrepreneurs in the food-service industry, first as market people and then as street food vendors and cook- and food-shop owners. In 1736, in Providence, R.I., Emanuel Manna Bernoon opened the first African-American catering establishment with the capital from his wife's illegal whiskey distillery business. One of the leading caterers of nearby Newport was "Dutchess" Quamino, a pastry maker who conducted her business in a small house. The catering activities of blacks in these towns placed Rhode Island at the center of African-American enterprise and contributed significantly to the state's early development as a resort area.

One of the most renowned innkeepers in eighteenth-century America was Samuel Fraunces (1722–1795). While there is some dispute whether Fraunces was of African descent, there is no doubt that he was a West Indian who migrated to New York City in the 1750s. His tavern and inn, which opened in 1761, earned him a reputation as a leading restaurateur with "the finest hostelry in Colonial America." Four years later Fraunces established Vaux-Hall (named after the famous English pleasure gardens), a resort with hanging gardens, waxworks, concerts, fireworks, and afternoon dances, which set the standard for pleasure gardens in colonial America; during the 1780s, when New York City was the nation's capital, Fraunces' Tavern in lower Manhattan served as a meeting place for the new government and was the site of George Washington's farewell to his troops.

A number of northern blacks were successful tradesmen or artisans. Peter WILLIAMS, SR., who was born a slave in New York and helped found the AFRICAN METHODIST EPISCOPAL ZION CHURCH in 1800, was a successful tobacconist. With the profits from his earnings, Williams purchased his freedom in 1786. African-born Amos FORTUNE (1710–1801) purchased his freedom at age sixty and established a successful tannery business with a clientele that extended to New Hampshire and Massachusetts.

Black entrepreneurs were also to be found at the American frontier. In 1779 Jean Baptiste Pointe DU SABLE established a trading post on the site of what later became the city of Chicago. In addition to importing merchandise from the East, Du Sable owned a bake house, mill, dairy, smokehouse, and lumberyard. His mercantile activities serviced a wilderness hinterland with a two-hundred-mile radius.

Beginning in the late eighteenth century, blacks developed enterprises in sports and music. In Newport, R.I., African-born Occramer Marycoo, later known as Newport Gardiner (1746–?), established a successful music school based on his reputation as a musician and composer. In 1780 Gardiner cofounded the African Union Society, which kept community records, found training and jobs for black youth, and supported members in time of financial need. Gardiner led thirty-two other African Americans to Liberia, with support from the AMERICAN COLONIZATION SOCIETY, in 1826. The most famous late-eighteenth-century black sports figure was boxer Bill RICHMOND (1763–1829), who achieved recognition in both America and England. Born a slave in New York, Richmond left for London during the Revolution, where his fame in boxing grew. Upon retiring from the ring, he established a popular inn in London known as the Horse and Dolphin and opened a boxing academy.

1790–1865

The entrepreneurial efforts of African Americans became increasingly pronounced in the early national and antebellum years. Throughout this period African-American entrepreneurs were prominent in crafts and personal services, which required limited capital for the development of enterprise. Blacks also established profitable businesses in transportation, manufacturing, personal services, catering, restaurants and taverns, real estate, finance, commercial farming, merchandising, mining, and construction. Unlike later black entrepreneurs, most antebellum businessmen had a consumer base that was primarily white. By the advent of the Civil War, at least twenty-one black entrepreneurs had accumulated holdings of over $100,000.

A prominent figure in transportation and commodity distribution was Paul CUFFE (1759–1817), a native of New Bedford, Mass., who founded a shipping line, owned several vessels, and held an interest in several others. Cuffe purchased his first ship in 1785 and had constructed a wharf and warehouse by 1800. His shipping enterprises extended from whaling to coastal and transatlantic trade vessels, which carried cargo and passengers to the West Indies, Africa, England, Norway, and Russia. Cuffe's most notable voyage was undertaken in 1815, when he transported thirty-eight African Americans to Sierra Leone at his own expense. He died two years later and left an estate valued at $20,000. Like Cuffe, the Philadelphia entrepreneur James FORTEN (1766–1842) actively supported the abolitionist movement and agitated for the rights of free blacks. Forten, whose estate was valued at $100,000, invented a new sail-making device and ran a factory that employed over forty workers, both white and black. Other antebellum inventors and manufacturers included Henry BOYD (c. 1840–1922) and William Ellison (1790–1861). Boyd, a native of Cincinnati, patented a bedstead and employed some thirty people in his bedmaking factory. Slave-born William Ellison of South Carolina established a successful cotton gin factory after he was freed. He invented a device which substantially increased the gin's efficiency, and his market extended to most of the South's cotton-producing regions. He invested his profits in slaves and real estate holdings.

Antebellum blacks became leading innovators in the personal-service and hair-care industry, establishing luxurious barbershops, bathhouses, and hotels. In Mississippi, where there were fewer than a thousand free blacks and over four hundred thousand slaves, slave-born William Johnson (1809–1851) purchased his freedom and founded a successful barbershop and bathhouse in Natchez. Johnson used his profits to develop other enterprises, such as money brokerage, real estate leasing, a toy shop, a drayage business, and agriculture. He owned slaves, some of whom worked in his barbershop and on his plantation, while others were hired out. The most successful hairdresser in the North was Joseph Cassey of Philadelphia, whose estate was valued at $75,000 in 1849. Cassey's wealth also included profits from moneylending enterprises.

Another prominent African American in the hair-care business and an early African-American philanthropist was Pierre TOUSSAINT (1766–1853), a Haitian immigrant who became one of New York's leading hairdressers. Toussaint was generous in his support of the Roman Catholic church and the education of young men studying for the priesthood. During the 1840s the three Remond sisters, Cecilia, Maritcha, and Caroline Remond Putnam—members of a prominent African-American abolitionist and business family (their mother was a successful caterer)—established the exclusive Ladies Hair Works Salon in Salem, Mass. In addition to promoting the sale of Mrs. Putnam's Medicated Hair Tonic and other products both locally and nationally (through mail-order distribution), they opened the largest wig factory in the state.

Black entrepreneurs also flourished in the clothing industry, as African-American tailors and dressmakers became leading designers in American fashion.

Perhaps best known was Mary Todd Lincoln's dressmaker, Elizabeth KECKLEY (1818–1907), who employed twenty seamstresses at the height of her enterprise.

During the antebellum period Philadelphia and New York became the leading centers for black catering businesses. The most prominent caterers of Philadelphia were Robert Bogle, Peter Augustine, the Prossers, Thomas DORSEY, Henry MINTON, and Eugene Baptiste. Much of the $400,000 in property owned by free Philadelphia blacks in 1840 belonged to caterers. New York's Edward V. Clark was listed as a jeweler in the R. G. Dun mercantile credit records; yet he operated a successful catering business, which included lending out silver, crystal, and china for his catered dinners. In 1851 Clark's merchandise was valued at $5,000.

During the War of 1812, Thomas Downing established a famous oyster house and restaurant on Wall Street, which became a noted attraction for foreign tourists and the haunt of the elite in business and politics. In 1844 Thomas's son, George T. Downing (1819–1903), founded the Sea Girt Hotel, housing businesses on the first floor and luxury rooms above. Twelve years after the Civil War, Downing expanded his food-service business to Washington, D.C., where he was known as "the celebrated colored caterer."

Samuel T. Wilcox of Cincinnati, who established his business in 1850 and relied primarily on the Ohio and Mississippi riverboat trade, was the most successful black entrepreneur in wholesale food distribution. Before the Civil War Wilcox's annual sales exceeded $100,000; his estate was valued at $60,000. Solomon Humphries, a free black in Macon, Ga., owned a grocery valued at $20,000. In upstate New York William Goodridge developed a number of diverse enterprises, including a jewelry store, an oyster company, a printing company, a construction company, and a large retail merchandise store, while running a train on the Columbia Railroad. In 1848 Goodridge earned a reported business capital of $20,000 in addition to real estate holdings in both New York and Canada. In Virginia the slave Robert Gordan managed his owner's coal yard and established a side business whose profits amounted to somewhere around $15,000. After purchasing his freedom, Gordan used the capital to start a profitable coal business in Cincinnati and by 1860 reported annual earnings of $60,000 from coal and real estate profits.

The extractive industries proved to be a source of wealth for slave-born Stephen Smith (1797–1873), a Pennsylvania lumber and coal merchant, bank founder, and investor in real estate and stock who was known as "Black Sam." The R. G. Dun mer-

Elizabeth Keckley, a dressmaker, purchased her freedom in 1855 through a loan from her customers. She eventually moved from St. Louis to Washington, D.C., where she became one of the capital's elite dressmakers and in 1868 worked in the White House as Mary Todd Lincoln's dressmaker. (Moorland-Spingarn Research Center, Howard University)

cantile credit records list his wealth at $100,000 in 1850 and $500,000 in 1865. Smith, whose wife ran an oyster house, obtained his start in business as the manager of his owner's lumberyard. William Whipper (1804–1876), Smith's partner in the lumber business from 1835 to 1836, started out in the steam-scouring business. Whipper, who, like Smith, had extensive real estate holdings, was a cashier in the Philadelphia branch of the Freedman's Savings Bank from 1870 to 1874, with reported assets (registered in the 1870 census) amounting to $107,000. Both men were leaders in abolitionist activities and provided financial support to black institutions.

Eight of the wealthiest antebellum African-American entrepreneurs were slaveholders from Lou-isiana who owned large cotton and sugar plantations. Marie Metoyer (1742–1816), also known as COIN-COIN, the daughter of African-born slaves, was freed in 1796 at the age of forty-six and acquired several hundred slaves as well as ten thousand acres of land. The Metoyer family's wealth amounted to several hundred thousand dollars. Urban black businessmen and women in Louisiana also owned productive slaves: CeCee McCarty of New Orleans, a merchant and money broker who owned a train depot and used her slaves as a traveling sales force, accumulated $155,000 from her business activities. Most of the wealthy black entrepreneurs lived in New Orleans: the Soulie Brothers, Albin and Bernard, accumulated over $500,000 as merchants and brokers; Francis La Croix, a tailor and real estate speculator, declared assets of $300,000; and Julien La Croix, a grocer and real estate speculator, reported assets totaling $250,000.

The developing frontier continued to provide entrepreneurial opportunities to African Americans. William LEIDESDORFF, a rancher and businessman in San Francisco during the last years of Mexican rule, died in debt in 1848; shortly afterward, gold was discovered on his property, and the value of his estate leaped to well over a million dollars. While still a slave, "Free" Frank McWorter (1777–1854) established a saltpeter factory in Kentucky during the War of 1812. Profits from the mining of crude niter, the principal ingredient used in the manufacture of gunpowder, enabled McWorter to purchase freedom for his wife in 1817 and for himself two years later. After he was freed, McWorter expanded his saltpeter enterprise and engaged in commercial farming and land speculation activities. In 1830 he moved to Illinois, where in 1836 he founded the town of New Philadelphia, the first town promoted by an African American, though both blacks and whites purchased New Philadelphia town lots. By the time he died, McWorter had been able to free a total of sixteen family members from slavery.

Antebellum blacks, both slave and free, profited significantly from the construction industry. The most resourceful slave entrepreneur in this field was Anthony Weston, who built rice mills and improved the performance of rice-thrashing machines. By 1860 Weston's property in real estate and slaves—purchased in his wife's name, since she was a free black—was valued at $40,075. Slave-born Horace King (1807–1885) worked as a covered-bridge builder in Alabama and Georgia. After being freed in 1846, King established a construction company that was eventually expanded to include construction projects for housing and commercial institutions. After King's death the company was renamed the King

Brothers Construction Company and overseen by his sons and daughter.

1865–1929

By the time the Civil War ended in 1865, over twenty-five hundred African-American businesses had been established by slaves and free blacks. Despite the difficulties that blacks experienced with regard to continuing social, political, and economic inequalities, the end of slavery did bring about a much wider range of prospects for budding African-American entrepreneurs. It was during this time that the first black millionaires emerged.

Health and beauty-aid enterprises, real estate speculation, and the development of financial institutions such as banks and insurance companies provided the basis for the wealth accumulated by many of the most successful black entrepreneurs. The food- and personal-service industries continued to be sources of income. Durham, N.C., and Atlanta, Ga., became the commercial centers for black America. The numbers of blacks involved in business steadily increased: In 1890, 31,000 blacks were engaged in business; their numbers rose to 40,455 in 1900 and to 74,424 in 1920.

Many leading black entrepreneurs of this era were either slave-born or had slave-born parents. Others had only limited formal educations and often started as unskilled workers or laborers. A number of African-American businesses were farm related. In 1900 Junius C. Graves, who owned five hundred acres of Kansas land valued at $100,000, became known as the Negro Potato King. Perhaps the most successful black entrepreneur of the Reconstruction era was Benjamin Montgomery (1819–1877), a slave of Joseph Davis (brother of the Confederate president, Jefferson Davis). In 1866 Joseph Davis sold his cotton plantations to Montgomery for $300,000. In addition to establishing a retail store on the Davis plantation in 1842, Montgomery had managed the Davis plantation from the 1850s on. In 1871 Dun gave Montgomery—who continued to run both enterprises with his sons as commission merchants—an A credit rating, ranking his family among the richest planter merchants and noting: "They are negroes, but negroes of unusual intelligence & extraordinary bus[iness] qualifications." The Montgomerys registered a net worth of $230,000 in 1874 but suffered severe setbacks several years later when crops failed and cotton prices declined. In 1881 the family was unable to make payments on interest and capital and the property reverted to the Davis family by auction. In 1887 Benjamin Montgomery's son Isaiah MONTGOMERY migrated to Mississippi and founded the all-black town of MOUND BAYOU, where black enterprise was encouraged and where, in 1904, Charles Banks (1873–1923) founded the Bank of Mound Bayou and the Mound Bayou Loan and Investment Company.

By the turn of the century, some of the most successful black entrepreneurs had already begun to discover a national black consumer market. In 1896 Richard H. BOYD, a Baptist minister (1843–1922), established the National Baptist Publishing House in Nashville, Tenn., with a printing plant that covered half a city block. In 1910 the annual company payroll amounted to $200,000. Under Boyd's management the publishing house earned $2.4 million in just under ten years and by 1920 was one of the largest black businesses in the nation. But Boyd did not limit his business enterprises to religious publishing. His holdings included the One Cent Savings and Bank Trust, which he founded in 1904 (and which became the Citizens Savings Bank and Trust in 1920), the *Nashville Globe* (established in 1905), the National Negro Doll Company (1909–1929), the National Baptist Church Supply Company, and the Union Transportation Company. Union Transportation owned five steam-driven buses and fourteen electric buses, carrying twenty passengers each. This company was founded in 1905 to support a black bus boycott in response to the segregated streetcar ordinance that Nashville had passed that year. By 1993 four generations of Boyds had continued their ownership of the publishing house and Citizens Bank; as of that year the assets of the bank alone totaled $118.3 million.

Urban real estate investment and speculation ventures continued to be the major source of wealth for some of the leading black entrepreneurs during this era. In New Orleans Thomy La Fon (1810–1893), whose real estate activities began before the Civil War, left an estate valued at over $700,000. In St. Louis slave-born James Thomas (1827–1913) used the profits from his exclusive barbershop to invest in real estate; his property holdings exceeded $400,000 by 1879. In Memphis slave-born Robert CHURCH (1839–1912) accumulated over $700,000 from real estate investments and speculation. His first enterprises were a bar, gambling hall, and pawnshop. Church Park, which he developed on Beale Street as a recreation center, included an auditorium used for annual conventions of black organizations and a concert hall that featured black entertainers. Church also founded the Solvent Bank and Trust Company.

The late nineteenth century marked the founding of large-scale black banks and insurance companies. In 1899 slave-born John Merrick (1859–1919) of Durham founded the NORTH CAROLINA MUTUAL and Provident Company, which as of 1993 still ranked first on *Black Enterprise*'s list of black-owned insurance companies with assets of nearly $218 million. Merrick had little formal education and was a barber by trade; his initial business activities included a chain of barbershops as well as real estate investments. He also founded a land company, the Mechanics and Farmers Bank (1907), and the Durham Textile Mill. Indeed, while Chicago and New York were only emerging as important centers of African-American enterprise in the early decades of the twentieth century, Durham's black business district had come to be known as the Capital of the Black Middle-Class. "At the turn of the century," John Sibley Butler noted, "commentators were as excited about North Carolina as they are today about the Cuban-American experience in Miami." Atlanta was also rapidly rising to prominence as a center for black business. Slave-born Alonzo Franklin Herndon (1858–1927), who founded the Atlanta Life Insurance Company in 1905, left an estate valued at more than $500,000. Herndon's real estate investments and lavishly appointed barbershops—which catered to an elite white clientele—provided profits for the start-up and expansion of Atlanta Life.

In 1923 C. C. Spaulding, one of the leading black businessmen of the first half of the twentieth century, became president of the North Carolina Mutual Life Insurance Company in Durham, N.C., the successor company to the North Carolina Mutual and Provident Association. (Photographs and Prints Division, Schomburg Center for Research in Black Culture, The New York Public Library, Astor, Lenox and Tilden Foundations)

In some cases, the overly rapid expansion of business enterprises led to bankruptcy. Atlanta businessman Edward Perry (1873–1929) established the Standard Life Insurance Company in 1913 and the Citizens Trust Bank in 1921. With the income from his Service Realty Company and Service Engineering and Construction Company, both founded in the 1920s, Perry purchased land on Atlanta's west side and constructed some five hundred homes. By 1925 he had established eleven different businesses together valued at $11 million and providing employment for twenty-five hundred people. Perry lost all of his holdings within four years. His contemporaries blamed his bankruptcy on imprudent expansion, limited capital reserves, and injudicious business decisions. An insurance company founder and winner of the NAACP's SPINGARN MEDAL in 1927, Anthony OVERTON (1865–1945) was another black businessman whose success in the early decades of the century was followed by bankruptcy in the depression years.

Real estate, an enterprise crucial to the growth of northern black communities, offered similar opportunities for rapid expansion, sometimes with disastrous results. Jesse Binga (1865–1950) began his real estate operations on the south side of Chicago in 1905. Three years later he founded the first black-owned bank in the North, which in 1921 became the Binga State Bank. In 1929 he constructed the five-story Binga Arcade to revitalize the deteriorating black business district. Later that year, when his bank failed, Binga's wealth was assesssed at more than $400,000; he was convicted of fraudulent bank practices in 1933 and spent three years in jail. Like Herman Perry and James Thomas, Binga spent the rest of his life in poverty and obscurity. The same fate befell Harlem's Phillip A. Payton, Jr. (1876–1917), who organized a consortium of black investors to found the Afro-American Realty Company in 1904. Within two years the company controlled $690,000 in rental properties. Payton was largely responsible for opening Harlem as a community to African Americans; subsequently, however, his stockholders charged him with fraudulent practices, and he went bankrupt.

Hair and beauty care, a less risky industry, proved especially profitable for black entrepreneurs. Annie M. Turnbo-Malone (1869–1957), founder of the Poro Company (1900) and a pioneer in the manufacture of hair- and skin-care products, is considered the first self-made American female millionaire. She began her business in Lovejoy, Ill., and eventually expanded to St. Louis, where she built a five-story manufacturing plant in 1917. The plant housed Poro College, a beauty school with branches in most major cities. In 1930 Turnbo-Malone moved her operations to Chicago and purchased a square city block on the South Side. She franchised her operations and, with national and international markets, reportedly provided employment opportunities for some seventy-five thousand people.

C. J. Sarah Breedlove WALKER (1867–1919) was a Poro agent before she initiated her own hair-care-products and cosmetics business in St. Louis in 1905. The "Walker system" for hair included an improved steel hot comb that revolutionized hair straightening for black women. The business strategies of the company—which employed over five thousand black women as agents who disseminated information on the Walker hair-care system in a marketing and employee-incentive program that utilized a national and international network of marketing consultants—presaged the practices of modern cosmetics firms.

The World War I era also witnessed the growth of black-owned publishing businesses. In 1905 Robert ABBOTT (1870–1940) founded the CHICAGO DEFENDER, the first black newspaper with a mass circulation. The *Defender* used sensationalized news coverage to attract a large audience and was outspoken in its condemnation of racial injustice. By 1920 it had a circulation of over 200,000, with national circulation exceeding local sales. At Abbott's death the *Defender* was valued at $300,000. Abbott's successor, his nephew John H. Sengstacke, went on to establish Sengstacke Enterprises, which, with the *Defender* and ten other papers, became the largest black newspaper chain in America.

As media opportunities grew, African Americans became increasingly visible in the entertainment industry. One of the most successful black entrepreneurs in this field was Harry Herbert PACE (1884–1943). After founding Pace and Handy Music (1917), a sheet music company whose publications included W. C. HANDY's "St. Louis Blues," he founded the New York–based Black Swan Record Company (1921), the first record company owned by an African American. Black Swan's first success was Ethel WATERS's "Oh Daddy" in 1921, which sold 600,000 copies in six months. Pace, who wanted to tap a national market for his records, refused to record Bessie SMITH because he thought her music "too colored." By 1923 Black Swan was cutting six thousand records a day. Pace sold the company, at a hefty profit, to Paramount later that year. In addition, Pace's creative management and financial strategies promoted the growth of several black financial institutions, including Robert Church's Memphis Solvent Savings Bank (whose assets he increased from $50,000 to $600,000 in the years from 1907 to 1911) and Herman Edward Perry's Standard Life Insurance Company. In 1929 Pace engineered the merger of three northern black insurance companies to form Supreme Liberty Life Insurance.

Even as African-American entrepreneurs were branching out into new lines of business, many remained active in the catering and hotel fields. James Wormley (1819–1884), a caterer and restaurateur who built the five-storied Wormley's Hotel (1871) in Washington, D.C., ranked among the most fashionable black hoteliers. Wormley's hotel was patronized by leading politicians and foreign dignitaries, and he left an estate exceeding $100,000 in assets. In Philadelphia the tradition of catering, long an African-American resource, reached a pinnacle with the Dutrieulle family. Their catering business, established by Peter Dutrieulle (1838–1916) in 1873, lasted for almost a century, flourishing under the management of his son Albert (1877–1974) until 1967.

African Americans also profited in new areas of the food industry. C. H. James & Company of Charleston, W.V., a wholesale food processing and distribution enterprise founded in 1883, lasted for four generations of family ownership. From the time of its inception, the company's suppliers and buyers were primarily white; it was initially headed by Charles Howell James (1862–1929) and included a traveling dry goods retail operation. However, once the family decided to abandon the retail operation (in 1916) and limit the enterprise solely to the distribution of wholesale produce, the profits escalated to over $350,000. After a brief period of bankruptcy—caused by the stock market crash of 1929—the company was resuscitated by Edward Lawrence James, Sr. (1893–1967), and began to show a profit by the end of the 1930s. The company's survival was due largely to innovations in wholesale food distribution methods. Now headed by Charles H. James III (1959–), it remains one of the most successful black businesses in the country.

Up to the onset of the Great Depression, black entrepreneurial efforts were concentrated primarily on the service industry, since in most cases African Americans could not gain access to the capital markets and financial resources needed for developing industrial enterprises. The few blacks who attempted to capitalize on the demand for such modern industries as auto manufactures, movie production, and airline companies did not succeed. Nevertheless, the Great Migration of the early twentieth century caused a dramatic rise in northern urban black populations, and entrepreneurs were quick to seize the opportunities afforded by a new and rapidly expanding African-American consumer base. This growth was not matched in the South, where Jim Crow laws and societal racist practices restricted black enterprise to the same, increasingly depleted markets.

1930–1963

During the Great Depression the number of black businesses declined from 103,881 in 1930 to 87,475 in

1940. Among the few who prospered in those years was Texan Hobart T. Taylor, Sr., who used family money from farm property to start a cab company in 1931. The company continued to flourish during World War II, and Taylor added considerably to his wealth by investing the proceeds in rural and urban real estate. By the 1970s Taylor's assets were valued at approximately $5 million.

The food-processing industries remained a fairly stable resource for black entrepreneurs before, during, and after World War II. In the late 1930s California businessman Milton Earl Grant (1891–) started companies in rubbish hauling and hog raising. In 1947 he founded the Broadway Federal Savings and Loan Association in Los Angeles. By 1948 Grant had grossed some $200,000 from the sale of hogs; he invested the profits in real estate, and by 1970 his holdings exceeded more than $1.5 million. In Buffalo, N.Y., Cornelius Ford founded the C. E. Ford Company, a cattle brokerage firm, during the 1920s. Ford's business survived the depression and in the 1950s was yielding over $1 million annually from livestock trade and sales. His company was one of the chief buyers for Armour and Company for some twenty-five years. In addition, Ford became president of the Buffalo Livestock Exchange (the fifth largest in the nation), speculated in the Canadian cattle market, and leased railroad yards from New York Central.

George McDermmod, a potato chip maker and chief executive officer of Community Essentials, established a manufacturing plant in Crescent City, Ill., and a distribution plant in Detroit during the 1940s. As of 1950 McDermmod was selling his products to fourteen hundred dealers in nine states with gross business receipts amounting to over $100,000 annually. In Chicago Kit Baldwin established an ice-cream company that catered primarily to the black community and was reporting annual business receipts of $75,000 by the late 1940s. During this same period Detroit entrepreneur Sydney Barthwell established a drugstore chain of nine stores and manufactured ice cream. In 1948 Barthwell reported a staff of eighty full-time employees and gross business receipts in excess of $1.5 million.

The hair-care and cosmetic-manufacturing business also continued to attract black entrepreneurs. In Harlem Rose Morgan and Olivia Clark established the Rose Meta House of Beauty in 1947. Three years later they were earning $3 million from the sale of cosmetics and hair-care products in national stores and via international mail. Morgan and Clark's chain of beauty shops proliferated in major American cities as well as in Monrovia, Liberia; Cayenne, British Guiana; Puerto Rico; Cuba; and Jamaica. In New York City alone, their three shops employed three hundred people.

One of the most successful and wealthiest black entrepreneurs of the World War II era was S. B. Fuller (1905–1988), whose Chicago business empire, Fuller Products, comprised health and beauty aids as well as cleaning products and real estate. Fuller's many investments included the famous Regal Theater, the PITTSBURGH COURIER, Fuller Guarantee Corporation, the Fuller Department Store, and various livestock operations. In 1947 he secretly purchased a cosmetic factory owned and operated by whites. By 1960 Fuller, who had begun his career in 1935 as a door-to-door salesman, reported a payroll of five thousand employees, white and black, and a three-hundred-product line that brought in over $10 million in sales. However, when Fuller's ownership of the cosmetic factory—the products of which were tailored to the needs of southern white consumers—was discovered in the early 1960s, his cosmetics were boycotted by whites, and he was unable to raise sufficient capital to offset his loses. In 1964 the SEC charged Fuller with the sale of unregistered securities and forced him to pay $1.5 million to his creditors. Although Fuller Products was resurrected from bankruptcy in 1972, it never recovered as a major black business.

Another financier who rose to prominence after the depression was Arthur George Gaston (1892–) of Birmingham, Ala. Gaston's business activities began with the founding of a burial society, which he incorporated in 1932 as the Booker T. Washington Insurance Company. Seven years later, with the proceeds from life and health insurance sales, Gaston established the Booker T. Washington Business College, the Gaston Motel, and the Gaston Construction Company. In 1952 he expanded his holdings with the Vulcan Realty and Investment Corporation, a real estate firm that financed the construction of office and apartment buildings, as well as the development of housing subdivisions. Gaston's Citizens Federal Savings and Loan Association—ranked seventeenth on the 1993 Black Enterprise list of financial companies—was founded in 1957. Additional enterprises included Booker T. Washington Broadcasting and a soft-drink bottling company. In 1987 Gaston sold ownership of his insurance, radio, and construction companies to the employees. In 1993 the Booker T. Washington Insurance Company ranked sixth on the Black Enterprise list of insurance companies, with assets over $43 million.

The 1940s and 1950s witnessed an increase in manufacturing opportunities for African-American entrepreneurs. The Grimes Oil Company of Boston, a petroleum products distributor, was founded in 1940 by Calvin M. Grimes; as of 1993, its sales had reached $37 million. In 1949 Dempsey Travis (1920–) founded the H. G. Parks Sausage Company in Baltimore. Subsequently, in 1990, Travis initiated the

The Rev. Jesse Jackson speaking at the *Black Enterprise* magazine twentieth-anniversary issue celebration. (Allford/Trotman Associates)

development of a middle-class townhouse project on Chicago's South Side.

1964–1994

The 1960s marked the emergence of a national network of large black businesses, many of which were founded on minute initial capital outlays. Johnson Publications began in 1942 with an investment of $250; the H. J. Russell Construction Company began in 1952 with a $150 truck; Berry Gordy started Motown for $700 in 1958. As the civil rights movement gathered momentum in the late 1950s and early '60s, it became easier for blacks to obtain more substantial business financing; however, undercapitalized joint ventures persisted as a major method in the founding and development of new enterprises by African-American entrepreneurs. With few exceptions enterprises founded by black entrepreneurs remain relatively small private or family-owned companies. As of 1993 only eleven of the *Black Enterprise* top 100 businesses employed more than a thousand people.

In 1964, for the first time in the history of this country, the federal government took steps to provide assistance to black entrepreneurs by creating the Office of Minority Business Enterprises (OMBE), a division of the Small Business Administration (SBA), which was overseen in turn by the Department of Commerce. In 1969 President Richard M. Nixon issued executive order no. 11458, calling for the "strengthening of minority business enterprise"; by 1976 surveys showed that over two-thirds of the top black businesses had been started with support from the SBA. However, under Presidents Reagan and Bush progress toward business parity for blacks was visibly slowed.

While African-American businesses have continued to tap an African-American consumer market, black entrepreneurs have slowly expanded sales to include mainstream national and international markets. One ironic consequence of black economic success has been that some of the most profitable black-owned companies—such as Johnson Products and Motown Records—have since been acquired by larger, white-owned organizations. The first black company to have its stock publicly traded was the Johnson Products Company, which was founded by George S. Johnson (1927–) in 1954; it was listed for the first time on the American Stock Exchange in 1969. Johnson Products greatly increased its sales when it introduced a non-lye-based hair relaxer, Ultra-Sheen (developed by George Johnson), into the market in 1966. During the late 1960s Johnson developed another best-selling hair product, Afro-Sheen, in response to the newly popular Afro hair style; so successful were these and other items that his company controlled the market in black hair products throughout the mid-1960s and into the early 1970s. By the mid-1970s, however, a series of setbacks—mostly in the form of competition from new black- and white-owned companies—cost Johnson the leading market share; in 1989 he lost control of the company to his ex-wife, Joan B. Johnson, who then sold Johnson Products to IVAX for $67 million dollars in 1993. In its final year as a black company, Johnson Products ranked twentieth in the *Black Enterprise* top 100 of 1992, registering $46.2 million in sales.

The most prominent rival for Johnson Products was Edward G. Gardner's (1925–) Soft Sheen Products, established in 1964. Soft Sheen's most successful product, Care Free Curl, was introduced in 1979. Like Johnson, Gardner also had to compete with white companies—most notably Revlon and Alberto Culver—which controlled 50 percent of a $1 billion black hair-care market in 1988. By this time black enterprises were seriously theatened with losing the market to white corporations that had only recently entered the field. Black manufacturers launched an aggressive campaign to prevent white companies from gaining control and received support from Jesse JACKSON's OPERATION PUSH, as well as from John H. JOHNSON, publisher of EBONY and JET magazines, and *Essence* founder Edward T. Lewis, both of whom refused to accept advertisements from white-owned companies in their publications. The white cosmetic giants escalated their strategies; by 1993 only five of the nineteen cosmetic companies in the black hair-care market were African-American owned. Black hair-care products remain an extremely profitable field. In 1993 Soft Sheen reported $96.6 million in sales and ranked ninth in the *Black Enterprise* top 100; Luster Products, reporting $46 million, ranked twenty-ninth; and Pro-Line, with $40.5 million, ranked thirty-fourth.

Berry GORDY's company, Motown Records, a subsidiary of Motown Industries, was the largest and most successful African-American enterprise in the entertainment field and the first to profit from the introduction of black music into the mainstream consumer market. Gordy's eight record labels, which recorded such groups as the Supremes and the Temptations, produced numerous hits on the pop and R&B charts. Almost from its inception Motown included Motown Productions, Hitsville, and the music publishing company Jobete. Most of Motown's holdings were sold to MCA Records for $61 million in 1988, and the company's listing was removed from *Black Enterprise.* As of 1993 Motown's gross business receipts totaled $100 million.

Motown's success served as a catalyst for African-American participation in the entertainment industry. Dick Griffey Productions, a concert-promotion and record company founded in 1975, has continued to flourish in recent years. Its founder, Dick Griffey (1943–) expanded into international markets by investing the company's proceeds in the African Development Public Investment Corporation, as well as in an African commodities and air-charter service, which he founded in 1985. In 1993 Dick Griffey Productions ranked fifty-seventh on *Black Enterprise*'s listing with sales of $26.5 million, while the African Development Corporation, registering sales of $57.8 million, ranked twenty-second.

Perhaps the most successful African-American entrepreneur of the postwar era was John H. Johnson (1918–), the owner of Johnson Publications. Johnson's business empire extends to various media corporations, Fashion Fair (a cosmetic company), radio stations, and television production companies. Founded in the 1970s, Fashion Fair has become the largest black-owned cosmetic company of the 1990s.

Black enterprise was greatly stimulated by an increasingly diversified African-American reading au-

dience. Essence Communications, the parent company of *Essence,* a black woman's magazine, was founded in 1970 by four African-American men. Edward T. Lewis (1940–), the company's publisher and CEO, also established a direct-mail catalogue business before joining with J. Bruce LLEWELLYN and Percy SUTTON in the purchase of an American Broadcasting Company (ABC) affiliate TV station in Brooklyn. In 1993 Essence Communications reported $71.1 million in sales.

In 1970 Earl G. GRAVES (1933–) launched *Black Enterprise,* a publication designed to address African-American interests in business and to report on black economic development. Soon afterward, Graves expanded his business interests by acquiring both a marketing and research company and EGG Dallas Broadcasting. In 1990 he joined Earvin "Magic" JOHNSON in purchasing the Washington, D.C., Pepsi-Cola franchise, of which Graves is CEO. In 1993 the franchise reported $49.3 million in sales, placing it twenty-sixth on the *Black Enterprise* listing; Earl G.

Earl Graves in 1970, founder of one of the most influential of black periodicals, *Black Enterprise,* has helped shape the thinking of the current generation of black professionals. (Photographs and Prints Division, Schomburg Center for Research in Black Culture, The New York Public Library, Astor, Lenox and Tilden Foundations)

Graves, Limited, ranked seventy-second, with sales of $22.4 million.

By the 1970s black entrepreneurs had managed to gain access to capital markets and were able to invest their wealth in a variety of business ventures. Some of the earliest black advertising agencies included the Chicago-based Proctor & Gardner Advertising, founded in 1970 by Barbara Gardner PROCTOR (1932–), and Burrell Communications Group, founded by Thomas J. Burrell (1939–) in 1971. In 1992 Burrell's client list included such megafirms as Coca-Cola, McDonalds, and Crest and registered assets in excess of $77 million.

One of the most promising businessmen to emerge during this period was New Yorker J. Bruce Llewellyn (1927–), who purchased FEDCO Foods Corporation, a Bronx chain of ten supermarkets, for $3 million. Llewellyn sold FEDCO for $20 million in 1984; the next year he joined basketball star Julius Erving and actor Bill COSBY in purchasing the Philadelphia Coca-Cola Bottling Company. Four years later Llewellyn bought Garden State Cable Television. By 1993 Garden State's assets registered $96 million, while Philadelphia Coca-Cola reported sales of $290 million, making it the third most profitable company on the *Black Enterprise* top 100 list.

Entertainment entrepreneur Percy E. Sutton (1920–) pursued a political career (he was Manhattan borough president for several years) in addition to founding the Inner City Broadcasting Company in 1970. Sutton, who controlled the Inner City Cable and the Apollo Theater Group, expanded his interests with Percy Sutton International, which has built manufacturing plants in such countries as Nigeria. In 1989 Sutton estimated his net worth at $170 million.

Black participation increased significantly in the area of finance. Perhaps the most profitable business enterprise was the TLC Group, established by securities lawyer Reginald LEWIS (1942–1993). Lewis purchased the McCall Pattern Company for $1 million in cash and $24 million in borrowed money; four years later he sold the company for $63 million. Aided by financing from Manufacturers Hanover Trust and Drexel Burnham Lambert, he then engineered a $985 million leveraged buyout of Beatrice International Companies, a large multinational corporation. Beatrice became the first billion-dollar black company, and in 1993 ranked first on the *Black Enterprise* top 100 list with $1.7 billion in sales (five times as much as the second company on the list).

Construction and land development executive Herman J. Russell (1930–), founder and CEO of H. J. Russell & Company of Atlanta, Ga., started out in 1952 as the owner of the H. J. Russell Plastering Company, a small private business. In 1959 Russell established the H. J. Russell Construction Company,

which specialized in building single-family homes and duplexes. His involvement in large-scale private-sector commercial projects began in 1969, when he was commissioned to construct the thirty-four story Equitable Life Assurance Building in Atlanta. In the 1970s Russell obtained financing from the Department of Housing and Urban Development (HUD) in order to construct twenty-nine housing projects with four thousand units for low- and middle-income families, while he maintained ownership of the properties. Other large-scale construction projects followed: the Atlanta Stadium, the Atlanta City Hall Complex, the Martin Luther King Community Center, and the Carter Presidential Center. In joint-venture projects with white construction companies, Russell built the parking deck for Atlanta's Hartsfield Airport, the Georgia Pacific fifty-two-story office building, and the addition to the Atlanta Merchandise Mart. He also joined with another African-American–owned construction company, C. D. Moody Construction, to place the winning bid for the $209 million Olympic Stadium contract in Atlanta for the 1996 games.

Russell has expanded his conglomerate to include many diverse businesses. H. J. Russell & Company is the parent company of several subsidiary firms, including Williams-Russell and Johnson, an engineering, architecture, and construction management firm. Russell also owns Russell-Rowe Communications, an ABC affiliate in Macon, Ga. In addition, the City Beverage Company and the Concessions International Corporation, which oversees food concessions in several major airports, are owned by Russell. In 1972 he secured the management rights to Atlanta's Omni sports-convention complex and a 10 percent ownership share of the National Basketball Association's Atlanta Hawks, anticipating by almost two decades the 37.5 percent interest, $8 million purchase of the Denver Nuggets by black entrepreneurs Bertram Lee and Peter Bynoe (1989).

During the past three decades many black athletes and entertainers have assumed entrepreneurial management positions by using their million-dollar salaries to develop new enterprises both inside and outside the sports and entertainment industries. For example, former Green Bay Packer football player Willie D. Davis (1934–) went on to earn an M.B.A. from the University of Chicago and found his own business, Willie Davis Distributing Company, in 1970. He sold the highly successful company (averaging annual sales of $25 million) in the late 1980s. Among Davis's multimillion-dollar enterprises are part ownership of five radio stations, significant shares in several companies, and the Alliance Bank of Culver City, Calif. Another successful athlete was football star Gale Sayers, who founded Crest Computer Supply in 1984, and by 1993 became the owner of a company whose annual sales amounted to $43 million.

One of the few very successful female entertainment entrepreneurs is television talk-show host Oprah WINFREY. In 1992 Winfrey became the highest paid U.S. entertainer, with earnings of $98 million. She has amassed a fortune of more than $250 million by controlling syndication of her talk show and founding the Harpo Production Company, a movie investment firm.

Naomi Sims (1949–), one of America's first successful black models, capitalized on the black hair-care-product market by designing and manufacturing wigs that approximated the hair texture of black women. In 1973 she established the Naomi Sims Collection. With sales of $5 million the first year, Sims expanded distribution to include an international market. A cosmetic line, Naomi Sims Beauty Products, Limited, was introduced in 1986, and by 1988 sales from those products exceeded $5 million.

Historically, black entrepreneurs have participated in the clothing industry as tailors and dressmakers

Naomi Sims, on a promotional tour for *All About Health and Beauty for the Black Woman* (1987). Since the days of Madame C. J. Walker, black beauty products have been a mainstay of black entrepreneurship. With the expansion of the market in the late twentieth century, many large cosmetic and beauty care companies have entered this lucrative field. (Photographs and Prints Division, Schomburg Center for Research in Black Culture, The New York Public Library, Astor, Lenox and Tilden Foundations)

but seldom as manufacturers of mass apparel. In 1989 Carl Jones (1955–) formed the first African-American–owned clothing manufacturing firm, the Los Angeles–based Threads 4 Life Corporation, doing business as Cross Colours. Cross Colours, which reported sales of $93 million in 1993, capitalized on the urban hip-hop, Afrocentric focus in dress, which came to prominence in the early 1990s. The company now has five clothing lines, including Cross Colour Classics, a line tailored to older and more conservative buyers. Jones's innovative Cross Colours Home, a home-furnishing line in which African fabrics and African-designed bed and table linens are featured prominently, is sold in Marshall Fields, I. Magnin, and Macy's.

New Jersey–based H. F. Henderson Industries, founded in 1954 by Henry F. Henderson (1928–), is an example of black participation in America's high-tech industries. Henderson specializes in automatic weighing systems, although most of the revenue for the company—which earned a reported $25.7 million in 1993—comes from defense contracts for the design and manufacture of control panels for the U.S. military. He began expanding his business in the 1970s with the Small Business Association's 8(a) program and a $125 million government contract; by the mid-1980s government contracts amounted to 50 percent of his business, with the private domestic sector accounting for 25 percent and the remaining 25 percent coming from an international market that included the People's Republic of China, Japan, Canada, Spain, and England.

Increasingly, black entrepreneurs are tapping markets on a global scale. Henderson, Sutton, Griffey, and George H. Johnson have all found international markets for their products. Soft Sheen's global expansion has taken place under the leadership of Edward G. Gardner's son, Gary, who purchased Britain's black-owned Dyke and Dryden, an import and manufacturing company that specializes in the distribution—primarily in Africa—of black personal-care products. Soft Sheen West Indies was also established in Jamaica. In the 1960s and '70s entrepreneur Jake SIMMONS, Jr. (1901–1981), had used his earnings from the southwestern petroleum industry to invest in oil leases in West Africa.

Despite the development of multimillion-dollar businesses by African-American entrepreneurs, black business-participation rates remain low; only 3 percent of all companies in the United States are black owned, and in 1987 earnings from African-American businesses comprised only 1 percent of American gross receipts. And while black entrepreneurial participation in manufacturing has increased, only 1 percent of all black businesses are involved in this area of the economy. Publicly traded black companies re-

Peggy Cockeran (center), from Atlanta, Ga., is the only female African-American car dealership owner in the United States. (Allford/Trotman Associates)

main few; indeed, only three black companies have taken this route. In 1971 Parks Sausage of Baltimore went public; it was taken over by a white private investment group in 1977 but was reacquired by the former black owners in 1980. In 1993 its sales reached almost $23 million. Robert Johnson, the founder of the Black Entertainment Channel, placed his company in public trading in order to expand his holdings. "It's time for African-Americans to think of company control in terms other than just percentage of black ownership," Johnson explained. "We should start thinking in terms of black control through the creation of value."

The future of privately held black businesses in the late twentieth century remains unclear. It has been argued that in the 1990s access to capital and strategic alliances has led some black-owned companies to either go public or become amalgamated within larger, interracial concerns. Whether exclusive black ownership of black enterprises will remain central to the black economy is one of many questions black entrepreneurship will face as it enters the twenty-first century.

REFERENCES

AMOS, WALLY, and LEROY ROBINSON. *The Famous Amos Story: The Face That Launched a Thousand Chips*. New York, 1983.
BAILEY, RONALD. *Black Business Enterprise*. New York, 1973.
BATES, TIMOTHY, and WILLIAM BRADFORD. *Financing Black Economic Development*. New York, 1979.
BUTLER, JOHN SILBEY. *Entrepreneurship and Self-Help Among Black Americans: A Reconsideration of Race and Economics*. Albany, N.Y., 1991.
CROSS, THEODORE. *Black Capitalism*. New York, 1969.
DU BOIS, W. E. B. *Economic Co-operation Among Negro Americans*. Atlanta, 1907.
———. *The Negro in Business*. Atlanta, 1899.
GATEWOOD, WILLARD. *Aristocrats of Color: The Black Elite, 1880–1920*. Bloomington, Ind., 1990.
GEORGE, NELSON. *Where Did Our Love Go? The Rise and Fall of the Motown Sound*. New York, 1986.
GREEN, SHELLEY, and PAUL PRYDE. *Black Entrepreneurship in America*. New Brunswick, N.J., 1990.
HAMILTON, KENNETH MARVIN. *Black Towns and Profit: Promotion and Development in the Trans-Appalachian West*. Urbana, Ill., 1991.
HARMON, J. H., JR. ARNETT G. LINDSAY, and CARTER G. WOODSON. *The Negro as Businessman*. 1929. Reprint. New York, 1969.
HARRIS, ABRAM L. *The Negro Capitalist: A Study of Banking and Business Among Negroes*. 1936. Reprint. New York, 1968.
HENDERSON, ALEXA BENSON. *Atlanta Life Insurance: Guardians of Black Economic Dignity*. Tuscaloosa, Ala., 1990.
———. "Henry E. Perry and Black Enterprise in Atlanta, 1908–1925." *Business History Review* 61 (Summer 1987): 216–242.
HUND, JAMES. *Black Entrepreneurship*. Belmont, Calif., 1970.
JOHNSON, FRANK J. *Who's Who of Black Millionaires*. Fresno, Calif., 1984.
JOHNSON, JOHN H., and LERONE BENNETT, JR. *Succeeding Against the Odds*. New York, 1989.
KINZER, ROBERT, and EDWARD SAGARIN. *The Negro in American Business: Conflict Between Separatism and Integration*. New York, 1950.
OAK, VISHNU V. *The Negro's Adventure in General Business*. Yellow Springs, Ohio, 1949.
OFARI, EARL. *The Myth of Black Capitalism*. New York, 1970.
OSBORNE, ALFRED. "Emerging Entrepreneurs and the Distribution of Black Enterprise." In *Managing Take-off in Fast Growth Companies: Innovations in Entrepreneurial Firms*. New York, 1986.
PIERCE, JOSEPH A. *Negro Business and Negro Business Education: Their Present and Prospective Development*. New York, 1947.
SCHWENINGER, LOREN. *Black Property Owners: The South, 1790–1915*. Urbana, Ill., 1991.
———, ed. *From Tennessee Slave to St. Louis Entrepreneur: The Autobiography of James Thomas*. Columbia, Mo., 1984.
WALKER, JULIET E. K. "Entrepreneurs, Slave." In the *Dictionary of Afro-American Slavery*. Westport, Conn., 1988.
———. "Entrepreneurs [Women] in Antebellum America." In *Black Women in America: An Historical Encyclopedia*. New York, 1993.

———. *Free Frank: A Black Pioneer on the Antebellum Frontier*. Lexington, Ky., 1983.

———. "Prejudices, Profits, Privileges: Commentaries of 'Captive Capitalists': Antebellum Black Entrepreneurs." *Economic and Business History* 8 (1990): 399–422.

———. "Racism, Slavery, and Free Enterprise: Black Entrepreneurship in the United States Before the Civil War." *Business History Review* 60 (1986): 343–382.

WASHINGTON, BOOKER T. *The Negro in Business*. 1907. Reprint. Chicago, 1969.

WEARE, WALTER B. *Black Business in the New South: A Social History of the North Carolina Mutual Life Insurance Company*. Urbana, Ill., 1973.

WHITTEN, DAVID O. "A Black Entrepreneur in Antebellum Louisiana." *Business History Review* 45 (1971): 210–219.

JULIET E. K. WALKER

Epidemics.   *See* Diseases and Epidemics; Epidemiology.

Epidemiology.   Reflections both on the social meaning of death and dying and on the etiology of disease have constituted core existential and societal dilemmas for African Americans from the seventeenth century onward. Historical epidemiologists and biological/medical anthropologists learn more daily about the scientific, social, and political factors that have contributed to patterns of health and disease alongside information about evolving cultural perceptions of contagion, illness, and death. The poor quality of vital statistical data on morbidity (nonfatal cases of disease) and mortality (deaths from a particular disease or from all causes) according to race before the early twentieth century has often hampered this investigation. Contemporary historians agree, however, even in light of fragile health data and varying interpretations of disease rates, that African-American experiences with death and dying as well as medical and lay expectations for prevailing trends diverged in significant ways from those of other Americans over the past three hundred years.

The Seventeenth and Eighteenth Centuries

Speculations about the meaning of race as a biological and behavioral determinant of disease and death dominated most medical writings on African-American health in the colonial and revolutionary eras. Northern and southern observers alike drew sharp distinctions between the etiology of black and white health outcomes. Physicians commonly theorized that unique anatomical and physiologic traits made African Americans more resistant to malaria, yellow fever and other epidemic diseases. In 1794 Richard ALLEN and Absalom JONES, in their lengthy essay *A Narrative of the Proceedings of the Black People, During the Late Awful Calamity in Philadelphia, in the Year 1793*, disputed the prevailing belief that blacks were immune to yellow fever and asserted that during a recent epidemic "we have suffered equally with the whites, our distress hath been very great, but much unknown to the white people."

The widespread appeal of biological arguments for differential racial immunity and susceptibility to particular diseases bolstered public support for the expansion of slavery in the Americas. Biologists have since identified the influence of a partial immunity conferred by the sickle-cell trait and other genetic factors in particular cases of malaria. Although the evolution and role of specific geographic and genetic factors in the health status of eighteenth-century African Americans remains a contested terrain in historical epidemiology, most researchers affirm that by 1800 the medical community rallied behind monocausal explanations that highlighted race as the sole determinant of black health status.

The Nineteenth Century

Biologic explanations of disease emphasizing racial factors continued to flourish during the early nineteenth century, particularly as southern proslavery physicians searched more zealously for distinguishing physical and anatomical characteristics to justify the social status of African Americans. Southern medical journals through the late nineteenth century traced pathological conditions associated with physical and mental disorders to racial differences in chest measurements, brain and lung size, and bodily "constitution." In many instances, slaveowners and white physicians ignored or downplayed the extent to which contagious diseases—cholera, whooping cough, scarlet fever, measles, and diphtheria, for instance—detrimentally influenced the health of slaves.

Slave narratives also offer a depiction of African-American health status, with vivid testimonies detailing poor environmental conditions on plantations. Overcrowded housing lots and poor drainage and waste-removal systems, for example, exacerbated an already high toll from visitations of cholera, pneumonia, typhoid fever, typhus, and a set of diarrheal, gastrointestinal, and respiratory diseases. A generally poor diet with deficiencies in protein, iron, and vitamins A, B, and C, historians have demonstrated, probably lowered resistance to disease and increased susceptibility to such common infections as consumption (later diagnosed as pulmonary tuberculosis) and parasites and worms. Slaves often intervened to stem the effects of illness and disease through alternative networks of lay healers and "conjurers," who employed a set of spiritual and material therapies to restore health. Africans in America believed that the entire spiritual journey from birth to death was connected to physical well-being and that ancestors and spirits systematically intervened in that process. Various herbs and teas made out of sassafras, chinaberry, sage, oak bark, and pokeberry—many of which have been found by modern scientists to have an effect on particular medical conditions—were also used extensively to address conditions ranging from persistent fever to blindness.

White physicians and the lay public in post-RECONSTRUCTION America questioned whether some diagnostic tests and therapies would work on blacks and believed that the community was headed toward extinction, in large part because of the high mortality and low fertility rates that were detailed in U.S. census reports after EMANCIPATION. This made it easier for some to argue that African Americans benefited under slavery. By the end of the nineteenth century, however, social scientists such as W. E. B. Du Bois, in *The Philadephia Negro* (1899), and domestic hygiene reformers criticized fatalistic predictions of death and the social scientific methods outlined in insurance company records, medical journals, and the popular press. A 1906 conference at Atlanta University also concluded that disease rates would decline with "improved education and better economic opportunities."

The Twentieth Century

The early twentieth-century public-health movement, with its emphasis on the germ theory of disease, the link between poverty and health, and local intervention in preventive health care gradually undermined monocausal explanations of African-American health. Health officials exposed the poor environmental conditions under which an increasingly urban black community lived, while single-city studies, such as John Daniels's *In Freedom's Birthplace: A Study of the Boston Negroes* (1914), consistently traced preventable morbidity and mortality to social and economic marginalization, racism, and limited access to health care. Although many medical and lay observers noted that African Americans shared in an overall decline in infant mortality and tuberculosis, for example, persistent differentials between black and white Americans attracted attention. Between 1900 and 1910 infant mortality for whites declined from 159.4 to 129.7 per 1000 population, while black rates declined from 344.5 to 261.9 per 1000. Rates for tuberculosis were also often triple and quadruple the rates for whites living in the same city. Langston

HUGHES, in his poem "The Consumptive," captured the debilitating clinical and social effects of this disease. *The Negro Year Book,* an annual with a large section on vital statistics, estimated in 1922 that 150,000 of these deaths and 45 percent of annual deaths from all causes were preventable.

During the 1920s and '30s black public-health nurses, physicians, and local activists made the public more aware of the rising incidence of and differentials in life expectancy from cancer and cardiovascular and other chronic diseases. The National Medical Association, the National Association of Graduate Nurses, and the NATIONAL URBAN LEAGUE, among others, pushed National Negro Health Week (begun in 1915) to battle poverty and the high prevalence of such contagious diseases as syphilis and gonorrhea, which increasingly became exposed with the refinement of diagnostic techniques. In 1932 President Hoover's Committee on the Cost of Medical Care traced lags in African-American health status to low socioeconomic status and served as an important catalyst for federal and state intervention in maternal and child health during the New Deal—for example, to reduce infant mortality. By the late 1940s and '50s blacks demanded more rapid integration of hospitals (and staffs) and access to preventive and curative services to address a range of medical conditions. Greater attention to sickle-cell anemia during the civil rights and social welfare movements of the 1960s brought an unprecedented agenda for preventive health education along with the health-care-insurance initiatives of the Great Society.

Despite prominent declines in particular diseases during the past half century, African American communities across the United States in the late twentieth century are still plagued by glaring health differentials in chronic and infectious diseases. Fluctuations in the economy and governmental support for local health care have often limited access to preventive health services, making dental care, immunization, prenatal care, and access to health insurance more difficult. Infant mortality among blacks in some cities remains three times as high as it is for white Americans. The Black Women's Health Project in Atlanta and Audre LORDE in *The Cancer Journals* (1980, 1987) suggest ways in which high breast-cancer rates among black women stem from the effects of a discriminatory health-care system and inadequate access to preventive services. According to the government's National Center for Health Statistics, life expectancy for African-American men and women continues to lag behind whites'. Most recently, HIV/AIDS infection rates have risen more rapidly among African Americans than among whites. Taken together, these disease events illustrate how African-American experiences with death and dying still diverge in marked ways from those of other Americans.

REFERENCES

BEARDSLEY, EDWARD H. *A History of Neglect: Health Care for Blacks and Mill Workers in the Twentieth-Century South.* Knoxville, Tenn., 1987.

JAYNES, GERALD DAVID, and ROBIN M. WILLIAMS, JR., eds. *A Common Destiny: Blacks and American Society.* Washington, D.C., 1989.

MCBRIDE, DAVID. *Integrating the City of Medicine: Blacks in Philadelphia Health Care, 1910–1965.* Philadelphia, 1989.

NUMBERS, RONALD L., and TODD L. SAVITT, eds. *Science and Medicine in the Old South.* Baton Rouge, 1989.

SECUNDY, MARIAN GRAY, ed. *Trials, Tribulations, and Celebrations: African-American Perspectives on Health, Illness, Aging and Loss.* Yarmouth, Maine, 1991.

WHITE, EVELYN C., ed. *The Black Women's Health Book: Speaking for Ourselves.* Seattle, 1990.

GERARD FERGERSON

Episcopalians. Although the first African-American Episcopal Church, St. Thomas African Episcopal Church in Philadelphia, was consecrated on July 29, 1794, with Absalom JONES as the first priest, the history of the African-American affiliation with the Episcopal Church began with the baptism of African slave children in seventeenth century Virginia, Maryland, and the Carolinas, where most eastern seaboard planters belonged to the Church of England. While some devout masters baptized slave children, others, suspecting that Christianity might legally or morally undermine their slaves' subordinate status, expressed indifference to religious training for slaves and resisted slave conversions. In spite of resistance in the colonies, several Anglican missionaries began training and baptizing slaves as early as 1695. The Church of England Christianized slaves and Native Americans through the English Society for the Propagation of the Gospel in Foreign Parts (SPG), which was founded in 1701. The first schools for blacks in the colonies were organized by the SPG in the early eighteenth century. Through the SPG, the Church of England became the first church to take Christianity to slaves in the British North American colonies and became the earliest denomination to train blacks to be missionaries.

During the colonial period the Church of England and the SPG established Sunday schools and catechetical schools for missionary training and adult education of slaves. Since baptism and religious instruction depended upon the masters' and mistresses'

attitude, SPG efforts to induce masters to send slaves to regular catechetical instructions met with inconsistent results. While some masters encouraged slave baptism and conversion, many other colonists and Anglican ministers continued to ignore the religious lives of slaves throughout the colonial period. Other colonists apprehensively questioned SPG activities, rejected slave presence at the communion table, and doubted the qualifications of African Americans for Christian salvation and church participation.

Though at midcentury the Church of England had the most extensive work of any denomination among slaves in the southern colonies, the AMERICAN REVOLUTION disrupted the church's work and led to the complete reorganization of the Church of England in America into a separate denomination, the Protestant Episcopal Church of America, in 1787. In addition to losing the momentum and experience of seven decades of work among slaves, the church lost the most influential catalyst for bringing slaves into the Episcopal Church: the large number of Anglican southern aristocrats who were British sympathizers and loyalists. This contributed to the decay and disestablishment of the church in the southern states and the subsequent decline of their membership and the rise of the Baptists and Methodists.

Whereas in the colonial period black participation in the Anglican Church had been centered among slaves in eastern seaboard cities and on plantations, antebellum black Episcopalians were predominantly

An Easter procession exiting an Episcopal church in Chicago in 1941. Black Episcopal congregations were favored places of worship of the black middle class. (Prints and Photographs Division, Library of Congress)

free blacks living in northern cities who saw themselves as role models of black achievement, activism, and independence for other blacks, and as members of a higher social class, differentiated from the masses of illiterate, rural slaves.

Given the identification of the Episcopal Church with the middle and upper classes, the bulk of the antebellum free black community rejected the Episcopal Church in favor of affiliation with the Methodists and Baptists, whose egalitarian message and ease of conversion offered greater access to membership and the ministry. Catechetical teaching and literacy requirements inhibited black membership in the Episcopal Church and especially denied African Americans access to the Episcopal ministry. With no literacy requirements for membership in Methodist and Baptist churches, blacks could not only join these denominations, they could become ministers to their own people. While Episcopalians recoiled at the emotional expressiveness of black worship in song, dance, and shout, the Methodist and Baptist evangelical traditions included these same worship styles. Free to lead their own congregations, black ministers could preach a message of liberation, and their congregations could claim this niche of cultural and political autonomy.

For the vast majority of antebellum blacks who were slaves, Methodist and Baptist membership and ministry were infinitely more accessible than Episcopalian affiliation on the expanding frontiers of plantation slavery. The farmers, planters, and slaves of Alabama, Mississippi, Tennessee, and other new states did not inherit the Anglican traditions of the eastern seaboard colonial aristocracy, but were instead claimed by the Second Great Awakening of Methodist and Baptist revivalism which not only brought slaves into Christianity in large numbers, but also provided fertile ground for the invisible slave church, led by black ministers and embraced by slaves who created African-American religious traditions.

By the end of the CIVIL WAR, these developments—limited access to membership and the ministry; rejection of African and evangelical traditions; and early geographic containment of the church on the eastern seaboard—placed black Episcopalians wishing to proselytize the freed slaves in the disadvantageous position of being in a church which required a highly literate ministry; rejected African folk traditions; afforded African Americans little independence or autonomy compared to the black Baptist church or the independent black Methodist denominations; and appealed to northern urban black communities rather than the majority of blacks in the rural South. Nonetheless, some of the most important leaders of African-American cultural and religious life were Episcopal priests, including James HOLLY (1829–1911), and Alexander CRUMMELL (1819–1898), both of whom, somewhat surprisingly given their denominational background, became ardent black nationalists.

In the two decades following the Civil War, the Episcopal Church's Freedman's Commission operated schools, hospitals, and churches, but failed to compete effectively against the missionary campaign launched by the predominantly black denominations whose membership swelled. To make matters worse, the black membership of the Episcopal Church drastically declined during RECONSTRUCTION when the Episcopal Church failed to accept black Episcopalians' demands for black ministers. For example, in South Carolina between 1860 and 1868 black membership in the Episcopal Church declined from 3,000 to less than 300.

By the 1880s, a slight increase in black membership from the small but growing black middle class in southern cities alarmed southern Episcopalians who had embraced the widespread reestablishment of white supremacy and segregation of the post-Reconstruction South. In 1883 the Sewanee Conference of Southern Bishops met in Sewanee, Tenn., and unanimously authorized diocesan segregation and placed the care of black congregations and ministers under missionary organizations. In response to this and other forms of church discrimination, Alexander Crummell, rector and founder of St. Luke's in Washington, D.C., founded the Conference of Church Workers Among Colored People in 1883 and the Women's Auxiliary to the Conference in 1894. Although the Negro Conference failed in its appeal to the General Convention to change the Sewanee Canon's endorsement of church segregation, they succeeded in getting the General Convention to appoint a Church Commission for Work Among the Colored People. The meetings of the Conference of Church Workers Among Colored People also provided black Episcopalians a forum in which they could meet each other, share their grievances, and formulate solutions to their ambiguous and limited role in the church.

As black Episcopalians entered the twentieth century, they confronted an ironic, complex dilemma which discouraged growth of black membership: While their own predominantly white denomination continued to discriminate against them by denying black clergy and lay persons full voting rights on diocesan councils and in the General Convention, the black denominations saw the majority of black Episcopalians as elite, privileged, and snobbish. From the 1880s to the 1930s, the Episcopal Church did not decide if black communicants should be separated into racial dioceses and missionary districts with their own bishops or if they should remain in a diocese and be given equal representation and perhaps a black suffragan bishop (a bishop without the right to become archbishop). In 1903 the Conference of Colored Workers asked that black churches be placed under the general church rather than the diocesan conventions composed of the same local white leaders who supported and upheld secular racial segregation and discrimination. Requests for redress of the inequality within the church at the 1905 General Convention went unanswered and revealed that sentiments among northern white Episcopalians were little better than those of the Sewanee Conference. Northern dioceses questioned African-American ordinations and promoted the idea of placing black congregations under the supervision of white parishes or under the direction of the bishop.

The question of independence was even more complicated, because black churches were not self-supporting. Black clergy salaries and black school supplies were paid by the Domestic and Foreign Missionary Society or the American Church Missionary Society and their auxiliaries until 1912. In 1918 Edward T. Demby and Henry B. Delany became the first black suffragan bishops.

By 1921 the Episcopal Church had two black bishops, 176 black ministers, 288 African-American congregations and 31,851 communicants concentrated along the eastern seaboard from New York to Georgia. The church had failed to respond adequately to requests for a black ministry, though it had established schools during the late nineteenth century—not only primary and secondary schools, but also schools to train teachers, ministers, and missionaries to go to Africa. Like the churches, the schools also had a welfare status and received at least half of their funding from the American Church Institute for Negroes, Inc., the agency that disbursed general church funds for black education. In spite of extensive efforts for black education, these schools created few black members, churches, or ministers. Black students felt no necessary allegiance to or affiliation with the Episcopal Church. Rather, their training led to secular jobs and their membership remained with the predominantly black denominations. After decades of training blacks, the church continued to impede African-American ordinations and to maintain the dependent status of black congregations as subordinate churches.

The large urban African-American migrations following World Wars I and II failed to increase the numbers of black Episcopalians. Rather, the rural folkways of black Southerners made black Episcopalians even more estranged from the black southern working class that filled northern cities. As ever larger numbers of black Southerners entered the urban North, black Episcopal scholars and clergy attacked the spontaneous, emotional music and folk traditions of rural black southern church culture in the Methodist and especially the Baptist churches.

The Civil Rights Movement of the 1950s and '60s and the Black Power movements of the 1960s and '70s evoked increasing racial consciousness among blacks within predominantly white denominations, including Episcopalians. Black Episcopalians confronted their historical dual identity crisis—one within the Episcopal church where black members and clergy had felt alienated, excluded, and invisible for almost two centuries, and the other in trying to identify with other black Christians, especially those in independent black churches.

Black Episcopalians responded to this new climate of racial awareness by forming the Episcopal Society of Cultural and Racial Unity and the General Convention Special Program in 1967. Formed out of the merger of the Conference of Colored Church Workers and Summer Schools of Religious Education, the Union of Black Episcopalians was founded in 1968 to confront the historically diminished role of African Americans in the Episcopal Church. More than twenty chapters in the United States serve 150,000 black members out of 3,500,000 Episcopalians. In 1972 the Union of Black Episcopalians had the church establish the Absalom Jones Theological Institute at the Interdenominational Theological Center in Atlanta. In 1973 the General Convention formed the Commission for Black Ministries, now the Office of Black Ministries, which compiles a directory of black clergy, convenes the Black Diocesan Executives, and acts as a clearinghouse for African-American clergy. In 1981 the church published an official supplementary hymnal *Lift Every Voice and Sing: A Collection of Afro-American Spirituals and Other Songs*. Since the 1960s a large influx of black Anglicans from the Caribbean and the development of new liturgies directed toward black parishioners have revitalized the African-American presence in the Episcopal Church.

Whereas the National Baptist Convention could claim a tradition of independence and the largest black Methodist denominations could embrace a strong tradition of protest, it seemed that the black Episcopal tradition could claim neither independence nor protest. Beginning in the 1960s black Episcopalians affirmed the strains of independence and protest within the African-American religious traditions by celebrating being Episcopalian and black. In recent years women have taken a more active role in the church. In 1976 the social activist, lawyer, and poet Pauli MURRAY became the first black female priest in the Episcopal Church; in 1980 Barbara HARRIS—a black woman—became the first female Episcopal bishop. Black Episcopal clergy joined the National

Council of Black Churches in its attack on white domination of the National Council of Churches and in its efforts to improve the lives of urban blacks. Since 1973 the Episcopal liturgical calendar has included the celebration of Absalom Jones, the first black Episcopal priest.

REFERENCES

BENNETT, ROBERT A. "Black Episcopalians: A History from the Colonial Period to the Present." *Historical Magazine of the Protestant Episcopal Church* 22 (1979): 312–321.

BRAGG, GEORGE F. *Afro-American Church Work and Workers.* Baltimore, Md., 1904.

———. *History of the Afro-American Group of the Episcopal Church.* Baltimore, Md., 1922.

BRYDON, GEORGE MacLAREN. *The Episcopal Church Among the Negroes of Virginia.* Richmond, Va., 1937.

HOOD, R. E. "From a Headstart to a Deadstart: The Historical Basis for Black Indifference Toward the Episcopal Church, 1800–1860." *Historical Magazine of the Protestant Episcopal Church* 51 (1982): 269–296.

SPENCER, JON MICHAEL. "The Episcopal Church." In *Black Hymnody: A Hymnological History of the African-American Church.* Knoxville, Tenn., 1993, pp. 165–181.

LILLIE JOHNSON EDWARDS

Equiano, Olaudah (c. 1750–April 30, 1797), autobiographer. Also known as Gustavus Vassa, Equiano was born the son of an Ibo chieftain in Benin, now part of Nigeria. He was eleven when he and his sister were kidnapped and sold to white slave traders on the coast. He was subsequently shipped to Barbados and later Virginia, where he was sold to a British naval officer whom he served for nearly seventeen years. On board ships and during brief intervals in England, he learned to read and write and converted to Christianity. His autobiography relates his several adventures at sea off the Canadian coast during the Seven Years' War and later with Admiral Boscawen's fleet in the Mediterranean. To his dismay, his master, who had promised him his freedom, sold him to an American shipowner who employed him in trading runs—sometimes with slaves as cargo—between the islands of the West Indies and the North American

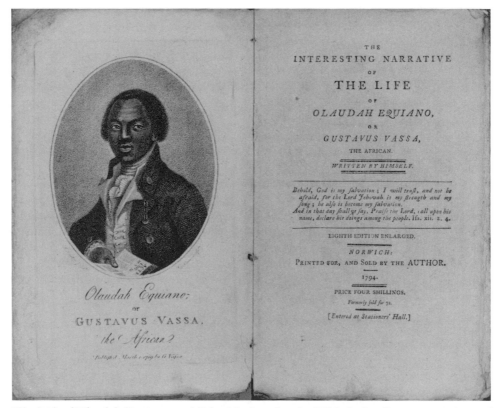

The Life of Olaudah Equiano, published in London in 1784, is the first masterpiece of African autobiography in English. Equiano provides an absorbing account of his African boyhood, his North American enslavement, and his subsequent struggles as a free black in the British Atlantic world. (Prints and Photographs Division, Library of Congress)

coast. Here Equiano records murders and cruel injustices inflicted on blacks, both free and enslaved.

In 1766, Equiano was at last able to purchase his freedom but elected to remain a seaman, although he passed some periods in England. Among other adventures, he sailed on the Phipps expedition to the Arctic in 1772–1773, and later worked as a manservant on a tour of the Mediterranean and as an assistant to a doctor with the Miskito Indians in Nicaragua. After 1777, he remained largely land-bound in the British Isles and assumed increasingly active roles in the antislavery movement. In 1787 he was appointed commissioner of stores for the resettlement of free Africans in Sierra Leone, but was dismissed after accusing a naval agent of mismanagement. His efforts to join an African expeditionary group or to do African missionary work also met with failure. In 1789 he published his autobiography under the title *The Interesting Narrative of Olaudah Equiano, or Gustavus Vassa the African, written by himself.* Three years later he married Susannah Cullen, an Englishwoman by whom he would have two children. Although several of his accounts have since been questioned, he saw nine editions of the book printed in his lifetime, thereby drawing invitations to lecture throughout the British Isles. Because Equiano infuses his autobiography with antislavery views and identifies enslaved blacks with biblical Hebrews, his work is generally regarded as a truer precursor of slave narratives written between 1830 and 1860 than other eighteenth-century Afro-American autobiographies.

REFERENCES

EDWARDS, PAUL. "Equiano's Narrative." Introduction to *The Life of Olaudah Equiano, or Gustavus Vassa the African,* edited by Paul Edwards. Harlow, U.K., 1988, pp. viii–xxxv.

OGUDE, S. E. "Facts into Fiction: Equiano's Narrative Revisited." *Research in African Literatures* 13 (1982): 31–43.

EDWARD MARGOLIES

Erving, Julius Winfield, II (February 22, 1950–), basketball player. Born in East Meadow, N.Y., Julius Erving, popularly known as "Dr. J," was one of the most exciting players in professional BASKETBALL. His hallmark move was a slam dunk that began with a tremendous leap from the foul line. As a basketball player at Roosevelt High School, Erving made the All-County and All–Long Island teams while maintaining a high scholastic average. Offered many athletic scholarships on graduation, he chose the University of Massachusetts. Dropping out after his junior year, he signed a four-year contract with the Virginia Squires of the American Basketball Association (ABA) and was voted rookie of the year in 1972. The following year Erving was traded to the New York Nets, and in his first season with the Nets he led the league in scoring and helped his team capture the ABA championship.

In 1976 Erving was sold by the Nets to the Philadelphia 76ers of the National Basketball Association (NBA). He retired from professional basketball in 1987, the same year in which he became the third player in NBA history to score 30,000 points. During his career, Erving was named to the NBA All-Star First Team eleven times (every year from 1977 to 1987), and in 1977 and 1983 was voted the All-Star Game's most valuable player. He was voted the most valuable player twice in the ABA (1974 and 1976) and once in the NBA (1981), and in 1980 was named to the NBA thirty-fifth anniversary All-Time Team.

Upon his retirement from basketball, Erving began to devote his energies to numerous business enterprises, including the Erving Group, Inc., "Dr. J" Enterprises, the Philadelphia Coca-Cola Bottling Company, and Garden State Cable. For his athletic and civic activities, he has been the recipient of honorary degrees from Temple University (1983) and the University of Massachusetts (1986, the same year in which he completed his undergraduate degree). Other awards include EBONY's Jackie Robinson Award for American Black Achievement (1983), American Express's Man of the Year Award (1985), and the Lupus Foundation of America Award (1985).

REFERENCES

New York Times, April 7, 1987, p. D35.
New York Times, April 20, 1988, p. D27.

KEITH ROONEY

Estes, Simon Lamont (February 2, 1938–), opera singer. The son of a coal miner and the grandson of a slave, Simon Estes was raised in a religious family in Centerville, Iowa. After entering the University of Iowa on a small athletic grant, he studied medicine, social psychology, and theology. When music professor Charles Kellis introduced bass-baritone Estes to opera, he soon began studying voice with Kellis, who remained his principal voice teacher. He continued his training on a scholarship at New York's Juilliard School. His operatic debut was as Ramfis in *Aida* at the Berlin Deutsche Oper (1965). In 1966, he won a silver medal at the first International Tchaikovsky Competition in Moscow, and achieved international recognition in 1978, when he sang *Der fliegende Holländer* at the Bayreuth Festival, becoming the first African-American man to sing there. After making his U.S. concert debut at Carnegie Hall in 1980, he made his Metropolitan Opera debut on January 4, 1982, as the Landgrave in *Tannhäuser*. Estes's repertoire includes spirituals, lieder, and almost ninety operatic roles, including Wotan in *Der Ring des Nibelungen* and King Marke in *Tristan und Isolde,* which rank among his favorites. Estes has also performed the roles of Ned in Scott JOPLIN's *Treemonisha* (1972) and Porgy in the Metropolitan Opera's first production of Gershwin's *Porgy and Bess* (1985).

REFERENCE

MATHEOPOULOS, HELENA. "Simon Estes." In *Bravo: Today's Great Tenors, Baritones, and Basses Discuss Their Roles.* London, 1986.

KYRA D. GAUNT

Eugenics. Eugenics is a scientific and social movement that advocates selective breeding to maintain racial "fitness." It did not gain widespread social appeal until after the publication of Charles Darwin's *On the Origin of Species by Means of Natural Selection; or the Preservation of Favoured Races in the Struggle for Life* in 1859, when biologists embarked on an unprecedented quest for mechanisms of human heredity. Francis Galton, a British biologist and first cousin of Darwin, coined the term "eugenics" in 1883 to describe his research on the heritability of intelligence, which he published in *Hereditary Genius* (1869) and *Natural Inheritance* (1889)—two precursors to later studies of IQ and race. Galton, who pioneered many statistical analyses in his correlations of brain and skull size with racial development, took it as axiomatic, as did other eugenicists, that genetic material produced different mental and moral capacities among racial and ethnic groups.

With the increased popularity of Social Darwinism—a philosophy that applied Darwin's principles of evolutionary struggle and survival to human affairs—ardent eugenicists in Britain and America argued that social policy initiatives would not benefit the poor or socially "unfit" since genes determined behavior through biological processes. The rediscovery of Gregor Mendel's laws of heredity in 1900 contributed to a more widespread appeal. Most eugenicists inferred from Mendel's work that single genes, rather than the complex interactions that we now know take place at the molecular level, produced specific human behaviors.

In their late nineteenth- and early twentieth-century call for scientific legitimacy, eugenicists basically espoused two types of prescriptions for the preservation of the more fit "stocks." "Negative eugenics" programs, they argued, would prevent reproduction among unfit racial stocks, while "positive eugenics" would encourage better breeding practices among the morally and mentally superior to remove the threat of deleterious traits and undesirable pedigrees. Highly successful in their social and political appeals to Victorian notions of womanhood with their equation of motherhood with racial purity, eugenicists heralded the publication of Victoria Woodhull's *The Rapid Multiplication of the Unfit* (1891), for instance, as a tract designed to transform reproductive behavior in society.

In this context, eugenics, or "racial hygiene," as it was often called, supplied scientific validation for America's nativist appeals for the maintenance of strict social segregation as well. Largely in response to early twentieth-century waves of immigration into the United States, eugenicists used plant and animal breeding studies to warn about the destabilizing effects of MISCEGENATION.

Although the first International Eugenics Congress was not held until 1912 in London, the social acceptance of eugenic ideas generated a global institutionalized movement from the turn of the century. The *Journal of Social and Racial Biology* was founded in Germany in 1904, three years after Karl Pearson, Walter Weldon, and Francis Galton founded *Biometrika*—a journal dominated by highly statistical eugenics investigations. Indiana became the first U.S. state to enact a sterilization law in 1907, just three years before a Eugenics Record Office opened in Cold Spring Harbor, Long Island, in 1910.

Headed by Charles Davenport, an eminent American biologist, the Eugenics Records Office promoted an aggressive negative eugenics campaign that championed sterilization measures and issued extensive reports on the mental deficiency of paupers, criminals, and various ethnic and racial groups. Davenport's subsequent publications, *Heredity in Relation to Eugenics* (1911) and *Race Crossing in Jamaica* (1929), published with Morris Steggerda, presented the strongest contemporary defense of eugenics and offered the decree that most disparities in health status were due to genetic factors and not socioeconomic status and other mitigating environmental conditions.

The proliferation of studies relating IQ to race after World War I, when the psychologist Henry Goddard, among others, identified marked disparities between black and white recruits, reflected a movement to define a genetic basis for intelligence. Indeed, the influence of eugenic investigations of mental capacity on public policy reached a prominent juncture in the

1927 *Buck* v. *Bell* Supreme Court case in which Justice Oliver Wendell Holmes ruled that the prospect of "three generations of imbeciles" warranted the forced sterilization of a Virginia woman who had been stigmatized by an IQ test. The Court's ruling legitimized thousands of sterilizations across the country.

In 1924, one year after the American Eugenics Society was founded, the eugenics movement witnessed perhaps its greatest victory with the passage of the Immigration and Restriction Act. Agitation for restrictive legislation persisted after the act's passage, but, following the congressional testimony of prominent American eugenic scientists who argued that foreign immigration promoted the deterioration of American racial stability, President Calvin Coolidge (1872–1933) signed an act that authorized a 2 percent cap on countries listed in the 1890 Census, thereby limiting the entrance of the "lesser" racial stocks of eastern and southern Europe. By the 1930s, however, a new generation of anthropologists and biologists had begun to critique rigid biological representations of race with new data on the prevalence of intra- and interracial genetic variation.

News of experiments conducted by the Nazis in Germany during World War II, in particular, bolstered popular and scientific skepticism of eugenic studies among younger geneticists. Since World War II, molecular biologists have firmly documented the biological insignificance of race. Contemporary psychologists have also demonstrated how earlier IQ studies ignored similarities in outcomes across racial groups. Although hereditarian arguments for a relation between IQ and race exist in contemporary scientific discourse alongside other static biological models of race, the acceptance of eugenic ideas has not reached the scale of earlier movements.

REFERENCES

DUSTER, TROY. *Backdoor to Eugenics.* New York, 1990.

GOULD, STEPHEN JAY. *The Mismeasure of Man.* New York, 1981.

KEVLES, DANIEL. *In the Name of Eugenics.* Berkeley, Calif., 1985.

PROCTOR, ROBERT N. *Racial Hygiene: Medicine under the Nazis.* Cambridge, Eng., 1988.

GERARD FERGERSON

Europe, James Reese (February 22, 1881–May 9, 1919), composer and conductor. Born in Mobile, Ala., Europe spent his formative years in Washington, D.C., where his father held a position with the

U.S. Postal Service. The family was unusually musical; his brother, John, became a noted ragtime pianist, and his sister, Mary, was an accomplished concert pianist, choral director, and music teacher in the Washington public schools. James Europe attended M Street High School and studied violin, piano, and composition with Enrico Hurlie of the Marine Corps Band and Joseph Douglass, grandson of Frederick DOUGLASS. Other musical influences included Harry T. BURLEIGH (especially his arrangements of African-American spirituals), organist Melville Charlton, and composer Will Marion COOK.

Like Cook and Burleigh—who had both studied with the celebrated Bohemian composer Antonín Dvořák while he was directing the Prague National Conservatory of Music—Europe accepted Dvořák's assessment of the importance of African-American folk music as a basis for an American national music. He did not believe, however, as did many at the time, that popular forms of musical expression were necessarily vulgar or "lowbrow" and therefore lacked potential musical value. He was a consistent champion of African-American music and musical artistry at every level and in any form, including those (like jazz) that had yet to emerge fully.

After moving to New York City in 1903, Europe established himself as a leading composer and music director in black musical theater, contributing to such productions as John Larkins's *A Trip to Africa* (1904), Ernest Hogan's *Memphis Students* (1905), Cole and Johnson's *Shoo-fly Regiment* (1906–1907) and *Red Moon* (1908–1909), S. H. Dudley's *Black Politician* (1907–1908), and Bert WILLIAMS's *Mr. Lode of Koal* (1910). In April 1910, Europe and several fellow professionals (including Ford Dabney, William Tyers, and Joe Jordan) formed the Clef Club, a union and booking agency that substantially improved the working conditions for black musicians in New York City. Europe was elected president and conductor of the club's concert orchestra, a 125-member ensemble whose unusual instrumentation (consisting primarily of plucked or strummed instruments) he felt to be better suited to the performance of authentic African-American music than that of the standard symphony orchestra. The orchestra's 1912 Concert of Negro Music at Carnegie Hall was a historic event, and Europe and the orchestra repeated their appearance on New York's most famous stage in 1913 and 1914.

In addition to developing "an orchestra of Negroes which will be able to take its place among the serious musical organizations of the country," Europe realized the practical importance to black musicians of taking advantage of the increasing demand for popular music to support the expansion of nightlife. Between 1910 and 1914, he built the Clef Club (and later, the Tempo Club) into the greatest force for organizing and channeling the efforts of black musicians in New York, providing musicians for vaudeville orchestras, hotels, cabarets, and dance halls, as well as for private society parties and dances. In 1913, as a result of his success in providing dance orchestras for the eastern social elite, Europe was recruited as musical director for the legendary dance team of Vernon and Irene Castle. Between them, they revolutionized American social dancing by making the formerly objectionable "ragtime" dances (turkey trots, one-steps, etc., which had been derived from traditional African-American dance practice) widely acceptable to mainstream America. The most lasting of the Castle dances, the fox-trot, was conceived by Europe and Vernon Castle after a suggestion by W. C. HANDY. Europe's association with the Castles led to a recording contract with Victor Records, the first ever for a black orchestra leader.

Late in 1916, Europe enlisted in the Fifteenth Infantry Regiment (Colored) of New York's National Guard and was commissioned as a lieutenant. Largely as an aid to recruitment, he organized a regimental brass band that became, when the Fifteenth was mobilized and sent overseas, one of the most celebrated musical organizations of World War I. As a machine-gun company commander, Europe also served in the front lines and was the first black American officer in the Great War to lead troops into combat. Upon his return to the United States in early 1919, he was hailed as America's "jazz king" for incorporating blues, ragtime, and jazz elements into his arrangements for the band. He received another recording contract and embarked upon a nationwide tour. During a performance in Boston, however, Europe was cut in a backstage altercation with a mentally disturbed member of the band. The injury did not appear serious at first, but his jugular vein had in fact been punctured, and he died before the bleeding could be stopped. Europe's funeral was the first public funeral ever held for an African American in New York City; he was buried with full military honors in Arlington National Cemetery.

Though Europe was not a composer of major concert works, his more than one hundred songs, rags, waltzes, and marches include several ("On the Gay Luneta," "Castle House Rag," "Castle Walk," "Hi There," "Mirandy") that exhibit unusual lyricism and rhythmic sophistication for their day. But it was as an organizer of musicians, as a conductor who championed the works of other African-American composers, and as an arranger and orchestrator that his genius was most pronounced and his influence the greatest. In this regard, Europe may properly be seen as an original catalyst in the development of orchestral jazz, initiating a line of development that would eventually lead to Fletcher HENDERSON and Duke EL-LINGTON. Among the many individuals who acknowledged his pioneering influence were Eubie BLAKE and Noble SISSLE (whose epoch-making 1921 musical *Shuffle Along* helped restore black artistry to the mainstream of American musical theater) and composer George Gershwin.

REFERENCES

BADGER, R. REID. "James Reese Europe and the Prehistory of Jazz." *American Music* 7 (1989): 48–68.
WELBORN, RON. "James Reese Europe and the Infancy of Jazz Criticism." *Black Music Research Journal* 7 (1987): 35–44.

R. REID BADGER

Evans, Ernest.   *See* Checker, Chubby.

Evans, Mari E. (July 16, 1923–), poet. Born in Toledo, Ohio, Mari Evans attended high school and college locally. Though she enrolled at the University of Toledo to study fashion design, she soon substituted her initial interest for writing poetry. Now recognized as a major contemporary African-American poet, Evans has been published in over two hundred anthologies and textbooks.

Evans credits her father with encouraging her to express herself creatively. She recalls that he praised her for her first story, written in the fourth grade and published in the school paper. The seed once planted, Evans began writing poetry as a means of highlighting both the triumphs and the failures of her community. Her poetry reflects a growing attempt to analyze and suggest resolutions for her community's concerns. Evans, who believes that a poet must be socially and politically responsible, has published several volumes of poetry, including *Where Is All the Music?* (1968), *I Am a Black Woman* (1970), *Whisper* (1979), and *Nightstar: 1973–1978* (1981). Her interest in black youth led to the publication of several esteem-building juvenile pieces, including *JD* (1973), *I Look at Me!* (1973), *Rap Stories* (1973), *Singing Black* (1976), and *Jim Flying High* (1979). Evans's landmark book, *Black Women Writers (1950–1980): A Critical Evaluation* (1984), brings together a collection of essays examining the work of fifteen of her contemporaries.

Evans combines writing with teaching and has held several posts in academia, including Purdue University, Indiana University at Bloomington, Northwestern University, Washington University in St. Louis, Cornell University, and the State University of New York at Albany. She has won a host of awards, including a John Hay Whitney Fellowship in 1965, a Woodrow Wilson Grant in 1968, a Black Academy of Arts and Letters Award in 1970, and a National Endowment of the Arts Creative Writing Award in 1981.

REFERENCES

"Mari Evans." In *Contemporary Authors*, NRS, vol. 2.

PEPPERS, WALLACE R. "Mari Evans." In Trudier Harris and Thadious Davis, eds. *Afro-American Poets since 1955: Dictionary of Literary Biography*, vol. 41. Detroit, 1985.

ELIZABETH BROWN-GUILLORY

Evans, Minnie Jones (1890–December 1987), painter. Minnie Jones Evans's artistic style has been characterized as semi-surrealistic. Born in rural Pender County, N.C., she spent most of her life in nearby Wilmington, where she attended school through the sixth grade, but never received any artistic instruction. She married Julius Evans and was the mother of three sons. Her earliest drawings, executed almost exclusively in wax crayons, were completed around 1925. Evans's multihued paintings were clearly influenced by the numerous botanical specimens at Airlie Gardens, where she worked as an admissions attendant for many years. The genesis for a number of her designs is a human face surrounded by curvilinear and spiral plant and floral forms and eyes merging with foliate patterns. The ubiquitous eyes in her paintings were equated by her with the omniscience of God, and the figures are sometimes portraits of ancient wise men and women and ancestral visitors who peopled her visions, or angels, demons, and chimerical creatures. Around 1966, Evans began creating collage-paintings by cutting out her earlier small wax-crayon designs, pasting them on cardboard backgrounds, and using them in combination with oils and watercolors. Her paintings are surrealistic without a conscious aesthetic and are the works of an artistic visionary who equated God with nature, color with divine presence, and dreams and visions with reality. The final six years of Evans's life were spent in a nursing home in Wilmington, where she died.

REFERENCES

STARR, NINA HOWELL. "The Lost World of Minnie Evans." *Bennington Review* (Summer 1969): 40–57.

"What It Is: Black American Folk Art from the Collection of Regina Perry." Virginia Commonwealth University, Richmond, Va., 1982.

REGENIA A. PERRY

Evans, William.   *See* Lateef, Yusef.

Evers, James Charles (September 11, 1922–), civil rights leader. Charles Evers gained national prominence in 1969 when he was elected mayor of Fayette, Miss. Fayette was then a town of two thousand, of whom twelve hundred were African-American. Evers's victory helped open the way for many black candidates who had long desired political office but who had been restricted by racial discrimination. Since Reconstruction, white Southerners had prevented African Americans not just from campaigning for public office, but even from exercising their constitutional right to vote. Born in 1922 to an impoverished farm family in Decatur, Miss., Evers became the first black mayor since Reconstruction of a biracial Mississippi town.

In 1971, Evers was unanimously nominated by the Mississippi Democratic party as its candidate for governor. Although he lost the election, he was the first African American in the history of the state to be a gubernatorial candidate. From 1973 to 1981 and from 1985 to 1987, Evers served as mayor of Fayette.

Evers first attained national recognition when he replaced his slain younger brother Medgar EVERS

Charles Evers giving a speech. (Photographs and Prints Division, Schomburg Center for Research in Black Culture, The New York Public Library, Astor, Lenox and Tilden Foundations)

(widely believed to have been assassinated by a white supremacist) as NAACP Mississippi field secretary. The elder brother, who had been in business in Chicago, returned to his home state to devote his life to the nonviolent struggle for racial equality and social justice. Toward these ends, Evers successfully led numerous boycotts and voter-registration drives. He has also served as Jefferson County, Miss., chancery clerk administrator.

REFERENCES

BERRY, JASON. *Amazing Grace: With Charles Evers in Mississippi.* New York, 1973.
EVERS, CHARLES, and GRACE HASKELL, eds. *Evers.* New York, 1971.

LOIS LYLES

Evers, Medgar Wylie (July 2, 1925–June 12, 1963), civil rights activist. Born in Decatur, Miss., Medgar Evers served in World War II, graduated from Alcorn Agricultural and Mechanical College, and became an insurance agent. Refused admission to the University of Mississippi's law school, he became the first Mississippi field director of the NATIONAL ASSOCIATION FOR THE ADVANCEMENT OF COLORED PEOPLE.

Evers's job entailed investigating murders of blacks, including that of Emmett TILL; local police generally dismissed such cases as "accidents." A clear target for violence, Evers bought a car big enough to resist being forced off the road, roomy enough to sleep in where motels were segregated, and powerful enough for quick escapes. His family owned guns and kept their window blinds drawn. Evers received daily death threats, but always tried reasoning with callers.

He led voter registration drives and fought segregation; organized consumer boycotts to integrate Leake County schools and the Mississippi State Fair; assisted James MEREDITH in entering the University of Mississippi; and won a lawsuit integrating Jackson's privately owned buses. He also began a similar effort with Jackson's public parks.

In May 1963, Evers's house was bombed. At a June NAACP rally he declared, "Freedom has never been free . . . I would die, and die gladly, if that would make a better life for [my family]."

In the middle of the night on June 12, Evers arrived home. His wife heard his car door slam, then gunshots. He died that night; his accused murderer was acquitted, despite compelling evidence. Evers was buried at Arlington National Cemetery.

The grave of Medgar Evers in Arlington National Cemetery in Virginia. Evers, the state chair of the NAACP for Mississippi, was murdered in the driveway of his home by white supremacists in 1963. (AP/Wide World Photos)

REFERENCES

EVERS, MYRLIE, with William Peters. *For Us, the Living.* Garden City, N.Y., 1967.
WILLIAMS, JUAN. *Eyes on the Prize: America's Civil Rights Years, 1954–1965.* New York, 1987.

ELIZABETH FORTSON ARROYO

Exodusters. The Exodusters were about 20,000 southern African Americans who migrated spontaneously to Kansas from Mississippi, Louisiana, Texas, Kentucky, and Tennessee in the spring of 1879 in fear that they would be reenslaved when Democrats consolidated control as RECONSTRUCTION ended. The Exodus to Kansas was the most spectacular manifestation of a widespread anxiety among southern freedpeople who sought bodily safety, personal autonomy, and their rights as citizens. They had seen enough of their former masters' conception of freedom to realize they were in danger.

Even before the violent campaigns that ended Reconstruction made hundreds of former slaves into refugees, white supremacists had inflicted frightful injustices upon freedpeople; farming arrangements and credit practices kept black families poor and landless. Political violence subverted attempts to engender meaningful democracy in state that had been run as oligarchies by the rich. The rights to vote, hold office, and send children to school all came under intense pressure—much of it blatantly illegal. The withdrawal of federal support, after the Panic of 1873, signaled to white supremacists that the freedpeople were fair game. Thus began a process, called "Redemption," that wrested control of southern states from blacks and Republicans by any means necessary.

To overthrow Reconstruction, white supremacists used murder, rape, arson, fraud, and intimidation. These terrorist campaigns indicated that after Reconstruction, not only would black men not be able to vote, but black people generally would lose the relative autonomy they had come to identify with freedom. Many blacks saw only one alternative to literal or virtual reenslavement: migration. In the late 1870s, black Southerners began a process of interstate migration that would eventually take one-half of the African-American population out of the South.

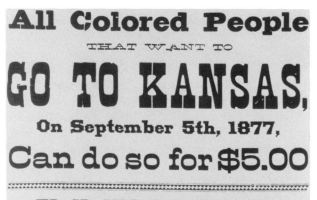

An immigration poster inviting people to join a colony in Kansas for the sum of one dollar. (Photographs and Prints Division, Schomburg Center for Research in Black Culture, The New York Public Library, Astor, Lenox and Tilden Foundations)

Exodusters headed to KANSAS, which they knew as the quintessential free state, in hopes of homesteading on free government land and becoming independent farmers. To people who vividly recalled the oppression of slavery, farming their own land meant being their own masters. Although few of the migrants of the Kansas Fever Exodus (as it was called at the time) were able to claim and keep land as homesteaders in the long term, as Kansans they were able to achieve much more economic and political autonomy than they would have in the South. Given that Kansas eventually became a segregated state (one of the five U.S. Supreme Court cases that together are known as BROWN V. BOARD OF EDUCATION, which paved the way for the desegregation of American life after 1954, originated in Topeka, Kans.), the Exodus to Kansas was qualified, though a real success.

Some confusion exists over the issue of leadership of the Exodus to Kansas. The migration of 1879 was a leaderless, unplanned, millenarian movement, in which migrants trusted in God and the federal government to restore their rights as citizens. But Benjamin "Pap" Singleton (1809–c. 1889) of Kentucky and Henry Adams (1843–?) of Louisiana are often identified as its leaders. Both were champions of migration and poor men who had been slaves.

Singleton was a cabinetmaker from Nashville, Tenn., who had come to advocate migration to Kansas in the early 1870s—a sentiment he shared with Sojourner TRUTH, who visited Lawrence, Kans., in 1871. Although Truth did not actually guide migrants to Kansas, Singleton and his co-workers had some success in the business of migration. He made three trips to Kansas from Tennessee and in 1879 established the Singleton Colony in Dunlap, Morris County. His faith in migration out of the South continued in the 1880s, as he vainly sought refuge for his people overseas.

Henry Adams was a traditional healer, businessman, and political organizer from Caddo Parish, La., who turned to migration only after realizing that hundreds of blacks in northern Louisiana had lost their lives trying to vote or organize politically. In and around Shreveport, Adams and his fellow Union army veterans set up two grassroots networks during Reconstruction: The first, called simply the Committee, rallied voters and kept account of the casualties of white supremacist terrorism; its successor, the Colonization Council, corresponded with the American Colonization Society toward the goal of moving black Southerners to Liberia. Kansas was never Adams's destination of choice, for he remained convinced that only West Africa offered a safe haven for American blacks. Unlike Singleton, who felt his wisdom was divinely inspired, Adams was a tireless political activist whose work came to an end when political violence drove him into exile in New Orleans.

Both Singleton and Adams testified before a joint committee of the United States Senate designated to investigate the Exodus. While these two figures did not lead the Exodus to Kansas, they symbolized black Southerners' well-founded conviction that Democratic rule was against their best interests. After Reconstruction, blacks throughout the South sought sanctuary in Kansas, Indiana, and West Africa. The spectacular, millenarian Exodus of 1879 was merely the most visible indication that black Southerners had no faith in the self-designated "wealth and intelligence," the would-be natural leaders of the southern states.

In 1879, black and white observers divided over whether to support the Exodus to Kansas. In general, old abolitionists and radical Republicans of both races supported the Exodusters' bid for freedom, but often with reservations. Blacks, especially, approved of migration out of the South, given the facts of political violence and economic exploitation, yet many would have preferred a carefully planned movement with educated leadership. While Henry Highland GARNET, Wendell Phillips, Sojourner Truth, William Lloyd Garrison, George T. Downing, John Mercer LANGSTON, and Richard T. GREENER supported the Exodus, the grand old man among black statesmen, Frederick DOUGLASS, was its unbending critic. Douglass had fled Maryland as a fugitive slave in 1838, but by 1879 he had become a high-ranking federal official; he excoriated the Exodusters for acting out of cowardice. Former confederates first denigrated the Exodusters as dupes, then attempted to persuade them to come back home and work. In general, the Exodusters' supporters were most concerned with what happened to black people. Critics thought in terms of the interests of the South as an economic whole that depended on the very low wage labor of black families who had no political rights.

REFERENCES

ATHEARN, ROBERT G. *In Search of Canaan: Black Migration to Kansas, 1879–80.* Lawrence, Kans., 1978.

PAINTER, NELL IRVIN. *Exodusters: Black Migration to Kansas After Reconstruction.* New York, 1976.

NELL IRVIN PAINTER

Expatriates. Expatriation has been an important part of the African-American experience at least since the eighteenth century, when fugitive or newly freed slaves fled to Canada, Mexico, France, and England. Escaping the racism of American society has been the most significant motivation for African Americans seeking to live elsewhere, but the search for political and artistic freedom has also motivated expatriation. Although what constitutes expatriation is the subject of dispute, many consider only those figures who have made an explicit or implicit political statement by their decision to live outside the United States to be expatriates.

Many of the first noteworthy African-American expatriates were abolitionists, and they moved abroad not only to escape racism in the U.S., but to propagandize against it. Paul CUFFE, a prosperous merchant seaman, saw repatriation to Africa as furthering the cause of abolition, and transported thirty-eight African Americans to Sierra Leone in 1815. The pioneering African-American newspaper editor John Brown RUSSWURM worked as an abolitionist editor starting in 1829 in Liberia, later worked as a Liberian government official, and died there in 1851. The abolitionist William Wells BROWN fled to Great Britain in 1849 while still technically a slave, and only returned to the United States in 1854, when friends purchased his freedom. Ellen and William CRAFT, fugitive slaves who fled to England in 1850, spoke out there against American slavery until their return to the United States in 1868.

Religious and missionary work in Africa or the Caribbean also inspired many early black expatriates. Alexander CRUMMELL was a missionary in Great Britain from 1848–53, and lived the next twenty years in Liberia. Henry Highland GARNET, a clergyman and abolitionist, lectured in Germany, Great Britain, and Jamaica from 1850–1856 before moving to Liberia, where he died in 1882. James Theodore HOLLY was an Episcopalian-affiliated bishop in Haiti, where he lived from 1865 until his death in 1911. Amanda Berry SMITH, a religious leader and missionary, began a twelve-year mission in 1878 to Great Britain and West Africa, spending eight of those years in Liberia.

In the late nineteenth and early twentieth centuries, politics continued to motivate expatriatism. Cuffe's vision of mass repatriation was kept alive by Henry McNeal TURNER, a Methodist theologian and early civil rights activist who founded African Methodist Episcopal (AME) Conferences in West and South Africa in the 1890s, and died in Windsor, Ontario, in 1915. Marcus GARVEY's "Back to Africa" movement inspired some African Americans to settle in Liberia in the years following World War I. Although W. E. B. DU BOIS spent most of his life fighting for black civil rights in the United States, in 1961 he settled in Ghana, where he spent the last two years of his life. The political pressures of the Cold War led many black intellectuals, particularly those with COMMUNIST PARTY sympathies, to live abroad. The U.S. government prohibited the political activist and actor Paul

ROBESON from leaving the country in the early and mid-1950s. Eventually, in 1958, he moved to London, where he remained for five years, and visited the Soviet Union frequently.

In more recent years, many militant civil rights leaders have spent time in exile, in some cases fleeing legal charges. Former BLACK PANTHER Stokely CARMICHAEL, now known as Kwame Touré, has lived in Guinea since 1969. Former Black Panther Eldridge CLEAVER fled the United States in 1969, and lived in Algeria from the early 1970s until 1979. Huey NEWTON lived in Cuba from 1974 to 1977. Assata SHAKUR, formerly known as Joanne Chesimard, escaped from prison in 1979 and has since lived in Cuba. Former Black Panther Elaine Brown has lived in Paris since the early 1980s.

Entertainers, writers, and artists often settled in England, France, and northern Europe starting in the nineteenth century, because of the respect bordering on adulation that they received there. The greatest of the nineteenth-century MINSTREL show dancers, William Henry "Juba" LANE, travelled to England in 1848, and died there, at the age of twenty-seven, in 1852. The minstrel comedian Billy McClain lived in Paris from 1906–13. Tap dancer Buddy BRADLEY lived and worked in London starting in 1930. Lavinia WILLIAMS spent more than two decades in Haiti starting in 1954, founding the Haitian Academy of Folklore and Classical Dance. Tap dancer Jimmy SLYDE and ballet dancer Sylvia WATERS both lived in Paris in the 1970s and '80s.

Expatriate actors include Ira ALDRIDGE, who moved to England in 1824, became a British citizen in 1863, and died on tour in Poland in 1867. The best known of all African-American expatriates, Josephine BAKER, moved to Paris in 1925 and quickly became the most popular entertainer in Europe. Her declaration of love for her two homelands, "J'ai deux amours, mon pays et Paris"—"I Have Two Loves, My Country and Paris"—was a hit song in the 1920s. Baker became a French citizen in 1937, and worked in the underground during World War II. She died in Paris in 1975. The Shakespearean and popular actor Earl HYMAN has lived and performed on and off in Norway since 1957. The filmmaker Melvin VAN PEEBLES spent time as an actor and writer in Holland and Paris for a decade starting in 1959.

Europe welcomed African-American writers as early as Phillis WHEATLEY, who visited London in 1773. France has been particularly important to African-American writers, at first because of the presence of French culture in New Orleans in the nineteenth century. The dramatist Victor Séjour lived in France from 1834 until his death forty years later. The poet Camille Thierry moved to Paris and lived there and in Bordeaux until his death in 1875.

The twentieth century brought an extraordinary cross-fertilization between the racial pride of the HARLEM RENAISSANCE writers and the French NÉGRITUDE movement. Claude MCKAY, one of the central writers of the Harlem Renaissance, lived from 1922 to 1934 in France, Spain, and Morocco. The novelist Richard WRIGHT lived in Paris from 1947 until his death in 1960. The novelist James BALDWIN, stigmatized because of his race as well as his homosexuality, lived in France from 1948 until his death in 1987. William DEMBY lived in Italy, France, and Spain starting in 1947, and was followed in the 1950s by a wave of young writers. Chester HIMES lived in Paris until the early 1970s, as did William Gardner SMITH until his death in 1974. From 1953 until his death in 1993 novelist Frank YERBY lived in Spain. The novelist Ronald Fair has lived in Finland since the mid-1970s. Poet James Emanuel has worked in Europe off and on for almost three decades.

Europe was not the only destination for expatriate African-American writers in the postwar years. Willard MOTLEY lived in Mexico City until his death in 1965. Poet Ted JOANS has divided his time between Paris, Africa, and the United States since 1960. Maya ANGELOU lived in Cairo, Ghana, and Sweden in the 1950s.

Jazz musicians traveled to Europe even before the term jazz was popularized, and there found a degree of racial acceptance, artistic acclaim, and economic comfort not possible in the United States. Saxophonist Sidney BECHET travelled to Europe in 1919 with Will Marion COOK's celebrated Southern Syncopated Orchestra, and returned several times before settling in Paris from 1951 until his death in 1959. Drummer Louis Mitchell, who first performed in Europe in 1914, lived and worked with his own ensemble, the Jazz Kings, in Paris and Brussels until 1924. Singer Alberta HUNTER lived in London from 1923 to 39 before World War II forced her return to the United States. Cornetist Johnny Dunn lived in Paris from 1928 to 1938. In 1934 Coleman HAWKINS, then the most important tenor saxophonist in the United States, took a job in London and remained in Europe until 1939.

After World War II, some of America's leading Jazz musicians moved to Europe, among them tenor saxophonist Don BYAS, who lived in Holland from 1946 until his death in 1972. Stride pianist Joe TURNER lived and worked in Europe from 1948 until his death in Paris in 1990. In 1956 drummer Kenny CLARKE moved to Paris, where he lived until his death in 1985. Scandinavia and northern Europe also became a popular destination for jazz expatriates. Pianist Kenny Drew lived in Copenhagen from 1964 until his death in 1993. Tenor saxophonist Ben WEBSTER lived in Amsterdam and Copenhagen from 1964 until his death in 1973. Saxophonist Dexter GORDON, who in 1986 acted the role of a jazz expatriate in the film *Round Midnight*, lived in France and Denmark from 1964 until his death in 1990. Other jazz musicians who went to Europe in the 1960s include Arthur Taylor, who moved to France, pianist Mal Waldron, who moved to Germany, and trumpeter Art Farmer who went to Austria. In the late 1960s and early 1970s, many members of the new generation of avant garde musicians from Chicago, including pianist Muhal Richard ABRAMS and saxophonist Anthony BRAXTON, lived in Paris.

Jazz musicians have also emigrated to Asia. Pianist Teddy Weatherford played piano and led bands starting in 1926 in Singapore, Manila, Shanghai, Bombay, Ceylon, and Calcutta, where he died in 1945. Trumpeter Buck Clayton lived and worked in Shanghai, China, from 1934 to 1936. Although jazz has often explicitly embraced African musical themes, relatively few jazz musicians have expatriated themselves to Africa. The most prominent to do so is saxophonist Yusef LATEEF, who has lived in Nigeria since the mid-1970s.

Although expatriation has been particularly popular among jazz musicians, other types of African-American musicians have also lived overseas. In 1959 the members of the Golden Gate Quartet vocal gospel group relocated to France, and subsequently lived and worked in Germany. Since the late 1970s, folk singer Nina SIMONE has lived in and worked in Europe, Paris in particular. Blues singer and pianist Champion Jack Dupree made his home in London, and blues singer Memphis Slim lived in Europe for many years.

Overseas tours have always been essential to building the careers of African-American classical musicians. The composer Edmond Dédé lived in Mexico in the 1830s, and in France from the 1850s to 1903. Tenor Roland HAYES lived in London and worked throughout Europe from 1917 to 1923. Soprano Marian ANDERSON lived in Europe in the 1920s and '30s, building her career there before returning to the United States. Conductor Dean DIXON lived in Europe from 1949 until 1970, conducting in Sweden, Germany, and Australia. Soprano Reri Grist moved to Berlin in the 1960s and lives in Austria. Soprano Barbara Hendricks has lived in Switzerland for many years. Among his other activities, James DEPREIST became conductor of the Malmö Symphony Orchestra in Sweden in 1991.

The attraction of Paris as the art capital of the world has been strong for many black artists. The painter Henry O. TANNER lived and worked in France from 1893 until his death in 1937. Sculptor Nancy Elizabeth PROPHET worked in Paris from 1922 to 1930. The painter Palmer HAYDEN worked in Paris from 1926 to 1932. Painter William H. JOHNSON lived in Paris from 1926 to 1929 and spent 1930 to 1938 in Denmark. In 1946 painter Herbert GENTRY moved to France and later to Sweden. Cartoonist Ollie HARRINGTON and the painters Larry Potter and Walter Coleman all lived in Paris in the 1950s. Painter Beauford DELANEY moved to Paris in 1953 and stayed until his death in 1977. Sculptor and novelist Barbara CHASE-RIBOUD moved to Paris in 1960.

Many African Americans have expatriated for reasons other than politics or the arts. In 1809 a black servant named Nelson visited Russia with then Minister to Russia John Quincy Adams, and remained there in the czar's service. Norbert RILLIEUX, a scientist and engineer who invented the vacuum evaporating pan used in sugar refining, moved to France in the 1820s, and except for a period from 1840 to 1854 in New Orleans, lived in Paris until his death in 1894. In 1883 the American lawyer and Methodist pastor Thomas McCants STEWART began a three-year term as professor of law at the College of Liberia, and he returned in 1906 as an associate justice of Liberia's Supreme Court. He left in 1915 and moved to England, dying in St. Thomas, Virgin Islands, in 1923.

In the 1980s and 1990s, changing racial and political tensions in the United States and throughout the world have had an impact on African-American expatriation. While many African Americans still prefer to live abroad, many, including James Baldwin, have preferred to be called "transatlantic commuters" rather than expatriates. Those like James Emanuel, for whom racism is a compelling reason to flee the United States in order to live and be buried elsewhere, are now exceptions.

REFERENCES

DUNBAR, ERNEST. *The Black Expatriates*. New York, 1968.

FABRE, MICHEL. *From Harlem to Paris: Black American Writers in France, 1840–1980*. Urbana, Ill., 1991.

MOODY, BILL. *The Jazz Exiles: American Musicians Abroad*. Reno, 1993.

MICHEL FABRE

F

Fagan, Eleonora. *See* Holiday, Billie.

Fagan, Garth (1940–), dancer and choreographer. Garth Fagan was born in Jamaica, West Indies. The son of an educator, his father had once been Jamaica's chief education officer. Fagan came to the United States at age twenty to attend college after training and performing with Ivy Baxter and the Jamaica National Dance Theater in his teens.

In the United States, he first settled in Detroit, where he directed the All-City Dance Company and danced with the Detroit Contemporary Dance Company and the Dance Theater of Detroit. He studied with Martha Graham, José Limón, Mary HINKSON, and Alvin AILEY before accepting a professorship at the State University of New York at Brockport in 1969. He also taught at the SUNY-affiliated Educational Opportunity Center in Rochester (preparing mostly minority, disadvantaged youth for college).

In 1970 Fagan started his own dance company, based in Rochester, N.Y. Because the dancers consisted of inner-city youth and students who came late to dance, the company was originally called The Bottom of the Bucket, But . . . Dance Theater. As the dancers improved and the company gained stature, the name was changed to The Bucket Dance Theater in 1981, and by the company's twentieth year they had become simply Garth Fagan Dance.

Over time, Fagan developed a unique, signature movement style and vocabulary, combining elements of modern dance and BALLET with African and Caribbean rhythms and postures. After extensive training with him, Fagan's dancers, like those of George Balanchine, achieve a certain look, regardless of the body they started with: long, lean, leggy, muscular, yet retaining their individuality onstage, his dancers move quickly with precision and energy from stork-like balances to fluid leaps and spiraling jumps that spring from no apparent preparation.

Fagan has been acclaimed for his dances for couples, such as the 1990 *Until, By & If.* Fagan's couples wrap around one another creating sensuous and electric dynamics. Music for a Fagan work is often live and has included collaborations with JAZZ pianist Don Pullen and jazz composer and trumpeter Wynton MARSALIS. Fagan worked with Marsalis and sculptor Martin PURYEAR for his 1991 *Griot New York.* In *Mask Mix Masque* (1986), an interview with fellow Jamaican Grace Jones is interspersed with her song, "Slave to the Rhythm." Popular works in the repertory include an early men's trio, *Oatka Trail,* named for a wilderness park between Rochester and Buffalo, and *Prelude* (1981). Both works aptly illustrate the key Fagan elements of balance and discipline.

REFERENCES

EMERY, LYNNE FAULEY. *Black Dance from 1619 to Today.* 2nd ed. Princeton, N.J., 1988, pp. 309–311.

THORPE, EDWARD. *Black Dance*. Woodstock, N.Y., 1990, pp. 153–156.

JULINDA LEWIS-FERGUSON

Fair Employment Practices Committee (FEPC). African Americans who served in the armed forces during World War I were disappointed when their expectations for improvement in their status following the war did not materialize. With the approach of World War II, the bitter lessons learned twenty years earlier persuaded leaders of the African-American community that the time to gain concessions for exemplary service to the nation was before and not after the fact. In the spring of 1941, A. Philip Randolph, the president of the Brotherhood of Sleeping Car Porters, began to organize a massive march on Washington to compel the federal government to institute legislation banning discriminatory hiring practices in the war industry.

With preparations for the march under way, and Randolph promising a turnout of more than 100,000 protestors, President Franklin Delano Roosevelt sought to head off what he saw as a potential embarrassment. After a series of discussions between Randolph and the Roosevelt Administration, Randolph canceled the march in exchange for Roosevelt's promise to issue an executive order redressing in-equalities in the war industry. On June 25, 1941, Roosevelt signed Executive Order 8802, which forbade discrimination in employment in federal government and in defense industries, and established the Fair Employment Practices Committee (FEPC), which was charged with investigating complaints and conditions in public and private enterprises deemed necessary for the war effort. The four members of the original committee included two African Americans, Earl Dickerson, a Chicago Alderman, and Milton Webster, first international vice president of the Brotherhood of Sleeping Car Porters.

While the FEPC was empowered to investigate discrimination, in its first two years its enforcement powers were never defined and thus were extremely limited. The FEPC, as the sole agency devoted entirely to the elimination of discrimination, acted in a sense as a gadfly to government and private war agencies by conducting investigations and issuing recommendations. The primary historical importance of the FEPC lies in the very fact of its establishment, for it represented a major step forward in the government's recognition of and commitment to racial equality. It was hailed by black leaders as evidence of the power of united action by African Americans.

The composition of the FEPC was never satisfactory for African-American leaders, who decried the preponderance of white businessmen and politicians with minimal commitment to civil rights on the

Charles A. Houston and Charles L. Horn (far left, left to right), recently appointed by President Roosevelt to the committee on Fair Employment Practices, are shown attending their first FEPC meeting in Washington, March 1944. (Photographs and Prints Division, Schomburg Center for Research in Black Culture, The New York Public Library, Astor, Lenox and Tilden Foundations)

commission. Dickerson, one of the FEPC's most outspoken members, was the only original member not retained when the committee was reorganized in May 1943. His replacement as one of two African-American representatives on the committee, P. B. Young, publisher of the *Norfolk Journal and Guide,* was considered by civil rights leaders to be an accommodationist on issues of segregation and discrimination.

However, Roosevelt's reorganization of the FEPC under Executive Order 9346 gave the committee explicit right to conduct hearings, make findings of fact, issue employment policy directives to war agencies and industries, and recommend to the chairman of the War Manpower Commission measures to be used in eliminating discrimination. Besides Young, the two new members added by Roosevelt were white industrialists with no record of opposition to discrimination.

The impact of the FEPC is hard to gauge. The number of black federal employees tripled in the 1940s, yet this was in large part due to a labor shortage brought on by the war. Similarly, from 1942 to 1944, black employment in the war industry rose from three percent to eight percent, but it is impossible to ascertain the FEPC's direct responsibility for this increase. Some of its most notable achievements came in the private and municipal sectors, where several employers began to hire or promote African Americans after FEPC intervention, including the New York Telephone Company and public transit corporations in Chicago, Philadelphia, and Los Angeles.

To clarify the committee's jurisdiction and powers in view of the war's end, President Truman, shortly after VJ Day, issued Executive Order 9664, which removed the committee's power to issue directives and mandated it to "investigate, make findings and recommendations, and report to the President, with respect to discrimination in industries engaged in work contributing to the production of military supplies or to the effective transition to a peacetime economy." Thus the committee was reverted to its original role as a fact-finding agency. Walter WHITE, chief executive of the NAACP, termed the order a "tremendous disappointment" and remarked that the time for "fact-finding on Negro discrimination is past," and that, instead, "immediate vigorous federal action is necessary."

The FEPC was never made a permanent committee despite recommendations made by African-American leaders and liberal politicians during the Truman Administration. The Senate, led by southern Democrats, successfully filibustered one bill for a permanent committee in February 1946 and in May rejected a one-year appropriation for the FEPC, thus bringing to an end the committee's life. Despite its death at the federal level, by the end of 1946 five states (New York, New Jersey, Massachusetts, Connecticut, and Washington) had enacted Fair Employment Practices acts. Subsequent bills for the establishment of a permanent federal FEPC were blocked by the Senate in 1950 and again in 1952.

REFERENCES

RUCHAMES, LOUIS. *Race, Jobs, and Politics: The Story of the FEPC.* New York, 1953.
SITKOFF, HARVARD. *A New Deal for Blacks: The Emergence of Civil Rights as a National Issue.* New York, 1978.

CHRISTINE A. LUNARDINI

Faison, George (December 21, 1945–), dancer and choreographer. George Faison was born in Washington, D.C., where he attended Dunbar High School. While in high school, he studied dance with the Jones-Haywood Capitol Ballet and Carolyn Tate of Howard University. Faison entered Howard to study dentistry in 1964, but left in 1966, after a performance by the Alvin AILEY company inspired him to pursue a career in dance.

Faison moved to New York City in 1966 and became an immediate success in the dance world. That same year, he was chosen as Lauren Bacall's dance partner in a television special. Faison joined the Alvin Ailey American Dance Theater in 1967 as a dancer and remained through 1969. He left Ailey to begin his own group, George Faison Universal Dance Experience, in 1971. The company's roster of dancers included Debbie ALLEN, Renee Rose, Gary DeLoatch, and Al Perryman. Faison served as dancer and choreographer, creating original work for the company. One of Faison's best-known works is *Suite Otis* (1971), set to the music of Otis REDDING. The dance is for five couples and combines elements of ballet and contemporary dance. Faison also created pieces with a historical and political bent, among them works inspired by the memory of MALCOLM X. *Poppy* (1971) dealt with the problem of drug addiction.

Faison made his choreographic debut on Broadway with the show *Don't Bother Me, I Can't Cope* in 1972. In 1974 he choreographed *The Wiz,* the successful all-black musical retelling of *The Wizard of Oz.* Faison won a Tony Award for his choreography, the first for an African American in that category. By the mid-1970s the George Faison Universal Dance Experience had disbanded, and Faison was choreographing music concerts for such artists as Stevie WONDER; Earth, Wind & Fire; and Gladys

KNIGHT and the Pips. This was in addition to his work in musical theater. Faison has choreographed more than thirty plays and musicals, including the short-lived Broadway musical *1600 Pennsylvania Avenue* (1967) with music by Leonard Bernstein; a Radio City Music Hall production of *Porgy and Bess* (1983); and *Sing, Mahalia, Sing* (1985) at the Shubert Theater in Philadelphia. Faison has also worked in television, and in 1989 he conceived and produced a television special "Cosby Salutes Ailey" for the thirtieth anniversary of the Alvin Ailey American Dance Theater. He won an Emmy Award for his choreography of the HBO special *The Josephine Baker Story,* which aired in 1991.

REFERENCES

DUNNING, JENNIFER. *New York Times,* November 27, 1977, p. B6.

McDONAGH, DON. *The Complete Guide to Modern Dance.* Garden City, N.Y., 1976.

ZITA ALLEN

Family: African Roots.

In the 1990s it is taken for granted that the roots of African-American family structure can be traced to AFRICA. Fifty years ago, however, the prevailing view was quite different. E. Franklin FRAZIER's authoritative book *The Negro Family in the United States,* published in 1939, argued that blacks enslaved in America had been "nearly completely stripped of [their] social heritage." He said of the black family, ". . . there is no reliable evidence that African culture has had any influence on its development." (Frazier, pp. 8 and 15).

Before Frazier, W. E. B. DU BOIS, the century's most prominent African-American scholar, looked at the African-American family in a different light. His pioneering 1908 book *The Negro American Family* noted the importance of connecting "present conditions with the African past." He recognized that while "Negro Americans are [not] Africans, there is a distinct nexus between Africa and America, which, though broken and perverted, [should] not be neglected by the careful student." (Du Bois, p. 9).

Du Bois's views on the connection between African and African-American family structure had no influence on Frazier. By the time Frazier wrote *The Negro Family in the United States,* he had already published two other books in which he criticized those who traced African-American family structure back to Africa (Glazer 1966, p. viii).

To Frazier, the origins of the African-American family were rooted in SLAVERY. He saw the evolution of the black family after slavery as a response or adaptation to the economic, political, and social environment in the United States. Referring to articles Du Bois and others had written extolling their African ancestors, Frazier said these were "scraps of memories, which form only an insignificant part of the growing body of traditions in Negro families. (Frazier, p. 15). Frazier considered nothing in the African heritage to be important to an understanding of the organization or development of the African-American family.

Although Frazier's position on the origin of African-American family structure remained the dominant one for decades, it did not go unchallenged. Melville J. Herskovits, anthropologist and authority on the cultures of Africa and the Caribbean, sought to refute Frazier's thesis in his equally well-known book *The Myth of the Negro Past* (1941). Rejecting Frazier's claim that African Americans had been stripped of their African past, Herskovits provided numerous examples of the survival of African cultural patterns in the areas of kinship and the family, religion, folklore, art, music, and other aspects of African-American life.

Frazier had argued that because the institution of slavery prevented stable marital bonds, "matriarchial" or "maternal" families (later termed "matrifocal families," "female-headed families," and "female-headed households") became the dominant form of African-American family organization. Herskovits made the counterargument that the origins of these families could be traced to the central place of the mother in African polygynous families—i.e., those where men had more than one wife.

Although Frazier asserted that the "maternal" family was the dominant form of the black family during slavery, he cited statistics showing that it was not the most prevalent form of the black family at the time he wrote (Frazier, p. 103). Yet, he and Herskovits focused their analyses on the "maternal" family because they both saw in it features that they considered most clearly to distinguish "Negro family structure in the United States . . . from the family organization of the white majority" (Herskovits, p. 167). These features they characterized as "the dominant role of the mother," and "ease of separation and divorce," and "a high rate of illegitimacy" (Frazier, pp. 89–126; Herskovits, p. 167).

By focusing their analysis on a form of the family that was *not* typical of the majority of African Americans, Frazier and Herskovits inadvertently laid the foundation for many of the inaccuracies and stereotypes found in later scholarship on the African-American family. Not until Herbert Gutman published his monumental study entitled *The Black Family in Slavery and Freedom* (1976) was it definitively established that even during slavery, at least three-fourths of all black families were headed by couples, not by single women.

Thus, while Frazier looked to slavery and Herskovits to Africa for the roots of the African-American family, both of them took an atypical form of that family as the starting point for their analyses. As a result, they overlooked the importance of the *extended family*, briefly mentioned by Herskovits, as the key to the link between African-American families and their African antecedents.

To understand the origins of African-American family structure, the most important consideration is *not* whether a family or household is headed by a male or female, or two parents or one. Rather than focus on household heads, one must look at household composition, kinship networks that link families in different households, values and obligations associated with kinship, definitions of kin and nonkin, and the relationship between kinship and residence.

Approached from this perspective, it becomes clear that there are important features common to African-American families, whether they are headed by women or by married couples. These features, in turn, distinguish them from the idealized Anglo-American family that came to be regarded as the "typical" American nuclear family, comprising a married couple and their children.

At some point in their developmental cycles, most African-American families that reside in a single household will be *extended* to include relatives beyond the nuclear family. For example, families headed by married couples may include their grandchildren and other relatives. Households headed by an unmarried woman might include one or two of her adult daughters or sisters, along with their dependent children.

In other words, historically, the *isolated nuclear* family, comprising only a couple and their children, has been far less common among African Americans than among Americans of European descent. When this is realized, it becomes clear that understanding the dynamics of the *extended family* is the key to understanding African-American family organization (Sudarkasa 1975, 1980, 1981, 1982).

Scholars familiar with African extended family organization can readily see how this was transformed in the United States in response to conditions that existed during slavery and beyond. Thus, Herskovits could see myriad examples of African "survivals" (or "retentions and reinterpretations" as he would later call them) in the African-American family as well as in other areas.

These "survivals" were not so apparent to scholars of African-American history who had little or no knowledge of the societies and cultures of West Af-

rica, from which most African Americans are descended. No less a scholar than Herbert Gutman, whose painstakingly researched book on the black family is replete with data that confirm the link to Africa, could not see the connection. Instead, he speaks about an "adaptive slave culture" without realizing that what was being adapted were institutions that came from Africa (Gutman 1976, especially Chapter 8).

While the debate over the African origins of African-American families was being revisited by Gutman and other scholars in the 1970s, the publication of Alex HALEY's autobiographical novel *Roots* (1976), convinced many skeptics in the general public that African Americans could actually document family connections to Africa. Because *Roots* generally heightened American interest in the African past, in the 1990s Frazier's rejection of any connection to Africa seems strangely uninformed and anachronistic. Scholars and laypersons alike no longer ask *if* there is a connection to Africa, they want to see the evidence of that connection, and to understand it.

One of Herskovits's most important contributions to African-American studies was to document the cultural continuity and long history of culture contact in the contiguous areas of West Africa from which most African Americans came. Thus, while many scholars stressed the multiplicity of "tribes" (i.e., ethnic groups) represented in the population enslaved in America, Herskovits emphasized the commonalities in their cultural backgrounds (Herskovits, pp. 1–85). Nowhere were these commonalities more obvious than in the area of kinship and family organization.

The most characteristic and widespread element in traditional African kinship is the LINEAGE. This is a group of kin who trace their relationship to each other and to a common ancestor through the motherline (in the case of matrilineages) or the fatherline (in the case of patrilineages), but not through both. With the exception of matrilineal Ashanti and other Akan-speaking people of Ghana, most West African societies are traditionally patrilineal. Every person is a member of his or her lineage from birth to death. Each person must marry outside the lineage. Through the practice of polygyny (marriage to more than one wife) and through divorce and remarriage, over a lifetime a person might have marital ties to a number of lineages.

The distinguishing features of African family organization derive from the primacy of the lineage in its kinship structure. The ties of descent that separate each lineage from the other, and the ties of marriage that link them together create the large and complex extended families known in Africa from early historical times to the present. All the adults in a lineage in a given locality, plus their spouses and children make up an extended family that traditionally lived together in a cluster of houses known as a *compound.* These compounds range in size from twenty or thirty to hundreds of people.

Not all members of any given individual's extended family will reside together. Each individual's extended family network cuts across different compounds. For example, in a patrilineal society, children live with their parents in the compound of their father's lineage and extended family. Members of their mother's lineage and extended family (other than those who have married into the same compound as she) would reside in another compound somewhere else.

African extended families may be conceptualized as divisible in two ways. First, there is the division between the "core group" that belongs to the lineage and the "outer group" compromised of the spouses married to members of the lineage. In a patrilineal society, members of the "outer group" are the "wives of the house," who are at the same time the "mothers of the children of the house."

Extended families are also divisible into smaller constituent families comprising parents and their children. These families are roughly analogous to the nuclear families of the West. One major difference, however, is that traditionally, African males could have more than one wife at the same time. Another difference is that the frequent "absorption" of the children of relatives or friends into the African conjugal family tends to make its boundaries more fluid than those of Western nuclear families (Sudarkasa 1981, pp. 41–42).

Over fifty years ago, Ralph Linton (1936) observed that all human families are built around a core group of kin related by consanguinity (ties based on "blood") or conjugality (ties created by marriage). For centuries in Europe, except in the case of royalty, conjugality appears to have been the dominant principle in family organization. In Africa, on the other hand, the principle of consanguinity defined the core group around which extended families were built. Consanguinity rather than conjugality served as the primary basis for family stability over time. In other words, the stability of the African family derived from the stability of the lineage, a kin group that existed in perpetuity. Divorce could dissolve a conjugal union within the extended family, but it did not signal the dissolution of the family, as is the case with Western nuclear families. After a divorce, the in-marrying spouse returned to his or her natal compound. The spouse who was already at home would simply marry another person; or a male in a polygynous union would simply continue with one less wife.

Children or divorced couples normally continued to reside in their natal compounds except under special circumstances. In patrilineal societies, for example, a divorced woman would leave her older children in their father's compound to be reared by his mother, one of his brothers' wives, or perhaps one of her former co-wives. Very young children would usually remain with their mother until they were old enough to move back to their father's compound. There does not appear to have been any problems with "visitation rights," as parents were apparently free to visit their children and vice versa, wherever they resided. On special occasions such as weddings or funerals, divorced wives would even return to their former husband's compound to help with arrangements "on behalf of their children."

One no longer hears the naive argument that Africans came to these shores stripped of their culture just as they had been stripped of their freedom. Obviously, they came with memories, some more vivid than others, of what they left behind. In the context of slavery, they established family groupings that reflected both the African families in which they had previously lived *and* the constraints placed upon them by the slave regime under which they were currently forced to exist.

African extended families were groupings that provided economic assistance, socialization, social control, and social security for their members. It is not surprising that African Americans sought to recreate them on the plantation (Kerri 1979; Shimkin and Uchendu 1978; Genovese 1974; Blassingame 1979; and Owens 1976). These networks helped enslaved blacks to rear their children, handle work assignments, respond to events such as birth and death, and, where possible, escape from slavery.

Like the extended families in Africa, African-American family networks were built around consanguineal kin. According to Gutman, spouses were incorporated into the networks to varying degrees, and "the pull between ties to an immediate [conjugal] family and to an enlarged kin network sometimes strained husbands and wives" (1976, p. 202). Living quarters for the enslaved, such as they were, favored the evolution of separate conjugal families rather than co-residential extended families, as in Africa. There is no doubt, too, that the American preference for the nuclear family also helped to encourage that institution among the enslaved population. Yet, Gutman and others show that husbands and wives on the plantation commonly extended their meager housing to grandchildren and others, both kin and nonkin.

Female-headed households, which had been rare except in matrilineal societies in Africa, constituted only about one-fourth of the African-American families that existed during slavery. Frazier was probably right, however, in attributing the origins of these "maternal" families to conditions of slavery that destabilized marriages and/or made widows of many relatively young women.

Herskovits stretched the evidence when he argued that these female-headed households were the analogues of the mother-child dyads within African polygynous families. The distinct responsibilities women had for their own children within the polygynous family may have helped to socialize them for the responsibilities of heading a household. But the fact is, those mother-child dyads were not separate households. They were an integral part of the polygynous family *and* the extended family that included the various polygynous families (Sudarkasa 1980, pp. 43–46; 1981, p. 46).

Looking at the totality of kin and family relations among African Americans during slavery, it is obvious that even though there are few instances of direct institutional transfer from Africa to America, the examples of institutional transformation are too numerous to ignore or discount (Sudarkasa 1980, 1981). Not only are there examples of what Herskovits called African "retention and reinterpretations" in the structure and functioning of African-American families, but also in the particular use of kinship terminology and the ideology and values governing that kinship.

In reference to the former, the earliest observers of plantation etiquette remarked on the practice of addressing nonkin by the kinship terms of "aunt" and "uncle." The practice of calling siblings by the kinship terms "brother" and "sister" rather than by their given names also derives from the African practice of using terms of reference as terms of address.

An entire essay could be written on the evidence for the perpetuation of African values through the medium of kinship. The family offered a network of security, but it also imposed a number of obligations. Seven basic values emphasize and reinforce the requirements as well as the rewards associated with kinship. A common thread in these seven Rs—respect, restraint, responsibility, reciprocity, reverence, reason, and reconciliation—is the notion of a commitment to the group, often made at the expense of what Americans regard as the rights of the individual (Sudarkasa 1980, 1990).

All studies of the black family in America document what might be called the imperative of kinship, particularly kinship based on consanguineal ties. Thus, writers such as Billingsley (1968), Aschenbrenner (1973, 1975) and Stack (1974) have documented the strong ties of mutual obligation that exist between mothers and sons, mothers and daughters, brothers and sisters, and other consanguineal kin. The focus on the growing number of "absent fathers" in black families has caused many observers to overlook the important role that fathers do play in these families (J. McAdoo 1988). This has also obscured the important roles of sons, brothers, and uncles within the consanguineally based extended family (Sudarkasa 1988).

The great migrations of African Americans from the rural South to the urban North would have been impossible had there been no kin networks to provide housing and other forms of support for the newcomers. The strong ties of kinship within the immediate and extended families still make it possible for most elderly blacks to be cared for without recourse to nursing homes. Extended families still provide most of the child care needed by mothers who cannot take care of their children by themselves. In all these instances, we see evidence of the persistence of African traditions, albeit in ways modified by the American environment in which those traditions have survived.

Conclusion

The African roots of the African-American families are irrefutable. Nevertheless, like all human institutions, African-American families have changed over time in response to the social, economic, political, and demographic environments in which they have found themselves (see, for example, essays in H. McAdoo, ed. 1981 and 1988). Obviously, too, African family organization has also undergone changes over the centuries since the two systems began to diverge as a result of the population upheavals caused by the trans-atlantic slave trade. The pace of change in Africa has been greatly accelerated in the twentieth century, as a result of the forces associated with colonialization, urbanization, and the spread of the market economy, and the emergence of many new nations.

One of the great research topics to be tackled on a longitudinal basis is the comparative study of African and African-American families in their changing contemporary contexts. The fact of their divergence will no doubt be recorded. Convergence in structure is also likely to emerge. Many of the forces operating in contemporary Africa are changing Africa's families in ways similar to those already experienced by Africa's descendants in America.

REFERENCES

ASCHENBRENNER, JOYCE. "Extended Families among Black Americans." *Journal of Comparative Family Studies* 4 (1973): 257–268.
———. *Lifelines: Black Families in Chicago.* New York, 1975.
BILLINGSLEY, ANDREW. *Black Families in White America.* New Jersey, 1968.

BLASSINGAME, JOHN W. *The Slave Community: Plantation Life in the Antebellum South*. New York, 1972.

DU BOIS, W. E. B. *The Negro American Family*. 1908. Reprint. New York, 1969.

FRAZIER, E. FRANKLIN. *The Negro Family in the United States*. 1939. Reprint. Chicago, 1966.

GENOVESE, EUGENE D. *Roll Jordan Roll: The World the Slaves Made*. New York, 1974.

GLAZER, NATHAN. "Foreword." In *The Negro Family in the United States*. Chicago, 1966, pp. vii–xviii.

GUTMAN, HERBERT. *The Black Family in Slavery and Freedom, 1750–1925*. New York, 1976.

HALEY, ALEX. *Roots: The Saga of an American Family*. Garden City, N.Y., 1976.

HERSKOVITS, MELVILLE, J. *The Myth of the Negro Past*. 1941. Reprint. Boston, 1958.

KERRI, J. N. "Understanding the African Family: Persistence, Continuity, and Change." *Western Journal of Black Studies* 3 (1979): 14–17.

LINTON, RALPH. *The Study of Man*. New York, 1936.

MCADOO, HARRIETTE P., ed., *Black Families* (1st and 2nd eds.), Beverly Hills, Calif., 1981 and 1988.

MCADOO, JOHN. "The Roles of Black Fathers in the Socialization of Black Children." In *Black Families*. 2nd ed. Beverly Hills, Calif., 1988, pp. 257–269.

OWENS, LESLIE H. *This Species of Property: Slave Life and Culture in the Old South*. New York, 1976.

SHIMKIN, D., and V. UCHENDU. "Persistence, Borrowing, and Adaptive Changes in Black Kinship Systems: Some Issues and their Significance." In *The Extended Family in Black Societies*. The Hague, Netherlands, 1978, pp. 391–406.

STACK, CAROL. *All Our Kin*. New York, 1974.

SUDARKASA, NIARA. "African and Afro-American Family Structure." *The Black Scholar*, (November–December 1980): 37–60.

————. "An Exposition on the Value Premises Underlying Black Family Studies." *Journal of the National Medical Association* 17 (1975): 235–239.

————. "Interpreting the African Heritage in Afro-American Family Organization." In *Black Families*. Beverly Hills, Calif., 1981, pp. 37–53; 2nd ed., 1988, pp. 27–43.

————. "Reassessing the Black Family: Dispelling the Myths, Reaffirming the Values." *Sisters Magazine* (Summer 1988): 22–23, 38–39.

————. "Roots of the Black Family." *LSA Magazine of the College of Literature, Science & the Arts* 5, no. 3 (1982): 16–19.

NIARA SUDARKASA

Fantasy.   *See* Science Fiction.

Fard, Wallace D. (?–c. 1934), religious and political leader. Little is known about the mysterious Wallace D. Fard, credited with founding the NATION OF ISLAM. Only the years of 1930 to 1934 are clearly documented. He claimed to have been born in Mecca, a member of the tribe of Kureish, to which the Prophet Muhammad belonged, and to have been educated in England and at the University of California. His detractors claimed he had been jailed in California for dealing in narcotics. Neither of these accounts of his life was ever confirmed.

Fard appeared in Detroit some time before 1930, peddling silks and raincoats and declaring that he was on a mission to secure justice, freedom, and equality for American blacks. He professed that he was an Islamic prophet and that redemption would come through Islam. Fard quickly gained a following, especially among recent immigrants from the South who were undergoing severe economic hardship. In 1930, he set up permanent headquarters for what he called the "Lost-Found Nation of Islam" in the Temple of Islam. He also organized the Fruit of Islam, a defense corps; the Muslim Girls Training Corps Class; and the University of Islam, a radically unconventional elementary and high school that Muslim children attended instead of public schools. Fard began the practice of substituting *X* for black Muslims' last names—disavowing their identities as slaves. The names were intended to be replaced later by their "original" Arabic names.

Fard asserted that blacks were the first people on Earth, indicating their superiority to whites, whom he castigated as devils. Fard was a reputed nationalist, calling for racial separatism and self-determination in the form of an independent black republic within current U.S. borders.

The Nation of Islam gained mainstream public attention in Detroit in November 1932 when one of its members, Robert Karriem, "sacrificed" his boarder by plunging a knife into his heart. Press reports tried to link this crime to his involvement in the Nation of Islam. The movement, however, continued. After converting an estimated 8,000 Detroit blacks to the Nation of Islam, Fard disappeared in late 1933 or 1934. His followers used the mysterious circumstances of Fard's disappearance to deify him further, maintaining that he was God, although his successor as the Nation's head, Elijah MUHAMMAD, claimed to have accompanied him to the airport when he was deported.

While Wallace Fard clearly was important in the 1930s, his legacy in the large and influential Nation of Islam is most significant. Although his tenure with the organization was short, he continued to be revered as its spiritual leader. The Nation of Islam stated in an official publication in 1942, "We believe that Allah appeared in the person of Master W. Fard Muhammad, July 1930; the long-awaited 'Messiah' of the Christians and the 'Mahdi' of the Muslims."

REFERENCES

EVANZZ, KARL. *The Judas Factor: The Plot to Kill Malcolm X.* New York, 1992.

WHITE, JOHN. *Black Leadership in America: From Booker T. Washington to Jesse Jackson.* New York, 1990.

SIRAJ AHMED

Farmer, James (January 12, 1920–), civil rights leader, educator. James Farmer was born in Holly Springs, Miss., where his father was a minister and professor at Rust College. The family moved when Farmer's father took a post at Wiley College in Marshall, Tex. Farmer grew up in Marshall and was educated at Wiley College and at HOWARD UNIVERSITY, where he received a bachelor of divinity degree in 1941. During this time, he became interested in the philosophy of nonviolence espoused by Mahatma Gandhi in his movement for India's independence. Farmer refused to become ordained to serve a segregated Methodist congregation (he was committed to interracial forums), and his pacifist ideas and opposition to Army segregation led him to oppose the wartime draft. Exempted from service by his ministerial background, Farmer dedicated himself to pacifist and civil rights causes.

Shortly after graduating from Howard in 1941, Farmer took a job as race-relations secretary of the pacifist group Fellowship of Reconciliation (FOR). In 1942, while living in Chicago, he drew up plans for a civil rights group operating on Gandhian principles, and set up an organization with aid from some University of Chicago students. Farmer became the first executive director of the Chicago-based organization named the CONGRESS OF RACIAL EQUALITY (CORE). Farmer was a committed integrationist, and CORE's early leadership was predominantly white. The Congress remained small, and in 1946, Farmer tired of bureaucratic struggles with FOR and gave up his leadership role to work as a labor organizer for trade unions, and later as a civil rights campaigner for the NAACP. He remained involved with CORE as a field worker.

In 1960, after the MONTGOMERY BUS BOYCOTT and the SIT-INS had made nonviolent protest a widespread civil rights tool, Farmer returned to leadership of CORE, by now based in New York City. In spring of 1961, he organized the first freedom rides, which were designed to desegregate buses and terminals in the South and publicize denials of civil rights. During the effort Farmer was jailed for forty days—the first of many such imprisonments during the days of the civil

James Farmer was executive director of CORE from 1960 to 1966, the period of its greatest influence. Throughout his career, Farmer remained a strong and impassioned advocate of integration as a goal of the civil rights movement. (Photographs and Prints Division, Schomburg Center for Research in Black Culture, The New York Public Library, Astor, Lenox and Tilden Foundations)

rights movement as CORE contingents participated in strikes, sit-ins, voter education programs, and demonstrations, both in the South and in the North. As CORE's national director, Farmer was one of the foremost leaders of the civil rights movement and participated in its major campaigns. His eloquent speaking voice and manner made him a popular lecturer and debater. He wrote many articles and essays, and in 1965 published *Freedom, When?*, a book dealing with the problem of institutionalized inequality and the debate over nonviolence as a protest tactic.

One of Farmer's significant efforts during his years in CORE was his ongoing attempt to improve the position of blacks in the job market and in labor unions. Realizing that African Americans faced disadvantages in schooling and training, Farmer pushed the idea of "compensatory" action by employers and government, including programs for the hiring of proportionate numbers of black workers with a labor pool, and their training in job skills, when necessary. These ideas were a major ingredient in the formation of affirmative action policies.

By 1966, as CORE turned away from its original integrationist goals and nonviolent tactics in civil rights action, Farmer decided to leave the organization. For two years, he taught social welfare at Lincoln University in Penn. In 1968, Farmer, who had long been active in New York's Liberal Party, ran for Congress in Brooklyn on the Liberal and Republican tickets, but was defeated by African-American Democrat Shirley Chisholm.

The following year, Farmer faced a storm of criticism when he accepted the post of Assistant Secretary of Health, Education, and Welfare (HEW) in Richard Nixon's Republican administration. Farmer, who felt blacks should reach out to all political parties, was given the job of increasing minority participation in government. He soon grew dissatisfied with his role in HEW, however, and resigned in 1971.

In 1972, Farmer set up the Council on Minority Planning and Strategy, a black think tank, but was unable to secure sufficient funding. In 1975, he became active with the Fund for an Open Society, and from 1977 through 1982 served as Executive Director of the Coalition of American Public Employees. Starting in 1982 and continuing through the early 1990s, he taught at Mary Washington College in Fredericksburg, Va. He continued to be a strong speaker for black equality, although he remained out of the political arena. In his later years, Farmer developed retinal vascular occlusion, a rare eye disease, and lost all vision in one eye and some vision in the other. Still, he managed to complete a volume of memoirs, *Lay Bare the Heart,* in 1985. Farmer's forceful leadership and eloquence combined with his dedication to nonviolent principles made him one of the central figures of the civil rights movement in the 1960s.

REFERENCES

FARMER, JAMES. *Lay Bare the Heart: An Autobiography of the Civil Rights Movement.* New York, 1985.

MEIER, AUGUST, and ELLIOT RUDWICK. *CORE: A Study in the Civil Rights Movement.* New York, 1973.

STEVEN J. LESLIE

Farrakhan, Louis Abdul (May 17, 1933–). Louis Eugene Walcott was born in the Bronx, N.Y., but was raised in Boston by his West Indian mother. Deeply religious, Walcott faithfully attended the Episcopalian church in his neighborhood and became an altar boy. With the rigorous discipline provided by his mother and his church, he did fairly well academically and graduated with honors from the prestigious Boston English High School, where he also participated on the track team and played the violin in the school orchestra. In 1953, after two years at the Winston-Salem Teachers College in North Carolina, he dropped out to pursue his favorite avocation of music and made it his first career. An accomplished violinist, pianist, and vocalist, Walcott performed professionally on the Boston nightclub circuit as a

singer of calypso and country songs. In 1955, at the age of twenty-two, Louis Walcott was recruited by MALCOLM X for the NATION OF ISLAM. Following its custom, he dropped his surname and took an *X,* which meant "undetermined." However, it was not until he had met Elijah MUHAMMAD, the supreme leader of the Nation of Islam, on a visit to the Chicago headquarters that Louis X converted and dedicated his life to building the Nation. After proving himself for ten years, Elijah Muhammad gave Louis his Muslim name, "Abdul Farrakhan," in May 1965. As a rising star within the Nation, Farrakhan also wrote the only song, the popular "A White Man's Heaven is a Black Man's Hell," and the only dramatic play, *Orgena* ("A Negro" spelled backward), endorsed by Mr. Muhammad.

After a nine-month apprenticeship with Malcolm X at Temple No. 7 in Harlem, Minister Louis X was appointed as the head minister of the Boston Temple No. 11, which Malcolm founded. Later, after Malcolm X had split with the Nation, Farrakhan was awarded Malcolm's Temple No. 7, the most important pastorate in the Nation after the Chicago headquarters. He was also appointed National Spokesman or National Representative after Malcolm left the Nation in 1964 and began to introduce Elijah Muhammad at Savior Day rallies, a task that had once belonged to Malcolm. Like his predecessor, Farrakhan is a dynamic and charismatic leader and a powerful speaker with an ability to appeal to masses of black people.

In February 1975, when Elijah Muhammad died, the Nation of Islam experienced its largest schism. Wallace Dean Muhammad, the fifth of Elijah's six sons, was surprisingly chosen as supreme minister by the leadership hierarchy. In April 1975 Wallace, who later took the Muslim title and name of Imam Warith Deen Muhammad, made radical changes in the Nation of Islam, gradually moving the group toward orthodox Sunni Islam. In 1975 Farrakhan left the New York Mosque. Until 1978 Farrakhan, who had expected to be chosen as Elijah's successor, kept silent in public and traveled extensively in Muslim countries, where he found a need to recover the focus upon race and black nationalism that the Nation had emphasized. Other disaffected leaders and followers had already formed splinter Nation of Islam groups— Silas Muhammad in Atlanta, John Muhammad in Detroit, and Caliph in Baltimore. In 1978, Farrakhan formed a new organization, also called the Nation of Islam, resurrecting the teachings, ideology, and organizational structure of Elijah Muhammad, and he began to rebuild his base of followers by making extensive speaking tours in black communities. Farrakhan claimed it was his organization, not that of

Louis Farrakhan (center), the controversial leader of the Nation of Islam, addressing a rally at Madison Square Garden in New York City in 1985. Farrakhan revived the influence and the popularity of the Nation of Islam after the death of Elijah Muhammad. (Shawn Walker)

Wallace Muhammad, that was the legitimate successor to the old Nation of Islam.

In 1979, Farrakhan began printing editions of *The Final Call,* a name he resurrected from early copies of a newspaper that Elijah Muhammad had put out in Chicago in 1934. The "final call" was a call to black people to return to Allah as incarnated in Master Fard Muhammad or Master Fard and witnessed by his apostle Elijah Muhammad. For Farrakhan, the final call has an eschatological dimension; it is the last call, the last chance for black people to achieve their liberation.

Farrakhan became known to the American public via a series of controversies which were stirred when he first supported the Rev. Jesse JACKSON's 1984 presidential campaign. His Fruit of Islam guards provided security for Jackson. After Jackson's offhand, seemingly anti-Semitic remarks about New York City as "Hymietown" became a campaign issue, Farrakhan threatened to ostracize *Washington Post* reporter Milton Coleman, who had released the story in the black community. Farrakhan has also become embroiled in a continuing controversy with the American Jewish community by making anti-Semitic statements. Farrakhan has argued that his statements were misconstrued. Furthermore, he contends that a distorted media focus on this issue has not adequately covered the achievements of his movement.

Farrakhan's Nation of Islam has been successful in getting rid of drug dealers in a number of public housing projects and private apartment buildings; a national private security agency for hire, manned by the Fruit of Islam, has been established. The Nation has been at the forefront of organizing a peace pact between gang members in Los Angeles and several other cities. They have established a clinic for the treatment of AIDS patients in Washington, D.C. A cosmetics company, Clean and Fresh, has marketed its products in the black community. Moreover, they have continued to reach out to reform black people with the Nation's traditional dual emphases: self-identity, to know yourself; and economic independence, to do for yourself. Under Farrakhan's leadership, the Nation has allowed its members to participate in electoral politics and to run for office, actions that were forbidden under Elijah Muhammad. He has also allowed women to become ministers and public leaders in the Nation, which places his group ahead of all the orthodox Muslim groups in giving women equality. Although the core of Farrakhan's Nation of Islam continues to be about 20,000 members, his influence is much greater, attracting crowds of 40,000 or more in speeches across the country. His group is the fastest growing of the various Muslim movements, largely through the influence of RAP groups like Public Enemy and Prince Akeem. International branches have been formed in Ghana, London, and the Caribbean. In the United States throughout the early 1990s, however, Farrakhan has remained an immensely controversial figure.

REFERENCES

ESSIEN-UDOM, E. *Black Nationalism: A Search for an Identity in America.* Chicago, 1962.

FARRAKHAN, LOUIS. *Seven Speeches by Minister Louis Farrakhan.* New York, 1974.

———. *A Torchlight for America.* Chicago, 1993.

LINCOLN, C. ERIC. *The Black Muslims in America.* Boston, 1963.

LOMAX, LOUIS F. *When the Word is Given.* New York, 1963.

MAMIYA, LAWRENCE H. "From Black Muslim to Bilalian: The Evolution of a Movement." *Journal for the Scientific Study of Religion* 21, no. 2 (1982): 138–151.

MARSH, CLIFTON E. *From Black Muslims to Muslims: The Transition from Separatism to Islam, 1930–1980.* Metuchen, N.J., 1984.

MUHAMMAD, WARITH DEEN. *As the Light Shineth From the East.* Chicago, 1980.

LAWRENCE H. MAMIYA

Farrow, William McKnight (April 13, 1885–1967), painter, printmaker, and writer. William McKnight Farrow was born in Dayton, Ohio, and spent most of his working life in Chicago. He maintained a twenty-four-year association with the Art Institute in Chicago, where he studied from 1908 to 1917 under Ralph Clarkson and Karl Buehr, conducted gallery lectures, and worked as superintendent of the print shop and as an exhibition designer. Farrow also taught art at the Art Institute (he was one of the school's first black instructors), the Carl Schurz Evening School and Museum (1923–1934), and the Northwestern University Settlement. He wrote articles on the work of African-American artists in Chicago for journals like OPPORTUNITY, *Southern Workman,* the CRISIS, and the CHICAGO DEFENDER; in the latter, he contributed a regular column, "Art in the Home." Farrow served as president of the Chicago Art League, an organization founded by black artists in 1925.

Farrow became well known for his landscapes in oil and watercolor; one of his watercolors, *Mother Nature's Mirror* (n.d.), was accepted for the International Water Color Exhibition in 1923. In the late 1920s he also worked as a commercial artist, designing a poster series for Pathé phonographs and Kimball Piano Studios, selling his illustrations to the *Crisis* and illustrating vocational training texts for the Chicago Board of Education. He ran his own Christmas-card business, and three of his card illustrations—prints depicting snowy, small-town landscapes—were exhibited by the Harmon Foundation in 1928. Farrow's lithograph *Peace on Earth* was cho-

sen as one of the fifty best American prints by the American Art Dealers Association in 1933. His etchings also won him the Chicago Art League's Eames MacVeagh Prize in 1928 and its Charles P. Paterson Prize in 1929. An early oil painting, *Portrait of Paul Laurence Dunbar* (1923), reveals Farrow to be a fine historical portraitist, capable of conveying the solemn dignity of the formally dressed poet through the subtle use of contrasting light and coloring.

Farrow's work was shown at many national exhibitions, including the Lincoln Exhibition in 1915 where he won a prize, the Chicago "Century of Progress" World Exposition (1934), the Harmon Foundation (1928–1936), and the Harmon Foundation College Art Association traveling exhibition (1934–1935). In 1935 a solo show of his prints, oils, and watercolors traveled throughout the United States. Little is known about his life after the mid-1930s. Farrow died in 1967.

REFERENCES

LOCKE, ALAIN. *The Negro in Art: A Pictorial Record of the Negro Artist and of the Negro Theme in Art.* Washington, D.C., 1940.

REYNOLDS, GARY A., and BERYL J. WRIGHT. *Against the Odds: African-American Artists and the Harmon Foundation.* Newark, N.J., 1989.

THERESA LEININGER-MILLER

Father Divine (c. 1880–September 10, 1965), minister. Born George Baker to ex-slaves in Rockville, Md., he endured poverty and segregation as a child. At age twenty he moved to Baltimore, where he taught Sunday school and preached in storefront churches. In 1912, he began an itinerant ministry, focusing on the South. He attracted a small following and, pooling his disciples' earnings, moved north and purchased a home in 1919 in the exclusively white Long Island community of Sayville, N.Y. He opened his doors to the unemployed and homeless.

By 1931, thousands were flocking to worship services in his home, and his white neighbors grew hostile. In November they summoned police, who arrested him for disturbing the peace and maintaining a public nuisance. Found guilty, he received the maximum fine and a sentence of one year in jail. Four days later, the sentencing judge died.

The judge's sudden death catapulted Father Divine into the limelight. Some saw it as evidence of his great powers; others viewed it as sinister retribution. Although Father Divine denied responsibility for the death, the incident aroused curiosity, and throughout the 1930s the news media continued to report on his activities.

The charismatic religious leader Father Divine, at the peak of his popularity, leading his followers during a parade in Kingston, N.Y., in 1936. (AP/Wide World Photos)

Father Divine's Peace Mission Movement grew, establishing extensions throughout the United States and in major cities abroad. He relocated his headquarters to Harlem, where he guided the movement, conducted worship services, and ran an employment agency. During the Great Depression, the movement opened businesses and sponsored a national network of relief shelters, furnishing thousands of poor people with food, clothes, and jobs.

Father Divine's appeal derived from his unique theology, a mixture of African-American folk religion, Methodism, Catholicism, Pentecostalism, and the ideology based on the power of positive thinking, New Thought. He encouraged followers to believe that he was God, to channel his spirit to generate health, prosperity, and salvation. He demanded they adhere to a strict moral code, abstaining from sexual intercourse and alcohol. Disciples cut family ties and assumed new names. His worship services included a banquet of endless courses, symbolizing his access to abundance. His mind-power theology attracted many, especially those suffering from racism and economic dislocation, giving disciples a sense of control over their destinies in a time filled with chaos and confusion.

His social programs also drew followers. Although rigid rules governed the movement's shelters, they were heavily patronized. An integrationist, Father Divine campaigned for civil rights, attracting both African-American and Euramerican disciples. Challenging American racism, he required followers to live and work in integrated pairs.

With economic recovery in the 1940s, Father Divine's message lost much of its appeal; membership in the movement declined and Peace Missions closed. In 1946 he made headlines with his marriage to a white disciple named Sweet Angel. He spent his declining years grooming her for leadership. Upon his death in 1965, she assumed control of the movement, contending that Father Divine had not died but had surrendered his body, preferring to exist as a spirit. The movement perseveres with a small number of followers and businesses in the Philadelphia area.

REFERENCES

WATTS, JILL. *God, Harlem U.S.A.: The Father Divine Story*. Berkeley, Calif., 1992.
WEISBROT, ROBERT. *Father Divine and the Struggle for Racial Equality*. Urbana, Ill., 1983.

JILL M. WATTS

Fauset, Arthur Huff (January 20, 1899–September 2, 1983), folklorist and educator. Arthur Fauset, born in Flemington, N.J., received his primary and secondary education in the public schools of PHILADELPHIA. He completed all of his postsecondary education—B.A. in 1921, M.A. in 1924, and Ph.D. (anthropology) in 1942—at the University of Pennsylvania. From 1918 to 1946, Fauset was an educator and administrator in the Philadelphia public school system, including many years as the principal of the Douglass Singerly School. His older half sister, Jessie Redmon FAUSET, was a Phi Beta Kappa graduate of Cornell and a well-known novelist. Arthur Fauset was married to Crystal Bird Fauset for almost ten years; they divorced in 1944.

Fauset's first important essay appeared in 1925, when he published "American Negro Folk Literature" in Alain LOCKE's famous collection *The New Negro* (1925). Also interested in fiction, Fauset won first prize in a short story competition sponsored by *Opportunity* magazine in 1926. He is best known, however, for his anthropological works, which remain an important contribution to understanding the history and culture of African-American life. During a research trip to Nova Scotia, Fauset collected material for *Folklore from Nova Scotia* (1931), which includes folk tales, ballads, rhymes, riddles, and verses as related by black Nova Scotians. He also collected material on folklore from the Mississippi Delta. Other publications include *For Freedom: A Biographical Story of the American Negro* (1927), *Sojourner Truth: God's Faithful Servant* (1938), and *America, Red, White, Black, and Yellow* (with Nella Bright, 1969).

Fauset's best known work is *Black Gods of the Metropolis: Negro Religious Cults of the Urban North* (1944), which was based on his Ph.D. thesis. This study examines the prevalence of religious cults and discusses such leaders as FATHER DIVINE of the Father Divine Peace Mission Movement, Bishop Grace of the United House of Prayer for All People, and Prophet F. S. CHERRY of the Church of God (a sect of the Black Hebrews or Black Jews). It remains one of the most important efforts to explore African-American urban culture. Fauset died on September 2, 1983, at the age of eighty-four.

REFERENCES

BROWN, STERLING A., ARTHUR DAVIS, and ULYSSES LEE, eds. *The Negro Caravan.* New York, 1947.
LOW, AUGUST W., and VIRGIL A. CLIFT, eds. *Encyclopedia of Black America.* New York, 1981.

JOHN C. STONER

Fauset, Crystal Dreda Bird (June 27, 1893–March 27, 1965), elected official. Born in Princess Anne, Md., the daughter of Benjamin O. and Portia E. Bird, Crystal Bird was orphaned at age six and moved to Boston to be raised by her aunt, Lucy Groves. She attended Boston Normal School, and in 1914 began to teach in Boston. In 1918 she became the national secretary for younger Negro girls of the YOUNG WOMEN'S CHRISTIAN ASSOCIATION (YWCA), and traveled the country studying the condition of blacks. Already an experienced public speaker, she received further public visibility in 1927 when the American Friends Service Committee (AFSC) asked her to tour and give lectures on black aspirations. She went on to study at Teachers College, Columbia University, where she earned a B.S. degree in 1931. That year, she was made a social worker and administrator of Negro affairs of the New York and Philadelphia YWCAs. Two years later she helped found the Swarthmore College summer Institute of Race Relations, and became the executive secretary. Catalyzed by the GREAT DEPRESSION and passionate about the need to redress economic inequality, she became active in the DEMOCRATIC PARTY. In 1935, the same year she married Arthur Huff FAUSET, she became director of Negro women's activities for the Democratic National Committee and became assistant personnel director for the Philadelphia office of the WORKS PROJECT ADMINISTRATION (WPA).

In 1938, Democratic leaders persuaded Fauset to run for the Pennysylvania House of Representatives,

Crystal Dreda Bird Fauset during World War II, when she served as special consultant on Negro affairs in the Office of Civilian Affairs. In 1938, with her election to the Pennsylvania House of Representatives, Fauset became the first black woman elected to a state legislature. (Prints and Photographs Division, Library of Congress)

from a heavily white district. There had been few, if any, African-American female elected officials. Minnie Harper had briefly sat in the West Virginia Legislature in 1927, but only as a replacement for her deceased husband. In November 1938, Fauset was elected, becoming the first African-American woman elected to a state legislature. She only served for a year, however, before resigning her seat. Hoping to improve economic conditions for both blacks and whites, she became assistant director of education and recreation programs for the Pennsylvania WPA. In October 1941, with the aid of her friend Eleanor Roosevelt, she was appointed special consultant on Negro affairs in the Office of Civilian Defense in Washington, D.C.

During World War II, Fauset broke with the Democratic party over their treatment of blacks and joined the REPUBLICAN PARTY. She spent the postwar years concentrating on world affairs. In 1945, she helped establish the United Nations Council (now the World Affairs Council) of Philadelphia and traveled to San Francisco to attend the founding of the United Nations. In 1953, she founded the Korean-American Foundation, for which she was awarded a Meritorious Service Medal by Pennsylvania's Governor John

S. Fine. Fauset died in Philadelphia in 1965, following a heart attack.

REFERENCES

BOGIN, RUTH. "Crystal Dreda Bird Fauset." In *Notable American Women—The Modern Period: A Biographical Dictionary*. Cambridge, Mass., 1980.

FRANKLIN, V. P. *The Education of Black Philadelphia: The Social and Educational History of a Minority Community, 1900–1950*. Philadelphia, 1979.

GREG ROBINSON

Fauset, Jessie Redmon (April 27, 1884–April 30, 1961), writer and teacher. As literary editor of the CRISIS, the official journal of the NATIONAL ASSOCIATION FOR THE ADVANCEMENT OF COLORED PEOPLE (NAACP), Fauset published the early writings of Arna BONTEMPS, Langston HUGHES, and Jean TOOMER. She promoted the work of poets Georgia Douglas JOHNSON and Anne SPENCER. But, although she is more often remembered for her encouragement of other writers, she was herself among the most prolific authors of the HARLEM RENAISSANCE. In addition to her poems, reportage, reviews, short stories, and translations that appeared regularly in the *Crisis,* she published four novels in less than ten years.

Born in what is now Lawnside, N.J., Fauset grew up in Philadelphia. Her widowed father, a minister, was the primary influence on her childhood. Her outstanding academic record won her admission to Cornell University, where she was elected to Phi Beta Kappa; she graduated in 1905. She taught high school French and earned an M.A. from the University of Pennsylvania, before W. E. B. DU BOIS hired her for the *Crisis* in 1919.

Her contributions to the *Crisis* were numerous and diverse: biographical sketches of blacks across the diaspora, essays on drama and other cultural subjects, and reports on black women activists and political causes. One of the few women to participate in the 1921 Pan-African Congress (*see* PAN-AFRICANISM, Fauset recorded her vivid impressions of that meeting. Several of her best essays describe her travel to Europe and North Africa during 1925 and 1926. She reviewed and translated works by Francophone writers from Africa and the Caribbean.

Although she subtitled one of them "A Novel without a Moral," all of Fauset's books convey strong messages. *There Is Confusion* (1924) depicts the struggle of an educated, idealistic young woman to achieve her professional goal of becoming a concert singer without compromising her personal and racial pride. Fauset's best novel, *Plum Bun* (1929),

Jessie R. Fauset, one of the first successful black female novelists, was literary editor of *The Crisis* from 1919 to 1926, a position she used to encourage many of the new writing talents of the Harlem Renaissance. (Prints and Photographs Division, Library of Congress)

uses the subject of "passing" to explore issues of race and gender identity. Its protagonist, another aspiring artist, learns that no success is worth betraying one's selfhood. In the foreword to *The Chinaberry Tree* (1931), Fauset explains that her purpose is to write about the "breathing-spells, in-between spaces where colored men and women work and love and go their ways with no thought of the 'problem.'" Blacks and whites were not so different after all. But as her final novel, ironically titled *Comedy: American Style* (1934), demonstrates, she did not ignore the problems of racism and sexism endemic to early twentieth-century American life. In general, however, Fauset's novels present sentimental resolutions to the complex problems they raise.

After resigning from the *Crisis* in 1926, Fauset returned to teaching. In 1929 she married businessman Herbert Harris and later moved to Montclair, N.J.

She ceased thereafter to play a public role. Yet even after her death in 1961, her example continued to inspire. Not only had she probably published more than any black American woman before her, her fiction confirmed that not all the drama in African-American life revolved around interracial conflict.

REFERENCES

MCDOWELL, DEBORAH E. Introduction to *Plum Bun* by Jessie Redmon Fauset. Boston, 1990.
SYLVANDER, CAROLYN W. *Jessie Redmon Fauset, Black American Writer.* Troy, N.Y., 1981.

                                CHERYL A. WALL

Fax, Elton C. (October 9, 1909–May 13, 1993), artist and author. Elton Fax was born in Baltimore and was a graduate of Syracuse University, with a B.A. in art in 1931. In 1932 he began writing for the Baltimore newspaper *Afro-American* and painting murals for the city's Dunbar High School. He taught art at Claflin College in South Carolina from 1935 to 1936 and in 1936 he relocated to New York City to teach at the Harlem Community Art Center (1936–1941).

Through the 1940s Fax illustrated magazine articles, created a weekly black history cartoon called "They'll Never Die," which was distributed to twenty-five black newspapers, and gave talks and sketching presentations to high school students across the United States. From 1953 to 1956 Fax lived with his wife and two children in Mexico, and in 1955 he joined the State Department's Program of Overseas Educational and Cultural Exchange and traveled extensively in Latin America and the Caribbean.

In 1956 Fax returned to New York and three years later traveled to West Africa where he wrote and illustrated for the black weekly newspaper *The New York Age* and illustrated his first book, *West African Vignettes* (1960). As a representative of the State Department and the American Society of African Culture, Fax returned to West Africa and visited East Africa in the early 1960s, often speaking before groups of young people about American policy in Africa and about being black in the United States.

Fax began publishing books of his writings and illustrations in the late 1960s, including *Black and Beautiful* (1969), *Contemporary Black Leaders* (1970), *Seventeen Black Artists* (1971), and *Garvey: Story of a Pioneer Black Nationalist* (1972). During the 1970s Fax was one of eight black writers to travel to the U.S.S.R. as a guest of the Soviet Writers Union; he published several books documenting his impres-

sions, including *Through Black Eyes: Journey of a Black Artist to East Africa and Russia* (1974) and *Elyuchin* (1984). Beginning in the 1970s Fax was a guest lecturer at many American universities. He spoke regularly at the Langston Hughes Library and Cultural Center in Queens, N.Y., and was a board member of the library until his death in 1993.

REFERENCES

ETHRIDGE, JAMES and BARBARA KOPALA, eds. *Contemporary Authors: A Bio-bibliographical Guide to Current Authors and Their Works.* Detroit, 1967.
FAX, ELTON. "It's Been a Beautiful But Rugged Journey." *Black American Literature Forum* 20, no. 3 (Fall 1986): 273–288.

                                RENEE NEWMAN

Federal Art Projects.   The GREAT DEPRESSION of the 1930s had enormous consequences for the visual arts in America. Because it was considered a luxury, art suffered in those hard times. When economic survival became a basic issue after the stock market crash of 1929, the market for painting and sculpture disappeared overnight. Artists were forced to give up their profession and seek work elsewhere. For this reason, the Roosevelt administration set up programs designed to preserve and maintain artists' "usable" skills during the crisis. Almost as a by-product of that mission, however, the art created for public places at government expense also brought beauty, hope, purpose, and a sense of national identity into the drab lives of those who saw it. Ironically, hard times brought art and artists a new prestige, especially among ordinary people in the community to whom the high-cultural apparatus of dealers, openings, and the like meant little.

As the Great Depression deepened and the New Deal agencies matured, some kept the focus squarely on human need while others worried about the quality and content of emergent federal art. The programs that would prove most significant to the African-American artist, already at an economic disadvantage because of prejudice, were those devoted primarily to the welfare of the unemployed. The short-lived Public Works of Art Project (1933–1934) and the Federal Art Project (FAP) of the WORKS PROJECT ADMINISTRATION (1935–1942, under several titles) selected personnel on the basis of need and paid low weekly wages to discourage the practice of making the projects a career. In theory, at any rate, selection premised on means tests discouraged racial bias. Other agencies, like the Treasury Department's

Section of Fine Arts (1934–1943), concentrated on the work of art—especially murals and sculpture for new government buildings—and selected artists for fairly lucrative commissions through anonymous competitions. Again, the published rules discouraged exclusion on the basis of race, although the stylistic preferences of agency juries often made it difficult for those without a history of training and exhibition in the established realist mode to compete effectively.

Despite formidable obstacles, the depression ultimately provided fresh opportunities for many whose access to the mechanisms for making and appreciating art relevant to their own lives had been restricted even in good times. Along with women, the old, and the young, African-American artists became major beneficiaries of federal patronage. Like the HARMON FOUNDATION, the FAP in particular helped black artists to begin and build active professional lives in the absence of adequate private support from sales. A good case in point is the FAP in Cleveland. Photos of the project studio taken there in 1936 show a very young Elmer W. Brown—obviously an apprentice consigned to undemanding work—decorating ceramic statuary with a group of older, white women. As the 1930s wore on, however, Brown learned and grew. He came into his own on the project both as a sculptor and printmaker. Eventually, in 1940, he painted a pair of powerful murals for a local housing project showing a multiracial city back on the road to economic health. Brown himself was pictured brandishing his palette and brushes among the workers. The self-portrait demonstrates Brown's pride in his professional standing as an artist—a status directly attributable to federal support for the jobless. Hughie LEE-SMITH, who worked as a lithographer on the Cleveland FAP, made a series of telling prints entitled *The Artist's Life* (1938–1939), underscoring the importance of having the financial and spiritual support necessary for observation, contemplation, and creativity.

Brown, Lee-Smith, Charles Sallee, and other major African-American talents nurtured by the Cleveland project were also the beneficiaries of a strong local tradition of black artists and iconography maintained by KARAMU HOUSE (founded in 1915), a community center eventually funded and strengthened by the WPA. Across the nation, it was the cities with strong African-American cultural institutions like Karamu House that produced the greatest outpouring of New Deal art with a black emphasis. These were, for the most part, the industrial cities of the North and Midwest. In New York, for instance, the Harlem Art Workshop had sponsored regular shows at the 135th Street branch of the public library since 1921, and Harlem's professional artists, such as Ver-

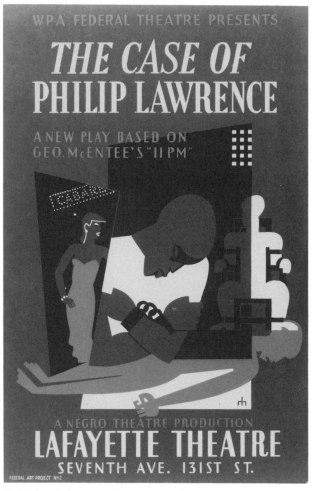

A Federal Arts Project poster by Harry Herzog advertising the 1937 production of *The Case of Philip Lawrence* presented by the Negro Theater. (Prints and Photographs Division, Library of Congress)

tis Hayes, Aaron DOUGLAS, and Augusta SAVAGE, had opened their own studios to interested students from the neighborhood. The first free art classes sponsored by the federal government in New York during the 1930s were, in fact, held in Savage's garage studio, and a consortium of local artists that came together in 1935 as the Harlem Artists' League to lobby for additional funding was directly responsible for the WPA-financed Harlem Community Art Center, which opened in 1937. Chicago's South Side Community Art Center, an FAP project launched in 1941 with a ceremony that included Dr. Alain LOCKE and Eleanor Roosevelt, also grew from the fundraising efforts of a local collective.

In one sense, prominent black community centers in New York, Ohio, Michigan, and Florida invited federal funding because they were self-segregated units that posed no threat to established white institutions. But because the local audience became the artists' de facto patron when the government paid the bills, this art also tended to be a direct, unmediated response to community values. Whereas the HARLEM RENAISSANCE of the 1920s had been premised on the taste of white connoisseurs in search of black exoticism, New Deal funding allowed African-American artists to set their own agenda with the help of their neighbors, who flocked to exhibitions and classes in enormous numbers (by actual count, 70,592 visitors toured the Harlem Center in one sixteen-month period).

The roster of major black artists affiliated with the FAP centers is impressive: Archibald MOTLEY, Charles SEBREE, Margaret BURROUGHS, and Gordon PARKS, SR., in Chicago; Hale WOODRUFF on the Atlanta University project in Georgia and William H. JOHNSON and Jacob LAWRENCE in Harlem. In Philadelphia, in the absence of such support, Dox THRASH, Claude Clark, Raymond Steth, and Samuel BROWN all rose to prominence in the only fine-print workshop organized by the FAP. Thrash, who invented the velvety Carborundum print process during his tenure on the project, was appointed head of the entire Philadelphia graphics division, supervising the work of white workers who were shocked, at first, by the inversion of the established racial hierarchy. His prints and the works of his African-American colleagues of the 1930s remain arresting by virtue of the aesthetic confidence with which the vitality of black culture is affirmed by its own aspiring creators.

It is possible to argue that the art projects of the Roosevelt years accomplished little in the long run. The murals are mostly faded curiosities. Many of the prints and paintings have disappeared. Many artists who survived the 1930s on federal paychecks—black and white alike—later drifted into other jobs. But the ideal of art as a community-based activity and a matter of great collective importance to African-American men and women remains a powerful and compelling critique of the market-driven aesthetic still dominant in American high culture today.

REFERENCES

Black Printmakers and the W.P.A. Exhibition catalog. Lehman College Art Gallery. New York, 1989.

DRISKELL, DAVID C. Two Centuries of Black American Art. Exhibition catalog. Los Angeles Museum of Art. New York, 1976.

MARLING, KARAL ANN, et al. Federal Art in Cleveland. Exhibition catalog. Cleveland Public Library. Cleveland, 1974.

O'CONNOR, FRANCIS V., ed. Art for the Millions: Essays from the 1930s by Artists and Administrators of the WPA Federal Art Project. Greenwich, Conn., 1973.

KARAL ANN MARLING

Federal Bureau of Investigation (FBI). Founded in 1908, the investigative arm of the United States Department of Justice was originally known as the Bureau of Investigation (the word "Federal" was added in 1935). With a statutory mandate to investigate violations of federal civil rights law and a controversial internal security mandate to investigate dissident political activity, the FBI has been near the center of African-American history since its founding during the last year of Theodore Roosevelt's administration.

Under J. Edgar Hoover, bureau director from 1924 to 1972 in eight administrations (Coolidge through Nixon), the FBI pursued its civil rights mandate reluctantly. Hoover objected to civil rights enforcement on legal and constitutional grounds. With some justification, he argued that federal statutes provided little authority for federal agents to usurp the law-and-order responsibilities of state and local police. (Many scholars agree that this was so during the decades prior to the Civil Rights Act of 1964 and the VOTING RIGHTS ACT of 1965.) On a more practical level, civil rights enforcement threatened the FBI's bipartisan constituency. Hoover's traditional enemies were communists and criminals, uncontroversial targets in twentieth-century America. The director could scarcely move on the civil rights front, in contrast, without alienating one side or the other. Less than energetic enforcement brought down the wrath of liberals, while any movement at all enraged the white South. The FBI's much-talked-about immunity to criticism during Hoover's day, often attributed to his voluminous files and veiled blackmail threats, broke down in the 1960s. It did so precisely because the bureau could no longer avoid civil rights work in that decade.

Whether the issue was segregation of lunch counters and buses or police brutality aimed at civil rights activists in particular and African Americans in general, the FBI director was unsympathetic. In public and private discourse, he adopted the manner and language of state's rights. "The Constitution," he told the NATIONAL ASSOCIATION FOR THE ADVANCEMENT OF COLORED PEOPLE'S (NAACP) Walter WHITE, after the Stork Club in New York refused to serve Josephine BAKER in 1951, "does not deal in general with the relationships between one private individual and another."

Preferring the familiar comforts of dossier collecting to the alien business of civil rights enforcement, Hoover's FBI fully mobilized only on the internal security front. With a consensual mandate to follow members of the COMMUNIST PARTY OF THE U.S.A. and communist sympathizers, the bureau used a communist-infiltration rationale to justify spying on virtually anyone interested in the state of race relations in the United States. It did not matter that there were no laws whatsoever on which to base these investigations. Never content with mere intelligence gathering, moreover, Hoover's agents invariably moved from intelligence to counterintelligence. They targeted for "neutralization" (the bureau's word)—that is, destroying the political effectiveness—much of the black leadership from Marcus GARVEY to MALCOLM X and from the Rev. Dr. Martin Luther KING, Jr., to Jesse JACKSON.

From 1910 to 1920, the FBI recognized civil rights jurisdiction only in the area of peonage (involuntary servitude and slavery). This was hardly surprising, given the William Howard Taft administration's position: The federal government, Taft claimed, had "no authority . . . to protect citizens of African descent in the enjoyment of civil rights generally." Other than peonage, the closest the FBI came to civil rights work involved voting fraud investigations. Rioting in East St. Louis in 1917 and elsewhere somehow convinced the Wilson administration that the REPUBLICAN PARTY was manipulating the votes of recent black migrants from the deep South.

World War I led to homefront surveillance of dozens of black groups, from the moderate NAACP to the militant African Blood Brotherhood. The FBI recruited so-called "reliable Negroes" as informants and had them report on such things as attitudes toward "social equality" and "equal rights." More generally, FBI agents visited black communities to assess attitudes toward the draft and investigate rumors of subversion. One rumor the FBI investigated involved the infamous Zimmermann telegram, made public in February 1917, in which Germany offered to help Mexico regain territory lost seventy years before in the Mexican War. German agents were supposedly organizing a Mexican and African-American army to fight a rearguard action in the southwest on Kaiser Wilhelm's behalf. No matter how farfetched the assertion, the FBI approached African Americans with the underlying negative assumption that their loyalty was suspect.

J. Edgar Hoover's first major African-American case came after the war. Its subject, Marcus GARVEY, was among the century's most important black leaders. Concluding in 1919 that this Jamaican-born founder of the UNIVERSAL NEGRO IMPROVEMENT ASSOCIATION needed to be jailed, Hoover searched for an appropriate crime. After failing to prove that Garvey was an operative of the British and Canadian governments, he began an investigation into whether Garvey had violated the Mann Act of 1910, which made it a federal crime to transport a woman across a state line for immoral purposes (i.e., prostitution). Although the charge was baseless, the FBI had used this law successfully in the past—most notably in

1912 against Jack JOHNSON, the first black heavyweight boxing champion of the world. This proved ineffective because of a total lack of evidence, and Hoover moved on to other fields. In 1923, he gathered enough information to support an indictment on the charge of using the mails to defraud while raising money for the Black Star Steamship Line. Garvey got five years in 1925, serving two before President Calvin Coolidge pardoned him and ordered his deportation as an undesirable alien.

The gathering world crisis of the late 1930s and the coming of World War II led to another expansion of the FBI's security responsibilities. Field agents gathered intelligence on "Negro organizations," and officials at headquarters lumped their findings with reports on "Communism" and "German, Italian, and Japanese" saboteurs. Files on individuals included those of Olympic hero Jesse Owens and First Lady Eleanor Roosevelt. Information-gathering techniques included burglaries and wiretaps. One target of electronic surveillance, A. Philip RANDOLPH's MARCH ON WASHINGTON movement, was the subject of regular reports to the Roosevelt White House in 1941. By 1942 the FBI had launched a nationwide survey of "foreign-inspired agitation" in "colored areas and colored neighborhoods." Hoover wanted to know "why particular Negroes or groups of Negroes . . . have evidenced sentiments for other 'dark races' (mainly Japanese) or by what forces they . . . adopted un-American ideologies." From World War I to World War II, assumptions about African-American loyalties remained consistent.

FBI civil rights enforcement responsibilities also expanded during the war years. Attorney General Frank Murphy, a former NAACP board member, provided the catalyst by creating a special Civil Liberties Section in the Justice Department. Renamed the Civil Rights Section in 1941 (and upgraded to full division status in 1957), the new section rarely acted aggressively. There were exceptions, however, especially after Pearl Harbor, when one of Murphy's successors, Francis Biddle, ordered FBI agents to investigate the Cleo Wright lynching in Sikeston, Mo. There had been nearly 4,000 LYNCHINGS between 1889 and 1941, and this was the first to attract official Justice Department and FBI interest. Ultimately, the Civil Rights Section was more important as symbol than sword. It legitimized, for the first time in the twentieth century, the idea that the federal government bore responsibility for closing the gap between the nation's democratic ideals and white-over-black reality.

Following the Supreme Court's decision in BROWN V. TOPEKA, KANSAS BOARD OF EDUCATION (1954) and the growth of the CIVIL RIGHTS MOVEMENT, pressure on the FBI to investigate civil rights violations escalated. When in 1961 Attorney General Robert F. Kennedy ordered the bureau to recruit African Americans as special agents, Hoover held out for nearly two years and then made only a token gesture. (Before 1962, there were only a handful of black "special agents," and they functioned as servants. The "agents" were in fact on-the-job chauffeurs and elevator operators to move Hoover from point to point, and at-home gardeners and handymen to keep up his property.) Similarly, when the attorney general ordered the FBI to gather the registration data needed to prosecute voting rights cases, the director responded with bureaucratic obfuscation. He also embraced a "no arrest" policy, this time with the Kennedy administration's concurrence, in which the FBI agents merely gathered information on antiblack activities. This stance meant that southern sheriffs and KU KLUX KLAN members could beat voter registration workers while the FBI watched. Given the widespread media coverage of the movement, television camera crews sometimes filmed the assaults. Still, a taped account meant little. Indictments were rare, prosecutions more so, convictions practically nonexistent.

In line with Hoover's notions of federalism, the FBI kept local police posted on civil rights demonstrations. This policy held in instances where the Klan had infiltrated the department in question. During the May 1961 Freedom Rides, for example, the bureau gave a Birmingham, Ala., police officer the Riders' itinerary knowing full well that the officer was a Klansman. In addition, the bureau knew that Commissioner of Public Safety Eugene "Bull" Connor had promised the Klan twenty minutes to break heads once the Freedom Ride bus arrived. Gary Thomas Rowe, an FBI informant in the Klan, participated in those beatings. Four years later, during the Selma voting rights march in 1965, Rowe was with the Klansmen who murdered Viola Liuzzo, a white Detroit housewife and civil rights volunteer.

Hoover and his senior staff watched with alarm in the spring and summer of 1963 as the Birmingham demonstrations and March on Washington pushed the civil rights movement onto the nation's main political stage. They responded, in effect, by declaring war on the movement and its principal leader. Hoover's men wiretapped the Rev. Dr. Martin Luther KING, Jr. (with Robert Kennedy's approval), planted microphones in his hotel rooms, broke into his offices and the offices of his associates, and generally pursued him with pants-leg ferocity. Hoover, who called King in 1964 "the most notorious liar in the country," hated King with a vehement and personal passion. Under the leadership of William Sullivan, an assistant director, the FBI disseminated derogatory information about King to the White House, Congress, the media, fellow activists (the NAACP's Roy WILKINS, among others), and King's wife. At the height of this campaign, Sullivan dreamed of replacing the prince of nonviolence with the "right kind" of black leader. His candidate, Samuel R. PIERCE, Jr., a talented, conservative attorney, later joined the cabinet of President Ronald Reagan as secretary of housing and urban development.

Before the 1960s urban rioting in Watts, Newark, and Detroit, and the emergence of a militant black power movement, FBI counterintelligence action was informal. Perhaps the best known case, other than the actions aimed at King, involved the NATION OF ISLAM rift between Elijah MUHAMMAD and MALCOLM X. "It's time to close his eyes," Elijah Muhammad said of Malcolm X, in a comment picked up by an electronic surveillance crew. Hoover's agents acted as agent-provocateurs, encouraging Elijah Muhammad's rage until the day Malcolm X died at the hands of five gunmen from the Nation of Islam's Newark mosque. While the FBI probably played no role in the assassination, its conduct was controversial enough. For its own ends, the nation's principal law-enforcement agency tried to manipulate what it called a "violence-prone Negro cult" knowing full well that the Nation of Islam had no real mechanism for handling personal, political, or doctrinal schisms peacefully.

Rather than reevaluate such tactics, FBI officials institutionalized them in 1968 with COINTELPRO-Black Hate Group. This formal program intended to check "[the] *growth* of militant black nationalist organizations" and "the *coalition* of [such] groups." If left unchecked, the bureau concluded, these organizations "might be the first step toward a real 'Mau Mau' in America." FBI officials also intended to "pinpoint potential troublemakers," "neutralize them before they exercise their potential for violence," and finally, "prevent the *rise of a [black] messiah*" from their radical midst. Initial targets included the familiar (King and Muhammad) and the new (Stokely CARMICHAEL and H. Rap BROWN of the STUDENT NONVIOLENT COORDINATING COMMITTEE, and Maxwell Stanford of the REVOLUTIONARY ACTION MOVEMENT). Over the next few years, Jesse Jackson's name and hundreds of others would be added to the list.

Ultimately, the BLACK PANTHER party took the brunt of this formal FBI counterintelligence program. One especially controversial action in 1969 resulted in the death of Chicago Panther Fred Hampton. In the manner of the Muhammad–Malcolm X rift, the bureau also encouraged a bloody California feud between the Panthers' revolutionary political nationalists and Maulana Karenga's US (as opposed to "them") organization of revolutionary cultural nationalists. At least six Panthers were killed, and to convince the survivors to retaliate, the FBI laboratory produced forged handbills, flyers, underground newspaper copy, and letters that had Karenga bragging about the body count: "US—6, Panthers—0."

Simultaneously, the FBI organized BLACPRO and Ghetto Informant Programs to cover black communities from Brooklyn's Bedford-Stuyvesant to the Texas towns Odessa and Pecos. New York informants reported on such things as "Subversive and/or Communist Links Between Harlem and Africa." By the end of Richard M. Nixon's first term, bureau agents operated some 7,500 paid ghetto informants. Most were black. Many received up to $400 a month for services rendered. With war raging in Vietnam, the FBI again had doubts about African-American loyalty.

Since J. Edgar Hoover's death in May 1972, several forces have tempered the FBI. Notably, the Church Committee's intelligence-community investigations in the Senate in 1975; a special House Assassination Committee probe of the King and Kennedy murders in 1977; amendments to the Freedom of Information Act of 1966 allowing limited access to the files; lawsuits filed by persons harassed or otherwise targeted for neutralization; and charges of discrimination brought by the bureau's own black special agents. Twenty years after Hoover's death, African Americans headed 1 of 56 field offices and held 3 of 166 senior executive staff positions and only 68 supervisory jobs bureau-wide. To avoid a class-action lawsuit on behalf of 520 black agents (4.8 percent of the total agent force), FBI Director William Sessions negotiated a settlement in January 1993 that drew praise from Coretta Scott King and Andrew YOUNG and criticism from in-house opponents of affirmative action. The settlement, which granted a federal judge limited supervision over personnel practices, polarized the bureau and led to a clash between Sessions and his own executive staff which ultimately cost the director his job.

The FBI's internal-security and civil rights enforcement mandates have also remained intact in the decades since Hoover's death. While denying the existence of a new program to target elected black officeholders (supposedly called "Frühmenschen," for "primitive man"), bureau agents continued to investigate discrimination and police brutality cases. The latter included the federal civil rights charges brought against the Los Angeles police officers who pounded Rodney Glenn King in 1992. Every FBI agent who worked that case had an institutional legacy to overcome, a legacy that Hoover stated starkly in a 1966 conversation with Senator Birch Bayh (Dem.–Ind.). Reacting to newspaper photographs and television news footage of police officers beating civil rights

workers, the director said he stood with the "officers above" and their nightsticks, not the "Negro on the ground." That view ruled unchallenged in the FBI for half a century.

REFERENCES

BELKNAP, MICHAEL R. *Federal Law and Southern Order.* Athens, Ga., 1987.

CARSON, CLAYBORNE. *Malcolm X: The FBI File.* New York, 1991.

EVANZZ, KARL. *The Judas Factor: The Plot to Kill Malcolm X.* New York, 1992.

GARROW, DAVID. *The FBI and Martin Luther King, Jr.* New York, 1981.

GENTRY, CURT. *J. Edgar Hoover: The Man and the Secrets.* New York, 1991.

NAVASKY, VICTOR. *Kennedy Justice.* New York, 1971.

O'REILLY, KENNETH. *"Racial Matters": The FBI's Secret File on Black America, 1960–1972.* New York, 1989.

SULLIVAN, WILLIAM C., with Bill Brown. *The Bureau: My Thirty Years in Hoover's FBI.* New York, 1979.

THEOHARIS, ATHAN. *The Boss: J. Edgar Hoover and the Great American Inquisition.* Philadelphia, 1988.

UNGAR, SANFORD. *FBI.* Boston, 1976.

U.S. Congress. House Select Committee on Assassinations. *The Final Assassinations Report.* New York, 1979.

KENNETH O'REILLY

Federal Elections Bill of 1890.   Introduced to the House of Representatives in June 1890 by Massachusetts Rep. Henry Cabot Lodge, the Federal Elections Bill, or "Force Bill" as it was popularly known, was an attempt by northern Republicans to respond to the disenfranchisement of African Americans in southern states. As such, it called for federal supervision of congressional elections in any district where such supervision was requested by 500 or more voters. Violently opposed by southern whites, the Force Bill caused more alarm and excitement in the South than had any federal measure since the first Enforcement Act of 1870, which was also enacted to prevent infringement of the right to vote. Following a United States Supreme Court decision in 1876 (*United States* v. *Reese*) that severely limited the scope of the first Enforcement Act, black voting rights were systematically stripped away in one southern state after another through poll taxes, literacy tests, restrictive registration laws that were selectively enforced, and outright violence and fraud. Thus, African Americans throughout the South were included in census counts to determine allocation of congressional seats, yet were not allowed to vote in elections. (*See also* SUFFRAGE, NINETEENTH–CENTURY)

The Force Bill was considered by its supporters to have been a principled stand for full black suffrage, yet it was also in part a partisan tactic to weaken the grip that Democrats had held on southern states since the end of Reconstruction. The bill was passed in the House of Representatives by a narrow margin by the Republican majority. In the Senate, however, it was met with obstruction and finally of filibuster led by southern Democrats. This last serious effort by Congress to arrest the wholesale erosion of black voting power in the post-Reconstruction South was cast aside without a vote when even its strongest supporters backed down in the face of this opposition.

REFERENCES

GARRATY, JOHN. *Henry Cabot Lodge: A Biography.* New York, 1953.

WOODWARD, C. VANN. *Origins of the New South.* New Orleans, 1971.

JOSEPH W. LOWNDES

Federal Writers' Project. The Federal Writers' Project (FWP) was an arm of the New Deal's WORKS PROJECT ADMINISTRATION (WPA) that gave employment between 1935 and 1939 to some 4,500 American writers, 106 of them (as of 1937) African-American. The great majority of FWP writers were hired to work on the American Guide Series, a collection of state guidebooks describing the distinctive folkways and histories of the country's different regions, both rural and urban.

A number of prominent African-American writers participated in the FWP. The Illinois project hired Margaret WALKER, Richard WRIGHT, Willard MOTLEY, Frank YERBY, William ATTAWAY, Fenton JOHNSON, Arna BONTEMPS, and Katherine DUNHAM. The New York projected hired Wright, Claude MCKAY, Ralph ELLISON, Tom Poston, Charles Cumberbatch, Henry Lee MOON, Roi Ottley, Helen Boardman, Ellen Tarry, and Waring Cuney. Zora Neale HURSTON briefly directed the Florida project, and Charles S. JOHNSON contributed to the *Tennessee State Guide.*

Because of the cutoff in federal funding in 1939, after which various FWP projects reverted to individual states, much FWP material never saw publication. But in addition to the sections on Negro history in several state guides, a number of important studies of black culture were generated by FWP writers on FWP-based research. Urban studies include: McKay, *Harlem: Negro Metropolis* (1940); Wright,

Twelve Million Black Voices (1941); Ottley and William Weatherby, *New World A-Comin': Inside Black America* (1943); Ottley, *The Negro in New York: An Informal History* (1967); Bontemps and Jack Conroy, *Anyplace but Here* (1966); St. Clair DRAKE and Horace CAYTON, *Negro Metropolis: A Study of Negro Life in a Northern City* (1945); Moon, *Balance of Power: The Negro Vote* (1948); and Gilbert Osofsky, *Harlem: The Making of a Ghetto* (1965).

Rural studies, drawn from the FWP's massive interviewing project of over two thousand ex-slaves from eighteen states, include the North Carolina project's *These Are Our Lives* (1939); the Savannah project's *Drums and Shadows: Survival Studies among the Georgia Coastal Negroes* (1940); Roscoe Lewis, *The Negro in Virginia* (1940); Benjamin Botkin, *Lay My Burden Down: A Folk History of Slavery* (1945); Charles L. Perdue, *Weevils in the Wheat: Interviews with Virginia Ex-Slaves* (1976); and George P. Rawick's nineteen-volume *The American Slave: A Composite Autobiography* (1972), subsequently supplemented (1977, 1979) by twenty-two additional volumes.

The materials gathered in the slave narrative collection, while flawed, continue to be widely used in studies of U.S. slavery. Sterling BROWN, the FWP's national editor of Negro affairs, encountered resistance from various state project heads who were reluctant to hire black interviewers or to adhere to Brown's goal of eliminating "racial bias . . . [that] does not produce the accurate picture of the Negro in American social history" (Gabbin 1985, p. 69). But Brown received support from other project directors and managed to insert substantial material about African-American history and culture into many state guides, as well as to foster the ex-slave interviewing project.

Some historians of slavery insist that because most of the FWP interviewers were white, the former slaves engaged in a self-censorship that "lead[s] almost inevitably to a simplistic and distorted view of the plantation as a paternalistic institution where the chief feature of life was mutual love and respect between masters and slaves" (Blassingame 1975, p. 490). Other historians, however, argue that "a blanket indictment of the interviews is as unjustified as their indiscriminate or uncritical use" and that the interviews constitute "the single most important source of data used to examine the 'peculiar institution' and its collapse" (Yetman 1984, pp. 189, 209).

In addition to contributing to the state guides and the slave narrative collection, a number of African-American writers wrote and published works of their own during their FWP tenure. Hurston published *Their Eyes Were Watching God* (1937), *Tell My Horse* (1938), and *Moses, Man of the Mountain* (1939); At-

Zora Neale Hurston holding a copy of *American Stuff* at the Federal Writers' Project booth at the *New York Times* Bookfair, November 1937. (Photographs and Prints Division, Schomburg Center for Research in Black Culture, The New York Public Library, Astor, Lenox and Tilden Foundations)

taway worked on *Blood on the Forge* (1941); Wright published *Uncle Tom's Children* and wrote *Native Son* (both in 1940); Bontemps published *Drums at Dusk* (1939); Walker wrote an unpublished novel about Chicago ghetto life, *Goose Island,* as well as an early draft of *Jubilee* (eventually published in 1966).

The FWP experience did not simply provide these writers with financial support but significantly shaped the content and perspective of their writing. The project provided Hurston with recording equipment and transportation, enabling her to deepen her already established interests as a folklorist. Attaway's *Blood on the Forge* and Wright's *Twelve Million Black Voices,* which depict the cultural dislocation of southern sharecroppers in the industrial North, reflect central concerns of the Illinois project. Wright's *Native Son* was profoundly shaped by the FWP-based urban sociology of Cayton's and Drake's emerging Chicago School. Ellison's *Invisible Man* (1953), which treats black experience as both distinctly African American and broadly human, reflected the FWP's characteristic insistence that the United States is a harmonious blend of distinct cultural particularities.

The work performed by black writers in the FWP showed the project's preoccupation with the nation's diverse folkways. The FWP's distinct approach to diversity cannot be fully understood, however, apart from the influence of the cultural politics espoused by the Left—specifically, the COMMUNIST PARTY of the United States—in the era of the Popular Front (1935–1939). The FWP was not, as was claimed in 1939 by House Un-American Activities Committee head Martin Dies, "doing more to spread Communist propaganda than the Communist Party itself" (Penkower 1977, p. 195). But a number of FWP writers, black and white, worked in the orbit of the Left. The admixture of localism and universalism pervading many works of the FWP was strongly influenced by the cultural Left's pluralistic project of seeking the "real America" in "the people."

REFERENCES

BLASSINGAME, JAMES W. "Using the Testimony of Ex-Slaves: Approaches and Problems." *Journal of Southern History* 41 (1975): 473–492.

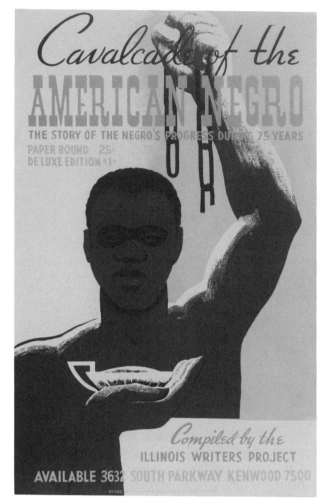

During the New Deal the Federal Writers' Project explored a number of aspects of African-American history, including the oral histories of former slaves. Among its publications was *Cavalcade of the American Negro* (1940), produced by the Illinois Writers' Project. (Prints and Photographs Division, Library of Congress)

GABBIN, JOANNE V. *Sterling A. Brown: Building the Black Aesthetic Tradition.* Westport, Conn., 1985.

MANGIONE, JERRE. *The Dream and the Deal: The Federal Writers' Project, 1935–1943.* Boston and Toronto, 1972.

PENKOWER, MONTY NOAM. *The Federal Writers' Project: A Study in Government Patronage of the Arts.* Urbana, Ill., 1977.

YETMAN, NORMAN R. "Ex-Slave Interviews and the Historiography of Slavery." *American Quarterly* 36 (Summer 1984): 181–210.

BARBARA CLARE FOLEY

Feelings, Thomas (May 19, 1933–), author and illustrator. Born in New York and raised in the Bedford-Stuyvesant neighborhood of Brooklyn,

Tom Feelings graduated from the George Westinghouse Vocational School in 1951 and the School of Visual Arts, where he studied cartooning from 1951 to 1953 and illustration from 1957 to 1960. His education was interrupted by four years in the air force, in which Feelings served in the graphic arts division.

In 1958, while still in school, Feelings published a comic strip, "Tommy Traveler in the World of Negro History," in the *New York Age.* The strip, featuring a boy educating himself about black history, was celebratory, pedagogic in intent, and directed largely at children—concerns that dominate all of Feelings's art. Upon graduation, he sought freelance work while occupying himself drawing pictures of black people and places in and around his Brooklyn neighborhood.

In 1960, Feelings joined the African Jazz Art Society, a group of musicians and artists inspired by the teachings of Marcus GARVEY. In 1964, unable to establish a freelance career, largely because black illustrators found it difficult to get assignments, Feelings emigrated to Ghana. He worked as an illustrator at the Government Printing House and also did freelance commissions. The Ghana experience changed Feelings's illustrative style: His previous drawings had been somber and mostly monochromatic; his new pictures were colorful and livelier. Following the 1966 coup in Ghana, the press where Feelings worked was closed and he lost his job. He returned briefly to the United States, then headed the children's book project at the Ministry of Education, in Guyana, from 1971 to 1974.

Since returning to the United States, Feelings has lived mostly in New York and has illustrated more than twenty books, winning numerous awards and citations in the process. In 1968, he illustrated Julius LESTER's *To Be a Slave. Mojo Means One: Swahili Counting Book* (1971) and *Jambo Means Hello: Swahili Alphabet Book* (1974), both works authored by his wife at the time, Muriel Feelings, seek to introduce the young African-American reader to a traditional, simple, communal black America. His 1972 autobiography, *Black Pilgrimage,* looks at what it means to be black and a minority in the United States as compared to being part of a majority in independent Africa.

In 1982 Feelings was awarded a National Endowment for the Arts (NEA) Visual Arts Fellowship. *Now Sheba Sings the Song,* a series of drawings of black women done over twenty-five years, accompanied by a poem by Maya ANGELOU was published in 1987. In 1990 Feelings became the artist-in-residence at the University of South Carolina in Columbia. *Soul Looks Back in Wonder,* his first full-color picture book, along with poems with uplifting messages chosen from some of the best African-American poets, appeared in 1993. Like almost all of Feelings's output, it celebrates the African and African-American experience for the benefit of a young audience.

REFERENCES

COLLIER, LAURIE, and JOYCE NAKAMURA, eds. *Major Authors and Illustrators for Children and Young Adults.* Detroit, 1993.

DUNBAR, ERNEST. *The Black Expatriates: A Study of American Negroes in Exile.* New York, 1968.

FEELINGS, TOM. *Black Pilgrimage.* New York, 1972.

HARRISON, BARBARA, and GREGORY MAGUIRE, eds. *Innocence and Experience: Essays and Conversations on Children's Literature.* New York, 1987.

QADRI ISMAIL

Female Benevolent Society of St. Thomas. *See* Early African-American Women's Organizations.

Feminism.   *See* Criticism, Feminist.

Fencing.   African-American participation in fencing began after World War II, but did not increase to significant numbers until the 1970s.

In 1951, Sophronia Pierce Stent became the first African American accepted into the Amateur Fencers' League of America. Stent, a native of Harlem, was also captain of the New York University (NYU) team. Bruce Davis became the first black fencer to earn an NCAA title when he won the 1957 foil competition. He won again in 1958. In 1964, Craig Bell of the University of Illinois won the NCAA saber title. In 1971, Tyrone Simmons of the University of Detroit captured the NCAA foil championship, and Edward Ballinger of NYU won the same title in the Intercollegiate Fencing Association (IFA). Simmons won again the following year, and with African-American teammates Ken Blake (saber) and Fred Hooks (épée), captured the NCAA three-weapon team championship. Randy Eggleton of the University of Pennsylvania won the NCAA épée championship in 1976.

Other black NCAA fencing champions include Peter Westbrook of NYU, who won the saber championship in 1973; Michael Lofton of NYU, who won the NCAA saber championship four times from 1984 to 1987; and Robert Cottingham of Columbia University, who won the saber title in 1988.

Black women have also achieved considerable success in the sport. In 1969, Ruth White of NYU was the first African American to win an Amateur Fencers' League of America national title; in 1971 and 1972 she captured the foil championship of the National Intercollegiate Women's Fencing Association (NIWFA). Nikki Franke became one of the most successful coaches in the 1980s, guiding the Temple University women's team to second place in the 1987 women's championship.

The first black member of a U.S. Olympic fencing team was Uriah Jones, who made the team for the 1968 games in Mexico City. In 1972, White, Bert Freeman, and Simmons competed in the Olympics. In 1976, three black men made the team: Westbrook, Ballinger, and Edward Wright. Westbrook fared the best, finishing thirteenth in the saber competition. In the 1984 games, Westbrook captured the first fencing medal for the United States since 1960 when he won the bronze in the saber competition. Michael Lofton, foil fencer Peter Lewison, and women's foil fencer Sharon Monplaisir also competed in the 1984 games. At the 1988 Olympics in Seoul, Westbrook and Lofton were joined by saber fencer Bob Cottingham. Once again, Lewison was a member of the foil team, and Monplaisir competed in women's foil. Monplaisir, Cottingham, Westbrook, and Lofton also represented the United States at the 1992 games in Barcelona.

REFERENCE

ASHE, ARTHUR R., JR. *A Hard Road to Glory: A History of the African-American Athlete.* 3 vols. New York, 1988.

BENJAMIN K. SCOTT

Ferdinand, Vallery.   *See* Salaam, Kalamu Ya.

Ferguson, Angela Dorothea (February 15, 1925–), pediatrician, hospital and health care developer. Born and raised in Washington, D.C., Angela Ferguson completed her undergraduate studies at HOWARD UNIVERSITY and entered Howard Medical School, receiving her M.D. in 1949. As an intern in the pediatric ward of Freedmen's Hospital in Washington, D.C., Ferguson was drawn to the medical conditions and needs of infants and children. She completed a two-year program in pediatrics. While visiting clinics she took special interest in children suffering from sickle-cell disease. She developed new methods for treating this inherited blood disease and prolonging the lives of sickle-cell victims. These methods included dietary changes and blood-thinning through heavy water-drinking to improve blood circulation.

In 1965, when a modern hospital was being planned to replace Freedmen's Hospital (which had been the major hospital for black Washingtonians since the post–Civil War days), Ferguson became director of programs and facilities. She oversaw the planning and construction of the new building and convinced the U.S. Congress to increase the funding for the hospital. After Howard University Medical Center opened in 1975 (replacing the former Freedmen's Hospital), Ferguson was promoted to the position of associate vice president of health affairs. Her work as a developer of Howard's medical complex continued as she spearheaded the creation of the new Seeley G. Mudd Building of the Howard College of Medicine (completed in 1979), and the Animal Research Center. She also oversaw the renovation of the College of Allied Health and Sciences and the College of Nursing.

After forty-two years in medicine, half in pediatrics and half in "bricks and mortar," Ferguson retired in June 1991. She had helped shape a vast medical complex—a 500-bed hospital facility that annually trains hundreds of health professionals and brings a full array of health services to the large African-American community in the nation's capital.

REFERENCES

HAYDEN, ROBERT C. *Eleven African-American Doctors.* Frederick, Md., 1992.
"Lady in the Hard Hat Built Howard University Hospital." *Women in Health at Howard University Hospital.* (Winter 1986): 2–3.

ROBERT C. HAYDEN

Ferrill, London (c. 1789–1854), minister. London Ferrill (also known as Loudin Ferrell) was born a slave in Hanover County, north of Richmond, Va. He was converted to Christianity at the age of twelve and started to preach the gospel, though his status as a slave prevented him from being ordained a minister in the Baptist Church. He was freed at the death of his owner, and moved to Kentucky, where he joined the white congregation of the First Baptist Church in Lexington in 1817. His preaching from the floor earned the admiration of some members of the First African Baptist Church, founded by a former slave preacher known as "the Old Captain." They asked Ferrill to become their minister, and established an all-black congregation annexed to First Baptist. This prompted the white Baptist leaders of the Elkhorn Association to meet in 1822 to decide whether they would allow the ordination of a free black man. Ferrill was ordained following their affirmative decision, and at the death of the unordained Old Captain he became minister of the First African Baptist Church, baptizing the former slave's followers.

Ferrill served as minister of the church until his death. Under his leadership, the congregation grew from approximately 280 members to more than 1,800, making First African the largest church in Kentucky. Ferrill was said to be the descendent of African royalty and, though he received no formal education, he had an authoritative demeanor and earned the respect of his congregation as well as of the white citizenry of Lexington. His influence over the black citizens of the city was so great that the town subsidized his salary. In the 1830s Ferrill established an educational program for the children of church members, and during the cholera epidemic of 1833, he cared for his sick parishioners. When a jealous citizen tried to have Ferrill removed for violating a Kentucky law that forbade nonnative freedmen the right to reside in the state longer than thirty days, Ferrill's white neighbors signed a petition to the state legislature which allowed an exemption to assure him of that right. Ferrill died in Louisville in 1854.

REFERENCES

HILL, SAMUEL S., ed. *Encyclopedia of Religion in the South.* Macon, Ga., 1984.
LUCAS, MARION B. *A History of Blacks in Kentucky: Vol. 1, From Slavery to Segregation, 1760–1891.* Frankfort, Ky., 1992.

LYDIA MCNEILL

Festivals.   From early colonial times to the present day, African Americans have created and observed an impressive calendar of celebratory and commemorative events: jubilees, festivals and anniversaries, "frolics" and seasonal feasts, fairs and markets, parades, and pilgrimages, not to speak of more private or secret ceremonies such as church meetings and revivals, family reunions, baptisms and funerals, and spiritual cults. These customs have received the casual or sustained attention of travelers, visitors, or local observers. They have been praised or disparaged, extolled as the epitome of a festive spirit that should prevail in any society and as the expression of an enduring, authentic culture, or dismissed as primitive, low-brow manifestations of a subculture, an unsophisticated, burlesque imitation of mainstream life, or, at best, an adaptation or appropriation of Euro-American customs.

This festive mood with which African Americans have been credited has encouraged the persistence of many prejudices and stereotypes fostered by the minstrel tradition (see MINSTRELS/MINSTRELSY), which represented blacks as a happy-go-lucky, careless, lighthearted people, prone to dancing and singing. This inclination for mirth has been interpreted as a sign that the predicament of slaves and their descendants should not be such a burden to the white mind and that their sufferings and the wrongs committed against them have been exaggerated.

Yet African-American celebrations, with all their unacknowledged complexities of forms and functions, are powerful symbolic acts that express, vehemently and with exuberance, not acquiescence to fate but needs, desires, and utopian will, disenchantment, anger, and rebelliousness. Communal, playful, or carnivalesque in character, they are events through which the community endeavors to build its identity, in self-reflective scrutiny and in constant confrontation with "the black image in the white mind," to question or challenge its basic assumptions. These feasts not only give the lie to and articulate the pain of certain truths, the ambivalence of a dream always deferred; they also define unexamined propositions in performances infused with subtle ironies and double entendre.

Among the "hallowdays" observed by northern slaves and free blacks, the coronation festivals or "negro elections" set the pattern for many civic feasts and festivals. Once a year in colonial New England, slaves were allowed to accompany their masters to election festivities where whites organized the election of their governors. In the 1750s, blacks started to organize their own similar celebrations, in which a leader, preferably African-born and of known royal ancestry, quick-witted and ready of speech, was elected king or governor, a title that endowed him with authority among both blacks and whites. (The title "king" or "governor" was used by blacks according to each New England colony's specific status: Governors were elected in colonies that were relatively autonomous, whereas kings were elected in colonies more closely tied to England. According to this custom, which endured through the 1850s, bondsmen confronted their African origin—the king was intermediary to the ancestors. Bondsmen also expressed their desire to have their separate institutions and to prove their ability for self-government.

Elections were prepared for by weeks of debates and meetings. A strong political message was conveyed to the community and to white rulers in a spirit that blended parodic intent and high seriousness. By ritually transferring power from the hands of the masters to those of one of their fellows, slaves were paving the way for their emancipation. Election days were perhaps the first freedom celebrations that combined the memory of the freedom and power Africans enjoyed before their capture with an anticipation of the freedom to come. The official recognition of African royalty and gentility reversed old stereotypes, which associated Africanness with savagery and lack of culture. The king was regarded as a civilized "negro" (the term "black" was not in usage as a noun then), composed and refined. These elections, prompted by the desire to counter forces of fragmentation and to ease conflicts, sought a consensus and struck a note of unity.

Coronation festivals were also indicative of white-black relations. The elected was often the slave of a prominent master, and slaves devised strategies to gain the support of masters to organize their ceremonies. The wealthier the slave owner, the greater the chance of having a grand festival, and, conversely, the greater the display, the stronger the evidence of the master's influence. While these feasts increased antagonism between blacks and poor whites, they offered an occasion to redefine slave-master relations, based on mutual claims and obligations. Negro kings held many roles as opinion leaders, counselors, justice makers, and mediators who could placate black insurgency or white fearfulness when faced with such a display of autonomy and self-rule.

There were other occasions when blacks gathered around a self-appointed leader. Pinkster is another well-known festival. Derived originally from the Dutch Whitsuntide celebration "pfingster," which the "Africs" took over in the late eighteenth century, the pinkster reached its peak in the early 1800s in Albany, N.Y. There the choice of a hill as the site for the celebration had many symbolic meanings. From the top of this hill, the low could look down on the world—an interesting reversal of the usual situation and a mock imitation also of the hills on which rulers like to set their capitols. Pinkster Hill was close to the place where many executions of blacks (accused in 1793 of having set fire to the city) had been staged. It was also close to the burial grounds, a military cemetery, and an all-black cemetery.

Thus death presided over the festivities, reminding blacks of the limits set on their freedom, of punishments inflicted on black rebels, of the failure to acknowledge or reward the achievements of black soldiers who had participated in the nation's wars, and of the intricate game of integration and segregation. The epitaphs and names inscribed on the graves emphasized the enduring character of African customs and rites. Cemeteries may have been the ultimate freedom sites, since only in death could blacks reach the absolute freedom they were celebrating.

Coronations and the pinkster exemplify a significant trend in the role granted to feasts: the official recognition of blacks' special gift for creating festive performances and their capacity for infusing it into other groups. (Native Americans, Germans, Dutch, and French attended the pinkster.) Feasts thus offered an arena for interaction and for the dream of a utopian and pluralistic order in a society divided by many social and political conflicts. Feasts were also an ironic comment on a republic that claimed to be dedicated to freedom but could still enslave part of its population, on the indignity of those who dared establish their power through the subjugation of others, and on the resilience of victims whose spirits could not be crushed.

Through the postrevolutionary era and in the antebellum years. African Americans evolved a tradition of emancipation celebrations that charted the different stages toward gradual, then complete liberation. This tradition, however, initiated at a time when blacks were experiencing a sense of betrayal and of the enduring precariousness of their situation, was conditional—the ought and the should prevailed. The future that was at stake was not only that of slaves and freed blacks, it was also the destiny of the nation and its aspiring democracy. These yearly occurrences were not marginal to black life; they were a political manifestation of jeremiad and claim making that was pursued deliberately, was announced and debated in the press, and involved major institutions, societies, and associations (churches, societies for mutual relief, temperance and benevolent societies, freemasons, etc.).

Emancipation celebrations were occasions for public appearances in marches and parades or at universal exhibitions. Many leaders, religious or political, seized these opportunities to address the world in sermons, speeches, orations, or harangues, developing race pride and race memory. There they assessed the contribution of black people in the building of the nation, their progress, their capacity for self-government, their commitment to liberty as a universal right. These feasts were not merely opportunities to celebrate on a large scale; they held out a promise to fashion new roles in a better world and wield new power, and they heralded a season of change, from enslavement and invisibility to liberation and recognition.

Both freedom and power were present in the ceremonies, not as mere allegorical figures but as fully developed ideas whose force needed to be conveyed to large audiences. Images and symbols were evolved and played out—in words, gestures, movements, and visual forms, with much ado and the will to adorn. The talents and gifts of black folks were put to use in a collective effort to stir and arouse consciousness and encourage action.

In the black calendar of feasts, Independence Day was the most controversial as well as the bleakest celebration. The solemnities of the Fourth of July encouraged African Americans to organize their own separate ceremonies and formulate their own interpretation of the meaning of these national commemorations. One is reminded here of Frederick DOUGLASS's famous 1852 address, "What Is to the American Slave Your Fourth of July?" Many black leaders urged their members not to observe that unholy day and proclaimed that persecution was not over and final emancipation still out of reach. July 4 thus became a menacing and perilous day, one on which blacks were more tempted to plan insurrection than to celebrate the republic, a day also when they were most exposed to violence, riots, arrests, and murder, as in New York in 1834 or New Hampshire in 1835. No wonder they looked for other sites and landmarks to construct an alternative memory.

After 1808, January 1 was adopted as a day of civic celebration. The time, New Year, coming right after the Christmas festivities, and the date, in commemoration of the official end of the SLAVE TRADE, seemed most appropriate. Yet, as in similar feasts, thanksgiving was tempered by ardent protest, and rejoicing by mourning and memories of the hardships of the Middle Passage. January 1 induced a heightened consciousness of Africa, where the black odyssey had begun. Africa became the central symbol and the subject of heated debate, especially when the colonization movement encouraging free blacks to return to Africa divided the community.

Curiously, January 1 never became a black national holiday. It was celebrated as such for only eight years in New York, was abandoned in the 1830s in Philadelphia, and only after general EMANCIPATION was proclaimed on January 1, 1863, did it assume new significance. The strengthening of the "peculiar institution," the development of the much dreaded domestic slave trade and its illegal perpetuation and that of the foreign trade, may explain the decline in popularity of this memorial celebration. Many states chose instead the days when emancipation law was passed into their constitutions: July 14 was adopted in Massachusetts, while after 1827 New York institutionalized July 5 as its freedom day, setting it apart from the American Fourth of July.

The abolition of slavery in the British West Indies by an act of Parliament on August 1, 1834, brought new hopes, and henceforth this memorable date became a rallying point for all freedom celebrations and for the black abolitionist crusade. State emancipations were indicted for having brought little improvement in the conditions of slaves and free blacks: The rights of blacks were trampled in the North, and racial violence and tensions continued to rise, while in the South slavery was entrenched more solidly than ever.

England and Canada became the symbols of the new celebration; the former (the perfidious and despotic tyrant at the time of the Revolutionary War) was praised for setting an example for the American republic, the latter was hailed as the land of the free and a refuge for the fugitives. Black orations became more fiery, urging the righting of wrongs and of all past errors. Orations also called for self-reliance, respectability, and exemplary conduct among blacks, for a distrust of whites, and for a stronger solidarity with the newly freed population of the West Indies and between the slaves and free blacks in the United States.

Increasingly, blacks sought sites that would commemorate events or figures more related to the African-American diaspora or to their community and its own distinctive history. Sometimes towns set the calendars—Baltimore for the Haitian Revolution, or Cleveland for NAT TURNER's REBELLION, or Boston in the late 1850s for Crispus ATTUCKS. In 1814, Wilmington, Del., created its own celebration, Big Quarterly, which has been observed until very recently. Held at the close of the harvest season, it honored the founder of the Union Church of Africa, Peter SPENCER.

Similar to religious revivals and patterned after the early meetings of the Quakers, Big Quarterly celebrated the struggles endured by leaders to achieve full ecclesiastical autonomy. This feast can be seen as the prototype of many religious services: praying, singing, the clapping of hands and stomping of feet, the beating of drums and tambourines, the playing of guitars, violins, and banjos. There was a characteristic use of space at such gatherings: The feast began in the church, then moved outside on the church grounds, and finally moved out to the open—Baltimore's famous French Street, for instance—where late in the century, as the feast grew more popular (in Baltimore attendance reached 10,000 in 1892, 20,000 in 1912), revival preachers took their stands to urge repentance from sin, and wandering minstrel evangelists played spirituals on odd instruments.

It was then also that educated "colored people" criticized the celebrations for giving way to weird cult practices and worldly pleasures, and for being outdated relics of old slavery times. In antebellum days, this religious feast was closer to a freedom celebration. Occurring in a region where slave-catching activities were intense, where slaves—who had to have a pass from the master to attend—were tempted to escape to Philadelphia or to the free states, Big Quarterly became a "big excursion on the Underground Railroad," with the presence among the pilgrims, who became potential fugitives, of both vigilant spies and marshals in addition to helpful railroad conductors.

In Syracuse in 1851 another major festival emerged in protest against the 1850 Fugitive Slave Law and after the rescue of a slave named Jerry (see FUGITIVE SLAVE LAWS). Jerry Rescue Day, which established Syracuse as the slaves' City of Refuge, embodied the spirit of defiance, of bold resistance to "iniquitous power" and to an infamous act that prevailed in the prewar years. Significantly, black leaders, rebels, warriors, and fugitives became heroic figures in celebrations and were chosen as signs that could demonstrate the unending fight against tyranny and for freedom. The oratory became more exhortative, the mood more impatient and indignant.

Freedom celebrations culminated in the early 1860s in Emancipation Jubilees and in the famous "Juneteenth" still observed today in Texas and surrounding states. In Texas, emancipation was announced to slaves eighteen months after its proclamation. This oddity of American history explains why Juneteenth and not January 1 became a popular celebration in those parts, in defiance of the official calendar and in reaction to the contempt in which part of the slave population had been held at a time when the proclamation event was a major breakthrough in the nation's history.

Thus, from Election Day to freedom celebrations, African Americans created a ritual tradition of religious and community life. Momentous appearances in public places became challenges to the established order, calling attention to the danger of overlooking or forgetting iniquities, setbacks, and sufferings as well as heroic acts. By reiterating a commonality of origin, goals, and strivings, feasts served to correct the inconsistencies of history and to cement a unity that was always in jeopardy.

Feasts also emphasized the necessary solidarity between the enslaved and the free, between African-born and American-born black people. Although most celebrations occurred in the North, they were symbolically and spiritually connected with slaves in the South, and a dense network of interaction was woven between various sites, places, and times. Former celebrations were often referred to and used as examples to follow or improve upon. The feasts themselves became memorable events to be passed on for generations to come and to be recorded in tales, song, and dance and in physical, verbal, kinetic, or musical images. The festive spirit became ingrained in African-American culture as something to celebrate in black speech, where it is inscribed in so many words, in the literature and the arts that bear incessant testimony to the tradition.

The tradition created by colonial and antebellum celebrations has continued well into the twentieth century, still in anticipation of a freedom and justice that general emancipation failed to accomplish. Numerous associations founded after the CIVIL WAR resorted to ceremonial and commemorative rites to continue to enforce the idea of freedom, and they patterned their meetings and conventions on earlier gatherings. Freedom celebrations remained a model for the great marches and demonstrations—the protest against the 1917 riots, or the parades of the Garvey movement (see Marcus GARVEY), or the marches of the CIVIL RIGHTS MOVEMENT. The persistence of the tradition attests to the participation of African Americans in the struggle for democracy and to the crucial significance of these ritual stagings in cultural, intellectual, and political life.

Yet civil celebrations underwent some dramatic changes. More and more they became occasions of popular rejoicings. Boisterous festivity, screened out at first, crept in. Abundance and plentifulness replaced the earlier sobriety. As they grew in scope (the most popular were in urban centers where the population was largest), they sometimes lost their original meaning and became essentially social occasions for convivial gatherings. It was the orator's and leader's duty and the role of the black press to remind participants of the seriousness of the purpose, and they did so with authority and eloquence. Nevertheless, the celebrations sometimes got out of control. With the changes brought by migration and demographic shifts, by the development of the media and of mass culture, and by the impunity of profit-seeking sponsors, some feasts turned into large commercial and popular events and lost their civil and political character, while others continued to meet white opposition and censure.

Rituals played an important role in celebrations and, whatever the occasion, shared certain features. They included the same speeches and addresses or sermons; parades and marches or processions; anthems, lyrics, and songs; banquets or picnics; dances and balls. They used all black people's skills—from the oratorical to the culinary, from the gift to adorn to polyrhythmic energy—to create their own modes, styles, and rhythms, always with an unfailing sense of improvisation and performance. And as they drew more people, many folkways, many rites of ordinary life (the habit of swapping songs, of cracking jokes, or "patting juba") found their way into the ceremonies, blending memories of Africa with New World customs and forms, in a mood that was both solemn and playful, sacred and secular, celebratory and satiric. In many respects also, feasts were a privileged space for the encounters between cultures, favoring reciprocal influences, mergings and combinations, syncretism and creolization.

Nowhere is the creolization of cultures more evident than in the carnivalesque tradition, which emerged in the New World in Brazil, Trinidad, Jamaica, and the other islands, is found in its earlier forms mostly in the South, and continues its modern forms in the great Caribbean festivals of Brooklyn and Toronto. These carnivals, perceived as bacchanalian revelry or weird saturnalia, were often associated with a special season and with rites of renewal, purification, or rebirth. Usually seen as more African, and therefore as more "primitive" and exotic, more tantalizing than the more familiar Anglo-European feasts, they have elicited ambiguous responses, ranging from outright disparagement on moral and aesthetic grounds (indecency and lewdness are judged horrid and hideous) to admiration for the exuberant display of so many skills and talents.

These "festivals of misrule" were often banned or strictly regulated by city ordinances and charged with bringing disturbances and misconduct—boisterous rioting and drunkenness, gambling and undue license of all sorts. The same criticism, phrased in similar words, was leveled by some members of the black community itself, especially those concerned with respectability and with the dignity of the "race," every time they suspected any feast of yielding too much to the carnivalesque propensity of their people.

Yet the carnivalesque is always present in festive rituals to correct excesses—of piety, fervor, power—and as an instrument of emancipation from any form of authority. In the African-American quest for liberation, it became an essential means of expression, allying humor, wit, parody, and satire. It had ancient roots in African cultures; and in North American society, where the weight of puritanism was strong, where work, industriousness, sobriety, and gravity were highly valued and had become ideological tools to enforce servitude, the carnivalesque tradition became part of the political culture of the oppressed. Artistically it developed also as a subversive response to the Sambo image that later prevailed in the minstrel tradition: It created, as coronation festivals did, possibilities for the inversion of stereotypes and challenged a system of representation that was fraught with ideological misinterpretations. Paradoxically, black carnivalesque performances may have nourished white blackface minstrelsy, providing it with the artistic devices on which it thrived.

The most notorious manifestations of the tradition are perhaps to be found in the North Carolina Jon-

Konnu (John Canoe) Festival or in the Zulu and Mardi Gras parades of New Orleans. JonKonnu probably originated in Africa on the Guinea coast, was re-created in Jamaica in the late seventeenth century, spread through the Caribbean, where it was widely observed, and was introduced by slaves in the States in isolated places, on plantations like Somerset Place, or in city ports like Wilmington, N.C., or Key West, Fla. Meant to honor a Guinean folk hero, the festival became an elaborate satirical feast, ridiculing the white world with unparalleled inventiveness and magnificence.

The festival could last weeks, but it climaxed on Christmas Day and was attended by huge crowds. The procession, which took a ragman and his followers from house to house and through the streets, came to be known as a unique slave performance. "Coonering," as it was called, was characterized most of all by spectacular costumes and by extravagant dance steps to the music of "sinful" tunes. The rags and feathers, the fanciful headdress and masks, the use of ox or goat horns and cow and sheep bells, and the handmade instruments wove a complex web of symbolic structure, ritualization, and code building. The dressing in white skin encouraged slaves to claim certain prerogatives, even to organize revolts. In many feasts an implicit analogy was established between the "beaten" skin of the (often forbidden) drums and that of whipped slaves.

Christmas, the season of merrymaking and mobility that favored big gatherings and intense communication, became a dreaded time for planters who tried to stifle the subversive and rebellious spirit of Coonering and to change a disquieting performance into a harmless pageant. Still held today but now mostly controlled and observed by whites, it has lost part of its magnificence. In its heyday, in antebellum America, the carnival was an artistic and political response of the slave population to its situation; it echoed in its own mode the freedom celebrations of the North. The lampooning liberty and grotesque parody of southern festivals turned them into arenas in which to voice anger and protest.

In New Orleans, when the carnival came into existence in the late 1850s, blacks were not supposed to participate. The Zulu parade, which grew out of black social life, was created by a section of the population concerned about publicly asserting its status. It developed into a wholly separate street event, a parody of the white Krewes. The African Zulu, a new king of misrule, precedes Rex and mocks his regal splendor. The carnival figures—shrunken heads of jungle beasts, royal prognosticator or voodoo doctor—the masked or painted faces, and the coconuts emphasize both the African and minstrel motifs. Nei-

ther elite nor low-brow, neither genuinely African nor creole, the Zulu parade came under attack as too burlesque; later, in the 1960s, it was criticized as exemplifying an "Uncle Tom on Wheels" and not fitting the mood of the times.

Yet the Zulu is a complex ritual that brings together several traditions: satire and masking, minstrelsy and vaudeville, brass bands, song, and dance. Another version of the coronation festival, the Zulu fuses elements of the European carnival with African, Caribbean, and Latin American practices. It establishes African Americans' rights to participate in the city's pageant, not as mere onlookers or indispensable entertainers, whose various skills as musicians and jugglers had often been used to increase the glamor of white parades, but as creators and full-fledged citizens who could thus demonstrate both their role in the city's history and their potential role in its future.

The Mardi Gras Indians, consisting of ritual chiefs, each with a spy, flagboys, and followers, march in mock imitation of the king's court and follow secret routes through the city. They enact their own rituals of violent physical and verbal confrontations between tribes. These wild warriors chant disquieting songs and speak in tongues, accompanied by haunting drumbeats and an array of other percussive sounds, as old as ancestral memories (in preference and contrast to the orderly military music of the official bands). They dance weird dance steps (e.g., the famous spy dance) and wear elaborate costumes made of beads, sequins, rhinestones, ribbons, and lace.

The tradition of Indian masking is old; originally found in Brazil, it appeared in the Caribbean in 1847. Meant to celebrate the Indian's fighting spirit and resistance, it also relates to communal rites of ancestral worship and to Dahomean ceremonial dances found also in jazz funerals. It is no accident that Mardi Gras Indians perform in the same area of New Orleans where jazz emerged out of the brass bands of Congo Square dances. Their festival may be a resurgence of the early drum gatherings that started in 1730 near the marshes of Congo Square, a market site where slaves bought merchandise from Native Americans and danced to African beats.

Now, the black Indians also appear on another festive day, March 19, at the intermission of the Lenten season. St. Joseph Day, originally an Italian Catholic feast that stylized altar building, blends the cult of saints (St. Joseph, "Queen Esther") with that of Indian heroes (Black Hawk) as well as that of voodoo spirits (see VOODOO). Thus religious and pagan rites, cult and carnival practices, indoor ceremonies and outdoor parades complement each other, converge, and merge.

The annual Caribbean Day Parade on Eastern Parkway, Brooklyn, on Labor Day, has become one of the largest and most colorful of New York City's many ethnic parades, shown here in 1974. (Shawn Walker)

Later in the year, Easter Rock, another feast that is still observed in rural Louisiana, celebrates the Resurrection and similarly blends pagan and Christian elements. Its hero and emblem is both son and sun. The Son of God's rise from the dead is likened to that of the sun "rocking from the earth." All night long, prayer, "the shout," and dance herald and accompany the rocking of the sun/son.

Although the South has been the cradle of a diverse black carnivalesque tradition, in the prejazz and jazz ages another form of carnival celebration found its way to the North. The modern West Indian festivals of Brooklyn, N.Y., and of Toronto, Canada, give further evidence of a process of Caribbeanization that has always been at work and that repeatedly intensified during periods of great migration. The importation of slaves from the Carib Basin, the arrival of many slaves from Santo Domingo after the Haitian Revolution in the early nineteenth century, and the late twentieth-century West Indian migration to the United States have all in various degrees brought many changes to "black" celebrations. They have intensified the creolization that brought together people of African, Hispanic, Indian, and French descent. The recent festivals are also generating a pan–West

Indian consciousness that expresses itself artistically through costumes, masks, music, and dance. On a much-contested terrain they enact their own rituals of rebellion, resistance and protest, inclusion and exclusion. Chaotic, playful, or violent, carnivals offer a delicate balance between many complementary or contradictory elements.

African-American celebratory performances are special occasions to celebrate freedom; they consist of various cycles of ritualized events that have rich semantic and symbolic meaning, fully a part of African-American and American history and culture. They invite us to reconsider stereotyped representations of "the race" and to revise the assumptions upon which conceptions of important figures, events, and places have themselves become objects of celebration and commemorative fervor. They are potent weapons and arenas through which to voice anger, strivings, and desire. They are efficacious and eloquent tools to educate, exhort, or indict. They are witty parodies and satires that help distance reality and change "mentalities." Crucial agents of change, celebratory performances demonstrate a people's faith in words and ideas, in the force of collective memory and imagination, in the necessity of finding powerful display. These entertaining and instructive ceremonies exhibit a gift for adornment and an inventiveness that emphatically proclaim the triumph of life over all the forces that tend to suppress or subdue "the souls of black folk."

REFERENCES

ABRAHAMS, ROGER, and JOHN SZWED, eds. *Discovering Afro-America*. Leiden, Netherlands, 1975.

BLASSINGAME, JOHN W. *The Slave Community: Plantation Life in the Antebellum South*. New York, 1972.

GENOVESE, EUGENE D. *Roll, Jordan, Roll: The World the Slaves Made*. New York, 1974.

LEVINE, LAWRENCE W. *Black Culture and Black Consciousness*. New York, 1977.

SOUTHERN, EILEEN. *The Music of Black Americans*. New York, 1971.

STUCKEY, STERLING. *Slave Culture*. New York, 1987.

GENEVIÈVE FABRE

Fiction.   *See* Children's Literature; Literature.

Fiction, Science.   *See* Science Fiction.

Field Hockey.   Several African-American women have had prominent careers in field hockey, a predominantly female sport. Relatively few historically black colleges and universities have competed in field hockey, and most black participants have been at predominantly white colleges.

Ketura "Kitty" Waterman Cox was the first notable black field hockey player, starring for New York University in the early 1940s. After her playing years, Cox devoted her professional career to the sport, coaching the field hockey team at Queens College in New York City from 1952 to 1976. Verneda Thomas was a member of the Northeast Field Hockey team in the 1940s and later became active on the national organizational level. Two prominent athletes from other sports were also accomplished field hockey players. C. Vivian Stringer, a basketball player and college coach, earned a spot on the Mid-East college field hockey team. Lacrosse player Tina Sloan Green participated on the U.S. national field hockey team in 1969 and coached the Temple University team from 1974 through 1979.

The most successful black field hockey player was Gloria Jean Byard, a player for Glassboro State College in New Jersey. In 1974, Byard became the first African American to play for the United States national team; she stayed with the team the following two years. She was also named first team All-College player for the 1974, 1975, and 1976 seasons.

REFERENCE

ASHE, ARTHUR R., JR. *A Hard Road to Glory: A History of the African-American Athlete*. 3 vols. New York, 1988.

THADDEUS RUSSELL
BENJAMIN K. SCOTT

Fields, Mary (ca. 1832–1914), stagecoach driver and businesswoman. Mary Fields's life in the old West gives a taste of the range of lifestyle and occupational possibilities for an adventurous African-American woman. Although not much is known about Fields's early life, it is known that she was born a slave in Tennessee and that she traveled throughout the West. By 1884 she had become associated with a group of Ursuline nuns in Toledo, Ohio, doing handy work in their convent. She followed them out to Helena, Mont., a few years later to assist in the construction of a mission school for Native American girls.

Fields's unconventional lifestyle raised the ire of some of those living near the mission. She was notorious for dressing in men's clothes, drinking, smoking, and engaging in gun duels. The Roman Catholic bishop for the region forced the Ursulines to send her away. After a brief attempt at operating a restaurant, she took a job as a stagecoach driver for the U.S. government.

By 1903, Fields had left her job as a driver and settled in Cascade, Mont., where she was the only African-American resident. Here she built a large laundry business and established herself as a fixture of the community. The townspeople of Cascade had no objections to her manner, and she was even welcomed by the men in the local saloon. She was honored regularly on her birthday by the townspeople, many of whom contributed to rebuild her business when it was destroyed by fire in 1912. Fields died in 1914 and is buried in Cascade.

REFERENCES

COOPER, GARY. "Stage Coach Mary: Gun Toting Montanan Delivered U.S. Mail." As told to Marc Crawford. *Ebony* 14 (October 1959): 97–100.

KING, ANITA. "Black Mary: A Westerner with Style." *Essence* 4 (January 1974): 23, 91.

JUDITH WEISENFELD

Fifteenth Amendment. The Fifteenth Amendment to the U.S. Constitution provides that voting rights shall not be abridged by the federal government or any state "on account of race, color, or previous condition of servitude." The amendment reflected the federal government's emergence during Reconstruction as the guarantor of civil rights against state intrusion.

Having granted most southern black men the right to vote, at least temporarily, by the Military Reconstruction acts of 1867, the Republican majority in Congress wanted to render black suffrage nationwide and permanent. Congressman George S. Boutwell of Massachusetts proposed a constitutional amendment in January 1869. Controversy arose over the wording, with many supporters of civil rights fearing that a vague amendment would permit later disenfranchisement through indirect means.

Other Republicans, however, insisted that northern states must remain able to restrict the suffrage on the basis of literacy of education, often for nativist reasons. In addition, some Congressmen feared granting unrestricted authority in the area to the federal government. In response to such concerns, a relatively limited form of the amendment passed Congress in February 1869, over vehement Democratic opposition. It was ratified by the states in March 1870, aided by the presence of Reconstruction governments in most southern states.

A more radical amendment, calling for an end to disenfranchisement based on "race, color, nationality, property, education, or religious beliefs," was rejected, as were feminist calls for women's suffrage. Furthermore, the amendment did not guarantee the right of blacks to hold office.

As feared, southern Democratic state governments did almost eliminate black voting through poll taxes, literacy tests, residency requirements, and similar means. The Fifteenth Amendment permanently secured voting rights in the northern states, several of which still did not permit black voting at the time. The amendment was also of long-term significance in that it declared equal suffrage an ideal, if not a reality, in the nation's fundamental law. The effort actually to secure black suffrage took more than this amendment. The NAACP fought successfully against the many abridgments to black suffrage in the early twentieth century, but it was not until the VOTING RIGHTS ACT OF 1965 that the vast majority of eligible southern blacks were registered to vote.

REFERENCES

FONER, ERIC. *Reconstruction: America's Unfinished Revolution, 1863–1877.* New York, 1988.

HYMAN, HAROLD M. *A More Perfect Union: The Impact of the Civil War and Reconstruction on the Constitution.* Boston, 1973.

MALTZ, EARL M. *Civil Rights, the Constitution, and Congress, 1863–1869.* Lawrence, Kans., 1990.

MICHAEL W. FITZGERALD

Fifty-fourth Regiment of Massachusetts Volunteer Infantry. The "Fifty-fourth Massachusetts Regiment" was the first regular army unit of African Americans raised in the North during the CIVIL WAR. For northern blacks, the Fifty-fourth assumed enormous significance: "The eyes of the whole world are upon you," one black newspaper announced, "civilized man everywhere waits to see if you will prove yourselves." Blacks hoped that the unit's valor would discredit charges of racial inferiority and advance the antislavery cause; failure might jeopardize the struggle for black freedom.

Massachusetts's abolitionist governor John A. Andrew organized the regiment between January and May 1863, choosing as officers white men with military experience who opposed slavery and embraced the idea of black military service. Andrew worked closely with black leaders such as Lewis Hayden to win the confidence of the African-American community and declared his own commitment to the regiment, announcing that his honor "as a man and a magistrate" would "rise or fall" with the Fifty-fourth. Enlistees came from across the North, including the well-educated sons of such black leaders as Frederick DOUGLASS, who overcame their initial resentment over the Lincoln administration's refusal to commission black officers. Black communities braved the threats and assaults of racist mobs to assist in recruitment efforts and to collect money and supplies for the troops.

The Fifty-fourth quickly proved its fighting ability in the South Carolina Sea Islands, in one case saving a white Union regiment from annihilation. The unit led the attack on FORT WAGNER, a key Confederate fortification in Charleston's defensive network. Although the July 18, 1863, assault failed—the Fifty-fourth's colonel, Robert Gould Shaw, was killed, and nearly half of the attacking forces became casualties—the unit's valor won the right for blacks to serve in the army. Approximately 178,000 African Americans subsequently enlisted and played a crucial role in the victory over slavery and the South.

The Wagner attack decimated the regiment; months passed before recruits filled the unit and its new colonel, Edward N. Hallowell—who was seri-

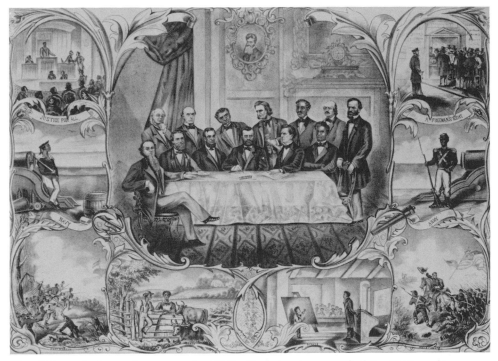

The Fifteenth Amendment to the U.S. Constitution, ratified in 1870 and guaranteeing that the right to vote would not be impeded by state or federal governments "on account of race, color, or previous condition of servitude." Its passage is hailed in these contemporary engravings. It would take a century, however, for the promise of the Fifteenth Amendment to be realized. (Prints and Photographs Division, Library of Congress)

ously wounded at Wagner—assumed command. The regiment's palmy first days never returned and many new officers lacked the commitment of the original ones, although Hallowell was a genuine abolitionist and closely identified with his men. Irksome fatigue duty preoccupied the regiment until February 1864, when it fought in the disastrous Olustee, Fla., campaign. More important, the unit led other black regiments in an eighteen-month pay strike against the federal government's offer of unequal pay. Although promised the same pay and benefits as whites, all blacks, regardless of rank, received less pay than white privates. Near-mutinous conditions prevailed in the Fifty-fourth until Congress bowed to pressure and adopted legislation equalizing the pay of black and white troops. In the closing months of the war, members of the Fifty-fourth were the first Union soldiers to occupy Charleston, the seat of secessionist fervor. The unit also destroyed valuable rail stock and liberated hundreds of slaves in the back country of northern Georgia and South Carolina before being mustered out in August 1865.

REFERENCES

ADAMS, VIRGINIA M., ed. *On the Altar of Freedom: A Black Soldier's Civil War Letters from the Front.* Amherst, Mass., 1991.

BURCHARD, PETER. *One Gallant Rush: Robert Gould Shaw and His Brave Black Regiment.* New York, 1965.

EMILIO, LUIS F. *A Brave Black Regiment: History of the Fifty-fourth Regiment of Massachusetts Volunteer Infantry, 1863–1865.* 1894. Reprint. New York, 1968.

DONALD YACOVONE

Film. Motion pictures and large numbers of African Americans arrived in American cities simultaneously in the late nineteenth century. Black Americans came to cities in flight from the southern peonage that had replaced the institution of slavery after the Civil War. Their Great Migration in turn coincided with a similar migration from Europe. Movies, in their "primitive" days, when techniques of cutting and editing as a means of conveying a narrative had not yet been perfected, became the first medium of mass communications for the poor, teeming populations that filled northeastern cities toward the end of the nineteenth century.

Movies had played the Cotton States Exposition in Atlanta in 1895, and in the following year opened at Koster and Bial's music hall in New York. Strikingly, in these early years African Americans often appeared on the screen in unmediated, unedited form, and therefore devoid of some of the worst stereotypes with which they had been maligned by decades of southern novels, advertising logos, and popular songs. A shot of, for example, black soldiers watering their horses or dockers coaling a ship appeared on the screen untrammeled by the pejorative images of the past.

These topical vignettes were the result of a rage for news of events in the corners of the world. Thomas Edison filmed life in the Caribbean; others caught black "buffalo soldiers" on their way to the Spanish-American War, tribal ceremonies in Africa, and Theodore Roosevelt on safari.

Gradually after the turn of the century, the medium changed, both technically and economically. As the prospects for a profitable future opened up, producers began to cultivate more sophisticated techniques that allowed them to edit scenes into narratives along the lines set down by novelists and dramatists. The trend pointed toward a future cinema that would play to middle-class rather than poor audiences, in picture palaces rather than storefront nickelodeons, and at length rather than in the brief snippets with which the medium had begun its life.

For African Americans, this meant a resumption of many conventions inherited from the nineteenth-century melodramatic, comic, and musical stage. Indeed, in 1903 William S. Porter brought UNCLE TOM'S CABIN to the screen, complete with overambitious attempts at spectacle—cakewalks, pursuits across ice floes, and even a race between miniature steamboats. Tom himself was more a figure drawn from the sentimental stage than from Harriet Beecher Stowe's staunch hero.

Other restorations of familiar racial material gradually dominated the screen just as the medium began to emerge from a primitive, limited visual rhetoric. In *A Bucket of Cream Ale* (1904), a stock, obstreperous black-faced servant appeared; *The Fights of Nations* (1907) featured a razor fight; and comedies about chicken thieving and life in "coontown" became routine. From 1911 through 1915, movies sentimentalized the Civil War during the five years of its semicentennial. Rarely was there an opportunity for a genuine black portrayal to show through in *A Slave's Devotion* (1913); *Old Mammy's Secret Code* (1913), or *For the Cause of the South* (1914). Typical of the era was D. W. Griffith's *His Trust* (1911) and its sequel, a tale of the Civil War in which a slave is first entrusted with managing his master's estate while the latter is away fighting and then, after the master dies a hero's death, gives his own "savings" toward sending the master's daughter to finishing school so that she may meet and marry someone in her class.

It was at this moment that African Americans took their first steps toward an indigenous cinema. Local black entrepreneurs in Lexington, Ky., as early as the first decade of the century booked all-black films in their theaters. By 1912, William Foster in Kansas made *The Railroad Porter* with a black audience as his target. About the same time in Florida, James Weldon JOHNSON wrote two scripts for a company bent upon making films with an African-American angle.

Unfortunately for small-time entrepreneurs, the economic setting of moviemaking had begun to rationalize into competing oligopolies, even "trusts," in which ever-fewer sellers drove out competition for customers who gradually included more demanding middle-class, urbane tastemakers. Edison's Motion Picture Patents Trust, for example, formed a pool of patents through which it hoped to control the entire nation's film output by licensing the use of cameras and projectors. In such a richly capitalized economic field, African Americans only a half century removed from slavery had little chance.

The Birth of a Nation
Then in 1915, D. W. Griffith—after years spent learning filmmaking and extending its range into techniques unforeseen in the primitive years—released his Civil War epic THE BIRTH OF A NATION. An evocative combination of conventional racial attitudes, a celebration of the Civil War and of the forbearance of the white South during Reconstruction, and a genuinely avant-garde piece of filmmaking, *The Birth of a Nation* galvanized African Americans and their white allies into a nationwide protest campaign. At issue were two major factors: first, its depiction of Reconstruction as a tale of black cupidity, corruption, and vindictiveness toward the prostrate white South, and second, the unprecedented nationwide advertising campaign, which further heightened the film's impact. It was this *combination* that nettled blacks. Most literate Americans believed the account of Reconstruction as portrayed therein, complete with its venal freedmen who did the bidding of scalawags and carpetbaggers (Woodrow Wilson had retold it in his multivolume history of the nation), but the couching of it in a blaring ad campaign and in an emotionally charged movie made the difference.

The NAACP fruitlessly conducted a national campaign against the movie, demanding cuts of scenes that "slandered" blacks, advocating strict legal codes against maligning races and groups, and instigating a plan to make its own movie, to be titled *Lincoln's Dream*. But despite the protesters' best efforts, by the end of 1915 *The Birth of a Nation* could be seen almost anywhere its makers wished, and *Lincoln's Dream* foundered for want of an "angel."

Nonetheless, the struggle against Griffith's film confirmed a number of African Americans in their embracing of a strategy of making movies alternative to those of the mainstream. Even Booker T. WASHINGTON, the famous founder of TUSKEGEE Institute and a reputed accommodationist in racial matters, took up the idea of making black movies. At first he feared that the makers of *The Birth of a Nation* might profit from the notoriety that would follow from a vigorous black protest, but soon, through his secretary Emmett J. SCOTT, he committed resources to a film eventually titled *The Birth of a Race*.

The Birth of a Race
Washington and Scott's movie seemed to possess everything: the endorsement of national worthies of the Republican party; a script that traced the progress of humankind, while allocating a prominent place in it for African Americans; and a panel of rich angels led by Julius Rosenwald, a Sears and Roebuck vice president. But things fell apart. First, Washington died on November 15, 1915. Then, acting on rumors of unscrupulous practices among the project's Chicago fund-raisers, Rosenwald and other prestigious figures withdrew. And finally, with the onset of World War I, the thrust of the already episodic movie veered wildly from a pacifist theme to its ideological opposite—a justification of the American entry into the war. Thus, after almost three years of scrabbling for money, shooting in Tampa, and cutting through the thicket of cross-purposed story lines, the project changed. And yet the completed movie reached a level of accomplishment never previously attained by black moviemakers. They had actually completed a feature-length film, albeit one burdened by seemingly endless title frames that slowed its pace and shouldered aside its African-American premise in favor of militaristic themes.

The Lincoln Company
Moreover, readers of the black press noticed. Indeed, one man in particular, a postman in Omaha named George P. JOHNSON, saw the film as more than a grand flop. Together with his brother Noble JOHNSON, a contract player at Universal, he assembled a circle of black investors in Los Angeles into the Lincoln Company. Between 1916 and 1922 they turned out an impressive string of films (of which only a fragment survives), all of them celebrations of the black aspiration embedded in one of the company's titles: *The Realization of a Negro's Ambition*.

Indeed, aspiration was emblazoned on the Johnsons' battleflags. It marked or guided everything they made, whether tales of black "buffalo soldiers" fighting Mexican *insurrectes* along the border or go-getters scoring successes in capitalist circles that few blacks would have had access to in the reality of American life. The Johnsons' rivals during the booming 1920s not only followed their example but extended its reach. Among these were the Frederick Douglass Company (with its Republican namesake on its letterhead), Sidney P. Dones's Democracy Company, and regional operations such as Gate City in Kansas, Ker-Mar in Baltimore, and Norman in Jacksonville and later Boley, Okla. In the pages of the African-American press there appeared dozens of announcements of additional companies, most of which did not survive long enough to see their first film to the screen.

Some studios, such as Norman, were conduits for the investments of white "angels" or were in fact white firms. Robert Levy's Reol Studio, for example, was a white-owned company that made films from well-known black classics such as Paul Laurence DUNBAR's *The Sport of the Gods*. To some extent this rush of activity merely testified to the wealth that had reached even black strata of urban life during the 1920s. But it also suggested the presence of a maturing film culture, drawing in a sector of the black population that was not only well off enough to buy tickets but also literate enough to read the growing amount of advertising copy, reviews, and show-business gossip that had begun to fill the pages of the African-American press.

The Black Audience

In other words, an audience had been formed by the black migrations to the urban centers of America, both North and South. The names of the theaters signaled the identity of the audience. No Bijous, Criterions, or Paramounts there. But rather a Douglass or an Attucks to honor famous heroes, a Lenox, Harlem, or Pekin to provide linkages to increasingly well-known centers of black urban culture. This sort of social, institutional, and cultural density suggested the nature of this newly arrived audience: urban, literate, employed, affiliated in a circle of lodges and clubs, and church members. In short, the audience constituted a thin layer of bourgeoisie to whom movies spoke of aspiration, racial pride, and heroism, and cautioned against the evils of drink and sloth—much like a Booker T. Washington commencement address with pictures.

We can sense these social traits not only from the themes of the movies themselves but also from the critics who wrote about them: D. Ireland Thomas in the Mississippi Valley, Lester Walton of the New York *Age,* Theophilus Lewis on several papers in the New York area, Billy Rowe on the PITTSBURGH COURIER, Romeo Daugherty in the AMSTERDAM NEWS, Fay Jackson for Claude A. BARNETT's Associated Negro Press service, and other regulars on the *Afro-American* chain (*see* BALTIMORE AFRO-AMERICAN) and even smaller papers. Augmenting their own acute criticism that seemed to be maturing

toward a genuine African-American posture toward cinema were the syndicated columnists, who wrote gossipy copy for the *Los Angeles Sentinel* and the *California Eagle*—Ruby Berkeley Goodwin, Harry Levette, and Lawrence LaMar.

Micheaux and the Colored Players

Playing to this emerging audience in the 1920s were the elite of "race" film companies, either staunchly black firms such as that of Oscar MICHEAUX or white firms with a feel for the audience, such as David Starkman's Colored Players in Philadelphia. Micheaux, a peripatetic author who sold his own novels from door to door, entered the movie business in 1919 after a failed negotiation with Lincoln to produce his autobiographical novel *The Homesteader*. For much of the ensuing quarter century and more, he audaciously if not always artfully reached for effects and messages left untouched by his forebears. In his *Body and Soul* (1924) he featured the singer Paul ROBESON in his only appearance in a race movie. In *Within Our Gates* (1921) he put his own spin on the infamous Leo Frank murder case in Atlanta. And throughout his career Micheaux played on themes of racial identity, often hinging his plots upon revelations of mixed parentage.

The Colored Players differed from Micheaux's group in that they not only calculatedly played to urban, eastern audiences but seemed to have a capacity for putting every dollar on the screen, with handsomely—even densely—dressed sets and more polished levels of acting. They did Dunbar's *A Prince of His Race* (1926), a black version of the temperance tract *Ten Nights in a Bar Room* (1926), and an original screenplay entitled *The Scar of Shame* (1927).

More than any other race movie, *The Scar of Shame* addressed the concerns of the urban black middle class. Although it teased around the theme of color caste snobbery among African Americans, its most compelling argument was a call to rise above the lot that blacks had been given and to strive for "the finer things" despite adversity. But at the same time, as critic Jane Gaines has argued, their poor circumstances were given them not by a natural order but by a white-dominated system that blacks knew as the real puppeteer working the strings off camera.

Hollywood's Blacks

For its part, Hollywood in the 1920s rarely departed from conventions it had inherited from southern American racial lore. Its high moments included *In Old Kentucky* (1926), in which the black romance was in the hands of the enduring clown STEPIN FETCHIT. In most movies blacks merely lent an atmosphere to the sets: Sam Baker as a burly seaman in *Old Ironsides,* Carolynne Snowden as an exotic dancer in Erich von

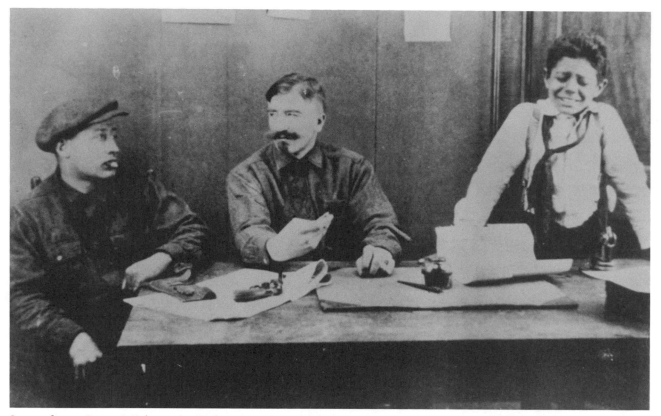

Scene from Oscar Micheaux's *Within Our Gates*. (Photographs and Prints Division, Schomburg Center for Research in Black Culture, The New York Public Library, Astor, Lenox and Tilden Foundations)

Stroheim's Ruritanian romances, and so on. The decade also produced its own obligatory version of *Uncle Tom's Cabin*.

But with the coming of the cultural crisis wrought by the Great Depression of 1929 and after, blacks and whites shared at least fragments of the same depths of despair and were thrust together in the same breadlines and federal programs such as the WORKS PROJECT ADMINISTRATION (WPA). In Hollywood the result was a run of socially and artistically interesting black roles, and even a couple of tolerable all-black homages to the hard life the race lived in the South: *Hallelujah!* and *Hearts in Dixie* (both in 1929).

At the same time, Hollywood had also matured into a corporate system that had rationalized moviemaking into a vertically integrated mode of production, distribution, and exhibition. The result was a manufactured product marked by so many family traits that it could be labeled by some historians "the classic Hollywood movie." Typically, such movies told an uncomplicated tale in which engaging characters embarked on a plot that obliged them to fill some lack, solve a mystery, or complete a quest resulting in a closure that wrapped all the strands into a fulfilling denouement.

Unavoidably, the African-American roles that filled out these plots owed more to the conventions of the moviemaking system than to the authentic wellsprings of everyday black life. Moreover, supporting this industrial/aesthetic system were the proscriptions set forth by Hollywood's self-censorship system, the Production Code Administration or "the Hays Office." These dos and don'ts discouraged full black participation in any plot forbidding racial slander or miscegenation, so that almost no African-American "heavy" or villain could appear. Nor could any black person engage in any sort of close relationship other than that of master and servant.

Stepin Fetchit, for example, enjoyed a flourishing career during the Great Depression, but one severely limited in its range. In *The World Moves On* (1934) he had a rare opportunity to play a soldier in the French army, but only as a consequence of following his master into combat; in *Stand Up and Cheer* (1934) he joined the rest of the cast in fighting off the effects of the depression, but was absent from pivotal scenes that centered on the white principals; and in the middle of the decade he appeared in a brief string of rural fables as a sidekick to Will Rogers's folksy *Judge Priest* or *David Harum*. Women had their moments as wise or flippant servants, notably Louise BEAVERS in *Imitation of Life* (1934) and Hattie MCDANIEL in *Alice Adams* (1935). Such a role eventually won McDaniel the first Oscar ever won by an

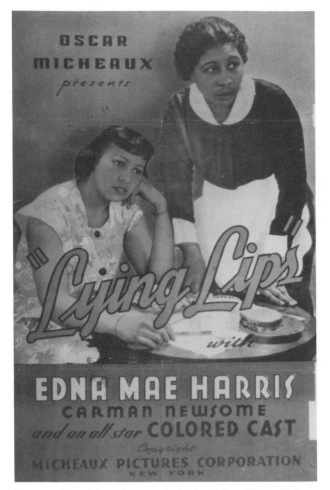

Poster advertising the movie *Lying Lips,* 1939. (Prints and Photographs Division, Library of Congress)

African American: her "Mammy" in *Gone with the Wind* (1939). Whenever the script called for a character of mixed heritage, such as Tondelayo in *White Cargo* or Zia in *Sundown,* the Hollywood self-censorship system, the Hays office, pressed the studios toward the cautious choice of casting white actors in the roles.

For African Americans, the combination of an increasingly factory-like Hollywood system and a lingering economic depression provided only scant hope of improved roles. And yet the coming of sound film technology opened a window of opportunity for black performers.

Already, theatrical audiences had been introduced to African-American musical performance in the form of rollicking revues such as the *Blackbirds* series and Marc Connelly's Pulitzer Prize fable *The Green Pastures,* which he had drawn from Roark Bradford's book of tales, *Ole Man Adam and His Chillun.* Fleetingly, two major Hollywood studios—Fox and Metro—had responded with *Hearts in Dixie* and *Hallelujah!* And both the majors and the independents offered hope for an African-American presence in

sound films in the form of a rash of short musical films that lasted well past the decade.

The most famous of these one- or two-reel gems were Bessie SMITH and Jimmy Mordecai's *St. Louis Blues* (1929)—which used not only W. C. HANDY's title song but incidental choral arrangements by J. Rosamond JOHNSON, who, with his brother James Weldon, had written the "Negro national anthem," *Lift Ev'ry Voice and Sing*—and Duke ELLINGTON's films *Black and Tan* and *The Symphony in Black* (1929 and 1935, respectively). Throughout the decade and beyond, stars of the jazz scene—Cab CALLOWAY, Louis ARMSTRONG, and the NICHOLAS BROTHERS, among others—appeared in these shorts, which culminated with Lena HORNE, the duo pianists Albert AMMONS and Pete Johnson, and the pianist Teddy Wilson in *Boogie Woogie Dream* (1944). By then such films had attracted the attention of white aesthetes such as the photographer Gjon Mili, who cast Illinois Jacquet, Sid CATLETT, Marie Bryant, and others in his *Jammin' the Blues* (1946), which became a *Life* magazine Movie of the Week.

Late Race Movies

As for race-movie makers, the times were harder. Of the African Americans only their doyen, Oscar Micheaux, worked through the entire decade of the 1940s, albeit as a client of white capital sources such as Frank Schiffman, manager of the Apollo Theater. Now and again a newcomer such as William D. Alexander's All America firm or George Randol with his *Dark Manhattan* (1947) entered the field, but race movies too had matured into a system led mainly by white entrepreneurs such as Ted Toddy of Atlanta, Alfred Sack of Dallas, Bert and Jack Goldberg of New York, and Harry and Leo Popkin of Hollywood, whose loose federation was modeled on the classic Hollywood system.

As a result, race movies soon imitated Hollywood genres such as the gangster film and the Western. *Paradise in Harlem* (1940), for example, featured a tale of a black gang bent upon taking over Harlem. The community, led by an actor (Frank Wilson), mounts a jazz version of *Othello* as a fund-raiser, and the play is so compelling that even gangsters are won over by its seductive beat and a black-themed Shakespeare. Westerns—*Two Gun Man from Harlem, Bronze Buckaroo,* and *Harlem Rides the Range*—also borrowed their formulas from Hollywood, particularly their satisfying closures that promised happy lives to the good people of the cast.

The Impact of World War II

No political event affected moviemaking more profoundly than did World War II. Even before the war reached America, Hollywood responded to it by forming an Anti-Nazi League and by cleansing its

Entrance to a movie house, Beale Street, Memphis, Tenn., October 1939. (Prints and Photographs Division, Library of Congress)

movies of the worst of racist traits, much as David O. Selznick tried to do when he told his writer to place African Americans "on the right side of the ledger during these Fascist-ridden times" as they began work on *Gone with the Wind*. Indeed, so successful was he that blacks were divided in their response to the Southern epic for which Hattie McDaniel became the first black ever to win an Oscar. In less splashy movies a similar impact of the war was felt. John Huston and Howard Koch included a strong black law student who stands up to a ne'er-do-well daughter of the southern gentry in their movie of Ellen Glasgow's Pulitzer Prize novel in *In This Our Life*. And Walter WHITE of the NATIONAL ASSOCIATION FOR THE ADVANCEMENT OF COLORED PEOPLE (NAACP) helped to adapt Walter Wanger's *Sundown* (1941) to fit the changing politics brought on by the war.

The war provided a cultural crisis that weighed upon African Americans in several ways: The Allies' war aims included anticolonialism, the nation needed black soldiers and war workers, and black journalists campaigned to insist on such linkages, as the *Pittsburgh Courier* did in calling for a "Double V," a simultaneous victory over foreign fascism and domestic racism. Together with the NAACP, liberals within the Office of War Information and the Pentagon joined in a campaign to make appropriate movies. Two new trends resulted: government pro-paganda such as *The Negro Soldier, Wings for This Man,* and *Teamwork,* which asserted a black place in the war effort, and Hollywood films such as *Crash Dive, Sahara, Bataan,* and *Lifeboat,* which often integrated the armed forces before the services themselves acted to do so. Along with federal measures such as a Fair Employment Practices Commission, the movies contributed to a new political culture that reintroduced the issue of racism to the arena of national politics.

After the war, filmmakers emerged from their military experience to form a new documentary film culture bent upon making films of liberal advocacy, much as they had done during the war. The NAACP continued to lead this movement by urging wartime agencies to send their surplus films to schools, trade unions, and civil rights groups, constituting audiovisual aids for, as Roy WILKINS of the NAACP said, "educating white people now and in the future." Thus, informational films such as *The Negro Soldier* entered the civilian marketplace of ideas. In the same period, a wartime antiracist tract by Ruth Benedict and Gene Weltfish became *The Brotherhood of Man,* an animated cartoon endorsed and distributed by the United Auto Workers. Another film of the era was *The Quiet One,* an account of a black boy of the streets who enters Wiltwyck School, an agency charged with treating such children. The fact that it enjoyed an unprecedented run in urban theaters perhaps contributed to Hollywood's decision to resume attention to the racial issues it had taken up during the war.

By 1949, Hollywood majors and some independent companies that had sprung up following the war produced peacetime versions of the war movies. The results were mixed. Louis DeRochemont's "message movie" *Lost Boundaries* focused on a New England village "black" family that had been passing as white, thereby blunting the main point, racial integration; Stanley Kramer's *Home of the Brave* did somewhat better by introducing a black soldier into an otherwise white platoon; Dore Schary's *Intruder in the Dust* faithfully rendered William Faulkner's book into film, including its portrayal of African Americans as icons of a sad past who could teach white people the lessons of history; Darryl F. Zanuck's *Pinky* provided a closure in which a black nurse learns the value of building specifically black social institutions; and Zanuck's *No Way Out* carried the genre into the 1950s, focusing tightly on a black family and neighborhood and their willingness to defend themselves against the threat of racism.

Postwar Hollywood

Taken as a lot, these message movies perpetuated the integrationist ideology that had emerged from the war and gave Sidney POITIER, James Edwards, Juano Hernandez, and others a foothold in Hollywood. Indeed, if anything, Hollywood only repeated itself in the ensuing decade, hobbling efforts to press on. Poitier, for example, after a few good films in the integrationist vein—*The Blackboard Jungle* (1954), *The Defiant Ones* (1959), and *Lilies of the Field* (1963)—was given few challenging scripts. Typical of the era was Alec Waugh's novel *Island in the Sun,* a book specifically about racial politics in the Caribbean, bought by 20th Century-Fox only to have its most compelling black spokesman written entirely out of the script. Black women fared little better, mainly because they were assigned only a narrow range of exotic figures, such as Dorothy DANDRIDGE's title role in the all-black *Carmen Jones* (1954).

Dorothy Dandridge as Carmen, and Harry Belafonte as Joe in *Carmen Jones,* 1954, directed by Otto Preminger. A version of George Bizet's opera *Carmen,* this film was among the most successful of the many all-black-cast adaptations of musicals and operas. (UPI/Bettmann)

Not until the era of the civil rights movement—when such events as the Greensboro, N.C., student SIT-INS of 1960 became daily fare on national television—would Hollywood try to catch up with the pace of events and TV's treatment of them. Even then, the most socially challenging themes were in movies made outside the Hollywood system, on East Coast locations or even in foreign countries. These included Shirley Clarke's harsh film of Harlem's streets *The Cool World* (1964); Gene Persson and Anthony Harvey's London-made film of Amiri BARAKA's *Dutchman* (1967); Larry Peerce's cautionary tale about the stresses of interracial marriage, *One Potato Two Potato* (1965); Marcel Camus's Afro-Brazilian movie of the myth of Orpheus and Eurydice, *Orfeo Negro* (1960); and Michael Roemer's *Nothing but a Man* (1964), a pastoral film that was named by *Black Creation* magazine as the "greatest" of black movies.

Parallel to the civil rights movement, Hollywood itself experienced key changes in its institutional structure. Its production system became less vertically integrated and more dependent on sound marketing; federal laws began to require the active recruiting of blacks into studio guilds and unions from which they had been excluded by "grandfather clauses"; the old Hays Office censorship gave way to legal challenges and eventually to a liberalized system of ratings; and television assumed the role of seeking the steady audiences that B movies once had done. All these factors would alter the ways Hollywood treated race, but TELEVISION had a particular impact.

In the 1960s television shows *East Side/West Side, The Store Front Lawyers, Mod Squad,* and *Julia,* social workers, idealistic attorneys, dedicated cops, and self-sacrificing hospital workers struggled on behalf of their clients, often against the social order itself. Television news and documentaries provided a

The Ku Klux Klan's revival in the 1950s was part of the resistance to the quickening pace of the civil rights movement. Organizations such as the Klan engaged in a wide range of tactics to frustrate demands for black equality, ranging from violence to relatively peaceful picketing and lobbying. Members of the Klan protest a Jacksonville, Fla., movie theater exhibiting a film depicting an interracial romance. (AP/Wide World Photos)

tougher image for Hollywood to strive to emulate. Daily camerawork from southern streets and courtrooms recorded the agony of the region as it resisted African-American challenges to the status quo. The documentaries, whether on commercial or public television, occasionally emerged from black origins, such as William Greave's BLACK JOURNAL. "TV Is Black Man's Ally," said the *Los Angeles Sentinel*, while *Variety* reported a new black stereotype: an "intensely brooding, beautiful black rebel."

"Blaxploitation" Films

Hollywood had little choice but to take the point, particularly since several studios were close to collapse. They stood on the verge of what came to be called the era of BLAXPLOITATION FILMS. Black youth flocked to this cycle of jangling, violent, and shrilly political movies. Timidly at first, the majors fell to the task. But first, there were easily digestible crossover movies, such as the pastoral tales *Sounder* and *The Learning Tree* (both 1968), the latter an autobiography by the photographer Gordon PARKS, Jr. Then came the urban, picaresque heroes most often thought of as "blaxploitation" icons, who combined the cynicism of 1940s film noir style with the kinetic yet cool mode of the black streets. The most famous and probably the highest earner of rentals was Parks's MGM film *Shaft* (1970). The movies that followed, such as Melvin VAN PEEBLES's *Sweet Sweetback's Baadasssss Song* (1971), constituted calls for direct and sometimes violent retribution against brutal police and exploitative mobsters.

Other movies in the cycle tried to remake white classics by reinventing them in African-American settings—*Cool Breeze* (from *The Asphalt Jungle*), *Blacula* (*Dracula*), *The Lost Man* (*The Informer*). Some were derived from original material angled toward blacks, such as the cavalry Western *Soul Soldier*.

Still another genre—"crossover" movies—sought a wider sector of the market spectrum in the form of material, such as biographies of performers—Billie HOLIDAY, Leadbelly (Huddie LEDBETTER)—who had enjoyed followings among whites.

Yet whatever their uneven merits, the blaxploitation movies lost touch with the market. Their place was taken by Chinese martial-art fables, the work of purveyors such as Raymond Chow and Run Run Shaw, featuring impossibly adept warriors whose revenge motifs touched a nerve in the psyches of black urban youth. Soon the domestic makers of blaxploitation movies lost their market entirely, so that African Americans reached the screen only as functionaries in conventional Hollywood features—police, physicians, and the like—or in prestigious, even reverent treatments of classics or successes from other media, such as Eli Landau's movie of Kurt Weill and Maxwell Anderson's South African musical *Lost in the Stars*, Charles FULLER's *A Soldier's Story*, and E. L. Doctorow's *Ragtime*.

Black Independent Film

Nonetheless, the era had revealed a previously unmeasured black marketplace that seemed ready for either the raffish or the political. Moreover, the combined impact of a thin wedge of black in the Hollywood guilds, an increase in African Americans' numbers in the university film schools, and the opening of television as a training ground resulted in a greater number of filmmakers and, eventually, a steady flow of independently made black films. Madeleine Anderson's combination of journalism and advocacy; St. Clair BOURNE's access to black institutions, as in *Let the Church Say Amen;* Haile Gerima's syncretism of the pace and rhythms of East African life and the stuff of African-American life, mediated by film school experience, resulting in his *Bush Mama;* and William MILES's classically styled histories such as *Men of Bronze* and *I Remember Harlem* reflected the catholicity of the movement.

In addition to this focused sort of journalism of advocacy, the 1980s also resulted in a black cinema of personal dimensions, represented by Ayoka Chenzira's *A Film for Nappy Headed People*, Charles BURNETT's *Killer of Sheep*, Kathleen Collins's *The Cruz Brothers and Miss Malloy*, and Warrington HUDLIN's *Streetcorner Stories* and *Black at Yale*.

By 1990 one of this generation of filmmakers, Spike LEE, had—most notably because of his flair for self-advertisement and for shrewd dealing with established Hollywood—crossed over into the mainstream system. A product of film school as well as the most famous African-American association of the craft, the Black Filmmakers Foundation, Lee managed to glaze his movies of black life with a certain universalist charm that earned the sort of rentals that kept Hollywood financing coming. Somehow he conveyed the urgency, extremity, and drama of the arcana of black life—courtship, Greek letter societies, neighborhood territoriality, the tensions of interracial marriage—into a crescendo of ringing cashboxes. From *She's Gotta Have It, School Daze, Do the Right Thing,* and *Jungle Fever,* he moved toward being entrusted with a Holy Grail of black filmmakers, a biography of MALCOLM X that had been stalled for almost a quarter of a century by fears that its protagonist's memory and mission would be violated if placed in the wrong hands.

More than at any other moment in African-American film history, Lee's access to black life, classical training, black associations, and commercial theaters promised the continued presence and vision of African Americans in cinema, rather than a reprise

Film director John Singleton. (Allford/Trotman Associates)

of the peaks and troughs of faddishness that had marked all previous eras of the medium.

The most insidious threat to their work continued to be that which touched everyone in Hollywood, not only the latest generation of African American moviemakers: the unyielding fact that Hollywood was a system, a way of doing business that obliged newcomers to learn its conventions and the rules of its game. This was how fads and cycles were made: an innovative spin placed upon a familiar genre revivified it, drew new patrons into the theaters, and inspired a round of sequels and imitators that survived until the next cycle drew attention to itself. After all, even the most dedicated outlaws, Oscar Micheaux and Melvin Van Peebles, either borrowed money from the system or used it to distribute their work. Unavoidably their benefactors expected to shape their products to conform to the codes of conduct by which all movies were made.

Spike Lee and his age-cohorts were particularly successful, since many of them had gone to film school where learning the trade meant in many ways learning the Hollywood system. Lee's *Malcolm X* was a case in point. In order to celebrate, render plausible, and retail his hero and his image, Lee was drawn into the dilemma of not only making a Hollywood "bioepic" but also marketing it as if it were a McDonald's hamburger. The result was remarkably faithful to its Hollywood model: its protagonist is carried along by his own ambition, revealing slightly clayed feet, as though more a charming flaw than a sin, faces implacable adversaries, is misunderstood by his friends and family, undergoes a revelatory conversion experience, is cast out by his coreligionists for having done it, and finally meets a martyr's death and a last-reel apotheosis. This formula, as stylized as a stanza of haiku poetry, in the hands of Lee was transformed into a vehicle for carrying a particularly reverential, yet engaging black political idiom to a crossover audience.

Could Lee's successors and age-mates not only endure but also prevail over their medium? Lee himself fretted over their future: "We seem to be in a rut," he told a black film conference at Yale in the Spring of 1992. His concern was not so much directed at the Hollywood establishment but rather to the young African-American filmmakers who had followed him to Hollywood: John Singleton, who at age twenty-three had made *Boyz N the Hood;* Matty Rich, who while still a teenager had made *Straight Out of Brooklyn;* and Lee's own cameraman, Ernest Dickerson, who had made *Juice;* each one of them set in a black ghetto, each centered on a protagonist at risk not so much from forces outside his circle but from within, and each marked by a fatalism that precluded tacking on a classic Hollywood happy ending.

Indeed, forces of daunting economic power seemed to hover over the new black filmmakers even as old-line Hollywood producing companies turned out attractive packages in which black themes and characters held a secure place. First, despite various gestures, the studios had hired woefully few black executives so that every project was pitched to persons uncommitted to its integrity. Second, the topmost owners of the system were more remote than ever, as in the case of the Japanese firm Sony which owned both Columbia Pictures and Tri-Star. Third, each new film, upon its release, faced a round of rumors of impending violence that would mar its opening. Fourth, some movies drawn from black material seemed lost in the welter of ghetto movies, much as Robert Townsend's chronicle of the careers of a black quintet of pop singers, *The Five Heartbeats,* sank from view without having reached the audience it deserved. Fifth, some black films, such as Julie Dash's *Daughter of the Dust,* a rose-tinted history of an African-American family in the Sea Islands of the Carolina low country, were so unique in texture, pace, and coloring that they were played off as esoteric art rather than popular culture. Sixth, Hollywood itself seemed ever more capable of portraying at least some aspects of black life or at least drawing black experiences into closer encounters with white. John Badham's *The Hard Way* (1992) featured the rapper LL Cool J (*see* RAP) as an undercover police-man of such depth that the actor felt "honored" to play him. Black critics almost universally admired the quiet depth of Danny Glover's role as a steady, rock-solid tow-truck driver in *Grand Canyon* (1992). And in the work of Eddie Murphy at Paramount (where he sponsored "fellowships" designed to add to the talent pool of minority writers) and in other movies such as *White Men Can't Jump,* the absurdities of race and racism in America were portrayed with arch humor.

At its height during the gestation period of Lee's *Malcolm X,* the trend toward a Hollywood-based African-American cinema seemed problematic and open either to a future of running itself into the ground as the moviemakers of the *Super Fly* era had done, falling prey to cooptation by the Hollywood system, or constantly searching out new recruits who might be the answer to Susan Lehman's rhetorical query in her piece in GQ (February 1991): "Who Will Be the Next Spike Lee?"

REFERENCES

BOGLE, DONALD. *Toms, Coons, Mulattoes, Mammies & Bucks.* New York, 1973.

BOURNE, ST. CLAIR. *The Making of Spike Lee's Do the Right Thing* (film). New York, 1989.

CARBINE, MARY. " 'The Finest Outside the Loop': Motion Picture Exhibition in Chicago's Black Metropolis, 1905–1928." *Camera Obscura* 23 (May 1990): 9–42.

CRIPPS, THOMAS. *Black Film as Genre.* Bloomington, Ind., 1978.

———. *Black Shadows on a Silver Screen* (film). Washington, D.C., 1976.

———. "*Casablanca, Tennessee Johnson,* and *The Negro Soldier*—Hollywood Liberals and World War II." In K. R. M. Short, ed. *Feature Films as History.* London, 1981, pp. 138–156.

———. "Making Movies Black." In Jannette L. Dates and William Barlow, eds. *Split Image: African Americans in the Mass Media.* Washington, D.C., 1990, pp. 125–154.

———. "Movies, Race, and World War II . . ." *Prologue: The Journal of the National Archives* 14 (Summer 1982): 49–67.

———. "*Native Son* in the Movies." *New Letters* 28 (Winter 1972): 49–63.

———. *Slow Fade to Black: The Negro in American Film, 1900–1942.* New York, 1977.

———. "*Sweet Sweetback's Baadasssss Song* and the Changing Politics of Genre Film." In Peter Lehman, ed. *Close Viewings: Recent Film.* Tallahassee, Fla., 1990, pp. 238–261.

———. "Winds of Change: *Gone with the Wind* and Racism as a National Issue." In Darden Asbury Pyron, ed. *Recasting: Gone with the Wind in American Culture.* Miami, 1983, pp. 137–153.

GAINES, JANE. "*The Scar of Shame:* Skin Color and Caste in Black Silent Melodrama." *Cinema Journal* 26 (Summer 1987): 3–21.

HALL, STUART. "Gramsci's Relevance for the Study of Race and Ethnicity." *Journal of Communications Inquiry* 10 (Summer 1986): 5–27.

HOOKS, BELL. "Black Women Filmmakers Break the Silence." *Black Film Review* 2 (Summer 1986): 14–15.

KLOTMAN, PHYLLIS RAUCH. *Frame by Frame–A Black Filmography.* Bloomington, Ind., 1979.

———. *Screenplays of the African American Experience.* Bloomington, Ind., 1991.

LEAB, DANIEL J. *From Sambo to Superspade: The Black Experience in Motion Pictures.* Boston, 1975.

MAYNARD, RICHARD A., ed. *The Black Man on Film: Racial Stereotyping.* Rochelle Park, N.J., 1974.

MEROD, JIM. "A World Without Whole Notes: The Intellectual Subtext of Spike Lee's *Blues.*" *Boundary* 2 (1991): 239–251.

PATTERSON, LINDSAY, ed. *Black Films and Filmmakers: A Comprehensive Anthology.* New York, 1975.

PEAVY, CHARLES D. "Black Consciousness and the Contemporary Cinema." In Ray B. Browne, ed. *Popular Culture and the Expanding Consciousness.* New York, 1973, pp. 178–200.

SAMPSON, HENRY T., comp. *Blacks in Black and White: A Source Book on Black Films.* Metuchen, N.J., 1977.

TAYLOR, CLYDE. "Visionary Black Cinema." *Black Collegian* (October/November 1989): 226–233.

WALLER, GREGORY A. "Another Audience: Black Moviegoing in Lexington, Ky., 1907–1916." *Cinema Journal* 31 (Winter 1992): 3–44.

WOLL, ALLEN L., and RANDALL M. MILLER, comps. *Ethnic and Racial Images in American Film and Television: Historical Essays and Bibliography.* New York, 1987.

THOMAS CRIPPS

First Amenia Conference.   *See* Amenia Conference of 1916.

First South Carolina Volunteer Regiment.

As the first Union regiment of ex-slaves organized in the South during the CIVIL WAR, the First South Carolina Volunteers assumed the burden of proving to a skeptical North that blacks could be effective soldiers. Although officially mustered on November 7, 1862, the regiment emerged from earlier independent efforts of Gen. David Hunter (1802–1886) to organize black troops in the Department of the

South. Hunter's unit never received authorization from the War Department, and within a few months he disbanded all but one company of his men. Gen. Rufus Saxton (1824–1908), supervisor of freed slaves in Hunter's department, took control of the unit, and on August 25, 1862, he gained Secretary of War Edwin M. Stanton's approval to enlist "volunteers of African descent as you may deem expedient, not exceeding five thousand." According to Stanton, the soldiers—and their families—would be granted their freedom and were entitled to receive "the same pay and rations as are allowed, by law, to volunteers in the service."

Thomas Wentworth Higginson (1823–1911), the fiery Massachusetts abolitionist, commanded the regiment and led it on daring raids from Port Royal, S.C., to Palatka, Fla. Higginson and his men understood that they "fought with ropes around their necks." They faced execution or enslavement if captured by Southerners, who considered black soldiers to be rebellious slaves and their white officers as treacherous criminals. Perhaps more galling, they were subjected to scurrilous charges of racial inferiority from the northern press. Nevertheless, Higginson sought to test his men in combat to dispel racist accusations that blacks could not or would not fight. The men, former slaves from South Carolina and Florida, quickly proved their ability and Higginson published stirring accounts of their exploits, laying the groundwork for full-scale black recruitment. Both Higginson and Saxton proclaimed that the men fought as bravely as any other regiment in the army. Moreover, Higginson maintained that the unit, the first to fight alongside whites under the same command in regular duty, helped to reduce racism in the army.

The regiment was authorized to draft former slaves into service, which led to some illegal impressments. But the overwhelming number of blacks volunteered for service to win freedom for themselves and their families. The government's refusal to grant the promised equal pay caused dissension in the "First," as it did among nearly all black regiments, but Higginson claimed that he never resorted to harsh measures to maintain discipline. The men, he believed, had joined out of the deepest sense of patriotism, a hatred of slavery, and "a love of liberty."

On February 8, 1864, the "First" was redesignated the Thirty-third United States Colored Troops (USCT) and subsequently took part in battles at Pocotaligo and James Island, in South Carolina. The Thirty-third USCT performed provost guard duty at Charleston, S.C., and Savannah, Ga., in February and March 1865, and was mustered out on February 9, 1866.

REFERENCES

CORNISH, DUDLEY TAYLOR. *The Sable Arm: Negro Troops in the Union Army, 1861–1865.* New York, 1966.
HIGGINSON, THOMAS WENTWORTH. *Army Life in a Black Regiment.* 1869. Reprint. Boston, 1962.

DONALD YACOVONE

First World War. *See* World War I.

Fisher, Rudolph John Chauncey (1897–1934), fiction writer, dramatist, and essayist. The youngest child of a Baptist minister, Fisher was born in Washington, D.C. He lived briefly in New York City as a small boy but was raised and educated largely in Providence, R.I., where he graduated from Classical High School and Brown University. An undergraduate of many talents, he was chosen by fellow students to be Class Day orator and by the faculty to be commencement speaker. He wrote his first published short story, "The City of Refuge" (1925), in his final year at Howard Medical School, initiating simultaneous vocations in literature and science. When Fisher's internship ended at Freedman's Hospital in Washington, D.C., a National Research Council Fellowship brought him to New York City in 1925 to work in bacteriology with Dr. Frederick P. Gay at the College of Physicians and Surgeons of Columbia University. At the pivotal moment of HARLEM RENAISSANCE in the mid-1920s, he consolidated his medical and literary careers with scientific articles in the *Journal of Infectious Diseases* and *Proceedings of the Society of Experimental Biology and Medicine* and short stories in the *Atlantic Monthly, Survey Graphic,* and *McClure's* magazine. He married Jane Ryder in 1925, and their son Hugh was born in 1926.

One of the more prolific writers of the Harlem Renaissance, Fisher produced in less than a decade fifteen published and seven unpublished short stories, two novels, half a dozen book reviews, a magazine feature article, and a play—while maintaining a medical practice, administering a private X-ray laboratory, and chairing the department of roentgenology at the International Hospital in Manhattan. Harlem is at the center of his literary project. "I intended to write whatever interests me. But if I should be fortunate enough to be known as Harlem's interpreter," he said in response to a radio interviewer's question on WINS in 1933, "I should be very happy." *The Walls of Jericho* (1928), his first novel, interweaves genre elements of color-conscious 1920s Harlem fiction—country-rooted southern migrants, slick

Rudolph Fisher. (Photographs and Prints Division, Schomburg Center for Research in Black Culture, The New York Public Library, Astor, Lenox and Tilden Foundations)

Harlemites, and West Indians with their distinctive dialects and repartee; block-busting scenarios; racist uplifters of the race; rival lovers and their Arcadian conflicts; passing—and brings it all together amid the converging vectors of social and racial distinction at a Harlem ball. His other novel, *The Conjure Man Dies* (1932), is regarded as the earliest example of a detective novel published in book form by an African-American author.

Fisher's place among the writers of the Harlem Renaissance rests, however, on the excellence of his short fiction. In short stories, focused on tensions between West Indians and native-born Americans ("Ringtail"); alienation and reconciliation ("Fire by Night" and "The Backslider"); divisions between youth and age, the modern and the traditional, spirituals and blues ("The Promised Land"); and black consciousness and jazz in a battle of the bands ("Common Meter"), he conveys what Arthur P.

Davis called a "fuller" picture of Harlem life viewed with "an understanding and amused eye," and what Sterling BROWN termed "a jaunty realism . . . less interested in that 'problem' than in the life and language of Harlem's poolrooms, cafes, and barbershops."

Two short stories in particular, "The City of Refuge" and "Miss Cynthic" (1933)—both anthologized in *The Best American Short Stories*—are Fisher's most highly regarded achievements. "The City of Refuge" concerns the arrival in Harlem of King Solomon Gillis, "a baby jess in from the land o' cotton . . . an' ripe f' the pluckin." Gillis is betrayed by everyone who seems to befriend him, yet when he is arrested by a black policeman, the symbol of Harlem's possibility he saw when he first arrived, Gillis, who "plodded flat-footedly" on "legs never quite straightened," can stand "erect" and "exhultant" as he submits to an icon of black authority. In "Miss Cynthie," Fisher's last published work, he matches his undisputed ability to evoke locale and character with what Robert Bone calls a newly discovered sense of "how to *interiorize* his dramatic conflicts, so that his protagonists have the ability to grow." Miss Cynthie struggles to embrace the success of the grandson she hopes is a doctor or at least an undertaker, but who turns out to be a song-and-dance virtuoso.

In 1934, Rudolph Fisher underwent a series of operations for an intestinal disorder—associated by some sources with his early work with X-rays—and died on December 26 of that year.

REFERENCES

BONE, ROBERT. "Three Versions of Pastoral." In *Down Home: A History of Afro-American Short Fiction from Its Beginnings to the End of the Harlem Renaissance*. 1975. Reprint. New York, 1988, pp. 139–170.
BROWN, STERLING. "The Urban Scene." In *Negro Poetry and Drama and The Negro in American Fiction*. New York, 1969, pp. 131–150.
DAVIS, ARTHUR P. "Rudolph Fisher." In *From the Dark Tower: Afro-American Writers, 1900–1960*. Washington, D.C., 1974, pp. 98–103.
McCLUSKEY, JOHN, JR. "Introduction." In *The City of Refuge: Collected Stories of Rudolph Fisher*. Columbia, Mo., 1987, pp. xi–xxxix.
PERRY, MARGARET. "The Brief Life and Art of Rudolph Fisher." In *The Short Fiction of Rudolph Fisher*. New York and Westport, Conn., 1987, pp. 1–20.

JAMES DE JONGH

Fisk Jubilee Singers, choral group.   The Fisk Jubilee Singers, a student choral group of former slaves at FISK UNIVERSITY, in Nashville, Tenn., was organized in 1867 by George L. White, Fisk's treasurer and vocal-music teacher. After several local appearances, the eleven-member group of men and women traveled north to raise money for the financially beleaguered young school. Barely meeting expenses and suffering prejudice and discrimination, the Singers worked their way through the Congregational and Presbyterian churches of Ohio. They began to achieve success with their appearance on November 15, 1871, at Oberlin College in a meeting of the National Council of Congregational Churches, constituents of the AMERICAN MISSIONARY ASSOCIATION, which had founded Fisk.

The Jubilee Singers' repertory of anthems, operatic excerpts, popular ballads, and temperance songs impressed their audiences, in part with the realization that African Americans could sing European music. The singers received their greatest popular response, however, when they sang spirituals, and it can be said that they introduced black music to a white audience. They made plantation hymns popular and even caused them to be written down and preserved. Endorsed by Henry Ward Beecher of Brooklyn's Church of the Pilgrims, the singers began winning praise and raising money in Connecticut and Massachusetts, especially with an audience of forty thousand at the World's Peace Jubilee in Boston in 1872. In Washington, they sang for President Ulysses S. Grant.

During a tour of the British Isles, the group sang for Queen Victoria and with the Moody and Sankey evangelistic campaign. They were popular with Quakers and other former abolitionists, as well as with both the aristocracy (Prime Minister William Gladstone invited them to lunch) and common people (they sang for an audience of 6,000 in Charles Spurgeon's London tabernacle). In 1875, Fisk graduated its first collegiate class and completed construction of Jubilee Hall, its first permanent building, paid for by the Jubilee Singers' tours. The Jubilee Singers have continued to exist until today at Fisk University.

REFERENCE

MARSH, J. B. T. *The Story of the Jubilee Singers with Their Songs.* Boston, 1881.

DORIS EVANS McGINTY

Fisk University.   Fisk University is a private, co-educational, and independent liberal arts institution in Nashville, Tenn. It was founded in October 1865 by Erastus Milo Cravath, field secretary for the AMERICAN MISSIONARY ASSOCIATION (AMA); John Ogden, superintendent of education, Freedmen's Bureau, Tenn.; and the Rev. Edward P. Smith, district secretary, Middle West Department, AMA, at Cincinnati. Cravath and Smith had been sent to Nashville by the AMA to establish an elementary school

Formed at Fisk University in 1867, the Fisk Jubilee Singers popularized the uniquely moving music of the Negro spiritual among nonblack audiences in the United States and Europe, raising much money for Fisk in the process. There were several incarnations of the Fisk Jubilee Singers; this photograph dates from about 1880. (Frank Driggs Collection)

for freedmen in the area. The two men joined forces with Ogden, who was named principal of the Fisk School, or the Fisk Free Colored School, when it opened on January 1, 1866, in former Union hospital barracks. The buildings and land had been purchased with much financial and moral support from the assistant commissioner of the Freedmen's Bureau for Tennessee and Kentucky, Gen. Clinton Bowen Fisk, for whom the school was named. The American Missionary Association and the Freedmen's Bureau also helped to fund the school.

Although at first it functioned mainly as an elementary and normal school, Fisk was incorporated as Fisk University on August 22, 1867, following the founders' desires for a "first-class college" to educate black teachers. The college curriculum was organized by Adam K. Spence, a Scottish-born professor of foreign languages who left the University of Michigan in 1870 to replace Ogden as principal. Fisk graduated its first four college students in 1875, awarding them the B.A. degree for successfully completing courses in such liberal arts subjects as classical and foreign languages, mathematics, natural sciences, philosophy, history, and political science. In keeping with Fisk's religious orientation, weekly Bible classes were also required.

Fisk's income derived primarily from sporadic donations, as well as what could be raised from the modest tuition rates. Under Spence's leadership it experienced dire financial problems, and had often to delay salary payments to its hardworking and dedicated teaching staff, which was originally composed primarily of white missionaries sent by the AMA. The buildings were deteriorating and in need of repair. George L. White, Fisk's treasurer and self-taught music instructor, set out on October 6, 1871, with a group of nine of his best students for a fundraising singing tour of the North and East. White named the group the Jubilee Singers.

The Jubilee Singers introduced "slave songs" or SPIRITUALS to audiences and returned the following year with $20,000 to purchase a forty-acre campus site. Groundbreaking ceremonies were held July 1, 1873, for the erection of Jubilee Hall, now a historic landmark. The Singers remained a Fisk tradition for many years.

In 1875, Erastus Milo Cravath became the first president of Fisk University when the position of principal was eliminated, and the AMA gave up direction of the institution, transferring titles and buildings to the Fisk trustees. Spence continued at Fisk as professor of Greek until 1900. He joined other members of Fisk's white faculty in enrolling his own child at the increasingly reputable university.

Under Cravath's presidency Fisk's reputation grew, and as early as 1875 black professors joined the staff. Among the students who came from the North to study at Fisk was W. E. B. DU BOIS, one of the university's most famous alumni, who received his B.A. in 1888. When Cravath died in 1900, Fisk had graduated more than 400 students who spread Fisk's fame across the U.S. in their careers as lawyers, professors, businessmen, ministers, and editors.

During the presidency of James G. Merrill (1900–1908), Fisk added a summer school for black teachers who wanted to improve their training, as well as many new science courses. When Merrill resigned, Fisk was again experiencing money troubles, since philanthropies at that time were more interested in investing in vocational and industrial schools such as the Tuskegee Institute. Many educators followed the line of reasoning that favored a "practical" education for blacks—training to enter the work force. But Fisk remained staunchly in favor of offering the best liberal arts education it could to blacks in order to produce leaders for the black community.

Under the administration of George A. Gates, president from 1909 to 1912, Fisk established the social science department for which it would become well known. It also began to receive considerable donations from such philanthropists as Andrew Carnegie, Julius Rosenwald, and John D. Rockefeller. These donations were largely results of tireless campaigning on behalf of the university by Booker T. WASHINGTON, whose wife and son were alumni of Fisk.

The presidency of Fayette Avery McKenzie, who took office after Gates's untimely death, brought with it an "expansion of the curriculum and raising of standards," as well as a $2 million endowment campaign. By July 19, 1924, McKenzie was successful in securing half of the endowment. Although the school showed growth, McKenzie's dictatorial administration and strict student discipline led in 1924 and 1925 to one of the first student rebellions on a black college campus. Du Bois fueled the fire of the revolt by speaking out to other alumni against McKenzie. McKenzie was especially resented for his ingratiating behavior toward prominent white citizens of Nashville, and his insistence on unobtrusive, passive behavior from the black students even in the face of antiblack violence. McKenzie resigned on April 16, 1925.

Thomas Elsa Jones, a Quaker missionary, became the last white president in 1926. His years are viewed as one of the most productive periods in Fisk history. He eradicated the stricter regulations imposed on students until then. The $2 million endowment was attained. Black faculty increased to more than one-half, and the first black dean, Ambrose Caliver, was named when Jones took office. Jones placed emphasis on increasing graduate studies at the university and

Like all historically black colleges and universities, Fisk University offered extensive precollege training. This junior preparatory class is from the early twentieth century. (Prints and Photographs Division, Library of Congress)

attracting research-oriented professors. One of these professors was Charles Spurgeon JOHNSON, who became the head of the department of social science in 1928 and established the Institute of Race Relations at Fisk in 1944, drawing white and black leaders to campus annually for intensive three-week conferences. In 1947 Johnson became Fisk's first black president, replacing Jones, who'd resigned to become president of his alma mater, Earlham College. Johnson's administration ended abruptly in 1956 when he died of a heart attack.

During these formative years, Fisk garnered a number of historical firsts among black colleges and universities. It was the first black college to gain full accreditation by the Southern Association of Colleges and Schools (1930); to be on the approved list of the Association of American Universities (1933); to establish a university archive (1948); to be approved by the American Association of University Women (1951); to be granted a chapter of the honorary society Phi Beta Kappa (1952); and to be accredited for membership in the National Association of Schools of Music (1954).

The 1960s brought an expansion in educational programs and buildings. A centennial celebration was held in 1966, and James Raymond LAWSON, an alumnus and scientist, was inaugurated as president, replacing Stephen Junius Wright, Jr., who had been named president after Johnson's death. Enrollment reached 1,559 in 1972, the largest in the University's history. In 1977, the campus was designated by the Department of the Interior as an historical site in the National Register of Historical Places by the National Parks Service.

Ironically, in the early 1970s, school desegregation had an adverse effect on Fisk's finances, as government funding was cut back and competition for students increased as formerly segregated schools lured potential black applicants. In July 1975, Fisk's financial situation reached a crisis point as eleven percent of full-time faculty and forty staff members were laid off. Those remaining took a twenty-percent salary abatement.

With the resignation of Lawson that same year, the school was without a president until 1977, when Walter Jewell Leonard, an attorney, was selected. Inheriting serious financial woes, Leonard's administration was also a target of faculty and student disgruntlement. Student enrollment dropped and a number of faculty resigned.

When a cold homecoming day on November 12, 1983, found dormitories without heat, it became public that the Nashville Gas Company had discontinued service in April because of an overdue bill of $157,000. The financial crisis worsened as the Nashville Electric Service threatened to cut off the university's electricity if $140,000 of their bill was not met immediately. At the same time the Internal Revenue Service was threatening to put a lien on Fisk's property, since the university owed $500,000 in back payroll taxes. When Leonard suddenly resigned on November 23, 1983, the school, which had been $2.2 million in debt at his inauguration, owed some $2.8 million.

The crisis alarmed the nation, and leaders rallied to "save Fisk." President Ronald Reagan donated $1,000, and the United States Secretary of Education, Terrel H. Bell, created a task force from the public and private sectors "to review financial difficulties facing Fisk University."

As in 1871, Fisk once again withstood the tide of financial disaster, receiving scores of donations from alumni and friends. Henry Ponder, an economist, took the reins of the beleaguered institution in July 1984 as the tenth president, and set out to pare back to a "bare-bones" operation.

Despite financial hardships, the university has continued to maintain its position as a flagship among historical black colleges and universities with a tradition of academic excellence. Fisk's $10 million Alfred Stieglitz Collection of Modern Art, presented to the university in 1949 by Georgia O'Keeffe, widow of Stieglitz, as well as its library of valuable research collections and rare books, attracts visitors from all over the world. Fisk alumni, among some of the most distinguished in the nation, include the aforementioned W. E. B. Du Bois, the historian Charles H. WESLEY, Congressman William Levi DAWSON, and the novelist Frank YERBY. Enrollment for 1993 numbered 861.

REFERENCES

COLLINS, L. M. *One Hundred Years of Fisk University Presidents.* Nashville, Tenn., 1989.
RICHARDSON, JOE M. *A History of Fisk University, 1865–1946.* 1980.

ANN ALLEN SHOCKLEY

Fitzbutler, Henry (1842–1901), physician. Born in Amherstburg, Canada West (now Ontario), Fitzbutler was the first African American to study at the Detroit Medical College (1869), the first to receive the M.D. degree from the University of Michigan Medical School (1872), and the first to practice medicine in the state of Kentucky. He founded the Louisville National Medical College in 1888 and was its dean from 1888 to 1901.

Before and during his medical studies, Fitzbutler worked as a farm hand, school teacher, lumberman, and surveyor to finance his education. In July 1872, after receiving his M.D., he moved to Louisville, Ky.

Race prejudice and discrimination barred Fitzbutler from practicing in the hospitals of Louisville. Furthermore, he was not allowed to attend lectures at the medical school. When he first arrived in Louisville he began training other blacks in medicine through apprenticeships. He developed a medical school program, and in 1888 the Kentucky legislature granted a charter for him (and Drs. W. A. Burney and R. Conrad) to open the Louisville National Medical College. In a rented hall his medical college opened with six

students. The school also provided nursing and pharmaceutical training. In 1895, with his own finances, he established the Auxiliary Hospital of the College. The school continued until 1912 and had seventy-five students during its twenty-four years of existence (*see* MEDICAL EDUCATION).

Along with his medical work, Fitzbutler was vehement in his demand for opportunities in public education for African-American children and youth and in the field of journalism to advance conditions for his race. In 1872, at a Kentucky state convention called to discuss the educational interests of African Americans, he volunteered to be chairman of a venture to push for a resolution demanding equal school privileges and resources for black students. He was a leading opponent of JIM CROW legislation.

Fitzbutler was also a journalist. He was editor of and chief financial investor in the *Planet* (founded by Alfred Froman) a civil rights publication that advocated the educational interests and rights of African Americans. From 1879 until his death in 1901, Fitzbutler published his own newspaper, the *Ohio Falls Express,* which became the first successful newspaper under black management in Kentucky.

REFERENCES

"Henry Fitzbutler," *Journal of the National Medical Association* (1952): 403–407.
"Henry Fitzbutler." In Martin Kaurman et al., eds. *Dictionary of American Medical Biography.* Westport, Conn., 1984, pp. 250–251.
MORAIS, HERBERT. *History of the Negro in Medicine.* New York, 1967, pp. 65–66.

ROBERT C. HAYDEN

Fitzgerald, Ella (April 25, 1918–   ), jazz vocalist. In a career lasting half a century, Ella Fitzgerald's superb pitch and diction, infallible sense of rhythm, and masterful scat singing have all become part of the fabric of American music, and she has been recognized as one "First Lady of Song." While her background and technique were rooted in jazz, she has always been a popular singer, with a soothing yet crystalline sound that brought wide acclaim. Born in Newport News, Va., she came north as a child to Yonkers, N.Y., with her mother. In 1934, on a dare, she entered a Harlem amateur-night contest as a dancer, but became immobile with stage fright when called on to perform. Instead, she sang two songs popularized by the Boswell Sisters, "Judy" and "The Object of My Affection," and won first prize.

After she had won several more amateur competitions, an opportunity came in February 1935, when she appeared at the Apollo and was spotted by Bardu ALI, the master of ceremonies for Chick WEBB's band, who persuaded Webb to hire her. Fitzgerald began performing with Webb's band at the Savoy Club, and cut her first record, "Love and Kisses," with them in June 1935. Inspired by a nursery rhyme, Fitzgerald cowrote and recorded "A-Tisket, A-Tasket" with Webb's group in 1938; it became one of the most successful records of the swing era and transformed the young singer into a national celebrity.

When Webb died suddenly in 1939, Fitzgerald assumed nominal leadership of his band, which broke up two years later. During the 1940s she gained prominence as a solo performer through hit records that showcased her versatility. Influenced by Dizzy GILLESPIE and bebop, in 1947 Fitzgerald recorded, "Oh, Lady Be Good" and "How High the Moon," two songs that utilized her scat singing, the wordless vocal improvising that became her signature style. By the early 1950s, she had appeared around the world with the star-studded Jazz and the Philharmonic tours organized by Norman Granz, a record producer and impresario who became her manager in 1954. Under his supervision and on his Verve label, she recorded *The Cole Porter Songbook* in 1956, followed by anthologies devoted to George and Ira Gershwin, Duke Ellington, Irving Berlin, and other popular composers. Heavily arranged and cannily designed to promote both songwriter and performer, Fitzgerald's "songbooks" extended her appeal.

By the 1960s, she was one of the world's most respected and successful singers. In the following years, she became something of an institution, regularly honored. She was named "Best Female Vocalist" by *Down Beat* magazine several times, and she has more Grammy Awards than any other female jazz singer. Following heart bypass surgery in 1986, she suffered from erratic health, but she intermittently recorded and gave concerts.

REFERENCES

COLIN, SID. *Ella: The Life and Times of Ella Fitzgerald.* London, 1986.

KLIMENT, BUD. *Ella Fitzgerald.* New York, 1988.

PLEASANTS, HENRY. "Ella Fitzgerald." In *The Great American Popular Singers.* New York, 1974, pp. 168–180.

BUD KLIMENT

Fitzhugh, H. Naylor (October 31, 1909–July 26, 1992), business and marketing adviser. H. Naylor Fitzhugh was born in Washington, D.C. He received a B.S. with honors from Harvard University in 1930 and in 1933 became the first black student to earn an M.B.A. from Harvard Business School. Fitzhugh continued postgraduate work at Columbia University (1939–1941) and American University (1959–1961) and received an L.L.D. from Virginia State College in 1971. Fitzhugh was an assistant professor of marketing at HOWARD UNIVERSITY from 1934 to 1965. At Howard he organized a small-business center and advised the student marketing association. In 1965 he became a vice president at Pepsi-Cola and was responsible for special markets targeting black consumers. He was founder and former president of the National Association of Market Developers (1967–1968, 1976–1977), former member of the American Marketing Association Census Advisory Committee (1972–1974), and chairman of the Harvard Business School Black Alumni Association (1977–1978). In 1975, Fitzhugh received a special award in black enterprise achievement from Vice President Nelson Rockefeller in a White House ceremony. In addition, he was the recipient of the Harvard Business School Distinguished Service Award (1987) and the Pioneer Award from the National Assault on Illiteracy Program (1988). He died after a prolonged illness on July 26, 1992.

REFERENCE

CLOYD, IRIS, ed. *Who's Who Among Black Americans.* Detroit, 1990.

SABRINA FUCHS

Flack, Roberta (1939–), popular singer. Born in Black Mountain, N.C., but raised in Arlington, Va., Roberta Flack learned to play piano on an upright salvaged from a junkyard. At fifteen she won a full scholarship to HOWARD UNIVERSITY. She graduated in 1958 with a degree in music education. After teaching for several years she began performing in 1967 at a Washington, D.C., nightclub and was spotted by jazz artist Les McCann, who helped arrange a contract for her at Atlantic Records. She was signed in 1969 and later that year released her debut album, *First Take,* distinguished by its broad range of material, plaintive folk-song style alongside up-tempo jazz. Included was a song that would become her breakthrough recording three years later, "The First Time Ever I Saw Your Face" (1972). That same year the song was featured in the film *Play Misty for Me,* propelling the single to the number-one place on the *Billboard* charts for six weeks, capturing Grammy Awards for Song and Record of the Year and for Best Pop Vocal—Female. In 1973, Flack recorded another

Soul singer Roberta Flack achieved enormous popularity in the 1970s with sensitive ballads such as "The First Time Ever I Saw Your Face" and "Killing Me Softly with His Song." (Photographs and Prints Division, Schomburg Center for Research in Black Culture, The New York Public Library, Astor, Lenox and Tilden Foundations)

number-one single, "Killing Me Softly with His Song," which topped the charts for five weeks. She won a Grammy for Song of the Year in 1973 and a trophy for Best Pop Vocal Performance—Female.

Besides doing solo work, Flack also recorded several hit duets with longtime collaborator Donny Hathaway, who died in 1979, including "Where is the Love," from 1972, and "The Closer I Get to You" from 1978. In the early 1980s, Flack teamed up with Peabo Bryson for a number of recording duets, producing in 1983 a top-twenty single, "Tonight I Celebrate My Love." Flack continued to release meticulously crafted albums such as *Oasis* (1988) and *Set the Night to Music* (1991), both full of ethereal, romantic vocals that characterized her work and won her a devoted listening audience.

REFERENCE

STAMBLER, IRWIN. *The Encyclopedia of Pop, Rock, and Soul.* Rev. ed. New York, 1989.

BUD KLIMENT

Fletcher, Thomas "Tom" (May 16, 1873–October 13, 1954), performer and historian of minstrelsy. Tom Fletcher was born and raised in Portsmouth, Ohio, a town that was frequently visited by minstrel shows, and it was there that he developed a love for the theater. He sang at local talent shows and festivals and by the time he was fifteen began traveling with some of the best-known minstrel groups, such as Howard's Novelty Colored Minstrels and Richard Pringle's Georgia Minstrels. As a self-described entertainer, Fletcher had diverse skills, and he often served as singer, dancer, drummer, comedian, stage manager, and booking agent of minstrel shows. He performed in vaudeville shows, in private upper-class homes, and also in films. In 1919 he toured with Will Marion COOK's New York Syncopated Orchestra in Europe, a show that featured such performers as Abbie MITCHELL and a young Sidney BECHET, who later achieved international fame as a jazz clarinetist. Fletcher remained active as a performer and bandleader in the 1920s and 1930s for various summer resorts and New York City–area affairs, notably the Cave Grill Orchestra (1924–1937) at the Mt. Washington Hotel in New Hampshire. In the 1940s, he performed in Ole Olsen and Chic Johnson's Broadway show *Laffing Room Only* (1944–1945) and was a consultant on ragtime dance for the Katherine Dunham Company's *Ballet Negro* (1946).

Fletcher is best known for his partly autobiographical *100 Years of the Negro in Show Business* (1954), one of the few sources documenting black entertainment history before 1930. His book recalls the day-to-day life of black theater performers in the late nineteenth and early twentieth centuries. Each chapter highlights anecdotes of minstrel life, includes lists of important performers and of where and when they appeared, and shows how America's economic climate influenced employment opportunities from decade to decade. *100 Years* is a basic source for the still largely untold history of blacks in show business.

REFERENCES

BLOOM, KEN. *American Song: The Complete Musical Theatre Companion.* Vol. 1. New York, 1985.
FLETCHER, TOM. *100 Years of the Negro in Show Business: The Tom Fletcher Story.* New York, 1954.

THEODORE R. HUDSON

Flexner Report. Based on a survey of over 150 medical schools, the Flexner Report, published in 1910, offered a severely critical analysis of the state of medical education in North America. Its recommendations, widely adopted, included a greater emphasis on the basic sciences, a more rigorous clinical approach, and the elimination of schools that could not meet basic standards. Five of the seven existing black medical schools became casualties of the report.

The author, Abraham Flexner, had been invited in 1908 to carry out the study under the auspices of the Carnegie Foundation for the Advancement of Teaching. Among the shocking conditions he observed were anatomy labs crowded with clucking hens and rotting cadavers. Only the medical department of the Johns Hopkins University, which Flexner cited as a model, escaped serious criticism.

The final chapter of the report is devoted to "The Medical Education of the Negro." A firm segregationist, Flexner expressed the view that black practitioners were needed to treat the black populace (never the white), and that it was in whites' self-interest to promote health education for blacks in order to protect themselves against diseases spread by blacks. He urged the disbanding of all but two black medical schools: HOWARD UNIVERSITY Medical College and Meharry Medical College. The others, he said, were "sending out undisciplined men, whose lack of real training is covered up by the imposing M.D. degree." Within a few years, these other schools had vanished. Knoxville Medical College was discontinued in 1910; Flint Medical College (New Orleans) in 1911; Louisville National Medical College in 1912; Leonard Medical School (Raleigh, N.C.), in 1918; and the medical department of the University of West Tennessee (Memphis) in 1923. Partly through Flexner's influence, Howard and Meharry attracted significant funding and became the focus of efforts to train black health professionals.

REFERENCES

EPPS, HOWARD R. "The Howard University Medical Department in the Flexner Era: 1910–1929." *Journal of the National Medical Association* 81 (August 1989): 885–911.

FLEXNER, ABRAHAM. *Medical Education in the United States and Canada: A Report to the Carnegie Foundation for the Advancement of Teaching.* Washington, D.C., 1910.

PHILIP N. ALEXANDER

Flipper, Henry Ossian (March 21, 1856–May 3, 1940), first African-American graduate of West Point. The son of Festus and Isabella Flipper, Henry O. Flipper was born a slave in Thomasville, Ga. Festus, a shoemaker and carriage trimmer, managed to save enough money to purchase the freedom of his wife and children; in 1865 he brought the family to Atlanta. Henry and his brothers were educated in AMERICAN MISSIONARY ASSOCIATION schools and attended Atlanta University. In 1873, his first year in the university's collegiate department, Henry applied for and received an appointment to the United States Military Academy at West Point. He was not the first African American appointed to West Point: Michael Howard and James Webster Smith entered the academy in 1870, but both were dismissed prior to graduation. Flipper, however, endured four years of ostracism and persecution. On June 15, 1877, he became the first black cadet to earn a commission, graduating fiftieth in his class of seventy-six. In 1878 Flipper published *The Colored Cadet at West Point,* an autobiographical account of his experiences at the academy.

That same year Flipper was assigned to the all-black Tenth Cavalry Regiment and served in Texas and the Indian Territory. In 1881, while serving as post commissary at Fort Davis, Tex., he was brought before a general court-martial and charged by his commanding officer, Col. William R. Shafter, with the embezzlement of $3,791.77 in commissary funds and with "conduct unbecoming an officer and a gentleman." Although he was acquitted of the first

Henry O. Flipper as a cadet. (Photographs and Prints Division, Schomburg Center for Research in Black Culture, The New York Public Library, Astor, Lenox and Tilden Foundations)

charge, the court found him guilty of the second. On June 30, 1882, he was discharged from the Army. Flipper claimed he was innocent of any misconduct and believed that his dismissal was motivated by white prejudice.

As a civilian, Flipper worked in Mexico and the American Southwest as a mining engineer and as a special agent of the Department of Justice in the Court of Private Land Claims. He became a recognized authority on Spanish and Mexican land law. While serving as an engineer for the Greene Gold-Silver Company in Chihuahua, Mexico, Flipper befriended Albert B. Fall. In 1919 Fall, then in his second term as a U.S. senator from New Mexico, asked Flipper to come to Washington, D.C., as a translator for the subcommittee on Mexican internal affairs of the Senate Committee on Foreign Relations. Two years later, Fall was appointed secretary of the interior in the Harding administration and named Flipper as an assistant. In 1923 Flipper left Washington to work as a consultant for the Pantepec Oil Company in Venezuela. During his seven years there, he published an important translation of that country's mining and land law. In 1930 Flipper retired to Atlanta to live with his brother Joseph, a bishop in the AFRICAN METHODIST EPISCOPAL CHURCH. He died of a heart attack in 1940.

Flipper spent most of his life trying to clear his name, but despite the many political connections he was able to make in the West and in Washington, D.C., his efforts were in vain. Finally, in 1976, the Army granted him a posthumous honorable discharge, and on May 3, 1977, West Point unveiled a bust commemorating its first black graduate.

REFERENCES

CARROLL, JOHN M., ed. *The Black Military Experience in the American West.* New York, 1977.

CULLOM, THEODORE HARRIS, ed. *The Western Memoirs of Henry O. Flipper.* El Paso, Tex., 1963.

FLIPPER, HENRY O. *The Colored Cadet at West Point.* 1878. Reprint. New York, 1969.

KATZ, WILLIAM L. *The Black West.* Seattle, Wash. 1987.

New York Times, May 4, 1977, p. B-2.

BENJAMIN K. SCOTT

Flood, Curtis Charles "Curt" (January 18, 1938–), baseball player. The youngest of six children, Curt Flood was born in Houston on January 18, 1938. Before he was three, his family moved to Oakland, Calif., where his parents, both hospital

After Curt Flood, a graceful fielder and fine hitter for the St. Louis Cardinals from 1958 to 1969 refused to accept a trade to the Philadelphia Phillies, he set in motion a series of events that eventually led to the overturning of the reserve clause. Flood saw the fight against the reserve clause, which gave management total control over the trading and salaries of players, as a part of the larger struggle for civil rights for all Americans. (UPI/Bettmann)

workers, held several jobs at once to support the family. Flood excelled at baseball from early childhood, becoming a standout on American Legion teams and at McClymonds and Oakland Technical high schools. Upon graduation in 1956, he signed with the Cincinnati Reds. At the time, many facilities were still segregated and many fans were still opposed to athletic integration. Yet Flood became a star in the Carolina and South Atlantic Leagues and was called up to the Reds. After two seasons in the minors, with brief stints with the Reds in each season, he was traded to the St. Louis Cardinals for the 1958 season. He won seven consecutive Golden Glove Awards and established a reputation as one of baseball's finest defensive center fielders. In twelve seasons with St. Louis, he had a career batting average of .293 and helped the Cardinals win three National League pennants and two World Series championships (1964 and 1967).

On October 7, 1969, the Cardinals announced that Flood had been traded to the Philadelphia Phillies. In a letter to Commissioner Bowie Kuhn, Flood stated that he would not play for his new team and refused to report to Philadelphia. He brought a lawsuit against the National League, arguing that the reserve clause in his contract (and that of every major-league ballplayer), which made a player the exclusive property of one team until released or traded, violated antitrust laws by infringing on the rights of an employee to negotiate with multiple employers in an open market. Flood's position was widely shared by other players; in fact, the Major League Players Association voted unanimously to support his suit. After lower courts ruled against Flood, the U.S. Supreme Court held that, as established by precedent, baseball was not interstate commerce and, therefore, enjoyed special exemption from antitrust legislation. While his case was in the lower courts, Flood sat out the 1970 season, and the Phillies sent their absent star to the Washington Senators. Flood finally signed with Washington, but he played only ten games in 1971, and by the time his case was heard in the nation's highest court he had retired. Though Flood's challenge to the reserve system was unsuccessful, his efforts helped lay the groundwork for future gains in players' rights, including free agency and salary arbitration.

After leaving the Senators, Flood purchased a bar on the island of Majorca in Spain, which he managed until 1976, when he returned to Oakland. He found employment in the front office of the Oakland A's, provided radio color-commentary for the A's, and was named commissioner of Oakland's Little League. Flood later moved to Los Angeles, where he continued his work as a portrait painter and, through his participation in fantasy baseball camps, maintained his ties to baseball. He joined the old-timers' circuit, playing exhibition games in major league cities around the country. In 1987, he helped organize the Fantasy Major League Slo-Pitch Softball League. His autobiography, *The Way It Is,* written with Richard Carter, was published in 1970.

REFERENCES

BERRY, ROBERT C. et al., eds. *Labor Relations in Professional Sports.* Auburn House, Dover, Mass., 1986, Chapter 2.

PORTER, DAVID L., ed. *Biographical Dictionary of American Sports: Baseball.* Westport, Conn., 1987, pp. 185–187.

WHITFORD, DAVID. "Curt Flood," *Sport.* December 8, 1986, pp. 102–103.

BENJAMIN K. SCOTT

Florida.   Blacks have lived in Florida since shortly after the founding of St. Augustine by Spain in 1565. While plantation SLAVERY never became a dominant institution in Spanish Florida, enslaved blacks did play an important role in the history of the settlement. After English settlers created the Georgia colony in 1733, Spain offered freedom to runaway slaves from the British colonies, and the fortress of San Marcos became the destination of many of those slaves who sought freedom. Many maroons and freed slaves were armed and transfered to a fort called Mose (or Moosa) serving as a first line of defense against British raids. In 1738, despite a spirited defense by the black soldiers, Fort Mose fell to a British colonial invasion force. However, its garrison was later reconstituted, and it was operating as late as 1759.

In 1763 Spain surrendered Florida to Britain, and practically all its inhabitants—including at least 600 slaves and twenty-three free blacks—departed for Havana and other places. The new British population consisted primarily of planters and slaves from South Carolina. Their numbers were swelled by large numbers of loyalists and enslaved blacks who began arriving in 1781, as Britain experienced reverses in the AMERICAN REVOLUTION. The enslaved black population jumped from 2,000 to over 10,000 in a short time. However, in 1783 Spain regained Florida, and most of the British colonists departed. Spanish Florida included the land within the approximate boundaries of the present state, known as "East Florida," as well as "West Florida," encompassing Mobile and other areas. One of the few colonists who remained through both the Spanish and British eras was Francisco Sánchez, a planter and slave holder who had married a black woman and had seven baptized children with her.

During the second period of Spanish rule, slavery in Florida was a minor institution, though Pensacola developed as an important port with some 300 black inhabitants, and several slave plantations sprang up near Jacksonville. St. Augustine developed a large free black population, and in 1795 the colonial governor ruled that slave owners in the city had eight days to claim slaves or they would be considered free. Blacks without freedom papers, meanwhile, were required to obtain work permits under the threat of enslavement to the King of Spain.

Florida remained a source of conflict between Spain and the United States, which denounced Spain for protecting runaway slaves in Florida and sponsoring raids by maroons and Seminoles on American soil. The United States claimed West Florida under the Louisiana Purchase, and during the WAR OF 1812 American forces seized its central city of Mobile. Soon after, under the pretext that Spain was allowing

Great Britain to base its fleet in Pensacola, American forces led by Andrew Jackson invaded and occupied that city. In 1816, Jackson attacked and burned "Fort Negro" (Fort Blount), a nearby base constructed by the British and later occupied by groups of escaped African Americans and Creek Indians. Spain was forced to recognize United States claims to West Florida.

Following the war's end, Jackson launched a series of attacks on Seminole forces in East Florida. Fearing an American takeover, Spain sold Florida to the United States in 1819. In the 1830s the Americans sent armed troops to reenslave the maroons. Slavecatchers captured the African-American wife of Seminole chief Osceola in 1835, sparking a bloody seven-year phase in the Seminole Wars.

Once under American control, Florida developed an agricultural economy based on slave labor. Although most of the territory remained unsettled, northern Florida, with the city of Tallahassee as its hub, was settled by planters from neighboring southern states in the 1820s. They brought or purchased large numbers of African Americans (and some Africans, via the illegal Atlantic SLAVE TRADE) to cultivate cotton. By the time Florida achieved statehood in 1845, its culture and economy were solidly allied with those of its neighbors. However, it stayed isolated and backward throughout the antebellum period, and its population remained small. Despite high growth rates in the slave population, which represented almost half the state's total by 1860, fewer slaves lived in Florida than any other slave state except Delaware. The free black population never exceeded 932 persons, but free blacks helped found Jacksonville's First Bethel Baptist Church in 1838.

In 1861 Florida seceded from the Union. Most of its white population was solidly pro-Confederate. There was relatively little action in Florida during the CIVIL WAR. In 1862 Union troops took over St. Augustine, and fortified it with the hired labor of the

The 1904 graduating class of the Florida State Normal and Industrial School, predecessor to Florida A & M University. (Florida State Archives)

town's free black population and of slaves who fled to freedom behind Union lines. In 1864 federal forces, including the Eighth U.S. Colored Troops and the Fifty-fourth Massachusetts Volunteers, took Jacksonville and moved on towards Tallahassee. They were met near Olustee by Confederate gunfire, which killed 300 of the black soldiers occupying the North's front line. Despite heroic resistance by the Fifty-fourth, the Union troops were driven back.

RECONSTRUCTION brought a reordering of Florida's political system. In 1866 the state legislature passed a restrictive "black code" which limited the freedom of contract and movement of African Americans. In 1867 Congress dissolved the Florida government, granted African-American males the vote, and called a new constitutional convention. Following a white conservative boycott, only 11,000 whites registered to vote, against 15,000 blacks. While eighteen of the forty-six delegates to the convention were black, they were outvoted on most issues. The new constitution provided for black voting and public schools, but otherwise limited black political control. Terror groups such as the KU KLUX KLAN opposed black self-assertion. The Klan was so powerful that in 1868 and 1870 Gov. Reed vainly requested federal troops to suppress it. By the time it was disbanded in 1871, it had committed 235 murders in the state.

Meanwhile, veterans and ex-slaves from other southern states poured into Florida, and the state's black population increased. The Freedmen's Bureau and northern charities opened schools. By 1866, there were sixty-five black schools in Florida. Blacks' desire for autonomy and distance from whites in the daily conduct of religious affairs led them to withdraw from "biracial" congregations to form their own churches. African Americans throughout Florida built independent communities, such as the "Africa" district south of St. Augustine.

A few African Americans rose to positions of prominence. Josiah T. WALLS, an educated ex-slave from Virginia, migrated to Florida after the Civil War. While in Florida he practiced law, edited two newspapers, was named brigadier-general of the state militia, and served in the state legislature. In 1870 Walls was elected Florida's lone U.S. representative, and he won another term before his Democratic opponent successfully challenged his election in 1873. John Wallace, originally from North Carolina, served two terms in each branch of the Florida state legislature. Jonathan C. Gibbs was named Florida's secretary of state in 1868 and later built up the state's public school system as superintendent.

Jacksonville, which had a reputation as a liberal Southern city throughout the late nineteenth century, developed a small and exclusive black middle class of ministers, doctors, and other professionals. Among those raised in the community were editor T. Thomas FORTUNE, composer J. Rosamond JOHNSON, and his brother, writer and activist James Weldon JOHNSON (principal of the city's Stanton Grammar School for Negroes and editor of the *Daily American* newspaper during the 1890s).

Once conservative Democrats regained control of the state in 1876, blacks quickly lost the scant legal protections they had managed to build. The black vote was reduced through violent harassment and fraud. In 1895 it was largely restricted by a poll tax, then eliminated in 1901 by a "white primary." Public accommodations, beginning in 1887 with railroad cars, were rigidly segregated by law. Even Jacksonville, long a haven of tolerance, passed a law segregating streetcars in 1901. Blacks in the city, led by ministers, responded by organizing a successful boycott. In 1905, Florida passed a statewide streetcar law, ultimately defeated in court, which sparked boycotts in Jacksonville and Pensacola.

Most blacks, unable to purchase or retain land holdings, were forced to seek agricultural work. An oppressive sharecropping system soon took hold in the state. The only other labor available was in lumber and turpentine production. Black laborers worked long hours doing unpleasant and often dangerous work for little pay, with no way of escaping company control. Blacks formed groups such as the Florida Colored Farmer's Alliance and Co-operative Union, launched in Ocala in 1890 by Rev. J. L. Moore to secure better treatment and political rights. A few all-black towns were set up, notably Eatonville, immortalized in native Zora Neale HURSTON's novel *Their Eyes Were Watching God* (1937).

Public education—and private education, after 1895—was strictly segregated, and in most of Florida black schools were nonexistent. A few small colleges were created by churches or by secular educators, including Florida Normal College, a Baptist institution in Jacksonville and St. Augustine (now part of Florida Memorial College in Miami), and the State Normal College for Colored Students (later Florida Agricultural & Mechanical University), established in 1887 in Tallahassee. The state's most unusual institution of black higher learning, BETHUNE-COOKMAN COLLEGE in Daytona Beach (established as the Daytona Educational and Training School), was founded in a garbage dump in 1904 by Florida native Mary McLeod BETHUNE, who built up facilities through funds raised from bake sales and aid from wealthy northern visitors.

By the turn of the century, the state's entire culture had begun to change. Railroads were built and new towns such as Palm Beach, Miami, and Boca Raton were created. African Americans both benefitted and suffered from the commercial development of South

Florida. Although racial exclusion was universal, local whites kept racial violence to a minimum so as not to antagonize wealthy northern visitors. Blacks found employment clearing land, as construction workers, and in the burgeoning farm industry of South Florida. However, they were often forgotten once projects were finished. Black neighborhoods, such as the "Styx" in Palm Beach, were no sooner created than rising property values prompted white landowners to evict their black tenants. Many blacks left Florida, and between 1900 and 1940 the percentage of blacks in the state's population dropped from 44 percent to 27 percent.

Conditions for blacks in Florida remained harsh through the first half of the twentieth century. The Florida land boom of the early 1920s brought large numbers of black Floridians to the southern portion of the state. However, beaches and public areas throughout the state were strictly segregated (one result of this was the creation of all-black beaches and resorts such as Jacksonville's American Beach). The new black communities such as Miami's Liberty City and Boca Raton's Pearl City were threatened by bombings and random violence. After a hurricane in 1926, Miami blacks were randomly conscripted into work brigades by U.S. Marines to clean up the damage. The resurgent Ku Klux Klan was active throughout the state. In 1923, after a white woman fraudulently accused three African Americans of rape in Rosewood, local whites rioted, killing four blacks and burning down much of the black community. Once the land boom collapsed in the mid-1920s, Florida entered a sustained depression, which lasted until the coming of military bases and the growth of the citrus industry during World War II. After 1945, the expanding economy drew African Americans southward, and led to an increase in the already substantial migration of Caribbean blacks.

The black struggle for equality in Florida, never abandoned, took on new life in the 1940s. In the late 1930s, blacks began winning important court victories. The U.S. Supreme Court ruling in *Chambers* v. *Florida* (1940) struck down the conviction of defendants based on coerced confessions in criminal trials. In *Shepherd* v. *Towner* (1951), the Court overturned a death penalty conviction in a sensational rape case because of racial prejudice in jury and venue selection. In 1944, following the U.S. Supreme Court's *Smith* v. *Allwright* decision, a federal judge ordered the registration of thousands of voters. Under the leadership of state NAACP head Harry Tyson MOORE, the Florida Voters League was created to encourage black voter registration, which jumped from 20,000 in 1944 to over 128,000 in 1954. He also campaigned to desegregate public beaches and equalize funds for black education. Moore was killed in a bombing attack on his house in Mims, Fla., on Christmas night, 1951.

The next victories came in the field of education. In 1949 Virgil Hawkins applied to the University of Florida Law School, and was rejected on racial grounds. After he challenged the ruling in court, Florida created a separate black law school at Florida A & M University. He then appealed to the U.S. Supreme Court, which in 1954 ordered him admitted based on their just-announced ruling in BROWN V. BOARD OF EDUCATION, TOPEKA, KANSAS. The state court stalled, but the University of Florida was forced to open its doors to blacks in 1958 by a federal court order. In primary public education, progress was slower. While Florida's reaction to *Brown* was at first restrained, and Gov. Leroy Collins appointed a biracial committee to supervise compliance, the Florida Board of Education refused to admit any black pupils to white schools until 1959, when the Orchard Villa School in Miami admitted its first black pupils. Thereafter, pupil assignment plans limited desegregation. At the same time, a segregated junior college system was created, not to be fully integrated until the 1970s.

The Tallahassee Bus Boycott was a significant turning point in civil rights struggles in Florida. It began on May 27, 1956, when Wilhelmina Jakes (age twenty-six) and Carrie Patterson (age twenty), both students at Florida A & M University, refused to vacate seats in the "white" section of a Cities Transit Company Bus. The following day a mass meeting of students voted unanimously to boycott the buses. The students were joined by the interdenominational Tallahassee Ministerial Alliance, led by minister and professor James A. Hudson. When negotiations with the bus company and the city failed, the Inter-Civic Council, a new umbrella group, was formed to organize boycott efforts. On December 16, 1956, following the precedent of the Montgomery Bus Boycott, bus segregation was struck down in court, and the boycott ended. Seating difficulties remained, and total desegregation did not occur until 1958. Nevertheless, the boycott shaped new leaders, and proved not only that Montgomery was no fluke but, more importantly, that black masses could be organized for protest in smaller cities as well as larger ones.

The sit-in movement came to Florida in 1959, when activists from the CONGRESS OF RACIAL EQUALITY (CORE) protested at department stores and public beaches in Jacksonville, and succeeded in opening parks, swimming pools, and public facilities to blacks. Meanwhile, sit-ins began in Deland, Tallahassee, Tampa, St. Petersburg, Daytona Beach, Sarasota, Miami, Orlando, Sanford, and St. Augustine, with mixed results. Blacks in Jacksonville protested the selling of a municipal golf course to private interests to prevent integration. Sit-ins in the city sparked local whites to riot, injuring at least fifty blacks. Jacksonville and St. Petersburg also closed public swimming pools rather than admit blacks. Despite the sit-ins, housing and jobs in Florida's cities remained almost completely segregated. Jacksonville became a center for the Ku Klux Klan, and several black homes and businesses were bombed. In March 1964, after a black school had to be evacuated following a bomb threat, students vented their anger and threw stones at police and reporters. Ultimately, 200 blacks were arrested.

St. Augustine provided a chilling example of white resistance to equality. The movement in the city, a center of terrorist violence by Klansmen and militant white supremacists, gained widespread attention in 1963, when NAACP leader Dr. Robert Hayling began leading large protests against racial discrimination, in the face of heavy white resistance and police brutality. The city refused to appoint a biracial committee to supervise voluntary desegregation. The movement grew enormously in early 1964, when Hayling invited to St. Augustine activists from the SOUTHERN CHRISTIAN LEADERSHIP CONFERENCE (SCLC), led by Rev. Dr. Martin Luther KING, Jr. In April, SCLC leaders started a campaign of protest marches to integrate city beaches and public spaces. On May 28, Klansmen and white thugs rioted, beating demonstrators at the city's former slave market. City authorities refused to curb the terror campaign, and violence continued. It peaked on the night of June 25, when 350 marchers celebrating passage of the 1964 Civil Rights Act, were met by a group of 800 white extremists. The whites attacked the marchers with clubs and bricks, and also beat reporters and onlookers, including children. The crowd was dispersed by police with tear gas. Florida Gov. Farris Bryant, who had previously claimed, "I don't intend to collect taxes and I don't propose to enforce civil rights," supported the segregationists and banned night marches. He promised to appoint a biracial committee, but no action was taken, and threats and violence continued for many months.

Florida's tense race relations led to several racial uprisings during the 1960s, including seven in 1967 alone. The largest racial rebellion took place in Tampa. Although blacks constituted almost 20 percent of Tampa's population in 1960, none served on the city council, the school board, the fire department, and only seventeen blacks served on the 511-member police force. In 1967, 60 percent of Tampa's blacks lived in dilapidated rental housing, black unemployment rates were double those of whites, and school dropout rates were high. On June 11, 1967, a white policeman shot nineteen-year-old Martin Chambers, following a break-in at a photo supply house. Rumors spread that Chambers had been shot after surrendering, and rioting broke out across the city. The riot lasted four days, and led to sixteen injuries and 111 arrests.

Between 1970 and 1990, as Florida's sunbelt economy was boosted by military contracts, retirees, and industry, the state's black population increased from 1,041,651 to 1,759, 354, though due to the enormous white population growth it declined as a percentage of the state's total. By 1990, seven Florida cities had black populations of 30,000 or more: Jacksonville, Miami, Tampa, St. Petersburg, Orlando, Fort Lauderdale, and Tallahassee. However, problems of poverty and police harassment continued to plague Florida's African-American community. In rapidly changing Miami, blacks lived uneasily alongside whites and among the city's large Cuban and Haitian populations. The city's black areas such as Liberty City, once considered "model neighborhoods" for upwardly mobile black entrepreneurs, seethed with the frustration and anger of African Americans hemmed in by poverty and discrimination. Riots broke out in 1968 and 1970. On May 16, 1980, large-scale violence erupted in Miami when four Dade County policemen with extensive histories of citizen complaints and internal review probes were acquitted of the shooting death of Arthur McDuffie, a black motorist.

While the quest by African Americans for equality in Florida remained far from complete, blacks did succeed in breaking into the state's government. In 1968 Democrat Joe Lang Kershaw became the first African American in the Florida legislature in eighty years. During the following decade, the number of black elected officials grew from sixteen (including Kershaw and eight city council members) to ninety-one, including Mrs. Gwen Sawyer Cherry of Miami, the first black woman to sit in the legislature. In 1992 veteran state legislator Carrie Meek became the state's first black woman to be elected to Congress.

While each Southern state has produced black writers, poets, musicians, and leaders in abundance, Florida has been home to some of the most sensitive and influential interpreters of black life and folk culture, notably Zora Neale HURSTON, folklorist, novelist, and journalist, who did research on Florida black folklore for her study *Mules and Men* (1935). The list of other well-known and important black Floridians includes: African Methodist Episcopal Bishop Abram Grant, born a slave in Lake City; labor leader and activist A. Philip RANDOLPH, born in Crescent City in 1889; preacher and theologian Howard THURMAN, born in Daytona; Harry V. Richardson, scholar of African-American religion, born in Jacksonville in 1901; JAZZ musicians Fats NAVARRO, born in Key West, Archie SHEPP, born in Fort Lauderdale, and

Nat and Julian "Cannonball" ADDERLEY of Tampa; GOSPEL singer Marion WILLIAMS of Miami; poet and painter Stephen Henderson of Key West; sculptor Augusta SAVAGE of Green Cove Springs; baseball star Dwight Gooden of Tampa; and anthropologists and college presidents Niara Sudarkasa of Fort Lauderdale and Johnnetta Betsch Cole of Jacksonville.

REFERENCES

COLBURN, DAVID R. *Racial Change and Community Crisis: St. Augustine, Florida, 1877–1980.* New York, 1985.

COOPER, ALGIA R. "*Brown v. Board of Education* and Virgil Darnell Hawkins: Twenty-Eight Years and Six Petitions to Justice." *Journal of Negro History* 64 (Winter 1979): 1–20.

EVANS, ARTHUR B. *Pearl City, Florida: A Black Community Remembers.* Boca Raton, Fla., 1980.

MCDONOGH, GARY W., ed. *The Florida Negro: A Federal Writers' Project Legacy.* Jackson, Miss. 1993.

MORRIS, ALDON D. *The Origins of the Civil Rights Movement: Black Communities Organizing for Change.* New York, 1984.

PORTER, BRUCE, and MARVIN DUNN. *The Miami Riot of 1980: Crossing the Boundaries.* Lexington, Mass., 1984.

PRICE, HUGH DOUGLAS. *The Negro and Southern Politics: A Chapter of Florida History.* New York, 1957.

SHOFNER, JERRELL H. *Nor Is It Over Yet: Florida in the Era of Reconstruction, 1863–1877.* Jacksonville, Fla., 1974.

SMITH, CHARLES U., ed. *The Civil Rights Movement in Florida and the United States: Historical and Contemporary Perspectives.* Tallahassee, Fla., 1989.

SMITH, JULIA FLOYD. *Slavery and Plantation Growth in Antebellum Florida, 1821–1860.* New York, 1973.

ROBERT L. HALL

Folk Arts and Crafts.

The folk arts and crafts created by African Americans are, perhaps, the least acknowledged of their cultural traditions. Worldwide recognition of black achievement in music and dance has overshadowed significant accomplishments in the area of material culture so that while black Americans are seen as gifted performers, they are rarely described as even adequate producers of objects.

Vernacular Traditions

In times past, black artisans were numerous, and they are to be credited with making a wide array of artifacts, particularly in the southern states. It is important to recall that during the preindustrial era most rural people made things: tools, utensils, containers, clothes, food, houses, toys. Whether as slaves or as free people, blacks created a multitude of necessary, useful, and sometimes beautiful, objects.

The reasons why African Americans would be skilled at making domestic arts and crafts are not hard to fathom. On plantations they often had little choice when they were ordered to learn particular trades by their owners. But more often, because they were provided with so few domestic items, they either had to make most of their furnishings and utensils, or do without. After Emancipation the folk arts and crafts that blacks had developed in the plantation setting continued to prove useful. Reduced to a condition of near servitude by continued racial exploitation and poverty, African-American artisans used their traditional skills to get themselves and their families through tough times, and some still do today. Folk arts and crafts have always played dual roles in the black community, serving both as a means of making a living and as a means for creative self-expression. While many items of folk art and craft produced by African Americans are indistinguishable in form, technique, and style from works produced by white Americans, there is a stream of African inspiration that runs through traditional black material culture in the South. The most distinctive works of African-American black folk art, in cultural terms, are those that manifest a linkage to African origins. This article provides a survey of these expressions.

BASKETRY

Coiled-grass baskets have been produced in the United States by black artisans for more than three centuries. Once integral items on plantations, particularly along the so-called "rice coast" that once extended from North Carolina to Florida's northern border, the craft is today most publicly on display in and around Charleston, S.C. Here hundreds of "sewers" are at work fashioning baskets. Using "sweetgrass," rush, pine needles, and strips of leaves from the palmetto tree as their primary materials, they produce a seemingly limitless variety of forms which they sell on street corners, in the central open-air market, and at more than fifty stands along the main highway entering the city.

What one sees here are "show baskets," a subgenre within this tradition that was initiated probably in the mid-nineteenth century. Included under this category are all sorts of decorative containers: flower baskets, serving trays, purses, sewing baskets, casserole holders, umbrella stands, and cake baskets. As is evident from this partial inventory, the show basket is intended to be used in the home where it will be prominently displayed. As these items are made, then, to be fancy, the basketmakers explore, at every opportunity, new creative possibilities in form and decoration. A show basket is a highly personalized artwork shaped extensively by individual imagination.

Yet matriarch basketmaker Mary Jane Manigault explains, "All baskets begin as a hot plate," meaning that all works, no matter how imaginative and seemingly without precedent, trace back to a common ancestry rooted in basic forms and techniques: all coiled baskets start out as a disk form. The oldest African-American coiled baskets were "work baskets." They were made with bundles of stiff rushes and often sewn with strips of oak. With coils generally an inch in diameter, these were tough, durable baskets intended to be used outside, either in the fields or in the farmyard. They are easily distinguishable from the lighter, more delicately formed show baskets. Most work baskets were large, heavy, round containers made to carry produce; they all had flat bottoms and straight walls that flared out slightly from the base. One specialized work basket, the fanner, was a large tray about two feet in diameter, with a low outer rim. Primarily an implement for processing the rice harvest, it was also used as a basic kitchen tool. Rice could not be properly cooked unless it had first been fanned to separate the kernels from the husks.

These baskets were but one element in a set of African practices upon which the production of rice was based. Planters specifically sought out slaves from the rice-growing regions of West and Central Africa and with these people came not only a knowledge of rice cultivation, but also the basic technology for its harvest and preparation as food. While planters were generally wary about allowing overt African expressions among their slaves, they tolerated this mode of basketry when they realized that it basically enhanced the productivity of their estates.

Unwittingly, then, these planters actually facilitated the maintenance of decidedly African tradition. While the end of the plantation era understandably brought an end to the work basket tradition, it did not cause coiled basketry to disappear altogether. These baskets remained a feature of home craft on small black farms in the area and there was from 1910 to 1950 an attempt at the Penn School on St. Helena Island to revive the practice. While this particular effort ended with disappointing results, the tradition was able to flourish in the Charleston area, where show baskets became exceedingly popular among tourists who assiduously sought them as souvenirs of their visits.

The basketmaking tradition was necessarily transformed as artisans shifted from a rural to an urban venue as artisans made baskets more often for sale than for domestic use. Yet venerable traditions were still honored. The sewing baskets and serving trays were old-time baskets, too, even if their origins did not trace all the way back to Africa, as did those of the work baskets. But the entrepreneurial energies that were released in this commercial effort led mainly to freewheeling displays of personal imagination. Soon basketmakers were as proud of new unprecedented forms that they called "own style baskets" as they were of more conventional flower baskets or clothes hampers.

But even within this spirited and open-ended creativity there are still signs of historical memory. Fanner baskets, for example, can occasionally be found for sale in the Charleston market, albeit as lightweight show basket facsimiles. But more important, the techniques for coiling and stitching remain unchanged regardless of the type of basket. This continuity of process allows contemporary basketmakers to place themselves in the flow of a tradition that traces back through time and space to African roots. The personal satisfaction that these artisans derive from making coiled baskets is amplified by a keen awareness of that history, and as a result they are all the more motivated to preserve this custom.

BOATBUILDING

That African-American competence in agriculture was matched by maritime abilities should not be surprising. Most African slaves were captured, after all, from either coastal or riverine environments, and thus they had extensive experience with a variety of small craft. When set to work on plantations, often located near coasts or along prominent rivers, these Africans had ample opportunity to display their navigation skills. Eighteenth-century commentators were quick of acknowledge how adept slaves were in paddling log canoes, which often proved difficult to maneuver in swift currents and to keep upright. In the Charleston area, black watermen working out of hewn dugouts called "pettiaugers" (an Anglicized version of the French *piroques*) had by 1750 achieved almost complete domination of the local fishing trade. White people depended on black boating skills from Georgia to Maryland as slaves literally provided the backbone for the local transportation system during the period when there were few roads.

In this context, slaves also built boats, and while their surviving descriptions tend to be somewhat vague with respect to details, it seems that West Indian watercraft, and thus in some measure African-derived maritime traditions, provided the basic models. The pettiauger was a well-known Caribbean vessel with a hull consisting of a log dugout extended by the addition of extra planks. Fitted with sails for open-water voyaging, it could also by propelled by teams of oarsmen. Boats of this sort are described repeatedly as the usual type of plantation "barge" used to ferry people, supplies, and produce. A second type of plantation vessel was a canoe hewn from a single log. Derived from either African or Native American precedents, it was less than twenty feet in length and relatively light due to the thinness of the hull. This was an excellent vessel for navigating the shallow marshes and streams surrounding the barrier islands of the South Carolina and Georgia coasts. Plantation mistress Fannie Kemble recorded in 1838 that two slave carpenters on her Butler Island estate had made such a canoe which they sold for the sum of $60. A type of multilog dugout, common to the waters of the Chesapeake Bay, is credited to a slave from York County, Va., remembered only as Aaron. In form this craft, a log canoe with a hull shaped from as many as nine logs, seems related to the West Indian pettiaugers.

In Virginia and Maryland, African Americans were extensively involved in a full range of shipbuilding trades as ship's carpenters, caulkers, sailmakers, and blacksmiths. A remarkable account from the *Raleigh Star* in 1811 describes how a brig launched in Alexandria, Va., was "drafted by a coloured man belonging to Col. Tayloe and under his superintendence built from her keel to her topmast." Here the design sources were unquestionably Anglo-American, but the fact that a slave was given such broad authority suggests that he was working in a context in which most of the men under his command must have been slaves as well. This event suggests that blacks might have been able to do quite well as shipbuilders had they simply been afforded the chance. But there were few opportunities as African-American waterman were diverted mainly to fishing and oyster dredging, where they would be employed for their brawn rather than their designing and woodworking skills.

MUSICAL INSTRUMENT MAKING
In the testimony of former slaves there is frequent mention of homemade musical instruments. Litt Young from Mississippi recalled exciting events around 1860, when "Us have small dances Saturday nights and ring plays and fiddle playin' and knockin' bones. There was fiddles made from gourds and banjos from sheep hides." The inventory here of stringed and percussive instruments identifies two of the main classes of musical instruments frequently made by African-American artisans. To Young's short list one can add rattles, gongs, scrapers, fifes, whistles, pan pipes, and drums. All of these had verifiable African antecedents, as did many of the songs they were used to play and the dances the instruments were intended to accompany.

The drums that were so essential not only to African musical performance but to religious and healing rituals were frightening to slave holders, for they realized that these instruments could be used to send private messages that they would not be able to de-

cipher. Laws were passed in South Carolina after the STONO REBELLION of 1739 and later in other colonies banning the playing of drums expressly to eliminate this means of communication. But such prohibitions were less than effective as deterrents, and well into the nineteenth century, slaves, particularly those who were more recently arrived from Africa, were still making drums. They commonly affixed some type of animal skin with thongs or pegs across the open end of a hollowed log or large gourd. Apparently such drums were made often enough that even as late as the 1930s elderly blacks living in the coastal regions of Georgia could still describe the practice in detail. Even though the custom was fast fading into obscurity by that time, a few of these informants claimed even to have made drums themselves.

The banjo is a very old black folk instrument that continues to enjoy considerable popularity among white aficionados of so-called "country music." This is an instrument which, according to no less an authority than Thomas Jefferson, black people "brought hither from Africa." In the earliest examples, the body of the instrument was shaped from gourd sliced in half lengthwise that was then covered with a stretched animal skin. A fretless neck was inserted at one end and four gut strings were run from its top to the base of the gourd. Today's banjos made in factories are different in every respect, except that they continue to have membrane-covered drums underneath the strings. Thus when the instrument is strummed one can still hear the distinctive combination of melodic tone and percussive thrump that was present in the original plantation instruments. The mainstay of African-American folk music through the early twentieth century, when it was largely supplanted by the blues guitar, the banjo is rarely played today by black musicians, and the only reported contemporary makers of banjos with gourd bodies are white.

The experience among fife makers, however, is more positive. In the delta area of northwestern Mississippi a small number of families continue to play fifes or, as they might say, "blow canes," as the entertainment at local picnics and barbecues. These people make their fifes as well. The process seems relatively simple: A foot-long section of bamboo cane is hollowed out and a mouth hole and four finger holes are pierced into it with a red-hot poker. There is considerable difficulty in calculating the correct placement for the holes so that notes of the correct pitch can be played. Considerable experimentation is required, since each piece of cane has a slightly different tonal range. In Mississippi, the fife is played as the lead instrument together with an ensemble of drums; it is a performance that resonates with similar performances among the Akan peoples of Ghana.

POTTERY

Slave potters made two very different types of wares. The earliest were earthenware vessels shaped by hand and fired to very low temperatures in open bonfires. These pots, recovered from the sites of many eighteenth-century plantations in South Carolina and Virginia, consisted mainly of small, round-bottomed bowls suitable for eating and drinking and larger round-bottomed cooking vessels. For decades these sorts of vessels were believed to be Native American in origin and thus were labeled as "Colono-Indian wares." Subsequent investigation has shown that given the sheer quantity of Colono shards at the sites of slave occupation and their relative absence in Indian villages during the same period, there can be no other conclusion than that this type of pottery was being made by slave artisans. Comparisons with African wares lend further support to the claim of slave manufacture so that some of this eighteenth-century eathenware is now referred to as Afro-Colono pottery. Many plantation-made bowls have a cross or an "X" scratched into their bases. While the function of these intriguing marks remains open to speculation, these are signs that have mystical association in Central Africa, where they are used in acts of prayer, particularly in summoning the protective power of ancestral spirits. As scholars have puzzled through the significance of these marks, they have surmised that the first slaves must have looked to their own inventory of cultural forms when they had to find an adequate way to feed themselves and they simply turned to a familiar African craft tradition. When slaves next discovered that their owners would not interfere in their efforts, some of these Africans may have gone even further and used their African pots to regenerate their interrupted religious traditions.

By the middle of the nineteenth century, the production of earthenware on plantations had ended. There were by then relatively few Africans in the slave population left to carry on the practice. More important, slave owners were now providing more food preparation items like cast-iron cooking pots. The first quarter of the nineteenth century witnessed as well an upsurge in the production of stoneware pottery, a durable type of ware shaped on a potter's wheel and fired to very high temperatures in a kiln. This type of pottery was produced mainly at small family-run shops. Occasionally slaves were employed in these shops, but chiefly as the laborers who cut the firewood or dug and mixed the clay; the more prestigious role of potter or turner was reserved for a white artisan. There was, however, one site where blacks were allowed more extensive participation, and it is there that one can identify a nineteenth-century tradition for African-American pottery.

About 1810, Abner Landrum, a prosperous white man living in the Edgefield District of west-central South Carolina, opened a pottery shop and was soon producing high-quality wares recognized as superior to any in the region. His shop would quickly grow into a booming industrial village and before long Landrum was selling stock in his operation. His financial success, however, did not go unchallenged. Other entrepreneurs also set up potteries in the area, luring away many of Landrum's skilled artisans. When he solved this crisis by training slaves to make pottery, other pottery owners soon followed his example.

Most of these African-American artisans remain unnamed, but various records suggest that about fifty slaves were employed at various shops throughout the Edgefield District. The best known of this group was a man named Dave who had once belonged to Abner Landrum. Trained first as a typesetter at Landrum's newspaper, Dave continued to display the fact that he was literate on his pots by signing and dating them and occasionally inscribing them with rhymed couplets. These vessels, unlike most, carry terse captions describing the time of manufacture and their maker's identity. More important, that they publicly carry words at a time when it was illegal for slaves to be literate makes these pots statements of overt resistance. Other slaves, upon seeing Dave's works, were likely to know that one of their own was mocking the white man's law, and they may have derived some measure of inspiration from his audacious example.

Certainly many would have noticed Dave's pots, for he made some of the largest vessels known in Edgefield. The largest one, inscribed "Great and Noble Jar," has a capacity of almost forty-five gallons and stands thirty inches in height. Many of his other pots are in this same size range and are distinctively shaped, with walls that flare boldly from a relatively narrow base to a wide shoulder close to the top of the vessel. While white potters also made large storage jars, none of their works seem as daring. With their widest sections nearer their middles, they appear to squat safely on the floor, while Dave's pots seemingly leap up and threaten to teeter back and forth. The form of Dave's pot thus emphasizes the rebelliousness signaled by his inscriptions.

Even though Dave's work is a reflection of commonplace African-American experiences of chattel slavery in the South, his pieces, as objects, are basically expressions of European ceramic traditions. The pot forms for which he is now so famous appear to take their lines ultimately from the bread pots of northeastern England, and his use of pottery wheels, kilns, and glazes are all manifestations of standardized Anglo-American ceramic technology. Yet within the community of black potters in Edgefield there were opportunities for artisans to revisit ancestral aesthetic forms. In series of small vessels, averaging about five inches in height, slave potters were apparently able to rekindle memories of African sculpture.

Pots decorated with faces are known in every ceramic tradition on the globe, but those attributed to black people in Edgefield have several attributes not seen elsewhere. Their most distinctive feature is the use of a different clay body to mark the eyes and teeth: White porcelain clay contrasts sharply with the dark glaze covering the rest of the stoneware vessel. The riveting gaze and seeming snarl that results from this mode of decoration recalls the mixed-media approach to sculpture found in West and Central Africa, where all sorts of contrasting materials are applied to a wooden form for dramatic effect, particularly in the rendering of eyes and teeth on statues and masks. That a white substance is used in Edgefield is very significant, for the same visual effect might have been achieved by simply coloring the eyes and teeth with a light colored slip. That the look of an Edgefield face jug was created by the rather difficult technique of embedding an entirely different clay body into the walls of the pot suggests that both the material and the behavior are both charged with important symbolic meanings. In Central Africa, homeland to 75 percent of all slaves imported into South Carolina, white clay has sacred associations with ancestral authority.

Among the Central African Kongo people, for example, white is the color of the dead, so that white objects are offered to them and effigies of the dead are marked with white eyes. The strong stylistic affinities between Kongo sculpture and Edgefield vessels suggest that the enslaved artisans took advantage of their access to ceramic technology and used it to enhance African-inspired religious ceremonies held on the plantations in the region. These rituals could be carried on without detection because during the antebellum period blacks outnumbered whites in the Edgefield District by more than four to one. The Africanity of slave life in this area was ironically sustained as well by constant illegal smuggling operations of new African captives into the area; in fact, one of the last known cargoes of slaves to the United States was a group of Kongo captives landed on the Georgia coast, carried up the Savannah River, and sold into Edgefield County in 1858. The face vessels of Edgefield are evidence, then, of how African-American artisans could, when circumstances allowed, counter the assimilationist trajectory of their experiences and use new foreign means to reestablish ties to their African roots.

WOODCARVING

The prodigious woodcarving skills of African artisans are widely recognized, and their masks and statues are granted honored places in first-rank museums along with noteworthy masterpieces of western art. Since these works, so abundant in Africa, seem to be noticeably absent in the United States, assessments of African-American culture often begin by lamenting the loss of these skills. However, this carving tradition, while diminished in scale, is not altogether absent.

African slaves seem to have remembered their traditions for woodcarving. According to an old African-American man from Georgia who was interviewed in the late 1930s: "I remember the African men used to all the time make little clay images. Sometimes they like men, sometimes they like animals. Once they put a spear in his hand and walk around him and he was the chief. . . . Sometimes they try to make the image out of wood." In 1819 a banjo was seen in Congo Square in New Orleans by architect Benjamin Latrobe, which had an unmistakable African figure carved at the top of the instrument's neck just above the tuning pegs. A remarkable table was built sometime in the 1850s on a plantation in north-central North Carolina with each of its legs carved into figures highly reminiscent of African figures. A drum, now in the collections of the British Museum, was collected in 1753 in Virginia that is in every respect an excellent example of an Akan-Ashanti *apentemma* drum. However, since it was carved from a piece of American cedar, it is American rather than African in origin. From this smattering of examples, one can conclude that African proclivities for working creatively in wood did not simply end upon Africans' arrival in the Americas. These skills were carried on when and wherever possible.

Most often, African woodcarving skills were turned in other directions—generally to the production of useful household objects like bowls, trays, mortars and pestles, and handles for various metal tools. The severely functional nature of these items did not provide much of an opportunity for creative expression even if the artisan did his work with diligence and commitment. Yet in the carving of wooden canes some degree of African inspiration was seemingly able to reemerge. Numerous walking sticks carved by African Americans, from the nineteenth century to the present, sometimes bear distinctive marks that may relate to African traditions kept alive mainly among country people. These canes are often decorated with a wide range of media, including brass tacks, colored beads and marbles, aluminum foil, and other shiny materials. In one case from Mississippi, the carver attached a silver thermometer to the handle of a cane that was already elaborately carved with figures of humans and serpents. Yet it was not judged as complete without the bit of flash that a seemingly incongruous temperature gauge could provide. While this decorative gesture could be nothing more than a whimsical act of personal innovation, the fact that such acts are so commonplace among African-American canemakers in the South implies the presence of a shared style. Certainly one senses in the construct of these decorated canes a parallel to the African use of mixed-media assembly in sculpture.

Closer African affinities are seen in the selection of certain motifs. Reptiles dominate the shafts of most of the walking sticks that have clear attributions to African-American carvers; in addition to snakes (which are common to decorators of canes everywhere), black carvers also render alligators, turtles, and lizards, and as they are often combined with figures of human beings, the contrast may be read as symbolic of supernatural communication. According to widely held African beliefs, reptiles are appropriate symbols of messages between the spirit and human domains because they are creatures able to travel in two realms (in the water and on the land, or underground and above ground). They, like spiritual messages, move between the human environment and another, unseen place. The chief linkage between this symbolism and African-American traditions in woodcarving may lie in the fact that throughout the nineteenth century, traditional healers or "root doctors" are said to have carried carved walking sticks decorated with reptiles as a sign of their authority. Since their cures are likely to have been based on African practices, it follows that the rest of their paraphernalia (which was often as instrumental in affecting a cure as the medicines administered) was also African-derived. Consequently, when an African-American carved a snake or an alligator on a walking stick, it may have carried a different meaning and function than a similar animal carved by a white artisan.

QUILTING
Quilted bedcovers are objects that are unknown and unnecessary in tropical Africa. However, some West African ceremonial textiles are decorated with colorful appliqué figures, and large pieces of cloth for everyday use are assembled by sewing narrow strips together. Thus enslaved African women may have been somewhat prepared to make quilts since they already had the requisite skills needed to piece quilt tops from scraps and remnants. While the actual quilting process was, for the most part, new and dif-

ferent—that is, the binding of two large pieces of cloth together with a layer of batting in between by means of thousands of geometrically patterned stitches—extant quilts alleged to be slave-made show that these women were certainly capable of mastering the task.

Very little about the oldest surviving African-American quilts seems to demonstrate any affinity for African textile traditions. Mainly what one sees is the strict guidance of the plantation mistress. However, during the last decades of the nineteenth century, Harriet Powers of Athens, Ga., produced two quilts filled with images that seem to come straight out of Dahomey, a prominent kingdom on the West African coast. While her links to Africa are less than certain and would have been, at best, indirect, the figures on her two "bible" quilts compare closely with appliqué figures found on sewn narrative textiles of the Fon people. More commonplace and perhaps even more profoundly associated with African textiles are the so-called "strip quilts," which appear with great regularity wherever African Americans make quilts. In this type of bedcover, long, thin strip units are sewn edge-to-edge to form the large square or rectangular quilt top. The "strips" may be single pieces, or may be assembled from blocks, from thin remnants called "strings," or from assorted remnants. Regardless of the technique, the overall linear composition of the top cannot be missed. Since most contemporary African-American quilters claim that quilts of this type are the oldest pattern they know, there is a good possibility that such quilts were made during slavery. Certainly they resemble in form and technique the strip cloths of West and Central Africa. These textiles are assembled from narrow pieces about five inches wide and eight feet long that are sewn edge-to-edge to create a large rectangular panel. This tradition is seemingly perpetuated in a modified form in the African-American strip quilt.

Even if this mode of quilt assembly proves not to be African in origin, it is certainly a marker of African-American style. While such quilts are made by white quilters, too, they will usually protest that they were a simple type made when they were "just learning" or they were quilts merely "thrown together" and thus were nothing to be proud of. Black quilters, on the other hand, celebrate strip patterns as among the most significant in their repertories and produce them from childhood to old age. They constantly work at refining the form as they explore the nuances of the genre. These quilters are fully aware of the geometric patterns common in Euro-American quilting, patterns usually generated from block units, but they prefer to use strips. The strip format is by nature innovative and open-ended, and thus, unlike

Euro-American quilt genres, is considerably less bound by formal conventions. There is, then, a sense of design permission about strip quilts, even a sense of liberation. In all of its variety, African-American folk art is a vital and enduring contribution to the artistic achievement of the United States.

Twentieth-Century Folk Art

The names of only a handful of early African-American folk artists have survived. By the middle of the nineteenth century, however, there are increasing numbers of artists whose names have been recorded. Two of the most impressive examples of nineteenth-century African-American carved walking sticks were made by a slave blacksmith named Henry Gudgell (c. 1826–1895) in Livingston County, Mo., during the 1860s. They are in the collections of the Yale University Art Gallery and of Allan and Anne Weiss, Louisville, Ky. Each version has a slender, tapering shaft with a handle carved in powerful spiral grooves and depicts a slender serpent carved in relief and entwined around the bottom of the stick. A lizard and a tortoise appear near the top of the shaft in each example, and a series of carved bands may be seen directly below the handle. The combination of motifs on the Gudgell walking sticks is undoubtedly African, and their existence was sometimes related to African beliefs in witchcraft, healing, and conjuring.

EARLY TWENTIETH-CENTURY AFRICAN-AMERICAN FOLK ART

The earliest national recognition of an individual African-American folk artist occurred when the limestone sculptures of William EDMONDSON (1882–1951), a tombstone carver from Nashville, Tenn., were exhibited in 1937, at the Museum of Modern Art in New York. Although the show consisted of only ten objects and no catalogue was published, it was the first one-man exhibition of works by an African-American artist to be held at the Museum of Modern Art.

The most celebrated early twentieth-century African-American folk artist is Horace PIPPIN, (1881–1946), who lived in West Chester, Pa. Pippin began painting ca. 1930, following a World War I–related disability, and was represented by the Carlen Gallery in Philadelphia. Widely collected during his lifetime, the majority of Pippin's paintings are in the permanent collections of major museums. He was the subject of the first monograph on an African-American artist. *Horace Pippin: A Negro Artist in America* by Seldom Rodman was published in 1947, the year following Pippin's death. In 1972, a revised, updated edition, *Horace Pippin: The Artist as a Black American,* was published by Seldon Rodman and Carole Cleaver.

CONTEMPORARY AFRICAN-AMERICAN FOLK ART

A revival of interest in African-American folk art occurred in 1982, when the Corcoran Gallery of Art in Washington, D.C., mounted the exhibition "Black Folk Art in America, 1930–1980," which included the works of twenty African-American artists. This exhibition was the first comprehensive show of African-American folk art to be mounted by a major museum.

Within the broad spectrum of contemporary American folk art, works produced by African Americans exist as a unique category with distinct characteristics. The majority of African-American folk artists were born and lived in the deep South. States that have produced unusually large numbers of African-American folk artists are South Carolina, Georgia, Alabama, Mississippi, Louisiana, and Texas. Many prominent African-American folk artists who live in northern and midwestern cities moved there from the South. They usually began producing art late in life, following retirement, widowhood, or a work-related disability. Some produced art sporadically: however, it is usually not until their retirement that their styles reach maturity.

A deep religiosity is one of the most common characteristics of African-American folk art. Many of the artists are ministers, missionaries, and self-styled prophets, and others insist that God instructed them to produce art. They credit their intuitive artistic abilities to God, and state that He is actually producing art through their hands. One of the most private and enigmatic examples of African-American religious folk art is *The Throne of the Third Heaven of the Nation's Millennium General Assembly,* created in a downtown Washington, D.C., garage by James HAMPTON (1911–1964) over a period of fourteen years. The throne is an assembly of furniture, light bulbs, and other discarded objects that were carefully covered with silver and gold metallic paper. There are few known facts concerning Hampton or his motivation for creating the throne. The glittering monument was virtually unknown before Hampton's death, and has now been permanently installed at the Smithsonian Institution, National Museum of American Art. Religious subjects occur frequently in works by African-American folk artists who are not vocally expressive of their religious convictions. The church has always been a powerful institution in African-American communities, and the belief in an afterlife is frequently more fervent among African Americans than among those of other ethnic groups, owing to its perception by them as a sphere of material comforts not attainable on earth.

A predilection for bird, animal, and serpent imagery is also a common denominator of African-American folk art. Many of the artists state that they are recalling the barnyard menageries of their childhood in the rural South. Entwined serpent and reptile motifs on carved canes and staffs are similar to examples carved in Africa many centuries ago. Animals, birds, and reptiles fashioned from tree trunks and limbs are conceived as protector figures related to a spirit world often understood only by the artist. The paramount role of animals in West African religions, folklore, and mythology suggests that the predominance of animal themes in African-American folk art is another example of African "survivals" in America.

An unusual ingenuity for transforming cast-off and scrap objects into artifacts is another general characteristic of African-American folk art. Originating from the necessity of surviving from cast-offs and leftovers, such improvisational practices can be traced back to slavery. African-American slave cooks converted cast-off pork parts into "soul food" delicacies, and leftover rice and stale bread scraps into moist, succulent puddings. Scraps of calico were converted into quilts and bedcovers. In a similar display of creativity, African-American folk artists frequently employed unusual materials in the creation of their art. These materials include chewing gum, styrofoam trays and packing panels, sawdust, mud, roots and tree trunks, animal and fish bones, broken glass, umbrella frames, costume jewelry, bottles, wooden spools, house paint, scrap pieces of masonite and paneling, bottle caps, aluminum beverage cans, and other commonplace objects which are converted into art.

Figures associated with emancipation and civil rights appear frequently in African-American folk art. George Washington, Abraham Lincoln, the Rev. Dr. Martin Luther King, Jr., John F. Kennedy, and Robert Kennedy are the most frequently represented subjects. President John F. Kennedy is the most frequently depicted nonblack subject in African-American folk art. Most African-American folk artists are keenly aware of both their African heritage and their American heritage. Elderly African-American folk artists often produced scenes of slavery, slave auctions, cotton picking, and other scenes of plantation life which are commentaries on their own feelings. Louisiana artist Clementine HUNTER (1885–1988) rarely depicted whites in her paintings, even in her religious figures, evidencing a rare and astonishing expression of black pride for a rural woman from the deep South who lived beyond the century mark.

African-American folk art is deeply reflective of childhood experiences. An endless repertory of baptisms, funerals, weddings, parties, barnyard scenes, cotton pickings, slavery scenes, Saturday shindigs, honky-tonk scenes, and other events which are remembered or relayed by parents and grandparents are visually recorded by African-American folk artists. This art is vibrant, pulsing with rhythm, and little attempt is made to model form three-dimensionally. Scale relationships are frequently inaccurate, and vertical perspective is usually employed.

Indulgence in flights of fantasy and desire to satisfy unfulfilled lifelong career ambitions often motivate African-American folk artists. Leslie Payne (1907–c. 1985) of Reedsville, Va., was fascinated by airplanes and ships. He dreamed of a career as a pilot and built an airplane, powered by an automobile engine, that he hoped to fly. When the plane would not lift off, Payne drove it—automobile-style—and indulged in imaginary flights which he carefully recorded in a log book. John Landry (1912–1986) grew up in New Orleans, was fascinated by Mardi Gras floats since his childhood, and often competed with other youths for the coveted positions of carrying flambeaux in Mardi Gras parades. Following his retirement as a longshoreman, Landry began fashioning miniature replicas of Mardi Gras floats using wire and discarded Mardi Gras beads. These carefully constructed shoebox-sized floats have wheels which roll, and their durability attests to Landry's desire to become an architect.

Simplicity and unpretentiousness are two of the inherent characteristics which contribute to the widespread appeal of African-American folk art. No tedious academic or intellectual mental exercises are necessary to comprehend or enjoy it. Childlike but not childish, simplistic but not always simple, twentieth-century African-American folk art is a spontaneous and untutored mode of expression. Because it is free from influences of academic art and "mainstream" movements, it is not surprising to note that a number of academically trained African-American artists have been influenced by folk art forms of African Americans.

REFERENCES

BENBERRY, CUESTA. *Always There: The African-American Presence in American Quilts.* Louisville, Ky., 1992.

CHASE, JUDITH WRAGG. *Afro-American Art and Craft.* New York, 1971.

Dallas Museum of Art. *Black Art—Ancestral Legacy: The African Impulse in African American Art.* Dallas, 1989.

FERGUSON, LELAND. *Uncommon Ground: Archaeology and Early African America, 1650–1800.* Washington, D.C., 1992.

FERRIS, WILLIAM H., ed. *Afro-American Folk Art and Crafts.* New York, 1993.

Georgia Council for the Arts and Humanities. *Missing Pieces: Georgia Folk Art 1770–1976.* Atlanta, 1977.

Greenville County Museum of Art. *Early Decorated Stoneware of the Edgefield District, South Carolina.* Greenville, S.C., 1976.

HORNE, CATHERINE WILSON, ed. *Crossroads of Clay: The Southern Alkaline-Glazed Stoneware Tradition.* Columbia, S.C., 1990.

LEON, ELI. *Who'd A Thought It: Improvisation in African-American Quiltmaking.* San Francisco, 1987.

LIVINGSTON, JANE, and JOHN BEARDSLEY (with a contribution by Regenia Perry). *Black Folk Art in America, 1930–1980.* New York, 1982.

MYERS, LYNN ROBERTSON, and GEORGE D. TERRY. *Carolina Folk: The Cradle of a Southern Tradition.* Columbia, S.C., 1985.

———. *Southern Make: The Southern Folk Heritage.* Columbia, S.C., 1977.

PERRY, REGENIA. *Selections of Nineteenth-Century Afro-American Art.* New York, 1976.

———. *Spirits or Satire: African American Face Vessels of the 19th Century.* 1985.

———. *What It Is: Black American Folk Art from the Collection of Regenia Perry.* Richmond, Va., 1982.

ROSENGARTEN, DALE. *Row Upon Row: Sea Grass Baskets of the South Carolina Low Country.* Columbia, S.C., 1986.

SEIBELS, EUGENIA, and JoANNE McCORMICK. *Southern Folk Arts.* Columbia, S.C., 1988.

THOMPSON, ROBERT F. "African Influences on the Art of the United States." In Armistead L. Robinson, et al., eds. *Black Studies in the University.* New York, 1969, pp. 128–177.

———. *Flash of the Spirit: African and Afro-American Art.* New York, 1983.

VLACH, JOHN MICHAEL. *The Afro-American Tradition in the Decorative Arts.* 1978. Reprint. Athens, Ga., 1990.

———. *By the Work of Their Hands: Studies in Afro-American Folk Life.* Charlottesville, Va., 1991.

WEBB, ROBERT LLOYD. *Ring the Banjar!: The Banjo from Folklore to Factory.* Cambridge, Mass., 1984.

WOOD, PETER H. *Black Majority: Negroes in Colonial South Carolina from 1670 through the Stono Rebellion.* New York, 1974.

REGENIA A. PERRY
JOHN MICHAEL VLACH

Folklore. African-American folklore is a mode of creative cultural production that manifests itself in expressive forms such as tales, songs, proverbs, greetings, gestures, rhymes, material artifacts, and other created products and performances. Although African-American folklore is most often thought of in terms of these expressive forms, it is in reality a dynamic process of creativity that arises in performative contexts characterized by face-to-face interaction. The performative aspects of this folklore is what distinguishes it from other modes of creative cultural production within an African-American context. In other words, unlike other modes of African-American creative cultural production, such as literary and popular culture, folklore gains its meaning and value as a form of expression within unmediated performances on an ongoing basis in African-American communities.

Although African-American folklore should be conceptualized as a performed medium, it has an important historical dimension as well. That is, its performance even in contemporary settings entails the creative manipulation of historical forms of indefinite temporal origin. As such, it is intricately linked to processes of black culture-building in that it has historically served as an important means of communicating shared cultural attitudes, beliefs, and values of and within an ever-changing African community in the United States. As interrelated phenomena, African folklore creation and culture-building are both dynamic creative processes with roots in the diverse African cultures from which contemporary African Americans originated.

Among scholars of African-American folklore, however, the existence of a dynamic relationship between African and African-American processes of folklore creation has historically been controversial. The controversy arose in large part from the intricate link that folklorists envisioned between folklore creation and culture-building. Early in the study of African-American culture and folklore, scholars postulated that African people were so traumatized by the process of enslavement that they arrived in the New World culturally bankrupt and, therefore, dependent on Europeans for new cultural capital. In early studies, this view of a lack of African cultural retention contributed to a conception of the products of African-American folklore as mere imitations of European expressive forms. Although this view has been challenged over the years by the discovery of African cultural forms in the United States, these cultural expressions have been disparaged further by being identified as "Africanisms," isolated cases that somehow survived in the New World despite the trauma of enslavement. In fact, however, "Africanisms" represent the most obvious evidence that African culture and cultural forms have had a profound influence on black culture-building and folklore creation in the United States (Roberts 1989, p. 9).

Historically, the difficulty of appreciating and recognizing the influence of African culture and cultural forms on African-American folklore has been exacerbated by the fact that Africans brought to the United States as slaves did not themselves share a coherent culture. Only recently have scholars begun to realize the irrelevance of this perspective to an understanding of black culture-building in African communities throughout the New World. For example, Sidney Mintz and Richard Price (1972, p. 5) have suggested that although Africans enslaved in the New World did not share a common culture or folk tradition upon arrival, they did share "certain common orientations to reality which tended to focus the attention of individuals from West African cultures upon similar kinds of events, even though the ways of handling these events may seem quite diverse in formal terms." While these "common orientations to reality" may not have been sufficient to support the re-creation of African cultural institutions in their pristine form, they could and did serve as a foundation for culture-building in a new environment.

African people who were forcibly unrooted from their homelands and transplanted in America as slaves brought with them cherished memories of their traditional lifestyles and cultural forms that served as the foundations of African-American folk tradition. To understand the dynamic processes that characterized the development over time of an African-American folk tradition, we must recognize that both black culture-building and folklore creation have proceeded as recursive rather than linear processes of endlessly devising solutions to both old and new problems of living under ever-changing social, political, and economic conditions. While both culture-building and folklore creation are dynamic and creative in that they adapt to social needs and goals, they are also enduring in that they change by building upon previous manifestations of themselves. Cultural transformation is a normative process experienced and carried out by all groups. In the process, the institutional and expressive forms by which a group communicates and upholds the ideals by which it lives are equally subject to transformation.

As James Snead (1984, p. 61) has argued, however, the failure to recognize the dynamic and transformational properties of African cultures in the New World has been influenced historically by the view that African cultures are static. Only by recognizing that such cultures are and always have been dynamic (i.e., capable of transforming themselves in response to the social needs and goals of African people) is it possible to envision African-American folklore as a continuous process of creativity intricately linked to a historical tradition of black culture-building with roots in Africa. During the period of black SLAVERY in the United States, enslaved Africans began the process of building a culture based on their "common orientations to reality." Despite their lack of a sense of shared identity and values upon arrival, the similarity of the conditions and treatment that they faced in the slave system facilitated their ability to envision themselves as a community. To communicate their shared identity and value system, they transformed

many of their African cultural forms by focusing on the common elements within them. In the process, their creative efforts as well as the final expressive products that they created were greatly influenced by the differences in their situations in the United States from those they had known in Africa. In other words, the transformation of African cultural forms involved a process of creating new forms based on common elements from diverse African cultures and their infusion with insights and meanings relevant to contemporary situations in the United States. That these new forms did not always resemble some African original did not negate the debt they owed to African cultural roots.

The beginnings of an African-American folk tradition can be traced to the slavery period and to the efforts of African people from diverse cultural backgrounds to maintain a sense of continuity with their past. Throughout the period of slavery, scattered references to African-American folklore appeared in written records. Systematic efforts to collect and study such folklore, however, did not begin until the late nineteenth century. The earliest efforts to collect it were carried out primarily by white missionaries who flocked into the South following Emancipation to assist black freedpeople. Although these early efforts were motivated in large part by a desire to use African Americans' creative cultural production to demonstrate their humanity and fitness for freedom, such activities nevertheless preserved for posterity a vast body of African-American oral tradition.

An equally important motive for early collectors of black folklore was the prevalent belief in the late nineteenth century that folklore as a mode of creative cultural production as rapidly disappearing. In the case of African Americans, many envisioned the growing rate of literacy among freedpeople as a sure sign that the African-American folk tradition would soon disappear. Although contemporary folklorists realize the falsity of this perspective, it nevertheless provided a primary impetus for the collection of African-American folklore in the late nineteenth century and influenced a concentration on those forms that had obvious roots in slavery. During this productive period of African-American folklore gathering, collectors focused most of their attention on three forms: SPIRITUALS, animal-trickster tales, and folk beliefs.

Spirituals received a great deal of attention, especially from northern missionaries, in the late nineteenth century. The first book-length collection of African-American folklore published was *Slave Songs of the United States* which primarily contained spirituals. The spiritual song tradition of African Americans developed during the late eighteenth and early nineteenth centuries with the conversion of large numbers of enslaved African-Americans to Christianity. Spirituals as a body of songs were developed primarily around the actions of Old Testament figures whose faith in God allowed them to be delivered from bondage and persecution in dramatic ways. The songs followed a pronounced leader/chorus pattern known as call and response, which in performance created a kind of communal dialogue about the power of faith and belief in an omnipotent God. While the songs often portrayed Heaven as the ultimate reward of faith in God, their primary focus was on earthly deliverance from bondage and persecution. Through analogy to Old Testament stories of persecution and divine deliverance, the songs constantly reiterated the power of God to deliver the faithful.

Spirituals provided enslaved Africans with an alternative expressive form for communicating their vision of the power of God and the rewards of faith in Christianity to that offered by the slavemasters. As enslaved Africans freely and often testified, the masters frequently attempted to use slave's Christian conversion and participation in white religious services to reinforce the masters' view of enslavement. The dominant message that enslaved Africans received from white preachers was "Servants, obey your masters." In the spirituals, enslaved Africans were able to convey to members of their community a more empowering and liberating vision of God and the Christian religion. Of equal importance, the creation and performance of spirituals allowed them to incorporate more of their African cultural heritage into Christian worship. Despite general prohibitions against unsupervised worship, enslaved Africans created opportunities for separate worship in slave cabins, "hush harbors," and even their own churches, where they created and performed spirituals in a style and manner that incorporated African performance practices. These practices included the development of the "shout," a religious ritual characterized by a counterclockwise shuffling movement reminiscent of African ritual dancing. The primary purpose of the "shout" was to induce spirit possession, a form of communion with the supernatural valued by many people of African descent.

In the late nineteenth century, the collection of spirituals was rivaled only by the collection of animal-trickster tales. With the publication of Joel Chandler Harris's *Uncle Remus: His Songs and Sayings* in 1881, the collection of animal-trickster tales by various individuals escalated. By the end of the nineteenth century, literally hundreds of these tales had been collected and published. Early collectors of black folktales often expressed amazement over the variety of animal-trickster tales created by enslaved Africans. That tales of the animal trickster would become central in the narrative performances of en-

slaved Africans is not surprising, however. In the cultures from which enslaved Africans originated, folktales in which clever animals acted as humans to impart important lessons about survival were ubiquitous. Although various animals acted as tricksters in different African traditions, the tales of their exploits showed important similarities throughout sub-Saharan Africa. In fact, even the same plots could be found in the trickster-tale traditions of diverse African groups (Feldmann 1973, p. 15).

In the United States, the animal trickster was most often represented by Brer Rabbit, although other animals acted as tricksters in some tales. Although a number of trickster tales found in the repertory of enslaved Africans retained plots from African tradition, many transformed the African trickster in ways that reflected the situation of enslavement. The impetus for transforming the African trickster was not only the need to create a single tradition out of many but also the differences in the situations faced by Africans in the New World from those in Africa that had given the exploits of tricksters there meaning and value. In the trickster tales of enslaved Africans, the trickster was an actor particularly adept at obtaining the material means of survival within an atmosphere similar to that in which enslaved Africans lived. Unlike African tricksters, whose behavior was often conceptualized as a response to famine or other conditions in which material shortage existed, the trickster of enslaved African Americans acted in a situation of material plenty.

The primary obstacle to the acquisition of the material means of survival for the trickster of enslaved Africans was the physical power and control wielded by the dupe. This situation reflected the conditions under which enslaved Africans lived, in which the material means of survival were readily available but were denied by the control of the slavemasters. In these tales, the trickster was portrayed as developing clever strategies for obtaining material goods, especially food, despite the efforts of his dupes to deny access. As historians of the slave experience have noted, the concern with the acquisition of food was a common one during slavery (Blassingame 1972, p. 158; Genovese 1976, pp. 638–639). In tale after tale, Brer Rabbit proved to be a masterful manipulator of his dupes, who appeared most often in the guise of the wolf or the fox. The tales often portrayed situations in which cleverness, verbal dexterity, and native intelligence or wit allowed the trickster to triumph over the dupes. For enslaved Africans, this provided a model of behavior for dealing with the power and control of the slavemasters over the material means of survival.

Often reported as case studies, the folk beliefs of enslaved Africans also seemed widespread to collectors in the late nineteenth century. In many ways, the concerns of collectors reflected a stereotypical view of many white Americans that African Americans were inordinately superstitious. The collection of folk beliefs centered primarily around the practice of conjuration. At the core of this practice was the conjurer, a figure transformed by enslaved Africans but based on African religious leaders such as medicine men. While the conjurer in different parts of the South was known by different names, including root doctor, hoodooer, and two-heads, the practice of conjuration was remarkably similar wherever it was found (Bacon and Herron 1973, pp. 360–361). In most instances, conjurers were believed to be individuals possessed of a special gift to both cause and cure illness. Although the source of the conjurer's powers was usually believed to be mysterious, some believed it came from an evil source, others believed it came from God, and still others believed it could be taught by those possessed of it.

During the period of slavery, conjurers played a prominent role among enslaved Africans, especially as healers. Although most slavemasters attempted to provide for the health needs of enslaved Africans, their efforts often fell short. In general, the state of scientific medicine during the period of slavery was so poorly developed that, even under ideal conditions, doctors were ineffective in treating many diseases. The importance of conjurers for enslaved Africans also had to do with beliefs about the causes of illness, beliefs deeply influenced by their African cultural heritage. Like their ancestors, many enslaved Africans continued to believe that illness was caused by the ill-will of one individual against another through an act of conjuration. Individuals could induce illness either through their own action or by consulting a conjurer, who could be persuaded to "lay a spell." In these cases, only the power of a conjurer could alleviate the illness.

In their practices, conjurers used both material objects, such as charms and amulets, and verbal incantations in the form of curses and spells. However, theirs was primarily an herbal practice; hence, the common name of root doctor for these practitioners. The frequent use of verbal incantations derived from African beliefs about the power of the spoken word to influence forces in nature for good or ill. Although conjurers have often been associated with unrelieved evil, their role was a culturally sanctioned one. Within the belief and social system that supported the practice of conjuration, social strife, believed to be the dominant cause of illness, was seen as disruptive to the equilibrium and harmony of the community. The conjurer's role was to discover the identity of the individual responsible for the disruption and to restore harmony. For both the social and physical well-being of enslaved Africans, the conjurer's abilities in this regard proved beneficial. Not only did the presence of conjurers provide them with a means of tending to their own health needs, it also provided a mechanism for addressing issues of social strife within the group without the intervention of slavemasters.

Although spirituals, trickster tales, and folk beliefs were the focus of most early collecting, the folklore of enslaved Africans included more than these genres. Collectors seldom noted other vibrant genres that developed during slavery, including proverbs, courtship rituals, prayers, sermons, and forms of folktale other than trickster narratives. But while there was no concerted effort to collect these genres, examples sometimes found their way into collections. In addition, folklorists and other scholars have begun to utilize various kinds of records, including plantation journals, slave narratives, and diaries of various sorts in an effort to better understand the nature of black vernacular creativity during the slave period (Joyner 1984; Ferris 1983). These types of resources have proven particularly useful in the study of black material culture. Because slavemasters were generally responsible for the material needs of enslaved Africans, the importance of knowledge possessed by Africans and applied to the production of various material objects has generally been overlooked. However, African skill and knowledge were responsible for the production of many material objects used in everyday life on farms and plantations. It has become evident, for example, that African knowledge and skill in rice cultivation were responsible for the profitable rice industry that thrived along the coast of Georgia and South Carolina. In addition, African knowledge of basketry and textiles was responsible for the development of a unique tradition of basketry and quilting that continues to be practiced today (Ferris, 1983, pp. 63–110 and 235–274). Of equal importance, many enslaved Africans who served as blacksmiths, carpenters, cooks, and seamstresses on farms and plantations used African techniques in the production of the material products for which they were responsible.

Despite early predictions of the demise of an African-American folk tradition with the advent of freedom and literacy, African Americans have continued to create and perform various genres of folklore. In many ways, the success of early collectors was a testament to the vibrancy and importance of vernacular creativity among African Americans. Although Emancipation brought about important changes in lifestyle, it did not alter many of the conditions that had made the forms of folklore created by enslaved Africans meaningful. In the post-Emancipation era, the development of the sharecropping system and the imposition of JIM CROW laws created patterns of economic and social oppression similar to those that had existed during slavery. In fact, the similarities in the conditions of freedpeople in the late nineteenth and early twentieth centuries to those endured by enslaved Africans allowed them to simply alter many of the forms they had created during slavery to reflect new realities.

As the conditions that would influence black culture-building in the post-Emancipation era became clear, African Americans began the process of both transforming existing forms and creating new ones to communicate their perceptions of the economic, social, and political realties that informed their lives as freedpeople. With the failure of Reconstruction and growing patterns of segregation following Emancipation, African Americans came to realize that conditions imposed on them that inhibited their progress in society had to be addressed differently. In a general sense, the powerful role that the law played in the lives of freedpeople made many of the strategies developed during slavery for dealing with white power and control no longer effective or in the best interest of African Americans. For example, the tales of the animal trickster, which had provided an important model of behavior for dealing with white economic exploitation and social oppression during slavery, gradually lost their effectiveness as the expressive embodiment of a strategy for freedpeople. In some animal-trickster tales collected in the late nineteenth century, contests between the animal trickster and dupe were settled in the courts.

Despite the decline of animal-trickster-tale narration, African Americans retained the trickster as a focus for folklore creation. In the late nineteenth and early twentieth centuries, the trickster was transformed into the badman, a character whose primary adversary was the law, personified by the white policeman or sheriff (Roberts 1989, pp. 171–220). The emergence of white lawmen as powerful and often brutal defenders of white privilege made it extremely problematic for African Americans to retaliate directly against whites for their exploitation. At the same time, the proliferation of patterns of segregation and economic exploitation and the rise of Jim Crow laws made the black community an arena for the actions of badmen. Therefore, although badmen spent much of their energy attempting to elude the law, they found their dupes in members of the black community. As tricksters, they attempted to dupe members of the black community into participating in illegal activities such as gambling, bootlegging, prostitution, numbers-running, and drug-dealing. That is, badmen as tricksters sought material gain by outwitting both African Americans and the

law. In this sense, the black badmen of the post-Emancipation era faced a double bind not unknown to many African Americans.

Folklore creation surrounding black badmen in the late nineteenth and early twentieth centuries reflected changed conditions faced by African Americans in society. As the law in both its abstract and personified forms became a powerful force in maintaining white privilege, African Americans were forced to turn increasingly to their own communities for solutions to their economic and social oppression. Because the law was often brutal in its treatment of African Americans, they made avoidance of the law a virtue and attempted to keep the law out of their communities. In so doing, they assumed a great deal of responsibility for maintaining harmony and peace among themselves. In economically deprived black communities, however, the means of enhancing one's economic status were extremely limited. The rise of secular entertainment establishments such as jukes and bars served as a focus for many of the activities associated with black badmen. In these establishments, many African Americans found activities by which they had the potential to enhance their economic well-being, such as gambling and numbers-playing, as well as offering psychological escape in whiskey and drugs from the oppressive conditions of their lives. Despite their illegal nature, these activities posed little danger to the black community as long as individuals who participated in them played by the unwritten rules. However, the consumption of alcohol and the existence of games of chance created an environment in which violence often erupted and the law intervened.

The exploits of black badmen typically unfolded in jukes and bars. The badman emerged in folklore as an individual who, in defense of his trade, committed an act of murder. The badman's exploits were celebrated in legends and ballads, narrative songs that told of their deeds. For example, the notorious gambling badman Stackolee purportedly shot Billy Lyons, who was cheating him in a card game. Duncan shot the white policeman, Brady, to end his bullying of patrons at Duncan's bar. Invariably caught and punished, the badman was treated sympathetically in folklore. The sympathy engendered by the badman derives from the importance to some members of the black community of the activities with which he became associated, as well as the individuals he killed. The badman's victims were usually cheaters or bullies whose actions threatened to bring the power and force of the law down on the community. In the late nineteenth and early twentieth centuries, many African Americans endured economic conditions that made the activities identified with black badmen important to their material well-being. At the same time, they recognized the potential and real consequences of participating in these activities.

In many ways, the focus of folklore creation surrounding black badmen reflects the nature of black folklore since Emancipation. In a profound sense, expressive celebration of the black badman reflected a general pattern of forms that focused on conditions faced by African Americans on a recurrent basis yet suggested that the solutions lie within the black community. The most common types of folktale performed by African Americans since Emancipation attempt to identify the origins of conditions that inhibit black progress in society. These often humorous narratives attempt through suggestion and persuasion to address intragroup attitudes and behaviors perceived as responsible for the conditions faced by African Americans. At the same time, they suggest that when African Americans recognize their own role in maintaining behaviors not in their best interest, they gain the ability and power to change them.

In many narratives the focus of the tales is on the origins of certain animal characteristics. These tales were developed during slavery and usually involved animals from the trickster cycle. In some instances, the animal trickster is made the dupe. The best known of these tales purport to explain why the rabbit has a short tail or the buzzard a bald head. While these tales often seem to be naive explanations for the physical characteristics of different animals in reality they impart useful lessons about African-American moral and social values. In most instances, the tales reveal that the acquisition of the physical characteristics came about as a result of obsessive pride and vanity, or a failure to evaluate the motives of one known to be an adversary.

The didactic intent of African-American origin tales is even more evident in those that involve human actors. Many of these tales, which also originated in slavery, continue to be performed in African-American communities today (Dance 1978, pp. 7–11). The focus is on the development of certain physical features associated with African Americans as a race. For example, the performer purports to explain why African Americans have big feet or hands, nappy hair, black skin, etc. The stories are invariably set at the beginning of time when God, a principal actor in the tales, gave out human traits. African Americans are envisioned as always getting the "worse" characteristics because they arrived late, were playing cards and did not hear God calling them, or were too impatient to wait for God. Despite the humor often evoked in these tales, they speak to African Americans about certain negative patterns of behavior stereotypically associated with the race—

laziness, tardiness, impatience, etc. Rather than being self-deprecating, as some scholars have suggested, these tales attempt in a humorous way to call attention to certain behavioral patterns perceived by some members of the black community as inhibitive to the advancement of African Americans. In addition, they reveal one of the ways in which African Americans have historically attempted to communicate in intragroup contexts the nature and consequences of negative stereotypes of them.

Closely associated with tales of origin is a large group of tales that revolves around the character of "Colored Man" (Dorson 1956, pp. 171–186). These tales often purport to explain the origins of conditions experienced by African Americans in society. From all internal evidence, Colored Man tales are a post-Emancipation invention that thrived in the early and mid–twentieth century. In this group of tales, Colored Man is pitted in a contest with White Man and a member of another racial or cultural group, either Jew or Mexican. In some instances, the three actors are given a task by God, usually involving the selection of packages of different sizes; in others, they are involved in a scheme of their own making. In the former case, Colored Man makes the wrong decision, whether he selects the largest or the smallest package. His choices are most often conceptualized as a result of his greed, his ability to be deceived by appearances of easy gain, his laziness, or even his efforts not to be outsmarted. The tales almost invariably revolve around some stereotype associated with African Americans. By portraying situations in which a generic African American acts out a stereotype, the performers of these tales implicitly call for critical self-examination. On the other hand, by setting these tales at the beginning of time, performers suggest that conditions experienced by African Americans in the present result from systemic sources.

Throughout the twentieth century, African Americans have created and performed folktales that deal realistically with their situation in society. Many function as jokes that revolve around stereotypes. However, these tales function to constantly remind African Americans that one of the most problematic aspects of their existence in American society derives from negative images of them held by other groups. In many of these tales, the African American appears as the dupe of the nonblacks, who use stereotypes to manipulate him into making bad choices. In other tales, African-American performers celebrate certain stereotypical images that seem to allow them to gain an advantage over other groups. This type of narrative usually revolves around sexual stereotypes; blacks triumph over members of other groups because they demonstrate superior sexual prowess or larger sexual organs. In their celebration of an image of self generally evaluated negatively in society, African Americans reveal an interesting ambivalence about such images and possibly a different value orientation.

Besides narrative, other forms of African-American folklore created since Emancipation reveal an intimate concern with intragroup problems and solutions. Of the genres created and performed by African Americans, the BLUES is concerned directly with conditions and situations within the black community. As a body of song, the blues touches on various problematic areas of black life like unemployment, homelessness, sharecropping, police brutality, and economic exploitation (Titon 1977; Keil 1966; Oliver 1963). However, it concentrates primarily on the problems of black male/female relationships. Although the blues celebrates the joys of being in a successful relationship, it most often focuses on the problems involved in sustaining one. These problems often revolve around economic issues, especially the inability of black males to provide for the material well-being of lover, wife, or family.

In the late nineteenth century and the early decades of the twentieth, the blues served as an ongoing commentary on conditions faced by many African Americans. As an expressive form, the blues did not often propose solutions to the problems it identified but rather focused on defining the contours of situations shared by large numbers of African Americans. When the blues did offer a solution, it most often proposed mobility: either moving out of a troubled relationship or moving out of town. It might be suggested that the idea of mobility as a solution to problematic situations often found in the blues simply reflected a solution embraced by thousands of African Americans in the early twentieth century. During the heyday of the blues, African Americans witnessed the migration of thousands from the rural South into urban centers in search of better economic and social conditions (see MIGRATION/POPULATION).

For many African Americans, the blues reflected much about the nature of black culture-building in the early twentieth century. It emerged as the first solo form of musical expression created by African Americans and signaled the growing diversity of the black population. In the midst of the Great Migration and other changes in black life, the blues revealed the difficulty of speaking about a common African-American experience in post-Emancipation America. It envisioned a community beset by various problems of identity, values, and even beliefs arising from mobility as well as economic and social upheaval. Although blues performers spoke from a first-person point of view, their popularity derived

from their ability to use personal experience as a metaphor for shared realities. Despite its popularity with a large segment of the black population, however, the blues was not valued by all members of the community. Due to its association with secular entertainment establishments in which drinking alcohol, dancing, gambling, and often violent crimes occurred, as well as to its often sexually explicit lyrics, it was sometimes strongly disparaged by religious and socially conscious members of the black community.

However, in the early twentieth century, the blues had its expressive and religious counterpart in the emergence of GOSPEL MUSIC (Heilbut 1975; Allen 1991). The development of modern gospel can be attributed to two interrelated influences, which can be conceptualized as, on the one hand, musical and, on the other, social and religious. Although spirituals continued to be performed well after Emancipation, the message of deliverance from bondage and persecution through analogy to Old Testament figures and events lost much of its meaning for freedpeople. In addition, performance of spirituals in the post-Emancipation era was greatly influenced by efforts of some African-American religious leaders to make black religious practices more closely resemble those of white Americans. As a result, many black churches banned the "shout," an important context for spiritual song performance, and began to encourage the singing of European hymns to the neglect of spirituals. At the same time, the emergence of Europeanized arrangements and performances of spirituals proliferated, especially with touring college choirs such as those organized at Fisk University and Hampton Institute. The success of these choirs, as well as the barbershop-quartet craze of the nineteenth century, influenced the organization of hundreds of black harmonizing quartets that sang primarily arranged spirituals.

While these changes in the religious and musical life of African Americans in the South greatly influenced the attitude toward and performance of spirituals, the Great Migration confronted many African Americans with a new lifestyle and environment that threatened their ability to maintain the spiritual values that many had traditionally associated with black religion. In urban areas, many African Americans embraced not only new social and economic patterns but also modes of worship in churches that did not fulfill social and spiritual needs as southern churches had. In both South and North, many African Americans in the late nineteenth and early twentieth centuries turned to the newly developing SPIRITUAL CHURCH MOVEMENT and HOLINESS MOVEMENT and the STOREFRONT CHURCHES that arose to house them. In these churches, many African Americans found patterns of worship more conducive to their religious sensibilities, and an emerging musical style that came to be known as gospel. Unlike the spirituals of enslaved Africans, gospel songs tended to emphasize the New Testament message of love and faith in God as the solutions to human problems. As such, gospel relies less on analogy to Old Testament personalities and events and more on the abstract New Testament promise of rest and reward for the faithful.

In an important sense, gospel, like the blues, envisions a diverse black community, whereas spirituals relied on the existence of a coherent community sharing a single condition: slavery. As such, gospel songs tend to abstract the nature of the problems for which Christian faith provides a solution. In essence, the lyrics of gospel songs seldom identify specific conditions but, instead, speak of burdens, trials, and tribulations and offer faith in God as a solution. In this regard, gospel is genre that gains its meaning in performance. Through performance, its apparent abstract message is concretized in messages delivered as sermons, prayers, and testimonies, which provide numerous illustrations of the situations of which gospel music speaks. Although gospel songs are usually written by individuals and recorded by commercial companies, a development that goes back to the 1920s and 1930s, gospel remains a vernacular form performed in African-American communities in churches and concert halls throughout the United States on a regular basis.

The study of African-American folklore in the twentieth century remains vital. The focus of collection in recent years has turned from the rural South to urban communities in both North and South where viable traditions of African-American oral expressive culture continue to thrive. In the process, folklorists continue to produce important collections of African-American folklore reflective of both historical and contemporary concerns. For example, the toast tradition, which involves the recitation of long narrative poems revolving around the actions of black badmen, has been collected extensively (Jackson 1974; Wepman, Newman, and Binderman 1976). These poems, which have been collected in prisons and on the streets, chronicle the lives of individuals involved in criminal activities and warn of the consequences of their behavior. Although a large number of toast texts have been published, the toast as a genre is not widely known among African Americans. In fact, it seems to be known and performed primarily by individuals who participate in a criminal lifestyle or individuals who have connections with it. While toasts seem to celebrate criminality and the peculiar brand of "badness" associated with it, these poems tend to be highly moralistic and realistic in terms of the consequences of criminal activity. In addition—despite their often offensive language, violent imagery, and seeming disregard for legal and moral authority in the black community and society—toasts give expressive embodiment to behavioral and economic strategies and reflect attitudes embraced by some individuals in African-American communities with regard to drug-dealing, prostitution, gambling, and other so-called victimless crimes.

Although not primarily or exclusively an urban genre, the DOZENS has been the focus of much study in recent years (Abrahams 1970). The dozens is a generic name for a form of verbal artistry known variously in African-American communities as joning, wolfing, busting, breaking, and cracking, and by a host of other names. Although the art of playing the dozens is generally associated with adolescent males, the practice in different ways is one that knows no age limit or gender. Generally speaking, younger males tend to play more often and to rely more on formulaic rhymes and phrases in their performances. Often discussed as verbal exchanges that disparage the mother through implications of sexual impropriety, playing the dozens just as often involves apparent insults to one's opponent. While playing the dozens has been associated with the acquisition of verbal skill, especially among young African-American males, it also serves as an intragroup mechanism for communicating information with negative import for individuals. Regardless of who plays the dozens or how it is played, the content of the exchanges focuses on behaviors that violate certain norms generally accepted by African Americans, whether they relate to sexual activity, personal habits, physical characteristics, modes of dress, etc.

A concern with playing the dozens in recent years has been accompanied by a general focus on other forms of African-American folklore that reveal a rich tradition of verbal play. Forms such as signifying, marking, and loud-talking have been discussed as a reflection of the art of everyday life in African-American communities (Mitchell-Kernan 1972). The artistry of these forms derives from the ability of individuals to encode messages with serious import in humorous and witty forms. In addition, the rise of RAP music, which transforms many African-American expressive forms into a flourishing narrative tradition, reflects the continuing verbal artistry in black communities. Rap, which exists as both a narrative and a musical tradition, reflects a continuing concern in African-American expressive culture with identifying conditions and situations that impact negatively on the black community. Though a diverse group, rap songs frequently point to the need for self-evaluation, criticism, and change in the black community itself without denying the impact of systemic causes for many of the conditions it identifies.

African-American folklore reflects many of the ways in which African Americans have historically communicated their attitudes, beliefs, and values in artistic forms in everyday life. Although the roots of the study of this folklore lie in beliefs about its ultimate demise, the African-American tradition of vernacular creativity and performance remains vital. While the genres that constitute the African-American folk tradition are too numerous to be examined in a short discussion, the basic categories of narrative, song, verbal artistry, and material culture suggest the tradition's contours. With African culture and cultural forms providing the tradition-rich source of African-American folklore, it has been endlessly transformed to both aid and reflect black culture-building in the United States. On an everyday basis, African-American folklore continues to provide individuals with a rich creative outlet for expression and performance.

REFERENCES

ABRAHAMS, ROGER. *Deep Down in the Jungle: Negro Narrative Folklore from the Streets of Philadelphia.* Chicago, 1970.

ALLEN, RAY. *Singing in the Spirit: African-American Sacred Quartets in New York City.* Philadelphia, 1991.

ALLEN, WILLIAM F., CHARLES P. WARE, and LUCY MCKIM GARRISON. *Slave Songs of the United States.* 1867. Reprint. New York, 1951.

BACON, ALICE M., and LEONORA HERRON. "Conjuring and Conjure-Doctors." In Alan Dundes, ed. *Mother Wit from the Laughing Barrel: Readings in the Interpretation of Afro-American Folklore.* Englewood Cliffs, N.J., 1973.

BLASSINGAME, JOHN W. *The Slave Community.* New York, 1972.

DANCE, DARYL C. *Shuckin' and Jivin': Folklore from Contemporary Black America.* Bloomington, Ind., 1978.

DORSON, RICHARD M. *American Negro Folktales.* Greenwich, Conn., 1956.

FELDMANN, SUSAN. *African Myths and Tales.* New York, 1973.

FERRIS, WILLIAM. *Afro-American Art and Crafts.* Boston, 1983.

GENOVESE, EUGENE. *Roll, Jordan, Roll: The World the Slaves Made.* New York, 1976.

HARRIS, JOEL CHANDLER. *Uncle Remus: His Songs and Sayings.* 1881. Reprint. Detroit, 1971.

HEILBUT, TONY. *The Gospel Sound: Good News and Bad Times.* Garden City, N.Y., 1975.

JACKSON, BRUCE. *Get Your Ass in the Water and Swim like Me: Narrative Poetry from Black Oral Tradition.* Cambridge, Mass., 1974.

JOYNER, CHARLES. *Down by the Riverside: A South Carolina Slave Community.* Urbana, Ill., 1984.

KEIL, CHARLES. *Urban Blues.* Chicago, 1966.

LOVELL, JOHN, JR. *Black Song: The Forge and the Flame.* New York, 1972.

MINTZ, SIDNEY W., and RICHARD PRICE. *An Anthropological Approach to the Afro-American Past: A Caribbean Perspective.* Philadelphia, 1972.

MITCHELL-KERNAN, CLAUDIA. "Signifying, Loud-Talking, and Marking." In Thomas Kochman, ed., *Rappin' and Stylin' Out.* Urbana, Ill., 1972.

OLIVER, PAUL. *The Meaning of the Blues.* New York, 1963.

ROBERTS, JOHN W. *From Trickster to Badman: The Black Folk Hero in Slavery and Freedom.* Philadelphia, 1989.

SNEAD, JAMES. "Repetition as a Figure in Black Culture." In Henry Louis Gates, Jr., ed. *Black Literature and Literary Theory.* New York, 1984, pp. 59–80.

TITON, JEFF TODD. *Early Downhome Blues: A Musical and Cultural Analysis.* Urbana, Ill., 1977.

WEPMAN, DENNIS, RONALD B. NEWMAN, and MURRAY B. BINDERMAN. *The Life: The Lore and Folk Poetry of the Black Hustler.* Philadelphia, 1976.

JOHN W. ROBERTS

Folk Medicine.   Folk medicine has been a significant feature of the cultural and social heritage of African Americans since colonial times. Its origins trace back to traditions brought to the New World by slaves. African-based religious and medical customs were often closely intertwined, reflecting an effort to understand relationships between metaphysical and physical phenomena and to apply this knowledge in promoting the health and well-being of an individual or community. "Root doctor" is perhaps the best-known type of folk practitioner. Other types include "witch doctor," "hoodoo doctor," and "voodoo doctor." While the practice of folk medicine involves a complex, eclectic array of belief systems and therapies, the most common ingredient is a combination of incantations (the spiritual element) and herbal concoctions (the physical element).

Prior to Emancipation, planters tolerated and sometimes encouraged folk practice in order to save the expense of hiring white practitioners to treat slaves. Thus, a special class of folk practitioner evolved within the slave community. A number of these practitioners were women, the so-called "Negro doctoresses," entrusted with health-care responsibilities ranging from midwifery to minor surgery and the preparation and dispensing of medicines.

After Emancipation, folk practitioners were confronted by two major obstacles. The first concerned developments in modern medicine, particularly the evolving notion of disease as a largely physical process involving specific tissues and organs, and distinct from religious or spiritual traditions. Second, mainstream practitioners erected legal, educational, and other hurdles as part of the effort to increase professionalization of the field and to reduce competition from those using alternative approaches. The mainstream medical press highlighted instances of alleged malpractice by "unqualified" folk practitioners. In 1899, for example, the *Journal of the American Medical Association* noted: "A colored 'voodoo doctor' . . . was put on trial for manslaughter during the past week. In a raid of the man's house by the police, there was found a weird collection of things, including animal remains, herbs, charms, and medicines."

Despite such pressures, folk practices continued to play a significant role in health care in the twentieth century. Deeply rooted in cultural experience, they provided options for those whose access to health care was otherwise limited. Tensions between folk practitioners and advocates of "community standards" in religious and health practice persist, as in legal actions in Florida, for example, against the Santeria cult for violation of animal-sacrifice statutes during the late 1980s and early 1990s. A common thread that links these worlds—the promotion and preservation of health—is often buried under disputes over philosophy and methodology. Nevertheless, connections occur in unexpected ways, especially within the African-American community, where folk traditions run deep. Numa Pompilius Garfield Adams, a graduate of Rush Medical College (1924) and the first African-American dean of the Howard Medical School, always acknowledged the influence of his grandmother, Mrs. Amanda Adams, in his choice of a career. Mrs. Adams, a folk practitioner and midwife in rural Virginia, had introduced him as a child to the therapeutic properties of herbs.

REFERENCES

Hurston, Zora Neale. *Mules and Men.* 1935. Reprint. Bloomington, Ind., 1978.

Journal of the American Medical Association 33 (December 16, 1899): 1559.

Puckett, Newbell Niles. *Folk Beliefs of the Southern Negro.* 1926. Reprint. Montclair, N.J., 1968.

Watson, Wilbur H. *Black Folk Medicine: The Therapeutic Significance of Faith and Trust.* New Brunswick, N.J., 1984.

KENNETH R. MANNING

Folk Music. African-American folk music embraces sacred songs known as spirituals and many kinds of secular music, both vocal and instrumental. These include work songs that regulated the rate of work, street cries, field "hollers" that enabled workers to communicate over long distances, lullabies, and various kinds of dance music—all known before the Civil War. The musical elements that characterized African music described by European traders in the early seventeenth century were common in African-American folk music.

Africans did not arrive in the New World culturally naked, despite many statements to that effect. Historians and anthropologists now agree that many elements of African culture converged with surrounding European influences to form a new African-American culture. In their free time, blacks continued to perform the songs and dances they had had in Africa. Early contemporary descriptions depicted the same musical elements previously described in Africa: polyrhythms; a strained, rasping vocal quality; variable pitches; singing accompanied by bodily movement in which everyone participated; and the extremely common call-and-response form of singing, in which leader and chorus overlapped. African instruments also came to the New World: drums, banjo, a kind of flute, and the balafo, a kind of xylophone. Improvised satiric or derisive singing was used to regulate the rate of work in rowing, grinding grain, and harvesting, in both Africa and the Americas. Strong rhythms were accentuated by stamping, hand-clapping, and other percussive devices. Although European music shared some of these elements, contemporary observers emphasized the exotic qualities, not the similarities that were later cited erroneously as evidence of European origin. Until the invention of sound recording, the only means of preserving music was transcription into a notational system designed for European forms. In the process, many distinctive elements were lost, and what was transcribed *looked* like European music. Performance style and sound could not be captured, but until the mid-twentieth century, musicians tended to regard transcription as the equivalent of the music as it was performed.

African instruments reached the New World through the practice, common in the slave trade, of providing instruments aboard slave ships to encourage singing and dancing, a recognized means of combating depression, suicide, and revolt. As early as 1693, a slaving captain reported that music and dance provided exercise in a limited space, raising the captives' spirits. Some captains collected African instruments before sailing, thus transmitting African instruments to the New World.

When the Africans landed, concern for the continued health of their new possessions led some plantation owners to make efforts to acclimate them gradually to their new circumstances. Contemporary accounts describe the welcome of the new arrivals by older slaves, who sang and danced with them in a style characterized by Europeans as "exotic" or "barbaric."

African instruments were described in the West Indies from the mid-seventeenth century, but reports from the mainland came later because of the relatively small number of blacks there until the mid-eighteenth century. As early as February 18, 1755, the *Virginia Gazette* printed an advertisement for a runaway slave who played well on the "Banjar," while Thomas Jefferson in his *Notes on the State of Virginia* (1781) described the "banjar, which they [blacks] brought hither from Africa."

The official report of the Stono, S.C., slave revolt of 1739 described "dancing, Singing and beating Drums" as the means used by the rebels to attract more blacks to their ranks. An African drum from Virginia was purchased in 1753 by the British Museum, where it remains today. In many mainland colonies the playing of drums or other loud instruments, being forbidden by law, was surreptitious, but drum-making continued; as late as the 1930s, it was observed in Georgia by Federal Writers' Project interviewers. In place of drums, other percussive devices were used to provide rhythmic support for singing and dancing—stamping, hand-clapping, and the less threatening sound of the banjo.

An African xylophone, the balafo (or barrafou), was reported in Virginia in 1775 by a schoolmaster, John Harrower, in his *Journal,* and in a news item in Purdie's Williamsburg *Virginia Gazette* in 1776. Blacks also learned to play European instruments such as the fiddle, the French horn, and the flute. As early as the 1690s, Accomack County records in Virginia reported a court case involving a slave fiddler. During the eighteenth century, reports of blacks fiddling for white dances were common, an indication of the progress of acculturation.

Most of the music blacks played for the dancing of whites consisted of conventional European country dances and minuets, but reports from the eighteenth century also described whites dancing "Negro jigs" as a change from the more formal dances. Published versions of these "jigs" show few African characteristics; how the music sounded in performance is conjectural.

With the beginning of evangelical efforts to convert blacks to Christianity in the mid-eighteenth century, reports of African dancing became less frequent except in New Orleans, where such activities continued into the nineteenth century in a specially designated area called Place Congo.

From a musical point of view, the characteristics of sacred and secular music were similar. In many instances, songs regulating work in the fields or on the water that originally had secular words were adapted to sacred texts when the singers joined churches that proscribed secular songs.

Learning to play European instruments and to sing Protestant hymns was part of a process of accultur-

Josh White (right), with bass player. (Photographs and Prints Division, Schomburg Center for Research in Black Culture, The New York Public Library, Astor, Lenox and Tilden Foundations)

ation, along with learning the English language and the ways of the white captors. But African ways were not forgotten. Even though new arrivals from Africa virtually stopped in 1808, many old customs persisted in secret, rarely witnessed by the whites who were the primary source of contemporary reports. Political and social pressures also influenced these nineteenth-century accounts, tending to divide them into two patterns: either to describe the singing and dancing as proof that the slaves were happy, or to deny that the slaves had any secular music, depicting them as singing only hymns. Pro-slavery arguments and the minstrel-theater tradition fit into the first pattern, while the abolitionists tended to the latter. Neither pattern conformed fully to reality. Contemporary accounts of slaves singing and dancing demonstrate beyond dispute that increasingly acculturated secular music and dance continued without interruption, despite the undeniable suffering of the slaves.

Songs to regulate the rate of work in Africa were easily adapted to the fields of the New World for planting, cultivating, and harvesting crops, whether they were sugar, rice, indigo, corn, tobacco, or cotton. These songs frequently were a dialogue between a leader and a chorus, although the chorus could play a relatively minor role in providing a rhythmic background. Later, such songs were adapted to the pace of railroad gangs for laying track. This kind of singing was observed in southern prison camps, where isolation and long association led to a higher development of the relation between leader and chorus.

Incredible as it seems, a belief that blacks had no secular music coexisted with the immense popularity of the white minstrel theater, which, initially at least, purported to show plantation life. The early shows were relatively simple, and it is not known how much the early minstrels knew of slavery. Dan Emmett, the reputed composer of "Dixie," had toured the southern states in a circus, but the extent of his contact with blacks is unknown. Little has been written about black secular folk music in the post–Civil War era, but it must have thrived to have produced a generation of talented black performers who themselves played in minstrel shows and popular theater.

Another form of improvised folk music was the BLUES. Its origins are obscure, but blues probably developed among rural blacks during Reconstruction. In contrast to the spiritual, which was usually a group performance with solo and chorus alternating, the blues was a solitary expression of loneliness and misery. It incorporated some elements of the so-called field holler and the gapped scales, blue notes, and syncopation of African music. As improvised utterances, the earliest blues songs were never written down and were lost. By the time blues achieved publication and recording, it had become to some extent professional.

Collections of black folk songs, as distinct from spirituals, began to be published after World War I. Natalie Curtis Burlin edited the *Hampton Series of Negro Folk Songs* (1918–1919), based on the singing of students at the Hampton Institute. Camille Nickerson of New Orleans specialized in Creole French folk songs. John Wesley WORK III produced an important collection, *American Negro Songs and Spirituals,* in 1940. A very different collection was Lawrence Gellert's *Negro Songs of Protest* (1936), described as "the living voice of the otherwise inarticulate resentment against injustice." Initially, such songs were received with suspicion as reflecting an outside political motivation, but the civil rights struggle of the 1960s testified to their legitimacy.

The civil rights movement, beginning with the Montgomery, Ala., bus boycott in December 1955, produced a group of songs that played a more important role in a political and social movement than any since the antislavery songs of a century earlier. "We Shall Overcome," based at least in part on a spiritual, "No More Auction Block for Me," was only the most famous of the freedom songs that inspired and inspirited a great movement.

In southern Louisiana, French-speaking blacks had made their own music for many years, unnoticed by the world outside. Only in the post–World War II period did the whole country become aware of it, largely through sound recordings. Zydeco, as it is called, has not been much published, for little has been written down, but it has become known through recordings.

No form of popular music in the United States, commercial or noncommercial, has remained uninfluenced by black folk music—its rhythmic drive, syncopated beat, gapped scales, and blue notes. The potency of this influence is now worldwide.

In the era after the Civil War, SPIRITUALS became the dominant form of black music in the thinking of the general public, both in Europe and in North America, since many writers denied the existence of black secular folk music. This misconception was due in part to the influence among many blacks of religious sects that denounced secular music and dancing as sinful. The many reports of blacks who refused to participate in dancing or to sing anything but sacred songs, persuaded many whites outside the South that blacks had no secular music.

The origins of the spiritual are still uncertain. Conversion of the slaves to Christianity proceeded very slowly in the eighteenth century because of the opposition of some slave owners, who worried that baptism might interfere with work or even lead to freedom. Moreover, missionaries were few and plantations far apart. Gradually, ministers took an interest in converting slaves, who learned European psalms and hymns with alacrity. At the beginning of the nineteenth century, the camp-meeting movement brought whites and blacks together in large, emotional crowds where mutual influence in styles of singing was unavoidable. It is likely that a blending of African performance style with Protestant hymnody grew out of these encounters. The public in the North first became aware of spirituals through the concert tours in the 1870s of the FISK JUBILEE SINGERS and other groups, such as the Hampton Singers.

Among very pious slaves, the only form of dancing permitted was the "shout," or holy dance, performed after a church service. Witnesses described it as a circle dance in which the legs were not crossed, while the feet edged backward and forward or right and left, without being lifted from the floor. Music was provided by a separate group of singers who "based" the dancing with "shout" songs or "running" spirituals (Epstein 1977, pp. 278–287).

REFERENCES

ALLEN, WILLIAM FRANCIS, CHARLES PICKARD WARE, and LUCY MCKIM GARRISON. *Slave Songs of the United States.* New York, 1867.

COURLANDER, HAROLD. *Negro Folk Music, U.S.A.* New York, 1963.

EPSTEIN, DENA J. *Sinful Tunes and Spirituals: Black Folk Music to the Civil War.* Urbana, Ill., 1977.

KREHBIEL, HENRY EDWARD. *Afro-American Folksongs: A Study in Racial and National Music.* New York, 1914.

DENA J. EPSTEIN

Folk Religion. The folk religious traditions of blacks in the United States have roots in a number of sources, but it is their African origins that have left the most indelible and distinctive cultural imprint. Of the 400,000 Africans who were held in bondage on the North American mainland during the SLAVE TRADE, most if not all were influenced by some indigenous philosophical or sacred system for understanding and interpreting the world. Religion for Africans, however, was more a way of life than a system of creeds and doctrines. The African religious experience allowed for meaningful relations between members of the human community and personal interaction with the world of ancestors, spirits, and divinities, who closely guided mortal existence and provided their adherents with explanations and protections within the realm of earthly affairs. African religions, although differing according to their national origins, provided an overall theological perspective in which spirituality was infused into every aspect of life.

In the colonies, Africans came into contact for the first time with the customs and cultures of white Europeans and Native Americans. Although strange and unfamiliar, the perspectives of these groups did share certain aspects, particularly in the realm of beliefs surrounding the supernatural. Both whites and Indians had worldviews that encompassed mythical perceptions of the universe and powers that pervaded human life and nature. Spiritual beings, holy objects, and the workings of the enchanted world were thought to be powerful and efficacious. Evil and misfortune were perceived as personalized agents of affliction.

Such beliefs were expressed, for the most part, in folklore and legend. Africans themselves had corresponding ideas concerning the supernatural that included sacred entities, charms, and places—although it is difficult to disengage these beliefs from their primary religious framework. We can speculate that from their initial periods of contact, blacks, whites, and Indians exchanged and adopted compatible ideas and visions of the world, each group drawing from the cultures of the others.

It was during the colonial era that enslaved Africans were first exposed to Christian missionary activity, although up to the mid–eighteenth century few blacks were actually converted. Evangelical revivalism, exploding among white Americans in the early national period, had a significant impact on blacks. Adopting their own interpretations and understandings of the message of the Christian faith, black preachers and laypersons developed unique and creative styles of religious devotion. It is here that one of the prominent strands of African-American folk religion developed.

African-American religion, however, was characterized by diversity from the start. Scattered references to the activity of "sorcerers," "doctors," and "conjurers" from the 1700s and early 1800s indicate that black religious beliefs were miltifaceted. Traditional African spirituality recognized the roles of individuals who were sacred practitioners, diviners, and healers, dynamic intermediaries between the unseen realm of spirits and the world of the living. Although they had been separated from the structures and institutions of their national homelands, African specialists recreated aspects of their religious identities within New World environments. Adapting their native beliefs and practices to the American context, these early black practitioners formed yet another thread in the evolving tapestry of African-American religion.

By the antebellum era, the second generation of blacks born in the United States had developed an indigenous culture. Although the overseas slave trade was declared illegal by 1808, most black Americans in the mid–nineteenth century had some knowledge or acquaintance with recently arrived or native-born Africans who recalled the traditions and ways of their homeland. To the American-born slaves, these Africans represented the presence and mystery of a powerful sacred past. While some blacks converted to Christianity and a few adhered to Islam, others maintained the beliefs of their forebears through their observance of modified African ceremonies. Accordingly, the religion of slaves consisted of widely differing innovations of traditions and beliefs.

African-American folk religion thus emerged as a composite creation, drawn from scattered elements of older cultural memories and grafted New World traditions which were later passed on from generation to generation. An "invisible institution," the folk Christianity of the slave quarters developed as a religion of the vernacular. As a community, slaves prayed, sang, "shouted," and preached to one another in the manner and styles reminiscent of their African heritage. The emphasis on the verbal medium in performance generated the distinctive vocal traditions that became characteristic of African-American liturgy, including the inventive oral repertory of chanted sermon and song.

Other traditions made real the power and presence of the supernatural in human life. Belief in a variety of mysterious beings, including hags, witches, and ghosts, suggests that for many African Americans the spiritual world was alive and immediate, active with forces ominous and threatening. Sacred folk beliefs were derived from Old and New World sources: local variations of Haitian-derived vodun (see VOO-DOO), the interpretation of signs, the usage of charms, and the mystical knowledge of conjurers, root workers, and hoodoo practitioners, who tapped supernatural forces for prediction and protection. Although many of these traditions were deeply embedded in black folklore, they reflected viable perspectives on spirituality, the need for control and explanation that leads to religious thought.

Healing, another prominent dimension of African-American folk religion, was practiced by specialists who combined knowledge of traditional remedies with holistic therapy. As in Africa, the onset of sickness was understood by many blacks to have both physical and spiritual implications. Folk religion undergirded African-American faith in skilled practitioners who were able to counteract ailments with herbal and natural medicines, as well as techniques such as prayer. Folk beliefs also offered a theory of explanation for why such afflictions might occur. For example, illness was often thought to be caused by negative spiritual forces. In the early twentieth century, some of these latter impulses would find their way into sectarian Christianity, within groups like the HOLINESS MOVEMENT, and PENTECOSTALISM, churches that emphasized faith healing and physical wholeness through spiritual power.

With the drastic demographic shifts and movements in black life during the late nineteenth and early twentieth centuries, from South to North and from countryside to city, African-American folk religion took on a broader significance. The "old-time" revivalist traditions of worship in the rural churches would no longer be restricted to the South, as thousands of migrants made their way to northern urban areas. Relocating in search of new prospects and new lives, they brought their local traditions and beliefs with them, establishing new religious institutions within storefronts and homes (see STOREFRONT CHURCHES). Many of these transplanted folk churches recalled features of African religion, especially the emphasis on emotional styles of worship, call and response, spirituals, and Holy Ghost spirit possession.

The folk religion of blacks also lived on in noninstitutionalized forms within urban centers. African-American conjurers, healers, and other specialists underwent a metamorphosis, some reemerging as leaders within the so-called cults and sects of the cit-ies, and others setting up within occult shops and botanicas as spiritual advisers. This vast network of urban practitioners attracted devotees from diverse religious backgrounds, including members of the mainstream Christian denominations, who found in these traditions resolution and assistance for day-to-day concerns.

Although black folk religion continues to be varied and eclectic in its manifestations, it demonstrates a common orientation toward spirituality that is dynamic, experimental, and intensely pragmatic. Characterized by pluralism, folk beliefs fulfill diverse needs and functions that cut across doctrinal barriers and creedal differences. They constitute a way of life that is at the heart of the African-American religious experience.

REFERENCES

FAUSET, ARTHUR HUFF. *Black Gods of the Metropolis: Negro Cults in the Urban North*. Philadelphia, 1944.
HURSTON, ZORA NEALE. *The Sanctified Church*. Berkeley, Calif., 1981.
LEVINE, LAWRENCE. *Black Culture and Black Consciousness: Afro-American Folk Thought from Slavery to Freedom*. New York, 1977.
PUCKETT, NEWBELL NILES. *Folk Beliefs of the Southern Negro*. Chapel Hill, N.C., 1926.
RABOTEAU, ALBERT J. *Slave Religion: The Invisible Institution in the Antebellum South*. New York, 1978.

YVONNE P. CHIREAU

Food.   African-American cooking is in many ways inseparable from both African and southern traditions, with considerable cross-influence from black and white food customs on both continents. The West African diet was dominated by starches such as rice, cassava, and yams, as well as by coconut, kidney beans, black-eyed peas, and other nuts and beans. Fruits and vegetables native to Africa included watermelon and okra, and many West Africans supplied their need for protein with eggs, goats, chicken, and fish. African slaves brought many of these foods to the New World and combined them with beef, pork, corn, potatoes, and other foods found here, which they transformed through African methods of harvesting, preparing, and cooking. The result was a uniquely African-American cuisine that came to be known as "soul food." Slaves cooked most of the food their owners ate, introducing many African and African-American foods and cooking styles into southern white culture. However, the slaves themselves were forced to develop their diets from the castoffs of those meals. Africans had traditionally utilized all edible parts of both plants and animals, and this cultural knowledge became necessary for survival in the United States.

There came to be profound regional differences in African-American cooking styles. The Chesapeake Bay's rich supply of crab encouraged cooks in the region to develop numerous specialties, while the ease of cultivating rice in the Carolina lowlands made that grain a staple there. Shrimp was largely limited to coastal regions such as the New Orleans area, where there was a complex interaction between French, Spanish, African-American, and Native-American cultures; the result was CREOLE and cajun cuisines characterized by rich, spicy foods such as gumbo and jambalaya.

There have been important changes in black cooking over time. During the Great Migration to the cities of the North (see MIGRATION/POPULATION), African Americans brought along their foods and cooking methods, preserving them with the help of markets specializing in black foods, soul food restaurants, and, of course, in family kitchens. The availability of fresh, frozen, or prepackaged foods has largely effaced whatever distinctions existed between northern and southern soul food, or between different styles of southern cooking.

In precolonial and colonial West Africa, beef was rarely eaten. Instead, chicken, goat, and fish were the primary animal foods, often cooked in soups or stews, or over an open flame. In contrast, African Americans often fried meat, a European practice that perhaps derived from the need to preserve dishes for hours without refrigeration. The extreme heat of the southern United States thus helps explain the popularity of fried chicken, often packed in a shoe box for carrying on long journeys. Despite the fact that chicken has been a part of the American diet since the seventeenth century, fried chicken did not become a popular dish until the mid-nineteenth century. Well into the twentieth century, chicken was considered something special and was served only on Sunday—hence the habit of calling a breakfast meal of grits and chicken "Sunday breakdown." In other parts of the South, blacks sometimes referred to chicken as the "preacher's bird" because it was often served to visiting preachers. Fried chicken is often associated through a common stereotype with American blacks who as slaves were sometimes allowed to raise their own chickens. Actually it was a popular dish among all southerners and it quickly became a favored dish throughout the entire United States. Even in the South, there is more than one way to fry a chicken, although coating the chicken parts with flour or batter, and then cooking them in a heavy iron skillet with bacon grease or lard is the most distinctly southern method. Fried chicken is sometimes served "smothered" in a gravy made from flour and the remnants of the frying, often with bits of the chicken gizzard or giblet added.

Until the price of beef began to fall during the twentieth century, pork was the most common meat in African-American diets. All of the pig was used, including the stomach or maw, thighs or hocks, snout, ears, ribs, feet, and tail—"everything but the oink," according to a popular saying. One of the best known African-American pork dishes, chitterlings or "chitlins," are the small intestines of the pig, prepared by boiling and then frying them. Chitterlings were sometimes called "Kentucky oysters," in an attempt to obscure their humble origins. African Americans and white Southerners also eat the entire leg of the pig, in particular the ham hocks. A special dish on New Year's Eve—intended to bring good luck in the coming year—is boiled and seasoned pig's feet. Pig fat was often used for seasoning and as a cooking oil in traditional African-American cooking, but the emphasis in recent decades on decreasing the amount of fat in the American diet has reduced the use of lard, which is rendered fatback grease, and "cracklins"—the fried, crispy residue of pork fat.

Game animals were also popular among African Americans, and included deer, bear, geese, woodcock, pigeons, and squirrels, as well as two nocturnal creatures, the raccoon and the oppossum. A dish of raccoon seasoned with gin and served with mashed potatoes was called "drunk coon" by Louisiana blacks. Oppossum or 'possum, which has all but disappeared from tables, was once eaten stewed or roasted. Reptiles eaten in rural southern communities included snakes and alligators.

Depending on the proximity of waterways, fish was an important part of early African-American diet. Meat or chicken could be expensive to buy and inconvenient, laborious, or prohibited to raise, but slaves could easily fashion inexpensive fishing rods and catch their own fish. Fried butterfish, catfish, and porgies served as the centerpiece of the weekend or holiday gathering known as the neighborhood fish fry. In the 1990s the fish sandwich, served with hot sauce and a slice of white bread, remains a popular dish in African-American communities. Less popular is turtle, also known in the South as "cooter," from the Kongolese "nkuda"; both the green turtle and the various species of snapping turtles are used in stews and soups.

Another important public meal is the barbecue, a method of cooking food over an open flame. The word barbecue, or "bar-b-q," originates from the Spanish or Haitian Creole word "barbacoa," meaning framework of sticks, and was used in America as early as 1709. Africans had a history of cooking food outdoors on a spit over a fire. In West Africa, fish, goat, and chicken were roasted and served with a spicy sauce on the side rather than being basted during cooking. Both methods are traditional in African-American communities, and recipes for barbecue sauce are fiercely guarded. Among African-Americans and white southerners, the wood "barbecue" most often refers to barbecued pork, particularly ribs, but chicken and beef are also cooked in this fashion.

African Americans are often credited with making fruits and vegetables a more central part of American cooking. As with meats, they tended to use all parts of plant foods, introducing the practice of eating "greens" into American cuisine. Slaves ate the leaves of turnips, sweet potatoes, and yams, in addition to collard and mustard greens, simmering them with oil, peppers, and spices to be eaten alone or added to sauces. The liquid left over from cooked greens is known as potlikker, sometimes as "pot liquor." It is often served alone as a soup or used as a dipping broth for bread.

Since plantation owners provided slaves with corn more frequently than any other food, corn was a staple of early African-American diets. With typical resourcefulness, early African Americans found many uses for the plant through various methods of processing and cooking corn. Cornbread, rather than bread made of wheat or other grains, was a staple of African-American meals. Hominy, a corn product made from bleached and hulled kernels of corn, is first mentioned in the early seventeenth century as an ingredient for porridge, and became popular among slaves who used it to make the cereal or side dish known as grits. A traditional southern dish, grits are still served as they were in the nineteenth century—as a breakfast food, boiled and served with a generous dollop of butter. Another product of the corn plant, cornmeal, provided slaves with the basis for many forms of breads, including hoe-cakes, which were made from a paste of cornmeal and water placed on the blade of a hoe and held over a fire until it solidified. This batter was also rolled into balls and deep-fried with onions and spices to form hush puppies, traditionally served with fried fish. Lore has it that these balls of dough were originally made as scraps to appease dogs who whined with hunger when they smelled food cooking. Corn pone, often eaten after being dunked into potlikker, derives from an Indian bread made with cornmeal, water, and salt.

Blacks also ate many varieties of the peas, beans, and nuts which they had eaten in Africa; in some cases they brought these to the United States, kidney beans, lima beans, and pigeon peas among them. Most varieties were prepared by simmering the beans slowly with a piece of meat for flavor. Black-eyed peas (also known as cowpeas), a plant native to Africa, are not actually peas, but beans. They are frequently eaten in "Hoppin' John," a mixture of rice and black-eyed peas traditionally eaten on New Year's Day for good luck. Peanuts are indigenous to South America, but it was not until the arrival of slaves from Portugal's African colonies, where the nuts were propagated, that peanuts appeared in North America. An African-American slang word for peanut, "goober," derives from a West African word for the nut. Peanuts are used in a variety of ways by African Americans including peanut pie and peanut soup, a variation of which is sometimes called Tuskegee soup after its inventor, George Washington CARVER.

Rice formed a crucial part of the African-American diet in the Carolinas, particularly because of the ease of cultivation there. Although African slaves were not responsible for the introduction of rice into the New World, their experience with raising rice in Africa is said to have made the successful, large-scale cultivation of the crop possible throughout the Carolina lowlands and the Gulf Coast. In Louisiana, the leftover hambone from a Sunday dinner was used to flavor the traditional Monday meal of red beans and rice, sometimes made with kidney beans.

The okra plant originated in West Africa and became a staple of southern diet, either fried or boiled. Its best-known use is in gumbo, which can be traced to seventeenth-century Africa; the recipe called for the okra to be boiled, drained, and mixed with shrimp, onions, spices, and other vegetables. While gumbo is commonly associated with Louisiana cuisine, okra itself is a popular food throughout the southern states.

Another staple of the early African-American diet was the sweet potato or yam. There are actually two varieties of sweet potato, both of which are native to North America. The yam is a third, distinct plant, found almost solely in Africa, which lent its name to the American sweet potato because slaves called the latter by various related African words meaning "to eat," including the Gullah *njam*. Sweet potatoes are cooked in a variety of ways—roasting, boiling, frying, baking. Sweet potatoes also provide a starchy raw material for breads, pies, and cakes. Sweet-potato pie is still a popular southern dessert and is very similar to pumpkin pie, which it often replaces at the Thanksgiving table.

In addition to sweet-potato pie, there are many typical African-American desserts often sweetened with molasses, including pralines and shortening bread. Another traditional dessert, but only during the summer, is watermelon, which is native to Africa and was brought to the New World by slaves. The watermelon, also known as "August ham," was so popular among slaves that slaves became derogatorily as "watermelons," a tenacious racist slur that persists into the 1990s.

Perhaps the most significant development in African-American cooking in the twentieth century has been the rise of a commercial market. For decades, numerous companies have produced canned or frozen African-American foods, and northern cities have seen the establishment of many world-famous soul food restaurants, including Sylvia's in New York. Many African-American chefs are among the nation's most renowned: Patrick Clark at the Cafe Luxembourg in New York, Leah Chase of Dooky Chase Restaurant in New Orleans, Carlisle Frazier at New York's Le Perigord, John Harrison at Bookbinder's in Philadelphia, and Edna Lewis of Gage and Tollner's in Brooklyn, N.Y. These are among the black chefs who have achieved prominence not only in soul food restaurants, but in hotel restaurants, grand French cafés, and even in the White House.

African-American cooking, which has remained relatively constant even through the enormous social changes of emancipation and urbanization, has continued to embrace other foods and cooking styles of African descent. Of particular importance have been the Ethiopian, West African, and West Indian cooking traditions that have become popular as changes in immigration patterns have brought huge numbers of immigrants from the Caribbean and Africa into the larger African-American community of the United States.

REFERENCES

HARRIS, JESSICA B. *Iron Pots and Wooden Spoons: African Gifts to New World Cooking.* New York, 1989.

KAISER, INEZ. *Soul Food Cookery.* New York, 1968.

MARIANI, JOHN F. *The Dictionary of American Food and Drink.* New York, 1983.

MENDES, HELEN. *The African Heritage Cookbook.* New York, 1971.

PIERSEN, WILLIAM DILLON. *Black Legacy: America's Hidden Heritage.* Amherst, Mass., 1993.

KENYA DILDAY

JONATHAN GILL

Football. American-style, intercollegiate football emerged from the English sport of rugby during the 1870s and 1880s. Almost immediately, African Americans distinguished themselves on college gridirons.

Black Pioneers at Predominantly White Colleges, 1889–1919

William Henry LEWIS and William Tecumseh Sherman Jackson were two of the first blacks to play football at a predominantly white college. Both of these Virginians played for Amherst College from 1889 through 1891. Jackson was a running back, while Lewis was a blocker. In 1891 Lewis served as captain of the Amherst squad. After graduation, he attended Harvard Law School, and because of the lax eligibility rules of the time, played two years for Harvard. In 1892 and 1893, Yale coach Walter Camp named Lewis to the Collier's All-American team at the position of center. After his playing days, Lewis became an offensive line coach at Harvard, the first black coach at a predominantly white college. He left football when President William Howard Taft appointed him as United States Assistant Attorney General in 1903.

William Arthur Johnson, George Jewett, and George Flippin were other early black players. Johnson appeared as a running back for MIT in 1890. That same year, Jewett played running back, punter, and field-goal kicker for the University of Michigan. Flippin, who played running back for the University of Nebraska from 1892 to 1893, was an intense athlete who would not tolerate foul play. The press reported that in one game he "was kicked, slugged, and jumped on, but never knocked out, and gave as good as he received." Flippin went on to become a physician. Other African Americans who played in the 1890s included Charles Cook (Cornell), Howard J. Lee (Harvard), George Chadwell (Williams), William Washington (Oberlin), and Alton Washington (Northwestern).

After the turn of the century, numerous blacks played football for northern and midwestern schools. Two of the most talented stars were Edward B. Gray of Amherst and Robert Marshall of the University of Minnesota. A halfback and defensive end, Gray earned selection to Camp's All-American third team in 1906. Marshall was another skillful end and field-goal kicker who played from 1903 to 1906. In 1904, Minnesota defeated Grinnell College 146–0. Marshall scored 72 points in that contest, a record that still stands. He was named to the second All-American team in 1905 and 1906.

As intercollegiate football gained in popularity during World War I, two black players won national acclaim. Frederick Douglass "Fritz" Pollard entered Brown University in 1915. By mid-season, the 5'6" freshman had excelled as a kicker, runner, and defensive back. He helped take his team to the second Rose Bowl game in 1916, a 14–0 loss to Washington State. The following year also proved successful. Pollard starred in games against Rutgers, Harvard, and Yale, scoring two touchdowns in each contest. In naming Pollard to the All-American team in 1916, Walter Camp described him as "the most elusive back of the year, or any year. He is a good sprinter and once loose is a veritable will-o'-the-wisp that no one can lay hands on."

The son of a Presbyterian minister, Paul ROBESON of Princeton, N.J., enrolled at Rutgers University in 1915 on an academic scholarship. Tall and rugged (6'3", 225 pounds), he played tackle and guard as a freshman and sophomore. In his final two seasons he was switched to end, where he gained All-American honors. Walter Camp described him in 1918 as "the greatest defensive end who ever trod a gridiron." Besides football, Robeson lettered in track, baseball, and basketball. He also excelled academically, earning election to Phi Beta Kappa. Although he was excluded from the college glee club for racial reasons, he was named to Cap and Skull, a senior society composed of four men "who most truly and fully represent the finest ideals and traditions of Rutgers." After graduation, he played professional football to finance his way through Columbia Law School. He also began an acting and singing career which brought him international recognition.

Almost all of the pioneer African-American players experienced both subtle and overt forms of discrimination. Pollard was forced to enroll at several universities before he found one willing to let him play football. Often black players were left off their squads at the request of segregated opponents. And football, a violent game at best, provided ample opportunities for players to vent racial animosities at black players. Paul Robeson, for example, suffered a broken nose and a dislocated shoulder as a result of deliberately brutal tactics by opposing players. Despite the drawbacks, there probably was no venue of major sporting competition of the era that had as few impediments to black participation as major collegiate football.

Pioneers at Black Colleges, 1889–1919

The first football game between black colleges occurred in North Carolina in 1892 when Biddle defeated Livingstone, 4–0. Owing to inadequate funding, it took nearly two decades for most black colleges to establish football programs. On New Year's Day in 1897, as a forerunner of the bowl games, Atlanta University and Tuskegee Institute met in what was billed as a "championship game." But major rivalries eventually developed between Fisk and Meharry in Tennessee, Livingstone and Biddle in North Carolina, Tuskegee and Talladega in Alabama, Atlanta University and Atlanta Baptist (Morehouse), and Virginia Union and Virginia State. By 1912, Howard and Lincoln in Pennsylvania, Hampton in Virginia, and Shaw in North Carolina had organized the Colored (later Central) Intercollegiate Athletic Association (CIAA).

The black press began to select All-American teams in 1911. Two of the players on that first team were Edward B. Gray, a running back from Howard who had played the same position from 1906 to 1908 at Amherst, and Leslie Pollard, older brother of Fritz, who had played halfback for one year at Dartmouth before resuming his career at Lincoln University. Two other standout athletes who played for black colleges were Floyd Wellman "Terrible" Terry of Talladega and Henry E. Barco of Virginia Union.

Pioneers: Black Professionals, 1889–1919

Charles Follis of Wooster, Ohio, is credited with being the first African-American professional football player. He was recruited by the Shelby, Ohio, Athletic Club, where he played professionally from 1902 to 1906. One of his teammates during the first two years was Branch Rickey, who would, as general manager and president of the Brooklyn Dodgers in 1947, desegregate major league baseball by signing Jackie ROBINSON. A darting halfback, Follis often experienced insults and dirty play. In one game in 1905 the Toledo captain urged fans to refrain from calling Follis a "nigger." By 1906 the abuse had become unendurable and Follis quit the game. He died of pneumonia in 1910, at the age of 31. Three other blacks appeared on professional club rosters prior to 1919. Charles "Doc" Baker ran halfback for the Akron Indians from 1906 to 1908, and again in 1911. Gideon "Charlie" Smith of Hampton Institute appeared as a tackle in one game in 1915 for the Canton Bulldogs. And Henry McDonald, probably the most talented black professional during the early years, played halfback for the Rochester Jeffersons from 1911 to 1917. In one game against Canton in 1917, Earle "Greasy" Neale hurled McDonald out of bounds and snarled, "Black is black and white is white . . . and the two don't mix." Racial incidents and segregation would become even more severe in the interwar years.

Black Stars at Predominantly White Colleges, 1919–1945

Following World War I, a number of blacks gained national celebrity for their football skills. John Shelburne played fullback at Dartmouth from 1919 through 1921. During those same years, Fred "Duke" Slater was a dominant tackle at the University of Iowa. In the early 1920s, Charles West and Charles Drew played halfback for Washington and Jefferson (in Washington, Pa.) and Amherst, respectively. West became the second African American to appear in a Rose Bowl game. After their football careers, both men became medical doctors. Drew achieved international acclaim for perfecting the method of preserving blood plasma. Toward the end of the decade, David Myers appeared as a tackle and end for New York University and Ray Kemp played tackle for Duquesne.

Although scores of blacks played football for major colleges, they constantly faced racial prejudice. Some colleges denied blacks dormitory space, thus forcing them to live off campus. Others practiced a quota system by limiting the number of black players on a squad to one or two. Others benched minority athletes when they played segregated southern schools. In 1937, Boston College surrendered to southern custom when it asked Louis Montgomery to sit out the Cotton Bowl game against Clemson. One sportswriter complained that "even Hitler, to give the bum his due, didn't treat Jesse Owens the way the Cotton Bowl folk are treating Lou Montgomery—with the consent of the young Negro's alma mater. . . ." African Americans also encountered excessive roughness from white players. Jack Trice of Iowa State was deliberately maimed by Minnesota players in 1923 and died of internal bleeding. Finally, minority players were snubbed by white sportswriters. No blacks were named first-team All-Americans from 1918 to 1937, including Duke Slater, probably the best tackle of that era.

In the 1930s, dozens of black players had outstanding careers. The Big Ten Conference featured a number of gifted running backs, especially Oze Simmons of Iowa and Bernard Jefferson of Northwestern. Talented linemen included William Bell, a guard at Ohio State, and Homer Harris, a tackle at the University of Iowa. Two of the best black athletes at eastern colleges were Wilmeth Sidat-Singh, a rifle-armed quarterback at Syracuse, and Jerome "Brud" HOLLAND, an exceptional end at Cornell. Named first-team All-American in 1937 and 1938, Holland was the first black to be so honored since Robeson two decades earlier. In the West, Joe Lillard was a punishing running back at Oregon State in 1930 and 1931. And Woodrow "Woody" Strode and Kenny Washington starred for UCLA from 1937 to 1940. Strode was a 220-pound end with sure hands and quickness. Washington, a 195-pound halfback, was one of the nation's premier players. In 1939, he led all college players in total yardage with 1,370, but failed to win first-team All-American honors.

During the war years, there were five exceptional African-American college players. Marion Motley was a bruising 220-pound fullback at the University of Nevada. Two guards, Julius Franks of the University of Michigan and Bill Willis of Ohio State, were named to several All-American teams. And Claude "Buddy" Young was a brilliant running back at the University of Illinois. As a freshman in 1944, the diminutive, speedy halfback tied Harold "Red" Grange's single-season scoring record with 13 touchdowns. He spent the next year in the armed service, but continued his career after the war. Finally, Joe

Kenny Washington, a teammate of Jackie Robinson on UCLA's football teams of the late 1930s, preceded Robinson in breaking the color barrier in major professional sports when he played with the NFL's Los Angeles Rams in 1946. (Photographs and Prints Division, Schomburg Center for Research in Black Culture, The New York Public Library, Astor, Lenox and Tilden Foundations)

Perry was a standout running back at Compton Junior College in southern California.

Black College Play, 1919–1945

Although black colleges lacked sufficient funds for equipment and stadiums, football grew in popularity after World War I. Black conferences sprang up throughout the South, but the CIAA, created in 1912, fielded the most talented teams. In the immediate postwar period, Franz Alfred "Jazz" Bird of Lincoln was the dominant player. A small but powerful running back, Bird was nicknamed "the black Red Grange."

Morgan State University was the dominant black college team of the 1930s and early 1940s. Coached by Edward Hurt, Morgan State won seven CIAA titles between 1930 and 1941. Running backs Otis Troupe and Thomas "Tank" Conrad were the star athletes for the Morgan State teams. In the deep South, Tuskegee Institute overwhelmed its opponents, winning nine Southern Intercollegiate Athletic Conference (SIAC) titles in ten years from 1924 through 1933. Tuskegee's team was led by Benjamin Franklin Stevenson, a skilled running back who played eight seasons from 1924 through 1931. (Eligibility rules were not enforced at the time.) In the more competitive Southwest Athletic Conference (SWAC), Wiley University boasted fullback Elza Odell and halfback Andrew Patterson. Langston College in Oklahoma, which won four championships in the 1930s, featured running back Tim Crisp. The Midwestern Athletic Conference (MWAC), started in 1932, was dominated by Kentucky State, which topped the conference four times in the 1930s. Its key players were ends William Reed and Robert Hardin, running back George "Big Bertha" Edwards, and quarterback Joseph "Tarzan" Kendall. During the war years, fullback John "Big Train" Moody of Morris Brown College and guard Herbert "Lord" Trawik of Kentucky State were consensus picks for the Black All-American team.

Black Professionals, 1919–1945

In 1919 several midwestern clubs organized the American Professional Football Association, the forerunner of the National Football League (NFL) created two years later. The first African Americans to play in the NFL were Robert "Rube" Marshall and Fritz Pollard. Over forty years old, Marshall performed as an end with the Rock Island Independents from 1919 through 1921. Pollard appeared as a running back with the Akron Pros during those same years. Racial incidents were commonplace. Pollard recalled fans at away games taunting him with the song "Bye, Bye, Blackbird." Occasionally, they hurled stones at him. Even at home games, fans sometimes booed him. Besides playing, Pollard served as the first black NFL coach, directing Akron in 1920, Milwaukee in 1922, Hammond in 1923 and 1924, and Akron again in 1925 and 1926. Other blacks who performed in the NFL during the 1920s were Paul Robeson, Jay "Inky" Williams, John Shelbourne, James Turner, Edward "Sol" Butler, Dick Hudson, Harold Bradley, and David Myers. Those athletes did not compete without incident. In 1926, the New York Giants refused to take the field until the Canton Bulldogs removed their quarterback, Sol Butler, from the game. Canton obliged. The last three minority athletes to play in the desegregated NFL were Duke Slater, Joe Lillard, and Ray Kemp. An exceptional tackle who often played without a helmet, Slater performed for Milwaukee (1922), Rock Island (1922–1925), and the Chicago Cardinals (1926–1931). Joe Lillard also starred for the Cardinals from 1932 to 1933. He was a skillful punt returner,

kicker, and runner, but his contract was not renewed after the 1933 season. Ray Kemp, a tackle with the Pittsburgh Pirates (later renamed the Steelers), met a similar fate.

In 1933, NFL owners established an informal racial ban that lasted until 1946. The reasons for the exclusionary policy are not entirely clear. Probably NFL moguls were attempting to please bigoted fans, players, and owners. In addition, professional football hoped to compete with baseball for fans and adopted that sport's winning formula on racial segregation. Southern-born George Preston Marshall, who owned the Boston franchise, was especially influential in the shaping of NFL policy. A powerful personality with a knack for innovation and organization, Marshall in 1933 spearheaded the reorganization of the NFL into two five-team divisions with a season-ending championship game. Four years later, he moved his Boston team to Washington, D.C., a segregated city. Marshall once vowed that he would never employ minority athletes. Indeed, the Redskins was in fact the last NFL team to desegregate, resisting until 1962.

Other owners implausibly attributed the absence of African-American athletes to the shortage of quality college players. The NFL draft was established in 1935, but owners overlooked such talented stars as Oze Simmons, Brud Holland, Wilmeth Sidat-Singh, Woody Strode, and Kenny Washington. Owners also lamely argued that they purposely did not hire blacks in order to protect them from physical abuse by bigoted white players.

Denied an opportunity in the NFL, blacks formed their own professional teams. The New York Brown Bombers, organized in 1935 by Harlem sports promoter Hershel "Rip" Day, was one of the most talented squads. Taking their nickname from the popular heavyweight fighter Joe LOUIS, the Brown Bombers recruited Fritz Pollard as coach. Pollard agreed to coach, in part, to showcase minority athletes. He signed Tank Conrad, Joe Lillard, Dave Myers, Otis Troupe, Hallie Harding, and Howard "Dixie" Matthews. The Bombers competed mainly against semipro white teams such as the New Rochelle Bulldogs. Pollard coached the Bombers to three winning seasons, but he resigned in 1937 when the team was denied use of Dyckman Oval Field in the Bronx. The Brown Bombers continued for several more years as a road team and then disappeared.

During the war years, blacks played professionally on the West coast. In 1944 both the American Professional League and the Pacific Coast Professional Football League fielded integrated teams. Kenny Washington starred for the San Francisco Clippers and Ezzrett Anderson for the Los Angeles Mustangs.

In the Pacific Coast League, Jackie Robinson, who would integrate major league baseball, represented the Los Angeles Bulldogs, and Mel Reid performed for the Oakland Giants. The following year the two leagues merged into the Pacific Coast League. The Hollywood Bears, with Washington, Anderson, and Woody Strode, won the title.

The Postwar Years: Blacks at Predominantly White Colleges

World War II and the Cold War proved instrumental in breaking down racial barriers. After all, how could Americans criticize Nazi Germany and then the Soviet Union for racism and totalitarianism when blacks were denied first-class citizenship in the United States? During the 1940s and 1950s, blacks worked diligently to topple segregation in all areas, including athletics. In football, their efforts met with considerable success.

During the postwar years, several minority athletes performed admirably at big-time schools. Buddy Young returned to the University of Illinois and helped lead his team to a Rose Bowl victory over UCLA. Levi Jackson, a fleet running back, became the first African American to play for Yale and was elected team captain for 1949. Wally Triplett and Denny Hoggard became the first blacks to play in the Cotton Bowl when Penn State met Southern Methodist in 1948. And Bob Mann, Len Ford, and Gene Derricotte helped the University of Michigan trounce the University of Southern California in the 1949 Rose Bowl, 49–0.

Blacks continued to make their mark in intercollegiate football in the 1950s. Ollie Matson excelled as a running back at the University of San Francisco from 1949 through 1951. The following year he won two medals in track at the Olympics in Helsinki. Jim Parker was a dominant guard at Ohio State. In 1956 he became the first African American to win the Outland Trophy, awarded to the nation's foremost collegiate lineman. Bobby Mitchell and Lenny Moore starred at halfback for the University of Illinois and Penn State, respectively. Prentiss Gautt took to the gridiron for the University of Oklahoma in 1958, the first black to perform for a major, predominantly white southern school. And Jim BROWN, perhaps the greatest running back in the history of the game, debuted at Syracuse University in 1954. There, Brown lettered in basketball, track, lacrosse, and football and was named All-American in the latter two sports. As a senior, he rushed for 986 yards, third highest in the nation. In the final regular season game he scored 43 points on 6 touchdowns and 7 conversions. In the 1957 Cotton Bowl game against Texas Christian University, he scored 21 points in a losing cause and was named MVP. Brown would go on to have a spectacular career in the NFL.

Literally and figuratively, African Americans made great strides on the gridiron in the 1950s. Yet barriers continued to exist. Dormitories at many colleges remained off limits. Blacks were denied access to most major colleges in the South. They were virtually excluded from some football positions, especially quarterback. And they were not seriously considered for the Heisman Trophy, an award presented to the best collegiate player.

In the 1960s, a landmark decade in the advancement of civil rights, black gridiron stars abounded. Ernie Davis, Brown's successor at fullback for Syracuse, was an exciting and powerful runner who shattered most of Brown's records. As a sophomore in 1959, Davis averaged 7 yards per carry and helped lead Syracuse to its first undefeated season. Ranked first in the nation, Syracuse defeated Texas in the Cotton Bowl and Davis was named MVP. The following year, Davis gained 877 yards on 112 carries and scored 10 touchdowns. As a senior, he had another outstanding season and became the first African American to win the Heisman Trophy. Tragically, he was diagnosed with leukemia in 1962 and never played professional football. He died at the age of twenty-three.

The 1960s produced a number of sensational black running backs. Leroy Keyes of Purdue and Gale SAYERS of Kansas twice earned All-American recognition. Floyd Little and Jim Nance proved worthy successors to Brown and Davis at Syracuse. And Mike Garrett and O. J. SIMPSON, both of USC, won Heisman awards. The decade's greatest breakaway runner, Simpson rushed for 3,295 yards and 22 touchdowns in only 22 games. Blacks also excelled as linemen, receivers, and defensive backs. Bobby Bell and Carl Eller both won All-American acclaim as tackles with the University of Minnesota. Bell also captured the Outland Trophy in 1962. Bob Brown of Nebraska and Joe Greene of North Texas State also were All-American tackles. Paul Warfield was a crafty wide receiver for Ohio State. And George Webster of Michigan State twice earned All-American distinction as a defensive back. Also from Michigan State was the feared defensive end Charles "Bubba" Smith, who joined the Baltimore Colts in 1967.

In the 1960s bastions of bigotry collapsed. The last three lily-white college conferences—the Southwest, Southeast, and Atlantic Coast—all desegregated. Blacks, too, put the lie to the stereotype that they lacked the intellectual necessities to perform as quarterbacks. Sandy Stephens was voted an All-American at Minnesota and Marlin Briscoe and Gene Washington called signals at the University of Omaha and

Stanford, respectively. Yet the NFL showed little or no interest in Stephens, and the other two were converted to wide receivers.

During the 1970s, 1980s, and 1990s, major colleges actively recruited African-American athletes. Considered essential to the success of the football program, blacks at some schools were illegally offered monetary and material inducements. Meager grade-point averages and low graduation rates also brought accusations that universities were exploiting minority athletes. After all, the vast majority of varsity players do not go on to enjoy lucrative professional athletic careers. To blunt the criticism, the NCAA instituted Proposition 48 in 1983. That directive required entering freshman varsity athletes to achieve a combined score of 700 on the Scholastic Aptitude Test (SAT) and to maintain at least a C average.

From 1970 through the 1993 season, blacks have won the Heisman Trophy 17 times. The vast majority of selectees have been running backs. Beginning with Ohio State's Archie Griffin in 1974 and 1975, minority athletes won the Heisman ten consecutive years: Tony Dorsett (1976), Earl Campbell (1977), Billy Sims (1978), Charles White (1979), George Rogers (1980), Marcus Allen (1981), Herschel Walker (1982), and Michael Rozier (1983). Running backs Bo JACKSON (1985) and Barry Sanders (1988) also were recipients. The only non–running backs to capture the prize were receivers Johnny Rodgers (1972), Tim Brown (1987), and Desmond Howard (1991), and quarterbacks Andre Ware (1989) and Charlie Ward (1993). Outland trophy winners for the best interior lineman have included Rich Glover (1972), John Hicks (1973), Lee Roy Selmon (1975), Ross Browner (1976), Greg Roberts (1978), Mark May (1980), and Bruce Smith (1984).

Blacks have only slowly been hired as collegiate coaches. The first African-American head coach at a major college football program was Dennis Green, who was head coach at Northwestern (1981–1985) and at Stanford (1989–1991) before being named head coach of the Minnesota Vikings in the NFL. In the early 1990s the only African-American coaches at Division 1-A colleges were Ron Cooper at Eastern Michigan University, Ron Dickerson at Temple University, and Jim Caldwell at Wake Forest University.

Black College Play in the Postwar Era

Although football programs at black colleges continued to be strapped financially, they still produced some superb players and coaches. Eddie Robinson of Grambling, Ed Hurt and Earl Banks of Morgan State, and Jake Gaither of Florida A & M were four of the most successful black college coaches. Each won several conference titles and sent numerous players to the NFL. Morgan State produced three premier NFL players—Roosevelt Brown, a guard with the New York Giants in the mid-1950s, Leroy Kelly, a running back with the Cleveland Browns in the mid-1960s, and Willie Lanier, a linebacker with the Kansas City Chiefs from 1967 to 1977—among numerous other stars. Florida A & M yielded Willie Gallimore, a running back with the Chicago Bears (1957–1963), and Bob Hayes, a sprinter who played wide receiver for the Dallas Cowboys (1965–1974). Grambling has sent more than seventy players to the NFL, including quarterback James Harris, running backs Paul Younger and Sammy White, wide receiver Charlie Joiner, defensive tackles Ernest Ladd and Junious "Buck" Buchanan, defensive backs Everson Walls, Roosevelt Taylor, and Willie Brown, and the outstanding defensive end for the Green Bay Packers, Willie Davis.

Two of the greatest offensive players in NFL history graduated from black colleges in Mississippi. NFL career rushing leader Walter PAYTON attended Jackson State before joining the Chicago Bears in 1975, and the San Francisco '49ers' Jerry Rice, the holder of the career record for touchdown receptions, graduated from Mississippi Valley State in 1985. Other notable products of black colleges include defensive specialists David "Deacon" Jones and Donnie Schell from South Carolina State, defensive end Elvin Bethea from North Carolina A & T, wide receivers John Stallworth and Harold Jackson of Alabama A & M and Jackson State, respectively, and guard Larry Little of Bethune Cookman. Prairie View A & M produced safety Ken Houston and wide receiver Otis Taylor. Maryland State delivered defensive back Johnny Sample and two dominant linemen, Roger Brown and Art SHELL. Savannah State yielded tight end Shannon Sharpe.

The NFL in the Postwar Years

The democratic idealism of World War II and the emergence of a rival professional league, the All-America Football Conference (AAFC), proved instrumental in the toppling of the racial barrier in 1946. That year the Los Angeles Rams of the NFL hired Kenny Washington and Woody Strode, and the Cleveland Browns of the AAFC signed Marion MOTLEY and Bill Willis. Washington and Strode were beyond their prime, but Motley and Willis were at their peak. They helped lead the Browns to the first of four consecutive league championships. Both athletes were named first-team All-Pros, an honor which became perennial. Both would also be inducted into the Pro Football Hall of Fame.

Cleveland fullback Marion Motley (left, number 76), gets a first down for the Browns against the Los Angeles Rams in the game for the National Pro Football League championship, December 24, 1950. (AP/Wide World Photos)

The success of the Browns prompted desegregation among other teams, especially in the AAFC, which lasted until 1949. The football New York Yankees signed Buddy YOUNG and the gridiron Brooklyn Dodgers took Elmore Harris of Morgan State. The Los Angeles Dons recruited Len Ford, Ezzrett Anderson, and Bert Piggott. Ford would go on to star as a defensive end for the Cleveland Browns. The San Francisco '49ers, originally an AAFC team, in 1948 signed Joe Perry, who would, in his second season, lead the league in rushing. After the '49ers joined the NFL, he became the first back to amass back-to-back thousand-yard rushing seasons in 1953 and 1954.

Among NFL teams, only the Rams, the New York Giants, and the Detroit Lions took a chance on African-American athletes in the 1940s. The Lions signed Melvin Grooms and Bob Mann, and the Giants acquired Emlen Tunnell, one of the sport's greatest safeties. In the early 1950s, the Giants also obtained Roosevelt Brown, a superior tackle. The Baltimore Colts acquired Buddy Young from the Yankees, and the Chicago Cardinals signed Wally Triplett, Ollie Matson, and Dick "Night Train" Lane. Matson was a crafty runner and dangerous receiver who rushed for 5,173 yards and caught 222 passes in 14 NFL seasons. He was inducted into the Pro Football Hall of Fame in 1972. Dick Lane, another Hall of Fame inductee, excelled as a cornerback for the Cardinals and Lions. The Washington Redskins, the last NFL team to desegregate in 1962, acquired Bobby Mitchell from the Cleveland Browns for the draft rights to Ernie Davis. Mitchell was a gifted wide receiver and an explosive kick returner. He, too, was elected to the Pro Football Hall of Fame in 1983.

Jim Brown, Lenny Moore, and John Henry Johnson were all premier running backs in the 1950s and early 1960s. In nine seasons with Cleveland, Brown led the NFL in rushing eight times, amassing 12,312 yards and 126 touchdowns, a career record. He was selected Rookie of the Year in 1957, and MVP in 1958 and 1965. He was also voted to nine All-Pro teams. At 6'2" and 230 pounds, Brown ideally combined power, speed, and endurance. Lenny Moore was the epitome of a runner-receiver. He gained 5,174 yards as a halfback and another 6,039 yards as a receiver. He was named Rookie of the Year in 1956 and helped propel the Baltimore Colts to NFL championships in 1958 and 1959. He was elected to the Pro Football Hall of Fame in 1975. John Henry Johnson, a powerful running back and ferocious blocker, played for San Francisco, Detroit, and Pittsburgh (1954–1966). In 13 seasons, he totaled 6,803 yards on 1,571 carries.

The formation of the American Football League (AFL) in 1959 presented opportunities on the new teams for scores of African Americans. Prior to its merger with the NFL in 1966, the AFL produced many exciting black players. Carlton "Cookie" Gilchrist of the Buffalo Bills became the league's first thousand-yard rusher in 1962. Other excellent running backs included Abner Haynes of the Dallas Texans, Paul Lowe of Oakland, Jim Nance of Boston, and Mike Garrett of Kansas City. Lionel Taylor of Denver, Art Powell of Oakland, and Otis Taylor of Kansas City were all gifted receivers. Willie Brown and Dave Grayson were prominent defensive backs for Oakland. And three future Hall of Famers all played for Kansas City: Buck Buchanan, Bobby Bell, and Willie Lanier.

Minority athletes also excelled in the NFL during the 1960s. Roosevelt Brown of New York and Jim Parker of Baltimore were frequent All-Pros on the offensive line. The successful Green Bay teams were anchored on defense by Willie Davis at end, Herb

Cleveland Browns' fullback Jim Brown breaking through the line and running for a touchdown against the Philadelphia Eagles in 1965. Brown, noted for his intimidating style of play, later had a career as an actor in action films such as *The Dirty Dozen*. (AP/Wide World Photos)

Adderly at cornerback, and Willie Wood at safety. Other defensive standouts were Roger Brown and Dick Lane of Detroit, Abe Woodson of San Francisco, Roosevelt "Rosey" Grier of New York and Los Angeles, and Carl Eller and Alan Page of Minnesota.

Gale Sayers of the Chicago Bears was probably the most electrifying offensive star of the 1960s. A graceful back with breakaway speed, he won Rookie of the Year honors in 1965, scoring 22 touchdowns. The following year, he led the NFL in rushing with 1,231 yards. After leading the league in rushing for a second time in 1969, injuries ended his career. The decade also yielded two superior pass receivers: Paul Warfield and Charlie Taylor. Playing 13 seasons for Cleveland and Miami, Warfield caught 427 passes for 8,565 yards. Another Hall of Famer, Taylor played his entire thirteen-year career for Washington, totaling 649 passes for 9,140 yards.

The 1970 merger of the AFL and NFL set the stage for the emergence of professional football as America's most popular spectator sport. Since the merger, the NFL has been split into two divisions, the National Football Conference (NFC) and the American Football Conference (AFC). During the era of the unified league, African Americans have managed to topple virtually every existing sports barrier. In football, they have continued to dominate the skill positions of running back, receiver, and defensive back. In the 1970s, Orenthal James "O. J." Simpson became the dominant back. A slashing and darting runner for the Buffalo Bills, Simpson led the AFC in rushing in 1972, 1973, 1975, and 1976. In 1973 he shattered Jim Brown's single-season record by rushing for 2,003 yards. In eleven seasons he rushed for 11,236 yards and caught 232 passes for 2,142 yards. Walter "Sweetness" Payton became the game's most statistically accomplished running back, establishing an NFL record of 16,726 yards in 13 seasons with the Chicago Bears. A durable player who missed only four of 194 games, he also holds the record for most thousand-yard seasons (10), most hundred-yard games (77), most yards rushing in a single game (275), and is second to Jim Brown for most touchdowns (125).

Erick Dickerson led the NFC in rushing with the Los Angeles Rams in 1983, 1984, 1986, and with the Indianapolis Colts in 1988. In 1984 he broke Simpson's record by gaining 2,007 yards in a single season. Earl Campbell, a barrel-thighed fullback with the Houston Oilers, led the AFC in rushing from 1978 to 1981. In 1978 he captured both the Rookie of the Year and the MVP awards. In eight seasons he gained 9,407 yards. Tony Dorsett of the Dallas Cowboys was another leading ground-gainer who accumulated more than 10,000 yards rushing. In a game

Chicago Bear Walter Payton carrying the football in his last regular-season game in 1987. Payton, a graduate of Jackson State University in Mississippi, a historically black college, is the all-time NFL leader in rushing yardage. (AP/Wide World Photos)

against Minnesota in 1983 he sprinted for a 99-yard touchdown run, establishing an NFL record. In the 1970s, Franco Harris helped spark the Pittsburgh Steelers to four Super Bowl victories, and in the 1980s, Marcus Allen helped the Oakland Raiders win the Super Bowl in 1984. The following year Allen led the NFL in rushing and was named MVP. Ottis Anderson, Roger Craig, and Herschel Walker have been successful ground-gainers and pass receivers. Thurmond Thomas of the Buffalo Bills is another quality dual-purpose back. In the early 1990s, three of the NFL's most gifted runners were Thomas, Barry Sanders of Detroit, and Emmitt Smith of Dallas, who won rushing titles in 1991, 1992, and 1993.

A number of blacks have gained recognition as receivers. Possessing both blocking and pass-catching ability, Kellen Winslow, Ozzie Newsome, Shannon Sharpe, and John MACKEY have served as model tight ends. Mackey was elected to the Pro Football Hall of Fame in 1991—an honor long overdue and probably denied him earlier because of his union fights against

management and the NFL office. Notable wide receivers have included Otis Taylor, Paul Warfield, Harold Jackson, Cliff Branch, Drew Pearson, Mel Gray, Lynn Swann, John Stallworth, Isaac Curtis, James Lofton, Charlie Joiner, Mike Quick, Art Monk, Al Toon, Andre Rison, Andre Reed, John Taylor, Ahmad Rashad, Mark Duper, Mark Clayton, Michael Irvin, and Sterling Sharpe. In 1993, Sharpe of the Green Bay Packers caught 112 passes, surpassing his own single-season record established the year before. Sure hands, breathtaking quickness, and an incomparable ability to run with the ball make Jerry Rice of the '49ers a peerless receiver. In Super Bowl XXIII against Cincinnati, Rice won the MVP by catching 11 passes for a record 215 yards. The following year, in Super Bowl XXIV against Denver, he caught 7 passes for 148 yards and 3 touchdowns. Barring injury, Rice seems certain to break Jim Brown's record for career touchdowns and Art Monk's record for career pass interceptions.

Blacks have also distinguished themselves as defensive backs, interior linemen, and linebackers. Art Shell, Gene UPSHAW, Bob Brown, Leon Gray, Reg-

Gene Upshaw, executive director of the National Football League Player's Association, speaks to reporters at the Touchdown Club in Washington, D.C., about the union's proposal to end the NFL strike, October 1987. (AP/Wide World Photos)

gie McKenzie, Anthony Munoz, and Larry Little all have excelled on the offensive line. Little was selected to the Pro Football Hall of Fame in 1993. A frequent All-Pro selection, Dwight Stephenson of the Miami Dolphins became the first outstanding black center in the mid-1980s. Claude Humphrey, Leroy Selmon, Joe Greene, Bruce Smith, Reggie White, and Charlie Johnson have all been standout defensive linemen. Defensive backs include Ronnie Lott, Mel Blount, Lem Barney, Jimmy Johnson, Emmitt Thomas, Donnie Schell, Louis Wright, Mike Haynes, Albert Lewis, and Ron Woodson. And some of the best linebackers in the game have been minority athletes such as George Webster, David Robinson, Willie Lanier, Robert Brazille, Lawrence Taylor, Mike Singletary, Cornelius Bennett, Seth Joyner, Hugh Green, Andre Tippett, Derrik Thomas, Vincent Brown, Junior Seau, and Rickey Jackson.

Blacks, too, have dispelled the myth that they lack the intellectual gifts to play certain positions, especially quarterback. In 1953 the Chicago Bears signed a black Michigan State signal caller appropriately named Willie Thrower. He appeared in several games but did not distinguish himself and was released at the end of the year. George Taliaferro of Indiana University appeared as a quarterback for Baltimore in 1953, but he also failed to make an impression. Two years later, the Green Bay Packers signed Charlie Brackins from Prairie View A & M, but he was used sparingly. Marlin Briscoe of the University of Omaha quarterbacked several games for the Denver Broncos in 1968, but was released the following year and became a wide receiver for Buffalo. James Harris of Grambling took snaps for Buffalo in 1969, and led the Los Angeles Rams to a division title in 1974. Joe Gilliam played adequately for Pittsburgh in 1974, but lost the job to Terry Bradshaw, who became the offensive leader of the Super Bowl champions.

The performance of Doug Williams for the Washington Redskins in the 1988 Super Bowl against Denver demonstrated that a black possessed the athletic and intellectual necessities to direct an NFL football team. In Super Bowl XXII Williams captured the MVP award by completing 18 of 29 passes for a record 340 yards and 4 touchdowns. Nonetheless, within a year Williams was out of professional football, receiving little reward or lasting recognition for his accomplishment.

In 1988, Randall Cunningham demonstrated dazzling running and passing ability and directed the Philadelphia Eagles to their first division title since 1980. And in the early 1990s, Warren Moon, leader of the high-powered "run and shoot" Houston Oiler offense, was one of the most accomplished passers in football. In 1990, his receiving corps of Haywood Jeffries, Drew Hill, Ernest Givens, and Curtis Dun-

Art Shell, the first African-American head coach in the NFL, watches his team, the Los Angeles Raiders, during a playoff game in 1990. (AP/Wide World Photos)

can each caught more than 65 passes, an unparalleled gridiron feat.

While distinguishing themselves at every playing position and earning salaries commensurate with their performances, blacks in football management positions are still a novelty. There are no black owners and few African Americans in NFL front office jobs. Minority head coaches are rare, even though by the 1990s sixty percent of the players were black. Art Shell was named head coach of the Los Angeles Raiders in 1989, becoming the first black NFL coach since Fritz Pollard. The Raiders also hired a minority candidate, Terry Robiskie, to become their offensive coordinator. In 1992, Minnesota appointed Dennis Green, formerly the coach of Northwestern and Stanford, to direct the team. Green named Tony Dungy as defensive coordinator. And that same year, the Green Bay Packers employed two black coordinators, Sherman Lewis and Ray Rhodes. Gene Upshaw was elected president of the NFL Players Union, but he came under fire when he led the membership in an unsuccessful one-game strike against the owners in 1987.

The status of African Americans in football in recent decades has been impressive, though many problems remain. Their entrance into leadership roles has been slow. The adjustment to the high-pressure world of top-level collegiate and professional football has proved difficult for many. Too many African Americans have developed drug problems, or have become burnt-out cases after their football careers have ended. For many, the adjustment to the largely white world of professional football has been jarring. In recent years football players have been more willing to speak out about racial problems. When the state of Arizona decided not to recognize the Martin Luther King, Jr., holiday, blacks helped persuade the NFL to transfer the site of the 1993 Super Bowl from Phoenix to Los Angeles.

In the past, high-salaried minority players have been criticized for being aloof. In part, blacks have been reluctant to speak out for fear of alienating the white majority. "A lot of people, myself included," Lawrence Taylor once observed, "don't want to give up their status in white America. You learn how to deal with certain situations, how to play the game." But Taylor and other highly visible minority athletes are increasingly speaking out on social issues in order to improve the human condition for athletes and nonathletes alike.

REFERENCES

AHSE, ARTHUR R., JR. *A Hard Road to Glory: A History of the African-American Athlete, 1619–1987.* 3 vols. New York, 1988.

CARROLL, JOHN M. "Fritz Pollard and the Brown Bombers." *The Coffin Corner* 12 (1990): 14–17.

CHALK, OCANIA. *Black College Sport.* New York, 1976.

———. *Pioneers of Black Sport.* New York, 1975.

EDWARDS, HARRY. "Black Athletes and Sports in America." *The Western Journal of Black Studies* 6 (1982): 138–144.

HENDERSON, EDWIN B. *The Black Athlete: Emergence and Arrival.* New York, 1968.

———. *The Negro In Sports.* Washington, D.C., 1949.

JOHNSON, WILLIAM OSCAR. "How Far Have We Come?" *Sports Illustrated* 75 (August 5, 1991): 39–46.

PENNINGTON, RICHARD. *Breaking the Ice: The Racial Integration of Southwest Conference Football.* Jefferson, N.C., 1987.

ROBERTS, MILTON. "Black College All-Time, All-Star Football Team." *Black Sports* (June 1976): 47–50.

SMITH, THOMAS G. "Civil Rights on the Gridiron: The Kennedy Administration and the Desegregation of the Washington Redskins." *Journal of Sport History* 14 (1987): 189–208.

———. "Outside the Pale: The Exclusion of Blacks from the National Football League." *Journal of Sport History* 15 (1988): 255–281.

SPIVEY, DONALD. "The Black Athlete in Big-Time Intercollegiate Sports, 1941–1968." *Phylon* 44 (1983): 116–125.

THOMAS G. SMITH

Foote, Julia (1823–1900), minister. On May 20, 1894, Julia Foote became the first woman to be ordained a deacon in the AFRICAN METHODIST EPISCOPAL ZION CHURCH, a goal for which she had struggled for over fifty years. Foote, born and raised in upstate New York, became a member of an African Methodist Episcopal (AME) church as a teenager. After her marriage to George Foote, a sailor, she settled with him in Boston and joined the African Methodist Episcopal Zion church. Like her ministerial colleagues Jarena LEE and Zilpha ELAW, Julia Foote argued for women's right to preach and be ordained by the church. Despite the opposition of her husband, her minister, and many other church members, Foote took up a public career as an itinerant preacher and organized prayer meetings in her home. Because of her activities, she was excommunicated from her church in Boston.

In 1879 Foote published a narrative called *A Brand Plucked from the Fire, an Autobiographical Sketch.* In the work she describes her spiritual development and testifies to her call to preach the gospel. Foote, like the many other AME preaching women in the nineteenth century, based her argument for the right to preach on firm theological grounding. God called her to preach, she insisted, and no human could deny this. She further emphasized that the stories of holy women in the Bible testify to a tradition of God working through women.

While most AME preaching women in this period remained unable to gain inclusion in the leadership structure of the church, Foote broke through that barrier with her ordination as a deacon. In 1900 she became the second woman to be ordained an elder in the AME Zion church.

REFERENCES

ANDREWS, WILLIAM, ed. *Sisters of the Spirit: Three Black Women's Autobiographies of the Nineteenth Century.* Urbana, Ill., 1986.

DODSON, JUALYNNE. "AME Preaching Women in the Nineteenth Century: Cutting Edge of Women's

Inclusion in Church Polity." In Hilah Thomas and Rosemary Keller, eds. *Women in New Worlds.* Nashville, 1981.

JUDITH WEISENFELD

Ford, Harold Eugene (May 20, 1945–), politician. Harold Ford was born in Memphis, Tenn., the eighth child of Newton J. Ford and Vera Ford. He received a B.S. degree in business administration at Tennessee State University in 1967 and proceeded to Philadelphia to work for IBM. He soon returned to Memphis to work in his family's funeral business.

In 1970, Ford ran successfully for the Tennessee state legislature, holding the same Shelby County seat his great-grandfather had occupied in the 1890s. During his four years in the Tennessee House of Representatives, Ford was chosen to be Majority Whip. In 1974, he ran for the U.S. House of Representatives and won, becoming the first black Tennessean elected to Congress. Through the election of 1994, Ford has been reelected ten times.

During his years representing Tennessee's Ninth Congressional District, a majority African-American area within the city of Memphis, Ford has emphasized welfare reform as well as such other urban problems as public housing, jobs, and education. Ford became the youngest member of Congress ever to chair a subcommittee of the House Ways and Means Committee: the Subcommittee on Human Resources.

A fiery speaker, master of constituent service, astute politician, and meticulous organizer, Ford has constructed a powerful political organization which has not only assisted him in his own bids for reelection but has made him a prominent presence in local elections in his district. In March 1991, Ford organized more than one hundred black civic, religious, and political leaders to choose a united candidate for mayor of Memphis; later that year, the group's endorsement and Ford's own efforts helped elect W. W. Herenton as the city's first African-American mayor.

Ford's organization and constituent backing have permitted him to withstand legal as well as electoral challenges. Starting in the early 1980s, Ford faced persistent charges of corruption and unethical activities. Ford denied any wrongdoing, claiming the attacks were a racially motivated attempt to unseat Tennessee's only black representative. In 1990, Ford was indicted and brought to trial on federal bank fraud and conspiracy charges. The prosecution charged that he and three other defendants had accepted bank loans they had no intention of repaying. The trial was acrimonious. Ford publicly accused

Rep. Harold Ford of Memphis, Tenn., speaking at a Capitol Hill press conference in 1993. (AP/Wide World Photos)

prosecutors of racism, and his supporters demonstrated outside the courtroom. The jury split along racial lines, and a mistrial was declared. In 1992, Ford was brought to trial a second time on the charges, this time before a jury selected outside Memphis. There was only one black juror, and Ford later denounced the presiding judge as biased. Nevertheless, in April 1993, the jury cleared Ford of all criminal charges.

REFERENCE

BERNSEN, CHARLES. "The Fords of Memphis: A Family Saga." *Memphis Commercial Appeal,* July 1–4, 1990.

MARCUS D. POHLMANN

Ford, James W. (December 22, 1893–June 21, 1957), Communist party official. James Ford was born in Pratt City, Ala. He worked on railroads and in steel mills while in high school. In 1913, Ford entered Fisk University in Nashville, Tenn., but before receiving his degree enlisted in the Army and served in France during World War I. Following the war he returned to Fisk and completed his degree in 1920.

Ford then moved to Chicago, where he went to work with the postal service. He joined the Chicago Postal Workers Union and the American Negro Labor Congress, both affiliated with the COMMUNIST PARTY, USA (CPUSA), and through these organizations was recruited into the party in 1926. Ford demonstrated considerable bureaucratic skill and political savvy, and he rose rapidly in the party hierarchy. In 1928 he was selected as a delegate to the Congress of the Communist Trade International, or Profintern, held in Moscow. Ford stayed in the Soviet Union for nine months and was elected to the executive committee of the Profintern. In 1930 he moved to Hamburg, Germany, where he cofounded the International Conference of Negro Workers and became the first editor of its *Negro Worker*.

Ford returned to the United States in 1931 and was selected to be the party's leading spokesperson on "the Negro question." Shortly after his return from Europe, Ford was made vice president of the party's League of Struggle for Negro Rights, and in 1932 he became the first black member of the American Politburo. Ford received national attention in 1932 when he was selected as the party's vice presidential candidate, becoming the first African American to appear on the ballot for national executive office. He and his running mate, party chairman William Z. Foster, received 102,991 votes.

In 1933, Ford was installed as leader of the party's section in Harlem. Through the 1930s, Ford transformed the Harlem party from a relatively decentralized, iconoclastic communist organization into a model of Stalinist orthodoxy. He quickly undercut the power of several black leaders in Harlem, including such leading black communists of the period as Cyril BRIGGS, Richard MOORE, and Harry HAYWOOD. In particular, Ford set out to rid the Harlem section of black nationalism, which had gained considerable currency among the membership. In his first year in Harlem, Ford terminated communist participation in campaigns to boycott those Harlem stores that did not hire African Americans, arguing that such a strategy of local black empowerment would exacerbate divisions between black and white workers. Ford redirected Harlem communists to boycott only institutions with unionized workers whose unions supported the campaign, a strategy that proved successful in desegregating several private businesses and government agencies located in Harlem. Ford was also successful in expanding the Harlem party, which in the first two years of his leadership increased its black membership from 87 to more than 300 and its general membership from 560 to 1,000.

In 1936, Ford helped found the NATIONAL NEGRO CONGRESS, a civil rights organization closely aligned with the Communist party. In that year he was again selected to be the CPUSA's vice presidential candidate, this time as a running mate with new party chairman Earl Browder. Ford and Browder ran again in 1940, but received fewer than 50,000 votes.

During World War II, Ford's power within the national party diminished as he was eclipsed by the more dynamic Benjamin J. DAVIS as the party's leading black spokesman. Ford was deposed from the National Committee (the renamed Politburo) at the party's congress in 1945 and was selected as chairperson of a newly formed internal security committee, though he remained the leader of the Harlem party.

After World War II, Ford languished as an obscure party bureaucrat, escaping the federal prosecution that sent many of the Communist party's leadership to prison. In the 1950s he served as executive director of the National Committee to Defend Negro Leadership, a party group set up to support black members convicted under federal antisubversion laws. Ford died in New York in 1957.

REFERENCES

KLEHR, HARVEY. *Biographical Dictionary of the American Left*. Westport, Conn., 1986.
———. *The Heyday of American Communism: The Depression Decade*. New York, 1984.

THADDEUS RUSSELL

Foreign Policy.   Attempts by African Americans to influence United States foreign policy in the twentieth century, though often forceful, have been circumscribed by social conditions unique to black Americans. During this period, attacking the legacy of white racism—lynching, segregation, disenfranchisement, poverty, and unemployment—was the focus of African-American political agitation. In addition, Elliott Skinner has noted that United States foreign policy has been run by a tiny elite, and shaping policy requires access to the white elite, to which African-American leaders have generally been antagonistic. Nevertheless, arguing that the fate of blacks outside the United States impacts upon the situation of blacks inside, many African-American leaders have tried to influence U.S. foreign policy—particularly with respect to Haiti, the decolonization of Africa, the VIETNAM WAR, and the formerly apartheid South Africa. These efforts have resulted in some significant successes, especially in the second half of the century.

The first major mobilization of African-American opinion on a foreign issue was against the U.S. occupation of Haiti from 1915 to 1934. President

Woodrow Wilson said he invaded Haiti to protect U.S. lives and business interests in a situation of civil unrest, and due to fears of German expansionism during WORLD WAR I. However, underlying Wilson's decision was the belief, shared by him and his closest advisers, that blacks could not govern themselves. U.S. Secretary of State Robert Lansing, for instance, wrote that "The African race . . . [has an] inherent tendency to revert to savagery."

To W. E. B. DU BOIS, on the other hand, Haiti was "a continuing symbol of Negro revolt against slavery and oppression, and capacity for self-rule." Thus, Du Bois led NAACP agitation against the invasion. Beginning in 1915, the civil rights organization (see NATIONAL ASSOCIATION FOR THE ADVANCEMENT OF COLORED PEOPLE) demanded to visit Haiti, but was not given permission until 1920. James Weldon JOHNSON's subsequent report called attention to the "atrocities" of U.S. marines against the natives, especially to the massacres of thousands of Haitian peasants who resisted U.S. rule and to the conscription of hundreds of others into forced labor gangs, which Johnson compared to slavery. Consequently, the forced labor policy was abandoned. Throughout the period of the occupation, the NAACP, together with black leaders like Rep. Oscar DEPRIEST of Illinois, organized protests against it. Their efforts had some effect on the U.S. decision to leave Haiti in 1934.

Idealistic and domestic considerations also motivated the enthusiastic participation of the African-American elite in the Pan-Africanist movement and struggles for decolonization in Africa (see PAN-AFRICANISM). At the end of WORLD WAR I, many black leaders were hopeful that the United States would take charge of efforts to decolonize Africa. Buoyed by President Wilson's commitment to the self-determination of the colonies, Du Bois asked him to include blacks in the U.S. delegation to the Paris peace conference of 1919. Wilson, partly fearing international exposure of the treatment of black troops by the U.S. Army during the war, refused.

Backed by the NAACP, and fearing that Africa would become an afterthought at the peace parley, Du Bois went to Paris that year, to investigate the conditions of black soldiers and organize a Pan-African Congress. He was joined there by other radical African-American leaders, including William Monroe TROTTER and William JERNAGIN, all of whom were denied passports by the Wilson administration and had to devise various means of getting to France. The Congress, which met in Paris in February 1919, with delegates from fifteen countries, petitioned the peace conference to improve the social and political conditions of blacks, especially in Africa, and argued that educated Africans and African-

Americans should oversee the process. The peace conference ignored the petition and the Africanist lobby, as did Wilson. While this episode denotes a clear failure on the part of black leaders to influence U.S. foreign policy, it also shows that when their interests were at stake, they went to great lengths to be heard.

Black leaders agitated again following the 1935 Italian invasion of Ethiopia, then one of only two independent countries in sub-Saharan Africa (the other was Liberia). The failure of the United States to actively oppose Italy angered many black leaders, who took their protest to the League of Nations. Partly consequent to the invasion, the Council of African Affairs was created in 1937 by Paul ROBESON, Ralph BUNCHE, and others, as an organization that would lobby the U.S. government on African issues. During WORLD WAR II, however, it did not have much impact.

At the end of the war, black leaders hoped that Africa would finally be decolonized. These hopes did not materialize—this time despite the efforts of Ralph Bunche, a committed anticolonialist, who in 1946 became head of the United Nations Trusteeship Division. Supported by an expectant African-American leadership, Bunche followed what he thought was the stated policy of President Franklin D. Roosevelt and his successor Harry Truman, and endeavored to place as many colonies as possible under U.N. trusteeship—as a first step toward independence. The British and French governments, and the U.S. Navy, which wanted control over those Pacific islands captured from the Japanese, opposed such moves and Bunche's positions were ignored.

Later African-American efforts to improve U.S. relations with the decolonizing world also failed. In 1955, Rep. Adam Clayton POWELL, JR., asked the Eisenhower administration to send an official observer to the Bandung, Indonesia, conference of Third World countries, which led to the formation of the nonaligned movement. The government refused, and Powell, who attended the conference himself, argued upon his return that the United States should support the efforts of nations battling to end colonialism. The advice was not heeded. By then, the United States was leading the Western alliance in the Cold War, and the Third World as a bloc was seen as pro-Soviet.

At no other period was the gulf between U.S. foreign policy and African-American responses to it greater than during the Vietnam War in the 1960s. No single individual personified this gulf more than Muhammad ALI, world heavyweight boxing champion and conscientious objector. Following the passage of the VOTING RIGHTS ACT OF 1965, Martin Luther KING, Jr., began involving the strong and organized CIVIL RIGHTS MOVEMENT in antiwar protests. By this time, King's attention was focused on social and economic issues pertaining to the black community, and he argued that massive war expenditure contributed to the further neglect of black concerns. The other major issue was the disproportionate number of black men who were drafted to fight, and die, in Vietnam. King was opposed by more conservative black leaders, like Bunche and Whitney YOUNG, Jr., of the NATIONAL URBAN LEAGUE, and it was not until 1967 that he became prominent in the antiwar movement. By then, with the rise of militant black nationalists like Stokely CARMICHAEL, who regarded Vietnam as part of a larger white war against all people of color, the African-American movement, itself and the antiwar movement as a whole were not united. Nevertheless, the sustained efforts of the antiwar movement, however tenuously allied it components were, in the long run forced the withdrawal of U.S. forces from Vietnam.

The next major foreign policy success for African-Americans came with South Africa. The mass movements of the 1960s had popularized foreign affairs within the black community and, in any case, apartheid was an issue with which black Americans could easily identify. Like the Vietnam protests, not just politicians but cultural and sports figures, students, and others demanded divestiture and tighter U.S. and international sanctions against the apartheid regime, both of which contributed directly to its downfall. South Africa was one foreign policy area on which there was little conflict between African Americans and official U.S. policy.

The South African agitation saw the emergence into prominence of the CONGRESSIONAL BLACK CAUCUS, established in 1971, which led the divestiture movement. The existence for the first time of a black group within the U.S. government in a position to influence foreign policy led to a marked improvement in the ability of African Americans to get their issues heard. The first chair of the caucus, Charles DIGGS of Michigan, also chaired the House Sub-Committee on African Affairs from 1970 to 1976. Although he failed to get U.S. aid to Africa increased, Democrats as well as Republicans have acknowledged the importance of the group and tried, on occasion, to work with it. In 1975, for instance, Secretary of State Henry Kissinger personally briefed black leaders on U.S. policy in Angola and Mozambique.

In the 1990s, the caucus and other black leaders lobbied against the North American Free Trade Agreement and demanded a say in the reformulation of U.S. immigration policy. The most notable success came with Haiti. Following the 1991 overthrow of President Jean-Bertrand Aristide by the military, the caucus was instrumental in persuading the Clinton administration to pressure the Haitian junta with the threat of military intervention to enable Aristide's return to office.

Overall, African-American attempts to influence United States foreign policy in this period shows that, as crucial aspects of their domestic agenda were taken care of, and black politics got better organized, blacks were in a better position to shape and change these policies.

REFERENCES

DeBenedict, Charles. *An American Ordeal: The Anti-War Movement of the Vietnam Era.* Syracuse, N.Y., 1990.

Horne, Gerald. *Red and Black: W. E. B. Du Bois and the Afro-American Response to the Cold War, 1944–1963.* Albany, N.Y., 1986.

Logan, Rayford W. *Haiti and the Dominican Republic.* New York, 1968.

Lynch, Hollis. *Black American Radicals and the Liberation of Africa.* Ithaca, N.Y., 1984.

Miller, Jake C. *Black Presence in American Foreign Affairs.* Washington, D.C., 1978.

Mullen, Robert W. *Blacks and Vietnam.* Washington, D.C., 1981.

Rivlin, Benjamin, ed. *Ralph Bunche: The Man and His Times.* New York, 1990.

Skinner, Elliott. *African-Americans and U.S. Policy Toward Africa, 1850–1924.* Washington, D.C., 1992.

QADRI ISMAIL

Foreman, George Edward (January 22, 1948–), boxer, minister, and actor. Born in Marshall, Tex., George Foreman grew up in a poor Houston neighborhood, where he dropped out of school in the tenth grade, drifted into petty crime and heavy drinking, and gained a reputation as a mean street fighter. In August 1965, Foreman joined the Job Corps, where Charles "Doc" Broadus introduced him to boxing. At the 1968 Olympic Games in Mexico City Foreman won the gold medal as a heavyweight. After his victory he waved an American flag in the ring, an action which contrasted dramatically with the behavior of two other black athletes at the games, sprinters John Carlos and Tommie Smith, who had protested racial injustice by raising black-gloved fists during the playing of the national anthem.

Foreman turned professional in 1969. He won his first thirty-seven professional fights, and in Kingston, Jamaica, on January 22, 1973, knocked out the reigning champion Joe FRAZIER in two rounds to take the title. Foreman successfully defended his championship against Jose "King" Roman and Ken NORTON, but on October 30, 1974, he lost it to Muhammad ALI in Kinshasa, Zaire. In that fight, billed as the "Rumble in the Jungle," Ali used an unorthodox "rope-a-dope" strategy, allowing Foreman to tire himself out by throwing most of the punches as Ali leaned back against the ropes and protected his head. By the eighth round, Foreman had tired significantly, and Ali was able to knock him out. Foreman won a number of fights in succeeding years, including a second match with Frazier. But he dropped a twelve-round decision to Jimmy Young in San Juan, Puerto Rico, on March 17, 1977, and retired, disheartened.

After his retirement from boxing, Foreman experienced a religious conversion and became a self-ordained evangelical preacher and pastor of the Church of the Lord Jesus Christ in Houston. He also straightened out his personal life, which he described as a "total mess," including four failed marriages and a flamboyant lifestyle. In 1984 he established the George Foreman Youth and Community Center in Aldine, Tex.

In 1987, at the age of thirty-nine and badly overweight (267 pounds, compared to 217½ when he beat Frazier), Foreman returned to the ring in what was originally described as an effort to raise funds for his youth center. Many observers found it difficult to take his comeback seriously, but, after beating twenty-four lesser-known opponents, he gained credibility by making a good showing in a close twelve-round loss to Evander HOLYFIELD on April 19, 1991, in Atlantic City, N.J. After winning several more fights, Foreman faced Tommy Morrison in a match for the World Boxing Organization title in Las Vegas, Nevada, on June 7, 1993, but lost in a unanimous twelve-round decision. After that fight, Foreman's career record stood at 73 wins (including 67 knockouts) and 4 losses. In a stunning reversal Foreman regained the heavyweight crown in 1994, fully twenty-one years after he first won it.

By that time, Foreman had become something of a media celebrity. His easygoing and cheerful attitude, his unique appearance (besides his girth, Foreman's shaved head made him easily recognizable), and his unlikely status as a boxer in his forties, made Foreman a favorite with many fans. He appeared on television in advertisements for a number of products, and in the fall of 1993 he briefly had his own television program on ABC, a situation comedy called "George," in which Foreman played a retired boxer who ran a youth center.

REFERENCES

ASHE, ARTHUR R., JR. *A Hard Road to Glory: A History of the African-American Athlete Since 1946.* New York, 1988.

BERGER, PHIL. "Body and Soul." *New York Times Magazine,* March 24, 1991, pp. 41–42, 62–64.

DANIEL SOYER

Forman, James (October 4, 1928–), civil rights activist, author. Born in Chicago, James Forman spent his early childhood with his grandmother in Marshall County, Miss. He eventually returned to Chicago with his parents, attended Wilson Junior College in Chicago, and served in the Air Force from 1947 to 1951. In 1953, Forman returned to Chicago and attended Roosevelt University, earning a degree in public administration in four years. He began to teach and also worked as a reporter for the CHICAGO DEFENDER, a leading African-American newspaper.

In 1960, Forman became active in the Emergency Relief Committee—an affiliate of the CONGRESS OF RACIAL EQUALITY (CORE) that gave assistance to black farmers in Tennessee who were evicted for registering to vote. Later that same year, he traveled to Monroe, N.C., in an interracial "freedom ride." He was arrested and beaten because of his civil rights activities. These experiences with racial injustice solidified his commitment to the cause of black civil rights, and in September 1961, he joined the STUDENT NONVIOLENT COORDINATING COMMITTEE (SNCC) in Atlanta.

SNCC was a young organization with a weak operational apparatus when Forman joined. Older and more experienced than most SNCC activists, he was appointed executive secretary almost immediately. He assumed full-time responsibility for fund-raising and hired and directed a support staff for SNCC activists. Due to his tenacity, commitment, and organizational skills, SNCC developed into a viable and durable civil rights organization.

Along with his administrative responsibilities, Forman participated in mass protests. He was active in the Albany movement—a coalition of civil rights groups in Albany, Ga.—in 1961, and in 1963 he was one of the leaders of a march in Greenwood, Miss., aimed at precipitating federal intervention. He gave many speeches on the subject of racial justice and was an outspoken critic of U.S. involvement in Vietnam.

As SNCC fell prey to divisive debates about tactics, strategies and goals in the mid-1960s, Forman was at the center of factional conflict. His often heavy-handed attempts to shape SNCC into a tightly

James Forman, executive director of the Student Nonviolent Coordinating Committee, speaking at the Bethel AME Church in Cambridge, Md., June 19, 1963. (AP/Wide World Photos)

structured organization were criticized by those who, like Robert MOSES, believed that SNCC's role was to serve as a catalyst for mass organization. By 1966, these pressures, coupled with ailing health, forced Forman to resign as executive secretary. He remained active within the organization, and played an integral role in promoting an alliance between SNCC and the BLACK PANTHER PARTY in 1967. When SNCC opted for a more collective leadership structure in 1968, Forman was elected as one of nine deputy chairmen. A year later, disheartened and exhausted by the years of factional infighting, he left the fragmenting organization.

He turned his energies toward black economic development. In 1969 he organized the National Black Development Conference (NBDC) in Detroit which produced the BLACK MANIFESTO, demanding that $500 million in REPARATIONS for slavery be given to African Americans by white churches and synagogues. Forman's bold and unannounced disruption of services at the Riverside Church in New York City to read the manifesto thrust him in the center of national publicity. The NBDC received over $1 million in donations from various white organizations. The money was used to establish Black Star Publications, a press controlled by Forman that published posters, pamphlets, and one book entitled *The Political Thought of James Forman* (1970). Funding was also given to the LEAGUE OF REVOLUTIONARY BLACK WORKERS, a Detroit-based militant organization made up of black industrial workers and others who

adhered to a socialist ideology. Forman was active in the League and was the guiding force behind the creation of the Black Workers Congress, a vehicle that was used to try to develop organizations similar to the League in other cities.

In 1972 Forman published the first edition of his autobiography, *The Making of Black Revolutionaries.* (A revised edition appeared in 1985.) In the mid-1970s he served as president of the Unemployment and Poverty Action council. From 1977 to 1980, he pursued a masters degree in African and African-American studies at Cornell University in Ithaca, New York. In 1982, he received a Ph.D. from the Union of Experimental Colleges and Universities (in corporation with the Institute for Policy Studies) in Washington, D.C. Out of his studies came a theoretical book, *Self Determination: An Examination of the Question and Its Application to the African-American People* (1984). Forman has continued to write and speak about issues of black empowerment and against oppression and discrimination. In 1990, he received the National Coalition of Black Mayors' Fannie Lou Hamer Freedom Award.

REFERENCES

CARSON, CLAYBORNE. *In Struggle: SNCC and the Black Awakening of the 1960s.* 1981.
FORMAN, JAMES. *The Making of Black Revolutionaries.* 1985.

JEANNE THEOHARIS

Forrest, Leon (1937–), novelist and educator. Leon Forrest was born in Chicago to Leon and Adeline Forrest, who came from two different African-American traditions—the Protestant deep South (Mississippi) and the Creole Catholic heritage of New Orleans, respectively. Both these traditions helped shape Forrest's imagination and are strongly reflected in his novels. His own experiences growing up in the city of Chicago, and his study of modern literature, particularly the fiction of Dostoyevsky, Joyce, and Faulkner and the drama of Eugene O'Neill, were additional influences on his development. Like Ralph ELLISON and Toni MORRISON, Forrest was one of those African-American writers of the second half of the twentieth century who adapted the forms and techniques of modern literature to the traditions of African-American fiction.

Forrest went to elementary and secondary schools on the South Side of Chicago and attended Roosevelt University and the University of Chicago before entering the U.S. Army in 1960. His army service in Germany as a public-information specialist from 1960 to 1962 helped launch him on a journalistic career.

Beginning as a reporter on a small Chicago neighborhood paper, the *Woodlawn Observer,* he became an associate editor of *Muhammad Speaks,* the newspaper of the Black Muslim movement, in 1969, rising to managing editor in 1972. In 1973 he was appointed associate professor of African-American studies at Northwestern University, where he later became professor and director of the African-American studies program.

Forrest's most important literary creation is the Forest County series, which consists of four novels published from 1973 to 1992. These novels, like those of William Faulkner's Yoknapatawpha saga, are quite different in form and style from each other, yet are interrelated in setting, characters, and themes. As a whole, the Forest County novels express a rich vision of African-American life, history, and culture in the United States as influences on the lives of characters in Forest County, an imaginative transformation of Chicago, during the 1960s and 1970s.

The first three Forest County novels—*There Is a Tree More Ancient Than Eden* (1973), *The Bloodworth Orphans* (1977), and *Two Wings to Veil My Face* (1983)—deal with a young African American's confrontation with his heritage. In *There Is a Tree,* Nathaniel Witherspoon faces the knowledge of loss and suffering in both his personal life and the consciousness of his heritage as an African American. In *The Bloodworth Orphans,* the same character learns about the tragic doom of a family whose history of miscegenation, incest, and orphanhood exemplifies the African-American heritage of racism and oppression and its catastrophic consequences. Finally, in *Two Wings to Veil My Face,* Nathaniel learns of his family's history in slavery from his adoptive grandmother, Sweetie Reed, who is one of Forrest's most memorable creations.

Forrest's most recent novel in the series, *Divine Days* (1992), is a comic epic of considerable range and variety that describes a crucial week and a day in which the aspiring young dramatist Joubert Jones encounters characters and experiences that reveal to him his true vocation as a writer.

In addition to his novels, Forrest has written a number of plays and librettos, as well as a collection of essays on such topics as William Faulkner, Billie HOLIDAY, and Elijah MUHAMMAD.

REFERENCES

FORREST, LEON. *The Furious Voice of Freedom: Collected Essays.* Mt. Kisco, N.Y. In preparation.

GRIMES, JOHANNA L. "Leon Forrest." In *Afro-American Fiction Writers After 1955,* Vol. 33 of *Dictionary of Literary Biography.* Detroit, 1984, pp. 77–83.

JOHN G. CAWELTI

Fort, Syvilla (July 3, 1917–November 8, 1975), dancer and dance teacher. Born in Seattle, Syvilla Fort began studying dance when she was three years old. After she was denied admission to several ballet schools because she was black, Fort's early dance education took place in her home and in private lessons. By the time she was nine years old, Fort was teaching ballet, tap, and modern dance to small groups of neighborhood children who could not afford private lessons.

Fort attended the Cornish School of Allied Arts in Seattle as their first black student after graduating from high school in 1932. After spending five years at the Cornish School, Fort decided to pursue her dance career in Los Angeles, and in 1939 her neighbor, black composer William Grant STILL, introduced Fort to dancer Katherine DUNHAM. Several weeks later, Fort began dancing and touring with the Katherine Dunham Company and learning the Dunham technique, which was rooted in the dance traditions of Africa, Haiti, and Trinidad. Fort danced with the company until 1945 and was included in the well-known film *Stormy Weather* (1943).

While dancing with the Dunham Company, Fort neglected a serious knee injury which prevented her from performing professionally by the mid-1940s. In 1948, Dunham appointed Fort as chief administrator and dance teacher of the Katherine Dunham School of Dance in New York, a position Fort retained until 1954 when the school closed because of financial problems. In 1955, Fort joined her husband Buddy Phillips, another Dunham dancer, to open a dance studio on West 44th Street in New York. In this studio Fort developed what she called the "Afro-Modern technique" which fused the Dunham approach with modern styles of dance that Fort learned in her early education. She continued to use this method in her work as a part-time instructor of physical education at Columbia University's Teachers College from 1967 to 1975.

The studio on 44th Street thrived until 1975 when Fort began struggling against breast cancer and was unable to solve the school's financial problems. Her staff and students found a new studio for Fort on West 23rd Street where she taught through the summer of 1975. Fort shaped three generations of dancers and among her best-known students were Marlon Brando, James Dean, Jane Fonda, James Earl JONES, Eartha KITT, José Limón, Chita Rivera, and Geoffrey HOLDER.

Five days before her death from breast cancer on November 8, 1975, Fort attended a tribute to her life's work which was organized by the Black Theater Alliance and hosted by her student Alvin AILEY and by Harry BELAFONTE. In 1992, Fort's work was honored again when dancers from several companies performed an evening of her choreography at New York's Symphony Space.

REFERENCES

ALEXANDER, J. B. "Syvilla Fort: Mother to 3 Generations of Dance." *New York Post,* October 28, 1975.

DUNNING, JENNIFER. "Syvilla Fort—A Life Benefitting Dance." *So-Ho Weekly News,* November 13, 1975.

———. "Tribute to a Choreographer." *New York Times,* May 21, 1992.

"Syvilla Fort, a Dance Teacher Who Inspired Blacks, Is Dead." *New York Times,* November 9, 1975.

ZITA ALLEN

Forten, James (September 2, 1766–March 15, 1842), businessman and abolitionist. Born free in Philadelphia in 1766, James Forten attended a Quaker school in Philadelphia headed by abolitionist Anthony Benezet. At the age of fourteen he went to sea and became a powder boy on the *Royal Louis,* a colonial privateer under the command of Captain Stephen Decatur, father of the nineteenth-century naval hero of the same name. After one successful sortie against the British, the *Royal Louis* was captured by a group of British ships; Forten and the rest of the crew were taken prisoner. Had he not befriended the son of the British captain, Forten, like many African Americans in his situation, might have been sent into slavery in the West Indies. Instead the British captain ensured that Forten would be transferred to the *Jersey,* a prison hulk in New York harbor; after seven months, Forten was released. On the prison hulk, many succumbed to rampant disease; Forten luckily avoided serious illness.

Shortly after his release, Forten began to work under the tutelage of Robert Bridges, a Philadelphia sail maker. Forten's skill and aptitude guaranteed his success in the industry: by the age of twenty he was the foreman of Bridges's shop. Upon Bridges's retirement in 1798, Forten became the undisputed master of the shop and developed a reputation for excellent service and innovative sail handling techniques. His business grew; some estimates suggest that he had a fortune of over $100,000 by the early 1830s.

Forten used both his fortune and his fame to forward his agenda for the destruction of slavery. One of the most prominent and vocal Philadelphians on the issue, Forten was a lifelong advocate of immediate abolition. In 1800 he was a petitioner to the U.S. Congress to change the terms of the 1793 Fugitive Slave Law which permitted suspected runaways to be seized and arrested without a warrant and access to

due process. Forten refused to rig sails for ships that had participated in or were suspected of participating in the slave trade. In 1812, along with well-known Philadelphians Richard ALLEN and Absalom JONES, he helped raise a volunteer regiment of African Americans to help defend Philadelphia were the city to be threatened by the British.

In September 1830, Forten was a participant in the first National Negro Convention in Philadelphia. Its goal was to "consider the plight of the free Negro" and to "plan his social redemption." At the next annual convention, Forten used his influence to oppose funding for the American Colonization Society which supported black emigration to Liberia; at other times, however, Philadelphia's black elite, including Forten, had advocated emigration to Haiti and Canada.

In 1832 Forten and several other African Americans forwarded another petition to the Pennsylvania legislature asking it not to restrict the immigration of free blacks into the state nor to begin more rigorous enforcement of the 1793 federal Fugitive Slave Law. Much of their argument was based on two main principles: a moral argument based on the evils of slavery and an economic argument—that free blacks were extremely productive members of the Philadelphia and Pennsylvania communities. As one of the organizers of the AMERICAN ANTI-SLAVERY SOCIETY in 1833, Forten provided support, especially economic, to abolitionist activities. Forten's generous support greatly aided the continuing publication of William Lloyd Garrison's abolitionist *Liberator* (see ABOLITION). Around 1838 he also went to court in a vain attempt to secure the right to vote.

Forten was a founder and presiding officer of the AMERICAN MORAL REFORM SOCIETY. The society stressed temperance, peace, and other Garrisonian ideals, which included the full and equal participation of women in antislavery activism and society in general. Forten's reputation for good works was well known: he received an award from the city of Philadelphia for saving at least four, and perhaps as many as twelve, people from drowning in the river near his shop. When he died in 1842, thousands of people, many of whom were white, reportedly attended his funeral.

Even before his death in 1842, the legacy of Forten's deep belief in abolition was carried on by his family. Forten's children, and later his grandchildren, would figure as prominent abolitionists and civil rights activists throughout the nineteenth century. Forten's son James, Jr., and his son-in-law Robert PURVIS were very active in the abolitionist movement from the 1830s onwards, and often collaborated with the elder Forten in his various activities. All of Forten's daughters were involved in antislavery affairs, and Charlotte Forten GRIMKÉ, Forten's grand-daughter, became a well-known author, educator, and activist for civil rights.

REFERENCES

APTHEKER, HERBERT, ed. *A Documentary History of the Negro People in the United States.* New York, 1951, pp. 126–133.

"The Forten Family." *Negro History Bulletin* 10, no. 4 (January 1947): 75–79.

PURVIS, ROBERT. *Remarks on the Life and Character of James Forten Delivered at Bethel Church, March 30, 1842.* Philadelphia, 1842.

WINCH, JULIE. *Philadelphia's Black Elite: Activism, Accommodation, and the Struggle for Autonomy, 1787–1848.* Philadelphia, 1988.

EVAN A. SHORE

Forten, Robert Bridges

Forten, Robert Bridges (c. 1814–April 1864), abolitionist and businessman. Robert Bridges Forten was born in Pennsylvania, the son of a freeman, James FORTEN, Sr. Robert Forten inherited his father's abolitionist zeal and prosperity. As a young man he spoke at abolitionist rallies and joined his father's sail-making concern. Robert Forten was so angered by Philadelphia's segregated schools that he educated his daughter, Charlotte Forten (*see* Charlotte Forten GRIMKÉ), at home until she was ready to live with his friend, Charles Lenox Remond, and attend an interracial school in Salem, Mass. Just before the CIVIL WAR, Forten moved his wife, son, and business to Britain in order to escape discrimination in the United States.

When the Civil War began, however, he felt it his duty to return and fight for the emancipation of African Americans. Although educated, prosperous, and fifty years old, Forten enlisted as a private in the 43rd U.S. Colored Infantry. He was quickly promoted to the rank of sergeant-major under Col. S. M. Bowman, Chief Mustering and Recruiting Officer for Colored Troops in the state of Maryland. In April 1864, approximately one month after his enlistment, Forten died of erysipelas, an acute infection of the skin. He was buried with a full military ceremony in Philadelphia, the first African American to receive such an honor.

REFERENCES

FORTEN, CHARLOTTE L. *The Journal of Charlotte L. Forten,* ed. Ray Allen Billington. London, 1953.

"The Forten Family." *The Negro History Bulletin* 10 (January 1947): 75–79.

Obituary. "Burial of a Colored Soldier." *The Liberator,* May 13, 1864, p. 80.

PETER SCHILLING

Fort Pillow, Tennessee

Fort Pillow, Tennessee, site of one of the most controversial battles of the CIVIL WAR, on April 12, 1864. The earthworks commanded a portion of the Mississippi River from a bluff forty miles north of Memphis. The 292 black troops from the Sixth United States Colored Heavy Artillery and the Second United States Colored Light Artillery, and 285 southern white Unionists from the Thirteenth Tennessee Cavalry, faced 1,500 Confederates under Nathan Bedford Forrest. Outnumbered and outmaneuvered, the Union forces nevertheless rejected Forrest's demand for surrender. Confederates easily overwhelmed the post, slaughtering many of the defenders within the fortification and sending scores of others fleeing down the bluff, into the river, and into a lethal crossfire. Some were shot as they bobbed in the water; many more were killed after surrendering.

Although Forrest and his defenders denied that a deliberate massacre occurred, a United States congressional inquiry and several Union survivors provided chilling testimony of wanton murder by Confederate troops. Forrest's superior generalship and the inexperience of the Union soldiers contributed to the ghastly federal defeat, but cannot account alone for the astounding Union losses. Confederates suffered only about 13 killed and 60 wounded, while inflicting over 331 Union casualties. Although President Abraham Lincoln belatedly threatened to retaliate for such atrocities, the policy was never implemented. Blacks temporarily spurned military service, fearing that their government could not or would not protect them from southern retribution. But black recruitment soon resumed its former levels, buoyed by the rallying cry "Remember Fort Pillow."

REFERENCES

CIMPRICH, JOHN, and ROBERT C. MAINFORT, JR. "Fort Pillow Revisited: New Evidence about an Old Controversy." *Civil War History* 28 (December 1982): 293–306.

MANESS, LONNIE E. "The Fort Pillow Massacre: Fact or Fiction." *Tennessee Historical Quarterly* 45 (Winter 1986): 287–315.

DONALD YACOVONE

Fortune, Amos

Fortune, Amos (1710?–1801), philanthropist. Amos Fortune was born a slave in New England. In 1725 he was sold to Caleb Copeland and his family in Boston. He remained there for fifteen years before being sold to Ichabod Richardson of Woburn, Mass., from whom he learned the tanner's trade. In 1770 he bought his freedom and set up shop in Woburn, where he purchased a half-acre lot. In 1779 he bought and married Violate Baldwin. Two years later they left Massachusetts and settled in Jaffrey, N.H. Fortune opened a successful tanning business, while his wife worked weaving cloth, and they became leading citizens. In 1789 Fortune bought land and built a house. In 1796 he joined the local library and began binding all its books. He died in 1801 and was buried in Jaffrey.

Fortune is chiefly known as a philanthropist. During his lifetime, he helped support local African Americans and trained poor black and white apprentices in the tanning trade. He also defended them in legal matters. At his death, he left an estate worth nearly $800, a large sum for the time. Almost all his possessions went to his wife. After her death, the money was earmarked for the support of the local school and church, and during the nineteenth century the money was used to help support a local school. In 1928, after the school closed down, the town of Jaffrey began an annual student public speaking competition, with part of the money as the prize. In 1946 the contest was transformed into a summer lecture series named the Amos Fortune Forum. It takes place every year in the Old Meeting House, where Fortune worshipped and is buried.

REFERENCE

KAPLAN, SIDNEY, and EMMA NOGRADY KAPLAN. *The Black Presence in the Era of the American Revolution, 1770–1800.* Washington, D.C., 1973.

GREG ROBINSON

Fortune, Timothy Thomas (October 3, 1856– June 2, 1928), journalist, civil rights activist. T. Thomas Fortune was born a slave in Marianna, Fla., in 1856, to Emanuel and Sarah Jane Fortune. After EMANCIPATION his father, active in Republican politics, was forced by white violence to flee to Jacksonville, where young Fortune became a compositor at a local newspaper. In the winter of 1874, Fortune enrolled at Howard University with less than three years of formal education behind him. But financial troubles compelled him to drop out, and he began working for a black weekly paper. Fortune married Carrie C. Smiley in the late 1870s and returned to Florida, where he worked on several newspapers. Chafing under southern racism, Fortune gladly moved to NEW YORK CITY in 1881 to accept a position with a white-owned weekly publication.

In New York, Fortune joined with other African Americans who had founded a tabloid called *Rumor* (soon known as the New York *Globe*), and he became managing editor. Fortune set the *Globe*'s militant tone in his editorial advocacy of black civil rights and self-defense; he also shared Henry George's critique of monopoly and endorsed his land distribution program. Moreover, at a time when most black newspapers backed the Republican Party, Fortune favored political independence. He expanded on these radical themes in his book, *Black and White: Land, Labor, and Politics in the South,* published in 1884.

The *Globe* folded in early November 1884. Just two weeks later, however, Fortune was producing the *Freeman* (soon called the *New York Freeman*), a four-page weekly whose circulation stood at 5,000 by the end of its first year. In October 1887 Fortune left the *Freeman,* which became the *New York Age* and began to court Republican support. (Fortune had supported Democratic presidential candidate Grover Cleveland in 1888.) He returned as editor in February 1889, renouncing his past alliance with the Democrats but continuing to criticize the Republicans' inaction on racial issues. He supplemented his income by writing for the *New York Sun,* a leading newspaper.

T. Thomas Fortune. (Photographs and Prints Division, Schomburg Center for Research in Black Culture, The New York Public Library, Astor, Lenox and Tilden Foundations)

Fortune was also a key figure in the Afro-American League (AAL), an early and important vehicle for civil rights agitation. In May 1887, Fortune proposed the formation of a nonpartisan organization to challenge lynch law in the South and to demand equal opportunities in voting, education, and public accommodations.

He also issued the call for the AAL's first national convention; at the January 1890 meeting, he was elected secretary. The AAL planned to fight JIM CROW through legal means; after Fortune himself was refused service at a New York hotel bar, the AAL sued the proprietor and won. But without adequate resources to mount regular legal challenges, and lacking support from prominent black Republicans, by 1893 the organization had sunk into decline.

Fortune continued to expose racist abuses, particularly in the South. After Ida B. Wells's (*see* Ida B. WELLS-BARNETT) Memphis newspaper office was destroyed by a mob, he offered her work on the *Age* and published her stunning exposé of lynching. In 1894–95, Fortune himself toured the South and reported on worsening conditions there. Despite the revival in 1898 of the old AAL as the Afro-American Council (AAC), Fortune had by then grown deeply pessimistic about the possibilities for securing racial justice.

During this period of disaffection, Fortune solidified his relationship with Booker T. WASHINGTON. The two had first come into contact in the early 1880s and, despite their differences, Fortune helped launch the accommodationist Washington as a national figure. He not only publicized Tuskegee Institute (*see* TUSKEGEE UNIVERSITY) in the *Age,* but also employed his literary talents to polish and promote Washington's views; he wrote a long introduction to *Black-Belt Diamonds* (1898), a collection of Washington's speeches, and he edited and revised Washington's *The Future of the American Negro* (1898). Because Fortune's only income came from journalism, the remuneration he received for these efforts, as well as emergency loans from Washington, helped tide him over through hard times.

As Washington rose in national stature, he relied increasingly on Fortune—his closest ally in the North—to advance his political agenda. Fortune, aware that Washington occasionally backed legal challenges to Jim Crow behind the scenes, tried to make Washington's views more palatable to a northern black audience. Fortune served as chair of the executive committee of the NATIONAL NEGRO BUSINESS LEAGUE (NNBL), formed by Washington in 1900. As AAC president in the early 1900s, Fortune helped squelch anti-Washington sentiment spearheaded by William Monroe TROTTER of the *Boston Guardian.*

One reason for Fortune's efforts on Washington's behalf was that he hoped for a political appointment to resolve his financial difficulties. He did manage, in late 1902, to secure a six-month post as Special Immigrant Agent of the U.S. Treasury Department, investigating racial conditions in Hawaii and the Philippine Islands. Evidence suggests, however, that Washington thwarted Fortune's future aspirations, possibly because he realized a government position would increase Fortune's economic independence.

Fortune's greatest usefulness to Washington had been as an "independent" journalist, and observers had grown skeptical of his independence; as early as 1902, the *Guardian* had written scathingly that "much of the fat that now greases the way for the *Age,* comes out of the Tuskegee larder." Moreover, Fortune continued to take militant political stances that were not in line with Washington's own positions.

In February 1907, Washington secretly acquired direct control of the *Age,* and his heavy-handed management contributed to Fortune's nervous breakdown later that year. Believing he had been called by God to preach to the race, Fortune sold his shares in the *Age* to Fred R. Moore (1857–1943), a Washington loyalist, who claimed a "white friend" had backed the transaction. Unknown to Fortune, it was Washington's money that had clinched the deal.

Fortune left for Chicago and sought unsuccessfully to reestablish himself. With little to lose, he disclosed Washington's financial interest in the *Age* and was lauded by Washington's rivals. But this did nothing to resolve his deepening financial crisis. His marriage had collapsed by 1906; now he lost his home. Suffering from alcoholism and unable to obtain steady work, he scraped by for years on whatever intermittent journalistic employment he could find.

The *Age,* meanwhile, deteriorated dramatically in quality, and Washington lured Fortune back in the fall of 1914. While the compensation was poor and Fortune's editorial independence limited, he remained with the *Age* for three years. Thereafter he worked for papers in Philadelphia, Indianapolis, Washington, D.C., and elsewhere.

The early 1920s ushered in new political possibilities for African Americans and brought Fortune back from the edge of destitution and despair. In 1923 he became editor of the *Negro World,* the organ of Marcus GARVEY's UNIVERSAL NEGRO IMPROVEMENT ASSOCIATION. While Fortune never embraced the Garvey movement, he had become deeply disillusioned by black people's failure to attain equality and justice by means of the political process. Through his work for the *Negro World,* he was able to regain his self-respect. In the late 1920s Fortune's colleagues in the National Negro Press Association (over which he himself had presided some thirty years before) lauded him as the "dean" of Negro journalists. He edited the *World* until his death on June 2, 1928, at the home of his son Fred in the Philadelphia area.

Fortune's erratic career has somewhat obscured his own historical importance. Before Booker T. Washington's ascent as a national figure began in 1895, Fortune himself was acknowledged as the major spokesperson for black America. His leadership role in the late nineteenth-century civil rights movement was instrumental in shaping the debate over how African Americans would respond to their legal and social oppression in the decades to come.

REFERENCES

HARLAN, LOUIS R. *Booker T. Washington: The Wizard of Tuskegee, 1901–1915.* New York, 1983.
PENN, I. GARLAND. *The Afro-American Press and its Editors.* 1891. Reprint. Salem, N.H., 1988.
THORNBROUGH, EMMA LOU. *T. Thomas Fortune, Militant Journalist.* Chicago, 1972.
WOLSELEY, ROLAND E. *The Black Press, U.S.A.* Ames, Iowa, 1971.

TAMI J. FRIEDMAN

Fort Wagner, South Carolina. On July 18, 1863, the FIFTY-FOURTH REGIMENT OF MASSACHUSETTS VOLUNTEER INFANTRY led the Union assault on Fort Wagner, an impregnable sand redoubt on Morris Island at the mouth of Charleston harbor. Gen. Quincy A. Gillmore planned the ill-fated attack as a tactical move in the larger northern effort to capture Charleston. Despite a failed first assault on July 11 and one of the most intensive land and naval bombardments of the CIVIL WAR, Wagner sustained little damage. The Fifty-fourth led the second charge, withstood harrowing defensive fire, overcame a spike-filled moat, surmounted the walls, and occupied a portion of the fort's eastern wing. But the Union's failure to provide reinforcing troops compelled the regiment to withdraw.

The costly defeat—1,515 Union casualties before the Confederates quietly abandoned the fort on September 7—left the Fifty-fourth shattered (the defenders suffered only 181 casualties). Fourteen of its officers and 256 enlisted men had been killed, wounded, or captured—nearly half of the regiment's attacking force. Some were mistakenly shot by fellow white soldiers during the assault, while others were murdered in retreat by racist Union troops. The regiment's much-honored commander, Col. Robert Gould Shaw, was killed on Wagner's parapets and buried by the Confederates in a mass grave with his men—who were laid face down—as an intended insult. But the Fifty-fourth's undeniable heroism

(Sgt. William H. CARNEY received the Congressional Medal of Honor) dispelled racist allegations that blacks could not fight and cleared the way for the recruitment of about 178,000 blacks into the Union Army.

REFERENCES

BURCHARD, PETER. *One Gallant Rush: Robert Gould Shaw and His Brave Black Regiment.* New York, 1965.
EMILIO, LUIS F. *A Brave Black Regiment: History of the Fifty-fourth Regiment of Massachusetts Volunteer Infantry, 1863–1865.* 1894. Reprint. New York, 1968.

DONALD YACOVONE

Forty Acres and a Mule. After the CIVIL WAR, many freedmen expected the federal government to provide them with enough land (forty acres) to establish themselves as independent farmers. This, they felt, was owed to them as restitution for their past labor. The hope for land redistribution sprung from a number of sources, including the wartime experiments at the Sea Islands of South Carolina and at Davis Bend. Expectations were also sparked by Union Gen. William T. Sherman's victorious march through Georgia. On January 12, 1865, Sherman and Secretary of War Edwin Stanton met with twenty leaders of the black community in Savannah, Ga. Four days after the meeting, Sherman issued Special Field Order No. 15, which set aside a thirty-mile portion of the low-country rice coast from South Carolina to Georgia for settlement by blacks. Families of freedmen would receive forty acres and, possibly, the loan of a mule—many historians claim this to be the origin of the phrase. Further indication that the government would assist blacks in their effort to become independent farmers came with the formation of the Freedmen's Bureau (*see* BUREAU OF REFUGEES, FREEDMEN, AND ABANDONED LANDS) in March 1865. Along with distributing food and clothing, the bureau was authorized to divide abandoned and confiscated land into forty-acre plots for rental to freedmen and loyal refugees. Complicating these efforts was the fact that the federal government's legal title to southern land was still not clear.

In the summer of 1865, President Andrew Johnson ordered land in federal hands to be returned to former owners. Thaddeus Stevens, Charles Sumner, and other Radical Republican congressmen tried to pass a bill upholding the Sherman land titles; however, it was vetoed by Johnson. In July 1866 Congress ratified another attempt at land redistribution, with the Southern Homestead Act. Unfortunately, this, too, proved to be of little help to the freedmen. Many blacks had signed long-term restrictive labor contracts, and others were unable to afford the implements, seed, and rations needed to work the land. By mid-1867, Radical Republican congressmen had limited their focus to securing political rights for blacks (in particular the right to vote), rather than sweeping land reform.

The phrase "forty acres and a mule" has been used since the nineteenth century for a number of black causes. It suggests that African Americans deserve restitution for the work of black slaves. More generally, the term suggests empty promises made by the U.S. government and the debt owed to its black citizens.

REFERENCE

OUBRE, CAUDE F. *Forty Acres and a Mule: The Freedmen's Bureau and Black Land Ownership*. Baton Rouge, La., 1978.

WALTER FRIEDMAN

Foster, Andrew "Rube" (September 17, 1879–December 9, 1930), baseball player and executive. Andrew "Rube" Foster was the man most responsible for the creation of the first Negro National League (*see* BASEBALL), the African-American baseball league of the 1920s. Born in Calvert, Tex., the son of an elder in the Methodist Episcopal Church, Foster attended school through the eighth grade. His baseball career started in 1897 with the traveling black club the Waco Yellow Jackets. A confident pitcher, Foster moved on to Chicago's Leland Giants in 1902, but soon jumped to Otsego, Mich., to play on a white semipro team. By the end of the year, he had joined Philadelphia's Cuban X-Giants, the best black team in the East. In 1903, when the Cuban X-Giants played the Philadelphia Giants for the "Colored Championship of the World,' Foster starred, pitching and winning four of five games. In 1904, he moved to the Philadelphia Giants, and helped them beat his old team, the Cuban X-Giants, in the playoff series.

In 1907 Foster joined the Cleveland Giants; three years later he and most of the other players left the Giants to start their own team. In 1911, Foster and John Schorling, a white tavern owner and son-in-law of Chicago White Sox owner Charles Comiskey, founded a new club, the Chicago American Giants. They made an oral agreement to split profits equally. The Giants soon became the finest team in black baseball, and one of the most profitable. Foster was not only a player for the Giants, until his retirement from active play around 1915, but he was the team's manager and agent. According to fragmentary surviving statistics, in 174 innings pitched he allowed just 135 hits and struck out 82 batters. In the four playoff games he pitched, Foster was 3-1, and struck out 26 batters in 36 innings.

During the 1910s, Foster began serving as booking agent for other black and white semipro teams in the Chicago area. However, around 1919, attendance began to drop. Bookings for the important East coast clubs were controlled by Nat Strong, a white booking magnate. Unable to compete, Foster agitated for the creation of an African-American league.

In February 1920, Foster met in Kansas City with the owners of six black teams. Foster suggested forming a league which would both professionalize black baseball and offer financial advantages to ballclub owners such as a world series. Appointed temporary president, he showed his partners a league charter he had written, which had already been incorporated in six states. After speedily writing a league constitution, Foster was formally elected president and treasurer of the League of Professional Baseball Clubs, otherwise known as the Negro National League (NNL). On May 2, 1920, the Chicago Giants lost to the Indianapolis ABCs in the league's first game.

Since he was both President of the NNL and owner of the Chicago American Giants, Foster worked a long day. He accepted no salary as league president, and most of the 5 percent of gate receipts he collected went for league expenses. While his autocratic leadership alienated the other owners, they supported him whenever he offered to resign. Under the stress of his heavy schedule, Foster suffered a nervous breakdown in 1926 and entered an Illinois state asylum. He never recovered, and he died there in 1930. His body lay in state in Chicago for three days as crowds poured in to mourn him. After Foster's death, his partner in the Chicago American Giants, John Schorlin, refused to honor the profit-sharing agreement the two had devised, and Foster's wife was left destitute.

Foster was elected to the Baseball Hall of Fame in 1981.

REFERENCES

PETERSON, ROBERT. *Only the Ball Was White*. New Jersey, 1970.

ROGOSIN, DONN. *Invisible Men: Life in Baseball's Negro Leagues*. New York, 1983.

GREG ROBINSON

Foster, Frank Benjamin, II (September 23, 1928–), saxophonist and bandleader. Frank B. Foster started taking clarinet lessons at the age of eleven.

By the age of nineteen, when he matriculated at Wilberforce University in Ohio, he had learned to play alto saxophone, started writing his own big band arrangements, and fronted his own twelve-piece band. While at Wilberforce, Foster switched from alto to tenor saxophone.

He left college after two years and began performing with Snooky Young. He was drafted in 1951, and after his discharge in 1953, he joined the Count BASIE Band around the same time as fellow saxophonist Frank Wess. The two of them helped to revitalize the Basie band during the 1950s. Foster contributed both his abilities as a saxophonist and as composer/arranger. The most famous of his compositions for the Basie band is "Shiny Stockings" (1956).

In 1963, Foster left the Basie band in order to expand his horizons as a player. He organized and played in various ensembles throughout the 1960s and '70s, including that of Elvin JONES in the late 1960s. He was commissioned to write the *Lake Placid Suite* for the 1980 Winter Olympics. He continues to compose and perform, chiefly as the leader of the Count Basie Orchestra, which he has led since 1986.

REFERENCES

BASIE, COUNT, with Albert Murray. *Good Morning Blues: The Autobiography of Count Basie.* New York, 1985.
VOCE, STEVE. "Frank Foster." *Jazz Journal International* 36, no. 2 (1983): 15–17.

TRAVIS JACKSON

Foster, Robert Wayne "Bob" (December 15, 1938–), boxer. Bob Foster was born and raised in Albuquerque, N. Mex. He excelled in football at his local high school and was offered a scholarship at the University of New Mexico. But instead of pursuing a football career after high school, Foster enlisted in the U.S. Air Force and was stationed at Billings, Mont. He began his organized boxing career while in the military, winning the All-Air Force light heavyweight championship four times and the All-Service title once.

Soon after his discharge in 1961, Foster began his professional career as a light heavyweight. At 6 feet 3½ inches, Foster usually fought at 173 pounds, with a powerful left hook as his main weapon. After seven years as a professional, with a hiatus in 1965 caused by discouragement with his career, Foster finally earned a title match with light heavyweight champion Dick Tiger in 1968. Foster knocked out Tiger in the fourth round. He then went on to successfully defend his light heavyweight crown a record four-

teen times, ten by knockout. From 1966 through the summer of 1970, Foster dominated the light heavyweight class with a record of twenty consecutive wins, nineteen by knockout.

Foster's victories led to unsuccessful heavyweight title shots against Joe FRAZIER in 1970 and Muhammad ALI in 1972. In 1973 he had two fights with Pierre Fourie, a South African, in back-to-back light heavyweight title bouts. The first meeting, held in Albuquerque, ended in a fifteen-round decision for the champion. The rematch, which was the first ever professional contest between black and white boxers held in South Africa, also ended with a fifteen-round decision for Foster. In 1974 Foster announced his retirement and went to work as a deputy sheriff in Bernalillo County, N. Mex.

Foster staged another successful comeback between 1975 and 1978, winning five consecutive bouts. His boxing career finally came to an end in 1978, however, after he lost successive matches by knockout to Mustapha Wassaja and Bob Hazelton. Foster's professional career included 56 victories, 46 by knockout, 1 draw, and 8 losses. In 1990 he was elected to the Boxing Hall of Fame in Canastota, N.Y.

REFERENCES

ASHE, ARTHUR, JR. *A Hard Road to Glory: A History of the African-American Athlete Since 1946.* New York, 1988.
GOLDMAN, HERBERT G., ed. *The Ring 1984 Record Book and Boxing Hall of Fame.* New York, 1984.
PORTER, DAVID L. *Biographical Dictionary of American Sports: Basketball and Other Indoor Sports.* New York, 1989.

THADDEUS RUSSELL

Four Step Brothers, The, acrobatic tap dance act. Unlike many other brother acts of the mid-twentieth century, the Four Step Brothers were not blood brothers, but a troupe of talented dancers who worked together. While working as a newsboy in New York City in the mid-1920s, Maceo Anderson (September 3, 1910–) spent most of his spare time at the Hoofers Club, headquarters of tap dance, located next to the Lafayette Theatre in Harlem. Anderson saw Al Williams (1910–1985) and Happy Johnson perform at an amateur night competition at the Apollo. The three formed a trio in 1925. When they convinced Duke ELLINGTON to introduce them during an intermission at the COTTON CLUB, they ended up staying there as performers for several years. By 1930, Sherman Robinson joined the group, and they became a quartet. Their electrifying style of flash tap was made even more exciting by their use of the tap challenge, a form of ritualized one-upmanship, during which they egged each other on and set tempos by clapping their hands and stomping their feet. The act was famous for its trademark "Bottle Dance," and for a furious finale in which the dancers jumped over each other in wild flips and splits. Billed as the "Eight Feet of Rhythm," they played in Europe, and worked in many nightclubs and theaters in the United States, in addition to appearing in a number of films, including *It Ain't Hay* (1943), *Rhythm of the Islands* (1943), and *Here Come the Girls* (1953).

The Four Step Brothers was one of the longest lived of acrobatic tap dance acts. Over the years the act changed in personnel; in addition to Maceo Anderson and Al Williams, who remained with the group until it disbanded in the mid-1970s, the act featured such talented dancers as Rufus "Flash" McDonald, Sherman Robinson, Sylvester Johnson, Prince Spencer, Sunshine Sammy, Freddie James, and Norman Rowe. Extremely diversified in scope, the quartet incorporated comedy, song, Afro-Cuban movement, acrobatics, and a boogie-woogie style of rhythm tapping.

REFERENCES

FRANK, RUSTY. *Tap!* New York, 1991.
STEARNS, MARSHALL, and JEAN STEARNS. *Jazz Dance: The Story of American Vernacular Dance.* New York, 1968.

CONSTANCE VALIS HILL

Fourteenth Amendment. Coming approximately ten years after the DRED SCOTT DECISION had ruled that all slaves and their descendants were not citizens of the United States, the Fourteenth Amendment, ratified on July 28, 1868, granted both state and federal citizenship to "all persons born or naturalized in the United States" (with the notable exception of Native Americans living on reservations). It also pledged that no state shall "abridge the privileges or immunities" of citizens, nor "deny to any person within its jurisdiction the equal protection of the laws." Along with the FIFTEENTH AMENDMENT, which sought to extend the franchise to all blacks, the Fourteenth Amendment was drafted by Radical Republican members of Congress, who were uneasy with President Andrew Johnson's lenient policies toward the South in the wake of the CIVIL WAR. These Republicans aimed at giving meaning to the freedom which had been legally granted to slaves by the THIRTEENTH AMENDMENT. In particular, they hoped to invalidate the discriminatory black codes that had been passed by various state legislatures.

Radical Republicans were also concerned that, with the emancipation of slaves, southern representation in Congress would dramatically increase when the former Confederate states reentered the Union—according to Article I, Section 2 of the Constitution, only three-fifths of the slave population had previously been counted for purposes of representation. To ensure that newly freed blacks would have a voice in choosing their political leaders, Section 2 of the amendment promised to reduce congressional representation proportionately for each male citizen denied suffrage. (Despite severe restrictions placed on black suffrage, however, this section was never applied.)

Section 3 of the Fourteenth Amendment excluded former Confederates from holding political office even if they had previously taken an oath to support the U.S. Constitution. This section aimed at keeping former Confederate officers from regaining political office. It had only a temporary effect. Section 4 declared the government of the United States not liable for the Confederate debt.

The intentions of the Radical Republicans were undermined by a series of conservative Supreme Court decisions. In the *Slaughterhouse Cases* (1873), the Court held that state law, rather than federal law, controlled the basic civil liberties of citizens. Further, it interpreted the "privileges and immunities" of citizens in a narrow way, covering such matters as protection on the high seas. The Court also declared that states were not required to enforce the liberties guaranteed in the Bill of Rights. In the 1883 Civil Rights cases, the Court ruled that the Fourteenth Amendment did not ensure citizens equal access to public accommodations, and in PLESSY V. FERGUSON (1896), that racial segregation of railways was not a violation of the amendment's "equal protection" clause.

After World War II, a different interpretation of the Fourteenth Amendment evolved from a less conservative Supreme Court. The "equal protection" clause began to be used to fight racial discrimination in such cases as BROWN V. THE BOARD OF EDUCATION OF TOPEKA, KANSAS (1954), against school segregation, and the *Reapportionment Cases* (1964), against unfairly drawn state legislative districts. As well, the Court came to hold a broader interpretation of the civil rights protected under the Fourteenth Amendment. *Shelley* v. *Kraemer* (1948) outlawed racially restrictive covenants in housing. *U.S.* v. *Guest* (1966) applied the Fourteenth Amendment to cover private violence that was racially motivated. Under Chief Justice Earl Warren, the Court ruled, in a series of cases, that most of the Bill of Rights had to be respected by the states. The liberal Court of the late 1960s and early '70s found other rights guaranteed by the amendment, such as the right to use birth control devices (*Griswold v. Connecticut,* 1965) and the right to an abortion (*Roe v. Wade,* 1973). The appointees of several conservative Republican presidents from the 1970s and 1980s, however, have interpreted the rights protected under the amendment more narrowly.

It took approximately a century before the federal government was willing to enforce the provisions of the Fourteenth Amendment as its authors had envisioned. The amendment will no doubt continue to be interpreted in ways that will either broaden or narrow federal protection of civil rights, according to the political climate of the nation and the makeup of the Court.

REFERENCES

BERGER, RAOUL. *The Fourteenth Amendment and the Bill of Rights.* Norman, Okla., 1989.

NELSON, WILLIAM E. *The Fourteenth Amendment: From Political Principle to Judicial Doctrine.* Cambridge, Mass., 1988.

WALTER FRIEDMAN

Four Tops, The. The Four Tops is a popular soul quartet whose classic recordings for MOTOWN in the 1960s helped to establish the Detroit label's reputation and success. All of the members of the group—Renaldo "Obie" Benson, Abdul "Duke" Fakir, Lawrence Payton, and lead singer Levi Stubbs—grew up in Detroit's North End, where they played sports together but sang in different groups. They first sang together in 1952 at a mutual friend's party, and their lineup has since remained unchanged. At first they called themselves the Four Aims. Chess Records, which released their first single, "Kiss Me Baby," in 1956, changed their name to the Four Tops to avoid confusion with the Ames Brothers. Following incidental recordings for other labels, including "Ain't That Love?" (1960) and "Where Are You?" (1962), and years of personal appearances opening for such acts as Billy ECKSTINE, Brook Benton, and Della Reese, the group signed with Motown in 1963. By then, they were already seasoned performers. After contributing background vocals to a number of other artists' records, success came when they were paired with Motown's trio of composer-producers, Brian and Eddie Holland and Lamont Dozier, who created songs and arrangements highlighting and propelled by Stubbs's dramatic, impassioned voice. Between 1964 and 1967 the group released a steady stream of hits, including "Baby, I Need Your Loving" (1964), "Standing in the Shadows of Love" (1966), "Bernadette" (1967), and two songs that reached the top of

the national pop charts: the bouncy, driving "I Can't Help Myself" (1965) and "Reach Out I'll Be There" (1966), widely considered a pop masterpiece for its epic sound and innovative instrumentation, including oboes, flutes, and Arab drums. When Holland-Dozier-Holland left Motown in 1967, the Four Tops had marginal success working with other producers, but they left the label in 1972. They recorded the hit song "Ain't No Woman" in 1973, and two years later released *Night Lights Harmony.* In the 1980s and 1990s the Four Tops continued their busy international touring and recording schedule, including *Tonight!* (1981), *Magic* (1985), and *Indestructible* (1988).

REFERENCES

GEORGE, NELSON. *Where Did Our Love Go?: The Rise and Fall of the Motown Sound.* New York, 1985.

HIRSHEY, GERRY. *Nowhere to Run: The Story of Soul Music.* New York, 1984.

BUD KLIMENT

Foxx, Redd (December 9, 1922–October 11, 1991), comedian. Redd Foxx was born John Elroy Sanford in St. Louis, Mo., the second son of Fred Sanford, an electrician, and Mary Alma Hughes Sanford, a minister. Foxx's father deserted the family when Foxx was four, and Foxx was raised first by his grandmother, and then in Chicago by his mother, who at that time was employed as a domestic.

Foxx quit high school after one year to play in a washtub band with two friends, Lamont Ousley and Steve Trimel. In 1939, they ran away to New York City, called themselves the Bon-Bons, and earned money performing on street corners and in subways. World War II broke up the band, and Foxx, rejected by the military, began to play in a tramp band act at the APOLLO THEATER with Jimmie LUNCEFORD.

About this time, Foxx adopted his professional name. Called "Red" because of his red hair and light complexion, he added an extra "d" to "Red" and took the name "Foxx" with the term "foxy" (and the baseball player Jimmy Foxx) in mind. He began landing nightclub jobs, where he developed his stand-up routine.

After four years of teaming with comedian Slappy White (1947–1951), Foxx worked on the West Coast. In 1956, he recorded the first of what would become more than fifty "party records"—comedy albums specializing in raunchy humor.

Although Foxx had never done any straight acting, he accepted the small role of Uncle Bud in the 1969 film *Cotton Comes to Harlem.* Executives at NBC developed the character into the situation comedy

Sanford and Son, and cast Foxx in the title role of a cantankerous junk dealer who spent more time malingering and badgering his son than working. The program, which premiered in 1972 and ran through 1977, brought Foxx considerable acclaim and popularity. He attempted to recreate his role as Fred Sanford in a series that ran in 1980, but was unable to revive the original program's appeal.

While *Sanford and Son* made Foxx wealthy, in 1983 he filed for bankruptcy protection, citing mounting debts. In 1985, the Internal Revenue Service claimed Foxx owed almost $3 million in taxes, interest, and penalties, and seized many of his possessions, including his home in Las Vegas.

Foxx was working on the set of a new NBC series, *The Royal Family,* when he suffered a heart attack and died on October 11, 1991.

REFERENCES

BOGLE, DONALD. *Blacks in American Films and Television.* New York, 1988.

MAPP, EDWARD. *Directory of Blacks in the Performing Arts.* Metuchen, N.J., 1990.

SUSAN MCINTOSH
MICHAEL PALLER

Franklin, Aretha Louise (March 25, 1942–), singer. Known as "Lady Soul" and "The Queen of Soul," Aretha Franklin brought the undiluted power of black gospel singing to American popular music beginning in the late 1960s (see GOSPEL). Born March 25, 1942, in Memphis, Tenn., and raised in Detroit, Mich., she was the fourth of five children of Barbara Siggers Franklin and the well-known gospel preacher and singer, the Rev. C. L. FRANKLIN of Detroit's New Bethel Baptist Church. Her mother, also a gospel singer, left her husband and children in 1948 when Aretha was six, and died shortly thereafter.

Aretha's formative years were spent singing in her father's church choir and traveling with him on the gospel circuit. Numerous jazz and gospel figures visited the Franklin's home, and James CLEVELAND boarded with the family and worked with Aretha as she practiced playing the piano and singing. Clara Ward sang at an aunt's funeral, and Franklin was so moved she decided to become a professional singer herself. At fourteen she recorded a selection of gospel songs including Thomas A. Dorsey's "Precious Lord, Take My Hand." She became pregnant at fifteen and dropped out of school.

At eighteen Franklin was brought to the attention of John Hammond, the producer at Columbia Records who had "discovered" Bessie SMITH, Billie

Aretha Franklin, daughter of a well-known Detroit preacher, saw her career soar after 1967 when she signed with Atlantic Records, which produced a number of hit recordings that stand as the definitive examples of female soul singing. Franklin was an active performer for a number of years before her breakthrough to great popular success; this photograph dates from 1963. (Frank Driggs Collection)

HOLIDAY, and other African-American musicians. Hammond praised Franklin's voice as the best he had heard in twenty years. Franklin signed with Columbia and moved to New York but achieved only marginal success as a pop singer because of Columbia's material and arrangements, a confused hodgepodge of jazz, pop, and standards.

Her breakthrough came in 1966 when her Columbia contract expired and she signed with Atlantic Records, where she was teamed with veteran producer Jerry Wexler. He constructed simple, gospel-influenced arrangements for her, often based on her own piano playing. In these comfortable musical settings her true voice emerged with intensity and emotion. Wexler said, "I took her to church, sat her down at the piano, and let her be herself." Franklin's first record with Wexler was "I Never Loved a Man (The Way I Love You)" in February 1967. It was an immediate success and topped *Billboard*'s charts. Her second hit, "Respect," was sung with such conviction it became a call for black and feminist pride and empowerment.

Often compared to Ray CHARLES for her fusion of sacred and secular styles, Franklin came to personify African-American "soul" music. She produced a series of top records including "Chain of Fools," "Think," and "Don't Play That Song." She has won fifteen Grammy Awards, three American Music Awards, and a Grammy Living Legend Award. With thirty-five albums, she has had seventeen number one rhythm-and-blues singles, and more million-selling singles than any other woman singer. In 1980 she switched to the Arista label.

Throughout her career, her dominant public voice has been contrasted with her private, even reclusive, personality, although she carefully monitors her career and the music industry. Her personal life has at times been difficult, with her mother's abandonment, her own pregnancy at age fifteen, several unsuccessful marriages, and, particularly, the fact that her father, to whom she was very close, spent five years in a coma from a gunshot wound in 1979 until his death in 1984.

REFERENCE

BEGO, MARK. *Aretha Franklin: The Queen of Soul.* New York, 1989.

                                          BUD KLIMENT

Franklin, Clarence LaVaughn

Franklin, Clarence LaVaughn (January 22, 1915–July 27, 1984), minister. C. L. Franklin, father of the singer Aretha FRANKLIN, was the most popular African-American preacher of his generation. Born in Sunflower County, Miss., near Indianola, he was raised by his mother, Rachel, and stepfather, Henry Franklin, a sharecropper, near Cleveland, Miss. The segregation, discrimination, and material poverty of that time and place made an enduring impression on him, but so did his mother's constant love and support. At about the age of nine, he was converted, joined St. Peter's Rock Baptist Church in Cleveland, and sang in the church choir, eventually becoming a soloist. Inspired by the preaching of Dr. Benjamin J. Perkins, then president of the State Baptist Convention, he himself felt that God had called him to preach. A dream or vision in which he saw a burning plank confirmed the call; he preached his first sermon at age fifteen or sixteen, was ordained by St. Peter's Rock Church two years later, and began preaching regularly. He left his parents' farm and moved to Cleveland, then to Clarksdale, where he pastored

several rural churches and married. He and his wife, Barbara, moved to Greenville, where he attended Greenville Industrial College, a combined seminary and trade school, supporting his new family by preaching. In his early twenties the Franklins moved to Memphis, Tenn., and for three years he pastored two churches while attending LeMoyne College as a special student, taking courses in literature and social science. His next pastorate was Friendship Baptist Church in Buffalo, N.Y. Although he liked the congregation, he regretted that Buffalo was outside the mainstream of African-American culture and resolved to look elsewhere. In 1946 he became pastor of New Bethel Baptist Church in Detroit, a position he held until his death.

A handsome man of uncommon intelligence and theological insight, and a brilliant orator with a rich, forceful delivery and masterful powers of organization and concentration, Franklin became a national celebrity as a result of sermon recordings and groundbreaking preaching tours. Joe von Battle, an entrepreneur within the Detroit black community, recorded Franklin's Sunday sermons at New Bethel beginning in the early 1950s, and for the next twenty-five years these were issued on long-playing records, played on black radio programs, and distributed throughout the nation. From about 1953 through the mid-1960s, until his health could no longer stand the strain, he combined time at New Bethel with preaching tours that took him to almost every city in the United States. The programs began with gospel singing and concluded after he delivered a sermon. Millions of people bought his records and heard him preach at churches, city auditoriums, and stadiums. His sermon recordings were (and still are) used in seminaries, and his influence on other African-American preachers was enormous. It is said that every preacher either tried to imitate him or tried to avoid doing so. New Bethel's membership grew to more than ten thousand, and visitors to Detroit made it a point to hear him preach, swelling the congregation until his sermons had to be broadcast to crowds gathered in the city blocks near the church.

Franklin's sermons were well informed historically and theologically, and he sought to instruct as well as inspire his listeners. He thought about his subjects and planned his sermons in advance, but he delivered them extemporaneously. Always based on a passage from the Bible, each sermon brought biblical characters and theological insights to life in historical and contemporary contexts, with special relevance to African-American experience. A consummate orator, Franklin began his sermons as interactive rhetorical demonstrations, making theological concepts plain and incorporating traditional African-American biblical storytelling and dramatic monologues while members of the congregation responded aloud, punctuating his phrases with encouraging cries. After these expositions, Franklin changed his delivery to "whooping" (intonational or chanted preaching), often carrying on to the climax of a story with shouts and moans amid a poetic eloquence that brought congregations to their feet, shouting, moaning, and dancing in response. His sermons thus combined traditional African-American subjects and techniques with modern theological insight (he left Fundamentalism behind in Mississippi) and appealed to people over a broad spectrum of age and experience.

Although best known as a gospel preacher, Franklin participated in the CIVIL RIGHTS MOVEMENT and helped African Americans obtain political office. Many black political figures, including Detroit mayor Coleman YOUNG and Michigan congressman John CONYERS, were close to Franklin and campaigned in New Bethel. Against much opposition from the white power structure, Franklin organized the 1963 civil rights march in Detroit, which drew a quarter-million people and where the Rev. Dr. Martin Luther KING, Jr., first presented his "I Have a Dream" speech. King invited Franklin to preach at the 1968 Poor People's Campaign in Washington, where he electrified the assembled crowd.

In the 1970s, Franklin ceased his preaching tours and concentrated on his New Bethel ministry. He was shot by robbers in 1979 and remained in a coma until he died in 1984. His most popular recorded sermons were "The Eagle Stirreth Her Nest," "Give Me This Mountain," "Dry Bones in the Valley," and "The Prodigal Son." They rank among the most outstanding documented sermons in the English language.

REFERENCE

TITON, JEFF TODD, ed. *C. L. Franklin, Give Me This Mountain: Life History and Selected Sermons.* Urbana, Ill., 1989.

JEFF TODD TITON

Franklin, John Hope (January 2, 1915–), historian and educator. John Hope Franklin was born in Rentiesville, Okla., an exclusively African-American town. At an early age he came to be introduced to white custom, law, and justice in the South. His father, a lawyer, was expelled from court by a white judge who told him that no black person could ever practice law in his court. Young Franklin was himself ejected, along with his mother (an elementary school teacher) and sister, from a train because his mother refused to move from the coach designated for whites. After moving to Tulsa in 1926, Franklin attended Booker T. Washington High School and learned the meaning of a "separate but equal" education—inferior facilities and a sharply limited curriculum. His avid interest in music introduced him to the JIM CROW seats in the local concert hall. He went on to receive his B.A. at FISK UNIVERSITY in 1935 and his Ph.D. in history at Harvard University in 1941.

Throughout his career, Franklin combined scholarship with social activism. As student body president at Fisk University, he protested the lynching of a local black man to the mayor, the governor, and President Franklin D. Roosevelt. Having once been barred from entering the University of Oklahoma to pursue graduate studies, he readily agreed to the NAACP's request that he be an expert witness for a black student seeking admission to the graduate program in history at the University of Kentucky. At the request of Thurgood Marshall, he served on the research team whose work led to the Supreme Court's BROWN V. BOARD OF EDUCATION decision outlawing school segregation. In 1965, he joined more than thirty other historians on the civil rights march into Montgomery, Ala.

Like Carter WOODSON and W. E. B. DU BOIS, Franklin demonstrated to a skeptical or indifferent

John Hope Franklin. (Photographs and Prints Division, Schomburg Center for Research in Black Culture, The New York Public Library, Astor, Lenox and Tilden Foundations)

profession that the history of black Americans was a legitimate field for scholarly research. His first book, *The Free Negro in North Carolina, 1790–1860* (1943), explored the anomalous position of free blacks in the slave South. *Reconstruction After the Civil War* (1961) was a revisionist treatment of the unique experiment in biracial democratic government in the postwar South, particularly in its depiction of blacks as active participants and leaders, not simply as victims or passive tools of white politicians. In *The Militant South* (1956) and *A Southern Odyssey* (1976), Franklin explored different facets of the southern experience and varieties of southern white expression. His Jefferson Lecture in the Humanities for 1976, *Racial Equality in America,* probed that troubled and elusive search. In a turn to biography, his *George Washington Williams* (1985) traced the life of a historian who wrote in the 1880s the first substantial and scholarly history of black Americans. For hundreds of thousands of students, Franklin's *From Slavery to Freedom* (first published in 1947) introduced them to African-American history. In *Race and History* (1989), he brought together his most important essays and lectures, including his autobiographical sketch and reflections, "A Life of Learning."

In his books, as in his teaching, Franklin transcends the distinction between African-American and American history. He has underscored the unique quality of the history of African Americans even as he has viewed that history as an intimate part of American history, inseparable from and a central theme in the national experience. Rejecting the need to replace old distortions with new myths and eulogistic sketches of heroes and heroines, he has demonstrated his full appreciation of the complexity and integrity of the American and African-American past.

His early teaching career included Fisk University, St. Augustine's College, North Carolina Central College, and HOWARD UNIVERSITY. In 1956 he went to Brooklyn College as chairman of the department of history—a department of fifty-two white historians. (The appointment made the front page of the *New York Times*; Franklin's troubled search for housing did not.) In 1964, he joined the history faculty of the University of Chicago, serving as chair from 1967 to 1970 and as the John Matthews Manly Distinguished Service Professor from 1969 to 1982. Moving to Durham, N.C., he chose to diversify rather than retire, becoming the James B. Duke Professor of History and professor of legal history in the law school at Duke University.

Franklin has been elected to the presidencies of the American Studies Association, the Southern Historical Association, the United Chapters of Phi Beta Kappa, the Organization of American Historians, and the American Historical Association. More than

seventy colleges and universities have awarded him an honorary degree. He has served on numerous national commissions, and in 1980 was a United States delegate to the 21st General Conference of UNESCO. In 1978 the state that initially forced John Hope Franklin to undergo the humiliating rites of racial passage elected him to the Oklahoma Hall of Fame.

REFERENCE

FRANKLIN, JOHN HOPE. *Race and History: Selected Essays, 1938–1988,* especially "John Hope Franklin: A Life of Learning," Baton Rouge, La., 1989, pp. 277–291.

LEON F. LITWACK

Franklin, Martha Minerva (October 29, 1870–September 26, 1968), nurse. Born in New Milford, Conn., Franklin graduated from Meriden Public High School in 1890, and, in 1895 enrolled in the Woman's Hospital Training School for Nurses in Philadelphia. She received her diploma in 1897 and was the only black student in her graduating class. She then returned to Connecticut, where she worked as a private-duty nurse.

At that time, African-American nurses had minimal access to training and hospital positions, and were not allowed membership in the American Nurses' Association (*see* NURSING). In 1906, Franklin sent 1500 letters to other black nurses to collect information on racial discrimination in the profession. One of the respondents was Adah Belle Samuels THOMS, the pioneering black nurse who was president of the Lincoln Hospital School of Nursing Alumnae Association. Thoms invited the correspondents to meet as guests of her association in New York City. In 1908, Franklin chaired a three-day conference and the National Association of Colored Graduate Nurses (NACGN) was born. It was decided that only those nurses who had state registration and had graduated from schools approved by the NACGN would be given membership. Franklin was elected its president, and was reelected when the NACGN met in Boston the following year. She refused reelection the third year, but was named honorary president for life and permanent historian of the NACGN.

In the 1920s, Franklin went on to a six-month postgraduate nursing course at Lincoln Hospital in New York City, becoming a registered nurse and working for many years as a nurse in the city's public school system. Her lifelong dedication to her profession is demonstrated by the fact that at the age of fifty-eight she enrolled for two years in the Department of Practical Arts (now the Department of Nursing Education) at Teachers College of Columbia University. Franklin retired at New Haven, Conn., where she died at the age of ninety-eight. In 1976, she was posthumously inducted into the Nursing Hall of Fame.

REFERENCES

BULLOUGH, VERN L., OLGA MARANJIAN CHURCH, and ALICE P. STEIN, eds. *American Nursing: A Biographical Dictionary*. New York, 1988.

HINE, DARLENE CLARK, ed. *Black Women in America*. Brooklyn, N.Y., 1993.

LYDIA MCNEILL

Fraternal Orders and Mutual Aid Associations.

Fraternal orders and mutual aid associations were among the first and most durable organizations established by African Americans. The earliest black lodges and societies were formed toward the end of the eighteenth century. Although their heyday came between the CIVIL WAR and the GREAT DEPRESSION, many remained active into the final years of the twentieth century. Throughout their history, lodges and societies offered important material benefits to their members, as well as arenas for social interaction, the development of leadership skills, and the cultivation of economic and political networks. In size and influence, they have often rivaled the black church as the most significant organizations within African-American community life.

As a general category, fraternal organizations include both local societies and multibranch orders operating on a regional or national scope. Local mutual aid societies offer their members benefit packages that might include financial support in times of sickness; a funeral and burial in a society cemetery; cash payments or pensions for windows and orphans, and low-cost loans.

Beginning in the late nineteenth century, some of the national orders provided their members with formal life insurance policies, as well as other types of economic assistance. The larger orders generally took the from of secret societies, developing elaborate rituals, symbols, regalia, and hierarchical structures of "degrees," or levels of membership and esoteric knowledge. Elaborate ritual was less important for the local groups than for the larger orders. Nevertheless, the line between the two types of such organizations was indistinct; the local groups sometimes also adopted elements of fraternal ritual and a number of them grew into multibranch fraternal orders.

Since the founding of the first African-American Masonic lodge by Prince Hall in Boston in 1775, fraternal organizations have played an important role in African-American communal life and group cohesion. (Photographs and Prints Division, Schomburg Center for Research in Black Culture, The New York Public Library, Astor, Lenox and Tilden Foundations)

Some of the societies limited membership to men, but there were many women's organizations and mixed groups as well. Although the majority of the more ritualistic secret orders, such as the Masons, included only men, women played a larger role in African-American fraternal orders and mutual aid societies than in similar organizations in other ethnic communities, perhaps because black women played a more prominent role as wage earners and providers for their families than their counterparts in other groups. Moreover, even the all-male orders usually had affiliated women's auxiliaries.

African-American mutual aid societies first took shape in the 1780s and '90s in cities of both the North and the South with large communities of free blacks. Perhaps the earliest such association was the African

Union Society of Newport, R.I. Founded in 1780, its activities included "assisting members in times of distress," arranging apprenticeships and compiling vital records of the black population. As similar organizations arose in other cities, notably Boston and Philadelphia, the African Union Society also established contact with them—at one point urging them to consider its endorsement of black emigration to Africa.

One of the organizations with which the Newport group maintained friendly relations was Philadelphia's Free African Society, founded in 1787. Led by Absalom JONES and Richard ALLEN, its members pledged to "support one another in sickness and [provide] for the benefit of their fatherless children." It was closely associated with the group of African Americans who left St. George's Methodist Episcopal Church the same year, and later was instrumental in the establishment of both Jones's St. Thomas African Episcopal Church and Allen's Bethel African Methodist Episcopal Church. Other early societies also had close religious associations.

In the opening decades of the nineteenth century, mutual aid societies became the most widespread form of organization among free blacks. Their importance is illustrated by figures from Philadelphia, where, by 1848, some 106 such societies enrolled a combined membership of about 8,000—nearly half of all free black adults in the city. The societies' prominence and visibility was also enhanced by their acquisition of property. The New York African Society for Mutual Relief, for example, erected its own building on Orange (now Baxter) Street in 1820, using it as a meeting hall, a school, and a stop on the UNDERGROUND RAILROAD.

In the South, conditions were less conducive to organization. Nevertheless, free blacks in such cities as Charleston, S.C., New Orleans, Washington, and Richmond maintained associations. In Baltimore, there were 30 organizations with memberships ranging from 35 to 150 in 1835. At times when laws restricted meetings by African Americans, these organizations often continued to operate clandestinely. Sometimes, however, white authorities tacitly allowed them to function, or, as in Baltimore, officially exempted them from repressive legislation. Slaves were forbidden to organize, but there is some evidence that they, too, formed secret burial and mutual aid societies. Slaves sometimes joined the associations of free blacks in the cities. Frederick DOUGLASS, for example, was a member of the East Baltimore Improvement Society before his emancipation.

Provisions for membership and benefits varied, especially in the early years. But by the 1820s and 1830s, they were becoming more standardized, assuming a form also common among similar societies formed by members of other ethnic groups. The 1825 constitution of the New York African Clarkson Association, named after an English abolitionist, delineated a more or less typical set of membership requirements and benefits. Prospective members were

Arthur Schomburg (top row, far right) with other members of the Masons. (Photographs and Prints Division, Schomburg Center for Research in Black Culture, The New York Public Library, Astor, Lenox and Tilden Foundations)

required to be "free persons of moral character" between the ages of twenty-one and forty in good health, who would not "in any probability become . . . charge[s] to the Association." After a candidate was proposed by a current member, a committee would investigate his character, and, if he was found to be suitable, the members voted on whether to admit him. The new member paid an initiation fee, signed the constitution, and pledged fealty to the organization. Dues were twenty-five cents a month, in return for which sick members were entitled to $2 a week for up to three months and $1.50 a week for three additional months. The society provided up to $15 to bury deceased members, whose widows and children received pensions of $20 a year. Members could be fined for being out of order at a meeting and expelled for a criminal conviction. The organization met once a month and, in addition to its material assistance, aimed to provide its members with "improvement in literature."

At times, membership requirements for societies reflected color and class divisions within the African-American society. Founded in 1790, the Brown Fellowship Society of Charleston, S.C., admitted only light-skinned members of the local, free African-American elite. Those excluded formed the Free Dark Men of Color (later the Humane Brotherhood), which cooperated with the Ladies Union Benevolent Society. The Brown Fellowship Society survived into the twentieth century, after changing its name in 1890 to the Century Fellowship Society.

Women's societies were among the earliest black mutual aid associations. In some cases, these groups formed when men's or mixed societies refused to grant equal rights to female members. This was the case, for example, in Newport, where women split from the African Benevolent Society in 1809. By 1830, there were twenty-seven women's benefit societies in Philadelphia, including such venerable groups as the Female Benevolent Society of St. Thomas (founded in 1793) and the Benevolent Daughters (founded 1796). The New York Benevolent Branch of Bethel was a women's organization, which, in 1843, offered its members a sick benefit of $1.50 a week for up to six weeks and six shillings a week for another six weeks.

Alongside the local mutual aid associations, a parallel tradition of black fraternal orders arose during the last decades of the eighteenth century. Freemasonry was, for African-Americans as for whites, both the first secret order and the source for much of the internal culture that characterized the other fraternal orders that came later.

African-American Freemasonry originated in 1775, when Prince HALL, a prominent black Bostonian, was initiated into Masonry together with fourteen other free blacks by a lodge attached to the British military in Boston. Barred from local white lodges, the African-American Masons met separately as a provisional lodge until they were issued a charter as African Lodge No. 459 by the Mother Grand Lodge of England in 1784. (Although the charter was dated 1784, it was not actually received by the Bostonians until 1787.) Later, the black group constituted itself as a grand lodge independent of other (white) Masonic grand lodges, and instituted a number of subordinate lodges that came to be known as Prince Hall Masonry.

Freemasonry appealed to many middle-class African-American men with its emphasis on the principles of universalism and international brotherhood. For the most part, however, black Masons found that their erstwhile white brothers were unwilling to acknowledge the legitimacy of black lodges, much less to admit individual blacks into white ones. From time to time, individual white Masons and lodges spoke out for equality within the movement, and a handful of lodges even initiated light-skinned African-American members. However, such efforts usually met with condemnation by the great majority of white Masons and their institutions. Whites paid little heed to black arguments that the undeniable authenticity of the first African Americans' initiation into the order justified the recognition of Prince Hall Masonry.

Nevertheless, black Freemasons maintained an abiding faith in the ability of Masonic ideals to overcome even the most vicious racism. This faith was vindicated to some degree by Prince Hall Masonry's ability to circumvent the white American lodges and establish friendly relations with lodges in England and continental Europe. The depth of this belief is also illustrated by widespread stories of white Masons coming to the aid of black Masons in times of danger or need. One such account concerns three free blacks kidnapped in 1788 from Boston and shipped to the West Indies for sale as slaves. When a slave owner and prospective buyer—himself a Mason—saw one of the men give the secret Masonic signal for distress, he saw to it that they were freed and returned home. In the nineteenth and twentieth centuries, similar signals were said to have helped turn back lynch mobs and prompted sympathetic treatment by jailers and judges. Some degree of plausibility is lent these accounts by C. L. Dellums, a leader of the BROTHERHOOD OF SLEEPING CAR PORTERS in the early twentieth century, who related that he obtained his first job on the railroad when a white employment clerk noticed his Masonic insignia and put him ahead of other applicants.

With the exception of a short period in the early nineteenth century, the Prince Hall Masons were never united in a common national grand lodge. Rather, each state's grand lodge operated independently. By the time of Emancipation, Prince Hall Masonry was active in fourteen states and the District of Columbia, as well as Canada, Liberia, Haiti, and the West Indies. The order expanded quickly after the Civil War, enrolling 46,000 members in 1904. After explosive growth in the early decades of the twentieth century, Prince Hall Masonry contracted in the 1930s. Although it recovered in the 1940s and 1950s, growth was uneven in later decades. Nevertheless, Prince Hall Masonry claimed about 500,000 members in 1980.

Prince Hall Masonry was a prestigious organization within the African-American community, deriving its status from its exclusivity and the charitable works it performed. The membership was largely middle class, consisting of professionals, small-business executives, skilled workers, and unskilled and semiskilled workers with stable employment with the government and railroads. Many of the most prominent African-American politicians, businessmen, religious leaders, and civil rights activists have been members. Indeed, fully half of the men listed in *Who's Who in Colored America* for 1930–1932 were Freemasons.

Like their white equivalents, the Prince Hall Masons developed an array of auxiliary organizations. Women who were relatives of Masons could join the Prince Hall Grand Chapter of the Eastern Star, the Heroines of Jericho, and the Order of the Golden Circle. Thirty-second-degree Masons and Knights Templar were eligible for membership in the Ancient Egyptian Arabic Order of the Nobles of the Mystic Shrine for North and South America, the "Shriners," organized in 1893. The women's auxiliary of the Shrine was called the Daughters of Isis.

The influence of Freemasonry on fraternal culture went beyond numbers or the prestige of individual members. Prince Hall Masonry emphasized that strand of Masonic thought that traced the "craft's" roots back to ancient Egypt and King Solomon, whom the Prince Hall order viewed as black. Many subsequently established orders adopted elements of Masonic ritual and symbolism into their own systems. The Grand United Order of Galilean Fishermen, established in Washington, D.C., in 1856, for example, used such Masonic emblems as the fish, passion cross, and rose. Members of the Independent Order of St. Luke, founded in Richmond, Va., in 1866, wore aprons during ceremonies and evergreen sprigs during funerals. The order's symbols included the Masonic all-seeing eye. Many fraternalists belonged to two or more societies, and the overlapping affiliations helped to spread ritual elements throughout the fraternal world.

Like the Prince Hall Masons, the black Grand United Order of Odd Fellows received its charter directly from the English Grand Lodge of the order. In 1842, two local societies, the Philomathean Institute of New York and the Philadelphia Company and Debating Society, appealed to the New York Grand Lodge of the Odd Fellows for a lodge charter citing the "need for mutual aid and protection in case of sickness and distress." When they were rejected, a black sailor named Peter Ogden, who had been initiated into a lodge in Britain, helped the African-American group acquire a charter from the English Grand Lodge in 1843. Eventually, the Odd Fellows were to become the largest black fraternal order, claiming 304,000 members in more than 7,500 lodges in 1922. The Sojourna [sic] Household of Ruth, a women's auxiliary, was then affiliated with the Odd Fellows.

Two other African-American fraternal orders that paralleled similar white organizations were established during the heyday of fraternalism in the decades after the Civil War. The Knights of Pythias of North and South America, Europe, Asia, and Africa was formed after a group of African Americans was denied a charter by the New York Grand Lodge of the white Pythians in 1870. Apparently, a number of African Americans who could pass for white were nonetheless initiated into the order and thereby gained access to the secret rituals. By 1880, they had established their own grand lodge and begun chartering local lodges. The origins of the black Pythian order were therefore somewhat irregular by fraternal standards, but were justified by its members on the grounds that their exclusion from the older group violated the order's principles of benevolence and brotherhood. By 1905, the black Knights of Pythias claimed 70,000 members in 1,628 lodges.

The origins of the Improved Benevolent and Protective Order of Elks of the World were even more irregular, but the organization proved to have enduring appeal to African Americans. The order began in 1897 when Arthur J. Riggs, a railroad porter from Covington, Ky., somehow became familiar with the Elks' ritual. Together with B. F. Howard, he founded the Improved Order in Cincinnati, copyrighting the ritual—something the white Elks had neglected to do. The white Elks made several attempts to suppress their black counterparts—once in 1906 by having the New York State legislature make it illegal for nonwhites to use the name "Elks," and another time by suing successfully in court. The Improved Order simply ignored these attacks and became the fastest-growing black fraternal order in the 1920s and '30s. Known for a membership with a large working-class element, the Elks reported 400 lodges and more than 100,000 members in 1932 and 500,000 members in 1,000 lodges in 1946. A sister organization, Daughters of the Improved Benevolent Protective Order of Elks of the World, was founded earlier, in 1902.

Other fraternal orders, founded both before and after the Civil War, had no equivalents among whites. The Grand United Order of Galilean Fishermen, which grew out of a local benevolent society, was one such organization. In 1897, it claimed 56,000 members. The International Order of the Twelve Knights and Daughters of Tabor, founded in Independence, Mo., in 1871 by the Rev. Moses DICKSON, was another (see TWELVE KNIGHTS OF TABOR.) In 1902, Booker T. Washington identified twenty national secret orders operating in the African-American community. In addition to those already noted, these included the Grand United Order of True Reformers, the United Brothers of Friendship and Sisters of the Mysterious Ten, the Benevolent Protective Herd of Buffaloes of the World, the Foresters, the Independent Order of Good Samaritans, the Nazarites, the Sons and Daughters of Jacob, the Seven Wise Men, the Knights of Honor, and the Mosaic Templars of America.

The Grand United Order of True Reformers was exemplary of a new kind of secret benefit order that became popular in the late nineteenth century among both blacks and whites. These orders combined the fellowship, ritualism, and mutual aid of the traditional orders with a formal life insurance policy that provided a fixed amount of between $500 and $1,000 to a member's survivors at the time of his death. The True Reformers, founded by William Washington Browne in Richmond, Va., in 1881, built a business empire that included a bank, a regalia factory, a printing house, a real estate office, a hotel, and a funeral home. At the time of Browne's death in 1900, the True Reformers operated in eighteen states and had approximately 70,000 members. Its business interests had collapsed by 1910, but the order continued to exist on a smaller scale.

The Independent Order of St. Luke also developed extensive economic interests under the leadership of its Right Worthy Grand Secretary, Maggie Lena WALKER. Uniquely among the ritualistic fraternal orders, the Order of St. Luke not only admitted women as members, but elected them to top leadership positions. Walker became the order's top officer in 1899; in 1901 the executive board consisted of six women and three men. By 1913, the Independent Order of St. Luke had become identified as a "woman's organization, broad enough, liberal enough, and unselfish enough to accord equal rights and equal opportunity to men."

Under Walker's leadership, the Independent Order of St. Luke grew from a membership of 1,080 in fifty-seven local councils to 100,000 members in 2,010 councils and twenty-eight states. Based in Richmond, Va., the order's business interests included a newspaper and printing plant, the St. Luke Penny Savings Bank (which later merged with several other black-owned institutions to form the Consolidated Bank and Trust Company), and a department store called the Emporium. By the second decade of the twentieth century, the Independent Order of St. Luke was a major employer in Richmond, especially of women in clerical and sales positions.

In principle, orders such as the Masons preferred a less formal system under which local lodges proffered aid to needy members and their survivors on an ad hoc basis as an expression of brotherly love. They resisted the implementation of standard life insurance benefits, which they viewed as a commercial intrusion into the fellowship of the lodge. The popularity of the insurance orders, however, forced them to reconsider this position. Beginning with Arkansas in 1892, a number of Masonic state grand lodges, particularly in the South, added insurance to the benefits of membership. In some states, Masons had the option of joining separate Masonic benefit associations nominally independent of the grand lodges.

In addition to the national fraternal orders, the period following the Civil War saw the establishment of thousands of new local benefit societies, especially among the newly freed former slaves in the South. These societies offered their members benefits similar to those provided by their antebellum predecessors, particularly assistance in times of illness and death. In the absence of large-scale government social-welfare programs, and with the exclusion of blacks from many of those that did exist, benevolent associations bore a major part of the responsibility for the economic well-being of the African-American community. Membership was widespread in both North and South, in rural and urban areas. In 1909, for example, W. E. B. Du Bois estimated that 70 percent of African Americans in Philadelphia's 7th Ward belonged to a fraternal or mutual aid society. The following year, Howard Odum estimated that such societies in Mississippi had a combined membership of more than 80,000—almost equal to the membership of black churches in the state.

Societies formed on the basis of neighborhood residence, occupation, religion, and ethnicity. Catholic African Americans established the Knights of Peter Claver in 1909. Like their counterparts from Europe and Asia, black immigrants (mostly from the English-, Spanish-, and French-speaking Caribbean) had their own mutual aid associations. Many of these, like the Trinidad Benevolent Association and the Sons and Daughters of Nevis, both of New York, carried the names of their members' former homelands. The Jamaican Progressive League even played an active role in old-country politics. Some associations, like the Sociedad la Unión Martí-Maceo, an Afro-Cuban organization founded in Tampa, Fla., in 1904, kept their distance from both white compatriots and the local African-American community.

The burgeoning fraternal orders and mutual aid societies came in for criticism from a number of quarters. Some southern whites feared that independent black organizations, some of which met in secret, would harbor conspiracies against the racist regime. Despite the fact that many of the benefit associations were actually affiliated with churches, some black ministers resented the growing influence of independent lodges and societies, which they believed were drawing members away from their congregations. On the other hand, while W. E. B. Du Bois criticized the extravagance of some fraternal ritualism, both he and Booker T. Washington generally praised the organizations not only for the material assistance they afforded their members, but also for encouraging savings and investment, and fostering business and leadership skills among African Americans.

Many lodges and societies dedicated themselves to the social uplift of their members and attempted to regulate their morals and behavior. The organizations encouraged temperance and discouraged fighting and the use of vulgar language. Members who sustained injuries or fell ill due to drunkenness or other activities seen as immoral were denied benefits, and violators of the rules of decorum were liable to be fined or even expelled. Following the lead of the prestigious Masons, some organizations excluded anyone convicted of a crime from membership. The Humane Brotherhood of Charleston, however, recognized that African Americans sometimes found themselves in prison through no fault of their own. Its constitution extended benefits to those unfortunate enough to "fall into prison, without injuring or rendering impeachable their moral character."

The benefit orders and societies of the late nineteenth and early twentieth centuries played an important role in the rise of black-owned commercial INSURANCE COMPANIES. In some cases, the societies themselves evolved into commercial companies. This was true, for example, of the Atlanta Mutual Aid Association, which, under the leadership of A. F. Herndon, became the ATLANTA LIFE INSURANCE COMPANY. In other cases, entrepreneurs who gained experience in the fraternal sector went on to found private companies. Former True Reformer leaders S. W. Rutherford and John Merrick, for example, established the NORTH CAROLINA MUTUAL LIFE INSURANCE COMPANY.

Fraternal societies also played an important political role. One order that predated the Civil War,

the Independent Order of Good Samaritans, was founded in 1847 as an arm of the temperance movement. The Samaritans originally included both white and black members and organized in separate lodges, with leadership in the hands of the whites. As the proportion of black members grew after the Civil War, however, whites withdrew. When the order elected a black Grand Sire, the remaining whites left and the organization remained exclusively black. In the twentieth century, the Independent Order of St. Luke actively campaigned for women's suffrage and opposed segregation and lynching. (The order's leader, Maggie WALKER, was the Virginia Lily-Black Republican Party candidate for state superintendent of public instruction in 1921.) Such black political movements as the left-wing nationalist AFRICAN BLOOD BROTHERHOOD and Marcus GARVEY's UNIVERSAL NEGRO IMPROVEMENT ASSOCIATION adopted many of the trappings of Masonry and other secret orders. The Knights of the Invisible Colored Kingdom was organized in Chattanooga, Tenn., in 1923 to counter the KU KLUX KLAN (itself a secret fraternal benefit order).

The mainstream orders also contributed to the CIVIL RIGHTS MOVEMENT. The Elks were particularly active in this regard, establishing a civil liberties department in 1926. The following year, one of the department's first efforts was aimed at ending segregation in high schools in Gary, Ind. Likewise, the Prince Hall Masons supported national antilynching legislation and voting rights movements in the South. In 1951, the International Conference of Grand Masters, a Masonic organization, created the Prince Hall Masons Legal Research Fund under the control of Thurgood MARSHALL (himself a Mason) and the NATIONAL ASSOCIATION FOR THE ADVANCEMENT OF COLORED PEOPLE (NAACP).

By the 1920s, the importance of fraternal insurance had begun to decline as many blacks, especially those in urban areas, turned to commercial insurers instead. Not only had the number of black-owned companies increased, but the larger white-owned firms had begun to issue low-cost insurance policies and become more willing to sell them to African Americans. Moreover, many of the fraternal organizations unsoundly financed their insurance benefits, oblivious to proper actuarial principles.

As memberships aged, organizations frequently collapsed under the weight of mounting payments and decreasing income. The economic hardship of the Great Depression further contributed to the decline of the fraternal orders and societies by making it more difficult for large numbers of African Americans to afford membership dues. In addition, the government social programs initiated by the New Deal supplanted many of the benefits provided by the societies. Small mutual benefit societies, in particular, played an increasingly marginal role, though they continued to exist albeit in smaller numbers toward the end of the twentieth century, especially throughout rural areas of the South and among many immigrant groups.

Although larger, more established black fraternal orders, such as the Masons, Elks, and Odd Fellows, regained many members after World War II, most fraternal organizations have experienced a steady decline in membership since the 1930s. In the early 1990s, two-thirds of all fraternal members were more than fifty years of age, forcing the organizations to redefine and reorient themselves in an effort to attract younger members. Nevertheless, the Masons, Elks, and Odd Fellows continued to enroll a combined membership of more than one million. Together with several smaller orders, they remained an important presence within the African-American life, with extensive social, charitable, and civil rights activities.

See the Appendix in the final volume of this encyclopedia for a list of major fraternal organizations.

REFERENCES

BROWN, ELSA BARKLEY. "Womanist Consciousness: Maggie Lena Walker and the Independent Order of Saint Luke." *Signs* 14, no. 3 (Spring 1989): 610–633.

BROWNING, JAMES. "The Beginnings of Insurance Enterprise Among Negroes." *Journal of Negro History* 22 (1937): 417–432.

DU BOIS, W. E. B. *Some Efforts for Social Betterment Among Negro Americans*. Atlanta, 1909.

FRAZIER, E. FRANKLIN. *The Negro in the United States*. New York, 1949.

GREENBAUM, SUSAN. "A Comparison Between African-American and Euro-American Mutual Aid Societies in 19th Century America." *Journal of Ethnic Studies* 19 (Fall 1991): 95–119.

———. "Economic Cooperation among Urban-Industrial Workers—Rationality and Community in an Afro-Cuban Mutual Aid Society, 1904–1927." *Social Science History* 17, no. 2 (Summer 1993): 173–193.

HARRIS, ROBERT. "Early Black Benevolent Societies, 1780–1830." *Massachusetts Review* 20 (Autumn 1979): 603–628.

KUYK, BETTY. "The African Derivation of Black Fraternal Orders in the United States." *Comparative Studies in Society and History* 25, no. 4 (1983): 559–592.

MURASKIN, WILLIAM, *Middle Class Blacks in a White Society: Prince Hall Masonry in America*. Berkeley, Calif., 1975.

ODUM, HOWARD. *Social and Mental Traits of the Negro*. New York, 1910.

PALMER, EDWARD NELSON. "Negro Secret Societies." *Social Forces* 23, no. 2 (December 1944): 207–212.

PORTER, DOROTHY, ed. *Early Negro Writing, 1760–1837*. Boston, 1971.

SCHMIDT, ALVIN J. *Fraternal Organizations*. Greenwood Encyclopedia of American Institutions. Westport, Conn., 1980.

SCOTT, ANN FIROR. "Most Invisible of All: Black Women's Voluntary Associations." *Journal of Southern Studies* 56, no. 1 (February 1990): 3–22.

SPENCER, C. A. "Black Benefit Societies and the Development of Black Insurance Companies in Nineteenth-Century Alabama." *Phylon* 46 (September 1985): 251–261.

THOMAS, BERT J. "Historical Functions of Caribbean-American Benevolent/Progressive Associations." *Afro-Americans in New York Life and History* (July 1988): 45–58.

WALKER, JOEL. The Social Welfare Policies, Strategies and Programs of Black Fraternal Organizations in the Northeast United States, 1896–1920. Ph.D. diss., 1985.

WHALEN, WILLIAM J. *Handbook of Secret Organizations*. Milwaukee, 1966.

WILLIAMS, LORETTA. *Black Freemasonry and Middle Class Realities*. Columbia, Mo., 1980.

WOODSON, CARTER G. "Insurance Business Among Negroes." *Journal of Negro History* 14, no. 2 (April 1929): 202–226.

PETER SCHILLING
DANIEL SOYER

Fraternities and Sororities. "Greek-letter" organizations, so called because each takes a series of three letters from the Greek alphabet for its name, have played an important role in African-American college life.

Devoted primarily to socializing among members (women in sororities and men in fraternities), campus chapters provide young people with a structured environment in which to adjust to college life and, often, to form lasting friendships. African-American fraternities and sororities share with similar white organizations a culture that features exclusiveness (members must be invited to join and meet both objective and subjective requirements regarding scholastic achievement and desirable personal and social qualities); secret rituals, grips, and passwords; humiliating and sometimes even physically dangerous initiation rites (though these have been discouraged by the national organizations at least since the 1930s); and an emphasis on parties and socializing for their own sake. However, they also encourage good scholarship, teach their members social skills, and instill a sense of character and service to society. In doing so these organizations have constituted one of the chief training grounds of what has been called the "community of striving blacks."

Moreover, many college graduates remain active in alumni chapters, swelling the ranks of the national organizations and giving them a central place in the institutional infrastructure of the black middle class. Graduate members usually provide the leadership of the national organizations, which over the years have distinguished themselves in both the provision of social services and the struggle for civil rights. Sorority and fraternity presidents have included such significant figures as Sadie T. M. ALEXANDER and Dorothy I. HEIGHT (both of Delta Sigma Theta) and Charles WESLEY, Rayford W. LOGAN, and Ernest Morial (All of Alpha Phi Alpha). Patricia Roberts HARRIS was Delta Sigma Theta's first executive director before she went on to become the first black woman cabinet secretary. Marian ANDERSON, Violette Anderson, Countee CULLEN, W. E. B. DU BOIS, John Hope FRANKLIN, John HOPE, Lena HORNE, Barbara JORDAN, Thurgood MARSHALL, Ralph METCALFE, Jesse OWENS, Adam Clayton POWELL, SR., Leontyne PRICE, Paul ROBESON, Georgiana Simpson, and Walter WHITE were just a few of the prominent blacks to join African-American fraternities and sororities.

Nevertheless, critics such as the eminent sociologist E. Franklin FRAZIER have taken the Greek-letter organizations to task for their elitism, social snobbishness, and frivolity, which, as Frazier charged in *Black Bourgeoisie,* "divert the students from a serious interest in education." Moreover, their detractors argue, black fraternities and sororities have at times reinforced pernicious class and color divisions within the black community. In particular, some have accused the Greek-letter organizations of favoring light-skinned candidates for membership. Those with darker complexions, they charge, are forced to demonstrate superior academic, athletic, or social prowess to gain admittance. The organizations themselves, however, have denied harboring this sort of prejudice.

Administrators at black colleges originally opposed the establishment of fraternities and sororities on their campuses, fearing that secret societies would divide student bodies and distract students from the Christian and literary activities preferred by the administrators. In 1910, for example, the trustees of ATLANTA UNIVERSITY voted to "disapprove entirely" of secret organizations and gave the administration and faculty the right to do whatever they deemed necessary to suppress such groups. Before 1925 FISK UNIVERSITY also prohibited fraternities. Both of these schools eventually lifted their bans on Greek-letter societies, but a similar prohibition remained in effect at SPELMAN COLLEGE until at least 1964.

Despite their critics, however, Greek-letter organizations have provided many important benefits to their members. Although popular also at historically black colleges and universities, the social and cultural opportunities offered by fraternities and sororities were especially important for African Americans at predominantly white schools at a time when black students were few in number and excluded from general campus activities. Chapter houses provided housing for many students; at times this was the only adequate housing available to blacks barred from regular dormitories. On the campuses of black colleges, Greek-letter organizations often formed formidable political machines, dominating student government and controlling access to coveted positions in student clubs and publications. While this provoked the opposition of some, it also influenced others to seek membership.

The first African-American Greek-letter organization was not, strictly speaking, a college fraternity, though it was patterned after existing white societies. Sigma Pi Phi was founded in Philadelphia in 1904 by two physicians, a dentist, and a pharmacist. Open only to those with college degrees, it aimed to provide a space for social interaction for the most successful men in the African-American community. Self-consciously elitist, Sigma Pi Phi quickly spread to other cities, but its membership remained small— 177 in 1920, 500 in 1954. Each chapter was called a *boulé,* a Greek term referring to a deliberative body, and the national organization soon also became known informally as Boulé. (Other sororities and fraternities use this word to describe their national conventions.) In 1992 Sigma Pi Phi claimed three thousand members in ninety-one chapters.

The years between 1906 and 1922 saw the founding of all of the eight major African-American Greek-letter student societies. Five of the eight were established at HOWARD UNIVERSITY, though in most cases they quickly spread to white campuses as well. These were Alpha Kappa Alpha Sorority (1908), Omega Psi Phi Fraternity (1911), Delta Sigma Theta Sorority (1913), Phi Beta Sigma Fraternity (1914), and Zeta Phi Beta Sorority (1920). The other three, Alpha Phi Alpha Fraternity (1906), Kappa Alpha Psi Fraternity (1911), and Sigma Gamma Rho Sorority (1922), were established at Cornell (Ithaca, N.Y.), Indiana (Bloomington, Ind.), and Butler universities (Indianapolis), respectively.

Alpha Phi Alpha, the first black Greek-letter fraternity, was established by a group of seven students at Cornell University in 1906, emerging out of a literary society founded earlier. In 1907 students at Howard formed the fraternity's second chapter, and in 1908 a chapter at the University of Toronto made Alpha Phi Alpha an international organization (the Toronto chapter lasted until 1912). Also in 1908, the fraternity held its first convention, adopting as its stated ideals, "manly deeds, scholarship, and love for all mankind."

Founded at Howard on January 15, 1908, Alpha Kappa Alpha became the first black sorority and the first Greek-letter organization established at a black school. The nine founders were all students in the university's School of Liberal Arts. Their leader, Ethel Hedgeman, was encouraged in this undertaking by Ethel Robinson, a graduate of Brown University who had been a sorority sister there. In its first year Alpha Kappa Alpha set standards for membership, requiring that candidates complete the first half of their sophomore year and maintain an average of 75 percent or better. The organization's early activities centered on concerts and cultural events, often relying on the talents of the members themselves.

Two fraternities were formed in 1911, Kappa Alpha Psi at Indiana University and Omega Psi Phi at Howard. The former typified the strength of fraternities and sororities among African-American students on predominantly white Midwestern campuses, where they were greater in numbers than at Eastern white schools but faced social isolation. The founders of Omega Psi Phi, on the other hand, received encouragement from Ernest E. JUST, a biologist and prominent member of the Howard faculty.

By 1913 dissatisfaction had spread among some members of the Howard chapter of Alpha Kappa Alpha who wanted to put more emphasis on involvement in community affairs and building a national organization. They also opposed the pompous Greek titles given officers (basileus, anti-basileus, grammateus, epistoleus, tamiouchos). Based largely in Howard's Teachers College, many of the dissident members were also members of a circle of friends that included men in Omega Psi Phi. After an unsuccessful attempt to reform the older organization, twenty-two women left Kappa Alpha and founded a new sorority called Delta Sigma Theta.

The following year, Howard saw the founding of a new fraternity, Phi Beta Sigma, which adopted the motto "Culture for service and service for humanity." In 1920 members of Phi Beta Sigma played an important role in the establishment of a new sorority, Zeta Phi Beta, which became a sister organization to the fraternity from which it took part of its name and on whose constitution it based its own. Finally, in 1922 Sigma Gamma Rho Sorority became the last of the major black Greek-letter organizations to be founded. Originally established at Butler University as a professional sorority for teachers and students of education, Sigma Gamma Rho expanded beyond this constituency by the end of the decade. By the early 1920s the African-American fraternities and sororities claimed a total membership of several thousand in dozens of chapters.

Competition for members and honors characterized the interaction among the various Greek-letter societies on campus. The close relationship between Alpha Kappa Alpha and Delta Sigma Theta led to an especially heated rivalry that became part of the sororities' traditions. Attracting the boyfriend of a member of the other organization was considered a particular coup. Each group strove to best the other in academic pursuits as well; when Alpha Kappa Alpha established an award for the woman graduating from Howard with the highest grade point average, Deltas made a special effort to win the prize—and often did. Partly in an effort to control this sort of rivalry, black sororities and fraternities founded the National Interfraternal Council in 1922. The council also sought to develop common membership standards for the Greek-letter organizations. It was replaced in 1930 by the National Pan-Hellenic Council, which, in addition to setting academic standards for membership, worked to secure black representation in predominantly white interfraternal organizations and fought discrimination in dormitory housing.

Social service and the promotion of education have provided the national organizations with their main focus of activities. Together with both campus and graduate chapters, they have sponsored a variety of projects in the United States and abroad (especially in Africa).

Alpha Phi Alpha pioneered with its annual campaign to promote higher education among black youth. Inaugurated on a national level in 1916, this effort was broadened in 1919 under the title "Go to High School, Go to College." Carried out each year during the first week in June, this campaign featured the dissemination of literature, speeches by fraternity members, and counseling sessions with individual students and parents. Under the influence of its education director, the noted historian Rayford W. Logan, Alpha Phi Alpha replaced "Go to High School, Go to College" in 1933 with "Education for Citizenship." Designed to inform blacks of both the "rights" and the "responsibilities" of citizenship, Logan hoped that the campaign would help African Americans challenge their disfranchisement by preparing them to vote. Similarly, Kappa Alpha Psi established its "Guide Right Program" to help youth with "discovering and developing their potentials."

The sororities, in particular, initiated a number of notable social welfare programs. Alpha Kappa Alpha, for example, began its Mississippi Health Project in 1935. Continued for eight years, the project sent teams of doctors and nurses to rural areas of the state to provide treatment and education. In the 1940s and 1950s Sigma Gamma Rho sponsored "Teen Towns," where black youths ages thirteen to seventeen could spend their leisure time at "worthwhile activities." In 1937 Delta Sigma Theta initiated its National Library Program to send bookmobiles throughout the South. Ten years later the Detroit chapter of Delta Sigma Theta opened the Delta Home for Girls to provide a residential alternative to the local juvenile detention home.

Since 1965 Alpha Kappa Alpha has operated the Jobs Corps Center in Cleveland under contract with the government. In the 1970s Phi Beta Sigma initiated Project SAD (Sigma Attacks Defects) to promote infant health by educating men concerning the importance of proper prenatal and neonatal health care, as well as the dangers of tobacco, alcohol, drugs, and venereal disease. Both sororities and fraternities continued to sponsor a wide range of social welfare programs into the 1990s.

The sororities also took a particular interest in international affairs. In the late 1940s Alpha Kappa Alpha became an accredited observer at the United Nations. In Africa Sigma Gamma Rho started Project Africa to provide agricultural assistance to African women and ran several campaigns to send books to educational institutions on the continent. Alpha Kappa Alpha chapters "adopted" more than three hundred African villages in conjunction with the international-aid organization Africare. And in 1965 Zeta Phi Beta opened a Domestic Science Center in Monrovia, Liberia. Delta Sigma Theta has aided hospitals and other projects in Kenya and Uganda, as well as in India and Haiti.

All the Greek-letter organizations encouraged education among young African Americans by providing scholarships and fellowships to both members and nonmembers. They also sponsored essay contests and other competitions for high school and college students, ran tutoring, counseling, and placement programs and undertook leadership training seminars for college members and graduates. Phi Beta Sigma had an affiliated Sigma Beta Club for young men in high school. Alpha Phi Alpha's Education Foundation encourages scholarship, promotes research, and aids the publication of works by African Americans. Over the years the fraternities and sororities have also contributed millions of dollars to educational, scientific, charitable, and civil rights causes, including the United Negro College Fund, and many individual black schools.

African-American fraternities and sororities have differed from their white counterparts in their stress on political involvement, particularly in support of civil rights. One of Delta Sigma Theta's first public activities after its founding in 1913 was to participate in the mass march on Washington for women's suffrage. (Later that year the sorority sent a delegate to the national conference of the Intercollegiate Socialist Society, where, as the only African-American present, she was called upon to comment on the question of civil rights for blacks.)

By the 1930s many of the organizations put considerable emphasis on civil rights work, lobbying for progressive legislation, participating in litigation, and working closely with such organizations as the NATIONAL ASSOCIATION FOR THE ADVANCEMENT OF COLORED PEOPLE (NAACP), the NATIONAL URBAN LEAGUE, the Joint Council on National Recovery, and the NATIONAL COUNCIL OF NEGRO WOMEN. Alpha Phi Alpha helped initiate Donald Murray's legal battle for admission to the law school of the University of Maryland. Following his court-ordered admission in 1936, the fraternity paid Murray's tuition and book costs. After campaigning actively for the Costigan-Wagner Anti-Lynching Bill, Alpha Kappa Alpha Sorority established a full-time civil rights lobby in 1938. In 1948 Alpha Kappa Alpha (which, ironically, had been viewed as too insular and conservative by the members who had split off to form Delta Sigma Theta in 1913) invited the seven other major African-American Greek-letter societies to join it in forming the American Council for Human Rights (ACHR), whose aim it was to eliminate racial discrimination and inequality. The ACHR pressed for fair employment legislation, desegregation in the armed forces, bans on poll taxes and lynching, and the integration of transportation and public accommodations in Washington, D.C. The council was dissolved in 1963.

In the late 1940s several of the organizations removed any reference to color or race from their membership requirements, enrolling a small number of students of non-African descent. Nevertheless, they remained overwhelmingly African-American and committed to work in the black community. The societies also continued to educate the public on the achievements of black men and women. In the 1940s Delta Sigma Theta produced a series of publications on black heroes, and in the 1960s Alpha Kappa Alpha published a series on black women in the judiciary, politics, business, medicine, and dentistry.

In the late-1960s, a period in which black and student militancy converged, sororities and fraternities suffered a decline in popularity among students who disdained their elitism and stress on purely social activities. Even within the organizations themselves, members advocated reforms that would deemphasize their exclusive nature. Several societies, for example, did away with the minimum-grade-point-average requirements that had helped define their elite character. However, society members were often in the forefront of the black campus activism of the era. Cultural historian Paula Giddings, who joined Delta Sigma Theta at Howard University in 1967, recalls that most of the leaders of the student revolt there the following year were members of Greek-letter organizations.

By the early 1980s observers noted the resurgence of student interest in fraternities and sororities. To some extent, this was a consequence of collegians' increased concern for personal advancement and the realization that society membership could help them fulfill their aspirations in this regard. At the same time, however, organizational leaders, both on campus and among graduates, sought to reemphasize the societies' commitments to political action and social service within the black community and overcome their negative image as "noncaring, social-activity prone" groups. During this period Alpha Kappa Alpha carried out its "Black Faces in Public Places" campaign to build monuments to important African Americans in parks and government buildings. It also supported "Black Family Month" and "Black Dollar Day," the latter as part of an effort to encourage African Americans to patronize black-owned businesses.

Despite their temporary dip in popularity in the late 1960s and early 1970s, black sororities and fraternities have grown steadily since their inception, as more and more African Americans have attended college and as graduate members have accumulated. By 1990 the eight major black fraternities and sororities claimed a membership of more than 700,000 in thousands of campus and alumni chapters. In 1981 the Council of Presidents was established to promote better relations among organizations on campus and augment its constituents' political influence.

In addition to the major college-based fraternities and sororities, there have been a number of much smaller Greek-letter societies recruiting from among practitioners and students of particular professions. These organizations provide their members with social activities, professional enrichment, and in some cases, scholarships and loan funds. They also sponsor charitable programs and recruit young people to their respective professions. These include Alpha Pi Chi Sorority (business and professional women, established in 1963), Chi Delta Mu Fraternity (physicians, dentists and pharmacists, est. 1913), Chi Eta Phi Sorority (registered and student nurses, est. 1932), Eta Phi Beta Sorority (businesswomen, est. 1942), Iota Phi Lambda Sorority (est. 1929), and the National Sorority of Phi Delta Kappa (women in education, est. 1923). In 1990 they ranged in membership from six hundred fifty to eight thousand.

REFERENCES

Baird's Manual of American College Fraternities. Various editions, authors, and publishers, 1898–1968.
"A Dramatic Comeback on Campus." *Ebony* (December 1983): 93–98.
DREER, HERMAN. *The History of the Omega Psi Phi Fraternity.* Washington, D.C., 1940.

TABLE 1. **Major African-American College Sororities and Fraternities**

Organization	Place and Date of Founding	Headquarters	Membership[*]	Number of Chapters[†]
Alpha Kappa Alpha *Sorority*	Howard 1908	Chicago	110,000	Campus: 410 Alumni: 420
Alpha Phi Alpha *Fraternity*	Cornell 1906	Chicago	100,000 (since founding)	Campus: 290 Alumni: 274
Delta Sigma Theta *Sorority*	Howard 1913	Washington, D.C.	175,000	Active: 760
Kappa Alpha Psi *Fraternity*	Indiana 1911	Philadelphia	80,000	Active: 323 Alumni: 308
Omega Psi Phi *Fraternity*	Howard 1911	Washington, D.C.	50,000	Active: 511 Alumni: 259
Phi Beta Sigma *Fraternity*	Howard 1914	Washington, D.C.	65,000	N.A.
Sigma Gamma Rho *Sorority*	Butler 1922	Chicago	50,000[†]	Active: 350[†]
Zeta Phi Beta *Sorority*	Howard 1920	Washington, D.C.	75,000	550 (College and alumnae)

[*] As reported in Julia C. Furtaw, ed., *Black Americans Information Directory 1992–93,* 2nd ed. (Detroit, 1992).
[†] As reported in Darren L. Smith, ed., *Black Americans Information Directory 1990–91,* (Detroit, 1990).

GIDDINGS, PAULA. *In Search of Sisterhood: Delta Sigma Theta and the Challenge of the Black Sorority Movement.* New York, 1988.

LITTLE, MONROE. "The Extra-Curricular Activities of Black College Students, 1868–1940." *Journal of Negro History* (September 1980): 135–148.

PARKER, MARJORIE. *Alpha Kappa Alpha Through the Years, 1908–1988.* Chicago, 1990.

WESLEY, CHARLES. *The History of Alpha Phi Alpha: A Development in Negro College Life.* Washington, D.C., 1948.

———. *History of Sigma Psi Phi.* Washington, D.C., 1954.

WHITE, PEARL SCHWARTZ. *Behind These Closed Doors—a Legacy: The History of Sigma Gamma Rho Sorority.* Chicago, 1974.

WRIGHT, CHARLES. "Phi Beta Sigma Fraternity: Yesterday's Tradition—Tomorrow's Innovation." In Lennox S. Yearwood, ed. *Black Organizations: Issues on Survival Techniques.* Washington, D.C., 1980.

WRIGHT, WILLIE J. "The Role of the Omega Psi Phi Fraternity in the Survival of Black Organizations." In Lennox S. Yearwood, ed. *Black Organizations: Issues on Survival Techniques.* Washington, D.C., 1980.

YA SALAAM, KALAMU, and BRENDA REESE. "Is Pledging Passé?" *Black Collegian* (November–December 1974): 50–53.

DANIEL SOYER

Frazier, Edward Franklin (September 24, 1894–May 17, 1962), essayist and activist. Born in Baltimore in 1894, the year in which W. E. B. DU BOIS was completing his doctoral degree at Harvard and 135 blacks were lynched in the South, E. Franklin Frazier was encouraged in his formative years by his parents, especially his working-class father, to seek upward mobility and social justice through education. With a scholarship from Colored High School he went on to Howard University, where he graduated *cum laude* in 1916 after four years of rigorous education and political activism at the "capstone of Negro education." For the rest of his academic career, he taught primarily in segregated, African-American schools and colleges, first in the South in the 1920s and early '30s, then for most of his career in Howard's sociology department. In between teaching jobs, he received scholarships that enabled him to get a master's degree at Clark University (1920) and a Ph.D. in sociology from the University of Chicago (1931). Despite his election as the first African-American president of the American Sociological Association (1948) and his recognition by UNESCO in the 1950s as a leading international authority on race relations, Frazier was never offered a regular faculty appointment by a predominantly white university.

With minimal institutional and foundation support, Frazier managed to produce eight books and over one hundred articles. He is best known for his pioneering studies of African-American families, especially *The Negro Family in the United States* (1939), which demonstrated that the internal problems of black families were socially created within and by Western civilization, not by the failure of Africans to live up to American standards. Building upon Du Bois's 1908 essay, *The Negro American Family,* Frazier refuted the prevailing social scientific wisdom which, in his words, "most often dealt with the pathological side of [black] family life. . . ." In contrast, Frazier's family is a broad spectrum of households, constantly in a process of change and reorganization, sometimes disorganized and demoralized, sometimes tenacious and resourceful. To Frazier the serious problems within African-American families—"the waste of hu-

E. Franklin Frazier. (Photographs and Prints Division, Schomburg Center for Research in Black Culture, The New York Public Library, Astor, Lenox and Tilden Foundations)

man life . . . delinquency, desertions, and broken homes"—was not due to cultural backwardness, but rather to economic exploitation and the social damage inflicted by racism.

Frazier also made a variety of other important intellectual contributions: as an ethnographer and historian of everyday life in black communities; as a trenchant and subtle critic of the dynamics and etiquette of racism; as an influential consultant to Gunnar Myrdal's *An American Dilemma* (1944); as the author of the first systematic textbook on *The Negro in the United States* (1949); and as a critic of overly specialized, narrowly conceived studies in the social sciences. Frazier's popular reputation was made by *Black Bourgeoisie* (first published in the United States in 1957), but he explored the controversial relationship between class, politics, and culture all his life, beginning with a polemical essay on "La Bourgeoisie Noire" in 1928 and ending with his scholarly assessment of *Race and Culture Contacts in the Modern World* (1957). In this body of work he challenged monolithic portraits of African-American communities and documented their socioeconomic diversity; in particular, he exposed the collaborative and opportunistic role played by the black middle class in holding back the struggle for social equality and ensuring that "bourgeois ideals are implanted in the Negro's mind." Instead of being "seduced by dreams of final assimilation," Frazier called upon black leaders to envision "a common humanity and a feeling of human solidarity" in which "racial and cultural differentiation without implications of superiority and inferiority will become the basic pattern of a world order."

Frazier was part of a cadre of activists, intellectuals, and artists who after World War I formed the cutting edge of the NEW NEGRO movement that irrevocably changed conceptions of race and the politics of race relations. Though a loner who distrusted organizations, Frazier had close and respectful relationships with civil rights leaders such as W. E. B. Du Bois, Paul ROBESON, and A. Philip RANDOLPH, as well as with scholars, such as Ralph BUNCHE and Abram HARRIS, who tried to bridge the gap between university and community, theory and practice. From his undergraduate days at Howard, when he was a vigorous opponent of U.S. entry into World War I, until his last years, when he welcomed a revitalized civil rights movement, Frazier was a politicized intellectual who believed that "a moral life is a life of activity in society."

REFERENCES

EDWARDS, G. FRANKLIN, ed. *E. Franklin Frazier on Race Relations.* Chicago, 1968.

FRAZIER, E. FRANKLIN. *The Negro in the United States.* New York, 1949.

———. *The Negro Family in the United States.* Chicago, 1939.

PLATT, ANTHONY M. *E. Franklin Frazier Reconsidered.* New Brunswick, N.J., 1991.

ANTHONY M. PLATT

Frazier, Joseph William (January 12, 1944–), boxer. "Smokin' " Joe Frazier was the World Heavyweight Boxing champion from 1970–1973. Born in Beaufort, S.C., Frazier grew up in Philadelphia and began BOXING at a Police Athletic League gym. After he won Golden Gloves titles in 1962, 1963, and 1964, as well as a gold medal in the 1964 Olympics in Tokyo, Japan, a consortium of investors, incorporated as Cloverlay, Inc., sponsored Frazier's professional career.

Frazier was only 5'11½" high and 205 pounds, small for a heavyweight. Managed by Yancey Durham, Frazier adopted a crowded and hard-hitting style that compensated for his relative slow-footedness. Beginning with a one-round knockout of Woody Goss in August, 1965, Frazier won by knockouts his first eleven professional bouts, none of which went beyond six rounds, and he won thirty-one straight fights before being defeated by George FOREMAN in 1973.

After Muhammad ALI gave up his title in 1970, Frazier won the World Heavyweight Championship, defeating Jimmy Ellis in a five-round knockout. Ali, who had been stripped of his title after the U.S. government convicted him of draft evasion (later overturned), also claimed to be the heavyweight champion because he had never retired or been defeated.

On March 8, 1971, in New York City's Madison Square Garden, Frazier defeated Ali after fifteen rounds of such ferocious boxing that both men entered hospitals after its conclusion; they would later fight twice more, both times with great intensity. After the first fight with Ali, Frazier did not fight a title bout again for ten months. He then defended his championship twice, winning both bouts, but on January 22, 1973, George Foreman knocked him out in the second round of a heavyweight title bout.

Having lost his title to Foreman, Frazier again fought Ali in a non-title bout in New York City on January 28, 1974, and lost in twelve rounds. Frazier had fights with two lesser boxers, both of whom he knocked out, then faced Ali for the heavyweight title on October 1, 1975, in the Philippines. The fight, dubbed by Ali "The Thrilla in Manila," was a hard-fought contest. Ali knocked Frazier out in the fourteenth round.

Frazier followed the Manila bout with a second fight against Foreman on June 15, 1976. He was knocked out by Foreman early in the fight. Frazier then retired from the ring. He made a brief appearance, playing himself, in the movie *Rocky* (1976) and tried unsuccessfully to build a singing career with a group called the Knockouts. In 1981 he attempted a comeback, but was defeated by Floyd Cummings. Of his 37 career bouts, Frazier won a total of 32 fights—27 by knockouts. He then managed his son Marvis's short boxing career. In 1980 Frazier was elected to the Boxing Hall of Fame.

REFERENCE

ASHE, ARTHUR R., JR. *A Hard Road to Glory: A History of the African-American Athlete Since 1946.* New York, 1988.

GREG ROBINSON

Frazier, Walter, II (March 29, 1945–), professional basketball player. Born in Atlanta, Ga., Walt Frazier attended David T. Howard High School, where he excelled in both basketball and football. Recruited by colleges in both sports, he accepted a basketball scholarship from Southern Illinois University in Carbondale, Ill., partly because he realized that as a black quarterback he faced barriers to a professional football career. Frazier had three outstanding years with the Southern Illinois "Salukis" (he missed the 1965–1966 season as a result of academic ineligibility). In 1967 he led Southern Illinois to victory in the National Invitational Tournament and was named the tournament's most valuable player.

The New York Knickerbockers (commonly known as the Knicks) selected the 6′4″ Frazier in the first round of the 1967 National Basketball Association (NBA) draft. During his thirteen-year professional career (1967–1968 through 1979–1980), including ten years with the Knicks and parts of three with the Cleveland Cavaliers, Frazier was considered one of the game's best defensive guards. He was especially admired for his remarkable ability to steal the ball from opposing players as they dribbled it. Frazier earned a spot on the NBA's All-Defensive team for seven consecutive seasons (1968–1969 through 1974–1975).

Frazier was also an outstanding offensive player, leading the Knicks in scoring five seasons, and in assists all ten that he spent with the team. He helped the Knicks to NBA championships in 1968–1969 and 1972–1973, and played in the league All-Star game seven times between 1970 and 1976. (He was the All-Star game's most valuable player in 1975.) During his playing days, Frazier was almost as famous for his flamboyant style off the court as on. Driving a Rolls-Royce and given to wearing fur coats and broad-brimmed hats, he acquired the nickname "Clyde" after the bank robber Clyde Barrow.

Retiring after the 1979–1980 season, Frazier ran Walt Frazier Enterprises, which represented other athletes. He also became a commentator on the radio broadcasts of Knick games over WFAN. As a broadcaster he amused some listeners and irked others with his frequent use of rhyme and obscure words to describe play.

Frazier was elected to the Pro Basketball Hall of Fame in 1986.

REFERENCES

FRAZIER, WALT, and JOE JARES. *Clyde.* New York, 1970.
FRAZIER, WALT, with Neil Offen. *One Magic Season and a Basketball Life.* New York, 1988.

DANIEL SOYER

Frederick, Rivers (May 22, 1874–September 9, 1954), physician. Rivers Frederick was born in New Roads, Pointe Coupée Parish, La. He graduated from New Orleans University and earned an M.D. (1897) from the University of Illinois. Frederick spent the next two years serving as a surgical clinician in Chicago. In 1899, he returned to New Orleans to practice as a private physician.

Frustrated by the lack of opportunities for black doctors in the United States, Frederick moved to Honduras in 1901. There he was made chief surgeon of the government hospital at El Rio Tan, where he served until 1904. Little is known about his departure from Honduras except that he was involved in a failed attempt by a revolutionary movement to overthrow the incumbent government there.

Back in New Orleans in 1904, Frederick worked as a private physician until 1907, when he became associate professor of surgery at Flint Medical College, also in New Orleans. In 1911, he left Flint to become chief surgeon at Sarah Goodridge Hospital. From 1913 to 1932, he also served as surgeon for the Southern Pacific Railroad. In 1932, when Sarah Goodridge Hospital merged with Flint Medical College, Frederick taught postgraduate courses for physicians at the new Flint-Goodridge Hospital.

Frederick was a fellow of the International College of Surgeons. He was also a member of the executive committees of both the American Cancer Society and the Tuberculosis Association, and served on the mayor's Advisory Committee of Race Relations in New

Orleans. As an active member of the NAACP, he worked against health-care discrimination faced by African Americans. Frederick was also charter member and cofounder of the black-owned Louisiana Industrial Life Insurance Company, and in 1936, served as its president. In 1951, he received the Distinguished Service Medal from the National Medical Association; that same year, he was made a member of the Society Tosca-Umbra di Italia at the annual assembly of the International College of Surgeons in Florence, Italy. Frederick's published articles include "Acute Intestinal Obstruction" (1935), "Primitive Surgeons in Modern Medicine" (1946), and "The Treatment of Toxic Goiter" (1951), all in the *Journal of the National Medical Association*. At the time of his death in New Orleans in 1954, Frederick was chief emeritus of the surgical department of the Flint-Goodridge Hospital.

REFERENCES

"Dr. Rivers Frederick Receives Distinguished Service Award for 1951." *Journal of the National Medical Association* (November 1951): 400.
KAUFMAN, MARTIN, STUART GALISHOFF, and TODD L. SAVITT, eds. *Dictionary of American Medical Biography*. Westport, Conn, 1984.

ROBERT C. HAYDEN

Frederick Douglass's Paper, abolitionist newspaper. It was founded in December 1847 by Frederick DOUGLASS as the *North Star* in Rochester, N.Y. Douglass renamed his paper when it merged with the *Liberty Party Paper* of Syracuse, N.Y., in June 1851. During its thirteen-year history, several black intellectuals collaborated with Douglass, including Martin R. DELANY, William C. NELL, William J. Watkins, and James McCune SMITH. Douglass also received assistance from a British abolitionist, Julia Griffiths. She helped him hone his writing skills and, as the paper's business manager, organized fund-raising fairs and lecture tours in England and the United States. The success of Douglass's newspaper can be attributed in large part to an elaborate network of support. Contributions from British abolitionists encouraged him to start the paper in 1847. Later, women's auxiliaries in several cities organized antislavery fairs and bazaars on his behalf.

Douglass recognized the symbolic as well as practical antislavery value of a viable black press. He gave the paper his own name to emphasize to a skeptical public that a former slave could master the editor's craft. His paper followed the eclectic approach of the antebellum reform press, but it was first and foremost an antislavery organ, and carried the bold imprint of one man's thought. He directed his message beyond the black community to the broader Anglo-American reformist audience. Despite financial difficulties and criticism from white reformers and black leaders, Douglass succeeded in making his weekly publication the most influential black newspaper of the antebellum period.

REFERENCES

RIPLEY, C. PETER, et al., eds. *The Black Abolitionist Papers, Volume 3: The United States, 1830–1846.* Chapel Hill, N.C., 1991.
———. *The Black Abolitionist Papers, Volume 4: The United States, 1847–1859.* Chapel Hill, N.C., 1991.

MICHAEL F. HEMBREE

Frederick Wilkins Slave Rescue. After the passage of the Fugitive Slave Act by the U.S. Congress in May 1850, control over the fate of alleged runaways passed from local and state officials to the federal government (*see* FUGITIVE SLAVE LAWS), through commissioners appointed by the President. The act had an enormous potential impact on many northern cities that had large FUGITIVE SLAVE populations. One of those cities was Boston, where it was estimated that as many as 400 out of a total city black population of 2,000 could be considered runaway slaves by the definition of the new legislation.

While Boston as a whole was not favorable to ABOLITION, the city was a center of abolitionist activism, and the abolitionist network was several times galvanized into operation to hinder or prevent the enforcement of the law. One instance of successful opposition was the case of Frederick "Shadrach" Wilkins, a waiter at a local coffeehouse about whose life little is known, but whom a slave owner from Norfolk, Va., claimed was his property.

Wilkins was arrested in February 1851, while waiting on tables in the coffeehouse. One of the arresting officers later bragged how "we got a nigger." As they dragged Wilkins to the courthouse, he vowed he would not allow himself to be returned to Virginia alive. An angry crowd of at leasts two hundred, mostly black, gathered to denounce the proceedings. Some of them threatened to take the law into their own hands to prevent Wilkins's rendition to Virginia. His court-appointed lawyers tried to have Justice Lemuel Shaw, Chief Justice of the Massachusetts Supreme Court, free Wilkins on the ground that no proper cause had been given for holding the alleged runaway, but Shaw ruled that the arrest was proper under the Fugitive Slave Act.

Just as the court session was concluding, some fifty blacks rushed the door, charged into the courtroom, and grabbed Wilkins before any of the surprised police officials could respond. The shocked but thankful Wilkins was rushed into a waiting carriage attended by Louis Hayden, one of Boston's leading black citizens and the city's best-known conductor on the UNDERGROUND RAILROAD. Wilkins was soon safe in Canada, where his subsequent history is obscure.

Many participants in the rescue plan were arrested, on demand of President Millard Fillmore. The arrested included Hayden and Robert Morris, the first black to pass the bar in Massachusetts. However, the government soon realized that in the inflamed atmosphere of Boston, juries would sympathize with the defendants, and no one was ever convicted of any crime connected with the rescue. Abolitionists, as well as other Bostonians who considered the Fugitive Slave Act a threat to individual liberty, rejoiced over the successful rescue. The fiery West Roxbury abolitionist minister Theodore Parker described the incident as "the noblest deed done in Boston since the destruction of the tea." More importantly, the rescue demonstrated the ineffectiveness of the Fugitive Slave Act in the face of concerted black and white resistance, and hinted at the growing power of Northern opposition to slavery.

REFERENCES

HORTON, JAMES O. and LOIS E. HORTON. *Black Bostonians: Family Life and Community Struggle in the Antebellum North.* New York, 1979.
PEASE, JANE H. and WILLIAM H. *They Who Would Be Free: Blacks' Search for Freedom, 1830–1861.* New York, 1974.
ROBBOY, STANLEY J. and ANITA W. "Lewis Hayden: From Fugitive Slave to Statesman," *The New England Quarterly,* 46, no. 4, pp. 597–613.

DONALD M. JACOBS

Free African Society. The Free African Society (FAS) was a mutual aid society founded in Philadelphia in 1787 by free blacks. Although it had close ties to the Quakers—and to the Methodist Church, to which belonged its two black founders, Richard ALLEN and Absalom JONES, and its principle white patron, Benjamin Rush—the Free African Society was religiously oriented but nondenominational and run entirely by African Americans. The Free African Society sought to improve the lives and the treatment of blacks on this continent, and was a supporter of abolition and an opponent of repatriation schemes such as those supported by the Free Union African Society of Newport, R.I. The Free African Society petitioned both state and federal governments to abolish the slave trade. In addition, members of the society attempted to foster goodwill toward African Americans by volunteering as nurses and undertakers during the deadly yellow fever epidemic in 1793, in part because of the mistaken belief that Africans were immune to the disease.

The society required members to pay regular dues and live soberly. Following the example of the Quakers, the society formed a visiting committee to ensure that all members conformed to its rules of decorum, sobriety, and fidelity. It kept marriage records, and penalized members who were known to engage in adulterous acts.

From the outset, the Free African Society was a quasi-religious organization, but there was considerable disagreement over the issue of formal denominational affiliation. The institutional and religious connections to the Quakers became more pronounced in November 1789, when the Society voted to begin meetings with fifteen minutes of silent prayer. This was too much for the Methodist Richard Allen, who left the Society with a group of supporters. They later formed the Bethel African Methodist Episcopal Church, which became the "mother church" in the AFRICAN METHODIST EPISCOPAL denomination. By 1790, the Society was conducting nondenominational religious meetings under Absalom Jones's leadership and had began to consider establishing a broadly Christian African Church of Philadelphia, though the elements of Methodist and Episcopalian liturgy used in its services alienated Quaker supporters of the FAS. With its decision in early 1792 to build a formal church (as its minutes of 1792 indicate), the Free African Society came to an end and the African Church began. The Society returned to its members the money it had collected and gave each member the option of offering it to the new church, the African Episcopal Church of St. Thomas, led by Absalom Jones.

REFERENCES

DOUGLASS, WILLIAM. *Annals of the First African Church in the United States of America, Now Styled the African Episcopal Church of St. Thomas, Philadelphia.* Philadelphia, 1862. Reprint. Westport, Conn., 1990.
NASH, GARY, B. *Forging Freedom: The Formation of Philadelphia's Black Community, 1720–1840.* Cambridge, Mass., 1988.

PETER SCHILLING

Free Blacks in the North. As in the South, free blacks in the northern states prior to the Civil War straddled the boundaries of SLAVERY and freedom. While searching for the social, legal, and political liberties whites enjoyed, free blacks in the North reached back to help liberate African-American slaves. Whites in the North used every measure of control to squeeze black liberty, making free black existence akin to slavery. Still, such people were free, earned their own livelihood, created their own cultural and religious institutions, and formed a shadow political order dedicated to the overthrow of the slavocracy.

Slavery constantly affected free black life in the North. It existed in all northern colonies until the American Revolution. In the states with the largest black populations—Pennsylvania, New Jersey, and New York—the gradual introduction of emancipation meant that servitude affected the lives of African Americans into the antebellum era. Although the numbers of free blacks grew steadily, from a few in the colonial era to virtually the entire black population in the antebellum period, they were denied political equality; hampered by poverty and by segregation in work, housing, and property ownership; and buffeted by worsening racism. Free blacks, organizing of churches and benevolent societies and their indefatigable struggle against slavery and racism combated white presumptions of racial inferiority. By the Civil War, free blacks in the North established strong church-based communities in the urban areas, owned hard-won farm property, and created a distinguished, politically minded intelligentsia.

Enumeration of free blacks in the colonial era is difficult because censuses did not differentiate between slave and emancipated. In New England, where the vast majority of blacks were slaves working in the seaports, the African-American population reached its zenith of 15,400, or 2.6 percent of the area's population of 581,100, in 1770. Blacks in New England gained freedom by working as indentured servants. A Rhode Island statute of 1652 limited servitude to ten years. Masters grateful for good service manumitted some, while keen-minded slaves used legal loopholes to win freedom from their masters in court, or negotiated an end to slavery through private contract. A few purchased their liberty. Estimates of the free black population included about 2,000 in Massachusetts in 1764 and 500 (a rough estimate) in Rhode Island in 1774.

The enactment of gradual emancipation laws in New England after the American Revolution immediately multiplied the free black population. Among the most notable was sea captain Paul CUFFE. In 1790 in Massachusetts, New Hampshire, Maine, and Vermont, free blacks outnumbered slaves by 6,804 to 157. Slavery retained a stronger grip in Rhode Island, with 3,484 free blacks to 958 slaves. Only in Connecticut did slavery retain real consequence, with 2,771 slaves to 2,648 free blacks. Although the last slaves were not completely freed in New England until 1840, the words *free* and *black* became firmly linked. On the eve of the Civil War, more than 23,000 free blacks lived in New England.

New Jersey, New York, and Pennsylvania—the middle colonies—had a larger enslaved population of 35,000 in 1770; nearly 21,000 of these lived in and around New York City. The oldest free black population in colonial America emerged in the 1640s in New Amsterdam, later New York. This original group expanded to about 100 people living in the city and its hinterlands. Traces of the first group of free black settlers existed in rural New York and New Jersey throughout the slavery era. Present in New Amsterdam, slavery became codified in the half century after the English conquest in 1664. Struggling against the tightening noose of bondage, blacks used loopholes in the law and sued successfully for their freedom.

In 1713, the colonial government stymied emancipations by requiring a £200 insurance bond and sharply restricting blacks' property rights. Despite these legal curbs, about 140 blacks were freed by wills from 1667 to 1770. The English government freed an additional 100 Spanish slaves in court decisions affected by international diplomacy between 1747 and 1760. Other, very rare means of obtaining freedom included financial redemption, military service, and special grants. The QUAKERS' antislavery position began to erode slavery during the AMERICAN REVOLUTION, as over 100 blacks became free through testaments. British proclamations exchanging freedom for military service freed about 600 New York and New Jersey blacks during the American Revolution. At the end of the war in 1783, these black loyalists left for Nova Scotia and Great Britain (*see* LOYALISTS IN THE AMERICAN REVOLUTION).

After 1783, blacks gained freedom through favorable court decisions, confiscation of Loyalist estates, self-purchase, and a rising political antislavery sentiment. The abolition of slavery was contentious in New York and New Jersey; Dutch slave owners were the most recalcitrant. In 1790, slaves in the two states outnumbered free blacks by 32,616 to 7,444. Gradual emancipation in 1799 in New York and 1804 in New Jersey made long-term chances for freedom better, but as late as 1830, New Jersey had 2,254 slaves out of a black population of 20,557. On the eve of the Civil War, 75,000 free blacks and 18 slaves lived in the two states.

Conditions for free blacks in New York and New Jersey were characteristic of those in northern states. Both states curtailed black suffrage, harbored hostile social attitudes, openly practiced discrimination in work and housing, tolerated murderous disease climates, and encouraged free blacks to emigrate to

Liberia. Rioters periodically attempted to destroy black institutions.

Despite depressing social conditions, a staunch black middle class constructed a community in New York City. By 1830, three years after final abolition, New York's blacks could proudly point to significant churches in all denominations except the Dutch Reformed and to schools, newspapers, and a politically progressive intelligentsia from the clergy and antislavery activists. The 1830s was the decade of an African-American renaissance in New York as blacks battled slavecatchers, conducted an UNDERGROUND RAILROAD, published magazines and newspapers, wrote poetry, and opened schools. The successes of the middle class did not always ameliorate poverty for the mass of free blacks. Although black activists constantly railed against inequality, basic jobs such as carting were segregated and factories rarely hired blacks. Mortality rates were far higher than those of whites, and few blacks lived past fifty years of age. New York's free black population rose to 49,005 by 1860, but the percentage of blacks in the total population dipped to less than 5 percent. In New Jersey, free blacks lived more constricted lives as lack of opportunity, tenant farming, and residual bigotry blighted their freedom. The persistence of slavery, which did not end in New Jersey until passage of the THIRTEENTH AMENDMENT in 1865, meant that most free blacks lived and worked as employees on white farms. With few prospects, the young left for the cities. As late as 1860, only 25,318 free blacks lived in New Jersey.

Pennsylvania was more liberal to free blacks. While Quaker antislavery agitation became more effective by 1760, free blacks were few in the eighteenth century. Political and economic restrictions were powerful impediments. By 1770 there were about 300 free blacks in Philadelphia; in the next six years, masters freed another 175. British enticements and black opportunism helped at least 80 Philadelphians to gain freedom and leave for Nova Scotia. In 1780, Pennsylvania enacted gradual emancipation. Despite limits to immediate freedom, by 1790 freepeople outnumbered slaves in Pennsylvania by 6,531 to 3,707. Freedom by degrees meant that even in 1840 there were 64 slaves in the state, but Philadelphia in particular became a beacon for free blacks. As in New York, community was based on church. Richard ALLEN and Absalom JONES established important congregations. Philadelphia became a city of refuge for already free, newly freed, and fugitive slaves. By 1810, 9,653, or 40 percent, of the state's blacks lived in Philadelphia. Proprietors, artisans, mariners, and domestics composed a fragile middle class. As in New York City, there was a free black serving the community in every trade. Less segregated than New

York, Philadelphia offered better support to the unskilled black.

Pennsylvania became cooler to free blacks by the 1820s. Racism, competition for jobs, and the steady stream of unskilled fugitives from the South tested the limits of the state's egalitarianism. Riots, nasty public attitudes, and stark discrimination made the state gradually less attractive. But despite rising bigotry, the middle class flourished intellectually and spiritually. Richard Allen headed the first conventions of black Methodists and, later, the first Colored National Conventions between 1830 and 1833. Aiming at the extinction of slavery, black activists welcomed fugitive slaves and fought for black civil rights.

By the 1850s, the issues of slavery and its aftermath consolidated free black aims in the North. Working with sympathetic whites, black political and abolitionist societies lobbied for the emancipation of slaves in the South and advancement of black civil liberties in the North. For ordinary people, the Fugitive Slave Act of 1850 (see FUGITIVE SLAVE LAWS), the DRED SCOTT DECISION of 1857, and bigotry's unceasing irritant made life in the North less palatable. The allure of the city faded in the antebellum period as other free blacks sought refuge and land in the West, Canada, or Liberia. As the Civil War unfolded, northern free blacks beseeched Abraham Lincoln to enroll them in the Union army. After 1863, tens of thousands of northern blacks served with distinction and courage in the war to end slavery. Passage of the thirteenth, fourteenth and fifteenth amendments validated their efforts and those of their ancestors to earn full citizenship.

See also FREE BLACKS, 1619–1860.

REFERENCES

COTTROL, ROBERT J. *Providence's Black Community in the Antebellum Era.* Westport, Conn., 1982.

CURRY, LEONARD P. *The Free Black in Urban America, 1800–1850.* Chicago, 1981.

HORTON, JAMES O., and LOIS E. HORTON. *Black Bostonians: Family Life and Community Struggle in the Antebellum North.* New York, 1979.

LITWACK, LEON. *North of Slavery.* Chicago, 1961.

NASH, GARY B. *Forging Freedom: The Formation of Philadelphia's Black Community.* Cambridge, Mass., 1987.

NASH, GARY B., and JEAN SODERLUND. *Freedom by Degrees: Emancipation in Pennsylvania and Its Aftermath.* New York, 1991.

WHITE, SHANE. *Somewhat More Independent: The End of Slavery in New York City, 1770–1810.* Athens, Ga., 1991.

ZILVERSMIT, ARTHUR. *The First Emancipation: The Abolition of Slavery in the North.* Chicago, 1967.

GRAHAM RUSSELL HODGES

Free Blacks, 1619–1860. In 1860, some half a million free people of African descent resided in the United States. Known alternately as free Negroes, free blacks, free people of color, or simply freepeople (to distinguish them from post–Civil War freedpeople), they composed less than 2 percent of the nation's population and about 9 percent of all black people. Although the free black population grew in the centuries before the universal EMANCIPATION that accompanied the CIVIL WAR, it generally increased far more slowly than either the white or the slave population, so that it was a shrinking proportion of American society.

But free blacks were important far beyond their numbers. They played a pivotal role in American society during slave times and set precedents for both race relations and relations among black people when slavery ended. Their status and treatment were harbingers of the postemancipation world. Often the laws, attitudes, and institutions that victimized free blacks during the slave years—political proscription, segregation, and various forms of debt peonage—became the dominant modes of racial oppression once slavery ended. Similarly, their years of liberty profoundly influenced the pattern of postemancipation black life. Free people of African descent moved in disproportionate numbers into positions of leadership in black society after emancipation. For example, nearly half of the twenty-two black men who served in Congress between 1869 and 1900 had been free before the Civil War.

Although free blacks have been described as more black than free, they were not a monolithic group. Their numbers, status, and circumstance changed from time to time and differed from place to place, in some measure based on their origins, their social role, and relations with the dominant Euro-American population, on the one hand, and the enslaved African-American population, on the other.

Before the AMERICAN REVOLUTION, few free blacks could be found in colonial North America. The overwhelming majority of these were light-skinned children of mixed racial unions, freed by birth if their mother was white, as colonial law generally provided that a child's status followed that of its mother. Others were manumitted (i.e., freed) by conscience-stricken white fathers. A 1775 Maryland census, the fullest colonial enumeration of free blacks, counted slightly more than 1,800 free people of African descent, 80 percent of whom were people of mixed racial origins. Like Maryland whites, about half of these free black people were under sixteen years old, and, of these, almost nine in ten were of mixed racial origins. Few black people of unmixed racial parentage enjoyed freedom in colonial Maryland; the free black population was not only light-skinned but also getting lighter. Unlike slaveholders in the Caribbean and South America, Maryland slave owners emancipated their sons as well as their daughters with equal—if not greater—facility. The sex ratio, following that of slaves, generally favored males. In addition, about one-sixth of adult free blacks were crippled or elderly persons deemed "past labor," whom heartless slaveholders had discarded when they could no longer wring a profit from them. In all, free black people composed 4 percent of the colony's black population and less than 2 percent of its free population. Almost a century after slavery had been written into law, the vast majority of Maryland black people remained locked in bonded servitude. The routes to freedom were narrow and dismal.

Fragmentary evidence from elsewhere on the North American continent suggests that free black people were rarely a larger proportion of the population than in Maryland. In most places, they made up a considerably smaller share of the whole, and in some places they were almost nonexistent.

Although their numbers were universally small, the status of free people of African descent differed from place to place in colonial North America. In Spanish Florida and in French and (after 1763) Spanish Louisiana, black people generally gained their freedom as soldiers and slavecatchers in defense of colonies vulnerable to foreign invasion and domestic insurrection. Playing off the weakness of European colonists, free African and Afro-American men gained special standing by taming interlopers, disciplining plantation slaves, and capturing runaways. However grossly discriminated against they were, service in the white man's cause enabled some free black men to inch up the social ladder, taking their families with them.

Spanish authorities first employed black men, many of them runaways from English colonies, in defense of St. Augustine in the late seventeenth century. Eager to keep the English enemy at bay, Spanish officials instructed the fugitives in the Catholic faith, allowed them to be baptized and married within the Church, and then sent them against their former enslavers in raids on the English settlements at Port Royal and Edisto. Black militiamen later fought against the English in the Yamassee War and protected Spanish Florida against retaliatory raids. During the eighteenth century, Spanish officials stationed black militiamen and their families at Gracia Real de Santa Teresa de Mose, a fortified settlement north of St. Augustine. Mose became the center of free black life in colonial Florida until its destruction in 1740. Thereafter, free blacks were more fully integrated into Spanish life in St. Augustine. They married among themselves, with Native Americans, and with African and Afro-American slaves; worked as craftsmen, sailors, and laborers; purchased property; and enjoyed a degree of prosperity and respectability. The free black settlement at Mose was rebuilt in the 1750s, and it once again became a center of free black life in colonial Florida until the Spanish evacuated the colony in 1763.

French authorities in Louisiana first enlisted black soldiers in quelling an Afro-Indian revolt in 1730. Thereafter, officials incorporated black men into Louisiana's defense force and called upon them whenever Indian confederations, European colonial rivals, or slave insurrectionists jeopardized the safety of the colony. On each such occasion—whether the Chickasaw war of the 1730s, the Choctaw war of the 1740s, or the threatened English invasion of the 1750s—French officials mobilized black men, free and slave, with slaves offered freedom in exchange for military service. By 1739, at least 270 black men were under arms in Louisiana, of whom some 50 were free.

The black militia played an even larger role in Spanish Louisiana than it had under the French. Spain gained control of the colony in 1763, as part of the settlement of the Seven Years' War. Finding themselves surrounded by hostile French planters, Spanish authorities embraced free people of African descent as an ally against internal as well as external foes. They recommissioned the Louisiana free black militia, adopting the division between *pardo* (light-skinned) and *moreno* (dark-skinned) units present elsewhere in Spanish America. Officials clad the free black militiamen in striking uniforms and granted them *fuero militar* rights, thereby exempting the black militiamen from civil prosecution, certain taxes, and licensing fees—no mean privileges for free black men in a slave society.

The free black militia thrived under the Spanish rule, becoming an integral part of the colony's defense force. When not fighting foreign enemies, free black militiamen were employed to maintain the levees that protected New Orleans and the great riverfront plantations, to fight fires in the city limits, and to hunt fugitive slaves. As the value of the free black militia to Spain increased, so did the size and status of the class from which the militia sprang. In 1803, when the Americans took control over Louisiana, the free black militia numbered over five hundred men.

The central role of free black men in defense of colonial Florida and Louisiana allowed them to enlarge their numbers and improve their place within those colonies. Black militiamen employed their pay and bounties to secure the freedom of their families and a modest place in societies that were otherwise hostile to free people of African descent. From their strategic position, they entered the artisan trades, frequently controlling many of the interstitial positions as shopkeepers, tradesmen, and market women—occasionally even as plantation overseers and midwives.

In English seaboard colonies, white nonslaveholders served as soldiers and slavecatchers and monopolized the middling occupations as artisans, tradesmen, and overseers. Free blacks, as a result, were confined to the most marginal social roles. They had few opportunities to advance themselves, accumulate property, gain respectability, and buy their loved ones out of bondage. Their status fell far below that enjoyed by free blacks in the Gulf region.

The American Revolution transformed the free black population. But because the Revolution took a different course in different places and because of differences within the extant slave and free black populations, the reformation of black life moved in different directions in different parts of the new republic. Post-Revolutionary free black life can best be understood from a regional perspective. During the antebellum years, there were three distinctive groups of free blacks in the United States: one in the northern or free states, a second in the Upper South, and a third in the Lower South. Each had its own demographic, economic, social, and somatic characteristics. These differences, in turn, bred different relations with whites and slaves and, most important, distinctive modes of social action.

First, the Revolution transformed the North from a slave to a free society, greatly enlarging its free black population. But slavery died hard in the northern states, and the gradualist process by which northern courts and legislatures abolished slavery left some black people in bondage until the eve of the Civil War. Still, post-Revolutionary emancipation ensured that eventually all northern blacks would be free, and by the first decade of the nineteenth century the vast majority had emerged from slavery. To their number were added immigrants from the South, most of them fugitive slaves. In 1860, about a quarter of a million blacks, slightly less than half of the nation's free blacks, lived in the free states.

But universal emancipation in the North did not transform the economic status or social standing of black people—except perhaps for the worse. Before the Revolution, northern slaves had been disproportionately urban in residence, black in color, and unskilled in occupation. Free blacks followed that pattern, becoming in fact more urban and unskilled during the antebellum years, as they increasingly migrated to cities and found themselves pushed out of artisan trades by European immigrants.

Nevertheless, post-Revolutionary emancipation allowed black people certain rights. Because the abolition of slavery freed northern whites from the fear of slave revolts, they did not look upon every gathering of black people as the beginning of a revolution. They limited the political rights of free blacks, but they allowed them to travel freely, organize their own institutions, publish newspapers, and petition and protest. Black men and women transformed these liberties into a powerful associational and political tradition. African churches, schools, fraternal organizations, and literary societies flourished in the northern states. The AFRICAN METHODIST EPISCOPAL and AFRICAN METHODIST EPISCOPAL ZION denominations and the Prince Hall Masons, the Grand United Order of Odd Fellows, and the Knights of Pythias were among the largest of these, extending their reach to all portions of the North (see also FRATERNAL ORDERS AND MUTUAL AID ASSOCIATIONS). Every black community also supported a host of locally based institutions and organizations. Members of these institutions, national and local, joined together to hold regional and national conventions that protested discrimination and worked for group improvement. From Richard ALLEN to Frederick DOUGLASS, the black leaders forged a tradition of protests that demanded full equality.

As in the North, the free black population in the Upper South was largely a product of the American Revolution. But in this region, the ideas and events—along with the economic changes—of the Revolutionary era merely loosened the fabric of slavery by increasing MANUMISSION, self-purchase, and successful suits for freedom. Slavery survived the challenge of the Revolutionary years, and indeed flourished. Nevertheless, the free black population grew rapidly, so that by 1810 the Upper South contained nearly 100,000 free blacks, who composed about 8 percent of the black population in the region and almost 60 percent of all free people of African descent. Thereafter, the tightening noose of slavery slowed the growth of the free black population, and the proportion of free black people residing in the region declined.

The free black population in the Upper South was the product of two patterns of manumissions. The first and most important occurred on a large scale; it was indiscriminate, and rooted in ideological and economic changes of the Revolutionary era. The second, smaller and more selective, originated in personal relations between master and slave. The first wave of manumissions produced a population that, like the slave population, was largely rural and black in color. To the extent, however, that post-Revolutionary emancipation was selective—with masters choosing whom they would free—it produced a free black population that was more skilled and lighter in color than that of the North. In the course of the nineteenth century, manumission became even more selective, so that freepeople of the Upper South became increasingly skilled in occupation, urban in residence, and light in skin color. The absence of large-scale European immigration to the slave states and a long-standing reliance on black labor allowed Upper South free blacks to enjoy a higher economic standing than those in the free states. In 1860, a quarter to a third of free black men practiced skilled trades in Nashville, Richmond, and other Upper South cities.

But if the presence of slavery helped elevate their economic status, it severely limited the freepeople's opportunities for political or communal activism, for southern whites looked upon free black people as the chief inspiration and instigators of slave unrest. White southerners not only prevented free black people from voting, sitting on juries, and testifying in court but also barred them from traveling without permission and meeting without the supervision of some white notable. These constraints circumscribed political and organizational opportunities. No black newspapers were published and no black conventions met in the South. There were no southern counterparts of Allen or Douglass. Black churches, schools, and fraternal societies were fragile organizations, often forced to meet clandestinely. With limited opportunities for political outlets, free black men and women poured their energies into economic opportunities, and, as tradesmen and artisans, made considerable gains.

This tendency toward economic advancement at the expense of political activism was present in an even more exaggerated form in the Lower South, particularly the port cities of Charleston, Mobile, and New Orleans. These places were largely untouched by the egalitarian thrust of the Revolutionary era. Moreover, when the United States gained control of Louisiana and Florida, American officials decommissioned and dispersed the free black militias, and slaveholder-dominated legislatures subjected the existing free black population to considerable restrictions. The free black population increased slowly in the nineteenth century, its growth the product of natural increase and sexual relations between masters and slaves. Almost all free blacks were drawn from the small group of privileged slaves who had lived in close contact with their owners, connections that often bespoke family ties. As a result, former slaves were overwhelmingly urban and light-skinned, a quality that earned them the title "free people of color," or in New Orleans gens de couleur. Although comparatively few in number, most were far more skilled than free blacks in the Upper South. In some places, such as Charleston and New Orleans, over three-quarters of the free men of color practiced skilled crafts, and they monopolized some trades on the eve of the Civil War. A handful of wealthy free people of color even purchased slaves and moved into the planter class.

As in the Upper South, the presence of slavery in the Lower South prevented free people of color from translating their higher economic standing into social and political gains. Denied suffrage and proscribed from office, they found a political voice only by acting through white patrons—their manumittors, their customers, and occasionally their fathers. Their own organizations remained private, exclusive, and often shadowy, especially in comparison to the robust public institutions created by free black people in the North. Although some were well traveled and highly educated, as much at home in Paris and Glasgow as in New Orleans and Charleston, they dared not attack slavery or racial inequality publicly. Many feared to identify with slaves in any fashion. Rather, they saw themselves—and increasingly came to be seen by whites—as a third caste, distinct from both free whites and enslaved blacks.

With the general emancipation of 1863, free people of African descent carried their diverse histories into freedom. Although Civil War emancipation liquidated their special status, their collective experience continued to shape American race relations and Afro-American life.

REFERENCES

BERLIN, IRA. *Slaves Without Masters: The Free Negro in the Antebellum South*. New York, 1974.

BREEN, T. H., and STEPHEN INNES. *"Myne Owne Ground": Race and Freedom on Virginia's Eastern Shore, 1640–1676*. New York, 1980.

CURRY, LEONARD P. *The Free Black in Urban America, 1800–1865: The Shadow of the Dream*. Chicago, 1987.

DEAL, DOUGLAS. "A Constricted World: Free Blacks on Virginia's Eastern Shore, 1680–1750." In Lois Green Carr, Philip D. Morgan, and Jean B. Russo, eds. *Colonial Chesapeake Society*. Chapel Hill, N.C., 1988.

FONER, LAURA. "The Free People of Color in Louisiana and St. Dominque: A Comparative Portrait of Two Three-Caste Societies." *Journal of Social History* 3 (1970): 406–430.

JOHNSON, MICHAEL P., and JAMES L. ROARK. *Blacks Masters: A Free Family of Color in the Old South*. New York, 1984.

LITWACK, LEON F. *North of Slavery: The Negro in the Free States, 1790–1860*. Chicago, 1961.

STERKX, HERBERT. *The Free Negro in Ante-Bellum Louisiana, 1724–1860*. Rutherford, N.J., 1972.

IRA BERLIN

Freedman's Bank. The short history of the Freedman's Bank, officially titled the Freedman's Savings and Trust Company, exemplifies both the promise and the frustrations of African-American economic development immediately after the CIVIL WAR. The Freedman's Bank was incorporated by Congress on March 3, 1865, absorbing the military banks that had been established by the Union Army during the Civil War in Norfolk, Va., Beaufort, S.C., and New Orleans to provide depository services for African-American troops. John W. Alvord, superintendent of schools and finances for the federal Freedmen's Bureau, spearheaded the drive to establish the bank and organized the bank's original founders, a group of white businessmen, philanthropists, and humanitarians.

Created as a missionary endeavor to promote thrift among the freed slaves, the Freedman's Bank was to serve as a mutual savings bank for the benefit of the black community. The first interstate bank established after the charter of the Bank of the United States expired in 1836, the Freedman's Savings and Trust Company was a nonprofit organization. Its original charter made no provisions for loans but stated that it would receive deposits from freedmen and women, invest them in government securities, and return the profits to the depositors in the form of interest.

Although the bank remained a legally private corporation, its concurrent establishment with the Freedmen's Bureau and the appointment of many Freedmen's Bureau officers as bank trustees misled many African Americans into believing that the federal government had assumed responsibility for the institution's financial solvency. Hoping to attract black support for the bank, the trustees used the bank's advertisements to reinforce the public's belief that the bank had government backing. Principal control of the bank came from the bank's all-white trustees operating at the national headquarters, located first in New York City and then in Washington, D.C. However, the bank gradually hired local black leaders, usually politicians, ministers, and businessmen, as cashiers and as members of the advisory boards in a further attempt to win the trust of the black community.

Encouraged by the bank's government charter and the endorsement by the commissioner of the Freedmen's Bureau, many African Americans deposited funds in the bank. Thirty-four branch offices eventually were established, covering every southern state, as well as Washington, D.C., Philadelphia, and New York City. By 1874, 72,000 depositors had entrusted over $3,000,000 to the bank.

Buoyed by its success and seeking to increase interest payments, the bank's predominantly white board of trustees amended the bank's charter in 1870, allowing the trustees to invest half of its deposits allotted for government securities in speculative stocks and bonds and on real estate. Led by the chairman of the Finance Committee, Henry Cooke, the bank invested heavily in Washington real estate in the 1870s and made several large, unsecured loans. Among these loans was one for $50,000 to Jay Cooke and Company, run by Henry Cooke's brother and business partner, Jay Cooke, to finance the Northern Pacific Railroad. This loan, along with a number of other unsecured investments, left the bank severely overextended and vulnerable when the banking firm of Jay Cooke and Company failed in 1873. The ensuing national financial panic crippled the bank, forcing it to sacrifice its best securities and borrow at ruinous rates in order to remain solvent.

The 1870 amendment to the bank's charter was intended to increase the profits of the depositors and was restricted principally to the Washington office. This policy ensured that the majority of the bank's investments would go to white business ventures. In addition, the collateral requirements for blacks requesting loans were far more stringent than those for whites. As a result, few blacks were able to borrow from the bank, and very little money was invested in the black community. Many blacks were vocal about their dissatisfaction with the bank's limited lending policies and its failure to stimulate black business and economic development, but the trustees did not persuade Congress to amend the charter until June 1874. This amendment would have allowed money to be returned to the branch offices for investment, but its late passage prevented its implementation.

With the onset of the Panic of 1873, most of the bank's white trustees resigned, leaving the bank's black trustees, whose numbers had increased steadily since the original appointments made in 1867, in control of the institution. Among the active black trustees in 1874 were Charles B. PURVIS, John Mercer LANGSTON, and A. T. AUGUSTA. Along with the other remaining trustees, they made a desperate effort to save the bank and to restore the confidence of depositors by electing Frederick DOUGLASS as president in 1874. Even his efforts to reorganize the bank, however, could not make up for years of mismanagement and the devastating effects of the national economic crisis. Careless lending, incompetence of certain bank officials, and poor management proved an insurmountable legacy. The failure of the bank struck a deep blow to African-American economic development after the Civil War.

Although there was a good deal of support for a bill introduced into Congress that would have reimbursed the depositors in full with federal funds, the legislation never passed. Only by selling off its assets was the bank able to begin reimbursing its depositors in 1875, offering each 20 percent of their total deposits. Many of the small depositors, however, could

not be located and thus lost everything. By 1883 less than one quarter of the depositors had received complete reimbursements, which only amounted to 62 percent of their original deposits. The bank's collapse and the government's unwillingness to shoulder responsibility for the depositors' investments left a legacy of suspicion and distrust among the black community. The bank's monetary losses were especially tragic because they represented one of the first attempts of the newly freed slaves to grasp economic security and equal citizenship.

REFERENCES

FLEMING, WALTER. *The Freedman's Savings Bank: A Chapter in the Economic History of the Negro Race.* Chapel Hill, N.C., 1927.
OSTHAUS, CARL. *The Freedman's Savings Bank: Philanthropy and Fraud.* Urbana, Ill., 1976.

LOUISE P. MAXWELL

Freedmen's Bureau. *See* Bureau of Refugees, Freedmen, and Abandoned Lands.

Freedmen's Hospital. Originally established in 1862 at Camp Barker, a Washington, D.C., army barracks, to serve displaced former slaves and other CIVIL WAR refugees, this medical facility was named Freedmen's Hospital in 1863. Alexander T. AUGUSTA, a black army physician, served as its surgeon-in-chief for a short time, succeeding Dr. Daniel Breed. Augusta was the first of many staff physicians to complain about the substandard physical conditions of the hospital. Freedmen's would continue to struggle to serve its indigent clients in the face of economic hardship and outdated equipment.

In January 1865, Dr. Robert Reyburn assumed the leadership of Freedmen's Hospital. The following year Reyburn was appointed to the Medical Faculty of the proposed HOWARD UNIVERSITY, establishing the longstanding connection between the two institutions. In 1869 the hospital moved to buildings newly built by the Freedmen's Bureau on the university campus. This relationship kept the hospital alive past 1872 when the Freedmen's Bureau was officially dismantled. However, the staff of the hospital fought to retain their autonomy as the university sought to gain control of the facilities, which served the important function of a teaching hospital for black nursing and medical students.

After the demise of the Freedmen's Bureau, the hospital was placed under the Department of the Interior. In 1873 a black doctor, Dr. Charles B. PUR-

VIS, was named surgeon-in-chief. In 1894, Dr. Daniel Hale WILLIAMS, the black physician credited with performing the first open-heart surgery, replaced Purvis. In 1897 he was replaced by Dr. Austin M. CURTIS, who was succeeded four years later by Dr. William A. Warfield.

In 1892, Congress passed a law requiring the District of Columbia commissioners to contribute half of the hospital's funding and to control financing while the Department of the Interior continued to manage the hospital. This complicated arrangement proved inefficient, and the condition of the hospital worsened under it.

In 1903 Congress authorized $350,000 for the construction of a new hospital. Two years later it put the hospital completely under the Department of the Interior, with a new arrangement whereby the hospital would contract in advance for an estimated allotment of patients. The number of patients admitted, however, always exceeded the number allowed for in the contract, and the hospital administrators were forced to run the facility under a financial deficit.

On February 26, 1908, the new facilities were occupied. On June 26, 1912, a law was passed allowing the hospital, which until this time had been restricted to treating indigents, to admit paying patients.

In 1936 Dr. T. Edward Jones was named Freedmen's surgeon-in-chief. His successor, in 1944, was Charles Richard DREW. These two leaders had to negotiate the hospital's conflicting purposes of providing medical care to its indigent clients, one third of whom were white, and providing medical training to black students who continued to be denied access to white hospitals.

In 1955 a government study deploring the substandard physical conditions recommended that a new hospital be built and turned over to Howard. On September 15, 1961, President John F. Kennedy signed a bill officially placing Freedmen's Hospital under Howard University's control and authorizing the construction of a new facility. On March 2, 1975, the Howard University Medical Center was opened, replacing Freedmen's Hospital.

REFERENCES

HOLT, THOMAS, CASSANDRA SMITH-PARKER, and ROSALYN TERBORG-PENN. *A Special Mission: The Story of Freedmen's Hospital, 1862–1962.* Washington, D.C., 1975.

LOGAN, RAYFORD W. *Howard University: The First Hundred Years, 1867–1967.* New York, 1969.

LYDIA MCNEILL

In 1893, Daniel Hale Williams performed the first successful open-heart surgery. Williams was also involved in establishing programs for nursing and medical education for blacks. In this 1897 photograph he sits near center with nurses and interns studying at Freedmen's Hospital in Washington, D.C. (Moorland-Spingarn Research Center, Howard University)

Freedom Democratic Party, Mississippi.
See Mississippi Freedom Democratic Party.

Freedom National Bank. In 1964, baseball great Jackie ROBINSON led a group of black and Jewish entrepreneurs in the founding of Freedom National Bank at 275 West 125th Street in Harlem. One of the first black-owned banks in New York City, it was meant to provide low-cost loans to Harlem home owners and small businesses who had difficulty obtaining loans from large banks. Freedom National experienced little growth during its early years and, after having written off $2 million of its $19 million loan portfolio as losses in 1974, it required an investment of $3.7 million from a consortium of eleven major banks to avoid failure in 1975. In 1977, Sharnia Buford became president. During his presidency, which ended with his resignation in January 1987, Freedom National's assets grew from $35 million to $125 million, making it one of the nation's largest black-owned banks. It also opened a branch in the Bedford-Stuyvesant section of Brooklyn.

In the mid-1980s, members of the board of directors pushed for a more aggressive growth strategy in opposition to Buford's conservative approach. From 1985 to 1987, Freedom National made loans to minority entrepreneurs who did not have adequate collateral. Consequently, the bank lost $1.9 million in 1988, $1.8 million in 1989, and had projected losses of $2 million for 1990. Beginning in 1988, the federal government told Freedom National to protect its reserves against default by obtaining more capital, but it was unable to do so. In November 1990, facing the threat that the federal government would close Freedom National, its board of directors attempted to merge it with the black-owned Boston Bank of Commerce, while a group of city politicians, black clergy, and black businessmen, led by U.S. Rep. Charles B. RANGEL (D–N.Y.), attempted to find investors. But on Friday, November 9, amid charges that it had not given the community sufficient notice, the federal government closed Freedom National, which at the time had $90.8 million in deposits, $101.9 million in assets, and two branches in Brooklyn.

The Federal Deposit Insurance Corporation (FDIC) claimed that it had unsuccessfully contacted scores of banks to take over Freedom National. Unlike the FDIC's treatment of large commercial bank failures of the 1980s, it chose not to fully reimburse accounts above the $100,000 insurance limit, arguing that Freedom National's failure would not have the same impact on the national economy. This was widely criticized in the black community. The fed-

eral government was also criticized for not placing Freedom National in a period of conservatorship, a period of time during which depositors could have transferred their accounts. Of Freedom National's 22,000 accounts, 100 had a total of $11 million above the $100,000 insurance limit. Some of these large depositors were protected against loss. But because the FDIC agreed to pay only 50 cents on every uninsured dollar, many account holders, including nonprofit organizations, stood collectively to lose millions of dollars, until a $6 million bill to refund the uninsured accounts was passed by Congress in 1991.
See also BANKING.

REFERENCE

New York Times, December 3, 1990, p. A1.

SIRAJ AHMED

Freedom's Journal, newspaper. Founded in March 1827, *Freedom's Journal* was the first African-American weekly newspaper. The idea of a black press arose among New York City blacks who sought a public voice to respond to racist commentary in local white newspapers. Samuel E. CORNISH, a Presbyterian minister, and John B. RUSSWURM, a graduate of Bowdoin College, took charge of the enterprise. *Freedom's Journal* followed a format common to antebellum reform newspapers by using current events, anecdotes, and editorials to convey the message of moral reform. The editors also focused on issues of interest to northern free blacks: racial prejudice, slavery, and particularly the threat of colonization—the efforts by the AMERICAN COLONIZATION SOCIETY to expatriate free blacks to Africa. The newspaper received widespread support from blacks outside New York City. Over two dozen authorized agents, including David WALKER in Boston, collected subscriptions and distributed the paper. Within a year, *Freedom's Journal* reached an audience in eleven northern and southern states, upper Canada, England, and Haiti.

When Russwurm assumed total control of *Freedom's Journal* in September 1827, he gradually shifted the paper's editorial position on colonization. Few readers knew that he had actually developed an interest in colonization during his college days, and his announced "conversion" to colonization in 1828 severely damaged the paper's credibility and eroded its base of support. In March 1829 it ceased publication, and Russwurm departed for the American Colonization Society's settlement in Liberia. Cornish attempted to revive the newspaper in May as *The Rights of All,* but he succeeded in publishing only six monthly issues.

REFERENCES

GROSS, BELLA. "Freedom's Journal and the Rights of All." *Journal of Negro History* 17 (1932): 241–286.

JACOBS, DONALD M., ed. *Antebellum Black Newspapers.* Westport, Conn., 1976.

MICHAEL F. HEMBREE

Freedom Summer.   In the summer of 1964, the COUNCIL OF FEDERATED ORGANIZATIONS (COFO)—a Mississippi coalition of the CONGRESS OF RACIAL EQUALITY (CORE), the STUDENT NONVIOLENT COORDINATING COMMITTEE (SNCC), and the NATIONAL ASSOCIATION FOR THE ADVANCEMENT OF COLORED PEOPLE (NAACP) invited Northern white college students to spearhead a massive black voter registration and education campaign aimed at challenging white supremacy in the deep South. This campaign, which became known as Freedom Summer, was the culmination of COFO's efforts to attack black disfranchisement in Mississippi. COFO had been formed in 1962 in response to the Kennedy administration's offer of tax-exempt status and funding from liberal philanthropies to civil rights organizations that focused their activities on increasing black voter registration. The considerable success of COFO activists in sparking the interest of black Mississippians in voter registration during the summer of 1963 prompted them to propose an entire summer of civil rights activities in 1964 to focus national attention on the disfranchisement of blacks in Mississippi, and to force the federal government to protect the civil rights of African Americans in the South.

SNCC played the largest role in the project and provided most of its funding. Robert MOSES of SNCC was the guiding force behind the summer project, and the overwhelming majority of COFO staff workers were SNCC members who were veterans of the long fight for racial equality in Mississippi.

Approximately 1,000 northern white college students, committed to social change and imbued with liberal ideals, volunteered to participate in the Freedom Summer campaign. Under the direction of SNCC veterans, these volunteers created community centers that provided basic services such as health care to the black community, and initiated voter education activities and literacy classes aimed at encouraging black Mississippians to register to vote. SNCC activists also directly challenged the segregated policies of the all-white Mississippi Democratic party by

supporting the efforts of local black leaders to run their own candidates under the party name MISSISSIPPI FREEDOM DEMOCRATIC PARTY (MFDP). The MFDP efforts encouraged over 17,000 African Americans to vote for the sixty-eight delegates who attended the national Democratic Convention in Atlantic City in the summer of 1964 and demanded to be seated in replacement of the regular Democratic organization. The MFDP challenge, though unsuccessful, focused national attention on Mississippi and propelled Fanny Lou HAMER, a local activist, into the national spotlight.

Another focus of the Freedom Summer was institutionalized educational inequities in Mississippi. Thirty COFO project sites created "Freedom Schools," administered under the direction of

SNCC, CORE, and the SCLC combined forces to direct the Freedom Summer of 1964, a coordinated effort to register and empower black Mississippians. One of the most successful programs of the Freedom Summer were freedom schools, in which black and white college students taught classes in basic reading skills, citizenship and politics, and black history. (Photographs and Prints Division, Schomburg Center for Research in Black Culture, The New York Public Library, Astor, Lenox and Tilden Foundations)

Staughton Lynd, a white Spelman College history professor, to provide an alternative education to empower black children to challenge their oppression. These schools provided students with academic training in remedial topics, as well as in more specialized subjects like art and French. A key goal of the schools was to develop student leadership and foster activism through discussions about current events, black history, the philosophy behind the civil rights movement, and other cultural activities. Despite the overcrowding and the perennial lack of facilities, over 3,000 African-American students attended the Freedom schools.

Violence framed the context of all COFO activities and created a climate of tension and fear within the organization. White supremacists bombed or burned sixty-seven homes, churches, and black businesses over the course of the summer, and by the end of the project, at least three civil rights workers—James CHANEY, Michael Schwerner, and Andrew Goodman—had been killed by southern whites, four had been critically wounded, eight hundred had been beaten, and over a thousand had been arrested. The reluctance of the state government to prosecute the perpetrators of these acts of violence and the failure of the federal government to intervene to provide protection for civil rights workers left many activists disillusioned about the federal government's ability or desire to ensure racial justice.

The impact and legacy of the Freedom Summer stretched far beyond the borders of Mississippi. Many Freedom Summer programs lived on when the project ended and COFO disbanded. Freedom Summer community centers provided a model for federally funded clinics, Head Start programs, and other War on Poverty programs. Freedom schools served as models for nationwide projects in alternative schooling. The barriers to black voting uncovered and publicized during the summer project provided stark evidence of the need for the VOTING RIGHTS ACT OF 1965, which made literacy tests and poll taxes illegal.

The Freedom Summer facilitated the development of a radical new political consciousness among many white volunteers, who found the summer to be a powerful experience of political education and personal discovery. At least one-third of the volunteers stayed on in Mississippi to continue the struggle for black equality. Many volunteers who returned to the North were disillusioned with the promises of the federal government and became activists in the New Left and the antiwar movement. Mario Savio, a Free-

Students in a freedom school. Such schools educated thousands of black children. (UPI/Bettmann)

dom Summer veteran, emerged in the fall of 1964 as the principal spokesperson of the free speech movement at the University of California at Berkeley, a key event in the emergence of the New Left.

The Freedom Summer experience was also an important catalyst for the women's liberation movement. Group consciousness of gender oppression among white women grew markedly during the summer as male volunteers were assigned more visible organizing tasks. In November 1964, at a SNCC staff meeting in Waveland, Miss., Mary King and Casey Hayden, two white staff members, presented an anonymous position paper criticizing the enforced inferiority of women in the Freedom Summer project and their exclusion from the decision-making process. This memo was one of the first discussions of the issues that would form the basis of the emerging women's movement within the New Left.

The experience of the Freedom Summer also radicalized black civil rights workers—though in quite different ways from white radicals. The summer helped steer black radicals in SNCC away from interracial movements and toward a suspicion of white participation that came to characterize the black power movement. Subsequent debates in the CIVIL RIGHTS MOVEMENT about the doctrine of interracialism were fueled by what the Freedom Summer revealed about the successes, and inherent limitations, of interracial civil rights activity. From the inception of the project, some black SNCC activists contested the Freedom Summer's premise that national attention could only be garnered by exposing white people to the violence and brutality that black people faced daily. These blacks were veterans of the long battle with white racists that SNCC had waged in Mississippi since 1961, were increasingly skeptical of liberal politics, and believed that the presence of white volunteers—who often tended to appropriate leadership roles and interact with black people in a paternalistic manner—would undermine their goal of empowering Mississippi blacks and hamper their efforts to foster and support black-controlled institutions in Mississippi. Tensions and hostility between black and white COFO activists were further inflamed by interracial liaisons which were often premised on the very racial stereotypes and misconceptions that they sought to surmount.

However, the Freedom Summer's most enduring legacy was the change of consciousness it engendered among black Mississippians. The Freedom Summer succeeded in initiating thousands of African Americans into political action, providing thousands of black children with an antiracist education and creating black-led institutions like the Mississippi Freedom Democratic Party. Fannie Lou Hamer provided a fitting testament to the impact of the Free-

dom Summer when she stated in 1966, "Before the 1964 summer project there were people that wanted change, but they hadn't dared to come out. After 1964 people began moving. To me it's one of the greatest things that ever happened in Mississippi."

REFERENCES

CAGIN, SETH, and PHILIP DRAY. *We Are Not Afraid: The Story of Goodman, Schwerner, and Chaney and the Civil Rights Campaign for Mississippi.* New York, 1988.
McADAM, DOUG. *Freedom Summer.* New York, 1988.
WEISBROT, ROBERT. *Freedom Bound: A History of America's Civil Rights Movement.* New York, 1990.

ROBYN SPENCER

Freeman, Harry Lawrence (October 9, 1869–March 24, 1954), composer and conductor. Harry Freeman began his musical activities at an early age; he organized a boys' quartet at the age of ten and became the organist in his family's church at age twelve. He later studied piano with Edwin Schonert, and theory and composition with Johann H. Beck, the founder of the Cleveland Symphony Orchestra. Around 1892, he moved to Denver, where he wrote numerous dances and marches. Freeman is known primarily as the first African-American composer to produce a substantial number of operas. The first of these works was *The Martyr* (1893), produced by the Freeman Grand Opera Company in September 1893.

After teaching at Wilberforce University from 1902 to 1904, Freeman became involved in black musical theater. In Chicago, he served as musical director for Ernest Hogan's *Rufus Rastus* (1905) and the Pekin Theater Company, for which he wrote the musical score *Captain Rufus* with Joe Jordan and J. Tim Brymm. He then moved to New York, where he participated in the company of *The Red Moon,* by Bob COLE and the Johnson brothers (*see* James Weldon JOHNSON and J. Rosamond JOHNSON). In 1910 he left the company and established the Freeman School of Music in New York City and organized the Negro Grand Opera Company, where he produced his two operas *Vendetta* (1923) and *Voodoo* (1928). In total, five of his operas were staged between 1893 and 1947, including a concert version of *The Martyr* at Carnegie Hall in 1947. His works are in a post-romantic style and incorporate folk songs of African Americans.

REFERENCES

HIPSHER, EDWARD E. "Harry Lawrence Freeman." In *American Opera and Its Composers.* New York, 1978, pp. 189–195.

SOUTHERN, EILEEN. *Biographical Dictionary of Afro-American and African Musicians.* Westport, Conn., 1982, p. 138.

WILLIE STRONG

Freeman, Morgan (June 1, 1937–), actor. Morgan Freeman was born and raised in rural Greenwood, Miss. He first acted in an elementary school production of *Little Boy Blue* and won a statewide acting competition in junior high school. Upon graduating from high school, Freeman worked as a radar technician in the Air Force. He moved to California, where he took acting lessons at the Pasadena Playhouse and dancing lessons in San Francisco. In 1964, Freeman moved to New York and danced at the World's Fair. Three years later, he made his Off-Broadway debut in *The Nigger Lovers.* His first Broadway appearance was in an all-black production of *Hello, Dolly!* in 1967, and from 1971 until 1976 he portrayed the character Easy Reader on Public Television's *The Electric Company.* He continued to do theater work on and off Broadway and received Obie Awards in 1980 for the title role in *Coriolanus,* and in 1984 for his role as the preacher in *The Gospel at Colonus* (1983). Freeman also won a Drama Desk Award and a Clarence Derwent Award (as a promising newcomer) for his role as a wino in *The Mighty Gents* (1978). He received a third Obie Award for his role as a soft-spoken southern chauffeur for a Mississippi Jewish widow in *Driving Miss Daisy* (1987), which was adapted for the screen in 1989.

Freeman made his film debut in 1980, playing minor roles in *Harry and Son* and *Brubaker.* He also appeared in *Eyewitness* (1981), *Death of a Prophet* (1983), *Teachers* (1984), *Marie* (1985), and *That Was Then, This Is Now* (1985). He gained recognition with his motion picture appearance in *Street Smart* (1987) with Christopher Reeve, for which Freeman received an Oscar nomination. In 1988 he played a reformed drug addict who counsels Michael Keaton in *Clean and Sober.* The following year was a turning point in Freeman's career. In 1989 he had starring roles as the school principal Joe Clark in *Lean on Me,* as the chauffeur in the movie adaptation of *Driving Miss Daisy,* for which he received an Oscar nomination, and as the first black sergeant of a northern black regiment during the Civil War in *Glory.* In 1991, he appeared in *Robin Hood,* and the following year he fulfilled a lifelong ambition to play a cowboy by starring in the Oscar-winning western *Unforgiven,* opposite Clint Eastwood. In the fall of 1993, Freeman made his directorial debut with *Bopha!,* a film set in South Africa and filmed in Zimbabwe, about the 1976 Soweto uprisings.

Actor Morgan Freeman (left) is pictured here with Joe Clark, the controversial law-and-order high school principal from Paterson, N.J., whom Freeman portrayed in the 1989 film *Lean on Me.* (AP/ Wide World Photos)

REFERENCES

MAPP, EDWARD. *Dictionary of the Performing Arts.* 2nd ed. Metuchen, N.J., 1990.
WETZSTEON, ROSS. "Morgan Freeman Takes Off." *New York* (March 14, 1988): 54–56.
WHITAKER, CHARLES. "Is Morgan Freeman America's Greatest Actor?" *Ebony* (April 1990): 32–34.

SABRINA FUCHS

Freeman, Paul Douglas (January 2, 1936–), conductor. Paul Freeman was born in Richmond, Va. He began studying the piano at age five, the clarinet at eight, and the cello at thirteen. He studied at the Eastman School of Music (B.M., 1956; M.M., 1957; Ph.D., 1963) with interludes at the Hochschule für Musik in Berlin (1957–1959) as well as private study with Richard Lert, Ewald Lindemann, and Pierre Monteux.

Early in his professional career (1961–1966), Freeman was conductor of the Opera Theater of Rochester, N.Y., moving then for three years to conduct the San Francisco Conservatory Orchestra and that city's Little Symphony. As associate conductor of the

Dallas Symphony (1968–1970), he attracted national attention with a televised concert of works by contemporary African-American composers. He was engaged in 1970 as conductor in residence by the Detroit Symphony Orchestra. In addition to his activities in Detroit, Freeman joined with Dominique-René de Lerma to establish the Black Composers Series for Columbia Records, a nine-volume anthology of primarily orchestral works by composers from three centuries and three continents, subsequently reissued by the College Music Society.

That relationship also resulted in annual concerts and lectures on black music held in Baltimore (1973), Houston (1974), Minneapolis (1975), Detroit (1976), and with the New York Philharmonic (1977). From 1974 to 1976 he served as principal guest conductor of the Helsinki Philharmonic but conducted and recorded extensively elsewhere in Europe. In 1968 he presented Wagner's *Tristan und Isolde* at Spoleto, in Italy. In 1977, he was also affiliated with National Opera Ebony, the first full-fledged black grand opera company.

Freeman left Detroit in 1979 to become music director of the Victoria Symphony Orchestra in British Columbia, where he gave particular attention to Canadian performers and composers, but continued his European career. He returned to the United States in 1988 to found the Chicago Sinfonietta, an ensemble with a large minority membership, whose success quickly established its musical significance, justifying European tours. By this time, Freeman had performed as guest conductor of most major orchestras in the United States and London and many on the Continent.

REFERENCES

GRAY, JOHN. *Blacks in Classical Music: A Bibliographic Guide to Composers, Performers, and Ensembles.* Westport, Conn., 1988.

SOUTHERN, EILEEN. *Biographical Dictionary of Afro-American and African Musicians.* Westport, Conn., 1982.

DOMINIQUE-RENÉ DE LERMA

Freeman, Robert Tanner (c. 1847–June 14, 1873), dentist. Robert Freeman was born in North Carolina of slave parents. His interest in dentistry was sparked when he worked as an office assistant to H. B. Noble, a leading dentist in Washington, D.C., with offices on Pennsylvania Avenue between Eleventh and Twelfth streets. Freeman's application to two dental schools, however, was rejected on racial grounds.

In 1867, Freeman was accepted at the newly established dental school at Harvard University. This was the first dental school in the United States founded on a nonproprietary basis and attached to an institution of higher learning. Freeman's admission to the program was the subject of debate among the faculty, which decided on consensus that "right and justice should be placed above expediency, and that intolerance must not be permitted." On March 6, 1869, he received a D.M.D. (Doctor of Dental Medicine) degree, together with the other five students in Harvard's first dental class. (Also in 1869, the first African Americans, Edwin Clarence Joseph HOWARD and George L. Ruffin, graduated from the Harvard medical and law schools, respectively.)

Freeman was the first African American to earn a dental degree. He returned to Washington, D.C., and practiced dentistry until his death on June 14, 1873. The next fully qualified black dentists to practice in Washington were William S. Lofton and Walter Sleubey Over, who took their degrees at Howard University in 1888. The first black dental society, the Washington Society of Colored Dentists (founded November 14, 1900), subsequently adopted the name Robert T. Freeman Dental Society. Freeman was the grandfather of Robert C. WEAVER.

REFERENCE

DUMMETT, CLIFTON ORRIN. *The Growth and Development of the Negro in Dentistry in the United States.* Chicago, 1952.

PHILIP N. ALEXANDER

Fugitive Slave Laws. From the colonial period to the adoption of the THIRTEENTH AMENDMENT, African Americans sought to escape their bondage. Masters found the recovering of runaways to be time-consuming, expensive, and often impossible. Colonial governments occasionally agreed to help recover slaves from other jurisdictions, but generally such cooperation was ineffective.

During the American Revolution, those states dismantling slavery usually exempted fugitive slaves from their emancipatory schemes. The Articles of Confederation (1781) did not obligate the states to return fugitive slaves, but in 1787 the Confederation Congress adopted the first national fugitive slave law as part of the Northwest Ordinance. The ordinance prohibited slavery in the Northwest Territory but also provided that a fugitive slave "may be lawfully reclaimed and conveyed to the person claiming his or her labor or service."

Late in the Constitutional Convention of 1787, without serious debate or a recorded vote, the delegates adopted what became the fugitive slave clause, providing that "No Person held to Service or Labour in one State, under the Laws thereof, shall, in Consequence of any Law or Regulation therein, be discharged from such Service or Labour, but shall be delivered up on Claim of the Party to whom such Service or Labour may be due" (U.S. Constitution, Art. IV, Sec. 2, Par. 3). The framers apparently contemplated enforcement by state and local governments, or through individual action. The location of the clause in Article IV, with other clauses dealing with interstate relations, supports this analysis.

However, in the Fugitive Slave Act of 1793 Congress spelled out procedures for returning runaway slaves. This law emerged from a controversy between Pennsylvania and Virginia over the status of a black named John Davis. In 1788 three Virginians seized Davis in Pennsylvania, claiming him as a fugitive slave, and took him to Virginia. When Virginia's governor refused to extradite the three men charged with kidnapping in Pennsylvania, the governor of Pennsylvania complained to President Washington, who brought the problem to Congress. This eventually led to the 1793 law, which regulated both the extradition of fugitives from justice and the return of fugitive slaves.

Under this law, the slave owners or their agents (claimants) seized runaways and brought them to any federal, state, or local judge or magistrate and presented "proof to the satisfaction" of the judge that the person seized was the claimant's fugitive slave. A claimant could establish this proof orally or through a certified "affidavit taken before . . . a magistrate" of the claimant's home state. If the judge upheld the claim, he issued a certificate of removal to the claimant. Anyone interfering with the seizure or rendition of a fugitive slave was subject to a five-hundred-dollar penalty, plus the value of any slaves lost and any costs a master incurred trying to reclaim the slave.

This law never worked well. All responsibility for capturing slaves rested with owners, who were not guaranteed any aid from police officials. Northern judges sometimes declined to participate in fugitive slave cases. In *Jack* v. *Martin* (1835), New York's highest court declared the federal law unconstitutional but returned Jack to slavery under the constitutional clause itself. In 1836, in an unpublished opinion, New Jersey's Chief Justice Joseph Hornblower declared the 1793 law unconstitutional and also freed the black before him.

Starting in the 1780s, northern legislatures passed "personal-liberty laws" to protect free blacks from kidnapping or mistaken seizure. These laws also pro-

vided state procedures to facilitate the return of bona fide fugitives. Laws passed after 1793 often added procedural and evidentiary requirements to the federal law. The northern states balanced protecting free blacks from kidnapping with fulfilling their constitutional obligation to return fugitive slaves.

In 1837 a local judge in Pennsylvania refused to take cognizance of a case involving an alleged fugitive slave named Margaret Morgan and her children. Edward Prigg, a professional slavecatcher, then acted on his own, taking Morgan and her children to Maryland in violation of Pennsylvania's 1826 personal-liberty law. In *Prigg* v. *Pennsylvania* (1842), United States Supreme Court justice Joseph Story held the 1793 law constitutional and determined that state personal-liberty laws interfering with rendition were unconstitutional. Story characterized the fugitive slave clause as "a fundamental article" of the Constitution necessary for its adoption, even though the history of the clause, by that time available to Story, shows this was not true. Story urged state officials to continue to enforce the 1793 law, but stated they could not be required to do so. A number of states soon passed new personal-liberty laws, prohibiting their officials from acting under the federal law.

Congress amended the 1793 law as part of the COMPROMISE OF 1850. Under this act, alleged fugitives could not testify on their own behalf or have a jury trial. In reaction to state refusals to participate in the rendition process, the Fugitive Slave Act of 1850 provided for enforcement by federal commissioners to be appointed in every county in the country. They received five dollars if they decided that the black before them was not a slave, but were paid ten dollars if they found in favor of the claimant. Popular opposition to the law increased after the publication of Harriet Beecher Stowe's fictional attack on slavery, UNCLE TOM'S CABIN (1852), which partially centered on the fugitive slave Eliza.

The 1850 law led to riots in Boston; Syracuse, N.Y.; Oberlin, Ohio; and elsewhere. Federal prosecutions of rescuers often failed. In Christiana, Pa., federal officials obtained treason indictments of over forty men after a group of fugitives fought their would-be captors and killed a slave owner. The prosecutions failed when United States Supreme Court justice Robert Grier ruled in *United States* v. *Hanway* (1851) that opposition to the fugitive slave law did not constitute treason. After these incidents, the Fugitive Slave Act was a dead letter in much of the North. In *Ableman* v. *Booth* (1859) the Supreme Court affirmed the constitutionality of the 1850 law and the supremacy of the federal courts.

Peaceful enforcement of the 1850 law was more common than violent opposition. Some removals required a show of federal force and the use of troops.

Over nine hundred fugitives were returned under the act before 1862. However, Southerners estimated that as many as ten thousand slaves escaped during that period.

Ultimately, the fugitive slave laws did little to protect southern property, but did much to antagonize sectional feelings. Southerners saw the North as unwilling to fulfill its constitutional obligation. Northerners believed the South was trying to force them to become slavecatchers, and in the process undermining civil liberties in the nation. In 1864, after the issuance of the Emancipation Proclamation, Congress repealed both the 1793 and 1850 laws.

REFERENCES

FINKELMAN, PAUL. An Imperfect Union: Slavery, Federalism, and Comity. Chapel Hill, N.C., 1981.
———. "The Kidnapping of John Davis and the Adoption of the Fugitive Slave Law of 1793." Journal of Southern History 56 (1990): 397–422.
———, ed. Articles on American Slavery. Vol. 6, Fugitive Slaves. New York, 1989.
MORRIS, THOMAS D. Free Men All: The Personal Liberty Laws of the North, 1780–1861. Baltimore, 1974.
WIECEK, WILLIAM M. The Sources of Antislavery Constitutionalism in America, 1760–1848. Ithaca, N.Y., 1977.

PAUL FINKELMAN

Fugitive Slaves. Many of the stories of fugitive slaves who managed to reach the free states in the antebellum period have entered the realm of legend. The dangers and sacrifice inherent in their efforts to reach free soil have been acknowledged and have become part of the historical record. Most scholars would agree, however, that only a small minority of the runaway slave population in any given year even attempted to reach the free states. Their stories are much more difficult to tell. This article will discuss the individual histories of fugitive slaves; a separate article discusses FUGITIVE SLAVE LAWS.

The principal source for the study of fugitive slaves is the advertisements published in local newspapers. (There is little reason to assume, however, that all slave runaways were advertised.) Information can also be gleaned from the diaries, logbooks, correspondence, and other personal papers of slave owners. Newspapers in both free states and slave states gave a great deal of attention to the more spectacular cases where violence or the threat of violence occurred in the recovery process. Newspapers also gave considerable coverage of efforts to subvert legal process in the return of fugitive slaves, particularly in the decade before the CIVIL WAR. Part of the record

has also been preserved in legal documents and court records. The owners dispassionately, and in considerable detail, described the personal characteristics of the fugitives and noted whether or not they were habitual runaways, the names of their previous owners or employers, their motives for running away, and whether they were expected to be fleeing beyond state lines.

The advertisements provided elaborate descriptions noting age, height, date of running away, date of the advertisement, home county or city, any scarring, four or five gradations of skin color, marital status, literacy, speech impediments, whether the runaway had been charged with a crime, motivations, and work skills, along with the names of employers and previous owners by county. The advertisements of sheriffs and town jailers revealed the date and county of incarceration of those who had been "taken up."

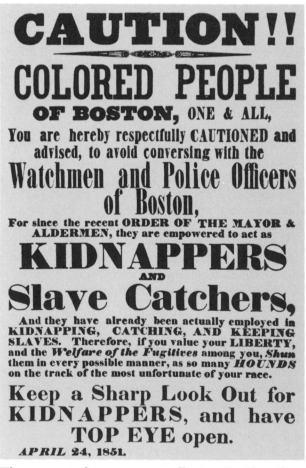

The passage of a new, more effective Fugitive Slave Law in 1850 ushered in a decade of anxiety for many northern blacks. This poster appeared in April 1851, two months after Shadrach, an escaped ex-slave from Virginia, was liberated from his imprisonment by Boston blacks. (Prints and Photographs Division, Library of Congress)

Some of the participants in the Oberlin-Wellington Rescue of 1858, when several hundred whites and thirty to forty blacks in the abolitionist stronghold of Ohio's Western Reserve rescued fugitive slave John Price from incarceration. Charles Langston, twelfth from left, arrested for his participation in the rescue, told the court that he was proud of his defiance of immoral laws. (Prints and Photographs Division, Library of Congress)

The owners of fugitive slaves usually described their runaways with great care. Distinguishing marks were carefully noted. In the *Richmond Enquirer*, Robert Lewis, of Albemarle County, Va., described his runaway in the following manner:

EIGHTY DOLLARS REWARD—Ran away from the Subscriber on the 4th of April, in the city of Richmond, a mulatto fellow, about 30 years of age, 5 feet 6 or 8 inches high; is remarkable on account of having red curly hair & grey eyes which generally appear to be sore; one of his legs somewhat shorter than the other, though scarcely to be perceived without nice observation; when standing, is very apt to stand fast on his right leg, and rather extend the left. In pronouncing the word whiskey, which he is very fond of, and apt to call for at a public house, he pronounces it whisty. He is a very humble, obedient fellow, and when spoken to, has a down-look. It is not improbable that he may obtain free papers, to endeavor to pass as a free man, having absconded from his boat in the basin at Richmond, with about $120 in cash (June 24, 1817).

Scholars have often noted the frequency of stuttering or other speech impediments in the runaway slave population. In the Virginia sample, the frequency was 7 percent, seven times greater than the norm for the population as a whole.

The interpretations of this phenomena are controversial. Kenneth Stampp (1956) suggested that the "down look" and the speech impediments were caused by stress resulting from fear (pp. 381–382). While Eugene Genovese (1974) did not disagree that slaves had been conditioned to fear white men, he argued that the stuttering was also an expression of "smoldering anger and resentment" (p. 647). John W. Blassingame (1979) disagreed. He argued that the incidence of stuttering and other speech impediments may have resulted from the slaves' "unfamiliarity with European languages, missing teeth, and other physical infirmities" (p. 203). Another plausible explanation for the speech impediments is that stuttering was an acceptable form of aggression, a result of which was to make the listener suffer.

An analysis of the 1,433 fugitive advertisements in the Richmond *Enquirer* published between 1804 and 1830 revealed an interesting profile. In this record, 84.9 percent were males; 13.02 percent were females. Only 2 percent were children. James Benson Sellers, in *Slavery in Alabama* (1964), reported that of 562 fugitives advertised between 1820 and 1860, 84.1 percent were males; and 15.4 percent were females (p. 293). Eugene D. Genovese noted in *Roll, Jordan, Roll* that, between 1850 and 1860, the percentage of North Carolina runaways was 82 percent male (p. 798, note 2). The percentage of female runaways from New Orleans in 1850 was higher. Judith Kelleher Schafer reported in *The Journal of Southern History* that 31.7 percent were women (1981, pp. 33–56). All the sources seem to agree that the great majority of fugitives was made up of relatively young men. The average age in the Virginia sample was 27.

A possible explanation for the preponderance of males is suggested by the dangers inherent in running away. Successful flight demanded planning, ingenuity, bravery, and opportunity. In most southern states, the law provided that any black person could be stopped and checked for documentation of free status or possession of a "free pass." Any slave beyond a given distance from home without a "free pass" could be taken into custody and returned. The law also provided that the owner was obligated to pay a prescribed reward, based upon mileage, for the return of his slave. Even if those dangers were avoided, slave patrols had to be eluded and slave catchers frustrated. The rigor of successfully avoiding arrest and the fear of returning to face certain punishment were such that women, especially those with children, were discouraged from running away.

Although they were predominantly male, the runaways represented fieldhands, skilled artisans, the more privileged, and the less privileged. Roughly one-third of the fugitives were skilled or had some training and education. Fieldhands represented 70 percent of the Virginia slaves. Owners advertised for the return of runaways in Virginia every month, but the most popular months were between May and August. The least popular month was November. Owners demonstrated no hurry to advertise their runaways. A time lapse of six weeks to six months occurred between the date of running away and the date of advertisement. In January 1811, for example, Archer Hankins reported that his slave George had run away the previous July. In April 1811, John S. Payne of Campbell County reported that three of his slaves had absconded in January. The most plausible reason for the delay in advertising runaways was the assumption that the slaves would return of their own accord. Several instances on the record indicate that an owner knew where his slave was lurking; but rather than go after the fugitive himself, he offered a reward for someone else to return his slave to him, or "secure him in jail so that I get him again." Whatever the motivation for running away, large numbers returned of their own accord or were apprehended within days, or sometimes in weeks. Of 1,151 runaways advertised in Virginia, 831 were single men and 111 were single women. Married men numbered 154 and married women 55. The advertisements in the Richmond *Enquirer* also made a point of identifying fugitives by color: black, mulatto, tawny, yellow, and "pass for white." Only about 2.5 percent of the Virginia sample could read or write.

The motivations for running away discussed in the literature are complex. Gerald W. Mullin (1972) classified motives by objective. The first group were lit-

tle more than truants who ran off to visit wives, friends, or family on other plantations. The second group included those slaves who absconded to the towns and cities to find employment and pass as free men. A third smaller group was made up of those slaves who preferred freedom to bondage and attempted, by whatever means, to reach the free states (p. 106). Stampp argued that slaves had a heightened sense of dignity that was easily insulted. Running away was a means of expressing a personal grievance (Stampp 1956, p. 112). There is general agreement on an extended list of reasons for running away that include fear of sale, loneliness resulting from sale out of state, the desire to reestablish family ties, to escape overwork, and simply to be free. In the Virginia advertisements, the single most important reason for running away was the desire not to be free, but to "pass as free."

Motivation for slaves who ran away was in many cases a great mystery to their owners. Kenneth Stampp (1956) reported several owners who stated that their slaves had run away for no apparent reason and without provocation (pp. 111–112). But William K. Scarborough has argued that a more common explanation was fear of the whip (Scarborough 1984, pp. 89–90). The cruelty of some masters and overseers in the treatment of slaves is well documented. While only a small minority of slaves in the Virginia sample was described as scarred, the scars were often noteworthy. Robert Dickenson of Nottoway County described the scars of Isaac, an "habitual" runaway. He had a scar "over his right eye and . . . a lump as large as the finger on the fore part of the right shoulder." The scars, he said, were "caused by whipping" (*Richmond Enquirer*, December 23, 1809). Many of the slaves had been scarred by smallpox. A few of the scars were inflicted with branding irons. A recently purchased slave of John Sanders had been "lately branded on the left hand" (*Richmond Enquirer*, March 12, 1814). Thomas Coleman of Lunenburg County branded his slave, Charles, on the forehead, on each cheek, and his chest with the letter C (*Richmond Enquirer*, July 1, 1823).

The treatment of runaway slaves was often callous; but occasionally the advertisements expressed concern for the welfare of the fugitive, especially the younger ones. Edmund Lewis had taken a thirteen-year-old boy into custody in Buckingham County. The boy told his captor that he had been stolen from his father, George Belew, when "very young" and thought he had been sold "about ten times." The object of the notice, said Lewis, was to notify "his parents or friends to attend to his case," which was pending before the court of Buckingham County (*Richmond Enquirer*, October 27, 1818). Samuel Carter of Halifax County expressed concern for a ten-year-old whom he had "taken up" after being lost from a slave-trading expedition. Carter did not place the boy in jail because he was too ill and too young (*Richmond Enquirer*, April 18, 1817).

A large category of fugitives comprised those who had been hired out. Because of the surplus of slave labor in Virginia, many slaveholders were forced either to sell their surplus slaves or to hire them out. The services of the slaves were usually rented for six months or a year, and many of them ran away during that time. Slaves were hired as boatmen on the river and laborers in the coal pits, brick yards, and rope walks. Some were hired because they had special skills. They worked as ostlers, carriage drivers, and house servants.

Those who hired slaves did not always find it a happy experience. P. V. Daniel of Richmond hired the services of John Brown, who was a "good house servant, ostler and driver, and a pretty good barber." One evening, Brown requested a pass to go into town and had not been heard from since (*Richmond Enquirer*, July 8, 1823). Nelson Patterson of Kanawha County hired John and Reuben from Thomas Logwood of Gloucester County. Patterson "carried them" to Buckingham County to make salt. At the first opportunity, they ran away (*Richmond Enquirer*, December 19, 1816).

The advertisements contain frequent expressions of fear that slaves had been "enticed off" by a white man or some other person. William B. Johnson could explain Isabella's elopement in no other way for "such was her attachment for her mistress and fellow-servants, that she would not have eloped had she not been taken off by some white man." Nathaniel Price believed that Kitty had been "inveigled off by her husband" (*Richmond Enquirer*, June 17, 1808).

A few African Americans engaged in an interesting racket. Lewis informed his owner William Fisher of Chesterfield County that a white man with whom Lewis had worked the previous year tried to decoy him off by promising to sell him and then later meet at some designated place, divide the money, and thus continue on (*Richmond Enquirer*, September 19, 1826). Jerman Baker in Cumberland County had a similar experience when a young fellow who called himself John Irvin came up to Baker's plantation on foot with two African-American men. He claimed that his horse had foundered on the road and that he was on his way to Richmond to deliver one of the slaves. The other slave, he said, belonged to his father, a merchant in Campbell County. Baker bought this slave for $430. He gave Irvin a horse valued at $130, paid $100 in cash, and gave him a note for $200. The slave absconded shortly thereafter, and adding insult to injury, took a horse with him. Baker warned: "I forewarn all persons from trading for the note I executed to said John Irvin" (*Richmond Enquirer*, March 3, 1812).

White people aided and abetted relatively few slaves in their escapes. Some slaves received permission to visit their wives or families in other locations and never returned. Without help from other slaves, runaways could not remain away from their owners

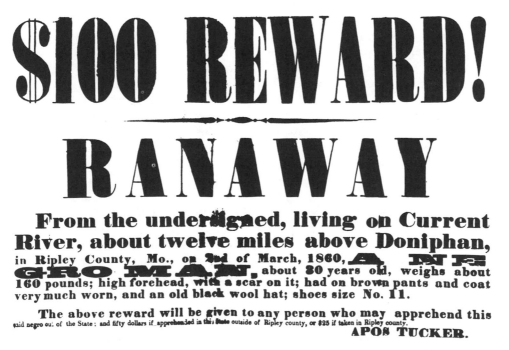

An advertisement for runaway slaves, dated 1860. (Prints and Photographs Division, Library of Congress)

for long periods of time. Literate slaves provided forged passes that made it possible for fugitive slaves to lurk around the smaller towns or simply disappear in the larger cities. Owners could do little to prevent such aid. Free papers could be checked against the court records in the fugitive's home county; but if he was caught and returned to his master, another opportunity to escape usually presented itself.

The objective of the fugitives who remained within the state was usually the larger towns. Spencer Roane of Hanover complained that Betsy, one of his servants, "was so much pleased with Richmond, as to abscond, when his family returned from thence" (*Richmond Enquirer*, July 26, 1811). Joseph Ingraham sent Billy into Richmond with a load of wheat. Billy sold the wheat for $40 and disappeared (*Richmond Enquirer*, October 1, 1824). The chances of being detected in the cities were considerably reduced. In Virginia, Richmond, Manchester, Petersburg, Williamsburg, and Norfolk were the principal towns for which many fugitives aimed. Work could more readily be secured in the towns, and the townspeople were less suspicious of a strange black face. Hiding in the cities was easier and less dangerous than in the countryside.

Methods used to deter running away varied. William Scarborough has argued that overseers were more inclined to use harsh discipline in order to create fear. At least two overseers resorted to shooting their "recalcitrant" runaways (Scarborough 1984, pp. 90–91). A more common deterrent was the use of dogs. The practice of running away was so widespread that some men became professional slave-catchers who used hounds to hunt down fugitives. This practice was more likely to be used in the deep South than in the border states. Other methods were less violent. For example, in South Carolina, one planter restricted the privileges of the slaves who did not run away in order to induce the runaways to return (Scarborough 1984, p. 92).

All slave states enacted laws both to deter and to aid in the recovery of fugitive slaves. The laws in Virginia were fairly typical. The laws to suppress runaway slaves before the Revolution were extremely harsh. In 1680 a law was passed making it lawful to kill any fugitive who resisted arrest. A 1723 law provided for punishment by "dismembering, or any other way not touching life." Laws designed to restrict the movement of slaves were amended very little over the years; only refinements were added. These laws required slaves who were away from the plantation to have written permission. The unfortunate slave without such permission was subject to punishment of ten lashes for every offense. In 1748, slave stealing was defined as a capital offense punishable by "death without benefit of clergy." Laws that made it a crime to transport a slave out of the colony

or state without the consent of the owner were enacted and amended many times. A Virginia law enacted in 1805 prohibited a master of a vessel from taking any African American on board without checking his status. The penalties for violation of this law were severe. If the master of a vessel was convicted, his fine was to be $500 for every African American found on his vessel without a pass. The master was also liable for an additional $200 fine: "one third thereof shall go to the master or owner of such slave, one third to the informer, and one third to the overseers of the poor, for the use of the poor." Upon conviction of removing a slave out of the county, the master could be imprisoned for a period of up to four years.

Laws for the apprehension and return of fugitive slaves depended upon the goodwill and support of the white population. The function of these laws was to ensure, so far as possible, the return of the runaway to his master. A schedule of rewards was established by state legislatures to encourage compliance. Usually a basic fee was required, plus mileage. If a fugitive was caught in Maryland or Kentucky, the reward was to be $25 plus $0.25 per mile for traveling to the residence of the owner, or the jail to which the fugitive was committed. The reward for apprehending runaways in Delaware, New Jersey, New York, Pennsylvania, or Ohio was to be $50. Between 1800 and 1830 in Virginia, rewards offered for the return of fugitive slaves ranged from $3 to $150.

A system of confining and selling unclaimed runaways developed during the years preceding the AMERICAN REVOLUTION. After 1726, it was permissible to hire out such slaves with an iron collar around their necks stamped with the letter "P.G." (for "Public Gaol"). This procedure of confining slaves and hiring them out changed little except that after the Revolution, treatment of runaways became somewhat less stringent. After 1782, slaves were forbidden to hire themselves out in order to pay their masters money in lieu of services. After 1807, the owner became liable to a fine of $10 to $20 for permitting his slaves to hire themselves out.

Every free African American was forced to register with the county clerk and obtain a copy of the register certifying that he or she was free. This law facilitated the recognition of runaways and placed the burden of enforcement on the free population and not on the slaves. The fine for employing or harboring an African American without a pass was $5 for each offense, and the offender was liable to a suit for damages by the aggrieved party. The most severe penalties were reserved for those convicted of "enticing off" or stealing slaves. As late as 1799, the penalty was still death "without benefit of clergy." After 1805, however, the punishment for slave steal-

Fugitive slaves crossing the Rappahannock River, in Virginia, August 1862. (Prints and Photographs Division, Library of Congress)

ing was reduced to a fine of between $100 and $500 and imprisonment for not less than two years and not more than four. The convicted felon was also required to pay the owner an amount double the value of the slave, plus double the amount of costs.

The literature on fugitive slaves provides extended discussion of slave crime. Stampp (1956) argued that petty theft was almost universal. Other crimes discussed were arson, deliberate injury and self-mutilation, and acts of violence. The most frequent targets for arson were the slave quarters, cotton gins, and other farm buildings. Some slaves were willing to suffer personal injury and great pain rather than return to slavery. Attempts to arrest and return fugitive slaves frequently resulted in violence. A few slaves even resorted to murder (pp. 124–132). Genovese (1974) argued that some caution must be excercised concerning charges of arson. He asserted that in many cases, planters simply assumed that the arsonists were slaves. He further contended that arson committed by slaves was more likely to occur in the cities than on the plantations (pp. 613–615). Slaves were capable of the most violent crimes if provoked. A servant shot and killed Virginia Frost of Richmond, Va., when reproached for "insolent language" (Genovese 1974, pp. 361–362). In the period between 1710 and 1754, Mullin found evidence that only 2 slaves had been tried for murder before county courts (Mullin 1972, p. 61). Only 26 fugitives were charged with crimes in the Virginia advertisements between 1800 and 1830: 17 for theft, 1 for arson, 6 for robbery, 1 for assault, and 1 for murder. In Richmond, a double murder was committed when a runaway name Jack broke into the home of Daniel Ford. Both

Ford and his wife were shot and killed (*Richmond Enquirer*, October 17, 1820). However outrageous these crimes were perceived to be, the percentage of runaways charged with crime in Virginia was low. The number of crimes runaways committed after absconding is not known.

The fugitives who were believed by their owners in Virginia to be headed out of state were much more diligently pursued. The record indicates that, in many cases, the owners had a fairly clear idea of their runaway slaves' destinations. Mullin found a high correlation between the estimates of fugitives' destinations and the counties where they were intercepted and incarcerated (Mullin 1972, pp. 188–189). If the owners' estimates can be believed, only a small percentage of the runaways advertised in Virginia between 1800 and 1830 were headed north. In a sample of 1,253 fugitives, only 113, or 9 percent, were thought to be headed for the Mason-Dixon Line. During that period, 294, or 23.4 percent, were captured. Twelve northward-bound fugitives were advertised in 1823. Typical was an advertisement in January. John Taylor of Brunswick County, Va., advertised in the *Richmond Enquirer* for his runaway named Granderson. Granderson, "a first rate house and body servant," had been hired the previous year to Gen. Robert R. Johnson of Warrentown, N.C., from whom he had run away. Taylor believed that the slave was headed for Petersburg, "where it is feared he will attempt to procure a conveyance to the north" (January 14, 1823). Thirteen were thought to be headed north in 1826. Abner Mitchell of Richmond had hired a slave named Robin, alias Robert Chamberlayne, from his owner in New Kent

County. Mitchell asserted that the fugitive "will endeavour to get to New-York, or some other Northern cities" (January 3, 1826). In 1826, 56 fugitives were advertised, and 20, or 35.7 percent, were captured and placed in jail. It must be understood that the 20 fugitives who were captured in 1826 had not necessarily run away that year.

Between the founding of the Republic and the Civil War, there is good reason to believe that many thousands of slaves slipped their shackles and successfully made their way to the free states; many went on to Canada. Despite the most stringent efforts of both the state and national governments to deter the efforts of slaves to become free, the flow of fugitives to the North continued (*see also* UNDERGROUND RAILROAD). The numbers of fugitives going north was only a small portion of the runaways. However, the impact of fugitive slaves on the African-American and white communities in the North and their role in shaping the antebellum anti-slavery discourse were out of proportion to their numbers.

REFERENCES

BLASSINGAME, JOHN W. *The Slave Community: Plantation Life in the Antebellum South.* Revised and enlarged edition. New York, 1979.

CAMPBELL, STANLEY W. *The Slave Catchers: Enforcement of the Fugitive Slave Law, 1850–1860.* Chapel Hill, N.C., 1970.

FINKELMAN, PAUL. *An Imperfect Union: Slavery, Federalism, and Comity.* Chapel Hill, N.C., 1981.

GENOVESE, EUGENE D. *Roll, Jordan, Roll: The World the Slaves Made.* New York, 1974.

MULLIN, GERALD W. *Flight and Rebellion: Slave Resistance in Eighteenth-Century Virginia.* New York, 1972.

Richmond Enquirer. September 1804–December 1830.

SCARBOROUGH, WILLIAM KAUFFMAN. *The Overseer: Plantation Management in the Old South.* Athens, Ga., 1984.

SCHAFER, JUDITH KELLEHER. "New Orleans Slavery in 1850 as Seen in Advertisements." *Journal of Southern History* 47 (1981): 33–56.

SELLERS, JAMES BENSON. *Slavery in Alabama.* New York, 1964.

STAMPP, KENNETH M. *The Peculiar Institution: Slavery in the Antebellum South.* New York, 1956.

SYDNOR, CHARLES. *Slavery in Mississippi.* New York, 1933.

STANLEY W. CAMPBELL

Fuller, Charles Henry, Jr. (March 5, 1939–), playwright and short-story writer. Born in Philadelphia to Charles H. Fuller, Sr., a printer, and Lillian Anderson Fuller, Charles Fuller attended Villanova College from 1956 to 1958, and he served for four years as an Army petroleum laboratory technician in Japan and Korea. He returned to Philadelphia, attended La Salle College from 1965 to 1968, and completed his degree.

Although he had been writing since he was a teenager, Fuller began writing in earnest in the 1960s, usually at night, while attending school or holding a number of jobs, from bank loan collector to counselor at Temple University to housing inspector from the city of Philadelphia. His early writing was mostly poetry, essays, and stories. Realizing that his stories were composed mostly of dialogue, Fuller turned to playwriting. His first short plays were written for the Afro-American Arts Theatre of Philadelphia, which he cofounded and codirected from 1967 through 1971. In 1970 he moved to New York City and devoted himself to writing full-time.

His first full-length play, *The Village: A Party,* was produced at the McCarter Theater in Princeton, N.J., in 1968. The play illustrates the conflicts inherent in a racially integrated community. When the black head of the community falls in love with a black woman, the other racially mixed couples in the community feel threatened and destroy him.

Other Fuller plays include *In the Deepest Part of Sleep,* which was produced at St. Marks Playhouse in New York in 1974, and *The Brownsville Raid,* also produced in New York, at the Negro Ensemble Company, in 1976. It was based on a 1906 incident

Playwright Charles Fuller, 1981. (Reprinted from *In the Shadow of the Great White Way: Images from the Black Theatre,* Thunder's Mouth Press, © 1957–1989 by Bert Andrews. Reprinted by permission of the Estate of Bert Andrews)

involving a black United States Army regiment that was dishonorably discharged for allegedly inciting a riot in Brownsville, Tex.

In 1981, Fuller won an Obie Award as well as an Audelco Award for *Zooman and the Sign,* a play about inner-city violence in Philadelphia. The play dramatizes the accidental death of a young girl and its effects. In 1982, Fuller became the second black playwright to win a Pulitzer Prize for drama for *A Soldier's Play,* for which he also received a New York Drama Critics Award, an Audelco Award, a Theatre Club Award, and an Outer Circle Award for best off-Broadway play. In *A Soldier's Play,* which centers on the investigation of the murder of a black sergeant at an army base in Louisiana during World War II, Fuller explores racial prejudice by a white southern community as well as self-hatred by black soldiers. The play was adapted for the screen and released as *A Soldier's Story* by Columbia Pictures in 1984.

In 1987, CBS televised Fuller's adaptation of Ernest J. Gaines's novel *A Gathering of Old Men;* in 1988, two related one-act plays, *Sally* and *Prince,* were produced first in Atlanta by the First National Black Arts Festival and then in New York by the Negro Ensemble Company. The first parts of a projected five- or six-part cycle chronicling the experience of African Americans from the Civil War through the end of the nineteenth century, the plays relate the life of Prince Logan, an educated former slave. In *Sally,* he participates in the rebellion of the country's first all-black Army regiment during the Civil War when they learn they are to be paid three dollars less per month than white Union soldiers. In *Prince,* former slaves working a plantation discover there is little difference between their condition as free men and women under northern sponsorship and as slaves before the war: they remain victims of economic, political, and social exploitation, and realize the promise of freedom had been an illusion.

Fuller has been a Rockefeller Foundation Fellow (1975), a National Endowment for the Arts Fellow (1976), and a Guggenheim Fellow (1977–1978). In addition to playwrighting, Fuller wrote and directed a radio talk show about the black experience in Philadelphia (1970–1971). He has also contributed both fiction and nonfiction to such magazines as *Black Dialogue, Liberator,* and *Negro Digest.*

REFERENCES

DAVIS, THADIOUS M., and TRUDIER HARRIS, eds. *Dictionary of Literary Biography: Afro-American Fiction Writers After 1955,* Vol. 38. Detroit, 1984.
METZGER, LINDA, ed. *Black Writers.* Detroit, 1989.

SABRINA FUCHS
MICHAEL PALLER

Fuller, Meta Vaux Warrick (June 9, 1877–March 18, 1968), sculptor. Named for one of her mother's clients (Meta, daughter of Pennsylvania senator Richard Vaux), Meta Vaux Warrick Fuller was born in Philadelphia, the youngest of three children of William and Emma (Jones) Warrick, prosperous hairstylists. She enjoyed a privileged childhood, with dancing and horseback-riding lessons. While attending Philadelphia public schools, Fuller took weekly courses at J. Liberty Tadd, an industrial arts school. At eighteen, she won a three-year scholarship to the Pennsylvania Museum and School for Industrial Art. In 1898 she graduated with honors, a prize in metalwork for her *Crucifix of Christ in Anguish,* and a one-year graduate scholarship. The following year, she was awarded the Crozer (first) Prize in sculpture for *Procession of the Arts and Crafts,* a terracotta bas-relief of thirty-seven medieval costumed figures.

From 1899 to 1903, Fuller studied in Paris, at first privately with Raphael Collin, and then at the Colarossi Academy. Among her supporters in France were expatriate painter Henry O. TANNER and philosopher W. E. B. DU BOIS, who encouraged her to depict her racial heritage. Fuller produced clay, painted-plaster, and bronze figurative works based on Egyptian history, Greek myths, French literature, and the Bible.

In 1901, sculptor Auguste Rodin praised Fuller's clay piece *Secret Sorrow* (or *Man Eating His Heart*). With his sponsorship, Fuller began to receive wider notice. Art dealer Samuel Bing exhibited twenty-two of her sculptures at his L'Art Nouveau Gallery in June 1902. *The Wretched,* a bronze group of seven figures suffering physical and mental disabilities (as well as other macabre pieces, such as *Carrying the Dead Body* and *Oedipus,* in the latter of which the figure is blinding himself), earned Fuller the title "delicate sculptor of horrors" from the French press. She later enlarged a plaster model of *The Impenitent Thief,* which she had shown at Bing's gallery. Although she never finished the piece, Rodin saw that it was exhibited at the prestigious Société National des Beaux Arts Salon in April 1903.

Upon Fuller's return to Philadelphia, she established a studio on South Camac Street in a flourishing artistic neighborhood. Her sculptures were exhibited at the Pennsylvania Academy of Fine Arts in 1906, 1908, 1920, and 1928. In 1907 the Jamestown Tercentennial Exposition commissioned Fuller to create fifteen tableaux of 24-inch-high plaster figures depicting African-American progress since the Jamestown settlement in 1607. She received a gold medal for *The Warrick Tableaux,* a 10-foot-by-10-foot diorama.

The artist's career slowed considerably after her marriage in 1909 to the Liberian neurologist Solo-

"The Talking Skull," by Meta Vaux Warrick Fuller. (National Archives)

mon C. FULLER and a fire in 1910 that destroyed the bulk of her work in storage. By 1911, Fuller was the devoted mother of two sons (the last was born in 1916), an active member of Saint Andrew's Episcopal Church, and host to prominent guests who frequently visited the family in the quiet town of Framingham, Mass.

Fuller began to sculpt again in 1913, when Du Bois commissioned a piece for New York state's celebration of the fiftieth anniversary of the Emancipation Proclamation. *The Spirit of Emancipation* represented Humanity weeping for her freed children (a man and woman) as Fate tried to hold them back. Positive public response promoted Fuller to continue working. In 1914, the Boston Public Library exhibited twenty-two of her recent works. Among the numerous requests and awards that followed from African-American and women's groups were a plaster medallion commissioned by the Framingham Equal Suffrage League (1915); a plaster group, *Peace Halting the Ruthlessness of War* (for which she received second prize from the Massachusetts branch of the Women's Peace Party in 1917); and a portrait relief of the NAACP's first president, Moorfield Storey, commissioned by Du Bois in 1922. The same year, the New York Making of America Exposition displayed Fuller's *Ethiopia Awakening,* a one-foot-high bronze sculpture of a woman shedding mummy cloths. This Pan-Africanist work symbolized the strength of

womanhood, the emergence of nationhood, and the birth of what Alain LOCKE would call three years later the "NEW NEGRO." One of Fuller's most poignant works, *Mary Turner: A Silent Protest Against Mob Violence* (1919), commemorates both the silent parade of ten thousand black New Yorkers against lynching in 1917 and the lynching of a Georgian woman and her unborn child in 1918. Fuller never finished the piece because she believed Northerners would find it too inflammatory and Southerners would not accept it. She created numerous other works that depicted symbolic and actual African and African-American culture, including her celebrated *Talking Skull* (1937), based on an African fable. She also produced portrait busts of friends, family members, and African-American abolitionists and other black leaders, such as educator Charlotte Hawkins BROWN, composer Samuel Coleridge Taylor, and Menelik II of Abyssinia. The HARMON FOUNDATION exhibited Fuller's work in 1931 and 1933. She later served as a Harmon juror.

Fuller participated in numerous local organizations; she was a member of the Boston Art Club, an honorary member of the Business and Professional Women's Club, chair of the Framingham Women's Club art committee, and the only African-American president of Zonta, a women's service club. Additionally, she designed costumes for theatrical groups and produced "living pictures": re-creations of artistic masterpieces with actors, costumes, sets, and lighting.

In the 1940s, Fuller's husband went blind and became increasingly ill. She nursed him until his death in 1953, then contracted tuberculosis herself and stayed at the Middlesex County Sanatorium for two years. She wrote poetry there, too frail to create more than a few small sculptures.

By 1957, Fuller was strong enough to continue her work. She produced models of ten notable African-American women for the Afro-American Women's Council in Washington, D.C. She also created a number of sculptures for her community, including several religious pieces for Saint Andrew's Church, a plaque for the Framingham Union Hospital, and the bronze *Storytime* for the Framingham Public Library. For her achievements, Livingstone College (her husband's alma mater) awarded her an honorary doctorate of letters in 1962, and Framingham posthumously dedicated a public park in the honor of Meta and Solomon Fuller in 1973. Since then, Fuller's sculptures have been included in numerous exhibitions.

REFERENCES

GORDON, JOY L., and HARRIET FORTE KENNEDY. *An Independent Woman: The Life and Art of Meta Warrick Fuller.* Framingham, Mass., 1985.

KERR, JUDITH NINA. God-Given Work: The Life and Times of Sculptor Meta Vaux Warrick Fuller, 1877–1968. Ph.D. diss., University of Massachusetts, 1986.

THERESA LEININGER-MILLER

Fuller, Solomon Carter (August 11, 1872–January 16, 1953), psychiatrist, researcher. Solomon Carter Fuller was born in Monrovia, Liberia. His parents were coffee planters and government officials. In 1889 he traveled to the United States and that fall entered Livingstone College in Salisbury, N.C., where he received a bachelor's degree in 1893. Fuller began his medical studies at Long Island College Hospital, in Brooklyn, N.Y., and completed them at Boston University in 1897. He began an internship at Westborough State Hospital in Westborough, Mass., in 1897, and in 1899 was promoted to resident pathologist. That year he also joined the faculty of Boston University's School of Medicine, where he served as professor of, at various times, pathology, neurology, and neuropathology until 1933; he was one of the first African-American physicians to serve on the faculty of a predominantly white American medical school.

Fuller, considered the first African-American psychiatrist, studied and researched degenerative mental illnesses early in his career. He completed postgraduate work at New York's Carnegie Laboratory in 1900 and in Germany at the University of Munich's Psychiatric Clinic and Pathology Institute from 1904 to 1905. In Germany Fuller worked with Emil Kraepelin, an influential taxonomist of psychiatric disorders. Fuller wrote on *dementia praecox,* Kraepelin's term for what was later known as schizophrenia, as early as 1909. In Munich he also studied brain disorders with Alois Alzheimer, for whom Alzheimer's Disease is named. Fuller was one of the first Americans to study and write on this daunting phenomenon. While it was widely believed that arteriosclerosis was the main cause of Alzheimer's Disease, Fuller suggested in his article "Alzheimer's Disease (*Senilium Praecox*): The Report of a Case and Review of Published Cases" (1912) that this assumption was false; it was not until 1953 that researchers demonstrated conclusively that he was correct.

Fuller married renowned sculptor Meta Warrick in 1909 (see Meta Vaux Warrick FULLER). In 1913 he edited the *Westborough State Hospital Papers,* a journal that specialized in mental disorders. In 1923 Fuller participated in a program sponsored by the National Medical Association, the country's main African-American association of the medical profession, to recruit and train young black doctors to staff Tuskegee Veterans Hospital. He also remained on the staff at Westborough State Hospital until 1944. Besides stints as visiting neurologist at Boston's Massachusetts General Hospital and the Massachusetts Memorial Hospital, Fuller ran a private practice from his home in Framingham until his death in 1953. The Solomon Carter Fuller Mental Health Center in Boston is named in his honor. Additionally, the American Psychiatric Association honors prominent African Americans with its Solomon Carter Fuller Award.

REFERENCES

MORAIS, HERBERT MONTFORT. *The History of the Negro in Medicine.* New York, 1967.

SAMMONS, VIVIAN OVELTON. *Blacks in Science and Medicine.* New York, 1990.

ALLISON X. MILLER

KEVIN PARKER

G

Gabriel Prosser Conspiracy. During 1800 Gabriel Prosser worked in secret to recruit and organize thousands of enslaved Virginians. He sketched out an elaborate plan to overthrow the slavery regime, and it came within hours of execution. But on the chosen day—Saturday, August 30—a hurricane destroyed bridges and flooded roads. The violent downpour washed out the proposed attack on the state capitol at Richmond, allowed time for word of the plan to leak to white authorities, and foiled what could have become a brilliant move in the dangerous chess game to force an end to SLAVERY.

Gabriel was born into bondage about 1775 around the time that white Virginians declared their political independence. The authorities who executed him said he showed "courage and intellect above his rank in life." As the property of tavernkeeper Thomas Prosser, he worked regularly as a blacksmith in the Richmond area, where, inspired by stories of the recent HAITIAN REVOLUTION, he framed his desperate plan. Aided by his wife and his brothers Martin and Solomon, he worked to procure weapons and rally recruits (Martin, a preacher, found recruits at funerals and secret religious gatherings, where he employed biblical accounts of the Israelites' escape from Egypt to inspire potential conspirators). According to testimony in subsequent trials, from two to ten thousand African Americans knew of the design and looked to Gabriel as their leader to, in Solomon's words, "conquer the white people and possess ourselves of their property." The insurrectionists intended to spare METHODISTS, QUAKERS, and local Frenchmen because of their emancipationist leanings, and they expected poor whites and nearby Catawba Indians to join their cause when it gathered strength.

The plan called for several hundred participants (advised by a veteran from the successful siege at Yorktown) to gather at a spot outside Richmond. Behind a banner invoking the American, French, and Haitian Revolutions with the words Death or Liberty, they would march on the city in three contingents. One group would light fires in the dockside warehouses to divert whites from the heart of the city, while the other two groups would seize the capitol armory and take Gov. James Monroe hostage. When the "white people agreed to their freedom," Gabriel "would dine and drink with the merchants of the city," and a white flag would be hoisted above the capitol, calling other blacks in the countryside to join them.

Betrayal by informers presented a huge danger, with so many persons approached about such an overwhelming plan. When torrential rains forced last-minute postponement of the march on Richmond, several slaves had already alerted whites to the impending action, and Gov. Monroe moved swiftly. The state militia arrested scores of suspects, and several dozen persons were executed. Prosser took refuge on the schooner *Mary,* captained by a sympathetic white Methodist. But in late September he was betrayed by two slave crewmen and captured in Norfolk. After a brief show trial in which the leader remained silent, he was hanged on October 7.

In the aftermath of the foiled insurrection, the Virginia Assembly acted to restrict the movement of all blacks—enslaved and free—and to set up a white public guard in Richmond. Such precautions proved ineffective, however. In 1802 authorities discovered further black plans to fight for freedom in Virginia and North Carolina. In 1936 the publication of Arna Bontemps's novel *Black Thunder* offered an interesting literary treatment of Prosser's revolt.

REFERENCES

EGERTON, D. R. "Gabriel's Conspiracy and the Election of 1800." *Journal of Southern History* 56 (1990): 191–214.
MARSZALEK, JOHN F. "Battle for Freedom: Gabriel's Insurrection." *Negro History Bulletin* 39 (1976): 540–543.
MULLIN, GERALD W. *Flight and Rebellion: Slave Resistance in Eighteenth-Century Virginia*. New York, 1972.

PETER H. WOOD

Gaines, Clarence Edward "Bighouse" (May 21, 1923–), basketball coach. Clarence Gaines was born and raised in Paducah, Ky. In 1941 he entered Morgan State College in Baltimore, where he excelled as an offensive tackle on the football team, graduating in 1945. In 1946 Gaines took a position as athletic director and basketball coach at Winston-Salem Teachers College in North Carolina, a historically black institution renamed Winston-Salem State University in 1969. Gaines was expected to develop Winston-Salem's basketball program, although at the time of his hiring the school's student population was 575, of which only seventy-five were men. He quickly established a winning program, posting an 80–55 record over his first five seasons. Gaines built the program by establishing a network of former players in the Midwest and along the East Coast who served as recruiters. To augment his coaching and teaching skills, Gaines in 1950 earned a master of arts degree from Columbia University.

In 1961 the Winston-Salem Rams, with Gaines as coach and led by star guard Cleo Hill, won the Central Intercollegiate Athletic Association championship with a 26–5 record. In 1963 Gaines recruited Earl Monroe, who during his senior year led the Rams to the 1967 National Collegiate Athletic Association (NCAA) Division II championship, making Gaines the first black coach to win an NCAA division championship. (Monroe went on to the National Basketball Association's Baltimore Bullets, New York Knicks, and the Basketball Hall of Fame.)

In 1982 Gaines was inducted into the Naismith Memorial Basketball Hall of Fame in Springfield, Mass. In 1990 new NCAA rules forced Gaines to vacate the athletic director's position. Gaines retired from coaching after the 1992–1993 season with a lifetime record of 828 victories and 430 losses. His victory total is second only to Kentucky's Adolph Rupp for career victories.

REFERENCES

PORTER, DAVID L., ed. *Biographical Dictionary of American Sports*. Westport, Conn., 1987.
WILEY, RALPH. "Bighouse." *Sports Illustrated* (November 19, 1990): 116–120.

THADDEUS RUSSELL

Gaines, Ernest J. (1933–), writer. The oldest son of a large family, Ernest Gaines was born on January 15, 1933, on the River Lake Plantation in Point Coupée Parish, La. His parents separated when he was young, and his father's absence led to a permanent estrangement. More important than his parents in his childhood was a maternal great-aunt who provided love and served as an example of strength and survival under extreme adversity. The older people in the close-knit community of the plantation "quarters" exemplified similar qualities, passing on to the child the rich oral tradition that figures prominently in his fiction.

At the age of fifteen Gaines moved from this familiar environment to Vallejo, Calif., where he could receive a better education. Lonely in these new surroundings, he spent much of his time in the town's public library and began to write. After high school he spent time in a junior college and the military before matriculating at San Francisco State College. An English major, he continued to write stories and graduated in 1957. Encouraged by his agent, Dorothea Oppenheimer, and (while in the creative writing program at Stanford) by Malcolm Cowley, Gaines committed himself to a literary career. In 1964 he published his first novel, *Catherine Carmier*. His subsequent books are *Of Love and Dust* (1967), *Bloodline* (1968), *The Autobiography of Miss Jane Pittman* (1971), *In My Father's House* (1978), and *A Gathering of Old Men* (1983). In a collection of interviews published as *Porch Talk with Ernest Gaines* (1990), he discussed his work in progress, a novel about an uneducated black man on death row and a black teacher in a Louisiana plantation school titled *A Lesson Before Dying*.

In the 1960s and '70s, except for a year at Denison University, Gaines lived and wrote in San Francisco. Since the early 1980s he has been associated with the University of Southwestern Louisiana, although he has continued to summer in San Francisco.

Novelist Ernest Gaines in 1993, shortly after the publication of *A Lesson Before Dying*. (AP/Wide World Photos)

South Louisiana, the region of Gaines's youth and literary imagination, is beautiful and distinctive with unique cultural, linguistic, and social patterns. Like George Washington Cable and Kate Chopin before him, Gaines has been fascinated by the interplay of caste and class among the ethnic groups of the area: blacks, mixed-race Creoles, Cajuns, white Creoles, and Anglo whites. Once fairly stable as subsistence farmers, blacks and mixed-race Creoles have been dispossessed of the best land or displaced altogether by Cajuns, who are favored by the plantation lords because they are white and use mechanized agricultural methods. Under such socioeconomic conditions, young blacks leave, as Gaines himself did, though they often find themselves drawn back to Louisiana.

Such is the case in *Catherine Carmier*. In this novel the protagonist is the educated and alienated Jackson Bradley, who returns to his native parish to claim the love of the title character, daughter of a mixed-race Creole whose racial exclusivism, attachment to the land, and semi-incestuous feelings toward her cannot condone such an alliance. Nor do Jackson's fellow blacks approve. Jackson cannot recapture his love or his homeland because, for all its pastoral charm, the

world of his childhood is anachronistic. In *Of Love and Dust* Gaines moves from Arcadian nostalgia to a tragic mode. Marcus Payne, the rebellious protagonist, defies social and racial taboos by making love to the wife of a Cajun plantation overseer, Sidney Bonbon, after being rejected by Bonbon's black mistress. As Marcus and Louise Bonbon prepare to run away together, the Cajun, a grim embodiment of fate, kills him with a scythe.

If *Catherine Carmier* is a failed pastoral and *Of Love and Dust* a tragedy, *The Autobiography of Miss Jane Pittman* is a near-epic account of a centenarian whose life has spanned slavery, RECONSTRUCTION, JIM CROW, and the CIVIL RIGHTS MOVEMENT. Her individual story reflects the experience of oppression, resistance, survival, and dignity of an entire people. Although the protagonist of *In My Father's House* is a minister and civil rights leader in Louisiana and his unacknowledged son is an urban militant, this work's central theme is more private than public—the search for a father who has abdicated parental responsibility. In this grim tale, the son commits suicide and the father survives but without dignity. The mood of *A Gathering of Old Men,* on the other hand, is more comic than grim, but the old men who gather with shotguns to protect one of their own from unjust arrest achieve in this act of resistance the dignity that has been missing from their lives. White characters, too, achieve moral growth as social and racial change finally catches up with the bayou country. It is Gaines's most hopeful novel and in some ways his best.

In 1972 Gaines received the BLACK ACADEMY OF ARTS AND LETTERS Award. He was given the annual literary award of the American Academy and Institute of Arts and Letters in 1987.

REFERENCE

BABB, VALERIE MELISSA. *Ernest Gaines*. Boston, 1991.

KENNETH KINNAMON

Gaither, Alonzo Smith "Jake" (April 11, 1903–February 18, 1994), football coach. Alonzo "Jake" Gaither was born in Dayton, Tenn., and graduated from Knoxville College in 1927. He then worked for ten years as a high school coach and teacher in Knoxville. After receiving a master's degree from Ohio State University in 1937, he was hired as an assistant football coach at Florida A & M College in Tallahassee, a historically black institution renamed Florida A & M University in 1953.

Gaither took over as head coach and athletic director in 1945 and quickly established a successful and innovative football program. From 1945 to his retirement from coaching in 1969, Gaither's teams compiled a 203–36–4 record, an .844 winning percentage that is the highest for college coaches with 200 or more victories. During Gaither's tenure, Florida A & M won seventeen Southern Intercollegiate Athletic Conference championships, a record number of conference titles for black coaches. Gaither sent more than thirty players to the NFL, including Bob HAYES, who became an All-Pro wide receiver with the Dallas Cowboys.

Gaither was widely considered an unorthodox but brilliant football strategist. His annual summer football clinics were attended by major college coaches from across the country and his innovative "split-line T" offensive formation was copied by coaches at every level of college football. After retiring as head coach in 1969, Gaither continued as athletic director until 1973. Gaither died in Tallahassee.

REFERENCES

ASHE, ARTHUR R., JR. *A Hard Road to Glory: A History of the African-American Athlete Since 1946.* New York, 1988.

THOMAS, ROBERT M., JR. Obituary. *New York Times,* February 19, 1994.

THADDEUS RUSSELL

Gantt, Harvey Bernard (January 14, 1943–), architect, politician. Harvey Gantt was born in 1943 in Charleston, S.C. He helped his father, a self-taught carpenter, to build his family's house. Gantt became further interested in buildings during his young career as a delivery boy; he was often intrigued by the designs of the town houses he frequented in the Charleston area. He combined this fascination with the drawing abilities he cultivated in grade school. While Gantt was in the ninth grade, he observed an architect directing an addition being made to his school. The sight of this architect at work so fascinated Gantt that he decided to become an architect.

As he approached the end of his high school career, Gantt realized that there were no black colleges in South Carolina offering architectural programs. However, South Carolina would pay the travel and tuition costs for a student studying architecture in another state. Gantt therefore enrolled in Iowa State University in 1960, but he subsequently sued for and won transfer to Clemson University in South Carolina. He received his bachelor's degree in architecture at Clemson in 1965 and went on to earn a master's degree in architecture at Massachusetts Institute of Technology in 1970.

In 1971, Gantt cofounded a private architectural firm, Gantt Huberman Architects, in Charlotte, N.C. Throughout the 1970s, Gantt sought not only to establish a viable African-American architectural firm in the South but also to encourage other minorities to enter the profession. He served as lecturer at the University of North Carolina at Chapel Hill from 1970 to 1972 and was a visiting critic at Clemson University. In 1981, Gantt entered local politics when he became mayor pro tempore of Charlotte. He filled this interim position until 1983, when he won election to the mayoralty in his own right, serving as mayor until 1987. In 1990, Gantt ran against the incumbent Jesse Helms for a Senate seat from North Carolina. The election was marked by an intense and bitter debate over racial hiring quotas. Gantt and the media claimed that his narrow defeat was due to race baiting on the part of Helms's organization.

Following this election, Gantt returned to private practice at his firm. His electoral defeat was in part assuaged by the completion of one of his most notable architectural works, the addition to the C. G. O'Kelly Library at Winston-Salem State University. Opened in 1990, the entrance to the addition featured such classical motifs as the grand arched portal with columns, but adapted to a contemporary style. Gantt took a similar approach to the classically inspired grand stairwell of the library's interior.

In 1993, Gantt announced his plans to run again for election to Helms's Senate seat in 1996.

REFERENCES

SULLIVAN, JACK. "Helms Foe Blames Loss on Use of Race as Issue." *Boston Globe,* December 7, 1990, p. 49.

TRAVIS, JACK, ed. *African-American Architects in Current Practice.* New York, 1991.

DURAHN TAYLOR

Gardner, Charles W. (1782–1853), abolitionist and clergyman. Charles W. Gardner was born near Shoemakerstown, N.J. He began his ministerial career at age twenty-seven as an itinerant preacher for several Methodist congregations in the Chesapeake region of Delaware and Maryland. Gardner brought his abolitionist convictions to the pulpit, and local authorities, irritated by his outspoken criticism of slavery and colonization, resorted to threats and harassment to force him from the area.

In 1836, Gardner took charge of the First African Presbyterian Church in Philadelphia and quickly attained a prominent position among the city's black elite. He participated in the African-American national convention movement and in the American Moral Reform Society. In 1837 he became the first black invited to address the AMERICAN ANTI-SLAVERY SOCIETY's annual convention. He also participated in the founding of the Pennsylvania Anti-Slavery Society. In 1838, he assisted the Pennsylvania Abolition Society in compiling a census of Philadelphia blacks. He later referred to this detailed record to demonstrate the progress of free blacks and their economic contributions to society.

Although a member of the American Anti-Slavery Society, Gardner was troubled by the Garrisonians' radical social and religious doctrines. When the society underwent a schism in 1840, he went over to the newly organized AMERICAN AND FOREIGN ANTI-SLAVERY SOCIETY. Shortly thereafter he joined other black Presbyterian and Congregational clergymen in founding the Union Missionary Society. From the late 1840s, Gardner held positions in black churches in Hartford, Conn., Princeton, N.J., and Newport, R.I. He spent his last years as pastor of the Second Presbyterian Church in Harrisburg, Pa.

REFERENCES

RIPLEY, C. PETER, et al., eds. *The Black Abolitionist Papers.* Vol. 3, *The United States, 1830–1846.* Chapel Hill, N.C., 1991.

WINCH, JULIE. *Philadelphia's Black Elite.* Philadelphia, 1984.

MICHAEL F. HEMBREE

Garnet, Henry Highland (1815–1882), clergyman and abolitionist. Henry Highland Garnet was one of the most formidable African-American leaders of the mid-nineteenth century. He was born on a slave plantation in New Market, Md., where his grandfather, likely a former Mandingo chief, was a leader of the slave community. At the age of nine, he escaped from slavery with his family to New York City, where he was reared in an African-American community committed to evangelical Protestantism, "mental and moral improvement," and the antislavery cause. Young Garnet, whose father was a shoemaker and a leader of the AFRICAN METHODIST EPISCOPAL CHURCH, received an excellent education for a black youth in Jacksonian America in schools established by abolitionists, black and white. Beginning in 1825, he attended the famous African Free School on Mulberry Street. After several years as a seaman, followed by an apprenticeship to a Quaker farmer on Long Island (whose son became his tutor), Garnet in 1832 entered the Canal Street High School, which was directed by Theodore S. WRIGHT and Peter

WILLIAMS, JR., two of the leading black clergymen and abolitionists of the era. Wright, who had been educated at Princeton, became his mentor, and in 1833 Garnet joined Wright's First Colored Presbyterian Church, a church that Garnet himself was later to pastor.

In 1835, Garnet, along with Alexander CRUMMELL and another black youth, matriculated at the newly opened Noyes Academy in Canaan, N.H. Not long after their arrival, following a harrowing journey on segregated transportation, a mob of neighboring farmers, angered by the boys' presence and their participation in local abolition meetings, dragged the makeshift school building into a nearby swamp and forced them to leave. The next year, Garnet enrolled in Oneida Institute at Whitesboro, N.Y., from which he graduated in 1839.

In 1843, Garnet became an ordained minister in the Presbyterian church, although he had already pastored the Liberty Street Presbyterian Church in Troy, N.Y., since 1840, turning the church into a center of abolitionism and black self-help in the Troy area. He

Henry Highland Garnet's 1843 "Call to Rebellion" was among the most radical and controversial statements by any black abolitionist. The Presbyterian minister was later active in encouraging American blacks to settle in Africa. (Prints and Photographs Division, Library of Congress)

made his church an important station on the underground railroad; he set up a grammar school at the church, for education was the key to black progress; he preached temperance because drink undermined black advancement; and he edited two short-lived antislavery newspapers, the *Clarion* (1842) and the *National Watchman* (1847), in order that African Americans should have their own voice. He also urged African Americans to leave the cities and pursue the greater independence of farm ownership.

During his Troy years, Garnet became heavily involved in radical antislavery politics. Shortly after joining in 1841, he became a leader in the newly formed Liberty party, which pledged to end slavery through participation in the political process, an approach that contrasted with the moral suasionist, antigovernment approach of William Lloyd Garrison and his followers. At the same time, Garnet played a leading role in the struggle—unsuccessful until 1870—to eliminate property restrictions on the black franchise in New York State. In addition to state conventions, Garnet was active in the national Negro conventions movement, designed to establish policies on problems of slavery and race. It was at the Buffalo, N.Y., meeting in 1843 that he delivered his provocative "Address to the Slaves of the United States of America." In it he urged them to meet their moral obligation to the just God who had created all people in his image by using whatever means the situation dictated to throw off the oppressor's yoke. Garrisonians, led by Frederick DOUGLASS, who interpreted Garnet's remarks as a call for slave rebellion, opposed a resolution authorizing the convention to distribute the speech. After heated debates, the resolution was defeated. Garnet reintroduced the speech in the Troy convention in 1847 and shortly afterward published it, together with David WALKER's *Appeal to the Coloured Citizens of the World* (1829), from which he had drawn some of the ideas contained in the "Address." By 1849, Douglass himself, no longer a Garrisonian, was stating publicly that he welcomed news of a rising of the slaves.

In 1850, following two years of successful mission work in Geneva, N.Y., Garnet left for England to lecture in the free-produce movement, whose major object was to strike at slavery through the boycott of goods produced by slave labor. Garnet remained in the British Isles until 1853 and then served as a missionary in Jamaica until illness forced his return to the United States in 1856. He then was named pastor at the Shiloh (formerly First Colored) Presbyterian Church in New York City and remained there until 1864, when he was called to the Fifteenth Street Presbyterian Church in Washington, D.C.

Garnet's restless search for ways to liberate African Americans from the bonds of slavery and color prej-

udice took another turn in 1858, when he became president of the newly formed and black-led AFRICAN CIVILIZATION SOCIETY (ACS). Its grand design was the development of an "African nationality" through the "selective" emigration of African Americans to the Niger valley, there to embark upon the civilizing mission of introducing evangelical Protestantism, expanding trade and commerce, and cultivating cotton and other crops that would compete with slave-grown produce to undermine slavery. His incipient PAN-AFRICANISM was enhanced by his early contacts with Africans in New York City and his years in Jamaica, and it is likely that only illness prevented him from shifting his ministry to Africa in 1856, following the example of his longtime friend Alexander Crummell, who had earlier undertaken a mission to Liberia. Although opposed by anticolonizationists such as Frederick DOUGLASS, Garnet eventually won the support of many African nationalists, including Martin DELANY, who joined the African Civilization Society in 1861. Even as the ACS gradually turned its missionary impulse toward meeting the relief and educational needs of the freed people during and after the Civil War, Garnet never relinquished his vision of African redemption.

Garnet also viewed the Civil War as a grand opportunity for African Americans, who were destined for freedom, to lead in the redemption of the United States. This faith was sorely tested, however, by the NEW YORK CITY DRAFT RIOTS in July 1863, which took a heavy toll on black lives and property, endangering Garnet's life and resulting in the sacking of his church. He was a leader in the organized effort to aid victims of the violence. Undeterred, he continued at great personal risk to recruit black volunteers for the Union armies. Soon after he became minister to Washington, D.C.'s Fifteenth Street Presbyterian Church in 1864, he took up missionary work among the recently freed slaves flocking into the national capital. In February 1865, he was invited to deliver a memorial sermon in the U.S. House of Representatives commemorating passage of the THIRTEENTH AMENDMENT, the first African American so asked. His message was a call for national atonement: "*Emancipate, enfranchise, educate, and give the blessings of the gospel to every American citizen*" (Garnet's italics).

After the Civil War, those who had long been in the forefront of the liberation struggle were gradually replaced by another generation. Garnet left Washington in 1868 to assume the presidency of Avery College in Pittsburgh; he remained there for a year before returning to Shiloh Presbyterian. His beloved wife, Julia, died in 1871, and in 1878 he married Sarah Thompson, a feminist and educator. During the 1870s, he continued to champion civil rights and other reform causes, notably the emancipation of blacks in Cuba. He also grew increasingly disillusioned by the failures of RECONSTRUCTION and was especially upset by the government's refusal to distribute land to the freedpeople. And he came to believe that his lifelong efforts in the cause of liberation had gone largely unappreciated by his own people. In 1881, tired, in ill health, and against the advice of friends, he accepted the appointment as American minister to Liberia. He died in Liberia on February 12, 1882, and as was his wish, he was buried in the soil of Africa.

REFERENCES

LITWACK, LEON F., and AUGUST MEIER, eds. *Black Leaders in the Nineteenth Century.* Chicago, 1988.

MILLER, FLOYD J. *The Search for a Black Nationality: Black Colonization and Emigration, 1787–1863.* Urbana, Ill., 1975.

OFARI, EARL. *Let Your Motto Be Resistance: The Life and Thought of Henry Highland Garnet.* Boston, 1972.

PEASE, JANE H., and WILLIAM H. PEASE. *Bound with Them in Chains.* Westport, Conn., 1972.

SCHOR, JOEL. *Henry Highland Garnet: A Voice of Radicalism in the Nineteenth Century.* Westport, Conn., 1977.

STUCKEY, STERLING. *Slave Culture: Nationalist Theory and the Foundations of Black America.* New York, 1987.

SWIFT, DAVID E. *Black Prophets of Justice: Activist Clergy Before the Civil War.* Baton Rouge, La., 1989.

OTEY M. SCRUGGS

Garrison, Zina (November 6, 1963–), tennis player. Zina Garrison was born in Houston, Tex., in 1963. At the age of seventeen she won the junior women's singles titles at Wimbledon and the U.S. Open. In 1982 she turned professional and by the end of the year was ranked the sixteenth best woman TENNIS player in the world. Over the next decade Garrison remained one of the world's top twenty women players, reaching as high as number four in May 1990.

Although Garrison has not won a grand slam tournament, in 1985 she reached the semifinals at Wimbledon and the quarterfinals at both the Australian and U.S. Open. In 1988 Garrison beat Martina Navratilova in the U.S. Open quarterfinals and stopped Chris Evert's attempt at a comeback in the quarters the following year. At the 1988 Seoul Olympics Garrison earned a bronze medal in women's singles and, with her partner, Pam Shriver, a gold in women's doubles. In 1988 she also won the mixed doubles at Wimbledon with Sherwood Stewart (who became her coach in 1990). Garrison's greatest success as a player came at Wimbledon in 1990: she defeated Monica Seles and Steffi Graf in the quarters and semis to face Navratilova in the final. Though she lost, the tennis world took notice, as did equivalent sponsors, and the top-ranked U.S. woman player received a clothing and shoe contract with Reebok. In 1993 Garrison and her husband, Houston businessman Willard Jackson, founded the All Court Tennis Academy for Houston's inner-city children.

REFERENCES

ASHE, ARTHUR R., JR. *A Hard Road to Glory,* New York, 1988, pp. 176, 257.

PORTER, A. P. *Zina Garrison: Ace.* Minneapolis, Minn., 1991.

SHIPHERD REED

Garvey, Amy Ashwood (January 18, 1897–May 3, 1969), Pan-Africanist. Amy Ashwood was born in Port Antonio, Jamaica. Educated in Panama and Jamaica, she first met Marcus GARVEY in 1914 while attending high school in Jamaica. Garvey launched the United Negro Improvement Association (UNIA) a few days after the two met; Ashwood, considered by some a cofounder of the organization, was at least its second member. An excellent public speaker, she worked actively to establish and promote the incipient movement in Jamaica and served as its executive secretary.

Ashwood left for Panama in 1916 and did not meet Garvey again until 1918, when she came to New York. In the United States, she busied herself with UNIA work: traveling across the country making speeches and recruiting new members, working on its journal, *Negro World,* and helping manage the new Black Star Line Steamship Corporation. In 1919, she is reported to have saved Garvey's life by placing her body between him and a disgruntled former employee who wanted to shoot him and then wrestling the would-be assassin to the ground.

Ashwood married Garvey in New York City at Liberty Hall on December 25, 1919. However, by the middle of the following year, the marriage ended acrimoniously. There were accusations of infidelity on both sides. Garvey, in addition, charged Ashwood with misappropriating funds; she countered that the UNIA leader was politically inept. Garvey received a divorce in 1922, which Ashwood later contested, and promptly married his secretary and Ashwood's childhood friend, Amy Jacques.

Following the breakup with Garvey, Ashwood left the UNIA but remained a committed Pan-Africanist all her life (*see also* PAN-AFRICANISM), taking Garvey's message to many parts of the world. In 1924, she helped found the Nigerian Progress Union in London. In New York, in 1926, she collaborated with Caribbean musician Sam Manning on the musicals *Brown Sugar, Hey! Hey!,* and *Black Magic,* intended to introduce calypso to Harlem audiences. In 1929, she left with Manning for London, where she lived until 1944.

In London, Ashwood's Pan-African activities resulted in friendships with people like C. L. R. James, George Padmore, Kwame Nkrumah, and Jomo Kenyatta; all of them frequented the West Indian restaurant she ran from 1935 to 1938, which became a famous Pan-Africanist meeting place. In 1935, she was active in organizing protests against the Italian invasion of Ethiopia. In 1945, she chaired the sessions of the fifth Pan-African Congress in Manchester along with W. E. B. DU BOIS.

Ashwood returned to New York briefly in 1944 and campaigned hard on behalf of Adam Clayton POWELL, JR., who was seeking his first term in the House of Representatives. Ashwood spent the next few years in West Africa. In 1947, she went to Liberia on the invitation of President William Tubman. The two became close friends, and, with Tubman's help, Ashwood wrote an official history of Liberia, which has never been published. In 1949, she spent some time in Ghana and researched her Ashanti roots.

Ashwood divided the rest of her life between the United States, England, the Caribbean, and West Africa. A lifelong feminist, she paid greater attention to women's issues in the later years of her life. She also continued antiracist agitation in England, forming a chapter of the Association for the Advancement of Colored People in London in 1958.

Ashwood was in England in 1964 when Garvey's body was returned to Jamaica; she participated in the official ceremonies marking the occasion. During these years she also tried, unsuccessfully, to find a publisher for her biography of Garvey and the movement, which is yet to be published. Ashwood died destitute in London.

REFERENCES

MARTIN, TONY. *Amy Ashwood Garvey: Pan-Africanist, Feminist and Wife No. 1.* Dover, Mass., 1988.
YARD, LIONEL M. *Amy Ashwood Garvey.* New York, 1987.

KEVIN PARKER

Garvey, Amy (Euphemia) Jacques (December 31, 1896–July 25, 1973), journalist. Amy Jacques Garvey was the second wife of Marcus Mosiah GARVEY, founder of the UNIVERSAL NEGRO IMPROVEMENT ASSOCIATION (UNIA). She was born in Kingston, Jamaica, to Charlotte and George Samuel Jacques, who were from the Jamaican middle class. Plagued by ill health, Amy Jacques, in need of a cooler climate, migrated in 1917 to the United States. She became affiliated with the UNIA in 1918 and served as Marcus Garvey's private secretary and office manager at the UNIA headquarters in New York. After Marcus Garvey divorced his first wife, Amy Ashwood Garvey, he married Amy Jacques on July 27, 1922, in Baltimore, Md.

During Marcus Garvey's several periods of incarceration for alleged mail fraud (1923–1927), Amy Jacques Garvey assumed an unofficial leadership position, though she was never elected to a UNIA office. She nevertheless functioned as the major spokesperson for the UNIA and was the chief organizer in raising money for Marcus Garvey's defense. In addition, she served as the editor of the Woman's page, "Our Women and What They Think," in the *Negro World,* the UNIA's weekly newspaper, published in New York. Amy Jacques Garvey's editorials demonstrated her political commitment to the doctrine of Pan-Africanism and also her belief that women should be active within their communities.

After Marcus Garvey's deportation from the United States in 1927, Amy Jacques Garvey packed their belongings and soon thereafter joined her husband in Jamaica. After Marcus Garvey died on June 19, 1940, in London, Amy Jacques Garvey continued to live in Jamaica and to serve the UNIA headquartered in Cleveland, Ohio. Her edited books include *The Philosophy and Opinions of Marcus Garvey* in two volumes (1923, 1925). Her biographical memoir *Garvey and Garveyism,* published in 1963, helped to stimulate a rebirth of interest in Garveyism. Amy Jacques Garvey was awarded a prestigious Musgrave Medal in 1971 by the Board of Governors at the Institute of Jamaica for her distinguished contributions on the philosophy of Garveyism.

REFERENCE

HILL, ROBERT, ed. *The Marcus Garvey and Universal Negro Improvement Association Papers.* 7 vols. Los Angeles, 1984.

ULA Y. TAYLOR

Garvey, Marcus Mosiah (August 7, 1887–June 10, 1940), founder and leader of the Universal Negro Improvement Association (UNIA), the largest organized mass movement in black history. Hailed in his own time as a redeemer, a "black Moses," Garvey is now best remembered as champion of the Back-to-

Africa movement that swept the United States in the aftermath of World War I.

Garvey was born on August 17, 1887, in the town of St. Ann's Bay on the north coast of the island of Jamaica. He left school at fourteen, worked as a printer's apprentice, and subsequently joined the protonationalist National Club, which advocated Jamaican self-rule. He participated in the printers' union strike of 1912, and following its collapse, he went to Central America, working in various capacities in Costa Rica, Honduras, and Panama. He spent over a year in England during 1913–14, where he teamed up for a time with the pan-Negro journalist and businessman Duse Mohamed Ali, publisher of the influential *African Times and Orient Review*. After a short tour of the European continent, he returned to England and lobbied the Colonial Office for assistance to return to Jamaica.

Garvey arrived back in Jamaica on the eve of the outbreak of World War I. He lost little time in organizing the UNIA, which he launched at a public meeting in Kingston on July 20, 1914. Content at first to offer a program of racial accommodation while professing strong patriotic support for British

Within a decade of founding the Universal Negro Improvement Association (UNIA) in Jamaica in 1914, Marcus Garvey built the UNIA into the largest independent African-American political association. (Prints and Photographs Division, Library of Congress)

war aims, Garvey was a model colonial. He soon aspired to establish a Tuskegee-type industrial training school in Jamaica. In spring 1916, however, after meeting with little success and feeling shut out from political influence, he came to America—ostensibly at Booker T. Washington's invitation, though Garvey arrived after Washington died.

Garvey's arrival in America was propitious. It coincided with the dawn of the militant NEW NEGRO era, the ideological precursor of the Harlem Renaissance of the 1920s. Propelled by America's entry into World War I in April 1917, the New Negro movement quickly gathered momentum from the outrage that African Americans felt in the aftermath of the infamous East St. Louis race riot of July 2, 1917. African-American disillusionment with the country's failure to make good on the professed democratic character of American war aims became widespread.

Shortly after his arrival in America, Garvey embarked upon a period of extensive travel and lecturing that provided him with a firsthand sense of conditions in African-American communities. After traveling for a year, he settled in Harlem, where he organized the first American branch of the UNIA in May 1917.

With the end of the war, Garvey's politics underwent a radical change. His principal political goal now became the redemption of Africa and its unification into a United States of Africa. To enrich and strengthen his movement, Garvey envisioned a black-owned and -run shipping line to foster economic independence, transport passengers between America, the Caribbean, and Africa, and serve as a symbol of black grandeur and enterprise.

Accordingly, the Black Star Line was launched and incorporated in 1919. The line's flagship, the SS *Yarmouth,* rechristened the SS *Frederick Douglass,* made its maiden voyage to the West Indies in November 1919; two other ships were acquired in 1920. The Black Star Line would prove to be the UNIA's most powerful recruiting and propaganda tool, but it ultimately sank under the accumulated weight of financial inexperience, mismanagement, expensive repairs, Garvey's own ill-advised business decisions, and ultimately, insufficient capital.

Meanwhile, by 1920 the UNIA had hundreds of divisions and chapters operating worldwide. It hosted elaborate annual conventions at its Liberty Hall headquarters in Harlem and published the *Negro World,* its internationally disseminated weekly organ that was soon banned in many parts of Africa and the Caribbean.

At the first UNIA convention in August 1920, Garvey was elected to the position of provisional president of Africa. In order to prepare the groundwork for launching his program of African redemption, Garvey sought to establish links with Liberia. In

1920 he sent a UNIA official to scout out prospects for a colony in that country. Following the official's report, in the winter of 1921 a group of UNIA technicians was sent to Liberia.

Starting in 1921, however, the movement began to unravel under the economic strain of the collapse of the Black Star Line, the failure of Garvey's Liberian program, opposition from black critics, defections caused by internal dissension, and official harassment. The most visible expression of the latter was the federal government's indictment of Garvey, in early 1922, on charges of mail fraud stemming from Garvey's stock promotion of the Black Star Line, though by the time the indictment was presented, the Black Star Line had already suspended all operations.

The pressure of his legal difficulties soon forced Garvey into an ill-advised effort to neutralize white opposition. In June 1922 he met secretly with the acting imperial wizard of the Ku Klux Klan in Atlanta, Ga., Edward Young Clarke. The revelation of Garvey's meeting with the KKK produced a major split within the UNIA, resulting in the ouster of the "American leader," Rev. J. W. H. Eason, at the August 1922 convention. In January 1923 Eason was assassinated in New Orleans, La., but his accused assailants, who were members of the local UNIA African Legion, were subsequently acquitted. Following this event and as part of the defense campaign in preparation for the mail fraud trial, Garvey's second wife, Amy Jacques Garvey (1896–1973), edited and published a small volume of Garvey's sayings and speeches under the title *Philosophy and Opinions of Marcus Garvey* (1923).

Shortly after his trial commenced, Garvey unwisely assumed his own legal defense. He was found guilty on a single count of fraud and sentenced to a five-year prison term, though his three Black Star Line codefendants were acquitted. (The year following his conviction, Garvey launched a second shipping line, the Black Cross Navigation and Trading Co., but it too failed.)

Thanks to an extensive petition campaign, Garvey's sentence was commuted after he had served thirty-three months in the Atlanta federal penitentiary. He was immediately deported to Jamaica upon release in November 1927 and never allowed to return to America. A second and expanded volume of *Philosophy and Opinions of Marcus Garvey* was edited and published by Amy Jacques Garvey in 1925 as part of Garvey's attempt to obtain a pardon.

Back in Jamaica, Garvey soon moved to reconstitute the UNIA under his direct control. This move precipitated a major split between the official New York parent body and the newly created Jamaican body. Although two conventions of the UNIA were held in Jamaica, Garvey was never able to reassert control over the various segments of his movement from his base in Jamaica.

Although he had high hopes of reforming Jamaican politics, Garvey went down to defeat in the general election of 1930 in his bid to win a seat on the colonial legislative council. He had to content himself with a seat on the municipal council of Kingston. Disheartened and bankrupt, Garvey abandoned Jamaica and relocated to London in 1935. A short time after arriving in England, however, fascist Italy invaded Ethiopia, producing a crisis that occasioned a massive upsurge of pro-Ethiopian solidarity throughout the black world, in which movement UNIA divisions and members were at the forefront. Garvey's loud defense of the Ethiopian emperor Haile Selassie soon changed to scathing public criticism, thus alienating many of Garvey's followers.

Throughout the thirties Garvey tried to rally his greatly diminished band of supporters with his monthly magazine, *Black Man*. Between 1936 and 1938 he convened a succession of annual meetings and conventions in Toronto, Canada, where he also launched a school of African philosophy as a UNIA training school. He undertook annual speaking tours of the Canadian maritime provinces and the eastern Caribbean.

In 1939 Garvey suffered a stroke that left him partly paralyzed. The indignity of reading his own obituary notice precipitated a further stroke that led to his death on June 10, 1940. Although his last years were spent in obscurity, in the decades between the two world wars, Garvey's ideology inspired millions of blacks worldwide with the vision of a redeemed and emancipated Africa. The importance of Garvey's political legacy was acknowledged by such African nationalists as Nnamdi Azikiwe of Nigeria and Kwame Nkrumah of Ghana. In 1964 Garvey was declared Jamaica's first national hero.

While he failed to realize his immediate objectives, Garvey's message represented a call for liberation from the psychological bondage of racial subordination. Drawing on a gift for spellbinding oratory and spectacle, Garvey melded black aspirations for economic and cultural independence with the traditional American creed of success to create a new and distinctive black gospel of racial pride.

REFERENCES

CRONON, EDMUND DAVID. *Black Moses: The Story of Marcus Garvey and the Universal Negro Improvement Association.* Madison, Wis., 1955.

HILL, ROBERT A., ed. *The Marcus Garvey and Universal Negro Improvement Association Papers.* Los Angeles and Berkeley, 1983–1991.

JACQUES-GARVEY, AMY, ed. *Philosophy and Opinions of Marcus Garvey.* New York, 1923–1925. Reissued with an introduction by Robert A. Hill. New York, 1992.

LEWIS, RUPERT. *Marcus Garvey: Anti-Colonial Champion.* Trenton, N.J., 1988.

MARTIN, TONY. *Race First: The Ideological and Organizational Struggles of Marcus Garvey and the Universal Negro Improvement Association.* Westport, Conn., 1976.

STEIN, JUDITH. *The World of Marcus Garvey: Race and Class in Modern Society.* Baton Rouge, La., 1986.

VINCENT, THEODORE G. *Black Power and the Garvey Movement.* 2nd ed. Trenton, N.J., 1992.

ROBERT A. HILL

Garvey Movement. *See* Universal Negro Improvement Association.

Gary Convention. From March 10 to 12, 1972, eight thousand African Americans from every region of the United States attended the first National Black Political Convention in Gary, Indiana. Organized largely by Michigan congressman Charles C. DIGGS, Mayor Richard Hatcher of Gary, and the writer and activist Amiri BARAKA, who chaired the event, the convention sought to unite blacks politically—"unity without uniformity" was the theme—and looked toward the creation of a third political party. Hatcher, who had been elected mayor in 1968, was the keynote speaker. Many delegates had been elected in conventions in their home states. The convention approved a platform that demanded reparations for slavery, proportional congressional representation for blacks, the elimination of capital punishment (which resulted in executions of a disproportionate number of African Americans), increased federal spending to combat crime and drug trafficking, a reduced military budget, and a guaranteed income of $6,500 (a figure above the then-current poverty level) for a family of four.

After much debate and some walkouts by delegates, the convention also rejected integration as an idea, supporting local control of schools instead, and passed a resolution favoring the establishment of an independent Palestinian state. However, the convention took no position on any of that year's presidential candidates, including black congresswoman Shirley CHISHOLM, who was then running for the Democratic nomination. Chisholm had been left out of the convention planning, and believing that many black male leaders did not support her, she did not attend the Gary convention. Roy WILKINS and the

NAACP denounced the convention as "openly separatist and nationalist." The mainstream media, which had been barred from the event, were also critical.

The National Black Assembly, not a third political party, emerged from the convention. It met in October 1972 and again in March 1973. A second National Black Political Convention was held in 1974 in Little Rock, Ark., with follow-up meetings the next year. Thereafter, interest in further conventions petered out.

REFERENCES

HAMPTON, HENRY, and STEVE FAYER. *Voices of Freedom.* New York, 1990.

LOW, W. AUGUSTUS, and VIRGIL A. CLIFT, eds. *Encyclopedia of Black America.* New York, 1981, 1984.

JEANNE THEOHARIS

Gaye, Marvin (Gay, Marvin Pentz) (April 2, 1939–April 1, 1984), singer and songwriter. Marvin Gaye grew up in Washington, D.C., and began his musical career singing in the choir and playing organ in the church where his father, Marvin Gay, Sr., was a Pentecostal minister. In a radical rejection of his father's expectations, the younger Gaye became a secular musician.

Gaye's career as a professional musician began in 1958 when he became friendly with Harvey Fuqua, a record promoter for Chess Records who was impressed with his performance at a local high-school talent contest. After hearing Gaye's 1957 recordings with a group called the Marquees ("Wyatt Earp" and "Hey Little Schoolgirl") on the Columbia rhythm and blues label Okeh, Fuqua invited Gaye to Chicago and signed him to the Chess label in 1959. From the beginning of his career Gaye altered his last name, adding an *e* to the end for reasons he never explained.

In 1960 Gaye and Fuqua relocated to Detroit, where Fuqua established contacts with Berry Gordy, founder of the fledgling MOTOWN Records. In the next year, Gaye and Fuqua married two of Gordy's sisters (Anna and Gwen, respectively), Fuqua joined Motown, and Gaye was signed to the label. Even though Gaye was part of the Gordy family, it was several years before he began recording as a Motown solo artist. From 1960 to 1962 he was a backup singer and session drummer for various Motown performers. In 1962 Motown released his debut solo album, *The Soulful Mood of Marvin Gaye,* a collection of jazz-influenced, middle-of-the-road ballads. It was two years until Gaye had a hit single with "Hitch Hike" (1964). That same year he released "Pride and Joy," which climbed to the top ten on both the pop and the rhythm-and-blues charts.

During his time with Motown, Gaye recorded such hit records as "Ain't That Peculiar" (1965), "It Takes Two" (1967), "Your Precious Love" (1967), "Ain't Nothing Like the Real Thing" (1968), "You're All I Need to Get By" (1968), and, most successful of all, "Heard It Through the Grapevine" (1968) and "What's Going On" (1971). As one of Motown's soul-music emissaries, Gaye perfected the style, its ballad idiom, emotional lyrics, and use of gospel techniques in a secular context.

Gaye's most successful album was *What's Going On* (1971), which included three Top Ten hits ("Inner City Blues," "Mercy Mercy Me," and the title song). As Motown's first "concept album," *What's Going On* was musically diverse and a forum for Gaye to articulate his views on contemporary political issues, with particular attention to pollution in the nuclear age and the challenges facing inner-city blacks.

The year *What's Going On* was released, Gaye received honors from *Billboard* and *Cashbox* magazines as trendsetter and male vocalist of the year, respectively. He also won an Image Award from the NAACP. Motown released his next album, *Let's Get It On,* in 1973, and the title song immediately reached number one on the charts as Gaye's most successful single.

The last ten years of Gaye's life were marked by his divorce from Anna Gordy, marriage to Janis Hunter, relocation to Europe because of tax debts, dismissal from Motown in 1981, and increased dependence on drugs. His long-term feuds with his father and ongoing depression erupted on April 1, 1984, when an argument between the men resulted in

In 1983, Marvin Gaye received the first Grammy Awards of his career for his album *Sexual Healing*. (AP/Wide World Photos)

Gay shooting and killing his son in Los Angeles. Gaye's father was acquitted because a brain tumor contributed to his irrational and violent behavior.

Gaye's soulful aesthetic, with his light, crooning tenor voice full of emotion, earnestness, and often guttural sensuality, was ideally suited to both his contemplative and ecstatic performance modes. In 1983, the year before his death, Gaye continued to reveal his gifts as a performer, winning two Grammy Awards, for best male vocalist and best instrumental performance, with his gold record "Sexual Healing."

REFERENCES

GEORGE, NELSON. *Where Did Our Love Go: The Rise and Fall of the Motown Sound.* New York, 1985.
HARDY, PHIL, and DAVE LAING. *Encyclopedia of Rock.* London, 1987.
PARELES, JON, and PATRICIA ROMANOWSKI. *The Rolling Stone Encyclopedia of Rock & Roll.* New York, 1986.
RITZ, DAVID. *Divided Soul: The Life of Marvin Gaye.* New York, 1985.

MICHAEL D. SCOTT

Gay Men. The history of African-American gay men is far from a linear progression in status from social pariahs to more or less accepted and acceptable members of both the black and gay communities. Rather, it is a troubling and often painful story of the attempt to find an identity and build a visible community within the white and heterosexual power structures. On the one hand, the post–World War II economic boom and the gains of the CIVIL RIGHTS MOVEMENT have contributed to increased financial stability and social mobility of many black Americans. At the same time, relatively relaxed attitudes toward sex have prevailed in contemporary society. These have led to a broader range of the totality of black gay identity becoming visible and have reduced in some respects the stigma on such activity. However, black gays and lesbians experienced the large increase in poverty, drug addiction, homelessness, and other ills that afflicted other blacks during the 1980s and early 1990s; moreover, they have been plagued by antigay violence and by the epidemic of AIDS.

Although black civil rights leaders and elected officials have sometimes pushed for legal protections for gays and lesbians, homosexuality was not and is not generally accepted in the black community, which shares white society's negative attitudes toward sexual minorities. Various explanations have been propounded for the black community's response to homosexuality. First, the black church, as an important and historically independent institution, has had great prominence in African-American life, and its ministers and clergy have traditionally evinced a patriarchal, homophobic stance. For instance, in 1993 black minister Eugene Lumpkin, a member of San Francisco's Human Rights Commission, referred to homosexuality as an "abomination." (He was forced to resign soon after.) The same year, conservative black ministers in Cincinnati played a crucial role in overturning a local antidiscrimination ordinance covering sexual orientation. At the same time, the black church's music, ritual, and message of love and community have served an important nurturing role for the many gay men who retain a strong bond with their church and community.

Another example of homophobia is the traditional disdain of homosexuals as effeminate. Ironically, large numbers of black men, particularly those in prison, have same-sex contact but remain strongly antihomosexual and refuse to consider themselves gay. Black militant politics has often had a homophobic side, a famous example being Eldridge CLEAVER's attack on James BALDWIN, and numerous militant cultural figures, such as rap musicians, have included antigay slurs in their work. Many African Americans who tolerate private same-sex conduct oppose public affirmation of homosexuality. They fear it is an embarrassment to the larger black community, which is trying to overcome white stereotyping of black crime, immorality, and sexual excess (a notable example is civil rights activist Bayard RUSTIN's dismissal from the SOUTHERN CHRISTIAN LEADERSHIP CONFERENCE in the early 1960s, due in part to concern over his homosexuality).

Perhaps the most crucial element in the black community's homophobia is the widespread assumption that gayness and gay men are white ("the white man's weakness" as Amiri BARAKA termed it in 1970). Since many blacks do not realize that their own friends and relatives can be gay, they have no reason to change their negative outlook and resent the gay movement's appropriation of the civil rights movement's tactics and rhetoric as an attempt to divert attention from the cause of African-American liberation. All too often, white gay activists reinforce this belief by projecting a white image for the gay community and by refusing to incorporate black leadership and culture. In 1993, when the subject of admitting gays and lesbians into the military was being nationally debated, the contributions and the important legal precedent of Sgt. Perry Watkins, an African American who had successfully litigated his discharge on grounds of sexual orientation, were largely ignored by activists and the media.

Some black scholars claim that same-sex desire is the result of the alienating forces of modern life or

Perry Watkins, inducted into the Army in 1968, was discharged in 1984 after he acknowledged his homosexuality. After a lengthy legal fight, he was ordered reinstated in 1990 and later settled with the Army for back pay. In 1993, in recognition of his fight for gay service in the military, Watkins was a grand marshal in the Gay Pride Day march in New York City. (AP/Wide World Photos)

merely a more or less recent white intrusion into and against "African" values. Nevertheless, while we know little about its early history, same-sex contact by African Americans has existed since at least as far back as 1646, when Jan Creoli, "a Negro" in New Netherland (now New York State) was sentenced to be "choked to death, and then burned to ashes" for a second sodomy offense. Similarly, in 1712 Massachusetts authorities executed "Mingo, alias Coke," the slave of a magistrate, for "forcible buggery" (presumably sodomy). Through the nineteenth century the subject remained almost completely hidden except for what can be gathered from criminal records or the shrill exhortations of elite editors and writers in antebellum black newspapers warning blacks to curb both their sexual appetites and their tendency toward revelry and erotic abandon. In 1892 a report on "perversion" by Dr. Irving Rosse discussed such topics as African Americans arrested for performing oral sex in Washington D.C.'s Lafayette Square (still a popular cruising area in the 1990s) and the rituals of a "band of Negro men of androgynous character." In 1916 Dr. James Kiernan reported on blacks who solicited men in Chicago cafés and performed fellatio and sometimes "pederasty" on them in a "resort" under a popular dime museum.

The Great Migration of the 1910s and '20s and the consequent urbanization of African Americans led to the creation and expansion of gay spaces—bars, dance clubs (including "drag balls," dances where men dressed as women), bathhouses, and theaters—in the black communities of larger cities. These served as meeting places for black gay men and sometimes for white gay men trying to escape the rigid sexual mores of white society or seeking black male prostitutes. Popular songs such as "Foolish Man Blues" and "Sissy Man Blues" (sung by such singers as Ma RAINEY and Bessie SMITH, both bisexual women), though disdainful in tone, testified to the existence and attractiveness of homosexuals.

At the same time, black gay men assumed important positions in American cultural and intellectual life, a primacy they have maintained ever since. Cultural movements—notably that brief concatenation of artists and intellectuals known as the HARLEM RENAISSANCE—were heavily gay flavored. Socialite hostess A'Lelia WALKER surrounded herself with gay

Alderman Keith St. John, the first openly gay African-American elected official in the United States, Albany, N.Y., 1993. (AP/Wide World Photos)

men whose work she promoted, and Carl Van Vechten, a gay white man, helped sponsor the movement's artistic products. Countee CULLEN, Alain LOCKE, Wallace THURMAN, Lawrence BROWN, Claude MCKAY, and Richard Bruce Nugent were gay and bisexual men who were some of the renaissance's brightest lights. Significantly, Nugent published the first explicit piece of black gay literature, "Smoke Lilies and Jade," in the short-lived renaissance journal *Fire*. Claude McKay's novel *Home to Harlem* (1928) features a scene in a recognizably gay bar.

Despite the high visibility of gay men in black culture, many aspects of gay life itself remained secret, forbidden, and indeed alienating to many black gay men themselves. The idea that black gays actually composed a community that intersected, but was not subsumed in, either the black or gay communities would have seemed altogether odd to earlier generations of black gay intellectuals. James Baldwin, a literary giant of the latter part of the twentieth century whose works included homosexual characters and complex meditations on sexuality and race, commented as late as 1984 that he felt uncomfortable with the label "gay" and presumably with the idea of belonging to a (black) gay community. "The word 'gay' has always rubbed me the wrong way . . . I simply feel it's a world that has very little to do with me, with where I did my growing up. I was never at home in it."

Despite the presence of such openly gay individuals as Baldwin and science fiction writer Samuel DELANY during the 1950s and '60s, the emergence of gay African Americans as a political group did not occur until the late 1960s and 1970s, when the success of the civil rights movement in empowering and enfranchising blacks led other groups to struggle publicly for their liberation. Fittingly, African Americans had a large hand in the Stonewall rebellion, traditionally considered the founding event of the gay liberation movement. In June 1969, the Stonewall Inn, a New York gay bar, was raided by police. Many of the patrons were black, largely drag queens and effeminate gay men. Tired of police harassment, they fought back, throwing bottles and bricks. News of the incident quickly spread and led to the formation of political groups, notably the short-lived Gay Liberation Front (GLF). Sensitive to the revolutionary nature of the gay struggle, the GLF formed alliances with radical black groups, such as the BLACK PANTHER PARTY. However, as most gay political groups abandoned their radical beginnings and reverted to a predominantly white, middle-class outlook and membership, gay black activists became alienated from and less involved in their activities. Many blacks continue to feel unwelcome in the white gay community. Bars, dance clubs, and other spaces in gay areas sometimes discourage black patronage through discriminatory "carding" and harassment policies.

Split between the black and gay communities, many African-American homosexuals continue to feel obliged to choose. Writers such as Max C. Smith and Julius Johnson have noted the rough division of African-American homosexuals into two groups, "black gays" and "gay blacks." Black gays remain primarily active in the black community and have mostly black male friends and lovers. Many of them remain private about their gayness, and some lead bisexual "front lives." Gay blacks, on the other hand, identify with the gay community. They more frequently date and socialize with whites, and they tend to be more open about their sexuality.

Black gays and lesbians have worked to create a community and to mold a distinctively black gay culture. An important ingredient of the drive has been to construct independent black gay institutions. Black gay men, often in cooperation with black lesbians, have, since the late 1970s, created a number of political, social, and cultural institutions. The founding of the National Coalition of Black Gays (later the National Coalition of Black Lesbians and Gays) in 1979 demonstrated a profound belief in the viability of the black lesbian and gay community. Indeed, the creation of such a national coalition by a handful of Washington, D.C.–based activists showed just how secure some black gays had become in their assumption of black gay cultural and political unity. This initial effort was followed by the founding of black gay organizations throughout the country, including several black gay churches (the Pentecostal Faith Temple of Washington, D.C., among them); a writers collective called Other Countries; music groups, such as the Lavender Light Gospel Choir; and a number of social institutions, including Gay Men of African Descent (New York), Black Gay Men United (Oakland), Adodi, and Unity (both of Philadelphia). A notable example of organizing within the larger black community was the organization of a gay student group at HOWARD UNIVERSITY, the first of several gay organizations at historically black colleges. Black gay men have also branched out into fighting racism in the gay community through work in such groups as Men of All Colors Together (formerly Black and White Men Together), and they have also been active in AIDS education, Philadelphia's Blacks Educating Blacks About Sexual Health Issues (BEBASHI) being a noted example. Bars, bathhouses, and restaurants catering mainly to a black gay clientele have been set up, and black gay men have organized plays, musical performances, and dances (including the drag balls immortalized in white filmmaker Jennie Livingston's 1991 documentary *Paris Is Burning*).

In addition, there has been an explosion since the early 1980s of black gay (and lesbian) literature. Black gay and lesbian literature was regularly collected in special issues of gay and lesbian magazines. Moreover, a number of independent black gay and lesbian publications—namely, *Habari Daftari, Other Countries Journal, Pyramid Review, Blacklight, Blackheart, BLK, Yemonja, Black/Out, Moja: Black and Gay, B,* and *Real Read*—were started with the express purpose of providing an outlet for the broadest possible group of black gay and lesbian writers. Indeed, it is striking that two of the most prominent and successful pieces of black gay literature to date, *In the Life* and *Brother to Brother,* have been anthologies. As Joseph Beam wrote in the opening piece of the former, "Together we are creating and naming a new community while extending a hand to the one from which we've come."

Several black writers have become prominent outside the community. Randall Kenan's *Visitation of Spirits* (1989) and *Let the Dead Bury Their Dead* (1992), and Melvin Dixon's *Vanishing Rooms* (1991) were published by major presses. Essex Hemphill has not only had his 1992 collection *Ceremonies* published by a major press, but he has also achieved renown through his appearance in Marlon Riggs's popular nonfiction films, such as *Tongues Untied* (1991). At the same time, black gay publishing concerns produced some two dozen pieces of literature during the period, such as Donald Woods's *The Space,* Philip Robinson's *Secret Passages,* Roy Gonsalves' *Evening Sunshine* and *Perversions,* Rory Buchanan's *Taboos,* Lloyd "Vega" Jeffries's *Men of Color* and *A Warm December,* Alan Miller's *At the Club,* Hemphill's *Earthlife* and *Conditions,* and Assotto Saint's *Stations* and *Triple Trouble.* Saint also edited the 1991 collection, *The Road Before Us,* an anthology of one hundred black gay poets.

Black gay artists and intellectuals have established inroads into areas of expression outside of literature. Alvin AILEY helped revolutionize modern dance with his integration of black folk music and motifs and strong sensual elements, while Bill T. JONES was a pioneer in New Wave—including openly gay—choreography. Films such as Isaac Julien's *Looking for Langston* and Marlon Riggs's *Anthem* and *"Non, Je Ne Regrette Rien,"* have been enthusiastically received by gay and straight audiences throughout the world. Thomas Harris's two short videos, *Splash* and *Black Body,* have established a strong black gay presence in video, while his brother Lyle Harris has enriched the field of photography through such works as *Confessions of a Snow Queen.* The San Francisco performance troupe Pomo Afro Homos has offered a powerful testimony on the black gay experience. RuPaul has become a major singer and cultural icon. In an attempt to focus and unify critical study of these diverse artists and genres, black literary and cultural critics have been brought together at the Los Angeles–based African-American Gay and Lesbian Studies Center, founded by Gil Gerard in 1992.

As the twentieth century draws to a close, the dilemma facing black gays, particularly black gay artists and intellectuals, is whether they will be able to maintain and develop their autonomous institutions while continuing to push into the mainstream of American political and cultural life. Already very serious questions have been raised about who can and should control the image of the black gay man. For example, black critics bell hooks and Robert Reid-Pharr have questioned the political and cultural imperatives underpinning the representation of black gay men in *Paris Is Burning*. Kobena Mercer and Essex Hemphill have challenged the gay community's celebration of photographer Robert Mapplethorpe, asking whether his photographs of black men do not reinscribe the image of the sexual animal on the gay black body. The question "Whither the black gay community?" is still very much open to debate. Such questions are being asked in an atmosphere of intense ambiguity and uncertainty, marked on the one hand by a huge amount of gay political and cultural activity, with a particular explosion of representations of black gay men, and on the other hand by extremes of violence, disease, poverty, and despair.

REFERENCES

BEAM, JOSEPH, ed. *In the Life: A Black Gay Anthology,* Boston, 1986.

CLEAVER, ELDRIDGE. *Soul on Ice.* New York, 1968.

D'EMILIO, JOHN. *Sexual Politics, Sexual Communities: The Making of the Homosexual Minority in the United States, 1940–1970.* Chicago, 1983.

DUBERMAN, MARTIN, MARTHA VICINUS, and GEORGE CHAUNCEY, JR., eds. *Hidden from History: Reclaiming the Gay and Lesbian Past.* New York, 1990.

HEMPHILL, ESSEX, ed. *Brother to Brother: New Writings by Black Gay Men.* Boston, 1991.

HOOKS, BELL. "Is Paris Burning?" *Black Looks: Race and Representation.* Boston, 1992.

KATZ, JONATHAN NED. *Gay/Lesbian Almanac.* New York, 1983.

PETERSON, JOHN L. "Black Men and Their Same-Sex Desires and Behaviors." In Gilbert Heratt, ed. *Gay Culture in America: Essays from the Field.* Boston, 1992.

REID-PHARR, ROBERT. "The Spectacle of Blackness." *Radical America* 24, no. 4 (Winter 1992).

SMITH, MICHAEL, ed. *Black Men/White Men: A Gay Anthology.* San Francisco, 1983.

ROBERT REID-PHARR
GREG ROBINSON

Gay Women. *See* Lesbians.

Genius of Universal Emancipation, abolitionist newspaper. "That this abomination of abominations, the system of slavery, *must* be abolished, is as clear as the shining of the sun at noon-day." This declaration from the inaugural issue of the *Genius of Universal Emancipation* represented a new and potent voice against American slavery. Published between 1821 and 1839, the *Genius* was the first newspaper to champion African-American rights and helped to lay the foundation for the radical abolitionist movement (*see* ABOLITION) before the Civil War. The paper's founder and resolute editor, Benjamin Lundy, an Ohio Quaker, won the enduring support of blacks for his courageous stand against "injustice, tyranny, and despotism." At a time when few Americans questioned the institution of slavery and most whites denigrated blacks as inferior, Lundy's *Genius* denounced slavery as immoral, called for its gradual end, and insisted upon the repeal of all laws that discriminated against blacks.

Angry public opposition to abolitionism and the *Genius,* coupled with the paper's financial instability, forced Lundy to repeatedly uproot his press. First published in Mount Pleasant, Ohio, the *Genius* moved to Tennessee in 1822; between 1824 and 1833 it shuttled between Baltimore and Washington, D.C. After five years in Philadelphia, it went to Hennepin, Ill., where dwindling resources and Lundy's declining health led to the paper's demise in 1839. During its life the *Genius* publicized not only the international and domestic abolitionist movements but also free black opposition to slavery. More important, the paper provided a national forum for debate just as Americans began to reconsider the morality of slavery.

REFERENCES

BLASSINGAME, JOHN W., and MAE G. HENDERSON, eds. *Antislavery Newspapers and Periodicals.* Vol. 1, pp. 31–39. Boston, 1980.

DILLON, MERTON L. *Benjamin Lundy and the Struggle for Negro Freedom.* Urbana, Ill., 1966.

DONALD YACOVONE

Gentry, Herbert (July 17, 1919–), painter. Born in Pittsburgh, Gentry grew up in New York City and was introduced to art through the WORKS PROJECT ADMINISTRATION program at Roosevelt High School in New York City from 1938 to 1939.

He then attended New York University (1940–1942) and thereafter served in World War II (1942–1945).

After the war, Gentry moved to Paris because he saw the city as a place where he could work unhindered by racial prejudice. In Paris, Gentry said, "We were free . . . even if we did not have much materially. We had time to sit down and talk for hours. That was why we were there, to express ourselves freely."

Gentry studied at the Académie de la Grande Chaumière and at the École des Hautes Études from 1946 to 1949 in Paris. In 1948, he opened a gallery club called Chez Honey, named after his wife and located on the rue Jules Chaplin. The club featured art exhibitions and jazz performances and became a popular place for African-American musicians abroad to visit. Performers such as Don Byas, Kenny Clarke, James Moody, Duke Ellington, Jimmy Davis, and Lena Horne played at Chez Honey.

From 1949 to 1952, Gentry's work was displayed in over a dozen exhibits in Paris at such galleries as Galérie Hult (1950), Salon d'Automne (1951), and Salon de Mai (1952). In the 1950s his work was shown at the Burr Gallery (New York), but beginning in the 1960s, his paintings were most often displayed in Copenhagen and Stockholm, after he relocated to Malmö, Sweden. Gentry has been included in group shows at the Studio Museum in Harlem (1984) and at the National Museum of American Art in Washington, D.C. (1991). Despite his success and continued residence in Europe, during the 1980s and early 1990s Gentry has spent more time in the United States, often spending half of each year in New York City. From 1980 to 1982 he was a visiting professor at Montclair State College (New Jersey), and in 1987 he began teaching at Rutgers University. Throughout his career, Gentry has worked in an abstract expressionist style. He uses color and flat planes to create a mood in his work rather than to communicate representationally. His paintings often feature biomorphic forms made from rhythmic brushstrokes which convey a sense of movement and released energy. His best-known works include *Actual 75* (1975), *The Chase* (1981), *The Real World* (1981), and *Blue Garden* (1987).

REFERENCES

Afro-American Artists Abroad. Catalog. University Art Museum of the University of Texas, March 29–May 31, 1970.
BONAMI, ASAKE, and BELVIE ROOKS, eds. *Paris Connections: African American Artists in Paris.* San Francisco, 1992.
An Ocean Apart: American Artists Abroad. Catalog. Studio Museum in Harlem, New York, 1982.

MICHEL FABRE

George, David (c. 1742–1810), minister. Born a slave in Essex County, Va., David George twice escaped his abusive master to Indian territory on the Chattahoochee River along the present-day border of Alabama and Georgia. He hid with the Creeks as a servant to their chief, Blue Salt. Captured by his first master's son, he again escaped and persuaded King Jack, chief of the Natchez, to take his services in exchange for security. These Indians likely held him as a slave, for he was bought by George Galfin, a trader with the Indians, in the early 1770s. On Galfin's estate at Silver Bluff, S.C. (about twelve miles downriver from Augusta, Ga.), he taught himself to read with the help of his master's children. George was also baptized during this time. Accounts differ as to exactly who baptized him, but all agree that it was an African American, probably a slave. Encouraged by other religious slaves, George began to preach on the plantation in a mill that Galfin provided, eventually gathering a congregation of about thirty slaves. By 1775 these slaves had established what was likely the first African-American Baptist Church.

In 1778 Galfin fled when British troops began a major campaign against South Carolina and adjoining areas of North Carolina and Georgia. George thus sought the freedom British officers had promised blacks in return for work in the English war effort and their loyalty to the Crown. George ran a butcher stand behind British lines until he decided to evacuate to Nova Scotia in 1782. Nova Scotia proved no haven for black refugees, however. Although free, blacks were not allowed the rights of citizens and were subject to numerous forms of discrimination. George's first attempts at building a congregation at Shelburne were met with open hostility from whites there. In spite of this opposition, so many Nova Scotians, both black and white, were intrigued by the newness of George's style of preaching and singing that he had to hold his open-air meeting every day. After he baptized two wealthy white converts, however, hostile townspeople and discharged soldiers ran him out of town. Settling nearby, his reputation grew quickly, and by 1786 he was asked to preach or baptize in numerous communities of free African-American Christians. Despite his popularity, some white Nova Scotians continued to harass him and threatened to sell him back into slavery.

When John Clarkson, the governor of Nova Scotia, offered him religious work in colonizing Sierra Leone, he accepted. The colony was a part of abolitionist ambitions to end slavery by resettling former slaves, usually converts to Christianity, in West Africa. In 1792 George settled there as one of the founding fathers of Sierra Leone, establishing a Baptist church in the settlement of Freetown. The chapel also served as a political center for the town, and George became an informal leader, organizing the colonists to fight against higher taxes and rents levied upon them by the British. His chapel had grown to nearly two hundred members by the time of his death in 1810 in Freetown.

REFERENCES

CAPPON, LESTER J., et al. *Atlas of Early American History*. Princeton, N.J., 1976.

FREY, SYLVIA. *Water from the Rock: Black Resistance in a Revolutionary Age*. Princeton, N.J., 1991.

FYFE, CHRISTOPHER. *A History of Sierra Leone*. Aldershot, U.K., 1968, 1993.

KAPLAN, SIDNEY, and EMMA NOGRADY KAPLAN. *The Black Presence in the Era of the American Revolution*. Amherst, Mass. 1989.

LOGAN, RAYFORD W., and MICHAEL R. WINSTON, eds. *Dictionary of Negro Biography*. New York, 1982.

LORD, CLIFFORD L., and ELIZABETH LORD. *Historical Atlas of the United States*. New York, 1953.

MACKERROW, P. E. *A Brief History of the Coloured Baptists of Nova Scotia*. Halifax, Nova Scotia, 1895.

SOBEL, MECHAL. *Trabelin' On: The Slave Journey to an Afro-Baptist Faith*. Westport, Conn., 1979.

LYDIA MCNEILL

George, Zelma Watson (December 8, 1903–July 3, 1994), civic leader, musicologist, singer. Zelma George, née Watson, was born in Hearne, Tex., the daughter of a baptist minister and a college teacher. She spent her childhood and adolescence in Topeka, Kans. After receiving a bachelor of philosophy degree from the University of Chicago in 1924, George worked as a social caseworker for Associated Charities and as a probation officer for Chicago's juvenile court. During this time, she studied the pipe organ at Northwestern University (1924–1926) and voice at the American Conservatory of Music (1925–1927). In 1932, George accepted a position as dean of women at the Tennessee Agricultural and Industrial State University, a black college, where she remained for five years. During her tenure at Tennessee State, she began researching black music, a subject for which she became well known. In 1937, she moved to Los Angeles and founded the Avalon Community Center. George was appointed a research fellow at the Rockefeller Foundation in New York City in 1942 and earned an M.A. in personnel administration from New York University in 1943. She married Clayborne George, a lawyer, in 1944. Ten years later, she completed her thesis, an annotated bibliography of African-American folk and art music, for an Ed.D. degree in sociology at New York University.

In addition to lecturing on music and politics, George performed professionally as a soprano, and in 1949, she sang the leading role of Madame Flora in an all-black production of Gian Carlo Menotti's *The Medium*. When Menotti learned of her performance, he insisted that she play the part when the opera opened on Broadway. The following year, George became the first black woman to assume a leading role in a Broadway show. She performed in another Menotti opera, *The Consul,* at the Cleveland Playhouse in 1951 and sang the role of Mrs. Peachum in Kurt Weill's *The Threepenny Opera* at Cleveland's Karamu Theater in 1955.

In addition to being named one of the ten men and women of the year in both 1950 and 1951 by the Cleveland Press, George—a prominent Republican and Baptist—received a merit award from the NATIONAL ASSOCIATION OF NEGRO MUSICIANS in 1950 and the NATIONAL URBAN LEAGUE citizenship award in 1951. From 1955 to 1958, she was appointed to Secretary of Defense Charles E. Wilson's advisory committee on women in the armed services. At the request of President Dwight D. Eisenhower and Vice President Richard M. Nixon, she participated in several national conferences on minority and youth education and employment programs. In 1959, she was appointed goodwill ambassador by the State Department and spent six months traveling around the world on a government-sponsored lecture tour.

The following year George made news headlines when she was appointed by Eisenhower as an alternate delegate to the Fifteenth General Assembly of the United Nations. The only black member of the United States delegation, she was forced to resign after she leaped to her feet and spontaneously applauded the passage of a resolution calling for an end to colonialism in Africa and Asia. The resolution had been originated by Nikita Khrushchev and was passed without the support of the U.S. delegation, which abstained on the final vote.

Some years later, George returned to Cleveland as director of that city's Job Corps Center for Women. She continued to lecture on music, sociology, and civic affairs and sat on a number of committees, including the American Red Cross, the Cleveland Girl Scouts, and the Cleveland Conference of Christians and Jews. In 1972, George was the recipient of Fisk University's annual humanitarian award; two years later, Cleveland State University awarded her an honorary doctorate of humane letters. Although she retired as director of the Job Corps, she remained active as a lecturer and community leader until her death from heart failure in 1994.

REFERENCES

MORITZ, CHARLES W., ed. *Current Biography Yearbook.* New York, 1961.

SAXON, WOLFGANG. Obituary. *New York Times,* July 3, 1994, p. D3.

PAMELA WILKINSON

Georgia. In the 1730s and '40s, Georgia was officially a slave-free society, founded in 1733 as a sanctuary for poor white Englishmen and as a military outpost against Indians and Spanish, and thus unique among European colonies in the New World. In 1751, however, Georgia officially became a slave society and began to emulate South Carolina, its rich sister colony across the Savannah River.

For the next hundred years and more, Georgia, like South Carolina, relied on slave labor to produce mounting quantities of rice and cotton. The number of Georgia slaves rose from about five hundred in 1750 to perhaps fifteen thousand on the eve of the American Revolution. Growth took place mostly through migration, whether it was slaves coming from West Africa or accompanying planters from South Carolina and the West Indies. Men greatly outnumbered women, and young adults outnumbered the young and the old alike. During the AMERICAN REVOLUTION, black Georgians' lives were disrupted as each side stole slaves from the other. Meantime, some slaves fought on the British side in the defense of Savannah, and many sailed away from Georgia when the British evacuated. After the Revolution, the international SLAVE TRADE resumed, and Georgia, like South Carolina, insisted at the Philadelphia convention in 1787 that the United States Constitution leave the trade a question of state policy until 1808. The state constitution of 1798 declared an end to slave importation into Georgia the next year.

In the years between the Revolution and the CIVIL WAR, Indians were forced to cede new areas, and central and southwest Georgia opened to King Cotton. Georgia's population, already 36 percent black in 1790, rose to 42 percent black by 1810, and it held between about 41 and 44 percent black for the next half century. In absolute numbers, between 1790 and 1860, Georgia's slave population rose steadily and rapidly, from 29,264 to 462,198. Family life became increasingly significant in slaves' lives; in reciprocal fashion, ever larger numbers of slave children were born in Georgia, and native-born generations had sex ratios near parity. Movement from the Chesapeake region, together with natural increase, propelled almost all of the nineteenth-century growth of Geor-

gia's slave population. Free black Georgians, who numbered 3,500 in 1860, were concentrated in the cities of Savannah and Augusta. In rural Georgia, a number of counties had black majorities, and virtually all blacks were slaves. In 1860, coastal Camden County was 76 percent slave, the highest in the state, while three other coastal counties—Glynn, Liberty, and McIntosh—had populations that were 73 percent slave, as did southwest Georgia's Dougherty County. By the time the Civil War began, more slaves toiled in Georgia than in any other state, even Virginia.

Between the Revolution and the Civil War, Protestant Christianity became a powerful part of the culture of most Georgia slaves, and one of the oldest black congregations in North America was organized in Georgia in the 1770s. Though facing the constant threat of the whip, the slave trade, and sexual exploitation, black Georgians established families and communities under slavery. Freedom, for those few black Georgians who were not slaves, did not exempt them from most of the laws that governed slaves, including one that prohibited anyone from teaching blacks how to read and write. Some Georgia slaves successfully escaped to the North, among them George and Ellen CRAFT in 1848, but most had to wait until the Civil War made freedom possible.

During the Civil War, slaves contributed immensely to the Confederate cause by growing the corn that fed the troops, growing the cotton that clothed them, and working on railroads and defensive works. Increasingly, however, many tens of thousands of Georgia slaves helped bring Union victory about, whether by withdrawing their labor from the support of the Confederacy, or even, as thirty-five hundred did, joining the Union military and taking up arms.

Union Gen. William T. Sherman's march from Atlanta to Savannah in late 1864 brought EMANCIPATION to a wide swath of Georgia's plantation region, and events over the next few months brought a formal end to slavery in the rest of the state. Changes in politics and education suggest the meaning of freedom. Already in the summer of 1865, schools for black Georgians—promoted by the Freedmen's Bureau and supported by such northern groups as the AMERICAN MISSIONARY ASSOCIATION—were opening up everywhere. The beginnings of Atlanta University date from the first postwar years: Morehouse College was founded for men in 1867, and Spelman College for women in 1881; at about the same time, Methodists founded Clark College, and the AFRICAN METHODIST EPISCOPAL CHURCH established Morris Brown College. Black Georgians first voted in 1867. Among the black delegates elected to the 1867–1868

The Poor People's Mule Train arrives at Atlanta, Ga., city limits as it travels along I-20. The mule train was permitted to use the highway by Gov. Lester Maddox despite a law that forbids nonmotorized vehicles on the roadway. The mule train traveled from Mississippi to Washington, D.C. (AP/Wide World Photos)

state constitutional convention and the 1868 legislature was Henry M. TURNER.

After 1870, black representation proved scant, though coastal McIntosh County elected a black legislator, William H. Rogers, as late as 1907. By 1872, political Reconstruction had come to an end, as Democrats regained control of all major public offices and both branches of the state legislature. But by that time, too, the state had undertaken to establish a system of public schools that, though completely segregated between black children and white, was open to students of both races. Increasingly, black teachers staffed black schools. To obtain training to become teachers, some black Georgians attended Atlanta University, which for nearly twenty years received black Georgians' share of the state's land-grant funds. Funds were withdrawn from the Atlanta school on the grounds that it admitted a few white students and thus violated the state's segregation policy, but the Second Morrill Act, passed by Congress in 1890, increased the level of land-grant funds and mandated that a portion go to a school open to black students. In 1890, the legislature established Georgia Normal and Industrial Institute in Savannah (now Savannah State College) as Georgia's black land-grant school. State funding for black education continued, though

funding for white schools grew at much faster rates. With disfranchisement widespread as early as the 1870s and nearly complete after 1908, black Georgians found themselves excluded from either making or administering public policy. In the late nineteenth century, as conditions grew ever less promising, Henry M. Turner, as a bishop in the African Methodist Episcopal Church, promoted emigration to Africa.

In the twentieth century, thousands of black Georgians found themselves driven by sharecropping, the boll weevil, lynching, and disfranchisement—and pulled by perceptions of better opportunities elsewhere—off the farms and into town, out of Georgia and to the North and West. The GREAT DEPRESSION, the New Deal, and agricultural mechanization also led to the departure of many tenants from lands they had worked. Between the 1910s and the 1970s, the percentage of the nation's black residents who lived in Georgia dropped from 12 to 6, as black Georgians participated in the Great Migration. After reaching a total of 1.2 million in 1920, the number of black residents of Georgia dropped by 11 percent in the 1920s, barely changed in the 1930s and 1940s, and stayed below the 1920 figure until the 1970s, but it then rose to 1,746,565 by 1990. Georgia's population dropped from 47 percent black in the 1880s and 1890s, and 45 percent as late as 1910, to only 26 percent black by 1970 and 27 percent in 1980 and 1990.

Between 1910 and 1970, while Georgia's total black population showed almost no growth, blacks in Atlanta, the state's largest city, quintupled in number and grew to 21 percent of all black Georgians, up from 4 percent. For Atlanta natives and migrants alike, the city became a major center of black business, professional advancement, social life, educational opportunity, cultural activity, and political protest. Former slave Alonzo F. Herndon founded the Atlanta Life Insurance Company in 1905, for example, and Heman Perry established the Standard Life Insurance Company and the Citizens Trust Bank a few years later. Black Atlanta had its newspaper, the *World*; its musicians, including Ma RAINEY; and its baseball team, the Black Crackers. Beginning in the 1930s, Martin Luther King, Sr., served for many years as pastor of the Ebenezer Baptist Church, and in the 1960s the Rev. Dr. Martin Luther KING, Jr., headed the SOUTHERN CHRISTIAN LEADERSHIP CONFERENCE. When black students from Atlanta University began their SIT-INS in 1960, white observers professed surprise that there were so many black college students at all.

The 1940s brought the beginnings of change in politics and public policy, including an end to the total exclusion of African Americans from Democratic primary elections. Black Georgians began to reenter politics, particularly in Atlanta, where, following a court-ordered reapportionment that gave Atlanta more representation, Leroy Johnson was elected to the state senate in 1962, the first black legislator in a former Confederate state in the modern era. Until 1972, when Andrew YOUNG gained election to the U.S. House of Representatives, no black candidate had been elected to Congress from any southern state since the 1890s, and the only black Congressman ever elected from Georgia had been Jefferson F. LONG, who had served for a few weeks in early 1871. In 1973, Maynard H. JACKSON was elected Atlanta's first black mayor. In 1961, meanwhile, Charlayne Hunter and Hamilton Holmes forced the desegregation of the University of Georgia, first by getting a federal court order, and then by walking courageously through the hostile crowd that greeted them when they entered campus to begin their studies. In the 1980s, by contrast, Heisman Award winner Herschel Walker earned the cheers of black and white spectators alike by his performance on the school's football field. Court-ordered public school desegregation and the Civil Rights Act of 1964 sapped JIM CROW's strength. Working to take advantage of the VOTING RIGHTS ACT OF 1965, black Georgians throughout the state voted in increasing numbers and, for the first time in generations, won elective office.

Georgia native Jackie ROBINSON desegregated major league BASEBALL in 1947. Other African Americans from Georgia who achieved prominence in the half century after WORLD WAR II were singer "LITTLE RICHARD" Penniman; civil rights activists John Lewis and Julian BOND; Clarence THOMAS, appointed Supreme Court justice; and Alice WALKER, Pulitzer Prize–winning writer. Among the recordings of RHYTHM AND BLUES singer Ray CHARLES is his version of Georgia's state song, "Georgia on My Mind."

REFERENCES

DITTMER, JOHN. *Black Georgia in the Progressive Era, 1900–1920.* Urbana, Ill., 1977.

MOHR, CLARENCE L. *On the Threshold of Freedom: Masters and Slaves in Civil War Georgia.* Athens, Ga., 1986.

REIDY, JOSEPH P. *From Slavery to Agrarian Capitalism in the Cotton Plantation South: Central Georgia, 1800–1880.* Chapel Hill, N.C., 1992.

TRILLIN, CALVIN. *An Education in Georgia: Charlayne Hunter, Hamilton Holmes, and the Integration of the University of Georgia.* 1964. Reprint. Athens, Ga., 1991.

WALLENSTEIN, PETER. *From Slave to New South: Public Policy in Nineteenth-Century Georgia.* Chapel Hill, N.C., 1987.

WOOD, BETTY. *Slavery in Colonial Georgia, 1730–1775.* Athens, Ga., 1984.

PETER WALLENSTEIN

Gibbs, Mifflin Wister (April 17, 1823–July 11, 1915), entrepreneur, lawyer, abolitionist. Born free in Philadelphia, Gibbs attended grade school until his father died in 1831. To help his invalid mother support his three siblings, Gibbs drove a doctor's carriage before becoming a carpenter's apprentice at the age of sixteen and then a journeyman contractor on his own in 1840. Throughout this period he was a member of the Philomathean Institute, a colored men's literary society, and he was active in the UNDERGROUND RAILROAD with William STILL and others. In 1849, Gibbs was prominent enough in the ABOLITION movement to accompany Frederick DOUGLASS on a speaking tour for that cause in western New York.

In 1850, Gibbs relocated to San Francisco, where racial prejudice forced him to abandon carpentry. With savings earned as a shoeshiner, Gibbs opened a successful imported clothing store and quickly rose to prominence. While in California, he became a delegate to the state Negro Convention in 1854, 1855, and 1857, and he served in 1855 as editor of the *Mirror of the Times*, an abolitionist newspaper. Gibbs left California in 1858 for British Columbia, hoping to prosper from recently discovered gold in that area. While there, he acquired a small fortune in real estate and other trades, became a director of the Queen Charlotte Island Coal Company, and was twice elected to the Victoria Common Council (1866 and 1867).

Gibbs returned to the United States briefly in 1859 to marry Maria A. Alexander and again in 1869 to begin studying law at Oberlin College. Two years later, he opened his own practice in Little Rock, Ark. Gibbs was appointed county attorney in 1873 and was elected municipal judge of Little Rock later that year, thereby becoming the first African-American judge in the United States. In 1877, President Rutherford B. Hayes appointed Gibbs registrar of United States lands in Arkansas, a position he held until 1889. Gibbs was an active member of the RE-PUBLICAN PARTY, attending as a delegate all but one Republican national convention between 1868 and 1896. Gibbs was also appointed consul at Tamatave, Madagascar, where he served from 1898 until 1901. Upon his return to Little Rock, Gibbs continued his involvement in business, remained active in the civil rights movement, and published his autobiography, *Shadow and Light* (1902), which contained an introduction written by his friend and colleague Booker T. WASHINGTON.

Throughout his long and diverse career, Gibbs advocated the creation of a skilled African-American middle class through the acquisition of property and independent control of agriculture and industry. In an attempt to further this cause, Gibbs financed a conference in 1885 aimed at establishing industrial schools for blacks and supported the expansion of African-American business opportunities throughout his career.

REFERENCES

GIBBS, MIFFLIN W. *Shadow and Light*. 1902. Reprint. New York, 1968.

WHEELER, B. GORDON. *Black California: The History of African-Americans in the Golden State*. New York, 1992.

JEFFREY L. KLEIN

Mifflin W. Gibbs. (Photographs and Prints Division, Schomburg Center for Research in Black Culture, The New York Public Library, Astor, Lenox and Tilden Foundations)

Gibson, Althea (August 25, 1927–), tennis player. Althea Gibson was the first black tennis player to win the sport's major titles. Born in Silver, S.C., to a garage hand and a housewife, she came to New York City at age three to live with an aunt. The oldest of five children, she was a standout athlete at Public School 136 and began playing paddleball under Police Athletic League auspices on West 143rd Street in Harlem. In 1940, she was introduced to tennis by Fred Johnson, a one-armed instructor, at the courts (now named after him) on 152nd Street. She was an immediate sensation.

Gibson became an honorary member of Harlem's socially prominent Cosmopolitan Tennis Club (now defunct) and won her first tournament—the American Tennis Association (ATA) junior girls title—in 1945. (The ATA is the oldest continuously operated black noncollegiate sports organization in America). Though Gibson lost in the finals of the ATA women's singles in 1946, she attracted the attention of two black physicians: Dr. Hubert Eaton of Wilmington, N.C., and Dr. R. Walter Johnson of Lynchburg, Va., who tried to advance her career.

In September 1946 Gibson entered high school in Wilmington while living with the Eatons, and she graduated in 1949. She won the ATA women's single title ten years in a row, from 1947 to 1956. As the best black female tennis player ever, she was encouraged to enter the U.S. Lawn Tennis Association (the white governing body of tennis) events. Jackie Robinson had just completed his third year in major league baseball, and pressure was being applied on other sports to integrate. Though she was a reluctant crusader, Gibson was finally admitted to play in the USLTA Nationals at Forest Hills, N.Y., on August 28, 1950.

Alice Marble, the former USLTA singles champion, wrote a letter, published in the July 1950 issue of *American Lawn Tennis* magazine, admonishing the USLTA for its reluctance to admit Gibson when she was clearly more than qualified. Gibson's entry was then accepted at two major events in the summer of 1950 before her Forest Hills debut. She was warmly received at the Nationals, where she lost a two-day, rain-delayed match to the number-two–seeded Louise Brough in the second round.

Gibson's breakthrough heralded more to come. The ATA began a serious junior development program to provide opportunities for promising black children. (Out of that program came Arthur ASHE,

Althea Gibson holding a large gold plate presented to her as the winner of the women's singles tennis title at Wimbledon, England, July 6, 1957. She was the first black to win a Wimbledon championship. (AP/Wide World Photos)

who became the first black male winner of the sport's major titles.) Sydney Llewelyn became Gibson's coach, and her rise was meteoric. Her first grand slam title was the French singles in Paris in 1956. Before she turned professional, she added the Wimbledon and the U.S. singles in both 1957 and 1958, and the French women's doubles and the U.S. mixed doubles. She was a Wightman Cup team member in 1957 and 1958. After her Wimbledon victory, she was presented her trophy by Queen Elizabeth II, she danced with the queen's husband, Prince Philip, at the Wimbledon Ball, and New York City accorded her a ticker-tape parade.

The poise she showed at Wimbledon and at other private clubs where USLTA-sanctioned events were played was instilled by Dr. Eaton's wife and by her time spent as an undergraduate at Florida A&M University in Tallahassee, Fla. Jake Gaither, FAMU's famed athletic director, helped secure a teaching position for her in physical education at Lincoln University in Jefferson City, Mo. In the winter of 1955–56, the State Department asked her to tour Southeast Asia with Ham Richardson, Bob Perry, and Karol Fageros.

In 1957 Gibson won the Babe Didrickson Zaharias Trophy as Female Athlete of the Year, the first black female athlete to win the award. She also began an attempt at a career as a singer, taking voice lessons three times a week. While singing at New York City's Waldorf-Astoria Hotel for a tribute to famed songwriter W. C. HANDY, she landed an appearance on the *Ed Sullivan Show* in May 1958. Moderately successful as a singer, she considered a professional tour with tennis player Jack Kramer, the American champion of the 1940s. She also became an avid golfer, encouraged by Joe LOUIS, the former world heavyweight champion, who was a golf enthusiast. Louis had also paid her way to her first Wimbledon championships.

The Ladies Professional Golfers Association (LPGA) was in its infancy and purses were small. But Gibson was a quick learner and was soon nearly a "scratch" player. She received tips from Ann Gregory, who had been the best black female golfer ever. Gibson, a naturally gifted athlete, could handle the pressure of professional sports. But the purses offered on the LPGA tour were too small to maintain her interest.

In 1986, New Jersey Governor Tom Kean appointed Gibson to the state's Athletic Commission. She became a sought-after teaching professional at several private clubs in central and northern New Jersey and devoted much of her time to counseling young black players. The first black female athlete to enjoy true international fame, Gibson was elected to the International Tennis Hall of Fame in 1971.

REFERENCES

GIBSON, ALTHEA. *I Always Wanted to Be Somebody.* New York, 1958.

GIBSON, ALTHEA, with Richard Curtis. *So Much to Live For.* New York, 1968.

ARTHUR R. ASHE, JR.

Gibson, Joshua "Josh" (December 21, 1911–January 20, 1947), baseball player. If any one man personified both the joy of Negro League BASEBALL and the pathos of major league baseball's color line, it was catcher Josh Gibson, black baseball's greatest hitter. Born to sharecroppers Mark and Nancy (Woodlock) Gibson in Buena Vista, Ga., Josh moved to Pittsburgh in 1924 when his father found employment at the Homestead Works of the Carnegie-Illinois Steel Company. On the diamond, the solidly built Gibson astounded fans and players with his feats for two decades, but he never got the chance to play in the major leagues.

As a youth on the Northside of Pittsburgh, Gibson attended a vocational school where he prepared for the electrician's trade. But it was on the city's sandlots, playing for the Gimbel Brothers and Westinghouse Airbrake company teams, that he prepped for his life's work. Joining the Pittsburgh Crawfords in 1927 when this team of local youths was still a sandlot club, Gibson soon attracted the attention of Homestead Grays owner Cumberland Posey.

Gibson starred for the Grays in the early 1930s, returning to the Pittsburgh Crawfords for the 1934–1936 campaigns. By then, the Crawfords were owned by numbers baron Gus Greenlee, who remade them into the 1935 Negro National League champions. With future Hall of Famers Gibson, Satchel PAIGE, Judy JOHNSON, Oscar CHARLESTON, and "Cool Papa" BELL on the team, the Crawfords were quite possibly the best team ever assembled.

In 1937, after breaking his contract and joining many of his Crawford teammates in the Dominican Republic, Gibson was traded back to the Grays. There, he and Buck LEONARD were considered black baseball's equivalent to Babe Ruth and Lou Gehrig. The Grays won nine NL pennants in a row after Gibson returned, a mark equaled only by the Tokyo Giants.

Although a fine defensive catcher, the muscular 6'1", 215-pound Gibson is remembered best for his legendary swings at the plate. Perhaps the greatest slugger ever, he hit balls out of parks across the United States and the Caribbean basin, where he played each winter between 1933 and 1945. His home runs at Forbes Field and Yankee Stadium are thought to have been the longest hit at each. During his career, Gibson never played for a losing team.

His lifetime .379 batting average in the Negro and Caribbean leagues is the highest of any Negro Leaguer. He won batting championships, most-valuable-player awards, and/or home run titles in the Negro Leagues, Cuba, Mexico, the Dominican Republic, and Puerto Rico. His home run blasts are still recalled throughout these lands.

The second-highest-paid Negro Leaguer, Gibson also was its second-best attraction, behind Satchel Paige in both categories. Promoters often advertised for Negro League games by guaranteeing that Gibson would hit a home run. He rarely let them down.

Although fellow Negro Leaguers remember Gibson with fondness and a respect that borders on awe, his personal life was touched by tragedy. His young bride, Helen, died delivering their twin children, Josh, Jr., and Helen, in 1930. Gibson himself died in 1947, soon after the Brooklyn Dodgers signed Jackie ROBINSON. He was only thirty-five at the time. In 1972, he joined batterymate Satchel Paige in the Baseball Hall of Fame.

REFERENCES

HOLWAY, JOHN B. *Josh and Satch: A Dual Biography of Josh Gibson and Satchel Paige.* Westport, Conn., 1991.

RUCK, ROB. *Sandlot Seasons: Sport in Black Pittsburgh.* Champaign-Urbana, Ill., 1987.

ROB RUCK

Gibson, Robert "Bob" (November 9, 1935–), baseball player. Born in Omaha, Neb., Bob Gibson had a childhood plagued by a variety of chronic illnesses. He nonetheless starred in baseball and basketball at Omaha Technical High School and went on to play both at Creighton University. He was drafted by the St. Louis Cardinals in 1957, and that autumn played basketball with the HARLEM GLOBETROTTERS. Gibson moved into the baseball minor leagues in 1958 and then went back and forth between the minors and the Cardinals in 1959 and 1960. He established himself in the majors in 1961 and 1962, with records of 13–12 and 15–13.

One of the finest pitchers of the postwar era, Gibson played his entire career (1959–1975) with the St. Louis Cardinals. With a blazing fastball and a vicious slider, Gibson became one of the game's greatest strikeout pitchers, finishing his career with 3,117 strikeouts. Throughout the 1960s Gibson posted remarkable statistics, and in 1968 he completed one of the best seasons by a pitcher in the modern era with

St. Louis Cardinal Bob Gibson, an intimidating force on the pitcher's mound, led his team to three World Series in five years. (Photographs and Prints Division, Schomburg Center for Research in Black Culture, The New York Public Library, Astor, Lenox and Tilden Foundations)

son was elected to the Hall of Fame on the first ballot. Since then he has worked as a pitching coach for the New York Mets and as a pitching coach and announcer for the Atlanta Braves.

REFERENCES

ASHE, ARTHUR R., JR. *A Hard Road to Glory: A History of the African-American Athlete Since 1946.* New York, 1988.
GIBSON, BOB. *From Ghetto to Glory: The Story of Bob Gibson.* Englewood Cliffs, N.J., 1968.
PORTER, DAVID L., ed. *Biographical Dictionary of American Sports: Baseball.* Greenwood, Conn., 1988.

THADDEUS RUSSELL

Giles, Roscoe Conkling (May 6, 1890–February 19, 1970), surgeon and civic activist. Roscoe Giles was born in Albany, N.Y., the son of Francis Fenard Giles, a minister and attorney, and Laura Caldwell Giles. A Cornell graduate (A.B., 1911), he became the first African American to earn an M.D. degree at Cornell University Medical College (1915). He interned at Provident Hospital, Chicago (1915–1917) and later (1930–1931) pursued postgraduate studies in surgery at the University of Vienna. In 1917, Giles established in Chicago a private practice in general surgery that lasted over fifty years. He performed 2,457 major surgical procedures during the first thirteen years of his career. He was an attending surgeon at Provident Hospital (1917–1970) and served on the faculty at the University of Chicago (1946–1970). In 1953, he became the first black to hold the rank of attending surgeon at Cook County Hospital in Chicago.

Giles carried on a lifelong campaign against racial discrimination in the medical profession. In 1915, partly through his initiative, a policy excluding black interns from programs in New York's municipal hospitals was modified. He chaired a committee of the National Medical Association (a black organization) charged with persuading the predominantly white American Medical Association to drop its use of "col." to designate, or stigmatize, black physicians in the *American Medical Directory.* The practice ceased with the 1940 edition. During World War II, from his position as chief of medical services at Fort Huachuca, Ariz., Giles pressed for the opening of military hospitals to black officers.

The first black surgeon certified by the American Board of Surgery (1938), Giles was elected a fellow of the American College of Surgeons and became a charter fellow of the International College of Sur-

a record of 22–9, a league-leading 268 strikeouts and 13 shutouts, and an earned-run average of 1.12, the lowest recorded for a starting pitcher since 1913. He won the Cy Young and Most Valuable Player awards in 1968 and the Cy Young again in 1970, when he posted a 23–7 record. He was chosen for the National League All-Star team eight times.

Gibson's postseason record is no less impressive, with a combined record of 7–2 in three World Series (1964, 1967, and 1968). In the first game of the 1968 championship, Gibson set a series record by striking out seventeen batters.

A fierce competitor and one of the most intimidating figures in the game, Gibson was known for his willingness to knock down an aggressive batter with a high, hard fastball. Gibson attributed his angry demeanor to the social injustice he felt as an African American. In 1968, amid the black uprisings in northern cities, he stated that, "In a world filled with hate, prejudice, and protest, I find that I too am filled with hate, prejudice, and protest."

Gibson retired as a player in 1975 and became an announcer for the St. Louis Cardinals. In 1981 Gib-

geons (both in 1945). In 1937, he served as the thirty-eighth president of the National Medical Association. His wife, Frances Reeder Giles, a registered nurse, attended the Provident Hospital and Training School.

REFERENCE

COBB, W. MONTAGUE. "Roscoe Conkling Giles, M.D., F.A.C.S., F.I.C.S., 1890–1970." *Journal of the National Medical Association* 62 (May 1970): 254–256.

PHILIP N. ALEXANDER

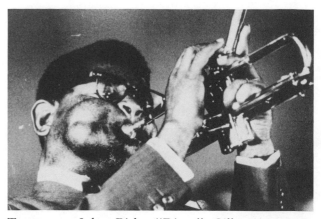

Trumpeter John Birks "Dizzy" Gillespie, was a cocreator, with Charlie Parker, of the innovative and frequently controversial jazz style known as bebop. (© Ken Heyman/Black Star)

Gillespie, John Birks "Dizzy" (October 21, 1917–January 6, 1993), jazz trumpeter and composer. Born in Cheraw, S.C., John Birks Gillespie, or Dizzy, as he was later known, took up trombone in his early teens and began playing trumpet shortly thereafter. When he began to play trumpet, he puffed out his cheeks, a technical mistake that later became his visual trademark. Starting in 1932, Gillespie studied harmony and theory at Laurinburg Institute, in Laurinburg, N.C., but in 1935 he broke off studies to move with his family to Philadelphia. Frank Fairfax gave Gillespie his first important work, and it was in Fairfax's band that Gillespie earned his nickname, Dizzy, for his clowning onstage and off.

In 1937 Gillespie moved to New York and played for two years with Teddy Hill's band. Through the early 1940s his experience was mostly with big bands, including those of Cab CALLOWAY, Ella FITZGERALD, Benny CARTER, Charlie Barnet, Les Hite, Lucky Millinder, Earl HINES, Duke ELLINGTON, and Billy ECKSTINE. Among his important early recordings were "Pickin' the Cabbage" (1940) with Calloway and "Little John Special" (1942) with Millinder. Gillespie, who married Lorraine Willis in 1940, began leading small ensembles in Philadelphia and New York shortly thereafter. In 1945 he joined with saxophonist Charlie PARKER to lead a bebop ensemble that helped inaugurate the modern JAZZ era.

Although in the early 1940s younger jazz musicians had played in a bebop style in big bands and in after-hours jam sessions at clubs in HARLEM, it was not until Parker and Gillespie's 1945 recordings, including "Dizzy Atmosphere," "Shaw 'Nuff," and "Groovin' High," that the new style's break from swing became clear. Bebop reacted to the at times stodgy tempos of the big bands and was instead characterized by adventurous harmonies and knotty, fast lines played in stunning unison by Gillespie and Parker, with solos that emphasized speed, subtlety, and wit.

Gillespie's trumpet style during this time was enormously influential. By the mid-1940s he had broken away from his earlier emulation of Roy ELDRIDGE and arrived at a style of his own, one which he maintained for the next five decades. He had a crackling tone, and his endless flow of nimble ideas included astonishing runs and leaps into the instrument's highest registers. Although many of Gillespie's tunes were little more than phrases arrived at spontaneously with Parker, Gillespie composed many songs during this time that later became jazz standards, including "A Night in Tunisia" (1942), "Salt Peanuts" (1942), and "Woody 'n' You" (1943). In addition to his virtuosity on trumpet, Gillespie continued to display his masterful sense of humor and instinct for gleeful mischief both onstage and off. Starting in the mid-1940s he affected the role of the jazz intellectual, wearing a beret, horn-rimmed glasses, and a goatee. He popularized bebop slang and served as the hipster patriarch to the white beatniks.

After his initial successes with Parker in the mid-1940s, Gillespie went on to enormous success as the leader of a big band. He hired Tadd DAMERON, George Russell, Gil Fuller, and John LEWIS as composers and arrangers; some of the band's recordings include "Things to Come" (1946), "One Bass Hit" (1946), and "Our Delight" (1946). The band's celebrated appearance at the Salle Pleyel in Paris, France, in 1948 yielded recordings of " 'Round About Midnight," "I Can't Get Started," and "Good Bait." The latter date included the Cuban percussionist Chano Pozo, and during this time Gillespie began to explore Afro-Cuban rhythms and melodies. Gillespie's composition "Manteca" (1947) and his performance of George Russell's "Cubana Be, Cubana Bop" (1947) were among the first successful integrations of jazz and Latin music, followed later by his composition

"Con Alma" (1957). In the late 1940s and early '50s Gillespie also continued to work on small group dates, including reunions with Charlie Parker in 1950, 1951, and 1953 and a return to the Salle Pleyel as a leader in 1953.

Although Gillespie never lost his idiosyncratic charm and sense of humor—after 1953 he played a trumpet with an upturned bell, supposedly the result of someone having bent the instrument by sitting on it—he outgrew the role of practical joker and instead became a figure of respect and genial authority. He released "Love Me" and "Tin Tin Deo" in 1951 on his own short-lived Dee Gee record label and became a featured soloist on many performances by the popular traveling sessions known as Jazz at the Philharmonic (JATP). In 1956 Gillespie's integrated band became the first to tour overseas under the sponsorship of the U.S. State Department, and in the following years he took them on tours to the Middle East, South America, and Europe. In 1959 Gillespie, always an outspoken opponent of segregation, performed at the first integrated concert in a public school in his hometown of Cheraw, S.C. The next year he refused to back down when Tulane University in New Orleans threatened to cancel a concert unless he replaced his white pianist with an African American. Gillespie's political activities took another twist in 1964 when he went along with a tongue-in-cheek presidential campaign. During this time Gillespie continued to record, both with small groups (*Swing Low, Sweet Cadillac*, 1967) and with big bands (*Reunion Big Band*, 1968). He also worked extensively in film and television.

In the 1970s and '80s, Gillespie maintained his busy schedule of touring and recording both in the United States and abroad as a leader of small and large bands and as a guest soloist. He appeared with the Giants of Jazz tour (1971–2) and recorded with Mary Lou WILLIAMS (1971), Machito (1975), Count BASIE (1977), Mongo SANTAMARIA (1980), Max ROACH (1989), and often with his trumpet protégé, John Faddis. During this time he also appeared on television shows such as *Sesame Street* and *The Cosby Show*. In 1979 he published his autobiography, *To BE or Not to BOP*, in which he explained his longstanding interest in Africa, which influenced his politics, music, and style of dress, and also recounted his involvement in the Baha'i faith, to which he had converted in the late 1960s.

By the late 1980s Gillespie had long been recognized as one of the founding figures of modern jazz. In 1989 he won the U.S. National Medal of the Arts and was made a French Commandeur d'Ordre des Arts et Lettres. Although his instrumental style was largely fixed by the mid-1940s, he won four Grammy Awards in the 1970s and '80s, and his career as a trumpeter ranked in influence and popularity with Louis ARMSTRONG and Miles DAVIS; along with Armstrong he became jazz's unofficial ambassador and personification around the world. Gillespie, who lived in Queens, N.Y., and then in Camden, N.J., continued giving hundreds of concerts each year in dozens of countries until his death at the age of seventy-four.

REFERENCES

GILLESPIE, DIZZY, and AL FRASER. *To BE or Not to BOP.* New York, 1979.

GITLER, IRA. *Jazz Masters of the Forties.* New York, 1966.

HORRICKS, RAYMOND. *Dizzy Gillespie.* Tunbridge Wells, U.K., 1984.

JONATHAN GILL

Gilliam, Sam (November 30, 1933–), artist. Born in Tupelo, Miss., Sam Gilliam began painting at an early age and received his B.A. and M.A. from the University of Louisville. Most of Gilliam's works are hanging or drooping canvases laced with pure color pigments bunched in abstract configurations. In 1966, he was awarded a National Endowment for Humanities fellowship. He received the Norman Walt Harris prize in 1969 and a Guggenheim Fellowship in 1971. In 1980, he was commissioned, with thirteen other artists, to design an artwork for the Atlanta airport terminal. This was the first contemporary artwork for public viewing at any American airport. Gilliam presented one-man shows at the Washington Gallery of Modern Art, the Jefferson Place Gallery, the Speed Museum, the Museum of Modern Art, the Walker Art Center in Minneapolis, and the Whitney Museum of American Art. Gilliam has also been represented in many group exhibitions, among them the first World Festival of Negro Arts in Dakar, Senegal (1966), "The Negro in American Art" at UCLA (1967), and the Whitney Museum's American Art Annual (1969). Gilliam's work is represented in permanent collections in over forty-five museums around the United States. Notable works include *Watercolor 4* (1969); *Herald* (1969); *Carousel Change* (1970); *Mazda* (1970); and *Plantagenets Golden* (1984).

REFERENCES

MATNEY, WILLIAM, ed. *Who's Who Among Black Americans.* 2nd ed. Northbrook, Ill., 1978.

PLOSKI, HARRY A., ed. *The Negro Almanac.* New York, 1982.

NEIL GOLDSTEIN

Gilpin, Charles Sidney (November 20, 1878–
May 6, 1930), actor and singer. Born and raised in
Richmond, Va., Charles Gilpin worked as an apprentice in the *Richmond Planet* print shop before finding his vocation in the theater and becoming one of
the most highly regarded actors of the 1920s.

Gilpin first appeared onstage as a singer when he
was only twelve. In 1896, he joined a MINSTREL show
and left Richmond, thus beginning the life of an itinerant performer that he would lead for many years.
Between engagements in restaurants, variety theaters, and fairs, he worked at various odd jobs and
was, among other things, a printer, barber, boxing
trainer, and railroad porter.

In 1903, Gilpin joined the Canadian Jubilee Singers
of Hamilton, Ontario. In 1905 and 1906, he performed with the Abyssinia Company and the Original Smart Set, two traveling musical troupes. From
1907 to 1911, he appeared with Robert Motts's Pekin
Theatre in Chicago, where he played his first dramatic roles and became a well-known character actor. He toured Canada and the United States with the
Pan-American Octette from 1911 to 1913. Afterward
he performed for one season with Rogers and Creamer-
er's Old Man's Boy Company in New York.

In 1915, Gilpin joined the Anita BUSH players, one
of the first black stock companies in New York City,
as its star performer. He accompanied the troupe
when it moved within the year from the Lincoln Theater in Harlem to the neighboring Lafayette Theatre,
where it became known as the Lafayette Stock Company and eventually launched the careers of many
famous black performers.

In January 1916, Gilpin made a memorable appearance in whiteface as Jacob McCloskey, a slave overseer and villain of Dion Boucicault's *The Octoroon*.
He starred in several more successful productions before leaving the company over a salary dispute in
April 1916. As a result of the reputation Gilpin earned
with the Lafayette players, he was given the role of
the Rev. William Custis, modeled after Frederick
DOUGLASS, in the 1919 Broadway premiere of John
Drinkwater's *Abraham Lincoln*.

Gilpin's first Broadway role led to a far greater
one: Eugene O'Neill saw him in *Lincoln* and recommended Gilpin for the lead in his new play, *The Emperor Jones*. The play opened in November 1920 in
Greenwich Village and, following favorable reviews,
moved to the Princess Theatre on Broadway. Gilpin,
having beaten out numerous white actors for the part,
became famous overnight. He played the title role for
four years to great critical and popular acclaim. *The
Emperor Jones* marked O'Neill's first great success
and, more important, it greatly advanced the case for
the public acceptance of black performers in serious
drama.

One of the first African Americans given the chance
to perform substantial dramatic parts in the mainstream theater was Charles Gilpin, shown here in the
title role in Eugene O'Neill's *The Emperor Jones*, a
part he created in 1920. (Prints and Photographs Division, Library of Congress)

For his work in *The Emperor Jones*, the Drama
League of New York named Gilpin in 1920 as one of
the ten people who had done the most for the American theater. Gilpin was the first African American so
honored. His invitation to the league's presentation
dinner, however, created a public controversy that
ended with his attendance, following the Drama
League's refusal to rescind the invitation and Gilpin's

refusal to decline it. Gilpin received a standing ovation of unusual length on accepting the award.

In 1921, the NAACP awarded Gilpin its SPINGARN MEDAL for his achievement, and he was received at the White House in a private audience by President Warren G. Harding. In 1922, the Dumas Dramatic Club (now the Karamu Players) in Cleveland renamed itself the Gilpin Players in his honor.

In 1924, Gilpin starred as the Rev. Cicero Brown in Nan Steven's *Roseanne,* a drama about black life in the South, produced in Greenwich Village in New York City. In 1925, he appeared in a brief run of J. B. Totten's *So That's That.*

Although he never again achieved the success he had with his portrayal of Brutus Jones, Gilpin continued to perform after 1926, mainly in revivals of *The Emperor Jones.* Gilpin was on the road with the play when his health failed in 1929. He died of pneumonia a year later in Eldridge Park, N.J.

REFERENCES

HUGHES, LANGSTON, and MILTON MELTZER. *Black Magic: A Pictorial History of the African-American in the Performing Arts.* New York, 1967.

ISAACS, EDITH. *The Negro in the American Theatre.* New York, 1947.

MONROE, JOHN G. "Charles Gilpin and the Drama League Controversy." *Black American Literature Forum* (Winter 1982): 139–141.

THOMPSON, FRANCESCA. "The Lafayette Players." In Errol Hill, ed. *The Theatre of Black Americans.* New York, 1987.

ALEXIS WALKER

Gilpin Players. *See* Karamu House.

Giovanni, Yolanda Cornelia "Nikki" (June 7, 1943–), poet. Nikki Giovanni was born in Knoxville, Tenn. Her father, Jones Giovanni, was a probation officer; her mother, Yolanda Cornelia Watson Giovanni, was a social worker. The Giovannis were a close-knit family, and Nikki felt a special bond with her younger sister, Gary, and her maternal grandmother, Louvenia Terrell Watson. Watson instilled in Giovanni a fierce pride in her African-American heritage.

After graduating from Fisk University in 1967, Giovanni was swept up by the Black Power and BLACK ARTS movements. Between 1968 and 1970 she published three books of poetry reflecting her preoccupation with revolutionary politics: *Black Judgment* (1968), *Black Feeling, Black Talk* (1970), and *Re: Creation* (1970).

But *Re: Creation* also introduced more personal concerns. In the spring of 1969, Giovanni gave birth to a son, Tom. The experience, she said, caused her to reconsider her priorities. Her work through the middle 1970s concentrated less overtly on politics and confrontation and more on personal issues such as love and loneliness. Yet Giovanni would always deny any real separation between her "personal" and her "political" concerns. During this time she began writing poetry for children. *Spin a Soft Black Song: Poems for Children* appeared in 1971, *Ego-Tripping and Other Poems for Young People* in 1973, and *Vacation Time: Poems for Children* in 1980.

In the 1970s, Giovanni expanded her horizons in other ways. Between 1971 and 1978 she made a series

One of the most popular poets to emerge from the Black Arts Movement of the 1960s, Nikki Giovanni's militant political verse sometimes overshadowed her gift for lyrical introspection. (Photographs and Prints Division, Schomburg Center for Research in Black Culture, The New York Public Library, Astor, Lenox and Tilden Foundations)

of six records, speaking her poetry to an accompaniment of gospel music (the first in the series, *Truth Is on Its Way,* was the best-selling spoken-word album of 1971). She published essays and two books of conversations with major literary forebears: *A Dialogue: James Baldwin and Nikki Giovanni* (1973) and *A Poetic Equation: Conversations Between Nikki Giovanni and Margaret Walker* (1974). She was also a sought-after reader and lecturer.

Critical reaction to Giovanni's work has often been mixed. While some have praised her work for its vitality and immediacy, some have felt that her early popularity and high degree of visibility worked against her development as a poet. Others have criticized her work as politically naive, uneven, and erratic. Some of these reactions were due in part to Giovanni's very public growing up as a poet and the diversity of her interests. These criticisms have never bothered Giovanni, who believes that life is "inherently incoherent."

Other works of Giovanni's include *My House* (1972), *The Women and the Men* (1972), *Cotton Candy on a Rainy Day* (1978), *Those Who Ride the Night Winds* (1983), and a collection of essays, *Sacred Cows and Other Edibles* (1988).

REFERENCES

BAILEY, PETER. "I Am Black, Female, Polite, . . ." *Ebony* (February 1972): 48–56.

TATE, CLAUDIA. *Black Women Writers at Work.* New York, 1983.

MICHAEL PALLER

Globetrotters, Harlem. *See* Harlem Globetrotters.

Gloucester, John (1776–May 2, 1822), minister. Gideon Blackburn, a Presbyterian missionary, gave ministerial training to his slave John Gloucester and brought him before Union Presbytery in Tennessee, where he was later ordained. The Presbyterian Evangelical Society of Philadelphia, impressed by Gloucester's preaching and singing, requested that Blackburn emancipate him for a street ministry in the ghetto of South Philadelphia. Gloucester was released to become the founder and pastor of the First African Presbyterian Church, the first in the nation.

First African Presbyterian Church was formed in 1807 with twenty-two members. The presbytery received the congregation in 1811 with 123 members, but it never exceeded 300 and Gloucester was obliged to spend much of his time raising funds to support his ministry, as well as $1,500 to purchase the freedom of his wife and four children. Three sons became Presbyterian ministers.

In characteristic Presbyterian fashion, Gloucester emphasized liberal-arts education, and he conducted a school for black youth that attracted white support. After his death the First Church split. In 1824, Samuel CORNISH declined to serve the minority that withdrew to form the Second African Presbyterian Church under Gloucester's eldest son, Jeremiah.

GAYRAUD S. WILMORE

Glover, Danny (July 22, 1947–). Born in San Francisco, the son of two postal workers who were both union organizers and members of the NAACP, Danny Glover attended San Francisco State University, where he majored in economics. During the 1960s, he became a student activist, and he worked as an economic planner for the city after graduation. He began taking acting classes in the 1960s at the Black Actor's Workshop sponsored by the American Conservatory Theatre in Oakland. In the 1970s he acted with Sam Shepard's Magic Theater, the San Francisco Eureka Theater, and the Los Angeles Theater and made guest appearances on such television series as *Lou Grant, Chiefs,* and *Gimme a Break.*

In 1979, Glover made his New York theater debut in Athol Fugard's *The Blood Knot,* for which he won a Theater World Award. He also played in the 1982 Broadway production of Fugard's *Master Harold . . . and the Boys,* where he was seen by writer and director Robert Benton, who cast him as a sharecropper in the motion picture *Places in the Heart* (1984). Glover also appeared in Fugard's *A Lesson from Aloes* (1986) at the Steppenwolf Theater Company in Chicago.

In 1985 Glover appeared in three films: *Witness, Silverado,* and *The Color Purple,* Steven Spielberg's adaptation of Alice Walker's novel, in which he appeared as the sadistic "Mister," opposite Whoopi GOLDBERG. In 1987, Glover starred as a Los Angeles detective who is partners with Mel Gibson in *Lethal Weapon.* The action-adventure movie was a major commercial success and led to two sequels.

In 1990 Glover produced and starred in Charles BURNETT's *To Sleep with Anger,* a film about middle-class black life in South-Central Los Angeles. The same year he was inducted into the Black Filmmakers Hall of Fame and received the Phoenix Award from the Black American Cinema Society. Glover appeared in *Predator 2* (1991) and *The Saint of Fort Washington* (1992), and in 1993, he starred as a police officer in *Bopha!,* a film set in South Africa and filmed in Zimbabwe, about the 1976 Soweto uprisings. Glover has been the recipient of two NAACP Image Awards, both in 1987, for his performance in *Lethal Weapon* (1987) and in HBO's *Mandela* (1987), for which he also received an ACE Award.

REFERENCES

"Danny Glover." *Current Biography* 53 (April 1992): 29–32.

"Danny Glover." In Michel L. LaBlanc, ed. *Contemporary Black Biography,* vol. 1. Detroit, 1989, pp. 86–87.

SABRINA FUCHS
SUSAN MCINTOSH

Godbolt, James.   *See* Slyde, Jimmy.

Goldberg, Whoopi (November 13, 1950–), actress. Whoopi Goldberg was born Caryn Johnson in New York City and raised in a housing project by her mother. She received her earliest education at a parish school, the Congregation of Notre Dame. She gained her first stage experience at the Helena Rubinstein Children's Theatre at the Hudson Guild, where she acted in plays from the age of eight to ten.

In the mid-1960s Goldberg dropped out of high school and worked on Broadway as a chorus member in the musicals *Hair, Jesus Christ Superstar,* and *Pippin.* She was married briefly in the early 1970s and had a daughter from the marriage, Alexandrea Martin.

In 1974 Goldberg moved to Los Angeles and has since maintained California residence. She became a founding member of the San Diego Repertory Theatre and later joined Spontaneous Combustion, an improvisation group. It was about this time that she adopted the name Whoopi Goldberg.

In 1981 Goldberg, with David Schein, wrote the extended comedy sketch *The Last Word.* The eclectic ensemble of characters in her sketches include a self-aborting surfer girl, a panhandling ex-vaudevillian, a junkie, and a Jamaican maid. Goldberg's style, a blend of social commentary, humor, and improvisation, earned her both critical acclaim and a large audience. In 1983 she developed an hour-long piece entitled *The Spook Show,* which played in London and New York to great acclaim. After appearing in Berkeley, Calif., in a one-woman show called *Moms,* based on the life of comedian Moms MABLEY, Goldberg opened on Broadway in 1984 in a new version

of her comedy sketches, *Whoopi Goldberg,* produced by Mike Nichols.

The following year Goldberg starred as Celie in Steven Spielberg's film of Alice WALKER's *The Color Purple.* She received an Academy Award nomination for her performance, which propelled her into the Hollywood mainstream. She subsequently starred in such films as *Jumping Jack Flash* (1986), *Burglar* (1987), *Fatal Beauty* (1987), *Clara's Heart* (1988), and *The Long Walk Home* (1990). She appeared in a continuing role on the television series *Star Trek: The Next Generation* from 1988 through 1993. In 1990 she received an Academy Award for best supporting actress for her role as a psychic in *Ghost.* Goldberg became only the second black woman—the first since Hattie McDaniel in 1939—to win an Oscar in a major category. Subsequently she appeared in *Soapdish* (1991), *Sister Act* (1992), and *Sarafina!* (1992), becoming the first African-American to star in a film shot on location in South Africa.

In 1992 Goldberg cofounded the annual comedy benefit "Comic Relief" on the cable television network Home Box Office to raise money for the homeless. That same year she launched her own syndicated television talk show. In 1993 Goldberg appeared in the films *Sister Act 2* and *Made In America,* a comedy about an interracial relationship.

REFERENCES

HINE, DARLENE CLARK. *Black Women in America.* Brooklyn, N.Y., 1993, pp. 491–493.

MORITZ, CHARLES. *1985 Current Biography Yearbook.* New York, 1993.

SUSAN MCINTOSH

Golf.   Despite limited access to public courses, exclusion from private clubs, and the absence of professional role models, substantial numbers of African Americans have played the game of golf since its introduction to America. They have also established and maintained many of the social institutions associated with the sport. According to a 1990 study by Mediamark Research, of the nearly eighteen million adults in the United States who play golf, about 2.5 percent, or 450,000, are black Americans.

Ironically, considering the elitist origins of golf in this country, one of the first American-born golf professionals was an African American—John Shippen, who competed in the 1896 U.S. Open, held at Shinnecock Hills on Long Island. Shippen, then eighteen years old, worked as an assistant to Willie Dunn, the professional at Shinnecock Hills. His participation was protested by a group of foreign-born professionals who threatened to withdraw if Shippen and Oscar Bunn, a Shinnecock Indian golfer from the reservation, were allowed to play. Theodore Havemeyer, the president of the United States Golf Association (USGA), informed the disgruntled golfers that the tournament would be run even if Shippen and Bunn were the only competitors.

Shippen shot a 78 in the morning round of the thirty-six-hole, one-day event and was tied for the lead. In the end, he tied for fifth. He played in four other U.S. Opens, continued to compete in local and national tournaments, and became the golf professional at several black-run clubs in Philadelphia and in Laurel, Md. For thirty-five years he served as the professional at the Shady Rest Country Club in Scotch Plains, New Jersey. He died at the age of ninety in a nursing home in Newark, N.J., in 1968.

Most African-American golfers developed an interest in the game through caddying. In the early 1920s, a golf boom fueled a demand for caddies at both private and public courses. Traditionally, clubs allowed caddies to play golf one day a week when the course was closed to members for maintenance. This allowed some black teenagers the chance to play on courses at clubs that would not have allowed them as members.

While blacks were able to gain limited access to America's golf courses, they faced many obstacles when they attempted to make a living at golf. The original Professional Golfers' Association (PGA) constitution in 1934 stipulated that only "golfers of the Caucasian race" were eligible for membership. Dewey Brown, who was playing golf in the 1920s,

became the first black member of the PGA. However, there is no indication of the exact date or explanation of how he was exempted from the "Caucasian clause." He served as golf professional at several black clubs but was most closely associated with the Buckwood Inn at Shawnee-on-the-Delaware.

Despite this limited opportunity to play golf, enough African Americans developed an interest in the game to support a number of black-operated clubs by the second decade of the twentieth century. One was the Shady Rest Golf Club in Westfield (now Scotch Plains), N.J., established in 1921, which is generally considered to be the first black country club—that is, a club incorporating golf and tennis with a full schedule of social events. A colony of black resident cottages had sprung up on either side of what was the Westfield Country Club, and eventually the course itself was sold to a group of African Americans and renamed Shady Rest. The membership, according to the *New York Sun* in July 1922, consisted of "prosperous Negro merchants, lawyers, doctors, Pullman porters, waiters and janitors."

At about the same time, black golfers in Washington, D.C., found it difficult to gain access to courses in the area. So strong was their interest in the game that, during the 1920s, several of them secured summer cottages in Stow, Mass., where they established the Mapledale Country Club, one of the significant early black golf courses. Other black-owned clubs included Sunset Hills Country Club in Kankakee, Ill.; Lincoln Country Club in Atlanta; and the Asbury Park Course in New Jersey.

In 1926, Robert Hawkins (a resident of Stow) invited players from black clubs throughout the United States to a tournament at Mapledale. On Labor Day weekend of that year, thirty-five black golfers came to play the seventy-two-hole tournament. The winners of the professional division, Harry Jackson of Washington, D.C., and Marie Thompson of Chicago, were paid one hundred dollars each; the amateurs received medals. The tournament was repeated in 1927 and 1928, when the players came together to establish the UNITED GOLFERS ASSOCIATION (UGA). Through UGA tournaments, a number of black golfers gained prominence; they included Robert "Pat" Ball (who won the UGA title in 1927, 1929, 1934, and 1941) and Walter Speedy of Chicago; Howard Wheeler (who won the UGA title five times between 1933 and 1958) of Atlanta; John Dendy of Asheville, N.C.; and A. D. V. Crosby and R. G. Robinson of Ann Arbor, Mich.

Black women also demonstrated a strong desire to gain access to golf facilities. In 1937, an all-black women's club, Wake Robin Golf Club, was formed in Washington, D.C., followed soon afterward by the

Lee Elder became the first black golfer to play in the prestigious Masters Tournament, Augusta, Ga., April 1975. (AP/Wide World Photos)

Renee Powell. (Photographs and Prints Division, Schomburg Center for Research in Black Culture, The New York Public Library, Astor, Lenox and Tilden Foundations)

Chicago Women's Club. Lucy Williams of Indianapolis and Laura Osgood of Chicago emerged as leading women golfers, as did Thelma Cowan (who won the UGA national tournament in 1947, 1949, 1954, and 1955), Anne Gregory (who won in 1950, 1953, 1957, 1965, and 1966), and Ethel Funches, who won seven times, beginning in 1959.

While the UGA provided an opportunity for black club pros and amateurs to test their skills against other club players, it had little success in introducing black golfers into the white mainstream. The USGA did not reserve any place in its annual championship for members of the UGA (as the United States Lawn Tennis Association did for the all-black American Tennis Association). There was little interaction between the USGA and the UGA. It wasn't until 1959 that any USGA championship was won by an African American. In that year, Bill Wright won the Public Links Championship. In 1982, Charles Duhon won the USGA Senior Amateur Championship.

Military service and black colleges were two other avenues for the development of black golfers. For some, the Army offered the only opportunity to play on an eighteen-hole course that approached championship caliber. Pvt. Calvin Searles (who subsequently died in World War II) played in the 1944 Tam O'Shanter All American event. This was the only mainstream tournament that allowed blacks to compete during the war years. Other prominent players during the 1940s included Ed Jackson and Bennie Davis of Detroit; Calvin Ingram and Frank Radcliffe of Chicago; Peter Fortunes of Suffolk, Va.; and Hoxey Hazzard of Montgomery, Ala.

The only black college with its own course was TUSKEGEE INSTITUTE, which had a three-hole course built in 1920 that was expanded to nine holes approximately a decade later. Tuskegee sponsored the first black intercollegiate tournament in 1938 and, on a larger scale, established a national intercollegiate event in 1940.

African Americans were also making efforts to increase access to public courses. In a number of court cases around the country, blacks sued to gain equal access to public facilities, paralleling other civil rights efforts of the period. A black dentist, P. O. Sweeny, sued the Louisville, Ky., Parks Department in 1947 for the right to play unrestricted on local municipal courses. The decision ruled, in essence, that the courts could not enforce social equality, and the suit was dismissed. Other lower court cases yielded similar results or, in some, modified rules for access. There were some exceptions, however. A federal judge in Baltimore opened city courses to African Americans in 1948, and in 1950 the U.S. Supreme Court overturned a Florida State Supreme Court ruling that had restricted black access to local courses to one day per week. Finally, in 1955, the U.S. Supreme Court reaffirmed its rejection of "separate but equal" accommodations for public golf and recreational facilities. In this decision, the Court vacated a ruling by a lower court that allowed Atlanta to legally segregate blacks and whites if the facilities were of equal quality. However, the ruling did not immediately open up public courses to black golfers.

A similar struggle occurred over the integration of professional organizations. In 1948, Ted RHODES, Bill Spiller, and Gunter Madison, accomplished black golfers, forced the PGA to rethink its exclusionary rule. These golfers brought suit against the PGA for discrimination when they were not allowed to compete in the Richmond Open in Richmond, Calif. The case was settled out of court in September 1948 when the PGA, through attorney Dana Murdock, declared that it would not discriminate or refuse tournament-playing privileges to anyone because of color. But discrimination on the professional tour continued.

At the 1952 San Diego Open, former boxing champion Joe LOUIS, himself an accomplished ama-

Calvin Peete (left), confers with his caddy Dolphus "Golfball" Hall during the Tournament Players Championship golf tournament, March 30, 1985. (AP/Wide World Photos)

teur golfer, was invited by a local Chevrolet sponsor to participate in the tournament. A PGA committee notified Louis that he was banned from participation. While the PGA constitution prohibited non-Caucasians from membership, Louis had been invited, according to the rules, by the local sponsor as one of five amateur golfers allowed, without the need for qualification. Non-Caucasians were prohibited from membershp in the PGA, but an individual sponsor could invite up to five members or nonmembers (amateurs or pros) to compete.

Horton Smith, PGA president, polled the members of the executive committee to gain an exemption for Louis to compete. The PGA added a clause to its bylaws that allowed one PGA-approved "Negro" amateur (under five handicap) and one PGA-approved "Negro" professional of "recognized standing and ability" to be designated by local sponsors to compete in its events. Louis accepted these conditions because at the time he had no other choice. Despite the national attention afforded the San Diego Open racial controversy, it would be nine years be-

fore the PGA would officially rescind its "Caucasian only" clause.

In 1960, after receiving a letter protesting PGA policies from black tour professional Charles SIF-FORD, the attorney general of California, Stanley Mosk, announced, "We intend to take every step available to us, both in and out of the courts, to force the PGA either to eliminate this obnoxious restriction or to cease all activity of any kind within our state" (*New York Times,* November 23, 1960). Eventually, the executive committee of the PGA voted to eliminate racial restrictions for membership. The full membership ratified the committee's decision in November 1961.

Charles Sifford was the most prominent black professional golfer of the postwar decades. Other than John Shippen, he accomplished the most "black firsts" in golf. After dominating the annual UGA professional championship, winning a record five championships in a row between 1952 and 1956, he became the first black player to win a significant title in a predominantly white event, the Long Beach (California) Open, in 1957. While Pete BROWN, another early black professional, also helped pave the way for black professional golfers by being the first black pro to win a PGA tournament, the 1964 Waco Turner Open, Sifford was the first black player to win a major PGA event, the 1969 Los Angeles Open.

The Ladies Professional Golfers Association (LPGA) was established in 1948, and although there was no written clause in its constitution barring blacks from membership and tournament play, it was not until 1963 that an African-American tennis champion, Althea GIBSON, competed on the LPGA tour, and not until 1967 that an African American, Renee Powell, became a regular member of the tour.

The black golfer who played the most prominent public role in bringing African-American golf to the attention of the sporting world was Lee ELDER. After competing mainly in UGA tournaments, Elder earned his PGA card in 1967. He is best known as the first black golfer to compete in the Masters, the tournament most symbolic of the inability of African-American golfers to break into major tournament golf. Throughout the early 1970s, Elder was the focal point of the effort to obtain equality in entrance to the Masters. In 1971 the Masters changed earlier policies, which had invited players on the basis of a complicated point system and by ballot of former Masters champions. The new policy granted an invitation to anyone who won a PGA tournament in the year prior to the Masters. In 1974, Elder won the Monsanto Open, which qualified him to compete in the 1975 Masters.

By the early 1990s, the most successful black golfer by far was Calvin PEETE. In 1982 Peete became the first black multiple winner, capturing the Greater Milwaukee Open for the second time, the Anheuser-Busch Classic, the BC Open, and the Pensacola Open and had his best finish in a grand slam event, placing third in the PGA championship.

Despite considerable progress by black golfers on the professional tour, African Americans are still denied equal access to private country-club memberships. During an interview before the 1990 PGA championship at the Shoal Creek Country Club in Alabama, Hall Thompson, president of Shoal Creek, openly stated that his club did not allow black members. The ensuing controversy prompted both the PGA and the USGA to review site-selection policies for all future championships and coaxed several discriminatory clubs to open their doors. This open public discussion has exposed the racial intolerance that has long been associated with the game of golf but has at least begun the exploration of ways to eliminate the barriers that have restricted African-American golfers.

REFERENCES

ASHE, ARTHUR R., JR. *A Hard Road to Glory: The History of the Black Athlete.* Vol. 2. New York, 1988.

BARKOW, AL. *The History of the PGA Tour.* New York, 1989.

GRAFFIS, HERBERT. *The PGA: The Official History of the Professional Golfers Association.* New York, 1975.

HANNIGAN, FRANK. "A Champion Against the Odds." *U.S.G.A. Journal* (August 1982): 38–41.

JONES, GUILFORD. "Past Greats." *Black Sports* (July 1973): 65–68.

McRAE, FINLEY F. "Hidden Traps Beneath the Placid Greens." *American Visions* (April 1991): 26–29.

MARTIN, H. B. *Fifty Years of American Golf.* London, 1966.

WILLIAMS, LENA. "Renee Powell on Tour." *Black Sports* (July 1973): 43–45.

YOUNG, A. S. *Negro Firsts in Sports.* Chicago, 1963.

LAWRENCE J. LONDINO

Gordon, Dexter Keith (February 27, 1923–April 25, 1990), jazz tenor saxophonist. Dexter Gordon was born in Los Angeles and began his musical training on the clarinet at the age of thirteen. When he was fifteen, he began study on alto saxophone with Lloyd Reese, a member of the Les Hite Orchestra. He switched to tenor saxophone two years later, when he began touring with Lionel HAMPTON and his orchestra. Gordon recorded with Hampton in 1941, and in late 1943 he recorded under his own name with a group that included Nat "King" COLE and

Harry "Sweets" Edison. Other recordings from the early 1940s included broadcast performances made in Los Angeles and New York with Fletcher HENDERSON and Louis ARMSTRONG.

Gordon came to prominence between 1944 and 1946, when he was with the Billy ECKSTINE Orchestra, an organization that from time to time included other leading jazz artists of the bebop movement. Gordon recorded his first solo, "Blowing the Blues Away," while with the group. He was one of the first tenor saxophonists to play bebop, but his later style incorporated the modal styles of the post-bop era as well. He continued to play both in New York and on the West Coast during the late 1940s and early 1950s, leading his own groups and recording with artists such as Wardell Gray, with whom he staged friendly tenor-saxophone duels.

Due to problems with drug addiction, the 1950s were a period of limited productivity for Gordon. He released a small number of recordings and was imprisoned on drug-possession charges in 1952. In the

After his early success as a bebop tenor saxophonist in Los Angeles in the 1940s, Dexter Gordon moved to Europe. Upon his return to the United States in the mid-1970s, his American career underwent a revival, which culminated in his portrayal of an expatriate jazz musician in *'Round Midnight* in 1986. (© Leandre Jackson)

1960s he moved to Europe, where he remained for fifteen years, first in Paris and later in Copenhagen. There he made a number of memorable recordings for the Blue Note label with Bud POWELL, Kenny Drew, and Johnny Griffin. In 1976, Gordon returned to the United States and confirmed his status as one of the most important tenor saxophonists in jazz history. He was elected to the Jazz Hall of Fame in 1980 and named *Down Beat*'s Musician of the Year in 1978 and 1980. He starred in the 1986 film *'Round Midnight,* about an expatriate jazz musician in Paris, a role, based loosely on his own life, that earned him an Academy Award nomination for best actor. Gordon had a profound influence on subsequent tenor saxophonists, including Johnny Griffin, John COLTRANE, and Sonny ROLLINS.

REFERENCE

BRITT, STAN. *Long Tall Dexter: A Critical Musical Biography of Dexter Gordon.* London, 1989.

GUTHRIE P. RAMSEY, JR.

Gordon, Odetta Holmes Felious. *See* Odetta.

Gordy, Berry, Jr. (November 28, 1929–), music executive. Born in Detroit, Berry Gordy, Jr., the third in his family to carry that name, was attracted to music as a child, winning a talent contest with his song "Berry's Boogie." He also took up boxing, often training with his friend, Jackie Wilson. Gordy quit high school to turn professional; however, he soon gave up that career at the urging of his mother. After spending 1951 to 1953 in the Army, Gordy married Thelma Louise Coleman and began to work in the Gordy family printing and construction business.

In 1953 Gordy opened a JAZZ record store in Detroit. However, since RHYTHM AND BLUES records were more in demand, the business closed after only two years. Gordy then began working at a Ford Motor Co. assembly line, writing and publishing pop songs on the side, including "Money, That's What I Want" (1959). During this time Gordy, who had separated from his wife, wrote some of Jackie Wilson's biggest hits, including "Lonely Teardrops" (1958), "That Is Why I Love You So" (1959), and "I'll Be Satisfied" (1959). He also sang with his new wife, Raynoma Liles, whom he had married in 1959,

Motown Records founder and longtime president Berry Gordy after his 1988 induction into the Rock and Roll Hall of Fame. (AP/Wide World Photos)

on a number of records by the Detroit singer Marv Johnson. In the late 1950s Gordy met and worked with Smokey ROBINSON and the Matadors, who at Gordy's suggestion became the Miracles. Gordy recorded them on their first record, "Got a Job" (1958).

During this period Gordy became increasingly dissatisfied with leasing his recordings to larger record companies, who often would take over distribution. At the urging of Robinson, Gordy borrowed $800 and founded Tamla Records and Gordy Records, the first companies in what would become the Motown empire. He released "Way Over There" (1959) and "Shop Around" (1961) by the Miracles. Gordy began hiring friends and family members to work for him, and he began to attract young unknown singers, including Diana ROSS, Marvin GAYE, Mary WELLS, and Stevie WONDER. The songwriting team of Eddie Holland, his brother Brian, and Lamont

Dozier began to write songs for Gordy, who had formed a base of operations at 2648 Grand Boulevard in Detroit. From that address Gordy also formed the publishing and management companies that would constitute the larger enterprise known more generally as Motown. Over the next ten years, Motown, with Gordy as chief executive and chief shareholder, and often producer and songwriter as well, produced dozens of pop and rhythm-and-blues hits that dominated the new style known as soul music.

In the mid-1960s Gordy began to distance himself from the company's day-to-day music operations, spending more and more time in Los Angeles, where he was growing interested in the film and television industries. He divorced Raynoma in 1964, and married Margaret Norton, whom he also later divorced. (Gordy again married in 1990, but that marriage, to Grace Eton, ended in divorce three years later.)

In the late 1960s, many Motown performers, writers, and producers complained about Gordy's paternalistic and heavy-handed management of their finances. Some of them—including the Jackson 5, Holland-Dozier-Holland, and the Temptations—left the company, claiming that Gordy had misled and mistreated them. By this time he was also quite wealthy, living in a Los Angeles mansion that contained a portrait of himself dressed as Napoleon Bonaparte. He resigned as president of the Motown Records subsidiary in 1973 in order to assume the chair of Motown Industries, a new parent corporation. The following year he completed what had been a gradual move of Motown to Los Angeles and produced several successful television specials. His film ventures—including the Diana Ross vehicles *Lady Sings the Blues* (1973), *Mahogany* (1975), and *The Wiz* (1978)—were not as successful.

Despite the departure of its core personnel over the years, the company Gordy presided over in the 1980s remained successful, with more than $100 million in annual sales in 1983, making it the largest black-owned company in the United States. In 1984 Gordy allowed MCA to begin distributing Motown's records, and the company bought Motown in 1988 for $61 million. Gordy kept control of Gordy Industries, Motown's music publishing, film, and television subsidiaries. His net worth in 1986, as estimated by *Forbes,* was more than $180 million, making him one of the wealthiest people in the United States. In the late 1980s and '90s Gordy branched out into other fields, including sports management and the ownership and training of racehorses.

Although Gordy, who was inducted into the Rock and Roll Hall of Fame in 1988, began his career as a successful songwriter and producer, his greatest achievement was selling soul music to white pop audiences, thus helping to shape America's youth into a single, huge, multiracial audience.

REFERENCES

GEORGE, NELSON. *Where Did Our Love Go? The Rise and Fall of the Motown Sound.* New York, 1985.
WALLER, DON. *The Motown Story.* New York, 1985.

JONATHAN GILL

Goreleigh, Rex (September 2, 1902–October 28, 1986), painter. Rex Goreleigh was born in Penllyn, Pa. He became interested in art at an early age because images helped him communicate and overcome shyness, which resulted from a childhood speech impediment. When Goreleigh was fifteen, his mother died, and he left Penllyn for Philadelphia. In 1918, Goreleigh went to live in Washington, D.C., where he attended Dunbar High School for two years. At the age of eighteen, Goreleigh moved to New York City, where he saw his first display of African-American art at the Harmon Foundation exhibition at International House. The show inspired him to take drawing lessons while he worked as a waiter. In 1933, after waiting on the table of Mexican muralist Diego Rivera, Goreleigh was invited to watch Rivera work on the murals he was mounting at Rockefeller Center. Goreleigh claimed that Rivera put him "on the road to becoming an artist."

In 1934, Goreleigh applied for work with the WORKS PROJECT ADMINISTRATION (WPA) in New York, where he worked for a short time as a muralist with Ben Shahn. From 1935 to 1936 Goreleigh traveled and studied art in Europe. When he returned to New York, Goreleigh taught painting for the Federal Art Project at the Utopia Neighborhood Settlement House, and by the end of 1936 Goreleigh was teaching art at the Harlem branch of the YOUNG MEN'S CHRISTIAN ASSOCIATION (YMCA) where he remained through 1937.

In the late 1930s the Art Project of the WPA assigned Goreleigh and African-American artist Norman LEWIS the job of establishing an art center for African Americans in Greensboro, N.C. When his contract at the art center expired, Goreleigh remained in the town and married a local librarian. The couple moved to Chicago in 1940, where Goreleigh attended classes at the University of Chicago and worked as an art coordinator for the Schreiner-Bennet advertising agency. From 1944 to 1947, Goreleigh directed the Chicago Southside Community Art Center.

Throughout a long career as a painter and printmaker, Rex Goreleigh often depicted images of proud black women and men, as in this untitled 1975 silkscreen. (The Studio Museum in Harlem)

In the late 1940s, Goreleigh moved to Princeton, N.J., where he worked as an artist and art teacher until his death in 1986. From 1947 to 1953, he directed Princeton Group Arts, a community arts center that provided art lessons and organized concerts, lectures, and exhibits. In 1955, he opened his Studio-on-the-Canal art school, which served adults and children in Princeton into the 1970s.

Goreleigh's paintings are representational, and he utilizes an exceptionally vibrant palette. His best-known paintings, such as *Dean's Alley* (1938) and *Tomato Pickers* (1962), depict the everyday life of migrant workers. He also has created religious paintings (*Misery,* 1940), landscapes (*Quaker Bridge Road,* 1967), and still lifes (*Sunflower,* 1967).

Goreleigh's work has been exhibited at the Art Museum in Raleigh, N.C. (1940); South Side Community Art Center, Chicago (1940); Pyramid Club, Philadelphia (1942, 1948, 1949); Trenton Trust Company, Trenton (1965); Trenton State College (1975); Boston Museum (1976); Studio Museum in Harlem (1976); and Gallery 100, Princeton (1977). In 1979, his paintings were featured in a retrospective at Montclair State College in New Jersey.

REFERENCES

FAX, ELTON. *Seventeen Black Artists.* New York, 1971.

McELROY, GUY C., RICHARD J. POWELL, and SHARON F. PATTON. *African-American Artists 1880–1987: Selections from the Evans-Tibbs Collection.* Seattle, Wash., 1989.

WILLIS, JOHN RALPH. *Fragments of American Life: An Exhibition of Paintings.* Princeton, N.J., 1976.

JANE LUSAKA

Gospel Music. The African-American religious music known as gospel, originating in the field hollers, slave songs, spirituals, and Protestant hymns sung on southern plantations, and later at camp meetings and churches, has come to dominate not only music in black churches, but singing and instrumental styles across the spectrum of American popular music, including jazz, blues, rhythm and blues, soul, and country. Exemplified in songs such as "Take My Hand, Precious Lord" and "Move On Up a Little Higher," gospel music encourages emotional and jubilant improvisation on songs of thanksgiving and praise as well as sorrow and suffering.

Musically, gospel is distinguished by its vocal style, which in both male and female singers is characterized by a strained, full-throated sound, often pushed to guttural shrieks and rasps suited to the extremes of the emotion-laden lyrics. Melodies and harmonies are generally simple, allowing for spontaneity in devising repetitive, expressive fills and riffs. The syncopated rhythms of gospel are typically spare, with heavy, often hand-clapped accents.

The Founding Years

Although the roots of gospel can be traced to Africa, and the earliest arrival of Africans in the New World, the main antecedent was the "Dr. Watts" style of singing hymns, named for British poet and hymnist Isaac Watts (1674–1748), who emphasized a call-and-response approach to religious songs, with mournful but powerful rhythms. Thus, in the nineteenth century, African-American hymnody in mainstream denominations did not differ considerably from music performed in white churches. The earliest African-American religious denominations date back to the late eighteenth century, when black congregations split off from white church organizations in Philadelphia. In 1801 the minister Richard ALLEN, who later founded the AFRICAN METHODIST EPISCOPAL (AME) denomination, published two collections of hymns designed for use in black churches. These collections were the forerunners of similar collections that formed the basis for the music performed in most nineteenth-century black churches, yet they were quite similar to the slow-tempo, restrained white Protestant hymnody. Around the middle of the nineteenth century a new type of music known as "gospel hymns" or "gospel songs" was being composed in a new style, lighter and more songlike than traditional hymnody, written by white composers such as Dwight Moody (1837–1899), Ira Sankey (1840–1908), Philip Paul Bliss (1838–1876), Robert Lowry (1826–1899), and William Batchelder Bradbury (1816–1868).

Another important nineteenth-century influence on gospel music was the idea, increasingly popular at a minority of nineteenth-century black churches, that spiritual progress required a deeper and more directly emotional relationship with God, often through the singing of white "gospel hymns," although gospel as an African-American form would not take that name for decades. These congregations, often led by charismatic ministers, began searching for a religion based on "Holiness or Hell" and were early participants in the Latter Rain movement, which sought to "irrigate the dry bones" of the church. The first congregation known to accept this doctrine, based on the activities of the Day of Pentecost (though, confusingly, this is *not* what is now called Pentecostalism) was the United Holy Church of Concord, S.C., which held its first meeting in 1886 and had its first convention in 1894 under the leadership of Brother L. M. Mason (1861–1930). Another early congregation to accept that doctrine and encourage early forms of gospel music was the Church of the Living God, in Wrightsville, Ark., under the leadership of William Christian (1856–1928) in 1889.

The Holiness doctrine proved controversial within black churches, as did the music associated with Holiness. In 1895 Charles Harrison MASON and Charles Price JONES were forced from the Baptist church, and together they proceeded to organize the CHURCH OF GOD IN CHRIST in Lexington, Miss., where the music was heavily influenced by the performance style at Los Angeles's Azusa Street Revival, a black congregation that marked the beginning of PENTECOSTALISM, under the leadership of William Joseph SEYMOUR. The Azusa Street Revival featured highly charged services involving "speaking in tongues" as a manifestation of the Holy Ghost. Such activities were eventually integrated into the mainstream of black church activity, but around the turn of the century, Holiness-style services, and even the singing of spirituals, were strenuously opposed by conservative black church elders who had fought to "elevate" the musical standards of their congregations. Jones, for example, was opposed to the Azusa Street style, and eventually split from Mason to organize the Church of Christ, Holiness.

Early forms of gospel music such as sung or chanted testimonials and sermons were used to complement prayers in Holiness churches. Drawing on the call-and-response tradition that dated back to slavery times, members of a congregation would take inspiration from a phrase from the sermon or testimony and out of it spontaneously compose a simple melody and text. A chorus of congregants would repeat the original phrase, while the leader interpolated brief extemporized choruses. For example, in Charles Harrison Mason's 1908 "I'm a Soldier," the leader and congregation begin by alternating the following lines: "I'm a soldier/In the army of the Lord/I'm a soldier/In the army." Succeeding choruses differ only in the lead line, with the leader interpolating such phrases as "I'm fighting for my life," "I'm a sanctified soldier," or "I'll live and I'll die," and the congregation repeating "In the army" as a refrain. The length of such songs often stretched to fifteen minutes or more. Along with simple "homemade" harmonies came hand-clapping, foot-stomping, and holy dancing, also known as "shouting."

Holiness, Sanctified, and Pentecostal congregations sprang up rapidly all over the South, particularly in rural, poor communities, starting around the turn of the century, and in less than a decade gospel music, then known as church music, was being sung in Baptist and Methodist congregations as well. During this time the most popular gospel hymns were by a new generation of black composers, including William Henry Sherwood; Jones, who composed "Where Shall I Be? and "I'm Happy with Jesus Alone"; Mason, who in addition to "I'm a Soldier" wrote "My Soul Loves Jesus" and the chant "Yes, Lord"; and Charles Albert TINDLEY, who composed "What Are They Doing in Heaven," "Stand by Me," and "I'll Overcome Someday," which was the forerunner of the civil rights anthem "We Shall Overcome." Since at this time there were no publishing houses for black gospel, these composers began to establish their own. They also depended on recordings and traveling preachers to spread their music. Preachers who popularized their own songs included J. C. Burnett ("Drive and Go Forward," 1926), Ford Washington McGhee ("Lion of the Tribe of Judah," 1927), J. M. Gates ("Death's Black Train Is Coming," 1926), and A. W. Nix ("The Black Diamond Express to Hell," 1927).

The Birth of Gospel Music

The 1920s were a crucial time in the development of gospel music. In 1921 the National Baptist Convention, USA, the largest organization of black Christians in the world, not only formally recognized gospel as a legitimate sacred musical form but published a collection of hymns, spirituals, and gospel songs under the title *Gospel Pearls,* edited by Willa A. Townsend (1885–1963). That hymnal contained six songs by Tindley, the first gospel composer successfully to combine the conventions of white evangelical music with the simple, often sentimental melodies of black spirituals. The 1921 convention also marked the emergence of the composer Thomas A. DORSEY (1899–1993), who would go on to become the Father of Gospel because of his indefatigable songwriting, publishing, organizing, and teaching. Three years later the National Baptist Convention published the *Baptist Standard Hymnal,* another important step toward bringing gospel into the mainstream of African-American church worship. Other important gospel composers who came to prominence during this time were Lucie Campbell (1885–1963) and William Herbert Brewster (1897–1987).

Despite the publication of these hymnals and the dissemination of individual songs in both print and by record, it was by word of mouth that gospel spread, particularly in working-class communities in the rural South. In Jefferson County, Ala., workers in coal mines and factories used their lunch hours to organize quartets to sing this new type of religious song. In some respects these groups were inspired by the tradition of the secular FISK JUBILEE and Tuskegee vocal quartets, but the new groups emphasized the powerful emotional experiences of conversion and salvation. One of the first such groups, the Foster Singers, organized in 1916, stressed equality between the vocal parts. However, it was a Foster Singers spinoff group, the Birmingham Jubilee Singers, led by one of the members of the Foster Singers, that inspired GOSPEL QUARTETS that soon started all over the South. The Birmingham Jubilee Singers allowed the bass and tenor more prominence and freedom, raised tempos, and used more adventurous harmonies, including "blue" notes. The vocal quartets organized in this style in the 1920s include the Fairfield Four (1921), which as of 1992 still included one of its original members, the Rev. Samuel McCrary; the Blue Jay Singers (1926); the Harmonizing Four (1927); and the Dixie Hummingbirds (1928). In the 1930s, new quartets included the Golden Gate Quartet (1934), which went on to become the most popular group of the 1930s and '40s, and the Soul Stirrers (1936). The following year, Rebert H. Harris (b. 1916) joined the groups, and over the next fourteen years he became their most famous singer. In 1938 Claude Jeter Harris (b. 1914) organized the Four Harmony Kings, who later changed their name to the Swan Silvertones to acknowledge their sponsorship by a bakery.

By the 1930s, gospel music had been firmly planted in northern cities. This was due not only to the Great Migration of rural blacks following World War I but also to the fact that, increasingly, record companies and publishing houses were located in northern cities, and particularly in Chicago, then the focal point for gospel music. Thomas Andrew Dorsey opened his publishing house in 1932, the same year he composed "Take My Hand, Precious Lord" (popularly known as "Precious Lord, Take My Hand"). Through composing, publishing, organizing, and teaching gospel choirs, Dorsey was given the sobriquet Father of Gospel.

Starting in the 1920s, gospel music was taken up by many different types of ensembles, in addition to vocal quartets. In urban areas, blind singers often came to prominence by performing on street corners and in churches. One of the most important of these was Connie Rosemond, for whom Lucie Campbell composed "Something Within Me." Others were Mamie Forehand and the guitarists and singers Blind Joe Taggard and Blind Willie Johnson. The blind Texan singer Arizona DRANES accompanied herself on piano and is credited with introducing that instrument to recorded gospel music. Among the gospel singers who sang with piano accompaniment as early as the 1920s were Willie Mae Ford SMITH, Sallie MARTIN, Clara Hudmon (1900–1960), Madame Ernestine B. Washington (1914–1983), and guitarist and singer Sister Rosetta THARPE, the first important performer to find a large audience outside the gospel circuit. Male-accompanied singers included Brother Joe May (1912–1973) and J. Robert Bradley (b. 1921). The greatest of the accompanied singers was Mahalia JACKSON, who was born in New Orleans and found her calling in Chicago at age sixteen. Her 1947 recording of "Move On Up a Little Higher," by Herbert Brewster, featuring her soaring contralto, came to define the female gospel style.

In the late 1930s, accompanied gospel ensembles consisting of four to six women, four or five men, or a mixed group of four to six singers, became popular. Clara Ward (1924–1973) organized the earliest notable accompanied ensemble, the Ward Singers, in 1934. The year before, Roberta MARTIN had joined with composer Theodore Frye (1899–1963) to form the Martin-Frye Quartet, later known as the Roberta Martin Singers. Sallie Martin organized the Sallie Martin Singers in 1940. Three years later the Original Gospel Harmonettes were formed, with pianist Evelyn Stark. They later came to prominence when singer Dorothy Love Coates joined the group and introduced "hard" gospel techniques, such as singing beyond her range and straining the voice for dramatic effects. Other accompanied ensembles included the Angelic Gospel Singers and the Davis Sisters, with pianist Curtis Dublin.

During this time vocal quartets and quintets continued to be popular. Archie Brownlee (1925–1960) organized the Five Blind Boys of Mississippi in 1939, the same year that Johnny L. Fields (b. 1927) formed the Five Blind Boys of Alabama, featuring Clarence Fountain (b. 1929). James Woodie Alexander (b. 1916) began leading the Pilgrim Travelers in 1946.

In the years between the wars, women, who from the start had been pillars of African-American religious institutions, became increasingly involved as publishers and organizers. In 1932, Dorsey, Sallie Martin, and Willie Mae Ford Smith formed the National Convention of Gospel Choirs and Choruses. Roberta Martin, the composer of "God Is Still on the Throne," opened her own publishing house in 1939. Sallie Martin opened hers along with Kenneth Martin (1917–1989), the composer of "Yes, God Is Real," in 1940.

The Golden Age

By 1945, gospel was becoming recognized not only as a spiritual experience but also as a form of entertainment, and this became known as gospel's golden era. Singers, appearing on stage in attractive uniforms, had established and refined a popular and recognizable vocal sound. Gospel pianists such as Mildred Falls (1915–1975), Herbert Pickard, Mildred Gay, Edgar O'Neal, James Herndon, and James Washington and organists such as Little Lucy Smith, Gerald Spraggins, Louise Overall Weaver, and Herbert "Blind" Francis were working in exciting styles derived from ragtime, barrelhouse, and the blues, with chordal voicing, riffs, and complicated rhythms. Finally a group of composers including Doris Akers (b. 1923), Sammy Lewis, and Lucy Smith could be depended on to come up with fresh material. Just as early gospel composers relied on traveling from church to church to popularize their songs, so too did the first early popular gospel singers find it necessary to go on the road. Sister Rosetta Tharpe performed at nightclubs and dance halls, but far more typical was the experience of Mahalia Jackson, who by 1945 had quit her regular job and joined a growing number of traveling professional gospel singers performing in churches and schools, moving on to auditoriums and stadiums. These singers were able to support themselves, and some, like Jackson, were quite successful, especially in the context of touring companies.

After the war the recording industry and radio played a large part in popularizing gospel. At first, small companies such as King, Atlantic, Vee-Jay, Dot, Nashboro, and Peacock were the most active in seeking out gospel singers. Apollo Records recorded Jackson and Roberta Martin before they moved to larger labels. The Ward Sisters, the Angelic Gospel Singers, and the Davis Sisters first recorded for Gotham Records. The Original Gospel Harmonettes recorded first for RCA Victor. With the proliferation of recordings, gospel radio programs became popular. In New York, the gospel disk jockey Joe Bostic was extraordinarily successful, as were Mary Manson in Philadelphia, Irene Joseph Ware in Chicago, Mary Dee in Baltimore, Goldie Thompson in Tampa, and John "Honeyboy" Hardy in New Orleans. Other cities with gospel shows in the postwar years included Atlanta, Los Angeles, Louisville, and Miami.

Among the more prominent performers and leaders who emerged during gospel's postwar golden era were Madame Edna Gallmon Cooke (1918–1967), Julius "June" Cheeks (1928–1981), who joined the Sensationales in 1946, "Professor" Alex Bradford (1927–1978), Robert Anderson (b. 1919), and Albertina Walker (b. 1930), who in 1952 formed the Caravans. Among the members of the Caravans were Shirley CAESAR and Inez Andrews (b. 1928), who had a hit record with "Mary, Don't You Weep." Marion WILLIAMS left the Ward Singers in 1958 to form the Stars of Faith. Willie Joe Ligon (b. 1942) organized the Mighty Clouds of Joy in 1959. Perhaps the best-known singer to emerge from the golden era was Sam COOKE, who joined the Soul Stirrers in 1950 and revitalized the male gospel quartet movement with his hits "Nearer to Thee" and "Touch the Hem of His Garment" before going on to fame as a popular singer starting in 1956.

The most significant figure from this time was the Rev. James CLEVELAND, who began singing in Dorsey's children's choir at the age of eight. By the age of sixteen, Cleveland had composed his first hit for the Roberta Martin Singers. He accompanied the Caravans, formed his own group, and in 1963 began recording with the Angelic Choir of Nutley, N.J. Cleveland's recordings were so successful that they sparked a new phase in gospel music dominated by gospel choirs. Prominent choirs following Cleveland's lead included those led by Thurston Frazier, Mattie Moss Clark (b. 1928), and Jessy Dixon (b. 1938).

By the end of the 1950s, gospel was becoming ubiquitous, not only in black communities but as a part of mainstream American culture. Mahalia Jackson recorded "Come Sunday" as part of Duke Ellington's *Black, Brown and Beige* in 1958 and the next year appeared in the film *Imitation of Life*. Langston Hughes, who in 1956 wrote *Tambourines to Glory: A Play with Spirituals, Jubilees, and Gospel Songs,* wrote the gospel-song play *Black Nativity* in 1961, for a cast that included Marion Williams and Alex Bradford. In 1961, a gospel category was added to the Grammy awards, with Mahalia Jackson the first winner. During the 1960s, costumed groups and choirs began to appear on Broadway, at Carnegie Hall, and in Las Vegas, as well as on television shows. In addition to

Sam Cooke, many singers trained in the gospel tradition helped popularize gospel-style delivery in popular music. Rhythm-and-blues doo-wop groups from the late 1940s and 1950s, such as the Ravens, the Orioles, and the Drifters, used close harmonies and a high-crooning-male-lead style borrowed from gospel. Singers such as Dinah WASHINGTON, Ray CHARLES, Al GREEN, Aretha FRANKLIN, James BROWN, LITTLE RICHARD, and Stevie WONDER used gospel techniques to cross over to enormous international popularity on the rock, soul, and rhythm-and-blues charts.

Gospel music was a crucial part of the civil rights movement. There had been a political thrust in sacred black music since the abolitionist hymnody of the nineteenth-century, and in the 1960s musicians such as Mahalia Jackson, Fannie Lou HAMER, Guy Carawan, the Montgomery Trio, the Nashville Quartet, the CORE Freedom Singers, the SNCC Freedom Singers, and Carlton Reese's Gospel Freedom Choir appeared at marches, rallies, and meetings. Gospel musicians had always reworked traditional material at will, and in the 1960s gospel songs and spirituals originally intended for religious purposes were changed to apply to secular struggles. For example, "If You Miss Me from Praying Down Here" became "If You Miss Me from the Back of the Bus." Other popular songs were "We Shall Overcome," "This Little Light of Mine," "We'll Never Turn Back," "Eyes on the Prize," "Ninety-Nine and a Half Won't Do," "O Freedom," and "Ain't Nobody Gonna Turn Me Around." For many leaders of the civil rights movement, such as Hamer, the Rev. Dr. Martin Luther King, Jr., and the Rev. Wyatt Tee Walker, gospel music was an essential part of their organizing work. "Precious Lord" was a favorite of Martin Luther King, Jr., and Mahalia Jackson sang the song at his funeral.

The Contemporary Sound and Beyond

The next phase in the history of gospel music came in 1969, when Edwin HAWKINS released his rendition of "Oh Happy Day," a white nineteenth-century hymn, in which he eschewed the gritty timbres of Cleveland in favor of smooth pop vocals, soul harmonies, and jazz rhythms, including a conga drum. The song, which became the number one song on Billboard's pop chart, represented a fusion of the traditional gospel style of Mahalia Jackson, Thomas Andrew Dorsey, and the Dixie Hummingbirds, with elements of jazz, rhythm and blues, and soul. Record producers, inspired by the crossover potential of what became known as contemporary gospel, began encouraging gospel groups toward a more contemporary sound, igniting a long-running controversy within the gospel community.

After Hawkins, one of the principal figures of contemporary gospel throughout the 1970s was the composer and pianist Andrae CROUCH, the cousin of critic Stanley Crouch. Also important were Myrna Summers, Danniebell Hall, Douglas Miller, Bebe and Cece Winans, the Clark Sisters, and the ensemble Commissioned. At the same time, gospel came to Broadway again in the widely acclaimed musical *Your Arms Too Short to Box with God* (1976).

In 1983 *The Gospel at Colonus* was a popular stage production in New York, and in the 1980s and '90s gospel, particularly contemporary, has continued to attract large audiences. The unaccompanied vocal sextet Take 6 combined gospel-style harmonies with mainstream jazz rhythms to achieve huge popular success in the late 1980s. Other popular contemporary singers from this time included Richard Smallwood, who uses classical elements in his songs, Bobby Jones, Keith Pringle, and Daryl Coley. Walter Hawkins (b. 1949), the brother of Edwin Hawkins, combines elements of traditional and contemporary styles, especially on recordings with his wife, Tremaine (b. 1957). The Hawkins style was taken up by the Thompson Community Choir, the Charles Fold Singers, the Barrett Sisters, and the Rev. James Moore, as well as mass choirs in Florida, New Jersey, and Mississippi. The choral ensemble Sounds of Blackness has been popular in recent years, as have contemporary vocal quartets such as the Williams Brothers, the Jackson Southernaires, and the Pilgrim Jubilees. These groups often use synthesizers and drum machines in addition to traditional gospel instruments. Prominent contemporary gospel composers include Elbernita Clark, Jeffrey LeValle, Andrae Woods, and Rance Allen.

Gospel-style singing, at least until the advent of rap music, dominated African-American popular music. One indication of the importance of gospel to the music industry is the fact that as of 1993 there were six Grammy categories devoted to gospel music. Gospel, which started out as a marginal, almost blasphemous form of musical worship, now has a central place in African-American church activity. Not only Holiness and Pentecostal churches but Baptist and Methodist denominations have fully accepted gospel music. Its striking emotional power has enabled gospel music to remain a vital part of African-American culture.

REFERENCES

BOYER, HORACE CLARENCE. "A Comparative Analysis of Traditional and Contemporary Gospel Music." In Irene W. Jackson, ed. *More Than Dancing: Essays on Afro-American Music and Musicians.* Westport, Conn. 1985.

BURNIM, MELLONEE V. "Gospel Music Tradition: A Complex of Ideology, Aesthetic and Behavior." In Irene W. Jackson, ed. *More Than Dancing: Essays on Afro-American Music and Musicians.* Westport, Conn., 1985.

HARRIS, MICHAEL W. *The Rise of Gospel Blues: The Music of Thomas Andrew Dorsey in the Urban Church.* New York, 1992.

HEILBUT, ANTHONY. *The Gospel Sound: Good News and Bad Times.* New York, 1971. Revised, 1985.

LOVELL, JOHN, JR. *Black Song: The Forge and the Flame: The Story of How the Afro-American Spiritual Was Hammered Out.* New York, 1972.

MAULTSBY, PORTIA K. *Afro-American Religious Music: A Study in Musical Diversity.* Springfield, Ohio, 1986.

REAGON, BERNICE JOHNSON, ed. *We'll Understand It Better By and By.* Washington, D.C., 1992.

RICKS, GEORGE R. *Some Aspects of the Religious Music of the U.S. Negro: An Ethnomusicological Study with Special Emphasis on the Gospel Tradition.* New York, 1977.

WALKER, WYATT TEE. *"Somebody's Calling My Name": Black Sacred Music and Social Change.* Valley Forge, Pa., 1979.

HORACE CLARENCE BOYER

Gospel Quartets. Four-part-harmony singing, usually performed in a religious setting, forms the foundation for gospel quartets. This genre developed in the rural South during Reconstruction and emerged from three principal sources: college jubilee singing groups, minstrel shows, and shape-note singing. By 1900, there were hundreds of community-based and church-related quartets performing an eclectic mixture of early folk spirituals, such as "Roll, Jordan, Roll," and newly penned gospel hymns. In 1902 the Dinwiddie Colored Quartette, of Virginia, became the first group to appear on record.

The early twentieth-century quartets became part of everyday African-American life, singing not only at church services but for picnics, at parties, and even during lunch hours at work. Companies and trade unions sustained quartets that sometimes performed at official functions. For example, the Norfolk & Western Railroad sponsored its own group, the N & W Quartet. These groups almost always performed a cappella. The lack of musical accompaniment encouraged the quartets to work out arrangements unencumbered by the inherent harmonic and rhythmic limitations of pianos, guitars, and other instruments.

Although this genre was ubiquitous throughout the South, by the 1920s several centers for quartet singing had emerged. Hampton Roads, Va. (Norfolk, Newport News, Virginia Beach, etc.), and Jefferson County, Ala. (Birmingham), arose as the two strongest areas for quartets. The recording of the Norfolk Jubilee/Jazz Quartet and the Birmingham Jubilee Singers sold well, though many other groups from these centers recorded during the 1920s and 1930s.

The commercial popularity of gospel quartets increased throughout the 1930s. Around the beginning of World War II, the Famous Blue Jay Singers of Birmingham were among the first quartets whose sound took its direction from the Holiness and Pentecostal churches with which they were closely associated. The most famous was the Golden Gate quartet, whose style was typified by close barbershop harmony.

Following the close of the war, interest in this music virtually exploded. From 1945 to 1960, "quartets," now most often accompanied by instruments (usually one or two guitars or piano, but sometimes a full rhythm section), often comprised five to seven members. To the barbershop harmonic background was added a lyric tenor or baritone lead singer who soloed in call-and-response manner with the vocal accompaniment. The most popular groups included the Soul Stirrers—whose lead singer, Robert H. Harris, introduced falsetto singing to the quartet style—the Dixie Hummingbirds, and the Swan Silverstones. The widespread acceptance of quartets peaked in the early 1950s, when hundreds of semiprofessional and professional groups went on the road. Many of them also took advantage of regularly scheduled fifteen-minute or half-hour radio broadcasts to solidify their popularity. Instead of performing in churches, professional quartets often sang at special "gospel programs" held in municipal auditoriums or other nonsacred venues.

After 1960, the gospel-quartet sound included loud vocal utterances—growls, screams—and more physical body movement, such as thigh slapping, to emphasize rhythmic accents. The Five Blind Boys of Alabama (led by Clarence Fountain), the Five Blind Boys of Mississippi (led by Archie Browntee), and the Sensational Nightingales (led by Julius "Jim" Cheeks) typified this style. The popularity of quartets eventually succumbed to the whims of commercial tastes and newly emerging trends in black religious music. Some of the more recognizable voices—those belonging to Sam COOKE and Lou RAWLS, for example—abandoned gospel for lucrative pop-music contracts. Larger ensembles, especially choirs like the one led by Rev. James CLEVELAND, and soloists such as Brother Joe May and Mahalia JACKSON stole some of the thunder from gospel quartets. Today, there are relatively few quartets still singing in the older styles.

REFERENCES

HEILBUT, ANTHONY. *The Gospel Sound: Good News and Bad Times.* 1971. Reprint. New York, 1985.
LORNELL, KIP. *"Happy in the Service of the Lord": Black American Gospel Quartets in Memphis.* Urbana, Ill., 1988.

KIP LORNELL

Gossett, Louis, Jr. (May 27, 1936–), actor. Louis Gossett, Jr., was born in Brooklyn, N.Y., the son of Louis, Sr., a porter, and Hattie Gossett, a maid. He was raised in Bath Beach, an ethnically mixed neighborhood of Jewish, Italian, and African-American residents.

In high school, Gossett was encouraged by his English teacher to pursue acting. In 1953, he captured a role in the Broadway play *Take a Giant Step* and won the Donaldson Award as best newcomer of the year

Lou Gossett, Jr., received the Academy Award for Best Supporting Actor for his performance in the 1982 film *An Officer and a Gentleman.* (AP/Wide World Photos)

for his performance. He helped support the family with his earnings from acting, allowing his mother to give up her work as a maid.

From 1956 to 1958, Gossett attended New York University on an athletic and drama scholarship. Though invited to try out for the New York Knickerbocker basketball team, he instead chose to accept the part of George Murchison in the 1959 Broadway premiere of *A Raisin in the Sun,* a role he assumed in the film version in 1961.

Gossett's most important roles include "Fiddler" in the television miniseries *Roots* (1977) and Sergeant Foley in the film *An Officer and a Gentleman* (1982), a part which was not written expressly for a black actor. When he received an Academy Award for best supporting actor for his portrayal of Sergeant Foley, he became only the third black actor ever to be so honored, after Sidney POITIER and Hattie MCDANIEL.

Gossett has starred in two short-lived television series, *The Powers of Matthew Star* (1982) and *Gidion Oliver* (1989). In the 1980s and early 1990s, Gossett played a hard-nosed military officer, modeled on the Sergeant Foley character, in the films *Iron Eagles* (1986), *Iron Eagles II* (1988), and *Aces: Iron Eagles III* (1992). In 1992 Gossett starred as an out-of-shape boxer who revives his career in the film *Diggstown.*

REFERENCE

BOGLE, DONALD. *Blacks in American Film and Television: An Illustrated Encyclopedia.* Westport, Conn., 1988.

ELIZABETH V. FOLEY

Grace, Charles Emmanuel "Sweet Daddy" (January 25, 1881–January 12, 1960), religious leader. Bishop Grace, better known as Sweet Daddy, was born Marceline Manoël de Graça in the Cape Verde Islands of mixed African and Portuguese descent. Around 1908 he immigrated to New Bedford, Mass., where he engaged in several occupations, including cranberry picking, before a journey to the Holy Land inspired him to found a church in West Waltham, Mass., around 1919. In religious revivals in Charlotte, N.C., in the mid-1920s, Daddy Grace gathered several thousand followers and in 1926 incorporated in the District of Columbia the United House of Prayer for All People of the Church on the Rock of the Apostolic Faith.

A flamboyant and charismatic leader, Grace wore his hair and fingernails long, the latter painted red, white, and blue. He baptized converts with fire hoses and sold his followers specially blessed products, such as soap, coffee, eggs, and ice cream. He specialized in

"Daddy Grace and Children," by photographer James VanDerZee, 1938. (Courtesy Donna VanDerZee)

acquiring expensive real estate, particularly mansions and hotels, but he also supported church members with housing, pension funds, and burial plans. At his death in Los Angeles in 1960, there was an estate of some $25 million, but it was unclear what was owned by the church and what was his personal estate. An Internal Revenue Service lien of $6 million in back taxes was settled for $2 million in 1961.

Sweet Daddy never overtly claimed the divinity his followers attributed to him. "I never said I was God," he once noted, "but you cannot prove to me I'm not." At Daddy's death in 1960, Bishop Walter T. McCullogh took over the House of Prayer following a successful lawsuit against rival James Walton.

REFERENCES

FAUSET, ARTHUR HUFF. *Black Gods of the Metropolis: Negro Religious Cults of the Urban North*. Philadelphia, 1944.

HALTER, MARILYN. *Between Race and Ethnicity: Cape Verdean American Immigrants, 1860–1965*. Urbana, Ill., 1993.

RICHARD NEWMAN

Gradual Emancipation Statutes. One of the most important by-products of the American Revolution for African Americans was the ending of SLAVERY in the North. At the beginning of the Revolution, slavery was legal in all thirteen colonies. By 1801 two of the newly independent states, Massachusetts and New Hampshire, had abolished slavery outright, while five others had adopted legislation to gradually end the institution. In *Commonwealth* v. *Jennison* (1783), Chief Justice William Cushing of Massachusetts charged a jury that a slave owner should be convicted for assault and false imprisonment of his own slave. Cushing based his charge on the Massachusetts constitution of 1780, which declared that all people in the state were born "free and equal." This clause and the *Jennison* case effectively ended slavery in Massachusetts. Slavery in New Hampshire, which was never very significant, faded away after the adoption of its 1784 constitution with a provision declaring all were "born equally free and independent."

The bulk of the slaves in the North lived south of Massachusetts. In 1780, Pennsylvania became the first state to take steps toward ending slavery through legislative action. The Pennsylvania gradual-emancipation statute of 1780 became the model for similar statutes adopted by Connecticut (1784), Rhode Island (1784), New York (1799), and New Jersey (1804).

In a startling preamble, Pennsylvania's lawmakers explained that the statute was a direct result of the Revolution. The legislators were adopting this statute after "contemplat[ing] our abhorrence of that condition, to which the arms and tyranny of Great-Britain were exerted to reduce us" and with "a serious and grateful sense of the manifold blessings" of freedom they had received "from the hand of that Being, from whom every good and perfect gift cometh." They "rejoice[d]" at the opportunity "to extend a portion of that freedom to others, which hath been extended to us, and release from that state of thraldom, to which we ourselves were tyrannically doomed."

The most important aspects of the law were its emancipatory provisions. Under the act, no slaves living in Pennsylvania gained their freedom. However, all children of slave women born after the passage of the law were free persons, though subject to an indenture until they turned twenty-eight.

As servants, the children of slave mothers had numerous rights their mothers lacked. Each of them was "entitled to relief" if "evilly treated by his or her master or mistress"; when they became free they were to be given "freedom dues," as white indentured servants got; and as free blacks (although subject to an indenture), they could testify against whites, including their masters, in trials. The statute implicitly obligated masters to prepare their servants for freedom by holding the masters financially liable if their servants became destitute after becoming completely free. A 1788 amendment to the law prohibited the removal from the state of any indentured free black; prohibited the removal of pregnant slaves, ensuring that their children could be born in a free state; and prohibited the separation of slave women from their slave husbands or their freeborn children.

These laws also had strict provisions, mandating that owners record the name, age, and sex of all slaves they held at the time the statute was adopted. Any slave not registered would be presumptively free. Pennsylvania courts often interpreted these provisions strictly. In one case a court freed a slave named Belinda because, while her master had properly registered her, he had neglected to indicate her sex.

Under the 1780 law, slaves brought into Pennsylvania became free after six months' residence. The only exception was for congressmen, senators, government officials, and diplomats. After 1788, slaves became free immediately if migrants intended to move to the state.

The other northern gradual-emancipation statutes contained provisions that were similar to those of Pennsylvania. The most important difference was in the number of years the children of slaves had to serve. Rhode Island freed male children at age 21 and females at 18; Connecticut freed both male and female children at 25; New York's age of freedom was 28 for men and 25 for women; New Jersey freed men at 25 and women at 21.

These laws led to a dramatic increase in the free black population and an equally dramatic decrease of slaves in the North. Pennsylvania, for example, had 3,737 slaves in 1790 and 6,537 free blacks. By 1810 there were only 795 slaves in the state and 22,492 free blacks. By 1840 only 64 slaves remained, while the free black population stood at 47,584. In the 1840s Pennsylvania, Rhode Island, Connecticut, and New Jersey freed all of their remaining slaves.

New York acted more quickly. It passed its gradual-abolition act in 1799. In 1800 there were 20,343 slaves in the state but only 10,347 free blacks. A decade later the slave population was down to just over 15,000, while the free black population was over 25,000. In 1817 New York declared that as of July 4, 1827, all slaves in the state would be free. The 1830 census found 75 slaves somehow living there, alongside 44,870 free blacks.

These acts were attempts to balance competing claims to liberty and property in the revolutionary era. Masters claimed that their slaves were property, which they were entitled to own. They viewed the slaves as an investment that would produce what today would be called a capital gain through the children of their slave women. Slave owners also argued that pregnant slaves and nursing mothers were less productive and that small children were a net financial loss to them. They, the slave owners, claimed that the children of slaves cost them money, which they could not recoup if the children of all slaves were free. Cynical slave owners might be disinclined to provide the necessary support for the children of their slaves if they could get no value from them. Moreover, they might also permanently remove their slaves from the state, thus depriving future generations of their freedom.

By allowing masters to use the children of slaves until they reached anywhere from age eighteen to twenty-eight, these laws granted masters some recompense for the cost of raising the children. In Pennsylvania, the twenty-eight years of servitude probably paid for most of the costs that a master laid out during that period.

The children of slaves, on the other hand, gained their freedom, and their own children were completely free. The result was that the northern states peacefully, and with relatively little social dislocation, ended slavery between the 1780s and the 1840s.

REFERENCES

FINKELMAN, PAUL. *An Imperfect Union: Slavery, Federalism, and Comity.* Chapel Hill, N.C., 1981.

———, ed. *Slavery in the North and West.* New York, 1989.

ZILVERSMIT, ARTHUR. *The First Emancipation: The Abolition of Slavery in the North.* Chicago, 1967.

PAUL FINKELMAN

Grandfather Clause.

Grandfather Clause. The grandfather clause was among the legal devices designed by southern legislatures to limit African-American suffrage following RECONSTRUCTION. Literacy and property tests were imposed on potential voters, except for those who had been entitled to vote before black enfranchisement as well as their sons and grandsons. The grandfather clause was thus technically an exemption written into laws restricting suffrage but an exemption that allowed virtually all whites to retain the vote and that effectively disfranchised almost all African Americans.

The Mississippi constitution of 1890 represented the first attempt to eliminate black voting, and by World War I almost all the ex-Confederate states had adopted some form of black disfranchisement legislation. These included poll taxes, literacy requirements, property holding requirements, the white primary, and an array of similar provisions designed to circumvent the Fifteenth Amendment to the U.S. Constitution, which prohibits states from limiting suffrage on the basis of race.

In 1898 Louisiana introduced the first grandfather clause, which stated that "no male person who was on January 1st 1867 or at any date prior thereto entitled to vote . . . and no son or grandson of any such person . . . shall be denied the right to register and vote in this state by reason of his failure to possess the educational or property qualifications." Variants of this approach were the fighting grandfather clause, which exempted descendants of veterans, or Mississippi's "understanding" clause, which exempted those who could verbally interpret the state constitution to the satisfaction of white registration officials.

The grandfather clauses' effects were temporary. Only current white voters were exempted, and all new voters had to meet the literacy test. In practice, literacy tests resulted in a substantial reduction in white as well as black voting, since few whites would publicly proclaim their illiteracy to take the exemption. In 1914, the U.S. Supreme Court found grandfather clauses unconstitutional, and the southern states shifted to other forms of disfranchisement legislation.

REFERENCES

KEY, V. O., JR. *Southern Politics in State and Nation.* New York, 1949.

KOUSSER, MORGAN. *The Shaping of Southern Politics: Suffrage Restriction and the Establishment of the One-Party South, 1880–1910.* New Haven, Conn., and London, 1974.

MICHAEL W. FITZGERALD

Granger, Lester Blackwell (September 16, 1896–January 9, 1976), civic leader. Lester B. Granger was born in Newport News, Va., one of six sons of William Randolph Granger, a Barbadian-born physician, and Mary L. Turpin Granger, a teacher. Granger grew up in Newark, N.J. He attended Dartmouth College and graduated in 1918. After serving in the U.S. Army during World War I, Granger worked briefly for the Newark affiliate of the NATIONAL URBAN LEAGUE (NUL) and taught school in the South.

In 1922 Granger became an extension worker with a state vocational school for African-American youth in Bordentown, N.J.; except for a year-long hiatus in 1930, during which he organized the Los Angeles chapter of the Urban League, Granger remained with the school until 1934. At Bordentown he met Harriet Lane, whom he married in August 1923. Also in the early and mid-1920s, Granger briefly attended both New York University and the New York School of Social Work.

In 1934 Granger, then serving as business manager for the NUL's *Opportunity* magazine, was selected to oversee the organization's Workers Bureau. Through the creation of Workers' Councils, Granger led the NUL's efforts to promote trade unionism among African-American workers, as well as to challenge racial discrimination by employers and labor organizations alike. In October 1940, after serving for several years with the New York City Welfare Council, Granger was chosen as the NUL's assistant executive secretary in charge of industrial relations. He was named executive secretary effective November 1941; he was to lead the NUL for the next twenty years.

Although the NUL was predominantly a social service agency, during World War II Granger was an active, though at times hesitant, participant in the effort to eliminate racial segregation and discrimination in military service and defense employment. He joined the 1941 March on Washington movement, and in 1945 he served as a special adviser on race relations to then Secretary of the Navy James Forrestal. In December 1945, he received the U.S. Navy's highest civilian award. During President Harry S. Truman's administration, Granger pressed for integration of the remaining branch of the armed services. The NUL continued to emphasize employ-

Lester Granger, the leader of the National Urban League during the 1940s and '50s, primarily worked behind the scenes with white business and other large institutions to eliminate economic discrimination and other kinds of disadvantages faced by African Americans. (Photographs and Prints Division, Schomburg Center for Research in Black Culture, The New York Public Library, Astor, Lenox and Tilden Foundations)

ment and housing discrimination in the postwar period.

With the emergence of the CIVIL RIGHTS MOVEMENT in the 1950s, "dissident" local staff and executive board members called on the NUL to challenge racial problems more aggressively. Granger insisted that the NUL continue its strategy of "education and persuasion," and his position prevailed in the wake of an internal shakeup that led some board members to resign. The NUL did, however, take steps to ensure more black representation on the board and a greater voice for local affiliates.

Granger remained a leading figure in social work over the years. He served as president of the National Conference of Social Work (later the National Conference on Social Welfare) in 1952. In 1961 he became the first American to preside over the International Conference of Social Work (later the International Conference on Social Welfare).

In October 1961, Granger retired from the NUL. The following year, he joined the faculty of Dillard

University in New Orleans, La. In 1972 he was named Amistad Scholar in Residence at Dillard's Amistad Research Center. Granger died in Alexandria, La., on January 9, 1976.

REFERENCES

MOORE, JESSE THOMAS, JR. *A Search for Equality: The National Urban League, 1910–1961.* University Park, Pa., 1981.

PARRIS, GUICHARD, and LESTER BROOKS. *Blacks in the City: A History of the National Urban League.* Boston, 1971.

The Social Welfare Forum, 1952. Official Proceedings, 79th Annual Meeting, National Conference of Social Work, Chicago, Ill., May 25–30. New York, 1952.

TAMI J. FRIEDMAN

Granville, Evelyn Boyd (May 1, 1924–   ), mathematician, educator, and author. Evelyn Boyd was born in Washington, D.C., the second of two daughters of Julia Walker Boyd, a U.S. government employee, and William Boyd, an apartment building superintendent. William Boyd did not remain with the family; Evelyn Boyd was reared primarily by her mother and aunt. Boyd attended Dunbar High School and won a partial scholarship to study at Smith College in Northampton, Mass.

Boyd excelled in mathematics, and in 1945 she graduated summa cum laude from Smith, where she was elected to Phi Beta Kappa. She won several grants that allowed her to enter a graduate program at Yale University, from which she earned a Ph.D. with a specialty in functional analysis in 1949. She was one of the first two black female recipients of a doctorate in mathematics. She had a postgraduate fellowship at New York University and, in 1950, was appointed to the mathematics faculty of Fisk University in Nashville. She remained on the faculty for two years and inspired at least two young women to pursue a Ph.D. in mathematics. She left Fisk and spent sixteen years working in government and private industry. Some of her employers included the National Bureau of Standards, IBM, the Computation and Data Reduction Center of the Space Technology Laboratories, the Diamond Ordinance Fuze Laboratories, and the North American Aviation Company. Her work involved primarily celestial mechanics, trajectory and orbit computation, and associated numerical and digital computer techniques.

In 1967, Boyd was appointed to the faculty at California State University in Los Angeles. While there, she cowrote a book with Jason Frand, *Theory and*

Application of Mathematics for Teachers (1975). She accepted a position in 1985 at Texas College in Tyler, where she had purchased a farm with her husband, Edward V. Granville. Boyd Granville left Texas College in 1988 and, in 1990, was appointed to the Sam A. Lindsey Chair at the University of Texas in Tyler. In addition to teaching at the university level, Boyd Granville has taught in secondary school programs in the California and Texas public-school systems.

See also MATHEMATICIANS.

REFERENCES

HINE, DARLENE CLARK, ed., *Black Women in America.* Brooklyn, N.Y., 1993.

KENSCHAFT, PATRICIA. "Evelyn Boyd Granville." Louise Grinstein and Paul Campbell, eds. In *Women of Mathematics: A Bibliographic Sourcebook.*

SYLVIA TRIMBLE BOZEMAN

Graphic Arts. The category "graphic arts" encompasses a wide range of media and techniques. Traditionally employed to describe visual arts that are linear in character, the term often includes all drawing media, as well as art processes that allow artists to make multiple images—i.e., photography and all of the printmaking media (such as relief printing, engraving, etching, aquatint, silkscreen printing, and lithography). However, in this essay the term will be limited to the arts of printmaking.

Although the African forebears of African Americans had their own traditions of printed and/or multiple arts (as seen in the relief and resist textile-printing techniques of numerous West African peoples), there is no evidence that these printing traditions survived in the Americas. Therefore, a discussion of African Americans in the graphic arts rightfully belongs within the larger historical picture of printmaking in America.

Occasional African-American graphic artists emerged from the late eighteenth century to the end of the nineteenth century. Possibly the earliest known black American printmaker—and the most obscure—was Scipio MOORHEAD. Moorhead's talents were praised by a fellow black Bostonian, the famous Senegalese-born poet Phillis WHEATLEY, in her poem "To S.M., a Young African Painter, on Seeing His Work." A copperplate engraving of the poet, which appeared as the frontispiece to the 1773 London edition of her volume of poetry, has been attributed to Moorhead.

Moorhead, like many of the African-American artists who came after him, learned to paint and/or make prints through an apprenticeship with a sympathetic white artisan. Numerous black artists during the antebellum period, like Robert M. Douglass, Jr., and Patrick Reason, trained with artisans and cultivated clients from the growing ranks of northern white abolitionists. Reason's skillfully realized 1848 copper engraving of the runaway slave and antislavery lecturer Henry BIBB demonstrates that these black artists were capable of both mastering the intricacies of the various graphic arts techniques and making their work a part of the abolitionist movement.

In contrast to those antebellum black artists whose careers were linked with the struggle for black emancipation, many nineteenth-century artists of color avoided social issues altogether, choosing instead to do common portraiture, picturesque landscapes, and other forms of nonracial art. For example, Jules LION in New Orleans and James P. BALL in Cincinnati both headed thriving lithography businesses that catered to largely white clienteles. After the Civil War and continuing into the first decade of the twentieth century, African-American lithographer Grafton Tyler Brown produced numerous stock certificates, street maps, and landscapes, mostly of California, the Pacific Northwest, and the Nevada territories.

Henry Ossawa TANNER and his student William Edouard SCOTT, although known primarily as painters, were the first African-American graphic artists to move beyond commercial work and create fine art prints. Working through the first two decades of the twentieth century, Tanner and Scott borrowed art techniques learned from the French impressionists and applied these to their respective etchings and lithographs of landscapes, marine settings, and occasional portraits and genre scenes. Etchers William McKnight FARROW, Allan Randall FREELON, and Albert Alexander SMITH, though active at the height of the HARLEM RENAISSANCE and the Great Depression, also subscribed to this belated/modified form of visual modernism.

Two graphic artists who, during the period of the Harlem Renaissance, broke away from European-American artistic conventions and embraced more avant-garde, African design sensibilities were Aaron DOUGLAS and James Lesesne WELLS. Douglas's bold, angular renderings of African Americans, as seen in his series of relief prints illustrating the Eugene O'Neill play *The Emperor Jones* (1926), recalled the highly stylized and distorted representations of human anatomy found in traditional African sculpture. Similar approaches to the human figure and to two-dimensional design appeared in Wells's graphic works, such as his relief print *African Fantasy* (1929).

With the onset of the Great Depression, Douglas and Wells continued their experiments in design and form, but their innovations were tempered by the social and economic realities of the times. Conse-

quently, these graphic artists and others turned toward an art of social realism, an approach that placed humanity, social concerns, and the environment at the center of artistic matters.

A more socially engaged art scene in America, with the graphic arts playing a major role in this ideological shift, was further encouraged by the creation of the Works Progress Administration/Federal Arts Projects, or the WPA/FAP, in 1935. This government program, apart from helping to put Americans back to work, provided support for the creation of art in public places, the implementation of scholarly inventories of American design, the development of community art centers, and the establishment of artists' workshops. Significant numbers of African-American artists participated in WPA/FAP graphic workshops in Atlanta, Chicago, Cleveland, Philadelphia, New York, and Washington, D.C. A few of these black printmakers—such as the Philadelphia-based Dox THRASH, who helped develop a new printmaking process—were considered major figures in their respective art communities, regardless of race.

From the end of World War II to the historic signing of the Civil Rights Act of 1968, African-American art and culture underwent numerous shifts and emphases, which are reflected in the graphic arts of those transitional years. Toward the end of the 1940s, visual commentaries on the racial inequities in America were present in the prints of several black artists, most notably Elizabeth CATLETT in works such as her relief print *I Have Special Reservations* (1946). Concurrent with these images of black protest were the more idealistic and uplifting representations of an artist like Charles WHITE, whose relief print *Exodus #1* (1949) focuses on black aspirations and Afro-America's sense of racial pride.

By the 1950s and early 1960s, many African-American graphic artists worked with themes and stylistic approaches that differed radically from the political and/or culture-specific works of Catlett and White. Etcher/engraver Norma Morgan and relief printmaker Walter Williams, though two very different artists, developed essentially nonracial formulas for their work. Williams subscribed to a figurative expressionist sensibility, as seen in his relief print *Fighting Cock* (1957), while Morgan's copper engraving *David in the Wilderness* (1956) illustrates her adherence to a romantic realist agenda.

Beginning in the late 1960s, the rumblings of the civil rights movement and the strong identification with an African heritage propelled many African-American artists to revisit social themes and ethnic styles that had been pioneered by Elizabeth Catlett and James Lesesne Wells. The results were works that spoke to the issue of black solidarity, such as the silkscreen *Unite* (1970) by Chicago artist Barbara Jones-Hogu, and works that recalled African colors and imagery, like the relief print *Jungle Rhythms #2* (1968) by New York artist Ademola Olugebefola.

This atmosphere of a heightened racial consciousness ushered in an abundance of work from about 1968 to 1976 that reflected African-American sensibilities, most often in the form of a race-specific figurative art. This new black imagery among artists, coinciding with a newfound enthusiasm within the greater art world for the art of the print, resulted in many different examples of African-American graphic art. Among the many artists who produced important graphic works during this period were Samella Lewis, Ruth Waddy, Lev Mills, and Leon Hicks. *Injustice Case* (1970), a relief "body" print by David Hammons, and *The Get-A-Way* (1976), a lithograph by Margo Humphrey (b. 1942), show the wide range of approaches to the figure, as well as to issues of culture, that African-American graphic artists grappled with during the 1970s. Nonfigurative art was explored in depth during this period as well, as seen in the abstract prints of etcher and lithographer John E. Dowell, Jr.

The 1970s and 1980s, like the depression years, were a period in which graphic workshops among black artists proliferated. Apart from the important printmakers and printmaking activities based within college and university art departments (like the printmaking department at Howard University, headed by etcher Winston Kennedy [b. 1944]), several African-American–managed graphic arts workshops produced major works. These include Workshop, Inc., in Washington, D.C., founded by silkscreen artist Lou Stovall; WD Graphic Workshop, also in Washington, founded by etcher Percy Martin; Brandywine Graphic Workshop in Philadelphia, founded by lithographer Allan EDMUNDS, Jr.; and the Printmaking Workshop in New York, founded by master printmaker Robert BLACKBURN. Major African-American artists known primarily as painters and sculptors, such as Romare BEARDEN, Jacob LAWRENCE, Betye SAAR, Sam GILLIAM, Richard HUNT, and Mel EDWARDS, have all produced prints under the supervision of these workshop founder/directors. Since the 1980s, these workshops and others have provided many African-American artists with the opportunity to explore new graphic-arts techniques, as well as traditional printmaking media, in service to contemporary issues and ideas in the visual arts.

REFERENCES

PORTER, JAMES A. *Exhibition of Graphic Arts and Drawings by Negro Artists.* Washington, D.C., 1947.

———. *Modern Negro Art.* 1943. Reprint. New York, 1969.

POWELL, RICHARD J. "The Afro-American Printmaking Tradition." *PrintNews* 3, no. 1 (February/March 1981): 3–7.

———. "Current Expressions in Afro-American Printmaking." *PrintNews* 3, no. 2 (April/May 1981): 7–11.

———. *Impressions/Expression: Black American Graphics.* New York, 1980.

WYE, DEBORAH. *Committed to Print: Social and Political Themes in Recent American Printed Art.* New York, 1988.

RICHARD J. POWELL

Graves, Earl Gilbert, Jr. (January 9, 1935–), publisher. Born in Brooklyn, N.Y., Earl G. Graves attended Morgan State College in Baltimore, Md., receiving his B.A. in economics in 1958. Graves, who had been enrolled in the Reserve Officers' Training Corps, joined the U.S. Army immediately after graduation, and rose to the rank of captain. After leaving the Army in 1962, he sold houses and then worked for the Justice Department as a narcotics agent. In 1965 he was hired by New York Sen. Robert F. Kennedy as a staff assistant, charged with planning and supervising events. Graves occupied that position until Kennedy's death in 1968. That year he started his own business, Earl G. Graves Associates, a management consulting firm specializing in assistance to small businesses.

In 1970, using $150,000 borrowed from the Manhattan Capital Corporation, Graves became founder, editor, and publisher of *Black Enterprise,* the first African-American business magazine. An immediate success, the journal had sales of $900,000 by the end of its first year. By the beginning of the 1990s, the magazine had 250,000 subscribers and annual earnings of more than $15 million. *Black Enterprise* soon became a black community institution, widely known for its how-to advice on building minority business and its lists of the top 100 black-owned companies. Graves's monthly "publisher's page" served as a forum for examining politics and the black marketplace. The magazine developed two other special features. In 1975 Graves began the *Black Enterprise* Achievement Awards for successful African-American entrepreneurs. In 1982 he organized a board of economists to make periodic reports on the black economy.

While Earl G. Graves Publishing Company, Inc., which published *Black Enterprise,* remained the flagship property of Graves's company, Earl Graves, Ltd., Graves set up five other businesses over the following two decades: EGG Dallas Broadcasting, Inc.; B.C.I. Marketing, Inc.; a development firm; a market research firm; and a distribution firm. In

1990, in a notable deal, a limited partnership led by Graves and basketball star Earvin "Magic" JOHNSON acquired a $60 million Pepsi-Cola franchise in Washington, D.C. In addition to his business activities, Graves remained involved in social and political activism, and during the 1990s was active in the lobbying group TransAfrica, as national commissioner and member of the national board of the Boy Scouts of America, as a director of HOWARD UNIVERSITY, and as a member on several corporate and foundation boards.

REFERENCES

Black Enterprise 20th anniversary issue (August 1990).
DAVIS, TIM. "Graves Gets Serious." Beverage World 111 (October 1992): 80–84.

GREG ROBINSON

Graveyards. *See* Cemeteries and Burials.

Gray, William Herbert, III (August 20, 1941–), congressman and administrator. William H. Gray III was born in Baton Rouge, La., the son of William H. Gray, Jr., minister and president of Florida A&M University, and Hazel Yates, a high school teacher. In 1963 he received a B.A. from Franklin and Marshall College in Lancaster, Pa., in 1966 an M.Div. from Drew Theological Seminary in Madison, N.J., and an M.Th. from Princeton Theological Seminary in 1970. In 1964 he became pastor of Union Baptist Church, in Montclair, N.J., where he was active in helping to initiate low-income housing projects. In 1972, as both his father and grandfather before him, he became pastor of Bright Hope Baptist Church in Philadelphia where he developed a politically active ministry and continued his interest in housing and mortgage issues.

Gray was first elected to Congress from Pennsylvania's Second District as a Democrat in 1978. During his time in Congress, he served on the House Appropriations, Foreign Affairs, and District of Columbia committees. His most important post was chair of the House Budget Committee in 1985, from which he steered the passage of the country's first trillion-dollar budget through controversies and differences between Congress and President Ronald Reagan.

A centrist within the DEMOCRATIC PARTY, Gray's primary focus in domestic policy was federal support of black private-sector development. On foreign issues he served as a leading spokesman on U.S. policy toward Africa and was a congressional sponsor of the antiapartheid movement. Gray sponsored an emergency aid bill for Ethiopia in 1984 and helped secure passage of the Anti-Apartheid acts of 1985 and 1986, overriding presidential vetoes.

Gray's mainstream domestic politics and energetic party politicking helped pave the way for his ascendance to the Democratic leadership. In 1985 he was elected chairman of the Democratic caucus in the House, and in 1989 he became majority whip, the number three leadership position in the House and the highest rank held by an African-American congressman.

In 1991 Gray resigned from Congress to become president of UNITED NEGRO COLLEGE FUND (UNCF) in New York City. That year he oversaw the inauguration of the UNCF's Campaign 2000, a drive to raise $250 million by the year 2000. With the support of President George Bush and a $50 million gift from media magnate Walter Annenberg, the campaign raised $86 million in its first year.

In May 1994 Gray was named temporary envoy to Haiti by President Bill Clinton but retained his position at the UNCF.

REFERENCE

CLAY, WILLIAM L. Just Permanent Interests: Black Americans in Congress, 1870–1991. New York, 1992.

RICHARD NEWMAN

Great Depression and the New Deal. The Great Depression was a period of enormous economic upheaval that affected the lives of all Americans. Rich and poor alike experienced the hardships of a contracting economy. The political and economic status of African Americans made them particularly vulnerable; they felt the effects of the depression earlier than other groups. During the booming 1920s, blacks had made modest gains because there was a need for their labor. These gains were achieved even though the jobs available were, for the most part, unskilled, low-paying positions, jobs that white workers no longer wanted.

According to the 1930 census, 37 percent of working African Americans were employed as agricultural laborers and 29 percent as personal-service and domestic workers. Only 2 percent were classified as professionals (lawyers, doctors, teachers, and clergy). Because such a large proportion of black workers were involved in agriculture, the collapse of the cotton industry brought devastating results. As early as 1926, the NATIONAL URBAN LEAGUE was advising unemployed southern black workers not to come north unless they were certain they had a job. White workers were already displacing black workers in jobs that had traditionally belonged to African Americans.

Unemployment increased rapidly in the early 1930s. It was thought that approximately 15 percent of the workforce was unemployed in 1930, and this percentage increased as the depression lengthened. African-American organizations estimated that the percentage of unemployed black workers was at least twice the rate of the country as a whole. Private social-service agencies, as well as state and local relief organizations, became overwhelmed with requests for help from people seeking work and public assistance. President Herbert Hoover's administration paid little attention to the plight of those in need,

assuring the country that "prosperity is just around the corner."

Most of the country regarded Franklin D. Roosevelt's election as president in 1932 with hope and anticipation. He had run on a platform that promised to turn the economy around and put America back to work.

Roosevelt moved swiftly to enact legislation that would provide quick temporary measures to alleviate the economic distress experienced by the unemployed and to stimulate the private sector of the economy. This legislation seemed, at first, to be promising to the African-American population. Programs in his plan, known as the New Deal, that were of special interest to blacks included the NATIONAL RECOVERY ADMINISTRATION (NRA), the Agriculture Adjustment Administration (AAA), the Civilian

The Great Depression only intensified the severe poverty of many rural farmers. A thirteen-year-old sharecropper plows a field near Americus, Ga., 1937. (Prints and Photographs Division, Library of Congress)

Conservation Corps (CCC), the Public Works Administration (PWA), and the Civil Works Administration (CWA)—all federal programs created in 1933. In addition, the Federal Emergency Relief Administration (FERA) provided federal funds to the states to enable them to provide relief and work relief to the poor. This was the first federal program to give direct grants to the states; it included incentives that encouraged states to improve public-assistance policies.

The WORKS PROGRESS ADMINISTRATION (WPA) and the National Youth Administration (NYA) were created in 1935. The WPA provided work relief to those out of work but employable; meanwhile, the FERA was phased out, giving the responsibility for providing public assistance back to the states. The NYA provided work relief for young people living at home or attending college.

In addition, significant New Deal reform legislation was enacted during the Great Depression that was of great concern to African Americans. This included the Social Security Act of 1935, a watershed in social-welfare policy, which established old-age and unemployment insurance administered by the federal government and categorical relief programs administered by the states; the National Labor Relations Act of 1935, which gave considerable power to organized labor by guaranteeing the right of workers to organize on their own behalf without interference from employers; and the Fair Labor Standards Act of 1938, which established a minimum wage and maximum hours of work.

The National Industrial Recovery Act (NIRA) of 1933 was an omnibus act designed to stimulate the private-sector economy, relieve economic distress, and resolve conflicts between labor and management. African Americans believed that the NIRA had the potential to be very helpful. Several black organizations, including the National Urban League and the NAACP, tried unsuccessfully to have an antidiscrimination amendment attached to it. The NIRA created the National Recovery Administration; one of its immediate tasks was to establish industrial codes with minimum-wage rates and maximum hours of work in all industries, an anti-inflationary measure to control a wage-price spiral. The first problem that African Americans encountered in this program was the exclusion of domestic and agricultural workers from coverage. This meant that for two-thirds of the black workforce, there was very little hope of receiving any increase in wages or improvement in working conditions.

Furthermore, during the process of establishing codes, it became apparent that industries were submitting codes that amounted, in effect, to differential wages in occupations with a majority of black workers. The proposed wages were 20 percent to 40 percent lower than the wages in occupations whose workers were predominantly white. When Roosevelt issued a blanket "blue eagle" agreement to promote support of the codes, it caused widespread displacement of black workers, especially in the South, where employers refused to pay a minimum wage to them. In order to counteract these policies, the Joint Committee on National Recovery was founded, composed of twenty-two national African-American fraternal, civic, and church groups. The Joint Committee, cochaired by John P. Davis and Robert WEAVER, closely monitored the establishment of codes in all industries where there were a substantial number of black workers and submitted briefs against a different wage based on geographic areas.

Section 7A of the NIRA gave workers the right to organize and bargain collectively without interference from employers. Organized labor was able to use section 7A to expand its membership and help workers take advantage of collective bargaining, particularly in the coal industry and needle trades. Some African Americans had reservations about this policy, not because they were against the principle of collective bargaining, which they saw as very positive, but because of the policies of local unions that prevented blacks from becoming part of the organized labor movement (see LABOR AND LABOR UNIONS).

African-American organizations, especially the National Urban League and the NAACP, pressured the American Federation of Labor (AFL) to abolish segregation and discrimination, but these practices continued. As labor gained more control over jobs in New Deal work programs, more black workers were denied jobs because they were not union members. The Joint Committee, along with National Urban League officials Eugene Kinkle Jones and T. Arnold HILL and NAACP executive secretary Walter WHITE, argued that this was a violation of the NRA codes, but discrimination continued. In 1935, when the Supreme Court ruled that the NRA's regulation of the private sector was unconstitutional, African Americans did not regard this as a significant loss.

The Agricultural Adjustment Administration was established to alleviate the problems associated with depressed prices for farm products and mounting crop surpluses. The AAA had a decentralized administration that gave a great deal of power to local areas. In spite of clear federal guidelines as to how benefits were to be allocated between owner and tenant, there were great variations in the treatment of black sharecroppers—people who lived and farmed on land that was owned by another person and shared their earnings, based on acreage and production, with the landowner (see SHARECROPPING).

The extreme impoverishment caused by the Great Depression brought about a further decline in living standards for many southern blacks. A young girl looks out of a window in Gee's Bend, Ala., 1937. (Prints and Photographs Division, Library of Congress)

Too frequently, large landowners controlled the AAA benefits (incentives to reduce cotton acreage), and tenant farmers and sharecroppers were not given their fair share. The Southern Tenant Farmers' Union, an interracial organization, was formed to fight for fair treatment under the AAA and received considerable support from the NAACP. But it was difficult for these organizations to compete with the southern bloc of the Democratic party in Congress, and little was accomplished. The AAA was replaced by the Soil Conservation Act and the Domestic Allotment Act when, in 1936, the Supreme Court ruled that the AAA's processing tax was unconstitutional.

The Civilian Conservation Corps was one of the most enduring and popular New Deal work-relief programs, lasting until the 1940s. It served three purposes. It provided relief to young men and their families; it removed young people from the private labor market; and it provided basic education and job training. The young men lived in CCC camps run by the War Department and worked on conservation projects; one major project was reforestation.

African Americans did not have equal access to this program. Although it was federally financed and administered, local social-service staffs selected participants. In some areas, this resulted in the exclusion of African-American youths. Since the camps were administered by the War Department, the segregated policies of the armed forces were often followed. In addition, there was a racial quota that limited the number of black youth according to the proportion of blacks in the population. Since a larger proportion of black families than white families were on relief, the quota severely limited the participation of black youth.

Furthermore, the camps did not hire black personnel. Through pressure brought to bear by such African-American organizations as the National Urban League and the NAACP, some of these policies were changed. All-black camps were set up in areas where segregation was the law of the land; in other areas, the camps were integrated. Some black reserve officers were placed at all-black camps. In spite of these changes, local autonomy and quotas continued to limit the participation of African Americans.

The intent of the Public Works Administration in the Department of the Interior was to stimulate industry through the purchase of materials and wage payments. The program was designed to construct large projects such as dams, government buildings, and low-rent housing. It was a federal employment program that paid set wages based on levels of skill and prevailing wages in local areas. Federal administration was more likely to ensure that African-American workers would be treated fairly, but projects were awarded to local contractors who negotiated with organized labor for the selection of workers. This resulted in the exclusion of many black workers because local AFL craft unions did not admit blacks, and there was no enforcement against discrimination.

Robert Weaver, special adviser for Negro affairs in the Department of the Interior, proposed a plan to correct this situation based on the percentage of skilled and unskilled African-American workers in each of the cities involved in low-rent-housing construction. Eighteen months after the plan had been implemented, Weaver expressed the belief that it had helped to overcome discrimination against black workers. Unfortunately, the plan was never extended to other PWA projects or other New Deal programs.

The Federal Emergency Relief Administration was a relief and work-relief program administered by the states through federal grants. Designed as a temporary program to meet emergency needs, it had many attributes that promised to be helpful to African-American workers. It provided jobs with a specific wage rate based on skill; there was no racial quota; it had a white-collar component that provided work for black professionals; it funded self-help projects; and federal regulations attached to the program raised relief standards and discouraged discrimination. The FERA also established eligibility with means testing—i.e., one's income had to be below a set amount so that one could quality for benefits—which ensured that those most in need would be given priority.

But there was no rule to enforce nondiscrimination. Since eligibility was established locally, local prejudices prevailed, making it difficult for African Americans to participate. It was easier for them to get relief than to obtain work on FERA projects. The FERA's wage rates were established according to geographic zones and were disliked by many employers who thought the rates increased labor costs. A great deal of pressure to rescind or lower the wage rates came from the southern states, where the rates were above the average wage paid to most black workers in the private sector. African Americans were appalled when this pressure proved effective, arguing that one of the goals of the New Deal was to attain a decent standard of living for all Americans.

The Civil Works Administration was a temporary program that was created because the PWA was slow in getting work projects started. Winter was approaching, and many people faced extreme hardship because the CCC, the FERA, and the PWA were not meeting the needs of all the unemployed. The CWA had the capacity to provide four million jobs on projects that could be started quickly, were labor-intensive, and required minimal use of equipment and material. The program had a white-collar component but did not have racial quotas, and although it was not means-tested, it gave preference to those most in need. This initiative appears to have been more helpful to African Americans than other New Deal programs, but it was of short duration. It was created as a temporary measure to help the unemployed survive the winter of 1933, and it was slowly dismantled as the cold weather passed.

The National Youth Administration was established in 1935 to help young men and women who were living at home. It helped those young people who were not attending school to receive job training and those in school to continue their education. African-American youth fared fairly well under the NYA, in spite of a great deal of local autonomy in the administration of the programs. This relative success may have been the result of the influence of Mary McLeod BETHUNE, the head of the Negro Affairs section of the NYA, who was able to funnel thousands of dollars to black youths.

New Deal administrators began to fear that the FERA was creating a permanent dependent class. There was a general consensus that relief for the able-bodied unemployed should be in the form of work relief. Thus, the FERA was dismantled in 1935 and the Works Progress Administration (later known as the Work Projects Administration) was established to serve as a coordinating agency for work-relief programs in the states. Instead, it became a giant work relief program itself, assuming responsibility for providing work to over three and a half million people and emphasizing the desirability of work over relief. Responsibility for providing relief was returned to the states, many of which reverted to "poor-law standards" that had been in place prior to the FERA.

After the experiences that African Americans had had with earlier New Deal programs, they regarded the WPA very cautiously. It had attributes that appeared to be helpful, such as federal administration, an emphasis on work, a white-collar component, and set wage rates, and it gave preference to those most in need by establishing eligibility with means testing.

But the WPA also had policies that were disturbing to the black population, including wage rates that were lower than those in the private sector and with geographic differentiations. The states in the Southeast, where the majority of African Americans lived, had the lowest wage rate (sixty-five cents per day for unskilled workers). Although discrimination was forbidden, there was no enforcement mechanism to prevent it. It was a federal program, but most of the projects were developed at the local level and gave a great deal of control to local officials. Organized labor controlled hiring on many of the projects.

Since the WPA was not allowed to compete with private industry and the cost of materials was to be kept at a minimum, many of its jobs were regarded as make-work assignments, of very little value. Harry Hopkins, the administrator of the WPA, was creative in his development of projects and actually accomplished a great deal: The program built or improved hospitals, schools, farm-to-market roads, playgrounds, and landing strips. The white-collar component proved especially beneficial to African-American professionals. Hopkins created the WPA FEDERAL THEATRE PROJECT, which presented plays and dances for children and adults, many of whom had never seen a live production. The WPA FEDERAL WRITERS' PROJECT resulted in the development of numerous brochures, guides, and other publications such as the *Life in America* series; this included ethnic studies, one of which was *The Negro in Virginia*. The FEDERAL ARTS PROJECT gave jobs to unemployed artists, who taught at community centers, produced artistic works, and painted murals in government buildings. Many African-American actors, writers, and artists were employed in these WPA projects. Charles WHITE and Hale WOODRUFF, for example, were accomplished artists who taught in WPA programs in the South.

As the private sector expanded, WPA policies became more restrictive. Workers could not remain on projects longer than eighteen months. This was especially hard on black workers because the private labor market was not absorbing them as quickly as it was absorbing whites. The WPA was curtailed sharply in 1940, although over eight million people remained unemployed; they were forced to return to relief for help.

The National Urban League and the NAACP thought it imperative for African Americans to be gainfully employed and advocated some kind of permanent public-works program to provide jobs for those workers who could not find employment in the private sector. They predicted that a large proportion of African Americans would become permanently dependent on relief without a work program to help them remain employed. They also recognized that the WPA was costly and had its faults but thought that it was worth the price in the human dignity and self-respect that regular employment provided.

In addition to creating temporary programs to alleviate the economic distress and stimulate the private-sector economy, the New Deal produced some permanent, significant social-welfare legislation. Legislation of the greatest concern to African Americans included the National Labor Relations Act and the Social Security Act, both in 1935, and the Fair Labor Standards Act in 1938.

The National Labor Relations Act had its beginning with section 7A of the NIRA. When the NRA was ruled unconstitutional, many of the policies in section 7A were transferred to a labor bill that was introduced by Sen. Robert Wagner of New York in 1935. African Americans were especially concerned about a clause stating that "the employer and a labor organization may agree that an applicant for employment shall be required to join a labor organization as a condition of employment." They feared that this clause would have very negative consequences for black workers because it seemed to legalize closed shops. If this was to be the law, the African-American population believed it was mandatory to have a mechanism to prevent unions from discriminating against black workers.

T. Arnold Hill, industrial secretary of the National Urban League, testified against Wagner's labor bill, prefacing his testimony with a statement supporting the labor movement and the concept of collective bargaining. The crux of his testimony was that the league could not support the bill in its present form because it permitted closed shops; it denied black workers the right to engage in strikebreaking in occupations where they were also prohibited from joining the striking union; and it failed to protect them from racial discrimination by labor unions.

Wagner was very much aware of the discriminatory practices of organized labor, but he was reluctant to include any kind of antidiscrimination clause in the labor bill because he thought this would jeopardize its passage. The bill was passed without such a clause. This issue continued to be a major concern among blacks; enforcement against employment discrimination was finally accomplished with title 7 of the 1964 Civil Rights Act.

The passage of the Social Security Act was very significant: It established federal responsibility for a broad range of social-welfare programs to help individuals meet the loss of earnings or absence of income caused by unemployment, old age, death of a family's wage earner, and other hazards of life. The initial act provided old-age insurance, unemployment compensation, aid to destitute blind and elderly persons, and aid to destitute children in one-parent families. In 1939, the act was amended to include survivors' insurance.

This act was of special importance to President Roosevelt, whose primary concerns were old-age security and unemployment insurance. He insisted on worker contributions, because he thought this would make old-age insurance different from relief and ensure the permanence of these programs. Benefits would be regarded as a right by those who had contributed through the social security payroll tax, and the programs would be viewed as self-supporting. This would make it less likely for Congress, in later years, to dismantle them.

The Social Security Act has had a lasting and profound effect on African Americans because it created a two-tier social-welfare system. The first, and preferred, tier is a system to which workers and/or their employers contribute (old-age and survivors' insurance and unemployment compensation). The second tier is a stigmatized system that consists of public-assistance programs (aid to the poor elderly, the blind, and dependent children).

African-American organizations closely monitored the debates leading to the passage of the Social Security Act. The three issues that were of most concern to them were administrative responsibility, coverage, and methods of financing. They preferred federal administration of all programs, universal coverage, and financing by a means other than worker contributions. The original bill covered all workers, but the Treasury Department objected because of the difficulties involved in collecting a payroll tax from agricultural and domestic workers; they were thus excluded from coverage under the first tier. This exclusion may have been for political reasons also, since it was anticipated that farmers, especially in the South, would have strong objections to contributing to social insurance benefits for black farm laborers and would fight against passage of the bill.

African Americans testified while the bill was being debated in Congress, advocating the inclusion of domestic and agricultural workers, federal administration of all programs, and financing through general revenues. The exclusion of agricultural and domestic workers under the first tier meant that about two-thirds of the black workforce would not be eligible for old-age insurance or unemployment compensation. Such people would have to rely on public assistance when they were unable to support themselves by working. The act gave the states the administrative responsibilities for public-assistance programs under the second tier, something that was especially difficult for the African-American population in the Southeast. Local autonomy meant that many black individuals and families who were eligible for old-age assistance, blind assistance, or aid to dependent children would be denied it by local agencies with discriminatory policies. Many would be forced to work in the cotton fields without the protection of any labor statutes.

African Americans paid very little attention to the public-assistance components of the act. Their main concerns were the programs tied to employment. The NAACP and the National Urban League pointed out that relief rolls were no substitute; relief was a dole that stigmatized and robbed an individual of self-respect and initiative. These organizations continued to try to amend the act to provide coverage for agricultural and domestic workers under the first tier.

The Fair Labor Standards Act established a minimum wage and maximum hours of work. As with the NLRA, many aspects of this act had been part of the code policies under the NRA. The African-American population was generally in favor of the bill, although geographic wage differentials were seriously considered and it was quite likely that agricultural and domestic workers would once again be excluded. The National Urban League favored the bill but decided not to support it openly because of the likelihood of a racist backlash. The NAACP attempted to ally with the AFL, hoping that such an alliance would result in the inclusion of agricultural and domestic workers, but the AFL did not join it on this issue.

The bill barely passed because it had no strong backing from any group; indeed, it might never have been reported out of committee if Claude Pepper, who supported it, had not won a senatorial primary in Florida over a congressman who campaigned against the bill. It was then brought to the floor and quickly passed.

The Fair Labor Standards Act was very weak because too many concessions had been given to diverse groups to ensure its passage. This meant that several occupations had been excluded from coverage, including domestic and agricultural workers. It left the differential wage question to the administrator of the law. This eventually resulted in a federal set wage of 25 cents per hour and a maximum workweek of 44 hours; after two years, industry would reach a minimum wage of 40 cents and a 40-hour maximum workweek.

The New Deal administration was the first to include a substantial number of African Americans. Several black leaders served as advisers for Negro affairs in the various cabinet departments, a group frequently referred to as the "black cabinet" or the "black brain trust." Some of the prominent appointees were Robert Weaver, Mary McLeod Bethune, William HASTIE, Forrester Washington, Eugene Kinkle Jones, and Robert Vann. Historians are not in agreement regarding the amount of influence this group exercised. Black advisers were able to expand employment opportunities for black professionals in civil-service positions and perhaps, from time to time, focus some attention on civil rights. But for the most part, the black cabinet was not a cohesive group and never made any strong policy statements.

Advisers for Negro affairs were seldom involved in the formulation of policy. However, it is clear that the presence of such advisers was a positive force. Robert Weaver was able to devise policies that helped more black workers gain jobs under the PWA. Mary McLeod Bethune, head of the Negro Affairs section of the NYA, was a highly respected woman who was able to help thousands of black youths take advantage of NYA benefits. In addition, Bethune had a close relationship with Eleanor Roosevelt and explained the needs, concerns, and aspirations of the African-American population to her. Mrs. Roosevelt, as the president's wife, was perceived by the black community as a friend who was willing to intervene and be an advocate for them. She was sympathetic to the plight of African Americans but, like the president, did not believe that the government could eliminate racial obstacles.

The leadership that was most helpful to African Americans came from outside the administration, in the form of black organizations such as the National Urban League and the NAACP. These groups attempted to monitor the development of New Deal legislation and programs, to testify in favor of certain policies, to keep the African-American population abreast of New Deal initiatives, and to help them take advantage of the programs. These organizations frequently made attempts to mobilize the African-American population to support or fight against certain legislation. However, they were not very successful in persuading Congress to support policies that would have been more helpful to African Americans. This was largely due to a lack of political power.

Most African Americans who voted in 1932 were loyal to the Republican party, the party believed to be responsible for the emancipation of the slaves. By 1936, however, most of the voting black population had switched their loyalties to the Democrats. This switch occurred in spite of the fact that the Democratic party paid very little attention to the needs of blacks. The party tended to be beholden to its southern bloc, which was adamantly racist and against the federal government's exercising authority in matters traditionally left to the states. This meant, of course, that the southern states would be able to continue their segregation laws and patterns.

Yet New Deal legislation had the potential to provide more for blacks than had any recent Republican administration legislation. It did provide at least a segment of the black population with public-works jobs and with relief. There was an effort in at least some of the New Deal programs to prevent discrimination on the basis of race. More than any previous administration, it appointed African Americans to meaningful positions. These events appear to be a plausible explanation for the switch from the "party of Lincoln" to the Democratic party.

Even though most African Americans made this switch in 1936, they continued to lack the political clout needed to influence New Deal legislation because the largest proportion of the black population was in the South and disfranchised. Blacks in the South lived under a repressive political system; fear of lynching made it difficult to mobilize any southern protest movement. Throughout the 1930s, the NAACP strongly advocated legislation that would make lynching a federal crime, but its attempts were never supported by New Deal administrators. Nor did the New Deal support the NAACP's efforts to eliminate the poll tax in southern states, a tax designed to disfranchise the black population.

Throughout the depression decade, New Deal legislation had to meet a litmus test that would ensure the support of the southern bloc of the party. This was to the detriment of African-American workers because, too often, legislation was enacted with policies that limited their access to programs and entitlements. In 1940, as the WPA was dismantled, a substantial portion of the black population remained unemployed and on relief, and no significant change had occurred in discriminatory employment practices. The New Deal did not become the panacea the African-American population had hoped it would.

REFERENCES

CAYTON, HORACE, and GEORGE MITCHELL. *Black Workers and the New Unions*. Chapel Hill, N.C., 1939.

KIRBY, JOHN B. *Black Americans in the Roosevelt Era: Liberalism and Race*. Knoxville, 1980.

SITKOFF, HARVARD. *A New Deal for Blacks*. New York, 1978.

WEISS, NANCY J. *Farewell to the Party of Lincoln: Politics in the Age of FDR*. Princeton, N.J., 1983.

WOLTERS, RAYMOND. *Negroes and the Great Depression*. Westport, Conn., 1970.

DONA COOPER HAMILTON

Greaves, William (October 8, 1926–), actor, film director, writer, and TV producer. Born and raised in New York City, William Greaves attended Stuyvesant High School and later enrolled for a year as an engineering student at the City College of New York. Throughout the 1940s and early '50s, he worked in radio, television, and film and acted with the AMERICAN NEGRO THEATRE.

In 1950 Greaves was asked to play a stereotyped role in a Broadway revival and walked off the set, which led to an interest in studying film direction. He enrolled in film classes at the City College. Upon completion, he found most white studios unwilling to hire black apprentices, and in 1952 he left for work in Canada's more open film industry.

During his six years in Canada Greaves worked at the National Film Board (NFB), first in Ottawa and later in Montreal. He gained experience in both directing and editing. Yet, while the NFB afforded Greaves an opportunity to gain technical experience, it offered little chance for iconoclasm. After leaving the NFB Greaves founded and for two years directed a Canadian acting troupe. In 1960 he joined an agency of the United Nations, the International Civil Aviation Organization, as a public information officer. In 1963 Greaves moved back to New York.

The following year he took a position with the United States Information Agency (USIA). While there, he documented the historic summit of Pan-African artists and intellectuals in Dakar, Senegal, *The First World Festival of Negro Arts* (1966). In 1967 Greaves made a documentary entitled *Still a Brother: Inside the Negro Middle Class* for National Educational Television (NET). Around the same time, NET was developing BLACK JOURNAL, a show with a magazine-type format focusing on national black issues; Greaves became a cohost. After a power struggle between the program's white executive producer and its predominantly black staff, Greaves became the show's executive producer. In 1969 *Black Journal* received an Emmy Award.

While working on *Black Journal,* Greaves continued to operate William Greaves Productions, which he had established in 1964. Greaves's first independent feature-length film was the experimental *Symbipsycotaxiplasm: Take One* (1967), a movie within a movie depicting the creative and conflicting

William Greaves with Toni Morrison on the set of *Ida B. Wells: A Passion for Justice*. (William Greaves)

dynamics involved in acting and filmmaking. Though not commercially released at the time, the film enjoyed a critically praised release in the early 1990s. In 1970 Greaves left *Black Journal* to pursue his filmmaking interests. In 1971 he made the commercially successful "doutainment" *Ali the Fighter,* which was followed in 1972 by the lesser-known *Nationtime Gary* (about the National Black Political Convention in Gary, Ind.).

Greaves made several films for the Equal Employment Opportunity Commission, as well as *From These Roots* (1974), a documentary about the HARLEM RENAISSANCE that won twenty-two film festival awards. In 1981 he was executive producer for the Richard PRYOR comedy *Bustin' Loose*. Throughout the 1980s he directed, wrote, and/or coproduced documentaries on black historical figures and black issues, including *Black Power in America: Myth or Reality* (1986) and the multiaward-winning *Ida B. Wells: A Passion for Justice* (1989), narrated by Toni MORRISON, as well as works about Booker T. WASHINGTON (1982) and Frederick DOUGLASS (1984). In all, Greaves has been involved in the production of more than three hundred documentary films.

REFERENCES

CLOYD, IRIS and WILLIAM C. MATNEY, eds. *Who's Who Among Black Americans*. Detroit, 1990.

MUSSER, CHARLES, and ADAM KNEE. "William Greaves, Documentary Filmmaking and the African-American Experience." *Film Quarterly* 45 (Spring 1992): 13–25.

PETRA E. LEWIS
SHIPHERD REED

Green, Al (April 13, 1946–), singer and songwriter. Al Green was born in Forrest City, Ark., where at age nine he began singing in a family GOSPEL QUARTET called the Green Brothers. For six years the group toured gospel circuits, first in the South and then in the Midwest when the family relocated to Grand Rapids, Mich., first recording in 1960. Green formed his own pop group, Al Green and the Creations, in 1964 after his father expelled him from the gospel quartet for listening to what he called the "profane music" of singer Jackie WILSON. The group toured for three years before changing their name in 1967 to Al Greene and the Soulmates (the "e" was briefly added to Green's name for commercial reasons). That year Green made his record debut with the single "Back Up Train," which went to number five on the national soul charts in 1968. However, there were no follow-up successes, and Green was plunged back into obscurity, playing small clubs again.

While touring in Midland, Tex., in 1969, Green met Willie Mitchell, vice president of Hi Records in Memphis, Tenn. Mitchell produced Green's version of "I Can't Get Next to You," which went to number one on the national soul charts in 1971. Continuing to collaborate with Mitchell and drummer Al Jackson, Jr. (of Booker T. and the MGs), Green went on to record a string of million-selling singles and LPs throughout the early 1970s. Combining sensuous, emotive vocals with strings, horns, and hard-driving backbeats, Green helped define the sound of soul music in the 1970s. His hits included "Let's Stay Together" (1971), "Look What You've Done for Me" (1972), "I'm Still in Love with You" (1972), and "You Ought to Be with Me" (1972).

At the height of his career, Green began to reconsider his pop music orientation and shifted back toward gospel music. A turning point was an incident in 1974 in which his girlfriend scalded him with a pot of boiling grits before killing herself with his gun. When Green recovered from his burns, he became a minister, and in 1976 he purchased a church in Memphis and was ordained pastor of the Full Gospel Tabernacle, where he would perform services nearly every Sunday. He did not immediately give up pop music, but his attempts to mix gospel themes with secular soul music fared poorly.

In 1979, Green decided to sing only gospel music, and the next year he released his first gospel album, *The Lord Will Make a Way.* In 1982 he costarred in a successful Broadway musical with Patti LABELLE, *Your Arms Too Short to Box with God.* The lines between gospel music and love songs remained somewhat blurred for Green, who in his shows would lose himself in religious ecstasy one moment and toss roses into the audience the next.

Throughout the 1980s and early '90s, Green continued to record gospel records and pastor the Full Gospel Tabernacle. In 1994 he rerecorded a duet, "(Ain't It Funny) How Time Slips Away," on the compilation disc *Rhythm, Country, and Blues* with country-pop singer Lyle Lovett.

REFERENCES

HEILBUT, ANTHONY. *The Gospel Sound: Good News and Bad Times.* New York, 1985.
HOERBURGER, ROB. "The Gospel According to Al." *Rolling Stone* 27 (March 1986): 27–28.

JOSEPH W. LOWNDES

Green, Chuck (1918–), tap dancer. Born in Georgia, Chuck Green, when only six, won third place in an amateur dance contest where Noble SISSLE was the bandleader. Within a year Green was under contract and touring the South as a child tap dancer.

In his early teens, Green and his childhood friend, James Walker, formed the team of Chuck and Chuckles. While Green produced a continuous flow of cascading taps, Walker played the vibraphone and executed legomania (a dance form in which the legs are loose and rubbery, appearing to twine around each other in counterpoint with the fast-moving feet). Picking up lines of patter from blackface comedy acts, Green and Walker were groomed as a younger version of the headlining dance team of Buck and Bubbles. Indeed, Green's mature style was shaped by the dancing of John BUBBLES. Chuck and Chuckles toured with big bands across the United States, Europe, and Australia. Green developed a bebop-influenced style of rhythm tap that was improvised and up-tempo. However, Green's career, like most dancers', waned after the decline of the big bands.

Green made a memorable appearance in New York City at a tap dance challenge at the Village Vanguard in 1964. In 1969 he became an important part of tap's rebirth when he appeared with members of Harlem's Hoofer's Club for a series of "TapHappenings" produced in New York City. Green then went on to perform as a guest with the COPASETICS and to coach younger tap dancers. He was twice honored with a New York Dance and Performance Award (a Bessie) for his innovative achievements and technical skill in dance. His tap fluency is captured in the documentary *No Maps on My Taps* (1979), while his free-associational poetry of speech is captured in another documentary, *About Tap* (1987). In the 1990s Green continued his activity in New York City as a revered master of tap dancing.

REFERENCE

TREBAY, GUY. "Hoofing It." *Village Voice,* January 21, 1984.

CONSTANCE VALIS HILL

Green, Cora (December 10, 1895–?), entertainer. Cora Green was born in Baltimore, the daughter of Alexander and Elizabeth Sorrell Chambers. Educated in the Baltimore public schools, she was on the stage at age fourteen with the Southern Troubadours. She had a full-flavored contralto singing voice, somewhere "between sweet and jazz," Alberta HUNTER said. Green appeared in an act called Green and Pugh but first came to notice in Southside Chicago just before World War I at the notorious Panama Café. With Florence MILLS and Ada "Bricktop" SMITH, she constituted the Panama Trio with Tony Jackson on piano. When the police closed the Panama Café, the trio went into vaudeville; when they split up, Green worked in 1919 with Earl Dancer on the Keith circuit.

With the reintroduction of black musicals on Broadway, Green starred in Irvin C. Miller's 1921 revue *Put and Take* (originally entitled *Broadway Rastus*), which was castigated by the critics for discarding racial stereotypes and not being "colored" enough. She was featured the next year in *Strut Miss Lizzie,* which tried unsuccessfully to capitalize on the popularity of *Shuffle Along.* Green appeared in Florence Mills's *Dixie to Broadway* in 1924, where she sang one of her classic double-entendre numbers, "He May Be Your Man, but He Comes to See Me Sometimes." At Mills' death, Green replaced her in Lew Leslie's *Blackbirds of 1927* in England. In *Harlem Hotcha* (1932) at Connie's Inn, she sang Andy RAZAF and James P. JOHNSON's "Can't Take It Papa."

Green appeared in two films, both musical melodramas: *Swing* (1938), produced by the Micheaux Film Corporation, and Meteor Productions' *Moon over Harlem* (1939) with Sidney BECHET. At the end of 1938 she had a major role in Michael Ashwood's *Policy Kings* with music by James P. JOHNSON in

which she sang "Walking My Baby Back Home" and "You, You, You." She was well received, but *Variety* called the show "pitifully misguided," and it closed after only three performances at the Nora Bayes Theater. Details of the later life of one of Harlem's most popular torch singers are presently unknown.

REFERENCE

CUNARD, NANCY. *Negro: An Anthology.* New York, 1970.

RICHARD NEWMAN

Green, Frederick William "Freddie" (March 31, 1911–March 1, 1987), guitarist. Born in Charleston, S.C., Green taught himself guitar as a child and went on to anchor the rhythm section of the Count BASIE band for half a century. He first came to New York in 1930—where he remained for most of his life—performing as a banjoist. He was working for Kenny Clarke in 1936 when the critic and producer John Hammond heard him play at a Greenwich Village club. Hammond referred Green to Count Basie, who hired the guitarist in 1937, and except for brief intervals, Green remained with Basie for most of the next five decades. As part of the "all-American rhythm section," which accompanied Basie until 1941, Green rarely soloed; instead, he provided an unamplified and unassuming but steady presence on such Basie classics as "Good Morning Blues" (1937) and "Topsy" (1937) and the 1938 recordings with the Kansas City Six, which included Lester Young, Buck Clayton, and other members of the Basie band.

In addition to his work with Basie, Green also backed up Lester Young, Billie Holiday, Benny Goodman, Teddy Wilson, Benny Carter, Lionel Hampton, and Illinois Jacquet. Green recorded his first album as a leader, *Mr. Rhythm,* in 1955. He also composed several works for the Basie band, including "Down for Double," "Right On," and "Corner Pocket." His last major recording with Basie was *Kansas City Shout* (1980). Green, who continued to play in Basie's band after the bandleader's death, died in Las Vegas.

REFERENCES

JORDAN, STEVE, with Tom Scanlan. *Rhythm Man: Fifty Years in Jazz.* Ann Arbor, Mich., 1991.
RUSSELL, ROSS. *Jazz Style in Kansas City and the Southwest.* Berkeley, Calif., 1971.

MICHAEL D. SCOTT

Greener, Richard Theodore (January 30, 1844–May 2, 1922), diplomat. Born in Philadelphia in 1844 and raised in Cambridge, Mass., Richard T. Greener became, in 1870, the first black to graduate from Harvard College. He worked from 1870 to 1873 as a school principal, first at the Institute for Colored Youth in Philadelphia, then at the Preparatory High School for Colored Youth in the District of Columbia. In 1873 he accepted a professorship in metaphysics and logic at the University of South Carolina and studied there for the law degree he had always wanted. In 1876 he was admitted to the bar in South Carolina and in 1877 to the bar in the District of Columbia. In 1879 Greener became dean of Howard University's law school.

In 1877, at the Congress of the American Social Science Association held in Saratoga Springs, N.Y., Greener presented a paper advocating the migration of the freedmen to the western states. (Frederick DOUGLASS presented an opposing paper.) Greener supported other social causes besides that of black civil rights, including women's rights and the reform of the land system in Ireland. Yet he never became a confidant of either W. E. B. DU BOIS or Booker T. WASHINGTON and was never active in African-American affairs. He served on the 1880 Republican conference that nominated James A. Garfield for president and was secretary of the Grant Memorial Association in New York State from 1885 to 1892. A loyal Republican, he contributed to government-reform movements in New York City during the 1880s and '90s, serving from 1892 to 1899 as chief examiner of the city's municipal civil-service board.

However, financial and marital difficulties led him to seek work in the U.S. Foreign Service. In 1898 he was appointed the first U.S. consul to Vladivostok, Russia, a position he held until 1905. During that time he was decorated by the Chinese government for his famine relief work. As consul, he served as advocate for both Britain and Japan in the settlement of the Russo-Japanese War. He retired from his post in 1905, and in 1906 he settled in Chicago. Greener joined the Harvard Club and resumed his writing activities but failed to produce any major publications. He died in his Chicago home of a cerebral hemorrhage in 1922.

REFERENCES

LOGAN, RAYFORD W., and MICHAEL R. WINSTON, eds. *Dictionary of American Negro Biography.* New York, 1982.

SOLLORS, WERNER, et al., eds. *Blacks at Harvard: A Documentary History of African-American Experience at Harvard and Radcliffe.* New York, 1993.

LYDIA MCNEILL

Greenfield, Elizabeth Taylor (c. 1824–March 31, 1876), concert singer. Born a slave in Natchez, Miss., Elizabeth Taylor Greenfield was brought as an infant to Philadelphia by her mistress and later manumitted there. Her musical talent became apparent at an early age, and she studied voice briefly with a local amateur. In 1851 she moved to Buffalo, N.Y., and made her debut before the Buffalo Musical Association in October of that year. After that concert, the Buffalo press dubbed her "the Black Swan" (derived from the stage name for Irish soprano Catherine Hayes), and Greenfield retained this sobriquet throughout her career. From December 1851 through March 1853 she concertized in the northern United States and Canada under the management of Col. J. H. Wood. On March 31, 1853, she set sail for London for a concert tour and further training. The duchess of Sutherland and the writer Harriet Beecher Stowe befriended her there, and she studied with George Smart, organist and composer of the Royal Chapel. While in England, Greenfield gave concerts and performed before Queen Victoria at Buckingham Palace. She returned to the United States in July 1854 and resettled in Philadelphia, where she remained active for twenty years as a teacher and performer. During the 1860s, she directed an opera troupe.

Greenfield reportedly possessed a natural soprano voice of unusual range and flexibility. Her repertory included operatic arias, oratorio literature, and popular tunes. Critics often compared her with such European singers as Giulia Grisi, Jenny Lind, and Teresa Parodi.

REFERENCES

LABREW, ARTHUR. *The Black Swan, Elizabeth T. Greenfield, Songstress: Biographical Study.* Detroit, 1969.

SOUTHERN, EILEEN. *Biographical Dictionary of Afro-American and African Musicians.* Westport, Conn., 1982.

TROTTER, JAMES MONROE. *Music and Some Highly Musical People.* 1878. Reprint. New York, 1968.

JOSEPHINE WRIGHT

Greer, William Alexander "Sonny" (December 13, 1895–March 23, 1982), jazz drummer. Born in Long Branch, N.J., Greer played drums as a child and first performed professionally in local bands, including those of Wilbur Gardner and Mabel Ross. In 1919, while playing in Marie Lucas's orchestra at the Howard Theater in Washington, D.C., Greer met pianist Duke Ellington. Greer began working for Ellington the next year, an association that lasted more than three decades.

Greer had a reputation as a hard-drinking, extroverted showman, who at times hustled pool to retrieve his drums from pawnshops. Nonetheless, he eschewed flashy solos. Rather, he was a master colorist who depended on subtle brushwork, the cymbal, and chimes and gongs. Despite his erratic sense of swing, Greer was Ellington's preferred drummer, and he distinguished himself on the ragtime-rhythm "The Creeper" (1926), "Ring Dem Bells," a showpiece for tubular bells (1930), and *Liberian Suite* (1947). He first recorded as a leader in 1944 ("Ration Storm"). Greer left Ellington in 1951 and performed with saxophonist Johnny HODGES, trumpeter Henry "Red" Allen, and trombonist Tyree Glenn. In the 1960s he worked with saxophonist Eddie Barefield and trombonist J. C. Higginbotham, and in 1967 he led his own band, appearing in the film *The Night They Raided Minsky's*. He was also the subject of a short film, *Sonny* (1968). In the 1970s he performed with pianist Brooks Kerr. Greer, a longtime resident of New York, died in 1982.

REFERENCES

DANCE, STANLEY. *The World of Duke Ellington*. New York, 1990.
FISH, S. "Sonny Greer: The Elder Statesman of Jazz." *Modern Drummer* 8 (1981).

JOHN EDWARD HASSE

Gregory, Frederick Drew (January 7, 1941–), astronaut. Born and raised in Washington, D.C., Gregory graduated with a B.S. from the U.S. Air Force Academy in 1964. He then received pilot training at Randolph Air Force Base (AFB) and completed squadron officer school in 1965. In 1966, after a year as a helicopter pilot at the Central Aerospace Rescue and the Recovery Center at Vance AFB in Oklahoma, Gregory served as a helicopter pilot and rescue-crew commander in South Vietnam. Returning to the United States in 1967, Gregory was successively stationed at Whiteman AFB in Missouri, Randolph AFB, and Davis-Monthan AFB in Arizona. From 1971 to 1974, he was an Air Force research and engineering test pilot at Wright-Patterson AFB in Ohio. From 1974 to 1978 he was a NASA research test pilot at the Langley Research Center in Virginia.

In April 1975, Gregory returned to South Vietnam and flew helicopters to rescue refugees during the evacuation of Saigon. In 1978 he was accepted into NASA's astronaut program. He made his first space flight aboard the shuttle *Challenger* in April 1985. On that flight he became the first black astronaut to pilot a spaceship. He then served on the ground as lead capsule communicator and was in contact with the *Challenger* crew when the shuttle exploded on January 28, 1986. On November 22, 1989, Gregory became the first African American to command a space flight when *Discovery* was launched. He served again as commander aboard the space shuttle *Atlantis* in November 1991. In charge of a six-man crew, Gregory had to chart a new course in space in order to avoid colliding with a 3,200-pound Soviet rocket remnant. The flight was cut short by three days due to a failed navigation device, and Gregory successfully landed the spacecraft under manual control. In May 1992, NASA named Gregory to the post of associate administrator for the Office of Safety and Mission Quality. He was awarded an honorary doctor of science degree from the University of the District of Columbia in 1986; his other awards include the Defense Superior Service Medal, the Air Force Distinguished Flying Cross, the Air Force Commendation Medal, and the NASA Space Flight Medal.

REFERENCES

"Anacosta High's High Flyers." *Washington Post*. December 5, 1991, p. A22.
HAWTHORNE, DOUGLAS B. *Men and Women of Space*. San Diego, Calif., 1992.

LYDIA McNEILL

Gregory, George, Jr. (November 22, 1906–May 11, 1994), civic leader and athlete. George Gregory was born in New York City in 1906. A star athlete in three sports, he graduated from DeWitt Clinton High School in the Bronx in 1927. Gregory then attended Columbia University, supporting himself as a redcap at Pennsylvania Station. At Columbia he was an outstanding BASKETBALL player. He was captain of the 1930–1931 varsity team, which won its league championship. Only the second black to make Columbia's varsity, in 1931 Gregory became the first African-American basketball player to be named to the All-American team. He played semiprofessional basketball while he earned a law degree from St. John's University in New York City.

While at Columbia, Gregory began a career in public service as the boys' director for the Harlem Center of the Children's Aid Society. This led to work in settlement houses and youth clubs such as the Harlem Youth Center and the Forest Neighborhood House in the Bronx. In 1947 he was a founding member of the New York City Youth Board.

After WORLD WAR II Gregory became increasingly involved in urban redevelopment in Harlem and in projects that would create job opportunities for blacks. From 1950 to 1965, a time of enormous growth in public works in Harlem, Gregory chaired Community Planning Board 10. He served as a commissioner on the Municipal Civil Service Commission from 1954 to 1968. Gregory also helped to promote public JAZZ and art festivals, creating the "Jazzmobile," which brought top jazz talent to Harlem neighborhoods. He retired in 1970 after serving two years on what is now the Department of Environmental Protection. He died in New York City in 1994 at the age of eighty-eight.

REFERENCES

CHALK, OCIANIA. *Black College Sport*. New York, 1975.

LYONS, RICHARD D. "George Gregory, Jr., 88, Athlete and a Civic Leader in Harlem." Obituary. *New York Times,* May 12, 1994.

ALLISON X. MILLER

Gregory, Richard Claxton "Dick" (October 12, 1932–), comedian, activist, and rights advocate. Dick Gregory was born and raised in a St. Louis slum. Abandoned by his father when he was a child, Gregory worked at odd jobs to help support his family. In high school, he distinguished himself as a talented runner and demonstrated the quick wit and gift for satire that would ultimately catapult him toward stardom. With the aid of an athletic scholarship, he attended Southern Illinois University at Carbondale (1951–1954 and 1956), where he became a leading track star and began to dream of becoming a COMEDIAN.

Drafted into the army in 1954, Gregory returned briefly to Carbondale after completing his term of service in 1956 and then traveled to Chicago to pursue his goal of becoming a comedian. He admired and was influenced by Timmie Rogers, Slappy White, and Nipsey RUSSELL. In the late 1950s, Gregory worked in small black clubs like the Esquire Show Lounge, where he met his future wife, Lillian Smith, and struggled to gain popular recognition. His efforts won him a cameo appearance in "Cast the First Stone," a 1959 ABC television documentary.

Gregory's breakthrough occurred in January 1961, when the Playboy Club in Chicago hired him to replace the unexpectedly ill white comedian "Professor" Irwin Corey. Gregory's bold, ironic, cool, and detached humor completely disarmed and converted his audience, which included many white southern conventioneers. After this success, his contract with the Playboy Club was quickly extended from several weeks to three years. Against the backdrop of the intensifying pace of the CIVIL RIGHTS MOVEMENT, Gregory's candid, topical humor signaled a new relationship between African-American comedians and white mainstream audiences. By 1962 he had become a national celebrity and the first black comic superstar in the modern era—opening the doors for countless black comedians. He also became an author, publishing *From the Back of the Bus* (1962) and, with Robert Lipsyte, *Nigger: An Autobiography* (1964).

His celebrity status secured, Gregory emerged as an outspoken political activist during the 1960s. As an avid supporter of the civil rights movement, he participated in voter registration drives throughout the South, marched in countless parades and demonstrations, and was arrested numerous times. He also began to entertain at prisons and for civil rights organizations, using his biting humor as a powerful tool to highlight racism and inequality in the United States. The assassinations of John. F. Kennedy, the Rev. Dr. Martin Luther KING, Jr., and others led Gregory to believe in the existence of a large framework of conspiracies to thwart civil rights and liberties in the United States. He took to the lecture circuit, espousing the ideas of Mark Lane, a leading conspiracy theorist.

Gregory found numerous ways to dramatize his chosen causes. He fasted for lengthy periods to demonstrate his commitment to civil rights and to protest the VIETNAM WAR, the abuse of narcotics, and world hunger. In 1967 he campaigned unsuccessfully in a write-in effort to be mayor of Chicago, and in 1968 he was the presidential candidate for the U.S. Freedom and Peace party, a split-off faction within the Peace and Freedom party, whose candidate for president in 1968 was Eldridge CLEAVER. By the late 1960s, Gregory was increasingly devoting his attention to the youth of America, lecturing at hundreds of college campuses each year and making fewer and fewer night club appearances; he released his last comedy album, *Caught in the Act,* in 1973.

During the 1970s, Gregory wrote several books, including *No More Lies: The Myth and Reality of American History* (published as by Richard Claxton Gregory with James R. McGraw, 1971); *Code Name Zorro: The Murder of Martin Luther King, Jr.* (with Mark Lane, 1971); and *Dick Gregory's Political Primer* (1972). After moving with his wife and ten children to a farm in Massachusetts in 1973, he became a well-known advocate of vegetarianism. Often limiting himself to a regimen of fruit and juices, he became a nutritional consultant, often appearing on talk shows in his new role, and wrote (with Alvenia Fulton)

Dick Gregory's Natural Diet for Folks Who Eat, Cookin' with Mother Nature (1974). He also wrote *Up from Nigger,* with James R. McGraw, the second installment of his autobiography (1976).

In 1984 Gregory founded Health Enterprises, Inc., successfully marketing various weight-loss products. Three years later he introduced the Slim-Safe Bahamian Diet, a powdered diet mix that proved extremely popular, and expanded his financial holdings to hotels and other properties. These economic successes were abruptly reversed after the failure of a financing deal and conflicts with his business partners. Gregory was evicted from his Massachusetts home in 1992. In the same year, he returned to his home town of St. Louis to organize the Campaign for Human Dignity, whose stated purpose was to reclaim predominantly African-American neighborhoods from drug dealers and prostitutes. In October 1993, Gregory was arrested for illegally camping—along with members of his "Dignity Patrol"—in a crime-ridden park in Washington, D.C. In 1993 he also coauthored, with Mark Lane, *Murder in Memphis,* another book about the assassination of Rev. Dr. Martin Luther King, Jr.

After Gregory achieved the pinnacle of success in the world of stand-up comedy, he made a decision to place his celebrity status in the service of his fierce and uncompromising commitment to human rights. Throughout the various shifts and turns of his career for more than three decades, he has kept faith with those commitments.

REFERENCES

GREGORY, DICK, with Martin Lipsyte. *Nigger: An Autobiography.* New York, 1964.
GREGORY, DICK, with James R. McGraw. *Up from Nigger.* New York, 1976.
HENDRA, TONY. *Going Too Far.* New York, 1987.
WATKINS, MEL. *On the Real Side: Laughing, Lying and Signifying—The Underground Tradition of African-American Humor That Transformed American Culture from Slavery to Richard Pryor.* New York, 1994.

JAMES A. MILLER

Griffith-Joyner, Florence Delorez (December 21, 1959–), athlete. Florence Griffith was born in Los Angeles, the seventh of eleven children of an electronics technician and a garment worker. When she was four, her parents separated and she moved with her mother and siblings to the Jordan Downs housing project in the Watts section of Los Angeles. Griffith began running at age seven in competitions sponsored by the Jesse Owens National Youth Games for underprivileged youth and won races at ages fourteen and fifteen. She became a member of the track team at Jordan High School, where she set two school records before graduating in 1978.

In 1979 Griffith enrolled at California State University at Northridge, where she met assistant track coach Bob Kersee. However, she was forced to drop out of college the next year due to lack of funds. With the help of Kersee, who had moved to the University of California at Los Angeles (UCLA), Griffith won an athletic scholarship to UCLA and returned to college in 1981. Griffith competed on the track team, and in 1982 she won the NCAA championships in the two hundred meters. In 1983 she won the NCAA championships in the four hundred meters and graduated from UCLA with a major in psychology. In the 1984 Olympics in Los Angeles, she finished second to fellow American Valerie Brisco-Hooks in the two hundred meters.

After the Olympics Griffith worked as a customer-service representative for a bank during the day and as a beautician at night. In early 1987, however, she decided to train full-time for the 1988 Olympics. In October 1987 she married Al Joyner, brother of athlete Jackie Joyner-Kersee.

After strong showings in the world championships and the U.S. trials, Griffith-Joyner was a favorite for the 1988 Olympics in Seoul, Korea. Flo-Jo, as she was dubbed by the media, did not disappoint, winning three gold medals and one silver medal. Griffith-Joyner set an Olympic record in the one hundred meters and a world record in the two hundred meters. She ran the third leg for the American winning team in the four-by-one-hundred meter relay and the anchor leg for the American silver-medal winners in the four-by-four-hundred meter relay. Griffith-Joyner's outstanding performance and striking appearance (including long, extravagantly decorated fingernails and brightly colored one-legged running outfits) earned her worldwide media attention. She won the 1988 Jesse Owens Award and the 1988 Sullivan Award, given annually to the best amateur athlete.

Griffith-Joyner settled comfortably into post-Olympic life with numerous endorsements and projects, including designing her own sportswear line and a brief acting stint on the television soap opera *Santa Barbara* (1992). In 1993 President Bill Clinton named her cochairwoman of the President's Council on Physical Fitness and Sports.

REFERENCES

DAVIS, MICHAEL D. *Black American Women in Olympic Track and Field.* Jefferson, N.C., 1992.
HINE, DARLENE CLARK. *Black Women in America.* Brooklyn, N.Y., 1993.

CINDY HIMES GISSENDANNER

Griggs, Sutton Elbert (1872–1933), novelist and preacher. Born in Chatfield, Tex., Sutton E. Griggs was raised in Dallas, and attended Bishop College in Marshall, Tex. Following the path of his father, the Rev. Allen R. Griggs, he studied for the Baptist ministry at the Richmond Theological Seminary (later part of Virginia Union University) and was ordained in 1893. Griggs's first pastorate was in Berkley, Va., and he went on to serve more than thirty years as a Baptist minister in Nashville and Memphis, Tenn. In addition to his career as a pastor, he soon established himself as an author of novels, political tracts, and religious pamphlets. In the period following Reconstruction, marked by a fierce resurgence of segregation, disfranchisement, and antiblack violence in the South, Griggs—along with such African-American writers as Charles W. CHESNUTT, Paul Laurence DUNBAR, W. E. B. DU BOIS, and Frances Ellen Watkins HARPER—responded with positive portrayals of black Americans and demands for civil rights.

Griggs wrote more than thirty books, most of which he published himself and vigorously promoted during preaching tours of the South, as he describes in *The Story of My Struggles* (1914). His five novels are technically unimpressive, weakened by stilted dialogue, flat characterizations, and sentimental and melodramatic plot lines. Even as flawed polemics, however, they are distinguished by their unprecedented investigation of politically charged themes of African-American life in the South, such as black nationalism, miscegenation, racial violence, and suffrage. Above all else a religious moralist, Griggs was critical of assimilationist projects, calling instead for social equality and black self-sufficiency, but he was equally impatient with radical militancy in the quest for civil rights.

His fiction often centers on such ethical concerns. In *Imperium in Imperio* (1899), Griggs's best-known work and one of the first African-American political novels, the integrationist Belton Piedmont chooses to die rather than support a militaristic plot to seize Texas and Louisiana from the United States as a haven for African-Americans. In *Overshadowed* (1901), Astral Herndon, discouraged by the "shadow" of racial prejudice both in the United States and in Africa, chooses exile as a "citizen of the ocean." Dorlan Worthell in *Unfettered* (1902) wins the hand of the beautiful Morlene only by offering a plan for African-American political organization. *The Hindered Hand* (1905) is pessimistic about the possibilities of reforming southern race relations: The Seabright family encounters violent tragedy in striving to "pass" in white society in order to transform white racist opinions, and their one dark-skinned daughter, Tiara, flees to Liberia with her husband, Ensal, who has refused to participate in a "Slavic" conspiracy to destroy the Anglo-Saxons of the United States through germ warfare. While Baug Peppers attempts inconclusively to fight for voting rights for southern blacks before the Supreme Court in *Pointing the Way* (1908), Letitia Gilbreth, who believes that "whitening" the race through assimilation is the only way to effect racial equality, is driven mad when her niece refuses the mulatto Peppers and marries a dark-skinned man.

Similar themes also appear in Griggs's political treatises, most notably *Wisdom's Call* (1909), an eloquent argument for civil rights in the South that comments on lynching, suffrage, and the rights of black women, and *Guide to Racial Greatness; or, The Science of Collective Efficiency* (1923), with a companion volume of biblical verses entitled *Kingdom Builders' Manual* (1924); these together offer a project for the political organization of the African-American southern population, stressing education, religious discipline, employment, and land ownership. At the end of his life, Griggs returned to Texas to assume the position his father had held, the pastorate of the Hopewell Baptist Church in Denison. He soon departed for Houston and, at the time of his death, was attempting to found a national religious and civic institute there.

REFERENCES

FLEMING, ROBERT E. "Sutton E. Griggs: Militant Black Novelist." *Phylon* 34 (March 1973): 73–77.
GLOSTER, HUGH M. "Sutton E. Griggs: Novelist of the New Negro." *Phylon* 4 (Fourth Quarter 1943): 333–345.

BRENT EDWARDS

Grimes, Leonard Andrew (November 9, 1815–March 14, 1874), minister and abolitionist. Born in Leesburg, Va., Leonard Grimes moved to Washington, D.C., while still a boy and worked in a butcher shop and then in an apothecary. He next worked for a slave owner with whom he traveled throughout the South, witnessing the cruel conditions of slavery firsthand. When he was again living in Washington, he helped a family of slaves escape to Canada and was subsequently sentenced to two years in the state prison in Richmond, Va. Upon his release he returned to Washington, where he was baptized in 1840 by the Rev. William Williams. He embarked upon a career as a Baptist minister, helping to organize the American Baptist Missionary Convention in 1840, before moving to New Bedford, Mass. On November 24, 1848, he was ordained as the first minister of the Twelfth Street Baptist Church in Boston, having been recruited for the position by the new church's members. He held this position for a quarter of a century.

During his tenure, the church's membership grew from twenty-three to three hundred people, despite the fact that membership was often diminished due to the FUGITIVE SLAVE LAWS, whereby escaped slaves living in Massachusetts were returned to the South. Furthermore, during the Civil War, many people in Grimes's congregation joined the 54th Regiment of Massachusetts Volunteers. Grimes was invited to be the regiment's chaplain, but he preferred to remain in Boston, where he raised funds to aid the soldiers. He died suddenly at his Boston home on March 14, 1874, having just returned from New York, where he had delivered a contribution from his congregation to the board of the American Baptist Home Mission Society, of which he was a member.

REFERENCES

SIMMONS, WILLIAM J. *Men of Mark.* Cleveland, 1887.
WILIAMS, GEORGE W. *History of the Negro Race in America, 1618–1880.* New York, 1968.

NEIL GOLDSTEIN

LYDIA McNEILL

Grimké, Angelina Weld (February 27, 1880– June 10, 1958), writer. Born in Boston, Grimké was the daughter of Archibald GRIMKÉ and Sarah Stanley Grimké. She attended integrated schools in Hyde Park, Mass., and graduated in 1902 from Boston Normal School of Gymnastics, later part of Wellesley College. Grimké worked as a teacher in Washington, D.C., from that time until her retirement in 1926. In 1930, she moved to Brooklyn, where she lived for the rest of her life.

Grimké best-known work was a short play entitled *Rachel,* first presented in 1916 and published in book form in 1920. The play portrays a young African-American woman who is filled with despair and, despite her love of children, despondently resolves not to bring any of her own into the world. With its tragic view of race relations, *Rachel* was staged several times by the NATIONAL ASSOCIATION FOR THE ADVANCEMENT OF COLORED PEOPLE (NAACP) as a response to D. W. Griffith's racist 1915 film BIRTH OF A NATION.

But Grimké's most influential work was her poetry. Publishing first as a teenager, she initially wrote in the sentimental style of late nineteenth-century popular poetry. In the early years of the twentieth century, however, she began to display an interest in experimentation, both formal and thematic. She openly took up sexual themes, with a frankness that was not common among African-American poets of

Poet and playwright Angelina Weld Grimké was one of the most gifted of the young black writers who began their careers in the years around World War I. Her play *Rachel* was among the first works by a black dramatist to be staged professionally. (Moorland-Spingarn Research Center, Howard University)

her time. Only occasionally addressing racial issues, she nevertheless did so with a militance and subjectivity that looked toward the HARLEM RENAISSANCE. Although she was not to be a major figure in that movement, such work did much to contribute its foundations.

(Angelina Weld Grimké should not be confused with the nineteenth-century abolitionist Angelina Grimké Weld, though they were related. The former's father was the nephew of the latter.)

REFERENCE

HULL, GLORIA T. *Color, Sex and Poetry: Three Women Writers of the Harlem Renaissance.* Bloomington, Ind., 1987.

DICKSON D. BRUCE, JR.

Grimké, Archibald Henry (August 17, 1849–February 25, 1930), writer and activist. Born a slave in Charleston, S.C., Grimké was the nephew of the noted abolitionists Sarah Grimké and Angelina Grimké Weld. Receiving some education during his childhood, after EMANCIPATION he attended Lincoln University and, supported by his aunts, Harvard Law School, from which he graduated in 1874. In 1884, he became editor of the Boston *Hub,* a Republican newspaper. In 1886, disillusioned by the growing indifference of REPUBLICAN PARTY to the problems of African Americans and by the party's conservative economic program, Grimké switched allegiances. He soon became the most prominent African-American Democrat in Massachusetts.

After 1890, Grimké removed himself from politics and, focusing on scholarship, wrote major biographies of William Lloyd Garrison and Charles Sum-

Born a Charleston slave, Archibald H. Grimké was a leader of Washington's African-American community for many decades and a cofounder in 1879 of the American Negro Academy. (Photographs and Prints Division, Schomburg Center for Research in Black Culture, The New York Public Library, Astor, Lenox and Tilden Foundations)

ner. Then, in 1894, he was appointed consul to the Dominican Republic, where he served until 1898.

Upon his return to the United States, Grimké also returned to writing, and published widely on racial questions. In 1903, he became president of the leading African-American intellectual organization, AMERICAN NEGRO ACADEMY, a post he held until 1919. As an activist, he was deeply involved in the debate over the leadership of Booker T. WASHINGTON, although, despite a general opposite to Washington's views, he was unwilling to commit himself fully to either side.

But his activism became particularly notable when, in 1913, he became president of the District of Columbia branch of the NATIONAL ASSOCIATION FOR THE ADVANCEMENT OF COLORED PEOPLE (NAACP). The branch was the organization's largest, representing the NAACP on all issues involving federal legislation and policy. As president, Grimké led its efforts into the 1920s, lobbying Congress and federal agencies to inhibit the segregationist policies of Woodrow Wilson's administration, while fighting against discrimination in the Washington community itself. In 1919, in recognition of these efforts and of his lifetime of service defending the rights of African Americans, he received the Spingarn Medal, the NAACP's highest honor.

REFERENCES

Archibald Henry Grimké Papers. Manuscript Division, Moorland-Spingarn Research Center, Howard University, Washington, D.C.
BRUCE, DICKSON D., JR. *Archibald Grimké.* Baton Rouge, La., 1993.

DICKSON D. BRUCE, JR.

Grimké, Charlotte L. Forten (August 17, 1837–July 22, 1914), abolitionist, teacher, and writer. Charlotte Forten was born into one of Philadelphia's leading African-American families. Her grandfather, James FORTEN, was a well-to-do sail-maker and abolitionist. Her father, Robert Bridges FORTEN, maintained both the business and the abolitionism.

Charlotte Forten continued her family's traditions. As a teenager, having been sent to Salem, Mass., for her education, she actively joined that community of radical abolitionists identified with William Lloyd Garrison (*see* ABOLITION). She also entered enthusiastically into the literary and intellectual life of nearby Boston, and even embarked on a literary career of her own. Some of her earliest poetry was published in antislavery journals during her student years. And she began to keep a diary, published almost a century later, which remains one of the most valuable accounts of that era.

Completing her education, Forten became a teacher, initially in Salem, and later in Philadelphia. Unfortunately, she soon began to suffer from ill health, which would plague her for the rest of her life. Nevertheless, while unable to sustain her efforts in the classroom for any length of time, she did continue to write and to engage in antislavery activity. With the outbreak of the CIVIL WAR, she put both her convictions and her training to use, joining other abolitionists on the liberated islands off the South Carolina coast to teach and work with the newly emancipated slaves.

On the Sea Islands (*see* GULLAH), she also kept a diary, later published. This second diary, and two essays she wrote at the time for the *Atlantic Monthly,* are among the most vivid accounts of the abolitionist experiment. Like many teachers, Forten felt a cultural distance from the freedpeople but worked with dedication to teach and to prove the value of emancipation. After the war, she continued her work for the freedpeople, accepting a position in Massachusetts with the Freedmen's Union Commission.

She also continued her literary efforts, which included a translation of the French novel *Madame Thérèse,* published by Scribner in 1869. In 1872, after a year spent teaching in South Carolina, Forten moved to Washington, D.C., where she worked first as a teacher and then in the Treasury Department. There she met the Rev. Francis GRIMKÉ, thirteen years her junior, and pastor of the elite Fifteenth Street Presbyterian Church. At the end of 1878, they married.

The marriage was long and happy, despite the death in infancy of their only child. Apart from a brief residence in Jacksonville, Fla., from 1885 to 1889, the Grimkés lived in Washington, D.C. and made their Washington home a center for the capital's social and intellectual life. Although Charlotte Grimké continued to suffer from poor health, she maintained something of her former activism, serving briefly as a member of the Washington school board and participating in such organizations as the NATIONAL ASSOCIATION OF COLORED WOMEN. She did a small amount of writing, although little published. Finally, after about 1909, her failing health led to her virtual retirement from active life.

REFERENCES

Charlotte Forten Grimké Papers. In Francis James Grimké Papers, Manuscript Division, Moorland-Spingarn Research Center, Howard University, Washington, D.C.

COOPER, ANNA J. *Life and Writings of the Grimké Family.* 2 vols. 1951.

STEVENSON, BRENDA, ed. *The Journals of Charlotte Forten Grimké.* New York, 1988.

DICKSON D. BRUCE, JR.

Grimké, Francis James (October 4, 1850–November 11, 1937), minister, author. Francis Grimké was born on Caneacres, a rice plantation near Charleston, S.C. He was the son of Henry Grimké, a wealthy white lawyer, and his African-American slave Nancy Weston, who also bore him two other sons, Archibald (1849) (*see* Archibald Henry GRIMKÉ) and John (1853). Henry Grimké died in September 1852, and the mother and children lived for several years in a de facto free status. This ended in 1860 when E. Montague Grimké, the boys' half-brother, to whom ownership had passed, sought to exercise his "property rights." Francis Grimké ran away from home and joined the Confederate Army as an officer's valet. Montague Grimké eventually sold him to another officer, whom Francis Grimké served until EMANCIPATION. In 1866, he began his educational journey at Lincoln University (Pennsylvania), where he came to the notice of his white abolitionist aunts, Angelina Grimké Weld and Sarah Moore Grimké, who acknowledged his kinship and encouraged his further study, providing moral and material support.

Francis Grimké began the study of law at Lincoln after graduating at the head of his undergraduate class in 1870. He continued to prepare for a legal career, attending Howard University in 1874, but felt called to the ministry and moved to the Princeton Theological Seminary in 1875. Upon graduation from the seminary in 1878, Grimké began his ministry at the 15th Street Presbyterian Church in Washington, D.C., and married Charlotte L. Forten of Philadelphia (*see* Charlotte L. Forten GRIMKÉ). In 1880, Theodora Cornelia, their only child, died in infancy. From 1885 to 1889, Grimké served the Laura St. Presbyterian Church in Jacksonville, Fla. He returned to Washington and remained as pastor at the 15th Street Church until 1928, when he became pastor emeritus.

Grimké's pulpit afforded him access to one of the most accomplished African-American congregations in America; the members expected and received sermons that addressed issues of faith and morals with ethical insight, literary grace, and prophetic zeal. He practiced what he preached, earning himself the sobriquet Black Puritan. Through printed sermons and articles, Grimké encouraged a national audience to agitate for civil rights "until justice is done." He campaigned against racism in American churches, and helped form the Afro-Presbyterian Council to encourage black moral uplift and self-help. He also participated in the creation of organizations such as

Francis J. Grimké, a Presbyterian minister in Washington, D.C., and one of the most prominent African-American leaders at the turn of the century, tried to maintain a middle position between Booker T. Washington and W. E. B. Du Bois. (Prints and Photographs Division, Library of Congress)

the AMERICAN NEGRO ACADEMY, which nurtured African-American development.

While not normally an activist outside the church, Grimké was an active supporter of Booker T. WASHINGTON's self-help efforts. However, in the early years of the twentieth century, he joined the group of African-American "radicals" led by W. E. B. DU BOIS. He sided with Du Bois against Washington at the Carnegie Hall Conference (1906), which led to the schism between Washington and the radicals, and later became a strong and longtime supporter of the NAACP.

In 1923, Grimké aroused a storm of controversy by a Howard University School of Religion convocation address, "What Is the Trouble with Christianity Today?" in which he denounced groups such as the YMCA and the "federation of white churches" for their racist practices and challenged the sincerity

of the faith of former President Woodrow Wilson. Legislators, led by Rep. James Byrnes of South Carolina, protested the address, and tried to remove him from Howard's board of trustees by threatening Howard's federal budget appropriation. Grimké retired in 1925 and lived in Washington, D.C., until his death in 1937.

REFERENCE

WOODSON, CARTER G., ed. *The Works of Francis James Grimké*. 4 vols. Washington, D.C., 1942.

HENRY J. FERRY

Guardian, The (1901–1960), weekly newspaper. The *Guardian*, an African-American weekly newspaper, served primarily as a forum for its founder and editor, William Monroe TROTTER. Self-billed as "America's greatest race journal," it carried the motto "For Every Right with All Thy Might," setting the militant tone for its notorious page 4 editorials on racial issues. While the *Guardian* attracted a national audience by including social gossip from other major cities, its agenda was explicitly political, emphasizing integration, legal rights, and the importance of strong and persistent agitation. Trotter found it fitting that the *Guardian* came to occupy the very building where William Lloyd Garrison's abolitionist paper, the *Liberator*, had been produced.

Born into a wealthy Boston family, the Harvard-educated Trotter abandoned a successful business career, convinced that the pursuit of prosperity by African Americans was "like building a house upon the sands" so long as racial discrimination and persecution persisted. Trotter, with fellow Massachusetts Racial Protective Association member George W. Forbes, launched the *Guardian* on November 9, 1901, in order to challenge aggressively Booker T. WASHINGTON's accommodationist model of post-Reconstruction race relations (*see* ACCOMMODATIONISM).

Under Trotter's stewardship, the *Guardian*'s reportage featured his bellicose forays into the political arena, most prominently a public confrontation with Washington in 1903, which was dubbed the "Boston Riot." After the fracas, Forbes quit the paper, significantly weakening its literary quality. Soon thereafter, Washington himself launched a secret campaign to undermine Trotter's political legitimacy and the *Guardian* itself. But neither smear tactics nor infiltration of Trotter's circle of activists nor the subsidizing of rival publications succeeded in silencing Washington's nemesis. Even those who disagreed with Trotter's methods, such as W. E. B. DU BOIS, nonetheless expressed sympathy with his point of view.

The *Guardian* continued to reflect Trotter's commitment to independent politics, militant integration, and direct action. Presidential endorsements were based on candidates' records on race issues, not on party loyalties. The newspaper gave ample coverage to campaigns Trotter led or supported, including the NIAGARA MOVEMENT, the fight against racial discrimination in the armed forces during WORLD WAR I, and the public protests against D. W. Griffith's controversial film BIRTH OF A NATION (1915). In later years, the *Guardian* defended the Scottsboro Boys (*see* the SCOTTSBORO CASE) and supported New Deal economic policies.

The *Guardian*, said Trotter, was "not a mere money-making business, but a public work for equal rights and freedom." Intent on preserving the *Guardian*'s independence, he refused to sell shares in or incorporate the paper; because he relied on the black community for support, he did not raise the annual subscription rate until 1920. But the *Guardian* was Trotter's sole source of income, and he and his wife, Geraldine, made enormous personal sacrifices to keep the paper afloat, mortgaging and selling off property piece by piece until not even their house remained.

While the *Guardian* bore its founder's personal imprint—both politically and financially—for many years, it did survive him. After Trotter's death in 1934, his sister, Maude Trotter Steward, edited the *Guardian* until she died in 1957.

REFERENCES

BENNETT, LERONE, JR. *Pioneers in Protest.* Baltimore, Md., 1968.

CAMPBELL, GEORGETTA MERRITT. *Extant Collections of Early Black Newspapers: A Research Guide to the Black Press, 1880–1915, with an Index to the Boston "Guardian," 1902–1904.* Troy, N.Y., 1981.

FOX, STEPHEN R. *The Guardian of Boston: William Monroe Trotter.* New York, 1970.

TAMI J. FRIEDMAN
RENEE TURSI

Guillory, Ida Lewis "Queen Ida" (January 15, 1929–), zydeco singer and accordionist. Ida Lewis was born and raised in Lake Charles, La., and studied music with two of her uncles, who were musicians playing the popular Gulf Coast dance style known as ZYDECO. When she was seventeen, her family moved to Beaumont, Tex., and then to San Francisco, where she learned to play the accordion. She married Ray Guillory in 1949; for most of the next twenty years she was a housewife, occasionally working as a bus driver.

In the early 1970s she began to perform at private functions. In 1975, while attending a San Francisco Mardi Gras masquerade dance, she was called on-stage to perform as "the queen of Zydeco." That appearance started her career as Queen Ida, and she has since become one of the most famous and successful of all zydeco musicians, touring Europe, Africa, and Asia and recording prolifically. While she is an energetic and exciting singer, she is better known for playing the thirty-one-key accordion, an instrument that allows her greater melodic freedom than the button or piano accordion often used by zydeco musicians. Guillory has most often performed with the Bon Temps Band, an ensemble that has included her son and two of her brothers. Her albums include *Zydeco* (1976) and *On Tour* (1982), which won a Grammy Award. In 1989 she released an album, *Cookin' with Queen Ida,* and in 1990, a cookbook with the same name. Queen Ida is featured in the film *J'ai été au bal.*

REFERENCE

BROVEN, JOHN. *South to Louisiana: The Music of the Cajun Bayous.* New York, 1987.

ROSITA M. SANDS

Gullah. The Gullah are a community of African Americans who have lived along the Atlantic coastal plain and on the Sea Islands off the coast of SOUTH CAROLINA and GEORGIA since the late seventeenth century. Comprised of the descendants of slaves who lived and worked on the Sea Islands, Gullah communities continue to exist in the late twentieth century, occupying small farming and fishing communities in South Carolina and Georgia. The Gullah are noted for their preservation of African cultural traditions (*see* AFRICA), made possible by the community's geographic isolation and its inhabitants' strong community life. They speak an English-based CREOLE language also referred to as Gullah, or among Georgia Sea Islanders as Geechee.

The etymology of the term *Gullah* is uncertain. Among the most widely accepted theories is that it is a shortened form of Angola, a region of coastal central Africa (with different boundaries from the contemporary nation-state and former Portuguese colony of the same name). Many of South Carolina's slaves were imported from the older Angola. Equally plausible is the suggestion that the term is a derivation of the West African name *Golas* or *Goulah,* who were a large group of Africans occupying the hinterland of what is present-day Liberia. Large numbers of slaves were brought to South Carolina from both western and central Africa, lending both explanations credibility. The word *Geechee* is believed to have originated from *Gidzi,* the name of the language spoken in the Kissy country of present-day Liberia. Whatever the origins of these terms, it is clear that the Gullah community that developed in the Sea Islands embodied a mixture of influences from the coastal regions of West Africa.

The slave communities of the Sea Islands developed under unique geographic and demographic conditions that permitted them to maintain a degree of cohesion and autonomy denied slave communities in other regions of the South. A geographical shift in the production of rice within the South Carolina low country during the mid-1700s brought a major shift in population. South Carolina's slave population had been concentrated in the parishes surrounding Charleston, but in the 1750s, South Carolina rice planters abandoned the inland swamps for the tidal and river swamps of the coastal mainland. At the same time, new methods in the production of indigo stimulated settlement of the Sea Islands, where long-staple cotton also began to be produced in the late eighteenth century.

As a result, the coastal regions of South Carolina and the adjacent Sea Islands became the center of the plantation economy, and the demand for slave labor soared. Concurrent with this shift in agricultural production was a change in the African origins of the slaves imported into South Carolina. During the last half of the eighteenth century, imports from the Kongo-Angola region declined, and the majority of slaves introduced into the Sea Islands came from the Windward Coast (present-day Sierra Leone, and Senegal, and Gambia) and the Rice Coast (part of present-day Liberia). South Carolina planters apparently preferred slaves from these regions because of the Africans' familiarity with rice and indigo production. These African bondsmen and women brought with them the labor patterns and technical skills they had used in Africa. Their knowledge of rice planting had a major impact in transforming South Carolina's methods of rice production.

The geographic isolation of the Sea Islands and the frequency of disease in the swampy, semitropical climate of the region kept white settlement in the area to a minimum. Meanwhile, a constant, growing demand for slaves and their concentration on tremendous plantations created a black majority in the South Carolina coastal region. In 1770 the population in the South Carolina low country was 78 percent black, and the proportion of blacks along the coast and the Sea Islands probably was even higher.

The relative isolation and numerical strength of the slaves and their freedom from contact with white settlers permitted them to preserve many native African linguistic patterns and cultural traditions. The constant influx of African slaves into the region throughout the remainder of the eighteenth century (*see* SLAVE TRADE), likewise permitted the Gullah to maintain a vital link to the customs and traditions of West Africa.

The end of slavery brought significant changes to the Gullahs' traditional way of life, but the unique geographic and demographic conditions on the Sea Islands ensured that the Gullah community would retain its distinctiveness well beyond the CIVIL WAR. Blacks remained a majority in the South Carolina low country. In 1870, the population was 67 percent black; by 1900 it had decreased only marginally.

The Gullahs' experiences during and after the Civil War differed from those of blacks across the South. While the PORT ROYAL EXPERIMENT, established on the Sea Islands during the Union's wartime occupation to provide the Gullah with experience in independent farming, was ultimately a failure, many Gullah in the decades following the Civil War nevertheless were able to become independent farmers.

Due to the declining market for the Sea Islands' long-staple cotton, many white landowners began to desert the area shortly after the war's end. Agricultural production in the low country first suffered from war-related devastation of the land; then, in the early 1900s, competition from rice plantations in the western United States further crippled South Carolina's market position. As whites abandoned their former plantations and blacks took over the land, some cotton production for the market continued, but subsistence farming and fishing dominated the Sea Island economy.

Whites' abandonment of the coastal region and the Sea Islands left the Gullah even more isolated than before. While black residents of the Sea Islands during the first half of the twentieth century, like other African Americans across the South, were denied basic civil rights, they benefitted from their geographic isolation and numerical dominance. Unlike blacks in most other regions of the South, the Gullah were able to maintain cohesive, largely independent communities well into the twentieth century.

Most of what we know of the Gullah comes from studies conducted by anthropologists and linguists in the 1930s and '40s. The Gullah culture described by these observers reflects a blending of various African and American traditions. Gullah handicrafts such as basket weaving and wood carving demonstrate African roots, both in their design and their functionality. Wooden mortars and pestles, rice "fanners," and palm leaf brooms were introduced into the Sea Islands by the Gullah and were used in ways that reflected African customs. The Gullah, for example, used their palm-leaf brooms to maintain grass-free dirt yards—a tradition they still maintain in the late twentieth century. The Gullah diet similarly reflects the African origins of the original Gullah slave community. Based heavily on rice, the Gullah make gumbos and stews similar to West African dishes such as *jollof* and *plasas*.

The distinctiveness of the Gullah community is perhaps best reflected in its language. Gullah, or Geechee, a predominantly oral language, is the offspring of the West African Pidgin English that developed along the African Coast during the peak of the slave trade. Pidgin languages developed in Africa as a merger of the English language and the native languages spoken on the African coast and served as a means of communication among Africans and British slave traders. Many of the slaves from the coastal regions of West Africa that were brought to South Carolina in the eighteenth century were familiar with pidgin language and used it to communicate with one another in the New World. Over time, the pidgin mixed with the language spoken by the South Carolina planter class and took on new form. Gullah, the creole language that developed, became the dominant and native language of the slave community of the Sea Islands. Like most unwritten creole languages, Gullah rapidly evolved, and by the time it was first seriously studied in the 1930s, it undoubtedly had more in common with standard English than antebellum or eighteenth-century Gullah.

The Gullah language derives most of its vocabulary from the English language, but it also incorporates a substantial number of African words, especially from the Krio language of present-day Sierra Leone. The Gullah used names, for example, that reflected personal and historical experiences and that carried specific African meanings. Naming practices of the Gullah served, as they do for West Africans, as symbols of power and control over the outside world. The pronunciation of Gullah and its sentence and grammatical structures, moreover, deviate from the rules of standard English, reflecting instead West African patterns. Gullah is spoken with a Caribbean cadence, reflecting the common African background of the Gullah and West Indian slaves.

Gullah, though less widely spoken in the late twentieth century, remains prevalent throughout the Sea Islands. Lorenzo Dow TURNER, the first linguist to study Gullah speech in the 1940s, found a number of African words and phrases being used among the inhabitants of the Sea Islands in the 1940s. In 1993, William A. Stewart, a linguist at the City University of New York, estimated that 250,000 Sea Islanders still spoke Gullah and at least a tenth of this number spoke no other language. Gullah also has had a significant impact upon the language spoken among inhabitants across the southeastern region of the United States. Such Gullah words as *buckra* (a white person), *goober* (peanut), and *juke* (disorderly) can be found in the vocabulary of black and white southerners.

Other aspects of Gullah language observed by Turner and such scholars as Ambrose E. Gonzales and Guy B. Johnson also exhibit African roots. Gullah proverbs demonstrate an adaptation of the African tradition of speaking in parables, and the oral tradition of storytelling among the Gullah also has been identified with African patterns. Trickster tales such as those about Brer Rabbit, which were popularized in the late nineteenth and early twentieth centuries by the white folklorist Joel Chandler Harris, are still part of Gullah and Geechee folklore. These tales, often moral in tone and content, are an important form of entertainment.

Religion played a dominant role within the Gullah slave community and continued to regulate community life into the twentieth century. Church membership predicated membership in the community at large, and one was not considered a member of the plantation community until one had joined the "Praise House." Praise Houses, originally erected by planters in the 1840s as meetinghouses and places of worship for slaves, functioned as town halls among the Gullah well into the late twentieth century, possibly as late as the 1970s. The Praise House essentially took the place of the white-controlled Baptist churches as the slave community's cultural center. Even after blacks assumed control of their churches during and after the war, the Praise House remained the locus of community power.

Everyone in the community was expected to abide by the Praise House customs and regulations, enforced by a Praise House Committee, which held them to certain standards of behavior and trust. This method of defining the borders of the community reinforced the Gullahs' close-knit community structure; some argue that it mirrored West African traditions of establishing secret societies.

This utilization of the Praise House to fit the needs of the Gullah community illustrates the adaptive nature of the Gullah's religious practices. Gullah slaves applied a mixture of African customs and beliefs to Christian principles introduced by their masters to create a religion that served a vital function within their community. The Gullah incorporated certain African religious traditions into their Christian beliefs. While accepting Christianity, for example, they maintained their belief in witchcraft, called *wudu, wanga, joso,* or *juju,* and continued to consult "root doctors" for protection and for their healing powers.

The Gullahs' physical forms of worship also continued to follow West African patterns. Gullah spirituals, both religious and secular in nature, for example, incorporated a West African pattern of call-and-response. In addition to being sung in church and at work, these highly emotional spirituals often were used as accompaniments to the Gullah "ring shout," a syncretic religious custom that combined African-isms with Christian principles. During the ring shout, onlookers sung, clapped, and gesticulated, while others shuffled their heels in a circle. The performance started slowly but gained speed and intensity as it progressed. The ring shout, which has largely disappeared in the late twentieth century, served as a religious expression linked to natural and supernatural forces. While the trance like atmosphere of the ring shout is believed to be of West African origin, the practice itself and the way it functioned within the community are Gullah creations.

The strength and endurance of the Gullah community and culture is evident in the cultural traditions of the Seminole Blacks, a group strongly tied to the original Sea Island Gullah community. From the late 1700s to the early nineteenth century, Gullah slaves escaped from the rice plantations and built settlements along the remote, wooded Florida frontier. Over time, these maroon communities (*see* MAROONAGE) joined with other escaped slaves and surrounding Native Americans to form a loosely organized tribe with shared customs, food, and clothing. Along with the Native Americans, the escaped slaves were removed from Florida in the nineteenth century and were resettled on reservations in the West. During the late twentieth century, groups of these Seminole Blacks were found throughout the West, especially in Oklahoma, Texas, and Mexico. Some of these groups, who have retained numerous African customs, continue to speak Afro-Seminole, a creole language descended from Gullah.

While Gullah communities still exist in the Sea Islands of Georgia and South Carolina, they have begun to disintegrate in recent decades. The social cohesion of the community was first threatened in the 1920s when bridges were built between the mainland and the islands. Outmigration from the Sea Islands accelerated during WORLD WAR II as defense spending created new economic opportunities. During the 1950s and '60s, outside influence increased as wealthy developers began buying up land at cheap rates and building resorts on Hilton Head and other islands. While this development opened some job opportunities for black Sea Islanders, the openings tended to be in low-paying, service jobs with little opportunity for advancement.

One benefit of this development has been to break down the Gullah's isolation and to increase their awareness of trends within the larger African-American community. In the 1940s, Esau Jenkins, a native of Johns Island, led a movement to register voters, set up community centers, and provide legal aid to members of the island's African-American community. In an effort to register black voters, Jenkins, with the help of Septima Clark of Charleston, established the South's first Citizenship School on Johns Island in 1957. Jen-

kins' efforts helped break down the isolation of black Sea Islanders and involved them more directly in the struggle for civil rights among African Americans across the country.

The modernization of the Sea Islands and the Gullahs' subsequent loss of isolation, however, has caused the community to lose some of its cultural distinctiveness and cohesion. From a predominantly black population on Hilton Head in 1950, whites outnumbered blacks five to one by 1980. Many Gullah traditions, such as the ring shout, have largely disappeared, and many community members criticize the now predominantly white public schools for deemphasizing the history and culture of the Gullah people. In response to the negative impact of these modernizing changes, there have been efforts in recent years to increase public awareness of Gullah traditions and to preserve them.

In 1948, the Penn Center on St. Helena Island, S.C., formerly a school for freed slaves, was converted into a community resource center. It offers programs in academic and cultural enrichment and teaches Gullah to schoolchildren. In 1979, the Summer Institute of Linguistics, a professional society of linguists, and the nondenominational Wycliffe Bible Translators undertook projects on St. Helena Island to translate the Bible into Gullah, to develop a written system for recording Gullah, and to produce teaching aids for use in schools. The project director, Ervin Greene, a Baptist minister on nearby Daufuskie Island, estimated in 1993 that 75 percent of the New Testament already had been translated and that the New Testament would be completed by 1996, the Old Testament within five years of that date. In 1985, Beaufort, S.C., began an annual Gullah Festival to celebrate and bring recognition to the rich Gullah culture.

Increasingly, national attention has been focused on the Sea Islands. In 1989, "In Living Color," a dance-theater piece about Gullah culture on Johns Island, S.C., premiered in New York City at the Triplex Theater. Set in a rural prayer meeting, the piece offers a memoir of life among the Gullah during the late 1980s. *Daughters in the Dust,* a 1992 film about a Gullah family at the turn of the century, perhaps provided greatest national recognition for the Gullah. Written and directed by Julie DASH, whose father was raised in the Sea Islands, the film's dialogue is primarily in Gullah, with occasional English subtitles.

Such projects have helped increase public awareness of the importance of understanding and preserving Gullah traditions, and in 1994 the children's network, Nickelodeon, began work on a new animated series called *Gullah Gullah Island,* which focuses on a black couple who explore the culture of the Sea Islands. Black Sea Islanders hope that these efforts will bring the necessary national recognition to help protect the Gullah community from further cultural erosion.

REFERENCES

BURDEN, BERNADETTE. "A Bible to Call Their Own: Gullah Speakers Put Verses in Native Tongue." *Atlanta Journal and Constitution,* June 11, 1993, p. 6.

CREEL, MARGARET WASHINGTON. *"A Peculiar People": Slave Religion and Community-Culture Among the Gullahs.* New York, 1988.

CRUM, MASON. *Gullah: Negro Life in the Carolina Sea Islands,* 1940. Reprint. New York, 1968.

JACOBS, SALLY. "The Sea Islands' Vanishing Past." *Boston Globe,* March 24, 1992, p. 61.

JOYNER, CHARLES. *Down by the Riverside: A South Carolina Slave Community.* Urbana, Ill., 1984.

ROSE, WILLIE LEE. *Rehearsal for Reconstruction: The Port Royal Experiment.* New York, 1964.

TURNER, LORENZO D. *Africanisms in the Gullah Dialect.* Ann Arbor, Mich., 1949.

WOOD, PETER H. *Black Majority: Negroes in Colonial South Carolina from 1670 Through the Stono Rebellion.* New York, 1974.

LOUISE P. MAXWELL

Gumbel, Bryant Charles (September 29, 1948–), broadcaster. Born in New Orleans to Richard Dunbar Gumbel and Rhea LeCesne Gumbel, Bryant Gumbel was raised in Chicago, where his parents were active in Democratic party politics. Bryant received a bachelor of arts degree in history from Bates College in Lewiston, Me., in 1970. Gumbel is married to artist June Baranco. They have two children, Bradley Christopher and Jillian Beth.

Gumbel gained his first experience in journalism as a reporter and editor on the short-lived magazine *Black Sports.* In 1972 he accepted a position as sportscaster at KNBC-TV in Los Angeles. He soon became weekend sports anchor and, from 1973 to 1976, weeknight sportscaster. He was promoted to sports director (1976–1981) and hosted NBC's National Football League pregame shows from 1975 to 1982.

In January 1982 Gumbel became host of NBC's weekday morning *Today* show, one of the most visible positions in broadcast journalism. In 1986 he launched *Mainstreet,* a monthly magazine for teenagers. In 1989 he was writer, executive producer, and host of the two-part program "Racial Attitudes and Consciousness Exam (R.A.C.E.)." Gumbel has anchored *Today* from every continent. His broadcasts from the Soviet Union in 1984 won him the Edward R. Murrow Award for Outstanding Foreign Affairs Work and the Edward Weintal Prize for diplomatic reporting. In 1992 he took *Today* to sub-Saharan Africa for a week of on-location broadcasting. In 1993 Gumbel received TransAfrica's International Journalism Award, the U.S. Committee for UNICEF's Africa's Future Award, and the National Association of Black Journalists' Journalist of the Year award for this series. Gumbel's other honors include Emmys in 1976 and 1978 and the Golden Mike Award from the Los Angeles Press Club in 1988.

Bryant Gumbel is active in philanthropies and serves on the Board of Directors of the United Negro College Fund, United Way, and Xavier University.

REFERENCE

HAWKINS, WALTER L. *African American Biographies: Profiles of 558 Current Men and Women.* Jefferson, N.C., 1992, p. 177.

LILLIAN SERECE WILLIAMS

Gunn, Moses (October 2, 1929–December 17, 1993), actor. Moses Gunn was born in St. Louis, Mo., the eldest of seven children. The Gunn family splintered when his mother died, and Moses left home to ride the railroads when he was twelve. He returned to St. Louis to attend junior high school and, at seventeen, moved into the home of Jewel Richie, his high school teacher of English and diction. From 1954 to 1957, he served in the U.S. Army and obtained the post of assistant entertainment director while stationed in Germany. In 1959, he received his B.A. degree from Tennessee State University in Nashville. From 1959 to 1961, he studied at the University of Kansas at Lawrence in the graduate program in speech and drama, which belatedly awarded him an M.A. degree in 1989. After briefly teaching at Grambling State College in Louisiana in 1961, he moved to New York City to pursue an acting career.

Gunn began his career in 1962 as an understudy in the original New York production of Jean Genet's *The Blacks.* He next appeared in *In White America* by Martin Duberman in 1964 and Douglas Turner WARD's *Day of Absence* in 1965. In 1967, Gunn became a founding member of the Negro Ensemble Company (NEC). He performed in numerous NEC productions, including *Daddy Goodness* in 1968, *Sty of the Blind Pig* in 1972, and *The First Breeze of Summer* in 1975, for which he received an Obie award. Gunn also portrayed Othello at the American Shakespeare Festival Theater in Connecticut in 1970.

An intense cinematic presence, Gunn nevertheless was resigned to play character parts in film, beginning in 1964 with a small part in the much-lauded *Northing but a Man*. He gave a series of strong, stylized performances in *WUSA* (1970) and as a Harlem crime boss in *Shaft* (1971) and *Shaft's Big Score,* (1972). Gunn also appeared in *The Iceman Cometh* (1973), *Amazing Grace* (1974), and *Aaron Loves Angela, Cornbread, Earl and Me,* and *Rollerball*—all in 1975. In 1981, he portrayed Booker T. WASHINGTON in the film *Ragtime,* for which he received an Image award from the NAACP. He had small roles in *Firestarter* (1984), and *Leonard Part 6* (1987).

Gunn also appeared in a wide variety of television roles. In 1977, he received an Emmy nomination for his portrayal of Kintango, a tribal elder, in the miniseries "Roots." From 1981 to 1984 he portrayed miner Moses Gage on the television series *Father Murphy*. His television career also included appearances in *Little House on the Prarie* and *Maude* in the late 1970s, *The Women of Brewster Place* in 1989, and *Homicide* in 1992.

In 1993, Gunn costarred in productions of South African playwright Athol Fugard's *Blood Knot* and *My Children, My Africa*. He died in Guilford, Conn., that same year.

REFERENCES

BOGLE, DONALD. *Blacks in American Film and Television*. Westport, Conn., 1988.

MAPP, EDWARD. *Directory of Blacks in the Performing Arts*. Metuchen, N.J., 1990.

OBITUARY. *The New York Times,* December 20, 1993.

KENYA DILDAY

Actor Bill Gunn wrote plays and screenplays, including the 1976 film biography *The Greatest: The Muhammad Ali Story*. (Photographs and Prints Division, Schomburg Center for Research in Black Culture, The New York Public Library, Astor, Lenox and Tilden Foundations)

Gunn, William Harrison "Bill" (July 15, 1934–April 5, 1989), playwright, actor. Bill Gunn was born in Philadelphia. His father, William Harrison Gunn, was a composer and performer; his mother, Louise Alexander Gunn, cofounded Opportunities Industrialization Centers of America, a nationwide vocational training program, with the Reverend Leon SULLIVAN in 1964. In the early 1950s Gunn moved to New York, where he began a career as an actor. He made his Broadway debut in 1954 in *The Immoralist* and appeared in the 1959 film *The Sound and the Fury* and in several television programs. By 1960, he was developing a second career as a writer; after *All the Rest Have Died* (1964), a novel about a black man's success in the film industry, he turned to writing plays and screenplays.

While the subject of Gunn's work was the marginal place of the artist in American society, he usually placed this struggle within the context of race relations. Thus the play *Black Picture Show* (1975) depicts a black screenwriter compromising his ideals to survive in white-controlled Hollywood; *Rhinestone* (1982), a musical based on Gunn's 1981 novel *Rhinestone Sharecropping,* draws on his experience as screenwriter for the 1976 film biography *The Greatest: The Muhammed Ali Story*. It pits blacks (who several critics felt were made to look innocent to the point of naivety) against whites (who were thought to have been portrayed as little more than devils). His 1973 film about addiction, *Ganja and Hess,* which featured a black vampire, had greater critical success, however. It was the only American film among three hundred entries to be shown during Critics' Week at the 1973 Cannes Film Festival and acquired a cult following.

Gunn also wrote for television. Among his scripts, *Johannas* was singled out for an Emmy in 1972, and *The Alberta Hunter Story* was broadcast by the BBC in 1982. Gunn died of encephalitis in New York City on April 5, 1989, one day before his last play, *Forbidden City,* premiered at the New York Public Theatre.

REFERENCES

DAVIS, THADIOUS M., and HARRIS TRUDIER, eds. *Dictionary of Literary Biography.* Vol. 38. Detroit, 1985, pp. 109–114.

"Interview with Bill Gunn." *Essence* 4 (1973): 27.

GENETTE MCLAURIN

Guy, Rosa Cuthbert (September 1, 1925–   ), author. Born in Trinidad to Henry and Audrey Cuthbert, Rosa Cuthbert came to New York City as a young girl. After the death of her mother, she and a sister were raised by their father, with the help of a woman neighbor. Shortly before World War II, Rosa Cuthbert married Warner Guy. While he served in the army, she cared for their son, worked in a factory, and became involved in the American Negro Theater. Soon disappointed by roles available to black actresses, she turned to writing drama, and later, fiction. In the late 1940s, Guy and John KILLENS founded the HARLEM WRITERS GUILD, a much-needed forum for young black writers. The dissolution of her marriage forced Guy to work even harder at a variety of jobs, but she managed to continue writing and participating in guild workshops.

In 1966 she published her first book, *Bird at My Window,* about a black family that has fled the South only to be destroyed by racism in New York. The success of this novel allowed her to concentrate on writing, and she published work steadily for the next two decades. Titles include *Children of Longing,* as editor (1971); *The Friends* (1973); *Ruby* (1976); *Edith Jackson* (1978); *The Disappearance,* named to the Best Books for Young Adults 1979 list of the American Library Association; *Mother Crocodile,* translator, (1981); *Mirror of Her Own* (1981); *New Guys Around the Block* (1983); *Paris, Pee Wee and Big Dog* (1984); *And I Heard a Bird Sing* (1986); *The Music of Summer* (1992); and *The Ups and Downs of Carl David III* (1989).

Guy received perhaps her widest acclaim for *A Measure of Time,* which won the Prix du Livre Romantique Award (1988) in Cabourg, France. This 1983 bildungsroman is the story of Dorine Davis, a young maid who flees Alabama after a boss molests her. Guy vividly depicts 1920s Harlem in its glory of the HARLEM RENAISSANCE, but as an unschooled woman, and a minority excluded from respectable work, Dorine must turn to prostitution and later "boosting"—high-class shoplifting. This determined character takes on a foreign accent and a sophisticated manner. She steals all over the country, does time in prison, but eventually becomes a millionaire with a tavern business in New York.

A later work by Guy, *My Love, My Love; or, The Peasant Girl* (1985), also concerns a young heroine struggling against a society defined by race and class. This novella, based on Hans Christian Andersen's "The Little Mermaid," was the basis for *Once on This Island* (1990), a successful Broadway musical noted for its lush Caribbean sets and energetic music.

In a 1992 interview, Guy reflected on why so many of her books have focused on the plight of black children. "I always identified with orphans," she said. "Young people alone by themselves in society . . . the things that have happened to me, the things I've seen: children who were abused, children who couldn't walk or talk, children who were taken in to do housework . . . I wrote to incorporate the things I was learning. . . ." In recognition of her lifelong commitment to young people and their aspirations, the YMCA of the United States in 1993 selected Guy to give a nationwide series of readings at art centers traditionally underserved by the literary community.

REFERENCES

LAWRENCE, LEOTA S. "Rosa Guy." In *Dictionary of Literary Biography.* Vol. 33. Detroit, 1984, pp. 101–106.

RICH, FRANK " 'Once on This Island,' Fairy Tale Bringing Caribbean to 42nd Street." *New York Times,* November 17, 1990, pp. C1, C12.

SCHOFFMANN, STUART. "A Black Woman's Travails in Surviving." *Los Angeles Times Book Review,* August 24, 1983, p. 10.

WEINRAUB, JUDITH. "The Writer's Happily Ever After: Rosa Guy and the Musical with a Fairy Tale Ending." *Washington Post,* May 26, 1992, pp. D1, D6.

DEREK SCHEIPS

Gymnastics.   Black gymnasts first gained prominence in the 1970s and, by the early 1990s, were significantly represented on the U.S. Olympic women's team. Mike Carter, a three-time All-American at Louisiana State University, was the first black gymnast of national renown. During Carter's college career from 1973 to 1975, the LSU men's team went undefeated twice—in 1973 and 1975—and Carter achieved several top-ten finishes in national collegiate competitions. He finished third in the 1975 NCAA championship all-around event.

Ron Galimore, a star for LSU and Iowa State, was the most successful black gymnast of the 1970s.

He became the first gymnast to win NCAA individual titles in four different years and the first to achieve a perfect score of ten during the NCAA championships. Galimore won the NCAA vaulting championship in 1978, 1980, and 1981, was elected to the All-American team in 1980 and 1981, and was named to the 1980 U.S. Olympic team, which was denied participation in the Moscow games by a boycott imposed by U.S. President Jimmy Carter because of the Soviet invasion of Afghanistan.

Diane Durham was the first African-American woman to gain international standing; she was a heavy favorite to qualify for the 1984 U.S. Olympic team but was injured just before the competition. Durham had been the overall champion in the 1983 U.S. national championships.

The 1992 U.S. Olympic team carried three black gymnasts, signaling the ascension of African Americans in the sport on an international level. Betty Okino, a top balance-beam specialist, and Dominique Davis, a top contender in the floor exercise, competed for the women's team. Charles Lakes competed for the men's team. Though Okino and Davis were among the favorites in their events, none of the black gymnasts won medals.

REFERENCE

Ashe, Arthur R., Jr. *A Hard Road to Glory: A History of the African-American Athlete*. 3 vols. New York, 1988.

THADDEUS RUSSELL
BENJAMIN K. SCOTT